Privatization and Globalization

The Globalization of the World Economy

Series Editor: Mark Casson

Professor of Economics
University of Reading, UK

Future titles will include:

Globalization and the Location of Firms
John Cantwell

Wherever possible, the articles in these volumes have been reproduced as originally published using facsimile reproduction, inclusive of footnotes and pagination to facilitate ease of reference.

For a list of all Edward Elgar published titles visit our site on the World Wide Web at
www.e-elgar.com

Privatization and Globalization: The Changing Role of the State in Business

Edited by

Ram Mudambi

Associate Professor of Strategic Management and International Business
Temple University, USA

Reader in International Business
University of Reading, UK

THE GLOBALIZATION OF THE WORLD ECONOMY

An Elgar Reference Collection
Cheltenham, UK • Northampton, MA, USA

Published by
Edward Elgar Publishing Limited
Glensanda House
Montpellier Parade
Cheltenham
Glos GL50 1UA
UK

Edward Elgar Publishing, Inc.
136 West Street
Suite 202
Northampton
Massachusetts 01060
USA

A catalogue record for this book is available from the British Library.

Library of Congress Cataloguing in Publication Data

Privatization and globalization: the changing role of the state in business / edited by Ram Mudambi.
    p. cm. — (The globalization of the world economy ; 14)
  Articles selected from various sources.
  Includes bibliographical references and index.
  1. Privatization. 2. Deregulation. 3. Privatization—Europe. 4. Deregulation—United States. 5. Globalization—Economic aspects. I. Mudambi, Ram, 1954- II. Series.

HD3850.P7454 2003
338.9'25—dc21

2003054735

ISBN 1 85898 951 5

Printed and bound in Great Britain by MPG Books Ltd, Bodmin, Cornwall

Contents

Acknowledgements

The editor and publishers wish to thank the authors and the following publishers who have kindly given permission for the use of copyright material.

Academy of Management and the Copyright Clearance Center, Inc. for articles: Robert Grosse and Juan Yañes (1998), 'Carrying Out a Successful Privatization: The YPF Case', *Academy of Management Executive*, **12** (2), May, 51–63; Stuart Ogden and Robert Watson (1999), 'Corporate Performance and Stakeholder Management: Balancing Shareholder and Customer Interests in the U.K. Privatized Water Industry', *Academy of Management Journal*, **42** (5), October, 526–38; Ravi Ramamurti (2000), 'A Multilevel Model of Privatization in Emerging Economies', *Academy of Management Review*, **25** (3), July, 525–50; Shaker A. Zahra, R. Duane Ireland, Isabel Gutierrez and Michael A. Hitt (2000), 'Privatization and Entrepreneurial Transformation: Emerging Issues and a Future Research Agenda', *Academy of Management Review*, **25** (3), July, 509–24; Jonathan P. Doh (2000), 'Entrepreneurial Privatization Strategies: Order of Entry and Local Partner Collaboration as Sources of Competitive Advantage', *Academy of Management Review*, **25** (3), July, 551–71.

American Economic Association for articles: Jerry Hausman, Timothy Tardiff and Alexander Belinfante (1993), 'The Effects of the Breakup of AT&T on Telephone Penetration in the United States', *American Economic Review, Papers and Proceedings*, **83** (2), May, 178–84; William E. Taylor and Lester D. Taylor (1993), 'Postdivestiture Long-Distance Competition in the United States', *American Economic Review, Papers and Proceedings*, **83** (2), May, 185–90; Jonathan R. Hay and Andrei Shleifer (1998), 'Private Enforcement of Public Laws: A Theory of Legal Reform', *American Economic Review, Papers and Proceedings*, **88** (2), May, 398–403; James Peoples, Jr. and Wayne K. Talley (2001), 'Black-White Earnings Differentials: Privatization versus Deregulation', *American Economic Review, Papers and Proceedings*, **91** (2), May, 164–8; William L. Megginson and Jeffry M. Netter (2001), 'From State to Market: A Survey of Empirical Studies on Privatization', *Journal of Economic Literature*, **XXXIX** (2), June, 321–89.

Blackwell Publishing Ltd for article: Maxim Boycko, Andrei Shleifer and Robert W. Vishny (1996), 'A Theory of Privatisation', *Economic Journal*, **106** (435), March, 309–19.

Cato Institute for article: Hugh Thomas (2000), 'A Proposal to Deregulate Banking', *Cato Journal*, **20** (2), Fall, 237–53.

Elsevier Science for articles: Saul Estrin and David de Meza (1995), 'Unnatural Monopoly', *Journal of Public Economics*, **57** (3), 471–88; Harald Hau (1998), 'Privatization Under Political Interference: Evidence from Eastern Germany', *European Economic Review*, **42** (7), 1177–201; Igor Filatotchev, Mike Wright, Trevor Buck and Vladimir Zhukov (1999), 'Corporate

Entrepreneurs and Privatized Firms in Russia, Ukraine, and Belarus', *Journal of Business Venturing*, **14**, 475–92; David Jennings (2000), 'PowerGen: The Development of Corporate Planning in a Privatized Utility', *Long Range Planning*, **33** (2), April, 201–19; Daniel J. McCarthy, Sheila M. Puffer and Alexander I. Naumov (2000), 'Russia's Retreat to Statization and the Implications for Business', *Journal of World Business*, **35** (3), 256–74; David Dornisch (2001), 'Competitive Dynamics in Polish Telecommunications, 1990–2000: Growth, Regulation, and Privatization of an Infrastructural Multi-network', *Telecommunications Policy*, **25** (6), July, 381–407; Antonio Estache, Andres Gomez-Lobo and Danny Leipziger (2001), 'Utilities Privatization and the Poor: Lessons and Evidence from Latin America', *World Development*, **29** (7), 1179–98.

Elsevier Science, Inc. for article: Robert E. DeYoung, Joseph P. Hughes and Choon-Geol Moon (2001), 'Efficient Risk-taking and Regulatory Covenant Enforcement in a Deregulated Banking Industry', *Journal of Economics and Business*, **53**, 255–82.

Federal Reserve Bank of Cleveland for article: Paul W. Bauer (1986), '"Don't Panic": A Primer on Airline Deregulation', *Federal Reserve Bank of Cleveland Economic Review*, 4th Quarter, 17–24.

Financial Management Association for article: Raj Aggarwal and Joel T. Harper (2000), 'Equity Valuation in the Czech Voucher Privatization Auctions', *Financial Management*, **29** (4), Winter, 77–100.

Journal of International Affairs and the Trustees of the Columbia University in the City of New York for article: Jagdish Bhagwati (1998), 'Poverty and Reforms: Friends or Foes?', *Journal of International Affairs*, **52** (1), Fall, 33–45.

Journal of International Business Studies for article: Stefanie Ann Lenway and Thomas P. Murtha (1994), 'The State as Strategist in International Business Research', *Journal of International Business Studies*, **25** (3), 513–35.

Journal of Law and Economics, University of Chicago for articles: Harold Demsetz (1968), 'Why Regulate Utilities?', *Journal of Law and Economics*, **XI**, April, 55–65; Pablo T. Spiller (1990), 'Politicians, Interest Groups, and Regulators: A Multiple-Principals Agency Theory of Regulation, or "Let Them Be Bribed"', *Journal of Law and Economics*, **XXXIII** (1), April, 65–101; Messod D. Beneish (1991), 'The Effect of Regulatory Changes in the Airline Industry on Shareholders' Wealth', *Journal of Law and Economics*, **XXXIV** (2, Part 1), October, 395–419.

Kluwer Academic/Plenum Publishers for article: Ram Mudambi, Pietro Navarra and Chris Paul (2002), 'Institutions and Market Reform in Emerging Economies: A Rent Seeking Perspective', *Public Choice*, **112** (1–2), July, 185–202.

MIT Press for excerpt: John Vickers and George Yarrow (1988), 'Theories of Regulation', in *Privatization: An Economic Analysis*, Chapter 4, 79–120, references.

RAND for article: George J. Stigler (1971), 'The Theory of Economic Regulation', *Bell Journal of Economics and Management Science*, **2** (1), Spring, 3–21.

University of Chicago Press for article: Nicholas Barberis, Maxim Boycko, Andrei Shleifer and Natalia Tsukanova (1996), 'How Does Privatization Work? Evidence from the Russian Shops', *Journal of Political Economy*, **104** (4), August, 764–90.

Every effort has been made to trace all the copyright holders but if any have been inadvertently overlooked the publishers will be pleased to make the necessary arrangement at the first opportunity.

In addition the publishers wish to thank the Marshall Library of Economics, Cambridge University, the Library of the University of Warwick and the Library of Indiana University at Bloomington, USA for their assistance in obtaining these articles.

Introduction: Globalization and the Advance of Markets: Twin Forces Shaping the World Economy

Ram Mudambi

1. Introduction

One of the biggest economic questions since the industrial revolution concerns the role of the government in the economic system. Different systems have envisaged lesser or greater roles for the government, ranging from complete control in the totalitarian communist states to the minimalist 'night watchman' role advocated by classical liberals. Beginning with the Russian Revolution in 1918, the pendulum swung towards greater state control in the economy, with even most capitalist states dramatically increasing the role of the government during the Great Depression. This 'growth of government' was reflected in the inexorably rising share of government spending as a percentage of GDP. For example, the share of Federal spending in the United States has risen from about 3 per cent to almost 25 per cent of gross domestic product between the beginning and end of the 20th century (Sutter, 1998). The intellectual foundation for this movement can be traced to the victory of Keynesian ideas in the minds of policy-makers in the 1930s (Boettke, 1992). This intellectual foundation was reinforced by the heavy government expenditures involved in fighting World War II, so that by war's end in 1945, even countries with a strong free market orientation had economies that encompassed enormous state-controlled or state-regulated sectors.

Hayek argued persuasively that in capitalist economies, the government's role is two-fold – (i) to enforce the rules of 'just' conduct such as ensuring the safety of life and property; and (ii) to render additional 'highly desirable' services. Hayek considers such government service to be compatible with 'liberal' principles so long as 'the wants satisfied are collective wants of the community *as a whole*' (Hayek 1978, 1:111, italics added). Both of these roles involve the provision of public goods.[1] In the context of business, these principles may be interpreted as the promotion of competition where a market solution exists and the replacement of competition where the market fails.

It would be fair to say that there is a greater consensus regarding the state's role in the promotion of competition, as compared to its role in the replacement of competition. The promotion of competition, at least in theory, involves the enforcement of business 'rules of conduct' and these can increase the efficiency of markets. Examples include the unbiased enforcement of laws of contract and protecting efficient entrants from predatory behavior by incumbent firms. However, for the state to replace the market, it must be true that the market has failed. The bitterest debates concerning the role of the state in the economy relate to the extent of market failure.

Proponents of an activist state see market failure everywhere, while classical liberals tend to view it as a rare phenomenon. A good way to formalize the notion of market failure is to base it on Coasian transaction costs (Coase, 1937), i.e., the costs incurred in using the market mechanism. If transaction costs are zero, markets are efficient, Pareto optimality is achieved and state intervention is unnecessary. As transaction costs rise, markets become less efficient. When transaction costs become high enough, markets fail, in the sense that no gains from trade can be achieved. In a practical sense, market failure is rarely observable, so that government intervention is usually recommended on the basis of high transaction costs.

But as pointed out by Ricketts (2002), this argument is incomplete, since even in cases of high transaction costs government intervention is only one amongst several possible solutions. Both state activities and private responses are typically available to solve this problem. State activities usually involve the non-market delivery of a good or service, while private responses are usually based on either extending the scope of the firm or increasingly, on the emergence of new markets. However, private responses take time and their form is often unpredictable *a priori*. Until recently, these factors have meant that private responses have been the exception, rather than the rule in situations of high transactions costs.

2. Traditional Approaches

By the middle of the 20th century, approaches to situations of high transaction costs in market economies could be placed in two categories, the so-called US and European models. Both of these involved government intervention in the market. In addition, there were the countries of the communist bloc (with 'command economies') that formally eliminated markets and the private sector in their attempt to achieve an egalitarian distribution of goods and services. In these countries, the role of the state in the economy was pervasive. In virtually all countries of the world, the role of the government in the economy could be roughly described as being within one of these three categories.

In the US model of state regulation, the government guarantees provision of the good or service by granting a legal monopoly to a single firm. This single firm is prevented from extracting monopoly profits by direct or indirect control of its rate of return by the government. The ownership and management of assets remain in private hands and the firm is subject to monitoring by the stock market. In the European model of state ownership, the government guarantees the provision of the good or service by producing it within a state-run monopoly firm. The ownership and management of assets are now in public hands and there is no market-driven monitoring.

In practice, both these models had endemic problems. In the US model, setting the rate of return or 'rate-setting' remained a thorny problem, with the constant fear of 'regulatory capture', i.e., state regulators becoming advocates rather than monitors of the regulated firm (Stigler, 1971 – Chapter 7). Efficiency remained a difficult objective. However, by and large, the US model performed better than the European model, where the state-run firm not only ran up large deficits, but also became a vehicle for the implementation of a number of political objectives ranging from employment generation to income redistribution.

Most importantly, however, neither the US nor the European model could deal with rapid technological advance. As industry boundaries became eroded by technology, regulated private firms in the US and state-run firms in Europe increasingly had to be protected from competitive value propositions delivered by firms from outside the boundary of the traditional industry. Further, regulated firms, and even many state-run firms, began to see opportunities for leveraging their capabilities in new and rapidly growing industries and markets that their charters prevented them from entering.

Significant as the problems with the US and European models were, they paled in comparison to the problems faced by state enterprises in the command economies. By eliminating private enterprise, these countries had totally destroyed individual incentives and as a result, their economies became hopelessly inefficient. The gap between the market and command economies continued to grow between the 1950s and the 1980s, leading to the eventual collapse of the communist system as a whole, starting with the fall of the Berlin Wall in 1989. The fall of the Wall had far-reaching effects, perhaps none so important as the philosophical blow it dealt to the position of those advocating, in one way or another, a large role for the state in the economy. Attempts at rolling back the state that had until that point been largely confined to the US and the UK suddenly emerged in most countries of the globe.

3. A Taxonomy of Change

Arguably, the two most important forces affecting the world economy in the closing decades of the 20th century are the retreat of the state from the economic arena and globalization, which I use as a shorthand term for the increasing integration of the world economy. The former set of changes has affected the nature of economic and business systems within countries, while the latter has impacted the nature and extent of economic and business interactions across national borders.

The retreat of the state from the economy has occurred in all three contexts discussed above. First, and most spectacularly, the collapse of the state-run command economies has been followed by a wholesale movement away from central planning, universal public ownership and government management towards market systems (*transition*). Second, changes to the European model have involved the transfer of state-run operations to market governance in much of Western Europe and beyond (*privatization*). Such transfers have been implemented in a number of different ways, as shown in Table 1. Third and more subtly, changes to the US model have involved the dismantling of state controls and legal monopolies in some sectors (*deregulation*). Finally, an overarching theme running through all three contexts has been the opening up of sectors and whole economies to new competition, allowing and even encouraging the entry of foreign firms (*liberalization*).

Globalization, as defined here, has moved symbiotically with the spread of market-based systems and the growth and efficiency of multinational firms. The term itself may be taken to refer to the process of removing government-imposed restrictions on movements between countries in order to create an 'open, borderless' world economy, i.e., the process of international economic integration. Changes under this heading include the abolition of regulatory barriers to free movement of goods, capital and even, to a certain extent, of labor.

Table 1.   *Forms of Privatization*

Form	Description
Subcontracting	A public agency subcontracts some of its activities to a private sector company. This can cover an entire public service, such as trash collection, or part of an activity, such as electricity or water meter reading and billing.
Management contract	A temporary transfer of management responsibility, without transfer of ownership.
Leasing	The government leases a public organization to a private sector company to run.
Concession	This includes build, operate, transfer (BOT) contracts, where a private company agrees to build infrastructure, run it under license for a defined period, and then pass it to government ownership.

These two forces – the retreat of the state and globalization – have proceeded in parallel, but nonetheless have had significant interactions with one another. At the most basic level, the reduction in the role of the state has been fueled by efficiency of market-based systems and the inability of government-run systems to match them. The introduction of market forces in all three contexts has created opportunities for multinational firms to enter and operate in transition economies, and to enter sectors from which they were formerly barred, both in their home countries and abroad. This has created new challenges for governments as they move from the direct control of economic activity to designing and maintaining the institutional infrastructure to ensure the freedom of markets for the whole range of participants, from (foreign and domestic) firms, through workers to consumers and residents.

4. Normative Considerations

Are these powerful forces re-shaping the world economy for good or ill? Needless to say, there is an ongoing and vociferous debate on this question, with most participants starting from widely differing definitions of the same terms.[2] While actual declines, if any, in the share of GDP controlled by the government have been modest, it is nonetheless true that deregulation, privatization and transition have moved many formerly state regulated or controlled sectors into the private sector. Normative analyses can be carried out along two dimensions – within countries and across countries.

Within countries, we may consider industry and case studies in a number of countries, examining sectors before and after changes were implemented. In practice, the retreat of the state and the advance of markets are two separate changes and both changes have not always occurred simultaneously. The first change, by itself, is composed of the changes we have labeled deregulation, privatization and transition. The second change is what we have labeled liberalization. Theory predicts that replacing state with private control without introducing the disciplinary forces of the market is unlikely to yield large benefits. Private monopolies are likely to be only marginally more efficient than state ones, if at all. In addition, monopoly surpluses become concentrated in a few private hands, rather than being re-distributed. Many critiques of privatization focus on cases where it has occurred without liberalization and are thus flawed.

The introduction of the market nearly always creates winners and losers. Groups that were subsidized under state control generally lose and groups that paid the subsidies (e.g., in the form of higher prices) benefit. Typically, the gaining groups are larger than the losing groups, and liberalized markets increase efficiency, further boosting the gains from the change (Megginson and Netter – Chapter 18). This pattern can be observed right from the beginning with early deregulation like that of the US airlines (Bauer, 1986 – Chapter 14) and the break-up of AT&T (Taylor and Taylor, 1993 – Chapter 12, Hausman, Tardiff and Belinfante 1993 – Chapter 13).

Across countries, key tools of analysis are developed within the New Institutional Economics. While the precise nature of change and path of development cannot be predicted in detail, this literature suggests that a crucial determinant of the actual outcome of implemented policy is the institutional context. Following North (1990) and Furubotn and Richter (1991), institutions can be understood as rules or constraints that channel individuals' actions in specific directions. They can be formal or informal, depending on their genesis. Formal institutions are designed externally and imposed on a community from above by political action. They are made explicit by legislation and regulations and are formally enforced by an external authority such as the government or, more generally, the state.[3] Examples of this type of institution are civil law, the form of government and the electoral system. On the other hand, as analyzed by Young (1998), informal institutions evolve spontaneously from human experience. They develop gradually and tend to appeal to voluntary coordination amongst the members of a society. They tend to be flexible and the sanctions for their violation are not spelled out since they occur spontaneously. Examples of informal institutions are ethical manners, culture, conventions and customs.[4]

The findings of Olson (1996) regarding the inter-country competition among institutional systems are interesting. He shows that the low-income countries are poor not so much because of their lack of physical and human capital, but rather because of their institutions. Poor governance structures prevent them from obtaining the colossal gains from increased participation in the world economy through trade and foreign investment. Indeed, there is now evidence that multinational firms are strongly inclined to locate investment (and particularly, high value-added knowledge-intensive investments) in countries and even in regions of countries where the local political institutions support the functioning of markets by minimizing transaction costs (Mudambi and Navarra 2003; Ursprung and Harms, 2002).

De Soto (2000) also concludes that poor countries' incomes are far below their potential due to poor institutional structures. In contrast to Olson, he suggests that foreign investment would be unnecessary if poor countries were able to unlock their fixed capital through guaranteeing property rights. He points out that in Egypt the poor have accumulated wealth that is worth 55 times as much as the sum of all foreign direct investment ever recorded there, including that spent on building the Suez Canal and the Aswan Dam. However, such countries have yet to establish and normalize an institutional framework in the form of the invisible network of laws that turn assets from "dead" into "liquid" capital through financial markets.[5] In other words, the financial market multiplier whereby a relatively small base of wealth supports a huge superstructure of wealth-creating activities through credit is very weak. The web of property rights that gives individual agents the confidence to trust their wealth in the hands of other agents is virtually non-existent.

Thus, institutions that facilitate the working of markets and entrepreneurship have a better track record in terms of producing material prosperity than those that impede them (Zahra, Ireland, Gutierrez and Hitt – Chapter 28). The state has an important role to play in terms of developing and maintaining healthy institutions. Where does one draw the line in terms of the role of state regulation? The maintenance of a fair legal system is probably a valuable state function, the running of a national airline probably is not. A useful way of drawing the line is to ask whether the state is acting to achieve specific ends (e.g., maintenance of a national flag carrying airline) or whether it is acting to set up and enforce rules or laws to achieve general ends (e.g., providing a legal framework that encourages market transactions).

Many of the institutions that have the most profound effects on economic outcomes ranging from entrepreneurship to macroeconomic debts and deficits are political. When the citizenry wields political power, both individual well-being and business effectiveness are enhanced. Protection of individual property rights is one of the strongest forces guaranteeing the emergence and maintenance of economic welfare. A competitive institutional environment with outcome-based survival leads to institutional flexibility that selects against poor outcomes. Ricketts (2003) presents convincing evidence that with flexible institutions, multiple forms of economic and business organization compete with one another, with only the forms that best serve the interests of participants surviving.

However, there is a difference between institutional flexibility (deregulation and privatization) and institutional overhaul (transition). In the latter case, institutional design must precede market reform, since markets cannot function without some fundamental working institutions – law and order and guaranteed property rights. Transition does not automatically lead to institutional improvement. There are always some agents who gain from unfavorable institutional environments. In the words of Hobsbawm (1969):

> It is often assumed that an economy of private enterprise has an automatic bias toward innovation, but this is not so. It has a bias only toward profit. (p.40)

Transition presents opportunities for entrepreneurs of all types, only some of whose skills are productive. When the 'profit' or payoff to unproductive or destructive skills is high enough, institutional transition can be wealth destroying on a grand scale (Baumol, 1990). A society's material poverty is just as much the outcome of rational choice as is its prosperity.

Notes

1. A 'public good' is a good that can be produced at zero marginal cost and must be provided on a nonexclusive basis to everyone. Such goods include national defense, the provision of justice, the control of infectious diseases and pest control. The two fundamental properties of public goods are (a) 'non-exclusivity' and (b) 'non-rivalry'. In other words, no one can be excluded from the consumption of the good (the military cannot refuse to defend any one preference group of people, the health service cannot prevent anyone from enjoying the benefits of the eradication of a disease); and the consumption of the good by one person does not reduce the amount available for consumption by anyone else.

2.   There is even a small group that maintains that no changes whatsoever have taken place in the global economy. This school maintains that multinational companies remain deeply rooted in their home countries, that national governments remain all-powerful and that most 'global' institutions remain toothless. They maintain, moreover, that appearances of cultural homogenization are superficial and mask clashes in fundamental social values.
3.   The external imposition and enforcement of institutions by agents selected by the political process and acting from outside the society is known as the 'protective function of the state' (Buchanan, 1975).
4.   This distinction resembles the one between rules of organizations and rules of conduct (Hayek, 1973). The former are seen as designing the internal structure of organizations to serve their purposes, while the latter are viewed as coordinating the interactions of the members of a social group. The contrast between internal and external rules proposed by Kasper and Streit (1999) is similar.
5.   For example, in many underdeveloped countries, the poor store their assets in the form of precious metals in jewelry and the like, while the rich store their assets in offshore financial institutions. Neither of these practices results in the assets supporting credit and further wealth creation in the home economy.

References

Baumol, W.J. (1990), 'Entrepreneurship, Productive, Unproductive and Destructive', *Journal of Political Economy*, **98** (5), 893–921.

Boettke, P. (1992), 'F.A. Hayek: 1899–1992', *The Freeman*, August, 300–303.

Buchanan, J.M. (1975), *The Limits of Liberty: Between Anarchy and Leviathan*, Chicago: University of Chicago Press.

Coase, R.H. (1937), 'The Nature of the Firm', *Economica*, **4**, 386.

De Soto, Hernando (2000), *The Mystery of Capital: Why Capitalism Triumphs in the West and Fails Everywhere Else*, New York: Basic Books.

Furubotn, E. and Richter, R. (1991), *The New Institutional Economics*, College Station: Texas A&M University Press.

Hayek, F.A. (1973), *Law, Legislation and Liberty, Vol. 1, Rules and Order*, Chicago: University of Chicago Press.

Hayek, F.A. (1978), *New Studies in Philosophy, Politics and Economics*, London: Routledge and Kegan Paul.

Hobsbawm, E.J. (1969), *Industry and Empire from 1750 to the Present Day*, Harmondsworth: Penguin.

Kasper, W. and Streit, M.E. (1999), *Institutional Economics: Social Order and Public Policy*, Aldershot, UK and Brookfield, US: Edward Elgar.

Mudambi, R. and Navarra, P. (2003), 'Political Culture and Foreign Direct Investment: The Case of Italy', *Economics of Governance*, **4** (1), 37–56.

North, D.C. (1990), *Institutions, Institutional Change and Economic Performance*, New York: Cambridge University Press.

Olson, M. (1996), 'Big Bills Left on the Sidewalk: Why Some Nations are Rich and Others Poor', *Journal of Economic Perspectives*, **10**, 3–24.

Ricketts, M.J. (2002), *The Economics of Business Enterprise: An Introduction to Economic Organisation and the Theory of the Firm*, Aldershot, UK and Brookfield, US: Edward Elgar.

Ricketts, M.J. (2003), 'Corporate Governance and Capital Markets in the Two Capitalisms', in R. Mudambi, P. Navarra and G. Sobbrio (eds), *Economic Welfare, International Business and Global Institutional Change*, Aldershot, UK and Brookfield, US: Edward Elgar.

Sutter, D. (1998), 'Constitutions and the Growth of Government', *Journal of Economic Behavior and Organization*, **34** (1), 129–42.

Ursprung, H. and Harms, P. (2002), 'Do Civil and Political Repression Really Boost Foreign Direct Investment?', *Economic Inquiry*, **40** (4), 651–63.

Young, H.P. (1998), *Individual Strategy and Social Structure: An Evolutionary Theory of Institutions*, Princeton: Princeton University Press.

Part I
Introduction

[1]

THE STATE AS STRATEGIST IN INTERNATIONAL BUSINESS RESEARCH

Stefanie Ann Lenway* and Thomas P. Murtha*
The University of Minnesota

Abstract. No matter what strategy managers choose, cross-national differences in states' strategic capabilities and objectives affect multinational corporations' capabilities to manage interdependent operations. In this paper, we develop four attribute dimensions along which states' strategic economic capabilities vary. We then apply these dimensions to show how they contribute to familiar international business models of managerial process, MNC strategy and organizational structure, and country competitiveness.

In recent years, organizational researchers have increased their interest in the international aspects of organizing firms. In doing so, they have amplified themes, such as the intangible asset basis of firms' competitive advantages, that have long fascinated international business (IB) researchers. The organizational impact of firm/state strategic interaction, however, has not been among these themes. This seems surprising, given that operating across multiple political jurisdictions creates an important distinction between domestic and international management practice [Kogut 1985b, 1989; Behrman and Grosse 1990]. As mainstream organizational research begins to encompass IB issues, international firm/state relations should provide one of the more obvious areas of opportunity. Before this can happen, however, we believe that, as IB researchers, we must better specify the linkages between international firm/state relations models and models of international management, strategy and national competitiveness that have captured mainstream attention (e.g., Prahalad and Doz [1987]; Bartlett and Ghoshal [1989]; Porter [1990]).

This article takes steps toward specifying these linkages. In it, we offer a framework for understanding states that has a common intellectual lineage with the academic discourse on firms. Our argument relies on classical

---

*The authors are associate professors of strategic management and organization at the Carlson School of Management, University of Minnesota. Much of the research represented here took place at the University of Michigan, where Stefanie Lenway was a visiting scholar and Tom Murtha was assistant professor of international business.

We gratefully acknowledge comments and encouragement from Jean J. Boddewyn, Art Goldsmith, Sumantra Ghoshal, Stephen J. Kobrin, Robert T. Kudrle, David Ricks, Peter Smith Ring, Thomas Roehl, Alan Rugman, Michael P. Ryan and the anonymous referees. Responsibility for errors remains our own. The first author wishes to thank the McKnight Land Grant Fellowship program for financial support.

Received: April 1991; Revised: August 1992; July & December 1993; Accepted: January 1994.

514   JOURNAL OF INTERNATIONAL BUSINESS STUDIES, THIRD QUARTER 1994

sociological and political science conceptions of state and society that distinguish between political organization structures and groups of officials who govern [Weber 1978; Krasner 1978; March and Olson 1984; Benjamin and Duvall 1985]. We refer to the organization structures as "states" and to the groups of officials as "governments." [1] States embody country-specific governance capabilities that, together with national factor endowments, influence the international economic strategies that governments can implement. We define international economic strategies as government plans to allocate resources with intent to reach long-term national political and economic objectives, including growth, competitiveness, national security and state legitimacy. Thinking of states in this way lets us consider international firm/state relations as the interaction of organizational strategies and structures, largely driven by particular states' and firms' unique capabilities, objectives, economic resources, and teams of officials in charge.

The concern with firm/state relations in IB has generated a substantial literature. Among several broad topics, bargaining between multinational corporations (MNCs) and host states has advanced the farthest in paradigmatic development. Studies have documented how firm, industry and market conditions underlie governments' and MNCs' relative power to obtain their preferred conditions of market entry. They have also examined the causes of shifts in bargaining power over time: the dynamic that Vernon called "the obsolescing bargain" (see Vernon [1971]; Mikesell [1971]; Moran [1973]; Fagre and Wells [1982]; Lecraw [1984]; Teece [1986]; Kobrin [1987]; Kim [1988]; Grosse [1989]; Gomes-Casseres [1990]; Behrman and Grosse [1990]; Murtha [1991b, 1993]). Another related body of work examines how government policies influence firm strategy, decisions and performance. Some of these studies include managerial prescriptions for government relations [Boarman and Schollhammer 1975; Doz and Prahalad 1980; Robinson 1983; Doz 1986; Boddewyn 1988; Ring, Lenway and Govekar 1990; Behrman and Grosse 1990; Lecraw and Morrison 1991; Brewer 1993]. Another important segment of the literature concerns public policy process evaluation [Encarnation and Wells 1986; Brewer 1992], political risk assessment [Kobrin 1979; de la Torre 1981; Poynter 1982; Brewer 1985; Tallman 1988; Miller 1992], and managing the risk assessment function [Kobrin 1982]. Murtha [1991a], Murtha and Lenway [1994] and Stopford and Strange [1991] have discussed the impact of industrial strategies on MNCs' operations. Preston and Windsor's recent book [1992] has renewed the debate on how multilateral political economic arrangements, agreements and norms affect MNC strategy. Overall, the literature documents how government policies affect MNCs, taking into account aspects of industry, market, firm, political risk and interstate relations.

By linking what some IB scholars know about public policy with what other IB scholars know about corporate strategy, we believe that our perspective contributes to the field as a whole. It does this by using the concepts of strategy and organization structure to explain the limits and possibilities of governmental and managerial choice in different settings and to predict likely resulting patterns of MNC/state strategic interaction. We provide a framework for analyzing how state organizational attributes systematically associate with different state international economic strategy formulation and implementation capabilities. Knowledge of these state strategic capabilities, in turn, provides MNCs' managers with a basis to forecast the feasibility, likelihood and coherence of public policies, predict the relative consistency of these policies over time, and incorporate these expectations into the corporate strategy process.

Our framework consists of four attribute dimensions that distinguish among states in their impact on competitive advantage and on international coordination within MNCs. In the section below, we explain how we derived these dimensions by synthesizing sociological, political scientific and economic views of the state with IB perspectives on MNC/state relations. The following section shows the framework's practical relevance when incorporated within strategy frameworks that have reached broad audiences that include IB, corporate strategy and organizational studies researchers, as well as managers. We conclude by discussing the benefits for IB scholarship of drawing upon underlying disciplines to explicitly specify assumptions concerning the state.

STATE ORGANIZATION, POLITICAL INSTITUTIONS AND STRATEGIC INTERACTION BETWEEN STATES AND MNCs

Table 1 displays four dimensions of state organizational attributes that interact to affect international economic strategies. Dimension 1 concerns the domestic legal institutional basis and scope of states' strategic capabilities. Dimension 2 concerns the impact of ideology and domestic political interest groups. Dimension 3 pertains to states' foreign policy capabilities, particularly as related to territorial integrity. Dimension 4 concerns legitimacy. Each of the next four sections discusses one of these dimensions.

Dimension 1: Domestic Policy Capabilities: Authority vs. Markets

States' capabilities to implement international economic strategies rest largely on domestic policy instruments. These range in specificity from macroeconomic tools of monetary and fiscal policy, which affect entire economies, to micro tools such as loans or subsidies that target specific transactions. States vary in the specificity of the policy instruments most readily available to them. This variation reflects cross-national differences in the relative importance of political authority vs. market decisionmaking in domestic resource allocation [Lindblom 1977].

Chalmers Johnson's influential taxonomy of "regulatory" and "developmental" states [1982, p. 19] condenses key aspects of these differences. Regulatory states have minimal capabilities to formulate economic strategies, and few policy instruments with which to implement them. Developmental states

516   JOURNAL OF INTERNATIONAL BUSINESS STUDIES, THIRD QUARTER 1994

TABLE 1
States' Organizational Capabilities:
Eleven Attributes in Four Dimensions

---

1) Domestic policy capabilities: Authority vs. markets
   a) specification of property rights, including the mix of public and private sector discretion in macro- and microeconomic governance;
   b) ultimate authority to make and enforce laws, including those of contract;
   c) control of the courts, police and armed forces.

2) Policy networks and states' domestic autonomy: Individualism vs. communitarianism

   The ability of the government to act independently of domestic interest groups, taking into account
   a) ideology concerning the relative importance of individual vs. community interests;
   b) mechanisms of interest group formation;
   c) the nature of the policy network that links interest groups to the executive and legislature.

3) International autonomy and foreign policy capabilities: Economic vs. political objectives, including
   a) sovereign control of access to a territory;
   b) sovereign prerogatives in managing inter-state relationships;
   c) power and responsibility for safeguarding national security and autonomy within the international system.

4) Legitimacy and the balance of economic and noneconomic values: Equity vs. efficiency

   For any given state this substantially depends on the degree to which the dimensions above embody its society's political culture.

---

have capabilities to pursue "a strategic, or goal-oriented, approach to the economy." In practice all states display aspects of both regulatory and developmental approaches. We can categorize them only on the basis of their dominant tendencies.[2] Johnson [1982, p. 19] identifies the U.S. and Great Britain as examples of regulatory states and Japan as an example of a developmental state.

The economic capabilities of regulatory states reside in state agencies that set the rules of economic competition within countries. In the U.S., these agencies arose beginning in the late 19th century as a reaction to public perceptions that large corporations were exploiting the laissez-faire economy to gain market power and reduce competition. While these agencies developed capabilities to impose ex post sanctions on firms that overstepped the rules, they were not formed to lead economic development nor to directly influence corporate strategies. Regulatory approaches to national economic management assume that the competitive interplay of market forces ensures economic growth. States' roles are limited to running monetary and fiscal policies and to regulating private economic activity when markets fail.

Developmental states have organizational capabilities to formulate and implement strategies that target home firms to build their international competitiveness.

Johnson's [1982] characterization of the developmental state shares much with Gerschenkron's [1962] analysis of states' economic roles in those European countries that entered relatively late into the Industrial Revolution. Gerschenkron argued that late industrialization demanded that states play active economic roles, because capital would not finance the large investments needed to simultaneously start up and catch up to the leaders in production technologies. State agencies financed development using tools such as subsidies and equity ownership of enterprises in key economic sectors.

Over time, many developmental states increased their capabilities to influence firms' strategic decisions by establishing organizational subunits that collaborate with business while enjoying substantial independence from popular political oversight. Japan's Ministry of International Trade and Industry (MITI) provides a well-known example.[3] Political independence provides policymakers with considerable discretion to discriminate among property rights holders on the basis of industry, nationality or other criteria. This discretion, and an accompanying ideological propensity to discriminate, creates one of the most important, yet subtle, distinctions between regulatory and developmental states.

The distinction is subtle because all states use such inducements as tax holidays, training allowances and tax financing of infrastructural development to influence both domestic and foreign firms' location decisions (see Lecraw and Morrison [1991]; Moran [1992]; Murtha [1993]). The regulatory approach, however, makes such opportunities available to any firm able to show that a project fits general economic objectives such as increasing employment. Discrimination has primarily resulted from interest group pressures, and not from coherent programs to help domestic firms or industries.[4]

Developmental states, on the other hand, have the capabilities to discriminate either against or in favor of multinational investors to ensure that inward foreign direct investment (IFDI) supports their economic strategies. MITI, for example, officially discriminated against IFDI between World War II and the late 1960s, except where MNCs provided Japanese firms with key technologies.[5] Developmental host states have capabilities to unbundle the MNC package of capital, technology and managerial skills by targeting value chain activities[6] that best suit their economic strategies. For example, host countries may offer tax write-offs for research and development that MNCs might otherwise have performed elsewhere, subsidize local suppliers of inputs that MNCs might have produced themselves, or offer incentives for MNCs to license technology to local firms rather than establish their own facilities [Murtha 1991a, 1993; Wade 1990, pp. 151-57].

One common characteristic of such programs is that they lack contractual enforceability, since states control their own courts and are not subject to higher authority. Some probability always exists that governments will terminate programs on political or other grounds, creating negative consequences for MNCs.[7] Consequently, a state's credibility—which depends heavily upon

518   JOURNAL OF INTERNATIONAL BUSINESS STUDIES, THIRD QUARTER 1994

its reputation for following through on announced policies and sustaining them over time—becomes critical in evaluating a government's offers or demands. State credibility depends on institutionalized policy networks that link interest groups and governments [Murtha 1991a; Cowhey 1993]. The next section discusses this dimension of our framework.

Dimension 2: Policy Networks and State Autonomy: Individualism vs. Communitarianism

Many studies have associated states' strategic capabilities with countries' social cohesiveness, public/private intersectoral collaboration [Johnson 1982; Katzenstein 1985], state dominance [Gerschenkron 1962], or some combination of these factors [Doner 1991]. Johnson's developmental state, for example, relies on societal consensus to implement strategies for high speed economic growth [1982]. Katzenstein [1977] anticipated this research by asking whether variations in the "policy networks" that link governments with private interests explain variations in countries' economic strategies.

Lodge [1990] synthesized many of these studies in a bipolar typology of "individualistic" vs. "communitarian" political ideologies. These ideologies respectively inhibit and enable states' capabilities to forge domestic consensus around economic strategy. In an individualistic society, Lodge argues, the state exists primarily to "protect property, enforce contracts, and keep the marketplace open so that competition among firms may be as vigorous and as free as possible" (p. 15). Communitarian states, in contrast, "define and ensure the rights and duties of community membership, and play a central role in creating—sometimes imposing—consensus to support the direction in which they decide the community should move" (p. 16). Consensus increases the credibility of states' policies, because it unifies all political elements behind decisions. Majoritarian decisionmaking rules associated with individualism, on the other hand, create winners and losers. Unforeseen changes can result from the actions of intransigent minorities or from small groups changing sides.

Lodge's individualism encompasses the institutional fragmentation of Johnson's regulatory state and the interest group competition of pluralist democracy.[8] In the U.S. example, winner-take-all politics and adversarial public/private-sector interactions characterize the relationship between state and society. Narrow interest groups proliferate and compete with each other to lobby the Congress and executive branch. Regulatory agencies likewise proliferate, often with overlapping jurisdictions, in response to public policy problems of various eras. The constitution reserves substantial power to the states, while dividing federal powers among executive, legislative and judicial branches. Policies rarely target specific economic activities, firms or industries, except when particular interest groups gain political favor. Such policies are politically vulnerable because disfavored groups oppose them, and they conflict with individualist ideology. Consequently, the credibility of an individualist state generally covaries negatively with the specificity of the policies it attempts to implement. But, on the other hand, individualist states implement highly specific policies relatively infrequently.

Communitarianism has authoritarian and democratic variants. Authoritarian communitarian states impose their views of the national interest on society, often through corporatist political arrangements. Corporatist, authoritarian states charter interest groups and regulate their numbers by giving them exclusive franchises to represent particular constituencies, such as labor or industry. These groups then enjoy formal standing to join with state bureaucracies in collaborative economic decisionmaking.[9]

Democratic communitarianism also restricts competition among interest groups, but on a voluntary basis driven by corporatist norms of inclusiveness. Policy in democratic corporatist states derives from the "voluntary and informal coordination of conflicting objectives through continuous political bargaining among interest groups, state bureaucracies, and political parties" [Katzenstein 1985, p. 32]. Policy networks linking interest groups and government range from informal to state-mandated. Often, these networks provide forums for direct negotiation of compensation to groups forced to adjust to international competitive pressures. They also help states implement highly specific economic strategies and in some circumstances to influence firms' strategic decisions. In Japan, for example, MITI and the association of business enterprises (*Keidanren*) work together to address issues at economy, sector, industry, product market and enterprise levels [Hart 1992].

The targeting policies permitted by corporatist policy networks affect MNCs in at least two ways. First, they influence the investment decisions of MNCs' local suppliers, competitors and partners. Second, incentives may require MNCs to comply with states' strategic objectives in such areas as plant location, local purchases, local ownership, and exports. The theory of MNC-host state bargaining suggests that interactions over new investments take place within a range of solutions determined by each side's bargaining power and preferences [Kobrin 1987; Gomes-Casseres 1990; Behrman and Grosse 1990, pp. 7-8].[10] Once established, however, MNCs' facilities may function as hostages, strengthening governments' hands in renegotiations that typically emerge over such issues as local ownership [Vernon 1971; Fagre and Wells 1982; Lecraw 1984; Behrman and Grosse 1990], or benefits such as tax holidays [Murtha 1991b, 1993; Moran 1992]. Recent empirical research has also suggested that MNCs' relationships with subsidized suppliers can play out a similar dynamic, particularly when they involve difficult-to-replace inputs, or when MNCs rely on the subsidies to support a strategic price advantage in world markets [Murtha 1991a, 1991b, 1993].

Given this anticipated shift in bargaining leverage, what explains managers' willingness to commit resources to investments or relationships that are susceptible to host government intervention? Several studies have offered implications that shed light on this question. They share a degree of skepticism toward the classical IB assumption that managers fail to anticipate shifts in bargaining power from MNCs toward states during projects' lives. As early as 1973, Moran suggested tactics that extractive MNCs can use to reduce the efficacy of expropriation threats. These included precommitting output sales, encumbering host states with loan guarantees in world capital markets to cover new projects, and operating as management contractors rather than equity owners (Moran [1973]; see also Bergsten, Horst and Moran [1978]). Other studies have suggested that MNCs give more weight to stability of governments' policies than to preferences that governments might offer, since preferences can be rescinded [Grosse 1989; Moran 1992]. Similar considerations may have led MNCs to avoid responding to governments' investment and sourcing incentives, unless the prescribed behavior was consistent with their strategies [Robinson 1983].

These studies suggest that governments have little capacity to affect MNCs' strategies. Murtha [1991b, 1993] found statistical support, however, for propositions suggesting that governments' capabilities to affect MNCs' strategies vary with their states' reputations for following through on announced policies. Reputations, in turn, depended on attributes of national policy networks. Attributes that associate with corporatism, such as electoral rules that place a high value on legislative consensus, positively associated with managers' perceptions that government policies tended to persist in time. Where policy networks displayed attributes of interest group competition, managers placed high values on self-enforcement mechanisms that serve as credible commitments[11] for bargains involving governments [Murtha 1991a]. Examples included prepaid subsidies, site-specific infrastructural investments, and transaction-specific investments by subsidized local suppliers. Moran [1992] has argued that MNCs' preferences for precommitments rather than tax increment funding places less wealthy states at a disadvantage.

Our discussion of Dimensions 1 and 2 has focused on how domestic political institutions affect states' strategic capabilities, and on how these capabilities, in turn, affect MNCs' strategies. In the next section, we discuss how states' foreign policy capabilities affect and are affected by MNCs' strategies.

Dimension 3: International Autonomy and Foreign Policy Capabilities: Security vs. Prosperity

The existence of a state, in the classical view, requires a national territory and "physical force for its domination" [Weber 1978, p. 902]. This condition derives from sovereignty, which precludes the existence of any superseding authority within states' territories and defines them as autonomous, juridical equals in the international community. In practice, however, power asymmetry [Morgenthau 1971], economic interdependence [Keohane and Nye 1977], and common interest [Keohane 1984] may lead to cooperation among states or to relationships of dominance and dependence.

MNCs pose a challenge to sovereignty. Because they operate across borders, their networks can transmit national policies to other jurisdictions [Vernon 1971]. MNCs can also evade state authority by transferring operations among countries, shopping for policies that suit their strategies. States can counterbalance these MNC capabilities by cooperating to pursue joint policy objectives [Vernon 1971, 1981; Behrman and Grosse 1990; Preston and Windsor 1992].[12] For example, in provisions on trade-related investment measures (TRIMS) negotiated in the General Agreement on Tariffs and Trade (GATT) Uruguay round, states agreed not to impose local content, export quota or import offset requirements on MNCs. But cooperation may not, on average, dominate either economic or political power as a motivation for governments' policies toward MNCs. In addition to prosperity goals, states use MNCs to pursue international autonomy and security objectives [Kudrle and Lenway 1991; Kudrle 1991].

The United States, for example, continues to use MNCs to implement embargoes against adversaries. Kobrin [1989] has argued that sanctions have lost effectiveness as U.S. policy, in part because host countries do not recognize U.S. claims of extraterritorial jurisdiction over its MNCs' foreign affiliates. Sanctions have, however, gained greater currency as tools of multilateral diplomacy in instances such as the Persian Gulf Crisis of 1990-91. Unless all countries cooperate, sanctions reallocate market shares from participants' firms to those of nonparticipants. But even when sanctions enjoy broad international support, they subordinate national prosperity interests to security goals by reducing economic activity. Jacobson, Lenway and Ring [1993] show that sanctions also raise MNCs' internal coordination costs, reducing organizational efficiency.

Dimension 4: Legitimacy and the Balance of Economic and Noneconomic Values: Equity vs. Efficiency

States, in the classical view, require legitimacy [Weber 1978]. Benjamin and Duvall [1985, p. 36] suggested that states' policies derive legitimacy, in part, from "organizing principles addressed to the resolution or management of the tensions among conceptions of freedom, equality, order, and justice." They illustrate ways of resolving these tensions with examples that show how political and economic development interrelate as countries pass through different stages of industrialization. States in early stages of rapid industrialization, they argue (p. 39), "resolve the tensions unambiguously in favor of economic freedom and social order" (e.g., Singapore). Developing states may also less easily afford the dampened economic incentives that occur when tax systems subordinate property rights to income redistribution. Okun [1975] called this dilemma the equity vs. efficiency trade-off.

As countries industrialize, demands for income equality, political freedom and social justice offer increasingly potent challenges to order and property

522 JOURNAL OF INTERNATIONAL BUSINESS STUDIES, THIRD QUARTER 1994

rights (e.g., Korea, Taiwan, Thailand). States that value economic growth more than equitable distribution of the gains have often sacrificed political freedoms. Industrialized states, however, preserve their legitimacy only by responding to claims for fairness. Middle-class expansion brings demands for more comprehensive enfranchisement. Political freedom and social justice assume greater salience. So also do claims for compensation by society members who are adversely affected by international competition. As time passes, the equity/efficiency trade-off offers converging implications for industrialized and industrializing countries.

This dynamic has implications for MNCs. States in rapidly industrializing countries must strike a balance between local and foreign capital owners' interests, as citizens increase their claims on the gains from growth [Evans 1979]. MNCs often face regulations that require local partners, technology sharing, licensing, local content, or other arrangements that give host nationals access to their firm-specific advantages [Tang and Yu 1992]. Industrialized countries, on average, have placed fewer restraints on IFDI. In the U.S., where IFDI substantially exceeded OFDI in the late 1980s, political calls emerged for restrictions on inflows (see Graham and Krugman [1989]; Kudrle [1991]). These developments increase the complexity of global patterns of regulation and the political sensitivity of MNCs' operations, complicating managers' strategic tasks.

APPLYING THE FRAMEWORK

In the next two subsections, we apply our dimensions within strategy frameworks that address managerial, organizational and country levels of analysis. First, we examine our framework's relevance to managers and organizations by considering political aspects of frameworks in the process school of international organizational research (see Doz and Prahalad [1991]). These mutually consistent frameworks are most comprehensively presented by Prahalad and Doz [1987] and Bartlett and Ghoshal [1989], although they have many important antecedents. Then we suggest ways in which our framework intersects with Michael Porter's "diamond" model of country capabilities [1990].

Global Management and the State: States and MNCs as Interacting Authority Systems

Contemporary international management theory characterizes the principal task of multinational managers as a continual process of reconciling efficiency pressures for global integration with political and market forces that demand local responsiveness (see Prahalad and Doz [1987]). Governmental and managerial authority interact in the administration of national economies, as states and firms seek to balance local and global criteria for strategy implementation.

Domestic Capabilities: Authority vs. Markets. States and firms seek to optimize efficiency but for different objectives. Efficiency enhances national social welfare and creates the basis for international cost leadership strategies for MNCs (see Porter [1990]). MNCs and states have historically conflicted over efficiency, however, because minimum efficient scale production for many activities exceeded the size of most national markets. Responsive MNCs established inefficient plants in many countries to meet governments' demands for employment. MNCs could bury any resulting cost disadvantages in high prices made possible by product differentiation and/or protected markets. Local responsiveness and global integration seemed to function as a trade-off.

In a globalizing world economy, however, the interaction between efficiency and responsiveness has moved away from trade-off and conflict between MNCs and states toward synergy and collaboration. The boundaries of market segments rarely match the boundaries of countries, and even differentiated products have become subject to price competition. Governments still demand responsiveness. But any plants that MNCs establish must meet global standards of efficiency in order for countries to stay competitive [Stopford and Strange 1991]. The allocation of efficient production sites among countries and the pattern of trade that emerges for their outputs depends, in part, on firm/state interaction. Historically given political institutions influence states' capabilities to make credible, discriminating choices in these interactions.

Process research on international management suggests that MNCs can accommodate variation in states' capabilities and policies by differentiating management processes, headquarters/subsidiary relationships and organizational structures across affiliates. Functions and businesses within each MNC vary in the degree of integration and coordination necessary to conduct efficient operations. Most MNCs can maintain efficient networks that assign global responsibility for some activities to their home countries, assign other activities to every country where they operate, divide responsibility for others among just a few countries, and assign global responsibility for still others to single affiliates outside of the home country. The combination of decentralized production with global networking allows MNCs to satisfy multiple states' demands for facilities, but recover coordination and responsiveness costs through learning and information-cost economizing [Bartlett and Ghoshal 1989; Prahalad and Doz 1987].

Organizational differentiation and decentralization broadens the scope for local responsiveness in the context of integrated operations. As Kogut [1985b] points out, multiple siting also provides MNCs with flexibility to hedge against state interference in any one country, by retaining discretion to shift production. Multiple siting, however, has limitations. These include redundancy costs and requirements for stable local labor relations. More importantly, optimal activity assignments match MNCs' global needs with the organization-specific resources of national affiliates. These resources build up over time from the interaction of local factor endowments, MNCs' technologies and affiliate management team capabilities, as well as from the imprint of states' strategies on MNCs' local organizations. Arbitrary shifting of activities can waste these resources.

Our framework suggests that MNCs will design their networks to avoid exposing strategic activities to disruption by arbitrary government policy shifts. The complex networks envisioned in process research can structurally accommodate government policies that differ widely across countries. But networks operate most efficiently, once established, when public policies vary over relatively narrow ranges within countries. National institutions define these ranges and determine their stability.

Policy Networks and State Autonomy: Individualism vs. Communitarianism.
Unique and common attributes of national political institutions become easier to distinguish and less prone to distortion when they are viewed through appropriate ideological lenses. Both individualist and communitarian ideologies exert a normative influence on the strategies and organizational structures of home and incoming MNCs, because political enfranchisement requires that firms take part in national policy networks. Corporatist policy networks hold all participants, including MNCs, accountable for consultation with other participants and for meeting communitarian norms of social performance. Accommodation to local political realities may slow MNCs' decisionmaking processes and reduce their discretion over production location. Home MNCs also face pressure to keep production at home and concentrate FDI on downstream value chain activities such as marketing. The returns, in theory, include access to workforces that have been socialized to cooperate in industrial adjustment, in part through entitlements such as retraining allowances and relocation assistance [Katzenstein 1985; Freeman 1989]. MNCs' affiliates in corporatist host countries may face difficulties developing local political relationships and may experience unequal treatment compared to domestic counterparts. Alliances with local partners and indigenization of top management may help MNCs integrate into host policy networks. But these strategies cannot substitute for trust and relationship-specific knowledge, both of which take time to accumulate.

The pluralist policy networks that emerge in individualist political economies offer both foreign and home MNCs relatively open, equal access to the political process. But because individualist states rarely target specific firms, individual firms may face lower returns to political action than in communitarian systems. It is consistent with individualist ideology for states to implement policies that have economy-wide impact by, for example, supporting education or basic research. In these examples, firms that make astute choices in labor markets and new product applications benefit most.

The relatively noninterventionist postures of most individualist states does not mean that MNCs can overlook the potential impact of pluralist policy networks on their businesses. Individualist regulatory systems provide ample opportunities for interest groups, including home- and foreign-based firms, to exercise influence through petitions, litigation, hearings and lobbying for new regulations. Pluralist interest group competition requires MNCs to monitor not only governments' policies but also competitors' political strategies and those of such nongovernmental interests as consumers. MNCs have used political processes (particularly technical administrative procedures such as those provided in U.S. anti-dumping legislation) to raise competitors' costs, disrupt their production and marketing programs and divert their managerial resources. Opportunities to benefit from such strategies have emerged as firm-specific advantages, based on MNCs' value chain configurations, those of their competitors and the patterns of national regulations that affect them [Milner 1987; Yoffie 1988; Lenway and Schuler 1991; Salorio 1993].

Foreign Policy Capabilities and Targets: Political vs. Economic Objectives. MNCs' network configurations create patterns of leverage for home and host governments who might use embargoes on intrafirm transactions as foreign policy instruments. Understanding these patterns requires a systemwide perspective, not just pairwise analysis of the national interest of the home state as it relates to the interests of host states. As a firm becomes more internationalized, the potential effects of embargoes become more difficult to anticipate and evaluate. Intrafirm flows between non-belligerent countries may take on political significance because they affect business in third countries. The disruption of interdependencies among affiliates or with suppliers in an embargoed country may expose an entire MNC to disruption, involving countries with no obvious geopolitical linkage to a given set of belligerents (see Lenway and Crawford [1986]).

Understanding these exposures poses an increasing challenge to global strategy formulation. In the 1990s, superpower nuclear confrontation was replaced by a search for new instruments of control over proliferating small conflicts. Security policies to deal with these realities have not taken shape. As long as policymakers prefer economic pressure to military intervention, the threat of sanctions will retain considerable potential to disrupt MNCs' operations. In sourcing and location decisions, MNCs need to consider affiliates' abilities to function independently of parents or other affiliates that provide technologies and inputs [Jacobson, Lenway and Ring 1993].

Noneconomic Values: Equity vs. Efficiency. Each state's legitimacy has an historical basis in actions that successive governments have taken to sustain a social order consistent with the nation's values. Economic values and the maintenance of prosperity are important for all countries. But as countries reach prosperity, noneconomic values assume greater importance. Applying the process framework suggests that managers must do more than respond to these values on a country-by-country basis. They must also search for themes and criteria that cut across countries, create interdependencies, and demand a coordinated approach. Equity, environmental sustainability, and social justice are among the major areas of concern.

526   JOURNAL OF INTERNATIONAL BUSINESS STUDIES, THIRD QUARTER 1994

The years since World War II have seen increasing international economic openness, in part as a reaction to the damage that protectionism caused to global prosperity in the 1930s. The parallel development and diffusion of Keynesian economics also increased the importance that states place on domestic social welfare, including equity. States' support for global openness was set on a collision course with their domestic equity concerns when rapid increases in imports were perceived as "a threat by various national governments whose social and economic policies were upset by rising import penetration" [Bartlett and Ghoshal 1989, p. 10]. In many countries, interest groups will continue to demand policies to ease the discomfort of adjustment to international competition. If implemented, such policies would detract from managers' discretion to internationally allocate activities to optimize efficiency. Our analysis of Dimensions 1 and 2 is relevant to these prospects and the demands they place on firms.

The areas of environment and social justice offer MNCs greater scope for proactive policy choices that can enhance competitive advantage. Commitments to gender equality, racial equality and workforce diversity increase MNCs' discretion in local labor markets and ensure their capabilities to draw on global talent pools to fill positions. Although MNCs may implement country-specific social responsibility programs, they can generalize and internationally transfer policies that guide them. As international environmental and safety standards converge, empirical evidence suggests that MNCs that coordinate policies and technology have gained first mover advantages that raised their profits relative to those of more reactive competitors [Nehrt 1993].

Between Nations and Firms: Where Do States Fit?

Most strategy-oriented IB studies have adopted managers, firms and industries as principal units of analysis. Recently, however, interest has increased in studies of the contributions that country capabilities make to MNCs' international competitiveness (e.g., Porter [1990]; Kogut [1991, 1993]; Shan and Hamilton [1991]; Murtha [1991a]). The best-known among these studies, Porter's *The Competitive Advantage of Nations* [1990, p. 1], addresses the question, Why does a nation become the home base for successful international competitors in an industry? After comparing multiple industries across ten countries, Porter's research team concluded, "Competitive advantage is created and sustained through a highly localized process. Differences in national economic structures, values, cultures, institutions, and histories contribute profoundly to competitive success" (p. 19). The graphic visualization of the theory presents four principal determinants of country competitiveness as the points of a diamond. These determinants include factor conditions, demand conditions, related and supporting industries, and industrial organization as defined by firm strategy, industry structure and rivalry. The study refers to two additional determinants—government and chance—as outside forces.

Porter's new paradigm stands as a significant, empirically grounded critique that rejects monocausal explanations of competitiveness, among them government policy, in a world knit together by MNCs rather than by trade among unaffiliated parties. Government targeting, the study pointed out, created meaningful global competitive positions for only a few countries in a few industries. Even successful targeters also experienced failures. Government influence lacked any systematic pattern. Public policy appeared able to affect the elements of the diamond, but was not part of it (pp. 126-28).

Several studies have suggested that the Porter team erred by not including government policy as an element in the diamond (see Rugman [1991]; Stopford and Strange [1991]). Our framework suggests that a methodological issue may underlie this debate. The diamond's integrity as a causal framework, as opposed to an illustrative heuristic, depends on demonstrating a systematic association between its elements and competitiveness as a dependent variable. In our view, the diamond has, so far, failed to demonstrate systematic government effects because it operationalizes them as public policies. Public policy represents a different level of analysis from the other elements of the diamond. Differences in levels of analysis among elements of a model require the specification of causal mechanisms and rules of aggregation to account for cross-level effects. Otherwise, misspecification and fallacies of aggregation can result in specious inferences (see Roberts, Hulin and Rousseau [1978, pp. 81-109]; Arrow [1951]).

Since the Porter team examined the influence of lasting economy, firm and industry structures rather than of management teams' transient policies, consistency required that it examine the influence of state organization structures, rather than of governments' policies. Put another way, just as corporate resources for international competition do not arise from policies of governments and firms, but from "the outcome of thousands of struggles for competitive advantage . . . " [Porter 1990, p. 9], so do the political resources that matter accumulate in decisions made within evolving institutions that maintain the consistency of contemporary preferences with nations' historic values. In the discussion that follows, we apply our framework to demonstrate how cross-national differences in political institutions and state strategic capabilities can help systematize the effects of governments' policies within the context of the diamond model.

Domestic Capabilities: Authority vs. Markets. Our framework explains cross-national variations in industrial strategies as outcomes of differences in the organizational capabilities that political institutions provide to governments. These differences limit the transferability of strategies from one country to another. As institutions and economies evolve, the range of implementable strategies also changes. Any country's success with a particular strategy (say, providing export subsidies to heavy industries) depends on the match of strategy, organizational capabilities and timing, as well as on exogenous factors. No one policy can succeed for every country, and certainly not for all at the same time.

528   JOURNAL OF INTERNATIONAL BUSINESS STUDIES, THIRD QUARTER 1994

The Porter team's evolutionary stages theory of competitive development in national economies (Chapter 10) provides an interesting tableau on which to frame testable propositions that highlight synergies between our framework and the diamond. According to the study, government policies should help to "deploy a nation's resources (labor and capital) with high and rising levels of productivity," to build an economy that is "continually upgrading." Productivity improvement increases skills, incomes and living standards for a country's population (pp. 617-18). As countries upgrade, they incrementally build up and engage the sources of advantage in the diamond, passing through stages of factor-, investment-, and innovation-driven development. At a final, wealth-driven stage, competitive advantage ebbs. Obstacles to progress arise at transitions among the first three stages, in maintaining the innovation-driven stage, and in returning dynamism to economies at the wealth-driven stage. During such times, economic change threatens a relatively high proportion of a country's established firms.

Our framework suggests that developmental states may have a strategic advantage over regulatory states at the factor-driven stage and in implementing policies to promote transitions from the factor-driven to investment-driven stages. This transition implies a change from extractive, labor-intensive and commodity-producing industries toward large-scale industries that perform downstream processing and toward manufacturing industries that employ existing technology to make standardized products. At this stage, countries can acquire international advantage only in industries that require large capital investments, retain a large labor-cost component, and use production technology that can efficiently meet world demand with relatively few plants (p. 551).

The criteria for competitive industries in investment-driven development closely match those for targetable industries in economic models of strategic trade policy. In these models, government targeting of domestic firms constitutes a credible commitment that deters international competitors from retaliating for fear of provoking a price war in which the state's deep pockets predetermine the winner [Spencer and Brander 1983; Brander and Spencer 1985; Krugman 1984]. Developmental states may succeed in identifying industries to effectively target at the investment-driven stage, because there are relatively few industries to choose from that meet the criteria. This does not, however, guarantee against mistakes. Gomes-Casseres documented misjudgments in the Korean Government's attempt to imitate the success of Japan's early developmentalist policies targeting heavy industries [1988a, 1988b]. Korean labor costs had already risen too high, and its investments added out-of-date plant to existing global excess capacity. Subsequent efforts to leapfrog the investment-driven stage to enter the innovation-driven stage required more regulatory approaches to economic management.

Regulatory states may have a strategic advantage in transitions from investment- to innovation-driven growth. Innovation-driven growth depends on responding to market signals in fast-changing high technology industries. Optimal policies to support high technology fund workforce education, infrastructural development and basic research, while keeping markets competitive so that they reward entrepreneurship and innovation. The Porter study advocated these policies for all countries, implying that the team saw the global economy as a whole shifting toward innovation-driven growth.

Policy Networks and State Autonomy: Individualism vs. Communitarianism. When transitions and dynamism confront a high proportion of a country's firms with change, they also threaten a high proportion of its entrenched political interests. Governments face increased levels of political conflict as their policies promote resource flows from declining industries toward emerging industries.

Corporatist policy networks may have strategic advantages in factor-driven development and in resolving conflicts in transitions from factor- to investment-driven stages. These advantages associate with two types of state capabilities. First, corporatist networks enhance the target specificity of states' policy instruments. Second, tripartite wage/price bargains set by labor, business associations, and government help to maintain low labor costs, which are critical to success in both stages. These same capabilities become liabilities in transitions to innovation-driven development. Annual tripartite bargains obstruct industrial adjustment by reducing firm discretion and labor market flexibility. The complexity and dynamism of innovation-driven development outstrips the abilities of government decisionmakers to choose winners and losers. Capabilities to target at high degrees of specificity increase the chances that a government will intervene with consequences that distort markets. Pluralist policy networks may have advantages in innovation-driven development, as they tend to minimize states' economic roles.

Foreign Policy Capabilities and Targets: Political vs. Economic Objectives. Unlike our first two dimensions, states' foreign policy capabilities are not related to competitiveness in a systematic way. Neither national security contingencies nor governments' policy responses to them can ever be fully anticipated [Lenway and Crawford 1986; Jacobson, Lenway and Ring 1993]. It is possible, however, to demonstrate the historical impact of global security arrangements on the contemporary pattern of international competitive advantage. After World War II, the victorious Allies pressed for free trade, in the belief that strong economies in Europe and Japan would stop the spread of communism. The U.S. benefited from its leadership status in the early post-war era, as its MNCs expanded to provide capital goods for reconstruction and to support military forces based abroad. Inflows of foreign-made goods enriched U.S. consumers' choices and subjected domestic firms to stiff competition. But U.S. foreign policy has sometimes compromised the competitiveness of U.S. firms through export controls on high-technology products and prohibitions on trade with political adversaries [Lenway and Crawford 1986]. Other countries' firms expanded in the gaps. Bartlett [1992, p. 323], for example, argued that a U.S. embargo on a Caterpillar

530   JOURNAL OF INTERNATIONAL BUSINESS STUDIES, THIRD QUARTER 1994

pipe-laying equipment sale to Russia ceded a long-term advantage to a Japanese competitor.

Noneconomic Values: Equity vs. Efficiency. It is difficult to distinguish causal order between noneconomic values and the elements of the diamond. Equity generally requires redistribution, which becomes easier under economic conditions of growth [Okun 1975]. The Porter study's prescriptions were intended to foster these conditions. Competitiveness at advanced stages of development, however, requires flexibility. Workforce members may experience shorter hours and greater transience in employment than has typified advanced industrialized economies in the past [*New York Times* 1993, pp. 17, 29]. The expectation of equity seems a necessary condition for individuals to collaborate in a process that increases career uncertainty. The legitimacy of state institutions will play an important role in creating goodwill among groups and individuals to tolerate the dynamism of advanced industrial development.

CONCLUSION

Contributions to the literatures on sociology and political science have focused on "bringing the state back in" to models of social and political phenomena [Skocpol 1985]. International business scholarship, as applied social science, places a benchmark value on efficient international markets and tends to regard states as causes of deviation from this ideal. But the international economy links together domestic economies in which varied institutional arrangements govern exchange. Given these differences, states seek either to accommodate or shape MNCs' organizations, in light of the national interest.

Although MNCs often bring innovation and growth to countries, this does not mean that states can ignore the political consequences of economic change. Just as effective MNCs optimize competing, interdependent values of efficiency, responsiveness and learning [Bartlett and Ghoshal 1989], states must optimize efficiency, equity and security. Institutional arrangements whereby countries manage or fail to manage the political consequences of economic growth make a difference for the management of MNCs' relations with host and home states, and for internal MNC management.

Political organization creates the context for economic organization [Lindblom 1977; Freeman 1989], as the transitions in Asia and Central Europe make evident. Countries vary in their capabilities to implement new economic strategies without significant changes in social and political organization structures. National social and political structural evolution moves slowly, barring cataclysmic social revolution [Skocpol 1979]. Consequently, the attributes of such structures make powerful predictors of countries' economic strategies and implementation capabilities.

Incorporating political institutional attributes into IB frameworks lets us model state and government on a level of generality comparable to that of firm and management, using mutually consistent terminology and concepts. It strengthens an area of distinction for the IB research tradition and creates opportunities for IB and underlying social science disciplines to contribute to each other's development. It also improves our understanding of how state and corporate strategies interact to shape international business outcomes.

NOTES

1. State and government should be distinguished not only from each other, but also from country, which refers to the national territory or more comprehensively to that which is contained within it, and nation, which refers to a people. See Weber [1978].

2. A dominant regulatory orientation does not exclude the possibility that a state will intervene in economic affairs. Johnson [1982] suggests, however, that regulatory states may not have the institutional capacity to make this intervention effective.

3. MITI has the responsibility for devising and implementing Japan's industrial policy.

4. Bergsten and Graham listed notable discriminatory U.S. policies, including FDI restrictions in broadcasting, coastal shipping, nuclear energy, oil pipeline, and domestic transport industries [1992, p. 30]. These policies, however, have rarely associated with state-led investment strategies.

5. For example, Japan permitted IBM to establish a wholly owned affiliate only after it agreed to locally license technology [Encarnation and Mason 1990, pp. 26-29].

6. The terms "value chain" [Porter 1985] or "value-added chain" [Kogut, 1985a] have been widely adopted among strategy researchers to refer to the sets of linked organizational activities that firms perform in bringing their products to market. The generic value chain consists of primary and support activities. Primary activities include inbound logistics, production, marketing, outbound logistics; and service. Examples of support activities include human resources and finance. In practice, individual firms' value chains consist of any number of particular activities that fit into these categories. International strategies are often analyzed as a process of coordinating value chain activities matched to countries on the basis of cost and product differentiation opportunities (see Porter [1990, Ch. 2]).

7. In 1982, for example, Taiwan's economics minister withdrew a promise of import protection for a General Motors truck plant, citing efficiency concerns. Although the plant had just opened, GM pulled out [Wade 1990, p. 155].

8. Pluralist models assume that competition among interest groups yields public policies acceptable to all participants in the political process. States exist as interest group forums, with little independent policymaking capacity (see Krasner [1984, pp. 226-30]).

9. The German and Italian fascist regimes of the interwar era provide the most non-controversial examples of authoritarian corporatist regimes. In the years since World War II, many would agree that Franco's Spain and Pinochet's Chile exemplified the type. It is possible to array the many contemporary corporatist states of Latin America and Asia along a continuum from authoritarianism to democracy. For more on these distinctions, see, for example, the edited series by O'Donnel, Schmitter and Whitehead.

10. Behrman and Grosse [1990, p. 8] list host government bargaining power sources as control over market access, resource endowments, low-cost production factors, and government contracts. MNCs gain bargaining power from access to funds, technology, managerial skills, information, foreign inputs, and global markets.

11. The concept of a credible commitment is due to Schelling [1960] and may be defined as a self-evidently irrevocable action.

12. Preston and Windsor [1992, p. 4] argue that international policy regimes facilitate and regulate trade and investment flows as well as regulate the activities of domestic and multinational enterprises that participate in the global economy. They suggest (p.7) that the critical features of regimes include: (1) decisionmaking procedures and rules that allow the implementation of international agreements that may or may not involve formal institutional arrangements; (2) agreements on legitimacy and founding principles, e.g., the multilateral reduction of tariff barriers in the GATT; and (3) expected norms of behavior that support these principles.

532   JOURNAL OF INTERNATIONAL BUSINESS STUDIES, THIRD QUARTER 1994

REFERENCES

Arrow, Kenneth. 1951. Social choice and individual values. New Haven: Yale University Press.

Bartlett, Christopher A. & Sumantra Ghoshal. 1989. *Managing across borders: The transnational solution.* Boston: Harvard Business School Press.

_____. 1992. Komatsu Limited. In Christopher Bartlett & Sumantra Ghoshal, *Transnational management*, 311-26. Boston: Irwin.

Behrman, Jack N. & Robert Grosse. 1990. *International business and governments: Issues and institutions.* Columbia, S.C.: University of South Carolina Press.

Benjamin, Roger & Raymond Duvall. 1985. The capitalist state in context. In Roger Benjamin & Stephen L. Elkins, editors, *The democratic state*, 1-57. Lawrence, Kan.: University of Kansas Press.

Bergsten, C. Fred, Thomas Horst & Theodore H. Moran. 1978. *American multinationals and American interests.* Washington, D.C.: The Brookings Institution.

_____ & Edward M. Graham. 1992. Needed: New international rules for foreign direct investment. *International Trade Journal*, 7(1): 15-44.

Boarman, Patrick & Hans Schollhammer, editors. 1975. *Multinational corporations and governments.* New York: Praeger.

Boddewyn, Jean. 1988. Political aspects of MNE theory. *Journal of International Business Studies*, 19(3): 341-65.

Brander, James A. & Barbara Spencer. 1985. Export subsidies and international market share rivalry. *Journal of International Economics*, 18: 83-100.

Brewer, Thomas L., editor. 1985. *Political risks in international business: New directions for research, management, and public policy.* New York: Praeger.

_____. 1992. An issue-area approach to the analysis of MNE-government relations. *Journal of International Business Studies*, 23(2): 295-310.

_____. 1993. Government policies, market imperfections, and foreign direct investment. *Journal of International Business Studies*, 24(1): 101-20.

Cowhey, Peter F. 1993. Domestic institutions and the credibility of international commitments: Japan and the United States. *International Organization*, 47(2): 299-326.

de la Torre, Jose. 1981. Foreign investment and economic development: Conflict and negotiation. *Journal of International Business Studies*, 12(2): 9-33.

Doner, Richard F. 1991. *Driving a bargain: Automobile industrialization and Japanese firms in Southeast Asia.* Berkeley: University of California Press.

Doz, Yves L. 1986. Government policies and global industries. In Michael Porter, editor, *Competition in global industries*, 225-66. Boston: Harvard Business School Press.

_____ & C. K. Prahalad. 1980. How MNCs cope with host government intervention. *Harvard Business Review*, March-April: 149-57.

_____. 1991. Managing DMNCs: A search for a new paradigm. *Strategic Management Journal*, 12 (Summer Special Issue): 145-64.

Encarnation, Dennis J. & Louis T. Wells. 1986. Competitive strategies in global industries: A view from host states. In Michael Porter, editor, *Competition in global industries*, 267-90. Boston: Harvard Business School Press.

_____ & Mark Mason. 1990. Neither MITI nor America: The political economy of capital liberalization in Japan. *International Organization*, 44(1): 25-54.

Evans, Peter B. 1979. *Dependent development: The alliance of multinational, state and local capital in Brazil.* Princeton, N.J.: Princeton University Press.

Fagre, Nathan & Louis T. Wells. 1982. Bargaining power of multinationals and host governments. *Journal of International Business Studies*, 13(2): 9-23.

Freeman, John R. 1989. *Democracy and markets: The politics of mixed economies.* Ithaca: Cornell University Press.

Gerschenkron, Alexander. 1962. Economic backwardness in historical perspective. Cambridge: Harvard University Press.

Gomes-Casseres, Benjamin. 1988a. Korea's technology strategy. HBS case #9-338-137. Boston: Harvard Business School Publishing Division.

_____. 1988b. State and markets in Korea. HBS case #9-387-181. Boston: Harvard Business School Publishing Division.

_____. 1990. Firm ownership preferences and host government restrictions: An integrated approach. *Journal of International Business Studies*, 21(1): 1-22.

Graham, Edward M. & Paul R. Krugman. 1991. *Foreign direct investment in the United States.* Washington, D.C.: Institute for International Economics.

Grosse, Robert. 1989. *Multinationals in Latin America.* London: Routledge.

Hart, Jeffrey. 1992. *Rival capitalists: International competitiveness in the United States, Japan, and Western Europe.* Ithaca, N.Y.: Cornell University Press.

Jacobson, Carol, Stefanie Ann Lenway & Peter S. Ring. 1993. The political embeddedness of private economic transactions. *Journal of Management Studies*, 30(3): 454-78.

Johnson, Chalmers. 1982. *MITI and the Japanese miracle: The growth of industrial policy: 1927-1975.* Stanford, Calif.: Stanford University Press.

Katzenstein, Peter J., editor. 1977. *Between power and plenty: Foreign economic policies of advanced industrial states.* Madison: University of Wisconsin Press.

_____. 1985. *Small states in world markets.* Ithaca, N.Y.: Cornell University Press.

Keohane, Robert O. 1984. *After hegemony: Cooperation and discord in the world political economy.* Princeton, N.J.: Princeton University Press.

_____ & Joseph S. Nye. 1977. *Power and interdependence.* Boston: Little, Brown and Company.

Kim, W. Chan. 1988. The effects of competition and corporate political responsiveness on multinational bargaining power. *Strategic Management Journal*, 9(3): 289-95.

Kobrin, Stephen J. 1979. Political risk: A review and reconsideration. *Journal of International Business Studies*, 10(1): 67-80.

_____. 1982. *Managing political risk assessment.* Berkeley: University of California Press.

_____. 1987. Testing the bargaining hypothesis in the manufacturing sector in developing countries. *International Organization*, 41(4): 609-38.

_____. 1989. Enforcing export embargoes through multinational corporations: Why doesn't it work anymore? *Business in the Contemporary World*, Winter: 31-42.

Kogut, Bruce M. 1985a. Designing global strategies: Comparative and competitive value-added chains. *Sloan Management Review*, 26(4): 15-23.

_____. 1985b. Designing global strategies: Profiting from operational flexibility. *Sloan Management Review*, 27(1): 27-38.

_____. 1989. A note on global strategies. *Strategic Management Journal*, 10(4): 383-90.

_____. 1991. Country capabilities and the permeability of borders. *Strategic Management Journal*, 12 (Summer Special Issue): 33-48.

_____, editor. 1993. *Country competitiveness: Technology and the organizing of work.* New York: Oxford University Press.

Krasner, Stephen D. 1978. *Defending the national interest: Raw materials investments and U.S. foreign policy.* Princeton, N.J.: Princeton University Press.

_____. 1984. Approaches to the state: Alternative conceptions and historical dynamics. *Comparative Politics*, 16(2): 223-45.

Krugman, Paul R. 1984. Import protection as export promotion: International competition in the presence of oligopoly and economies of scale. In Henryk Kierzkowski, editor, *Monopolistic competition and international trade*, 180-93. Oxford, U.K.: Clarendon.

Kudrle, Robert T. & Stefanie Ann Lenway. 1991. Progress for the rich: An analysis of the Canada-U.S. free trade agreement. In Emmanuel Adler & Beverly Crawford, editors, *Progress in post-war international relations*, 235-72. New York: Columbia University Press.

_____. 1991. Good for the gander: Foreign direct investment in the United States. *International Organization*, 45(3): 397-424.

Lecraw, Donald J. 1984. Bargaining power, ownership and profitability of transnational corporations in developing countries. *Journal of International Business Studies*, 15(1): 27-43.

_____ & Allen Morrison. 1991. Transnational corporation-host country relations: A framework for analysis. *Essays in International Business*, No. 9. Columbia, South Carolina: Center for International Business Education and Research, University of South Carolina.

Lenway, Stefanie Ann & Beverly Crawford. 1986. When business becomes politics: Uncertainty and risk in east-west trade. In James Post, editor, *Research in corporate social performance and policy*, 29-53. Greenwich, Conn.: JAI Press.

_____ & Douglas A. Schuler. 1991. The determinants of corporate political involvement in trade protection: The case of the steel industry. In Robert Baldwin, editor, *Empirical studies in commercial policy*, 75-112. Chicago: University of Chicago Press for NBER.

Lindblom, Charles. 1977. *Politics and markets*. New York: Basic Books.

Lodge, George C. 1990. *Perestroika for America*. Boston: Harvard Business School Press.

March, James G. & Johan P. Olsen. 1984. The new institutionalism: Organizational factors in political life. *American Political Science Review*, 78(3): 734-49.

Mikesell, Raymond F. 1971. *Foreign direct investment in the petroleum and mineral industries*. Baltimore, Md.: Johns Hopkins Press.

Miller, Kent. 1992. A framework for integrated risk management in international business. *Journal of International Business Studies*, 23(2): 311-31.

Milner, Helen. 1987. Resisting the protectionist temptation: Industry and the making of trade policy in France and the United States during the 1970s. *International Organization*, 41(4): 639-66.

Moran, Theodore H. 1973. Transnational strategies of protection and defense by multinational corporations. *International Organization*, 27(2): 273-87.

_____. 1992. Strategic trade theory and the use of performance requirements to negotiate with multinational corporations in the third world. *International Trade Journal*, 7(1): 45-84.

Morgenthau, Hans. 1971 (fifth edition). *Politics among nations: The struggle for power and peace*. New York: Knopf.

Murtha, Thomas P. 1991a. Surviving industrial targeting: State credibility and public policy contingencies in multinational subcontracting. Journal of Law, Economics and Organization, 7(1): 117-41.

_____. 1991b. Credible enticements: Transactions costs analysis of MNCs' supplier arrangements in host-state-targeted industries. In Jerry L. Wall & Lawrence R. Jauch, editors, *Academy of Management Best Papers Proceedings*, 105-109.

_____. 1993. Credible enticements: Can host governments tailor multinational firms' organizations to suit their objectives? *Journal of Economic Behavior and Organization*, 20: 171-86.

_____ & Stefanie Ann Lenway. 1994. Country capabilities and the strategic state: How national political institutions affect multinational corporations' strategies. *Strategic Management Journal*, 15 (Summer Special Issue): forthcoming.

Nehrt, Chad. 1993. *Pollution control, investment and competitiveness: A multi-country study of the paper industry*. Unpublished Ph.D. dissertation, University of Michigan School of Business Administration, Ann Arbor.

New York Times. Facing up to global joblessness. July 10, 1993: 17, 29.

O'Donnel, Guillermo, Philippe Schmitter & Lawrence Whitehead, editors. 1986. Transitions from authoritarian rule, Vols. 1-4. Baltimore: Johns Hopkins University Press.

Okun, Arthur. 1975. *Equality and efficiency: The big tradeoff*. Washington, D.C.: The Brookings Institution.

Porter, Michael. 1985. *Competitive advantage*. New York: The Free Press.

_____. 1990. *The competitive advantage of nations*. New York: The Free Press.

Poynter, Thomas, A. 1982. Government intervention in less developed countries: The experience of multinational corporations. *Journal of International Business Studies*, 13(1): 9-25.

Prahalad, C.K. & Yves L. Doz. 1987. *The multinational mission: Balancing local demands and global vision*. New York: The Free Press.

Preston, Lee E. & Duane Windsor. 1992. *The rules of the game in the global economy: Policy regimes for international business*. Boston: Kluwer.

Ring, Peter S., Stefanie Ann Lenway & Michele Govekar. 1990. Management of the political imperative in international business. *Strategic Management Journal*, 11(2): 141-51.

Roberts, Karlene H., Charles L. Hulin & Denise M. Rousseau. 1978. *Developing an interdisciplinary
science of organizations*. San Francisco: Jossey-Bass.

Robinson, Richard D. 1983. *Performance requirements for international business: U.S. management
response*. New York: Praeger.

Rugman, Alan. 1991. Diamond in the rough. *Business Quarterly*, Winter.

Salorio, Eugene. 1993. Strategic use of import protection: Seeking shelter for competitive advantage.
In Alan Rugman & Alain Verbeke, editors, *Research in global strategic management*. Greenwich,
Conn.: JAI Press.

Schelling, Thomas. 1960. *The strategy of conflict*. Cambridge, Mass.: Harvard University Press.

Shan, Weijian W. & William Hamilton. 1991. Country-specific advantage and international cooperation. *Strategic Management Journal*, 12(6): 419-32.

Skocpol, Theda. 1979. *States and social revolutions*. Cambridge, U.K.: Cambridge University Press.

_____. 1985. Bringing the state back in: Strategies of analysis in current research. In Peter B. Evans,
Dietrich Rueschemeyer & Theda Skocpol, editors, *Bringing the state back in*, 3-43. New York:
Cambridge University Press.

Spencer, Barbara & James A. Brander. 1983. International R&D rivalry and industrial strategy. *Review
of Economic Studies*, 50 (October): 707-22.

Stopford, John & Susan Strange. 1991. *Rival states, rival firms: Competition for world market shares*.
Cambridge, U.K.: Cambridge University Press.

Tallman, Stephen. 1988. Home country political risk and foreign direct investment in the United States.
Journal of International Business Studies, 19(2): 219-34.

Tang, Ming-Je & Chwo-ming Joseph Yu. 1992. Regulating the entry of multinational enterprises:
Models and practices. *International Trade Journal*, 7(1): 131-50.

Teece, David. 1986. Transaction cost economics and the multinational enterprise: An assessment.
Journal of Economic Behavior and Organization, 7: 21-45.

Vernon, Raymond. 1971. *Sovereignty at bay*. New York: Basic Books.

_____. 1981. Sovereignty at bay: Ten years after. *International Organization*, 41(1): 1-26.

Wade, Robert. 1990. *Governing the market*. Princeton, N.J.: Princeton University Press.

Weber, Max. 1978. *Economy and society: An outline of interpretive sociology*. Guenther Roth & Claus
Wittich, editors. Berkeley: University of California Press.

Yoffie, David. 1988. The politics of business: How an industry builds political advantage. *Harvard
Business Review*, May-June: 82-89.

[2]

Private Enforcement of Public Laws: A Theory of Legal Reform

By JONATHAN R. HAY AND ANDREI SHLEIFER*

In the last several years, the countries of Eastern Europe and the former Soviet Union (FSU) have made tremendous progress in price liberalization, privatization, and macro-economic stabilization—the standard steps of the so-called shock therapy. Yet in the aftermath of these reforms, the East European countries have begun to grow rapidly, while the countries of the FSU, particularly Russia, are at best beginning to turn around. It is not possible to explain these differences in performance in terms of either having too much shock therapy or not enough of it, since the reforms that the different countries have pursued have been broadly similar.

A more plausible reason for the difference in performance is that institutional reforms, such as those of government regulation, the legal system, and the bureaucracy, have advanced much further in Eastern Europe than in Russia (Shleifer, 1997; Simon Johnson et al., 1997). Indeed, institutional failures have arguably deterred small-business formation, foreign investment, and enterprise restructuring in the FSU. For growth to take off, Russia and other FSU countries must radically improve the quality of their institutions.

In this paper, we discuss the principles of perhaps the key institutional reform, that of the legal system. The ideas we describe were developed at the Institute for Law Based Economy in Moscow. Since its inception in 1994, the Institute has been a key player in the Russian legal reform, and we were both involved in its work. Despite the Russian specificity of some of the analysis, we believe that these ideas apply to the problems of legal reform in the rest of the FSU, as well as in emerging economies more generally

* Ironwood Holdings and Department of Economics, Harvard University, Cambridge, MA 02138, respectively. We thank Edward Glaeser and Avner Greif for comments. This paper is dedicated to the memory of Albert Sokin.

I. The State's Failure To Provide and Enforce Laws

Business people in Russia use the state legal system a lot less than they feel they need to. In a survey of shopkeepers in Russia and Poland, for example, 45 percent of Moscow respondents said that they needed to use the courts in the last two years but did not, compared to only 10 percent of the Warsaw respondents who gave this answer (Timothy Frye and Shleifer, 1997). There are two apparent reasons why the state legal system is not used in Russia: the low quality of the services it provides and the unwillingness of business people to expose themselves to the legal system, and to the government, more generally.

The quality of the legal system is notoriously bad (Avner Greif and Eugene Kandel, 1995; Katharina Pistor, 1996). The legal rules are incomplete in crucial areas needed to support existing business activity, such as real-estate registration. When legal rules do exist, in many instances judges do not know what they are. Many judges, for example, are unfamiliar with the relatively new securities law, which comes up in securities-markets disputes. Even when the law speaks to a particular matter, judges may not have the resources or inclination to verify the relevant facts. And when the facts are available and the legal rules exist, judges may be biased, corrupt, or partial to political sentiment, and hence it is by no means certain how they will rule. Finally, once a judge rules, there are often no institutions to enforce his ruling. For example, contracts between Russian and Western partners often specify London courts as the venue for dispute resolution. When the Russian partner breaks the agreement and the London court rules against him, the Western partner is still left with absolutely no mechanism of collecting his claims.

VOL. 88 NO. 2   GOVERNMENT IN TRANSITION   399

A further reason that private parties in Russia refuse to use the legal system is that they operate to some extent extralegally to begin with and, hence, do not want to expose themselves to the government. The tax system in Russia is sufficiently arbitrary and draconian that private firms are either in violation of tax law or even operate unofficially. By some calculations (Johnson et al., 1997), over 40 percent of the Russian economy is unofficial. Given that many firms have both some official and some unofficial business, the majority of Russian businesses are probably in violation of some tax, customs, foreign-exchange, or regulatory rules and, hence, would not use the official legal system to resolve disputes for fear of exposure.

The consequence of this avoidance of the legal system is that private rather than state mechanisms are used to resolve disputes. These mechanisms range from social norms and pressures, to arbitration, to employment of private but legal protection agencies, to organized crime. In some cases, where parties interact repeatedly and the stakes in individual disputes are small compared to the value of long-term relationships, peaceful private mechanisms work extremely well (Robert Ellickson, 1991, Lisa Bernstein, 1992, Greif, 1996). For example, arbitration succeeded as a means of resolving disputes between brokers on Russia's commodity and stock exchanges, who interact repeatedly and can use the exchange to enforce the arbitrator's decisions (Frye, 1996). Even illegal private enforcement organizations that gain monopoly in dispute resolution in a particular area and manage to gain acceptance for their rules and enforcement mechanisms may be reasonably efficient. Why, then, has the private resolution of disputes left Russia with what is widely regarded as a dysfunctional legal system?

The trouble is that private dispute resolution often does not work efficiently. Many commercial disputes do not fit the nice picture of repeated interactions over long periods of time, where access to the system is a valuable asset that the trading parties would not give up. This is so with debt collection, where borrowers are too far underwater to worry about the future, or with big ownership disputes. In these and other cases, there needs to be some force in enforcement.

Moreover, private rules, including those for using force, are often neither known nor accepted by the disputing parties. If person A borrows money from person B and does not repay, A's protectors might think that the appropriate rule is to extend the period of repayment, whereas B's protectors might think the appropriate rule is to kill A. Once A is dead, there may be no public lesson to be learned about what the rules are, since the potential future borrowers from B or other lenders, including A's associates, would not even generally know what rule A has violated and why he was killed. Private rules are often unrecognized, unknown, and not enforced consistently, which makes it prohibitively expensive for private parties to rely on them to structure transactions.

Last but not least, private enforcement is unhelpful in legal disputes with the government. As a consequence, private parties remain vulnerable to the threat of discretionary regulation and extortion by public officials, without any effective legal recourse (see Shleifer and Robert Vishny, 1993). The standard function of the judicial system of providing a check, however rudimentary, on other branches of government is lost with purely private enforcement of private rules.

In sum, private enforcement of private rules in Russia has emerged as a market response to the failure of the state to provide and enforce its own rules, largely because of very weak incentives in the government to provide law and order. This private mechanism has the advantage that both the disputing parties and the enforcers have economic incentives to pursue enforcement. Yet it also has the major disadvantage that private rules are often different for different enforcers, insufficiently well known, and not legitimate enough for business people to rely on them in structuring their transactions. The result is that the legal system is viewed as a failure, and a lot of trade and production simply does not take place.

A common recommendation to address this problem, in line with the traditional economists' view that laws should be publicly enforced (Douglass North, 1981), is to beef up

400   *AEA PAPERS AND PROCEEDINGS*   *MAY 1998*

the state legal system, through administrative reforms of police and judicial system, accelerated production of laws, training of judges, and so on. Unfortunately, such recommendations often overlook the fundamental problem that the incentives in the government to reform itself are lacking, and hence these reforms may fail or even backfire. When the elite units of the Russian police obtained bigger guns to fight the mafia, they simply sold these guns to the mafia at higher prices than the previous, less powerful, weapons could fetch. The reforms of the tax bureaucracy have not gone well either, in part because no government official has enough authority to shake up a system that benefits, at least indirectly, other government officials. And increases in the power of tax police have led to greater arbitrariness, abuse, and corruption. Without a "benevolent" dictatorship, a common collective memory of law and order, or at least a very strong and unified democratically elected government (none of which describes the reality of Russia at the moment), strengthening the state's legal apparatus can do more harm than good. What, then, can be done in the interim to improve law and order?

II. Private Enforcement of Public Rules

The principal argument of this paper is that the appropriate legal-reform strategy for a country like Russia is private enforcement of public rules. Public rules can address the problems of multiplicity, obscurity, and illegitimacy that plague the private rules. Private enforcement of these rules introduces powerful incentives that the public sector does not have.

The strategy of private enforcement of public rules begins with the creation of legal rules that can be enforced jointly by an extremely limited public judicial system and the much more extensive private enforcement system. From the viewpoint of the state legal system, public laws can help well-intentioned judges to resolve disputes, and even restrict the discretion of the not-so-well-intentioned judges. To the extent that laws make judges more predictable, business will rely on these laws more and hence demand the services of the official legal system.

Even when disputes are ultimately resolved by courts, however, much of the benefit of public rules comes from private parties structuring their transactions so that courts become more usable. For instance, suppose that a rule completely prohibits, and actually annuls, certain "self-dealing" transactions by corporate managers, such as sales of corporate assets to affiliated parties. When this rule exists, large shareholders will try to institute procedures that allow them to review corporate transactions and to document who the buyers are. Most of the information collection will be done by private parties who have powerful incentives to verify violations, and who can then come to a court for a very simple decision based on verifiable information that the private parties themselves provide. All a judge has to do is annul the sale. The likelihood of such annulment would make managers wary of breaking the law, and buyers wary of losing their money. Moreover, when public rules exist and are clear, judges would come under public pressure to enforce them, rather than rule corruptly, politically, or arbitrarily. Without a specific rule, it is not clear what large shareholders need to do or to document in order to use the court. Public rules work because they tell private parties what they need to do to use the legal system and thus provide incentives for them to use it.

But public laws have a further, perhaps even more significant, benefit in an emerging economy: they become the focal point of totally private contract enforcement and dispute resolution. Unlike the private rules, public laws are public, and hence private enforcers can free ride on them to structure their own activities, and to create their own reputations. Public rules can thus coordinate the expectations of market participants even with little public enforcement, similarly to the idea of coordination of beliefs in Thomas Schelling (1960), Robert Sugden (1989), and Greif (1994). Public law is particularly attractive for belief coordination because in the eyes of many people law has a degree of legitimacy that private rules do not have. In an emerging economy, these coordination benefits of public rules may be enormous.

Take the case of reputation development by private enforcers. A public rule on loan de-

VOL. 88 NO. 2 GOVERNMENT IN TRANSITION 401

faults may encourage both A's (the borrower's) and B's (the lender's) protectors to use it to resolve the dispute. Suppose this rule is quite unfavorable to the lender, B. B's protectors may still accept it, because they can then become known for enforcing widely accepted public laws and thus further their public reputation. Indeed, it may no longer be in the interest of either A's or B's protectors to enforce their own rules, because these rules would be much less well understood, undermining their reputations, and hence the demand for their services. Indeed, if B's protectors try to enforce some other rules, A's protectors can tell all market participants that B's protectors are acting arbitrarily, thereby triggering some form of collective punishment or exclusion. Last, but not least, other borrowers (and lenders) can now structure their contracts with better knowledge of what happens when a borrower defaults. A's and B's protectors now have a larger share of a larger market.

Interestingly, private enforcement organizations in Russia often ask disputing private parties for copies of their written agreements. The enforcers do not want to enforce arbitrary claims; they want to establish reputations for resolving disputes according to rules, and public rules are a chosen focal point. As a further step, dispute resolution can proceed in the shadow of private law-enforcement organizations, but without their direct participation.

Through these mechanisms, public rules acquire a reputation and legitimacy of their own. In some cases, these rules are enforced by courts, though with significant efforts by private parties to simplify the courts' decision process. In other cases, these rules are enforced by private parties without any reliance on courts. In still other cases, the parties to a dispute agree to a resolution in line with these rules without any help with enforcement, since they know what is going to be enforced. In all these ways, private enforcement of public rules can work reasonably efficiently even when public enforcement remains ineffective.

III. Which Public Rules Encourage Private Enforcement?

So far, we have spoken of legal rules, and their coordination benefits, in general terms,

without distinguishing between good and bad rules. But, of course, good rules are more likely to be used by economic agents, as well as by both the private and the public enforcers, than bad rules. What, then, constitutes good legal rules?

In line with Section II, good legal rules are those likely to be adopted by private parties for both structuring and enforcing their transactions, as well as used by courts. In general, rules that are usable by private parties and those usable by courts are the same, since both types of users are looking for simplicity, consistency with standard business practice, efficiency, the ease of verification of violations, and most importantly, effectiveness of enforcing decisions.

The standard rule-making strategy is to borrow legal rules from advanced countries, rather than to reinvent the wheel. Indeed, virtually every country in the world has borrowed most of its commercial law from a few legal systems, particularly French and German civil law and English common law (Alan Watson, 1974; René David and John Brierley, 1985). But the decision to borrow does not end the story. Legal rules both within and across traditions vary enormously, and some rules facilitate trade better than others (Rafael La Porta et al., 1998). There is thus a question of which rules to pick. More importantly, rules are specific to other elements of the legal system. In particular, Western legal rules rely on vastly more extensive judicial verification and public enforcement mechanisms than are available in a transition economy. Western rules must therefore be adjusted to facilitate private enforcement.

On this basis, we suggest three general lessons for developing legal rules for a country like Russia. First, as argued by Bernard Black et al. (1996) and Hay et al. (1996), it is better to have "bright line" rules (i.e., rules that make it easy for judges, or private enforcers, to verify violations). For example, in an advanced economy, it may be best to have a flexible anti-self-dealing rule that allows managers to undertake transactions as long as (they can show in court) these are in the interest of shareholders. Such a rule would not work in Russia because a judge could not use it and is likely to side with the manager, or with whoever pays him more, in a dispute. A better rule for Russia would prohibit and annul all transactions between the corporation and any entity in which the manager has an interest. Violations of this rule are easier to verify and punish, even if it is less flexible.

A second idea, which has not had sufficient impact on Russian law-making, is that there needs to be a private right of action, and a clear private remedy, in a dispute. In the previous example, if shareholders have no clear right to sue for self-dealing and be rewarded through a higher value of their shares (or even a part of a fine), the likelihood of enforcement is negligible. Counting on an administrative agency to enforce the law is a mistake, since the agency is more likely to listen to corporate managers than to complaining shareholders. If, in contrast, a large shareholder can bring a specific violation to a court, he is more likely to monitor the managers. The role of private enforcement in making this law work is overwhelming.

Third, whenever possible, laws must agree with prevailing practice or custom. If public laws violate the practice, then private parties may refuse to enforce them either on their own or with ultimate reference to courts. The coordination benefit of public laws would then be lost. Alternatively, when laws absolutely must change the existing practice, it is crucial to write them keeping in mind what groups of private agents would enforce them. Thus the Russian mass privatization program relied on the incentives of corporate managers to implement its rules (Maxim Boycko et al., 1995), whereas the fledgling Russian corporate law relies crucially on the incentives of large private shareholders to control the managers.

To summarize, it is difficult but possible to construct legal rules, based on adjusting the best world practice, that become the focal point of both private and public enforcement, and that are usable even in a country with extremely limited public enforcement of laws, largely because they make private parties do most of the enforcing.

IV. Toward Public Enforcement

Although this paper has advocated the benefits of private enforcement of public laws, ultimately, as a country develops, the role of the public sector in law enforcement is likely to increase. The final question we address is what can be done to improve public law enforcement.

In many cases, public law enforcement is most likely to benefit from institutional reforms outside of the law-enforcement sector proper. In Russia, these reforms include tax reform and federalism reform (see Johnson et al., 1997; Shleifer, 1997). The simplification of tax rules, combined with the reduction of marginal rates, would draw firms out of the unofficial economy thus increasing the demand for official law enforcement and reducing the demand for unofficial services. Federalism reform can create the incentives for regional governments to provide high-quality courts to attract business and expand the tax base, as well as to improve police and other protective services for business. Indeed, these incentive-based reforms are likely to do more for law enforcement than the difficult-to-implement administrative reforms, which, as we mentioned earlier, can fail or even backfire.

Public enforcement is surely the ultimate goal of any legal reform. Yet it is important to remember that the strategy of private enforcement of public rules can serve Russia, and many other emerging economies, extremely well in the short and medium term.

REFERENCES

Bernstein, Lisa. ''Opting Out of the Legal System: Extralegal Contractual Relations in the Diamond Industry.'' *Journal of Legal Studies*, January 1992, *21*(1), pp. 115–57.

Black, Bernard; Kraakman, Reinier and Hay, Jonathan. ''Corporate Law from Scratch,'' in Roman Frydman, Cheryl Gray, and Andrzej Rapaczynski, eds., *Corporate governance in Central Europe and Russia*, Vol. 2. Budapest, Hungary: Central European University Press, 1996, pp. 245–302.

Boycko, Maxim; Shleifer Andrei and Vishny, Robert W. *Privatizing Russia*. Cambridge, MA: MIT Press, 1995.

David, René and Brierley, John. *Major legal systems in the world today*. London: Stevens, 1985.

VOL. 88 NO. 2 *GOVERNMENT IN TRANSITION* 403

Ellickson, Robert C. *Order without law*. Cambridge, MA: Harvard University Press, 1991.

Frye, Timothy. "Contracting in the Shadow of the State: Private Arbitration Courts in Russia." Mimeo, Harvard University, 1996.

Frye, Timothy and Shleifer, Andrei. "The Invisible Hand and the Grabbing Hand." *American Economic Review*, May 1997 (*Papers and Proceedings*), 87(2), pp. 354–58.

Greif, Avner. "Cultural Beliefs and the Organization of Society: A Historical and Theoretical Reflection on Collectivist and Individualist Societies." *Journal of Political Economy*, October 1994, 102(5), pp. 912–50.

_____. "Contracting, Enforcement, and Efficiency: Economics Beyond the Law," in Michael Bruno and Boris Pleskovic, eds., *World Bank Annual Bank Conference on Development Economics*. Washington, DC: World Bank, 1996, pp. 239–65.

Greif, Avner and Kandel, Eugene. "Contract Enforcement Institutions: Historical Perspective and Current Status in Russia," in Edward P. Lazear, ed., *Economic transition in Eastern Europe and Russia: Realities of reform*. Stanford, CA: Hoover Institution Press, 1995, pp. 291–321.

Hay, Jonathan; Shleifer, Andrei and Vishny, Robert W. "Toward a Theory of Legal Reform." *European Economic Review*, April 1996, 40(3–5), pp. 559–67.

Johnson, Simon; Kaufmann, Daniel and Shleifer, Andrei. "The Unofficial Economy in Transition." *Brookings Papers on Economic Activity*, 1997, (2), pp. 159–239.

La Porta, Rafael; Lopez-de-Silanes, Florencio; Shleifer, Andrei and Vishny, Robert W. "Law and Finance." *Journal of Political Economy*, 1998 (forthcoming).

North, Douglass C. *Structure and change in economic history*. New York: Norton, 1981.

Pistor, Katharina. "Supply and Demand for Contract Enforcement in Russia: Courts, Arbitration, and Private Enforcement." *Review of Central and East European Law*, 1996, 22(1), pp. 55–87.

Schelling, Thomas. *The strategy of conflict*. Cambridge, MA: Harvard University Press, 1960.

Shleifer, Andrei. "Government in Transition." *European Economic Review*, April 1997, 41(3–5), pp. 385–410.

Shleifer, Andrei and Vishny, Robert W. "Corruption." *Quarterly Journal of Economics*, August 1993, 108(3), pp. 599–618.

Sugden, Robert. "Spontaneous Order." *Journal of Economic Perspectives*, Fall 1989, 3(4), pp. 85–97.

Watson, Alan. *Legal transplants*. Charlottesville, VA: University of Virginia Press, 1974.

[3]

Poverty and Reforms: Friends or Foes?

Jagdish Bhagwati

As reforms in economic policy—generally centered on dismantling inward-looking policies on international trade and attracting equity investment—and the privatization of many public-owned enterprises have swept across the developing world, critics have charged that these reforms are inimical to the reduction of poverty. Thus, it is not unusual for a long-standing proponent of these reforms like myself to get into recurring debates on the question. Only a few months ago, I and Martin Wolf of *The Financial Times* teamed up to face two rather impassioned opponents in a BBC debate. Our opponents claimed that pro-globalization policies are responsible for the accentuation of poverty, while we argued exactly the opposite.

In fact, this debate is only a replay of the debate that we Indian economists and planners had almost four decades ago, with

---

...pro-globalization and pro-privatization economic reforms must be treated as complementary and indeed friendly to both the reduction of poverty and social agendas.

---

occasional argumentation thereafter, when we began planning for national poverty amelioration. India at the time had (and still has, precisely because of the policies that presently call for pro-globalization reforms) the misfortune of having a comparative advantage in poverty. Since policy economics is like literature and reflects the immediacy of one's experience, Indian economists have not surprisingly been at the forefront of debates about how to reduce poverty.

As I shall presently argue, this debate in India was precisely between those who maintained that growth reduced poverty and those who argued that it bypassed or even increased it. Proponents

---

Journal of International Affairs, Fall 1998, 52, no. 1. © The Trustees of Columbia University in the City of New York.

of the pro-growth strategy were divided into those who came to see the inward-looking import-substitution (IS) model toward trade and direct foreign investment (DFI) as the culprit that crippled growth and hence accentuated poverty (a minority in the 1960s and 1970s), and the vast majority that continued to cling to the increasingly implausible notion that these anti-globalization strategies were in fact pro-growth policies, despite compelling theoretical arguments and a growing body of evidence suggesting the opposite.

Since the 1980s, a majority of policy economists around the world have begun to favor economic reforms that increase global integration, in the strong belief that such reforms would, *ceteris paribus*, promote growth and would, both directly and indirectly (by raising resources for spending on social programs and in other ways discussed below), help to improve living standards among the poor. Today, the widespread view among Indian intellectuals and policymakers is that the absence of pro-growth economic policies for nearly three decades only served to accentuate Indian poverty. Ironically, the growth-retarding and hence poverty-enhancing policies in place throughout this time were adopted at the urging of those very economists who claimed that they were the virtuous ones who wished to attack poverty, while the rest of us were interested in growth for itself.[1]

Against this backdrop, I argue that pro-globalization and pro-privatization economic reforms must be treated as complementary and indeed friendly to both the reduction of poverty and social agendas. I maintain that poverty reduction and advancement of social agendas require not merely a policy focus on schooling, public health, etc., but also *simultaneous* attention to reforms aimed at improving the economic efficiency and growth of the economy. More precisely, I shall argue specifically in this paper that:

· Growth (or "development") has been regarded for several decades as a principal *instrument* for reducing poverty, rather than as an *objective* in itself. Hence the contention in some influential developmental circles and international agencies that poverty reduction has only recently been designated as an objective of development, displacing the earlier

---

[1]   See my critique of these economists and the hugely deleterious effects they had on India's poverty even as they were identified in the public eye as economists "more genuinely" concerned about poverty, in Jagdish Bhagwati, "A Machine for Going Backwards," *Times Literary Supplement*, reprinted in Jagdish Bhagwati, *A Stream of Windows: Unsettling Reflections on Trade, Immigration and Democracy* (Cambridge: MIT Press, 1998) chapter 56.

Jagdish Bhagwati

preoccupation with growth per se, is totally off the mark. The falsity of this argument is a cause for concern insofar as it encourages the harmful ethos that somehow growth is irrelevant, if not inimical, to poverty reduction and to the promotion of social agendas. Growth is, in fact, an important force for poverty alleviation and has been regarded as such, at least in Indian planning and policy circles, since the 1950s.

· Growth is properly regarded as an instrumental means of reducing poverty because, generally speaking, it moves poor unemployed and underemployed people into gainful employment. Growth can still have varying degrees of efficacy in terms of its impact on poverty, depending on the "structural" forms that poverty and growth take and on the political and social contexts in which the growth process unfolds.

· Increased integration into the global economy (through trade and DFI) and other reforms (such as privatization) currently being proposed in poverty-ridden countries can be fully expected to assist in poverty eradication.

· Growth attacks poverty in yet another way: economic prosperity alone increases tax revenues which, in turn, can be used to finance conventional anti-poverty programs such as the building of schools and the provision of clean water, electricity and health facilities for the poor. Without revenues, these expenditures cannot be sustained, let alone expanded. But this requires that these agendas be on the radar screen of governments: the availability of funds is no guarantee that they will be used for the right purposes.

· In this respect, there is a clear role for democracy to guarantee effective political participation among peripheral groups, nongovernmental organizations (NGOs) and social activists. There is also a profound need for a combination of government and private NGO work to maximize the impact of governmental expenditures on social and economic programs that target the poor. Growth will also support social and poverty-reduction agendas, since it will enhance the effectiveness of legislation aimed at helping the poor.

Thus, in conclusion, those who viscerally oppose economic reforms today as anti-poor are misguided and unfortunately accentuating poverty instead. We need to build bridges between economic reformers and anti-poverty campaigners, not burn them.

Journal of International Affairs

GROWTH AS AN ANTI-POVERTY STRATEGY, NOT AS AN OBJECTIVE IN ITSELF

In the mid-1970s and 1980s, I began to encounter assertions, from the International Labour Organization (ILO) and elsewhere, that growth had long been the primary objective of development planning and that poverty had been recognized as worthy of attention only recently. Such claims profoundly surprised me. A few dramatic examples of some of the untrue statements I was exposed to are illuminating.

First, I remember reading a biographical sketch of one of the South Asian architects of the Human Development reports of the United Nations Development Programme (UNDP). The thrust of these reports is that the UNDP deals with human beings, and hence with poverty and social agendas, whereas those of us who have worked at encouraging growth over the years are somehow tangential or inimical to those objectives. Such assertions prompted me once to mischievously inform the affable and dynamic UNDP head, Gus Speth, when he asked me at a party what I did, that I worked on Inhuman Development. The biographical sketch amusingly claimed that this particular economist had "dethroned the goddess of GNP from her pedestal."

I recall another example that took place several years ago when I was giving the keynote address at the 25th anniversary celebration of the Center for Development Studies in Antwerp, Belgium. In response to my comments on poverty, the Dutch economist Louis Emmerij (who had run the program on poverty at the ILO) said somewhat sarcastically that it was good to see Professor Bhagwati finally talking, not about free trade and growth, but about poverty and inequality. I could not resist retorting that I might have agreed with the statement were it not for the fact that, apropos of my speech that day, I was reading my best-selling 1966 book, *The Economics of Underdeveloped Countries*. The first chapter of that book is entitled "Poverty and Income Distribution."

In fact, many social scientists have responded with strongly disapproving commentary to the claim of some early development economists that pro-growth economists and policymakers ignored poverty. To cite one eminent sociologist, Gilbert Étienne, who has worked for decades on India's villages: "The claim that developmental strategies in the 1950s and 1960s overemphasized growth and increases of the GNP at the cost of social progress is a surprising one!...Equally peculiar is the so-called discovery of the

Jagdish Bhagwati

problem of poverty."[2]

GROWTH: A PULL-UP, NOT TRICKLE-DOWN, STRATEGY FOR REMOVING POVERTY

So, let me explain why we perceived growth at the time, and must continue to do so almost four decades later, as an effective anti-poverty strategy. This is because in countries such as India, where the poverty is immense, there are no simple answers like income redistribution (even if feasible politically) to bring poverty down. The problem is that redistribution would have little impact on poverty, even in the short-term. As the eminent Polish communist economist Mikhail Kalecki told me in India in 1962, the trouble with India is that there are too many exploited and too few exploiters. Moreover, governments need to pursue a sustained attack on poverty rather than a one-shot approach. With a rising population and stagnant growth, any favorable effects of redistribution on poverty would quickly erode.

Hence, Indian planners saw rapid growth as the principal component of an anti-poverty strategy. The idea was an activist program which would raise domestic savings and investment, assisted where possible by the influx of foreign funds through aid and investment in order to achieve accelerating growth that would move increasing numbers of people into gainful employment. The theoretical rationale was embodied in the well known Harrod-Domar growth model, in which employment rises with increasing capital stock and the chief policy instrument is a fiscal strategy to raise domestic savings.

All this was a far cry from the conventional liberal view in domestic debates within OECD countries, where growth is often presented as a *passive*, "trickle-down" process. Indeed, we thought of our strategy as an *active*, "pull-up" strategy requiring extensive savings mobilization, with the state playing a major (interventionist) role in that effort. Clearly, this was no conservative option.

Of course, not all growth has identical effects. Economists are ingenious enough to construct all kinds of scenarios. Thus, I am known for having demonstrated that growth can actually diminish economic well-being, as when it leads to losses from worsened terms

[2]   The Etienne quote is cited in my 1987 Vikram Sarabhai Memorial Lecture on Public Policy and Poverty, printed in *World Development*, 16, no. 5 (1988) pp. 539-555 and reprinted in Jagdish Bhagwati, *Political Economy and International Economics*, ed., Douglas Irwin (Cambridge: MIT Press, 1991) chapter 25.

of trade which outweigh the primary gains from growth.[3] To take another example, if rich farmers implement technical change, output increases and prices fall—and the poor farmers who did not innovate are hurt. For this reason, we used to say that the Green Revolution (which brought in new high-yield seeds) might lead to the Red Revolution! But these downside scenarios can be ruled out by suitable accompanying policies: in the former instance, an optimal tariff is the answer; in the latter, the government could adopt a price maintenance program or a policy to raise national investment, which would lead to a matching increase in demand for the added output of the high-yield grains.

Then again, it is obvious that growth may simply bypass certain pockets of poverty. Thus, for example, if tribal areas in India are not integrated into the main economy, growth occurring in the latter will not touch the former. This may well be the case internationally if an impoverished nation is not linked to the growing world economy and hence to profits from either trade or DFI. Indeed, such is the situation for many of the smaller, impoverished nations today (though, I would say, these "non-linkage" afflictions are, at least to some extent, a result of bad inward-looking policies over the years, and not an unfortunate external calamity of which poor countries are simply victims). Once again, supplementary programs are needed to accompany growth, so that it can act more effectively as a locomotive lifting people out of poverty.

If the efficacy of the locomotive depends on the nature of growth, there is enough evidence by now that the IS strategy harmed the poor, not just by slowing growth but also by affecting the horsepower of the locomotive. In a project for the National Bureau of Economic Research (NBER) that I and Professor Anne Krueger directed in the 1960s, we found that the IS strategy tended to reduce employment by biasing growth toward capital-intensive projects and choice of techniques, seriously limiting the assault on poverty as a result. This finding was reinforced by Krueger in a subsequent NBER Project, which focused more directly on the employment effects of the IS and the export promoting (EP) strategies.[4] Thus, the Far Eastern economies, with striking growth

---

[3] Jagdish Bhagwati, "Immiserizing Growth: A Geometrical Note," *Review of Economic Studies*, 25, no. 3 (June 1958) pp. 201-205.

[4] The volumes from the first project were published in 1978 by Ballinger and for the second project by University of Chicago Press in 1982. In addition, much important research-project-based work along these lines was done, in particular, by I.M.D. Little, Maurice Scott and Tibor Scitovsky for the OECD Development Center in the 1960s and by the late Bela Balassa for the World Bank. The findings of these projects and other research have been reviewed in Jagdish Bhagwati, "Export-Promoting Trade

Jagdish Bhagwati

rates over nearly three decades, had a substantial positive impact on the living standards of the poor because the development was based on labor-intensive production and exports. In India, on the other hand, the impact on poverty was handicapped, not merely by abysmally low growth rates, but also by the fact that the Indian economic planners—under the impetus of counterproductive theorizing that legitimated the use of capital-intensive techniques and the promotion of huge white elephants in heavy industry—biased the growth of the economy away from employment-creation.[5]

We may still ask whether the evidence demonstrates that in India, for instance, growth has pulled people out of poverty. After much debate, it seems that by now evidence of a favorable link has become more compelling. In the 1980s, when the Indian growth rate picked up from a range of 3 to 3.5 percent to around 5 percent, poverty reduction accelerated.[6] Evidence on the Green Revolution's spread has also shown it to be linked to improvements in poverty.

PRO-GROWTH REFORMS: GLOBALIZATION, PRIVATIZATION AND MARKET REFORMS

Against this backdrop, the recent wave of economic reforms in much of the developing world and in formerly socialist economies is to be regarded as an important long-run input toward the elimination of poverty. There are, however, two important caveats. First, the short-term effects of a *transition* to globalization, in which economies are opened up to integration into the world economy, may well exacerbate poverty. This is sometimes glossed over by ideologues. See, for example, the World Bank's 1996 *World Development Report* on the transition problems that the former-socialist countries face, entitled *From Plan to Market*. This report virtually dismisses, and even ignores, the problems concerning

---

Strategy: Issues and Evidence," *World Bank Research Observer*, 3, no. 1 (1988) pp. 27-57, reprinted in Bhagwati (1991) chapter 24.

[5]   Here, I have in mind the work on the choice of techniques in the 1960s by economists such as Amartya Sen, which did incalculable harm to the cause of growth and hence of poverty reduction by emphasizing the role of capital-intensive techniques in accelerating the growth rate by increasing savings. These conclusions came, of course, from the assumptions underlying the models built. But logical rigor is no substitute for wisdom; and, as the Oxford economist Thomas Balogh, adviser to Prime Minister Harold Wilson, used to say, rigor can lead to rigor mortis.

[6]   For a generally favorable assessment of the effect of growth on poverty reduction in India, see the recent World Bank, "India: Achievements and Challenges in Reducing Poverty," World Bank Country Study (Washington, DC: 1997).

unemployment and income distribution that attend such transitions. Moreover, it asserts without any serious response to the arguments advanced by scholarly opponents of the shock therapy model propounded by Jeffrey Sachs that these effects are desirable.[7] On the other hand, serious scholars of such transitions—chief among them Padma Desai of Columbia in her recent book, *Going Global: Transition from Plan to Market in the World Economy*, and John McMillan of the University of California at San Diego—have insightfully analyzed these problems associated with attempts at global integration.[8]

The second caveat is that all forms of globalization are not equally desirable, even from the viewpoint of efficiency and growth. Thus, it has become evident recently that the IMF's determination to push for capital account convertibility around the world has been hasty and, in fact, dangerous. The Asian financial crisis since 1997 has radically shifted opinion in the direction of halting the aggressive spread of such convertibility. Hence, the IMF is now conscious of what I have always argued, that free trade in widgets is not the same as free trade in dollars.[9] Unfortunately, public perception has likewise confused these two forms of globalization (goods vs. dollars); and now that the latter has once again caused a crisis, with incalculable economic and political consequences for the countries caught in the aftermath, there has been a tendency to condemn globalization per se, condemning the good form of globalization for the sins of the bad one.[10]

I would stress that the postwar experience has amply demonstrated the mutual gains to be made from trade liberalization. This is also true of equity investments, which bring

---

[7] In fact, one looks in vain even for references to the contributions of academic scholars who have opposed shock therapy.

[8] Padma Desai, *Going Global: Transition from Plan to Market in the World Economy* (Cambridge: MIT Press, 1997).

[9] See Jagdish Bhagwati, "The Capital Myth," *Foreign Affairs*, 77, no. 3 (May/June 1998) pp. 7-12. In explaining why free trade in widgets and in dollars were equated without justification, I also advance the view that a role has been played by what I call the "Wall Street-Treasury complex," an idea that has been picked up by the political scientist Robert Wade and others and needs further scholarly investigation.

[10] A particularly good example of this is a recent *Los Angeles Times* story by Tom Plate (May 12, 1998), citing my *Foreign Affairs* article on "The Capital Myth" and saying: "This Columbia University professor still swears allegiance to free-market philosophy in other respects [than free capital flows as with capital account convertibility], but his defection on this issue is on the order of a Vatican bishop turning up at a Presbyterian pulpit." The irony is that, not merely are the two forms of globalization, in free trade and in free capital flows, quite distinct from each other, but I have always been skeptical of free capital flows (as distinct from the advantages of equity investments).

Jagdish Bhagwati

into a country the benefits of capital, skills and technology. I would add the caveat, however, that energetic regression-prone economists such as Harvard's development experts Robert Barro and Sachs do not help us by turning out endless cross-country associations between growth rates and trade indicators. They even persuade financial journalists to reproduce these results as if they "proved" that globalization in trade, for instance, is immensely beneficial to liberalizing countries. In fact, they do not really do this.[11] My faith in the advantages of freer trade and eased restrictions on DFI inflows derives instead from sophisticated and nuanced studies of countries in which trade liberalization and DFI inflows are put into the appropriate context.

I should also add that privatization is now widely seen as conducive to economic efficiency. This view is not ideological, as it was when we were embarking on development and many of us had not pondered the deep-seated incentive problems that public enterprises would face, given the political context within which they would be operating, especially in developing countries. Political staffing, often excessive and of middling quality, the ability to ride out losses by resorting to subsidies and the absence of effective incentives for workers and managers to perform are among the key and ineradicable defects of public enterprises. Some unreformed proponents of the Marxist and Fabian preference for public ownership insist that suitable reforms could still salvage public enterprises as efficient economic entities. This logic, however, is like saying that if we put stripes on an elephant, it will become a zebra.[12]

GROWTH: ADDED REVENUES TO SUPPORT ANTI-POVERTY AND SOCIAL AGENDAS

Let me then turn to another reason why growth, aided and

---

[11]   In fact, such regressions are double-edged, since those opposed to trade can also play around with them, often leading to reversals of the "findings" by adding more variables, changing proxies, altering time periods or country coverage, etc. We are faced then with mutually assured destruction by opposed groups, each claiming scientific rectitude that serious econometricians and scholars would find unacceptable.

[12]   None of this is to say that all forms of privatization are good. Recently, for example, there has been much criticism of the Russian privatization. But few of the critics have faced up to the problem that all privatization programs must be politically and economically feasible, and unless they offer a better and feasible alternative, their critiques are not compelling. See, for example, Padma Desai, "Russian Privatization: A Comparative Perspective," *The Harriman Review*, 8, no. 3 (August 1995) pp. 1-34; and her review of Maxim Boycko, Andrei Shleifer and Robert Vishny, *Privatizing Russia* (Cambridge: MIT Press, 1995) in *Journal of International Economics*, 42, no. 1/2 (February 1997) pp. 244-246.

41

accelerated by reforms like those outlined above, can help. Without prosperity, the government will fall short of the funds needed to advance literacy, secondary schooling, health, sanitation and a host of programs aimed directly at the poor and conventionally described as "anti-poverty" programs in donor agencies and recipient countries. Of course, because it pulls the poor into gainful employment, growth is also to be seen as an indirect anti-poverty program, as I have already argued, and it is wrong to think otherwise. Indeed, to those who use the cliché of "development with a human face," I respond: "Yes, indeed. But remember that the face cannot exist by itself, except as a mask in a museum. It must be joined to the body; and if the body is emaciated, the face must wither no matter how much we seek to humanize and make it pretty."

For those who doubt this, it is perhaps necessary to reflect how, faced with a budget deficit, President Clinton turned away from social programs requiring funding, enraging in the process his liberal supporters who concluded that he had abandoned liberalism. As soon as the budget turned into a surplus, however, his liberal voice became loud and clear.[13]

Growth, Poverty and Social Agendas: All Bedfellows

Though revenues resulting from prosperity allow for spending on anti-poverty programs and on social agendas, this does not guarantee that they will be so spent. For this, it is necessary to identify processes and institutions that will generate and sustain the right "preferences," not just culturally but in terms of effective political demand. This is where we recognize the importance of democracy, with effective participation among the poor and minorities. Their vote enables their voice to be heard.[14] The introduction of democratic politics into poor countries should therefore be seen as "political reform" that complements the "economic reforms" that I have discussed so far.

The specific forms that such democratic politics may assume can be diverse. One important aspect is the growth of NGOs, which Indians call Social Action Groups. These NGOs help to ensure that in poor communities, still emerging in some cases from

---

[13]   Of course, nothing is uni-causal in the world of politics. Clinton's personal problems may have also intensified his need to rally the liberal Democrats around him. But he simply could not have done that without the necessary revenue surplus.

[14]   See my Rajiv Gandhi Memorial Lecture on "Democracy and Development," reprinted in Bhagwati (1998) chapter 40.

Jagdish Bhagwati

feudal social and political structures, the voice of peripheral groups is not silenced by intimidation despite formal democratic practices. I might add that the role of female education in the development of civil society has been phenomenal. In the early 1960s, when I was working on poverty at the Indian Planning Commission, I recall discussing with the great Indian planner, Pitambar Pant, the immense growth of women in higher education and wondering where they would all go and with what consequences. We came up with images of women engineers, doctors, scientists and scholars. But we had no idea that several of them would wind up as active members of NGOs, pushing social agendas in all directions. Indeed, both in rich and in poor countries (with higher education), NGOs are increasingly dominated by women.

In addition, it is important to emphasize that growth seriously enhances the efficacy of social legislation and anti-poverty programs. Take literacy, for instance. Political scientist Myron Weiner has beautifully noted that literacy has usually required that the incentive of poor parents to put children to work rather than sending them to school is outweighed by countervailing values. In the Lutheran religion, for example, everyone needed to know how to read the Bible instead of relying on a priest to act as a liaison to God. For economists, this countervailing pressure can come from the prospect of earning higher income as a result of education. Higher income, however, will come only when growth provides economic opportunities that allow increasing numbers of children to travel down the educational road. The few schools that do exist in India have had problems with attendance and thus work below potential output, largely because low growth over the decades has drastically reduced the chances that improved incomes will result from sending children to school.[15]

Moreover, in some instances, it can be argued that social agendas follow economic growth. Thus, for example, many political scientists and sociologists, among them Barrington Moore and Ralf Dahrendorff, have maintained that democracy emerges when growth has produced a middle class that seeks democratic rights. Similarly, movements for environmental protection, for children's and women's rights, etc., seem to gather steam as economies grow and their populations acquire information and ideas from other countries further up the development ladder.

I should note that this tendency is sometimes used by economists to argue, totally without justification, that economic growth will

---

[15]   As is always true, the full explanation of India's appalling illiteracy is more complex. Thus, in some cases, it is the teachers who do not turn up.

eventually take care of social and poverty concerns and that we therefore do not need to address them directly. I have a simple answer to that. If a hapless woman is being beaten by her husband and screams for help, it would be a bit ludicrous to say to her to hang in there, because growth will eventually change values and laws so that husbands are no longer able to abuse their wives. What you will want to do is immediately nail the guy to the wall. And so must social agendas for the poor and minorities move ahead, hand in hand with the growth process.

One final remark on the positive relationship between growth and poverty reduction is worth making. Sometimes, expenditures aimed at removing poverty can in turn promote growth. Thus many economists have recently argued that if credit market imperfections prevent the poor from investing in health, education and enterprises, then this can impede growth. Again, a malnourished labor force cannot be conducive to higher productivity: the "efficiency wage" theory, associated with economists James Mirrlees and Harvey Leibenstein, formalizes the idea that firms will sometimes pay more than the going wage if a productivity boost results from better nutrition enabled by higher incomes.

CONCLUDING OBSERVATIONS

And so, in many ways, the current reforms in developing countries must be seen as significant inputs into the important fight against world poverty. Unfortunately, in countries that face serious poverty, this is still not understood and reforms are considered to be a luxury for the rich and irrelevant to the poor. Having begun this essay with relevant reminiscences about India in the 1950s, let me conclude it with pertinent remarks about India in the 1990s.

Specifically, as we Indians try to move ahead with economic reforms to finally reduce poverty through rapid growth, let me express my astonishment, anguish and outrage over the following all-too-familiar criticism of reforms made by two influential economists:

> Debates on such questions as the details of tax concessions to multinationals, or whether Indians should drink Coca Cola, or whether the private sector should be allowed to operate city buses, tend to 'crowd out' the time that is left to discuss the abysmal situation of basic education and

44

Jagdish Bhagwati

elementary health care, or the persistence of
debilitating social inequalities, or other issues that
have a crucial bearing on the well-being and
freedom of the population.[16]

Mindful of the damage that such attitudes have done to the
cause of poverty reduction in India over a quarter of a century, I
was moved to respond, in a review essay:

Much is wrong here. No one can seriously argue
that there is a crowding out when the articulation
of Indians is manifest in multiplying newspapers,
magazines and books and the expression of a whole
spectrum of views on economics and politics; this
reviewer has noticed no particular shyness in
discussing social issues, including inequality and
poverty in India...But, more important, the put-
down of attention to multinationals misses the
point that India's economic reforms require
precisely that India join the Global Age and that
India's inward direct investments were ridiculously
small in 1991, around $100 million, and that this
was an important deficiency that had to be fixed.
The reference to Coca Cola is no better, serving as
a cheap shot against multinational investment; but
it also betrays the assumption that Coca Cola is
drunk by the elite or the Westernized middle class,
not by the truly poor. It is more likely, however,
that the former derive their caffeine from espresso
coffee as well whereas the poor are the ones who
must depend on coke instead![17]

In fact, the contemptuous reference to the privatization of bus
transportation in cities could only come from elitist economists
who travel by private car and are unaware that the common people
(especially the poor) travel by buses whose efficiency needs to be
improved by privatization. In short, we confront here the
spectacle of economists, who espouse the cause of the poor,
becoming unwitting accomplices in the perpetuation of poverty.
Ironic indeed. ✤

---

[16]   Jean Drèze and Amartya Sen, *India: Economic Development and Social Opportunity*
       (Oxford: Clarendon Press, 1995) p. vii.
[17]   Jagdish Bhagwati, *Economic Journal*, 108 (January 1998) pp. 198-199.

[4]

POLITICIANS, INTEREST GROUPS, AND REGULATORS: A MULTIPLE-PRINCIPALS AGENCY THEORY OF REGULATION, OR "LET THEM BE BRIBED"*

PABLO T. SPILLER
University of Illinois at Urbana-Champaign

I. INTRODUCTION

THE main thrust of the self-interest theory of regulation, as proposed by Stigler and Peltzman,[1] is that regulations develop as the result of demands from different interest groups for governmental intervention. There is no necessary divergence between politicians' optimal policies (as responses to interest groups' demands) and their implementation. Policies, however, are seldom implemented directly by the politicians themselves. Instead, they are delegated to regulatory agencies, departments, or the courts. In this article, I expand the self-interest theory of regulation to account for the potential agency problems between Congress and its regulators, and I subject the implications of the agency part of the framework to a preliminary empirical test.

Agency problems between politicians and regulators arise because regulators' actions are intrinsically unobservable. Thus, congressional (or

* This research was initiated while I was at the Hoover Institution on War, Revolution, and Peace. I would like to thank David Baron, Randy Calvert, Dennis Carlton, John Ferejohn, Ken Hendricks, John Lott, Mike Riordan, Jean Tirole, Barry Weingast, Ralph Winter, an anonymous referee, and participants at the 1987 Carnegie-Mellon Conference on Political Economy and at workshops at the University of California, San Diego, and at the University of Chicago, for very helpful comments and suggestions, to Ross D. Eckert for generously providing his data on regulatory commissioners' employment experience, and to Yeon Che and Johanna Rodgers for helpful library assistance. Financial support from the Center for Economic Policy Research at Stanford University is gratefully acknowledged.

[1] Sam Peltzman, Toward a More General Theory of Regulation, 19 J. Law & Econ. 211 (1976); George J. Stigler, The Theory of Economic Regulation, 2 Bell J. Econ. & Mgmt. Sci. 3 (1971).

[*Journal of Law & Economics*, vol. XXXIII (April 1990)]

presidential) delegation of regulatory authority generates agency discretion. Regulators, then, may pursue interests not aligned with those of the politicians who appoint them.[2] This insight has not gone unobserved by students of the political economy of regulation. Two main approaches have developed. One, coined the "Congressional Dominance" hypothesis, while recognizing the potential agency problems between Congress and its regulators, essentially assumes that congressional instruments are powerful enough to fully control its regulators.[3] The other approach, embedded in the naive capture or bureaucratic theories of regulation, implicitly assumes that agency problems are so acute that bureaucracies can work independently of congressional or presidential desires.[4] In this article, these two approaches are seen as particular (corner) solutions to a more general agency problem, where politicians and interest groups compete to influence regulators' decisions.[5]

I focus on congressional delegation of regulatory authority.[6] While the interests of congressmen and interest groups are related, they do not

---

[2] Throughout this article I will assume that congressional interests are well defined. This assumption would hold if, as will be the case here, the policies of the regulatory agency are unidimensional. If policies were multidimensional, then Congressional interests might not be well defined, and delegation of regulatory authority might in itself provide substantial scope for regulators pursuing their own interests. On this issue, see T. H. Hammond, J. S. Hill, & G. J. Miller, Presidential Appointment of Bureau Chiefs and the "Congressional Control of Administration" Hypothesis (mimeographed, Michigan State University, 1985).

[3] While implicit in Stigler, *supra* note 1, and Peltzman, *supra* note 1, this assumption appears explicitly in, among others, Barry Weingast, The Congressional-Bureaucratic System: A Principal-Agent Perspective (with Applications to the SEC), 44 Pub. Choice, 147 (1984); and Barry Weingast & M. J. Moran, Bureaucratic Discretion or Congressional Control? Regulatory Policymaking by the Federal Trade Commission, 91 J. Pol. Econ. 765 (1983). See T. M. Moe, Congressional Control of the Bureaucracy: An Assessment of the Positive Theory of Congressional Dominance (unpublished manuscript, Brookings Institution, 1985, for a critique of the congressional dominance hypothesis. While the congressional dominance hypothesis deals, naturally, with the role of Congress in the implementation of regulatory policy, this approach can be extended to other political institutions (for example, the relation between the president and the department secretaries).

[4] See, for example, William A., Niskanen, Jr., Bureaucracy and Representative Government (1971); or K. W. Clarkson & T. J. Muris, The Federal Trade Commission since 1970: Economic Regulation and Bureaucratic Behavior (1981).

[5] The unobservability of regulators' actions implies that regulators may shirk for two reasons. First, since regulators may dislike effort, they may shirk in order to reduce their effort. In contrast, the existence of an interest group not perfectly aligned with politicians' interests implies that interest groups will (implicitly or explicitly) offer compensation to the regulators for shirking. In this article I analyze the different implications of both sources of shirking.

[6] It should be clear from the outset, however, that a more complete analysis should take into account the role of the president in the appointment and control processes. For a discussion of this issue, see Randall Calvert, Matthew D. McCubbins, & Barry R. Weingast, A Theory of Political Control and Agency Discretion (unpublished manuscript, Hoover Institution, January 1987), and references therein.

necessarily coincide. The electoral connection suggests that congressmen take into account the electoral consequences of their actions.[7] Congressmen's interests, then, are related to those of a multiplicity of groups. Some may provide support through campaign contributions, while others may provide the necessary electoral support. Unless fully aligned with a particular interest group, congressmen will not pursue the interests of any single group. Interest groups, then, can influence regulatory outcomes through two channels: indirectly, through the electoral connection, and directly, by trying to influence the regulators. Hence, Congress and interest groups will usually compete for regulators' favors.

The competition for regulators' favors has several implications for the development of regulatory policies. First, since regulatory policies have nontrivial agency costs,[8] congressmen will balance those costs against the political benefits in assessing whether to undertake a certain regulatory policy. Second, competition between Congress and interest groups implies that, even if Congress's interests were exclusively aligned with a single interest group (that is, their direct constituency), the implementation of regulatory policies would take other interests into account.[9] This feature of the "agency" model presented here is what generates many of the results associated with the "self-interest" approach (that is, regulators cross-subsidize in a fashion similar to that found in Peltzman;[10] they mitigate changes in congressional demands for regulatory policies;[11] and they may make regulatory policies more proindustry in recessions and more proconsumer in booms).[12]

---

[7] D. R. Mayhew. Congress: The Electoral Connection (1974).

[8] The agency costs discussed here are different from the costs involved in regulating a firm with private information. See, for example, David P. Baron & Roger B. Myerson, Regulating a Monopolist with Unknown Costs, 50 Econometrica 911 (1982). Since these costs arise even in the absence of an "agency" problem between Congress and its regulators, it will be assumed in this article that the regulated firm cannot exploit private information.

[9] By assuming away the discrepancies in objectives between Congress and regulators, the traditional congressional dominance approach imposes on regulators an objective function that is characterized by some weighted average of consumer and producer interests (for example, Peltzman, *supra* note 1). See also Thomas W. Ross, Extracting Regulators' Implied Welfare Weights: Some Further Developments and Applications, 25 Q. Rev. Econ. & Bus. 72 (1985), for a method and applications to estimate the regulators' utility function weights. In contrast, the regulatory framework developed here endogenously determines the regulator's implicit weights. In this sense, this article can be seen as exploring the "black box" of Peltzman's "political-support" function.

[10] Peltzman, *supra* note 1.

[11] See Weingast & Moran, *supra* note 3, for a congressional dominance model with a similar implication.

[12] But changes in regulatory policy here are only partially the result of changes in congressional desires; they represent, rather, changes in the incentives faced by regulators. Congress, however, knowing those incentives, chooses its optimal policies accordingly.

The "agency" framework developed here has, however, particular implications for optimal regulatory budget policies and for the career path of
bureaucrats, which expands the set of empirical implications of the self-
interest theory of regulation. These particular implications allow a test of
the relevance of the agency part in the self-interest framework. This
model predicts that, to constrain regulators' actions, regulatory budgets
must fall following unfavorable outcomes for Congress.[13] A second set of
empirical implications is related to the career path of bureaucrats. Because of the competition between Congress and industry, it is shown that
regulators demand rents. Competition for regulators' jobs, then, implies
rent dissipation. Since congressmen can be seen as appointing regulators,
congressmen should be able to extract those rents from potential regulators.[14,15] Congressmen may collect the proceeds of the bidding process in
the form of campaign or staff work or in direct monetary contributions.
Limits on campaign contributions, however, implies that "working" for
congressmen may be the most common form of rent dissipation. Most
regulators, then, should have some public-sector experience. Similarly,
since interest groups should compensate regulators, the "agency" framework predicts that a high percentage of regulators should eventually have
postcommission jobs related to the regulated industry.

Finally, since agency costs increase when interest groups can influence
regulators' decisions, Congress could limit the extent by which interest
groups can influence regulatory outcomes. I present conditions, however,
under which Congress prefers to allow interest groups direct influence on
regulatory decisions.[16] While allowing interest groups to influence regula-

---

[13] This result formalizes the "fire alarm" approach suggested, among others, by Matthew
D. McCubbins & Thomas Schwartz, Congressional Oversight Overlooked: Police Patrols
vs. Fire Alarms, 28 Am. J. Pol. Sci. 165 (1984).

[14] While in principle the president appoints commissioners, Senate oversight committees
have to approve the appointments. Thus, congressmen have substantial power to determine
the pool from which potential appointees can be drawn.

[15] In what follows, I assume that Congress can be represented as a single agent. This
assumption requires some discussion. First, since I analyze regulatory policy as single
dimensional, committee majority rule would provide the rationale for this assumption. If,
however, regulatory policies were multidimensional, then this assumption would not be
sufficient to generate uniqueness of equilibrium. However, if Congress controls regulators
through committees, then this assumption requires either some measure of coordination
across congressional committees or that committees do not represent specialized constituencies. While committee members are able to capture regulators' rents through patronage, Congress as a whole has to agree to finance the agency's budget. Thus, unless
committee members are drawn from a random distribution of congressmen, some coordination among committees will be required to assure congressional approval of the regulators'
budgets.

[16] Recent public discussion of the "revolving door" at different governmental agencies
has raised the question of whether Congress should further restrict postgovernmental employment for senior government executives, which would impose stricter limits on the

tors reduces the extent of regulatory control, interest groups' influence may actually increase Congress's overall benefit from the regulatory process by increasing regulators' rents, which are appropriated by congressmen. In this sense, interest groups' influence on the regulatory process may be seen as indirect contributions to congressmen.

The article is organized as follows. Section II presents the basic model. Section III presents the general formulation of the Congress-industry-agency problem and presents the equilibrium when Congress can perfectly monitor its regulators. This section shows that simply delegating regulatory actions to an agent with limited liability may deter Congress from achieving its most desired regulatory outcome. Section IV analyzes the regulatory equilibrium that occurs when Congress cannot observe the regulator's actions. Two alternative institutional settings are analyzed, depending on whether or not transfers by the interest group are allowed. This section also analyzes the implications of allowing regulators to bid for their regulatory positions. It is shown that the main effect of this is to allow Congress to indirectly extract rents from the regulated firm. Sections V and VI explore, in the form of an example, the incentives that Congress may have to allow transfers from the interest groups to the regulators. Section VII explores the empirical implications of the agency framework. The data and preliminary results are discussed in Sections VIII and IX, and Section X concludes the article.

II. THE MODEL

Consider a three-player game: Congress, the interest group (which for convenience will be called "industry"), and the regulator. The model attempts to capture a situation where congressmen's interests are aligned with those of another, diffuse but electorally important, interest group (call them "consumers"). This interest group, however, is unable to directly influence the regulator's actions. Industry, in contrast, while being a concentrated group, may not be able to provide much electoral support.[17,18] It can, however, directly influence the regulator's incentives.

---

ability of interest groups to influence the design and implementation of regulatory policies. See U.S. General Accounting Office. DOD Revolving Door: Relationships between Work at DOD and post DOD Employment (1986).

[17] This model does not allow direct influence of industry on congressmen. A more general model would allow industry to make contingent transfers to congressmen as well, which could take the form of contingent (or retrospective) campaign contributions. If campaign contributions must be designed in a way similar to industry's transfers to the regulators, this extra layer of agency problem may not substantially change the nature of the problem since there will still be a need for direct industry transfers to regulators.

[18] This article assumes that industry is able to perfectly solve its free-rider problem in making transfers to regulators.

Privatization and Globalization

Congress's and industry's payoffs are functions of the regulator's actions. The regulator's actions are unobservable, but they affect the distribution of industry price, p, which has a binary distribution with values $\{p_1, p_h\}$.[19] The probability of observing a low price (p_1) is given by $\phi(x)$, where x is the unobservable action (effort) taken by the regulator.[20] Let $\phi'(x) > 0$. No regulation is equivalent to the regulator taking no regulatory action; that is, $x = 0$. In that case, the industry will charge p_h with probability one. Congress is assumed to prefer a low price, while industry prefers a high price. Given the form of the probability function $\phi(x)$, Congress's (industry's) preferences are increasing (decreasing) in x. Let Congress's preferences be given by consumer surplus minus the regulator's budget, and industry's preferences by profits net of transfers.

While this article uses as an example price regulation, the model is more general. The model could be directly applied to the analysis of nonprice regulation, like pollution control, or the regulation of safety in the workplace. The main requirement of the model is that Congress's preferences should not coincide with those of the interest group.[21]

Congress and industry try to influence the regulator's choice of x. Congress's sole instrument is assumed to be the regulator's budget, which can be made contingent on the observed regulatory outcome (in our case, the price).[22] Similarly, industry's single instrument is a direct transfer to the regulator, which may also be contingent on the observed price.[23]

---

[19] The regulator's actions can be thought of as avoiding price collusion among the firms or as monitoring their books. More effort implies that there is a higher probability of finding, say, collusion and hence of reducing the industry price to a lower level. Since this article does not deal with the use of private cost information by the industry, the analogy to cost regulation is only heuristic.

[20] In this model, x is unobserved by both Congress and industry. This assumption could be relaxed by letting industry have better information about x than Congress (that is, industry could observe a signal of x). While this assumption would make the model more realistic, it would increase its complexity without adding substantial new insights.

[21] Notice also that, since budgets enter into congressmen's preferences, the opportunity cost of a dollar is exactly one. Thus, there is a real utility cost for congressmen in providing large budgets to their regulatory agencies.

[22] The budget concept that I use here is the discretionary rather than the operational budget. The latter should also affect regulatory efficiency. That is, ϕ could, in principle, depend on the level of operational budget. Here it is assumed that ϕ depends only on the regulator's action x.

[23] For example, industry transfers could take the form of postgovernment employment. While I restrict industry's influence instrument to direct transfers, regulated industries may also use other methods to influence regulators. Bruce M. Owen & Ronald Braeutigam, The Regulation Game: Strategic Use of the Administrative Procedure (1978), analyze how regulated industries use administrative procedures to influence regulatory outcomes. In particular, by threatening to obstruct regulatory proceedings, the regulated industry may be able to provide incentives to the regulator to undertake favorable regulatory actions.

For any set of budgets and industry transfers, the regulator chooses the optimal action x (effort level), which in turn determines his expected utility. The regulator's utility function is assumed to be increasing in budgets and transfers, decreasing in the action x (effort), and separable in budgets, effort, and income (namely, industry's transfers).

The timing of the game between Congress, industry, and the regulator is as follows. First, Congress decides whether to allow industry transfers to the regulator. While in principle Congress could choose an optimal tax on industry's transfers, for simplicity I assume here that Congress either allows or prohibits transfers.[24] Congress makes public a budget offer to the regulator, which makes actual budgets contingent on the realized price. Second, if industry transfers are allowed, then, observing Congress's offer, industry chooses its best transfer offer, which also relates industry transfers to the realized price. Third, based on those offers, the regulator decides on an unobservable action, x. Following the regulator's action, a price is observed. Budgets and transfers follow.

Congress's optimal strategies (including its decision to prohibit industry transfers) anticipate the optimal industry offer to the regulator, as well as the optimal choice of x by the regulator. Similarly, industry's optimal transfer is calculated taking into account the optimal response by the regulator. Congress and industry can then be seen as two principals trying to influence a single agent (the regulator).[25] In this article, principals' strategies are constrained. In particular, budgets and transfers cannot be negative. Also, the equilibrium concept used here requires the principals to choose optimal sequential strategies, with Congress moving first.

Congress's strategies must satisfy the regulator's individual rationality constraint. That is, the regulator's expected utility must at least exceed

---

[24] Different regulatory agencies impose different restrictions on senior executives' post-agency employment. For example, the Federal Reserve Board allows board members to take industry jobs as long as they complete their full seven-year term. Other commissions, however, have less stringent requirements. Below, I discuss the rationale for congressional choice of different postagency employment restrictions.

[25] This model, then, captures parts of the multiple-principals/single-agent framework in B. Bernhaim & M. D. Whinston, Common Agency, 54 Econometrica 923 (1986); and the hierarchy framework developed in Jean Tirole, Hierarchies and Bureaucracies: On the Role of Collusion in Organizations, 2 J. L., Econ. & Org. 181 (1986). The hierarchy framework in this model is also related to that in Joel Demski & David E. Sappington, Hierarchical Regulatory Control, 18 Rand J. Econ. 369 (1987). While the focus of Demski and Sappington is on the role of private information by the regulatory agency, no consideration is given to the potential for third-party influence in the relation between the principal and its agent. In that sense, the framework in Demski and Sappington is in the traditional agency approach to regulation (see Baron & Myerson, *supra* note 8). See also David P. Baron, Noncooperative Regulation of a Nonlocalized Externality, 16 Rand J. Econ. 553 (1985); and John Ferejohn, Incumbent Performance and Electoral Control, 50 Pub. Choice 5 (1986), for analyses involving multiple principals.

his (known) reservation level (w^*). Industry's choice, in contrast, only takes into account the optimal choice of x by the regulator as a function of both Congress's and industry's offers.[26] Since industry benefits from no participation by the regulator. Congress must make sure that its offer provides the regulator enough utility to make his participation worthwhile for all feasible industry offers.[27] The game just described is formally presented in Appendix A.

The following notation and assumptions are used throughout the article: U_j, $j = 1, h$, represents Congress's utility from p_j; π_j, $j = 1. h$, is the industry profit derived from a price p_j; and $W(B, x) + T$ represents the utility of the regulator receiving a budget of B, a transfer of T, and performing the action x.[28]

$$W_B > 0. \quad W_x < 0. \quad W_{BB} < 0. \quad W_{BX} = 0. \quad W_{xx} < 0. \tag{1}$$

$$\phi'(x) > 0, \quad \phi''(x) \le 0, \quad \phi(0) = 0, \tag{2}$$

$$\Delta U = U_1 - U_h > \pi_h - \pi_1 = \Delta\Pi > 0. \tag{3}$$

Finally, when performing comparative statics with this model, the following assumptions will be made for computational simplicity:

$$\phi''(x) = 0, \tag{4}$$

$$W_{xxx} = 0. \tag{5}$$

III.   REGULATORY POLICY UNDER FULL INFORMATION

The thrust of this article is that informational problems are at the core of the relation between Congress and its regulators. To see the role of informational problems, it is worthwhile to analyze first the full informa-

---

[26] The equilibrium must also provide the principals with utility and profit levels above their nonparticipation levels. These constraints are assumed to be satisfied at the equilibrium.

[27] Alternatively, by withdrawing its transfer offer, industry could force the regulator to choose not to participate (that is, the regulator's individual rationality constraint will not be satisfied). Since in the absence of regulation a high price develops, industry would benefit from the no participation by the regulator.

[28] These assumptions are chosen so that the first-order approach to the principal-agent problem used here is valid. See William P. Rogerson, The First-Order Approach to Principal-Agent Problems, 53 Econometrica 1357 (1985); and Sandford J. Grossman & Oliver D. Hart, An Analysis of the Principal-Agency Problem, 51 Econometrica 7 (1983), for a discussion of the first-order approach and the sufficient conditions that make it valid.

tion solution to a game such as the one just described. In a full-information world, transfers from industry could be costlessly eliminated. Furthermore, industry will have no incentive to make transfers to the regulator. Instad, it will make direct transfers to Congress. Thus, industry transfers to regulators will play an important role only in an agency setting between Congress and the regulators. Since regulators' actions are observable, the only constraint Congress faces is that the contract offered to the regulator has to provide him with at least its reservation utility level. Observe, however, that, since the regulator is assumed to have disutility from effort, the equilibrium regulatory outcome implies a level of effort that may fall short of the one most preferred by Congress. In other words, simply delegating regulatory powers to an agency whose interests are not perfectly aligned with those of Congress may imply a regulatory outcome that takes other interests into account. That is, the equilibrium effort level is such that $\phi(x) \leq 1$.

The observability of the agent's actions imply that the risk-averse agent is provided with a constant payment (budget) while the single, risk-neutral principal (Congress) is allocated all the risk. Furthermore, because of the observability of the regulator's actions, he is driven to his reservation level, and Congress's welfare is maximized subject to those constraints. Consequently, the rates of substitution between effort and budget for both Congress and the regulator are equalized.[29] These results are formally presented in lemma B1 in Appendix B and are used in the next sections to compare the level of effort under full information with those achieved when the regulator's actions are not observable under the different institutional settings.

IV.   Equilibrium Outcomes

This section is organized in four parts. In the first part, I discuss the regulatory equilibrium that occurs when Congress effectively prohibits industry from making any type of transfer to the regulator. This equilibrium is then compared, in the two subsequent parts, to the situation that develops when industry transfers are allowed. Since in the latter game regulators obtain rents, I introduce, in the last part of this section, competition among the regulators for regulatory positions.

---

[29] This result suggests that Congress could benefit from appointing regulators with "better aligned" political and regulatory tastes (see Calvert *et al., supra* note 6). Once industry's transfers are introduced, however, different regulator's preferences would imply different industry transfer levels.

A. No Industry Transfers

If Congress is able to restrict industry from offering transfers to regulators, the game[30] becomes one between Congress and the regulator.[31] It is, then, a simple principal-agent problem. The equilibrium is then a pair (B, x), $B = (B_1, B_h)$, such that

$$x = \operatorname*{argmax}_{\{x\}} \{\phi(x)W(B_1, x) + [1 - \phi(x)]W(B_h, x)\}, \tag{6}$$

$$B = \operatorname*{argmax}_{\{B_1,B_h\}} \{\phi(x)[U_1 - B_1] + [1 - \phi(x)](U_h - B_h)\}, \tag{7}$$

subject to

$$x = \operatorname*{argmax}_{\{y\}} \{\phi(y)W(B_1, y) + [1 - \phi(y)]W(B_h, y)\}, \tag{8}$$

and

$$\phi(x)W(B_1, x) + [1 - \phi(x)]W(B_h, x) \geq w^*, \tag{9}$$

where (8) and (9) represent the constraints involving the regulator's optimal choice of effort and his participation decision (or individual rationality constraint), respectively, while (6) and (7) are the regulator's and Congress's problems, respectively.

In the usual way, the model is solved backward by first analyzing the regulator's problem given in (6). The first-order condition for the regulator, for any (B_1, B_h), is given by

$$\phi'(x)[W(B_1, x) - W(B_h, x)] + W_x(B_h, x) + \xi^{Rx} = 0, \quad x\xi^{Rx} = 0.^{32} \tag{10}$$

Equation (10) establishes a correspondence between x and the actual values of Congress's budgets. The internal solution to (10) is of the form

$$x = x(B_1, B_h), \tag{11}$$

with $x_{B1} > 0$ and $x_{Bh} < 0$.[33]

The solution to the game with no industry transfers is fully character-

---

[30] In what follows, I will refer to the "unrestricted' ("restricted") game as that where industry is (is not) allowed to make transfers to the regulator.

[31] This would be the case if, for example, Congress could impose a lifetime ban on private employment following governmental work and strictly control postagency earnings.

[32] The variable $\xi u2j$ are slack variables associated with first-order conditions with respect to the variable j. Thus, in eq. (10), ξ^{Rx} represents the slack variable associated with the regulator's first-order condition.

[33] Assumptions (1)–(3) guarantee the signs of the partial derivatives of $x(\cdot)$, with $x_{B1} = -\phi'W_B^1/[\phi''(W_1 - W_h) + W_{xx}]$, $x_{Bh} = \phi'W_B^h/[\phi''(W_1 - W_h) + W_{xx}]$, $W_j = W(B_j, x)$; W_B^j represents the derivative of $W(B, x)$ with respect to B evaluated at B_j.

ized in lemma C1 in Appendix C. A couple of results are worth noting here. First, from (10) we observe that for positive regulatory effort to be undertaken, budgets in low-price states must exceed those in high-price states. Second, Congress may find it optimal to provide zero budgets in high-price states. It is straightforward to see that, if in the equilibrium the regulator's individual rationality constraint is not binding, it does not pay Congress to provide a compensation to the regulator in high-price states. These results are at the core of the agency problem between Congress and its regulator. Compare them with the optimal budget levels under full information. In that case, Congress allocates a constant regulatory budget simply to provide the regulator with a level of utility equal to his reservation level. In the presence of informational problems, however, it becomes optimal for Congress to make budgets contingent on observable regulatory outcomes.

Finally, informational problems not only imply a different budget policy but also have an effect on the level of regulatory effort and on the level of expected regulatory budgets. Proposition D1, given in Appendix D, shows that under some conditions the full information level of regulatory effort is achievable. However, if Congress wants to achieve that level, it will have to provide, on average, larger budgets than under full information. Hence, the full information regulatory equilibrium is not an equilibrium to the restricted game. Consider now the case when Congress either chooses not to, or cannot, restrict industry transfer.

B. Equilibrium with Industry Transfers

When Congress is unable (or prefers not) to restrict industry's transfer to the regulator, competition between Congress and industry develops. The difference between the outcome to this game and the one where Congress prohibits industry transfers arises because $\pi_1 < \pi_h$ while $U_1 > U_h$. That is, the regulatory objectives of the two principals are contradictory. The opposite interests of industry and Congress imply that with positive industry transfers the regulator enjoys a utility level above his reservation level. Observe that the individual rationality constraint in (A3), in Appendix A, is calculated at the level of effort that the regulator would undertake if faced with $T = 0$, and $B = (B_h, B_1)$.[34] Otherwise, if with positive transfers the regulator was just obtaining its reservation utility level, industry would provide no transfer, and the regulator would choose not to participate. Thus, because industry prefers no regulation, we obtain the following corollary.

[34] This level of effort (x_0) is the equilibrium level only when the optimal industry transfer is in fact $T = 0$.

COROLLARY 1.   If the equilibrium involves positive transfers by industry, then the regulator's expected utility exceeds his reservation level.[35]

Since so far no entry barriers to regulatory positions have been introduced, the existence of regulatory rents implies that potential regulators would dissipate their rents. In the next subsection I analyze in more detail the incentives for Congress to create a rent-dissipation mechanism. Here, however, the analysis continues assuming that regulatory positions have already been assigned.[36]

Let us first analyze the regulator's problem in the unrestricted game, given in equation (A1) in Appendix A. The first-order condition for the regulator, for any (B, T), is given now by

$$\phi'(x)[W(B_1, x) + T_1 - W(B_h, x) - T_h] + W_x(B_h, x) + \xi^x = 0, \quad x\xi^x = 0. \tag{12}$$

COROLLARY 2.   Observe that, as in the game with no industry transfers, internal equilibria imply that the regulator must prefer a low-price to a high-price outcome. That is, $x > 0$, if and only if

$$W(B_1, x) + T_1 > W(B_h, x) + T_h.$$

Since it is shown below that $T_1 = 0$, corollary 2 implies, again, that budgets in low-price states must exceed budgets in high-price states. Here, however, the introduction of industry transfers provides further implications, which are described in lemma 1.

LEMMA 1.   The interior solution to the game with industry transfers is given by

$$T_1 = 0, \quad T_h \geq 0, \tag{i}$$

$$B_1 > B_h \geq 0, \tag{ii}$$

$$\text{if } \delta = 0, \quad \text{then } B_h = 0, \tag{iii}$$

$$\phi = 0 \text{ implies } B_1 = 0, \quad 1 - \phi = 0 \text{ implies } T_h = 0, \tag{iv}$$

and

$$EW = \phi(x)(W_1 - W_h - T_h) + [1 - \phi(x)](W_h + T_h) \geq w^*, \tag{v}$$

---

[35] This result does not imply that the individual rationality constraint in Congress's problem is never binding at the equilibrium since this constraint is calculated at zero industry transfers.

[36] As will become evident in the next subsection, regulatory rent dissipation has no implication for the actual level of budgets, transfers, or regulatory effort. Thus, the current omission of the mechanism to determine regulatory positions is, so far, innocuous.

with the inequality in equation (v) being strict when $T_h > 0$. The parameter δ, $0 \leq \delta \leq 1/W_B^h$, represents the Lagrange multiplier associated with the individual rationality constraint in Congress's problem.

The proof of lemma 1 is given in Appendix E. The intuition behind lemma 1 is that both industry and Congress will try to influence the regulator to take favorable actions. In the case of industry, such an action would be to undertake a low regulatory effort. This can be achieved by making the compensation to the regulator very large when there is a favorable outcome (a high price), while punishing him for unfavorable outcomes. Thus, both Congress and industry make low transfers in (the respective) unfavorable outcomes (items [i]–[ii]). Since transfers are restricted to nonnegative values, the worst punishment is a transfer of zero (items [i]–[iii]). Since industry does not have to guarantee the participation of the regulator, it will always make zero transfers in unfavorable states. Congress, however, may find it necessary to provide positive budgets in high-price states so that the individual rationality constraint of the regulator is satisfied, that is, so that the expected utility of the regulator exceeds its reservation level (item [v]).

Lemma C1 (in App. C) and lemma 1 show that budget restrictions follow unfavorable outcomes and, in the unrestricted game, are accompanied by industry transfers. Thus, corollary 3 follows.

COROLLARY 3.   Budget restrictions follow unfavorable outcomes for Congress and are accompanied by industry transfers.

This result arises exclusively because of the agency problems between Congress, industry, and the regulators. As discussed above, if Congress could costlessly control its regulators, budgets would be insensitive to regulatory outcomes and industry would make no transfers to regulators. Instead, industry influence could be achieved directly through transfers to congressmen. Thus, corollary 3 provides an empirically testable implication that is at the core of the agency part of the self-interest theory of regulation.

Lemma C1 and lemma 1 also show that the budget and effort allocations in the restricted and the unrestricted games are not the same.[37] In the game with no industry transfers, it can be seen as well that, for every budget offer, the optimal regulatory effort (x) exceeds that when transfers are allowed. The intuition is clear: when transfers are allowed, industry is able to compensate the regulator for high-price outcomes. Thus, given

---

[37] Substituting (B^*, x^*) (the solution to the equilibrium with industry transfers) into (10), we observe that the value for the left-hand side of (10) is positive. Thus, (B^*, x^*) is not a solution to the game without industry transfers.

any offer B, the regulator will tend to provide less regulatory effort.[38] Furthermore, proposition 1 shows that competition between Congress and industry generates social overexpenditure on regulation-related activities:

PROPOSITION 1.   In the presence of direct industry transfers, the total monetary expenditure on regulation exceeds the minimum required to achieve the equilibrium regulatory outcome.

The proof of proposition 1 is given in Appendix F.[39] Proposition 1 impiles that, if industry were allowed to make direct transfers to Congress *but not* to the regulators, then both industry and Congress could be made better off. Thus, corollary 4 follows.

COROLLARY 4.   If industry is not allowed to pay congressmen directly, social overexpenditure in regulation is an equilibrium outcome.

Observe that corollary 4 does not say that regulatory agency budgets are necessarily larger than would be if no industry transfers were allowed. Rather, total social expenditure on regulation is above what would be necessary if Congress and industry would coordinate their actions.[40] Whether actual budgets increase when industry transfers are allowed cannot be answered in general terms.[41]

C.. Comparative Statics in the Presence of Industry Transfers

While there are feasible corner solutions when industry transfers are allowed (that is, $T = B = x = 0$, or $B \geq 0$, $x > 0$, $T = 0$), here I concentrate on internal solutions. The parameters of the model are w^*, π_1, π_h, U_1, and U_h, while the endogenous variables are B_1, B_h, T_1, T_h, and x. When the individual rationality constraint is not binding, namely $\delta = 0$, the interior solutions are functions of the profit difference, $\Delta\Pi = \pi_h - \pi_1$, and of the consumer surplus difference, $\Delta U = U_1 - U_h$. By fully differentiating the first-order conditions (see App. E, eqq. [E1a–E2b]) and holding constant $\{p_1, p_h\}$, the following comparative statics are derived.

LEMMA 2.   If, in the game with industry transfers, the individual rationality constraint is not binding ($\delta = 0$), then

---

[38] The expected budget, however, may be higher in the unrestricted game.

[39] See Bernhaim & Whinston, *supra* note 25, for a general proof of this proposition. In Appendix F, I present a direct proof of the proposition.

[40] See Niskanen, *supra* note 4, for a different overexpenditure result.

[41] The presumption is that, since allowing industry transfers exacerbates the "agency" problem, Congress will try to control the regulator by offering him a riskier lottery (that is, Congress may want to increase the difference between B_1 and B_h). This result, while plausible, is not always correct. In Section VI, I present an example in which, when the regulator's individual rationality constraint is not binding, the equilibrium budget for the restricted and unrestricted case is the same.

$$\frac{dB_1}{d\Delta\Pi} = \frac{1}{\Omega} > 0, \qquad\qquad \frac{dB_1}{d\Delta U} = \frac{W_B^1}{\Omega} > 0,$$

$$\frac{dT_h}{d\Delta\Pi} = 1/2 + \frac{W_B^1}{2\Omega} > 0, \qquad \frac{dT_h}{d\Delta U} = \frac{(W_B^1)^2}{2\Omega} > 0,$$

$$\frac{dx}{d\Delta\Pi} = \frac{\phi'(x)[W_B^1 - (\Delta U - B_1)W_{BB}^1]}{2W_{xx}\Omega} < 0,$$

$$\frac{dx}{d\Delta U} = \frac{-\phi'(x)(W_B^1)^2}{2W_{xx}\Omega} > 0,$$

where $\Omega = 2W_B^1 - (\Delta U - B_1)W_{BB}^1 > 0$. The proof of lemma 2 is straightforward and is not presented here. It involves taking the full derivatives of the first-order conditions of the unrestricted game.[42]

Lemma 2 has several empirical implications that are similar to those originally developed in Peltzman.[43] Here, however, these results do not arise from the workings of Peltzman's "political wealth effect" but, rather, from competition between the two principals in an "agency" framework.[44] First, observe that, if the marginal utility of a dollar of budget (in the low-price state) is less than the marginal utility of a dollar of transfer ($W_B^1 < 1$), then budgets, transfers, and regulatory effort are more sensitive to changes in profit differentials ($\Delta\Pi$) than to changes in consumer-surplus differentials (ΔU). The rationale for this result is that, if in equilibrium $W_B^1 < 1$, then Congress compensates regulators with a relatively inefficient instrument, and a marginal increase in budgets increases regulatory effort by less than a marginal increase in transfers ($|dx/dB_1| = -\phi'(x)W_B^1/W_{xx} < -\phi'(x)/W_{xx} = |dx/dT_h|$). That would not be the case if Congress could make direct monetary transfers to its regulators. Thus, we can state proposition 2.

PROPOSITION 2. If, in the solution to the game with industry transfers, $W_B^1 < 1$, and if the regulator's individual rationality constraint is not binding ($\delta = 0$), then changes in budgets, transfers, and regulatory effort

---

[42] When $\delta > 0$, the comparative statics become much more complicated. Still, it can be shown that the following holds:

$$\frac{dB_1}{d\Delta U} > 0, \quad \frac{dB_h}{d\Delta U} < 0, \quad \frac{dT_h}{d\Delta U} > 0, \quad \frac{dx}{d\Delta U} > 0.$$

$$\frac{dB_1}{d\Delta\Pi} > 0, \quad \frac{dB_h}{d\Delta\Pi} < 0, \quad \frac{dT_h}{d\Delta\Pi} > 0, \quad \frac{dx}{d\Delta\Pi} < 0.$$

[43] Peltzman, *supra* note 1.

[44] That this model shares, under some conditions, many of Peltzman's results (see *id.*, *supra* note 1) is not surprising once it is realized that the regulator in the current model takes both Congress's (or consumers') and industry's interests into account.

are more sensitive to changes in profit differentials than to changes in consumer surplus differentials.

Proposition 2 also implies that the regulatory system will be less responsive to political changes (in Congress's ΔU) than to changes in technology (whch change $\Delta \Pi$ but not necessarily ΔU).

Most of Peltzman's main results can be derived from this framework by the introduction of some additional assumptions. For example, if the distribution of the potential outcomes of the regulatory activity (that is, $\{p_l, p_h\}$) remains constant, then an increase in marginal cost would increase the profit differential ($\Delta \Pi$) but not consumer surplus differential (ΔU). Consequently, an increase in marginal cost implies a reduction in regulatory effort, increasing the expected price. In contrast, an increase in demand increases both the profit and the consumer differential, which have opposite effects on the regulator's incentive to provide effort. Thus, increases in demand will increase both budgets and transfers, with a small effect on the equilibrium price distribution. A similar increase in the profit differential arising from a marginal cost increase will have a larger effect on expected prices.

Thus, from proposition 2 we obtain corollary 5.

COROLLARY 5.   The regulatory system dampens the effect of demand but magnifies the effect of costs on expected prices.

Furthermore, if during booms ΔU increases but $\Delta \Pi$ falls, with the opposite holding during recessions,[45] then lemma 2 predicts that regulatory effort will increase during booms and fall during recessions. The rationale for this result is that during booms Congress's willingness to pay for regulatory effort increases while industry's falls. Thus, corollary 6 follows.

COROLLARY 6.   If ΔU ($\Delta \Pi$) is procyclical (anticyclical), then regulations are oriented toward "consumer protection" during booms and toward "producer protection" during recessions.

From lemma 2 we also obtain that the regulation of industries with low costs will be more weighted toward "consumer protection" than that of high-cost industries. If regulated industries differ only in their productivity (more precisely, in their marginal cost), then the more productive industries will have lower $\Delta \Pi$s and will subject to higher levels of regulatory effort. Thus, while more productive industries may have higher profits, they may also be more heavily regulated. As in Peltzman,[46] profits and "industry capture" will be negatively correlated. Another similar

---

[45] This will be the case if during booms productivity increases while demand functions rotate outward and become more elastic.

[46] Peltzman, *supra* note 1.

implication[47] relates to Congress's incentives to regulate industries. In particular, since so far we have assumed that Congress cannot extract the rents from its regulators, its largest regulatory benefits arise from large-demand, low-cost industries. In those industries the profit differential is smaller, implying smaller regulatory agency costs. Thus, we can state lemma 3.

LEMMA 3. If Congress cannot extract the regulator's rents, and if in the equilibrium the individual rationality constraint is not binding ($\delta = 0$), then Congress's benefits from regulation are increasing in consumer surplus but decreasing on the profit differential.[48]

This result, however, may not follow if Congress is able to extract regulator's rents. In particular, see lemma 4.

LEMMA 4. If the individual rationality constraint is not binding, then regulators' rents increase with both ΔU and $\Delta \Pi$.[49]

The proofs of lemmas 3 and 4 are straightforward and are not presented here.

Lemmas 3 and 4 introduce the possibility that by extracting regulators' rents, Congress's benefits from regulation may actually increase with the extent of industry opposition to regulation (that is, with the industry's profit differential). In this case, Congress's incentives to restrict industry transfers may fall. These issues are analyzed next.[50]

---

[47] *Id.*

[48] It is straightforward to see that

$$\frac{dEU}{d\Delta\Pi} = \frac{[\phi'(x)]^2[W_B^1 - (\Delta U - B_1)W_{BB}^1]}{2W_{xx}[2W_B^1 - (\Delta U - B_1)W_{BB}^1]}$$

$$- \frac{\phi(x)}{[2W_B^1 - (\Delta U - B_1)W_{BB}^1]} < 0, \quad \frac{dEU}{d\Delta U} = \phi(x).$$

where $EU = \phi(x)(U_1 - B_1) + [1 - \phi(x)](U_h - B_h)$.

[49] That is, if in the solution to the game with industry transfers the individual rationality constraint is not binding, then

$$\frac{dEW}{d\Delta\Pi} = [1 - \phi(x)]/2 + [1 - \phi(x)]\frac{W_B^1}{[2W_B^1 - (\Delta U - B_1)W_{BB}^1]} > 0,$$

and

$$\frac{dEW}{d\Delta U} = \frac{(W_B^1)^2}{2[2W_B^1 - (\Delta U - B_1)W_{BB}^1]}[1 + \phi(x)] > 0.$$

where $EW = \phi(x)[W(B_1, x) - W(B_h, x) + T_1 - T_h] + W(B_h, x) + T_h - T_1$.

[50] Observe that the cases where Congress chooses to regulate industries with large $\Delta\Pi$ resemble extortion by regulation. That is, the equilibrium outcome implies low regulatory activity but large industry transfers, which Congress eventually appropriates. Thus, even if ΔU were very small, Congress may find it worth regulating, simply to extract rents. These issues are further discussed below.

D. Bidding for Regulatory Positions

As discussed above, if industry transfers are positive, regulators receive rents.[51] A bidding process, then, should develop by which potential regulators transfer all their expected rents to Congress. The actual bid, however, has no effect on the regulator's incentives once on the job. Thus, the bidding process by itself has no effect on the equilibrium budgets, transfers, or regulatory effort or on the regulator's individual rationality constraint.[52] I combine lemmas 3 and 4 to obtain corollary 7.

COROLLARY 7.   If potential regulators bid all their expected excess rents to Congress, and if in the equilibrium the regulator's individual rationality constraint is not binding ($\delta = 0$), then it is feasible that increases in the profit differential increase Congress's expected utility from the regulation.[53]

Corollary 7, then, implies that Congress may find it optimal not to restrict industry transfers. The following section analyzes conditions under which Congress may allow industry to make transfers to regulators.

V. OPTIMAL CHOICE OF RESTRICTIONS ON INDUSTRY TRANSFERS

The ability of industry to make transfers to regulators has two counterbalancing effects on congressional benefits from regulation. On the one hand, industry transfers exacerbate the "agency" problem between Congress and the regulator. On the other hand, regulator's rents are larger when industry transfers are allowed. Congress will then balance increased appropriation of regulator's rents against a lower level of direct regulatory

---

[51] This result holds even when the individual rationality constraint is binding.

[52] Would-be regulators are supposed to bid for their rights to become regulators. If regulatory appointments were allocated to the highest bidder, then the regulator that can capture the largest rent would obtain the position. Thus, the would-be regulator with the lowest w^* will obtain the position. If regulator's utility were also a function of the regulatory outcome, then regulatory rents would also depend on the characteristics of the regulator's utility function. Congress would then allocate regulatory positions on that basis. On a model trying to explore this insight, see Matthew D. McCubbins, Roger G. Noll, & Barry R. Weingast, Administrative Procedures as Instruments of Political Control (presented at the symposium on the Law and Economics of Procedure, Columbia Law School, New York, February 1987). Observe also that for regulators to be able to bid their expected rents, they must have either acess to credit markets or assets of equivalent value.

[53] Formally, under the conditions of corollary 7,

$$\frac{dEU^B}{d\Delta\Pi} = \frac{W_B^1[1 + \phi(x)] - 2\phi}{2[2W_B^1 - (\Delta U - B_1)W_{BB}^1]} + \frac{(1 - \phi)}{2} + \frac{(\phi')^2[W_B^1 - (\Delta U - B1)W_{BB}^1]}{2W_{xx}[2W_B^1 - (\Delta U - B_1)W_{BB}^1]}$$

$$\geq 0, \frac{dEU^B}{d\Delta U} = \phi + (1 + \phi) \frac{(W_B^1)^2}{2[2W_B^1 - (\Delta U - B_1)W_{BB}^1]} > 0,$$

where $EU^B = EU + EW - w^*$.

benefit. Thus, if the direct cost of lower regulatory effort is too large (namely, a large ΔU) then Congress should prefer to restrict industry transfers.

If the individual rationality constraint is binding in the restricted game, however, then in the absence of industry transfers there are no rents that Congress can appropriate from the regulators. Thus, the gains from allowing industry transfers may substantially exceed those that can be obtained when the individual rationality constraint is not binding in the restricted game. Therefore, we should expect less restrictions on industry transfers for regulators whose reservation utility levels are relatively high.

Proposition 3 shows that, if Congress cannot capture the regulators' rents, then in the absence of enforcement costs Congress will choose to prohibit industry from making transfer offers.

PROPOSITION 3. Under assumptions (1)–(5), in the absence of regulatory bidding, $EU^R > EU^U$, where EU^R (EU^U) represents Congress's expected utility when industry transfers are prohibited (allowed).

The proof of the proposition is given in Appendix G. The intuition for this proposition is clear. Industry transfers increase the cost of regulations, reducing Congress's expected gains from regulation. This proposition has implications for understanding the process of regulatory appointments and interest group influence. If Congress could not extract rents from the regulators, it would prefer to deter interest groups from directly influencing the regulatory process. Restricting interest groups, however, may be costly. In that case, partial restrictions may be optimal. They may be implemented in two different ways. First, all regulators may be deterred equally from employment in agency-related businesses. Alternatively, different regulatory agencies may stipulate different restrictions. The current model provides a direct rationale for Congress to impose different postagency employment restrictions across agencies. If the cost of enforcing those restrictions are independent of their benefits,[54] then agencies where the difference between EU^R and EU^U is not too large should have more permissive postagency employment restrictions. In the example given in Section VI, the larger ΔU, the larger the difference between EU^R and EU^U.[55] Also, for the same example, Table 1 shows that the larger w^*, the lower the difference between EU^R and EU^U. Observe, also, that regulatory effort increases with ΔU but falls with w^*. Thus, the industries for which it is optimal to relax postagency employment restric-

---

[54] Enforcement costs relate to those costs incurred in order to deter industry from making payments to regulators. These costs may involve the costs of examining former regulators' income tax returns, enforcing restrictions on postagency employment, and so on.

[55] This can be seen from Table 1 for the case of $w^* > \Delta U/12$ and from comparing lemmas 5 and 6, below, for the case when $w^* < \Delta U/12$.

TABLE 1

Simulation Results

ΔU (1)	w^* (2)	EU^{BU} (3)	EU^U (4)	EB^U (5)	EU^R (6)	EB^R (7)
2.2	.2	.610	.313	.179	.626	.358
	.4	.524	.204	.383	.429	.625
	.6	.324	.004	.583	.149	.762
	.8	.044	−.276	.863	−.191	.999
	1.0	−.316	−.636	1.223	−.600	1.327
2.6	.4	.648	.318	.464	.638	.852
	.6	.448	.118	.664	.328	.924
	.8	.168	−.162	.944	−.033	1.136
	1.0	−.192	−.522	1.304	−.458	1.448
3.0	.4	.775	.443	.506	.885	1.012
	.6	.578	.245	.765	.536	1.144
	.8	.298	−.035	1.045	.148	1.304
	1.0	−.062	−.395	1.405	−.295	1.591
3.6	.4	.965	.632	.506	1.265	1.012
	.6	.789	.465	.929	.916	1.516
	.8	.505	.186	1.262	.469	1.655
	1.0	.145	−.174	1.623	−.012	1.864
	1.2	−.295	−.614	2.062	−.547	2.212
4.0	.4	1.092	.759	.506	1.518	1.012
	.6	.944	.620	.929	1.239	1.859
	.8	.652	.358	1.431	.724	2.069
	1.0	.250	.000	1.999	.206	2.103
	1.2	−.190	−.440	2.439	−.352	2.404

Note.—We denote

$$EU^{BL} = \phi(U_1 - B_1) + (1 - \phi)(U_h - B_h) + EW - w^*,$$

and

$$EU^U, EU^R = \phi(U_1 - B_1) + (1 - \phi)(U_h - B_h),$$

where values are given by lemmas 5 and 6 for the restricted and the unrestricted case, respectively.

tions are also those where regulatory effort (in the absence of industry transfers) would not have been "too" large. Allowing transfers would further reduce the extent of regulatory effort. Thus, on average, the regulatory process should be more proindustry in cases for which Congress allows direct industry influence.

VI. Regulatory Bidding and Optimal Restrictions: An Example

The purpose of this example is to present, for a specific probability and regulatory utility functions, conditions under which Congress will allow industry transfers when regulators' jobs are obtained through bidding.

The regulator's utility and probability functions are specified as follows:

$$W(B, x) = \sqrt{B} - x^2, \tag{13}$$

$$\phi(x) = x, \quad 0 \le x \le 1. \tag{14}$$

Also, I normalize the problem by assuming

$$\Delta\Pi = \pi_h - \pi_1 = 2. \tag{15}$$

Below I analyze the solution to the games when Congress does and does not allow industry transfers. First, lemmas 5 and 6 present the equilibria under both regimes. Substituting assumptions into the first order conditions for the restricted and unrestricted games, we obtain the following results.[56]

LEMMA 5. Under assumptions (1)–(5) and (13)–(15), in the absence of direct industry transfers, the equilibrium is characterized by

$$x = (\sqrt{B_1} - \sqrt{B_h})/2, \quad \delta > (=) \quad 0 \quad \text{if } w^* > (<) \Delta U/12,$$

and, if $\delta = 0$, then

$$B_1 = \Delta U/3, \quad B_h = 0,$$

$$EU^R = (\Delta U/3)\sqrt{(\Delta U/3)} + U_h,$$

$$EW^R = \Delta U/12,^{[57]}$$

where $EU^R = \phi(U_1 - B_1) + (1 - \phi)(U_h - B_h)$, and $EW^R = \phi W(B_1, x) + (1 - \phi)W(B_h, x)$.

LEMMA 6. Under assumptions (1)–(5) and (13)–(15), in the presence of direct industry transfers, the equilibrium is characterized by

$$x = (\sqrt{B_1} - \sqrt{B_h} - T_h)/2,$$

$$T_h = (\sqrt{B_1} - \sqrt{B_h})/2,$$

$$T_1 = 0, \delta^c > (<) 0 \quad \text{if } w^* > (<) \Delta U/12,$$

and, if $\delta^c = 0$, then

$$B_1 = \Delta U/3, \quad B_h = 0,$$

$$EW^U = \Delta U/48 - \sqrt{(\Delta U/12)} > \Delta U/12 > w^*.$$

and

$$EU^U = (\Delta U/6)\sqrt{(\Delta U/3)} + U_h),^{[58]}$$

---

[56] See Appendix E for the first-order conditions of the game with industry transfers. The first-order conditions for the game without industry transfers can be similarly derived.

[57] If $\delta > 0$, then B_h and B_1 are implicitly determined by $\Delta U - 12(w^* - \sqrt{B_h}) + 8(w^* - \sqrt{B_h})\sqrt{(w^* - \sqrt{B_h})} - 4\sqrt{B_h}\sqrt{w^* - \sqrt{B_h}} = 0$, and $\sqrt{B_1} = \sqrt{B_h} + 2\sqrt{(w^* - \sqrt{B_h})}$.

[58] If $\delta^c > 0$, then $\sqrt{B_h}$ and $\sqrt{B_1}$ are implicitly given by $\sqrt{B_1} = \sqrt{B_h} + 2\sqrt{(w^* - \sqrt{B_h})}$, and $\Delta U - 12(w^* - \sqrt{B_h}) + 8(w^* - \sqrt{B_h})\sqrt{(w^* - \sqrt{B_h})} = 0$.

where EU^U (EW^U) represents Congress's (the regulator's) expected utility in the unrestricted case.

The proofs of lemmas 5 and 6 are derived from lemmas C1 and 1 and are not presented.[59]

I will now analyze congressional choice of restrictions, assuming that restrictions are chosen to capture regulators' rents. A bidding process, by which regulators bid up to their expected rents ($EW - w^*$), constitutes such a process.[60] The following proposition presents the result of the institutional comparison in the presence of regulatory bidding.

PROPOSITION 4.   Under assumptions (1)–(5) and (13)–(15), if regulators' jobs are obtained through bidding, then, if the individual rationality constraint is not binding (that is, $\delta = 0$ for $w^* < \Delta U/12$), then, for $\Delta U < 2.0663$, $EU^{BU} > EU^R$.

Variable EU^{BU} (EU^R) represents Congress's expected utility when transfers are (are not) allowed and regulators bid (do not bid) for their positions. When the individual rationality constraint is not binding, direct comparison of EU^{BU} and EU^R from lemmas 5 and 6 can be performed, showing the proposition.

The result presented in proposition 4 can be augmented by analyzing the simulation results presented in Table 1, columns 3 and 6. There it is seen that, when the individual rationality constraint is binding (that is, $w^* > \Delta U/12$), then, for each ΔU, there exists a $W^*(\Delta U)$ such that, for $w^* > W^*(\Delta U)$, $EU^{BU} > EU^R$.[61]

These results provide the strongest self-interest argument for Congress to allow direct industry transfers to regulators. By increasing regulator's rents, direct industry transfers increase the amount potential regulators are willing to bid for their positions, increasing congressmen's rents from the political process. Observe that allowing industry transfers may actually benefit the industry and hurt consumers. If consumers do not appropriate congressmen's rents, then proposition 3 implies that allowing trans-

---

[59] it is straightforward to see that the following comparative statics hold:

$$dT_h/dw^* \geq 0, \quad dB_1/dw \geq 0, \quad dB_h/dw^* \leq 0, \quad dEB/dw^* \geq, \quad dx/dw^* \geq 0,$$

and

$$dT_h/d\Delta U > 0, \quad dB_1/d\Delta U > 0, \quad dB_h/d\Delta U < 0, \quad dEB/d\Delta U > 0, \quad dx/d\Delta U > 0,$$

where EB represents the expected congressional budgetary allocation.

[60] If Congress captures the regulators' rents, then Congress's ex ante expected utility will be given by $EU^B = EU + EW - w^* = \phi(x)(U_1 - B_1) + [1 - \phi(x)](U_h - B_h) + \phi(x)(W_1 + T_1) + [1 - \phi(x)](W_h - T_h) - w^*$.

[61] Observe that, if there are enforcement costs, then the inequalities in proposition 4 should be further relaxed.

fers makes them worse off.[62] Industry, however, may benefit. Observe first that the equilibrium conditions for internal solutions require that industry's best response to a congressional budget offer be a positive transfer. Thus, in equilibrium, a positive transfer provides higher profits than a zero transfer. Budget offers, however, may differ across institutional arrangements, and, thus, it is conceivable that industry could be made worse off by allowing transfers.[63] In the example provided in this section, however, industry's profits are larger when transfers are allowed.[64,65] Thus, corollary 8 follows.

COROLLARY 8. If regulators bid for their jobs, Congress would prefer to allow industry transfers if regulators' reservation utility level is relatively high or if the costs from a lower regulatory effort level (ΔU) are relatively low.

VII. A TEST OF THE MODEL

The model presented in this article can be tested by analyzing the determinants of the career path of bureaucrats. The main implications of the agency model developed above are first, Congress and industry will reward regulators for favorable outcomes by increasing their transfers; second, regulators' rents are dissipated through bidding for regulatory positions. Appointments, then, take the form of patronage. Real politics, however, are not as simple as the model presented here. In particular, politicians have other instruments to reward regulators for favorable outcomes. Regulators may be appointed to more prestigious positions in the public sector (like cabinet positions) or rewarded with access to Congressmen, thereby increasing their general productivity. Since commissioners leave their agencies almost every year, Congress will use all its instruments to reward and punish its regulators. If there is a favorable outcome, the commission's budget will be increased, and those regulators that quit the agency will be provided with other nonbudgetary compensations.

---

[62] This result shows that there is also an important agency problem between voters and their own representatives that in a more general framework should also be addressed.

[63] In particular, if the equilibrium regulatory effort does not differ much under both institutional regimes, allowing transfers may imply a lower industry-expected profit. Hence, industry may find it worth supporting restrictions on its own transfers.

[64] It is easy to compute that, if the individual rationality constraint is not binding, then the increase in industry's expected profits from allowing transfers to the regulators equals $\Delta U/24$.

[65] Industry and consumers, however, could be made better off by allowng transfers only to congressmen. See proposition 1.

Similarly, industry does not have to provide the regulator with a job to compensate him for favorable outcomes. For example, the regulator may go to work for a law firm, with industry channeling some of its legal work through it.

Thus, the strongest empirical implication of the model is that, conditioned on a regulator quitting the commission, the probability of going to work (directly or indirectly) for the industry falls with the agency's budget during the regulator's last period at the agency.[66,67]

Eckert[68] shows that the typical career path for regulatory commissioners consists of coming to the agency with substantial previous public-sector experience and, in an important proportion, leaving the commission to work (directly or indirectly) for the industry they previously regulated. As Eckert suggests, this stylized fact cannot reject the specific-capital hypothesis—namely, that during their tenure at the commissions regulators acquire substantial industry-specific capital, making an industry-related position more attractive. The specific-capital hypothesis, however, does not share the main empirical implication of the agency framework. In particular, if the regulator's ability is unknown to the private sector, an augmented signaling-cum-specific-capital hypothesis would predict a positive, rather than negative, correlation between budgets and the probability of regulated industry jobs. A larger budget would imply that the regulator is an able and productive manager. Since he also has acquired industry-specific capital, larger budgets should be positively correlated with industry jobs.[69]

A second empirical implication of the model is the use of patronage. Clearly, not all regulatory appointments are patronage appointments. Many (and perhaps some of the most important) regulators have had no public service experience at all. The rationale for their appointment may not be to capture their potential economic rents but, rather, to appoint regulators whose ideological preferences or interests are similar to those

---

[66] It is clear that the decision to quit at a given period depends on (among other things) the available offers the regulator has received. Therefore, the optimal quitting time and post-agency employment will be related. While a general model that estimates simultaneously the optimal length of stay at the agency and the optimal career choice could be developed, it is beyond the scope of this work.

[67] The type of budget concept that I use is described in Section VIII.

[68] Ross D. Eckert, The Life Cycle of Regulatory Commissioners. 24 J. Law & Econ. 113 (1981).

[69] A positive correlation between industry jobs and budgets is further strengthened from a strategic consideration. Since industry prefers to be regulated by ineffective regulators, it may find it optimal to hire those commissioners that turn out to be efficient regulators. Thus, if a larger budget is a proxy for the regulator's unobserved ability, the probability of an industry job increases with the budget.

of congressmen. Those regulators, then, will be less receptive to industry offers. Thus, the probability of obtaining industry-related jobs should be smaller for nonpatronage appointments.[70]

A third empirical implication is derived from the passing, in 1978, of a broad government ethics bill (S.555) imposing new restrictions on senior government employees' postgovernment employment. Under the new bill, former employees could never lobby the government on matters they directly worked on. The bill also required a cooling-off period of one or two years in which former government employees would be restricted from contacting their former agencies.[71] Following the passage of the ethics bill, then, industry's cost of transfers would increase. Thus, the correlation between the probability of an industry job and budgets should be weakened following the introduction of the ethics bill. Furthermore, the overall probability of an industry job should fall following the ethics bill.[72]

A test of the model consists of estimating the determinants of the conditional probability of a regulator working for the industry following his tenure at a commission. While the empirical specification used here does not provide an estimate of the structural parameters of the model, the model will not be supported by the data if the probability of going to work for industry does not fall with the agency's discretionary budget during the last period of the regulator's tenure.

The empirical model to be used is a probit model, with $\text{prob}(\text{PostInd}_i = 1) = F(\mathbf{X}_i \beta)$, $i = 1, N$, where PostInd is a dummy variable taking a value of one if the regulator's job after the commission is directly or indirectly related to the regulated industry, $F(\cdot)$ is the normal cumulative distribution function, β is the vector of parameters to estimate, and $\mathbf{X}$ is a vector of exogenous variables given by $\mathbf{X}$ = (Patronage, Age, DBudget, Ethics, DBudget*Ethics, Other Dummies). Variable Patronage takes a value of one if the regulator had public-sector experience preceding his commission appointment; Age is the age of the regulator when leaving the commission; DBudget is a measure of the discretionary budget during the

---

[70] In contrast, it is conceivable that public-sector experience is a way for politicians to learn potential regulators' preferences. In that case, there may not be any difference between patronage and nonpatronage appointments, except that the former is a way for congressmen to extract the regulators' rents.

[71] The bill was first introduced in 1977 and drew substantial support in both the House and the Senate. The Senate passed an omnibus government ethics bill in June 1977, but the House's proliferation of ethics bills indicated that the final passage of the bill had to be postponed until 1978.

[72] Actually, since in early 1977 it was already clear that the bill would pass (see Cong. Q. Weekly Rep. 2353 (December 3, 1977)), the effect of the ethics bill should have started being felt then.

regulator's last year at the commission; and Ethics is a dummy taking a value of one if the regulator left the commission in 1977 or later. The other dummies are described in the next section.

VIII. The Data

The data set is composed of the career path of regulators for the Interstate Commerce Commission (ICC), Civil Aeronautics Board (CAB), and Federal Communications Commission (FCC) and a measure of discretionary budgets.

A. Career Path of Regulators

Most of the data on the career path of bureaucrats used here were generously provided by Professor Ross Eckert of Claremont McKeena College.[73] For each regulator, Eckert collected the period of his or her tenure at the commission, as well as his or her pre- and postagency experience. This data set consists of all regulators that were appointed until 1978. Following a methodology similar to Eckert's, I collected information for those commissioners who were appointed after 1978 and who completed their work at the commissions by 1984. I also checked and updated the information in Eckert's data set.

For each regulator, I have information on age, tenure at the commission, and pre- and postagency experience. I created a postindustry dummy (PostInd) equal to one if the postagency employment of the regulator is directly or indirectly related to the regulated industry. A direct relationship means being an employee of a regulated firm. An indirect relationship means working for a law firm that does industry work. Similarly, I created a patronage dummy equal to one if the regulator's preagency employment was in the public sector and a preindustry dummy that equals one if the preagency employment of the regulator was directly or indirectly related to the regulated industry.[74]

---

[73] Unpublished data, provided by Professor Ross Eckert, Dep't of Econ., Claremont McKeena College, 1985; specific information available from author on request.

[74] There are several recent examples of congressional staff members who became commissioners. For example, during the 1970s, ICC Commissioners Stafford, Gresham, O'Neal, and Gillian and FCC Commissioners Cox, T. Brown, Burch, Quello, and Fogarty were all congressional advisors or staff members prior to becoming commissioners. Many others were members of Congress (for example, ICC Commissioner Jackson), staff members of the commission (for example, CAB Commissioners Adams, O'Melia, and Johnson), or served as advisors to the executive branch (for example, FCC Commissioners Loevinger and Washburn and CAB Commissioners Gillilland and Kahn). Party activities and affiliation were extremely difficult to find. however, CAB Commissioner Schaffer seems to have been

For a regulator to be in the sample, the main requirement was to have a complete career path. Since I did not use the information on regulators who were incumbent as of 1985 or who died in office, not all regulators in Eckert's sample are in mine. Also, I did not include in the sample regulators for whom I was not able to find a specific post- or preagency activity (whether retired or still at work). Because of the need to have a consistent time series of discretionary budgets, my data set includes only those regulators who left the ICC after 1932, the CAB after 1943, and the FCC after 1939.[75]

The data sources were multiple and similar to those described in Eckert.[76] Multiple issues of the following *Who's Who* were used: *Who's Who in America, Who's Who in American Politics, Who's Who in Finance and Industry,* and *Who's Who in Government.*[77] Newspaper sources were the *New York Times* and the *Wall Street Journal.*[78] The source on law firm affiliation and nature of legal practice was the *Martindale-Hubbell Law Directory.*[79] Eckert also provided me with press releases of the different commissions listing the backgrounds of their current commissioners.[80] The information offices of the different agencies also provided information about some of their previous commissioners' postagency employment.[81]

B. *Discretionary Budgets*

For each agency, I collected the annual congressional appropriation. From this figure, I was interested in capturing the portion that is "discretionary." I define "discretionary" as unexplained by business cycle conditions, trends, or general movements in the federal civilian budget. Thus,

---

an active party member, as he was a delegate to the 1972 Democratic National Convention, and FCC Commissioner Ferris held several positions with the Democratic Policy Committee.

[75] The reason for selecting this sample is that the estimation of the budget equation uses lagged values of budgetary appropriations. Consequently, I include CAB and FCC regulators that left their commission not earlier than three years following the first congressional budgetary appropriation for their commission. To be able to have a comparable institutional framework for the three agencies, I included only ICC commissioners that left the ICC after 1932.

[76] See note 68 *supra.*

[77] For the years 1939–84, specific information is available from author on request.

[78] Numerous issues from 1939 to 1984 (especially the New York Times obituaries); specific information is available from the author on request.

[79] For the years 1939–84, specific information is available from the author on request.

[80] See note 73 *supra.*

[81] Telephone interviews, 1986; specific information is available from the author on request.

TABLE 2

PREAGENCY AND POSTAGENCY EMPLOYMENT OF REGULATORY COMMISSIONERS

	ICC (n = 46)	CAB (n = 35)	FCC (n = 48)	Total (n = 129)
Preagency employment:				
Regulated industry	9	1	10	20
Public sector	32	28	36	96
Other private sector	5	6	2	13
Postagency employment:				
Regulated industry	21	15	22	58
Public sector	7	7	8	22
Other private sector	18	13	18	49

SOURCE.—See text.

for each agency, I estimated a basic budget equation of the following form:

$$\text{Budget}_{ti} = a_{0i} + a_{1i}\text{NonDefense}_t + a_{2i}\text{Unemployment}_t$$
$$+ a_{3i}\text{Budget}_{it-1} + a_{4i}\text{Budget}_{it-2} + a_{5i}\text{Budget}_{it-3}$$
$$+ a_{6i}\text{Trend} + a_{7i}\text{Trend}^2 + e_{it}, \quad i = \text{CAB, FCC, ICC,}$$

where NonDefense represents total federal nondefense expenditures and Budget, the agency appropriation for the year. Both NonDefense and Budget are deflated by the consumer price index and are expressed in natural logarithms.

To obtain from the basic budget equation a measure of the discretionary budget during the last year of the regulator's tenure at the commission, I estimated the budget equation for that commission with the sample period, excluding the year in consideration. For a specific agency, the discretionary budget for that year was then defined as the (out-of-sample) prediction residual. To make the three time series of discretionary budgets comparable across agencies, I normalized them by dividing each constructed agency's time series by its standard deviation.[82]

IX. The Empirical Results

Table 2 presents the distribution of regulators by agency and occupation, and Table 3 presents the occupation matrix. Of the 129 regulators, three-quarters came to the agency with pubic-sector experience, and al-

---

[82] See Table 5 for the means and standard deviation of each agency's time series of discretionary budgets.

TABLE 3

Employment Transition Matrix

	Preagency Employment		
Postagency Employment	Public Sector	Regulated Industry	Other Private Sector
Public sector	18	2	2
	(.19)	(.10)	(.15)
Regulated industry	47	7	4
	(.49)	(.35)	(.31)
Other private sector	31	11	7
	(.32)	(.55)	(.54)
Total	96	20	13

Source.—See text.
Note.—Percentages are given in parentheses.

most half left to work directly or indirectly for the regulated industry. While 49 percent of patronage appointments went to work for industry following their tenure at the commission, only a third of the regulators that came from the private sector did so.[83] There were no major differences across agencies, except that, in this sample, only one CAB commissioner came from the regulated industry.

Table 4 presents the budget equations for the three agencies. All budgets were correlated with general nondefense expenditures and were sensitive to general business-cycle conditions. However, while CAB's and ICC's budgets increased with unemployment, FCC's budgets fell. There does not seem to be remaining serial correlation of the residuals.[84] Table 5 shows the distribution of the logarithm of discretionary budgets for the regulators in my sample. There is substantial variation in the logarithm of discretionary budgets, and their means are not statistically different from zero.

Table 6 presents the main empirical results. The main hypotheses being tested are whether larger discretionary budgets and the ethics bill of 1978 reduce the probability of obtaining a regulated-industry job and whether previous public employment increases the probability of obtaining a regulated-industry job. Different specifications are presented[85] trying to cap-

[83] Thus, as expected, this sample does not differ much from Eckert's, *supra* note 67.

[84] Since there are lagged-dependent variables in the right-hand side, Durbin's *h* test and the *t*-statistic for first-order serial correlation are reported.

[85] I tested whether the probit equation can be pooled across the different agencies. To perform the test, I estimated a probit equation where all parameters are allowed to vary across agencies and tested whether the restriction that all parameters are the same across

TABLE 4

BUDGET EQUATIONS, DEPENDENT VARIABLE: REAL BUDGETARY APPROPRIATION IN
LOGARITHMS

	ICC	CAB	FCC
Constant	−1.41	−.33	1.17
	(−1.18)	(−.44)	(1.21)
Real nondefense expenditures	.17	.22	.41
	(2.21)	(3.18)	(3.05)
BUDGET(−1)	1.13	.88	.64
	(9.36)	(5.74)	(4.74)
BUDGET(−2)	−.35	−.03	−.14
	(−1.93)	(−.17)	(−1.06)
BUDGET(−3)	−.06	−.23	−.28
	(−.41)	(−1.51)	(−3.50)
TREND	.04	.04	.6E-3
	(2.52)	(3.03)	(.08)
TREND2	−.3E-3	−.9E-3	12E-3
	(−2.63)	(−4.13)	(.79)
Unemployment	.01	.02	−.02
	(2.42)	(1.71)	(−3.30)
R^2	.91	.98	.97
D-W	2.006	1.958	1.905
Durbin-h	−.045	1.167	.949
t-statistic for AR(1)	−.446	.174	.443
No. of observations	53	42	48

NOTE.—Results are from ordinary least squares estimation; D-W is the Durbin-Watson statistic.

TABLE 5

DISTRIBUTION OF DISCRETIONARY BUDGETS

	ICC	CAB	FCC
Mean	−.01961	.00146	−.00796
Standard deviation	.09769	.08656	.10118

SOURCE.—Table 4.

---

agencies can be rejected. The test is given by −2(log LU − log LR), where log LR (log LU) is the logarithm of the restricted (unrestricted) estimation, and it is distributed as $\chi^2(q)$, with q being the number of restrictions. For the specification chosen, the statistic was equal to 9.322, which is smaller than the critical value for all normal confidence values. The specification on which this test was performed did not include the unemployment, female, or Republican variables.

TABLE 6

PROBIT EQUATION. DEPENDENT VARIABLE: REGULATORS' POSTCOMMISSION REGULATED INDUSTRY EMPLOYMENT (N = 129)

	(1)	(2)	(3)	(4)	(5)	(6)
Constant	5.40	6.13	5.99	6.44	6.51	4.67
	(2.17)	(2.41)	(2.37)	(2.55)	(2.61)	(2.00)
Patronage	.49	.58	.64	.54	.47	...
	(1.14)	(1.33)	(1.46)	(1.24)	(1.73)	...
Preindustry	.00	.14	.18	.18	...	...
	(.00)	(.26)	(.36)	(.28)		
Log age	−1.44	−1.63	−1.65	−1.68	−1.74	−1.20
	(−2.28)	(−2.54)	(−2.58)	(−2.62)	(−2.77)	(−2.05)
Discretionary Budget	...	−.25	−.18	−.26	−.22	...
		(−1.70)	(−1.41)	(−1.77)	(−1.64)	
DBUDGET*ETHICS	...	.20	...	.30	.35	...
		(.58)		(.88)	(1.11)	
Ethics bill	−.55	−.48	−.53	−.04	...	...
	(−1.43)	(−1.23)	(−1.38)	(−.13)		
Post-1965	.64	.63	.66	...	...	...
	(2.04)	(1.96)	(2.09)			
Republican	.38	−.35	−.37	−.13	...	...
	(1.46)	(−1.24)	(−1.44)	(−.51)		
Unemployment	−.01	−.03	...	−.03	...	...
	(−.34)	(−.87)		(−.89)		
Female	−1.19	−1.16	−1.14	−1.13	−1.20	...
	(−1.76)	(−1.67)	(−1.66)	(−1.66)	(−1.84)	
Log-Likelihood	−80.22	−78.71	−79.27	−80.70	−81.28	−86.62
χ^2	12.80*	15.82*	14.70*	11.84	10.68**	...
Degrees of freedom	7	9	7	8	4	...

NOTE.—Asymptotic t-statistics are in parentheses; see text for explanation of test.
* Rejects restriction at 10 percent.
** Rejects restriction at 5 percent.

ture the effects of various exogenous variables. General business conditions are proxied by the unemployment variable; the patronage and preindustry dummies capture the regulatory selection process; the Republican dummy captures any possible effects across different administrations; the post-1965 dummy captures the effect of the increase in regulations that followed the mid-1960s; the ethics dummy captures the effect of the ethics bill of 1978; the female dummy captures any potential sex differences in career paths, while the DBudget*Ethics variable captures the change in the cost of industry transfers following the ethics bill.

Column 1 of table 6 shows the results of estimating the probit equation where the set of explanatory variables does not include any of the budget variables. Patronage appointments and younger regulators have a higher probability of obtaining a regulated industry job; Republican administrations seem to reduce the probability of regulators working for the regulated industry; female commissioners go to work for the regulated industry in much lower proportions than their male colleagues;[86] and the ethics bill seems to have reduced the probability of working for industry.

Column 2 presents the estimation of the probit equation when all the variables are included, and columns 3–6 perform robustness tests by excluding selected variables.[87] Here, increases in discretionary budgets seem to reduce the probability of going to work for the regulated industry. The effect of discretionary budgets seems to differ following the ethics bill of 1978. While the change is insignificant, it is positive, implying that the effect of discretionary budgets may have fallen following the passage of the ethics bill. Macroeconomic considerations do not seem to significantly affect the decision to go to work for the regulated industry. Finally, the probability that regulators leaving their commissions obtain regulated industry jobs seem to be smaller during Republican administrations. This result may suggest either that Republican administrations enforce the conflict-of-interest laws more stringently or that they are able to lure regulators with better alternative compensations, thus reducing industry's ability to make transfers to regulators.[88] Column 6 presents the results of estimating the probit equation, excluding all variables except for age. This version is useful in order to test whether the coefficients of all other

---

[86] There are, though, only seven female commissioners in my sample.

[87] Since cols. 2–5 present qualitatively similar results, I will proceed with the discussion based on the results of col. 2. From col. 4, however, we see that the results concerning the ethics bill and the Republican coefficients (but not the coefficient of DBudget*Ethics) are sensitive to the inclusion of the post-1965 variable. Thus, inferences about the independent role of the ethics bill and of the party should be made with caution.

[88] See, however, col. 4, where this result does not hold if the post-1965 variable is excluded.

variables are, jointly, statistically significant. A χ^2 test is performed for each of the specifications in the table, with the results and the degrees of freedom being reported at the bottom of the table. The restriction that all coefficients, except for age, are jointly equal to zero is rejected at normal confidence levels. While the estimated coefficients are all of the predicted sign, and are jointly statistically significant, few estimates are, on their own, statistically significant at the percent level. With that caveat, these results suggest that discretionary budgets and postagency employment at the regulated industry are negatively correlated, with the correlation being reduced following the passage of the ethics bill.[89] Furthermore, the effect of discretionary budgets is not small. For example, at the sample mean, an abnormal budget increase of one standard deviation would increase the probability of postcommission employment at the regulated industry by approximately 9 percentage points, implying a 20 percent increase in the probability of regulated industry employment.[90] Congress, then, seems to have used budgets to discipline its regulators.

X.   Final Comments

In this article I present a multiple-principals/single-agent model of regulation. The model provides a framework to analyze Congress's incentives

[89] Observe that such a negative correlation will also arise even if Congress were to prohibit industry transfers. Lemma C1 implies that unfavorable regulatory outcomes (for Congress) are followed by lower budgets. Furthermore, if Congress is dissatisfied with the performance of commissioners, it will also restrict their future public employment. Thus, commissioners leaving the agency during periods of unusually low budgets would have a lower probability of finding public postcommission employment, and the probability of obtaining a private postcommission employment is increased. If the regulated industry does not provide transfers to regulators, then the determinants of the probability of moving to either a regulated or a nonregulated industry position should be the same. Consequently, the finding of a negative correlation does not necessarily provide support for the multiple-principals model, though it does for a single-principal (Congress) agency framework. A preliminary test of the single-principal hypothesis against the multiple-principals hypothesis can be performed by estimating the model of Table 6, col. 2, where the dependent variable is the probability of going to work for the nonrelated private sector. The estimated equation shows a positive and significant coefficient (*t*-statistic of 2.1) for the discretionary budget variable. Thus, the determinants of postcommission employment at the regulated and nonrelated private sector are different. While for the latter the human capital hypothesis may be relevant, that does not seem to be the case for the former. Thus, the data seem to provide some indirect support for the multiple-principals hypothesis against the single-principal hypothesis.

[90] The calculation of the change in the probability is as follows: dProb $= f(x\beta)*$coefficient$*dx$, where f($\cdot$) is the normal density function. Recall that, by construction, the standard deviation of the discretionary budget variable is one. Thus, $dx = 1$. Thus, the effect of a change in the discretionary budget of one standard deviation is simply the coefficient, $-.25$, times the value of the density function at the sample mean, .353, to give 8.83 percent. Also, the probability of postindustry employment at the sample mean is 45 percent.

to regulate industries, as well as to restrict the ability of interest groups to influence the outcomes of the regulatory process. It also provides empirically testable implications different from the traditional self-interest hypothesis. The empirical evidence provided here does not reject the existence of an agency problem between Congress and its regulatory agencies. While Congress seems to use its budgets to discipline regulators, congressional control does not seem to be perfect.

APPENDIX A

STATEMENT OF THE GAME

When Congress allows industry transfers to the regulator, then the solution to the game played by Congress, industry, and regulators is as follows.

The equilibrium is a triple $(\mathbf{B}, \mathbf{T}, x)$, with $\mathbf{B} = (B_1, B_h)$, $\mathbf{T} = (T_1, T_h)$, such that

$$x = \operatorname*{argmax}_{\{y\}} \{\phi(y)[W(B_1, y) + T_1] + [1 - \phi(y)][W(B_h, y) + T_h]\}, \quad (A1)$$

$$\mathbf{T} = \operatorname*{argmax}_{\{T_1, T_h\}} \{\phi(x)(\pi_1 - T_1) + [1 - \phi(x)](\pi_h - T_h)\}, \quad (A2)$$

subject to

$$x = \operatorname*{argmax}_{\{y\}} \{\phi(y)[W(B_1, y) + T_1] + [1 - \phi(y)][W(B_h, y) + T_h]\},$$

and

$$\mathbf{B} = \operatorname*{argmax}_{\{B_1, B_h\}} \{\phi(x)(U_1 - B_1) + [1 - \phi(x)](U_h - B_h)\}, \quad (A3)$$

subject to

$$x \text{ solves (RP),}$$

$$T \text{ solves (IP),}$$

and

$$\phi(x_0)W(B_1, x_0) + [1 - \phi(x_0)]W(B_h, x_0) \geq w^*, \quad (A4)$$

where

$$x_0 = \operatorname*{argmax}_{\{y\}} \{\phi(y)W(B_1, y) + [1 - \phi(y)]W(B_h, y)\},$$

and where w^* is the regulator's reservation utility level. That is, the solution to the game consists of simultaneously solving Congress's (eq. [A3]), industry's (eq. [A2]), and the regulator's (eq. [A1]) problems. The regulator's problem (eq. [A1] consists of maximizing its expected utility, subject to Congress's and industry's offers. Industry's problem (eq. [A2]) consists of maximizing its expected profits net of transfers, subject to Congress's budget offer and the regulator's first-order condition. Finally, Congress's problem (eq. [A3]) involves maximizing expected consumer surplus net of budgets, subject to (*a*) the regulator's optimal choice of *x* for any given set of budget and transfer offers, (*b*) the industry's optimal choice of transfers for any set of budget offers, which in turn depends on the optimal regulator's choice of effort, and (*c*) the regulator's individual rationality constraint evaluated at a level of zero industry transfers.

APPENDIX B

FULL INFORMATION REGULATORY POLICY

When no industry transfers are allowed, and x is observable, Congress's first-best outcome is obtained by solving equation B1:

$$\max_{\{B_1, B_h, x\}} \{\phi(x)(U_1 - B_1) + [1 - \phi(x)](U_h - B_h)\}, \qquad \text{(B1)}$$

subject to

$$\phi(x)[W(B_1, x)] + [1 - \phi(x)]W(B_h, x) \geq w^*.$$

Congress's first-best outcome is given by lemma B1.

LEMMA B1. In the absence of industry influence in the regulatory process, the full information effort and budget allocations are given by

$$B_1 = B_h = B, \qquad \text{(B1i)}$$

$$W(B, x) = w^*, \qquad \text{(B1ii)}$$

$$W_x(B, x)/W_B(B, x) = -\phi'(x)(U_1 - U_h). \qquad \text{(B1iii)}$$

The proof of the lemma is straightforward and is not presented. The intuition is discussed in the text.

APPENDIX C

The solution to the "no industry transfers" equilibrium is characterized by lemma C1.

LEMMA C1. The solution to (7) and (6) is given by

$$B_1 > B_h \geq 0, \qquad \text{(C1i)}$$

$$\text{if } \delta \leq 1/W_B^h, \text{ then } B_h = 0, \qquad \text{(C1ii)}$$

$$W_B^1/W_B^h = -\phi(1 - \delta W_B^1)/[(1 - \phi)(1 - \delta W_B^h)] \quad \text{for } B_h > 0. \qquad \text{(C1iii)}$$

$$\phi = 0 \Rightarrow B_1 = 0, \qquad \text{(C1iv)}$$

where δ is the Lagrange multiplier associated with the regulator's individual rationality constraint and W_B^j represents the derivative of $W(B, x)$ with respect to B evaluated at B_j. The proof of lemma C1 is similar to that of lemma 1 and is not given here.

APPENDIX D

PROPOSITION D1. In the absence of industry transfers,
(i) the full information regulatory effort level is achievable if and only if

$$\phi(x^*)(U_1 - U_h)W_B(B^*, x^*) \leq w^* - W(0, x^*). \qquad \text{(D1)}$$

(ii) Furthermore, if equation (D1) holds, then

$$B^* < \phi(x^*)B_1(x^*) + [1 - \phi(x^*)]B_h(x^*),$$

where (B^*, x^*) represent the first-best combination of budget and regulatory effort and $B_j(x^*)$, $j = 1, h$, represent the budget allocations needed to implement x^* in the restricted game.

The proof of proposition D1 involves finding a pair (B_1, B_h) so that x^* can be implemented as an equilibrium to the restricted game. Since in principle B_1 can be adjusted so that the regulator receives no rents, condition (D1) requires that the highest feasible punishment Congress can impose (a zero budget) should provide the regulator with a substantial relative disutility (compared to his reservation utility level) that will motivate him to undertake the optimal effort. Furthermore, since the regulator's expected utility equals w^*, assumption (1) implies point ii.

APPENDIX E

PROOF OF LEMMA 1. Industry first-order conditions are given by equations (E1):

$$x_{T1}\phi'(\pi_1 - T_1 - \pi_h + T_h) - \phi + \xi_{T1} = 0, \quad \xi_{T1}T_1 = 0, \quad \text{(E1a)}$$

and

$$x_{Th}\phi'(\pi_1 - T_1 - \pi_h + T_h) - (1 - \phi) + \xi_{Th} = 0, \quad \xi_{Th}T_h = 0, \quad \text{(E1b)}$$

where $x_{T1} = -\phi'/W_{xx}$, and $x_{Th} = \phi'/W_{xx}$ are derived from the regulator's first-order conditions. Equations (E1) imply $T_1 = 0$ since, for an internal solution, $\Delta\Pi > Th - T_1$. That $B_1 > B_h > 0$ can be derived from the first-order conditions for Congress that are given in (E2):

$$-\phi'^2(\Delta U - B_1 + B_h)W_B^1/(2W_{xx}) - \phi(1 - \delta\phi^0/\phi W_B^1) + \xi_{B1} = 0, \quad \xi_{B1}B_1 = 0, \quad \text{(E2a)}$$

and

$$\phi'^2(\Delta U - B_1 + B_h)W_B^h/(2W_{xx}) - (1 - \phi)[1 - \delta W_B^h(1 - \phi^0)/(1 - \phi)] + \xi_{Bh} = 0, \quad \xi_{Bh}B_h = 0. \quad \text{(E2b)}$$

Rearranging (E2a) and (E2b), we obtain $W_B^1 \leq W_B^h$, implying $B_1 \geq B_h$. Observe that as long as $T_h > 0$, $B_1 > B_h$ since $\phi^0 > \phi$ for $T_h > 0$. The derivation of equation (iii) is straightforward from (E2b). To see that $\phi = 0 \Rightarrow B_1 = 0$, assume an equilibrium with $x = \phi = 0$ but $B_1 > 0$. Then, by reducing B_1, Congress will experience no reduction in x and a welfare increase because of a budget reduction. Equation (v) is derived directly from corollary 1.

APPENDIX F

PROOF OF PROPOSITION 1. Assume that x^0 is the equilibrium regulatory effort. (B_h^0, B_1^0) and T_h^0 are spent to achieve that outcome. We want to show that the expected total amount, $\phi(B_1^0 + T_1^0) + (1 - \phi)(B_h^0 + T_h^0)$, exceeds the minimum required to obtain x^0, where the probability function is evaluated at x^0. The first-order conditions to minimize total expected expenditures subject to the individual rationality constraint and $x(B_1, T_1, B_h, T_h) = x^0$ are given by

$$\phi - \gamma x_{B1} - \delta\phi W_B^1 - \xi_{B1}^M = 0, \quad \xi_{B1}^M B_1 = 0, \quad \text{(F1)}$$

$$\phi = \gamma x_{T1} - \delta\phi - \xi_{T1}^M = 0, \quad \xi_{T1}^M T_1 = 0, \quad \text{(F2)}$$

$$(1 - \phi) - \gamma x_{Bh} - \delta(1 - \phi)W_B^h - \xi_{Bh}^M = 0, \quad \xi_{Bh}^M B_h = 0, \quad \text{(F3)}$$

and

$$(1 - \phi) - \gamma x_{Th} - \delta(1 - \phi) - \xi^M_{Th} = 0, \quad \xi^M_{Th} T_h = 0, \tag{F4}$$

where δ (γ) is the Lagrange multiplier associated with the individual rationality (constant effort level) constraint. Observe first that $W^1_B = 1$ is a solution to this problem. Since $x_{Th} < 0$ and $1/W^h_B \leq \delta \leq 1/W^1_B = 1$, we obtain $T_h = 0$. From (F2) we obtain $\delta = 1 + \gamma\phi'/(\phi W_{xx})$, which after some substitutions implies $W^1_B = 1 < W^h_B = (1 - \phi)/[1 - \phi + \gamma\phi'/(\phi W_{xx})]$. Thus, to achieve x^0 at minimum cost, compensations should make the regulator's rate of substitution between money and budget equal to one in low-price states but larger than one in high-price states. Since this allocation differs from the equilibrium one, the latter is not a cost-minimizing solution.

APPENDIX G

PROOF OF PROPOSITION 3.   Let $S^R = \{x, B_h, B_1 | \phi(x)(U_1 - B_1) + [1 - \phi(x)](U_h - B_h) \geq EU^{R*}\}$, where EU^{R*} represents the equilibrium expected-utility level for Congress in the restricted game. The term S^R represents the set of points in (x, B_h, B_1) that provide Congress with a level of expected utility which equals at least the level achieved in the restricted game. Call $X^R = \{x, B_h, B_1 | x = x(B_h, B_1, T_h = 0)\}$ where the function $x(\cdot)$ is derived from the first-order condition for the regulator. From assumptions (1)–(5) and the definition of equilibrium to the restricted game, $X^R \cap S^R$ consists of the restricted equilibrium values for (x, B_h, B_1) and is unique. Let $X^U = \{x, B_h, B_1 | x = x(B_h, B_1, T_h = T^{U*}_h)\}$, where T^{U*}_h is the equilibrium industry transfer in the unrestricted game. Since from the first-order condition for the regulator we know that $x(B_h, B_1, T_h = T^{U*}_h) < x(B_h, B_1, T_h = 0)$, then $X^U \cap S^R$ is empty. Thus, the unrestricted equilibrium cannot provide Congress with a utility level in excess of EU^{R*}.

[5]

Public Choice **112**: 185–202, 2002.
© 2002 *Kluwer Academic Publishers. Printed in the Netherlands.*

185

Institutions and market reform in emerging economies: A rent seeking perspective

RAM MUDAMBI[1], PIETRO NAVARRA[2] & CHRIS PAUL[3]*
[1]*Temple University, U.S.A. and University of Reading, U.K.;* [2]*Department of Economics, University of Messina, 98100 Messina, Italy; e-mail: navarrap@unime.it;* [3]*Georgia Southern University, U.S.A.*

Accepted 26 February 2001

Abstract. The role of institutions as determinants of rent seeking success is well established. In this paper, we focus on institutions that have received little attention in the literature, namely electoral institutions. We examine three measures of electoral institutional structure that are hypothesized to be instrumental in determining the level of rent seeking success. These are the type of electoral system, pluralistic or proportional; method of selection of the chief executive, presidential or parliamentary; and the number of electoral districts. An index of economic freedom is used as the metric for rent seeking opportunities created by governments. Theoretical implications of variation in these electoral institutions are developed. These implications are empirically tested employing data from 29 countries classified as having emerging market economies. Countries with emerging economies are expected to exhibit more institutional flexibility that more developed countries whose property rights are well established and defended. The empirical results are controlled for differences in a number of demographic and historical factors. Plurality electoral systems are more resistant to the political demands of rent seeking than proportional systems. Fewer election districts seem to reduce rent seeking opportunities. However, conditional on the type of electoral system, presidential systems are found to be no more resistant to rent seeking than parliamentary systems. Finally, we find strong control effects. Literacy increases a country's resistance to rent seeking while military spending and years of institutional entrenchment reduce it.

1. Introduction

In this paper we begin from the premise, well established in the economic regulation and public choice literatures, that special interests will seek to use the government to obtain economic advantage at the expense of the general population – the phenomenon known as rent seeking behavior. We apply the tools of economic theory to study the comparative politics of rent seeking in the context of economic reform. This investigation builds on some of our

  * The authors wish to thank Sebastiano Bavetta and Bernard Grofman stimulating discussions that greatly influenced this paper. Part of the paper was written while Pietro Navarra was Fulbright Research Scholar at Carnegie Mellon University. The comments of one of the anonymous reviewers greatly improved the paper. The usual disclaimer applies.

earlier work (Mudambi and Navarra, 1999) and follows the path suggested by Persson and Tabellini (1999). Several scholars have recently undertaken projects to study the political determinants of economic policy changes. Alesina and Drazen (1991) suggest interpreting the timing of stabilization policies and in particular their postponement as a "war of attrition". In this context, the expected time of stabilization is a function of characteristics of the economy including parameters meant to capture the degree of political polarization. In another important contribution, Fernandez and Rodrik (1991) construct a theoretical model in which politicians are seen as those resisting the implementation of economic reform because of the uncertainty over the distribution of gains and losses associated to the reform process itself. They use trade liberalization as an example to argue that there can be a bias toward the *status quo* in those cases in which the individual gainers or losers from the reform cannot be identified beforehand.

Our interest in this study is the political economy of economic policy reform in recently emerging market countries. Several bases have been used to describe economic policy choice and performance in such economies. These include international circumstances, cultural context or heritage, characteristics of the state of bureaucracy, organization of interest groups and the nature of the electoral and party systems. However, we limit our analysis to the following broad question: what are the effects of legislative and electoral institutions on the level and pace of the economic policy reform in emerging market countries? By economic reform we refer to market liberalization in general. Our contention is that differing electoral and legislative institutions can affect the pace of reform through their creation of differing levels of rent-seeking opportunities.

The paper is structured as follows. In Section 2 we discuss and specify our theoretical hypotheses. In Section 3 we describe the data used in the empirical analysis, present the econometric model and comment on the results of the empirical investigation. In Section 4 we discuss the implications of our findings. Finally, in Section 5 we offer some concluding remarks.

2. Theory: Three determinants of rent-seeking opportunities

Starting from the vote- or majority-maximizing model of representative behavior, we assume that in order to affect policy outcomes special interests must be able to effect election outcomes, i.e., the probability of a candidate winning. The extent to which rent seeking can take place is a direct function of the ability of interest groups to affect electoral outcomes and legislative response to the resulting incentives. Those institutional arrangements that reduce the threshold level of political support required to elect or displace a representative will result in an increased level of the rent-seeking opportunities being provided. The three principal differences in electoral institutions addressed here are proportional and plurality representation rules, the size of the electoral district, parliamentary and presidential regimes. For purposes of exposition, three sub-sections develop the theoretical impact of each.

Two electoral institutions, the number of seats (which is greatly influenced by whether the electoral system is governed by plurality or proportionality) and the number of districts are measure of district magnitude. As the number of seats increases or the number of districts increase district magnitude declines. District magnitude has been the primary focus of the study of electoral districts in the political science literature (for a detailed survey see, Taagepera and Shugart, 1989). However, the relationship between district magnitudes and policy outcomes has yet to be addressed. Larger district magnitudes give representative's greater autonomy from local or particularistic interest and the need to cultivate support by means of re-distributive programs, i.e., rent transfers (Weingast, Shepsle and Johnsen, 1981). Our expectation is that district magnitude and the creation of rent-seeking opportunities by legislators are inversely related.

A. The role of electoral systems: Proportionality versus plurality in electoral systems

The focus here is between two general classes of electoral systems, proportional representation (PR) and plurality representation (PL). The distinction between PR and PL electoral systems represents the difference between single-seat and multi-seat districts. In single-seat districts only one representative is elected to represent the entire electorate. In a multi-seat districts voters elect two or more representatives reducing the effective size of the district. Consequently, in PR electoral systems the district magnitude is greater the larger the number of elected representatives per district, *ceteris paribus*.

Single-seat and multi-seat districts present different electoral incentives. In the single-seat district, which will predominate under the PL system, a representative will campaign on more general issues that affect a larger proportion of voters. In other words, candidates in single-seat districts will move toward the center of the policy space as to do otherwise would mean surrendering the majority policy position and reducing the probability of election. In multi-seat districts, under the PR system, the candidate may select a policy position that benefits a minority interest group in the district's population. Indeed in PR systems a candidate may be elected by appealing to a particularistic segment of the electorate sufficient in size to win one of the seats awarded in the multi-member district (Hinich and Ordeshook, 1970; Navarra and Lignana, 1997). Since PR systems create incentives for politicians to satisfy the demands of the particularistic interest group that elected them, in PR systems policies that favor rent-seeking interest will be more likely to be supported by a majority of legislators. Obviously, this policy fragmentation results in PR systems being less likely to pass general interest economic reforms.

There is a large literature that concludes the behavior of legislators is motivated by their constituencies' particularistic objectives. For example, legislators intervene in the budgetary process to increase or defend particular programs that yield net benefits to their districts (Mayhew, 1974; Fiorina, 1977; Crain, Ferejohn and Fiorina, 1987). Marshall and Weingast (1988) employ an industrial organization model of legislatures to demonstrate how committees develop as a method to allow legislators to benefit from the gains to logrolling. In their model legislators bid for committee memberships that have influence over the programs that most benefit their own constituents. This results in committees dominated by "preference outliers", increasing the demand for government favors. The more specialized or particularistic the constituency the more polarized the policy stance of their representative. Thus, electoral systems should affect the types of policies selected and their durability.

A simple model may be used to demonstrate how the influence of particularistic interest groups increases as the effective size of interest groups declines. It is assumed that candidates are interested in generating a sufficient number of votes for election, or maximizing the probability of election. In the model the probability of election is positively related to the magnitude and allocation of rents to constituents, which benefit particularistic interest, and the level of economic reform undertaken, which benefits the general population. It is assumed that while the elected representative captures all the political support resulting from the provision of constituent services, reform generates benefits to the entire population regardless of whom they supported in the election. The number of seats in the electoral district is denoted by N, which takes a value equal to or greater than one. The representative's resource constraint is written as:

$$T = RS + GP \tag{1}$$

where RS is the effort allocated to providing particularistic constituent services or rent seeking opportunities and GP is the effort allocated to general interest policies. Since it is assumed that the representative's objective function is to maximize the probability of election, the probability of election is given by,

$$p = p[RS, GP/N] = p[T - GP, GP/N] \quad p_1 > 0, p_2 > 0, p_{11} < 0, p_{22} < 0 \tag{2}$$

Privatization and Globalization

Both RS and GP are positively related to the probability of re-election. However, the representative captures only $(1/N)^{th}$ of benefits of time allocated to general interest policies, since these function as non-rival public goods that benefit supporters and non-supporters alike.

Maximizing the re-election probability function with respect to the choice variable, GP, results in

$$p_2/p_1 = N^* \qquad (3)$$

Since both RS and GP are inputs into the probability of election function, as N increases, the marginal contribution of GP to the probability of election must rise and that of RS must fall. This means that an increase in the number of seats contested in a given electoral district will result in a reallocation of time away from the formulation of general interest policies to the generation rent seeking opportunities for particular groups of constituents. (This can be shown more formally by totally differentiating (3)).

Increasing the number of seats in a multi-seat district increases the incentive to support particularistic policies. Elected representatives in districts with a larger number of seats will, *ceteris paribus,* allocate a greater proportion of effort to the particularistic interest of constituents. This implies that PL systems with single-seat districts (N = 1) are less responsive to the rent-seeking demands of particularistic interest than PR systems with multi-seat districts.

B. The number of electoral districts

Since most countries organize political representation on a geographical basis, election winners are determined by both the quantity of votes cast for each party and the spatial distribution of votes. The interaction of the number of votes and their geographical distribution determines the distribution of political power between political parties, voter groups and geographical areas. The general rule is that larger district magnitudes result in a greater divergence of constituent interests.

As with increasing the number of seats in a given sized district, as district size declines polarization of party support increases, yielding increasingly homogeneous voter preferences. Larger districts will have a greater diversity of party support and a broader array of voter preferences. Smaller polarized districts will demand more particularistic legislation from elected representatives. As with multi-seat districts, smaller districts increase the incentives for elected representatives to support particularistic policies benefiting the narrow constituent interest. In both cases, particularistic electoral rules spawn particularistic politics (Kernell, 1991; Cowley and McCubbins, 1995; Ramsayer and Rosenbluth, 1993).

190

C. Presidential versus parliamentary systems

A fundamental difference between parliamentary and presidential election systems is that legislators select prime ministers while presidents are directly elected. As a consequence, in a presidential system with direct elections the chief executive will be more responsive to the general electorate, while in parliamentary systems where the prime minister is selected by the legislature, the chief executive will be more responsive to the demands of legislative representatives. Thus, in presidential regimes executive survival does not depend on support from a majority of representatives in the legislature. This reduces the incentives for the president to use policy legislation to maintain a stable coalition in the legislature. However, stable coalitions are crucial to the government's continuation in parliamentary systems. Coalition stability is depends on the behavior of elected representatives in the legislature. As discussed above, there is a large literature that concludes that legislators' behavior is driven by the particularistic interest of their constituencies. Persson and Tabellini (1999) have analyzed the effect of both the presidential-parliamentary and the pluralistic-proportional of electoral systems on government size. They find that presidential regimes and pluralistic election rules result in smaller government.

Our expectation is that directly elected presidents are more resistant to special interest demands for government intervention and are therefore more likely to support policies that benefit the general population over particularistic interest. Thus, presidential systems will have a lower incidence of rent-seeking opportunities. Conversely, parliamentary regimes are expected to have elected representatives who are motivated to create and consolidate government created rents for constituents and will resist economic reforms that threaten to dismantle the rent generating apparatus.

3. Data, estimation and results

Developed above were the theoretical relationship between three electoral institutions and the creation of rent-seeking opportunities. We turn now to the empirical testing of the hypothesized relationships.

We start with the basic contention, well accepted in the literature, that rent seeking opportunities are created by imposing restrictions on markets (Tullock, 1967; Krueger, 1974, 1992). Thus, the lower the level of restrictions on markets, and consequently, the higher the level of economic freedom, the lower the level of rent seeking opportunities. Thus, our dependent variable, the magnitude of rent-seeking opportunities, is a measure of economic freedom taken from Gwartney, Lawson and Block (GLB) (1996). This index

Table 1. Summary statistics

Variable	Mean	S.D.	Minimum	Maximum
REF	5.0448	1.3721	1.9	7.1
CREF	22.9655	34.4834	−39.0	114.0
PL	0.1034	0.3099	0.0	1.0
PRES	0.5172	0.5085	0.0	1.0
NDIST	53.7309	72.5326	1.0000	299.0000
LITER (%)	88.6379	9.3744	66.7	99.0
EASTEUR	0.1724	0.3844	0.0	1.0
LAT IN	0.4827	0.5085	0.0	1.0
MILSP (%)	2.5072	1.7393	0.9	8.0
YRSIND (years)	105.2759	75.4992	6.0	189.0

Note. The data are for 29 emerging market economies (See Appendix 2).

has 17 components divided across 4 categories: money and inflation, taxation, government regulation and international exchange. Complete details regarding the construction of the index are provided in Appendix 1.

We examine both the level of this index of freedom of the economy's markets as well as the amount of reform, measured as the change in this index over a period of time. The economic freedom measure is for 1995 and the economic reform is for the period 1990–1995. The data are for 29 countries in economic transition. The institutional and demographic variables were gathered from the CIA's *World Fact Book* (1998) and the World Bank's *Development Report* (1996). Summary statistics relating to the data set are presented in Table 1. The list of all countries in the data set is provided in Appendix 2.

Two equations were estimated, one with the level of economic freedom as the dependent variable and one with the change in economic freedom as the dependent variable. The two estimation equations are:

$$REF = f(POLINST, DEM) \qquad (4)$$

$$CREF = f(POLINST, DEM) \qquad (5)$$

where REF is the level of economic freedom in 1995 and the inverse of the level of rent seeking opportunities. CREF is the change in the level of economic freedom from 1990 through 1995 and is the inverse of the change in the level of rent seeking opportunities over this period. CREF can be viewed as a

192

measure of reform (or deterioration) over this period. POLINST is the vector of measures of political institutions. The three measures we are interested in are the system of electoral rules (PR vs. PL), the number of electoral districts and the organization of the executive (presidential vs. parliamentary). DEM is the vector of demographic control variables. The complete details of all variables used in the estimation are provided in Appendix 2.

Equations (4) and (5) are estimated with OLS. However, the countries in the sample substantially differ in size, ranging from Malta to Brazil, and there is strong evidence of heteroskedasticity. Consequently, White's heteroskedasticity-consistent variance-covariance was used to estimate standard errors. This procedure solves the problem, since the Breusch-Pagan test is now passed in all cases.

In estimating Equation (4), the regressand is REF, the level of economic freedom or the inverse of the level of rent seeking opportunities. However, we encounter a problem in that we find that the dummy variable for a plurality electoral system (PL) is highly correlated with the dummy variable for a presidential system of government (PRES). Hence when we use both of them as regressors, we expect that one or both of them will appear insignificant due to inflated standard errors. We designate the model that includes both PL and PRES as Model 1. The model that includes PL but excludes PRES is designated Model 2. The model that includes PRES but excludes PL is designated to be Model 3. The estimates of all three models are presented in Table 2.

We carry out a number of specification tests to choose amongst the three models. While all three models fit the data relatively well, all the specification tests point to Model 2, i.e., the inclusion of PL and the exclusion of PRES, as the appropriate specification. Model 2 provides the best fit to the data in terms of adjusted R^2 as well as the F statistic. The Akaike Information Criterion, a more stringent degrees-of-freedom test, also points to Model 2 as the best specification. Finally, we test the exclusion restrictions. We find that the exclusion of PRES from Model 1 cannot be rejected (the resulting F statistic has a probability value of over 49 percent). However, the exclusion of PL from Model 1 is conclusively rejected (the resulting F statistic has a probability value of less that 1 percent). Excluding PRES from Model 1 and including PL yields Model 2, our preferred specification. Thus, while PRES appears positive and highly significant in Model 3, in our data set we are unable to disentangle its effects from those of PL. We will discuss the results of Model 2 in detail. We begin by noting that our estimates are extremely good, both in terms of fit and in terms of statistical significance. The adjusted R^2 exceeds 66 percent and virtually all our regressors are found to be extremely statistically significant. We find that PL is positive and highly

Privatization and Globalization

Table 2. Estimating the level of reform in 1995: Heteroskedasticity-corrected OLS estimates[1]

Regressand: REF Regressor	Model 1 Coefficient ('t' stat.)	Model 2 Coefficient ('t' stat.)	Model 3 Coefficient ('t' stat.)
Constant	−3.675 (1.79)*	−4.333 (2.53)**	−5.794 (2.31)**
PL	2.937 (6.35)***	2.465 (6.37)***	–
PRES	−0.895 (1.25)	–	1.989 (3.31)***
NDIST	−0.0059 (2.99)***	−0.0048 (2.56)**	0.0011 (0.30)
LITER	0.111 (4.58)***	0.119 (5.82)***	0.139 (4.63)***
EASTEUR	−2.653 (4.47)***	−2.820 (5.40)***	−3.671 (5.24)***
LATIN	1.902 (2.90)***	1.011 (3.23)***	−1.020 (1.69)
MILSP	−0.0112 (2.84)***	−0.0112 (2.84)***	−0.0133 (2.51)**
YRSIND	−0.0084 (2.40)**	−0.0087 (2.73)***	−0.0111 (3.02)***
		Diagnostics	
Adjusted R^2	0.6597	0.6682	0.5212
F stat; (d.f.)	7.79***; (8,20)	9.06***; (7,21)	5.35***; (7,21)
Log-likelihood	−29.3045	−29.6456	−34.9637
Restricted log-likelihood	−49.8136	−49.8136	−49.8136
Sum of squared errors	12.8124	13.1174	18.9292
Exclusion restriction: $F(1,20)$	–	0.4761 (p=0.498)	9.5482 (p=0.006)
Akaike information criterion	2.6420	2.596	2.963
Breusch-Pagan test: χ^2; d.f.; ('p' value)	6.0045; (8); (0.6467)	4.4726; (7); (0.7240)	9.9741; (7); (0.1900)

Notes.
1. 't' statistics are computed using White's heteroskedasticity consistent variance-covariance matrix
2. * = coefficient significant at the 10% level
3. ** = coefficient significant at the 5% level
4. *** = coefficient significant at the 1% level

194

significant. Thus, a plurality electoral system creates a lower level of rent seeking opportunities than a proportional system, as measured by a higher associated level of economic freedom, i.e., reliance on markets. Second, the number of electoral districts (NDIST) is significant and negative. A larger number of electoral districts, *ceteris paribus*, reduce economic freedom and increase rent seeking opportunities.

Turning to the demographic control variables, we find that they are all statistically significant at the one-percent level in Model 2. First, increased literacy is associated with increased economic freedom and a reduced the level of rent-seeking opportunities provided by the government. A better-educated electorate is more knowledgeable about the actual intent and consequences of special interest legislation and therefore more resistant to it. This result lends additional support for the positive externality argument for subsidizing education. Second, the negative sign on the dummy variable for Eastern Europe is evidence of the early stages of transition from a directed economy. Indeed, the high level of government market intervention is a remnant of the former dominance of rent-seeking interests. Third, the positive sign on the Latin American dummy variable indicates that these countries have relatively lower levels of rent seeking opportunities. Fourth, the military's share of GDP is associated with significantly lower levels of economic freedom and higher rent-seeking opportunities. This may be evidence that military budgets are viewed as targets for rent seeking. Finally, increasing the years of independence, as a measure of the time rent seeking interests have had to influence government to create opportunities, reduces the level of economic freedom. This supports the contention that regardless of the other institutional arrangements, a stable set of special interest groups will be able to influence the government bring about creeping market intervention. Thus, the longer such special interests are undisturbed, the higher the associated level of rent seeking opportunities.

In estimating Equation (5), where the regressand is CREF or the change in the level of economic freedom over the 1990–95 period, we encounter the same specification problem with regard the regressors PL and PRES. As above, we set up three models – one including both PL and PRES, designated Model 4; one including PL, but excluding PRES, designated Model 5; and one excluding PL, but including PRES, designated Model 6. Carrying out a similar set of specification tests and we select Model 5, which includes PL and excludes PRES. Again, while PRES is significant and positive in Model 6, its effects cannot be disentangled from those of PL. All these results are presented in Table 3.

The estimation of Model 5 explains just over 35 percent of the variation in the dependent variable. The inferior performance of Model 5 relative to

Table 3. Estimating the change in the level of reform in 1990–1995: Heteroskedasticity-corrected OLS estimates[1]

Regressand: CREF Regressor	Model 4 Coefficient ('t' stat.)	Model 5 Coefficient ('t' stat.)	Model 6 Coefficient ('t' stat.)
Constant	−85.563 (1.51)	−88.603 (1.88)*	−118.519 (2.06)*
PL	45.659 (3.05)***	43.480 (5.78)***	−
PRES	−4.136 (0.21)	−	40.713 (3.96)***
NDIST	−0.299 (4.45)***	−0.294 (4.47)***	−0.190 (2.43)**
LITER	1.226 (1.63)	1.262 (1.95)*	1.662 (2.20)**
EASTEUR	40.751 (2.06)*	39.981 (2.26)**	24.928 (1.30)
LATIN	−0.054 (0.002)	−4.171 (0.29)	−45.493 (2.48)**
MILSP	−0.358 (2.94)***	−0.358 (2.93)***	−0.325 (2.46)**
YRSIND	−0.019 (0.15)	−0.021 (0.17)	−0.063 (0.51)
	Diagnostics		
Adjusted R^2	0.3214	0.3534	0.2945
F stat; (d.f.)	2.66**; (8,20)	3.19**; (7,21)	2.67**; (7,21)
Log-likelihood	−132.8137	−132.8195	−134.0849
Restricted log-likelihood	−143.3143	−143.3143	−143.3143
Sum of squared errors	16138.8	16145.3	27617.6
Exclusion restriction: $F(1,20)$	−	0.0080 (p=0.929)	14.2251 (p=0.001)
Akaike information criterion	9.780	9.712	9.799
Breusch-Pagan test: χ^2; d.f.; ('p' value)	6.4327; (8); (0.5989)	6.2712; (7); (0.5085)	4.4442; (7); (0.7274)

Notes.

1. 't' statistics are computed using White's heteroskedasticity consistent variance-covariance matrix
2. * = coefficient significant at the 10% level
3. ** = coefficient significant at the 5% level
4. *** = coefficient significant at the 1% level

196

Model 2 may be due to the fact that the independent variables are measured as levels rather then changes. However, in an absolute sense the fit is still very good and the F-statistic remains statistically significant.

For the variables of interest, the coefficient of the plurality system dummy, PL, is significantly positive while that of the number of electoral districts is significantly negative. Thus, plurality systems exhibit greater resistance to special interest manipulation than proportional systems in the speed of reform as well. Further, the number of electoral districts is positively related to the success of special interest groups in blocking reform and maintaining rent-seeking opportunities.

Turning to the demographic variables, we find that literacy remains significant, but only at the 10 percent level, while the East European dummy now is positive and significant at the 5 percent level. This suggests that while East European countries are starting from lower base level of economic freedom, they are making relatively more rapid progress in reducing rent seeking opportunities. Military spending as a percentage of GDP remains negative and highly significant, suggesting that larger military establishments increase resistance to economic reform. Neither the Latin American dummy nor the period of independence appears to have a significant effect on the pace of reform.

4. Discussion on our findings

We are interested in analyzing the important reality of the rising consequences of alternative legislative and electoral institutions on economic policy outcomes in terms of the opportunities for rent seeking. In this paper we apply economic theory and its methodological tools to study some of these effects. In particular, we analyze the impact of alternative legislative and electoral institutions on both the level and the pace of change of rent seeking opportunities (interpreted to be inversely related to market liberalization) in emerging market countries. We discover that a plurality system of representation and a smaller number of large electoral districts are both elements that favor the process of market liberalization in transition economies, and thus reduce rent seeking opportunities. On the other hand, a proportional system of representation and a greater number of small electoral districts hinder economic reform.

Our results are in line with the predictions of theory outlined in Section 2. Therefore they can be interpreted as the results of the different political incentives produced by alternative political institutions. Some legislative and electoral institutions generate greater incentives to implement particularistic policies to the detriment of the general interests of voters. Legislators confronted with such institutions are expected to hamper the path to economic reform. Efforts to free markets represent a reduction in politicians' ability to use the state to carve out divisible benefits for important constituents. When elected representatives are given incentives to serve particularistic interests, market liberalization directly threatens the viability of electoral strategies that are based on serving these interests

The empirical analysis was carried out for both the level and the pace of economic reform. Examining Tables 2 and 3, we note that the two variables that refer to electoral institutions (PL vs. PR and the number of electoral districts) maintain the expected sign and statistical impact on the market liberalization process. The difference in legislative institutions under observation (presidential vs. parliamentary regimes) cannot be disentangled from the electoral system measure in our data set. However, specification tests indicate that the electoral system (PL vs. PR) dominates the legislative regime in terms of its effects on the level and pace of reform. This suggests that election rules and the districting mechanism play a more important role than the organization of the executive in the dynamics of economic reforms.

This paper would be incomplete if we did not discuss our choice of the economic freedom index proposed by GLB (1996). We are aware of the large literature related to the measurement of freedom from Banks and Textor (1963) and Gastil (1972) to more recent works published by De Haan and Siermann (1995, 1998). This literature has focused on the relationship between economic liberty and economic growth, and has been dominated by a debate over two main related difficulties: the lack of a clear definition of economic freedom and of a unique methodology to measure it.[3] An analysis of this issue goes beyond the limited objectives of this paper. Therefore, we limit ourselves to very briefly explaining why we selected the GLB index. As opposed to most of the earlier and contemporary efforts, GLB aim at specifically measuring *economic* freedom separating it from political and social freedom. This is not to say that the latter are of less or more importance, but just that we have to be careful in understanding the conceptualizations which can be made about different schemes of values and use those which are most appropriate. In this paper we are concerned with market liberalization processes and therefore pay more attention to the elements of economic liberty rather than political and social liberty.

5. Concluding remarks

The empirical results support the theoretical predictions. Plurality electoral systems are more resistant to the political demands of rent seeking as compared to proportional systems. Fewer electoral districts reduce the incentives

198

of elected representatives to create rent seeking opportunities. However, the regime type, presidential or parliamentary, emerges as less important than the electoral system. This inquiry is seen as the first step in understanding the position of importance electoral systems play in determining the effectiveness of special interest group demands.

We have two recommendations for future research. First, a more complete modeling of electoral institutions with an emphasis on voting rules would significantly expand our understanding of the relationship between electoral rules and the effectiveness of particularistic interest in creating rent seeking opportunities. Second, testing the implication of electoral institutions with an expanded set of countries will determine if the empirical results reported here may be generalized or are unique to countries with emerging economies.

Our empirical results support the argument that the Eastern European countries are moving to a new equilibrium position with lower levels of market intervention (and associated rent seeking) as evidenced by the positive sign on a dummy variable for Eastern European countries in our estimation of reform. This is good news as it demonstrates the possibility of reversing rent gains and fostering the economic growth that results from reliance on the more efficient market mechanisms to coordinate economic activity. Our results re-emphasize the importance of high levels of literacy in maintaining the control of the citizenry over elected representatives. Finally, we suggest that military establishments have both direct costs in terms of explicit expenditures as well as indirect costs as targets of efficiency reducing rent seeking.

Notes

1. A number of studies linking alternative electoral systems with policy outcomes have appeared in the literature. We would like to mention two of them. Carey and Shugart (1995) lay out four different variables to measure the extent to which electoral rules create incentives to cultivate a personal vote: the extent of party control of the ballot, the level of vote pooling, the type of vote cast (i.e., whether voters vote for the party, for a single candidate or for multiple candidates) and the district magnitude. Following the path indicated by Carey and Shugart, Crisp (1997) analyzes 9 Latin American countries, and tests three hypotheses. First, the greater the party control over the ballot, the less the incentive for individual candidates to build a personal vote and the lower is government spending. Second, vote pooling should limit the incentive to cultivate a personal vote and correlates with lower spending. Third, the more the electoral rules put candidates from the same party in competition with one another, the higher government spending. The study offers support for the first and third hypotheses only and rejects the second: ballot access and type of vote cast impact on spending as expected, but vote pooling does not.
2. Huntington (1968) saw legislatures in countries undergoing modernization as clear examples of weak political institutions. They were typically dominated by landowning elites

and lacked the ability to channel demands for political participation by newly mobilized social groups. Much of the same view appears in Mezey (1985) who emphasizes the degree to which such legislatures act on particularistic demands due to the continued rural orientation of their economies. Waterbury (1992) suggests that privatization lags because the state-owned enterprise sector is especially useful for politicians seeking to build particularistic support networks among favored constituencies. He argues that the sale of state-owned enterprises might occur faster and more easily when the incentive to cultivate a personal vote is lower. Eaton (1998) evaluates the impact of electoral incentives on legislators' support for tax reforms that eliminate special exemptions and rates.

3. Papers by De Haan and Siermann (1995) and Scully and Slottje (1991) provide useful surveys of the literature on democracy and economic growth.

References

Alesina, A. and Drazen, A. (1991). Why are stabilisations delayed?. *American Economic Review* 81: 1170–1188.

Banks, A. and Textor, R. (1963). *A cross-polity survey*. Cambridge, MA: Cambridge University Press.

Cain, B., Ferejohn, J. and Fiorina, M. (1987). *The personal vote: Constituency service and electoral interdependence*. Cambridge: Cambridge University Press.

Carey, J. and Shugart, M. (1995). Incentives to cultivate a personal vote: A rank ordering of electoral formulas. *Electoral Studies* 14: 231–248.

Cowhey, P. and McCubbins, M. (1995). *Structure and policy in Japan and the United States*. New York: Cambridge University Press.

Crisp, B. (1997). Electoral rules and government spending patterns in Latin America: Institutional determinants of rational behavior. Paper presented at the annual meeting of the APSA, August 1997, Washington D.C.

De Haan, J. and Siermann, C.L.J. (1995). New evidence on the relationship between democracy and economic growth. *Public Choice* 86: 175–195.

De Haan, J. and Siermann, C.L.J. (1998). Further evidence on the relationship between economic freedom and economic growth. *Public Choice* 95: 363–380.

Eaton, K. (1998). *The politics of tax reform: Economic policy making in presidential democracy*. Ph.D. Dissertation, Yale University.

Fernandez, R. and Rodrik, D. (1991). Resistance to reform: Status quo bias in the presence of individual-specific uncertainty. *American Economic Review* 81: 1146–1155.

Fiorina, M. (1977). *Congress: Keystone of the Washington establishment*. New Haven: Yale University Press.

Gastil, R.D. (1972). *Freedom in the world: Political rights and civil liberties*. Westport, CT: Greenwood Press.

Grofman, B. and Reynolds, A. (2000). Electoral systems and the art of constitutional engineering: An inventory of main findings. In: R. Mudambi, P. Navarra and G. Sobbrio (Eds.), *Rules and reason: Perspectives on constitutional political economy*. New York: Cambridge University Press.

Gwartney, J., Lawson, R. and Block, W. (1995). *Economic freedom of the world*. Toronto: The Fraser Institute.

Gudgin, G. and Taylor, P.J. (1979). *Seats, votes and the spatial organization of elections*. London: Pion.

200

Haggard, S. and Kaufman, R. (1995). *The political economy of democratic transition.* Princeton: Princeton University Press.

Hausmann, R. (1998). *Latin America after a decade of reforms.* Washington D.C.: Inter-American Development Bank.

Hinich, M.J. and Ordeshook, P.C. (1970). Plurality maximization vs. vote maximization: A spatial analysis with variable participation. *American Political Science Review* 64: 772–791.

Huntington, S. (1969). *Political order in changing societies.* New Haven: Yale University Press.

Johnston, R.J. and Rossiter, D.J. (1982). Constituency building, political representation and electoral bias in urban England. In: D.T. Herbert and R.J. Johnston (Eds.), *Geography and the urban environment: Volume 5.* Chichester: Wiley.

Kernell, S. (1991). *Parallel politics: Economic policy-making in Japan and the United States.* Washington, D.C.: The Brookings Institution.

Kreuger, A.O. (1974). The political economy of the rent-seeking society. *American Economic Review* 64: 291–303.

Kreuger, A.O. (1992). *Economic policy reform in developing countries.* Cambridge, MA: Blackwell.

Marshall, W. and Weingast, B. (1988). The industrial organization of Congress, or why legislators, like firms, are not organized as markets. *Journal of Political Economy* 96: 132–163.

Mayhew, D. (1974). *Congress: The electoral connection.* New Haven: Yale University Press.

Mezey, M. (1985). Third world legislatures. In: *The handbook of legislative research.* Cambridge: Harvard University Press.

Mudambi, R. and Navarra, P. (1999). A complete model of strategic alliances in the context of electoral reform. *Discussion Papers in Economics and Management*, No.411, University of Reading, UK.

Navarra, P. and Lignana, D. (1997). The strategic behavior of the Italian left in a risk-sharing framework. *Public Choice* 93: 131–148.

Persson, T. and Tabellini, G. (1999). The size and scope of government: Comparative politics with rational politicians. *European Economic Review* 43: 699–735.

Ramseyer, M. and Rosenbluth, F. (1993). *Japan political marketplace.* Cambridge: Harvard University Press.

Scully, G.W. and Slottje, D.J. (1991). Ranking economic liberty across countries. *Public Choice* 69: 121–152.

Shugart, M. and Carey, J. (1992). *Presidents and assemblies.* New York: Cambridge University Press.

Taagepera, R. and Shugart, M. (1989). *Seats and votes: The effects and determinants of electoral systems.* New Haven: Yale University Press.

Taylor, P.J. and Gudgin, G. (1976). The statistical basis of decision making in electoral districting. *Environment and Planning A* 8: 43–58.

Tullock, G. (1967). The welfare costs of tariffs, monopolies and theft. *Western Economic Journal* 5: 224–232.

Waterbury, J. (1992). The hart of the matter? Public enterprise and the adjustment process. In: S. Haggard and R.R. Kaufman (Eds.), *The politics of economic adjustments.* Princeton: Princeton University Press.

Weingast, B.R., Shepsle, K.A. and Johnsen, C. (1981). The political economy of benefits and costs: A neo-classical approach to distributive politics. *Journal of Political Economy* 89: 642–664.

Appendix 1

Composition of the index of economic freedom

The index of economic freedom is based on the economic freedom survey conducted by Gwartney, Lawson and Block (1995). The index has 17 components divided across four categories: money and inflation, taxation, government operations and regulations and international exchange. Component weighting is a major challenge in constructing such indices. They construct three different indices following different component weightings. One weights each component equally. A second is based expert surveys of which components are most important, generally speaking. A third weights components according to the judgment of country experts regarding the importance of the different components. We used the average of the three different indices in this paper.

1. Money and inflation (protection of money as a store of value and medium of exchange):
   a. Average annual growth rate of the money supply during the last five years minus the potential growth rate of real GDP
   b. Standard deviation of the annual inflation rate during the last five years
   c. Freedom of citizens to own a foreign currency bank account domestically
   d. Freedom of citizens to maintain a bank account abroad
2. Government operations and regulations (freedom to decide what is produced and consumed):
   a. Government general consumption expenditures as % of GDP
   b. The role and presence of government-operated enterprises
   c. Price controls – the extent that businesses are free to set their own prices
   d. Freedom of private businesses and co-operatives to compete in markets
   e. Equality of citizens under the law and access of citizens to a non-discriminatory judiciary
   f. Freedom from government regulations and policies that cause negative real interest rates
3. Takings and discriminatory taxation (freedom to keep what you earn)
   a. Transfers and subsidies as % of GDP
   b. Top marginal tax rate (and income threshold at which it applies)
   c. The use of conscripts to obtain military personnel
4. Restraints on International Exchange (freedom of exchange with foreigners)
   a. Taxes on international trade as% of exports plus imports
   b. Difference between the official exchange rate and the black market rate
   c. Actual size of trade sector compared to the expected size
   d. Restrictions on the freedom of citizens to engage in capital transactions with foreigners

202

Appendix 2

Appendix 2. Variables used in the estimates and their sources

Variable	Definition and source
REF	level of economic reform – 1995 (Gwartney, Lawson and Block, 1995)
CREF	change in economic reform – 1990–1995 (Gwartney, Lawson and Block, 1995)
PL	dummy, 1 if PL , 0 if PR (Grofman and Reynolds, 2000)
PRES	dummy, 1 if presidential system, 0 if parliamentary system (Grofman and Reynolds, 2000)
NDIST	number of electoral districts per million registered voters (CIA *World Factbook*, 1998)
LITER	literacy rate – % of population over age 15 who can read and write (CIA *World Factbook*, 1998)
EASTEUR	dummy, 1 if East European country, 0 otherwise
LATIN	dummy, 1 if Latin American country, 0 otherwise
MILSP	1995 military spending as a percentage of GDP (CIA *World Factbook*, 1998)
YRSIND	years of independence (CIA *World Factbook*, 1998). Year of independence set as 1989 for East European countries

The countries in the data set are: Argentina Bolivia, Botswana, Brazil, Chile, Colombia, Costa Rica, the Czech Republic, Dominican Republic, Ecuador, Greece, Hungary, Iran, Jordan, Malaysia, Malta, Mexico, Panama, Paraguay, Peru, Poland, Romania, Slovakia, South Korea, Syria, Tunisia, Turkey, Uruguay and Venezuela.

Part II
Traditional Models and Theories

[6]

WHY REGULATE UTILITIES?*

HAROLD DEMSETZ
University of Chicago

CURRENT economic doctrine offers to its students a basic relationship between the number of firms that produce for a given market and the degree to which competitive results will prevail. Stated explicitly or suggested implicitly is the doctrine that price and output can be expected to diverge to a greater extent from their competitive levels the fewer the firms that produce the product for the market. This relationship has provided the logic that motivates much of the research devoted to studying industrial concentration, and it has given considerable support to utility regulation.[1]

In this paper, I shall argue that the asserted relationship between market concentration and competition cannot be derived from existing theoretical considerations and that it is based largely on an incorrect understanding of the concept of competition or rivalry. The strongest application of the asserted relationship is in the area of utility regulation since, if we assume scale economies in production, it can be deduced that only one firm will produce the commodity. The logical validity or falsity of the asserted relationship should reveal itself most clearly in this case.

Although public utility regulation recently has been criticized because of its ineffectiveness or because of the undesirable indirect effects it produces,[2] the basic intellectual arguments for believing that truly effective regulation is desirable have not been challenged. Even those who are inclined to reject government regulation or ownership of public utilities because they believe these alternatives are more undesirable than private monopoly, implicitly accept the intellectual arguments that underlie regulation.[3]

---

* The author is indebted to R. H. Coase, who was unconvinced by the natural monopoly argument long before this paper was written, and to George J. Stigler and Joel Segall for helpful comments and criticisms.

[1] Antitrust legislation and judicial decision, to the extent that they have been motivated by a concern for bigness and concentration, *per se*, have also benefited from the asserted relationship between monopoly power and industry structure.

[2] Cf., George J. Stigler and Claire Friedland, What Can Regulators Regulate? The Case of Electricity, 5 J. Law & Econ. 1 (1962); H. Averch and L. Johnson, The Firm under Regulatory Constraint, 52 Am. Econ. Rev. 1052 (1962); Armen Alchian and Reuben Kessel, Competition, Monopoly, and the Pursuit of Pecuniary Gain, in Aspects of Labor Economics 157 (1962).

[3] Thus, Milton Friedman, while stating his preference for private monopoly over public monopoly or public regulation, writes:

56   THE JOURNAL OF LAW AND ECONOMICS

The economic theory of natural monopoly is exceedingly brief and, we shall see, exceedingly unclear. Current doctrine is reflected in two recent statements of the theory. Samuelson writes:

Under persisting decreasing costs for the firm, one or a few of them will so expand their q's as to become a significant part of the market for the industry's total Q. We would then end up (1) with a single monopolist who dominates the industry; (2) with a few large sellers who together dominate the industry . . . or (3) with some kind of imperfection of competition that, in either a stable way or in connection with a series of intermittent price wars, represents an important departure from the economist's model of "perfect" competition wherein no firm has any control over industry price.[4]

Alchian and Allen view the problem as follows:

If a product is produced under cost conditions such that larger rates . . . [would] mean lower average cost per unit, . . . only one firm could survive; if there were two firms, one could expand to reduce costs and selling price and thereby eliminate the other. In view of the impossibility of more than one firm's being profitable, two is too many. But if there is only one, that incumbent firm may be able to set prices above free-entry costs for a long time. Either resources are wasted because too many are in the industry, or there is just one firm, which will be able to charge monopoly prices.[5]

At this point it will be useful to state explicitly the interpretation of natural monopoly used in this paper. If, because of production scale economies, it is less costly for one firm to produce a commodity in a given market than it is for two or more firms, then one firm will survive; if left unregulated, that firm will set price and output at monopoly levels; the price-output decision of that firm will be determined by profit maximizing behavior constrained only by the market demand for the commodity.

The theory of natural monopoly is deficient for it fails to reveal the logical steps that carry it from scale economies in production to monopoly price in the market place. To see this most clearly, let us consider the contracting process from its beginning.

Why must rivals share the market? Rival sellers can offer to enter into contracts with buyers. In this bidding competition, the rival who offers buyers the most favorable terms will obtain their patronage; there is no clear or necessary reason for *bidding* rivals to share in the *production* of

---

However, monopoly may also arise because it is technically efficient to have a single producer or enterprise. . . . When technical conditions make a monopoly the natural outcome of competitive market forces, there are only three alternatives that seem available: private monopoly, public monopoly, or public regulation. Capitalism and Freedom 28 (1962).

4 Paul A. Samuelson, Economics 461 (6th rev. ed. 1964).

5 Armen Alchian and William R. Allen, University Economics 412 (1st ed. 1964).

the goods and, therefore, there is no clear reason for competition in bidding to result in an increase in per-unit *production* costs.

Why must the unregulated market outcome be monopoly price? The competitiveness of the bidding process depends very much on such things as the number of bidders, but there is no clear or necessary reason for *production* scale economies to decrease the number of *bidders*. Let prospective buyers call for bids to service their demands. Scale economies in servicing their demands in no way imply that there will be one bidder only. There can be many bidders and the bid that wins will be the lowest. The existence of scale economies in the production of the service is irrelevant to a determination of the number of rival bidders. If the number of bidders is large or if, for other reasons, collusion among them is impractical, the contracted price can be very close to per-unit production cost.[6]

The determinants of competition in market negotiations differ from and should not be confused with the determinants of the number of firms from which production will issue after contractual negotiations have been completed. The theory of natural monopoly is clearly unclear. Economies of scale in production imply that the bids submitted will offer increasing quantities at lower per-unit costs, but production scale economies imply nothing obvious about how competitive these prices will be. If one bidder can do the job at less cost than two or more, because each would then have a smaller output rate, then the bidder with the lowest bid price for the entire job will be awarded the contract, whether the good be cement, electricity, stamp vending machines, or whatever, but the lowest bid price need not be a monopoly price.[7]

The criticism made here of the theory of natural monopoly can be understood best by constructing an example that is free from irrelevant complications, such as durability of distributions systems, uncertainty, and irrational behavior, all of which may or may not justify the use of regulatory commissions but none of which is relevant to the theory of natural monopoly; for this theory depends on one belief only—price and output will be at monopoly levels if, due to scale economies, only one firm succeeds in producing the product.

Assume that owners of automobiles are required to own and display

---

[6] I shall not consider in this paper the problem of marginal cost pricing and the various devices, such as multi-part tariffs, that can be used to approximate marginal cost pricing.

[7] The competitive concept employed here is not new to economics although it has long been neglected. An early statement of the concept, which was known as "competition *for* the field" in distinction to "competition *within* the field" is given by Edwin Chadwick, Results of Different Principles of Legislation and Administration in Europe; of Competition for the Field, as compared with the Competition within the Field of Service, 22 J. Royal Statistical Soc'y. 381 (1859).

new license plates each year. The production of license plates is subject to scale economies.

The theory of natural monopoly asserts that under these conditions the owners of automobiles will purchase plates from one firm only and that firm, in the absence of regulation, will charge a monopoly price, a price that is constrained only by the demand for and the cost of producing license plates. The logic of the example does dictate that license plates will be purchased from one firm because this will allow that firm to offer the plates at a price based on the lowest possible per-unit cost. But why should that price be a monopoly price?

There can be many bidders for the annual contract. Each will submit a bid based on the assumption that if its bid is lowest it will sell to all residents, if it is not lowest it sells to none. Under these conditions there will exist enough independently acting bidders to assure that the winning price will differ insignificantly from the per-unit cost of producing license plates.

If only one firm submits the lowest price, the process ends, but if two or more firms submit the lowest price, one is selected according to some random selection device or one is allowed to sell or give his contracts to the other. There is no monopoly price although there may be rent to some factors if their supply is positively sloped. There is no regulation of firms in the industry. The price is determined in the bidding market. The only role played by the government or by a consumers' buying cooperative is some random device to select the winning bidder if more than one bidder bids the lowest price.

There are only two important assumptions: (1) The inputs required to enter production must be available to many potential bidders at prices determined in open markets. This lends credibility to numerous rival bids. (2) The cost of colluding by bidding rivals must be prohibitively high. The reader will recognize that these requirements are no different than those required to avoid monopoly price in any market, whether production in that market is or is not subject to scale economies.

Moreover, if we are willing to consider the possibility that collusion or merger of all potential bidding rivals is a reasonable prospect, then we must examine the other side of the coin. Why should collusion or merger of *buyers* be prohibitively costly if an infinite or large number of bidding rivals can collude successfully? If we allow buyers access to the same technology of collusion, the market will be characterized by bilateral negotiations between organized buyers and organized sellers. While the outcome of such negotiations is somewhat uncertain with respect to wealth distribution, there is no reason to expect inefficiency.

Just what is the supply elasticity of bidders and what are the costs of colluding are questions to be answered empirically since they cannot be deduced from production scale economies. There exist more than one firm in every public utility industry and many firms exist in some public utility industries. And this is true even though licensing restrictions have been severe; the assertion that the supply of potential *bidders* in any market would be very inelastic if licensing restrictions could be abolished would seem difficult to defend when producing competitors exist in nearby markets. The presence of active rivalry is clearly indicated in public utility history. In fact, producing competitors, not to mention unsuccessful bidders, were so plentiful that one begins to doubt that scale economies characterized the utility industry at the time when regulation replaced market competition. Complaints were common that the streets were too frequently in a state of disrepair for the purpose of accommodating competing companies. Behling writes:

There is scarcely a city in the country that has not experienced competition in one or more of the utility industries. Six electric light companies were organized in the one year of 1887 in New York City. Forty-five electric light enterprises had the legal right to operate in Chicago in 1907. Prior to 1895, Duluth, Minnesota, was served by five electric lighting companies, and Scranton, Pennsylvania, had four in 1906 . . . . During the latter part of the nineteenth century, competition was the usual situation in the gas industry in this country. Before 1884, six competing companies were operating in New York City . . . . Competition was common and especially persistent in the telephone industry. According to a special report of the Census in 1902, out of 1051 incorporated cities in the United States with a population of more than 4,000 persons, 1002 were provided with telephone facilities. The independent companies had a monopoly in 137 of the cities, the Bell interests had exclusive control over communication by telephone in 414 cities, while the remaining 451, almost half, were receiving duplicated service. Baltimore, Chicago, Cleveland, Columbus, Detroit, Kansas City, Minneapolis, Philadelphia, Pittsburgh, and St. Louis, among the larger cities, had at least two telephone services in 1905.[8]

It would seem that the number of potential bidding rivals and the cost of their colluding in the public utility industries are likely to be at least as great as in several other industries for which we find that unregulated markets work tolerably well.

The natural monopoly theory provides no logical basis for monopoly prices. The theory is illogical. Moreover, for the general case of public utility industries, there seems no clear evidence that the cost of colluding is significantly lower than it is for industries for which unregulated market competition seems to work. To the extent that utility regulation is based on the fear of monopoly price, *merely because one firm will serve each market*, it is not based on any deducible economic theorem.

The important point that needs stressing is that *we have no theory that*

[8] Burton N. Behling, Competition and Monopoly in Public Utility Industries 19-20 (1938).

allows us to deduce from the observable degree of concentration in a particular market whether or not price and output are competitive. We have as yet no general theory of collusion and certainly not one that allows us to associate observed concentration in a particular market with successful collusion.[9]

It is possible to make some statements about collusion that reveal the nature of the forces at work. These statements are largely intuitive and cannot be pursued in detail here. But they may be useful in imparting to the reader a notion of what is meant by a theory of collusion. Let us suppose that there are no special costs to competing. That is, we assume that sellers do not need to keep track of the prices or other activities of their competitors. Secondly, assume that there are some costs of colluding that must be borne by members of a bidders' cartel. This condition is approximated least well where the government subsidizes the cost of colluding—for example, the U.S. Department of Agriculture. Finally, assume that there are no legal barriers to entry.

Under these conditions, new bidding rivals will be paid to join the collusion. In return for joining they will receive a pro rata share of monopoly profits. As more rivals appear the pro rata share must fall. The cartel will continue paying new rivals to join until the pro rata share falls to the cost of colluding. That is, until the cartel members receive a competitive rate of return for remaining in the cartel. The next rival bidder can refuse to join the cartel; instead he can enter the market at a price below the cartel price (as can any present member of the cartel who chooses to break away). If there is some friction in the system, this rival will choose this course of action in preference to joining the cartel, for if he joins the cartel he receives a competitive rate of return; whereas if he competes outside the cartel by selling at a price below that of the cartel he receives an above-competitive rate of return for some short-run period. Under the assumed conditions the cartel must eventually fail and price and output can be competitive even though only a few firms actually produce the product. Moreover, the essential ingredient to its eventual failure is only that the private per-firm cost of colluding exceeds the private per-firm cost of competing.

Under what conditions will the cost of colluding exceed the cost of competing? How will these costs be affected by allowing coercive tactics? What about buyer cartels? What factors affect how long is "eventually"? Such questions remain to be answered by a theory of collusion. Until such questions are answered, public policy prescriptions must be suspect. A market in which many firms produce may be competitive or it may be collusive; the large number of firms merely reflects production scale diseconomies; large numbers do not necessarily reflect high or low collusion costs. A market in

[9] However, see George J. Stigler, A Theory of Oligopoly, 72 J. Pol. Econ. 44 (1964).

which few firms produce may be competitive or it may be collusive; the small number of firms merely relects production scale economies; fewness does not necessarily reflect high or low collusion costs. Thus, an economist may view the many retailers who sell on "fair trade" terms with suspicion and he may marvel at the ability of large numbers of workers to form effective unions, and, yet, he may look with admiration at the performance of the few firms who sell airplanes, cameras, or automobiles.

The subject of monopoly price is necessarily permeated with the subject of negotiating or contracting costs. A world in which negotiating costs are zero is a world in which no monopolistic inefficiencies will be present, simply because buyers and sellers both can profit from negotiations that result in a reduction and elimination of inefficiencies. In such a world it will be bargaining skills and not market structures that determine the distribution of wealth. If a monopolistic structure exists on one side of the market, the other side of the market will be organized to offset any power implied by the monopolistic structure. The organization of the other side of the market can be undertaken by members of that side or by rivals of the monopolistic structure that prevails on the first side. The co-existence of monopoly *power* and monopoly *structure* is possible only if the costs of negotiating are differentially positive, being lower for one set of sellers (or buyers) than it is for rival sellers (or buyers). If one set of sellers (or buyers) can organize those on the other side of the market more cheaply than can rivals, then price may be raised (or lowered) to the extent of the existing differential advantage in negotiating costs; this extent generally will be less than the simple monopoly price. In some cases the differential advantage in negotiating costs may be so great that price will settle at the monopoly (monopsony) level. This surely cannot be the general case, but the likelihood of it surely increases as the costs imposed on potential rivals increase; legally restricting entry is one way of raising the differential disadvantages to rivals; the economic meaning of restricting entry *is* increasing the cost of potential rivals of negotiating with and organizing buyers (or sellers).

The public policy question is which groups of market participants, *if any*, are to receive governmentally sponsored advantages and disadvantages, not only in the subsidization or taxation of production but, also, in the creation of advantages or disadvantages in conducting negotiations.

At this juncture, it should be emphasized that I have argued, not that regulatory commissions are undesirable, but that economic theory does not, at present, provide a justification for commissions insofar as they are based on the belief that observed concentration and monopoly price bear any necessary relationship.

Indeed, in utility industries, regulation has often been sought because of the inconvenience of competition. The history of regulation is often written in terms of the desire to prohibit "excessive" duplication of utility distribution systems and the desire to prohibit the capture of *windfall* gains by utility companies. Neither of these aspects of the utility business are necessarily related to scale economies. Let us first consider the problem of excessive duplication of facilities.

Duplication of Facilities. Communities and not individuals own or control most of the ground and air rights-of-way used by public utility distribution systems. The problem of excessive duplication of distribution systems is attributable to the failure of communities to set a proper price on the use of these scarce resources. The right to use publicly owned thoroughfares is the right to use a scarce resource. The absence of a price for the use of these resources, a price high enough to reflect the opportunity costs of such alternative uses as the servicing of uninterrupted traffic and unmarred views, will lead to their overutilization. The setting of an appropriate fee for the use of these resources would reduce the degree of duplication to optimal levels.

Consider that portion of the ground controlled by an individual and under which a *utility's* distribution system runs. Confront that individual with the option of service at a lower price from a company that is a rival to the present seller. The individual will take into consideration the cost to him of running a trench through his garden and the benefit to him of receiving the service at lower cost. There is no need for excessive duplication. Indeed, there is no need for any duplication of facilities if he selects the new service, provided that one of two conditions holds. If the *individual* owns that part of the distribution system running under his ground he could tie it in to whatever trunk line serves him best; alternatively, once the new company wins his patronage, a rational solution to the use of that part of the distribution system would be for the utility company owning it to sell it to the utility company now serving the buyer.

There may be good reasons for using community property rather than private property to house the main trunk lines of some utility distribution systems. The placement of such systems under or over streets, alleyways, and sidewalks, resources already publicly owned (a fact taken as datum here), may be less costly than routing them through private property. The failure of communities to charge fees for the use of public property, fees that tend to prevent excessive use of this property, can be explained in three ways.

(1) There was a failure to understand the prerequisities for efficient resource use. Some public officer must be given the incentives to act as a rational conservator of resources when these resources are scarce.

(2) The disruption of thoroughfares was not, in fact, costly enough to bother about.

(3) The setting of fees to curtail excessive use of thoroughfares by utility companies was too costly to be practical.

The first two explanations, if true, give no support to an argument for regulating utility companies. The third explanation may give support to some sort of regulation, for it asserts that the economic effects that are produced by the placing of distribution systems are such that it is too costly to economize through the use of a price system. The costs of taking account of these effects through some regulatory process must be compared with the benefits of realigning resource use, and if the benefits are worth the costs some regulation may be desirable. Note clearly: scale economies in serving a market are not at issue. To see this, imagine that electrical distribution systems are thin lines of a special conducting paint. The placing of such systems causes no difficulties. They are sprayed over either public or private property. Nonetheless, suppose that the use of each system is subject to scale economies. Clearly, the desire to regulate cannot now be justified by such problems as traffic disruption, even though scale economies are present. "Excess" duplication is a problem of externalities and not of scale economies.

Let us suppose that it is desirable to employ some sort of regulation because it is too costly to use the price system to take account of the disruptive effects of placing distribution systems. Regulation comes in all sizes and shapes, and it is by no means clear what type of regulation would be most desirable.

A franchise system that allows only a limited number of utility companies to serve a market area was employed frequently. A franchise system that awarded the franchise to that company which seemed to offer the best price-quality package would be one that allowed market competition between bidding rivals to determine that package. The restraint of the market would be substituted for that of the regulatory commission.

An alternative arrangement would be public ownership of the distribution system. This would involve the collection of competing bids for installing the distribution system. The system could then be installed by the bidder offering to do the specified job at the lowest price. This is the same process used by communities to build highways and it employs rival bidding and not commissions to determine that price. The community could then allow its distribution system to be used by that utility company offering to provide specified utility services at lowest cost to residents. Again the market is substituted for the regulatory commission. Public ownership of streets may make public ownership of distribution systems seem desirable, but this does not mean that the use of regulatory commissions is desirable.

The Problem of Windfalls. We must now consider a last difficulty that has sometimes been marshalled to support the regulation of utilities. This argument is based on the fact that events in life are uncertain. The application of this observation to the utility business goes like this. After a buyer enters into an agreement with a utility company for supplying utility service, there may be changes in technology and prices that make the agreed upon price obsolete. In such cases, it is asserted, the price should be changed to reflect the current cost of providing utility services. The regulation by commission of prices on the basis of current costs is needed in the utilities industries because of the durability of original investments in plant and distribution systems. This durability prohibits the use of recontracting in the market place as a method for bringing about appropriate changes in price.

Problems of uncertainty create a potential for positive or negative windfalls. If market negotiations have misjudged the development of a better technology and if there is some cost to reawarding contracts to other producers once they are agreed upon, then an unexpected improvement in the technology used by those who are awarded the contracts may generate a price that is higher than per-unit cost, but higher by an amount no greater than the cost of reawarding contracts. In such cases, the firms now holding the contracts may collect a positive windfall for a short-run period. Or, if input prices increase by more than is expected, these same firms may suffer from a negative windfall. But the same thing is true of all markets. If a customer buys eggs today for consumption tomorrow, he will enjoy a positive windfall if the price of eggs is higher tomorrow and a negative windfall if the price is lower. The difference in the two cases is that, where long-term contracts are desirable, the windfalls may continue for longer periods. In such cases it *may* be desirable to employ a cost-plus regulatory scheme or to enter a clause that reserves the right, for some fee, to renegotiate the contract.

The problem faced here is what is the best way to cope with uncertainty. Long-term contracts for the supply of commodities are concluded satisfactorily in the market place without the aid of regulation. These contracts may be between retailers and appliance producers, or between the air lines and aircraft companies, all of whom may use durable production facilities. The rental of office space for ninety-nine years is fraught with uncertainty. I presume that the parties to a contract hire experts to provide relevant guesses on these matters and that the contract concluded resolves these issues in a way that is satisfactory to both parties. Penalties for reopening negotiations at a later date can be included in the contract. I presume that buyers and sellers who agree to contract with each other have handled the problem of uncertainty in a mutually satisfactory way. The correct way to view the problem is one of selecting the best type of contract. A producer may say, "if you agree to buy from me for twenty-five years, I can use facilities that are expected to produce the service at lower costs; if you contract five years, I will not invest much in tooling-up, and, hence, I will need a higher price to cover higher per-unit costs; of course, the longer-run contract allows more time for the unexpected, so let us include an escape clause of some kind." The buyer and seller must then agree on a suitable contract; durability of equipment and longer-term commitments can be sacrificed at the cost of higher per-unit costs, but there is no reason to expect that the concluded contract will be biased as to outcome or nonoptimal in other respects.

Cost-plus rate regulation is one way of coping with these problems, but it has great uncertainties of its own. Will the commission be effective? Does a well defined cost-plus arrangement create an inappropriate system of incentives to guide the firm in its investment and operating policies? Do the continual uncertainties associated with the meaning of cost-plus lead to otherwise avoidable difficulties in formulating investment plans? Rate regulation by commissions rather than by market rivalry may be more appropriate for utility industries than for other industries, but the truth of this assertion cannot be established deductively from existing economic theory. We do not know whether regulation handles the uncertainty-rent problem better or worse than the market.

The problem of coping with windfalls must be distinguished from the problem of *forecastable* rents. Suppose that it is known that buyers will incur considerable recontracting cost if they decide to change sellers after they are part way through an awarded contract. It would appear that the seller who wins the initial contract will be able to collect a rent as large as this recontracting cost. But this is not true if this recontracting cost is forecastable, that is, if it is not a windfall. The bidding for the initial contract will take account of the forecastable rent, so that if the bidding is competitive the rent will be forfeited by the lower bid prices to which it gives rise.

To what degree should legislation and regulation replace the market in the utilities or in other industries and what forms should such legislation take? It is not the objective of this paper to provide answers to such questions. My purpose has been to question the conventional economic arguments for the existing legislation and regulation. An expanded role for government can be defended on the empirical grounds of a documented general superiority of public administration in these industries or by a philosophical preference for mild socialism. But I do not see how a defense can be based on the formal arguments considered here; these arguments do not allow us to deduce from their assumptions either the monopoly problem or the administrative superiority of regulation.

In the case of utility industries, resort to the rivalry of the market place would relieve companies of the discomforts of commission regulation. But it would also relieve them of the comfort of legally protected market areas. It is my belief that the rivalry of the open market place disciplines more effectively than do the regulatory processes of the commission. If the managements of utility companies doubt this belief, I suggest that they re-examine the history of their industry to discover just who it was that provided most of the force behind the regulatory movement.

[7]

The theory of economic regulation

George J. Stigler

The University of Chicago

The potential uses of public resources and powers to improve the economic status of economic groups (such as industries and occupations) are analyzed to provide a scheme of the demand for regulation. The characteristics of the political process which allow relatively small groups to obtain such regulation is then sketched to provide elements of a theory of supply of regulation. A variety of empirical evidence and illustration is also presented.

■ The state—the machinery and power of the state—is a potential resource or threat to every industry in the society. With its power to prohibit or compel, to take or give money, the state can and does selectively help or hurt a vast number of industries. That political juggernaut, the petroleum industry, is an immense consumer of political benefits, and simultaneously the underwriters of marine insurance have their more modest repast. The central tasks of the theory of economic regulation are to explain who will receive the benefits or burdens of regulation, what form regulation will take, and the effects of regulation upon the allocation of resources.

Regulation may be actively sought by an industry, or it may be thrust upon it. A central thesis of this paper is that, as a rule, regulation is acquired by the industry and is designed and operated primarily for its benefit. There are regulations whose net effects upon the regulated industry are undeniably onerous; a simple example is the differentially heavy taxation of the industry's product (whiskey, playing cards). These onerous regulations, however, are exceptional and can be explained by the same theory that explains beneficial (we may call it "acquired") regulation.

Two main alternative views of the regulation of industry are widely held. The first is that regulation is instituted primarily for the protection and benefit of the public at large or some large subclass of the public. In this view, the regulations which injure the public—as when the oil import quotas increase the cost of petroleum products to America by $5 billion or more a year—are costs of some social goal (here, national defense) or, occasionally, perversions of the regulatory philosophy. The second view is essentially that the political process defies rational explanation: "politics" is an imponderable, a constantly and unpredictably shifting mixture of forces of the most diverse nature, comprehending acts of great moral virtue (the emancipation of slaves) and of the most vulgar venality (the congressman feathering his own nest).

The author obtained the B.B.A. degree from the University of Washington, the M.B.A. degree from Northwestern, and the Ph.D. degree from the University of Chicago. He is presently Charles R. Walgreen Distinguished Service Professor of American Institutions at the University of Chicago, and has published numerous articles and texts in the field of economics. Dr. Stigler is Vice Chairman of the Securities Investor Protective Commission.

why does not the powerful industry which obtained this expensive program instead choose direct cash subsidies from the public treasury? The "protection of the public" theory of regulation must say that the choice of import quotas is dictated by the concern of the federal government for an adequate domestic supply of petroleum in the event of war—a remark calculated to elicit uproarious laughter at the Petroleum Club. Such laughter aside, if national defense were the goal of the quotas, a tariff would be a more economical instrument of policy: it would retain the profits of exclusion for the treasury. The non-rationalist view would explain the policy by the inability of consumers to measure the cost to them of the import quotas, and hence their willingness to pay $5 billion in higher prices rather than the $2.5 billion in cash that would be equally attractive to the industry. Our profit-maximizing theory says that the explanation lies in a different direction: the present members of the refining industries would have to share a cash subsidy with all new entrants into the refining industry.[1] Only when the elasticity of supply of an industry is small will the industry prefer cash to controls over entry or output.

This question, why does an industry solicit the coercive powers of the state rather than its cash, is offered only to illustrate the approach of the present paper. We assume that political systems are rationally devised and rationally employed, which is to say that they are appropriate instruments for the fulfillment of desires of members of the society. This is not to say that the state will serve any person's concept of the public interest: indeed the problem of regulation is the problem of discovering when and why an industry (or other group of like-minded people) is able to use the state for its purposes, or is singled out by the state to be used for alien purposes.

1. What benefits can a state provide to an industry?

■ The state has one basic resource which in pure principle is not shared with even the mightiest of its citizens: the power to coerce. The state can seize money by the only method which is permitted by the laws of a civilized society, by taxation. The state can ordain the physical movements of resources and the economic decisions of households and firms without their consent. These powers provide the possibilities for the utilization of the state by an industry to increase its profitability. The main policies which an industry (or occupation) may seek of the state are four.

The most obvious contribution that a group may seek of the government is a direct subsidy of money. The domestic airlines received "air mail" subsidies (even if they did not carry mail) of $1.5 billion through 1968. The merchant marine has received construction and operation subsidies reaching almost $3 billion since World War II. The education industry has long shown a masterful skill in obtaining public funds: for example, universities and colleges have received federal funds exceeding $3 billion annually in recent years, as well as subsidized loans for dormitories and other construction. The veterans of wars have often received direct cash bonuses.

---

[1] The domestic producers of petroleum, who also benefit from the import quota, would find a tariff or cash payment to domestic producers equally attractive. If their interests alone were consulted, import quotas would be auctioned off instead of being given away.

4 / GEORGE J. STIGLER

We have already sketched the main explanation for the fact that an industry with power to obtain governmental favors usually does not use this power to get money: unless the list of beneficiaries can be limited by an acceptable device, whatever amount of subsidies the industry can obtain will be dissipated among a growing number of rivals. The airlines quickly moved away from competitive bidding for air mail contracts to avoid this problem.[2] On the other hand, the premier universities have not devised a method of excluding other claimants for research funds, and in the long run they will receive much-reduced shares of federal research monies.

The second major public resource commonly sought by an industry is control over entry by new rivals. There is considerable, not to say excessive, discussion in economic literature of the rise of peculiar price policies (limit prices), vertical integration, and similar devices to retard the rate of entry of new firms into oligopolistic industries. Such devices are vastly less efficacious (economical) than the certificate of convenience and necessity (which includes, of course, the import and production quotas of the oil and tobacco industries).

The diligence with which the power of control over entry will be exercised by a regulatory body is already well known. The Civil Aeronautics Board has not allowed a single new trunk line to be launched since it was created in 1938. The power to insure new banks has been used by the Federal Deposit Insurance Corporation to reduce the rate of entry into commercial banking by 60 percent.[3] The interstate motor carrier history is in some respects even more striking, because no even ostensibly respectable case for restriction on entry can be developed on grounds of scale economies (which are in turn adduced to limit entry for safety or economy of operation). The number of federally licensed common carriers is shown in Figure 1: the immense growth of the freight hauled by trucking common carriers has been associated with a steady secular decline of numbers of such carriers. The number of applications for new certificates has been in excess of 5000 annually in recent years: a rigorous proof that hope springs eternal in an aspiring trucker's breast.

We propose the general hypothesis: every industry or occupation that has enough political power to utilize the state will seek to control entry. In addition, the regulatory policy will often be so fashioned as to retard the rate of growth of new firms. For example, no new savings and loan company may pay a dividend rate higher than that prevailing in the community in its endeavors to attract deposits.[4] The power to limit selling expenses of mutual funds, which is soon to be conferred upon the Securities and Exchange Commission, will serve to limit the growth of small mutual funds and hence reduce the sales costs of large funds.

One variant of the control of entry is the protective tariff (and the corresponding barriers which have been raised to interstate movements of goods and people). The benefits of protection to an industry, one might think, will usually be dissipated by the entry of new domestic producers, and the question naturally arises: Why does the industry not also seek domestic entry controls? In a few industries

---

[2] See [7], pp. 60 ff.
[3] See [10].
[4] The Federal Home Loan Bank Board is the regulatory body. It also controls the amount of advertising and other areas of competition.

FIGURE 1

CERTIFICATES FOR INTERSTATE MOTOR CARRIERS

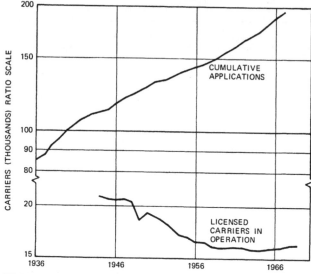

SOURCE: TABLE 5

(petroleum) the domestic controls have been obtained, but not in most. The tariff will be effective if there is a specialized domestic resource necessary to the industry; oil-producing lands is an example. Even if an industry has only durable specialized resources, it will gain if its contraction is slowed by a tariff.

A third general set of powers of the state which will be sought by the industry are those which affect substitutes and complements. Crudely put, the butter producers wish to suppress margarine and encourage the production of bread. The airline industry actively supports the federal subsidies to airports; the building trade unions have opposed labor-saving materials through building codes. We shall examine shortly a specific case of inter-industry competition in transportation.

The fourth class of public policies sought by an industry is directed to price-fixing. Even the industry that has achieved entry control will often want price controls administered by a body with coercive powers. If the number of firms in the regulated industry is even moderately large, price discrimination will be difficult to maintain in the absence of public support. The prohibition of interest on demand deposits, which is probably effective in preventing interest payments to most non-business depositors, is a case in point. Where there are no diseconomies of large scale for the individual firm (e.g., a motor trucking firm can add trucks under a given license as common carrier), price control is essential to achieve more than competitive rates of return.

☐ **Limitations upon political benefits.** These various political boons are not obtained by the industry in a pure profit-maximizing form. The political process erects certain limitations upon the exercise of cartel policies by an industry. These limitations are of three sorts.

TABLE 1

IMPORT QUOTAS OF REFINERIES AS PERCENT
OF DAILY INPUT OF PETROLEUM
(DISTRICTS I – IV, JULY 1, 1959 – DEC. 31, 1959)

SIZE OF REFINERY (THOUSANDS OF BARRELS)	PERCENT QUOTA
0–10	11.4
10–20	10.4
20–30	9.5
30–60	8.5
60–100	7.6
100–150	6.6
150–200	5.7
200–300	4.7
300 AND OVER	3.8

SOURCE: HEARING, SELECT COMMITTEE ON SMALL BUSINESS, U. S. CONGRESS, 88th CONG., 2nd SESS., AUG. 10 AND 11, 1964, [12] P. 121.

First, the distribution of control of the industry among the firms in the industry is changed. In an unregulated industry each firm's influence upon price and output is proportional to its share of industry output (at least in a simple arithmetic sense of direct capacity to change output). The political decisions take account also of the political strength of the various firms, so small firms have a larger influence than they would possess in an unregulated industry. Thus, when quotas are given to firms, the small firms will almost always receive larger quotas than cost-minimizing practices would allow. The original quotas under the oil import quota system will illustrate this practice (Table 1). The smallest refiners were given a quota of 11.4 percent of their daily consumption of oil, and the percentage dropped as refinery size rose.[5] The pattern of regressive benefits is characteristic of public controls in industries with numerous firms.

Second, the procedural safeguards required of public processes are costly. The delays which are dictated by both law and bureaucratic thoughts of self-survival can be large: Robert Gerwig found the price of gas sold in interstate commerce to be 5 to 6 percent higher than in intrastate commerce because of the administrative costs (including delay) of Federal Power Commission reviews [5].

Finally, the political process automatically admits powerful outsiders to the industry's councils. It is well known that the allocation of television channels among communities does not maximize industry revenue but reflects pressures to serve many smaller communities. The abandonment of an unprofitable rail line is an even more notorious area of outsider participation.

These limitations are predictable, and they must all enter into the calculus of the profitability of regulation of an industry.

☐ **An illustrative analysis.** The recourse to the regulatory process is of course more specific and more complex than the foregoing sketch

---

[5] The largest refineries were restricted to 75.7 percent of their historical quota under the earlier voluntary import quota plan.

suggests. The defensive power of various other industries which are affected by the proposed regulation must also be taken into account. An analysis of one aspect of the regulation of motor trucking will illustrate these complications. At this stage we are concerned only with the correspondence between regulations and economic interests; later we shall consider the political process by which regulation is achieved.

The motor trucking industry operated almost exclusively within cities before 1925, in good part because neither powerful trucks nor good roads were available for long-distance freight movements. As these deficiencies were gradually remedied, the share of trucks in intercity freight movements began to rise, and by 1930 it was estimated to be 4 percent of ton-miles of intercity freight. The railroad industry took early cognizance of this emerging competitor, and one of the methods by which trucking was combatted was state regulation.

By the early 1930's all states regulated the dimensions and weight of trucks. The weight limitations were a much more pervasive control over trucking than the licensing of common carriers because even the trucks exempt from entry regulation are subject to the limitations on dimensions and capacity. The weight regulations in the early 1930's are reproduced in the appendix (Table 6). Sometimes the participation of railroads in the regulatory process was incontrovertible: Texas and Louisiana placed a 7000-pound payload limit on trucks serving (and hence competing with) two or more railroad stations, and a 14,000-pound limit on trucks serving only one station (hence, not competing with it).

We seek to determine the pattern of weight limits on trucks that would emerge in response to the economic interests of the concerned parties. The main considerations appear to be the following:

(1) Heavy trucks would be allowed in states with a substantial number of trucks on farms: the powerful agricultural interests would insist upon this. The 1930 Census reports nearly one million trucks on farms. One variable in our study will be, for each state, trucks per 1000 of agricultural population.[6]

(2) Railroads found the truck an effective and rapidly triumphing competitor in the shorter hauls and hauls of less than carload traffic, but much less effective in the carload and longer-haul traffic. Our second variable for each state is, therefore, length of average railroad haul.[7] The longer the average rail haul is, the less the railroads will be opposed to trucks.

(3) The public at large would be concerned by the potential damage done to the highway system by heavy trucks. The better the state highway system, the heavier the trucks that would be permitted. The percentage of each state's highways that had a high type surface is the third variable. Of course good highways are more likely to exist where the potential contribution of trucks to a state's economy is greater, so the causation may be looked at from either direction.

---

[6] The ratio of trucks to total population would measure the product of (1) the importance of trucks to farmers, and (2) the importance of farmers in the state. For reasons given later, we prefer to emphasize (1).

[7] This is known for each railroad, and we assume that (1) the average holds within each state, and (2) two or more railroads in a state may be combined on the basis of mileage. Obviously both assumptions are at best fair approximations.

We have two measures of weight limits on trucks, one for 4-wheel trucks (X_1) and one for 6-wheel trucks (X_2). We may then calculate two equations,

$$X_1 \text{ (or } X_2) = a + bX_3 + cX_4 + dX_5 ,$$

where

X_3 = trucks per 1000 agricultural labor force, 1930 ,
X_4 = average length of railroad haul of freight traffic, 1930,
X_5 = percentage of state roads with high-quality surface, 1930.

(All variables are fully defined and their state values given in Table 7 on page 20.)

The three explanatory variables are statistically significant, and each works in the expected direction. The regulations on weight were less onerous; the larger the truck population in farming, the less competitive the trucks were to railroads (i.e., the longer the rail hauls), and the better the highway system (see Table 2).

□ The foregoing analysis is concerned with what may be termed the industrial demand for governmental powers. Not every industry will have a significant demand for public assistance (other than money!), meaning the prospect of a substantial increase in the present value of the enterprises even if the governmental services could be obtained gratis (and of course they have costs to which we soon turn). In some economic activities entry of new rivals is extremely difficult to control—consider the enforcement problem in restricting the supply of domestic servants. In some industries the substitute products cannot be efficiently controlled—consider the competition offered to bus lines by private car-pooling. Price fixing is not feasible where every

TABLE 2

REGRESSION ANALYSIS OF STATE WEIGHT LIMITS ON TRUCKS
(T VALUES UNDER REGRESSION COEFFICIENTS)

DEPENDENT VARIABLE	N	CONSTANT	X_3	X_4	X_5	R^2
X_1	48	12.28 (4.87)	0.0336 (3.99)	0.0287 (2.77)	0.2641 (3.04)	0.502
X_2	46	10.34 (1.57)	0.0437 (2.01)	0.0788 (2.97)	0.2528 (1.15)	0.243

X_1 = WEIGHT LIMIT ON 4-WHEEL TRUCKS (THOUSANDS OF POUNDS), 1932-33

X_2 = WEIGHT LIMIT ON 6-WHEEL TRUCKS (THOUSANDS OF POUNDS), 1932-33

X_3 = TRUCKS ON FARMS PER 1,000 AGRICULTURAL LABOR FORCE, 1930

X_4 = AVERAGE LENGTH OF RAILROAD HAUL OF FREIGHT (MILES), 1930

X_5 = PERCENT OF STATE HIGHWAYS WITH HIGH-TYPE SURFACE, DEC. 31, 1930

SOURCES: X_1 AND X_2: THE MOTOR TRUCK RED BOOK AND DIRECTORY [11], 1934 EDITION, P. 85-102, AND U.S. DEPT. OF AGRIC., BUR. OF PUBLIC ROADS, DEC. 1932 [13].

X_3: CENSUS OF AGRICULTURE, 1930, VOL. IV, [14].

X_4: A.A.R.R., BUR. OF RAILWAY ECONOMICS, RAILWAY MILEAGE BY STATES, DEC. 31, 1930 [1] AND U.S.I.C.C., STATISTICS OF RAILWAYS IN THE U.S., 1930 [18].

X_5: STATISTICAL ABSTRACT OF THE U.S., 1932 [16].

unit of the product has a different quality and price, as in the market for used automobiles. In general, however, most industries will have a positive demand price (schedule) for the services of government.

2. The costs of obtaining legislation

■ When an industry receives a grant of power from the state, the benefit to the industry will fall short of the damage to the rest of the community. Even if there were no deadweight losses from acquired regulation, however, one might expect a democratic society to reject such industry requests unless the industry controlled a majority of the votes.[8] A direct and informed vote on oil import quotas would reject the scheme. (If it did not, our theory of rational political processes would be contradicted.) To explain why many industries are able to employ the political machinery to their own ends, we must examine the nature of the political process in a democracy.

A consumer chooses between rail and air travel, for example, by voting with his pocketbook: he patronizes on a given day that mode of transportation he prefers. A similar form of economic voting occurs with decisions on where to work or where to invest one's capital. The market accumulates these economic votes, predicts their future course, and invests accordingly.

Because the political decision is coercive, the decision process is fundamentally different from that of the market. If the public is asked to make a decision between two transportation media comparable to the individual's decision on how to travel—say, whether airlines or railroads should receive a federal subsidy—the decision must be abided by everyone, travellers and non-travellers, travellers this year and travellers next year. This compelled universality of political decisions makes for two differences between democratic political decision processes and market processes.

(1) The decisions must be made simultaneously by a large number of persons (or their representatives): the political process demands simultaneity of decision. If A were to vote on the referendum today, B tomorrow, C the day after, and so on, the accumulation of a majority decision would be both expensive and suspect. (A might wish to cast a different vote now than last month.)

The condition of simultaneity imposes a major burden upon the political decision process. It makes voting on specific issues prohibitively expensive: it is a significant cost even to engage in the transaction of buying a plane ticket when I wish to travel; it would be stupendously expensive to me to engage in the physically similar transaction of voting (i.e., patronizing a polling place) whenever a number of my fellow citizens desired to register their views on railroads versus airplanes. To cope with this condition of simultaneity, the voters must employ representatives with wide discretion and must eschew direct expressions of marginal changes in preferences. This characteristic also implies that the political decision does not predict voter desires and make preparations to fulfill them in advance of their realization.

---

[8] If the deadweight loss (of consumer and producer surplus) is taken into account, even if the oil industry were in the majority it would not obtain the legislation if there were available some method of compensation (such as sale of votes) by which the larger damage of the minority could be expressed effectively against the lesser gains of the majority.

(2) The democratic decision process must involve "all" the community, not simply those who are directly concerned with a decision. In a private market, the non-traveller never votes on rail versus plane travel, while the huge shipper casts many votes each day. The political decision process cannot exclude the uninterested voter: the abuses of any exclusion except self-exclusion are obvious. Hence, the political process does not allow participation in proportion to interest and knowledge. In a measure, this difficulty is moderated by other political activities besides voting which do allow a more effective vote to interested parties: persuasion, employment of skilled legislative representatives, etc. Nevertheless, the political system does not offer good incentives like those in private markets to the acquisition of knowledge. If I consume ten times as much of public service A (streets) as of B (schools), I do not have incentives to acquire corresponding amounts of knowledge about the public provision of these services.[9]

These characteristics of the political process can be modified by having numerous levels of government (so I have somewhat more incentive to learn about local schools than about the whole state school system) and by selective use of direct decision (bond referenda). The chief method of coping with the characteristics, however, is to employ more or less full-time representatives organized in (disciplined by) firms which are called political parties or machines.

The representative and his party are rewarded for their discovery and fulfillment of the political desires of their constituency by success in election and the perquisites of office. If the representative could confidently await reelection whenever he voted against an economic policy that injured the society, he would assuredly do so. Unfortunately virtue does not always command so high a price. If the representative denies ten large industries their special subsidies of money or governmental power, they will dedicate themselves to the election of a more complaisant successor: the stakes are that important. This does not mean that every large industry can get what it wants or all that it wants: it does mean that the representative and his party must find a coalition of voter interests more durable than the anti-industry side of every industry policy proposal. A representative cannot win or keep office with the support of the sum of those who are opposed to: oil import quotas, farm subsidies, airport subsidies, hospital subsidies, unnecessary navy shipyards, an inequitable public housing program, and rural electrification subsidies.

The political decison process has as its dominant characteristic infrequent, universal (in principle) participation, as we have noted: political decisions must be infrequent and they must be global. The voter's expenditure to learn the merits of individual policy proposals and to express his preferences (by individual and group representation as well as by voting) are determined by expected costs and returns, just as they are in the private marketplace. The costs of comprehensive information are higher in the political arena because information must be sought on many issues of little or no direct concern to the individual, and accordingly he will know little about most matters before the legislature. The expressions of preferences in voting will be less precise than the expressions of preferences in the

---

[9] See [2].

marketplace because many uninformed people will be voting and affecting the decision.[10]

The channels of political decision-making can thus be described as gross or filtered or noisy. If everyone has a negligible preference for policy A over B, the preference will not be discovered or acted upon. If voter group X wants a policy that injures non-X by a small amount, it will not pay non-X to discover this and act against the policy. The system is calculated to implement all strongly felt preferences of majorities and many strongly felt preferences of minorities but to disregard the lesser preferences of majorities and minorities. The filtering or grossness will be reduced by any reduction in the cost to the citizen of acquiring information and expressing desires and by any increase in the probability that his vote will influence policy.

The industry which seeks political power must go to the appropriate seller, the political party. The political party has costs of operation, costs of maintaining an organization and competing in elections. These costs of the political process are viewed excessively narrowly in the literature on the financing of elections: elections are to the political process what merchandizing is to the process of producing a commodity, only an essential final step. The party maintains its organization and electoral appeal by the performance of costly services to the voter at all times, not just before elections. Part of the costs of services and organization are borne by putting a part of the party's workers on the public payroll. An opposition party, however, is usually essential insurance for the voters to discipline the party in power, and the opposition party's costs are not fully met by public funds.

The industry which seeks regulation must be prepared to pay with the two things a party needs: votes and resources. The resources may be provided by campaign contributions, contributed services (the businessman heads a fund-raising committee), and more indirect methods such as the employment of party workers. The votes in support of the measure are rallied, and the votes in opposition are dispersed, by expensive programs to educate (or uneducate) members of the industry and of other concerned industries.

These costs of legislation probably increase with the size of the industry seeking the legislation. Larger industries seek programs which cost the society more and arouse more opposition from substantially affected groups. The tasks of persuasion, both within and without the industry, also increase with its size. The fixed size of the political "market," however, probably makes the cost of obtaining legislation increase less rapidly than industry size. The smallest industries are therefore effectively precluded from the political process unless they have some special advantage such as geographical concentration in a sparsely settled political subdivision.

If a political party has in effect a monopoly control over the governmental machine, one might expect that it could collect most of the benefits of regulation for itself. Political parties, however, are

---

[10] There is an organizational problem in any decision in which more than one vote is cast. If because of economies of scale it requires a thousand customers to buy a product before it can be produced, this thousand votes has to be assembled by some entrepreneur. Unlike the political scene, however, there is no need to obtain the consent of the remainder of the community, because they will bear no part of the cost.

perhaps an ideal illustration of Demsetz' theory of natural monopoly [4]. If one party becomes extortionate (or badly mistaken in its reading of effective desires), it is possible to elect another party which will provide the governmental services at a price more closely proportioned to costs of the party. If entry into politics is effectively controlled, we should expect one-party dominance to lead that party to solicit requests for protective legislation but to exact a higher price for the legislation.

The internal structure of the political party, and the manner in which the perquisites of office are distributed among its members, offer fascinating areas for study in this context. The elective officials are at the pinnacle of the political system—there is no substitute for the ability to hold the public offices. I conjecture that much of the compensation to the legislative leaders takes the form of extra-political payments. Why are so many politicians lawyers?—because everyone employs lawyers, so the congressman's firm is a suitable avenue of compensation, whereas a physician would have to be given bribes rather than patronage. Most enterprises patronize insurance companies and banks, so we may expect that legislators commonly have financial affiliations with such enterprises.

The financing of industry-wide activities such as the pursuit of legislation raises the usual problem of the free rider.[11] We do not possess a satisfactory theory of group behavior—indeed this theory is the theory of oligopoly with one addition: in the very large number industry (e.g., agriculture) the political party itself will undertake the entrepreneurial role in providing favorable legislation. We can go no further than the infirmities of oligopoly theory allow, which is to say, we can make only plausible conjectures such as that the more concentrated the industry, the more resources it can invest in the campaign for legislation.

☐ **Occupational licensing.** The licensing of occupations is a possible use of the political process to improve the economic circumstances of a group. The license is an effective barrier to entry because occupational practice without the license is a criminal offense. Since much occupational licensing is performed at the state level, the area provides an opportunity to search for the characteristics of an occupation which give it political power.

Although there are serious data limitations, we may investigate several characteristics of an occupation which should influence its ability to secure political power:

(1) *The size of the occupation.* Quite simply, the larger the occupation, the more votes it has. (Under some circumstances, therefore, one would wish to exclude non-citizens from the measure of size.)

(2) *The per capita income of the occupation.* The income of the occupation is the product of its number and average income, so this variable and the preceding will reflect the total income of the occupation. The income of the occupation is presumably an index of the probable rewards of successful political action: in the absence of specific knowledge of supply and demand functions, we expect

---

[11] The theory that the lobbying organization avoids the "free-rider" problem by selling useful services was proposed by Thomas G. Moore [8] and elaborated by Mancur Olson [9]. The theory has not been tested empirically.

licensing to increase each occupation's equilibrium income by roughly the same proportion. In a more sophisticated version, one would predict that the less the elasticity of demand for the occupation's services, the more profitable licensing would be. One could also view the income of the occupation as a source of funds for political action, but if we view political action as an investment this is relevant only with capital-market imperfections.[12]

The average income of occupational members is an appropriate variable in comparisons among occupations, but it is inappropriate to comparisons of one occupation in various states because real income will be approximately equal (in the absence of regulation) in each state.

(3) *The concentration of the occupation in large cities.* When the occupation organizes a campaign to obtain favorable legislation, it incurs expenses in the solicitation of support, and these are higher for a diffused occupation than a concentrated one. The solicitation of support is complicated by the free-rider problem in that individual members cannot be excluded from the benefits of legislation even if they have not shared the costs of receiving it. If most of the occupation is concentrated in a few large centers, these problems (we suspect) are much reduced in intensity: regulation may even begin at the local governmental level. We shall use an orthodox geographical concentration measure: the share of the occupation of the state in cities over 100,000 (or 50,000 in 1900 and earlier).

(4) *The presence of a cohesive opposition to licensing.* If an occupation deals with the public at large, the costs which licensing imposes upon any one customer or industry will be small and it will not be economic for that customer or industry to combat the drive for licensure. If the injured group finds it feasible and profitable to act jointly, however, it will oppose the effort to get licensure, and (by increasing its cost) weaken, delay, or prevent the legislation. The same attributes—numbers of voters, wealth, and ease of organization—which favor an occupation in the political arena, of course, favor also any adversary group. Thus, a small occupation employed by only one industry which has few employers will have difficulty in getting licensure; whereas a large occupation serving everyone will encounter no organized opposition.

An introductory statistical analysis of the licensing of select occupations by states is summarized in Table 3. In each occupation the dependent variable for each state is the year of first regulation of entry into the occupation. The two independent variables are

(1) the ratio of the occupation to the total labor force of the state in the census year nearest to the median year of regulation,

(2) the fraction of the occupation found in cities over 100,000 (over 50,000 in 1890 and 1900) in that same year.

---

[12] Let n = the number of members of the profession and y = average income. We expect political capacity to be in proportion to (ny) so far as benefits go, but to reflect also the direct value of votes, so the capacity becomes proportional to ($n^a y$) with $a > 1$.

TABLE 3

INITIAL YEAR OF REGULATION AS A FUNCTION OF
RELATIVE SIZE OF OCCUPATION AND DEGREE OF URBANIZATION

OCCUPATION	NUMBER OF STATES LICENSING	MEDIAN CENSUS YEAR OF LICENSING	REGRESSION COEFFICIENTS (AND T-VALUES)		R^2
			SIZE OF OCCUPATION (RELATIVE TO LABOR FORCE)	URBANIZATION (SHARE OF OCCUPATION IN CITIES OVER 100,000*)	
BEAUTICIANS	48	1930	−4.03 (2.50)	5.90 (1.24)	0.125
ARCHITECTS	47	1930	−24.06 (2.15)	−6.29 (0.84)	0.184
BARBERS	46	1930	−1.31 (0.51)	−26.10 (2.37)	0.146
LAWYERS	29	1890	−0.26 (0.08)	−65.78 (1.70)	0.102
PHYSICIANS	43	1890	0.64 (0.65)	−23.80 (2.69)	0.165
EMBALMERS	37	1910	3.32 (0.36)	−4.24 (0.44)	0.007
REGISTERED NURSES	48	1910	−2.08 (2.28)	−3.36 (1.06)	0.176
DENTISTS	48	1900	2.51 (0.44)	−22.94 (2.19)	0.103
VETERINARIANS	40	1910	−10.69 (1.94)	−37.16 (4.20)	0.329
CHIROPRACTORS	48	1930	−17.70 (1.54)	11.69 (1.25)	0.079
PHARMACISTS	48	1900	−4.19 (1.50)	−6.84 (0.80)	0.082

SOURCES: THE COUNCIL OF STATE GOVERNMENTS, "OCCUPATIONAL LICENSING LEGISLATION IN THE STATES", 1952 [3], AND U.S. CENSUS OF POPULATION [15], VARIOUS YEARS.

* 50,000 IN 1890 AND 1900.

We expect these variables to be negatively associated with year of licensure, and each of the nine statistically significant regression coefficients is of the expected sign.

The results are not robust, however: the multiple correlation coefficients are small, and over half of the regression coefficients are not significant (and in these cases often of inappropriate sign). Urbanization is more strongly associated than size of occupation with licensure.[13] The crudity of the data may be a large source of these disappointments: we measure, for example, the characteristics of the barbers in each state in 1930, but 14 states were licensing barbers by 1910. If the states which licensed barbering before 1910 had relatively more barbers, or more highly urbanized barbers, the predictions

---

[13] We may pool the occupations and assign dummy variables for each occupation; the regression coefficients then are:

size of occupation relative to labor force: −0.450 ($t = 0.59$)
urbanization : −12.133 ($t = 4.00$).

Thus urbanization is highly significant, while size of occupation is not significant.

would be improved. The absence of data for years between censuses and before 1890 led us to make only the cruder analysis.[14]

In general, the larger occupations were licensed in earlier years.[15] Veterinarians are the only occupation in this sample who have a well-defined set of customers, namely livestock farmers, and licensing was later in those states with large numbers of livestock relative to rural population. The within-occupation analyses offer some support for the economic theory of the supply of legislation.

A comparison of different occupations allows us to examine several other variables. The first is income, already discussed above. The second is the size of the market. Just as it is impossible to organize an effective labor union in only one part of an integrated market, so it is impossible to regulate only one part of the market. Consider an occupation—junior business executives will do—which has a national market with high mobility of labor and significant mobility of employers. If the executives of one state were to organize, their scope for effective influence would be very small. If salaries were raised above the competitive level, employers would often recruit elsewhere so the demand elasticity would be very high.[16] The third variable is stability of occupational membership: the longer the members are in the occupation, the greater their financial gain from control of entry. Our regrettably crude measure of this variable is based upon the number of members aged 35–44 in 1950 and aged 45–54 in 1960: the closer these numbers are, the more stable the membership of the occupation. The data for the various occupations are given in Table 4.

The comparison of licensed and unlicensed occupations is consistently in keeping with our expectations:

(1) the licensed occupations have higher incomes (also before licensing, one may assume),

(2) the membership of the licensed occupations is more stable (but the difference is negligible in our crude measure),

(3) the licensed occupations are less often employed by business enterprises (who have incentives to oppose licensing),

(4) all occupations in national markets (college teachers, engineers, scientists, accountants) are unlicensed or only partially licensed.

---

[14] A more precise analysis might take the form of a regression analysis such as:
Year of licensure = constant

$$+b_1 \text{ (year of critical size of occupation)}$$
$$+b_2 \text{ (year of critical urbanization of occupation)},$$

where the critical size and urbanization were defined as the mean size and mean urbanization in the year of licensure.

[15] Lawyers, physicians, and pharmacists were all relatively large occupations by 1900, and nurses also by 1910. The only large occupation to be licensed later was barbers; the only small occupation to be licensed early was embalmers.

[16] The regulation of business in a partial market will also generally produce very high supply elasticities within a market: if the price of the product (or service) is raised, the pressure of excluded supply is very difficult to resist. Some occupations are forced to reciprocity in licensing, and the geographical dispersion of earnings in licensed occupations, one would predict, is not appreciably different than in unlicensed occupations with equal employer mobility. Many puzzles are posed by the interesting analysis of Arlene S. Holen in [6], pp. 492-98.

TABLE 4

CHARACTERISTICS OF LICENSED AND UNLICENSED
PROFESSIONAL OCCUPATIONS, 1960

OCCUPATION	MEDIAN AGE (YEARS)	MEDIAN EDUCATION (YEARS)	MEDIAN EARNINGS (50-52 WKS.)	INSTABILITY OF MEMBERSHIP*	PERCENT NOT SELF-EMPLOYED	PERCENT IN CITIES OVER 50,000	PERCENT OF LABOR FORCE
LICENSED:							
ARCHITECTS	41.7	16.8	$ 9,090	0.012	57.8%	44.1%	0.045%
CHIROPRACTORS	46.5	16.4	6,360	0.053	5.8	30.8	0.020
DENTISTS	45.9	17.3	12,200	0.016	9.4	34.5	0.128
EMBALMERS	43.5	13.4	5,990	0.130	52.8	30.2	0.055
LAWYERS	45.3	17.4	10,800	0.041	35.8	43.1	0.308
PROF. NURSES	39.1	13.2	3,850	0.291	91.0	40.6	0.868
OPTOMETRISTS	41.6	17.0	8,480	0.249	17.5	34.5	0.024
PHARMACISTS	44.9	16.2	7,230	0.119	62.3	40.0	0.136
PHYSICIANS	42.8	17.5	14,200	0.015	35.0	44.7	0.339
VETERINARIANS	39.2	17.4	9,210	0.169	29.5	14.4	0.023
AVERAGE	43.0	16.3	8,741	0.109	39.7	35.7	0.195
PARTIALLY LICENSED:							
ACCOUNTANTS	40.4	14.9	6,450	0.052	88.1	43.5	0.698
ENGINEERS	38.3	16.2	8,490	0.023	96.8	31.6	1.279
ELEM. SCHOOL TEACHERS	43.1	16.5	4,710	(a)	99.1	18.8	1.482
AVERAGE	40.6	15.9	6,550	0.117(b)	94.7	34.6	1.153
UNLICENSED:							
ARTISTS	38.0	14.2	5,920	0.103	77.3	45.7	0.154
CLERGYMEN	43.3	17.0	4,120	0.039	89.0	27.2	0.295
COLLEGE TEACHERS	40.3	17.4	7,500	0.085	99.2	36.0	0.261
DRAFTSMEN	31.2	12.9	5,990	0.098	98.6	40.8	0.322
REPORTERS & EDITORS	39.4	15.5	6,120	0.138	93.9	43.3	0.151
MUSICIANS	40.2	14.8	3,240	0.081	65.5	37.7	0.289
NATURAL SCIENTISTS	35.9	16.8	7,490	0.264	96.3	32.7	0.221
AVERAGE	38.3	15.5	5,768	0.115	88.5	37.6	0.242

(*) 1-R, WHERE R = RATIO: 1960 AGE 45-54 TO 1950 AGE 35-44.

(a) NOT AVAILABLE SEPARATELY; TEACHERS N.E.C. (INCL. SECONDARY SCHOOL AND OTHER) = 0.276

(b) INCLUDES FIGURE FOR TEACHERS N.E.C. IN NOTE (a)

SOURCE: U.S. CENSUS OF POPULATION, [15], 1960.

The size and urbanization of the three groups, however, are unrelated
to licensing. The inter-occupational comparison therefore provides
a modicum of additional support for our theory of regulation.

■ The idealistic view of public regulation is deeply imbedded in
professional economic thought. So many economists, for example,
have denounced the ICC for its pro-railroad policies that this has
become a cliché of the literature. This criticism seems to me exactly
as appropriate as a criticism of the Great Atlantic and Pacific Tea
Company for selling groceries, or as a criticism of a politician for
currying popular support. The fundamental vice of such criticism is
that it misdirects attention: it suggests that the way to get an ICC
which is not subservient to the carriers is to preach to the commissioners or to the people who appoint the commissioners. The only
way to get a different commission would be to change the political

3. Conclusion

support for the Commission, and reward commissioners on a basis unrelated to their services to the carriers.

Until the basic logic of political life is developed, reformers will be ill-equipped to use the state for their reforms, and victims of the pervasive use of the state's support of special groups will be helpless to protect themselves. Economists should quickly establish the license to practice on the rational theory of political behavior.

Appendix

TABLE 5

COMMON, CONTRACT AND PASSENGER MOTOR CARRIERS, 1935–1969[1]

YEAR ENDING	CUMULATIVE APPLICATIONS			OPERATING CARRIERS	
	GRAND-FATHER	NEW	TOTAL	APPROVED APPLICATIONS [3]	NUMBER IN OPERATION[2]
OCT. 1936	82,827	1,696	84,523	–	–
1937	83,107	3,921	87.028	1;114	–
1938	85,646	6,694	92,340	20,398	–
1939	86,298	9,636	95,934	23,494	–
1940	87,367	12,965	100,332	25,575	–
1941	88,064	16,325	104,389	26,296	–
1942	88,702	18,977	107,679	26,683	–
1943	89,157	20,007	109,164	27,531	–
1944	89,511	21,324	110,835	27,177	21,044
1945	89,518	22,829	112,347		20,788
1946	89,529	26,392	115,921		20,632
1947	89,552	29,604	119,156		20,665
1948	89,563	32,678	122,241		20,373
1949	89,567	35,635	125,202		18,459
1950	89,573	38,666	128,239		19,200
1951	89,574	41,889	131,463		18,843
1952	(89,574)[4]	44,297	133,870		18,408
1953	"	46,619	136,192		17,869
1954	"	49,146	138,719		17,080
1955	"	51,720	141,293		16,836
JUNE 1956	"	53,640	143,213		16,486
1957	"	56,804	146,377		16,316
1958	"	60,278	149,851		16,065
1959	"	64,171	153,744		15,923
1960	"	69,205	158,778		15,936
1961	"	72,877	162,450		15,967
1962	"	76,986	166,559		15,884
1963	"	81,443	171,016		15,739
1964	"	86,711	176,284		15,732
1965	"	93,064	182,637		15,755
1966	"	101,745	191,318		15,933
1967	"	106,647	196,220		16,003
1968	"	(6)	(6)		16,230[5]
1969	"	(6)	(6)		16,318[5]

SOURCE: U.S. INTERSTATE COMMERCE COMMISSION ANNUAL REPORTS [17].

1 EXCLUDING BROKERS AND WITHIN-STATE CARRIERS.

2 PROPERTY CARRIERS WERE THE FOLLOWING PERCENTAGES OF ALL OPERATING CARRIERS: 1944–93.4%; 1950–92.4%; 1960–93.0%; 1966–93.4%.

3 ESTIMATED.

4 NOT AVAILABLE; ASSUMED TO BE APPROXIMATELY CONSTANT.

5 1968 AND 1969 FIGURES ARE FOR NUMBER OF CARRIERS REQUIRED TO FILE ANNUAL REPORTS.

6 NOT AVAILABLE COMPARABLE TO PREVIOUS YEARS; APPLICATIONS FOR PERMANENT AUTHORITY DISPOSED OF (I.E., FROM NEW AND PENDING FILES) 1967-69 ARE AS FOLLOWS: 1967–7,049; 1968–5,724; 1969–5,186.

TABLE 6

WEIGHT LIMITS ON TRUCKS, 1932-33*, BY STATES (BASIC DATA FOR TABLE 2).

STATE	MAXIMUM WEIGHT (IN LBS.)		STATE	MAXIMUM WEIGHT (IN LBS.)	
	4-WHEEL[1]	6-WHEEL[2]		4-WHEEL[1]	6-WHEEL[2]
ALABAMA	20,000	32,000	NEBRASKA	24,000	40,000
ARIZONA	22,000	34,000	NEVADA	25,000	38,000
ARKANSAS	22,200	37,000	NEW HAMPSHIRE	20,000	20,000
CALIFORNIA	22,000	34,000	NEW JERSEY	30,000	30,000
COLORADO	30,000	40,000	NEW MEXICO	27,000	45,000
CONNECTICUT	32,000	40,000	NEW YORK	33,600	44,000
DELAWARE	26,000	38,000	NO. CAROLINA	20,000	20,000
FLORIDA	20,000	20,000	NO. DAKOTA	24,000	48,000
GEORGIA	22,000	39,600	OHIO	24,000	24,000
IDAHO	24,000	40,000	OKLAHOMA	20,000	20,000
ILLINOIS	24,000	40,000	OREGON	25,500	42,500
INDIANA	24,000	40,000	PENNSYLVANIA	26,000	36,000
IOWA	24,000	40,000	RHODE ISLAND	28,000	40,000
KANSAS	24,000	34,000	SO. CAROLINA	20,000	25,000
KENTUCKY	18,000	18,000	SO. DAKOTA	20,000	20,000
LOUISIANA	13,400	N. A.	TENNESSEE	20,000	20,000
MAINE	18,000	27,000	TEXAS	13,500	N. A.
MARYLAND	25,000	40,000	UTAH	26,000	34,000
MASSACHUSETTS	30,000	30,000	VERMONT	20,000	20,000
MICHIGAN	27,000	45,000	VIRGINIA	24,000	35,000
MINNESOTA	27,000	42,000	WASHINGTON	24,000	34,000
MISSISSIPPI	18,000	22,000	WEST VA.	24,000	40,000
MISSOURI	24,000	24,000	WISCONSIN	24,000	36,000
MONTANA	24,000	34,000	WYOMING	27,000	30,000

* RED BOOK [11] FIGURES ARE REPORTED (P. 89) AS "BASED ON THE STATE'S INTERPRETATIONS OF THEIR LAWS [1933] AND ON PHYSICAL LIMITATIONS OF VEHICLE DESIGN AND TIRE CAPACITY." PUBLIC ROADS [13] FIGURES ARE REPORTED (P. 167) AS "AN ABSTRACT OF STATE LAWS, INCLUDING LEGISLATION PASSED IN 1932."

1. 4-WHEEL: THE SMALLEST OF THE FOLLOWING 3 FIGURES WAS USED:

    (A) MAXIMUM GROSS WEIGHT (AS GIVEN IN RED BOOK, P. 90-91).

    (B) MAXIMUM AXLE WEIGHT (AS GIVEN IN RED BOOK, P. 90-91), MULTIPLIED BY 1.5 (SEE RED BOOK, P. 89).

    (C) MAXIMUM GROSS WEIGHT (AS GIVEN IN RED BOOK, P. 93).

EXCEPTIONS: TEXAS AND LOUISIANA—SEE RED BOOK, P. 91.

2. 6-WHEEL: MAXIMUM GROSS WEIGHT AS GIVEN IN PUBLIC ROADS, P. 167. THESE FIGURES AGREE IN MOST CASES WITH THOSE SHOWN IN RED BOOK, P. 93, AND WITH PUBLIC ROADS MAXIMUM AXLE WEIGHTS MULTIPLIED BY 2.5 (SEE RED BOOK, P. 93). TEXAS AND LOUISIANA ARE EXCLUDED AS DATA ARE NOT AVAILABLE TO CONVERT FROM PAYLOAD TO GROSS WEIGHT LIMITS.

TABLE 7

INDEPENDENT VARIABLES
(BASIC DATA FOR TABLE 2 — CONT'D)

STATE	TRUCKS ON FARMS PER 1,000 AGRICULTURAL LABOR FORCE	AVERAGE LENGTH OF RAILROAD HAUL OF FREIGHT (MILES)	PERCENT OF STATE HIGHWAYS WITH HIGH-TYPE SURFACE
ALABAMA	26.05	189.4	1.57
ARIZONA	79.74	282.2	2.60
ARKANSAS	28.62	233.1	1.72
CALIFORNIA	123.40	264.6	13.10
COLORADO	159.50	244.7	0.58
CONNECTICUT	173.80	132.6	7.98
DELAWARE	173.20	202.7	21.40
FLORIDA	91.41	184.1	8.22
GEORGIA	32.07	165.7	1.60
IDAHO	95.89	243.6	0.73
ILLINOIS	114.70	207.9	9.85
INDIANA	120.20	202.8	6.90
IOWA	98.73	233.3	3.39
KANSAS	146.70	281.5	0.94
KENTUCKY	20.05	227.5	1.81
LOUISIANA	31.27	201.0	1.94
MAINE	209.30	120.4	1.87
MARYLAND	134.20	184.1	12.90
MASSACHUSETTS	172.20	144.7	17.70
MICHIGAN	148.40	168.0	6.68
MINNESOTA	120.40	225.6	1.44
MISSISSIPPI	29.62	164.9	1.14
MISSOURI	54.28	229.7	2.91
MONTANA	183.80	266.5	0.09
NEBRASKA	132.10	266.9	0.41
NEVADA	139.40	273.2	0.39
NEW HAMPSHIRE	205.40	129.0	3.42
NEW JERSEY	230.20	137.6	23.30
NEW MEXICO	90.46	279.0	0.18
NEW YORK	220.50	163.3	21.50
NO. CAROLINA	37.12	171.5	8.61
NO. DAKOTA	126.40	255.1	0.01
OHIO	125.80	194.2	11.20
OKLAHOMA	78.18	223.3	1.42
OREGON	118.90	246.2	3.35
PENNSYLVANIA	187.60	166.5	9.78
RHODE ISLAND	193.30	131.0	20.40
SO. CAROLINA	20.21	169.8	2.82
SO. DAKOTA	113.40	216.6	0.04
TENNESSEE	23.98	191.9	3.97
UTAH	101.70	235.7	1.69
VERMONT	132.20	109.7	2.26
VIRGINIA	71.88	229.8	2.86
WASHINGTON	180.90	254.4	4.21
WEST VIRGINIA	62.88	218.7	8.13
WISCONSIN	178.60	195.7	4.57
WYOMING	133.40	286.7	0.08

(1) AVERAGE LENGTH OF RR HAUL OF (REVENUE) FREIGHT = AVERAGE DISTANCE IN MILES EACH TON IS CARRIED = RATIO OF NUMBER OF TON-MILES TO NUMBER OF TONS CARRIED. FOR EACH STATE, AVERAGE LENGTH OF HAUL WAS OBTAINED BY WEIGHTING AVERAGE LENGTH OF HAUL OF EACH COMPANY BY THE NUMBER OF MILES OF LINE OPERATED BY THAT COMPANY IN THE STATE (ALL FOR CLASS I RR'S).

(2) PERCENTAGE OF STATE ROADS WITH HIGH-QUALITY SURFACE: WHERE HIGH-QUALITY (HIGH-TYPE) SURFACE CONSISTS OF BITUMINOUS MACADAM, BITUMINOUS CONCRETE, SHEET ASPHALT, PORTLAND CEMENT CONCRETE, AND BLOCK PAVEMENTS. ALL STATE RURAL ROADS, BOTH LOCAL AND STATE HIGHWAYS SYSTEMS, ARE INCLUDED.

References

1. ASSOCIATION OF AMERICAN RAILROADS, BUREAU OF RAILWAY ECONOMICS. *Railway Mileage by States.* Washington, D. C.: December 31, 1930.
2. BECKER, G. S. "Competition and Democracy." *Journal of Law and Economics,* October 1958.
3. THE COUNCIL OF STATE GOVERNMENTS. "Occupational Licensing Legislation in the States." 1952.
4. DEMSETZ, H., "Why Regulate Utilities?" *Journal of Law and Economics,* April 1968.
5. GERWIG, R. W. "Natural Gas Production: A Study of Costs of Regulation." *Journal of Law and Economics,* October 1962, pp. 69-92.
6. HOLEN, A. S. "Effects of Professional Licensing Arrangements on Interstate Labor Mobility and Resource Allocation." *Journal of Political Economy,* Vol. 73 (1915), pp. 492-98.
7. KEYES, L. S. *Federal Control of Entry into Air Transportation.* Cambridge, Mass.: Harvard University Press, 1951.
8. MOORE, T. G. "The Purpose of Licensing." *Journal of Law and Economics,* October 1961.
9. OLSON, M. *The Logic of Collective Action.* Cambridge, Mass.: Harvard University Press, 1965.
10. PELTZMAN, S. "Entry in Commercial Banking." *Journal of Law and Economics,* October 1965.
11. *The Motor Truck Red Book and Directory,* 1934 Edition, pp. 85-102.
12. U. S. CONGRESS, SELECT COMMITTEE ON SMALL BUSINESS. *Hearings,* 88th Congress, 2nd Session, August 10 and 11, 1964.
13. U. S. DEPARTMENT OF AGRICULTURE, BUREAU OF PUBLIC ROADS. *Public Roads.* Washington, D. C.: U. S. Government Printing Office, December 1932.
14. U. S. DEPARTMENT OF COMMERCE, BUREAU OF THE CENSUS. *United States Census of Agriculture, 1930,* Vol. 4. Washington, D. C.: U. S. Government Printing Office, 1930.
15. ———. *United States Census of Population.* Washington, D. C.: U. S. Government Printing Office, appropriate years.
16. ———, BUREAU OF FOREIGN AND DOMESTIC COMMERCE. *Statistical Abstract of the U. S., 1932.* Washington, D. C.: U. S. Government Printing Office, 1932.
17. U. S. INTERSTATE COMMERCE COMMISSION. *Annual Report.* Washington, D. C.: U. S. Government Printing Office, appropriate years.
18. ———. *Statistics of Railways in the United States, 1930.* Washington, D. C.: U. S. Government Printing Office, 1930.

[8]

4.1 Introduction

We saw in the last chapter that in many circumstances the competitive
process provides an incentive system that impels private firms to behave in
ways that are broadly consistent with efficient resource allocation. But such
circumstances do not always hold, and in some industries the forces of
competition are inevitably weak or nonexistent. There is then a need for
regulatory policy to influence private sector behavior by establishing an
appropriate incentive system to guide or constrain economic decisions.
This need has arisen in several major industries involved in the U.K.
privatization program, where problems of monopoly power and various
kinds of externalities have been central issues. In later chapters we consider
in some detail the regulatory frameworks adopted in the U.K.
telecommunications, gas, and airports industries, and the framework
proposed for the water industry, but the purpose of the present chapter is to
examine some of the underlying principles of regulatory policy.

For the most part we will leave aside externality problems in order to
focus on regulation to constrain market power. To clarify the analysis
further, we will begin by assuming that competition in product and capital
markets is absent and cannot be stimulated. In other words, we will
suppose that the regulatory system is the only constraint upon the firm's
behavior apart from the fundamental conditions of demand and
technology. We can then examine how the firm would behave when faced
with various regulatory systems, and we can also address the broader
question of optimal regulatory policy.

It is useful to regard the problem as a game between the government (or
its agency) and the firm. With this perspective we need to specify the
players' possible strategies, their objectives, the move order, and the
information conditions of the game. As regards *possible strategies*, the firm
has to make decisions about prices, outputs, capital investment, product
quality, investment in cost reduction, product innovation, and so on. The
government might seek to regulate some of these variables (for example
prices, product quality, or profits) but, unless it is unusually well informed
about industry conditions and behavior, it is unlikely to be able to regulate
(as opposed to influence) other aspects of the firm's activities. This

information problem is crucial because the government can condition its policy only on what it knows. Indeed the asymmetry of information between government and firm will be a central theme of this chapter.

Turning now to decision-makers' *objectives*, there are several assumptions that can be explored. The traditional approach, which offers many useful insights, is to suppose that the firm is intent upon maximizing profits and that the government seeks to maximize social welfare defined as the (possibly weighted) sum of consumer and producer surplus in partial equilibrium analysis. However, we will also wish to pursue other approaches to company behavior—especially in view of the nature of much of the debate about the effect of privatization upon internal efficiency—by assuming that managers also attach importance to nonprofit objectives, for example the minimization of managerial effort or the enhancement of sales revenues. Similarly, we will not always suppose that governments or their regulatory bodies are imbued with the classical public interest objective. Political concerns affect governments, and the interests of regulatory agencies need not coincide with social wellbeing.

As regards *move order* and dynamics, there are again several analytical perspectives. A natural starting point is to suppose that the government has "first move" by virtue of its ability to design the regulatory framework, and that the firm then behaves as best it can in response to that framework. But this simple leader–follower approach has shortcomings. One is that regulatory policies are often more short-term in nature than some aspects of company behavior, notably investment in capital assets with long lives. In such circumstances government does not begin with a clean slate; rather, it responds to conditions shaped in part by decisions of the firm. A second and related point is that the government and firm each make a series of moves over time, and they interact strategically. Thus the firm may seek to influence the design of future regulatory policy by its current actions. Such behavior would not be surprising when—as in several U.K. privatizations—regulatory policy is explicitly temporary and periodically subject to major review. The dynamic nature of the problem also raises issues of credibility (sometimes known as "time-consistency" problems in other contexts). Thus government could not credibly adopt a policy that required it to act contrary to its interests in some future circumstances.

Finally we come to *information conditions*, in particular the asymmetry of information likely to exist between the regulator and the firm. We believe that this information problem is at the heart of the economics of regulation. A fully informed regulator equipped with suitable sanctions could simply command decision makers within the firm to behave in accordance with the first-best outcome. But in fact there are multifarious practical limitations to what the regulator can know, and hence to what outcomes he can bring about. We will pay particular attention to the case in which decision makers in the firm know more about conditions of technology and demand than the regulator. The problem for regulatory policy is one of incentive mechanism design—how to induce the firm to act in accordance with the public interest (which will depend on the state of technology and demand) without being able to observe the firm's behavior. This problem is precisely what agency theory is about, and below we will examine in detail several recent applications of that theory to the economics of regulation.

It will be clear even from these brief remarks about various objectives, strategies, dynamics, and information conditions, that regulation is a vast subject and that a full treatment of it would take us far beyond our present scope (see Kahn, 1970; Bailey, 1973; Schmalensee, 1979; Fromm, 1981; Breyer, 1982; Crew and Kleindorfer, 1986). This chapter therefore has the more limited aim of discussing a selected set of the problems and principles of regulatory policy towards dominant enterprises. The discussion will be organized under five headings:

(i) investment problems;

(ii) internal efficiency and asymmetric information;

(iii) the regulation of multiproduct firms;

(iv) collusion and capture;

(v) some relationships between competition and regulation.

4.2 Investment Problems

Investment problems pose fundamental problems for regulators in many industries. Although the direct object of regulation is often pricing policy, which is easily measured and readily changed, the effects of regulatory policy upon social welfare depends critically upon the investment behavior that it induces. Investment—whether in capacity, R&D, or whatever—is less easily quantified and typically cannot be altered in the short run because sunk costs are involved. The magnitude of the welfare effects is illustrated by investment in industries such as telecommunications (e.g. on network development and digital exchanges), gas (transmission, exploration, etc.), electricity (power stations, transmission grids, etc.), and water (pipelines, sewers, etc.).

Two general questions arise. First, do incentives exist for productive efficiency in the sense that capital investment minimizes the cost of producing the output(s) supplied? Secondly, is the scale of investment and production appropriate to the conditions of demand and technology? We address these questions by examining the regulatory theory stemming from the famous Averch and Johnson (A–J) (1962) paper on incentives for overcapitalization under rate-of-return regulation, and by analyzing a model in which price regulation cannot credibly be committed in advance of investment decisions. We discuss some dynamic issues, including regulatory lag, and we consider incentives for strategic behavior when regulator and firm interact over time. An example is the RPI − X style of regulation being adopted in the U.K., under which a bound for the path of prices (or an index thereof) is fixed for a given interval of time, at the end of which there is regulatory review. As that time approaches the firm might have an incentive to engage in socially inefficient strategic behavior designed to influence the outcome of the review. We also consider how private and social rates of discount might differ, especially when there exists the possibility of the return of the private firm to the public sector at some later date.

4.2.1   Rate-of-Return Regulation: the Averch–Johnson Effect

The fundamental problem for regulators is that they lack the information to determine what the firm's pricing and other policies ought ideally to be from the point of view of economic efficiency. Rate-of-return regulation offers the solution that price(s) should be such that an allowed "fair" rate of return on capital is earned. Three questions immediately arise. What is a "fair" rate? To what measure of the capital base should the allowed rate be applied? Will the firm make decisions affecting its capital base partly with a view to influencing the price(s) it is allowed to charge, and what distortions will result?

In their classic model of rate-of-return regulation Averch and Johnson (1962) provide an affirmative answer to this last question. Firms have an incentive to expand their capital base so as to achieve a greater absolute profit while staying within the constraint on their profit rate. An excellent review of early contributions to the debate stimulated by Averch and Johnson is provided by Baumol and Klevorick (1970), and in this section we rely heavily on their discussion.

The A–J model concerns a monopoly supplier of a single good produced with two inputs, labor L and capital K, according to production function $Q = F(L,K)$. Inverse demand is $P(Q)$, and $R(L,K) = F(L,K) P(F(L,K))$ in the revenue when the input levels are L and K. Labor and capital are available at factor prices w and r respectively, and profit is therefore

$$\pi(L,K) = R(L,K) - wL - rK. \tag{4.1}$$

The allowed rate of return is denoted by s, which is assumed to exceed r. (Otherwise the firm would wish to close down, at any rate in the long run.) Thus the constraint on the firm's behavior is that

$$[R(L,K) - wL]/K \leqslant s. \tag{4.2}$$

This constraint is assumed to bind—that is, s is not so generous that (4.2) is satisfied by pure monopoly behavior. The firm's problem is to maximize (4.1) subject to (4.2), and we form the Lagrangean

$$
\begin{aligned}
H(L,K,\lambda) &= \pi(L,K) - \lambda[R(L,K) - wL - sK] \\
&= (1-\lambda)[R(L,K) - wL] - (r - \lambda s)K. \tag{4.3}
\end{aligned}
$$

From the first-order conditions it follows that $\partial R/\partial L = w$, but that $\partial R/\partial K = r - \lambda(s-r)/(1-\lambda)$, which is less than r. (The second-order condition guarantees that $0 < \lambda < 1$.) Therefore excess capital is employed, and the firm produces its output in a manner that is too capital intensive and hence inefficient. The firm has no direct benefit from cost inefficiency, but it achieves a strategic gain by influencing the permitted price.

A diagrammatic method due to Zajac (1970) usefully illustrates this and related results. Figure 4.1 is a three-dimensional depiction of π as a function of L and K. The plane hinged on the L axis is the set of points such that $\pi(L,K) = (s-r)K$. The points on or beneath the plane are precisely those that meet constraint (4.2). Thus the firm's problem is to be as high as possible on the shaded "profit hill" without being above the "regulatory plane."

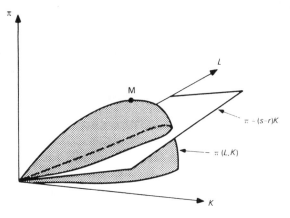

Figure 4.1   Rate-of-return regulation

Figure 4.2   The Averch–Johnson effect

The shaded area in figure 4.2 contains the feasible (L,K) combinations that satisfy the regulatory constraint. Since profit is proportional to capital where the constraint binds ($\pi = (s-r)K$), the profit of the regulated firm is greatest at point R, the rightmost point in the shaded area. Curve QQ is the isoquant passing through R. Note that it passes through the interior of the shaded area, which shows that, given output Q, profit and welfare could be higher. The cost of producing output Q is not minimized, because the capital stock is deliberately expanded by the firm. The efficient way to produce Q is at point Z where the "efficiency locus" ME intersects the isoquant. At Z the K/L ratio is lower than at R. Thus the output of the regulated firm is produced in a manner that is too capital intensive. An unregulated monopolist would operate at point M, where efficient production occurs; the unregulated firm has every incentive to minimize production costs.

To summarize, the effect on welfare of rate-of-return regulation in this model has two parts. The level of output is affected, and so too is the efficiency with which the output is produced. If—as is usually the case—regulation increases output, the two effects work in opposite directions, and there is a conflict between internal and allocative efficiency which will appear in several contexts in this chapter.

Without further assumptions on cost and demand conditions it is not necessarily the case that regulation has the effect of increasing output. If, for example, profit were maximized at point M′, output would be higher without regulation. Nor is it necessarily true that the K/L ratio under regulation is greater than that without regulation.

A final observation on the basic A–J model, which Baumol and Klevorick (1970, pp. 175–176) emphasize, is that the amount of capital employed by the regulated firm increases as s is set closer to the cost of capital r. A reduction in s would expand the shaded area in figure 4.2, and so the optimal K would rise. The cost inefficiency due to incentives to overcapitalize may well grow as s is set closer to r. Klevorick (1971) considers the *optimal* choice of s from the point of view of social welfare. Although intuition might suggest that $s = r$ was optimal, this is not in fact so. At $s = r$ the profit-maximizing firm is indifferent between all feasible input combinations that meet the regulatory constraint, because they all involve zero profit. But even if the firm has social welfare as a secondary objective (in the sense of lexicographic preferences) there is a wide range of cases in which some $s > r$ induces a superior outcome than $s = r$. Also, if the firm's secondary objective is to maximize K (e.g. because of managerial satisfaction), then it is generally true that $s > r$ is superior. The reason has already been indicated: s close to r can cause more productive inefficiency.

An extension of the A–J model which remains within its essentially static framework is to replace profit maximization by some other objective for the firm. For example, Bailey and Malone (1970) argue that, under a wide range of conditions, a firm maximizing sales revenue subject to rate-of-return regulation would produce its output in a way that was inefficient by being too labor intensive. This contrasts with Averch and Johnson's finding. However, Atkinson and Waverman (1973) contend that the sales-maximizing firm faces a minimum profit constraint as well as the regulatory restraint, and that various outcomes are possible depending on the interaction of the constraints and the basic conditions of demand. At any rate, this work illustrates that results can be sensitive to assumptions regarding the motivation of the firm.

4.2.2 Regulatory Lag

The A–J model provides a useful starting point, but it can be criticized for being too static in its formulation. Regulation does not occur in a continuous fashion. Typically prices are set for an interval of time, during which the firm is free to choose whatever input combinations it wishes, until the next price review occurs. Review might occur at some time specified in advance—for example the formula governing the pricing of British Telecom's telecommunications services in the U.K. will be reviewed in 1989—or its timing might be uncertain. In the latter case an important distinction must be made between exogenous and endogenous uncertainty. With endogenous uncertainty, the timing of the next review depends partly upon how the firm behaves in the meantime.

Bailey and Coleman (1971) extend the A–J model by supposing that regulators set prices after an interval of T periods. The firm, making its decisions at time zero, faces a trade-off between maximizing profits by producing more efficiently during the next T periods and overcapitalizing to induce a more favorable price when review eventually occurs. The balance is struck where

$$\frac{F_K}{F_L} = \frac{r}{w} - \frac{\rho^T}{1 - \rho^T} \frac{s - r}{w},$$

where ρ is the discount factor. It follows that it is optimal for the firm to overcapitalize to some extent (depending inversely upon T), but not as much as in the basic A–J model. A similar finding is obtained by Davis (1973) for a model in which price adjustment occurs continuously but only partially.

Baumol and Klevorick (1970, pp. 184–188) criticize the approach of Bailey and Coleman, and propose a model of regulatory lag which is of particular relevance to the style of regulation adopted in the major U.K. privatizations. They write (p. 184):

"While Bailey and Coleman regard the period before a regulatory review as a time when the firm suffers a loss because it is carrying an excessive amount of capital, now the period between reviews is regarded as the time when the firm has the possibility of earning a profit rate exceeding that specified by the constraint. When the regulatory review occurs, this excess is eliminated by the regulators' adjustment of the prices the firm can charge."

In our view this point has great force. Regulatory lag allows the firm to appropriate the benefits of improved cost efficiency until the next review occurs. A longer lag increases the firm's incentives to reduce its costs by innovation or superior organization of factors of production, but it delays the time at which consumers benefit from this greater efficiency. On the other hand, a shorter lag means that consumers benefit sooner, but the incentive to cut costs is reduced. This trade-off between static and dynamic efficiency has a close analogy in the literature on optimal patent life, and indeed Bailey (1974) analyzes the problem of innovation and regulatory lag in exactly that spirit (see also the debate between Lesourne (1976) and Bailey (1976)).

There is, however, a further point to consider. In the framework proposed by Baumol and Klevorick, price is brought into line with current costs at the time of each regulatory review. The RPI $-$ X style of regulation implemented in Britain is likely to fit this description. Although such a system provides good incentives for efficiency immediately after a review point, as time passes the firm's calculations will be increasingly affected by the benefit to be gained from influencing the outcome of the next regulatory review. As that time approaches, the firm will have little or no incentive to reduce costs if its future prices are positively related to its current cost level. Indeed, a point would then arise when the immediate gain from cost reduction was so short-lived as to be outweighed by the cost of having to face lower prices for the whole of the period until the following price review. In technical language, the second-order effect would be outweighed by the first-order effect, and the firm would come to favor *higher* costs when regulatory review is close at hand. We shall consider incentives for this kind of strategic behavior further in section 4.4 (see also Sappington, 1980).

These considerations suggest three lessons. First, the incentive effects of regulatory lag are not necessarily always benign. Strategic behavior designed to influence regulatory review could involve substantial losses in terms of allocative and productive efficiency, which would be offset against the initial spur to innovation provided by regulatory lag. Secondly, the potential losses from strategic behavior are reduced when regulatory review is less sensitive to current cost conditions. This points to the importance of the information available to regulators, especially information that is independent of the firm's decisions. We shall return later to this theme of the dangers of the firm's having a "monopoly of information." Thirdly, the timing of regulatory reviews is important—not only in terms of the length of regulatory lag, but also whether regulatory review occurs at regular intervals or stochastically.

We conclude this section by describing two models of stochastic regulatory review. (A discussion of further dynamic analysis is contained in section 4.4.) Klevorick (1973) examines a model in which for every period there is a given probability $\phi \in [0,1]$ of regulatory review. When review occurs, price is set so as to restore the "fair" rate of return s on the current capital stock. If ϕ were equal to 1, we would effectively have the A–J model, albeit in an explicitly dynamic setting, and if ϕ were equal to zero, regulatory lag would be infinite and the firm would have perfect incentives for productive efficiency. The intermediate case leads to overcapitalization, although not to the extent of that occurring in the A–J model.

Bawa and Sibley's (1980) more general model of *endogenous* stochastic regulatory review is more satisfactory. The probability of review in any period is a function $\phi(X)$ of current profit in excess (or deficit) of the level allowed by the rate of return s. Thus X_t is defined as

$$X_t = \pi_t - (s - r)K_t.$$

It is assumed that $\phi(0) = \phi'(0) = 0$, $\phi'(X) > 0$ for $X > 0$, and $\phi'(X) < 0$ for $X < 0$. If review does occur in period t, price is set at the level that yields rate of return s on the capital stock K_t until the next review takes place.

The model captures the idea that the firm has to balance its desire for short-run profits against the risk of jeopardizing future profits by triggering a review of its prices. Bawa and Sibley use techniques of stochastic dynamic programming to establish the following:

(i) the firm will overcapitalize, be efficient, or undercapitalize according to whether the allowed rate of return s exceeds, equals, or is less than the cost of capital r;

(ii) there is continuity in the sense that s close to r leads to approximate efficiency;

(iii) under fairly general conditions there is convergence to the price at which $X = 0$ and to cost minimization.

As well as having a more realistic formulation of the regulatory process, Bawa and Sibley's model yields more intuitive results than the basic A–J model. For example, $s = r$ leads to efficient production and $s < r$ involves undercapitalization, whereas in the A–J model we saw that $s = r$ has an outcome that is indeterminate (and, in terms of capital bias, undesirable) and $s < r$ leads to the shutdown of production. In the richer dynamic setting we therefore escape the welfare trade-off examined by Klevorick (1971) between allocative and productive efficiency as s approaches r: the conflict disappears.

4.2.3   Credibility, Commitment, and Underinvestment

So far we have paid little attention to one of the main features of much capital investment—the presence of sunk costs and adjustment costs. In the A–J model it is as though there exists a rental market for capital equipment that is a freely variable factor of production. But in fact there are typically major adjustment costs when the scale or nature of a firm's operations are changed, and capital costs are often sunk in the sense that the assets have significantly less value in their next alternative use. Much the same is true of certain types of labor when hiring, training, and firing costs are taken into account.

In contrast, variables such as price—the prime instrument of regulatory policy—are usually easier to alter. The resulting asymmetry of adjustment costs can have serious implications for regulatory policy, which we shall illustrate by way of two examples.

The first of these is a "dynamic consistency" problem (see Greenwald,

1984). Suppose for simplicity that the regulation game has three stages: (i) the regulator announces the price that the firm will be allowed to charge, (ii) the firm makes its investment decisions, which involve a large element of sunk costs, and (iii) the regulator reviews the previously announced pricing policy.

At stage (iii) a regulator seeking to maximize consumer benefits would wish to impose the lowest possible prices subject to encouraging the firm to produce (i.e. subject to covering the variable costs of production). Similarly, a regulator intent upon maximizing the sum of consumer and producer surplus would set $P = MC$, which in many regulated industries might imply that price is below (long-run) average cost. In sum there is a range of regulator's objectives for which the firm would be wary of committing large investment expenditures at stage (ii) for fear of what might happen at stage (iii), and the announcement of the price at stage (i) would then lack credibility. (The risk of renationalization on less than fair terms is a related problem, which we consider separately below.)

This credibility problem, which arises from the public interest mandate of the regulator, has the effect of undermining the public interest insofar as it inhibits investment at stage (ii), for example by increasing risk-adjusted private discount rates. The solution advocated by Greenwald (1984, p. 86) is as follows:

"Restricting regulators with an appropriate 'fairness' criterion may, therefore, be essential to the viability of the originally optimal equilibrium. The simplest way to do this would be to require by law that past regulatory promises must be honored in future proceedings. To maintain the flexibility of regulators to respond to unforeseen circumstances, however, the set of legally binding past promises should be minimally constraining. Since investors should be concerned only with future returns, the minimum acceptable set of legal constraints need only guarantee the value of future income implied by past promises."

Greenwald argues that in the United States "properly interpreted, the present structure of rate return regulation corresponds exactly to such a system." The credibility of a commitment to fairness is no doubt enhanced by wider share ownership, because the constituency opposed to "unfairness" is larger and more vocal. But this does not solve the problem completely, because whenever the credibility of the fairness constraint is below 100 percent, there is a risk factor that managers of a profit-maximizing firm would wish to take into account.

We now turn to our second illustration. Returning to the simple schema above, it is clear that the regulator at stage (iii) will be influenced by the investment decisions made by the firm at stage (ii). Thus the firm has an opportunity to influence the regulatory regime that it faces. For simplicity, suppose that expansion of the firm's capital stock is prohibitively costly in the relevant timescale. Assume that the regulator seeks to maximize the sum of consumer and producer surplus, and that there are no externalities. Then the regulator will set $P = $ MC given the cost curve resulting from the firm's prior investment decision.

More formally, let inverse demand be $P(Q)$ and let the cost function be $C(Q,K)$ where Q is output and K is the capital stock. It is reasonable to suppose that marginal cost C_Q is positive, increasing in Q for given K, and decreasing in K for given Q. Thus $C_Q > 0$, $C_{QQ} > 0$, and $C_{QK} < 0$. Also, we assume $C_{KK} > 0$. We are interested in at least two questions. Does the firm choose to operate on a scale that is suboptimally small? Does the firm produce its output in an efficient manner?

The regulator is assumed to impose marginal cost pricing. Thus

$$P(Q) = C_Q(Q,K). \tag{4.4}$$

The firm chooses K and Q to maximize profit $P(Q)Q - C(Q,K)$ subject to (4.4). The Lagrangean is

$$H(Q,K) = P(Q)\,Q - C(Q,K) + \mu[P(Q) - C_Q(Q,K)] \tag{4.5}$$

and the first-order conditions are

$$P + P'Q - C_Q + \mu(P' - C_{QQ}) = 0 \tag{4.6}$$

and

$$-C_K - \mu C_{QK} = 0. \tag{4.7}$$

Equations (4.4), (4.6), and (4.7) imply that

$$C_K = \frac{C_{QK}\,Q\,P'}{P' - C_{QQ}}, \tag{4.8}$$

which is negative. It follows that the regulated firm in this context produces its output inefficiently, and with a capital-to-output ratio (and hence a capital-to-labor ratio) that is too *low*. The firm holds back its capital stock in order to induce a more profitable price from the regulator. The result is undercapitalization. Moreover, the regulated firm produces less output than at the first best.

Figure 4.3 illustrates both points. Isoprofit curves for the firm in (Q,K) space are centered on point F, and isowelfare curves for the regulator are centered on point W. That point is northeast of F, representing the firm's interest in restricting output to the monopoly level. The efficiency locus defined by $C_K = 0$ slopes up and passes through both F and W. The

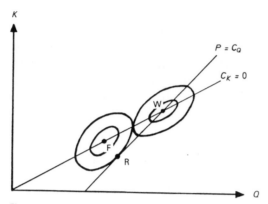

Figure 4.3 Strategic underinvestment

$P = $ MC locus also has an upward slope; it cuts isowelfare curves where they have a zero slope. The regulated firm operates at point R. Figure 4.3 shows how output is restricted below its optimal level and produced in an undercapitalized manner.

The diagram also suggests—and indeed it can be proved—that the welfare comparison between F and R is ambiguous. The pure monopoly point F is one of allocative inefficiency because $P > $ MC, but the monopoly output is produced at minimum cost. The regulated firm does not produce its output at minimum cost, but R is a point where there is allocative efficiency because $P = $ MC. Once again we see the conflict between internal (productive) efficiency and allocative efficiency.

Both models outlined in this section are rudimentary, but their purpose was simply to illustrate two dangers of underinvestment when considerations of commitment and dynamics are taken into account. In one case investment is inhibited by the fear of "unfair" future regulation. Unless the regulatory and/or political systems provide a credible means of commitment to future fairness, this fear is not entirely unreasonable in view of the objectives of regulators. In the second example, underinvestment was a strategic move by the firm seeking to obtain a more favorable regulatory regime. We will develop this point further, but now we address explicitly a major issue that has so far only been in the background of our discussion—the role of asymmetric information.

4.3 Regulation with Asymmetric Information

If a regulatory agency had as much knowledge about industry conditions

Privatization and Globalization

and behavior as the firm being regulated, it could simply direct the firm to implement its chosen plan, provided that the agency possessed sufficient powers to do so. Indeed, it would then be better simply to appoint the regulatory agency to run the enterprise rather than to leave decision-making authority with the managers of the firm. But of course decision makers within the firm are generally far more knowledgeable than regulators can be about the circumstances facing them, and the regulator can neither observe nor infer all aspects of the firm's behavior. Thus asymmetric information is one of the main features of the economics of regulation (of both public and private enterprise), and in this section we examine some recent contributions to the literature, notably those of Baron and Myerson (1982) and Laffont and Tirole (1986). An excellent survey of this topic is provided by Caillaud *et al.* (1985). Owing to its more technical nature, some of our discussion is contained in starred sections, which some readers might prefer to omit.

4.3.1 Principal–Agent Theory and Regulation

Principal–agent theory was introduced in chapter 2 as a way of examining the relationship between the (public or private) owners of a firm and its managers. The theory is concerned with the design of incentives for efficiency under conditions of asymmetric information. The principal (i.e. the owners in chapter 2) is less informed than the agent (i.e. the managers) about the conditions facing the firm, and may be unable to monitor the agent's behavior with precision. Asymmetry of information gives rise to imperfect incentives, and inefficiency is the result.

Principal–agent theory can be used in exactly the same fashion to study regulation. In this context the government or the regulatory authority is the principal, and (the management of) the firm is the agent. With this perspective, a system of regulation can be regarded as an *incentive mechanism*. The firm is better informed than the regulator about cost conditions for example, and the regulator seeks to induce the firm to make its pricing, output, and investment decisions in accordance with the public interest given the cost conditions that exist. But the firm is interested in maximizing (say) its profits and, whatever the scheme of regulation may be, it will act in its own interests.

Suppose for example that the government's objective is social welfare W defined as the sum of consumer surplus S and the firm's profit π. Let the firm's objective be to maximize profit. (The firm is taken to be risk-neutral.) Let θ be the unit cost level of the firm, which the regulator cannot observe, and let Q be the firm's level of output. To begin with let us assume that Q is observable by the regulator. He would like Q to be chosen so that price equals marginal cost, but he does not know θ. However, if he can make lump-sum transfers to (or from) the firm, it is in fact possible to bring about the optimal outcome in this example (see Loeb and Magat, 1979). The regulator should undertake to pay the firm an amount equal to the consumer surplus from output Q minus a constant sum. With this incentive scheme the firm receives its profit (i.e. producer surplus) plus the payment equal to consumer surplus minus the constant. It maximizes this objective if and only if it maximizes the regulator's objective. In this special case it is therefore possible to engineer the first-best outcome by an appropriate incentive scheme, even without knowing cost conditions.

Although this decentralized scheme might be neat in theory, it obviously has several overwhelming practical drawbacks (see Sharkey, 1979). First, although the scheme does not require cost information, the government needs to know the magnitude of consumer surplus—a much more demanding task. Although prices provide some information about *marginal* utility, they do not say much about the whole area under the demand curve (let alone income effects etc.). Secondly, the scheme runs the risk of bankrupting the firm when costs are high and consumer surplus is correspondingly low, unless the fixed element of the incentive scheme is so generous as to cushion the firm against any eventuality—in which case the firm will make huge profits in more favorable states of the world. Thirdly, the scheme depends on the government being indifferent to transfers between consumers or taxpayers and the firm, i.e. on its objective being $W = S + \pi$.

However, the government's objective cannot generally be represented simply as the sum of consumer surplus and profit (see section 2.3.2 above, and Caillaud *et al.* (1985, pp. 4–7)). A concern for distribution might cause less weight to be attached to profit than to consumer interests. In that case, an objective of the form $W = S + \alpha\pi$ would be appropriate, with $0 \leqslant \alpha < 1$. Indeed, we shall use that specification of government objectives in the following two sections. Secondly, costs to the economy of raising public funds can be represented by attaching a negative weight to lump-sum transfers to the firm. Thirdly, the interests of employees could be taken into account, although this is less likely to be an important factor for independent regulatory authorities than for politicians.

The next two sections describe versions of the models of regulation under asymmetric information examined by Baron and Myerson (1982) and Laffont and Tirole (1986). Our discussion is far from being rigorous, but it is somewhat more technical than usual. Some readers might prefer to go directly to section 4.3.4, which summarizes the main findings of the analysis.

4.3.2*   Regulation with Unknown Costs

In this section we present a simplified version of Baron and Myerson's (1982) model of regulation with unknown costs. The model is one of asymmetric information. The firm knows its unit cost level, denoted θ, but the regulator does not. We assume that θ is distributed uniformly on an interval $[\underline{\theta}, \overline{\theta}]$.

Consumer utility from output level Q is denoted $V(Q)$, and $P(Q) = V'(Q)$ is the inverse demand curve. Let $R(Q) = QP(Q)$ be the firm's revenue, and let T be the transfer (possibly negative) paid to the firm. Net consumer surplus is therefore $S = V - R - T$, and profit is $\pi = R - \theta Q + T$. The regulator's objective is taken to be $W = S + \alpha\pi$, where $0 \leqslant \alpha \leqslant 1$. We saw above that $\alpha < 1$ can be interpreted as reflecting a concern for distribution.

A regulatory mechanism will induce, for each value of θ, an associated level of output $Q(\theta)$ and transfer $T(\theta)$. The *revelation principle* (see Myerson, 1979; Dasgupta *et al.*, 1979) implies that, without loss of generality, we can consider the regulator's optimization problem as equivalent to the following. The regulator requires the firm to provide a report $\hat{\theta}$ of its cost level, and determines the output $Q(\hat{\theta})$ and the transfer $T(\hat{\theta})$ as a function of that report. The firm must have no incentive to report its cost level untruthfully given that Q and T are determined in that manner.

This truth-telling constraint involves no loss of generality, because if the firm found it optimal to lie by reporting $\hat{\theta}(\theta)$ when the truth was θ, the regulator could simply amend the mechanism to be $\overline{Q}(\theta) = Q[\hat{\theta}(\theta)]$ and $\overline{T}(\theta) = T[\hat{\theta}(\theta)]$, and the firm would then find it optimal to report the truth.

The revelation principle therefore allows us to consider the regulator's problem as one of choosing $Q(\theta)$ and $T(\theta)$ to maximize the expected value of W subject to (i) the firm's finding it optimal to report θ truthfully, and (ii) the firm's always being willing to operate—i.e. receiving nonnegative profits in all states of the world.

More formally, let

$$S(\theta) = V[Q(\theta)] - R[Q(\theta)] - T(\theta)$$

be the net consumer surplus in state θ, and let

$$\pi(\hat{\theta}, \theta) = R[Q(\hat{\theta})] - \theta Q(\hat{\theta}) + T(\hat{\theta})$$

be the profit in state θ when $\hat{\theta}$ is reported. Define $\pi(\theta) = \pi(\theta,\theta)$. Then we can state the regulator's problem as follows.

Choose $Q(\theta)$ and $T(\theta)$ to maximize

$$EW = \int_{\underline{\theta}}^{\bar{\theta}} [S(\theta) + \alpha\pi(\theta)]\,d\theta \qquad (4.9)$$

subject to

$$\pi(\theta) \geqslant \pi(\hat{\theta},\theta) \text{ for all } \theta \text{ and } \hat{\theta} \qquad (4.10)$$

and

$$\pi(\theta) \geqslant 0 \text{ for all } \theta. \qquad (4.11)$$

Conditions (4.10) and (4.11) correspond to (i) and (ii) above. We shall assume that (4.10) is characterized by the first-order condition

$$R'Q' - \theta Q' + T' = 0. \qquad (4.12)$$

The constraint (4.11) is binding only at $\underline{\theta}$, because for $\theta < \underline{\theta}$ we have

$$\pi(\theta) \geqslant \pi(\underline{\theta},\theta) > \pi(\underline{\theta}). \qquad (4.13)$$

The rent accruing to the firm from its monopoly of information derives from this fact.

The Lagrangean associated with the regulator's problem is

$$H = \int [S + \alpha\pi + \mu(R'Q' - \theta Q' + T')]\,d\theta$$

$$= \int [V - (1-\alpha)(R+T) - \alpha\theta Q + \mu(R'Q' - \theta Q' + T')]\,d\theta. \qquad (4.14)$$

For notational simplicity in (4.14) we suppress the dependence of Q, T, and the multiplier μ upon θ, and the range of integration $[\underline{\theta}, \bar{\theta}]$. Let I be the integrand [.]. Then the Euler optimization conditions are

$$\frac{\partial I}{\partial X} = \frac{d}{d\theta}\frac{\partial I}{\partial X'} \text{ for } X = Q, T \qquad (4.15)$$

The condition with respect to Q is

$$V' - (1-\alpha)R' - \alpha\theta + \mu R''Q' = \mu(R''Q' - 1) + \mu'(R' - \theta) \qquad (4.16)$$

and the condition with respect to T is

$$-(1-\alpha) = \mu'. \qquad (4.17)$$

Since we have a free-boundary problem we can choose $\mu(\underline{\theta}) = 0$, and (4.17) therefore implies that

$$\mu(\theta) = -(1 - \alpha)(\theta - \underline{\theta}). \tag{4.18}$$

Using (4.16) to (4.18), and recalling that $V' = P$, we have the central result that

$$P[Q(\theta)] = \theta + (1 - \alpha)(\theta - \underline{\theta}). \tag{4.19}$$

Under the optimal regulatory mechanism, price is equal to unit (and marginal) cost *plus* a mark-up depending on α and $(\theta - \underline{\theta})$. Note that optimality always involves marginal cost pricing when $\alpha = 1$, in keeping with the Loeb–Magat mechanism described above. But in general, when $\alpha < 1$, there is a loss of allocative efficiency because price exceeds marginal cost, except in the best state of the world $\underline{\theta}$.

It is optimal for the regulator to forego allocative efficiency to some extent because he is also concerned to minimize the size of the transfer T, which has a net cost of $(1 - \alpha)T$. He could induce marginal cost pricing, but only at the expense of a greater expected transfer to the firm. Optimality requires that a balance be struck between allocative efficiency and the minimization of the transfer.

If the regulator were as well informed as the firm—i.e. if he could observe θ—his problem would be to maximize (4.9) subject only to (4.11). The solution to this problem is $P[Q(\theta)] = \theta$ and $T = 0$ for all θ. In that event there is always allocative efficiency, and the firm always exactly breaks even. Therefore the partial loss of allocative efficiency is not the only reason why the regulator is adversely affected by the presence of asymmetric information. He also loses from the fact that the firm obtains a strictly positive payoff (in all but one state of the world). The asymmetry of information therefore causes two kinds of inefficiency to the detriment of consumers and the regulator's objective. However, the firm gains from the regulator's imperfect information because it obtains *money rent* in the form of transfers more than sufficient to meet its break-even constraint.

4.3.3*   Regulation with Unobservable Effort

We now present a model based (somewhat loosely) on the work of Laffont and Tirole (1986) which adds another dimension to the regulatory problem. In the Baron–Myerson model above it was assumed that the level of costs was given to the firm but that the regulator could not observe it. In contrast, we now suppose that costs are influenced by the firm's cost-reducing *effort*, and that the regulator can observe the cost level. However, costs are determined jointly by two factors—the state of nature and the firm's effort—neither of which is observable by the regulator. He therefore cannot tell whether (say) low costs are due to great efforts by the firm or to a favorable state of nature.

More specifically, let unit costs c depend upon the state of nature θ and the level of effort a as follows:

$$c = \theta - a.$$

The cost of effort is denoted $z(a)$, where $z(0) = z'(0) = 0$, $z'(a) > 0$ for $a > 0$, and $z''(a) > 0$. As before, θ is taken to be distributed uniformly on $[\underline{\theta}, \bar{\theta}]$. The notation for consumer utility, price, output, revenue, and the transfer is also as in the previous section. The regulator is again assumed to be concerned with welfare defined as $W = S + \alpha\pi$ with $0 \leqslant \alpha \leqslant 1$.

As before, a regulatory mechanism will induce an output level $Q(\theta)$, a cost level $c(\theta)$, and a transfer $T(\theta)$ for each value of θ. Invoking the revelation principle, we can consider the regulator's problem as choosing the three functions $Q(\theta)$, $c(\theta)$, and $T(\theta)$ to maximize expected welfare subject to (i) the firm's finding it optimal to report θ truthfully, and (ii) the firm's always being willing to operate in the sense of achieving nonnegative profits. It might be thought more natural to view the problem as one of choosing Q and T as functions of observed c, but the revelation principle is more convenient analytically and anyway accommodates the point. For if $\bar{Q}(c)$ and $\bar{T}(c)$ were an optimal regulatory scheme, and if $\bar{c}(\theta)$ was optimal for the firm facing that scheme, then by defining $Q(\theta) = \bar{Q}[\bar{c}(\theta)]$ and $T(\theta) = \bar{T}[\bar{c}(\theta)]$ we would have an optimal scheme satisfying (ii) and expressed in a more convenient form. Therefore no generality is lost.

The net consumer surplus in state θ is

$$S(\theta) = V[Q(\theta)] - R[Q(\theta)] - T(\theta),$$

and the profit in state θ when $\hat{\theta}$ is reported is

$$\pi(\hat{\theta}, \theta) = R[Q(\hat{\theta})] - c(\hat{\theta})Q(\hat{\theta}) - z[\theta - c(\hat{\theta})] + T(\hat{\theta}).$$

Define $\pi(\theta) = \pi(\theta, \theta)$. Then the regulator's problem is as follows.

Choose $Q(\theta)$, $c(\theta)$, and $T(\theta)$ to maximize

$$EW = \int_{\underline{\theta}}^{\bar{\theta}} [S(\theta) + \alpha\pi(\theta)] \, d\theta \tag{4.20}$$

subject to

$$\pi(\theta) \geqslant \pi(\hat{\theta}, \theta) \text{ for all } \theta \text{ and } \hat{\theta} \tag{4.21}$$

and

$$\pi(\theta) \geqslant 0 \text{ for all } \theta. \tag{4.22}$$

We shall assume that (4.21) is characterized by

$$R'Q' - c'Q - cQ' + z'c' + T' = 0. \tag{4.23}$$

Condition (4.21) binds only at $\bar{\theta}$, and $\pi(\theta) > 0$ for all $\theta \neq \bar{\theta}$ (see (4.12) above).

The Lagrangean associated with the regulator's problem is

$$\begin{aligned}
H &= \int [S + \alpha\pi + \lambda(R'Q' - c'Q - cQ' + z'c' + T')]\, d\theta \\
&= \int [V - (1-\alpha)(R+T) - \alpha cQ - \alpha z + \\
&\quad \lambda(R'Q' - c'Q - cQ' + z'c' + T')]\, d\theta.
\end{aligned} \tag{4.24}$$

For notational convenience we suppress the functional dependence of Q, c, T, and λ upon θ, and the range of integration $[\underline{\theta}, \bar{\theta}]$.

The Euler conditions with respect to Q, c, and T respectively are given in the following three equations:

$$V' - (1-\alpha)R' - \alpha c + \lambda(R''Q' - c') = \lambda(R''Q' - c') + \lambda'(R' - c) \tag{4.25}$$

$$-\alpha Q + \alpha z' + \lambda(-Q' - z''c') = \lambda[-Q' + z''(1-c')] + \lambda'(-Q+z') \tag{4.26}$$

$$-(1-\alpha) = \lambda'. \tag{4.27}$$

Since this is a free-boundary problem we can choose $\lambda(\underline{\theta}) = 0$, and (4.27) therefore implies

$$\lambda(\theta) = -(1-\alpha)(\theta - \underline{\theta}). \tag{4.28}$$

Equations (4.25) to (4.28) now imply the two central equations

$$P[Q(\theta)] = c(\theta) \tag{4.29}$$

and

$$\begin{aligned}
z'[\theta - c(\theta)] &= Q(\theta) - (1-\alpha)(\theta - \underline{\theta})z''[\theta - c(\theta)] \\
&< Q(\theta) \text{ except at } \underline{\theta}.
\end{aligned} \tag{4.30}$$

At the first best, where the regulator can observe effort, we have $P = c$ and $z' = Q$ for all θ. Equation (4.29) states that the optimum with asymmetric information has price equal to marginal cost, which is allocatively efficient *given* the level of costs. But (4.30) implies that cost-reducing effort is generally *less* than that required at the first best. Therefore costs are too high, and so price is higher than at the first best.

The firm in this example also enjoys some rent from its monopoly of information, but this rent comes partly in the form of *slack*—i.e. from suboptimally low levels of cost-reducing effort. Thus there is a precise sense in which the optimal regulatory mechanism involves X-inefficiency (see Leibenstein, 1966).

If the regulator did not have available the possibility of making a lump-sum transfer, he would of course have more problems. Price would have to exceed unit cost in order to cover the cost of effort. This would necessitate a departure from allocative efficiency, and would further attenuate incentives for cost reduction because gains from reducing unit costs would be spread across fewer units of output.

The analysis in the last two sections has been more technical than most of this book, but we must emphasize that it has not been at all rigorous. Our aim has been simply to try to convey the flavor of some of the methods used to analyze asymmetric information. A more exhaustive and rigorous treatment is given by Caillaud *et al.* (1985). Next we summarize the main findings of recent work on regulation under asymmetric information, and discuss some important extensions of the analysis.

4.3.4   Regulation with Asymmetric Information: Conclusions

Asymmetric information is at the heart of the economics of regulation. If the government and the firm's managers had access to the same information about industry conditions and the firm's behavior, then the regulatory problem could be solved by simply directing the managers to implement the socially optimal plan given the (common) information available. In reality, however, managers are much better informed about industry conditions than are the firm's owners and regulators, and their behavior can be monitored only imperfectly. The question is how to motivate managers to exploit their superior information to advantage despite the problem of imperfect monitoring. Note here the very close analogy between (a) the problem that a firm's owners (public or private) have in giving managers incentives to act in the owners' interests, and (b) the problem that government regulators have in giving a regulated firm (or its managers) incentives to act in the public interest.

Chapter 2 on ownership considered problem (a), while the present chapter is concerned with problem (b). Ideally we would like to combine (a) and (b) since the incentives of the managers of a regulated firm are influenced by both its owners and its regulators. However, that would raise very complex issues, and for the present we leave aside problem (a) by supposing that the managers of a regulated private firm act as profit maximizers.

Theories of regulation in the Averch–Johnson tradition do not explicitly take account of asymmetric information. Their purpose is to examine the consequences for firm behavior of given (and not necessarily optimal) regulatory schemes. The recent work reviewed in this section, which explicitly models asymmetries of information, addresses the question of what is the *optimal* regulatory mechanism given the information available. In doing so, it illuminates the trade-offs between internal and allocative efficiency that result from asymmetric information, and it reveals how the effectiveness of regulation depends critically upon the information available to the regulators.

In the model proposed by Baron and Myerson (1982) the government cannot observe the (exogenously given) cost structure of the firm. The government attaches more weight to consumer interests than to producer interests, and a scheme of the type suggested by Loeb and Magat (1979)—in which the firm receives consumer surplus minus a fixed amount—is therefore undesirable on distributional grounds because the firm would tend to make large profits. The government would like price to equal unit (variable) cost, but it cannot observe cost. If it imposed a low price, there would be some circumstances in which the firm would refuse to supply the market. In order to avoid this unpleasant result, the government's regulatory scheme must strike a compromise, and it turns out that price generally exceeds unit costs at the optimal compromise. Allocative inefficiency is the result. Furthermore, the firm generally makes a positive profit thanks to its "monopoly of information."

Laffont and Tirole (1986) extend the model by allowing costs to depend upon the firm's efforts as well as on given circumstances. The government is assumed to be able to observe the level of costs, but not the extent of cost-reducing effort. It cannot tell whether low costs are due to good luck or effort. The trade-off between internal efficiency (i.e. optimal effort given output) and allocative efficiency (i.e. optimal output given effort) is clear. Setting price equal to unit cost gives perfect incentives for allocative efficiency but no incentive for cost reduction. Setting price equal to a given constant gives perfect incentives for internal efficiency but poor allocative efficiency. The optimal compromise involves output being lower, and price higher, than at the optimum with symmetric information. The degree of cost reduction is too low, and so there is internal inefficiency. Once again the firm benefits from its "monopoly of information," and the government is doubly disadvantaged by the asymmetry of information. The outcome is inefficient, and the firm extracts a profit from its informational advantage.

Analyses of this kind can be extended in various ways. Baron and Besanko (1984) introduce the possibility of costly *ex post auditing* of the conditions facing the firm, which can enhance efficiency by diminishing the asymmetry of information between regulator and firm. The same authors (Baron and Besanko, 1987) examine regulation under asymmetric information in a *dynamic* setting. Over time the regulator may be able to learn about the cost conditions facing the firm, and choose a regulatory mechanism that uses the information that emerges. Much also depends on whether the regulator can commit his strategy in advance (see also Freixas and Laffont, 1985). Baron and Besanko examine intermediate degrees of commitment, in particular a "fairness" condition. For an excellent survey of all these matters and more, we again refer the interested reader to Caillaud *et al.* (1985).

4.4 Regulation of Multiproduct Firms

The economics of regulating multiproduct firms is central to an assessment of policy towards companies such as BT, British Gas, and the electricity supply industry (ESI), irrespective of how they are owned. It is obvious that BT supplies a wide range of products (telephone handsets, mobile phone services, private branch exchanges, etc.), and its principal activity (supplying telephone calls) is also a complex business. A call made at 10 a.m. on Monday is a separate product from one made at 4 a.m. on Sunday. A local call within Oxford is a different product from a long-distance call from Oxford to Glasgow (or to Washington). BT's pricing structure must reflect these differences between time and place, and their associated costs. This task is complicated by the fact that many costs are shared between various types of call, and the question arises of which consumers should bear them. Very similar issues are faced by energy utilities such as the electricity industry. Demand fluctuates between times of the day and year, and is influenced by the weather. Given the limitations on capacity and the difficulty of storing output, the electricity pricing structure must be sensitive to demand variation if rationing is to be avoided. Again the question arises of how to cover common costs (e.g. generating and distribution capacity).

Multiproduct pricing and investment problems are of course the subject of a large body of theory on public enterprise, which we have no wish to replicate here (see, for example, Atkinson and Stiglitz, 1980, chapter 15; Baumol and Bradford, 1970; Bös, 1986; Diamond and Mirrlees, 1971; Rees, 1984a,b). Rather, our aim is briefly to describe some work on the behavior of multiproduct profit-maximizing firms subject to regulatory constraint. In particular we will outline the dynamic regulatory adjustment mechanism proposed by Vogelsang and Finsinger (1979), but we begin by looking at the problem in its simpler static form.

Consider a multiproduct firm producing outputs $Q_1, Q_2, ..., Q_n$ for n markets. Let Q denote this vector of outputs. Let $P = (P_1, P_2, ..., P_n)$ be the vector of prices in the various markets. The demand Q_i for product i will depend on the price vector P. The firm's costs $C(Q)$ will depend on the output vector Q, which in turn depends on the prices P. We assume natural monopoly cost conditions. We can write the firm's profit as a function of prices:

$$\pi(P) = \Sigma P_i Q_i(P) - C[Q(P)] \tag{4.31}$$

The first term on the right-hand side is the sum of the firm's revenues in the various markets that it serves, and the second term is its costs. Note that we have not made very restrictive assumptions about the dependence of demand on prices, or the dependence of cost on outputs.

Let consumer surplus (the sum of the areas under each demand curve) plus profit be the social welfare objective. Consumer surplus will depend on the prices charged, and we will denote it by $S(P)$. A useful fact is that

$$\frac{-\partial S(P)}{\partial P_i} = Q_i(P). \tag{4.32}$$

If the price of product i is increased by a small unit, then the loss of consumer surplus is equal to that unit times the quantity of product i demanded.

Which pricing and production plan maximizes social welfare? The ideal solution (the first-best) has marginal cost pricing for each product:

$$P_i = MC_i = \frac{\partial C}{\partial Q_i}. \tag{4.33}$$

But marginal cost pricing entails losses when there are scale economies. If transfers from the government to the firm are impossible or undesirable, social welfare must be maximized subject to a break-even constraint. The problem then is equivalent to choosing P to

maximize $S(P)$ subject to $\pi(P) \geqslant 0$.

Under fairly mild assumptions about cost and demand conditions, the solution to this second-best problem requires that the term

$$\frac{P_i - MC_i}{MR_i - MC_i} \tag{4.34}$$

is the same in each market (MR_i denotes marginal revenue in market i). This is known as Ramsey pricing. The Ramsey formula implies that price–cost mark-ups are higher in markets where demand is less elastic.

Now let us turn to the profit-maximizing decision of a regulated private firm. Suppose that regulation takes the form of an average price constraint (this is roughly how BT is regulated). Suppose that a weighted average of its prices must be less than a given level $\bar{P}$:

$$\Sigma w_i P_i \leqslant \bar{P}, \tag{4.35}$$

where the w_i are positive weights that add up to unity. The firm maximizes $\pi(P)$ subject to (4.35). Everything now depends on how the weights and the price limit $\bar{P}$ are chosen. An important special case is when they are chosen in such a way that the firm can just break even, and when the weights are proportional to the demands for each product when there is Ramsey pricing. Given some assumptions about cost and demand conditions, it then turns out that *the regulated private firm chooses Ramsey pricing.*

Figure 4.4 attempts to illustrate why this is so in the two-product case. (See Vogelsang and Finsinger (1979) for a more rigorous account. The arguments depend on assumptions (e.g. about concavity) that we do not detail here.) The shaded region contains the price combinations that satisfy constraint (4.35) for a particular choice of the weights w_i and the limit $\bar{P}$. The diagram shows a consumer surplus indifference curve ($S(P) = $ constant) and an isoprofit curve tangential to the line representing the price constraint. Consumer surplus rises, but profit falls, nearer the origin. It is

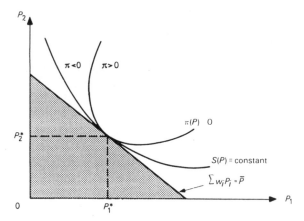

Figure 4.4 Regulation of multiproduct pricing

evident from the way that the diagram has been drawn that the price pair (P^*_1, P^*_2) maximizes consumer surplus subject to $\pi(P) \geqslant 0$. These are the Ramsey prices. The price constraint has been set so that the same price combination maximizes profit subject to prices obeying the regulatory price constraint. Thus the price constraint has induced Ramsey pricing.

How did the choice of w_i and $\bar{P}$ bring this about? The weights w_i determine the slope of the price constraint line, and $\bar{P}$ determines its distance from the origin. For given weights w_i it is easy to choose a level of $\bar{P}$ that causes the price constraint line to be a tangent to the $\pi(P) = 0$ locus. Weights proportional to the quantities demanded at Ramsey prices ensure that this point of tangency is also the point where the consumer surplus indifference curve is a tangent to the price constraint line. That is because the slope of the consumer surplus indifference curve at that point is

$$\frac{dP_2}{dP_1} = \frac{-\partial S(P^*)}{\partial P_1} \div \frac{\partial S(P^*)}{\partial P_2} = \frac{-Q_1(P^*)}{Q_2(P^*)}. \tag{4.36}$$

The first equality in (4.36) follows from totally differentiating $S(P^*) =$ constant, and the second equality follows directly from (4.32). If the weights are chosen so that w_i is proportional to $Q_i(P^*)$, it follows that the points of tangency coincide: maximizing profit subject to the appropriate price constraint delivers the same result as maximizing welfare subject to a break-even constraint.

The general reason why this form of price control produces the (constrained) optimal outcome can be outlined as follows. The problem of maximizing profit subject to the price constraint has the same solution as the problem of minimizing the cost of purchasing the consumption bundle demanded at Ramsey prices subject to the break-even constraint. (This follows from the weights' being proportional to Ramsey quantities.) The latter problem is equivalent to maximizing consumer surplus subject to the break-even constraint, because both involve minimizing the expenditure needed to obtain the consumers' preferred consumption bundle.

To summarize, private ownership of a multiproduct monopolist is no bar to allocative efficiency provided that the price control formula is aptly chosen. This proviso must be emphasized strongly, because the information about cost and demand needed to set the w_i and $\bar{P}$ correctly is very difficult to obtain. If the government possessed the information, it could just as well run the industry itself and implement optimal pricing directly. Before turning to dynamics there is one last point to make about the static case. There is a major difference between the average *price* constraint (4.35) and an average *revenue* constraint of the form

$$\frac{\Sigma P_i Q_i}{\Sigma Q_i} \leqslant \bar{P}. \tag{4.37}$$

The difference is that the weights in (4.35) are exogenous to the firm, whereas the weights (i.e. $Q_i/\Sigma Q_i$) in (4.37) depend on the firm's behavior. The optimality result for the average price constraint does not carry over to the average revenue constraint. In the latter case the firm has an incentive to behave strategically to alter the weights in its price control formula, and allocative inefficiency is the usual result (see section 9.2.4 for a discussion of this point in relation to the average revenue constraint facing British Gas).

The dynamic price control mechanism proposed by Vogelsang and Finsinger (V–F) (1979) is motivated by the limitation on the government's information that was mentioned in the paragraph above (and analyzed at some length in section 4.3). The government simply cannot know enough to design a price control formula that induces Ramsey pricing. Indeed, it does not know what the Ramsey prices are. The V–F mechanism is designed to enforce the eventual adoption of Ramsey pricing despite this lack of information about cost and demand functions.

The V–F mechanism allows the monopoly firm to choose its product prices in each time period subject to the condition that a weighted average of its prices should not exceed a given level. In particular, the prices charged in period t must be such that the revenues from setting the previous period's outputs at those prices must not exceed the total costs incurred in the previous period. In notation, the constraint is that the prices charged in period t must satisfy

$$\Sigma_i P_i^t Q_i (P^{t-1}) \leqslant C[Q(P^{t-1})], \tag{4.38}$$

where the superscripts (t and $t-1$) indicate time periods. It is assumed that the government can observe last period's prices, outputs, and costs, though it does not know the cost and demand functions. For a single-product firm the constraint is that the price in period t must not exceed the average cost in period $t-1$. (It is assumed that there are scale economies. Otherwise the firm would not be able to find a price that meets this constraint and makes a profit. Similarly, in the multiproduct case, it is assumed that there are decreasing ray average costs, i.e. the average cost of supplying a given bundle of goods decreases as the scale of output increases.)

It is assumed that the firm knows its cost and demand functions (which are constant across time), and that it maximizes profits in each period. It follows that its behavior subject to constraint (4.38) leads to an increasing level of social welfare over time. In the limit welfare converges to a level

$W^* = W(P^*)$ such that the optimal (Ramsey) conditions hold at P^*. Thus the V–F mechanism appears to have very desirable incentive properties, despite the limited information available to government. The mechanism gives the firm freedom over relative prices and uses a kind of regulatory lag. In the words of Vogelsang and Finsinger (1979, p. 170) "the regulated firm ... is encouraged to exploit both the potential for cost decreases and the consumers' willingness to pay. The firm converts these into profits. But both these advantages are turned over to the consumers in the next period."

However, the V–F mechanism has weaknesses, and a major problem is analyzed by Sappington (1980). The desirable welfare properties of the V–F mechanism are based on the assumption that the firm is a short-run profit maximizer, but (as Vogelsang and Finsinger themselves recognize) the firm may respond to the V–F mechanism strategically when it has longer-term aims. Sappington (1980, p. 360) argues that "pure waste, inefficient factor utilization, excessive research and development, and overinvestment in demand-increasing expenditures may be employed by a firm to increase long-run profits." Indeed, he shows that V–F regulation can be worse than no regulation at all. Sappington shows that the V–F mechanism can encourage the firm to engage in "pure waste," i.e. the deliberate raising of costs. The strategic advantage of pure waste today is that it increases the permitted level of prices tomorrow. The idea of a firm engaging in pure waste might be thought rather implausible, but the point applies more generally. For example, the firm might strategically slacken its efforts to cut X-inefficiency and there are many instruments that the firm might use in order to manipulate the prices that it can charge under the regulatory scheme.

In this section we have considered the *structure* (as well as the overall level) of prices chosen by a multiproduct monopolist subject to regulation. In a static framework we saw that a profit-maximizing firm can be induced to adopt a desirable pricing structure when regulation takes the simple form of a limit on a suitably weighted average of the prices of the firm's various products. The problem is that the authorities generally do not possess enough information to set the weights and the price limit at the right levels. The ingenious V–F dynamic mechanism can bring about the optimal constraint endogenously over time, but it relies on myopic behavior by the firm. Many regulatory schemes would work well if firms were myopic, but in fact they tend not to be, and the pervasive danger of inefficient strategic manipulation arises once again because asymmetric information rules out its effective prevention.

Many points made in this section are directly relevant to an assessment of the RPI − *X* method of price control that has been adopted for many privatized firms in Britain. This system essentially lays down a limit on the average price that the multiproduct firm can charge, and there is long regulatory lag. In principle the system could encourage an efficient price structure if the parameters of the allowed pricing formula were set correctly, but the authorities' relative paucity of information prevents this from happening, except perhaps by chance. Secondly, the system is vulnerable to inefficient strategic manipulation of costs by the regulated firm, especially as the time of regulatory review draws near (a problem which is shared by many regulatory schemes).

Finally, regulating a multiproduct firm by the RPI − *X* method faces further problems when the firm faces competition in some of its regulated product markets. In this section we have assumed that the firm is a pure monopolist, but companies like BT have some competitors even though they enjoy great market power. If the average price constraint covers markets in which there is some actual or potential competition, incentives for an efficient pricing structure can become distorted. The average price constraint encourages the firm to undercut its rivals in the competitive business segments by allowing it to recoup the costs of doing so elsewhere. This problem, which arises from averaging, calls for more product-specific regulation and for safeguards against anticompetitive conduct. These questions go beyond the scope of the present section, and we will return to them when discussing regulation in practice in later chapters.

4.5 Collusion between Regulator and Firm

So far we have discussed what are often called *public interest* theories of regulation. These theories take it as given that the purpose of regulation is the enhancement of economic welfare via improved efficiency in resource allocation, and that the established agencies faithfully pursue the implied allocative objectives. There is a second major strand in the U.S. literature, however, which explicitly challenges these assumptions. Work in this second tradition—often labelled the *economic* theory of regulation (to emphasize that it is concerned with the determinants of the supply of, and demand for, regulatory activities)—has developed from seminal papers by Stigler (1971), Posner (1971), and Peltzman (1976). This work has focused heavily upon the income-distribution consequences of regulatory processes and the incentives faced by the regulators themselves. The theories are intended to be nonnormative, and seek to explain how particular forms of regulation emerge and change by evaluating the gains and losses implied by alternative institutional arrangements for the various interest groups involved.

Some of the interest group pressures on regulators fixing the prices of monopolistic firms are clear enough: consumers benefit from lower prices and producers favor higher prices (up to the unconstrained monopoly level). There are other potentially important aspects of the problem, however, that may be relevant: trade unions may align themselves with management on the pricing issue, hoping to appropriate some of the monopoly returns in the form of higher wages or better working conditions; consumers tend to be less well organized as a lobby group than either management or labor; the greater frequency of contact between management and regulators could, over a period, make the latter more receptive to the firms' arguments; regulators may be influenced by the prospect of remunerative employment in the industry once their public service days are over.

The ways in which these various pressures filter through into regulatory policies are affected by the institutional arrangements of the agencies, and by the constraints placed on the latter in the form of delegated mandates and judicial decisions. In the United States most regulatory agencies have relatively vague mandates (requiring, say, that their rates be "just, reasonable and nondiscriminatory"), thus leaving commissioners with significant discretion as to their interpretation and thereby opening up more opportunities for pressure group lobbying.

The effect of such lobbying will also depend upon the terms of appointment of the commissioners. Factors such as length of service, whether commissioners are appointed or elected, restrictions on re-appointment or re-election, etc. vary considerably from agency to agency in the United States, illustrating the range of alternatives that have been considered appropriate in different circumstances.

There is particular reason to be concerned about the potential influence of producer groups on regulations dealing with new entry into the industry. The effects on consumers of entry restrictions are less visible than the effects of price fixing, and there is a public interest argument in favor of control of entry that could be used in self-serving ways by producer groups. Simply stated, it is that natural monopoly implies that efficiency is improved by having the goods or services in question supplied by a single firm, and that entry prohibition is necessary to guarantee this outcome.

We are, to say the least, highly skeptical of this argument in favor of entry restriction. In the first place, an efficient dominant firm, with significant sunk costs and subject to price regulation, is unlikely to be highly vulnerable to substantial entry threats. More importantly, given the inherent difficulty of actually establishing whether or not a given industry is subject to natural monopoly conditions, it is probable that entry restrictions would in many cases lead to supply by a single firm when the goods or services in question could be more efficiently provided by separate firms. This is particularly significant when technological change is rapid and cost conditions are constantly changing. Finally, if entry threats are removed there will be a corresponding loss of incentives for production efficiency and innovation on the part of the dominant firm.

A theoretical perspective on the possibility of collusion between regulator and firm is provided by work on *hierarchies*, i.e. principal–agent relationships consisting of several levels (see the discussion in chapter 2, and Caillaud *et al.* (1985, section 7)). In the previous section we examined the principal–agent relationship

regulator → firm,

and we supposed that the regulator had the public interest at heart. A generalization is the scheme

government → regulator → firm.

If members of the regulatory agency have interests that do not coincide with the public interest, we should consider the first link in this chain as well as the second. For example, the government might wish to limit the discretion of the regulator. This is what happens under the RPI $- X$ schemes of price regulation being introduced in Britain. The regulator has the duty of seeing that the firm complies with this general formula, but has no duty to intervene on specific pricing decisions.

A further generalization might be appropriate if it was felt that members of government are not necessarily fervent champions of the public interest. Then we might have

voters → government → regulator → firm.

Indeed it has been suggested in connection with the U.K. privatization program that it is government, rather than regulators, which has been partly "captured" by firms when designing regimes of competition and regulation for them. Related criticisms can be made of the control of nationalized industries. In chapter 5 below we will describe how the long-term development of nationalized industries in Britain has often suffered from government intervention and constraints motivated by short-term considerations. One of the advantages sometimes claimed for privatization is that it avoids problems of this kind. Whether or not it is the best way of doing so is another matter, to which we shall return later.

4.6   Competition and Regulation

In this section we examine three respects in which competition and regulation interact. The first is competition *for* monopoly, or franchising, which has indeed been used in a number of areas, for example local authority services in Britain where private operators have opportunities to outbid and displace public suppliers. Franchising has many attractive features especially where the product in question has a simple specification, but in industries of any complexity its merits are likely to be outweighed by problems of uncompetitive bidding, the handover of fixed assets, and contract monitoring. The second theme is competition via regulation, or "yardstick competition," in which regulated units in submarkets that are distinct (e.g. geographically) are brought into competition by the regulatory mechanism. For example, the price increase allowed in region A might be a function partly of cost performance in regions B and C. Thirdly we look at regulation in industries where there is some competition (actual or potential), as in the U.K. telecommunications industry for instance. The presence of competition influences the appropriate form of regulation, and regulation in turn affects the effectiveness of measures to permit or promote competition. Thus it is an important part of the task of regulatory authorities in the U.K. to try to guard against anticompetitive behavior. Here the overlap between regulatory and antitrust policies is most evident, and indeed it should always be remembered that regulatory mechanisms are just one element in the overall combination of public policies toward industrial organization and behavior.

4.6.1   Franchising

The dilemma for policy regarding natural monopolies is how to enjoy the cost benefits of single-firm production without suffering from monopolistic behavior. One answer is to have a competition—in the form of an auction—*for* the monopoly, with several firms competing to be the one that actually operates in the market. We will concentrate on an attractive form of franchising that was originally advocated by Edwin Chadwick, the Victorian social reformer, and developed by Demsetz (1969) in his famous article "Why regulate utilities?" According to the Chadwick–Demsetz (C–D) proposal, the franchise is awarded for a period of time to the competitor offering to supply the product or service at the lowest price(s), or, more generally, the best price–quality package (for a review of franchising in relation to natural monopoly, see Sharpe (1982)).

On the face of it, franchising appears to provide a very attractive way of combining competition and efficiency without any arduous burden for regulators. The competition for monopoly appears to destroy the undesirable monopoly of information that hinders traditional regulation, and price is set by competition, not by administrators. In practice, franchising has been successful in a number of fields. For example, a study in 1986 by the London Business School and Institute for Fiscal Studies showed that local authorities in Britain using private contractors have reduced costs by 22 percent on average while maintaining the standard of services. Local authorities have successfully used competitive tendering, which is a form of franchising, for subsidized bus services (see section 10.4). It goes almost without saying that franchising is widely used within the private sector.

However, there are many industries where franchising cannot work, at any rate in this simple form, and the industries described later in this book (energy, telecommunications, water, etc.) provide leading examples. We shall focus on three sources of difficulty—the danger that bidding for the franchise will be uncompetitive, problems of asset handover, and, most important, the difficulties of contract specification and monitoring.

There are two reasons why bidding for the franchise might fail to be competitive. First, there is a danger of *collusion* between bidders, especially if they are few in number (e.g. because the requisite skills or resources are rare) or if the firms are effectively in a repeated game with one another by virtue of frequent contacts of various kinds.

The second reason is that one firm might enjoy such *strategic advantages* in the competition for the franchise that other firms would be unwilling to compete with it. Suppose, for example, that firm A has recently been the holder of a franchise that is now up for renewal. If the experience gained by A from its past operation of the franchise has had the effect of reducing its costs of operation, then the future franchise is worth more to firm A than to other firms. This fact might deter the other firms even from competing with A for the future franchise because they know that they are unlikely to win the competition.

Another source of incumbent advantage can arise from asymmetries of information. If A is the incumbent operator of the franchise, then A's knowledge of cost and demand conditions is likely to be superior to that of any other firm. This will tend to deter others from competing with A for the future franchise. For if firm B outbids A for the franchise, it is likely that B has bid too much. The fact that the relatively ignorant firm B wins against the knowledgeable firm A is itself an indication that B has paid over the odds. This problem is sometimes known as the "winner's curse." Its effect is to deter competition with the knowledgeable firm, i.e. the incumbent. (Precisely how the effect operates depends, of course, upon the exact nature of the competition for the franchise. Although we do not present a formal model here, we believe that the verbal argument is sufficient to establish the general point. (See further Englebrecht-Wiggans *et al.* (1983) on the value of information in auctions.))

We now turn to problems of *asset handover*. Suppose that A has held the franchise until now, but that B has just defeated A in the competition for the franchise for the next interval of time. What happens to the assets hitherto used by A to operate the franchise? Unless sunk costs are zero (an extremely unlikely event) efficiency requires that B, the new operator of the franchise, takes over these assets from A. Otherwise there will be inefficient duplication of the assets. But how are the assets to be valued for this purpose? Here there is a problem of bilateral monopoly. If A had no alternative, it would accept as little as the scrap value of the assets. If B had no alternative, it would pay as much as their replacement value. The gap between replacement value and scrap value is likely to be large if the assets involve sunk costs, and the expense of bargaining or arbitration regarding the appropriate transfer price might well be considerable.

This fact in turn has implications for the nature of competition for the renewal of the franchise itself. Let X and Y denote the values to A and B respectively of operating the franchise in the future, aside from the cost of transferring the assets and bargaining costs. Let Z be the amount paid by B to A for the assets if B wins the future franchise, and let C_A and C_B be the bargaining costs of the two firms in that event. If A wins the franchise it receives X, and if A loses it receives $Z - C_A$. A's incentive to win is therefore $X - Z + C_A$. If B wins, it receives $Y - Z - C_B$ (which we initially assume to be positive), and if B loses it receives zero. Therefore A has a greater incentive than B if and only if

$$X + C_A + C_B > Y. \tag{4.39}$$

The condition for A to be a more efficient franchise operator than B is simply

$$X > Y. \tag{4.40}$$

A comparison of these two inequalities shows that the costs of bargaining $(C_A + C_B)$ have the effect of giving the incumbent firm A an advantage, because bargaining costs are avoided if the franchise does not change hands.

Note that Z, the amount paid to A for the assets if B wins, does not affect the *difference between* the incentives of A and B in the franchise competition (provided that $Z < Y - C_B$). This is because a higher level of Z reduces A's incentive to win just as much as it reduces B's incentive. However, if $Z \geqslant Y - C_B$, the level of Z *does* effect competition for the franchise, because B cannot make a positive profit whatever it bids and so would not compete. Thus A would be the only contestant. This consideration indicates that some form of regulation of the level of Z may be required.

Moreover the level of Z certainly influences the *level* of the bids that would be made in the auction for the franchise. If B could purchase A's assets at low cost, then B would be prepared to bid more than if the assets were more costly for B to acquire from A. Similarly, the incumbent firm A would compete less vigorously with B if B were required to pay more for the assets. Therefore the level of Z is bound to influence the size of incentives (if not the difference between them) and hence the efficiency of resulting pricing arrangements, especially if the auction is of the C–D type.

The level of Z, the amount paid for the assets of the displaced franchise, is also a critical determinant of the *investment* decisions of an incumbent firm. If it is thought likely that Z will be low (e.g. because the assets are of minimal value to an outgoing incumbent), then the existing incumbent will have an incentive to underinvest if there is any chance that he will fail to win future competitions for franchise renewal. On the other hand, if he were to receive an inflated price for the assets being passed on, he might have an incentive to overinvest.

More generally, there is likely to be considerable *uncertainty* about the level of Z *ex ante*. With risk-averse firms, this will affect investment strategies, bidding behavior, and perhaps even the decision to enter the competition for the franchise.

These numerous problems of asset valuation and handover perhaps suggest that investment decisions should be left to public authority and that the competition should be simply for an *operating* franchise. However, operating franchises allow market forces to act only to a limited extent, and the divorce of investment and operating decisions can lead to undesirable losses of coordination.

Finally we come to the important question of the *specification and administration of franchise contracts* (see in particular Williamson, 1976; Goldberg, 1976). If a franchise contract is for the provision of a well-defined product or service—for example the production of a thousand taxi license plates of a given specification at a given time—then the contract between franchisor and franchisee is a relatively simple affair that requires little effort to administer. But if there is technological or market uncertainty in relation to the product, then the specification of the franchise contract can be a very complex task, and the need to monitor and administer the contract during its life is certain to arise.

Williamson (1976) draws important distinctions between different types of franchise contract. A *complete* contract requires a franchise bidder to specify the terms on which he will supply the product or service at each future date during the life of the contract, and for every future contingency that might arise. A complete contract sensitive to future events would be impossibly expensive to write, negotiate, and enforce if uncertainty is present. But a complete contract does not have to take a complex form. For instance, a contract might simply say that the price charged will be such-and-such in all circumstances—i.e. whatever happens to demand, production costs, inflation, and so on. But an unconditional contract of this form faces two severe problems. First, the firm might be unable to fulfill the contract under some circumstances. The threat of inability or refusal to supply would probably lead to flexibility *ex post*, even though the original contract had been specified unconditionally. Therefore, unconditional contracts, especially if they are longer term, are likely to be infeasible. Moreover, unconditional contracts are undesirable. Considerations of efficiency require that price and quality adapt in response to changes in demand and technology.

Thus we are left with *incomplete* contracts, which do not make explicit what is to happen in every possible circumstance. With incomplete contracts there is a need for administration and monitoring of the (partly implicit) contract as time unfolds; a continuing contractual relationship exists, and this inevitably involves continuing costs. The alternative is for the franchisor to be left at the mercy of the franchisee.

The duration of the franchise contract must also be considered. The difficulties of contract specification and administration alluded to in the previous paragraph perhaps suggest that short-term contracts have advantages, because fewer future contingencies then need to be catered for. But the organization of frequent contests for the franchise also involves major costs. As well as the direct costs of holding more auctions, all the problems of asset valuation and handover (see above) occur more often, and the industry would frequently be in a state of turmoil.

The conclusion to be drawn is that, in industries where there is significant uncertainty about technology and demand, competition for monopoly by franchising does not have many of the advantages over regulation that it superficially appears to possess. Indeed franchising involves an implicit regulatory contract for all but the simplest products and services. As Goldberg (1976, p. 426) writes: "Many of the problems associated with regulation lie in what is being regulated, not in the act of regulation itself."

4.6.2 Yardstick Competition

One of the main themes emphasized in this chapter has been the importance of information for effective regulation. If the regulator is relatively uninformed about industry conditions, and especially if the firm being regulated has a monopoly of information, the regulatory mechanism is liable to become a blunt instrument that is insensitive to the basic parameters of cost and demand. Economic efficiency (in both allocative and internal terms) becomes impaired, and the firm extracts monetary or slack rent from its monopoly of information.

Yardstick competition is a method of promoting competition between regulated units indirectly via the regulatory mechanism. It has been proposed in the Littlechild Report (1986) on regulation of the U.K. water authorities. To take the simplest example, suppose that a national monopolist was split into separately owned northern and southern units, denoted N and S respectively, each with a natural monopoly in its geographical area. Suppose further that cost and demand conditions were very similar in the two regions, although the regulator might not know (say) the scope for cost reduction in either region. The two regional units could be brought into competition by the following kind of regulatory mechanism. The price that N could charge in a given period of time would depend on the level of costs achieved by S, and vice versa for the price allowed to firm S. Provided that N and S face very similar circumstances, and that they do not collude in any way, a method of this kind offers the prospect of combining both internal and allocative efficiency, and therefore of escaping the dilemma that usually exists between the two. Good incentives for internal efficiency exists because N keeps the benefits of its cost-reducing activities, for its price is linked to the cost performance of firm S. Allocative efficiency results if there is symmetry between firms, because industry prices are kept in line with industry costs. The promotion of competition via regulation overcomes the informational disadvantage of the regulator in an economical fashion, and shows again how competition can act as an efficient incentive mechanism.

Yardstick competition illustrates the general proposition that under asymmetric information, when a principal has many agents under his control, it is almost always the case that the optimal incentive scheme involves the reward of each agent's being contingent upon the performance of other agents as well as his own performance. The theoretical literature on this point includes Holmstrom (1982), Mookherjee (1984), and Nalebuff and Stiglitz (1983). It is particularly desirable to make reward contingent partly upon the performance of others when the uncertainties facing different agents are correlated to a high degree. If such correlation is absent, there is no advantage in linking reward to others' performance. Indeed, to do so would serve only to add "noise" in an undesirable way: the risk facing any agent would increase, and he would not be encouraged to behave as his circumstances warranted.

Shleifer (1985) examines a model of yardstick competition. In the basic version of the model there are n identical risk-neutral firms operating in a certain environment. Each faces demand curve $Q(P)$ in its market (the n markets are separate). A firm spending z on cost-reducing effort achieves unit cost level $c(z)$, with $c(0) = c_0$. The lump-sum transfer to the firm (if any) is denoted by T. Profit is therefore given by

$$\pi = [P - c(z)]Q(P) - z + T. \tag{4.41}$$

If the social welfare objective is the sum of consumer and producer surplus (and so is not affected by considerations of distribution or the cost of raising public funds), then the optimum subject to the nonnegative profit constraint has

$$P^* = c(z^*), \tag{4.42}$$

$$-c'(z^*)Q(P^*) = 1, \tag{4.43}$$

and

$$z^* = T^*. \tag{4.44}$$

In sum, price equals unit (and hence marginal) cost, efforts to reduce unit costs occur up to the point where their marginal cost ($= 1$) equals marginal benefit ($= -c'Q$, i.e. degree of cost reduction times volume of output), and the cost of effort is reimbursed by the lump-sum transfer.

However, this first-best outcome cannot be achieved if the regulator does not know the function $c(z)$, which describes the scope for cost reduction. Shleifer supposes that each firm is run by managers who like profits π but dislike effort z. In particular it is supposed that their preference ordering is lexicographic with profits preferred over leisure. This is the minimal extent to which some weight can be given to leisure in managers' preferences. Even so, a regulatory regime in which $P = c$ and $z = T$ (which is sometimes known as "cost of service regulation") induces no cost-reducing effort whatsoever. Profit is the same (i.e. zero) for all z, and so managers prefer to minimize z by setting it at zero, and the cost level is therefore c_0.

The key to efficiency is to break the dependence of the price for firm i upon its cost level. Let

$$\bar{c}_i = \sum_{j \neq i} c_j/(n-1) \tag{4.45}$$

and

$$\bar{z}_i = \sum_{j \neq i} z_j/(n-1) \tag{4.46}$$

be the average cost and effort levels of firms other than i. These provide yardsticks against which to compare i's performance. Shleifer (1985, proposition 1) shows that the following regulatory mechanism for all firms i induces first-best behavior:

$$P_i = \bar{c}_i \tag{4.47}$$

and

$$T_i = \bar{z}_i. \tag{4.48}$$

The profit of firm i is then

$$\pi_i = [\bar{c}_i - c(z_i)]Q(\bar{c}_i) - z_i + \bar{z}_i, \tag{4.49}$$

and the first-order condition is therefore

$$-c'(z_i)Q(\bar{c}_i) - 1 = 0. \tag{4.50}$$

There is a symmetric Nash equilibrium in which all firms choose $c_i = c^*$, in which case $P^* = c^*$ and $T^* = z^*$, and Shleifer shows that there exists no asymmetric Nash equilibrium. Therefore the equilibrium that sustains the first-best outcome is unique. This result in fact holds with pricing rules considerably more general than (4.47), but the simple example suffices to establish the main point. A related result holds even when lump-sum transfers are impossible. Yardstick competition can then induce the second-best outcome, i.e. the social optimum subject to $T = 0$.

The main shortcoming of the version of the model described so far is that it assumes that firms operate in *identical* environments. Of course this is quite unrealistic. The economics of water supply, for example, differs substantially between geographical regions. The water authority operating in the Welsh mountains faces conditions and uncertainties that are correlated by no means perfectly with those encountered by the authority operating in the plains of East Anglia. Shleifer examines the use of regression analysis based on observable characteristics to screen out at least part of the heterogeneity between firms that occurs in practice. *"Reduced-form" regulation* operates roughly as follows. Let θ be the vector of exogenous observable characteristics with respect to which firms differ. The regulator estimates a regression of unit costs against θ. With a linear functional form the regression equation is $c = \alpha + \beta\theta$. With $\hat{\alpha}$ and $\hat{\beta}$ denoting the estimated coefficients, the "predicted" unit cost level for firm i is $\hat{c}_i = \hat{\alpha} + \hat{\beta}\theta_i$, where θ_i is the observable characteristic of that firm. The regulator then imposes the price rule $p_i = \hat{c}_i$ and an associated transfer rule.

Reduced-form regulation works well if θ captures almost all of the variation between firms and if it is truly exogenous. If θ fails to capture the full extent of diversity, reduced-form regulation does not provide perfect incentives, and it causes there to be undesirable noise. The problem is especially acute if characteristics that are correlated with the observed characteristics θ are omitted, because omitted-variable bias is then introduced. Further difficulties arise if firms are able to manipulate the observed characteristics, because incentives then exist for strategic rent-seeking behavior and signaling. Similarly, reduced-form regulation has the disadvantage of encouraging endless argument about the appropriate way to conduct the regression analysis, which variables to include, and so on.

More problems arise if firms are able to collude and thereby frustrate competition via regulation. If firms tacitly agreed to slack to an equal extent, inefficiency would persist. Incentives to cheat might be weak if, as is probable, firms were few in number and well informed about each others' behavior.

Despite these difficulties, however, we believe that competition via regulation can provide good incentive systems in a number of industries. We know that the best regulatory mechanisms will exploit information from comparative performance in some form, but the question is *how* to do so in any particular case. It would be foolish to attempt generalization of this, since the degree of homogeneity between regional units differs from industry to industry, but the benefits to be gained from breaking the monopoly of information of a regulated firm could be substantial in individual cases. This is a factor which should be taken into account when considering the regional break-up of privatized companies.

4.6.3　Regulation to Maintain Effective Competition

Regulation is not only called for when competition is absent. Regulation designed to maintain freedom of *entry* is sometimes essential if threats of potential competition are to have force. We showed in section 3.2.2 that an incumbent firm with market power usually has at its disposal a variety of instruments of strategic entry deterrence, and that incentives for predatory behavior are likely to exist. Unless this sort of conduct (and the threat of it) are checked by suitable policy measures, market "liberalization" in the legal sense can be quite ineffective.

It can be argued that the sanctions of ordinary competition policy are sufficient to strike down anticompetitive behavior of this kind, but we disagree for several reasons. First, competition policy in the U.K. (and elsewhere) evolved at a time when dominant utility companies were in public ownership. The competition problems that arise in those industries were therefore not envisaged when policy was made, and so there is little reason why it should be expected to cope with them. Secondly, it can be argued that U.K. competition policy has weaknesses generally (see Sharpe, 1985). Certainly it has usually been less vigorous than U.S. antitrust policy. Thirdly, where the danger of particular anticompetitive practices can be foreseen, it makes sense to legislate against them in advance, and to give the specialist regulatory agency the duty of monitoring and enforcing the policy. This also reduces uncertainty. Finally, the agency has greater knowledge and expertise regarding industry conditions than a generalist competition authority can have. (A separate question, which we do not pursue here, is whether there should be one regulatory authority for all privatized utility companies, or one for each.)

In sum, we believe that the task of "regulation" to promote and maintain competition in industries with dominant privatized firms should belong to the regulatory authority for that industry. This is not to say that the general competition authority (the Monopolies and Mergers Commission (MMC) in the U.K.) has no role to play: the regulator should be able to refer cases to it, but he should also have sufficient power to deal swiftly with anticompetitive conduct if and when it occurs.

In section 3.2.2 we described some of the economics of anticompetitive behavior to deter entry. As regards practical policy measures to combat such conduct, we will pursue this question further when we come to consider the frameworks of competition and regulation that have been established for privatized industries in Britain.

4.7   Concluding Remarks

The purpose of this chapter has been to provide a theoretical perspective on the economics of regulation that will guide our assessment of U.K. regulatory policy in part II of the book.

We have focused on the *incentive* properties of various regulatory mechanisms to encourage both internal and allocative efficiency. We have seen how the regulator's relatively *imperfect information* can lead to an awkward trade-off between the two, and how the firm and its managers can enjoy rewards from their monopoly of information. This suggested that the social return from having better informed regulatory bodies could be high, and it indicated that the benefits from greater competition (potential if not actual) could extend to internal as well as allocative efficiency. We also emphasized the *dynamics* of regulation, and the *strategic interaction* between firm and regulator (or government) that can occur over time. We shall bear in mind all these themes when we come to the case studies of regulation in practice in the following chapters.

References

Atkinson, A.B. and J.E. Stiglitz (1980). *Lectures on Public Economics*. Maidenhead: McGraw-Hill.

Atkinson, A.B. and L. Waverman (1973). Resource Allocation and the Regulated Firm: Comment. *Bell Journal of Economics* 4: 283–287.

Averch, H. and L. Johnson (1962). Behavior of the Firm under Regulatory Constraint. *American Economic Review* 52: 1052–1069.

Bailey, E.E. (1973). *Economic Theory of Regulatory Constraint*. Lexington, MA: Lexington Books.

Bailey, E.E. (1974). Innovation and Regulation. *Journal of Public Economics* 3: 285–295.

Bailey, E.E. (1976). Innovation and Regulation: A Reply. *Journal of Public Economics* 5: 393–394.

Bailey, E.E. and R.D. Coleman (1971). The Effects of Lagged Regulation in the Averch–Johnson Model. *Bell Journal of Economics* 2: 278–292.

Bailey, E.E. and J.C. Malone (1970). Resource Allocation and the Regulated Firm. *Bell Journal of Economics* 1: 129–142.

Baron, D.P. and D. Besanko (1984). Regulation, Asymmetric Information, and Auditing. *Rand Journal of Economics* 15: 447–470.

Baron, D.P. and R.B. Myerson (1982). Regulating a Monopolist with Unknown Costs. *Econometrica* 50: 911–930.

Baumol, W.J. and D. Bradford (1970). Optimal Departures from Marginal Cost Pricing. *American Economic Review* 60: 265–283.

Baumol, W.J. and A.K. Klevorick (1970). Input Choices and Rate of Return Regulation: An Overview of the Discussion. *Bell Journal of Economics* 1: 162–190.

Bawa, V.S. and D.S. Sibley (1980). Dynamic Behaviour of a Firm Subject to Stochastic Regulatory Review. *International Economic Review* 21: 627–642.

Bös, D. (1986). *Public Enterprise Economics*. Amsterdam: North-Holland.

Breyer, S. (1982). *Regulation and its Reform*. Cambridge, MA: Harvard University Press.

Caillaud, B., R. Guesnerie, P. Rey and J. Tirole (1985). *The Normative Economics of Government Intervention in Production in the Light of Incentive Theory: A Review of Recent Contributions*. Technical Report 473, IMSSS, Stanford University, Stanford, CA.

Crew, M.A. and P.R. Kleindorfer (1986). *The Economics of Public Utility Regulation*. London: Macmillan.

Dasgupta, P. and J.E. Stiglitz (1985). *Sunk Costs, Competition and Welfare*. Mimeograph, St John's College, Cambridge.

Demsetz, H. (1968). Why Regulate Utilities? *Journal of Law and Economics* 11: 55–65.

Diamond, P. and J.A. Mirrlees (1971). Optimal Taxation and Public Production. *American Economic Review* 61: 8–27, 261–278.

Englebrecht-Wiggans, R., P.R. Milgrom and R.J. Weber (1983). Competitive Bidding and Proprietary Information. *Journal of Mathematical Economics* 11: 161–169.

Freixas. X. and J.J. Laffont (1985). Marginal Cost Pricing versus Average Cost Pricing under Moral Hazard. *Journal of Public Economics* 26: 135–146.

Fromm, G. (ed.) (1981). *Studies in Public Regulation*. Cambridge, MA: MIT Press.

Goldberg, V.P. (1976). Regulation and Administered Contracts. *Bell Journal of Economics* 7: 426–448.

Greenwald, B.C. (1984). Rate Base Selection and the Structure of Regulation. *Rand Journal of Economics* 15: 85–95.

Holmstrom, B. (1982). Moral Hazard in Teams. *Bell Journal of Economics* 13: 324–340.

Kahn, A.E. (1970). *The Economics of Regulation*, Vols I and 2. New York: Wiley.

Klevorick, A. (1971). The Optimal Fair Rate of Return. *Bell Journal of Economics* 2: 122–153.

Klevorick, A. (1973). The Behaviour of a Firm Subject to Stochastic Regulatory Review. *Bell Journal of Economics* 4: 57–88.

Laffont, J.J. and J. Tirole (1986). Using Cost Observation to Regulate Firms. *Journal of Political Economy* 94: 614–641.

Leibenstein, H. (1966). Allocative Efficiency versus *X*-Efficiency. *American Economic Review* 56: 392–415.

Lesourne, J. (1976). Innovation and Regulation: A Comment. *Journal of Public Economics* 5: 389–392.

Loeb, M. and W. Magat (1970). A Decentralized Method for Utility Regulation. *Journal of Law and Economics* 22: 399–404.

Mookherjee, D. (1984). Optimal Incentive Schemes with Many Agents. *Review of Economic Studies* 51: 433–446.

Nalebuff, B. and J.E. Stiglitz (1983). Prizes and Incentives: Towards a General Theory of Compensation and Competition. *Bell Journal of Economics* 14: 21–43.

Peltzman, S. (1976). Towards a More General Theory of Regulation. *Journal of Law and Economics* 14: 109–148.

Posner, R. (1971). Taxation by Regulation. *Bell Journal of Economics* 2: 22–50.

Rees, R. (1984a). *Public Enterprise Economics*. London: Weidenfeld and Nicholson.

Rees, R. (1984b). A Positive Theory of the Public Enterprise. In Marchand, M., P. Pestieau and H. Tulkens (eds), *The Performance of Public Enterprises*. Amsterdam: North-Holland.

Sappington, D. (1980). Strategic Firm Behavior under a Dynamic Adjustment Process. *Bell Journal of Economics* 11: 360–372.

Schmalensee, R. (1979). *The Control of Natural Monopolies*. Lexington: D.C. Heath.

Sharkey, W.W. (1979). A Decentralized Method for Utility Regulation: A Comment. *Journal of Law and Economics* 22: 74–75.

Sharpe, T. (1982). *The Control of Natural Monopoly by Franchising*. Mimeograph, Wolfson College, Oxford.

Sharpe, T. (1985). British Competition Policy in Perspective. *Oxford Review of Economic Policy* 1(3): 80–94.

Shleifer, A. (1985). A Theory of Yardstick Competition. *Rand Journal of Economics* 16: 319–327.

Stigler, G. (1971). The Theory of Economic Regulation. *Bell Journal of Economics* 2: 3–21.

Vogelsang, I. and J. Finsinger (1979). A Regulatory Adjustment Process for Optimal Pricing by Multiproduct Monopoly Firms. *Bell Journal of Economics* 10: 157–171.

Williamson, O.E. (1975). Franchising Bidding for Natural Monopolies—In General and with Respect to CATV. *Bell Journal of Economics* 7: 73–104.

[9]

ELSEVIER   Journal of Public Economics 57 (1995) 471–488

JOURNAL OF
PUBLIC
ECONOMICS

Unnatural monopoly

Saul Estrin[a], David de Meza[b,*]

[a]*London Business School, Sussex Place, Regents Park, London, NW1 4SA, UK*

[b]*Department of Economics, University of Exeter, Amory Building, Rennes Drive, Exeter, EX4 4RJ, UK*

Received May 1993, revised version received June 1994

Abstract

This paper investigates the merits of statutory monopoly as a means of preventing wasteful market fragmentation. The key result is that a public firm committed to price at cost may be unable to repel entry even when it is socially desirable that it should do so. Limited entry may be worse than either statutory monopoly or free entry. The robustness of results when competition stimulates a state firm to lower its costs is also examined.

Keywords: Statutory monopoly; Deregulation; Entry

JEL classification: L43

It is obvious for example, how great an economy of labour would be obtained if London were supplied by a single gas or water company instead of the existing plurality . . . were there only one establishment it could make lower charges consistently while obtaining the rate of profit now realised – J.S. Mill (1926, pp. 43).

There cannot be a doubt that if the law did not interpose its prohibition, the transmission of letters would be gladly undertaken by capitalists, and conducted on the ordinary commercial principles, with all that economy, attention to the wants of their customers, and skilful adaption of means to the desired end, which is usually practised by those whose interests are involved with their success. But the law constitutes the Post Office a monopoly. Its conductors are, therefore, uninfluenced by the ordinary motives to enterprise and good management; and however, injudiciously the institution may be conducted, however inadequate it may be to the

* Corresponding author.

472   *S. Estrin, D. de Meza / Journal of Public Economics 57 (1995) 471–488*

growing wants of the nation, the people must submit to the inconvenience: they cannot set up a Post Office for themselves – Rowland Hill (quoted by R.H. Coase, 1939, pp. 430).

1. Introduction

There are a few goods for which it is illegal for private producers to compete with the monopoly state supplier. The most notable current example is letter delivery, which in almost every country is the exclusive right of the state post office.[1] This paper investigates the circumstances in which there might be good reasons to take the drastic step of outlawing competition. The main finding is that in the presence of economies of scale, an average cost pricing public firm may be unable to deter the entry of lower cost private firms, but unless the cost advantage of the entrants is sufficiently great, consumers lose, whether or not the state firm is driven from the market. Even when the profits of the entrant are included in the social calculus, statutory monopoly may be justified.

The usual argument for prohibiting entry, as in the J.S. Mill quote above, is that the dissipation of economies of scale can thereby be avoided. In contrast, critics of statutory monopoly, exemplified by Rowland Hill, father of the Victorian penny post, invariably point to the stagnation of enterprise occurring, as Marshall puts it, "... under the deadly shades of official monopoly". Friedman (1962) amongst others claims that no policy dilemma is posed by these conflicting arguments. Either scale economies really are significant, in which case no entrant could succeed in competition with an efficient nationalised firm, and there is no need to legislate against entry; or, if despite economies of scale, the public firm proves vulnerable to entry due to its inefficiency, legislating against entry would be a harmful constraint on innovation and competition. On this view, statutory monopoly is never beneficial and is sometimes deleterious, at least from the point of view of consumers. Some analytical support for this 'survivability' test of the desirability at repeal is to be found in the theory of contestable markets according to which invisible hand results apply (with a few exceptions) even in the presence of economies of scale (Baumol et al., 1982).

In challenging these claims, this paper drops the 'hit and run' assumption required for a contestable market and instead allows all firms to adjust price and output after entry. It also recognises that a statutory monopoly is invariably a nationalised industry unconcerned with profit-maximisation per se. The relevant descriptive literature suggests that average cost pricing is the objective actually adopted by public sector enterprises in practice (see,

---

[1] Current exceptions include the United Kingdom for delivery priced at over £1.00 and Sweden.

S. Estrin, D. de Meza / Journal of Public Economics 57 (1995) 471–488   473

for example, Albon, 1987; Corby, 1979; Tulkens, 1968). In evaluating statutory monopoly, the first task is thus to find conditions under which private firms can profitably enter in the presence of a break-even price with economies of scale. If these conditions are met, the welfare consequences of entry are then examined.

The paper is organised as follows. Section 2 sets out the basic model and uses it to examine the trade-offs between the dissipation of scale economies and the gains from provision by a more efficient private firm. As long as the public firm survives, the repeal of the statutory monopoly either has no effect or, if entry occurs, price rises. Should the public firm be eliminated, or if it cuts its costs in response to the increased competition, results are not so clear cut. Section 3 investigates these issues using explicit functional forms. Even in the presence of quite modest economies of scale, inefficiency of the public firm must be substantial to justify repeal. The effects of multiple entry of private firms is considered in section 4. With freedom of entry, public and private firms tend not to co-exist though it is ambiguous whether this strengthens or weakens the case for statutory monopoly. Conclusions are drawn in Section 5.

2. The basic issues

Much public debate on liberalising the market in which public firms operate has centered on what is pejoratively termed 'cream skimming' or 'cherry picking'. This is a phenomenon of multi-product firms with the efficiency issue concerning an entrant invading only the high profit segment of the public firms' market. The loss of economies of scale forces the public firm to raise prices, eventually leading to an overall loss of consumer surplus. As with the single-product case, the question is whether fragmenting the market by permitting firms which may be more efficient to enter involves such a loss of scale economies as to be harmful on balance. The multi-product case adds realism and complexity but is conceptually a minor extension. In what follows, attention is therefore confined to the single-product case.

A literature on 'mixed' duopoly markets involving a private and a public enterprise has begun to appear (see Vickers and Yarrow, 1988; De Fraja and Delbono, 1990; and Bos, 1991, for surveys). Market structure has generally been taken as given and the issue has been the welfare properties of various duopoly solutions, e.g. Cournot–Nash equilibrium by Bos (1986), Stackelberg equilibrium by Beato and Mas-Colell (1984) and comparisons of the two by Cremer et al. (1989) and De Fraja and Delbono (1989). This paper differs from these works in its focus on the feasibility of entry and on its desirability.

474   S. Estrin, D. de Meza / Journal of Public Economics 57 (1995) 471–488

In a first-best world it is evident that if it is worth producing a good subject to economies of scale in production, it should be supplied by a single firm. Unfortunately, laissez faire cannot guarantee such a felicitous outcome, as illustrated by the basic free-entry Cournot–Nash model in which there is typically multiple entry involving the wasteful duplication of fixed costs. Suppose, for example, that market demand is of unitary elasticity and marginal cost is constant. If fixed costs are such as to allow five firms to enter, it can be shown that equilibrium price is 25% above marginal cost. With only one firm in the market, its break-even price is a mere 4% above marginal cost. Even so, prohibiting entry to all but approved firms may be undesirable. The obvious problem is that suppressing competition harms consumers, as illustrated by Seade's (1980) result that however great economies of scale are, in a stable Cournot–Nash equilibrium the fewer the number of firms the higher is their selling price. It seems plausible that this is why private firms are not normally given statutory protection against entry even when the existence of scale economies is not in doubt. When restrictions on entry are actually awarded to private firms,[2] regulation by an independent agency is the norm. However, as we have noted, governments do sometimes prohibit competition with public firms whilst imposing only limited external supervision of the resulting monopoly. It is presumably hoped that the dissipation of economies of scale and scope will thereby be avoided without running the risk of exploiting consumers or requiring a costly and inflexible bureaucracy.[3]

To explore the questions further, suppose a public firm, N, provides a single good subject to declining average cost. Its proximate goal is to maximise output subject to breaking even, behaviour reasonably in accord with the theoretical welfare literature (see Rees, 1984), public choice theories such as Niskanen (1971) and with at least British institutional practice (see Estrin and de Meza, 1988). Moreover, it is well known that break-even pricing achieves constrained social efficiency if N holds a monopoly position.

For now, we assume that there is but a single profit-maximising firm, M, capable of producing the good if the statutory monopoly were to be repealed. It also has declining average costs and may be more efficient than N. A two-stage game is specified. The firms first make simultaneous entry decisions, which involve sinking a fixed cost. If both enter, then at the next

---

[2] For example, in the United Kingdom to British Gas in the household market, to BT and Mercury in telecommunications and to taxi-cabs.

[3] Crew and Kleindorfer (1985) explore some of the issues.

S. Estrin, D. de Meza / Journal of Public Economics 57 (1995) 471–488   475

stage outputs are simultaneously chosen and variable costs are incurred.[4] The second stage is modelled as a regular Cournot game except that N still seeks to break even. Even in a mixed duopoly, this is the appropriate welfare objective for the public firm. This is because, given the standard assumptions leading to downward-sloping, profit-maximising, best-response functions and a unique equilibrium, as N expands, M contracts by less and so price falls.[5] Should N be unable to cover its total cost in the second stage, budgetary pressures from the government require that it does its best to break even and so make the greatest contribution to repaying fixed costs by maximising profit.

Fig. 1 shows the best-response functions for the second-stage game. If both firms were equally efficient and were to maximise profit, the best-response functions would be AA and BB and Nash equilibrium would be at $\hat{E}$. However, with average cost pricing, the response function of the public firm is modified. N will expand output whenever profit is positive along AA so as to eliminate the surplus. The best-response function of the public firm is thus ACD, where M^* is the highest private output consistent with N breaking even.[6] With break-even pricing by the public firm, the Nash equilibrium of the second-stage game is at E^*. Fig. 1 provides a basis for identifying the relevant properties of the subgame-perfect equilibrium, summarised in three propositions.

Proposition 1. A mixed duopoly is impossible if the public firm is at least as efficient as the private firm.

Proof. Inspection of Fig. 1 shows that average-cost pricing augments N's output relative to M's. Since N is at least as efficient and its output is higher, its realised average cost must be lower than M's. As price equals N's average cost, M must be loss-making. Hence, M would not enter. □

Proposition 1 does not resolve whether a mixed duopoly can exist when the public firm is less efficient than the private firm. Under these circumstances, N's response function shifts inwards as shown, for example, by

---

[4] Results are not dramatically altered if fixed costs are non-recurrent and have already been sunk by N prior to the game starting. Essentially, some equilibria in which only M operates are eliminated.

[5] Even if the entrant's profits are included in the social calculus, average cost pricing by the public firm is normally a constrained optimum (Cremer et al., 1989).

[6] Notice that because fixed costs are sunk, there is no discontinuity in the second-stage response functions at M^*.

476   S. Estrin, D. de Meza / Journal of Public Economics 57 (1995) 471–488

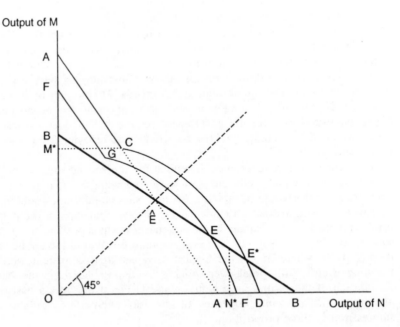

Fig. 1. Second-stage equilibrium.

FGF. The second-stage Nash equilibrium is at E, a public output below N^*, the output at which, because of fixed costs, the private firm breaks even. There is thus an equilibrium with both firms active. Cases of this sort will shortly be explored numerically. However, if entry does occur, the welfare consequences are immediate.

Proposition 2. Mixed duopoly is worse for consumers than statutory monopoly.

Proof. Eliminating the private firm from a mixed duopoly causes a rightward shift in the demand faced by the public firm. As average cost is falling and equal to price, consumers are better off under statutory monopoly. □
   By an obvious extension,

Proposition 3. The mixed duopoly price is higher the more efficient is the private firm.

S. Estrin, D. de Meza / Journal of Public Economics 57 (1995) 471–488 477

3. The benefits of competition

Propositions 1 and 2 indicate that statutory monopoly may have merit because, for some configurations of demand and cost parameters, it will be privately profitable for M to enter the market, even though the emergence of duopoly will reduce consumer welfare. Indeed, at first sight the case for protecting the public firm is compelling since, if repeal has any effect, it is harmful. What is omitted from the analysis, however, is the possibility that repeal eliminates the public firm. Moreover, the introduction of competition may also stimulate efficiency gains in N.[7] As results are now conditional, we explore possibilities numerically. In particular, market demand is assumed to be linear, marginal cost constant, and the declining average cost to be entirely due to a fixed cost. The modelling is detailed in the appendix.

The vertical axis of Fig. 2 shows the efficiency differential, λ, which is the common percentage by which the public firm's fixed and marginal costs exceed those of the private firm. The demand parameters are chosen so that if a fully efficient firm sets price equal to average cost, the price elasticity would be unity. The percentage of fixed costs in total cost at such a

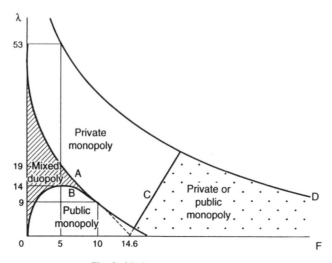

Fig. 2. Market-structure partition.

---

[7] Indeed, comparing Eastern Europe and Western Europe, this may be the major consequence of suppressing competition.

478   *S. Estrin, D. de Meza / Journal of Public Economics 57 (1995) 471–488*

configuration, F, is shown along the horizontal axis. As F varies, marginal cost is adjusted to preserve the efficient break-even average cost at unity.

In Fig. 2, locus A is the upper bound on λ such that the public firm can just cover its cost in a mixed-duopoly equilibrium. From Proposition 1, this threshold occurs where the public firm is inefficient relative to the private firm. When fixed costs are high, potential profits are low, so lowering the maximum inefficiency level consistent with the public firm covering its costs. Moreover, break-even pricing then makes less of a difference to the public firm's output and so lowers its strategic advantage. Hence, locus A is downward sloping. Break-even configurations are shown as Z in Figs. 3(a) and 3(b). What differs between the two cases is that in Fig. 3(a), Z lies to the left of N^*, the maximum public output at which the private firm can break even, whereas in Fig. 3(b), Z is to the right of N^*. In Fig. 3(a), as the efficiency of N increases and its response function shifts up, a stable equilibrium is reached at W, where M just covers its cost. Configurations of this kind are shown in Fig. 2 by locus B, the lower bound on the inefficiency of N consistent with M just surviving. Efficiency differentials intermediate between those implicit in the two response functions support mixed duopoly, and in Fig. 2 appear as the region enclosed by locus A and locus B. In Fig. 3(b) economies of scale are higher than in Fig. 3(a) and as the efficiency of N is raised, the stable equilibrium occurs to the right of W. So,

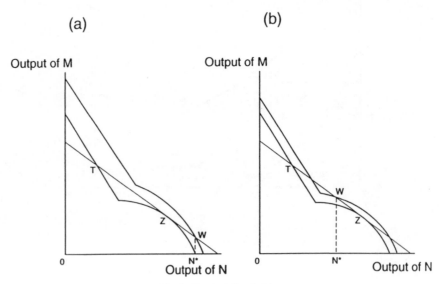

Fig. 3. Survival thresholds.

S. Estrin, D. de Meza / Journal of Public Economics 57 (1995) 471–488   479

if the efficiency of N is below that implicit in the lower response function, only M enters and if the firm's efficiency exceeds this level, it is the sole entrant. When F is sufficiently high there is no mixed duopoly zone. As shown in Fig. 2 this is the case when $F > 10\%$ and then locus A is the boundary between the two kinds of monopoly.

Notice that in both Fig. 3(a) and 3(b) there are also stable equilibria at T. If these are anticipated outcomes, only the private firm enters and price is higher than under mixed duopoly. In assuming these equilibria do not emerge, Fig. 2 does not report the strongest case for statutory monopoly. When the industry is a natural monopoly, which for our assumptions is the case when $F \geq 14.6\%$, the only second-stage equilibria are like T, so only one firm will be active. Locus C plots (λ, F) pairs where the private firm just breaks even and there is no equilibrium in which N covers cost. Finally, with locus D, the maximum λ at which a statutory monopoly can break even, the ingredients are assembled to enable the parameter space to be fully partitioned between the various possible market structures consistent with repeal of statutory monopoly.

The welfare consequences of repeal are summarised in Fig. 4, which is based on the same assumptions as Fig. 2 and reproduces the partitioning loci A and D. Recall that for benefits to flow, it is necessary that statutory monopoly is replaced by a private monopoly. In Fig. 4 locus E shows combinations of F and λ such that price is the same whether the supplier is public or private. Standard assumptions imply that on elimination of the public firm the private firm expands by less than enough to replace the lost output, hence locus E must lie above locus A. So only combinations above

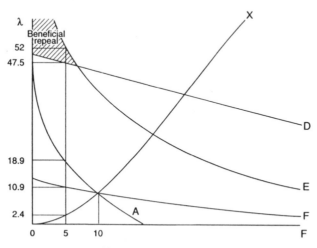

Fig. 4. Welfare partition.

480   S. Estrin, D. de Meza / Journal of Public Economics 57 (1995) 471–488

E and below *D* represent beneficial repeal. Economies of scale must be very low and inefficiency very high for entry to be desirable.

We have seen that if duopoly emerges, consumers are worse off provided that *N*'s cost function is unchanged. However, entry may force *N* to eliminate slack and this is a source of gain to consumers. Suppose that the post-entry efficiency differential is just large enough for *M* to cover its costs (i.e. is given by *B*). The locus *X* in Fig. 4 records the level of pre-entry *X* inefficiency of *N* such that, if wiped out when a mixed duopoly emerges, price remains the same as under statutory monopoly. To interpret *X* suppose that when *F* = 10%, prior to entry the public firm was operating with 19% inefficiency (the height of locus *B* in Fig. 2). Then as shown in Fig. 4, if 9% of this inefficiency were eliminated as a result of competition, mixed duopoly and statutory monopoly yield the same consumer surplus.

Public policy is more likely to be justified on the grounds that reform will benefit consumers than that it will boost profit. Nevertheless, it is of interest to look at the impact of repeal on the sum of profit and consumer surplus. In Fig. 5, locus *G* shows the threshold along which aggregate welfare is the same under mixed duopoly as public monopoly. Locus *F* represents points such that consumer surplus plus profit is the same under private monopoly as statutory monopoly. The regions under which repeal is strictly harmful are shaded. Including profit naturally eliminates some of the area where repeal is disadvantageous, but even with low scale economies and not too

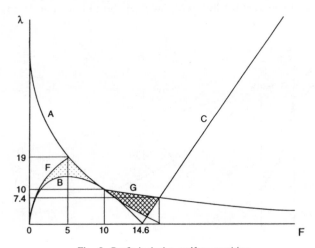

Fig. 5. Profit inclusive welfare partition.

S. Estrin, D. de Meza / Journal of Public Economics 57 (1995) 471–488 481

much inefficiency, there is a considerable area of the parameter space over which it is desirable to suppress competition. In particular, if there is a mixed duopoly with $F > 5\%$, statutory monopoly is always preferable.

We can now interpret the various curves in Figs. 2, 4 and 5 together. Consider, for example, the case of fixed costs 5% of the statutory monopoly's total cost. M does not enter if the post-entry efficiency differential is below 14%. If, $14 < \lambda < 18.9$, there is a duopoly and consumers lose, though if the entrants' profits are included, aggregate welfare is unchanged. For consumers to gain, the locus X shows that competition must have eliminated at least 2.4% of pre-entry inefficiency. When $\lambda > 18.9\%$ the only equilibrium is that the private firm is the sole producer. This is bad news for consumers unless the pre-entry efficiency differential exceeded 47.5%. Even if the criterion is consumer surplus plus profit, there will be welfare losses unless the efficiency differential exceeds 10.9%. Thus, according to Fig. 2, even quite modest economies of scale imply that repeal of the statutory monopoly is only beneficial with substantial inefficiencies.

4. Multiple entry

The analysis so far may seem to be biased in favour of statutory monopoly by a restriction to a single potential entrant. Replacement of a public monopoly by a private monopoly evidently leaves consumers vulnerable, but if repeal results in multiple entry, consumers will be protected by competition. This is particularly so since, in contrast to a regular private industry, in a mixed oligopoly more entry raises profits. The reason is essentially that to cover cost, the public firm must contract its output by more than the entrant produces.

Proposition 4. In the presence of a public firm, profit per private firm is increasing in the number entering.

Proof. In Fig. 5 the mixed duopoly equilibrium is at A. With two private firms, their aggregate output is higher, given that of N, than a single firm would produce. This is a standard property of Cournot–Nash equilibrium (see Seade, 1980) and the implied response function of a private sector comprising two firms is labelled as such in Fig. 6, yielding Nash equilibrium at D. To establish the properties of D note that total output is the same at A and B since both are on the 45° line. It follows that at B the public firm has lowered its output by what the private firm produced in the duopoly

482   S. Estrin, D. de Meza / Journal of Public Economics 57 (1995) 471–488

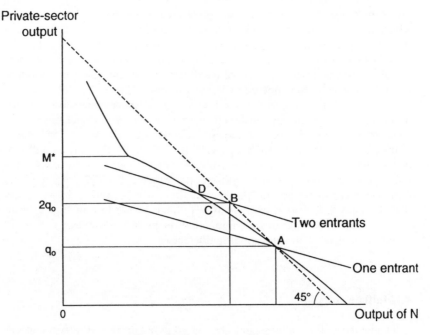

Fig. 6. Multiple entry equilibrium.

equilibrium. So at B, the residual demand of each private firm is the same as is faced by the single private firm in equilibrium at A. Hence, B is on the two-firm, private-sector response function. But at B the residual demand facing N is lower than at A since output by the rest of the industry is higher, implying that the average cost of N is higher at B than at A. As industry output and price are unchanged, it follows that B is not on N's best response function which, for break even, must lie to the left of B. The Nash equilibrium of the second-stage game is thus at D. Industry output is lower than at A and price is higher. As the output of each private firm exceeds that at A and average cost is declining, the profit of each of them is higher than under duopoly. □

Proposition 4 evidently implies that multiple equilibria are on the cards. Either no private firms enter or lots of them do. In fact, if a purely private industry were to support n firms, a mixed oligopoly must also have n active firms. So, if there is a mixed equilibrium there must also be an all private equilibrium, and public monopoly may also be an equilibrium.

S. Estrin, D. de Meza / Journal of Public Economics 57 (1995) 471–488 483

Proposition 5. The number of firms in a free-entry, mixed oligopoly is equal to the number of private firms entering if no public firm exists.

Proof. Suppose that the mixed oligopoly had fewer than n firms. For this to be an equilibrium it follows from Proposition 4 that the entry of another private firm causes the public firm to be loss-making. The extra firm is then sure to be profitable for it faces less competition than it would with $n - 1$ fully efficient profit maximisers. A contradiction also arises if the mixed oligopoly has more than n active firms. In such an equilibrium, the public firm is the budget producer. However, even if it produced the same output as the other firms, all the private firms would be loss-making since there is a private equilibrium with n firms. □

As consumers can only gain if an all private industry has an efficiency advantage more than enough to preclude the entry of the public firm, for welfare purposes it is enough to compare price under a free-entry private oligopoly with that under statutory monopoly. The number of firms entering depends on the level of fixed costs. For the various natural oligopoly intervals, Fig. 7 shows the combinations of λ and F yielding equal price. So above the line is where repeal is advantageous. Finally, notice that Figs. 2 and 7 show that limited entry may be worse than statutory monopoly or free entry. Suppose $\lambda = 6\%$ and $F = 6\%$. Then, from Fig. 2, allowing a single

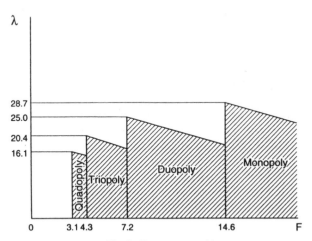

Fig. 7. Free-entry partition.

484   *S. Estrin, D. de Meza / Journal of Public Economics 57 (1995) 471–488*

entrant results in a disadvantageous mixed duopoly, but with free entry a welfare-enhancing quadropoly equilibrium exists.

5. Conclusion

The message of this paper is that in a simple quantity-setting Nash game it may be desirable to award a public firm statutory protection against entry.[8] In the absence of such a policy it is not true that a public firm can necessarily repel entry even when it is socially desirable that it should do so. Equally, there is a danger that statutory monopoly may preserve a public firm when it would be better that it is replaced by more efficient private enterprises. In short, there is merit in the views of both Hill and Mill. Matters cannot be decided a priori.

Acknowledgments

This paper is an extension of part of the theoretical and simulation work reported in Estrin and de Meza (1988). Polly Vizard provided excellent research assistance. We wish to thank two anonymous referees, John Black, Bob Gould, Ben Lockwood, Clive Southey, John Sutton, Hugh Wills, and participants in seminars at the Universities of Bristol, Exeter, Guelph, Quebec à Montreal, Western Ontario and the London Business School, for many helpful comments. Responses to earlier versions by Dobbs and Richards (1990) led to many corrections and modifications.

Appendix

The equations generating Figs. 2, 4, and 7 are derived from the following system:

$$C_M = F + cM , \tag{1}$$

$$C_N = (1 + \lambda)(F + cN) , \tag{2}$$

$$P = \alpha - \beta(M + N) . \tag{3}$$

---

[8] Alternatively, it may be better to follow the Demsetz (1968) proposal of allowing private firms to compete for the monopoly, awarding the franchise to the firm promising the lowest consumer price. There are well-known problems with this scheme, but the issues are not relevant here. Our focus is not on how to handle a natural monopoly but on the merit of the government in creating a monopoly when competition is feasible.

S. Estrin, D. de Meza / *Journal of Public Economics 57 (1995) 471–488* 485

Eqs. (1) and (2) are the total cost functions of the private and the public firm, and Eq. (3) is the inverse market demand curve. The output of an efficient break-even pricer is the largest root of

$$\alpha - \beta N = F/N + c . \tag{4}$$

Costs are normalised so that the solution of Eq. (4) is $N = P = 1$ and hence $\alpha = 1 + \beta$ is imposed. Moreover, the plotting is for the case that, with efficient break-even pricing, demand elasticity is unity, which requires $\alpha = 2$ and $\beta = 1$. As F varies, the price set by an efficient break-even pricer is maintained at unity by adjusting c. Thus,

$$c = 1 - F . \tag{5}$$

To put λ and F in percentage terms divide each by 100 in all equations.

A mixed-duopoly equilibrium requires that both firms be on their best-response functions. For the private firms this is the standard condition that

$$M = 0.5(2 - c - N) . \tag{6}$$

The public firm selects the highest output at which price equals average cost, which, from Eqs. (3) and (4), implies that

$$N = [2 - (1 + \lambda)c - M + \sqrt{((1 + \lambda)c - 2 + M)^2 - 4(1 + \lambda)F}]/2 . \tag{7}$$

Solving Eqs. (6) and (7) and picking the largest root yields the stable, mixed-duopoly equilibrium in the second-stage game. The output of the private firm is then

$$M = (-(12c - 8 - 8(1 + \lambda)c)$$
$$+ \sqrt{(12c - 8 - 8(1 + \lambda)c)^2 - 32(8(1 + \lambda)c - 8c + 4F(1 + \lambda) + c^2 4\lambda)}/16 . \tag{8}$$

Locus A. The public firm is at its survival threshold in a mixed-duopoly equilibrium so its response function is tangent to that of M. This requires that there is a single root to (8). Making use of Eq. (5) to substitute for c, the locus is

$$\lambda =$$
$$\frac{(1 - F)^2 + 2(1 - F) + 2F - \sqrt{((1 - F)^2 + 2(1 - F) + 2F)^2 - (1 - F)^2((1 - F)^2 + 4(1 - F))}}{2(1 - F)^2} - 1 . \tag{9}$$

Locus B. For M to break even in the mixed-duopoly equilibrium it follows from Eqs. (1), (3) and (6) that

$$M = \sqrt{F} . \tag{10}$$

486   S. Estrin, D. de Meza / Journal of Public Economics 57 (1995) 471–488

Setting the RHS of Eq. (8) equal to $\sqrt{F}$ and solving for λ yields locus B:

$$\lambda = \frac{2(1-F)-(1-F)^2 - F^{0.5}(3(1-F)-2)-2F}{2(1-F)+F-2F^{0.5}(1-F)-(1-F)^2} - 1 . \tag{11}$$

Locus C. When $F > 14.6$ and $\lambda > 0$ the public firm cannot cover its costs in the second-stage, mixed-duopoly equilibrium. This locus represents the value of λ just high enough for the private firm to cover its cost. Solving Eq. (5) and the analagous profit-maximising response function for the public firm, $N = (2 - \lambda c - M)/2$, yields the regular Cournot–Nash equilibrium

$$M = \{2 + c[1 - 2(\lambda - 1)]\}/3 . \tag{12}$$

Solving Eqs. (10) and (12),

$$\lambda = 1.5\sqrt{F} - F - 1 . \tag{13}$$

Locus D. Under statutory monopoly, the output of the public firm is the largest root of

$$2 - N = (1 + \lambda)(F/N + c) , \tag{14}$$

which is

$$N = 0.5(2 - (1 + \lambda)c + \sqrt{((1 + \lambda)c - 2)^2 - 4(1 + \lambda)F}) . \tag{15}$$

If the public firm is too inefficient it cannot cover its cost even under statutory monopoly. The relevant survival threshold occurs when there is a single root to Eq. (15), i.e. the expression below the square root sign is zero, which implies

$$\lambda = \frac{2 - 2\sqrt{1 - (1 - F)^2}}{(1 - F)^2} - 1 . \tag{16}$$

Locus E. If the private firm has a monopoly its output is

$$M = 1 - 0.5c . \tag{17}$$

Consumers are as well off as under statutory monopoly if the outputs determined by Eqs. (15) and (17) are equal, which requires

$$\lambda = \frac{(1 + F)^2 - 4}{2(1 - F) - 4(1 - F) - 4F} - 1 . \tag{18}$$

Locus X. Suppose that the public firm is just sufficiently inefficient for a mixed-duopoly to emerge, that is F and λ satisfy Eq. (11). As the private firm breaks even, its average-cost curve is tangent to its residual demand curve, which requires

S. Estrin, D. de Meza / *Journal of Public Economics 57 (1995) 471–488* 487

$$P = \sqrt{F} + c. \tag{19}$$

Now suppose that prior to entry the cost function of the public firm is $C_N = (1 + \lambda + X)(F - cN)$ so that X is the proportion of inefficiency eliminated by competition. Solving Eq. (15) for this augmented cost function and finding the associated price, it is set equal to the price determined by Eq. (19) to obtain

$$X = \frac{1 - F + 2F^{1.5} - F^2}{1 - F^{0.5} + F + F^{1.5} - F^2} - 1 - \lambda. \tag{20}$$

Finally, Eq. (11) is used to substitute for λ. So Eq. (20) gives the percentage by which entry must cause the public firm's cost to decline if a threshold mixed-duopoly leaves consumers just as well off as under statutory monopoly. Note that this is a lower bound on the X-inefficiency required to justify repeal in that if λ lies above locus B, the loss from mixed duopoly is greater so the offsetting efficiency gain must be larger if it is to offset the dissipatory effects of entry.

Locus F. The profit of a private monopoly is

$$\pi = 0.25(1 + F)^2 - F. \tag{21}$$

Making use of Eqs. (15) and (17) the difference between price under public and private monopoly is

$$\Delta = 0.5(1 - \lambda) + 0.5\sqrt{(\lambda c - 2)^2 - 4\lambda F}. \tag{22}$$

Adding the profit of the private firm to the loss of computer surplus, when a statutory monopoly is displaced by a private firm, aggregate surplus is unchanged if

$$\pi - 0.5\Delta^2 - N\Delta = 0. \tag{23}$$

Locus F is found by substituting Eqs. (15), (21), (22) in (23).

Locus G. This repeats the exercise of locus F for the mixed-duopoly case. Using Eq. (6), total output is $2 - c - M$, where M is given by Eq. (8). Price is then found from the inverse demand curve as $c + M$, so profit is $M^2 - F$. Relative to statutory monopoly, the increase in price is $2 - N - M - c$. With these redefinitions, locus G is the plot of Eq. (23).

Fig. 7. In a free-entry Cournot–Nash equilibrium with identical profit maximisers standard calculations give the number of active firms as the largest integer no greater than

$$n = (1 + F)F^{-0.5} - 1. \tag{24}$$

488   *S. Estrin, D. de Meza / Journal of Public Economics 57 (1995) 471–488*

Eq. (24) locates the various oligopoly intervals in the figure. Taking the total output of an industry of n private firms engaged in Cournot–Nash competition and setting it equal to output under statutory monopoly, as given by Eq. (15), yields the welfare partition of the figure:

$$\lambda = \frac{4(n-1)^2/(n+1)^2 + 4(1-F)^2(n/(n+1))^2 - 8(1-F)n(n-1)(n+1) - 4}{4(1-F)n/(n+1) - 4(1-F)(n-1)/(n+1) - 4(1-F) - 4F} - 1.$$

(25)

References

Albon, R., 1987, Privatise the post, Policy Study No. 82 (Centre for Policy Studies, London).

Baumol, W.J., R. Panzar and R.D. Willig, 1982, Contestable markets and the theory of industrial structure (Harcourt, Brace, Jovanovich, New York).

Beato, P. and A. Mas-Colell, 1984, Marginal cost pricing as a regulation mechanism in mixed markets, in: M. Marchand, P. Pestieu and H. Tulkens, eds., The performance of public enterprises (North-Holland, Amsterdam).

Bos, D., 1986, Public enterprise economics (North-Holland, Amsterdam).

Bos, D., 1991, Privatisation: A theoretical treatment (Clarendon Press, Oxford).

Coase, R.H., 1939, Rowland Hill and the penny post, Economica 6, 423–435.

Corby, M.E., 1979, The postal business 1969–79 (Kogan Page, London).

Cremer, H., M. Marchand and J.-F. Thiesse, 1989, The public firm as an instrument for regulation on oligopolistic markets, Oxford Economic Papers 41, 283–301.

Crew, M.A. and P.R. Kleindorfer, 1985, Governance costs and rate of return regulation, Journal of Institutional and Theoretical Economics, March.

Demsetz, H., 1968, Why regulate utilities?, Journal of Law and Economics 11, 55–65.

De Fraja, G. and F. Delbono, 1989, Alternative strategies of a public enterprise in oligopoly, Oxford Economic Papers 41, 302–311.

De Fraja, G. and F. Delbono, 1990, Game theoretic models of mixed oligopoly, Journal of Economic Surveys 4, 1–17.

Dobbs, I. and P. Richards, 1990, A critique of the DHL report on the monopoly, The Post Office.

Estrin, S. and D. de Meza, 1988, Should the Post Office's statutory monopoly be lifted?, London School of Economics, mimeo, September.

Friedman, M., 1962, Capitalism and freedom (University of Chicago Press, Chicago).

Mill, J.S., 1926, Principles of political economy (Largrass, London).

Niskanen, W.A., Jr., 1971, Bureaucracy and representative government (Aldine–Atherton, Chicago).

Rees, R., 1984, A positive theory of the public enterprise, in: M. Marchand, P. Pestieau and H. Tulkens, eds. The performance of public enterprises (North-Holland, Amsterdam).

Seade, J., 1980, On the effects of entry, Econometrica 48, no. 2, 479–489.

Tulkens, H., 1968, Programming analysis of the post service (Librarie Universitaire, Louvain).

Vickers, J. and G. Yarrow, 1988, Privatisation – an economic analysis (MIT Press, Cambridge, MA).

[10]

THE ECONOMIC JOURNAL

MARCH 1996

The Economic Journal, **106** (*March*), 309–319. © Royal Economic Society 1996. Published by Blackwell Publishers, 108 Cowley Road, Oxford OX4 1JF, UK and 238 Main Street, Cambridge, MA 02142, USA.

A THEORY OF PRIVATISATION

Maxim Boycko, Andrei Shleifer and Robert W. Vishny[1]

Public enterprises around the world have proved to be highly inefficient, primarily because they pursue strategies, such as excess employment, that satisfy the political objectives of politicians who control them. Privatisation of public enterprises can raise the cost to politicians of influencing them, since subsidies to private firms necessary to force them to remain inefficient are politically harder to sustain than wasted profits of the state firms. In this way, privatisation leads to efficient restructuring of firms. Moreover, privatisation is more effective when combined with a tight monetary policy, and when the new owners of firms are profit maximising investors, rather than their employees or even managers.

In the last decade, privatisation of state enterprises has swept the world. Thousands of state firms from Africa, Asia, Latin America, Western and Eastern Europe have gone private (Kikeri *et al.* 1992). A critical factor behind this move to privatisation is the well-documented poor performance of public enterprises. Donahue (1989) surveys multiple studies showing the significantly higher cost of public relative to private provision of municipal services in the United States. Lopez de Silanes (1993) documents the inferior profitability of state relative to private firms in Mexico in the 1980s. Mueller (1989) and Vining and Boardman (1992) survey dozens of studies of public and private firms around the world, most of which show that private firms are more efficient. More recent studies have actually shown that efficiency improves after privatisation (World Bank, 1992; Megginson *et al.*, 1994). In this paper, we develop a model of privatisation that explains the relative inefficiency of public firms and the improvements of efficiency after privatisation, as well as several other empirical findings concerning privatisation.

The starting point of our analysis is the commonplace observation that public enterprises are inefficient because they address the objectives of politicians rather than maximise efficiency. One key objective of politicians is employment: they care about votes of the people whose jobs are in danger and, in many cases, unions have significant influence on political parties. For example, Donahue (1989) describes evidence showing higher employment per unit of output in publicly provided municipal services. The British government for a long time refused to close grossly inefficient coal mines to preserve mining jobs. While excess employment is not the only politically demanded inefficiency of state firms (for example, Credit Lyonnais, the money losing French state

[1] This paper was presented by Shleifer as the Paish Lecture at the Royal Economic Society 1995 meeting. The authors are grateful to the Bradley, Sage and National Science Foundations for the support of this research, to Eric Maskin for very helpful comments, and to Ilya Segal for excellent research assistance.

bank, made its worst loans to the friends of the governing socialist party),[2] it is surely the most commonly noted one. Below, we focus on the implications of the political demand for excess employment by public enterprises.

In Section II, we present a simple model in which a spending politician, such as an industrial minister, who controls the decisions of a public enterprise, forces it, for political reasons, to spend too much on labour. This politician does not fully internalise the cost of the profits foregone by the Treasury and by private shareholders that the firm might have. The manager can bribe this politician to agree to lower employment, and in some cases corruption improves efficiency. However, corruption contracts are usually neither legal nor enforceable, so inefficiency is not necessarily cured by corruption.

This analysis raises a question: can a reformer make it more difficult for spending politicians to benefit from excess employment of public enterprises? A reformer in this model is a newly elected leader, such as Margaret Thatcher in Britain, Carlos Salinas in Mexico, or Vaclav Klaus in the Czech Republic, who derives political benefits not from excess employment in public enterprises, but from low spending and taxes. It is not that reformers are benevolent, but rather that their political constituents are taxpayers rather than the beneficiaries of public largesse. These reformers want to constrain the actions of their own spending ministries, or alternatively, to tie the hands of future governments (such as future Labour governments in Britain) that might be more inclined to spend money on public enterprise employment. In effect, these reformers represent the interests of the Treasury against those of the spending ministries.

Our paper discusses privatisation as a strategy available to the reformers to reduce inefficiency of public enterprises. By privatisation we mean a combination of the reallocation of control rights over employment from politicians to managers and the increase in cash flow ownership of managers and private investors.[3] At first glance, it seems that privatisation should reduce employment if managers maximise profits and have no interest in excess employment. However, a spending politician still wants to influence firms and can use government subsidies to convince their managers to keep up employment. In principle, there is nothing magic about privatisation: just as the spending politician was willing to give up profits of a public firm on excess labour spending, he is willing to subsidise a privatised firm to 'buy' excess labour spending. How, then, does privatisation serve the reformer's interests and separate the firm from the spending politician?

This question has been addressed by several authors. Schmidt (1990) argues that privatisation reduces the amount of information that politicians have, which may lead to the reduction of subsidies and restructuring. Shapiro and Willig (1990) make a clear case that privatisation must draw a line between politicians and firms, and like Schmidt, use an information argument to show how it works. We agree with the general approach of these papers, although we are not sure why privatisation necessarily changes the information of politicians.

---

[2] *The Economist*, April 9, 1994.
[3] Grossman and Hart (1986) stress the distinction between control and cash flow rights.

In this paper, we argue that it may be politically less costly for the politician to spend the profits of the firm on labour without remitting them to the Treasury than to generate new subsidies for the privatised firm. The public and the reformers may not be aware of the potential profits that a state firm is wasting, but they are keenly aware of the alternative uses of tax revenues, and would not wish to spend public money to subsidise private firms not to restructure. This difference between the political costs of foregone profits of state firms and of subsidies to private firms is the channel through which privatisation works in this paper. One important conclusion of this analysis is that a tough monetary policy makes privatisation much more effective.

In Sections I and II, we discuss a very simple model in which the only active players are the spending politician and the manager. In Section III, we consider the role of other potentially active players, such as the employees and the core investors. We discuss the effect of worker ownership and outside investor ownership on the likelihood of restructuring. In our model, different types of privatisation have different implications for efficiency.

Section IV concludes.

I. POLITICAL CONTROL OF FIRMS

A simple model

We consider a firm that only chooses its level of spending on labour E. It can spend an efficient amount L or a higher amount $H > L$. The higher spending comes from excess wages and employment. The restriction of only two levels of spending is introduced for simplicity.

There are two players in this model who have preferences over E: the politician and the manager. The manager here is assumed to represent private shareholders. We begin by assuming that the manager and shareholders own a fraction α of the firm's profits, while the Treasury owns a fraction $(1 - \alpha)$. The politician himself owns no equity. In a public firm, α is close to zero, whereas in a private firm, α is close to 1.

To begin, we assume that the objective function of the politician (in dollars) is given by:

$$Up = qE - m(1 - \alpha) E. \qquad (1)$$

The politician prefers higher labour spending since it is a source of political benefits, such as voting support from the employees and labour unions. The marginal benefit to him of an extra dollar of such spending is $q < 1$. But spending more on labour reduces the value of the Treasury's share of profits of the firm. The politician cares about these profits because the Treasury can impose sanctions on him if the firm loses (or fails to make) money. Importantly, the politician does not care directly about the share of the profits foregone by the manager and private shareholders, which matter only to the extent that angering shareholders reduces the net potential political benefit of excess employment q. The cost to the politician of a dollar of profits foregone by the Treasury as a result of spending on labour is m. We assume $m < 1$ because the politician cares less about the Treasury's income than he does about his own money. This, too, creates a bias for too much employment. The politician's objective function thus trades off the political benefits of higher employment against the political costs of the profits foregone by the Treasury.

The objective function of the manager (shareholders) is simply given by his share of profits:

$$Um = -\alpha E. \tag{2}$$

We can extend the model to allow the manager to care about employment directly; the results are very similar as long as the manager cares relatively more about profits than the politician does.

The critical parameter in this model is who controls labour spending. Initially, we assume that the firm is publicly controlled, meaning that E is chosen by the politician. This assumption accurately represents the situation with most public enterprises, where the government exerts substantial influence over their key decisions, particularly when political issues such as employment are involved. For example, the French government refused to back the management of Air France in its attempt to reduce labour costs, with the result that the management left and the employees stayed.

When the politician controls E, we assume he chooses $E = H$. Denote by $\Delta E = H - L$ the incremental gain in labour spending from switching from L to H. Then the assumption that the politician uses his control rights to choose $E = H$ can be rewritten as:

$$m(1 - \alpha) < q. \tag{3}$$

This condition says that political benefits per dollar of extra spending on labour exceed political costs per dollar of profits foregone by the Treasury from such spending. In this way, we illustrate the idea that political control leads to inefficiencies that benefit politicians at the expense of the Treasury and other shareholders.

Corruption

Even if the politician controls labour spending and (3) holds, it might be in the interest of the manager (and shareholders) to bribe the politician to cut the firm's labour spending. There are two ways of thinking about this bribe. First, it could be a payoff to change E (or some other decision that the politician imposes on the firm) from H to L. Second, it could be a payment to transfer the control rights over E from the politician to the manager. Since in this model the manager chooses $E = L$ once he gets control rights, the bribe necessary to buy control from the politician is the same as the bribe needed to get the politician to change his decision. We show below that corruption reduces the set of parameter values for which labour spending is excessive.

Denote the necessary bribe by b. With bribes, the politician's utility is given by:

$$Up = -m(1 - \alpha) E + qE + b, \tag{4}$$

and the manager's utility is given by:

$$Um = -\alpha E - b. \tag{5}$$

Since utility is transferable, the manager succeeds in bribing the politician to choose $E = L$ if their combined utility is higher at L than at H, i.e., if

$$m(1 - \alpha) + \alpha > q. \tag{6}$$

Both (3) and (6) can be satisfied simultaneously: the politician chooses H without corruption but is willing to be bribed and choose efficient labour spending. The bribe divides the surplus between the manager and the politician according to the Nash or some other bargaining solution.

This result illustrates the Coase theorem for our model. When side-payments in the form of bribes are allowed, the manager and the politician choose the outcome that, from their joint viewpoint, is the most efficient. If (6) holds, the 'jointly efficient' outcome coincides with the socially efficient one $E = L$, but if (6) fails, the two may differ. Condition (6) is different from social efficiency in two ways. First, when $m < 1$, the politician does not fully internalise the foregone profits from excessive labour spending. The Treasury is too soft to make him act as a full shareholder. Second, excess labour spending benefits the politician since it enables him to get votes away from other politicians, but it should not enter the social welfare function. Thus corruption generally raises efficiency, in that it allows private investors to buy their way out of some of the inefficiencies demanded by politicians, but it does not always lead to first best.[4]

There are, however, some problems with using corruption to renegotiate to a more efficient resource allocation, even if (6) holds. First, corruption in most societies is illegal, so both the giver and the receiver of a bribe risk going to jail. The illegality of corruption is a particular problem when the bribe-supported outcome leads to substantial losses by the workers, who have an incentive to expose the politician. For the same reason of illegality, the corruption contract is unenforceable in courts. After collecting a bribe, the politician can renew his demand that labour spending be kept at a high level, or ask for another bribe. Since the manager has no recourse to enforce the initial agreement, he might never offer a bribe in the first place. Of course, there are other mechanisms of contract enforcement, such as reputations, but in transition economies the horizons of politicians are often too short to develop a reputation for efficient bribe taking.[5] In this case, we are back to the case of the politician choosing the inefficient outcome as long as condition (3) holds.

II. PRIVATISATION

By privatisation we mean a combination of two changes undertaken by a reformer. The first is turnover of control from spending politicians to managers, often referred to as corporatisation. Such turnover can be implemented by a strong reform government that effectively suppresses the ministries and the bureaucracy, as happened in Czechoslovakia. Alternatively, such turnover can happen more spontaneously, as the power of bureaucracy to protect its control rights diminishes. Such slow turnover of control from politicians to managers occurred in Russia in the early 1990s.

The second change that is usually part of most privatisations is the reduction of the cash flow ownership by the Treasury and the increase of cash flow ownership of managers and outside shareholders. The Treasury can sell its

[4] See Leff (1964), Rose-Ackerman (1978), Shleifer and Vishny (1993, 1994).
[5] For a further discussion of this issue, see Shleifer (1994).

shares for cash, or it can give them away through vouchers or some other allocation scheme. Our model shows how both the reallocation of control rights and the increase in private cash flow rights contribute to restructuring.[6]

When the managers and shareholders interested in maximising profits get control over labour spending, they obviously choose $E = L$. This, however, is not the end of the story. For just as before a manager paid a politician with control rights to agree to $E = L$, the politician can now try to pay shareholders not to restructure. The mechanism that politicians use is typically not bribes, but subsidies from the Treasury to the firms, also known as soft budget constraints.[7] Indeed, this is the main question about privatisation: why would a politician fail to buy his way to high labour spending through subsidies? To show how privatisation leads to restructuring, we must establish conditions under which managers with control rights choose to restructure even when they must forego subsidies from the Treasury.

Denote the subsidy from the Treasury to the firm by t. Since the Treasury owns $(1-\alpha)$ of the cash flows, it gets the fraction $(1-\alpha)$ of this subsidy back, so the effective subsidy is αt. If the politician could ask the Treasury to subsidise the firm at no cost to himself, he would pay the firm infinite subsidies not to restructure and no restructuring will ever take place. But the Treasury has to raise the money for the subsidies through either taxes or inflation, both of which are unpopular. We denote the cost to the politician of making a (net) subsidy αt by $k\alpha t$. In the plausible case, $k < 1$, since subsidies are less expensive to the politician than bribes out of his own pocket, which correspond to $k = 1$.

This model has two parameters that reflect the cost to the politician of foregone Treasury revenue: m and k. The first measures the cost to the politician of profits foregone by the Treasury, the second measures his political cost of subsidies. If the Treasury suffers no illusions from the corporate veil, then $m = k$. However, it is more reasonable to suppose that it is easier for the politician to squander a firm's profits on inefficiencies than to get additional subsidies for it, in which case $m < k$. When a firm squanders its profits, most members of the government do not known that it is potentially profitable and hence do not claim a piece of its profits for the Treasury and indirectly for their own pet projects. As a result, the minister who oversees this firm can spend the profits on political benefits, such as employment at a relatively low political cost. In contrast, when a firm receives a subsidy, the minister must compete for the resources of the Treasury with all the other politicians who argue for their favourite projects. As a result, buying political benefits with the money that is already in the Treasury is more expensive than just spending the profits of the firm. We keep the two parameters k and m separate to be able to evaluate the effect of each on the likelihood of restructuring.

[6] An alternative model of privatisation is to keep control in the hands of politicians but also to give them personal cash flow rights. Such 'nomenklatura privatisation' is easy to analyse in our model, and can be shown to increase efficiency relative to political control with no cash flow rights. Although nomenklatura privatisation has sometimes been advocated for Eastern Europe, it is politically too unpopular to make it a viable privatisation strategy.

[7] Kornai (1979) is the classical study of soft budget constraints. More recent models include Dewatripont and Maskin (1990), Li (1992), and Schmidt (1990).

We assume that corruption is infeasible (bribes are equivalent to the case of $k = 1$), since we have already noted some problems with bribes, and we want to focus on new issues. The objective function of the politician is given by:

$$Up = -m(1-\alpha) E + qE - k\alpha t, \tag{7}$$

and the objective function of the manager is given by:

$$Um = -\alpha E + \alpha t. \tag{8}$$

We can compute the Nash bargaining solution to this problem. Without subsidies, the manager chooses efficient labour spending L. He and the politician then bargain and he chooses labour spending H if he is better off with H and a transfer than he is with L. The politician's incremental utility from switching to H is given by:

$$-m(1-\alpha) \Delta E + q\Delta E - k\alpha t \tag{9}$$

and the manager's incremental utility from switching to H is given by:

$$-\alpha\Delta E + \alpha t. \tag{10}$$

The Nash Bargaining solution is given by maximising the product of (9) and (10) over t, which yields the equilibrium transfer:

$$t = \Delta E[-m(1-\alpha) + q + k\alpha]/(2k\alpha). \tag{11}$$

This bargain fails to be struck if the manager (or the politician) is worse off with $E = H$ and transfer t than he is with $E = L$ and no transfer. The condition for neither of them benefitting from the switch [i.e. both (9) and (10) are negative with t given by (11)] is:

$$k\alpha + m(1-\alpha) > q. \tag{12}$$

When (12) holds, privatisation leads to restructuring in that the politician cannot successfully use subsidies to convince the manager to choose $E = H$.

The left hand side of (12) measures the cost to the politician of getting the firm not to restructure, in terms of both the foregone profits and the needed subsidies. The right hand side is the benefit to the politician of high labour spending. When the cost exceeds the benefit, the politician cannot convince the manager not to restructure. To understand why privatisation works in this model, we can compare (12) to (3) and (6).

The difference between (12) and (3) is the presence of the term αk in (12): the cost of getting the firm not to restructure is higher for the politician after privatisation. Privatisation works because, to convince the manager who has control rights to have high labour costs, the politician must compensate him (and shareholders) for foregone profits, which are proportional to the privatised cash flow stake α. In contrast, when the politician controls the firm, he does not need to pay for the profits foregone by the private investors. The politician pays for the profits foregone by the private shareholders with subsidies, and the cost to him of a dollar of subsidies is k. The term αk thus measures the cost to the politician of convincing the manager with control rights not to restructure.

The difference between (12) and (6) is that (12) has αk where (6) has α. When the manager bribes the politician to allow low labour spending, his foregone profits from high labour spending are also fully internalised, except now the cost of a dollar of foregone profits is exactly a dollar. With privatisation rather than bribes, the cost of a dollar of foregone profits is k rather than a dollar, so privatisation is not quite as effective as corruption [(12) is harder to satisfy than (6)]. However, corruption and privatisation work in similar ways: they get the politician to internalise the cost of profits foregone by the manager and outside shareholders. Since corruption has its own problems, privatisation may be the best available way to stimulate restructuring.

When does (12) hold and (3) fail? First, even for a fixed α and $k = m$, the left hand side of (12) is higher than that of (3) because, once control rights are turned over from the politician to the manager, the politician has to compensate the manager for the foregone profits if he wants high employment. By making the politician internalise the cost of the inefficiency borne by the manager and shareholders, this transfer of control encourages restructuring.

Second, when $k > m$, the left hand side of (12) rises with α, and hence higher private ownership is conducive to restructuring. As cash flow ownership is transferred from the Treasury to the manager (and outside shareholders), the politician must pay for excess labour spending not in terms of relatively cheap to him profits foregone by the Treasury, but in terms of relatively expensive to him subsidies. As a result, as more cash flows are privatised, condition (12) is more likely to become satisfied even when (3) fails. When subsidies are costlier to the politician than foregone profits, privatisation of cash flows and not just the transfer of control rights raises the overall cost to the politician of preventing restructuring. In this case, which we regard as the most plausible, a high α is essential for the restructuring to take place.

A high k is naturally interpreted as a tough monetary policy stance. Because a tough monetary stance makes subsidies costly to the politician, it facilitates restructuring. Indeed, condition (12) shows that there is an interaction between k and α: the harder is the monetary policy stance, the lower is the management ownership necessary to bring about restructuring. This result may describe the restructuring in Poland of public but managerially controlled firms during the regime of a restrictive monetary policy, which occurred even before privatisation (see Pinto *et al.* 1993). At the same time, when monetary policy is extremely loose, as it was in Russian in 1993, even high management ownership does not induce managers to give up huge government subsidies and restructure. Indeed, if k is low, no α might be high enough to satisfy (12). More generally, both a high k, meaning a restrictive monetary policy, and a high α might be needed to assure restructuring. We have made this argument informally in our earlier paper on the Russian privatisation (Boycko *et al.* 1993).

We began this paper by asking: how does privatisation work? In this section, we proposed a channel through which privatisation widens the separation between the manager and the politician, and in this way stimulates restructuring. By transferring control from politicians to the managers, privatisation makes politicians accountable for the profits used on excess labour spending, since they need to subsidise the firm to convince managers to incur this spending. By transferring cash flow rights from the Treasury to the managers (and outside shareholders), privatisation forces politicians to pay for these foregone profits not through the relatively cheap mechanism of failing to remit profits to the Treasury, but through a more expensive mechanism of extracting subsidies from the Treasury. Privatisation thus works because, first, it makes politicians pay for the private share of profits, and, second, it raises the cost of such payments.

III. DESIRABLE OWNERSHIP STRUCTURES

In the previous sections, we examined two types of control over firms: that by politicians and that by managers. Managers were not distinguished from outside shareholders. The reality is more complicated. In many countries, enterprise employees get significant control rights even before privatisation. In addition, managers do not always have the same preferences as outside shareholders. In thinking about desirable control structures, we can rank potential shareholders in terms of their concerns for labour spending versus profits. Thus employees are even more concerned about labour spending relative to foregone profits than the politicians. After all, the politicians' interest in labour spending is derived from pressure from the unions and the (potentially) unemployed. Managers in reality are in between politicians and outside shareholders, since managers have some concern for empire building/employment whereas outsiders have none.

The fundamental implication of our analysis is that the closer are shareholders' tastes to those of the politicians, the less likely restructuring is to occur. When these shareholders get control rights, it is relatively cheaper for politicians to convince them not to restructure through the use of subsidies.

This simple logic has several implications. First, it suggests that worker control is bad for restructuring. Workers are unlikely to want layoffs necessary for restructuring to begin with, especially if they can get subsidies. Formally, if we replace the manager's objective function (2) by one that puts some weight on labour spending, it is easy to check that restructuring is less likely. This result confirms well established scepticism about worker control (as opposed to control-free cash flow ownership common in the United States and other countries – see Hansmann (1990)). It is also consistent with scepticism about significant worker ownership in privatisation (Lipton and Sachs, 1990; Boycko *et al.* 1993).

Second, very similar logic suggests that, from the point of view of restructuring, control by large outside investors, who are unlikely to care about employment, is superior to control by managers, who care about it more. The reason, as before, is that large investors are harder to convince through subsidies not to restructure since their tastes are farther away from those of the politicians. In addition, large outside investors, unlike managers, need not be cash constrained, and hence could afford a larger ownership stake α, which also makes effective subsidisation harder. This result suggests that the presence of large outside investors is conducive to efficiency (see Shleifer and Vishny, 1986). It accords well with recommendations for core investors for East European privatisation programmes (see Frydman and Rapaczynski, 1991; Lipton and Sachs, 1990, and Phelps *et al.* 1993), which also happens to be a common practice in other countries, such as Mexico and France.

The result on desirability of large shareholders should be interpreted carefully. The reason that outside shareholders promote restructuring is their interest in profits. If large shareholders are politicised, in the sense that they are pressured or bribed to bring their objectives in line with those of the politicians, they can become detrimental to restructuring. In Russia, for example, politicians want to create industrial holding companies that become core investors in privatised firms. This strategy is designed to increase political influence on firms, not to reduce it. Indeed, throughout the world, government holding companies come to represent the tastes of the politicians, and as a result, slow down rather than encourage restructuring.

A more subtle example of the same potential danger would be privatisation in Poland, in which several government-sponsored mutual funds are to become controlling shareholders of privatising companies through a free allocation of shares to these funds, which in turn are to be owned by Polish citizens. This programme is intended to be a quick way to bring core investors to privatised firms, provided that those investors maximise profits. If, in contrast, the government-regulated mutual funds come to represent the preferences of politicians, they might work to prevent restructuring rather than facilitate it. To be effective, large blockholders must be private parties whose objective is to maximise profits.

IV. CONCLUSION

This paper started with an empirically plausible assumption that the inefficiency of state firms results from their pursuing well specified objectives of politicians, such as excess labour spending. We have presented a model in which privatisation effectively drives a wedge between politicians and managers, i.e., depoliticises firms and leads to their restructuring, even when politicians can use subsidies to convince privatised firms not to restructure, In this model, privatisation and an effective stabilisation policy can work together to make restructuring more likely, by making it too costly for politicians to subsidise firms.

At a more general level, this paper tried to show that the critical agency problem that explains the inefficiency of public firms is the agency problem with politicians rather than that with managers. We believe that managerial discretion problems are usually minor relative to political discretion problems. Privatisation works because it controls political discretion.

Russian Privatisation Centre

Harvard University

University of Chicago

REFERENCES

Boycko, Maxim, Shleifer, Andrei and Vishny, Robert W. (1993). 'Privatizing Russia.' *Brookings Papers on Economic Activity*, no. 2, pp. 139–92.
Coase, Ronald H. (1960). 'The problem of social cost.' *Journal of Law and Economics*, vol. 3, pp. 1–44.
Dewatripont, Mathias and Maskin, Eric S. (1990). 'Credit and efficiency in centralized and decentralized economies.' Harvard University (mimeo).
Donahue, John D. (1989). *The Privatization Process.* New York: Basic Books.
Frydman, Roman and Rapaczynski, Andrzej (1991). 'Markets and institutions in large-scale privatization.' In *Reforming Central and Eastern European Economies* (ed. V. Corbo, F. Coricelli and J. Bossak). Washington, D.C.: The World Bank.
Grossman, Sanford J. and Hart, Oliver D. (1986). 'The costs and benefits of ownership: a theory of vertical and lateral integration.' *Journal of Political Economy*, vol. 94, pp. 691–719.
Hansmann, Henry (1990). 'When does workers' ownership work? ESOPs, law firms, codetermination and economic democracy.' *Yale Law Journal*, vol. 99, pp. 1749–816.
Kikeri, Sunita, Nellis, John and Shirley, Mary (1992). *Privatization: The Lessons of Experience.* Washington, DC: The World Bank.
Kornai, Janos (1979). 'Resource *vs.* demand-constrained systems.' *Econometrica*, vol. 47, pp. 801–19.
Leff, Nathaniel (1964). 'Economic development through bureaucratic corruption.' *American Behavioral Scientist*, vol. 8, pp. 8–14.
Li, Daokui (1992). 'Public ownership as the cause of a soft budget constraint.' Harvard (mimeo).
Lipton, David and Sachs, Jeffrey D. (1990). 'Privatization in Eastern Europe: the case of Poland.' *Brookings Papers on Economic Activity*, pp. 293–341.
Lopez de Silanes, Florencio (1994). 'Determinants of privatization prices.' Harvard (mimeo).
Megginson, William L, Nash, Robert C. and van Randenborgh, Mathias (1994). 'The financial and operating performance of newly privatized firms.' *Journal of Finance*, vol. 49, pp. 403–52.
Mueller, Dennis C. (1989). *Public Choice.* Cambridge: Cambridge University Press.
Phelps, Edmund S., Frydman, Roman, Rapaczynski, Andrzej and Shleifer, Andrei (1993). 'Needed mechanisms for corporate governance and finance in Eastern Europe.' *Economics of Transition*, vol. 1 (2).
Pinto, Brian, Belka, M. and Krajewski, S. (1993). 'Transforming state enterprises in Poland: evidence on adjustment by manufacturing firms.' *Brookings Papers on Economic Activity*, pp. 213–70.
Rose-Ackerman, Susan (1978). *Corruption: A Study of Political Economy.* New York: Academic Press.
Schmidt, Klaus (1990). 'The costs and benefits of privatization (mimeo), MIT.
Shapiro, Carl and Willig, Robert D. (1990). 'Economic rationales for the scope of privatization.' In *The Political Economy of Public Sector Reform and Privatization* (ed. E. N. Suleiman and J. Waterbury). London: Westview Press, pp. 55–87.
Shleifer, Andrei (1994). 'Establishing property rights.' *Proceedings of the World Bank Annual Conference on Development Economics*, pp. 93–117.
Shleifer, Andrei and Vishny, Robert W. (1986). 'Large shareholders and corporate control.' *Journal of Political Economy*, vol. 94, pp. 461–88.
Shleifer, Andrei and Vishny, Robert W. (1993). 'Corruption.' *Quarterly Journal of Economics*, vol. 108, pp. 599–618.
Shleifer, Andrei and Vishny, Robert W. (1994). 'Politicians and firms.' *Quarterly Journal of Economics*, vol. 109, pp. 995–1025.
Tirole, Jean (1991). 'Privatization in Eastern Europe: incentives and the economics of transition.' *NBER Macroeconomics Annual*, vol. 5, pp. 221–67.
Vining, Aiden and Boardman, Anthony (1992). 'Ownership *vs.* competition: efficiency in public enterprise.' *Public Choice*, vol. 73, pp. 205–39.

< *Academy of Management Review*
2000. Vol. 25. No. 3, 525–550.

A MULTILEVEL MODEL OF PRIVATIZATION IN EMERGING ECONOMIES

RAVI RAMAMURTI
Northeastern University

Why are so many emerging economies privatizing state-owned enterprises, and how does that affect their performance? I propose a dynamic multilevel model to answer these questions. Firm-level arguments need to be complemented by industry- and country-level arguments to explain why some enterprises are privatized but not others. Similarly, changes in firm governance resulting from privatization are only one determinant of postprivatization performance; changes in industry structure, regulation, and country-level variables are as important. Furthermore, changes introduced at all three levels in one round of reform influence the context within which subsequent privatizations occur.

In the last decade more than $700 billion in assets have been privatized around the world, with almost 40 percent of that occurring in emerging economies (EEs; World Bank, 1998). Although the literature on privatization has grown as well, the causes and consequences of this important policy shift still are not very well understood. In this article I offer an organizing framework to help understand (1) why some state-owned enterprises (SOEs) in some EEs have been privatized but not others; (2) how SOEs are privatized and why; and (3) how privatization affects the performance of firms, industries, and countries. For reasons discussed later, I restrict the discussion to EEs, a term that includes both developing and transitional economies.

Is a theory of privatization addressing such questions worth developing? After all, even if SOEs are a unique species of organizations, as they seem to be (Aharoni, 1986; Hafsi, Kiggundu, & Jorgensen, 1987; Lewin, 1981), once such firms are privatized, they should behave like other private firms, about which we do know a great deal from the mainstream literature in management and economics. And because everywhere the trend in ownership is from state to private hands, rather than the other way around, why

bother with the task of this article? There are four reasons.

First, there is considerable variation in the pace at which EEs have privatized SOEs. Despite all the rhetoric about privatization, only 10 percent of SOE assets in the developing world and 30 to 40 percent of the SOE assets in transitional economies had been privatized by 1996 (Ramamurti, 1999: 140), with much of that concentrated in about a dozen countries (World Bank, 1998). This raises the question of why some SOEs in some countries have been privatized but not others.

Second, we are often interested in how privatization will *change* the behavior of SOEs—for example, if it will improve their efficiency, quality, exports, or competitiveness. This, in turn, requires a baseline theory of how SOEs behave (Aharoni, 1986; Vernon & Aharoni, 1981) and a model of how and why performance changes because of privatization, neither of which has been well researched.

Third, the end result of privatization is not always the same type of private firm. Capitalist economies include private firms that are managed by owners, by salaried managers, by family-controlled business groups, by multinational corporations, or by combinations of the above. In addition, the state may itself retain a block of shares for some time after privatization, resulting in "mixed enterprises" or "public-private partnerships" (Boardman, Eckel, Linde, & Vining, 1983; Musolf, 1972). Business-group capitalism and public-private capitalism are particularly common outcomes of privatization in EEs,

I acknowledge helpful feedback from colleagues at Northeastern University and from participants—especially Don Lessard—at the Academy of International Business annual meeting in Charleston, SC. Thanks also to MIT's Sloan School of Management, where I was a visiting professor when this article was written.

and neither is well researched because of its rarity in the West (Amsden & Hikino, 1994). One would expect the postprivatization performance of SOEs to depend on the type of private capital attracted to the firm. An interesting corollary issue is which of these types of private buyers a government is likely to target in the course of privatization and why.

Fourth and finally, in developing and transitional economies, market-supporting institutions, such as property rights, capital markets, labor markets, and regulatory institutions, are not nearly as well developed as they are in the West (Shleifer, 1994, 1997). Indeed, a primary difference between EEs and industrialized countries is that such institutions are underdeveloped in the former (North, 1993). Others have argued that concepts developed in the West may not be generalizable to EEs (Sharp & Salter 1997). For these reasons, private firms operating in EEs may behave differently from similar private firms in the West. We need to understand better how these institutional differences affect a country's privatization strategy and results and, equally important, how in the long run privatization may help strengthen those institutions.

If the preceding discussion has convinced the reader of the value of a theory of privatization in EEs, it will also have revealed the ambitiousness of the task ahead. Privatization is a complex phenomenon because it covers a variety of organizational transformations occurring in diverse and underresearched contexts. It is a field still requiring much analytical development and empirical work. It is also a multidisciplinary phenomenon, studied by financial analysts, organizational experts, management consultants, economists, political scientists, public administration specialists, and lawyers. In this article I try to draw on all these disciplines to answer the three questions outlined in the opening paragraph. The main conclusion of the article is that the causes and consequences of privatization can be better understood using dynamic, multilevel models, rather than static, single-level models.

OVERVIEW OF THE MULTILEVEL MODEL

In this article I use *privatization* in both its narrow and broad definitions. The narrow definition is any measure that transfers some or all

of the *ownership* and/or *control* over SOEs to the private sector. This definition treats privatization as a continuous variable, with many possible intermediate forms of public-private partnership. The broad definition of privatization is any measure that increases the role of the private sector in the economy—for example, through *deregulation,* which permits private entry into markets previously reserved for SOEs; *economic liberalization,* which exposes them to greater competition (e.g., through lower tariffs or fewer restrictions on foreign investment); or *institution building,* which improves the functioning of private firms and markets. Privatization in one sense does not always imply privatization in the other sense, because countries can and have privatized SOEs without deregulating their industries, liberalizing the economy, or strengthening institutions, and at other times they have done the opposite (Vickers & Yarrow, 1988). Indeed, the relation between privatization in the narrow and broad senses is itself an important issue in this field.

Key Features

In Figure 1 I present the framework proposed in this article. The figure has two distinguishing features: it is multilevel and dynamic. It is multilevel because, to understand the causes of privatization and the manner in which it is implemented, I believe it is important to consider variables at three levels: firm, industry, and country. (The role of international actors, as promoters of privatization or as parties affected by it [e.g., see Vernon, 1979], is subsumed under the country category of variables.) In turn, privatization usually induces changes at the firm, industry, and country levels, and it is the combined effect of these reforms that changes the performance of firms, industries, and countries, as indicated in Figure 1.

Traditionally, political scientists tend to focus on country-specific (political) variables to the exclusion of all others; economists tend to focus on country- and industry-specific variables while treating firms as black boxes; and management theorists tend to focus on firm- and industry-specific variables, often ignoring country-level factors. Focusing on variables at only one or two levels can cause one to overlook important drivers of privatization and some of its consequences.

FIGURE 1
A Multilevel Model of Privatization

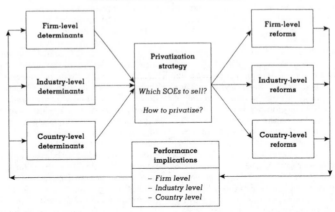

The other distinguishing feature of the model is that it is dynamic rather than static. It shows that privatization is not a one-shot *event* but a *process* that can occur in stages. As shown in the figure, a feedback loop is established wherein one round of privatization leads, with some time lag, to changes in firm, industry, or country variables that affect the dynamics of privatization in subsequent rounds. For example, the first set of actions might involve the government's selling minority shares in an SOE, allowing limited new entry into the SOE's industry, and creating a new law or regulatory agency for the sector. This may be followed some months or years later by full privatization of ownership and control, further deregulation, and measures to make regulation more effective. At the same time, the positive (or negative) experience with privatization in one sector may lead to more aggressive (less aggressive) reforms in another sector. Each privatization transaction might also strengthen one or more market-supporting institution at the margin; the cumulative effect of these marginal improvements in institutional infrastructure can be profound, thereby expanding the possibilities for privatizing more activities and sectors.

Distinctiveness of EEs

There is no widely accepted definition of EEs, although the term is generally used to refer to both developing and transitional economies. In this article I focus on two characteristics of EEs that are relevant to the study of privatization. First, I recognize that, compared to industrialized countries, institutional underdevelopment is a hallmark of developing and transitional economies (Alston, Eggertsson, & North, 1996; North, 1990), and I argue that this has important implications for the design and implementation of privatization programs (see, for example, Levy & Spiller, 1996). The smooth functioning of private firms and markets presupposes the existence of a variety of institutions, including laws (company, contract, bankruptcy, antitrust laws, and so on), specialized professions (auditors, accountants, financial analysts, management specialists, financial press, and so forth), and governmental agencies (capital market regulators, industry-specific regulators, independent courts, and so on).[1] Such institutions are far better developed in industrialized countries than in EEs.

---

[1] In his Nobel Prize acceptance speech, Douglass North defined institutions formally as "humanly devised constraints that structure interaction. They are made up of formal constraints (rules, laws, constitutions), informal constraints (norms of behavior, conventions, and self-imposed codes of conduct), and their enforcement characteristics. Together, they define the incentive structure of societies and specifically economies" (Alston et al., 1996: 344).

However, the boundaries between industrialized countries and EEs on this dimension are not sharp. Some countries that are often viewed as EEs (e.g., Singapore) in fact have highly developed institutions, whereas others that might be regarded as industrialized (e.g., European Union [EU] nations, such as Greece) are classified, by such sources as *The Economist*, as EEs. Equally important, institutional development varies considerably *among* EEs, especially between mixed-economy developing countries, whose economies have been predominantly private for decades, and transitional economies, whose economies were predominantly state owned for decades (DeCastro & Uhlenbruck, 1997: 137). The differences on this score are stark: in the late 1980s SOEs accounted, on average, for 15 percent of GDP in mixed-economy developing countries, compared to 70 to 95 percent of GDP in transitional economies (World Bank, 1995: 268–270).

If there were some way to collapse the complex, multidimensional concept of "market-supporting institutions" to a single measure, countries would probably lie on a *continuum*, from the least developed countries to transitional economies, to middle-income developing countries, and, finally, to the industrialized countries. A premise of this article is that the gap between industrialized countries and EEs on the institutional dimension is large enough for one to treat them as distinct types of countries. Alternatively, the reader may prefer to think of this article as focusing on institutionally underdeveloped countries, rather than EEs. At any rate, throughout the article institutional factors will figure as critical considerations in the design, implementation, and effectiveness of privatization programs.

A second distinctive characteristic of EEs is that they have opened up their economies dramatically in the last decade (Haggard & Webb, 1994), which has heightened competitive pressures on national firms, including SOEs. This exogenous increase in competition is itself a reason for privatization, as noted in the multilevel model that follows.

Although EEs have some distinctive characteristics, many other factors that drive privatization in industrialized countries also drive it in EEs. Therefore, many parts of the multilevel model presented in this article can be used to understand the causes and consequences of privatization in industrialized countries as well.

In the rest of the article, the model in Figure 1 will be used to organize the privatization literature. The primary purpose of the article is to convince the reader that the multilevel model is a useful conceptual scheme for understanding the causes and consequences of privatization in EEs. In addition, where the literature permits, I offer specific propositions about why some SOEs are privatized but not others, how privatization is implemented, and what factors determine the results of privatization. In some areas the variables in the model and their interaction will be relatively clear, but in others they will be fuzzy and the propositions conjectural; the latter represent opportunities for further research.

WHY ARE SOES BEING PRIVATIZED (OR NOT PRIVATIZED)?

The literature indicates a range of answers to this question, spanning all three levels of this multilevel model. I begin with the firm-level explanations.

Firm-Level Determinants

Most arguments in favor of privatization in the management and microeconomics literature are at the firm level and have to do with property rights and agency theory (Coase, 1988). Researchers have argued that under state ownership property rights are poorly defined. Because the SOE belongs to society as a whole, it ends up belonging to nobody (Boycko, Shleifer, & Vishny, 1995). As Aharoni puts it, the SOE is "an agent without a principal" (1982: 69). Moreover, some have argued that SOEs are not disciplined by the fear of takeovers, nor is bankruptcy a credible threat, because SOEs have access to bailout money from the treasury. The latter is sometimes also referred to as the "soft budget constraint" (Kornai, 1986; Majumdar, 1998a). Private owners, however, have every incentive to maximize the performance of their firms and are disciplined by threats of bankruptcy and takeover (Hanke, 1987).

Agency theory provides additional arguments for privatization in the scenario in which ownership is separated from management, as is usually the case when large firms are privatized. Because private firms have clearer goals, it is

2000   *Ramamurti*   529

believed to be easier for owners (principals) to hold managers (agents) accountable. For the same reason, incentive schemes can be designed to motivate managers to achieve the owners' goals. In contrast, SOEs have vague goals, such as maximizing the public interest (Morrison, 1933), which makes it harder for citizens (principals) to hold managers and ministers (agents) accountable or to motivate them through incentive schemes. Monitoring of managers by owners is also more effective under private ownership, since shareholders can signal their dissatisfaction with managers by selling their shares or by tendering them to takeover artists, but the only way shareholders of SOEs can show their dissatisfaction is through public protest or by not re-electing politicians when (and if) elections are held. The latter is a particularly blunt device, because elections are infrequent and involve a multitude of issues, of which SOE performance may be only one.

Although these arguments have merit, they run into one major problem: they do not fit the facts, in the sense that they do not tell the whole story. If, in fact, private ownership is superior to state ownership under all circumstances, as the above arguments imply, then why did so many countries create SOEs in the first place, why did they not begin privatizing them until the 1980s, and why even now are so many governments reluctant to privatize? The answers are to be found in other variables at all three levels of our multilevel framework (see Figure 2).

At the firm level, the literature indicates that two factors are positively related to the likelihood of privatization. First, firm size is relevant, because small SOEs can be privatized more easily than large SOEs. Local investors are more likely to be able to afford small firms, whose management also poses fewer managerial and technical challenges. The privatization of small firms also is likely to create fewer political problems, because such firms are less visible, their workers have less political clout, and their sale is unlikely to produce charges of selling the nation's "crown jewels" (Earle, Frydman, Rapaczynski, & Turkewitz, 1994). Empirical evidence shows that small firms usually were privatized

FIGURE 2
Which SOEs Will Be Privatized?

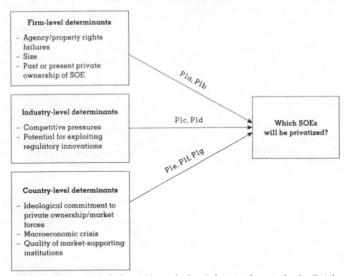

Note: The figure shows which variables at the firm, industry, and country levels affect the likelihood that an SOE will be privatized.

Academy of Management Review   July

before medium or large SOEs in both developing countries (Vuylsteke, 1983: 169–172) and transitional economies (World Bank, 1996: 56–58).

> *Proposition 1a: Small SOEs are more likely to be privatized than large SOEs.*

Second, SOEs that were once privately owned or are still partially privately owned are more likely to be privatized than SOEs that are wholly state owned or that were created afresh by the state as statutory public corporations. Most likely, the former came into existence when private firms were nationalized—for instance, when governments bailed out private banks that owned equity in other firms (e.g., in the Philippines after Marcos was overthrown), when governments bailed out an entire industry in crisis to save jobs (e.g., the textile industry in India), or when state-owned banks foreclosed on private firms that defaulted on loans (e.g., Brazil's BNDE). Such firms are easier to privatize or "denationalize," because their legal status as joint stock companies facilitates privatization, especially if they already have minority private shareholders (Nankani, 1990). In many transitional economies, governments returned some of these firms to their former owners through a process called *restitution* (especially in the Czech Republic and Estonia; see World Bank, 1996: 53).

> *Proposition 1b: SOEs that resulted from nationalization or that are still partially privately owned are more likely to be privatized than SOEs that are wholly state owned and/or were greenfield investments by the state.*

Industry-Level Determinants

The most persuasive justifications for state ownership arise from industry or country conditions—not on claims that it is a form of organization superior to private ownership. The industry-level arguments that follow apply to mixed-economy developing countries and not to the former communist countries. In the latter case, state or collective ownership was not limited to a few sectors but was all encompassing, including agriculture. Ideology, rather than economic pragmatism, dictated state/communal ownership, but this was

not the case in mixed-economy developing countries (Spulber, 1997: 41–65).

In the case of mixed economies, a distinction often is made between firms that operate in competitive markets and those that operate in highly imperfect markets, including monopolies (Kikeri, Nellis, & Shirley, 1992). Nowhere in the literature is there any theoretical argument in favor of state ownership of firms in competitive markets. The industry-level arguments in favor of state ownership have to do with market failures. In many industries, such as public utilities, there exists the natural monopoly problem, resulting in little or no competition (Aharoni, 1986: 106–107). In other industries, such as roads or water and sewerage, private firms are likely to ignore important externalities and therefore will underinvest when externalities are positive and overinvest when they are negative (Gomez-Ibanez, 1996: 317–320). Financial services, such as banking, present the moral hazard problem, wherein privately owned institutions might take excessive lending risks because they know the government will bail out depositors if their decisions turn out to be bad ex post. Natural resource industries, such as petroleum or copper, present opportunities for earning very high economic rents, which many countries believe belong to society as a whole, rather than to those who happen to own the land above those deposits (Vernon & Levy, 1982). The private sector is also regarded as myopic in its investment decisions and therefore unlikely to make long-term investments in infrastructure or human capital development. Jones and Mason (1982), among others, present strong evidence that SOEs in developing countries typically occur in lumpy, capital-intensive, long payback, monopolistic industries.

Governments could have used regulation, rather than state ownership, to correct for these kinds of market failures. In the event, many governments did not. Sappington and Stiglitz (1987) have explained this institutional choice using transaction cost economics, arguing that arm's-length regulation of private firms can be cumbersome and costly in a shifting, unpredictable world. In developing countries the risk of regulatory capture (Anderson, 1980) also is regarded as being higher. Indeed, in such regions as Latin America, governments nationalized infrastructure firms in the past, only after running into regulatory logjams with privately owned mo-

2000   *Ramamurti*   531

nopolies (Baer & McDonald, 1998; Wells & Gleason, 1995).

What, then, has happened in the last decade to reverse the power of these arguments? I propose two explanations at the industry level. First, many of the industries in which SOEs operate in EEs have become much *more competitive* than before, because of economic liberalization in the 1980s and 1990s, pursuant to agreements with such international institutions as the World Bank, the International Monetary Fund (IMF), and the World Trade Organization (WTO), or regional agreements, such as the North American Free Trade Agreement (NAFTA) and Mercosur. In addition, in service industries, such as telecommunications, competition has been brought about by technological change, which has eroded natural monopoly characteristics of local and long-distance service (Wellenius & Staple, 1996). In such industries as airlines, competition has come from international deregulation, often instigated by countries like the United States in pursuit of open-skies policies (Pustay, 1992). In such sectors as railroads, substitute modes of transportation—for instance, private trucking—have eroded the monopoly position that state railways used to have on long-distance shipments (Galenson & Thompson, 1994).

The agency failure arguments recounted earlier apply more strongly to SOEs in competitive markets, which expose the organizational weaknesses of SOEs and undercut traditional natural monopoly arguments for state ownership. Jones and Wortzel (1982), for instance, have argued that SOEs are particularly ill suited to businesses requiring quick adjustments, as is the case in competitive markets (Li & Simerly, 1995). Others have argued that SOEs are too mechanistic (Lawrence & Lorsch, 1967) to be effective in turbulent environments (Ramamurti, 1987). Privatization then emerges as a possible solution to improving the competitiveness of SOEs. In transitional economies, too, the first wave of privatization generally involved firms in competitive markets, such as hotels and retail stores (Earle et al., 1994). This leads to the following proposition.

> *Proposition 1c: SOEs in competitive markets or potentially competitive markets are more likely to be privat-*

> *ized than SOEs in monopolistic markets.*

Second, in the 1980s we witnessed several *regulatory innovations* that have expanded the potential role of private firms in such sectors as public utilities. We now recognize that public utilities consist of a mixture of natural and artificial monopolies. For example, in telecommunications, long-distance service is potentially competitive, even if local service is not (Wellenius & Staple, 1996); similarly, production of gas or electric power is potentially competitive, even if their transmission and distribution are not, and air transportation is competitive, even if airports are not (and so on). Recent experience has shown that vertical separation of these functions is feasible and that vertical coordination can be achieved despite fragmented ownership. Competition then can be introduced in areas that were artificial monopolies, and those activities also can be privatized (Bradshaw, 1997). The most famous American example of vertical separation is AT&T's breakup in 1984. The United Kingdom combined the vertical separation idea with privatization in many sectors, including gas, electric power, water, and railroads (Vickers & Yarrow, 1988). Privatization in EEs has been inspired partly by these American and British experiments.

There have been other regulatory innovations as well. Shleifer (1985) has proposed that local monopolies, such as gas or power distribution, can be regulated through "yardstick competition" and that state ownership is not the only option, even in the case of natural monopolies. The British also have introduced the price-cap method of price regulation (Baumol & Willig, 1989), wherein the regulated firm is allowed to raise its prices automatically over a multiyear horizon at a rate lower than actual inflation. Unlike the rate-of-return method of price regulation used widely in the past, the price-cap method gives the regulated firm strong incentives to lower costs, because it is not required to pass on immediately all such savings to consumers (Beesley & Littlechild, 1989; Brown, Einhorn, & Vogelsang, 1991). Price-cap regulation is also administratively simpler than rate-of-return regulation and, in many countries, has yielded large cost reductions that eventually have resulted in lower prices for consumers.

Proposition 1d: Monopolistic SOEs in sectors that can benefit from regulatory innovations like vertical and horizontal breakup, yardstick competition, or price-cap regulation are more likely to be privatized than those that cannot.

The importance of exogenous changes in competition and regulatory innovation as drivers of privatization varies across industries. For instance, competition is a key driver of privatization in airlines but regulatory innovation is not, whereas the opposite is true in water supply or port services, and both are important in the telecommunications industry. Therefore, telecommunications firms ought to be high on the list of firms to be privatized, which is, in fact, the case: telecommunications alone accounted for about 20 percent of all privatization revenues raised from 1988 through 1996 by emerging economies, according to data from the World Bank (1998).

Country-Level Determinants

In my view, country-level variables are the most important determinants of whether an SOE will be privatized. This is because privatization ultimately is a political rather than economic decision. No matter what the economic advantages of privatization, it will not happen in a country unless politicians in power are motivated to take on vested interests, such as labor unions, suppliers, or customers of SOEs, who benefit from state ownership of enterprises. At the country level, three variables stand out as drivers of privatization: (1) a change in ideology in favor of free markets (or, equivalently, the abandonment of the ideology in favor of central planning and state ownership), (2) the advent of macroeconomic crises, and (3) the level of development of a country's market-supporting institutions. The first two factors promote privatization, whereas the third usually is an obstacle to privatization, especially in transitional economies.

The power of a *change in ideology* in promoting privatization clearly can be seen in the case of the former communist countries after the collapse of the Berlin Wall. In several of those countries, privatization was part of the sweeping economic and political changes in favor of private ownership and markets. New political leaders came to power, many of them anxious to

move away from policies of the past as quickly as possible. Leaders in such countries as the Czech Republic wanted to privatize everything as soon as possible—among other things, to guarantee that economic and political changes made after the collapse of the Berlin Wall would be irreversible (Boycko, Shleifer, & Vishny, 1994, 1995). Ideological fervor in favor of privatization was stronger in some countries (e.g., Czech Republic, Hungary, Russia), however, than others (e.g., Poland, Slovakia, Bulgaria). The lack of this ideological commitment in such countries as Cuba and North Korea explains the absence of privatization in these countries, despite poor macroeconomic performance.

Ideology was less of a factor in mixed economies, with the exception of such countries as Chile under President Pinochet (Hachette & Luders, 1993), because, by definition, these countries already had large private sector firms that coexisted with SOEs. Yet, even in mixed economies, a new generation of leaders or senior policy makers, often Western educated, initiated privatization out of an abiding faith in private ownership and market mechanisms, even in monopolistic industries.

Proposition 1e: SOEs in countries where the political leadership is ideologically committed to private ownership and market forces are more likely to be privatized than those where the political leadership is committed to state ownership and/or central planning.

The second important driver of privatization at the country level is the advent of macroeconomic crises, as evidenced by hyperinflation or severe balance-of-payments problems. In the case of transitional economies, both a change in ideology and the onset of macroeconomic crises pushed governments toward privatization, whereas in the case of mixed economies, where no radical change in ideology occurred among the leadership (with a few exceptions), macroeconomic crisis was often the driving force. As long as governments could raise taxes or borrow at home and abroad to finance public spending and imports, including the needs of SOEs, painful reforms like privatization could be avoided. But when the limits of taxing and borrowing were reached, as was the case in many EEs in the 1980s, painful alternatives like privatization became politically desirable policies for achieving economic stability (Yarrow, 1999).

Normally, the beneficiaries of state ownership, such as employees, unions, and civil servants, are better organized than the widely dispersed groups that might benefit from reforming SOEs—for example, consumers or taxpayers (Olson, 1965). But when inflation gets out of control, politicians are willing to take on those organized interests as part of the struggle to kill inflation. Privatization is seen as one potent method for reducing the government's budget deficit, and thereby inflation as well.

In Latin America, Eastern Europe, and the former Soviet Union, balance-of-payments crises and plunging currencies worsened matters. On this front, too, privatization was seen as an effective remedy, because SOEs could be sold to foreign investors for hard currency. Countries in economic crisis also faced pressure to privatize from such international financial institutions as the IMF and the World Bank, to whom they turned for last-resort loans (Babai, 1988). The evidence clearly shows that most of the countries that privatized deeply did so in response to a macroeconomic crisis (Bruno, 1996; Ramamurti, 1992).

Conversely, countries that did not face macroeconomic crisis were generally slow to privatize (e.g., Asian countries, such as China, India, Indonesia, and Korea). Following the currency crises of 1997–1998, however, political leaders in many parts of East and Southeast Asia also came under pressure to privatize SOEs to bolster their foreign exchange reserves and satisfy IMF conditionalities. Predictably, such countries as Indonesia and Korea announced sweeping new privatization programs in 1998. And, to avoid economic problems similar to those of its neighbors, China announced for the first time in 1998 ambitious plans for restructuring and privatizing its SOEs.

> *Proposition 1f: SOEs in countries facing a macroeconomic crisis are more likely to be privatized than SOEs in countries with stable economies.*

Finally, countries' propensity to privatize is shaped by the quality of their *market-supporting institutions*—that is, the sophistication of the public and private institutions that underpin any market economy. As noted earlier, this includes protection for property rights, business laws, competent regulatory agencies to ensure fair competition or to protect minority shareholder rights, independent courts to enforce laws, financial institutions that can mobilize and loan out private savings, managerial and entrepreneurial talent, and so on.

Transitional economies were particularly underdeveloped in this regard, with limited private savings, weak financial intermediaries, shallow stock markets, ambiguous property rights, and underdeveloped legal systems (Child & Yuan, 1996; Steinfeld, 1998). Whereas in the typical mixed-economy developing country, SOEs accounted for 10 to 20 percent of GDP before privatization began, they accounted for 71.4 percent of GDP in Poland, 80.0 percent in China, and 95.9 percent in the Czech Republic (World Bank, 1995: 69). Thus, privatization created more daunting challenges in transitional economies than in mixed economies.

To be sure, there was considerable variation in the quality of market-supporting institutions, even among transition economies. Countries with a long industrial tradition before the turn to communism (e.g., the Czech Republic) and/or those bordering on advanced economies, such as the EU (e.g., the former East Germany, Hungary, or Poland), could create market-supporting institutions more rapidly than countries without those advantages (e.g., Bulgaria, Russia, Mongolia, and so forth). Likewise, China had the distinct advantage of having access to overseas Chinese with capital and technology who were comfortable operating in the country's institutionally underdeveloped environment.

In any case, as long as the SOEs in question were small and operated in competitive markets, they could be privatized, even if the institutional infrastructure was weak (Earle et al., 1994). Small firms did not suffer from the separation of ownership and management, their growth could be internally financed, and their markets did not have to be regulated; hence, they were privatized quickly after the collapse of communism. But weak institutional infrastructure presented serious problems in the case of large SOEs operating in imperfectly competitive markets; hence, their privatization was slow in mixed economies and even slower in transitional economies (see, for example, Regan & Hayes, 1994). Not surprisingly, 10 years after abandoning communism, the size of the SOE sector in Eastern Europe and the former Soviet

Union was three times that in the average mixed-economy developing country (World Bank, 1996: 53, Table 3.2). It is also easy to understand why transitional economies looked for innovative ways to get around some of their institutional constraints—for example, by pursuing mass privatization or voucher schemes (Boycko et al., 1994).

In contrast, institutions were stronger in such countries as Argentina, Brazil, and India, but they too required institution building at the margin when large SOEs were privatized, such as the creation of new industry-specific regulatory agencies (Levy & Spiller, 1996).

> *Proposition 1g: SOEs in countries with weak market-supporting institutions (e.g., many transitional economies) are less likely to be privatized than those in countries with stronger institutions, especially if they are large, monopolistic firms.*

HOW ARE SOES PRIVATIZED?

Once an SOE has been selected for privatization, several questions arise about how to im-plement that policy. In this section I propose a way of thinking about privatization strategies and then offer propositions about the circumstances under which particular options are likely to be pursued.

Firm-Level Reforms

At the firm level, the main change introduced by privatization is in governance arrangements, but the nature of the new governance mechanisms depends on how the SOE is privatized. Specifically, it will depend upon (1) the government's residual ownership after privatization and (2) the kind of private capital the firm attracts (see Figure 3). The discussion that follows is limited to the kind of buyer that the government is likely to target. Whether or not such buyers will, in fact, take up the government's offer is an interesting and important question but one that is beyond the scope of this article.

Consider first the government's residual ownership in privatized firms, which could be a majority or a minority stake. When the World Bank or Privatization International reports statistics on privatization, it includes in its totals firms

FIGURE 3
How Are SOEs Privatized? Firm-Level Reforms (Type of Buyer Targeted)

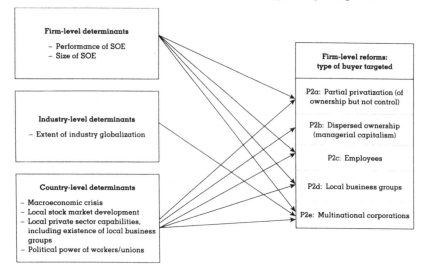

whose equity was only partially privatized. Such firms are actually public-private partnerships or "mixed enterprises" (Boardman et al., 1983). Perotti and Guney found, in a sample of five mixed-economy developing countries and three transitional economies, that staggered divestment of government shares was the predominant pattern, with governments tending to "retain a significant stake for long intervals of time" (1993: 84).

One must distinguish, however, between cases in which the government unwinds its holdings gradually and those in which it intends to retain ownership indefinitely. In the former case, control eventually passes on to the private sector, but by staggering divestment, the government reduces the amount of capital private investors have to raise in the short run while at the same time maximizing its long-run revenues, because the value of its shares often increases after control has been privatized and credibility for the privatization program has been established (Perotti & Guney, 1993: 84).

In other cases, however, the government privatizes a minority stake—not with a view to privatizing control later on but simply to let the SOE raise money by selling shares on the stock market or to strengthen its managerial autonomy, since listed SOEs are less vulnerable to political interference than wholly government-owned enterprises (Aharoni, 1982). This is with the assumption, of course, that the country has a functioning stock market, unless the SOE sells shares in a foreign stock exchange (Berg & Berg, 1997). Partial privatization also is more likely when a government is not strongly committed to privatization or prefers to privatize gradually; for instance, Chinese SOEs have been partially "privatized" through state-controlled joint ventures with local or foreign partners (Rosen, 1999). Countries privatizing to get out of a macroeconomic crisis are unlikely to take this sort of gradualistic approach (Berg & Berg, 1997). Partial privatization is also more likely in cases where the SOE's performance is relatively good and, therefore, not urgently in need of new management (Berg & Berg, 1997: 365). In such countries as Korea, Malaysia, and Singapore, large SOEs in the telecommunications, electricity, or airlines sectors were often partially privatized in this manner (Jomo, 1995).

Proposition 2a: Partial privatization (of ownership but not control) is more likely in countries that are not privatizing in the midst of a severe economic crisis, that have relatively well-developed stock markets, and if the SOEs in question are performing relatively well.

Managerial capitalism refers to the case in which ownership of the SOE passes into the hands of dispersed investors, who enjoy income rights but none of whom has, or is allowed to accumulate, sufficient ownership to exert control. Because takeover laws are not well developed, even in the more advanced developing countries, governments usually restrict the maximum percentage that can be owned by any single investor or by foreign investors as a group. Managerial capitalism works in the West because stock markets operate with a high degree of transparency, listed firms have to meet high accounting and auditing standards, and small shareholders are adequately protected—but these conditions do not hold for the stock markets of even the more advanced developing countries, not to mention transitional economies.

Although managerial capitalism has been a popular outcome of privatization in industrialized countries, it has been rare in EEs (*Wall Street Journal*, 1995: R4). Among the few exceptions, for instance, was the Argentine oil company, YPF, which the government put under a competent new management before privatization and intended to privatize fully through the stock market (Grosse & Yanes, 1998). But in 1999, as Argentina continued to face balance-of-payments problems, the government sold its final tranche of shares at an attractive price to the Spanish oil company, Repsol, and also allowed it to tender for all remaining shares. Thus, YPF turned from managerial capitalism to multinational capitalism. Examples of managerial capitalism perhaps will emerge in the future in such countries as Singapore, if and when such partially privatized firms as Singapore Airlines or Singapore Telecom are fully privatized through the stock market.

Proposition 2b: Governments in EEs are unlikely to target dispersed private investors as buyers of SOEs, because even middle-income mixed economies, not to mention transitional economies, do not yet have adequate laws or institutions to enforce good governance, fair takeover provisions, and the protection of small investors.

Employee capitalism, also known as management-employee buyouts, has occurred in many cases in the transitional economies, especially in small- or medium-size firms, which were within the financial reach of employees and managers (Thompson, Wright, & Robbie, 1990). This approach has political appeal, since it avoids the charge of "selling out" to foreigners or to local elites (Megyery & Sader, 1996: 16). Because of lack of funds, managers and workers usually get to buy at a discounted price and with deferred payment schemes (e.g., in Russia; see Boycko, Shleifer, & Vishny, 1996). Within transitional economies, employee capitalism has been popular in countries where workers were powerful after the collapse of communism (e.g., Poland, Russia) but less so where that was not the case (e.g., the Czech Republic). In countries such as Hungary, employees sometimes gained ownership of SOEs through "spontaneous privatization" (i.e., theft). Among employees, real control sometimes was in the hands of managers, whereas in other cases managers served at the pleasure of workers. In mixed economies workers often obtained some shares in the privatized firm but seldom enough to control the firm.

> *Proposition 2c: Governments are more likely to target employees as buyers—for example, through management-employee buyouts—in the case of small firms and in countries where workers/unions are politically powerful (e.g., several former communist countries).*

Business-group capitalism refers to the case in which SOEs are purchased by one of the country's business groups, which are diversified, family-controlled assemblages of firms held together by economic and social ties (Khanna & Palepu, 1997). Privatization provides business groups the opportunity to diversify still further into potentially attractive businesses—telecommunications, energy, banking, and transportation. It allows them to leverage their traditional strengths, which are usually home-country spe-

cific, such as familiarity with national laws and customs, ability to deal with local labor, and the ability to work closely with government.

In Latin America business groups have been major buyers of SOEs (Kuczynski, 1999). In Mexico local business groups bought the airlines, the telephone company, and all the banks, sometimes with foreign firms as junior partners. But in such countries as Argentina and Peru, and whenever large SOEs were privatized in transitional economies, *multinational capitalism* has been the rule. Why did governments use business-group capitalism in some countries and multinational capitalism in others? First, transitional economies had no business groups to begin with, and their citizens lacked capital; therefore, these countries had to rely more heavily on foreign investors to buy SOEs. Sader (1995) has reported that between 1988 and 1993, 57 percent of the privatization revenues in Europe and Central Asia was raised from foreign investors, whereas the same proportion for Latin America was only 30 percent (Sader, 1995: 34, 42). Also, in Argentina and Peru the performance of the SOEs involved was so dismal that only foreign firms were viewed as capable of turning them around. Second, such industries as telecommunications, airlines, chemicals, or electricity already were globalized or rapidly becoming so, and governments may have felt that multinational corporations (MNCs) were more likely to have the necessary technology or management skills.

> *Proposition 2d: Governments are likely to target local business groups as buyers (assuming they exist) if the SOEs in question are performing badly and need to be turned around.*

> *Proposition 2e: Governments are likely to target MNCs as buyers of SOEs if the SOEs in question are performing poorly and operate in industries characterized by extranational markets (i.e., global industries), even if local business groups exist that could by them.*

In summary, privatization can result in many organizational arrangements, with differing residual roles for government and differing kinds of private capital involved. Although I have speculated on the circumstances under which

2000   *Ramamurti*   537

each type of buyer may be sought, the main point of this section is that privatization results in quite different types of private firms, with differing governance arrangements, goals, and strategies.

Industry-Level Reforms

The discussion that follows applies to SOEs functioning under conditions of imperfect competition. As noted earlier, this is typically true of large SOEs in most countries. In these cases the SOE is the leading provider of the product or service—it may even enjoy a legal monopoly in those areas—and externalities are usually important. Before such firms are privatized, governments usually restructure them, trim their portfolio of businesses, do some financial window dressing, modify their labor contracts, and revise the regulatory regime under which they will operate (World Bank, 1995). To be sure, governments can take some or all of these measures without privatizing SOEs, but the converse is not true: it is hard for governments to privatize such SOEs without redefining competition and regulatory policies (see Figure 4). A fundamental difference between public divestiture (i.e., privat-

ization) and private divestiture is that in the former case the seller (i.e., government) has the power to modify market structure and regulation, whereas private sellers of firms have no such power (Jones, Tandon, & Vogelsang, 1990).

Changes in industry structure. Most large SOEs in EEs are horizontally and vertically integrated. A state-owned oil company is likely to be in exploration, transportation, refining, and distribution of oil products; a steel company is likely to have several plants and to be vertically integrated; an electricity company is likely to be in generation, transmission, and distribution; a bank is likely to have branches all over the country and to provide a broad range of services. These SOEs may also be the only licensed producers of some or all of these outputs. Therefore, at the time of privatization, it is natural for governments to wonder if such SOEs should be divided vertically or horizontally or if regulatory barriers to entry should be lowered.

Depending on how these restructuring options are exercised, industry structure may or may not be materially changed. If monolithic SOEs are broken up before privatization and their industries are deregulated, the resulting firms will be less powerful, competition will be stronger, con-

FIGURE 4
How Are SOEs Privatized? Industry- and Country-Level Reforms

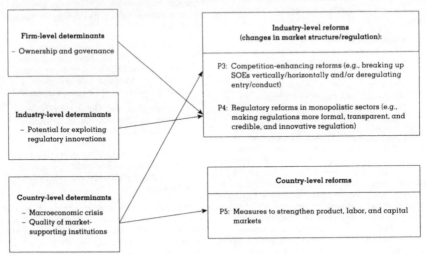

sumers will enjoy lower prices or better services, and public support for privatization will be stronger. There are also strong forces pushing governments in the opposite direction, however. Since privatization occurs in many countries at a time of macroeconomic crisis, governments want to privatize quickly to turn around their economies, but breaking up SOEs vertically or horizontally and redefining regulations take time. So does selling several constituent firms, rather than a single monolithic firm. More important, during economic crises, governments are strapped for funds and want to get the highest possible price for their SOEs (the so-called revenue objective); procompetition reforms, therefore, might be rejected, because a monopolistic, integrated firm will raise more money than a collection of smaller firms operating in competitive markets. Because of the crisis environment, private investors might need extra incentive to invest in risky emerging markets, and giving them monopoly power may be seen as the perfect solution. In many countries, transitional or otherwise, large SOEs have been privatized intact, with their monopoly power guaranteed for some number of years after privatization (Ramamurti, 1996).

A different dynamic seems to apply in EEs that have undertaken SOE reforms in the absence of a macroeconomic crisis. In precrisis Asia or in China, SOE reforms have been gradual, unlike in Eastern Europe, Russia, or Latin America. Under pressure from international trading partners, or volitionally (e.g., Malaysia), these countries have liberalized their economies, freeing up imports and foreign direct investment, which has exposed SOEs to greater competition. It is this heightened competition, rather than a macroeconomic crisis, that has produced SOE reform in many Asian countries (in the pre-Asian meltdown period—i.e., pre 1997). Because it is difficult for politicians to privatize SOEs in good economic times, however, they limit their reforms to deregulation—that is, allowing wider private participation in industries previously reserved for state enterprises, rather than privatizing SOEs.

> *Proposition 3: Countries that are in a macroeconomic crisis are likely to privatize without pursuing competition-enhancing policies, such as breaking up monolithic SOEs or deregulating*

their industries, in order to maximize revenues from privatization and implement the policy quickly. Conversely, countries not in a macroeconomic crisis are likely to pursue competition-enhancing policies without privatizing SOEs.

Changes in industry-specific regulatory regime. Part of the promise of privatization lies in the possibility that industry-specific regulation might be more effective after privatization than before it. One reason is that competition may be strengthened at the time of privatization through the methods discussed earlier, and the market is usually more effective at disciplining managers than regulators. But even if nothing else changes, government regulation of monopolies might be more effective when the firms involved are private, rather than state owned.

Part of this argument follows from the historical experience with SOEs: they are as capable as their private counterparts of capturing their regulatory masters to achieve the narrow goals of unions, suppliers, or customers. And regulatory flexibility, which was seen as an advantage of state ownership, is now seen more as a liability or as an example of "government failure" (Wolf, 1991). State ownership gives politicians and civil servants too much flexibility to change policies at whim, resulting in weak accountability of all parties (Willig, 1993). Most state monopolies are not governed by a formal set of rules or performance obligations, and the deals they cut with government regulators are not transparent. Even in cases in which governments have tried to formalize regulatory arrangements with SOEs through "performance contracts," both managers and ministers have broken their ends of the bargain with impunity (Nellis, 1991). Oddly enough, in many countries SOEs have come to be viewed as less concerned about the public interest than private firms. Thus, one advantage of privatizing monopolies, at least in the short run, is that it can lead to improved regulation.

Another reason why regulation may improve after privatization is that it gives regulators additional leverage in dealing with monopolistic firms. Consider first the case of franchising, wherein the government auctions the right to provide a monopoly service (e.g., operating airports) for a stipulated number of years. Although competition in the market is not feasible in

2000   Ramamurti   539

these cases, competition for the market is possible (Demsetz, 1968). But how can there be competition for the monopoly unless private firms are allowed to participate in and win such auctions? In large, decentralized countries, such as China or the United States, this competition might work within the public sector—that is, between provincial state enterprises that bid for contracts outside their home province. In practice, however, such competition seems not to occur when it is restricted to the public sector.

Another example of a regulatory innovation that works better with privatization is yardstick competition (Shleifer, 1985). This refers to the case in which regulators judge the performance of a local monopoly by comparing it with similar monopolies in other parts of the country. Such comparisons cannot be made when all the local monopolies are parts of a monolithic SOE. Even if such an SOE were spun off into several regional SOEs, one would expect more innovation and creativity if the constituent parts belonged to different private owners than if they all belonged to the public sector. For instance, when Argentina divided its monolithic telephone company into two regional monopolies and sold them to two different private consortia, it created a race between the two companies on such things as the rate of expansion, the rate of digitalization, and the quality of service (Petrazzini, 1996). Pitting private regional monopolies against one another in this manner makes the regulator's task a little easier, because it reduces the asymmetry in information and expertise that otherwise exists between regulators and the firms they regulate.

Finally, price-cap regulation, which seems to have worked better than rate-of-return regulation in motivating firms to reduce costs sharply, is harder to use with SOEs (Brown et al., 1991). The advantage of price-cap regulation is that, for a specified number of years, firms are allowed to retain all cost savings above a stipulated target (retail price inflation *minus* a productivity adjustment factor, also known as the RPI–X formula). This motivates firms to maximize cost savings, rather than to hide cost savings, as happens with rate-of-return regulation, and they are free to use those extra profits any way they wish (Littlechild, 1983). As a practical matter, it is difficult to extend the same idea to SOEs, because their managers are not owners of the firm and therefore cannot be given discre-

tion over how to use the extra cost savings. Even if a government promised to give SOE managers discretion over the use of these extra cost savings, the promise might not be credible; therefore, managers might not produce the extra cost savings in the first place (Beesley & Littlechild, 1989).

> Proposition 4: Privatization is likely to
> improve the regulation of monopolies
> by making it more formal, transparent, credible, and innovative than was
> possible under state ownership.

Country-Level Reforms

While discussing the drivers of privatization, I noted that institutional underdevelopment is the hallmark of EEs, especially in the former communist economies. In a book aptly titled *The Market Meets Its Match*, Amsden, Kochanowicz, and Taylor (1994) note the difficulties of creating "capitalism without capital" in such countries as Hungary and Poland. Therefore, as countries implemented individual privatization transactions, especially in the early years of reform, they also laid the foundation for the institutional infrastructure that was going to be necessary to create a market economy. For instance, when Poland listed its first SOE on the local stock market, it clarified how the country's revived stock exchange would operate; this paved the way for future listings on the exchange (Piper, 1994). Similarly, every privatization deal clarified some aspect of the laws that would apply in the country—for example, foreign investment laws, taxation laws, or property rights—and others helped build or strengthen such market-supporting institutions as the stock market, professional auditing, or reporting and disclosure standards. Ideally, market-supporting institutions ought to have been created before SOEs were privatized, but in practice the two had to be done in parallel, because privatization could not wait.

In mixed-economy developing countries the institutional infrastructure was stronger but still not as well developed as in the Organization for Economic Cooperation and Development (OECD) countries. In these countries property rights were well established, but capital, labor, and product markets had many flaws. Privatization turned the spotlight on these weaknesses and forced governments to address them. In the Jamaican, Malaysian, and Philippine mixed economies, governments tried to bring capitalism to the masses by encouraging citizens to buy shares in privatized firms, but this could not be done without strengthening the stock market to protect small investors. In Chile the government first privatized social security and then allowed the managers of privatized pension funds to invest in SOEs when they were divested; this augmented the stock of capital available for privatization while privatizing social security itself and promoting Chile's nascent long-bond market (Hachette & Luders, 1993). By the late 1990s privatized firms accounted for 19 to 58 percent of the market capitalization in a sample of Latin American countries (Kuczynski, 1999: 223). In addition, when large firms, such as the telephone companies in Argentina or Mexico, were listed on the New York Stock Exchange, they suddenly had to meet the Exchange's stringent accounting, auditing, and disclosure standards, which raised local capabilities in these service sectors (Khanna & Palepu, 1999).

Equally important, in most countries governments could not privatize large firms without getting unions to agree to greater flexibility in labor contracts or to schemes for downsizing the workforce, typically in exchange for generous severance payments and/or shares in the privatized firm (Biond, 1997; Kikeri, 1995). One of the biggest impediments to privatization in India in 1999 was the lack of an "exit policy"—that is, a policy to govern the dismissal of redundant workers. Therefore, while privatization was inching its way forward, mostly through small sales of shares, a debate raged about what the country's exit policy ought to be. In Mexico the government's strong-handed approach to labor issues in privatizing the state airline, Aeromexico, set the stage for labor cooperation in subsequent privatizations. As a result, labor contracts were simplified, and a productivity-based system for setting wages became standard practice (Tandon, 1995).

Another important example of institutional development often occurring concurrently with privatization is the creation of new regulatory institutions to supervise the privatized firm(s) in various sectors. In Argentina, Brazil, Chile, and Mexico, new industry-specific regulatory institutions were created in telecommunications, en-

ergy, transport, and banking at about the time that SOEs in these sectors were privatized (on telecommunications, see Levy & Spiller, 1996). Ramirez (1998) found that privatization was accompanied by significant regulatory reform in Chile and Mexico.

> *Proposition 5: Each privatization transaction in EEs, especially in the early years, is likely at the margin to strengthen the institutions required for the efficient working of product, capital, and labor markets; in turn, these institutional improvements make the subsequent rounds of privatization a little easier to implement.*

HOW DOES PRIVATIZATION AFFECT PERFORMANCE?

It is beyond the scope of this article to review comprehensively the vast literature on how privatization affects performance (for excellent reviews, see Sheshinski & Lopez-Calva, 1999; Tandon, 1993; and Vickers & Yarrow, 1988). Instead, I limit the discussion to showing that the literature supports the multilevel model presented here—that is, postprivatization performance is explained more fully by variables at all three levels, rather than one or two. My main concern in this section is with firm-level performance changes, and I discuss only briefly how privatization affects industry- and country-level performance.

Firm-Level Performance

Much of the early work on the ownership-performance relationship consisted of cross-sectional studies, in which scholars compared the technical efficiency of state-owned and private firms in the same country. These studies were inconclusive, with some researchers asserting that private firms are more efficient than SOEs (e.g., De Alessi, 1980; Majumdar, 1998b) and others concluding that there is no systematic difference (e.g., Borins & Boothman, 1985; Boyd, 1986). From my point of view, these studies have two limitations. First, most of them are based on data from industrialized countries, such as Canada or the United States. Second and more important, the researchers do not always control for industry differences, including the level of competition. Tandon notes that "if we simply look at public versus private firms without controlling for the market structure, then on average private firms are going to appear more efficient because they operate on average in more competitive markets" (1993: 2).

After surveying several studies on the ownership-performance relationship in mixed economies and industrialized countries, Vickers and Yarrow (1988) concluded that in competitive markets private firms outperform SOEs. Ayub and Hegstad (1987) reached a similar conclusion after comparing the performance of the 500 largest non-U.S. firms, as did Megginson, Nash, and van Randenborgh (1994), who found that after privatization the operating efficiency of SOEs in competitive markets rose more than that of SOEs in noncompetitive markets. Even if SOEs do well in competitive markets, Yarrow is "skeptical that the pressure (to perform well) could be maintained over long time periods" (1992: 338). Kikeri et al. (1992) raise the same question about the sustainability of good performance by SOEs operating in competitive markets in developing

countries. This leads to the following proposition (see Figure 5).

> *Proposition 6a: In markets where competition is strong, privatization alone is likely to improve firm performance (efficiency, profitability, and rate of growth of output).*

In most of the studies cited above, the researchers did not distinguish between different types of private firms (exceptions include Boardman et al., 1983, and Boardman & Vining, 1989), nor did they make sophisticated adjustments for industry or national differences. In more recent studies, however, scholars have tended to adjust privatization for industry or governance conditions (e.g., Boubakri & Cosset, 1998). Besides, with the passage of time, many researchers have compared the performance of the same firm before and after privatization, which automatically controls for variables like size and industry. Nevertheless, even in these cases, privatization might be accompanied by liberalization, output price changes, regulatory reforms, and institutional

FIGURE 5
Multilevel Reforms and Firm Performance

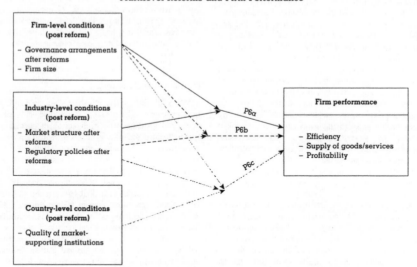

Note: Interaction effects between variables at two or more levels are indicated by intersecting arrows.

reforms. For instance, Megginson et al. (1994) concluded that privatization improved efficiency (sales per employee) by 10 percentage points and profitability by about 25 percentage points, but they did not control for contemporaneous changes in economic conditions, pricing, or competition. D'Souza and Megginson (1997) concluded, from an analysis of the pre- and postprivatization performance of sixty-eight firms, that privatization is a powerful tool for promoting growth and operating efficiency, but they did not adjust for firm-specific price revisions or regulatory changes. This is a serious shortcoming, because more than half their sample consists of firms in regulated industries.

After reviewing several studies on the subject, Vickers and Yarrow (1988) concluded that in noncompetitive markets, privatization would make less of a difference than competition or regulatory reform. Consistent with this conclusion, Caves and Christensen (1980) found that state-owned Canadian railroads were more efficient than privately owned U.S. railroads, because the former operated in a more deregulated environment than the latter. Similarly, other studies have shown that privatization without competition or regulatory reform produces less performance improvement than when all these reforms are combined (Ramamurti, 1996; Ros, 1999). In their study, Galal, Jones, Tandon, and Vogelsang (1994) were most careful to separate the effects of ownership from those of other reforms. They compared the actual results of privatization with the counterfactual case of what would have happened if the SOE had not been privatized and concluded that, even in the case of monopolies, privatization improved performance, partly because of regulatory reforms accompanying privatization. I likewise concluded (Ramamurti, 1996) that privatization, competition, and regulation are loosely coupled variables (Orton & Weick, 1990) and that ownership interacts positively with competition and regulatory reform. For example, I argued that certain regulatory reforms are feasible only with privatization (e.g., price-cap method or franchising). Thus, the following proposition emerges.

Proposition 6b: In imperfectly competitive markets, reforms that inject more competition or improve regulatory incentives (e.g., through such innovations as franchising, yardstick compe-

tition, or the price-cap method) are more likely to improve performance than privatization alone. Combining ownership, competition, and regulatory reforms will produce the greatest performance improvement because of, among other things, positive interaction between ownership and competition and between ownership and regulatory reform.

In most studies of privatization in mixed economies, researchers ignore the role of institutional factors in shaping performance, but that is scarcely possible when looking at transitional economies, where institutional failures in corporate governance, for instance, have stymied policy makers and often have led to disappointing results (Blasi et al., 1997; Filatotchev, 1997). The only exception seems to be the very small firms—for instance, retail shops and small businesses—which recorded significant performance improvement after privatization in Russia (Barberis, Boycko, Shleifer, & Tsukanova, 1996) and Central Europe (Earle et al., 1994). Even the World Bank (1996) admits that the performance of many mid-size or large privatized firms in transitional economies, such as Russia's, is hard to distinguish from that of erstwhile SOEs, because so little has changed in these firms. The same conclusion is echoed by Wintrobe, who notes that in Russia

> little emphasis was paid to the question of how to design appropriate institutions to ensure the transferability of ownership and to discipline managers . . . . The result has been a form of capitalism . . . in which managers are entrenched in the enterprises in a way that they never were under the old central planning system (1998: 604).

Even mass privatization schemes, which were seen as a quick and simple way to create private owners in transition economies (World Bank, 1996: 53), produced serious scandals in several countries, including the Czech Republic (Regan & Hayes, 1994; Wallace, 1996), Albania (Bohlen, 1997; Luthans & Riolli, 1997), and Russia (Blasi, Kroumova, & Kruse, 1997). The rules for accumulating shares or taking over firms either were ambiguous or abused by managers and fly-by-night mutual fund managers, leaving most small shareholders out in the cold. China's experience with partial privatization of SOEs likewise seems to have produced dubious benefits, because managerial accountability was weak (Steinfeld, 1998). Nevertheless, because China paid more attention to strengthening market-supporting institutions first and privatizing later, its reforms may in the end prove to be more effective than that of transitional economies in Eastern Europe or the former Soviet Union (Naughton, 1994; Nolan & Xiaoqiang, 1999).

> *Proposition 6c: Except in the case of very small firms operating in highly competitive markets, privatization will bring about less performance improvement (and possibly no improvement) in countries with weak market-supporting institutions than in countries with stronger market-supporting institutions.*

The main conclusion from the above studies is that to explain performance changes in firms, one must consider variables at all three levels of the multilevel model. Park, Li, and Tse (1997), in a study of Chinese firms—SOEs, community-owned firms, and private firms—found that variations in their performance could be explained more completely by considering ownership, industry, and institutional factors. Studies in which researchers do not control for industry- and country-level variables are apt to over- or underestimate the importance of the ownership variable. Likewise, policy advice is likely to be sounder when the contribution that variables at all three levels can make to performance improvement is recognized.

Industry- and Country-Level Performance

In this section I discuss the implications of privatization for industry- and country-level performance measures, but I offer no testable propositions since these issues are not the focus of this article.

Nonetheless, it should be noted that because many SOEs dominate their industries, privatization significantly can affect industry-level performance. When privatization is accompanied by procompetition and regulatory reforms, industry performance can improve still further because of new entry, greater rivalry, and stronger incentives than before for firms to innovate or reduce costs (Ramamurti, 1997). In studies in the telecommunications sector, researchers have found that after privatization, industry output

grew at two to three times historic rates, labor productivity rose fourfold or more, quality of service improved, and new services were introduced at an unprecedented rate (Ramamurti, 1996; Tandon, 1995; World Bank, 1995). In the case of Chile, privatization transformed a stodgy state monopoly into a fiercely competitive industry, with some of the lowest long-distance rates in the world (Cuervo-Cazurra, 1998). Similarly, in the case of airlines, privatization and/or deregulation produced sharp improvements in performance in Chile (Paredes-Molina & Ramamurti, 1996), Mexico, Malaysia, and the United Kingdom (Galal et al., 1994). In all of these cases, however, firm-level reforms in ownership were accompanied by procompetition policies and regulatory reforms. Where the SOE was privatized without deregulation or the introduction of incentive regulation—as in Jamaican telecommunications—output expanded rapidly and industry profits rose (because the private monopoly was able to charge higher prices), but neither labor productivity nor efficiency improved as rapidly (Wint, 1996).

The positive link between privatization and country performance is suggested in many studies of mixed economies (for a review, see Sheshinski & Lopez-Calva, 1999), although the relationship is hard to establish conclusively because of confounding factors (Miller, 1995). It has been claimed that privatization lowers the government's budget deficit and helps accelerate GDP growth (World Bank, 1995: 45); that it increases foreign investment inflows and, thus, stabilizes the balance of payments (Sader, 1995); and that it helps build the local capital market, as seen in the growth in stock market capitalization (McLindon, 1996). In transitional economies improvements in country performance have been recorded in Hungary, Poland, and (to a lesser extent) the Czech Republic, but in countries farther east—Bulgaria, Romania, or the former Soviet Union—that have especially weak institutions, the results have been far less encouraging (Nellis, 1998).

DYNAMIC EFFECTS

Up to this point, within each stage of the model, this analysis has been static. In reality, of course, countries' privatization programs unfold in stages over several years. I turn next to a brief discussion of the dynamic aspects of the multilevel model. Owing to space constraints, I only illustrate that aspect with a few examples.

The main feedback path, as shown in Figure 1, is through the results of one round of reforms, which are fed back to left side of the model, thereby changing the context within which the next round is implemented. I illustrate that feedback process at two levels: first, within a single industry and, second, across industries.

Consider first the dynamics within an industry, such as a monopolistic, public utility sector (e.g., telecommunications, electricity, gas). I noted in Proposition 3 that countries in a macroeconomic crisis are likely to privatize monopolistic SOEs without breaking them up vertically or horizontally or deregulating their markets, in order to obtain a higher sale price and implement privatization quickly (Ros, 1999; Vickers & Yarrow, 1988). The change in ownership alone is likely to produce some improvement in firm-level performance, especially if it is accompanied by regulatory reforms, but almost always not as much improvement as was expected at the time of privatization, because competitive pressure on the privatized firm is still weak or absent. In addition, the industry as a whole shows little dynamism, because no new players are allowed into it. The resulting disappointment in postprivatization performance, especially among consumers, creates political pressure to strengthen competition in the sector. Even if the government were reluctant to allow competition when the SOE was privatized, it would be liable to view the matter differently later. Once the SOE has been sold, the government has little to lose and a lot to gain (i.e., popularity) by opening the industry to new players (Smith, 1989). This kind of dynamic is clearly seen in sectors such as telecommunications, where Chile and Mexico went from state monopoly to private monopoly and, eventually, to a competitive structure with only privately owned firms (see Cuervo-Cazurra, 1998, and Wellenius & Staple, 1996).

But a similar dynamic works in EEs that undertake reforms in the absence of a macroeconomic crisis. In the 1980s and 1990s, many Asian countries were also concerned about making their economies more competitive in all areas, including infrastructure. In the absence of an economic crisis, however, it was difficult for leaders to force privatization down the throats of SOE employees and other opponents of the pol-

icy; therefore, they deregulated these sectors instead. The financial performance of SOEs operating in such sectors worsened, they lost market share to the new private entrants, and their inferior service was plainly visible for all to see. Political pressure built up to "do something" about the SOEs, such as privatizing them. The existence of alternative private providers also undermined the ability of unions to veto privatization, because there were credible alternatives for delivering the necessary services. In the changed circumstances, privatization of the SOE became feasible, even if that was not the case earlier. Many Asian countries, including China and India, have gone through this kind of evolution in a number of industries, as did Chile's airline industry in the 1980s (Paredes-Molina & Ramamurti, 1996).

Thus, whether or not a country's reforms begin with privatization or with deregulation, pressure builds, over time, on the government to embrace both policies. The long-run result, therefore, is a competitive industry structure with several private players; the only difference is that some countries pass through an intermediate stage of private monopoly, whereas others pass through an intermediate stage of SOE-private competition. Research shows this kind of dynamic evolution in the telecommunications sector in several Latin American countries (Ramamurti, 1996: 38–40). Hence, I offer the following proposition.

> *Proposition 7a: Privatization and deregulation are mutually reinforcing policies; pursuing one within a monopolistic industry is likely to lead eventually to pressures on the government to pursue the other in the same industry.*

Just as performance feedback may escalate reforms within a sector, so too can it escalate reforms across sectors. Argentina and Mexico provide excellent examples of this sort of *escalation in commitment* to privatization. The initial reforms were driven largely by the macroeconomic crisis the two countries faced, as well the resulting pressure from international agencies to privatize and deregulate a few key sectors, including telecommunications. The positive impact of the reforms on the quality and availability of services in those sectors and on the budget deficit, however, increased public support for the policy, which, in turn, strengthened the leadership's commitment to proprivate and promarket policies, long after the macroeconomic crisis had eased. By 1995 both countries had implemented some of the deepest privatization programs in the world (on Argentina, see Alexander & Corti, 1993; on Mexico, see Rogozinski, 1998).

A government's commitment to privatization can escalate over time for other reasons as well. Market-supporting institutions may become stronger over time because of cumulative reforms undertaken independently or concurrently with individual privatization transactions. Learning may occur within the government about how best to manage the privatization process so that deals are closed more quickly and without controversy. As noted before, the redefinition of labor's role and the clipping of its wings in the early privatizations (e.g., in Mexico) can make it easier to gain unions' support for privatization in later rounds (Tandon, 1995). Likewise, after the first few firms are listed on the local stock market or in foreign stock markets, it becomes easier to repeat those tactics in subsequent privatizations (Khanna & Palepu, 1999; Regan & Hayes, 1994). Learning of this sort and escalation of political commitment to privatization are evident in many countries, including China, India, and Malaysia (see, for example, Jomo, 1995). The feedback process is especially important in countries that privatize gradually, because it can help legitimize privatization and allow for learning-by-doing (Ramamurti, 1999). Conversely, if the initial rounds of privatization do not deliver the expected benefits, as was the case with voucher schemes in Albania's, the Czech Republic's, Russia's, and Slovakia's transitional economies, political commitment to privatization and marketization will wane (Nellis, 1998; World Bank, 1996: 56).

> *Proposition 7b: Positive (negative) results at the firm, industry, and country levels in one round of reforms tend to escalate (de-escalate) political commitment to privatization in subsequent rounds.*

CONCLUSIONS

In this article I have argued that privatization in EEs is a complex phenomenon because it encompasses a variety of organizational transformations in a variety of settings. Both the complexity of the context in which privatization occurs and the complexity of means through which it is implemented require that the phenomenon be analyzed in terms of a dynamic multilevel model of the kind proposed here. More specifically, I have argued that the causes of privatization, the manner in which it is implemented, and its consequences all can be understood more fully by considering variables at the firm, industry, and country levels. For instance, I contend that whether or not an SOE is privatized depends not only on the potential for firm-level improvements in governance but also on the potential for introducing competition in its markets and improving regulation, and on country-level variables, such as the prevailing political, economic, and institutional conditions. Similarly, privatization not only changes firm-level governance arrangements but also industry-level competition and regulatory variables, as well as country-level institutions, such as labor and capital markets. Performance improvement, which is often the goal of reform, is also determined by variables at all three levels and interactions among them. Focusing on variables at only one or two levels can cause one to overlook important drivers of privatization and some of its consequences.

I have argued as well that privatization should be viewed as a *process* in which firm-, industry- and country-level reforms are implemented in stages, rather than as a one-shot *event* in which all reforms are implemented fully and simultaneously. The feedback from one round of reform influences the context within which the next round is designed and implemented. In this way the scope of privatization expands or contracts, within and across industries, depending on whether the initial results are positive or negative and whether or not political commitment and market-supporting institutions have become stronger. Small changes made at the firm or industry level in individual privatizations can add up over time to large changes in country variables, such as GDP growth, productivity growth, quality of market-supporting institutions, or international competitiveness.

I believe both policy makers and managers can make better choices if they think of privatization in dynamic, multilevel terms. Unfortunately, in practice, policy making often has been dominated by variables at only one or two lev-

546 *Academy of Management Review* July

els. For instance, much of the popular controversy over privatization shows too much of a focus on the (firm-level) ownership issue—public versus private—without sufficient regard for attendant market structure, regulatory, or country-level reforms. In hindsight it is now clear that many Western advisers, including such international institutions as the World Bank and the IMF, did not pay sufficient attention to strengthening market-supporting institutions in transition economies, believing that unleashing market forces (e.g., freeing prices) and privatizing ownership would by themselves produce dramatic performance improvement (Nellis, 1999). These same actors also tended to overlook the importance of other country-level factors, such as political commitment to implementing privatization in a sound and sustained manner (Shafik, 1996).

In addition to the multilevel model, I have presented tentative propositions that relate the variables in the multilevel model to the causes, modalities, and consequences of privatization. Here, we are in the early stages of developing testable propositions. In a few areas, such as the first section, in which I discussed which SOEs are likely to be selected for privatization, our understanding of the phenomenon is deep enough to offer testable propositions, but in other areas our understanding is limited and the propositions more conjectural.

This leads directly to the limitations of the synthesis attempted in this article. Listed below are three areas in which those limitations are particularly severe. Each is phrased as a question that, hopefully, can be addressed in future research on this topic.

1. Under what circumstances are governments likely to select each type of private capitalism discussed in the article? In particular, when and why do governments switch from state capitalism to public-private capitalism, business-group capitalism, multinational capitalism, employee capitalism, or (occasionally) managerial capitalism? How do goals, governance arrangements, and strategies vary across these different forms of capitalism?

2. How does institutional underdevelopment affect the privatization strategy of EEs, and, equally important, how does privatization affect the evolution of these institutions? This promising research topic tends to fall between the cracks, because neither economists nor man-

agement specialists pay sufficient attention to it. Accordingly, in this article my treatment of institutional issues has been superficial: we lack a solid grasp of what this multidimensional concept means and, even more important, of precisely how it varies across rich, poor, and transitional economies. Fortunately, a new multidisciplinary association, called the International Society for New Institutional Economics, has been formed to study such issues.

3. How do firm-level changes in governance arrangements interact with industry-level changes in competition policy and regulation and with country-level variables (especially institutions) to shape the performance measures of interest to managers and public policy makers? More empirical research is needed in which scholars use variables at all three levels to explain postprivatization performance. Likewise, researchers need to look more at the dynamic evolution of privatization in EEs.

I hope in future research scholars will examine questions such as these to develop a more robust theory of privatization in EEs.

REFERENCES

Aharoni, Y. 1982. State-owned enterprise: An agent without a principal. In L. P. Jones (Ed.), *Public enterprise in less-developed countries:* 67–76. Cambridge: Cambridge University Press.

Aharoni, Y. 1986. *The evolution and management of state-owned enterprises.* Cambridge, MA: Ballinger.

Alexander, M., & Corti, C. 1993. *Argentina's privatization program.* Washington, DC: World Bank.

Alston, L. J., Eggertsson, T., & North, D. (Eds.). 1996. *Empirical studies in institutional change.* Cambridge: Cambridge University Press.

Amsden, A., & Hikino, T. 1994. Project execution capability, organizational know-how, and conglomerate growth in late industrialization. *Industrial and Corporate Change,* 3: 111–147.

Amsden, A., Kochanowicz, J., & Taylor, L. 1994. *The market meets its match: Restructuring the economies of Eastern Europe.* Cambridge, MA: Harvard University Press.

Anderson, D. D. 1980. Who owns the regulators? *Wharton Magazine.* 4(4): 14–21.

Ayub, M. A., & Hegstad, S. O. 1987. Management of public industrial enterprises. *World Bank Research Observer,* 2: 88–127.

Babai, D. 1988. The World Bank and the IMF: Rolling back the state or backing its role? In R. Vernon (Ed.) *The promise of privatization:* 254–285. New York: Council on Foreign Relations.

2000   *Ramamurti*   547

Baer, W., & McDonald, C. 1998. A return to the past? Brazil's privatization of public utilities: The case of the electric power sector. *Quarterly Review of Economics & Finance,* 38: 503–523.

Barberis, N., Boycko, M., Shleifer, A., & Tsukanova, N. 1996. How does privatization work? Evidence from the Russian Shops. *Journal of Political Economy,* 104: 764–790.

Baumol, W. J., & Willig, R. D. 1989. Price caps: A rational means to protect telecommunications consumers and competition. *Review of Business,* 10, 4: 3–8.

Beesley, M. E., & Littlechild, S. C. 1989. The regulation of privatized monopolies in the United Kingdom. *Rand Journal of Economics,* 20: 454–472.

Berg, A., & Berg, E. 1997. Methods of privatization. *Journal of International Affairs,* 50: 357–390.

Biond, A. 1997. Implications that downsizing could have for public sector unions. *Journal of Collective Negotiations in the Public Sector,* 26: 295–301.

Blasi, J., Kroumova, M., & Kruse, D. 1997. *Kremlin capitalism: Privatizing the Russian economy.* Ithaca, NY: Cornell University Press.

Boardman, A. E., Eckel, C., Linde, M.-A., & Vining, A. 1983. An overview of mixed enterprises in Canada. *Business Quarterly* 48(2): 101–106.

Boardman, A. E., & Vining, A. R. 1989. Ownership and performance in competitive environments: A comparison of the performance of private, mixed, and state-owned enterprises. *Journal of Law & Economics,* 32: 1–33.

Bohlen, C. 1997. Albanian parties trade charges in pyramid scandal. *New York Times,* January 29: A3.

Borins, S. F., & Boothman, B. E. C. 1985. Crown corporations and economic efficiency. In D. W. McFetridge (Ed.), *Canadian industrial policy in action:* 77–135. Toronto: University of Toronto Press.

Boubakri, N., & Cosset, J.-C. 1998. The financial and operating performance of newly-privatized firms: Evidence from developing countries. *Journal of Finance,* 53: 1081–1110.

Boycko, M., Shleifer, A., & Vishny, R. 1994. Voucher privatization. *Journal of Financial Economics,* 35: 249–266.

Boycko, M., Shleifer, A., & Vishny, R. 1995. *Privatizing Russia.* Cambridge, MA: MIT Press.

Boycko, M., Shleifer, A., & Vishny, R. 1996. A theory of privatization. *Economic Journal,* 106: 309–319.

Boyd, C. 1986. The comparative efficiency of state-owned enterprise. In A. Negandhi, H. Thomas, & K. L. K. Rao (Eds.), *Multinational enterprises and state-owned enterprises: A new challenge in international business:* 179–194. Greenwich, CT: JAI Press.

Bradshaw, W. P. 1997. Competition in the rail industry. *Oxford Review of Economic Policy,* 13(1): 93–103.

Brown, L., Einhorn, M., & Vogelsang, I. 1991. Toward improved and practical incentive regulation. *Journal of Regulatory Economics,* 3: 323–338.

Bruno, M. 1996. *Deep crises and reform: What have we learned?* Washington, DC: World Bank.

Caves, D. W., & Christensen, L. R. 1980. The relative efficiency of public and private firms in a competitive environment: The case of Canadian railroads. *Journal of Political Economy,* 88: 958–976.

Child, J., & Yuan, L. 1996. Institutional constraints on economic reform: The case of investment decisions in China. *Organization Science,* 7: 60–77.

Coase, R. H. 1988. *The firm, the market, and the law.* Chicago: University of Chicago Press.

Cuervo-Cazurra, A. 1998. *Hypercompetition in the Chilean telecommunications industry.* Cambridge, MA: Sloan School of Management.

De Alessi, L. 1980. The economics of property rights: A review of the evidence. In R. O. Zerbe (Ed.), *Research in law and economics,* vol 2: 1–47. Greenwich, CT: JAI Press.

DeCastro, J. O., & Uhlenbruck, K. 1997. Characteristics of privatization: Evidence from developed, less-developed, and former communist countries. *Journal of International Business Studies,* 28: 123–143.

Demsetz, H. 1968. Why regulate utilities? *Journal of Law and Economics,* 11: 55–66.

D'Souza, J., & Megginson, W. L. 1999. The financial and operating performance of privatized firms during the 1990s. *Journal of Finance,* 54: 1397–1438.

Earle, J., Frydman, R., Rapaczynski, A., & Turkewitz, J. 1994. *Small privatization, the transformation of retail trade and consumer services in the Czech Republic, Hungary, and Poland.* Budapest: Budapest-Central European University Press; Oxford: Oxford University Press.

Filatotchev, I. 1997. Review article: Privatization and corporate governance in transitional economies. *World Economy,* 20: 497–510.

Galal, A., Jones, L., Tandon, P., & Vogelsang, I. 1994. *Welfare consequences of selling public enterprises: An empirical analysis.* Oxford: Oxford University Press.

Galenson, A., & Thompson, L. 1994. *Options for reshaping the railways.* Policy research working paper No. 926. Washington, DC: World Bank.

Gomez-Ibanez, J. A. 1996. Regulating private toll roads. In R. Ramamurti (Ed.), *Privatizing monopolies: Lessons from the telecommunications and transport sectors in Latin America:* 317–331. Baltimore: Johns Hopkins University Press.

Grosse, R., & Yanes, J. 1998. Carrying out a successful privatization: The YPF case. *Academy of Management Executive,* 12(2): 51–63.

Hachette, D., & Luders, R. 1993. *Privatization in Chile: An economic appraisal.* San Francisco: ICEG Press.

Hafsi, T., Kiggundu, M. N., & Jorgensen, J. J. 1987. Strategic apex configurations in state-owned enterprises. *Academy of Management Review,* 12: 714–730.

Haggard, S., & Webb, S. B. 1994. *Voting for reform: Democracy, political liberalization, and economic adjustment.* Oxford: Oxford University Press.

Hanke, S. H. 1987. The necessity of property rights. In S. H.

Hanke (Ed.), *Privatization and development:* 47–51. San Francisco: ICS Press.

Jomo, K. S. (Ed.) 1995. *Privatizing Malaysia: Rents, rhetoric, and reality.* Boulder, CO: Westview.

Jones, L. P., & Mason, E. S. 1982. Role of economic factors in determining the size and structure of the public enterprise sector in less-developed countries with mixed economies. In L. P. Jones (Ed.), *Public enterprise in less-developed countries:* 17–48. Cambridge: Cambridge University Press.

Jones, L. P., Tandon, P., & Vogelsang, I. 1990. *Selling public enterprises: A cost-benefit analysis.* Cambridge, MA: MIT Press.

Jones, L. P., & Wortzel, L. 1982. Public enterprise and manufactured exports in LDCs. In L. P. Jones (Ed.), *Public enterprise in less-developed countries:* 217–242. Cambridge: Cambridge University Press.

Khanna, T., & Palepu, K. 1997. Why focused strategies may be wrong for emerging markets. *Harvard Business Review,* 74(4): 41–51.

Khanna, T., & Palepu, K. 1999. The right way to restructure conglomerates in emerging markets. *Harvard Business Review,* 77(4): 125–134.

Kikeri, S. 1995. *Privatization and labor: What happens to workers when governments divest.* Technical paper No. 396. Washington, DC: World Bank.

Kikeri, S., Nellis, J., & Shirley, M. 1992. *Privatization: The lessons of experience.* Washington, DC: World Bank.

Kornai, J. 1986. The soft budget constraint. *Kyklos,* 39: 3–30.

Kuczynski, P.-P. 1999. Privatization and the private sector. *World Development,* 27: 215–224.

Lawrence, P. R., & Lorsch, J. W. 1967. *Organizations and environment.* Boston: Harvard Business School Press.

Levy, B., & Spiller, P. 1996. *Regulations, institutions, and commitment: Comparative studies of telecommunications.* New York: Cambridge University Press.

Lewin, A. 1981. Research on state-owned enterprise—introduction. *Management Science,* 27: 1324–1325.

Li, M., & Simerly, R. 1995. Reexamining the ownership and performance relationship: The moderating effect of environmental change. *Academy of Management Proceedings:* 27–31.

Littlechild, S. 1983. *Regulation of British telecommunications.* London: Her Majesty's Stationery Office.

Luthans, F., & Riolli, L. T. 1997. Albania and the Bora Company: Lessons learned before the recent chaos. *Academy of Management Executive,* 11(3): 61–72.

Majumdar, S. 1998a. Slack in the state-owned enterprise: An evaluation of the impact of soft-budget constraints. *International Journal of Industrial Organization,* 16: 377–394.

Majumdar, S. 1998b. Assessing comparative efficiency of the state-owned, mixed, and private sectors in Indian industry. *Public Choice,* 96: 1–24.

McLindon, M. P. 1996. *Privatization and capital market development.* New York: Praeger.

Megginson, W. L., Nash, R. C., & Van Randenborgh, M. 1994. The financial and operating performance of newly privatized firms: An international empirical analysis. *Journal of Finance,* 49: 403–452.

Megyery, K., & Sader, F. 1996. *Facilitating foreign participation in privatization.* Occasional paper No. 8. Washington, DC: Foreign Investment Advisory Service.

Miller, A. N. 1995. British privatization: Evaluating the results. *Columbia Journal of World Business,* 30(4): 82–98.

Morrison, H. S. 1933. *Socialisation and transport.* London: Counstable.

Musolf, L. D. 1972. *Mixed enterprise: A developmental perspective.* Lexington, MA: Lexington Books.

Nankani, H. B. 1990. Lessons of privatization in developing countries. *Finance & Development,* 27(1): 43–45.

Naughton, B. 1994. Chinese institutional innovation and privatization from below. *American Economic Review,* 84: 266–270.

Nellis, J. 1991. Contract plans: A review of international experience. In R. Ramamurti & R. Vernon (Eds.), *Privatization and control of state-owned enterprises:* 297–323. Washington, DC: World Bank.

Nellis, J. 1998. *Time to rethink privatization in transition economies?* IFC discussion paper No. 38. Washington, DC: World Bank.

Nolan, P., & Xiaoqiang, W. 1999. Beyond privatization: Institutional innovation and growth in China's large state-owned enterprises. *World Development,* 27: 169–200.

North, D. C. 1990. *Institutions, institutional change, and economic performance.* Cambridge: Cambridge University Press.

North, D. C. 1993. Epilogue: Economic performance through time. Nobel Prize presentation speech, Nobel Foundation. Reprinted in L. J. Alston, T. Eggertsson, & D. North (Eds.). 1996. *Empirical studies in institutional change:* 342–355. Cambridge: Cambridge University Press.

Olson, M. 1965. *The logic of collective action: Public goods and the theory of groups.* Cambridge, MA: Harvard University Press.

Orton, J. D., & Weick, K. E. 1990. Loosely couple systems: A reconceptualization. *Academy of Management Review,* 15: 203–223.

Paredes-Molina, R., & Ramamurti, R. 1996. Ownership and competition in Chile's airline industry. In R. Ramamurti (Ed.), *Privatizing monopolies: Lessons from the telecommunications and transport sectors in Latin America:* 177–202. Baltimore: Johns Hopkins University Press.

Park, S. H., Li, S., & Tse, D. 1997. *Determinants of firm performance in a transition economy: Institutional vs. economic effects in China.* Paper presented at the Academy of International Business annual meeting, Monterrey, Mexico.

Perotti, E. C., & Guney, S. E. 1993. The structure of privatization plans. *Financial Management,* 22(1): 84–98.

Petrazzini, B. 1996. Telephone privatization in a hurry: Argentina. In R. Ramamurti (Ed.), *Privatizing monopolies: Les-*

sons from the telecommunications and transport sectors in Latin America: 108–146. Baltimore: Johns Hopkins University Press.

Piper, T. 1994. *Ministry of privatization*. Boston: Harvard Business School Press.

Pustay, M. W. 1992. Toward a global airline industry: Prospects and impediments. *Logistics and Transportation Review*, 28: 103–128.

Ramamurti, R. 1987. *State-owned enterprises in high technology industries: Studies in India and Brazil*. New York: Praeger.

Ramamurti, R. 1992. Why are developing countries privatizing? *Journal of International Business Studies*, 23: 225–249.

Ramamurti, R. (Ed.). 1996. *Privatizing monopolies: Lessons from the telecommunications and transport sectors in Latin America*. Baltimore: Johns Hopkins University Press.

Ramamurti, R. 1997. Testing the limits of privatization: Argentine railroads. *World Development*, 25: 1972–1993.

Ramamurti, R. 1999. Why haven't developing countries privatized deeper and faster? *World Development*, 27: 137–155.

Ramirez, M. D. 1998. Privatization and regulatory reform in Mexico and Chile: A critical overview. *Quarterly Review of Economics & Finance*, 38: 421–439.

Regan, A. D., & Hayes, S. L. 1994. *Czechoslovakia's privatization: The fund phenomenon*. Case No. 9-292-124. Boston: Harvard Business School Case Services.

Rogozinski, J. 1998. *High price for change: Privatization in Mexico*. Washington, DC: Inter-American Development Bank.

Ros, A. 1999. Does ownership or competition matter? The effects of telecommunications reform on network expansion and efficiency. *Journal of Regulatory Economics*, 15: 65–92.

Rosen, D. 1999. *Behind the open door: Foreign enterprises in the Chinese marketplace*. Washington, DC: Institute for International Economics.

Sader, F. 1995. *Privatizing public enterprises and foreign investment in developing countries, 1988–1993*. FIAS occasional paper No. 5. Washington, DC: IFC and World Bank.

Sappington, D., & Stiglitz, J. E. 1987. Privatization, information, and incentives. *Journal of Policy Analysis and Management*, 6: 567–582.

Shafik, N. 1996. Selling privatization politically. *Columbia Journal of World Business*, 31(4): 21–29.

Sharp, D. J., & Salter, S. B. 1997. Project escalation and sunk costs: A test of the international generalizability of agency and prospect theories. *Journal of International Business Studies*, 28: 101–121.

Sheshinski, E., & Lopez-Calva, L. 1999. *Privatization and its benefits: Theory and evidence*. Cambridge, MA: Harvard Institute for International Development.

Shleifer, A. 1985. A theory of yardstick competition. *Rand Journal of Economics*, 16: 319–327.

Shleifer, A. 1994. Establishing property rights. *World Bank Research Observer*, Annual Conference Supplement: 93–117.

Shleifer, A. 1997. Government in transition. *European Economic Review*, 41: 385–410.

Smith, D. J. 1989. Will privatization lead to competition in the British power industry? *Power Engineering*, 93(11): 35–38.

Spulber, N. 1997. *Redefining the state: Privatization and welfare reform in industrial and transitional economies*. New York: Cambridge University Press.

Steinfeld, E. S. 1998. *Forging reform in China*. New York: Cambridge University Press.

Tandon, P. 1993. *The efficiency of privatized firms*. Paper prepared for the Operations Evaluation Department, World Bank, Boston.

Tandon, P. 1995. Welfare effects of privatization: Some evidence from Mexico. *Boston University International Law Journal*, 13: 329–347.

Thompson, S., Wright, M., & Robbie, K. 1990. Management buy-outs from the public sector: Ownership form and incentive issues. *Fiscal Studies*, 11(3): 71–88.

Vernon, R. 1979. The international aspects of state-owned enterprises. *Journal of International Business Studies*, 10(3): 7–15.

Vernon, R., & Levy, B. 1982. State-owned enterprises in the world economy: The case of iron ore. In L. P. Jones et al. (Eds.), *Public enterprise in less-developed countries:* 167–188. Cambridge: Cambridge University Press.

Vickers, J., & Yarrow, G. 1988. *Privatization: An economic analysis*. Cambridge, MA: MIT Press.

Vuylsteke, C. 1983. *Techniques of privatization of state-owned enterprises. Volume I: Methods and Implementation*. Technical paper No. 88. Washington, DC: World Bank.

Wall Street Journal. 1995. Milestones in privatization. October 2: R4.

Wallace, C. P. 1996. The pirates of Prague. *Fortune*, December 23: 78–86.

Wellenius, B., & Staple, G. 1996. *Beyond privatization: The second wave of telecommunications reforms in Mexico*. Discussion paper No. 341. Washington, DC: World Bank.

Wells, L. T., Jr., & Gleason, E. S. 1995. Is foreign infrastructure investment still risky? *Harvard Business Review*, 73(5): 44–45.

Willig, R. D. 1993. Public versus regulated private enterprise. *World Bank Research Observer*, Annual Conference Supplement: 155–180.

Wint, A. 1996. Pioneering telephone privatization: Jamaica. In R. Ramamurti (Ed.), *Privatizing monopolies: Lessons from the telecommunications and transport sectors in Latin America:* 49–71. Baltimore: Johns Hopkins University Press.

Wintrobe, R. 1998. Privatization, the market for corporate control, and capital flight from Russia. *World Economy,* 21: 603–611.

Wolf, C., Jr. 1991. *Markets or governments: Choosing between imperfect alternatives.* Cambridge, MA: MIT Press.

World Bank. 1995. *Bureaucrats in business: The economics and politics of government ownership.* Oxford: Oxford University Press.

World Bank. 1996. *From plan to market: World development report 1996.* Oxford: Oxford University Press.

World Bank. 1998. *World debt tables 1997.* Washington, DC: World Bank.

Yarrow, G. 1992. Privatization in theory and practice. *Economic Policy,* 2: 324–364.

Yarrow, G. 1999. A theory of privatization, or why bureaucrats are still in business. *World Development,* 27: 157–169.

Ravi Ramamurti is professor of business administration at Northeastern University, Boston. He received his DBA from Harvard University. He studies business-government relations and corporate strategy in emerging economies.

Part III
Deregulation: Industry Studies

A
The First Major Step – The Breakup of AT&T

[12]

Postdivestiture Long-Distance Competition in the United States

By William E. Taylor and Lester D. Taylor*

The breakup of the Bell System in 1984 initiated a succession of dramatic changes in the structure of the U.S. telecommunications industry. Divestiture of AT&T's operating telephone companies split the industry vertically into separate local and long-distance companies. Regulators actively encouraged entry and competition in the long-distance market, requiring that equal interconnections with the local network be provided to all long-distance competitors. Finally, new methods of regulating AT&T and the local telephone companies were implemented, including deregulation in some jurisdictions and price-cap regulation for interstate long-distance and carrier access services.

Since 1984, there have also been radical changes in the basic data that describe the interstate long-distance market. Capacity in the market has roughly tripled; where once there was one nationwide long-distance network, there are now nearly four backbone long-distance networks and roughly 500 providers. AT&T's share of interstate switched-services long-distance usage has fallen precipitously from 84 percent in 1984 to 63 percent at the end of 1991 (FCC, 1992b). Over the same period, real interstate long-distance prices fell by about 50 percent, and long-distance demand approximately doubled.

Several observers have attributed these changes to the pressures of competition. In its application to provide competitive long-distance service in Canada, Unitel (1991) pointed to the American example:

> By any standard, the American policy has been a success. Rates have fallen, innovation has increased and usage has grown.

Similarly, in a recent proposal to increase competition in local telephone markets, the U.S. Federal Communications Commission (FCC, 1991a ¶11) asserted that:

> ...competition in the provision of interstate long-distance service has led to sharply reduced rates, a larger variety of service options, and more rapid deployment of new technologies....

While it is tempting to ascribe lower prices and increased demand to the pressures of competition, careful analysis shows that this is not the case.

In this paper, we show that the overall reduction in interstate long-distance prices and expansion of interstate demand is *more than* explained by the reduction in the carrier access charges paid by the long-distance carriers to the local telephone companies.[1] Net of these payments, real interstate long-distance prices fell at about half the rate after 1984 than before. Moreover, regulated competition in the interstate toll market has not led to an expansion of demand. Despite the introduction of new services and massive advertising and marketing efforts, toll demand grew no more than would be ex-

---

* National Economic Research Associates, Inc., One Main Street, Cambridge, MA 02142, and Department of Economics, University of Arizona, Tucson, AZ 85721, respectively.

[1] Long-distance companies (e.g., AT&T, MCI) pay carrier access charges per minute of use to local telephone companies (e.g., New York Telephone) for originating and terminating traffic on their networks. These charges constitute a marginal cost to the long-distance companies.

pected based on changes in price, population, and consumer income. Thus, although the FCC's decision to reduce carrier access charges has resulted in enormous welfare gains for consumers, competition—or at least regulated competition—is not responsible for these benefits. The substantial price reductions and outward shifting of the toll demand curve that would be expected to arise from vigorous toll competition have yet to materialize.

I. The Effect of Competition on Prices

Real interstate long-distance prices fell in half from 1984 to 1991 and fell faster since divestiture than their long-run historical average. From 1984 to 1991, real interstate toll rate reductions averaged about 8.2 percent annually, using the Bureau of Labor Statistics (BLS) producer price index for interstate toll rates, deflated by the BLS GNP-PI. From 1972 to 1983, the longest predivestiture period over which interstate rate data are compiled by the Bureau of Labor Statistics, interstate toll rates declined at an annual average (real) rate of 2.7 percent. Since the postdivestiture period coincides with the period during which equal access became available and during which AT&T lost considerable market share, one might attribute these additional price reductions to increased competition among interexchange carriers. But that would be wrong.

Starting in 1984, the FCC began to rebalance local and toll prices in the United States, primarily through two related activities. First, it shifted recovery of local-telephone-company fixed costs that had previously been recovered from long-distance companies (through carrier access charges) to final consumers (through monthly subscriber line charges). Beginning in 1984, subscriber line charge revenues grew from approximately $1.296 billion to $6.069 billion during 1990–1991, and all of that revenue represented lower carrier access charges paid by the interexchange carriers (United States Telephone Association, 1990). Second, the FCC instituted a series of accounting changes which effectively reduced interstate costs while increasing intrastate costs. The net effect of these accounting changes (and other regulatory changes, including changes in income tax rates) was to reduce carrier access charges an additional $4.493 billion (annually) by 1990–1991. By 1990, carrier access charge expenditures were approximately $9.266 billion less per year because of these changes in federal regulatory policy, and by July 1992, AT&T was receiving annual reductions in access charges (and other exogenous costs) of approximately $10.86 billion.

At the same time, AT&T's cumulative *price* reductions produced only $8.22 billion less revenue per year, compared with 1984 (Taylor, 1992 [exhibit 1]). Thus, net of access charge changes, AT&T's tariffed prices actually grew in nominal terms at an annual rate of about 1.5 percent per year between 1984 and 1992. In real terms, they fell at about 2.2 percent per year. Paradoxically, in a period when AT&T was losing market share rapidly, it nonetheless increased nominal prices (net of access charges).

In addition, we observe much larger reductions in real interstate toll rates (net of access charges) during the period *before* divestiture, equal access, and AT&T's loss of market share. If we adjust interstate toll rates to account for the changes in the non-traffic-sensitive cost assignment in the Ozark Plan between 1972 and 1984, we observe that real interstate toll rates, net of changes in separations, fell at an annual rate of 6.28 percent.[2] Net of access charge changes, then, real interstate toll rates fell roughly twice as fast in the decade before divestiture than in the seven years after.

These findings are hardly consistent with the view that competition among interexchange carriers led to drastically lower prices. Beyond the mandatory reflection of access charge reductions in AT&T's rates (which were followed by the other long-distance providers), interexchange carriers initiated no significant price reductions for

---

[2] The earliest year for which BLS price data for interstate toll service are available is 1972.

toll services.[3] Since reductions in carrier access charges represent reductions in marginal cost for all long-distance companies, these data are more consistent with the presence of a regulated price umbrella than with a competitive market.[4]

The discussion thus far applies to AT&T's prices for tariffed services. During the same time period, large business customers began to substitute lower-priced bulk discount services (such as Megacom or SDN) for ordinary toll service, and high-volume residential customers were switching to optional calling plans (such as Reach Out America). Our estimate of the reduction in AT&T's tariff prices thus underestimates the reduction in the average price paid by AT&T's customers. While this effect is important for large business customers, it has a very small effect on aggregate prices.[5]

The explanation for this noncompetitive price behavior is not difficult to find. Regulated competition in the U.S. interstate toll markets differs in several important ways from unfettered free competition. The seven regional (former) Bell holding companies are barred from the market, and GTE is subject to a decree which regulates its participation. In addition, the FCC instituted a number of measures to protect new competitors in the market, including access-charge discounts for entrants to compensate for unequal access, non-cost-based access transport pricing which favored the smaller entrants to compensate for AT&T's locational advantage, and asymmetric regulation of AT&T which continues to this day.

II. The Effect of Competition on Demand

A second possible benefit from competition in the interstate toll markets was growth in demand due to more intensive marketing and the introduction of new services. Since divestiture, interstate switched access usage has grown at an annual rate of 11.81 percent (FCC, 1992a table 24), and this measure of demand probably understates demand growth, as it ignores demand served by bypass services, including services like SDN and Megacom.[6] During the 20 years before divestiture, annual growth in interstate usage averaged 10.5 percent (AT&T, 1983). While interstate toll demand did grow more rapidly after competitive entry, this growth was not due to additional new services, advertising, consumer awareness, and so on. The change in the growth rate is completely explained by changes in price, income, and population.

We compare the decade before divestiture (1972–1982) with the period after divestiture (1984–1988).[7] In each period, we

---

[3]This generalization applies to aggregate interstate toll service. There is evidence of competitive pressure reducing toll rates (i) paid by large business customers (e.g., through new services such as Megacom, Prism, and Ultra-WATS) and (ii) in the intrastate toll markets where long-haul rates fell and short-haul rates rose from 1983 to 1987 (Alan Mathios and Robert P. Rogers, 1989 p. 446).

[4]The gap in prices between AT&T and its competitors shrunk from 10–20 percent in mid-1984 to about 5 percent in 1987 when the unequal access discount was essentially eliminated (Michael E. Porter, 1987). Until equal-access facilities were available to interexchange carriers other than AT&T, those carriers received a 55-percent discount compared with the access prices paid by AT&T.

[5]AT&T calculates that during the 1989–1991 period, prices actually paid by customers fell at an annual rate of 0.9 percent due to the migration of customers to lower-priced services like SDN (Richard Schmalensee and Jeffrey H. Rohlfs, 1992 table II). Assuming conservatively that migration occurred at this rate since 1984, our estimate of AT&T's annual nominal price increase is lowered to 0.6 percent, and our estimate of AT&T's real annual price reductions is raised to 3.1 percent.

[6]Conventional switched long-distance service uses the switched access service of the local telephone company on both ends of the call. Services like Megacom and SDN use a private line to reach the customer on one end of the call, reducing the use of switched access service by half.

[7]We treat the postdivestiture period as the competitive period, although the same analysis as that described below yields the same qualitative results if applied to the 1972–1978 and 1979–1990 periods. To judge the effects of competition on demand growth, it is useful to note that MCI and Sprint advertising was less than $5 million in 1980 compared with $45 million for AT&T (measured in 1986 dollars). Between 1983 and 1984, total annual advertising for AT&T, MCI, and Sprint increased from about $100 million to about $150 million (in 1986 dollars) (Porter, 1987 figure 23).

divide actual demand growth into two parts:

1. *predicted growth*: a part due to changes in prices, income, and population;
2. *unexplained growth*: a (residually measured) part due to other changes—changes in taste, changes in the market place (such as competitive entry), and the like.

If competition shifts the demand curve outward due to advertising, the availability of new products or services, or a heightened awareness of the uses for telephone service, we would expect to see that shift as an increase in unexplained growth.

To explain growth in the demand for interstate switched services, we estimated a quarterly model for aggregate interstate switched access demand using data from the third quarter of 1984 through the second quarter of 1992. The results are in keeping with estimates obtained from other interstate toll demand models:

$$\ln Q_t = -8.70 + 0.565 \ln Q_{t-1} - 0.272 \ln P_t$$
$$(-1.84) \quad (4.99) \qquad (-3.61)$$

$$+ 0.422 \ln Y_t + 1.49 \ln POP_t$$
$$(1.87) \qquad (1.76)$$

where

$\ln Q$ = logarithm of total interstate switched access minutes

$\ln P$ = logarithm of the ratio of the CPI for interstate toll calls to the CPI for all goods and services

$\ln Y$ = logarithm of real disposable personal income

$\ln POP$ = logarithm of population size

and where t statistics are in parentheses. On 26 degrees of freedom, the R^2 of the model is 0.998, and the Durbin h statistic is -0.60. The long-run price elasticity of -0.63 agrees with other estimates, notably the -0.72 estimate used by the FCC in CC Docket 87-313 (Joseph P. Gatto et al., 1988).

Using this simple model, we calculate the rate of growth of unexplained demand. During the 1972–1982 period, demand was predicted to grow at an annual rate of 6.58

percent. Actual demand growth averaged 8.92 percent, leaving a growth rate of unexplained demand of 2.34 percent. During the 1984–1991 period, the model predicted that demand growth would average 10.79 percent, and actual demand growth averaged 11.81 percent. Thus the growth rate of unexplained demand during the 1984–1991 period averaged 1.02 percent. Growth in demand unexplained by changes in price, income, and population averaged 1.33 percentage points *lower* in the 1984–1991 period compared with the 1972–1982 period.[8]

One possible explanation of this reduction in the growth rate of unexplained demand after divestiture is the growth of bypass—provision of interstate toll minutes of use without using the switched access facilities of the local telephone companies. In our calculation, we measure interstate toll demand as interstate switched access demand after divestiture, and the growth of bypass demand (including services like Megacom and SDN) would mask growth in toll demand after divestiture. To adjust our results for the possibility of bypass, we use industry estimates of interstate bypass usage from 1984 through 1991 (FCC, 1991b) and add that usage to our measure of switched access demand (Taylor, 1992 [exhibit 3]). The annual growth rate of this measure of interstate toll demand averaged 12.90 percent during the 1984–1991 period, so that unexplained growth rose about 1 percentage point to 2.12 percent. Including the effects of bypass, unexplained demand still grew about 0.23 percentage points more slowly in the 1984–1991 period than in the 1972–1982 period.

III. Observable Effects of Competition

Competition in the postdivestiture period among interstate long-distance suppliers did not reduce prices or expand demand, but it did have perceptible effects, at least in cer-

---

[8] The results are not sensitive to the particular time period chosen or to the precise values of the elasticities. If the price elasticity is taken to be -0.72, (Gatto et al., 1988), unexplained demand growth slows even more after divestiture.

tain market segments. While AT&T's over-all market share of switched access minutes of use fell from 84.2 percent in the third quarter of 1984 to 62.8 percent in the fourth quarter of 1991, its share of the large business market fell to about 50 percent. Moreover, AT&T consistently set prices for its business services below their applicable cap under price-cap regulation, and evidence amassed by the FCC suggests that AT&T faces a substantially more elastic (firm) demand curve in the business-services market. Supply elasticities of competitive firms have increased during the period. About 58 percent of AT&T's switched business-services revenue comes from firms that also purchase services from a competitor, and MCI and Sprint together could absorb about 15 percent of AT&T's business traffic without expanding their capacity (FCC, 1991c ¶36, 40, 50). Of course, it is not surprising to observe more lively competition in the market for large business customers: having higher usage, large business customers are more likely to change carriers in response to a given price difference.

Using the aggregate FCC data discussed above, we specified individual-firm demand functions, treating the interstate market as comprising two firms, AT&T and "others." Although we obtained a reasonable market demand equation, we were unable to estimate individual-firm elasticities. These results may be due to poor price data and limited independent variation in those data for AT&T and its competitors, but they are also consistent with lackluster price competition in the market. This is not to say that there has not been competition, even fierce competition, in price in certain submarkets —only that such behavior cannot be isolated in the aggregate data. The conclusion, accordingly, is that meaningful estimation of firm demand functions in the interstate toll market must await the development of a comprehensive data set that is disaggregated by both submarkets and firms.

IV. Conclusions

Competitive entry into interstate long-distance service has undoubtedly resulted in vigorous competition in the large business market. In the aggregate interstate toll market, AT&T's market share has fallen and its (firm) demand curve has accordingly become more elastic. Nonetheless, competition since 1984 has not led to lower prices in the aggregate market or to lower prices for residential and small business customers. In addition, despite massive increases in marketing efforts and a flurry of new service offerings, aggregate interstate toll demand has not shifted outward. Changes in prices (and income and population) fully explain the growth in demand in the postdivestiture period. In sum, regulated competition and asymmetric regulation of AT&T have yet to bring the benefits of lower prices and expanded demand to all interstate telephone customers.

REFERENCES

Gatto, Joseph P., Langin-Hooper, Jerry, Robinson, Paul B. and Tyan, Holly, "Interstate Switched Access Demand Analysis," *Information Economics and Policy*, 1988, *3* (4), 283–309.

Mathios, Alan and Rogers, Robert P., "The Impact of Alternative Forms of State Regulation of AT&T on Direct-Dial Long-Distance Telephone Rates," *Rand Journal of Economics*, Autumn 1989, *20*, 437–53.

Porter, Michael E., "Competition in the Long Distance Telecommunications Market: An Industry Structure Analysis," report filed with AT&T's *Comments* in CC Docket 87-313, 19 October 1987.

Schmalensee, Richard and Rohlfs, Jeffrey H., "Productivity Gains Resulting from Interstate Price Caps for AT&T," report filed by AT&T in CC Docket 92-134, 1992.

Taylor, William E., "Effects of Competitive Entry in the U.S. Interstate Toll Markets: An Update," NERA report filed in CC Docket 92-141, 10 July 1992.

American Telephone & Telegraph Company, "Long Lines Statistics, 1960–1982," mimeo, American Telephone and Telegraph Company, 1983.

Federal Communications Commission, (1991a) "Expanded Interconnection with Local Telephone Company Facilities," notice of proposed rulemaking and notice of inquiry, filed in CC Docket 91-141, 6 May 1991.

_____, (1991b) "Monitoring Report," filed in CC Docket 87-339, July 1991.

_____, (1991c) "In the Matter of Competition in the Interstate Interexchange Marketplace," report and order, filed in CC Docket 90-132, 1 August 1991.

_____, (1992a) "Trends in Telephone Service," mimeo, Federal Communications Commission, February 1992.

_____, (1992b) "Long Distance Market Shares: Fourth Quarter, 1991," mimeo, Common Carrier Bureau, Industry Analysis Division, Federal Communications Commission, 24 March 1992.

United States Telephone Association, "Ex Parte," presentation to the FCC filed in CC Docket 87-313, 6 August 1990.

Unitel Communications Inc., "Argument of Applicant," application to provide public long distance telephone service before the Canadian Radio-Television and Telecommunications Commission, 29 July 1991.

[13]

The Effects of the Breakup of AT&T on Telephone Penetration in the United States

By Jerry Hausman, Timothy Tardiff, and Alexander Belinfante*

The breakup of AT&T in 1984 into a long-distance (and manufacturing) component and seven local-service companies, the Bell operating companies (BOC's), created the opportunity for billions of dollars of annual economic efficiency gains for the U.S. economy. These potential annual efficiency gains arise in part from the establishment of a rational price system for telephone services. At the time of the breakup (and to a lesser extent today) basic access to the telephone network received a large cross subsidy from other telephone services; that is, the price of basic access was well below its incremental (or marginal) cost. The largest component of this cross subsidy arises from the prices of long-distance services which are well in excess of their incremental cost. However, since the price elasticity of basic access is near zero while the price elasticity of long-distance services varies from about -0.25 to -1.2 depending on the type of service, a large economic efficiency loss occurs.

Why did regulation evolve in the United States to cause this extremely large distortion in prices? Numerous reasons can and have been put forward (see e.g., Peter Temin, 1987), but our favorite explanation arises from a combination of an outmoded

framework of telecommunications regulation and changing technology. Congressional legislation, which established the Federal Communications Commission (FCC) and remains the basic framework for telecommunications regulation, was the Communications Act of 1934. This legislation led to the current joint regulation of telephone companies by both the FCC and state public utility commissions (PUC's). The Communications Act codified the goal of universal service—the notion that all U.S. households should have telephone service. This policy has been quite successful with U.S. telephone penetration at 93.3 percent in 1990 according to the Current Population Survey (CPS). Yet the FCC is basically in charge of setting long-distance prices while state PUC's are in charge of setting basic access prices, both of which are important factors in telephone penetration. During the post-World War II period the technology was changing so that the cost of long-distance service was decreasing markedly while the cost of labor-intensive basic access continued to rise essentially in line with inflation. The so-called separations system of regulation, established to "divide the cost" of the public telephone network between federal and state regulatory jurisdictions, created increasing cross subsidies as the contribution from long distance grew with increases in both the price–cost ratio of long distance and increases in long-distance demand.

Economists were aware of this problem and in the 1970's recommended that long-distance prices be decreased and basic access prices be increased. Indeed, to a first approximation if the basic access price elasticity is zero, the first-best tax solution of a

†*Discussants:* Glenn A. Woroch, GTE Laboratories; Molly K. Macauley, Resources for the Future; Gerald Faulhaber, University of Pennsylvania.

*Department of Economics, Massachusetts Institute of Technology, Cambridge, MA 02139, National Economic Research Associates, 1 Main Street, Cambridge, MA 02142, and Federal Communications Commission, 1919 M Street, N.W., Washington, DC 20554, respectively. The ideas expressed in this paper do not necessarily represent the opinions or policies of the FCC.

lump-sum tax on basic access is available, which eliminates the loss in economic efficiency. Income-distribution problems arise, but these problems can be solved by a targeted subsidy to low-income households. Yet, state PUC's have been reluctant to raise basic access prices because they perceive that the very small basic access price elasticity could lead to some decrease in telephone penetration. In this paper we present a model of basic residential access demand which demonstrates that these fears are unfounded. Prior econometric estimates have specified models of basic access demand as a function of only its own price. Our estimates also find an important effect of long-distance prices on the demand for basic access. Indeed, the effect of long-distance prices is sufficiently large that a revenue-neutral rebalancing of telephone prices, which would reduce the subsidy for basic access and lower long-distance prices, would lead to both large gains in economic efficiency and *increased* telephone penetration in the United States. Thus, the perceived policy trade-off between economic efficiency and telephone penetration is unlikely to exist any longer.

I. Regulated Price Setting by the FCC and State PUC's

A. *FCC Regulation*

In regulating interstate telephone services, the FCC uses two main approaches to set prices to allow the local exchange carriers (LEC's) to cover their separated cost basis. The first approach is to set a lump-sum tax, called the subscriber line charge (SLC), which is currently $3.50 a month per residential access line. Each residential phone user pays this fee as part of the monthly basic exchange access bill. The other approach used by the FCC is to charge long-distance companies for access from the customer premises to the long-distance companies' network. These access charges are currently about $0.07 per minute of interstate long-distance usage. Access charges are quite substantial since they comprise about 40–50 percent of long-distance com-

panies' overall costs and are over five times the LEC's incremental cost of providing long-distance access. In total, the subscriber line charge plus access charges combine to cover about 25 percent of overall LEC costs, which is the FCC share of separated costs.

B. *State PUC Regulation*

State PUC's set prices for basic exchange access and for intrastate long-distance services. Basic exchange access, which is often offered bundled together with free unlimited local calling (flat-rate tariff) or provides access plus a per-call charge for local calls (measured-rate tariff), has a price which varies from about $8 per month in New Jersey and California to about $23 in West Virginia. When the FCC subscriber line charge is included, the monthly basic access price varies from about $12 to $27. (In October 1990, the FCC reported a national average flat rate of $17.79, including taxes and the subscriber line charge.) The incremental cost of basic access depends on geographical location, but its range is about $18–$24 per month for residential customers. Thus, in most states residential basic access service receives a significant cross subsidy.

Intrastate long-distance service comes in two varieties. IntraLATA long distance calls are provided by the BOC's and also by long distance companies such as MCI and AT&T where permitted by state regulation.[1] Regulated prices of intraLATA calls are set well in excess of the cost of providing these calls. The revenues from BOC-provided intraLATA long-distance service are used to cover BOC costs, including the cross subsidy used to help finance residential basic access. Companies such as MCI and AT&T provide intrastate interLATA long-distance services. Most states have adopted access charges for intrastate long-distance services similar in form to the access-charge frame-

---

[1] LATA's (local access and transport areas) were established in 1984 at divestiture. BOC's are restricted to providing telephone services only within LATA's.

work used by the FCC. The access charges are again well above cost so that they provide an important source of cross subsidy for residential basic access service.

C. Overall Effect on Telephone Service Prices

Basic exchange access is typically set well below its incremental cost and receives a significant cross subsidy. The size of the cross subsidy, at least from interstate toll calls, has decreased since the breakup of AT&T because of the use of the subscriber line charge and the decrease in long-distance access prices. At the state level the size of the cross subsidy may well have increased, since most state PUC's have not increased residential basic access prices along with inflation, while the large labor component of providing copper links from residences to the telephone network has led to increased costs. Since the breakup of AT&T, interstate long-distance prices have decreased by about 40 percent, primarily due to decreases in access charges by the FCC. However, a decrease in FCC access charges down to incremental cost would probably lead to a further reduction in long-distance prices of another 25 percent, at least. Thus, long-distance service continues to cross-subsidize basic-access service as it did before divestiture. We now discuss the likely outcome of a further reduction, or even the elimination, of the cross subsidy by an increase in basic access prices together with a decrease in long-distance access charges, which would cause reduced long-distance prices.

II. A Model of Basic Access Demand

A. Model Specification

The decision to purchase basic access service depends on its price as well as the demand for usage of the telephone by the residential consumer. This usage falls into three categories: local usage, intraLATA long-distance calls, and interLATA long-distance calls. Thus, we have a combined discrete-choice equation and continuous demand system for three services which arise from a common decision framework.[2] Here we are interested in the question of whether the household decides to purchase basic exchange service which arises from a partially indirect utility function:

$$(1) \qquad u = u(y, \mathbf{p}, \mathbf{q}, z, \varepsilon)$$

where y is household income, $\mathbf{p}$ is a vector of prices for basic exchange access which includes the one-time installation price and the monthly basic exchange price, $\mathbf{q}$ is a vector of prices of usage for local service (whose price is often zero), intraLATA service, and interLATA service, z is a function of household characteristics, and ε is a random parameter which is independently distributed across households.[3] Conditional on purchasing basic exchange access, the three demand equations can be derived via Roy's identity:

$$(2) \qquad x_j = \frac{\dfrac{\partial u(y - p_1 - p_2, \mathbf{q}, z, \varepsilon)}{\partial q_j}}{\dfrac{\partial u(y - p_1 - p_2, \mathbf{q}, z, \varepsilon)}{\partial y}}$$

Thus, efficient estimation would involve joint estimation of telephone penetration and the demand equation for telephone services. Since we do not have data on telephone service demand, we instead estimate the basic-exchange-access discrete-choice equation where a household purchases tele-

---

[2] Models with combined discrete and continuous demand functions arising from a common-decision framework have been estimated in other contexts by Hausman (1979) and by Jeffrey Dubin and Daniel McFadden (1984). Hausman (1985) estimates a further model with this structure and considers the general econometric framework for such models.

[3] A Hicksian composite commodity provides the numeraire price. The observant reader will realize that actually two interLATA prices exist for each household depending on whether a call is interstate or intrastate. We combine these two prices into a price index for interLATA long-distance calls.

phone service if

(3) $\bar{u}_1 = \bar{u}(y - p_1 - p_2, \mathbf{q}, z, \varepsilon)$

      $\geq \bar{u}(y, z, \varepsilon) = \bar{u}_2$

where u_1 is the partially indirect utility function where basic access price has been subtracted from household income and u_2 is the partially indirect utility function where all consumption is of the composite (non-telephone) commodity. An important finding of equations (1)–(3) is that the discrete choice equation should depend on the basic access price(s) and also on the usage prices. This specification is in marked contrast to almost all other specifications of basic access demand.[4]

B. Data and Estimation

To estimate the effect of telephone prices on basic residential access, we acquired data that were collected for and by the FCC for CC Docket No. 87-339. For the years 1984–1988, the data combine telephone penetration and demographic variables from the Current Population Survey with prices collected through the U.S. Telephone Association at the request of the FCC. The data are organized into about 200 geographic areas for the first two years and about 500 geographic areas for the last three years. For each area, information on telephone penetration, demographic variables, and telephone prices is available. The long-distance price variables include a measure of interstate toll prices and a combined measure for intrastate toll prices combining intrastate intraLATA and interLATA prices to form an overall toll-price index using the following procedure. First, for each state, we obtained the 1984 numbers of intrastate toll calls (A) and interstate toll calls (B) for use in a fixed-weight toll index. The index

was constructed as follows:

toll index

$$= \frac{B \times (\text{interstate index}) + A \times (\text{intrastate index})}{B + A}$$

The interstate index was included in the FCC data and the intrastate toll index was the national-level CPI for intrastate toll calls. Flat-rate access prices charged by Bell Telephone companies, which supplemented the lowest-priced access rates from the FCC data, were obtained from the National Association of Regulatory Utility Commissioners' annual publication of "Bell Telephone Companies' Exchange Service Telephone Rates."

The basic specification used is a binary logit model estimated in Berkson-Theil form where the left-hand-side variable is the proportion of households with telephone service and the right-hand-side variables are telephone prices and demographic variables of households.[5] Because of the panel-data structure of our sample, which varies across both time and states, we use a more general stochastic specification than the Berkson-Theil specification. One component of the stochastic disturbance is the usual deviation between the observed proportion and the model prediction which arises because of sampling error and is proportional to within-cell sample size; an additional component of the disturbance arises from a state-specific component of variance which is invariant across time, and the final component varies across both states and time and allows for general specification error. The model was estimated using a feasible generalized least-squares procedure.

The results of the logit model estimation are available from the authors upon re-

---

[4] Probably the best known of these prior models is Lewis Perl's (1984) model. The only prior exception is Belinfante (1990), in which basic exchange access demand is allowed to depend on interstate long-distance prices.

[5] Because of the high proportion of observations that are in the tail of the distribution, estimation was also done using a probit specification and an arcsine specification. Very similar results were found for all three specifications. The specification tests of Hausman and William Taylor (1981) comparing between and within estimates produced no statistically significant differences.

quest. At 1990 average U.S. prices and penetration levels, the relevant elasticities are as follows (standard errors are in parentheses): installation charge, -0.0206 (0.0032); basic access price for measured rate service, -0.0052 (0.0025); difference between flat and measured rate, -0.0027 (0.0018); intraLATA toll price, -0.0086 (0.0017); intrastate interLATA toll price, -0.0019 (0.0004); interstate interLATA toll price, -0.0055 (0.0011).

The estimated elasticity with respect to the basic access price, -0.005, is quite small, with a 10-percent price increase leading to a 0.5-percent decrease in penetration (approximately 0.005, given a penetration rate of about 0.93). The finding of a very small but significantly nonzero own-price elasticity for residential basic access demand is consistent with prior studies, with the best known paper being Perl (1984). The very small price-elasticity effect has led some regulators to resist raising basic access prices because of the negative effect on telephone penetration. The other important own-price determinant of demand is the installation charge. Note that the elasticity is about four times as large as the elasticity for the monthly price of basic access. Such a large elasticity implies a very large implicit discount rate of over 100 percent per year, which is consistent with previous findings of purchase decisions for consumer durables for low-income households in Hausman (1979) and the findings of Dubin and McFadden (1984).[6]

However, concentration on only the own price effect could lead to incorrect conclusions on the effects of rebalancing telephone service prices. Note that the cross-price elasticity of the demand for basic access service is -0.0086 with respect to the price of intraLATA toll service and it is -0.0055 with respect to the interstate toll

price, which demonstrates the complementary nature of basic access demand and local and long-distance telephone usage. The higher estimated cross-price elasticity of intraLATA toll service is consistent with the general finding that own-price intraLATA toll elasticities are smaller in magnitude than interLATA toll elasticities and with the relative expenditures across bill categories. Thus, an increase in basic access prices combined with a decrease in long-distance toll prices (via a decrease in long-distance access prices) could well lead to an *increase* in telephone penetration, rather than a decrease as has been assumed by many regulators.

III. Postdivestiture Price Changes and Telephone Penetration

During the period 1984–1990, FCC and state pricing policies were accompanied by a gain in U.S. telephone penetration from 91.4 percent to 93.3 percent. Ten million additional households subscribed to telephone service, and households without telephone service decreased by 1.1 million. These results are inconsistent with the view that raising basic access price will necessarily lead to decreased penetration when long-distance prices are decreasing.[7]

The SLC accounts for about one-third of the average price of measured-rate basic access in the United States. Thus, use of the own-price elasticity only would lead to a prediction of a decrease in penetration of -0.18 percent. However, the decrease in interstate long-distance prices during the same time period, where 1984 real prices were approximately double 1990 prices, had

---

[6] A goal of many regulators to increase telephone penetration could well be advanced by allowing new customers to pay the installation charge over an extended period, say 12 months (with interest), instead of requiring an up-front payment.

[7] The results refute definitively the claims by some consumer advocates who predicted that when basic exchange rates increased because of the SLC that large numbers of households would drop off the telephone network. For instance, the Consumer Federation of America and the U.S. Public Interest Research Group predicted in 1985 that 6 million subscribers would cease telephone service between 1984 and 1986. The actual change in subscribers was an increase of about 4.1 million subscribers during this period.

a positive effect on penetration of approximately three times the magnitude of the increase in basic exchange access prices. Overall, the net effect of the increase in basic exchange access prices due to the SLC and decreases in interstate long-distance prices was to increase telephone penetration in the United States by 0.45 percent according to the model estimates.

In addition to the price changes attributable to FCC interstate access-charge policy, prices for basic access and intrastate toll also fell in real terms. In particular, monthly basic-services prices fell by about $0.85,[8] the installation charge fell by about $2.80, and real intrastate toll prices fell by about 30 percent. When these changes are included with the changes from FCC access-charge policy, the model estimates a gain in penetration of 1.3 percentage points, compared to the actual gain of 1.9 percentage points.[9]

The results are consistent with the fact that even low-income (lifeline) customers pay a substantial portion of their monthly bill for toll services. For example, using a sample of actual May 1991 bills from Pacific Bell for California, we calculate that toll calls account for 64.9 percent of the total bill. Thus, any analysis of the effect of price changes on network penetration needs to account for both the price of toll calls and the basic exchange access price.

IV. Conclusion

Economists have long realized that significant gains in economic efficiency would occur if telephone prices were more cost-based and if the cross subsidy for basic residential access were reduced or eliminated. However, the fear of regulators that such a change would lead to decreased telephone penetration has acted as an absolute constraint to proposed changes in many instances. Our model estimates demonstrate that increased economic efficiency need not lead to decreased penetration.

Indeed, the evidence from the period after the breakup of AT&T during the 1980's tends to show that increased penetration resulted in part from the combined effect of higher monthly basic access charges and lower long-distance prices. Further efficiency gains are likely to arise if the procedure continues to eliminate the cross subsidy received by basic exchange access and if long-distance prices are lowered.[10] These changes can come about in either (or both) of two ways. State PUC's can allow LEC's to change their pricing structures. While many state PUC's have set this change as a goal, very few have actually made much progress, in part because of the opposition of consumer advocacy groups. In addition, the FCC could raise the residential subscriber line charge and lower interstate long-distance access charges, although this change may require Congressional approval. Thus, either set of changes may be difficult to implement. However, the current combination of federal and state policy toward regulation of telephone service in the United States has an efficiency loss in the billions of dollars and retards the advancement of the "Information Age" which many individuals believe will increase productivity and lead

---

[8]Therefore, the net impact of the SLC and the reduction in basic access rates is a real price increase of about $2.20.

[9]Changes in demographic characteristics, particularly income, probably account for the additional increase in telephone penetration. For example, Perl's (1984) model produces an income elasticity of about 0.10. Thus, the change in real family income of about 8 percent between 1984 and 1990 according to CPS data (where both median family income and income of the lowest quintile increased by about 8 percent) would imply about a 0.8-percentage-point gain in penetration. Added to the 1.3-percentage-point gain implied by price changes, the total effect is about 2.1 percentage points, which is close to the actual gain of 1.9 percentage points.

[10]Of course, these changes need to be accompanied by a targeted subsidy program for low-income households. However, almost all states now have well-developed programs for such households.

to many new services for telephone consumers.

REFERENCES

Belinfante, Alexander, "A Dynamic Analysis of Telephone Penetration," mimeo, Federal Communications Commission, 1990.

Dubin, Jeffrey A. and McFadden, Daniel L., "An Econometric Analysis of Residential Electric Appliance Holdings and Consumption," *Econometrica*, March 1984, *52*, 345–62.

Hausman, Jerry A., "Individual Discount Rates and the Purchase and Utilization of Energy Using Durables," *Bell Journal of Economics*, Spring 1979, *10*, 33–54.

_____, "The Econometrics of Nonlinear Budget Sets," *Econometrica*, November 1985, *53*, 1255–82.

_____ and Taylor, William E., "Panel Data and Unobservable Individual Effects," *Econometrica*, November 1981, *49*, 1377–98.

Perl, Lewis, "A New Study of Economic and Demographic Determinants of Residential Demand for Basic Telephone Service," mimeo, National Economic Research Associates, White Plains, NY, 1984.

Temin, Peter, *The Fall of the Bell System*, Cambridge: Cambridge University Press, 1987.

B
Deregulating Airlines in the US

[14]

"Don't Panic"[1]: A Primer on Airline Deregulation

by Paul W. Bauer

The old dictum says that if the Devil did not exist, the Church would have had to invent him. Similarly, if the regulator didn't exist, the airline industry would have had to invent him—and did in 1938. A current question is what would happen to the industry were it totally deregulated. One thesis is that there would be a rush by existing and new entrants to those routes thought to be profitable. Other routes would be abandoned. Price competition would be destructive. With the essential link between economics and safety there would be an inevitable major air disaster, possibly involving a prominent Member of Congress. Public outcry and congressional responses would lead to the re-establishment of regulation. Since this was the sequence of events in the mid-30's, why re-learn that lesson? This thesis has been challenged, but the lesson of history ... cannot be totally ignored.

Secor D. Browne, Chairman
Civil Aeronautics Board
(January 1972)[2]

Paul W. Bauer is an economist at the Federal Reserve Bank of Cleveland.

The author would like to thank Randall W. Eberts, Joe A. Stone, and others who provided useful comments on an earlier draft of this paper.

17

Introduction

Former Civil Aeronautics Board (CAB) Chairman Browne's statement 15 years ago can scarcely be interpreted as an unqualified endorsement of the government's current policy of airline deregulation. It does remind us, however, that the issue of airline regulation has been controversial for quite some time.

The Civil Aeronautics Act (CAA) of 1938, enacted to counteract the alleged conditions of competitive instability of an industry then in its infancy, began 40 years of pervasive government regulation by the now-defunct CAB. With passage of the Airline Deregulation Act (ADA) of 1978, the federal government completed an about-face in policy and reintroduced competitive forces into the market.

For eight years now, the airline industry has been experiencing a great deal of turmoil, as evidenced by the large number of entries, mergers, and bankruptcies. Much of this turmoil, however, is not the result of deregulation, but rather of the fuel price increase in 1979,

of the recession in the early 1980s, and of the air traffic controllers' strike in August 1981. Even so, the regulation debate is heating up again as the events predicted by Mr. Browne seem to be unfolding—with such examples as the recent bankruptcy of Frontier Airlines, the financial problems of People Express and Eastern Airlines, and the crash of the Aeromexico airliner in southern California in August 1986.

This paper analyzes the conditions that prevailed under CAB regulation and that led to the Airline Deregulation Act of 1978. These conditions are contrasted with the effects of deregulation observed so far. Finally, an attempt is made to predict the future evolution and performance of the U.S. airline industry under deregulation.

I. The U.S. Airline Industry Under CAB Regulation

Between 1938 and 1978, the CAB maintained strict control over the two most important decisions airlines had to make: where to fly and how much to charge. This meant that airlines could only compete with one another by offering a higher quality of service (primarily more frequent flights

---

1   Sound general advice from *The Hitchhiker's Guide to the Galaxy* by Douglas Adams.

2   Foreword to R.E.G. Davies' *Airlines of the United States Since 1914*, Putnam & Company Limited, London (1972).

and other amenities). Studies have shown that CAB regulation led to more frequent flights and to lower load factors (the proportion of seats on a flight that are filled by paying passengers) than would be normal in a competitive airline industry.[3]

Since these actions resulted in higher costs for the airlines, and since the CAB was charged with maintaining the financial health of the industry (that is, preventing losses), it follows that fares were higher. In fact, the interstate carriers subject to CAB regulation marked up fares 20 to 95 percent more than the intrastate carriers not subject to CAB regulation for similar routes.[4] The General Accounting Office (GAO) estimated that passengers could save up to $2 billion dollars or more per year with competitive fares.[5]

II. The Theory Behind Deregulation

Given fare markups of these magnitudes, why were the airlines' earnings so mediocre? The answer appears to be that regulated industries do not have sufficient incentives to control costs. Given the CAB's mandate to maintain the health of the industry by raising fares whenever the airlines experienced hard times and the lack of a threat of competitive entry (the CAB had not allowed the formation of a single new trunk airline from 1938 to 1978), a strong prima facie case exists for inadequate cost control. Using data from 1972 to 1978, Bauer (1985) found that, on average, airline costs during that period were 48 percent over the minimum cost of providing the same service.

Another example of the poor incentive structure can be found by analyzing labor costs. Providing a service product—transportation between two points—airlines could not stockpile their output in anticipation of a strike. Any output diverted by one carrier (either to other carriers, or to other transportation modes) as a result of the strike is a permanent loss to that carrier. Further, even when the strike is settled, the airline may lose some of its customers to other carriers. Regulated airlines could not offer large discounts and free flights to lure their customers back, as United Airlines did after a strike in 1979. Under CAB regulation, strikes were very costly to the airlines, but higher labor costs could be

absorbed by CAB fare increases or CAB approval to enter some profitable new route. Thus, there was little incentive for airlines to endure strikes.

Given the evidence on fare markups and the suspicions about airline inefficiency, proponents of deregulation became convinced that elimination of CAB regulation, and a move towards more competition in the industry, would be beneficial to travelers and, ultimately, to the industry itself. Two basic tenets drive the model of the industry that proponents of deregulation had in mind: one, that the minimum efficient scale size is reached at a relatively low level of output and, two, that new entry and the threat of new entry into the industry would ensure sufficient competition to hold fares close to marginal cost and only allow firms to earn a normal profit.[6]

Numerous studies performed prior to deregulation, using various data sets from the late 1950s forward, found that larger airlines had no significant unit-cost advantage (measured in passenger miles) over smaller airlines. This research implied that there was plenty of room in the U.S. airline industry for anywhere from 20 to 100 efficiently sized airlines (see White [1979]), and that there was little chance of concentration increasing in the industry if it were deregulated.

The second tenet, that freedom of entry would severely limit any market power that an airline may have, was being strongly supported by the new theory of contestable markets (see Baumol, Panzar, and Willig [1982]). Simply stated, this theory predicts that if market entry and exit involves no irrecoverable costs and can occur quite rapidly, the threat of entry is sufficient to ensure that firms in this market earn no more than a normal profit.

The following illustrates how this result occurs. Suppose the firms in a contestable market decided to collude and to raise their prices. Although the strategy might work in the very short run, soon new firms not party to this agreement would recognize the opportunity for above-normal profits and would enter the industry, driving prices back down. In a contestable market, even a monopolist would thus earn a normal profit, because if it tried to take full advantage of its monopoly power to earn more than a normal profit, another firm would enter and charge the lower price, capturing the entire market for itself.

Clearly, not all industries in the economy can be considered contestable (the auto industry, for example, is definitely not). However, deregulation proponents considered

3 Douglas, George W. and James C. Miller, (1974) *Economic Regulation of Domestic Air Transport: Theory and Policy*, Brookings Institution, Washington, D.C.

4 T. E. Keeler, "Airlines Regulation and Market Performance," *Bell Journal of Economics* 3 (Autumn 1972), pp. 339-434.

5 General Accounting Office, Report to Congress, *Lower Airline Costs per Passenger Are Possible in the United States and Could Result in Lower Fares*, February 1977, p. 11.

6 A normal profit is the minimum return required to keep the firm from shifting resources out of the industry.

the airline industry a good candidate for contestability—once the artificial barriers to entry created by the CAB were eliminated.

The following market characteristics were considered to promote contestability:

• Inputs used by the airline industry are all relatively mobile when compared to most other industries. Labor, energy, and materials can either be employed or let go on fairly short notice, as in most industries, but capital is much more mobile than in almost any other major industry.

• Airlines can quickly shift planes from one route to another as the need arises. Further, since there is a ready secondary market for used aircraft—in fact, many carriers rent a significant portion of their fleets—planes are fairly mobile from one carrier to another.

• Ground facilities are usually rented, making them fairly disposable (acquisition is another matter, and will be discussed later).

These properties are thought to make it relatively easy for incumbent airlines to begin service on new routes, so that if fares are too high on a given route, other airlines will enter those markets at lower passenger fares. These properties are also thought to facilitate the start-up of new airlines if existing lines are making more than a normal profit.

Thus, according to the contestable market view, there was little to fear on the part of consumers from airline deregulation. Even if the industry did evolve into a handful of firms, the contestable market theory predicted that they could only earn a normal profit and fares would be as low as possible.

In summary, the proponents of deregulation predicted sharply lower coach fares, as fare markups would be bid down and airlines would strive to reduce their costs in the face of observed and potential competition. There would be some deterioration in service quality as flight frequencies would be reduced. However, this would in turn lower airline costs (by increasing load factors), thus further lowering fares, and passengers would receive the fare-service mix that they prefer. It was felt that there was no need to worry about increased concentration in the airline industry, because the minimum efficient scale would be small enough to make room for many carriers. Besides, the threat of entry would be sufficient to hold fares down and service quality up, even on routes with few carriers.

III. The Effects of Airline Deregulation
The actual effects of airline deregulation, while being generally beneficial to date, have not materialized precisely as the proponents predicted.

This divergence of prediction and reality can be traced to changes in the airlines' operating strategies that were induced by the increased freedom given to them by the elimination of CAB regulation. These changes in strategy occurred in the two areas mentioned earlier: where to fly and how much to charge. Market competition seems to have induced even more innovation than industry experts foresaw, leading to predominately beneficial changes in airline behavior.

Fares
As the CAB's authority over fares was diminished, the airlines gradually developed a more complex fare structure to replace the relatively simple first-class and coach-fare structure that existed under regulation. While an element of price discrimination certainly exists, most of the variation in fares is based on differences in the cost of serving the various classes of passengers.[7] Fares are lower for travel outside the periods of peak demand. Examples include flying on weekends, flying in the middle of the day or late evening, and flying to locations that are out of season. A prime example of fare differences based primarily on cost is found between those who can book and pay for tickets in advance and those who cannot. It is costly for airlines to fly planes with empty seats, yet they intentionally have some slack in their systems so that they can accommodate last-minute travelers—for a higher price.

These pricing strategies have enabled the airlines to increase both traffic and revenue far more than if a uniform pricing policy had been followed. The increase in the industry's revenue passenger miles (RPM) and average load factor are plotted over time in figure 1. Both have increased since deregulation, although the effect of the recession in the early 1980s is clearly evident. Traffic increased 33 percent just from 1977 to 1979.

As a result of this shift in pricing strategy, the average fare that passengers actually paid (adjusted for inflation) has fallen about 20 percent in the last 10 years, even though the standard coach fare has fallen very little. Though this is a far cry from the drop that had been expected given the fare markups and inefficiency that existed under regulation, it does represent a

19

. . . .

7 For example, whether one stays over a Saturday night on a round trip has no effect on the airline's cost of providing the service, yet it provides a very useful screening device enabling the airlines to charge higher fares to business travelers (who generally cannot meet this restriction) and lower fares to pleasure travelers (who usually can). Thus the airlines can price discriminate between the two classes of consumers, taking advantage of the business travelers' higher price elasticity of demand (and the leisure travelers' lower elasticity of demand) to increase their revenue and profits.

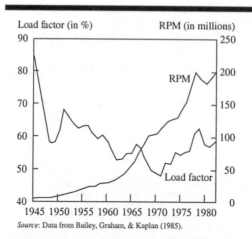

Figure 1

20

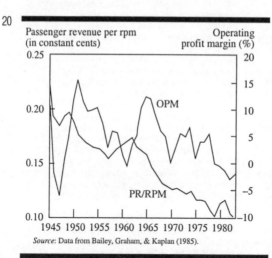

Figure 2

quency on most routes (as a result of the increase in traffic) and by the lower fares (for those who could qualify for the discount fares); and the airline industry was able to increase its profits over what they would have been under regulation as the increase in load factors lowered costs.

Routes

The other fundamental change in the airlines' strategies concerns the decision of where to fly. Few people inside or outside the industry foresaw the shift of the airlines to what is now known as a hub-and-spoke system. Since deregulation, instead of serving a hodgepodge of routes as dictated by the CAB, airlines organized their routes so that most of their flights now converge on one or two hubs. These hubs collect traffic from the "rim" cities, then the passengers change planes at the hub to go out on other flights to their final destinations. The potential benefits of this system were demonstrated to a small extent by Delta Airlines, which had a hub in Atlanta even under regulation.[8]

The hub-and-spoke system has enabled airlines to increase their load factors on flights both into and out of the hub, thus lowering their costs and enabling them to lower their fares. An important side benefit is that flights can be scheduled more frequently because of the higher traffic density. Thus, instead of flight frequencies decreasing under deregulation, as was generally predicted, they actually increased. Passengers are also more likely to be able to complete their entire trip on one airline (which is advantageous to the airlines) and to avoid the inconvenience of changing planes at busy airports (which the passengers like). Another benefit is that passengers can fly from almost any city to almost any other city without having to endure multi-stop flights. Usually a one-stop flight can be found, and routes with sufficient traffic density still receive nonstop service.

How much are these innovations worth to consumers? Morrison and Winston (1986) estimated the total benefit of deregulation to consumers to be $5.7 billion a year. For the average passenger, the benefits per trip were $11.08 and came from the following sources: a gain of $4.04 from lower fares, a loss of $0.96 from slightly increased travel time, and a gain of $8.00 from increased flight frequency. Morrison and Winston further estimate that airline profits would have been $2.5 billion higher than they were under regulation. Thus, airline earnings would have

considerable savings to travelers. A measure of the average fares paid by travelers, the average passenger revenue per RPM, is plotted along with the average operating profit in figure 2.

All parties benefited to some extent by this new fare structure. The super-low fares enabled many leisure travelers to take trips they would not have considered before; business travelers gained by the increase in flight fre-

....

8 The joke then was, "It does not matter whether you are going to heaven or hell; you have to go through Atlanta first."

been even worse than they actually were (as reported in figure 1) had CAB regulation continued. These are substantial aggregate benefits.

Passenger Concerns

Even so, the gains of deregulation have not been shared equally by all travelers and, in fact, some may be worse off. Travelers who do not qualify for the discount fares and who must pay the full coach fare are probably worse off, unless the benefit from the increase in flight frequency is sufficient to offset this effect. Also, due to the oversupply of wide-body jets, which are ideally suited to carrying passengers coast to coast, fares for flights between 2,000 and 2,999 miles have fallen much more than other fares, so that travelers on these routes have benefited proportionately more than travelers on shorter routes. This is a temporary benefit, however, and will last only until the airlines adjust their fleets. Finally, travel time for most flights involving large hubs has increased due to the increase in traffic.

One of the early concerns of opponents and even of some supporters of deregulation centered on the availability of air service to small communities. Provision was made in the ADA for subsidies to help support air service to small communities for a period of up to 10 years, but many communities were not covered by these provisions. However, most small communities, far from losing service, have gained service. In general, hedgehopping, multi-stop flights have been eliminated (lowering travel time), and flight frequencies have been increased. Travel time for trips involving nonhubs has fallen from one to six percent on average.[9] While service by trunk airlines has been replaced with service by commuter airlines in many cases (which is seen as less desirable), most of these commuter lines have their schedules coordinated with a major carrier at the connecting hub. When there is provision for online ticketing, travelers can save approximately 25 percent over the interline fare. The few communities that have lost all service have not had enough traffic to support scheduled carrier service by any class of carrier. In these cases, service could be restored by government subsidies if the affected taxpayers deemed it desirable to do so.

Beyond the basic issues of where to fly and how much to charge, there is the issue of whether the skies have become less safe under deregulation. Generally, the argument is that competition gives airlines an incentive to cut corners on

maintenance and to force pilots to fly more hours than is prudent. Under regulation, it was claimed that this was not a problem because the CAB ensured that the airlines were financially healthy so that they would not be as tempted to cut corners.

So far, the safety record of the airlines is as good as ever, but there is the charge by some that the country has simply been lucky. There are two responses to this charge. First, it is bad for an airline's business for its aircraft to be involved in an accident that is shown to be a result of its own negligence. Not only is the public likely to avoid the airline, but the airline would also have lost a plane worth millions of dollars and exposed itself to even greater claims of liability.[10] Second, and more important, one sure way of forcing the airlines to perform proper maintenance is to step up inspections by the Federal Aviation Administration (FAA). There may be a problem in doing this, however. The number of airlines and aircraft in service has risen dramatically since 1978, but the number of FAA inspectors has remained the same due to federal budget constraints.

A related problem is that the number and the level of experience of the nation's air traffic controllers has declined since deregulation as a result of the Professional Air Traffic Controllers' Organization (PATCO) strike in the summer of 1981. Thus, if there is a potential safety problem, it is likely to arise from inadequate attention to inspection and flight control, not from deregulation.

Industry Concerns

As one might have surmised from the earlier discussion of strikes, labor leaders were also concerned about the effects of deregulation. In fact, however, overall employment in the industry is up and compensation has kept pace with inflation. According to data presented by Morrison and Winston (1986), from 1975 to 1984, pilots' average real income fell a modest $500, dropping to $47,720 in 1977 dollars, while that of flight attendants increased $1800 to $14,428, and that of mechanics increased about $500 to $19,775.

Industry employment has increased since the early 1970s. Employment declined from a 1980 peak until 1983 when it rebounded and continued the upward trend it followed from 1971 to 1978 (see Morrison and Winston [1986]). Though the average worker has not suffered

21

---

9   An airport is classified as a "nonhub" if its total enplaned revenue passenger miles represents less than 0.05 percent of the total U.S. market.

10   It is assumed, of course, that the idea of preserving life also enters into the issue.

under deregulation, many union workers have been forced to take wage- and work-rule concessions, and some have had their careers interrupted as they have been either laid off or let go by airlines performing poorly in the new competitive environment. Two-tiered labor contracts have also been introduced. All this and the growth of the nonunion sector of the industry among the entering airlines have induced wide, and sometimes surprising, wage differentials between workers for different airlines, so that aggregate data on the welfare of workers is somewhat misleading.[11]

Finally, some firms may not have benefited from deregulation. There have been a number of bankruptcies in the airline industry since deregulation, most notably Braniff Airlines and Continental Airlines, which are both still flying after Chapter 11 reorganizations. Another airline (Frontier) is not flying, but is being acquired by Texas Air. In addition, there have been numerous mergers, particularly in the last year. Currently pending are two large mergers involving Continental-Eastern-People Express-Frontier (by Texas Air) and Delta-Western, that would create the first- and fourth-largest airlines in the U.S., respectively. While business failures impose some costs, such as uncertainty and inconvenience on the part of consumers, the loss of jobs on the part of workers, and the financial loss to creditors and stockholders, failures are a necessary force to ensure that firms operate efficiently in providing the services that consumers desire at a cost they are willing to pay.

IV. Future Evolution of the Industry

The current merger wave could be regarded as a natural process leading toward a competitive airline industry. Travelers prefer to have nonstop or one-stop flights with one carrier, rather than take a flight that would require them to endure two or more stops, or to change airlines at a busy airport. Providing such service requires a national route network with several regional hubs. In addition to the benefits for travelers, there also might be cost advantages to operating such a large hub network. Though the cost studies performed during the regulatory period indicated that there were no scale economies in the airline industry, the cost inefficiencies present in the regulatory era may have distorted these estimates. Bauer (1985) used an econometric procedure that allowed for these inefficiencies and found evidence of substantial returns to scale (contrary to

the cost studies that did not allow for inefficiency). This issue aside, there are definitely cost advantages to the extent that large hub-and-spoke systems lead to higher load factors. Currently, only United Airlines and American Airlines operate such networks. However, once the current wave of mergers subsides, there will be anywhere from six to eight such super-airlines, perhaps another four to six medium-sized carriers, and perhaps 10 to 30 regional carriers.

Should the public be concerned about the potential anti-competitive effects of these airline mergers? If the industry were perfectly contestable as discussed earlier, then the answer would be no. Many researchers have tested whether or not the implications of the theory of contestable markets hold exactly; unfortunately, no one has found that they have. Bailey, Graham, and Kaplan (1985), for example, found that on concentrated routes (routes served by only one or two carriers) airlines can raise fares five to 10 percent over what they could charge on nonconcentrated routes.

There are two reasons why actual and potential competition have not lived up to their promise in the airline industry. First, capital—both physical and human capital—may not have fully adjusted to the new deregulated environment. The number of merger proposals recently is evidence that the airline industry is not in a long-run equilibrium with respect to the number and size distribution of carriers. Given that it has been eight years since the formal deregulation process started, it appears that the transition from a regulated to a competitive market equilibrium will take longer than expected.

A second reason for the apparent lack of competition on some routes is that entry into some concentrated markets is not as easy as was first expected. Many airports across the country have severe problems with traffic congestion (for example, airports in Denver and Washington, D.C.); obtaining gates and takeoff and landing slots at these airports is difficult. Since gates and landing rights are "grandfathered" to the airline holding them as long as they are used, the airlines that have these scarce resources can earn monopoly returns from them. This creates a severe barrier to entry for airlines wishing to begin service on these routes. The importance of this problem was highlighted in the recent merger of Continental Airlines with Eastern Airlines. To get approval for the merger, slots at LaGuardia airport had to be sold to Pan-Am so that it could set up a competing shuttle service. Even at relatively uncongested airports, such as Cleveland Hopkins, airlines are reluctant to release unused gate space. Much of the impetus for the current merger wave is that airlines find it is easier to buy other airlines to expand (in an

22

---

[11] For example, unionized Western Airline workers earn less than Delta's nonunion workers. Also, United's unionized pilots earned 40 percent more than their ill-fated Frontier brethren.

effort to reach the most efficient size) than it is to grow internally (and be forced to try to obtain takeoff and landing slots on their own).[12]

Given that the contestable market theory does not seem to apply on all routes, should consumers worry about the increasing concentration of the industry? Currently, the national four-firm concentration ratio (CR), the sum of the market shares of the largest four firms in an industry, has remained unchanged at 47 from 1975 to 1986. Depending on how the current merger proposals are approved, it is likely that the resulting concentration ratio for the industry will be anywhere from 57 to 61. While this is high enough to cause concern, particularly in light of the fact that some individual city pairs now have even higher concentration ratios, there are reasons not to become alarmed just yet.

First, even though the industry has a fairly small number of firms, and concentration is relatively high, fare and route competition has been intense since deregulation. There have been no accusations that the industry as a whole is earning more than a normal profit. Furthermore, to the extent that only large airlines can provide the national route structure and the potential for nonstop and one-stop service that consumers prefer at the lowest cost, the level of concentration is only a reflection of the fact that there is only room for a limited number of efficiently sized airlines in the market.

If the ultimate effect of deregulation is a national market with six to eight huge airlines, there still would be a great deal of competition in the industry, even if many of the major cities are dominated by as few as two carriers. If one wants to fly from Cleveland to Los Angeles, for example, there may only be one or two airlines to choose from that provide nonstop service. However, one-stop service is a close substitute for nonstop service and, in that case, one would conceivably have six to eight choices depending upon which hub city he or she preferred to change planes. On shorter routes, such as Cleveland to Chicago, the smaller regional carriers would provide additional competition to the major carriers and thereby put a check on fares.[13] On still short-

er flights, Cleveland to Columbus for example, surface transportation provides some additional competition even if the market for air travel between those points is concentrated. Given the shortcomings of the contestable market theory as applied to the airline industry, however, the disciplining effect of potential competition may not be enough to ensure competitive behavior. It may still be necessary for the Departments of Transportation and Justice to enforce current antitrust laws.

In summary, at this point, the market for air travel in the U.S. is not perfectly contestable and, on some concentrated routes, airlines are able to charge modest fare markups on the order of between 5 and 10 percent. This situation is likely to continue for the foreseeable future, until steps are taken to alleviate the congestion problems at certain airports. The next few years will probably witness an increase in the concentration in the industry to the point where six to eight large airlines dominate the national market with a host of smaller regional and commuter lines filling a variety of special niches. There will be sufficient competition to ensure that travelers are better off than they were under regulation, but it remains to be seen how closely the industry will conform to the perfectly contestable ideal that was envisaged by proponents of deregulation.

V. Conclusion

Deregulation of the airline industry has been a painful experience for some travelers, workers, and firms. Large fuel price increases, the air traffic controllers' strike, and recessions have made the process even more difficult. On the whole, however, deregulation has been favorable. Far more individuals have benefited than have been hurt. Consumers are receiving better service for lower average fares; employment and compensation in the industry are up; and the airlines are generally earning higher profits than they would have under regulation. Yet, even eight years later, the industry is still adjusting to its new environment, and the final results of deregulation have yet to be determined.

There are several steps that can be taken to ensure that the gains to date are not lost and that the costs of adjustment to deregulation are minimized. First, airport expansion is needed to help reduce one of the few barriers to entry that remain in the industry. Deregulation, by greatly increasing air travel through lower fares, made the congestion worse. The solution, however, is not to reduce air travel, but to expand the system.

The federal government has a $3.5 billion fund that can be spent only on promoting air travel. This fund is financed by an 8 percent tax on air fares, but has become embroiled in the current federal budget problems. The money

23

. . . .

12 A further cause of the increased merger activity now is that the Department of Transportation (DOT) has authority over airline mergers for the next two years, at which time the Department of Justice (DOJ) will have that responsibility. The DOT has been much more lenient than the DOJ.

13 If they cannot obtain space at the major airports on the route in question, they have the aircraft that can effectively utilize the smaller regional airports which, in some cases, may be more convenient for passengers.

could be spent to expand airport facilities, to modernize the air traffic control system, and to hire more FAA inspectors. These expenditures would enhance the competitiveness of the system by lessening the incentives for airlines to merge, as well as by improving their safety and reliability.

Second, the U.S. Departments of Transportation and Justice should continue to enforce existing antitrust laws. While the competitive discipline that free-entry into the industry offers should not be ignored, it is important that these agencies not place too much faith in free-entry to the exclusion of other factors, particularly in the short run.

Finally, allowing foreign air carriers into the U.S. market (with reciprocal agreements for entry into their markets) should be considered as a way of further increasing industry competition. These policies would help the U.S. to maintain its position as having the world's foremost airline network.

REFERENCES

Adams, Douglas. *The Hitchhiker's Guide to the Galaxy.* New York, NY: Pocket Books, 1979.

Bailey, Elizabeth E., David R. Graham, and David P. Kaplan. *Deregulating the Airlines.* Cambridge, MA: The MIT Press, 1985.

Bauer, Paul W. "An Analysis of Multiproduct Technology and Efficiency Using the Joint Cost Function and Panel Data: An Application to the U.S. Airline Industry," Ph.D. Dissertation, University of North Carolina at Chapel Hill, 1985.

Davies, R.E.G. *Airlines of the United States since 1914.* London: Putnam & Company Limited, 1972.

Douglas, George W., and James Miller. *Economic Regulation of Domestic Air Transport: Theory and Policy.* Washington, D.C.: Brookings Institution, 1974.

Graham, David R., Daniel P. Kaplan, and David S. Sibley. "Efficiency and Competition in the Airline Industry," *Bell Journal of Economics,* vol. 14, no. 1 (spring 1983), pp. 118-138.

Keeler, Theodore E. "Airline Regulation and Market Performance," *Bell Journal of Economics and Management Science,* vol. 3, no. 2 (autumn 1972), pp. 399-424.

Meyer, John R., and Clinton V. Oster, Jr. *Deregulation and the New Airline Entrepreneurs.* Cambridge, MA: The MIT Press, 1984.

————. *Airline Deregulation: The Early Experience.* Boston, MA: Auburn House, 1981.

Morrison, Steven, and Clifford Winston. *The Economic Effects of Airline Deregulation.* Washington, D.C.: Brookings Institution, 1986.

U.S. General Accounting Office. "Lower Airline Costs per Passenger are Possible in the United States and Could Result in Lower Fares," Report to Congress, February 1977.

White, Lawrence J. "Economies of Scale and the Question of 'Natural Monopoly' in the Airline Industry," *Journal of Air Law and Commerce,* vol. 44, no. 3 (1979), pp. 545-573.

24

[15]

THE EFFECT OF REGULATORY CHANGES IN THE AIRLINE INDUSTRY ON SHAREHOLDERS' WEALTH*

MESSOD D. BENEISH

Duke University

I. Introduction

Five years of intense debate marked by hearings and deliberations in Congress and experimental regulatory actions by the Civil Aeronautics Board led, in October 1978, to the Airline Deregulation Act. Airline deregulation has attracted considerable attention in the academic literature, and researchers have examined the impact of deregulation in such areas as fares, welfare, and industry structure.[1] With the exception of Spiller's 1983 and 1986 studies, however, there has been little in the financial economics literature evaluating the effect of regulatory changes on airlines' profitability.[2] The purpose of this article is to examine the effect

---

* I have benefited from the comments of my dissertation committee: Dennis Carlton, Peter Easton, Bob Holthausen (chairman), Laurentius Marais, Katherine Schipper, and Mark Zmijewski. I have also received valuable suggestions from Campbell Harvey and Jim Anton and from workshop participants at State University of New York at Buffalo, Duke University, and the University of British Columbia. I thank the anonymous referee for many valuable suggestions. The usual disclaimer applies.

[1] See, among others, Theodore E. Keeler, Airline Deregulation and Market Performance, 3 Bell J. Econ. 399 (1972); George W. Douglas & John C. Miller III, Economic Regulation of Domestic Air Transport: Theory and Policy (1974); Arthur S. DeVany, The Effect of Price and Entry Regulation on Airline Output, Capacity and Efficiency, 6 Bell J. Econ. 327 (1975); Dennis W. Carlton, William M. Landes, & Richard A. Posner, Benefits and Costs of Airlines Mergers: A Case Study, 11 Bell J. Econ. 65 (1980); David R. Graham, Daniel P. Kaplan, & David S. Sibley, Efficiency and Competition in the Airline Industry, 14 Bell J. Econ. 118 (1983); Elizabeth E. Bailey, David R. Graham, & Daniel P. Kaplan, Deregulating the Airlines (1985); Steven A. Morrison & Clifford Winston, 30 J. Law & Econ. 53 (1987); Severin Borenstein, Hubs and High Fares: Dominance and Market Power in the U.S. Airline Industry, 20 Rand J. Econ. 344 (1989).

[2] Spiller's 1983 study focuses on three price regulatory changes: the March 1966 discount fare regulation, the 1974 domestic passenger fare investigation, and the June 1978 fare flexibility zone regulation. He provides evidence that the impact of price regulatory changes differs across eleven trunk airlines according to their demand characteristics. Pablo T.

[*Journal of Law & Economics*, vol. XXXIV (October 1991)]
© 1991 by The University of Chicago. All rights reserved. 0022-2186/91/3402-0001$01.50

of major events in the regulatory deliberation period on the expected profitability of airlines by analyzing the behavior of security prices at the time of those events.

This article studies the history of events leading to deregulation, identifies major events in the development of regulatory changes, estimates the economic effect of deregulation, and provides insights about the role of Congress and the Civil Aeronautics Board (CAB) in effecting regulatory reform. The study makes two contributions. First, I extend Spiller's 1983 and 1986 analyses by examining the impact of a broader set of regulatory actions on airline shareholders's wealth. The broader set includes regulatory actions by the CAB. These actions are important in assessing the effects of regulatory changes because the administration and Congress exerted pressure on the CAB to deregulate administratively the airline industry. As such, the inclusion of CAB actions increases the likelihood of capturing the impact of deregulation on shareholders' wealth.[3] Second, I examine the differential impact of regulatory changes on the expected profitability of individual airlines.[4] This analysis tests the hypothesis that airlines face differential costs of adjusting their route networks to operate efficiently in a deregulated environment.[5] Tests of this hypothesis focus on airline network characteristics responsible for positive effects. Focusing on network characteristics that minimize the costs of adjustment provides an indication of which airlines are expected to perform better post-deregulation.

The results in this article include the following. Regulatory changes in the airline industry had a negative impact on airlines' stock returns. The

---

Spiller, The Differential Impact of Airlines Regulation on Individual Firms and Markets: An Empirical Analysis, 26 J. Law & Econ. 655 (1983). In the 1986 study, Spiller examines the role of mobility barriers on the effect of regulatory changes on the profitability of airlines. Pablo T. Spiller, Mobility Barriers in the U.S. Airline Industry (working paper, Stanford Univ. 1986).

[3] Binder examines impact on shareholders' wealth of twenty regulatory changes from 1887 to 1978 and concludes that stock returns are not very useful in studying the effect of regulation. Binder's analyses, however, are conducted with monthly returns using dates of announcements relating to administration and congressional actions exclusively. This study uses daily returns and analyzes the impact of announcements by the CAB in addition to those by the administration and Congress. John J. Binder, Measuring the Effects of Regulation with Stock Price Data, 16 Rand J. Econ. 167 (1985).

[4] This follows the general theory of regulation that argues that the primary effects of regulation are distributional. See George J. Stigler, The Theory of Regulation, 2 Bell J. Econ. 3 (1971); and Sam Peltzman, Towards a More General Theory of Regulation, 19 J. Law & Econ. 211 (1976).

[5] A similar hypothesis is independently advanced by Spiller. He hypothesizes that there are mobility barriers in the airline industry and provides evidence that it is costly for airlines to adjust their networks to operate in a competitive environment. See Spiller, Mobility Barriers, *supra* note 2.

adverse effect is consistent with airlines facing costs to adjust their route networks to operate in a competitive environment. The costs of adjustment are shown to be lower when firms' networks are more readily adaptable. Airlines with higher ability to reorganize their operations around hubs, higher involvement in servicing first-class passengers, and higher borrowing ability are less adversely affected by deregulation. The lower adjustment costs associated with these airlines' characteristics are consistent with prior research findings and expectations about postderegulation airline performance: (i) hubbing has been shown to increase the efficiency of route networks as well as airlines' market power, (ii) the amount of first-class passengers has been shown to proxy for demand for quality of air travel, and (iii) borrowing ability is a proxy for both the firm's ability to shift capital resources to reorganize its operations and the speed with which such adjustments are effected.

The role of the participants in the deregulation process is also examined. Politicians exerted pressure on the CAB to deregulate administratively by criticizing the CAB policies at the Kennedy Hearings and by appointing CAB chairmen that supported a policy of deregulation. Since the impact of CAB regulatory actions on the expected profitability of airlines is substantial, the evidence suggests that failure to incorporate the agency's actions in the analysis leads to inaccurate inferences about the economic consequences of regulatory changes.

The remainder of the article is organized as follows. Section II describes the regulatory process leading to the Airline Deregulation Act. Section III describes the data and the methodology. Section IV discusses the empirical results. Section V contains the conclusions.

II. Regulatory Changes

The process leading to deregulation spans the five-year period from 1974 to 1978. Because this period contains both the economic effect of deregulation and revisions in the probability of its occurrence, I review the history of deliberations about the desirability and scope of airline deregulation to identify key announcements about administration, congressional, and CAB regulatory actions.[6] The event dates selected are listed in Appendix A.

---

[6] I draw on Morgan's account of the events that led to the Airline Deregulation Act. He examines the roles of Congress, the administration, and the Civil Aeronautics Board in instituting regulatory reform. See Ivor Morgan, Toward Deregulation, in Airline Deregulation: The Early Experience 41 (J. Meyer *et al.* eds. 1981). Additional events are identified by reference to Spiller, Mobility Barriers, *supra* note 2, and Civil Aeronautics Board, Bibliography of Important Civil Board Regulatory Actions, 1975–1979 (1979).

The role of the participants in the deregulation process is examined using the framework provided by Spiller, who expands the theory of regulation to account for potential agency problems between politicians and their regulatory agencies.[7] In this framework, budgets, hearings, and commissioner appointments are means for the administration and Congress to control the actions of regulatory agencies. Incentives to deregulate the airline industry stemmed from the poor profit performance of airlines in 1970–74 coupled with fare increases of 35 percent in this period. The visibility of the CAB's policy of fare regulation was heightened by the 20 percent increase in average ticket prices from 1973 to 1974. This increase stemmed from curtailment in discount fares and three general fare hikes approved by the CAB. With these incentives politicians wanted to reexamine the CAB's policies of regulation and effect regulatory reform.

The Kennedy Oversight Hearings allowed Congress to reexamine the CAB's administration of air transport regulation. Both the administration and Congress influenced the implementation of regulatory reform by appointing John Robson in 1975 to replace Robert D. Timms, a strong proponent of increased regulation, as CAB chairman and further appointing Alfred Kahn, a strong advocate of deregulation, as CAB chairman in 1977. These actions led the CAB to deregulate administratively.

A.   Administration and Congressional Actions

The beginning of the debate on regulatory reform is, following Spiller, traceable to President Ford's designation in 1974 of regulatory reform as a major policy element.[8] This event led to the February 1975 Oversight Hearings of the Civil Aeronautics Board Practices and Procedures.[9]

At the hearings, the CAB route policies came under severe criticism. From 1969 to 1974 the CAB rejected most applications for new routes by regulated carriers. This period became known as the "route moratorium" period. Senator Kennedy denounced this practice of thwarting competi-

---

[7] See Pablo T. Spiller, Politicians, Interest Groups, and Regulators: A Multiple-Principals Agency Theory of Regulation, or "Let Them Be Bribed," 23 J. Law & Econ. 65 (1990). See also Matthew D. McCubbins & Thomas Schwartz, Congressional Oversight Overlooked: Police Patrols vs. Fire Alarms, 28 Am. J. Pol. Sci. 165 (1984); and Barry Weingast, The Congressional Bureaucratic System: A Principal-Agent Perspective (with Applications to the SEC), 44 Pub. Choice 147 (1984).

[8] See Pablo T. Spiller, Quality, Capacity, and Regulation: An Analysis of the Airline Industry (unpublished Ph.D. dissertation, Univ. Chicago 1980).

[9] U.S. Congress, Senate, Committee on the Judiciary, Subcommittee on Administration Practice and Procedure, Oversight Hearings on the Civil Aeronautics Board Practices and Procedures, 94th Congress (1975).

tion as highly irregular because it had never been publicly announced. The unregulated intrastate carrier experience led the committee to believe that deregulation would bring a sizable reduction in the level of fares without affecting airlines' profitability.[10] The poor profit performance of airlines was put forward as evidence that regulation of air transport was inappropriate. The hearings also served as a catalyst for legislative reform as the Ford administration proposed to introduce legislation that would reduce the power of the CAB to regulate airlines.

In July 1975, a CAB task-force report recommending congressional action to deregulate the industry over a three- to five-year period was released. The CAB endorsed legislative reform and announced plans to experiment with route flexibility. In October 1975, the Ford administration introduced the "Aviation Act of 1975," which proposed total deregulation of the airline industry. The general push for deregulation of the airline industry by the administration, Congress, and consumer groups led the Senate Aviation Subcommittee, chaired by Senator Cannon, to hold hearings on regulatory reform in March and April 1976. The consensus of the testimony by various interest groups (airlines, airport administrations, and labor) at the hearings was that fare flexibility was desirable but that freedom of entry and exit would have disastrous effects.

In the period from October 1976 to mid-1979, the debate over the scope of deregulation continued, and, after nearly two years of congressional activity, the Airline Deregulation Act, which proposed gradual deregulation over fares and routes, was signed into law by President Carter on October 24, 1978. During this period, the CAB undertook route and fare actions to administratively deregulate the air transport industry. In awarding route authority, the CAB made low fares a major consideration, speeded hearing procedures, and adopted a multiple permissive entry policy (that is, a policy of granting authority to many applicants on a given route). Fare actions were geared toward permitting scheduled carriers to compete with charter carriers and allowing discount fares. The CAB actions considered in this study are discussed in the next section.

B. Civil Aeronautics Board Actions

The Civil Aeronautics Board actions selected are the policy-setting regulatory decisions made by the board after endorsing legislative reform.

---

[10] Eads analyzes the behavior of the unregulated intrastate airlines in California and Texas. He finds that, for a similar service, unregulated carriers were able to offer fares which were 40–90 percent lower than fares of regulated carriers depending on the length of the haul. Furthermore, unregulated carriers were profitable because of lower costs and a positive passenger response to lower fares. George C. Eads, The Local Service Airline Experiment (1976).

The majority of these actions were undertaken or decided under the chairmanship of Alfred Kahn from June 1977 to October 1978. Five major fare actions and five major route actions undertaken by the Civil Aeronautics Board after endorsing legislative reform are considered in this study.[11]

The five major fare actions selected are American's Supersaver, TWA's Super Jackpot, Delta's Aerobus, Western's No-Strings, and the board's charter carriers policy. With these actions, the CAB encouraged price competition by allowing discount fares and reductions in coach and first-class fares and by making it easier for scheduled carriers to compete with charter carriers.

The five major route actions selected are the Boston–Atlanta nonstop case, the Chicago-Midway low-fare case, the Chicago–Albany/Syracuse–Boston competitive route proceeding, the Baltimore/Washington–Houston low-fare case, and the Oakland service case. With these actions, the CAB set a procompetitive policy of allowing multiple permissive entry, made low fares an important consideration in route awards, and eliminated lengthy investigation procedures.

III.   DATA AND METHODOLOGY

A.   Data

To be included in the sample, a firm has to meet the following criteria. (1) The firm has to be an air carrier certificated by the Civil Aeronautics Board to perform passenger transportation services over specified routes.[12] (2) The firm's stock return data have to be available on the Daily Center for Research in Security Prices (CRSP) Tapes for the years 1974–79. There are twenty firms that satisfy criterion 1. Criterion 2 eliminates the following seven firms because of data availability: Aloha, Hughes Airwest, North Central, Piedmont, Texas International, and Wien Alaska.[13]

The eighteen firms that meet these criteria are listed in Table 1. The sample in this study is large relative to samples used in studies of the airline industry under regulation. These studies focused on eleven trunk carriers that, according to the CAB classification, are American, Braniff, Continental, Delta, Eastern, National, Northwest, Pan Am, TWA,

---

[11] These actions are highlighted in Civil Aeronautics Board, *supra* note 6. A more detailed description of both congressional and CAB actions is found in Messod D. Beneish, The Impact of Regulatory Changes in the Airline Industry on Shareholders' Wealth (unpublished Ph.D. dissertation, Univ. Chicago 1987).

[12] A carrier operating regularly scheduled flights over specified routes with aircraft weighing over 12,500 pounds had to receive authority from the CAB to provide this service.

[13] I checked the list of firms for which data are available on the NASDAQ tapes and did not find any of the airlines eliminated as a result of criterion 1.

REGULATORY CHANGES AND SHAREHOLDERS' WEALTH   401

TABLE 1

SAMPLE FIRMS

Company Name	Market Value of Equity* (1975 $ millions)
American†	626.1
Alaska	23.6
Braniff	99.5
Continental	228.1
Delta	699.2
Eastern	323.8
Frontier	108.9
Hawaiian	6.0
National	85.6
Northwest	103.5
Ozark	54.0
PSA	24.5
Pan Am	298.9
Southwest	15.8
TWA	132.9
United	523.2
US Air	151.4
Western	87.3
Mean	199.6
Standard deviation	218.3
Median	106.2
Minimum	6.0
Maximum	699.2
N	18

* Market value of equity is calculated as price times shares outstanding for the month of January 1975. The data are from the CRSP monthly master tape.

† The Civil Aeronautics Board classified eleven carriers as trunks on the basis of size and scope of operations. Trunk carriers are American, Braniff, Continental, Delta, Eastern, National, Northwest, Pan Am, Trans World, United, and Western. I use this classification in this study and designate the remaining seven sample firms as regional carriers (Alaska, Frontier, Ozark, US Air) and local carriers (Hawaiian, PSA, Southwest).

United, and Western. In addition to the eleven trunk carriers, seven local and regional carriers are included in the sample.

Table 1 also lists the market value of equity (January 1975) for each firm in the sample. If market value of equity (the product and price and shares outstanding) is an indicator of firm size, then sample airlines are large relative to the median ($62.4 million) firm traded in the New York and American Stock Exchanges. Sample firms' sizes range from $6 million (Hawaiian) to $699 million (Delta).

B. Methodology

To assess the effect of regulatory changes on airlines, I use a return-generating process that is a variant of the market model in that it conditions security returns on a market index return and includes variables that identify dates on which information is released about a regulatory change. The model allows for a shift in the intercept under the hypothesis that the return process is influenced by an unanticipated regulatory change. The variables allowing for a shift in the mean of the return process take the value of one on a date of information release about deregulation and zero on dates that contain no information.[14] Specifically, for each airline in the sample, I posit the following return-generating process:

$$R_{it} = \alpha_i + \beta_i R_{mt} + \sum_{j=1}^{J} \gamma_{ij} D_j + \epsilon_{it}, \qquad (1)$$

where R_{it} is the return for security i at time t, R_{mt} is the return at time t for the CRSP equally weighted index, and $D_j (j = 1$ to $J)$ are dummy variables identifying the dates of release of information about regulatory changes.

Equation (1) is estimated with ordinary least squares using daily returns from July 1974 to August 1979. Given the length of the period spanned by announcements of regulatory changes (1,300 trading days) as well as evidence in Spiller that such announcements alter firms' systematic risk, equation (1) is estimated on four subperiods of 325 trading days.[15] In each subperiod, the intercept α_i and systematic risk β_i are assumed constant and the effect of the announcements occurring in that subperiod is measured by the γ_{ij} coefficients. Estimation of equation (1) by subperiods relaxes the assumption of constancy of the α_i and β_i parameters and reduces the concern that changes in risk of firms alter the estimated regulatory change parameters.

I also considered the alternative methodology suggested by Spiller to adjust for risk changes.[16] The method differentiates risk-related from

---

[14] A similar methodology is used by Spiller (in 1980), Binder, and Schipper, Thompson, and Weil. In this study, I examine the stock price effect in the day preceding and the day of the announcement and also check for other firm-specific information simultaneously announced. The trade-off between the longer windows in Binder and Spiller and shorter windows is one of increased noise versus increased likelihood of capturing the effect of the regulatory change. Shorter windows and the elimination of confounding events are standard in recent event studies. Spiller, *supra* note 8; Binder, *supra* note 3; Katherine Schipper, Rex Thompson, & Roman L. Weil, Disentangling Interrelated Effects of Regulatory Changes in Shareholder Wealth: The Case of Motor Carrier Deregulation, 30 J. Law & Econ. 67 (1987).

[15] Evidence of risk changes is found in Spiller, *supra* note 8, and in Pablo T. Spiller, Assessing the Profitability Effects of Airline Deregulation, 14 Econ. Letters 369, 374 (1984). Each estimation subperiod covers approximately one and one-third calendar years and is similar in length to the period used in Spiller, Mobility Barriers, *supra* note 2.

[16] The methodology is presented in Spiller, *supra* note 8, and in Pablo T. Spiller, On Adjusting for Risk Changes When Assessing the Profitability Effects of Regulatory Changes, 10 Econ. Letters 263 (1982).

profit-releated changes at the time of regulatory change announcements. It is based on estimating risk shifts before and after regulatory changes announcements. In Appendix B, I present the results of tests that estimate profitability changes using equation (1) (specification 1) as well as applying the risk adjustment methodology suggested by Spiller (specification 2).

Comparing the results in both specifications indicates that, while the estimates of profitability changes differ in magnitude, they are similar in sign and significance for the portfolios of all airlines as well as trunk airlines. For the local and regional carriers the results differ substantially across specifications. Since estimates of systematic risk for the smaller local and regional airlines are more subject to sampling variation and infrequent trading biases, it is difficult to distinguish between changes in risk due to changes in economic conditions and changes due to the choice of estimation period. Thus, the profitability estimates adjusted for risk changes for locals and regionals appear unreliable. Given that the risk adjustment yields similar results for trunk airlines as well as the sample as a whole, the analysis in this article is based on the estimates of profitability changes as estimated from equation (1).

IV. EMPIRICAL RESULTS

The discussion of empirical tests follows two main lines. The impact of regulatory changes on airlines' expected profitability is examined in Section IV*A*. Section IV*B* presents evidence on determinants of differential impact of regulatory changes across airlines.

A. *Effect of Airline Deregulation on Shareholders' Wealth*

Ordinary least square estimates of the effect of announcements of regulatory changes (γ_{ij}) by the administration, Congress, and the Civil Aeronautics Board are presented in Table 2. In Table 3, these estimates are aggregated for individual and portfolios of airlines, and tests of linear combinations of coefficients across individual equations presented. The discussion is organized around the actions of the administration, Congress, and the CAB.

Announcements by the Ford and Carter administrations relate to the initiation of regulatory reform, the appointment of two new CAB chairmen, proposals for deregulation, and pressure on Congress to deregulate the airline industry. In Table 2, eight of the ten announcements by the administrations have a negative mean effect, but none of the individual announcements significantly alter the expected profitability of the industry. The lack of overall effect for each announcement may be attributable to effect of regulatory changes being distributional. On aggregate, how-

TABLE 2

Effect of Deregulation on Airline Stock Returns: Distributional Statistics on the Effect of Announcements by the Administration, Congress, and the Civil Aeronautics Board over the Period 1974–78

Date[a]	Description	N[b]	Mean	Standard Error	Maximum	Median	Minimum	F-Statistic for $H_0: \sum_{i=1}^{N} \gamma_{ij} = 0$[c]
Announcements by the administration:								
October 8, 1974	Ford Administration designs regulatory reform as a major policy element	17	−.008	.022	.046	−.013	−.036	1.11
February 7, 1975	Ford administration denounces CAB regulation of airlines at Kennedy hearings	17	−.003	.018	.039	−.002	−.039	.13
February 18, 1975	Ford administration proposes deregulation at hearings	17	.003	.024	.080	.001	−.028	.11
March 3, 1975	Ford administration appoints John Robson CAB chairman	17	.010	.021	.044	.016	−.030	1.99
October 9, 1975	Ford administration introduces Aviation Act of 1975	17	−.010	.016	.023	−.010	−.040	1.65
February 20, 1976	Ford administration publicizes study on benefits of deregulation	17	−.005	.021	.054	−.007	−.036	.38
January 13, 1977	Ford administration submits revised deregulation bill	18	−.005	.014	.023	−.006	−.035	.37
March 5, 1977	Carter urges Congress to deregulate	18	−.006	.015	.022	−.002	−.052	.59
May 20, 1977	Carter administration appoints Alfred Kahn CAB chairman	18	−.004	.018	.035	−.007	−.042	1.01
August 1, 1977	Carter pushes for stronger bill	18	−.004	.010	.018	−.005	−.023	.27

Announcements by Congress:								
February 27, 1975	Senator Kennedy criticizes CAB route policy	17	.041	.023	.088	.040	−.005	26.86*
March 5, 1977	Senators Kennedy and Cannon introduce legislation to deregulate airlines	18	−.002	.014	.035	−.002	−.029	.07
September 22, 1977	Senate mark-up amendment to eliminate automatic entry provisions	18	.001	.009	.015	.001	−.019	.03
October 13, 1977	Labor protection amendment adopted	18	.003	.013	.026	.003	−.030	.14
February 6, 1978	Senate reports bill S-2493	18	−.007	.009	.011	−.005	−.023	.76
March 8, 1978	Automatic Entry Provisions dropped by House Subcommittee	18	−.005	.017	.023	−.004	−.035	.38
April 19, 1978	Senate passes bill by 83–9 vote	18	−.010	.019	.032	−.007	−.013	1.62
May 15, 1978	Full House reaches compromise on weaker bill	18	−.002	.013	.019	.000	−.038	.09
May 19, 1978	HR 12611 reported	18	−.002	.026	.078	−.007	−.031	.04
September 21, 1978	HR 12611 passed by 363–8 vote	18	.009	.012	.040	.008	−.009	1.22
October 16, 1978	House and Senate agree to conference report	18	−.016	.012	.000	−.014	−.045	3.99*
Civil Aeronautics Board (CAB):								
General Announcements:								
July 8, 1975	CAB proposes to experiment with route deregulation	17	.037	.027	.093	.040	−.013	21.04*
August 6, 1975	Former CAB chairman warns of danger of deregulation	17	.002	.021	.027	.005	−.066	.08
January 9, 1976	CAB chairman proposes piecemeal approach to deregulation	17	−.001	.014	.021	−.001	−.031	.02
Announcements about fare actions:								
March 15, 1977	American Supersaver case	18	−.001	.012	.018	−.002	−.023	.02

continued overleaf

405

TABLE 2 (*Continued*)

Date[a]	Description	N[b]	Mean	Standard Error	Maximum	Median	Minimum	F-Statistic for $H_0: \sum_{i=1}^{N} \gamma_{ij} = 0$[c]
April 14, 1977	Petition for reconsideration of "super saver" case by Charter Companies denied	18	.003	.019	.062	−.001	−.019	.10
April 22, 1977	Extension of "super saver" to Northwest considered	18	.006	.010	.022	.008	−.014	.55
June 22, 1977	Local authorities to intervene in "super saver" case	18	−.013	.012	.012	−.015	−.036	2.76**
September 9, 1977	Extension of "super saver" to TWA and United considered	18	−.013	.014	.010	−.012	−.039	2.83**
September 30, 1977	Regional commission to intervene in "super saver" case	18	−.002	.011	.018	−.004	−.027	.05
February 27, 1978	Western Airlines applies for exemption to lower fares	18	.011	.010	.029	.010	−.004	1.90
March 27, 1978	Discount fares allowed on Florida–California routes	18	−.014	.010	.000	−.010	−.036	2.94**
April 6, 1978	National petitions to rescind Florida–California discount fares	18	.018	.015	.051	.019	−.005	5.14*
June 1, 1978	Investigation of TWA Super Jackpot fares dismissed	18	−.004	.012	.018	−.004	−.033	.22
June 29, 1978	Reporting requirements on discount fares case dismissed	18	−.008	.011	.018	−.009	−.027	.91
August 30, 1978	Fare setting flexibility allowed in major policy decision	18	−.008	.017	.016	−.005	−.041	.97
October 3, 1978	National's petition (4/6/78) dismissed	18	.007	.016	.038	.009	−.022	.81
Announcements about route actions: June 30, 1975	Institution of Boston–Atlanta service case	18	−.016	.011	.000	−.017	−.033	4.22*

June 16. 1976	Delta authorized to operate non-stop on Boston–Atlanta route	17	.012	.016	.054	.009	-.012	2.20
December 19. 1976	Institution of Chicago–Midway low-fare route case	18	-.007	.015	.030	-.009	-.034	.71
May 18. 1977	Chicago–Midway low-fare case: additional carriers considered	18	-.004	.010	.014	-.002	-.021	.26
December 12. 1977	Institution of Chicago–Albany–Boston competitive service case	18	.006	.012	.027	.004	-.018	.61
February 13. 1978	Hearings on Chicago–Midway case reported	18	.001	.012	.032	-.002	-.12	.01
March 20. 1978	Parties to Chicago–Midway case file position briefs	18	-.004	.012	.021	-.001	-.030	.21
April 11. 1978	Illinois congressional delegation supports certification in Chicago–Midway case	18	-.003	.016	.036	-.003	-.031	.13
May 23. 1978	Baltimore/Washington–Houston low-fare route case	18	-.008	.011	.012	-.007	-.31	.96
June 12. 1978	Local authorities support certification in Chicago–Albany–Boston case	18	-.003	.012	.018	-.002	-.025	.19
July 14. 1978	Awards eight city authorities to various airlines in Chicago–Midway case	18	.001	.013	.027	-.003	-.018	.02
July 31. 1978	Parties to Baltimore/Washington–Houston case file position briefs	18	-.001	.017	.029	-.001	-.028	.01
August 4. 1978	Parties to Chicago–Midway case file position briefs	18	-.007	.012	.010	-.009	-.024	.69
September 26. 1978	CAB policy to award authority to all qualified applicants in Oakland service case	18	-.004	.010	.015	-.002	-.021	.24
November 3. 1978	Awards route authority to two airlines in Baltimore/Washington–Houston case	18	-.007	.020	.037	-.014	-.047	.72
November 16. 1978	Initial decision on Chicago–Albany–Boston case reported	18	-.002	.012	.027	-.004	-.020	.08

continued overleaf

407

TABLE 2 (*Continued*)

Date[a]	Description	N[b]	Mean	Standard Error	Maximum	Median	Minimum	F-Statistic for $H_0: \sum_{i=1}^{N} \gamma_{ij} = 0$[c]
December 6, 1978	Release of preliminary report of December 5, 1978, in Oakland service case	18	−.005	.008	.013	−.007	−.019	.43
December 13, 1978	Release of prehearing report of December 12, 1978, in Oakland	18	.002	.018	.036	.003	−.030	.05
December 15, 1978	Notice to all applicants to complete applications for all markets in Oakland service case	18	−.008	.013	.019	−.009	−.030	1.01
January 23, 1979	Four airlines awarded authority on Chicago–Albany–Boston case	18	−.017	.022	.019	−.015	−.066	4.44*
March 19, 1979	Parties in Oakland service case file position briefs	18	−.006	.011	.023	−.007	−.022	.62
May 10, 1979	Grants authority to 17 airlines in Oakland service case	18	.006	.012	.028	.005	−.015	.66

[a] The source of the event dates used in the analyses is provided in Appendix A.

[b] The analysis is conducted on eighteen airlines except for some event dates when Southwest Airlines is excluded due to lack of security returns data. Southwest Airlines started trading on October 28, 1975.

[c] The null hypothesis that the sum of the event parameters is equal to zero ($H_0: \sum_{i=1}^{N} \gamma_{ij} = 0$) is tested as the restriction $AC = 0$ on the vector of coefficient estimates (C) using the test statistic in Theil (1971):

$$F = \frac{NT - NK}{Q} \cdot \frac{(a - AC)'(A(X'(\Sigma^{-1} \otimes I)X^{-1}A')^{-1}(a - AC)}{(R - XC)'(\Sigma^{-1} \otimes I)(R - XC)}$$

where N is the number of firms, T the number of observations, K the number of parameters estimated, Q the number of parameters estimated, K the number of restrictions, R the vector of security returns, X the matrix of explanatory variables, and Σ the true variance-covariance matrix of the system of equations. Following John J. Binder, Measuring the Effects of Regulation with Stock Price Data 16 Rand J. Econ. 167 (1985), and Katherine Schipper and Rex Thompson, The Impact of Merger-related Regulations Using Exact Distributions of Test Statistics, 23 J. Acct. Res. 408 (1985), the test statistic is distributed $F(1, 325 - k)$ where k, the number of estimated parameters varies by subperiod from 11 to 23. The cut-off points to evaluate significance at the 5 percent and 10 percent levels are 3.84 and 2.71, respectively.

  * Significant at the 5 percent level.

  ** Significant at the 10 percent level.

ever, announcements by the administrations negatively affected the stock return of fourteen out of eighteen airlines as displayed in Table 3. Among the four airlines positively affected are Southwest and PSA, the two interstate carriers whose superior performance was noted at the Kennedy Hearings, and Pan Am, which stood to benefit by obtaining fill-up rights on the domestic legs of its international flights. The effect of the administration announcements on the industry as a whole was −3.9 percent significant at the 10 percent level.

Overall, the evidence from announcements by both the Ford and Carter administrations indicates an adverse impact of regulatory changes on airlines' expected profitability. This is consistent with airlines incurring adjustment costs to change their operating structures in light of regulatory changes. Adjustment costs refer to (i) the costs of reorganizing their route networks, (ii) the costs of renegotiating labor contracts; and (iii) the costs of reorganizing their aircraft fleet in terms of aircraft size, range, and fuel efficiency. This view is supported by the lobbying behavior of airlines' management at the 1976 Senate hearings on deregulation because they feared "destructive" competition from other established airlines and from new entrants.[17]

Eleven announcements about regulatory changes by Congress are considered in the analysis. The first announcement (February 27, 1975) is Senator Kennedy's criticism of the CAB's management of route regulation. The impact of this announcement on airlines' profitability is 4.1 percent significant at the 5 percent level. The interpretation of this positive effect fits in Spiller's 1990 agency framework article, where hearings are a means for Congress to reduce the CAB's discretion in administrating the regulation of the industry. The criticism of the CAB route "moratorium" signals expected changes in the CAB route policy and shifts the blame of airlines' poor profit performance on the CAB. The positive effect is subject to two possible interpretations. Under the first interpretation, given greater route authority, airlines can improve their profit performance and demonstrate the viability of the present regulatory system, thus reducing the likelihood of costly regulatory changes. Under the second interpretation, route flexibility gives airlines the opportunity to reorganize their networks so as to be better prepared to face competition from potential entrants.

---

[17] Kahn reports that, in the 1976 Senate hearings, all air transportation firms testified against deregulation. See Alfred E. Kahn, Deregulation and Vested Interested: The Case of Airlines, in The Political Economy of Deregulation 132, table 8.1 (R. B. Noll & B. M. Bowen eds. 1983).

TABLE 3

CUMULATIVE EFFECT OF DEREGULATION ANNOUNCEMENTS BY THE ADMINISTRATION, CONGRESS, AND THE CIVIL AERONAUTICS BOARD (CAB) ON AIRLINE STOCK RETURNS

	Administration	Congress	Kennedy Hearings	CAB Experiments	CAB Fare Actions	CAB Route Actions
No. of events	10	11	3	3	13	22
Individual airlines:						
American	−.074	.025	.066	.032	.017	−.070
Alaska	.030	.083	.078	−.006	−.054	−.094
Braniff	−.053	.039	.098	.040	−.035	−.071
Continental	−.149	.032	.011	.063	−.043	−.202
Delta	−.048	.037	.021	.041	.033	−.003
Eastern	−.072	−.056	.051	.045	−.062	−.224
Frontier	−.054	.022	.014	.013	.032	.036
Hawaiian	−.035	.063	−.028	−.001	−.030	.084
National	−.049	.084	.039	.062	−.005	−.110
Northwest	−.060	−.028	.034	.055	.032	−.153
Ozark	−.088	.050	.001	.032	−.064	−.095
PSA	.041	.088	.024	.036	−.021	−.050
Pan Am	.135	.017	.183	−.011	−.063	−.009
Southwest	−.019	.013	−.005	−.007	−.001	.048

TWA	-.043	.047	.120	.038	-.053	-.086
United	-.106	.004	.016	.077	.028	-.123
US Air	-.035	.044	.002	.098	-.098	-.159
Western	-.105	-.031	.016	.070	.057	-.047
N positive	4	15	16	14	4	2
Portfolios:						
All (N = 18)[a]	-.039**	.029	.041*[b]	.037*	-.018	-.078*
Trunks (N = 11)	-.049**	.015	.059*[b]	.046*	-.009	-.099*
Regional (N = 4)[c]	-.036	.049	.023	.034**	-.046	-.096**
Local (N = 3)[d]	-.005	.054	-.003	.009	-.017	.027
Excluding Pan Am:[e]						
All (N = 17)	-.049*	.031	.03*	.041*	-.016	-.082*
Trunks (N = 10)	-.067*	.015	.047*	.052*	-.003	-.109*

[a] The null hypothesis that the sum of combinations of event parameters is equal to zero is tested using the F-statistic described in Henri Theil, Principles of Econometrics (1971); and in Table 2, note c.

[b] The Kennedy Hearings consist of three announcements: February 7, February 18, and February 27, 1975. The first two announcements are by the administration, the third by Congress.

[c] Regional airlines include Alaska, Frontier, Ozark, and US Air.

[d] Local airlines include Hawaiian, PSA, and Southwest.

[e] Portfolios excluding Pan Am are formed to assess the sensitivity of the effect of deregulation because Pan Am's domestic route authority consisted of legs on its international flights.

* Significant at the 5 percent level.

** Significant at the 10 percent level.

411

412   THE JOURNAL OF LAW AND ECONOMICS

The remaining ten announcements relate to the introduction of proposals for deregulation and mark-up on those proposals. It is of interest to note the positive mean effects associated with two announcements (September 22 and October 13, 1977) that reduced the scope of deregulation proposals. Of the eight remaining announcements, seven have negative mean effects on airline's profitability, and the announcement that the Senate and House agreed to a conference report had a significant negative impact of -1.6 percent on airlines' stock returns. The aggregate effect of congressional actions on the expected profitability of both individual and portfolios of airlines is not significant even after segregating announcements related to the Kennedy Hearings, which have a significant positive impact due to expected changes in CAB's administration of regulation.

A total of thirty-eight announcements by the CAB are included in the analysis.[18] Three announcements relate to the CAB commitment to experiment with deregulation, thirteen to the CAB fare policy, and twenty-two to the CAB route policy. The first three announcements relate to the response of the CAB to congressional pressures following the Kennedy Hearings and are made under the chairmanship of John Robson. One of the three announcements, the proposals by the CAB to experiment with route deregulation, had a significant positive impact of 3.7 percent on airline stock returns. The cautious approach to deregulation implicit in the announcement suggested a change from the route moratorium policy imposed by Chairman Timm and is consistent with the findings on the Kennedy Hearings announcements.

The remaining announcements relate to fare and route decisions adopted by the CAB under the chairmanship of Alfred Kahn. Kahn, a strong proponent of deregulation, took office in 1977. His nomination was yet another step politicians took to influence the CAB to deregulate administratively. Under Kahn, the CAB undertook fare and route actions designed to favor price competition and liberalize entry and exit into routes. Of the thirteen announcements about fare actions, eight are negative, and three that relate to supersaver and discount fares have a significant negative impact. The announcement of National's opposition and petition for cancellation of discount fares is associated with a significant positive impact. Sixteen of twenty-one announcements of CAB route actions have a negative average effect on airlines stock returns, and two announcements relating to the Boston–Atlanta and the Chicago–Albany/Syracuse–Boston cases have a significant negative effect. With these

---

[18] A total of forty announcements by the CAB are listed in Appendix A. The analysis excludes two announcements for which sample firms have confounding releases.

cases, the CAB first granted route authority in the post–route moratorium era and stressed that offers of fare reductions by applicants would be an important factor in the selection of applicants.

The aggregate effect of CAB fare actions on individual and portfolios of airlines is not significant. This result is consistent with fare liberalization imposing small or no costs of adjustment to airlines who would merely substitute price for service competition. In contrast, announcements of route actions have a negative impact on sixteen of eighteen airlines and represent a significant loss of shareholdlers' wealth of -7.8 percent. The two firms with a positive impact of CAB route actions were Southwest and Hawaiian. Southwest, a low-cost intrastate carrier, stood to benefit from greater route authority, and Hawaiian's interisland network was likely to remain protected by a geographical barrier to entry.

In summary, announcements of regulatory changes in the air transport industry had an adverse impact on airline shareholders' wealth. Congress influenced the adoption of deregulation by criticizing the CAB policies at the Kennedy Hearings and by appointing CAB chairmen who supported its goal to deregulate. The CAB then proceeded to deregulate administratively. Civil Aeronautics Board route actions had an impact of -7.8 percent, which is significantly larger at the 5 percent level than the impact of actions by the administration (-3.9 percent) and Congress (2.9 percent). The results presented have the following implication for research in the positive analysis of government regulation: if regulatory changes are delegated to regulatory agencies, researchers should focus not only on deliberations by Congress and the administration. Failure to incorporate the regulatory actions of the appropriate regulatory agency in the analysis may lead to inaccurate inferences about the economic consequences of regulatory changes.

B. Differential Impact

This section tests the hypothesis advanced by Spiller in his 1986 study of the existence of mobility barriers in the airline industry. The observed negative impact of regulatory changes on airlines' value reflects the costs of airlines' adjusting their route networks and cost structures to adapt to a competitive environment. Adjustment costs vary with characteristics of airlines' operations that proxy for airlines' relative abilities to operate in a deregulated environment. The differential impact of airline deregulation is examined with the following nonlinear estimation for (2):

$$R_{it} = \alpha_{0i} + \alpha_{1i}R_{mt} + \left(\sum_{j=1}^{J} \alpha_{2j}D_j \right) \left(1 + \sum_{k=1}^{K} \beta_k X_{ki} \right) + e_{it}, \qquad (2)$$

where R_{it}, R_{mt}, and D_j are as defined in equation (1) and X is a matrix of network characteristics. Equation (2) pools all airlines and allows for the direct estimation of the effect of network characteristics on the excess returns associated with the regulatory change announcements.[19]

The regression specified in (2) provides for tests of differential impact associated with characteristics of airlines' route networks and cost structures. Based on data availability and inclusion in previous research, five network characteristics are chosen: hub (+), first class (+), debt/assets (−), stage length (−), and labor cost/revenue passenger miles (RPM) (−).[20] Both the network characteristics and the expected direction of the effect (sign in parentheses) are described below. Descriptive statistics and a correlation matrix of network characteristics are presented in Table 4.

1. *Hubs (+)*. Hubbing consists of scheduling a large number of flights into and out of a central hub (airport). There are two major advantages to hubbing. First, an airline connects more city pairs together so that it can increase the number of passengers it serves. Second, carriers using hubbing operations can provide on-line service (where on-line service refers to passengers reaching their destination with connecting flights of the same carrier). This has two implications. First, the demand in a given market depends not only on the demand local to the points of origin and destination but also on the demand from feeds, that is, from points that connect with that market. Thus, airlines are able to increase load factors in any given market. And, second, since passengers value on-line service, airlines are likely to capture the demand of a larger number of passengers. Hubbing has been a widely used technique of route reorganization in the deregulation period. The measure used to proxy for hubbing is the percentage of departures at each airline's major airport in 1978.[21]

2. *First Class (+)*. Percentage RPM in first class is calculated as the ratio of RPM in first class to total carrier RPM. First-class passengers, in general, business travelers, have relatively price-inelastic demands for air travel and prefer service, such as convenient schedules, to cheaper

---

[19] I thank the referee for this suggestion. Equation (2) is estimated using the SYSNLIN procedure in SAS.

[20] I also considered the share of international passengers as a potential explanator of differential impact. Estimating eq. (2) with this additional network characteristic did not yield significant parameter estimates nor did it alter the estimates on the remaining variables. This finding is consistent with that in Spiller, Mobility Barriers, *supra* note 2.

[21] A more natural proxy would be the extent of involvement in hubbing. There were, however, no hubbing operations prior to deregulation because airlines did not have route flexibility to organize their operations around a hub. The known major airports during the regulation period (Atlanta, Chicago, Dallas, Denver, New York) have become major hubs.

TABLE 4

AIRLINES' NETWORK AND COST CHARACTERISTICS USED IN THE ANALYSIS OF THE
DIFFERENTIAL IMPACT OF DEREGULATION

	Mean	Standard Deviation	Median	Minimum	Maximum
A. Descriptive statistics:[a]					
HUB	.268	.104	.234	.144	.470
First class	.075	.035	.090	.000	.131
Debt/assets	.5453	.171	.561	.155	.787
Stage length	512.7	290.7	528.1	122.3	1,349.3
Labor cost/RPM	.0363	.0127	.0389	.0165	.0672

	Hub	First Class	Debt/Assets	Stage Length	Labor Cost/RPM
B. Correlation matrix:					
HUB	1.00				
First class	.24	1.00			
	(.33)				
Debt/equity	.18	−.05	1.00		
	(.48)	(.83)			
Stage length	−.17	−.13	.12	1.00	
	(.47)	(.61)	(.60)		
Labor cost/RPM	−.33	.12	−.55*	−.12	1.00
	(.17)	(.64)	(.02)	(.64)	

SOURCES.—Civil Aeronautics Board, Handbook of Airlines Statistics (1975–78); Civil Aeronautics Board, Air Carrier Traffic Statistics (1975–78); and Moody's Transportation Manual (1975–78).

NOTE.—*P*-values are in parentheses.

[a] Variable definitions: HUB is measured as the percentage of departures at an airline's major airport in 1978; first class is calculated as the ratio of Revenue Passenger Miles (RPM) in first class to total RPM; debt/assets is the ratio of long-term debt to total assets; stage length represents the average length of flights on airlines' route networks; labor cost/RPM is the ratio of labor costs to total RPM.

* Significant at the 5 percent level or lower (two-tailed test).

fares.[22] A higher proportion of first-class passengers in an airline's route network indicates a higher demand for quality of air travel. A higher demand for quality decreases the likelihood that passengers' traveling decisions are responsive to fare cuts. Thus, because first-class passengers have relatively inelastic demands and established airlines are at an informational advantage, airlines with high percentages RPM in first class are less adversely affected by deregulation.[23]

[22] Although elasticities of demand may vary across markets depending on the percentage of business travel, density, and other factors, there is evidence that the demand for air travel is elastic in most markets. DeVany estimates price elasticities of demand across markets and finds it to be between −1.6 and −1.9. See DeVany, *supra* note 1.

[23] Spiller finds that differential impact of price regulatory changes across airlines is a function of the availability elasticity of demand. The availability elasticity of demand repre-

3. *Debt/Assets (−)*.   The ratio of debt to assets is used to proxy for airlines' financial leverage. If the effect of regulatory changes is thought of as a tax on firm value with shareholders (as residual claimants) bearing the cost of the tax, then the effect on shareholder's wealth is proportionately higher the higher the firms' leverage. Alternatively, highly leveraged airlines have less flexibility to adjust their route networks because of a reduced borrowing ability.

4. *Stage Length (−)*.   Average stage length is the average flight distance on airlines' route networks. Caves, Christensen, and Tretheway provide evidence that costs decrease with average stage length.[24] The intuition behind the effect of average stage length on costs is that economies with respect to distance arise principally from (i) the "fixed cost" aspect of fuel consumption on takeoff and climbing to cruising altitude; (ii) the "fixed cost" aspect of hours paid to crew members before and after the flight; and (iii) the "fixed cost" of ticketing, boarding, and unloading a passenger and his baggage regardless of distance. Furthermore, since fares are based on an "equal fare for equal miles" basis without regard to the effect of distance on costs, then firms with higher average stage length route networks may face greater fare reductions under deregulation and be more adversely affected by deregulation.

5. *Labor Cost/RPM (−)*.   Labor costs represent 35–45 percent of airlines' total costs. Labor costs per RPM are a measure of labor costs per unit of output. Since airlines enter the deregulation period with different cost structures, I expect airlines with higher labor costs per unit of output to be more adversely affected by deregulation. Because regulation put upward pressure on costs, airlines enter the deregulation period with relatively high labor costs. Kahn suggests that airlines' employees, through collective bargaining, have diverted some of the benefits of suppressed competition to themselves in the form of higher wages and fringe benefits.[25]

Table 4, panel B, presents the correlation matrix between the five variables in equation (2). Only one of the correlation coefficients (debt/assets,

---

sents the effect of load factors on the choice between traveling first class or coach. Because load factors are related to availability and convenience of air travel, a high availability elasticity of demand in a given market or in a firm's route network increases the likelihood that potential passengers have relatively inelastic demands for air travel in that market or route network. Thus, firms having high availability elasticity of demand should be less affected by price regulation.

[24] See Douglas W. Caves, Laurits R. Christensen, & Michael W. Tretheway, Economies of Density versus Economies of Scale: Why Trunk and Local Service Airline Costs Differ, 15 Rand J. Econ. 471 (1984).

[25] See Kahn, *supra* note 17.

labor costs/RPM) is distinguishable from zero at the 5 percent level. To assess the effect of collinearity among regressors, I estimate equation (2) with and without the labor cost variable. I find that dropping the variable does not alter the results.

Table 5 contains nonlinear estimates of equation (2) for the percentage change in airlines' value associated with the administration, Congress, and CAB regulatory actions. Announcements by each participant in the regulatory process are aggregated to directly measure the effect of the network characteristics on the value of airlines associated with regulatory actions by each participant.[26] To assess the sensitivity of the estimates to the levels of aggregation, I estimated (2) with different combinations of information variables that included the separation of CAB actions into route and fare actions and the separation of congressional announcements from the Kennedy Hearings. I found that the sensitivity analysis yields similar results. I also estimated a full model and reduced model versions of equation (2). In the full model, the coefficient on the *jk*th interaction term is estimated as the product of two separate coefficient estimates $\gamma_j\beta_k$, whereas in the reduced form the coefficient on any interaction estimated as a single coefficient. A chi-square test could not reject the null hypothesis that the full and reduced model are equivalent.

The evidence in Table 5 indicates that the effect of both the administration and congressional announcements is not significantly related to airlines' network characteristics. Network characteristics, do however, influence the excess returns associated with announcements of CAB actions. The evidence provides fairly strong support that the adverse effect of deregulation is smaller the higher the airlines' ability to reorganize operations around hubs and the higher its involvement in servicing first-class passengers. These results are consistent with prior researchers who have documented that (i) a higher involvement in hubbing increases the efficiency of airlines' route network and their market power and (ii) a higher involvement in servicing first-class passengers is associated with a demand for higher quality of air travel.

The evidence also indicates that airlines were more adversely affected by deregulation the lower their borrowing capacity and the higher their average stage length. Airlines borrowing capacity affects both airlines' ability to shift capital resources to adjust their route networks and the speed with which they can affect these adjustments. Finally, the negative impact of stage length is consistent with expectations of greater expected price reductions on networks with longer flights since the policy of "equal

---

[26] See Spiller. Mobility Barriers, *supra* note 2.

TABLE 5

ANALYSIS OF DIFFERENTIAL IMPACT OF DEREGULATION ON THE VALUE OF AIRLINES

$$R_{it} = \alpha_0 + \alpha_1 R_{mt} + \left(\sum_{j=1}^{J} \alpha_{2j} D_j \right) \times \left(1 + \sum_{K=1}^{K} \beta_k X_{ki} \right) + \epsilon_{it}$$

Explanatory Variables[a]	Expected Sign	Coefficient Estimates	t-Statistic[b]
Constant		$-.002$**	-13.09
R_{mt}	+	1.490**	82.05
ADM		$-.012$	-1.10
ADM $\times$ HUB	+	$.013$	$.86$
ADM $\times$ first class	+	$.003$	$.14$
ADM $\times$ debt/assets	−	$.002$	$.31$
ADM $\times$ stage length (10^4)	−	$.006$	$.35$
ADM $\times$ labor cost/RPM	−	$.013$	1.05
CONG		$-.004$	$-.42$
CONG $\times$ HUB	+	$.014$	1.11
CONG $\times$ first class	+	$.041$	1.08
CONG $\times$ debt/assets	−	$-.004$	$-.47$
CONG $\times$ stage length (10^4)	−	$.016$	$.48$
CONG $\times$ labor cost/RPM	−	$-.067$	$-.61$
CAB		$-.002$	$-.03$
CAB $\times$ HUB	+	$.011$**	1.74
CAB $\times$ first class	+	$.074$**	1.67
CAB $\times$ debt/assets	−	$-.007$**	-1.64
CAB $\times$ stage length (10^4)	−	$-.089$*	-2.27
CAB $\times$ labor cost/RPM	−	$.009$	$.17$
N observations		$23,105$	
R^2		23.59	

[a] ADM, CONG, and CAB are information variables identifying announcements by the administration, Congress, and the Civil Aeronautics Board, respectively. Firm network characteristics are defined in Table 4, note a.
[b] The t-ratios are asymptotically valid.
* Significant at the 5 percent level (two-tailed test).
** Significant at the 10 percent level (two-tailed test).

fare for equal miles'' subsidized short travel at the expense of long travel. This finding is consistent with results in Spiller.[27]

In summary, the evidence indicates that the adverse impact of airline deregulation is smaller the greater the ability of airlines to reorganize their operations so as to compete in a deregulated environment. The evidence provides support for Spiller's hypothesis of the existence of mobility barriers in the airline industry and indicates which financial and network characteristics would improve airline performance in a deregulated environment.

[27] *Id.*

V. Conclusion

This article provides new evidence about the effect of airline deregulation on the expected profitability of airlines. In interpreting the evidence about the impact of regulatory changes, it should be considered that the results depend on (i) the assumption that event dates identified represent a substantial subset of information events relating to regulatory changes in the airline industry and (ii) the validity of the specification of the return-generating process. The article examines a broader set of regulatory changes than previous studies by analyzing the effect of regulatory actions by the CAB in addition to actions by the administration and Congress. The CAB actions are included because politicians exerted pressure on the CAB to deregulate administratively by critizing the CAB policies at the Kennedy Hearings and by appointing CAB chairmen who supported a policy of deregulation. Since the effect of CAB regulatory actions on expected profitability of airlines is substantial, the evidence suggests an important implication for research in the positive analysis of government regulation. If the administration of regulatory changes is delegated to regulatory agencies, failure to incorporate in the analysis the agency's actions may lead to inaccurate inferences about the economic consequences of regulatory changes.

Regulatory changes in the airline industry had a negative impact on airlines' stock returns. The adverse effect is consistent with airlines' facing costs of adjusting their route networks and cost structures to operate in a competitive environment. The costs of adjustment are smaller the higher the ability of airlines to reorganize operations. The evidence also indicates that the market expected airlines with higher ability to organize their route network around hubs, a higher proportion of first-class passengers, and higher borrowing ability to perform better in a deregulated environment.

C
Deregulating Banking in the US

[16]

A Proposal to Deregulate Banking
Hugh Thomas

Banks are the most highly regulated industry in the economy today because banks are viewed as special in their role of being the repository for society's money. This paper argues that the special role has outlived its usefulness and that full banking deregulation can be achieved through a democratization of access to the payments system.

The Banking Oligopoly

Money is the most liquid medium of exchange. Any commodity can be used by society as money but few have. The list includes gold and silver coins, deposit receipts for precious metals and coin, commercial drafts accepted for payment by the drawee, drafts accepted by banks, bank notes, government issued paper currency and, by far the most important in recent decades, bank deposits. Modern governments justifiably intervene to preserve the value of fiat money. Governments are also justifiably concerned that their payments system be run in the interests of society at large. Modern money and payments systems are technical monopolies enjoying strong economies of scale.

Money, as shown in Figure 1, is two-tiered. High-powered money, the venue of the payments system, is the claims of commercial banks on the central bank, and deposit money is the claims of the rest of society on commercial banks. (This discussion ignores the role of notes and coins, which, being issued by the central bank are effectively already sovereign risk money—the status to which this article argues all money should be elevated.) The majority of money is deposit money in the form of demand, notice, and time deposits. The transfer of commercial bank liabilities through the payments system at the request of depositors is the means of effecting payment in society. The potential breakdown of this payments system has pre-

Cato Journal, Vol. 20, No. 2 (Fall 2000). Copyright © Cato Institute. All rights reserved.
Hugh Thomas is Associate Professor of Finance at the Chinese University of Hong Kong and at McMaster University. He thanks Kenneth Chan, Mark Flannery, Will Roberds, Neil Wallace, Ingo Walter, and participants in the *Euromoney* Issuers and Investors Conference in Hong Kong for their helpful comments.

CATO JOURNAL

Figure 1

Two-Tiered Money

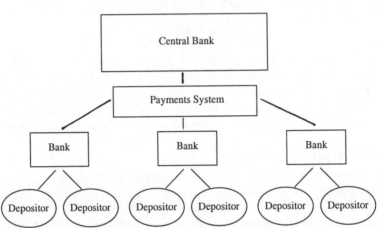

disposed governments to protect banks' restricted access to the payments system. In return, banks submit to strict regulatory oversight.[1]

Historically, banks enjoy restricted access to payments systems because they developed them. From the inception of banks in Italy in the 11th century through the 20th century, bankers would meet periodically to exchange customer requests to make payment (Kindleberger 1993: 42–54). These payment requests would be largely netted out so that only a small fraction of total claims actually resulted in the transfer of high-powered money (gold, silver, and claims on private clearinghouses in previous times, central bank deposits in our day) at the end of the day.

The sheer volume of transactions and the strict security requirements for this daily exchange used to mean that only a limited number of highly trustworthy bankers could feasibly participate in such a clearing system. The electronics revolution, however, has changed this requirement. In order to avoid the problem of systemic risk whereby one bank's intra-day failure would cause multiple failures of intra-day creditors in the payments system, clearing and settlement systems around the world have implemented real time gross settlement systems. Under RTGS, each large payment is made to the beneficiary's account with the central clearing authority in real time,

---

[1]By "banks" I mean all regulated deposit taking institutions including, in various countries, credit unions and credit union centrals, building societies, and postal savings banks.

A Proposal to Deregulate Banking

electronically, by gross, irrevocable settlement.[2] Because payment is irrevocable in real time, in the emerging RTGS payments environment, there is no intra-day credit risk between banks and, consequently, no need for the trust between banks that justified limited access to the payments system.[3]

In an RTGS system that does not allow intra-day overdrafts, a bank can only make a wholesale payment to another bank to the extent that it has, in real time, deposits with the central bank. Those deposits may be obtained through repurchase agreements (or, alternatively, collateralized loans) using specified government securities immobilized in a depository. The owner of the securities advises the depository that the securities should be made available to the RTGS to be used in repurchase agreements. Payments are made against those securities being sold back to the clearing authority.[4] With RTGS, one of the major reasons for having an oligopoly making payments in a two-tier monetary structure has disappeared. Thus, the first recommendation is to democratize the payments system.

Recommendation 1: Democratize the Payments System

On the wholesale level, RTGS can eliminate the intra-day credit risk management need to restrict access to the payments system.

---

[2]Fedwire in the United States, initiated in 1918 and subsequently periodically modified, was the first payments system in the world to give real-time credit for deposit transfers of member banks at the Federal Reserve, initially through the use of telegraph and later by computerized high speed links in the 1970s. RTGS systems were implemented in Sweden (1986), Germany (1987), Switzerland (1987), Japan (1988), Italy (1989), Belgium (1996), Great Britain (1996), France (1997), Hong Kong (1997), and The Netherlands (1997) (see Bank for International Settlements 1997).

[3]RTGS designs differ from system to system, yet all are structured to achieve finality from the point of view of the payee bank in real time. Under Fedwire, intra-day credit risk is still borne by the Federal Reserve, which guarantees payments made by members, effectively lending intra-day balances to its members (for a small fee). Clearly, with the central government maintaining intra-day credit risk, an incentive for bank regulation still exists. But other RGTS systems minimize or eliminate that risk. The Clearing House Interbank Payments System, a private clearinghouse through which most internationally originated U.S. dollar clearings are routed, achieves finality through a combination of bilateral limits, net debit caps, loss-sharing agreements, and collateral. CHIPS clears net payments through Fedwire at the end of the day. For a description of these arrangements, see *http://www.ny.frb.org/pihome/fedpoint/*. My discussion refers to an RTGS system that does not provide intra-day credit such as in force in Japan, Switzerland, and Hong Kong. There is a rapidly growing literature on the optimal configuration of RTGS systems, given the potential for intra-day gridlock and the incentives of participating banks to minimize early payments to reduce liquidity costs. See, for example, Kahn and Roberds (1998), who model the social cost-benefit analysis of the central bank providing intra-day liquidity.

[4]Interestingly, in RTGS systems that allow participants to obtain central bank balances by repo-ing eligible government securities, short-term government debt *is* a larger component of high-powered money than are commercial bank balances with the central bank (Yam 1998).

There is no reason why other financial institutions (FIs) or, indeed, any legal person with government securities (that are also immobilized in the same securities depository) cannot have an account with the clearing authority. Just as easily as a bank, such a person could give instructions to make payment to another account with the clearing authority. And the clearing authority would do so only if sufficient securities were present for the transaction to be effected. Given the ease of electronic data processing, there is no technical reason why a clearing authority would not maintain tens of thousands of clearing accounts, where today it only maintains dozens.

Full democratization of the payments system, however, would require hundreds of millions of retail clearing accounts. Implementing such retail access involves severe additional complications. Government securities are currently only produced in wholesale denominations, and the central banks of the world have no comparative advantage in catering to retail depositors. To overcome these complications, retail depositors could obtain access to wholesale deposits by using a money market mutual fund pooling mechanism. Each such fund (called a *money fund* in the following discussion) would place its securities in the depository and would transfer ownership over them on the instructions of its equity holders.[5] The manager of a money fund could be a former bank, bringing its wealth of knowledge of servicing retail customers to the new legal form. To the retail depositor, a money fund would seem very similar to a bank deposit of today but there would be a very great difference. The money fund manager would not have discretion over the placement of funds. They would have to be placed in government securities, giving the money fund depositor (i.e., the equity unit holder) access to the payments system. Figure 2 shows this recommended structure.

Recommendation 2: Demonetize Banking

As described above, only two activities define a bank: making payments and taking deposits from the public.[6] To protect society from

---

[5]Today, both bearer and registered securities are typically immobilized in depositories that record changes in ownership subject to electronic notification. Fedwire (for securities) in the United States, the Canadian Depository for Securities in Canada, and Cedel and Euroclear in the Euromarkets are examples of such depositories.

[6]U.S. banks under the federal Bank Holding Act used to be defined as "institutions that both accepted demand deposits and engaged in the commercial lending business." Since 1987, banks are defined rather circularly as any "insured bank as defined by section 3(h) of the Federal Deposit Insurance Act." The FDIC Act in turn defines an insured bank to be "a banking institution which is engaged in the business of receiving deposits, other than

A PROPOSAL TO DEREGULATE BANKING

Figure 2

Recommended System

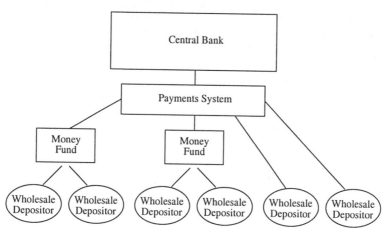

the costs of bank failure—that is, disruption of the payments system and destruction of deposit money—governments give substantial support to banks in the form of deposit insurance, liquidity from the central bank as lender of last resort, and protection from competitors. The term "bank" is often protected in law. Investors in banks are encouraged to feel that their investments are money and are therefore riskless. Banks thereby obtain funds at lower rates of interest than do nonbanks.

Current technology can eliminate the specialness of banks in the payments system. If regulators opened payments systems but left banks with the restricted power to take deposits, however, banks could continue to attract subsidized deposits to fund risky activities (Kwast and Passmore 1997). To avoid such continuing moral hazard, regulators should demonetize banks.

---

trust funds . . . and is incorporated as a bank under the appropriate jurisdictional laws." The FDIC Act's definition of "deposit" clarifies deposits as including sums from the receipt of monies "in settlement of checks, drafts, or other instruments forwarded to such bank or savings association for collection." Somewhat simpler definitions of banking in the British tradition simply refer to the taking of deposits and making of payments. In no jurisdiction that the author is aware of does the act of lending by itself qualify an institution as a bank. Banks do provide important delegated monitoring lending services (Diamond 1984) as well as underwriting, trading, dealing, trust, custodial, and advisory services. But these services are not unique to banks and the failure of a bank in these capacities does not cause society the distress of its failure to repay deposits or make ordered payments.

A demonetized bank would not forgo its funding activities, but it would have to give up the claim that it provided a riskless medium of exchange for what are, in fact, corporate debts. And to drive the point home to the public, it would have to give up the title "bank," becoming instead a nonbank FI. The FI could still issue risky short-term, retail debt, but it would have to advise creditors that their funds were at risk. To clarify the distinction between the new riskless money funds and risky investments such as FI short-term debt, FIs would be precluded from using any account but money funds to manage the receipt and remittance of payment for retail customers. FIs would manage money funds on a fee-for-service basis. With lines of credit, an FI could extend loans to customers to replenish their money funds as necessary. FIs, however, would have to maintain a clear distinction between riskless money—in money funds—and risky investments—in FI liabilities. It is precisely the lack of distinction between riskless money and risky investments that has caused many of the problems in many banking systems throughout history.

The Problems of a Monetized Banking System

As Alan Greenspan (1997) remarked, the U.S. government

> delegate[s] the use of the sovereign credit—the power to create money and borrow unlimited funds at the lowest possible rate—to support the banking system. It has done so indirectly as a consequence of deposit insurance, Federal Reserve discount window access, and final riskless settlement of payment system transactions.

Sovereign, domestic currency guarantees are very valuable. Rather than bearing commercial credit risk, the lender (here, a bank depositor) bears the risk that the country will not make payment with a medium (domestic currency) that the sovereign itself can create. In modern society, that risk is negligible. From the credit risk perspective of the guarantor, however, extending the guarantee to bank deposits is equivalent to extending a loan to the beneficiary bank in the same amount as the guaranteed deposits.

Academics have widely analyzed the moral hazard involved in deposit guarantees, the value of which increases with the risk of the project.[7] But there is a further cost to society in deposit guarantees. As guaranteed projects tend to displace unguaranteed projects, with

---

[7]See Merton (1977) for an analysis of the components of the value of deposit insurance. Estimates of the value of the guarantee are necessarily indirect. Kwast and Passmore (1997)

financial intermediation, banks, benefiting substantially from these subsidies, tend to displace other unguaranteed financial intermediaries. The tendency of banks to take maximum advantage of sovereign guarantees (both explicit and implied) increases the exposure of those governments who have been least able or willing to monitor and restrict lending of banks to the low-risk activities commensurate with the low-risk claims banks issue to depositors.

Governments often monitor banks ineffectively.[8] At least two-thirds of IMF countries experienced significant banking-sector problems from 1980 to 1996 (Lindgren, Garcia, and Saal 1996). The costs of each crisis ran from a few percentage points of GDP—as was the case in the U.S. Savings and Loan crisis which cost the taxpayer about $150 billion—to more than a quarter of GDP (Caprio and Klingebiel 1996: 48–52). The Asian financial crisis of 1997–98 shows that bank problems continue to plague economies.

Recommendation 3: Abolish Government Support for Banks

Once access to the payments system has been democratized and banks have been demonetized, then governments can credibly abolish the support they give to FIs. As part of this process, government supervision of FIs must also *decrease*. The reason for this paradox is that supervision leads to certification of financial health by the government. In the event that an FI that has been certified as healthy goes bankrupt, debt holders (i.e., the former depositors) might legitimately make claims against the government for losses sustained by relying on that certification.

Once a former bank's liabilities are not considered to be money, they can be more logically categorized as securities. The national public securities authority, not the former banking supervisor, should be responsible for oversight of the FI issuing securities. Public securities authorities emphasize the disclosure of information that the investors are responsible for analyzing. They do not need to prescribe

---

estimate that it exceeds the 40 to 100 basis points subsidy enjoyed by such government sponsored agencies as GNMA.

[8]In his discussion of systemic risk, Kaufman (1996) concludes that existing prudential regulations are frequently inefficient and counterproductive, exacerbating social losses from bank failures. His study uncovers little evidence of uninformed, contagious runs against otherwise healthy banks. Starting from the belief that retail deposit insurance is a fact of life that cannot be altered, he argues that much of the bank regulatory system is counterproductive and should be dismantled, being replaced by a structured early intervention and resolution program.

required levels of capital, asset quality, diversification, management quality, earnings, or liquidity, which banking supervisors use, often ineffectively, to reduce the risk of the banks.[9]

Without government supervision of and support for FIs, investors would look for other assurances that the funds they lent were safe. Less risky FIs would have a tremendous incentive to provide better financial disclosure. Yet most investors have neither the time nor the expertise to analyze even well-prepared, transparent financial statements. Thus, investors would most likely rely on the analysis of and ratings given by independent rating agencies. The regulatory burden currently borne by banks subject to government oversight would not really disappear. It would be shifted from centrally controlled government inspectors to market-driven ratings analysts.

Coordinated Implementation of Recommendations

If the proposed reform is to be successful, it is essential that the public understands the nature of the proposed reforms and believes the government's pledge not to rescue a large failing FI. The reforms would have to be implemented in concert. A piecemeal implementation—for example, opening the payments system without rescinding the implicit "too-big-to-fail" guarantee—would just increase the liability of the government. And the implementation would have to be accompanied by a public education campaign that explains the issues and emphasizes the following points:

- The word "bank" is to be revoked from appropriate FIs names, because the special protected status of their debts is being removed.
- Former bank supervisors (that emphasized risk control) are to be disbanded because the government is not in the business of controlling the risk of private corporations. It is up to the securities commissions (which emphasize disclosure) to see that the public is informed about the risk of debt securities.
- Investors are to sign a release for each non-money fund account saying that they understand that their funds are at risk. These releases should be in plain English, like the standard releases that investors in mutual funds currently sign.
- FIs are to strictly implement the principle that money funds be

---

[9]Flannery (1995) and Kaufman (1996) note that efforts of regulators to reduce the risk of banks are often inefficient and counterproductive, increasing the probability and cost of bank failures.

A Proposal to Deregulate Banking

the only vehicle for managing the remittance of funds for retail customers.

If these recommendations are implemented as a package, the public should be able to understand their importance. Public sympathy for banks has never been high. These reforms can honestly be presented to the public as a way to use technology to reduce public subsidies to banks at the cost of requiring that individuals make their own choices concerning the amount of financial risk they will bear.

Assume that a post-reform FI becomes distressed. The government would have ample opportunity to deny that it will provide funds to the failing FI. Sophisticated investors and competing FIs could assess the value in the distressed FI and purchase it or push it into liquidation as appropriate. Other FIs would raise their levels of capital if, because of such a competitor's distress, they reassessed upward their chances of distress. The collapse of the FI itself would not adversely affect others in the payments system. It would only compromise the debt holders of the investing public who had opted to purchase the FI's risky debt.

Objections to the Proposed Reforms

The reader can legitimately raise objections to these wide-ranging proposals for financial reform. Among these objections could be that the proposed reforms would cause monetary contraction, reduction of lending, shortage of eligible securities, loss of liquidity, increased financial-sector volatility, monopoly power going into the hands of the rating agencies, declining security of the payments system, and high implementation costs. The remainder of this article will address these concerns.

Objection 1: Monetary Contraction

Because bank loans are redeposited in other banks and (after subtracting a requirement for liquidity reserves) are lent out again and so on, deposit money is a multiple of high-powered money. One possible objection to the proposed reforms is that they ignore this money multiplier. By redefining money as only high-powered money, wouldn't the reforms force a massive monetary contraction?

This objection confuses two definitions of money: the theoretical and institutional. Monetary policy—generally carried out by a central bank—is one of the major tools of implementing economic policy. Central bankers attempt to keep the growth of money supply in line with economic growth and price stability and may use monetary

245

CATO JOURNAL

policy to stimulate the economy in times of recession. Although economists confidently write in their formulas "M" for money supply, in fact there is no clear line between assets that constitute money and assets that do not constitute money. Any asset that exhibits little price volatility and is traded in liquid, deep markets can be a money substitute. Although probably none of the current measures of the money supply correspond to true theoretical money, most are highly correlated with it. That is currently the case and would be the case under the reformed regime.

In the demonitized banking system outlined above, only high-powered money—coins, notes, and government securities available for repo (or collateralized borrowing) through accounts with the clearing authority (including the government security holdings of money funds)—would be legal money. And everyone would be able to hold this high-powered money.[10] This money would be greater in amount than current measures of high-powered money but would be lower than current M1, which includes all demand and notice deposits in the banking system.

In the new system, however, many persons would consider their short-term loans to top-rated FIs to be money substitutes, the same way that corporate treasurers today consider investments in commercial paper to be a cash substitute. Consumers may wish to keep 40 percent of their liquid savings in the money fund and 50 percent in the top-rated FI, to enjoy, for example, the 0.5 percent higher interest rate. They might also invest 10 percent in a C-rated FI to enjoy a higher interest rate. Because they consider the 50 percent (but not the 10 percent) to be liquid, it should theoretically be included in the money supply. Note, however, that although that 50 percent would *not* be calculated as part of money, it would be correlated with it. If the central bank finds that, with the current supply of money, prices are dropping rapidly and the value of its currency on foreign exchange markets is increasing, it can increase the supply of money. The theoretical money supply—whatever it truly is—would also increase, leaving the central bank with the means of adjusting the money supply to prevent contraction.

Of course, the old rules of thumb of central banking would no longer be applicable if the reforms are implemented. Once central

---

[10]This substitutability of debt securities for money has long been noted. Quoting Friedman (1959: 62) on monetary policy, "Since short-term debt is a closer substitute for money than long-term, the amount of money that would be consistent with price stability if long-term debt were sold would imply risking prices if the same amount of short-term debt were sold instead."

bankers learned how to navigate in the new regime, however, they would be no less able to control the money supply than they are today.

Objection 2: Reduction of Lending

Banks have been subsidized under the current system with the result that lending by depositors to banks and by banks to ultimate borrowers has been higher than it would have been in the absence of these subsidies. Objection 2 observes that the drop in lending implied by the reforms would cause economic contraction. The author acknowledges that a drop in lending would likely occur. I believe, however, that the real problem has not been the amount of debt (or equity) in society but its productivity.

To maximize the rate of economic growth of an economy, capital should be channeled into those activities that provide the best return. If the owners of capital are risk-averse, then the risk of those activities, as well as their expected returns, should be considered before investing. The owners of capital are the people best placed to honestly evaluate the risk and expected returns of projects. If they have neither the time nor the expertise to do so, they must find agents. FIs house those agents. But if the agents are removed from the risk-return preferences of the ultimate owners of capital by sovereign guarantees, the agents can hardly be expected to consider those risk-return preferences.

If a given, retail, capital owner—call her Miss Prudence—wishes simply to maintain her purchasing power without placing any of it at risk, she should be allowed to do so. Under the current banking system, she is not. Her savings can only be placed in a bank that then puts them at risk. If that risk is realized, she (along with other taxpayers) pays the cost of the central authority making good on its guarantee that her purchasing power, preserved in the bank, was indeed riskless.

Under the proposed reforms, risk-averse savers may place their funds in money funds, which will bid up the price of short-term government securities pledged in the clearing system so much that the short-term interest rate drops to zero. The government may find that if it issues more such securities it will engender inflation. If this were the case, then the incentive for investors to place funds in the securities of FIs and other corporations—which would offer attractive, positive rates of real return—would be greatly enhanced.

Investors other than Miss Prudence would seek better rates of return but, being aware that they were placing funds at risk, they would analyze (or pay agents to analyze) the link between promised returns to their funds and the risk of those funds.

Objection 3: Insufficient Government Securities

With governments' fiscal budgets increasingly in surplus, some may fear that the supply of specified government securities eligible for repurchase in the settlement system could be insufficient to meet the demand for high-powered money. This fear is misplaced because in the short run, there are sufficient securities, and in the long run either (1) the government can make available more securities to meet demand, or (2) other securities could be declared eligible.

Currently, there are sufficient securities in the United States. The U.S. public debt is now $5.72 trillion, down only marginally from $5.77 trillion in December 1999, and well above the levels of the early 1990s. That is about five times M1 (current transactions balances), nearly 38 percent more than M2 (which includes small-denomination time deposits and balances in retail money market mutual funds), and about the same size as M3 (which includes wholesale time deposits). That amounts to about $20,000 per capita, probably exceeding the requirements for individuals' riskless investments at today's substantially positive interest rates.

The treasury market is relatively efficient, with price equating supply and demand. There is considerable room for prices of government securities to be bid up (from increased demand following the reform) to reflect the true social demand for riskless funds before the interest rate on riskless debt hits zero percent.

If the interest rate actually does drop to zero, a government should be prepared to issue whatever amount of paper investors demand. In the unlikely event that interest rates did drop to zero, the government that raises funds by issuing debt, yielding zero percent, could achieve a positive return by investing the proceeds. In the interests of promoting liquidity, the government may choose to issue such securities prior to the riskless rate of interest dropping to zero. Note that in Hong Kong, the government has no net debt but the RTGS uses Exchange Fund bills and notes issued by the government nonetheless. The government issues that debt not to raise funds for fiscal spending but to provide liquidity in the money and fixed income capital markets. The government invests the funds in marketable securities for a profit. Note that these Exchange Fund bills and notes pay positive rates of interest.

If the government does not wish to provide this liquidity, the RTGS system could expand its definition of securities acceptable for collateralizing to include nondomestic government issues. The Bank of England currently allows payments in its RGTS to be collateralized by euro-area sovereign issues, not just U.K. sterling government issues. Conceivably, even high-quality, AAA-rated corporate or securitized

A PROPOSAL TO DEREGULATE BANKING

short-term securities could be used as collateral, with a margining percentage and the requirement that the securities' credit rating be maintained on a daily basis. Such a requirement, however, is not necessary in the short run because, as noted above, sufficient treasury securities are already available.

Objection 4: Loss of Liquidity

The fourth objection is as follows: banks issue liquid, short-term securities and book illiquid, long-term assets. If banks were eliminated, the economy's liquidity would be reduced. Because society values liquidity, the proposed reform would eliminate social value.[11] Note that I do not advocate the elimination of financial intermediaries (and the consequent loss of liquidity). Transformed banks, FIs under a different name and without the protection of the government, would continue to intermediate, but would separate that role from monopoly access to the payments system and narrowly defined money.

Liquidity is the characteristic of an asset that allows each investor to buy and sell large quantities (relative to the holdings of that investor) without seriously affecting the asset's price. Liquid assets are characterized by symmetric information: the buyers and sellers both have the same information about the assets. The electronics revolution, by allowing information to be disseminated cheaply and widely, has dramatically increased the liquidity of assets. The 21st century will be an era of rapidly rising liquidity, regardless of what is done to change the banking system. Rapid information flows allow worldwide, cheap access to (1) bid-ask prices of financial assets (2) information about issuers, and (3) models to price financial assets. Banks' and indeed other nonbank corporations' balance sheets are increasingly liquid, a fact which is reducing the need to give banks special regulatory consideration.[12]

Objection 5: Financial-Sector Volatility

Notwithstanding—or perhaps because of—the increase in liquidity, financial asset volatility has increased. Asset price volatility in-

---

[11]See Wallace (1996) for a critique on the *narrow banking proposal* based on Diamond and Dybvig (1983). It should be noted, however, that Diamond and Dybvig (1983) wrote the model partly to justify deposit insurance. They assume, rather than prove, FIs' liquidity role in society.

[12]Rajan (1998) points to three factors that have eroded the requirement for regulated banks: technology, information availability, and the property rights environment. These new factors have, in his view, obviated the need for banks as specially regulated financial intermediaries.

creases the chances of financial distress of leveraged banks. In a
volatile environment, an FI borrowing most of its capital may suddenly find that the value of its assets is less than the value of its
liabilities. Increasing financial system transparency will increase asset
liquidity and will reduce (subject to strict enforcement of rule of law)
the chances of embezzlement,[13] but it will also hasten the demise of
an FI that is insolvent. Under the proposed system, devoid of protection from a run, a former bank with high leverage would find that
its likelihood of bankruptcy increases.

This increased likelihood of bankruptcy would not increase systemic risk. First, democratizing the payments system and demonetiz-
ing banks would insulate the two critical components of the financial
system from the negative externalities of the FIs' collapse. Second,
investors would force FIs, without sovereign protection, to manage
their risks effectively or face an outflow of debt capital. Risk management can be effected through increasing the equity cushion, raising asset quality, and implementing sound-risk management principles.

To demonstrate their reduced risk, FIs would court the favors of
rating agencies. Instead of being forced by regulators to disclose their
condition, the most solvent would willingly disclose their risk management systems and conditions to the public in general and analysts
in particular.

Objection 6: Excessive Power for the Rating Agencies

Without a doubt, the reforms would increase the power of the
ratings agencies, but that increase in power does not equate to an
unacceptable concentration of power because rating agencies are not
by nature monopolistic.

There are two types of investors: those who simply accept the
ratings agencies' ratings and those who analyze companies themselves
as well as using the rating agencies. The first group ascribes para-
mount importance to ratings. The cost of reading a rating is near zero.
So investors usually look at more than one rating on which to base
their decisions. Seekers of capital, who pay to be rated, are aware of
this information diversification and seek ratings from more than one
source. On the other hand, investors, to minimize their work, rely on
the ratings of a very limited number of prestigious rating agencies.
Rating agencies can preserve their prestige only if they produce ac-

---

[13]Calomiris and Kahn (1991) discuss the liquidity risk booked by FIs not as a necessary
provision of liquidity to society but as a device for preventing bankers from embezzling
funds. Deposit insurance, however, eliminates the effectiveness of this monitoring.

A PROPOSAL TO DEREGULATE BANKING

curate ratings. Good analysts within the prestigious ratings agency—who themselves have personal reputations to protect—leave to join a competitor or to set up a new agency if their agency's reputation is compromised. Hence the ratings market is a contestable market where only a few can survive but where entry is inexpensive.

The second type of investor does primary credit analysis in addition to using ratings. These institutional and professional investors employ high-quality analysts themselves. By doing so, they maintain an external pool of analytical talent and an external standard against which the rating agencies are constantly judged.

Objection 7: Security of the Payments System

With the democratization of the payments system, any member of society would effectively have direct debit access to his or her holdings of high-powered money. While the idea of logging into the central bank may be daunting, the problems of security are the same as those that have been faced in implementing RTGS systems at the wholesale level for banks and debit card systems and ATMs at the retail level for the public in general. The same type of identifying procedures (ID numbers and passwords, limits to withdrawals, verification of transfers above certain amounts, denying of access if invalid information is input too frequently) provide appropriate guidelines for the design of secure systems.

But designing and implementing new systems is not cheap. Thus systems integrity is just one of the many components of the cost of implementing the proposed reforms.

Objection 8: Implementation Cost

Cost is the most valid objection to the proposed reforms. Any change to financial systems involves three sorts of costs: losses to former monopoly rent holders, systems implementation costs, and learning costs.

Even though the reforms would increase the efficiency of the capital and money markets, thereby giving net gains to society, the banks, who now enjoy monopoly rents from their low cost of funding and restricted access to payments systems, will lose out. Although many members of society would applaud cutting banks down to size, the falling bank stock prices; decreases in banking prestige, salaries and employment use; and disbanding of bank supervisory departments of governments would be painful. Banks, the very institutions that are required to implement these proposed reforms, can be counted on to resist them.

Systems implementation would also be expensive. Substantial legal, administrative, and advertising costs and systems investments would be required for redrafting of laws, changing corporate organization, reeducating society, and implementing new computer systems.

Financial market participants, from fund managers to retail depositors, would have to reappraise their borrowing, savings, and investment behavior. Moreover, as mentioned above, central banks would have to relearn how to control the money supply within a new structure. These learning costs are substantial, but very difficult to quantify.

Conclusion

In this article, I have argued that the democratization of the payments system, demonetization of banks, and repudiation of government guarantees can lead to substantial net savings for society. Increased efficiency in capital allocation, reduced regulatory burden, and reduced costs of government supervision would result. Like most reforms, the deregulation of banking also would involve costs. The task at hand is to analyze the cost of implementation and compare it with the expected benefits, bearing in mind the losses borne by society from banking crises in past years. If the expected benefits exceed the costs, then it is time to plan these fundamental reforms.

Today, however, there is no political will to mount the far-reaching reforms to banking proposed in this paper. Banking reform is neither popular nor well understood, and legislators are not keen to rewrite laws whose ink is still wet on the page. Yet the refrain "If it ain't broken, don't fix it" misses the point that it *is* broken. As the paper points out, the cost of built-in moral hazard has been large and recurring. We just do not see the effects every day. We may have to wait for the next crisis to appreciate the costs. But if we put the reforms suggested in this paper onto the social agenda, the next time support builds for banking reform of some kind, the appropriate solution will be apparent.

References

Bank for International Settlements (1997) *Real Time Gross Settlement Systems*. Report Prepared by the Committee on Payment and Settlement Systems of the Central Banks of the Group of Ten Countries. Basel: BIS.

Calomiris, C., and Kahn, C. (1991) "The Role of Demandable Debt in Structuring Optimal Banking Arrangements." *American Economic Review* 81 (3): 497–513.

Caprio G., and Klingebiel, D. (1996) "Bank Insolvencies: Cross-country Ex-

A PROPOSAL TO DEREGULATE BANKING

perience." Policy Research Working Paper 1620. Washington, D.C.: The World Bank.

Diamond, D. (1984) "Financial Intermediation and Delegated Monitoring." *Review of Economic Studies* 51: 393–414.

Diamond, D., and Dybvig, P. (1983) "Bank Runs, Deposit Insurance and Liquidity." *Journal of Political Economy* 91 (3): 401–19.

Flannery, M. (1995) "Prudential Regulation for Banks." In K. Sawamoto and H. Taguchi (eds.) *Financial Stability in a Changing Environment*, 281–318 New York: St. Martin's.

Friedman, M. (1959) *A Program for Monetary Stability.* New York: Fordham University Press.

Greenspan, A. (1997) Testimony before the Subcommittee on Financial Institutions and Consumer Credit of the Committee on Banking and Financial Services, U.S. House of Representatives, 13 February.

Kaufman, G. (1996) "Bank Failures, Systemic Risk, and Bank Regulation." *Cato Journal* 6 (1): 17–46.

Khan, C.M., and Roberds, W. (1998) "Real Time Gross Settlement and the Costs of Immediacy." Working Paper 98–21. Atlanta: Federal Reserve Bank of Atlanta.

Kindleberger, C. (1993) *A Financial History of Western Europe.* New York: Oxford University Press.

Kwast, M., and Passmore, W. (1997) "The Subsidy Provided by the Federal Safety Net: Theory, Measurement and Containment." Working Paper. Washington, D.C.: Board of Governors of the Federal Reserve System.

Lindgren, C., Garcia, G., and Saal, M. (1996) *Bank Soundness and Macro-economic Policy.* Washington, D.C.: International Monetary Fund.

Merton, R.C. (1977) "An Analytic Derivation of the Cost of Deposit Insurance and Loan Guarantees: An Application of Modern Option Pricing Theory." *Journal of Banking and Finance* 1: 3–11.

Rajan, R. (1998) "The Past and Future of Commercial Banking Viewed through an Incomplete Contract Lens." *Journal of Money, Credit and Banking* 30 (3): 524–50.

Wallace, N. (1996) "Narrow Banking Meets the Diamond-Dybvig Model." *Federal Reserve Bank of Minneapolis Quarterly Review* 20 (1): 3–13.

Yam, J. (1998) "Review of Currency Board Arrangements in Hong Kong." Hong Kong: Hong Kong Monetary Authority.

[17]

Journal of
Economics
& Business

NORTH-HOLLAND   Journal of Economics and Business 53 (2001) 255–282

Efficient risk-taking and regulatory covenant enforcement in a deregulated banking industry

Robert E. DeYoung[a],*, Joseph P. Hughes[b], Choon-Geol Moon[c]

[a]*Federal Reserve Bank of Chicago, 230 South LaSalle Street, Chicago, IL 60604, USA*
[b]*Department of Economics, Rutgers University, New Brunswick, NJ 08901-1248, USA*
[c]*College of Business and Economics, Hanyang University, 17 Haengdang-Dong, Seongdong-Gu, Seoul 133-791, South Korea*

Received 23 August 1999; received in revised form 19 January 2000; accepted 27 January 2000

Abstract

The deregulation of the U.S. banking industry has fostered increased competition in banking markets, which in turn has created incentives for banks to operate more efficiently and/or take more risk. We examine the degree to which supervisory CAMEL ratings reflect the *level of risk* taken by banks and the *risk-taking efficiency* of those banks (i.e., whether increased risk levels generate higher expected returns). Our results suggest that supervisors not only distinguish between the risk-taking of efficient and inefficient banks, but they also permit efficient banks more latitude in their investment strategies than inefficient banks. © 2001 Elsevier Science Inc. All rights reserved.

JEL classification: G21; G28

Keywords: Bank supervision; Bank efficiency

1. Introduction

Over the last twenty years, a variety of measures aimed at deregulating U.S. commercial banking have been enacted. For example, intrastate and interstate branching restrictions have been substantially relaxed, interest rate ceilings on time deposits have been abolished, and

---

* Corresponding author. Tel.: +1-312-322-5396; fax: +1-312-322-2357.
E-mail addresses: robert.deyoung@chi.frb.org (R. DeYoung), jphughes@rci.rutgers.edu (J.P. Hughes), mooncg@unitel.co.kr (C.-G. Moon).

0148-6195/01/$ – see front matter © 2001 Elsevier Science Inc. All rights reserved.
PII: S0148-6195(00)00044-8

256 . R. DeYoung et al. / Journal of Economics and Business 53 (2001) 255–282

thrift institutions have been permitted to enter product markets previously reserved for commercial banks. While the increased competition resulting from such measures can encourage banks to operate more efficiently, it can also increase banks' incentives to take risk, which can potentially threaten the safety of banks and the payments system.

Historically, barriers to competition supported banks' profitability, and the capitalized value of these profits increased the value of banks' charters. These high profits provided an important incentive for banks to limit their risk-taking to avoid insolvency and losing their valuable charters. But as increased competition has eroded both bank profits and charter values, banks have attempted to enhance their expected earnings by taking additional risk. The competition-induced incentives to increase risk can reinforce the already existing moral hazard incentives provided by the deposit insurance and discount window safety nets, which historically have not fully priced the risks that banks take. Thus, in a deregulated banking system, bank regulators face the challenge of monitoring and controlling banks' risk-taking, while at the same time not restricting competitive forces which can discipline banks and improve industry efficiency.

At the center of this regulatory challenge are banks' demand deposits—an unique form of demandable debt used by banks to finance their operations, and a key part of the economy's payments system. The regulation and supervision of banks' risk-taking protects the safety of bank deposits and, hence, the payments system. To a large degree, the role played by bank regulators is analogous to that of writing and monitoring debt covenants for the depositors, whose debt is not protected by standard covenants.[1] *Safety and soundness covenants,* such as minimum capital ratios and loan concentration limits, constrain banks' menu of feasible risk-return choices. When these safety and soundness covenants become binding, regulators can enforce *remedial* covenants, such as restricting asset growth or raising additional equity capital, that constrain the actions of banks further. Because *regulatory covenant enforcement* can impose substantial costs on banks that encounter financial distress, it provides an important incentive for banks to limit risk-taking.[2] If administered carefully, the threat of covenant enforcement can appropriately balance the risk-increasing incentives created by increased competition and mispriced safety nets.

Not all risk-taking is imprudent, and some banks are better at risk-taking than others. Banks that are more efficient risk-takers earn higher expected returns for the risks they take; that is, they enjoy a better menu of risk-return choices. Banks that are efficient risk-takers have a lower probability of experiencing financial distress, and have a higher probability of recovering from adverse exogenous circumstances that produce financial distress. Thus, effective regulation and supervision of commercial banks will distinguish efficient risk-taking from inefficient risk-taking, and will discourage the latter. In response to the risk-increasing incentives created by deregulation and increased competition, over the past decade bank regulators have introduced a number of measures that formally link the regulation of commercial banks to the level of risks they take. Risk-based capital requirements and risk-based deposit insurance premia are two prominent examples. More recently, regulators have changed the procedures for their annual examinations of bank safety and soundness to include an explicit assessment of banks' ability to manage risk.

In this study we look for evidence that, in formally linking regulation to risk, commercial bank regulators distinguish between a bank's level of risk and its efficiency at risk-taking.

R. DeYoung et al. / Journal of Economics and Business 53 (2001) 255–282   257

We ask, in effect, do bank regulators treat the risk-taking of efficient banks differently than the risk-taking of inefficient banks? Do regulators afford efficient banks more latitude in their investment strategies than inefficient banks? Do regulators create incentives for banks to improve the efficiency of their risk-taking? Our evidence answers, "Yes," to each of these questions. Our findings suggest that the increased opportunities for risk-taking in the deregulated banking industry are not encouraged equally for all banks. We also find that, despite this differential treatment of banks, regulators provide incentives for both efficient and inefficient banks to manage risk more efficiently.

To investigate these questions we focus on banks' CAMEL ratings, the annual supervisory assessment of a bank's overall financial condition and its compliance with safety and soundness covenants. *Because these ratings reflect the likelihood that supervisors will enforce remedial covenants and, in doing so, impose distress costs on banks, the ratings provide our investigation with the critical clues needed to look for differences in regulatory incentives for relatively efficient and inefficient risk-takers to trade return for reduced risk.*

We use a three-step procedure to investigate these questions. In the first step, we employ a structural model of production to obtain estimates of expected return and risk for the 356 national banks in our sample. Our model, developed by Hughes, Lang, Mester, and Moon (1995, 1996, 1999) and Hughes and Moon (1995), allows bank managers to trade expected return for reduced risk. The model employs the Almost Ideal Demand System (Deaton & Muellbauer, 1980) to recover managers' preferences for expected return and risk from cross-sectional price and production data for 1994. Using a production-based approach allows us to include both privately and publicly held banks in our tests and also allows us to estimate each bank's productive inefficiency. Each bank's expected return-risk combination establishes one point on its own risk-return frontier. In the second step, we fit a stochastic, envelope frontier to the 356 expected return-risk combinations. This produces an overall, best-practice risk-return frontier for all banks in the sample. We measure each bank's risk-return efficiency by its distance from this frontier. Finally, to consider how bank supervisors evaluate banks' risk-return trade-offs, we estimate an ordered logit model that relates each bank's CAMEL rating to its expected return, its risk, its risk-return inefficiency, and its size. By controlling for a bank's size and its risk-return choice, we can isolate the effect of its efficiency at risk-taking on its CAMEL rating. That is, we can reveal whether the likelihood that regulators enforce remedial covenants, and thus provide incentives for banks to exchange return for reduced risk, is related to the efficiency with which banks take risk.

The evidence we find is consistent with our hypothesis that a bank's regulatory treatment is influenced by how efficiently it manages risk. Among the least efficient banks in our sample, banks that take extra risk for a higher expected return are assigned worse CAMEL ratings, and the larger the bank, the stricter the standard that is applied to it. In contrast, among the most efficient banks in our sample, CAMEL ratings were related only to the degree of banks' efficiency, not to their risk-return choice or to their size. On one hand, our results suggest that if banks are relatively efficient at risk-taking, examiners provide incentives for further efficiency improvements, but tend not to discourage the "prudent" risks taken by these banks. On the other hand, our results also suggest that if banks are relatively inefficient at risk-taking, examiners not only penalize the choice of a higher risk-higher

258   *R. DeYoung et al. / Journal of Economics and Business 53 (2001) 255–282*

return strategy, but penalize size as well, perhaps because larger inefficient banks pose a greater threat to the payments system.

The principal contributions of our study are the following. First, we show that banks' efficiency at managing risk as well as banks' *ex ante* risk-return choices are important for explaining bank supervisors' assessments of their safety and soundness. Thus, the risk-increasing incentives created by increased competition may not compromise bank safety when bank supervision distinguishes efficient from inefficient risk-taking and discourages the latter. Second, the success of these measures in explaining CAMEL ratings demonstrates that it is important to account for risk when measuring banks' profit efficiency. Although there is a large literature on efficiency measurement in banking, only a handful of studies explicitly incorporate *ex ante* risk.[3] Finally, we introduce the techniques of efficiency measurement that incorporate risk to the literature on CAMEL ratings, which has to date generally focused on the relationship between CAMEL ratings and the market value of banks' debt and equity.

Section 2 that follows describes how the regulation of commercial banks in the United States influences the financial distress costs that they face and how distress costs affect their value-maximizing choice of expected return and return risk. Section 3 briefly reviews some of the literature on the effect of financial distress costs on bank risk-taking. Section 4 describes how a bank's exam scores, the CAMEL ratings, reflect the safety and soundness objectives of bank regulators. We present our three-step procedure for estimating expected return, risk, and efficiency in sections 5, 6, and 7. Because each stage of our analysis generates results that are interesting in their own right, we present the intermediate results at the end of each of these three sections. Lastly, we summarize our findings in section 8 and draw conclusions about the incentives that regulatory monitoring and covenant enforcement provide for banks to trade expected return for reduced risk and to manage risk efficiently.

2. The effect of distress costs on bank risk-taking

Trading expected return for reduced risk is a value-maximizing strategy whenever the occurrence of large losses would expose a firm to a costly episode of financial distress. Financial distress costs can include (i) constraints imposed on the firm when its debt covenants become binding; (ii) higher costs of borrowing that lead to suboptimal investment policy; (iii) the disruption of valuable relationships with customers and suppliers; and (iv) the sale of assets at depressed prices.

Financial distress costs play an important role in commercial banking. Not only are banks highly levered firms, but the nature of their leverage is unique in that a substantial portion of bank debt is demandable, and this demandable debt (i.e., bank deposits) is part of the economy's payments system. Banks' ability to monitor these demand deposits gives them an informational advantage over nonbank lenders in assessing credit risk and monitoring borrower behavior.[4] However, this informational advantage also means that the quality of banks' assets is not readily observable to outsiders, so depositors have the incentive to demand their funds when a bank appears to be taking excessive risks. Furthermore, because a run on one bank can spread to other banks, risk-taking at an individual bank can potentially disrupt the payments system.[5] Thus, episodes of financial distress are likely to impose a number of costs on commercial banks, including liquidity crises, the loss of valuable customer relationships, and, in the extreme case of insolvency, the loss of a valuable charter. Given the costs of these scenarios, banks may well find that trading current expected return for reduced risk—and thereby reducing the likelihood of distress and its expected costs—is a value-maximizing strategy.

Commercial banking is a highly regulated industry, and actions taken by bank regulators can strongly influence the distress costs at banks. Regulators monitor and constrain bank risk-taking, place limits on banks' investment activities and production plans, and have the power to remove bank officers and revoke bank charters. The regulatory process is analogous to writing debt covenants to control moral hazard and to enforcing these covenants when they become binding. Hence, the regulatory process guards the interests of demandable debtholders, who are not explicitly protected by the standard covenants of debt contracts. The regulatory process also protects the interests of the deposit insurer and insures the safety of the payments system.

Bank examinations are an integral part of monitoring and enforcing regulatory covenants. At the close of each examination, bank examiners assign a numerical rating of the bank's safety and soundness. This rating is based on objective measures of the bank's current condition and recent performance, and also reflects the examiners' subjective assessment of the bank's ability to respond to unfavorable future economic conditions. A bank's examination rating quantifies the likelihood that the supervisor will take action (i.e., enforce covenants) to protect depositors, the deposit insurer, and the payments system. In some cases the connection between the exam rating and covenant enforcement is direct, e.g., exam ratings enter into the formulae that determine capital requirements and deposit insurance premia. In other cases the connection is less direct, e.g., banks with poor exam ratings get examined more frequently and more rigorously.

Because the government has the power and the mandate to monitor banks' risk-taking, to enforce remedial covenants on banks that take imprudent amounts of risk, and to impose distress costs in the process, bank regulation and supervision may induce banks to choose less risky business strategies. When supervisors also distinguish the efficiency of banks' risk-taking from the level of their risk and impose higher expected distress costs on inefficient risk-takers, they give inefficient banks an incentive to become more efficient while they discourage inefficient risk-taking.

Banks that trade expected return for lower risk and that are more efficient at risk-taking reduce their likelihood of failure. The bank in Fig. 1 that chooses to produce at point A on its risk-return frontier rather than point B has traded return for reduced risk and has lowered its probability of failure. Risk-return combinations with the same probability of failure are indicated in Fig. 1 by the rays, which represent constant z-scores.[6] Because rays to the right represent lower z-scores and higher probabilities of insolvency, choosing to produce at A rather than B lowers the probability of financial distress and failure.

Unlike individual investors who purchase portfolios of market-produced assets and who face the same efficient risk-return trade-off, banks employ the informational edge afforded by their demand deposits to produce information-intensive assets, or loans, that constitute much of their portfolios. Since many of these loans are not generally marketable, individual

260   R. DeYoung et al. / Journal of Economics and Business 53 (2001) 255–282

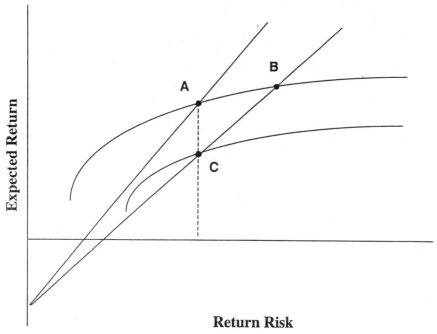

Return Risk

Fig. 1. Risk-return trade-offs.

banks do not face identical risk-return trade-offs. The bank in Fig. 1 whose frontier passes through point C may not be as well diversified geographically as the bank whose frontier includes A and B. Or, it may not manage risk and generate expected return as well. In any case, point C lies on the lower of the two z-score rays, so it is obvious that the inefficiencies that force a bank to operate at C rather than A also increase the probability of distress and failure.

Examination ratings summarize a bank's performance and reflect the likelihood that the supervisor will respond to poor performance by enforcing remedial covenants. In this study we investigate whether regulators assign better exam ratings to banks that choose point A in Fig. 1 over point B, sacrificing expected return for reduced risk and, hence, a lower probability of distress and failure. Similarly, we ask whether efficient banks at point A, with their higher expected returns and lower probabilities of distress, receive better exam ratings than inefficient banks at point C. To the extent that inefficiency and higher risk-return choices are associated with poorer exam ratings, the threat of remedial covenant enforcement will be greater and, hence, banks' incentives to trade expected return for reduced risk and to improve their efficiency will increase. Finally, we compare banks at points B and C and ask whether the more efficient banks at point B receive better exam ratings despite having the same likelihood of insolvency. To the extent that supervisors distinguish inefficiency from the level of risk and impose higher expected distress costs on inefficient risk-taking, supervisors both discourage inefficient risk-taking and they provide an incentive to improve efficiency.

R. DeYoung et al. / Journal of Economics and Business 53 (2001) 255–282   261

3. Evidence of the effect of distress costs on bank risk-taking

A number of recent studies have found relationships between banks' incentives to exchange return for reduced risk and the economic and market conditions under which banks operate. The studies have posited or established links between banks' risk-return trade-offs and the degree of market competition, the opaqueness of bank assets, banks' unusual liquidity risk, and the necessity of holding a valuable bank charter in order to be able to offer demand deposits.

The increased level of competition in the postderegulation banking industry has changed the incentives facing banks in several ways. Studies by Akhavein, Berger, and Humphrey (1997), DeYoung, Hasan, and Kirchhoff (1998), Hughes, Lang, Mester, and Moon (1999), and others suggest that the competition induced by deregulation has provided banks with an incentive to operate more efficiently. But increased competition can also increase banks' incentives to take risk, which can potentially threaten the safety of banks and the payments system. Keeley (1990) finds evidence that increasing competition in U.S. banking over the last several decades has eroded the value of a commercial bank charter and, consequently, has led banks to take greater risks to improve their expected earnings. A more recent study by Demsetz, Saidenberg, and Strahan (1996) draws similar conclusions. Kwan and Eisenbeis (1996) find that banks exhibiting large amounts of cost inefficiency earned low *ex post* returns, but tended to choose high-risk business strategies, and hypothesize that these inefficient banks had relatively low charter value. Finally, competition-induced incentives to increase risk may be reinforcing the existing moral hazard incentives provided by the deposit insurance safety net (Merton, 1977 and Marcus, 1984).

Banks with better asset quality can lower the cost of their uninsured, borrowed funds and reduce the probability of liquidity crises if they can credibly signal the quality to less informed creditors. To test this hypothesis, Lucas and McDonald (1992) develop a model in which value-maximizing banks signal asset quality with their holdings of riskless government securities. Hughes and Mester (1998) explore the role of equity capital as a signal of asset quality. Employing 1990 data on large U.S. banks, they estimate a cost function that is conditioned on the level of equity capital. Central to their model is the bank's demand for equity capital, which is derived from a managerial utility function so that banks do not necessarily choose the cost-minimizing level of capital. They find that equity capital behaves, not as an input, (i.e., a source of funds), but as a signal of both asset quality and the amount of resources devoted to risk management.

4. Interpreting CAMEL ratings

Regulatory monitoring and covenant enforcement might enhance incentives to trade return for reduced risk. The majority of commercial banks are examined annually for safety and soundness either by the Office of the Comptroller of the Currency, the Federal Deposit Insurance Corporation, the Federal Reserve System, or by a state regulator. The most important product of the annual exam is the CAMEL rating, which is a composite of five separate performance components: capital adequacy (C), asset quality (A), management or

administration (M), earnings (E), and liquidity (L). Each of these five performance components ranges in whole numbers from 1, indicating "strong performance," to 5, indicating
"unsatisfactory" performance. The composite CAMEL rating also ranges from 1, which
indicates that the bank is "basically sound in every respect," to 5, which warns of an
"extremely high, immediate or near-term probability of failure."[7]

Examiners determine the C, A, E, and L ratings based on a combination of objective
information and subjective judgment, with the primary focus on the former. Ratings in these
first four areas are based mostly on quantifiable measures of financial performance such as
capital ratios, profitability ratios, earnings retention, nonaccruing and nonperforming loans,
and deposit volatility. In contrast, the M rating is based to a large degree on the examiners'
subjective evaluation of nonquantifiable phenomena such as the adequacy of procedures and
policies, the demonstrated ability of managers to respond to unforeseen developments in the
four other performance dimensions, and any special circumstances that may be influencing
the bank's performance.[8]

Since many supervisory actions taken by regulators reflect the bank's current CAMEL
rating, not all banks receive the same supervisory treatment. These actions are aimed at
maintaining the solvency of the bank, and, although regulators often allow banks with
CAMEL ratings of 4 and 5 to fail, this general focus on safety and soundness suggests that
bank examiners may favor banks that trade return for reduced risk.

Because exam ratings are not disclosed to the public, most academic research using exam
ratings tests whether and how quickly financial markets discover this private information.[9]
In a recent study closely related to our investigation, Hall, Meyer, and Vaughan (1997)
regressed BOPEC ratings (the ratings that reflect regulators' assessment of bank holding
company risk) on a set of financial ratios for holding companies from the period 1988–93.
The authors also regressed estimates of risk from a two-factor market model (the market's
assessment of bank holding company risk) on the same variables. Regulatory risk assessments were strongly related to credit risk as well as capital levels, while the market risk
assessments were strongly related only to credit risk. The authors conclude that bank
regulators have a greater aversion to the risk of insolvency than do bank investors and are
therefore more likely to assign worse exam ratings to banks that take extra risk for more
return.

5. Estimating expected return and risk

In order to include banks in our sample that are privately as well as publicly held and in
order to measure banks' productive inefficiency, we estimate expected return and return risk
from a model of bank portfolio production developed by Hughes, Lang, Mester, and Moon
(1993, 1995, 1996, 1999) from earlier work by Hughes (1989, 1990), that allows bank
managers to choose levered portfolio production plans that trade profit for reduced risk.
Standard models of bank production assume that managers employ the combination of inputs
and outputs that maximizes profit. Hence, these models do not allow for the possibility that
managers would choose to trade profitability for a reduced risk of financial distress and
insolvency. In our model of bank production, however, managers choose their most preferred

levered portfolio production plan, which is the combination of inputs and outputs that maximizes their utility. This utility-maximizing production plan may or may not be the profit-maximizing plan.

Hughes and Moon (1995) show that the utility function's ranking of production plans is equivalent to a ranking of subjective probability distributions of profit that are conditional on the production plan. The connection between production plans and their implied probability distributions of profit follows from managers' beliefs about the probabilities of future economic states of the world and their beliefs about how profits will be generated by production plans in these future economic states. These beliefs link each production plan with a subjective, conditional probability distribution of profit and provide the foundation for managers' rankings of production plans. These rankings can be summarized by a utility function defined over production plans or, equivalently, defined over subjective, probability distributions that are conditional on the production plans. These rankings reflect not only the managers' beliefs about future economic conditions and their profit implications, but also the managers' risk preferences.

In the absence of distress costs, a value-maximizing manager ranks each production plan solely by the first moment of its implied conditional distribution of profit. Hence, the manager's highest ranked plan is the one that maximizes expected profit. In the presence of distress costs, however, maximizing the value of the bank requires the manager to trade expected current return for reduced risk. Thus, to rank a production plan which factors in consideration of distress costs, the manager will use, not just on its first moment (expected profit), but also its second moment (variance of profit) and, perhaps, higher moments of its conditional distribution of profit.

Hughes, Lang, Mester, and Moon (1993, 1995, 1996, 1999) adapt the Almost Ideal Demand System to represent these managerial preferences and use it to recover managers' rankings of production plans from data on input and output prices as well as other components of the economic environment. Hughes and Moon (1995) demonstrate how the most preferred production plan obtained in this fashion can be compactly expressed as the most preferred expected rate of return on equity (a first moment measurement) and the most preferred return risk (a second moment measurement) for each bank in the sample. They estimate a best-practice risk-return frontier for the banking industry as the stochastic upper envelope of the expected return and risk pairs of the individual banks, and identify each bank's risk-return efficiency as its "noise-corrected" distance from this frontier.

5.1. Producing an information-intensive, levered asset portfolio

Banks hold a portfolio of government securities and information-intensive loans. (Note that loans are produced outputs while securities are purchased outputs.) The loans are produced with labor and physical capital, both of which are used to gather information, assess credit risk, write loan contracts, monitor borrowers' behavior, and deal with borrowers' experiencing financial distress. The portfolio is funded with equity capital and levered with demandable debt and other borrowed funds. We designate the output or asset vector, y; the inputs that include labor, physical capital, demandable debt, and other borrowed funds, x; and equity capital, k. The bank's levered portfolio production plan is given by (y, x, k). The transformation function, $T(y,x,k) \le 0$, defines the feasible set of levered portfolio production plans.

Managers are assumed to have well-behaved preference orderings defined over profit, π, and the production plan, (y,x,k), that can be represented by the utility function, $U(\pi,y,x,k)$. If there are no distress costs and managers simply maximize profit, only profit has marginal significance in the utility function, and the production plan affects utility only indirectly through its effect on profit. Thus, the utility function ranks production plans and their implied subjective distributions of profit by the first moment of the distribution, expected profit. However, if there are distress costs and managers trade profit for reduced risk, the production plan will also have marginal significance in the utility function. In this case, the utility function's ranking of production plans will depend, not just on the first moment, but also on higher moments of the implied, subjective distributions of profit.

We condition the managerial utility function on asset or output quality, and use both *ex ante* and *ex post* proxies of output quality. Our *ex ante* measures are the risk premia on assets, given by the vector of asset returns, p, relative to the risk-free rate, r, and our *ex post* measure is the amount of nonperforming loans, n. Hence, the complete utility function is denoted by $U(\pi,y,x,k,p,r,n)$. Given asset quality, the utility maximizing production plan is the bank's choice of assets, liabilities, equity capital, labor, and physical capital and represents the bank's optimal levered portfolio of information-intensive assets.[10]

5.2. Choosing the most preferred production plan

We assume that managers maximize their utility by choosing profit and inputs, conditional on output quantities, output quality, and financial capital, and subject to the constraints imposed by the income statement and the production technology:

$$\max_{\pi,x} U(\pi,x;y,p,r,n,k) \tag{1}$$

$$s.t. \quad p \cdot y + m - w \cdot x - p_\pi \pi = 0 \tag{2}$$

$$T(x;y,k) \le 0, \tag{3}$$

where m is income from sources other than the output vector y, w is a vector of input prices, p_π is the price of a real dollar of after-tax profit, π, in nominal, before-tax dollars. Letting t be the tax rate on profit, we can write

$$p_\pi = 1/(1 - t). \tag{4}$$

Thus, $p_\pi \pi$ is before-tax, nominal profit. The solution to the problem defined by (1) through (3) is the manager's **most preferred production plan,** which is given by the most preferred input demand functions, $x(y,n,v,m,k)$, and the manager's most preferred profit function, $\pi(y,n,v,m,k)$, where $v = (w,p,r,p_\pi)$.

Three characteristics of the profit function make it distinctive. First, it is not necessarily maximum profit. Second, the input demand functions that underlie the profit function contain unusual arguments: fixed revenues (or, equivalently, fixed costs), m, and the tax rate on

R. DeYoung et al. / Journal of Economics and Business 53 (2001) 255–282   265

profit, embedded in p_π. These arguments affect the level of profit but not the values of inputs and outputs at which profit is maximized. Hence, they do not influence the input demands of the profit-maximizing (risk-neutral) firm. Yet, when managers trade profit for reduced risk, their production decisions are influenced by these variables. Accordingly, these variables can serve as a test of whether managers trade return for reduced risk. They also demonstrate the inadequacy of simply adding risk measures to the profit maximization and cost minimization problems. (See Hughes, Lang, Mester, and Moon (1996) for further details.) Finally, the profit function is conditioned on the level of equity capital, so it can be divided by equity capital to convert profit into a rate of return on equity.

5.3. Specifying the most preferred production plan

Just as a consumer's preferences for goods can be represented by a utility function, our approach describes bank management's preferences for production plans and profit in terms of a managerial utility function. And, just as the consumer chooses the most preferred, affordable bundle of goods, our approach characterizes the bank's management as choosing its most preferred, feasible production plan, where feasibility is determined by the bank's technology and its income statement. To obtain functional forms for the bank's most preferred or, equivalently, utility-maximizing demand functions for inputs and profit, we borrow the Almost Ideal (AI) Demand System from consumer theory and adapt it to represent managerial preferences. Although we have described managerial preferences by the utility function, the AI System employs the expenditure function, which is the dual characterization of preferences (just as the cost function is the dual characterization of technology). The managerial expenditure function is defined as the minimum expenditure on the "goods," profit π and inputs x, needed to obtain some given level of utility U^0, conditional on output quantities, output quality, and financial capital:

$$\min_{\pi,x} \quad w \cdot x + p_\pi \pi \tag{5}$$

$$s.t. \quad U^0 - U(\pi,x;y,p,r,n,k) = 0 \tag{6}$$

$$T(x;y,k) \leq 0 \tag{7}$$

The solution to (5) through (7) yields the constant-utility demand functions, $x^u(y,n,v,k,U^0)$ and $\pi^u(y,n,v,k,U^0)$. Substituting these demand functions into (5) gives the expenditure function $E(y,n,v,k,U^0)$. The indirect utility function, $V(y,n,v,m,k)$, is obtained by inverting the expenditure function. Since the expenditure minimization problem (5)–(7) is dual to the utility maximization problem (1)–(3), the maximum utility from the expenditure $(p \cdot y + m)$ is U^* while the minimum expenditure needed to achieve $U^0 = U^*$ is $(p \cdot y + m)$. Consequently, $E(y,n,v,k,U^0) = (p \cdot y + m)$.

When the Almost Ideal expenditure function is adapted to represent generalized managerial preferences, the following functional form is obtained:

$$\ln E(\cdot) = \ln P + U \cdot \beta_0 (\prod_i y_i^{\beta_i})(\prod_i w_j^{v_j}) p_\pi^\mu k^\kappa, \tag{8}$$

266 R. DeYoung et al. / Journal of Economics and Business 53 (2001) 255–282

where $\bar{p} = \sum_i p_i[y_i/\sum_j y_j]$, a weighted average of p, and

$$\ln P = \alpha_0 + \alpha_p \ln \widetilde{p} + \sum_i \delta_i \ln y_i + \sum_i \omega_j \ln w_j$$

$$+ \eta_\pi \ln p_\pi + \tau \ln r + \vartheta \ln n + \rho \ln k + \frac{1}{2}\alpha_{pp}(\ln \widetilde{p})^2$$

$$+ \frac{1}{2}\sum_i \sum_j \delta_{ij}\ln y_i \ln y_j$$

$$+ \frac{1}{2}\sum_s \sum_t \omega_{ij}^* \ln w_s \ln w_t + \frac{1}{2}\eta_{\pi\pi}(\ln p_\pi)^2$$

$$+ \frac{1}{2}\tau_{rr}(\ln r)^2 + \frac{1}{2}\vartheta_{nn}(\ln n)^2 + \frac{1}{2}\rho_{kk}(\ln k)^2$$

$$+ \sum_j \theta_{pj}\ln \widetilde{p} \ln y_j + \sum_s \varphi_{ps}\ln \widetilde{p} \ln w_s + \psi_{p\pi}\ln \widetilde{p} \ln p_\pi$$

$$+ \psi_{pr}\ln \widetilde{p} \ln r + \psi_{pn}\ln \widetilde{p} \ln n + \psi_{pk}\ln \widetilde{p} \ln k$$

$$+ \sum_j \sum_s \gamma_{js} \ln y_j \ln w_s + \sum_j \gamma_{j\pi} \ln y_j \ln p_\pi + \sum_j \gamma_{jr} \ln y_j \ln r$$

$$+ \sum_j \gamma_{jn} \ln y_j \ln n + \sum_j \gamma_{jk} \ln y_j \ln k$$

$$+ \frac{1}{2}\sum_s \omega_{s\pi}^* \ln w_s \ln p_\pi + \frac{1}{2}\sum_s \omega_{\pi s}^* \ln p_\pi \ln w_s$$

$$+ \sum_s \omega_{sr}\ln w_s \ln r + \sum_s \omega_{sn}\ln w_s \ln n + \sum_s \omega_{sk}\ln w_s \ln k$$

$$+ \eta_{\pi r}\ln p_\pi \ln r + \eta_{\pi n}\ln p_\pi \ln n + \eta_{\pi k}\ln p_\pi \ln k$$

$$+ \tau_{rn}\ln r \ln n + \tau_{rk}\ln r \ln k + \vartheta_{nk}\ln n \ln k.$$

Inverting the expenditure function gives the indirect utility function:

$$V(\cdot) = \frac{\ln(p \cdot y + m) - \ln P}{\beta_0(\prod_i y_i^{\beta_i})(\prod_j w_i^{\nu_i})p_\pi^\mu k^\kappa} \tag{10}$$

Applying Shephard's lemma to the expenditure function (8) and substituting the indirect utility function (10) into the resulting share equations yields the utility-maximizing, most preferred input and profit share equations:

R. DeYoung et al. / Journal of Economics and Business 53 (2001) 255–282   267

$$\frac{\partial ln\ E}{\partial ln\ w_i} = \frac{w_i x_i}{\mathbf{p} \cdot \mathbf{y} + m} = \frac{\partial ln\ P}{\partial ln\ w_i} + v_i[ln(\mathbf{p} \cdot \mathbf{y} + m) - ln\ P]$$

$$= \omega_i + \sum_s \omega_{si} ln\ w_s + \varphi_{pi} ln\ \widetilde{p} + \sum_j \gamma_{ji} ln\ y_j + \omega_{\pi i} ln\ p_\pi$$

$$+ \omega_{ir} ln\ r + \omega_{in} ln\ n + \omega_{ik} ln\ k$$

$$+ v_i[ln(\mathbf{p} \cdot \mathbf{r} + m) - ln\ P] \tag{11}$$

$$\frac{\partial ln\ E}{\partial ln\ p_\pi} = \frac{p_\pi \pi}{\mathbf{p} \cdot \mathbf{y} + m} = \frac{\partial ln\ P}{\partial ln\ p_\pi} + \mu[ln(\mathbf{p} \cdot \mathbf{y} + m) - ln\ P]$$

$$= \eta_\pi + \eta_{\pi\pi} ln\ p_\pi + \psi_{p\pi} ln\ \widetilde{p} + \sum_j \gamma_{j\pi} ln\ y_j + \sum_s \omega_{s\pi} ln\ w_s$$

$$+ \eta_{\pi r} ln\ r + \eta_{\pi n} ln\ n + \eta_{\pi k} ln\ k$$

$$+ \mu[ln(\mathbf{p} \cdot \mathbf{y} + m) - ln\ P]. \tag{12}$$

The conditions on parameter values that are implied by symmetry, homogeneity, and adding up are outlined in Hughes, Lang, Mester, and Moon (1996). Further parameter restrictions are obtained by adding a first-order condition for the most preferred level of equity capital:

$$\rho + \rho_{kk} ln\ k + \psi_{pk} ln\ \widetilde{p} + \sum_j \gamma_{jk} ln\ y_j + \sum_s \omega_{sk} ln\ w_s + \eta_{\pi k} ln\ p_\pi + \tau_{rk} ln\ r$$

$$+ \vartheta_{nk} ln\ n + \kappa[ln(\mathbf{p} \cdot \mathbf{y} + m) - ln\ P] = 0 \tag{13}$$

which is derived by maximizing the Lagrangean function from the utility maximization problem (1)–(3) with respect to k.

5.4. Estimating the most preferred production plan

We use nonlinear two-stage least squares, which is a generalized method of moments, to estimate a demand system consisting of the input share Eqs. (11), the profit share Eq. (12), and the first-order condition for equity capital (13). Because managers rank production plans based on their subjective assessments of future economic conditions and because these assessments and, hence, preferences are likely to change over time, we estimate this demand system using cross-section data. Since the risk-free rate r does not vary in a cross-section, it is omitted, and the homogeneity conditions are used to recover its associated coefficients.

We estimate the system for a sample of 356 national banks that range in asset size from $83.6 million to $120 billion. The sample includes all national banks that operate domestic and foreign offices plus all other national banks with at least $300 million in assets. We exclude special purpose banks. Balance sheet and income statement data are obtained from year-end 1993 and 1994 Consolidated Reports of Condition and Income. Asset and liability variables are the averages of the 1993 and 1994 year-end values, while flow variables are

Table 1
Summary of the Data

Variable	Mean	Std. Dev.	Minimun	Maximum
y1	1,207,759.46	3,575,432.41	57,456.00	45,654,000.00
y2	968,712.58	3,440,335.57	5,226.50	44,953,000.00
y3	532,052.01	1,460,527.84	4,711.00	22,005,000.00
y4	292,406.69	1,520,048.65	198.50	22,277,500.00
y5	1,381,093.30	3,945,076.35	22,675.50	50,381,000.00
p1	0.0815	0.0124	0.0273	0.1541
p2	0.0861	0.0223	0.0257	0.2209
p3	0.0961	0.0233	0.0426	0.2333
p4	0.0583	0.0259	0.0061	0.1897
p5	0.0577	0.0119	0.0338	0.1289
$\bar{p}$	0.0755	0.0108	0.0534	0.1392
w1	35.3983	7.8948	22.5157	75.8285
w2	0.3419	0.1789	0.0790	1.3439
w3	0.0166	0.0070	0.0057	0.0329
w4	0.0047	0.0239	0.0083	0.2398
w5	0.0437	0.0109	0.0169	0.0882
$p_\pi = 1/(1-t)$	1.6418	0.0917	4.5151	1.8706
share1	0.1950	0.0527	0.0480	0.3658
share2	0.0590	0.0195	0.0143	0.1293
share3	0.1552	0.0506	0.0149	0.3512
share4	0.0617	0.0496	0.0002	0.2839
share5	0.0397	0.0358	0.0031	0.2887
share6	0.4894	0.0792	0.2226	0.7899
n	52,161.03	285,667.12	238.50	4,557,000.0
k	504,672.14	1,706,694.61	25,741.00	21,410,000.0
m	73,827.85	308,263.66	134.00	4,490,000.00
assets	2,985,321.87	9,430,181.98	83,600.50	120,000,000.00

The variables y1, y2, y3, y4, y5, n, k, m, and assets are measured in 1,000's of 1994 dollars.

simply the 1994 year-end values. Compared with the late 1980s and early 1990s, 1994 was relatively stable, and the large majority of banks met regulatory capital standards. Although bank managers in 1994 knew that choosing a high risk production plan increased the probability of regulatory actions and financial distress, few banks in 1994 were operating under regulatory constraints that prevented them from choosing their most preferred production plans.

The data are summarized in Table 1. We define five outputs: y_1 is real estate loans; y_2 is commercial and industrial loans, agricultural loans, and lease financing; y_3 is individual loans; y_4 is other loans; and y_5 is cash and securities. We compute the output prices p_1 through p_5 by dividing the income recorded for accruing assets by the stock of accruing assets. Inputs are divided into six categories: equity capital, k, is the sum of equity, subordinated notes, and loan-loss reserves; x_1 is the quantity of labor, the number of full-time equivalent employees; x_2 is quantity of physical capital, measured by the dollar amount of fixed premises and assets; x_3 is insured deposits; x_4 is other borrowed money; and x_5 is uninsured deposits and foreign deposits. The average salary of labor, w_1, is the total labor expense divided by the number of full-time equivalent employees, x_1. The price of physical capital, w_2, is measured by the ratio of occupancy expenses to fixed premises and assets x_2. The average interest rates, w_3, w_4, w_5, are the ratios of the interest expense for each funding source to the amount of x_3, x_4, and x_5 respectively.

Nonperforming loans, n, is the amount of loans past due 90 days or more plus nonaccruing loans. Nonasset-based income, m, is measured by total noninterest income so that each bank's total revenue, $p \cdot y + m$, equals interest plus noninterest income.[11] Equity capital k is measured at its book value. Federal and state tax rates are used to calculate p_π. The state tax rates t were obtained from The Book of the States, published by the Council of State Governments, and from Significant Aspects of Fiscal Federalism, published by the U.S. Advisory Commission on Intergovernmental Relations.

5.5. Deriving expected return and risk

The fitted values from (12) are each bank's predicted or expected profit as a share of its total revenue.[12] Since these predicted profit shares are conditioned on the bank's level of equity capital, they can be converted into predictions, or expectations, of the return on equity simply by multiplying by total revenue and dividing by equity capital:

$$ER = s_\pi(\beta) \cdot [(p \cdot y + m)/k], \tag{14}$$

where $s_\pi(\beta)$ denotes the fitted profit shares and β denotes the estimated parameters in Eq. (12). ER is a proxy for the bank's prediction of its own return on equity, and this prediction is a function of its size and asset mix, its average return on assets, its cost of financial and nonfinancial inputs, the amount of nonperforming loans, its marginal tax rate on profit, and so on. The amount of confidence the bank has about this prediction is an indication of the amount of risk inherent in its most preferred production plan. A bank that chooses an *ex ante*, high-risk production plan will have less confidence in its prediction of earnings than a bank that chooses an *ex ante* low-risk production plan. We use a measure of the degree of uncertainty of the predicted return, the standard error of the prediction from (12), as a proxy for the bank's confidence in predicting its return on equity:

$$RK = [\hat{X} \text{ vâr}(\beta)\hat{X}']^{1/2} \cdot [p \cdot y + m)/k] \tag{15}$$

where the expression $[\hat{X} \text{ vâr}(\beta)\hat{X}']$ is the estimated asymptotic variance of the forecast $s_\pi(\beta)$, and $\hat{X} = \partial s_\pi(\beta)/\partial \beta$. This measure of return risk is a function of the bank's size and asset composition, its average return on assets, its costs of financial and nonfinancial inputs, its marginal tax rate on profits, its amount of nonperforming loans, and so on. Hughes and Moon (1995) and Hughes, Lang, Mester, and Moon (1998) show that expected profit ($ER \cdot k$) and profit risk ($RK \cdot k$) explain 96% of the variation in the market value of the publicly traded banks in their sample. In addition, the coefficient on profit is significantly positive while the coefficient on profit risk is significantly negative. Hence, these measures of profitability and risk derived from the most preferred model of production are priced by capital markets.

We do not impose homoskedasticity on the error terms in our estimation. Our nonlinear

270   *R. DeYoung et al. / Journal of Economics and Business 53 (2001) 255–282*

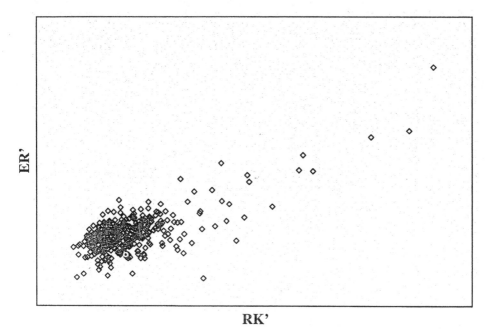

Fig. 2. Expected Return and Risk for Sample of 356 National Banks.

two-stage least squares estimation technique uses orthogonality conditions between instrumental variables and the error terms of our structural equation system. The resulting variance–covariance matrix vâr(β) is not based on a constant error variance across all banks, but instead captures how the error variance differs with different types of production plans. This estimation procedure allows the data to reveal the pattern of heteroskedasticity without imposing structure, which is consistent with our general approach of letting banks' choices of production plans reveal the amount of risk they prefer. Thus, for each bank in our sample, (14) provides the first moment of the distribution of the return on equity while (15) constitutes a proxy for the second moment. Note that *ER* and *RK* are *ex ante* measures of return and risk.

Fig. 2 is a scatter diagram of expected return and return risk for the 356 banks in our sample. The diagram is stated in terms of *ER'* and *RK'*, which are equal to the estimated values of *ER* and *RK* after rescaling by their respective sample standard deviations. We perform the remainder of our analysis using the rescaled values, *ER'* and *RK'*, which facilitates subsequent regression analyses without altering the empirical relationships among the variables.

6. Estimating efficiency and the best-practice frontier

Each pair (*ER, RK*) represents the trade-off that an individual bank has made between expected return and risk. Because not all banks are equally proficient at generating return and

R. DeYoung et al. / Journal of Economics and Business 53 (2001) 255–282   271

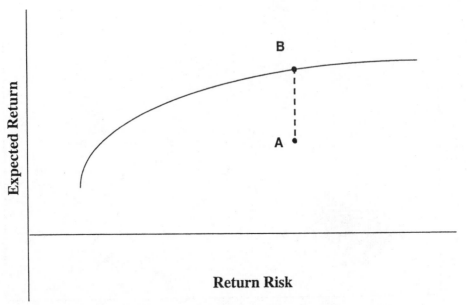

Fig. 3. Measuring Efficiency When Managers Trade Return for Reduced Risk.

controlling risk, the risk-return frontier of a relatively efficient bank will lie above the risk-return frontier of a relatively inefficient bank. This suggests that inefficient banks could potentially increase their expected return without taking more risk or, equivalently, reduce their risk without sacrificing return. By enhancing their risk-return profiles in this way, inefficient banks can move to higher risk-return frontiers, the highest of which is the best-practice frontier. Because the best-practice frontier may contain portions of the frontiers of many individual banks, it is the envelope of the frontiers of efficient banks or, more precisely, it is the envelope of their most preferred risk-return combinations.

Fig. 3 shows a stylized version of the envelope frontier. The bank positioned at point A is inefficient. Although its most preferred combination of return and risk is a point on its own frontier, its own frontier lies inside the best-practice envelope. The degree to which point A is inefficient can be measured by its distance from the frontier. Holding the level of risk constant at point A, we employ the difference between expected return at A and maximum return at B to gauge the inefficiency of point A. This shortfall in expected return, given a bank's choice of risk, can be readily estimated using econometric frontier techniques.

6.1. Estimating a stochastic risk-return frontier

Using techniques developed by Jondrow, Lovell, Materov, and Schmidt (1982), we estimate the best-practice risk-return frontier as the upper envelope of expected returns, given their associated levels of risk. Banks located below the estimated frontier are inefficient and

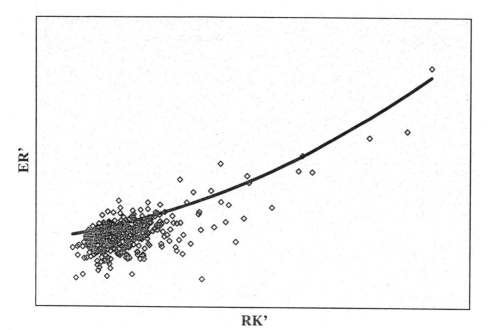

Fig. 4. The Best-Practice Stochastic Risk-Return Frontier for Sample of 356 National Banks.

their vertical distance from the frontier is their degree of inefficiency. We specify the frontier as

$$ER = a + b\,RK + c\,RK^2 + v - u \tag{16}$$

where

$$u_i \geq 0 \sim \text{IID N}(0, \sigma_u^2) \text{ truncated at } 0 \tag{17}$$

$$v_i \sim \text{IID N}(0, \sigma_v^2). \tag{18}$$

The error term consists of two components: v is a normally distributed, two-sided, term that allows for unmeasured randomness in the data generation process, and u is a one-sided, normally distributed, nonnegative term that measures vertical return inefficiency, the failure to achieve maximum return given the level of risk. After rescaling both ER and RK by their respective sample standard deviations, we estimate (16) using maximum likelihood techniques. The resulting envelope frontier is shown in Fig. 4, and is given by the equation,

$$ER' = 3.2204 + 0.2548*RK' + 0.0672*(RK')^2$$
$$\quad\;\; (0.2028) \;\; (0.1315) \qquad (0.0176) \tag{19}$$

where the standard errors of the coefficient estimates appear in parentheses. Note that some of the banks are located above the frontier in Fig. 4. This apparent superefficiency occurs when the random noise term, v_i, is positive and larger than the inefficiency term, u_i. Subtracting v_i from *ER* yields the "noise-adjusted" expected return, $ER - v_i$, which lies below the frontier.

The shape of the frontier in Fig. 4 has two striking features. First, its positive slope suggests that banks are not pure profit maximizers, but rather are trading return for reduced risk. To confirm this appearance, we applied a Wald test to the 31 conditions implied by profit maximization described in Appendix A. The value of the test statistic was 204.07 with 29 degrees of freedom (two of the restrictions are made redundant by the adding-up conditions). Thus, the hypothesis that these restrictions hold can be strongly rejected, i.e., the banks' behavior is not consistent with profit maximization. Second, the frontier is convex in risk. This convexity implies that there are combinations (e.g., mergers) of banks that would result in a better risk-return trade-off, that is to say, a concave frontier. Hughes and Moon (1995) hypothesize that because state and federal laws have historically restricted the geographic expansion of U.S. banks, individual banks have not been able to form mergers that would exploit these risk-return tradeoffs. Hughes, Lang, Mester, and Moon (1996) provide evidence in support of this hypothesis. They estimate a production-based, expected return-risk frontier that is identical to the one in Fig. 4 with one exception: they estimate it for a 1994 sample of large U.S. bank *holding companies,* i.e., firms that in many cases could legally circumvent geographic banking restrictions by organizing the geographically dispersed banks from our data set (along with other assets) into separate affiliates rather than merging them together. Strikingly, they obtain a frontier that is *concave* in risk, which suggests that the parent firms of the banks in our sample have in fact captured the improved risk-return tradeoffs that appear to be unexploited in Fig. 4. Nevertheless, we must employ the bank-level frontier to obtain efficiency scores since the CAMEL ratings are assigned to individual banks rather than to holding companies.

7. CAMEL ratings and banks' risk-return trade-offs

The last stage of our analysis focuses on the key questions: Do regulators assign better CAMEL ratings to banks that trade expected return for a reduced risk of financial distress, and do they treat the risk-taking of inefficient banks differently than the risk-taking of efficient banks? To investigate these questions, we estimate an ordered logit model that specifies each bank's composite CAMEL rating as a function of its risk-return trade-off.

The dependent variable in the ordered logit model is the most recent CAMEL rating for each national bank as of year-end 1994. For our sample of 356 national banks, 39.6% were 1-rated; 58.1% were 2-rated; 2.3% were 3-rated; and none were 4-rated or 5-rated. This distribution of CAMEL ratings suggests that national banks were substantially more safe and sound in 1994 than just a few years earlier, when nearly ten percentage of national banks had CAMEL ratings of 4 or 5 (DeYoung, 1998). However, note that our sample excludes domestic national banks with less than $300 million in assets, and those banks comprised the large majority of the 3,078 national banks operating as of year-end 1994.

On the right-hand side of the model, we include each bank's risk, its frontier expected return, its inefficiency, and its asset size. Risk and frontier expected return correspond to the

274   R. DeYoung et al. / Journal of Economics and Business 53 (2001) 255–282

Table 2
Composite CAMEL Rating

	all banks	50% most efficient	50% least efficient
	(intercept terms concealed to preserve the confidentiality of exam ratings)		
Assets ($bill)	.0239***	−.0019	.0244***
	(.0080)	(.0422)	(.0085)
Inefficiency	.6631**	4.1645**	.3926
	(.3315)	(1.6834)	(.5069)
Risk	1.8962**	0.6016	3.0392**
	(.8675)	(1.1225)	(1.2094)
Frontier Expected Return	−3.0461**	−1.1059	−4.6117**
	(1.3556)	(1.7057)	(1.8920)
N	356	178	178
chi-square statistic for -2*log(Lklihd)	28.006***	9.092**	24.214***

Ordered logit regressions for the full sample of 356 banks and for the more and less efficient halves of the sample. Dependent variable in all regressions is the composite CAMEL rating. Standard errors in parentheses. ***, **, * indicate significance at the 1, 5, and 10 percent levels.

coordinates of point B (the estimated values RK' and ER') in Fig. 3, while inefficiency (the estimated value of u_i) is the distance AB after adjusting for statistical noise. This specification allows us to test for the regulator's evaluation of banks' risk-return choices independent from its evaluation of bank inefficiency. We include bank asset size as a regressor since DeYoung (1998) found that exam ratings were significantly and positively related to bank size.

We estimate these regressions three times: for the entire sample of 356 banks, for the more efficient half of the sample (values of u_i below the median), and, finally, for the less efficient half of the sample. The results of these three sets of regressions are reported in Table 2. The contrasts among the full sample of 356 banks and the more and less efficient groups are striking. For the more efficient banks, CAMEL ratings appear to be unrelated to their risk-return trade-offs. In contrast, the risk-return trade-offs do matter to the regulator for the less efficient banks and for the full sample. This first impression suggests that bank supervisors are influenced not only by the banks' risk-return choices, but also by how efficiently banks make this trade-off.

7.1. The entire sample

The results for the full sample of 356 banks are displayed in the first column of Table 2. Since examiners assign numerically low CAMEL ratings to banks that they judge to be safe and sound, we would expect exam ratings to vary positively with risk and inefficiency and negatively with expected return. The coefficient on inefficiency is positive and significant,

R. DeYoung et al. / Journal of Economics and Business 53 (2001) 255–282   275

evidence that examiners penalize banks for operating below the best-practice frontier. CAMEL ratings also vary significantly and positively with risk, and significantly and negatively with expected return. The coefficient on asset size is positive and significant, evidence that national bank examiners set higher standards for larger banks.

A more intriguing question asks how the CAMEL rating responds when banks increase both risk and return along the efficient frontier. If we take the total differential of the estimated CAMEL rating equation, reported in the first column of Table 2, with respect to return and risk, holding asset size constant and the degree of inefficiency constant and equal to zero along the frontier, we obtain

$$d\,(CAMEL\ rating) = 1.8962\ d\,(RK') - 3.0461\ d\,(ER'). \tag{20}$$

Setting (20) equal to zero and rearranging, we obtain the slope of the iso-CAMEL-rating contours for efficient banks, holding asset size constant:

$$d\,(ER')/d\,(RK') = 1.8962/3.0461. \tag{21}$$

The iso-CAMEL-rating contours are linear and have positive slopes that are greater than the slope of the risk-return frontier, dER'/dRK' from (19), for 85% of the banks in our sample. In these cases, as a bank moves along the risk-return frontier to a higher return and higher risk position, it also moves to a less favorable iso-CAMEL-rating contour. (That is, the bank moves to an iso-CAMEL-rating *contour* that lies further to the right—a contour that is identified with a higher level of risk for any given level of expected return, and thus with a worse exam score.) Consequently, examiners penalize most banks that take extra risk for extra return by assigning them a worse CAMEL rating. The poorer rating implies that these banks are *relatively* less safe and sound and, thus, are more likely to experience remedial covenant enforcement.

7.2. Subsamples of efficient and inefficient banks

The second and third columns of Table 2 report the results from estimating the ordered logit model separately for the 178 most efficient (henceforth the "efficient") and the 178 least efficient (henceforth the "inefficient") banks. The results suggest a clear dichotomy in the way that examiners evaluate these two sets of banks. The risk-return trade-offs (i.e., the coefficients on RK' and ER') made by the efficient banks have no statistically significant effect on their CAMEL ratings. Examiners appear to be neutral toward the risk-return choices made by these banks, which operate relatively close to the frontier and efficiently manage risk and generate returns. In contrast, the trade-offs made by the inefficient banks do matter to bank supervisors. These banks are relatively inefficient at trading risk for return—that is, they operate along an inefficient risk-return frontier—and examiners appear to penalize them for taking greater risk for extra return. Hence, when relatively inefficient banks take extra risk for extra expected return, they are more likely to experience remedial covenant enforcement. This suggests that regulators impose greater discipline and higher distress costs on inefficient banks than on efficient banks.

Examiners also appear to treat asset size differently for efficient and inefficient banks. The

Table 3
Component CAMEL ratings

	C	A	M	E	L
	(intercepts concealed to preserve the confidentiality of exam ratings)				
Assets ($bill)	.0344***	−.0248***	.0161**	.0121*	.0317***
	(.0097)	(.0079)	(.0074)	(.0068)	(.0087)
Inefficiency	−.8103**	.3609	.9218***	−.16830***	−1.464
	(.3175)	(.3037)	(.3295)	(.3237)	(.3088)
Risk	1.3511***	1.5474**	.6000	1.1552	−.0773
	(.5003)	(.7822)	(.5310)	(.7250)	(.4827)
Frontier Expected Return	−1.5630**	−2.4486**	−1.0523	−1.9894*	.1882
	(.6488)	(1.2060)	(.7130)	(1.0984)	(.6270)
N	356	356	356	356	356
chi-square statistic for -2*log(Lklihd)	29.908***	24.994***	20.460***	43.663***	15.648***

Ordered logit regressions for the full sample of 356 banks and for the more and less efficient halves of the sample. Dependent variable in all regressions is the composite CAMEL rating
Standard errors in parentheses.
***, **, * indicate significance at the 1, 5, and 10 percent levels.

positive, significant coefficient on total assets for inefficient banks suggests that size counts against the bank if it is inefficient. In contrast, the results for the efficient-bank subsample indicates that examiners are neutral with respect to asset size for banks that demonstrate an ability to manage risk and produce return efficiently. Furthermore, the degree of inefficiency is the only significant explanatory variable for the efficient banks; that is, the higher the degree of inefficiency, the worse the exam rating.[13]

Regulatory covenant monitoring therefore appears to provide all banks—relatively efficient and relatively inefficient alike—with an incentive to improve the efficiency with which they manage risk. But, this treatment is asymmetric. When banks choose higher-risk production plans, relatively inefficient banks are more likely to experience remedial covenant enforcement than relatively efficient banks, and the larger the inefficient bank, the greater the likelihood of regulatory intervention. This distinction between the supervisory treatment of more and less efficient banks suggests that, in a more competitive and deregulated environment, opportunities for risk-taking will not be encouraged equally for all banks. However, even within this dichotomy, supervisors provide an incentive for all banks to become more efficient.

7.3. The CAMEL component ratings

In Table 3, we substitute the five individual CAMEL components into the left-hand-side of the full-sample ordered logit model. All five of these regressions suggest that examiners hold large banks to significantly higher standards than small banks. However, the coefficients on expected return, risk, and inefficiency vary across the five regressions in a manner that reflects the unique information contained in the C, A, M, E, and L ratings.

The C (capital adequacy) and A (asset quality) regressions produce results quite similar to the composite CAMEL regression. The coefficient on risk is positive and significant in both regressions, indicating that examiners prefer increased capital for high-risk banks and associate high amounts of risk with low asset quality. The coefficient on return is negative and significant in both regressions, indicating that examiners associate higher amounts of return with higher asset quality and are more likely to find capital levels at higher-return banks to be adequate. The coefficient on assets is larger in the C-rating regressions than in the other four regressions, perhaps because large bank failures are more disruptive than small bank failures and can lead to systemic problems. Although the significantly negative coefficient on inefficiency in the C-rating regression at first seems unintuitive, it probably reflects the relationship between financial leverage and return on equity. Banks with low amounts of leverage will have better C-ratings, but they will also be inefficient (by our measure) because they have reduced their expected return on equity without any compensating reduction in risk.

The M-rating (management quality) and E-rating (earnings quality) measure the two performance areas most directly related to inefficient operations, and the coefficient on inefficiency is positive and significant in both of these regressions. High quality managers can presumably run a bank more efficiently than can low quality managers, and an efficiently run bank will naturally generate larger expected earnings. Due to strong definitional similarities, the E-rating is significantly related in the expected direction to both expected return and inefficiency.

Neither the risk-return trade-off nor the degree of inefficiency has a significant impact on the L-rating (liquidity). In fact, asset size is the only significant coefficient, suggesting that examiners consider illiquidity at larger banks more disruptive to the payments system than illiquidity at smaller banks.

8. Conclusions

In an era of deregulation that seeks to increase banks' competition and to improve their efficiency, regulation has been linked to the risks that banks take, to address the increased incentives to take risk that are created by reduced charter values and mispriced safety nets. In addition, banks whose risk-taking leads to episodes of financial distress experience costly regulatory strictures that generally reduce the risk-taking incentives for all banks. Using CAMEL ratings that indicate the likelihood that such strictures will be imposed, we have asked if commercial bank regulators distinguish between a bank's level of risk and its efficiency at risk-taking in their ratings of banks. Do bank regulators treat the risk-taking of efficient banks differently than the risk-taking of inefficient banks? Do regulators afford efficient banks more latitude in their investment strategies than inefficient banks? Do regulators create incentives for banks to improve the efficiency of their risk-taking? We have offered evidence that answers, "Yes," to each of these questions.

The evidence seems to indicate that examiners draw a line between efficient banks and inefficient banks. Efficient banks are better at risk-taking, and when they take extra risk to increase their expected return, our results suggest that examiners do not penalize them with worse CAMEL ratings. Apparently, their "best-practice" ability to manage risk enables them to take extra risk without compromising their safety and soundness. Hence, the evidence implies that bank regulators impose lower distress costs on these banks and that the structure of these costs encourages efficiency but does not discourage efficient risk-taking.

For banks with less ability to manage risks or to enhance return, however, CAMEL ratings do reflect the risk-return trade-off. Examiners penalize these banks for taking increased risk. In addition, our results suggest that supervisors hold large inefficient banks (i.e., banks whose safety and soundness is most likely to have implications for the stability of the banking system) to higher standards than large efficient banks. Thus, the higher schedule of distress costs imposed on inefficient banks gives them the incentive to become more efficient and to take less risk, and the larger the inefficient bank, the greater these incentives. Thus, our evidence suggests that opportunities for risk-taking created in a more competitive, deregulated banking industry are not encouraged equally for all banks and that this differential treatment of banks encourages all banks to manage risk more efficiently.

Notes

1. See Dewatripont and Tirole (1994, p. 87) for an analysis of how bank regulation resembles debt covenant agreements.
2. Smith and Stulz (1985) demonstrate that the financial distress costs created by covenant enforcement make trading expected return for reduced risk a value-maximizing business strategy.
3. See Berger and Mester (1997) for a review of this literature. Hughes and Moon (1995) develop a production-based technique of efficiency measurement that accounts for *ex ante* risk and Hughes, Lang, Mester, and Moon (1996, 1999) apply this technique to interstate banking and to bank consolidation.
4. See, for example, Kane and Malkiel (1965), Black (1975), Fama (1985), and James (1987).
5. See Freixas and Rochet (1997), especially chapter 7.
6. A bank's z-score is the sum of its equity capital and expected profit, divided by the standard deviation of profit, and thus varies negatively with the bank's probability of insolvency. Equivalently, the z-score can be expressed as one plus the expected return on equity, divided by the standard deviation of return. When the z-score is a constant, say k, the expected return = (k*standard deviation − 1). Thus, loci of constant z-scores are rays whose slope equals k and which emanate from −1 on the y-axis.
7. Although the composite CAMEL rating is highly correlated *ex post* to each of the five performance ratings, it is not an arithmetic combination of the five ratings. In addition, a sixth performance rating, sensitivity to market risk (S), was added after our study was completed.
8. A detailed description of the conditions considered by national bank examiners when assigning the CAMEL ratings can be found in the "Uniform Financial Institutions Rating System," Examining Circular 159, Office of the Comptroller of the Currency (1979).

9. See Hirschhorn (1987); Cargill (1989); Simons and Cross (1991); Gilbert (1993); Berger and Davies (1994); Dahl, Hanweck, and O'Keefe (1996); O'Keefe and Dahl (1996); Flannery and Houston (1997); DeYoung, Flannery, Lang, and Sorescu (2001); Berger, Davies, and Flannery (1998); and Cole and Gunther (1998).

10. This formulation of the bank's production problem is consistent with portfolio-based models of banking. See Santomero (1984) for a discussion of these models.

11. Note that our measure of nonasset-based income, m, is a proxy for revenues that are unrelated to bank output, defined by the vector **y**. At most banks, m will be related to some extent to nonasset-based outputs that are not accounted for in our vector of outputs, whose definition reflects the role of banks as pure financial intermediaries.

12. The parameter estimates for the structural model are presented in the longer working paper version of this article (DeYoung, Hughes, and Moon 1998).

13. To test the robustness of these subsample results, we estimated an additional logit model for the entire sample of 356 banks. In this model, we replaced the continuous Inefficiency variable with a binary variable that distinguished between banks in the efficient and inefficient subsamples, and the variables Assets, Risk, and Frontier Expected Return entered the model both linearly and interacted with the binary variable. The results of this model (which are available from the authors upon request) were qualitatively similar in sign and significance to the results of the Table 2 subsample regressions.

Acknowledgments

The opinions expressed in this paper are those of the authors and do not necessarily reflect the views of the Federal Reserve Bank of Chicago, the Board of Governors of the Federal Reserve System, or their staffs. The authors thank Lee Cross, Kevin Jacques, Simon Kwan, Bill Lang, Tom Lutton, Joe Mason, Sherrill Shaffer, Paul Wilson, seminar participants at the Federal Reserve Board, and two anonymous referees for their helpful comments.

Appendix A. Testing for profit maximization

When managers maximize profit or, equivalently, minimize cost, the resulting input demands and before-tax profit are not affected by marginal tax rates on profits and by fixed charges and revenues. Using these propositions, Hughes, Lang, Mester, and Moon (1995) derive the parameter values implied by profit maximization and use them to test for managerial behavior consistent with profit maximization. We also apply these tests to our sample of national banks. Since the most preferred profit function is conditioned on the level of equity capital, maximizing profit in this case is equivalent to maximizing the rate of return on equity.

Using the implication of profit maximization that the marginal tax rate on profit will not influence the maximum before-tax level of profit, the coefficients associated with the price of profit, p_π, should all equal zero:

$$\eta_\pi = \eta_{\pi\pi} = \psi_{p\pi} = \gamma_{j\pi} = \omega_{s\pi} = \eta_{\pi n} = \eta_{\pi k} = 0 \quad \vee \text{ j,s.} \tag{P1}$$

Imposing (P1) on the most preferred production system (11)–(12), the profit share Eq. (12), becomes

$$p_\pi \pi/(p \cdot y + m) = \mu[\ln(p \cdot y + m) - \ln P]. \tag{A1}$$

Hughes et al. also note that the output price vector, **p**, summarized by its weighted average price, $\bar{p}$, cannot affect the profit-maximizing or cost-minimizing solution since the maximization problem is conditioned on the output vector. Hence, all coefficients associated with the average output price must also equal zero:

$$\alpha_p = \alpha_{pp} = \theta_{pj} = \varphi_{ps} = \psi_{p\pi} = \psi_{pn} = \psi_{pk} = 0 \quad \vee \text{ j,s.} \tag{P2}$$

In addition, fixed revenue or cost, *m*, cannot affect the profit-maximizing or cost-minimizing input demands, *x* and *k*. Thus, the numerators, $w \cdot x$, of the input share Eqs. (11) are invariant to m so that the only effect of a variation in *m* is on profit: $\partial(p_\pi \pi)/\partial m = 1$. If the share Eqs. (11)–(12) are differentiated with respect to ln *m* and these conditions are imposed, then the following parameter values are obtained:

$$\text{(P3)} \quad v_i = \partial(w_i x_i/(p \cdot y + m))/\partial\ln m = -w_i x_i/(p \cdot y + m), \tag{A2}$$

$$\mu_i = \partial(p_\pi \pi/(p \cdot y + m))/\partial\ln m = 1 - (p_\pi \pi/(p \cdot y + m)), \tag{A3}$$

while eliminating the influence of *m* on capitalization in the first-order condition, (13), requires that

$$\kappa = 0. \tag{A4}$$

Thus, the implications (P3) consist of (A2)–(A4).

Hughes et al. demonstrate that these conditions (P1)–(P3) reduce the most preferred profit and input revenue-share equations to the standard translog cost and input cost-share equations. Hence, when the parameter values implied by profit maximization or, equivalently, risk neutrality are imposed on the Almost Ideal input and profit share equations, they become equivalent to the standard translog cost function and input cost-share equations.

References

Akhavein, J. D., Allen N. Berger, & David Humphrey (1997). "The Effects of Megamergers on Efficiency and Prices: Evidence from the Bank Profit Function," *Review of Industrial Organization, 12,* 95–139.

Berger, Allen, N., & Sally M. Davies (1999). "The Informational Content of Bank Examinations," *Journal of Financial Services Research,* forthcoming.

Berger, Allen, N., Sally M. Davies, & Mark J. Flannery (1998). "Comparing Market and Regulatory Assessments of Bank Performance: Who Knows What When?" Federal Reserve Board of Governors FEDS working paper.

Berger, Allen, N., & Loretta J. Mester (1997). "Inside the Black Box: What Explains Differences in Efficiencies of Financial Institutions?" *Journal of Banking and Finance, 21,* 895–947.

Black, Fischer (1975). "Bank Funds Management in an Efficient Market," *Journal of Financial Economics, 2,* 323–339.

R. DeYoung et al. / Journal of Economics and Business 53 (2001) 255–282   281

Cargill, Thomas (1989). "CAMEL Ratings and the CD Market," *Journal of Financial Services Research, 3,* 347–358.

Cole, Rebel, & Jeffrey Gunther "Predicting Bank Failures: A Comparison of On- and Off-Site Monitoring Systems," *Journal of Financial Services Research,* forthcoming 1998.

Dahl, Drew, Gerald Hanweck, & John O'Keefe, "The Influence of Auditors and Examiners on Accounting Discretion in the Banking Industry," unpublished working paper, October 1996.

Deaton, Angus, & John Muellbauer (1980). "An Almost Ideal Demand System," *American Economic Review, 70,* 3, June, 312–326.

Demsetz, Rebecca, S., Marc R. Saidenberg, & Philip E. Strahan (1996). "Banks with Something to Lose: The Disciplinary Role of Franchise Value," Federal Reserve Bank of New York. *Economic Policy Review,* October, 2:2, 1–14.

Dewatripont, Mathias, & Jean Tirole (1994). *The Prudential Regulation of Banks,* Cambridge: MIT Press.

DeYoung, Robert (1998). "X-Efficiency and Management Quality in Commercial Banks," *Journal of Financial Services Research, 11,* 5–22.

DeYoung, Robert, Mark J. Flannery, William Lang, & Sorin Sorescu (2001). "The Informational Advantage of Specialized Monitors: The Case of Bank Examiners," *Journal of Money, Credit, and Banking,* forthcoming.

DeYoung, Robert, Iftekhar Hasan, & Bruce Kirchhoff (1998). "The Impact of Out-of-State Entry on the Cost Efficiency of Local Commercial Banks," *Journal of Economics and Business, 50,* 191–203.

DeYoung, Robert, Joseph P. Hughes, & Choon-Geol Moon (1998). "Regulatory Distress Costs and Risk-Taking at U.S. Commercial Banks," Working Paper, 98–1, Office of the Comptroller of the Currency, January.

Fama, Eugene (1985). "What's Different About Banks?" *Journal of Monetary Economics, 15,* 29–39.

Flannery, Mark, J., & Joel Houston (1994). "Market Responses to Federal Examinations of U.S. Bank Holding Companies," Working Paper, University of Florida, March.

Freixas, Xavier, & Jean-Charles Rochet (1997). *Microeconomics of Banking,* Cambridge: MIT Press.

Gilbert, R. Alton (1993). "Implications of Annual Examinations for the Bank Insurance Fund," *Economic Review,* Federal Reserve Bank of St. Louis, Jan./Feb, 35–52.

Hall, John, R., Andrew P. Meyer, & Mark D. Vaughan (1997). "Do Markets and Regulators View Bank Risk Similarly? An Empirical Investigation of Market-Based Risk Measures and Regulators' BOPEC Scores for Bank Holding Companies," Working Paper, February.

Hirschhorn, Eric (1987). "The Informational Content of Bank Examination Ratings," *Banking and Economic Review,* Federal Deposit Insurance Corporation, July/August, 6–11.

Hughes, Joseph, P. (1989). "Hospital Cost Functions: The Case of Revenues Affect Production," Working Paper No. 1990–01, Department of Economics, Rutgers University, November.

Hughes, Joseph, P. (1990). "The Theory and Estimation of Revenue-Driven Costs: The Case of Higher Education," Department of Economics, Rutgers University, February.

Hughes, Joseph, P., William Lang, Loretta J. Mester, & Choon-Geol Moon (1993). "Risk-Taking by U.S. Thrifts: Modeling Risk Indicative, Endogenous Interest Rates," Department of Economics, Rutgers University.

Hughes, Joseph, P., William Lang, Loretta J. Mester, & Choon-Geol Moon (1995). "Recovering Technologies That Account for Generalized Managerial Preferences: An Application to Non-Risk-Neutral Banks," Working Paper No. 95–8/R, Federal Reserve Bank of Philadelphia, September.

Hughes, Joseph, P., William Lang, Loretta J. Mester, & Choon-Geol Moon (1996). "Efficient Banking Under Interstate Branching," *Journal of Money, Credit, and Banking, 28,* 4, Nov (Part II), 1045–1071.

Hughes, Joseph, P., William Lang, Loretta J. Mester, & Choon-Geol Moon (1999). "The Dollars and Sense of Bank Consolidation," *Journal of Banking and Finance, 23,* 291–224.

Hughes, Joseph, P., & Loretta J. Mester (1998). "Bank Capitalization and Cost: Evidence of Scale Economies in Risk Management and Signaling," *Review of Economics and Statistics, 80,* 314–325.

Hughes, Joseph, P., & Choon-Geol Moon (1995). "Measuring Bank Efficiency When Managers Trade Return for Reduced Risk," Working Paper, Department of Economics, Rutgers University, September (revised September 1997).

James, Christopher (1987). "Some Evidence on the Uniqueness of Bank Loans," *Journal of Financial Economics, 19,* 217–235.

Jondrow, J., C. A. K. Lovell, I. S. Materov, & P. Schmidt (1982). "On the Estimation of Technical Inefficiency in the Stochastic Frontier Production Function Model," *Journal of Econometrics, 19,* 233–238.

Kane, Edward. J., & Burton G. Malkiel (1965). "Bank Portfolio Allocation, Deposit Variability, and the Availability Doctrine," *Quarterly Journal of Economics, 79,* 113–134.

Keeley, Michael, C. (1990). "Deposit Insurance, Risk, and Market Power in Banking," *American Economic Review, 80,* 5, Dec. 1183–1200.

Kwan, Simon, H., & Robert A. Eisenbeis (1996). "An Analysis of Inefficiencies in Banking: A Stochastic Cost Frontier Approach," Federal Reserve Bank of San Francisco. *Economic Review,* No. 2.

Lucas, Deborah, J., & Robert L. McDonald (1992). "Bank Financing and Investment Decisions with Asymmetric Information about Loan Quality," *RAND Journal of Economics, 23,* 1, Spring 86–105.

Marcus, Alan, J. (1984). "Deregulation and Bank Financial Policy," *Journal of Banking and Finance, 8,* 557–565.

Merton, Robert, C. (1977). "An Analytic Derivation of the Cost of Deposit Insurance Loan Guarantees," *Journal of Banking and Finance, 1,* 3–11.

Office of the Comptroller of the Currency (1979). "Uniform Financial Institutions Rating System," Examining Circular 159, Washington, DC.

O'Keefe, John, & Drew Dahl (1996). "The Scheduling and Reliability of Bank Examinations: The Effect of FDICIA," paper presented to the Financial Management Association, October.

Santomero, Anthony, M. (1984). "Modeling the Banking Firm," *Journal of Money, Credit, and Banking, 16,* 4, November; Part 2, 576–602.

Simons, Katerina, & Stephen Cross (1991). "Do Capital Markets Predict Problems in Large Commercial Banks?" *New England Economic Review,* Federal Reserve Bank of Boston, April/June 51–56.

Smith, Clifford, W., & Rene Stulz (1985). "The Determinants of Firms' Hedging Policies," *Journal of Financial and Quantitative Analysis, 20,* 4, December 391–405.

Part IV
Privatization and Transition:
International Evidence

[18]

Journal of Economic Literature
Vol. XXXIX (June 2001) pp. 321–389

From State to Market:
A Survey of Empirical Studies
on Privatization

WILLIAM L. MEGGINSON *and* JEFFRY M. NETTER[1]

1. *Introduction*

T HE POLITICAL AND economic policy of privatization, broadly defined as the deliberate sale by a government of

[1] Megginson: University of Oklahoma. Netter: University of Georgia. This paper was developed with financial support from the SBF Bourse de Paris and the New York Stock Exchange, and the assistance of George Sofianos, Bill Tschirhart, and Didier Davidoff is gratefully acknowledged. We appreciate comments received on this paper from Geert Bekaert, Anthony Boardman, Bernardo Bortolotti, Narjess Boubakri, Jean-Claude Cosset, Kathryn Dewenter, Alexander Dyck, Oleh Havrylyshn, Ivan Ivanov, Jonathan Karpoff, Ranko Jelic, Claude Laurin, Marc Lipson, Luis López-Calva, John McMillan (the editor), Sandra Sizer-Moore, Harold Mulherin, Rob Nash, John Nellis, David Newberry, David Parker, Enrico Perotti, Annette Poulsen, Ravi Ramamurti, Susan Rose-Ackerman, Nemat Shafik, Mary Shirley, Mike Stegmoller, Aidan Vining and three anonymous referees. We appreciate comments from participants at the NYSE/Paris Bourse Global Equity Markets conference (Paris, Dec. 1998), Harvard Institute for International Development Privatization Workshop (June 2000), International Federation of Stock Exchanges' Third Global Emerging Markets Conference (Istanbul, April 2000), World Bank and/or IFC meetings, OECD conferences (Paris and Beijing), 1999 Conference on Privatization and the Kuwaiti Economy in the Next Century, 1998 Financial Management Association meeting, 1999 European Financial Management Association meeting, Fondazione ENI Enrico Mattei (FFEM), Swiss Banking Institute and Credit Suisse, and seminars at City University Business School (London), London Guildhall University, and University of Oklahoma. All remaining errors are the authors' alone.

state-owned enterprises (SOEs) or assets to private economic agents, is now in use worldwide. Since its introduction by Britain's Thatcher government in the early 1980s to a then-skeptical public (that included many economists), privatization now appears to be accepted as a legitimate—often a core—tool of statecraft by governments of more than 100 countries. Privatization is one of the most important elements of the continuing global phenomenon of the increasing use of markets to allocate resources.

It is tempting to point to the spread of privatization programs around the world during the past two decades and conclude that the debate on the economic and political merits of government versus private ownership has been decided. But such a conclusion is flawed, since 25 years ago proponents of state ownership could just as easily have surveyed the postwar rise of state-owned enterprises and concluded that their model of economic organization was winning the intellectual battle with free-market capitalism. Instead of pointing to the spread of privatization and calling it destiny, our goal is to assess the findings of empirical research on the effects of privatization as a policy. Therefore, this paper surveys the rapidly growing literature on privatization,

322   *Journal of Economic Literature, Vol. XXXIX (June 2001)*

attempts to frame and answer the key questions this stream of research has addressed, and then describes some of its lessons on the promise and perils of selling state-owned assets. Throughout this survey, we adopt the perspective of an advisor to a government policymaker who is wrestling with the practical problems of whether and how to implement a privatization program. The policymaker asks "What does the research literature have to tell us about these aspects of privatization as an economic policy?" We attempt to answer these important questions.

This paper is organized as follows. Section 2 provides a brief historical overview of privatization. We examine the impact that privatization programs have had in reversing SOE involvement in the economic life of developed and developing countries. Section 3 briefly surveys the recent theoretical and empirical research on the relative economic performance of state-owned and privately owned firms. Section 4 details the different types of transactions that are labeled "privatization" in different regions. We draw particular attention to the structure and pricing selected for share issue privatizations. We also evaluate the various forms of "voucher" or "mass" privatizations that have been implemented. This section also examines whether less radical methods of improving the performance of SOEs, such as deregulation and allowing greater competition (or more routine steps such as using management performance contracts), can effectively substitute for outright privatization. In section 5, we examine the issue of whether, and by how much, privatization programs have actually improved the economic and financial performance of divested firms. Our discussion first evaluates privatization in industrialized and developing countries, and then assesses privatiza-

tion's overall impact in the transition economies. Section 6 asks whether domestic and international investors who purchase privatizing share offerings experience positive initial and long-term investment returns, and section 7 evaluates the impact of privatization on the development of non-U.S. capital markets over the past two decades. Finally, section 8 discusses how privatization programs have impacted the development of—and interest in—corporate governance practices around the world. Section 9 concludes and summarizes our survey.

2. How Large Has Privatization's Impact Been to Date?

Given the attention the press has given to the global movement toward markets, especially the privatization of state-owned enterprises, some might conclude that privatization has almost ended the involvement of state-owned enterprises in global economic activity.[2] This is a significant overstatement. To understand the impact of privatization on the state's role in different economies, we must first briefly review the history behind both privatization and its precursor, nationalization.

Throughout history, there has been a mixture of public (often including religious institutions) and private ownership of the means of production and commerce. Robert Sobel (1999) writes that state ownership of the means of production, including mills and metal working, was common in the ancient Near East, while private ownership was more common in trading and money lending. In

[2] Throughout this paper, we will use the World Bank's definition of state-owned enterprises, as described in World Bank (1995): "government-owned or government-controlled economic entities that generate the bulk of their revenues from selling goods and services."

ancient Greece, the government owned the land, forests, and mines, but contracted out the work to individuals and firms. In the Ch'in dynasty of China, the government had monopolies on salt and iron. Sobel notes that in the Roman Republic the *"publicani* (private individuals and companies) fulfilled virtually all of the state's economic requirements." Dennis Rondinelli and Max Iacono (1996) note that by the time of the Industrial Revolution in the western industrialized societies and their colonies, the private sector was the most important producer of commercial goods and was also important in providing public goods and services. This pattern, with more government involvement in some countries and less in others, continued into the twentieth century in western Europe and its colonies and former colonies. In the United States, there was less government involvement than in many other countries.

The Depression, World War II, and the final breakup of colonial empires pushed government into a more active role, including ownership of production and provision of all types of goods and services, in much of the world. In western Europe, governments debated how deeply involved the national government should be in regulating the national economy and which industrial sectors should be reserved exclusively for state ownership. Until Margaret Thatcher's conservative government came to power in Great Britain in 1979, the answer to this debate in the United Kingdom and elsewhere was that the government should at least own the telecommunications and postal services, electric and gas utilities, and most forms of non-road transportation (especially airlines and railroads). Many politicians also believed the state should control certain "strategic" manufacturing industries, such as steel and defense

production. In many countries, state-owned banks were also given either monopoly or protected positions, as discussed in Rafael La Porta, Florencio López-de-Silanes, and Andrei Shleifer (2000a).

Rondinelli and Iacono (1996) argue that government ownership grew in the developing world for slightly different reasons, primarily that government ownership was perceived as necessary to promote growth. In the post-colonial countries of Asia, Africa, and Latin America, governments sought rapid growth through heavy investment in physical facilities. Another reason for government ownership, often through nationalization, was a historical resentment of the foreigners who had owned many of the largest firms in these countries (see also Roger Noll 2000).

Thus there had been tremendous growth in the use of SOEs throughout much of the world, especially after World War II, which in turn led to privatizations several decades later.[3] Most people associate modern privatization programs with Thatcher's government. However, the Adenauer government in the Federal Republic of Germany launched the first large-scale, ideologically motivated "denationalization" program of the postwar era. In 1961, the German government sold a majority stake in Volkswagen in a public share offering heavily weighted in favor of small investors.[4] Four years later, the

[3] The historical overview of postwar privatizations is based on a longer historical discussion in Megginson, Robert Nash, and Matthias van Randenborgh (1994). Other discussions of the historical evolution of privatization include Timothy Jenkinson and Colin Mayer (1988), Shirley and John Nellis (1991), World Bank (1995), Josef Brada (1996), Paul Bennell (1997), and Daniel Yergin and Joseph Stanislaw (1998).

[4] Using a broader definition of privatization— one that encompassed reactively changing the policies of an immediate predecessor government— the Churchill government's denationalization of

government launched an even larger offering for shares in VEBA. Both offerings were initially received favorably, but the appeal of share ownership did not survive the first cyclical downturn in stock prices, and the government was forced to bail out many small shareholders. It was almost twenty years before another major western nation chose to pursue privatization as a core economic or political policy.[5]

Although the Thatcher government may not have been the first to launch a large privatization program, it is without question the most important historically. Privatization was not a major campaign theme for the Tories in 1979, but the new conservative government embraced the policy. Thatcher adopted the label "privatization," which was originally coined by Peter Drucker and which replaced the term "denationalization" (Yergin and Stanislaw 1998, p. 114). Early sales were strenuously attacked by the Labour opposition, which promised that if it were reelected it would renationalize divested firms such as British Aerospace and Cable and Wireless.[6]

---

the British steel industry during the early 1950s could well be labeled the first "privatization." We thank David Parker for pointing this out to us.

[5] Pan Yotopoulos (1989) describes and assesses the Chilean programs, which began before the program in the U.K. The Pinochet government of Chile, which gained power after the ouster of Salvador Allende in 1973, attempted to privatize companies that the Allende government had nationalized. However, the process was poorly executed and required very little equity investment from purchasers of assets being divested. Thus, many of these same firms were renationalized once Chile entered its debt and payments crisis in the early 1980s. Chile's second privatization program, which was launched in the mid-1980s and relied more on public share offerings than direct asset sales (in which the government often acted as creditor as well as seller) was much more successful.

[6] Ironically, a labor government partially privatized an SOE just before Thatcher came to power. In 1977, the Labour government sold a relatively small fraction of the government's shares in British Petroleum as a means of raising cash.

It was not until the successful British Telecom initial public offering in November 1984 that privatization became established as a basic economic policy in the United Kingdom. A series of increasingly massive share issue privatizations (SIPs) during the last half of the 1980s and the early 1990s reduced the role of SOEs in the British economy to essentially nothing after the Tories left office in 1997, from more than 10 percent of GDP eighteen years earlier.

We note that the objectives set for the British privatization program by the Conservatives were virtually the same as those listed by the Adenauer government twenty years before—and almost every government since. These goals, as described in Price Waterhouse (1989a,b), are to (1) raise revenue for the state, (2) promote economic efficiency, (3) reduce government interference in the economy, (4) promote wider share ownership, (5) provide the opportunity to introduce competition, and (6) subject SOEs to market discipline. The other major objective mentioned by the Thatcher and subsequent governments was to develop the national capital market.[7] We note these goals can be conflicting and we discuss the trade-offs further in the paper.

The perceived success of the British privatization program helped persuade many other industrialized countries to begin divesting SOEs through public share offerings. Jacques Chirac's government, which came to power in France in 1986, privatized 22 companies (worth $12 billion) before being ousted in 1988. The returning socialist government did not execute any further sales, but neither did it renationalize the divested firms. Beginning in 1993,

---

[7] Kojo Menyah, Krishna Paudyal, and Charles Inganyete (1995) and Menyah and Paudyal (1996) have more detailed discussions of the goals of the British privatization program.

the Balladur government launched a new and even larger French privatization program, which has continued under the Jospin administration. The Socialists, in fact, launched the two largest French privatizations ever, the $7.1 billion France Telecom initial public offering (IPO) in October 1997 and the subsequent $10.5 billion seasoned France Telecom issue in November 1998.

Several other European governments, including those of Italy, Germany, and, most spectacularly, Spain, also launched large privatization programs during the 1990s. These programs typically relied on public share offerings, and were often launched by avowedly socialist governments. Privatization spread to the Pacific Rim, beginning in the late 1980s. Japan has sold only a relative handful of SOEs during the past fifteen years (usually relying on SIPs), but many of these have been truly enormous. The three Nippon Telegraph and Telephone share offerings executed between February 1987 and October 1988 raised almost $80 billion, and the $40 billion NTT offer in November 1987 remains the largest single security offering in history. Elsewhere in Asia, governments have taken an opportunistic approach to SOE divestment, selling pieces of large companies when market conditions are attractive, or when money is needed to plug budget deficits. It is unclear how the economic difficulties that gripped the region during the late 1990s will impact privatizations in the future.

Two Asian countries deserve special attention. These two countries are already the world's second and fifth largest economies on a purchasing-power-parity basis, and promise to become even more important over time. The People's Republic of China launched a major economic reform and liberalization program in the late-1970s that has transformed the productivity of the Chi-

nese economy. While there have been numerous small privatizations, there have been relatively few outright sales of SOEs, thus the overall impact of privatization has been limited. Though the government recently (1999) reaffirmed its commitment to privatizing all but the very largest state enterprises, the fact that Chinese SOEs are burdened with so many social welfare responsibilities suggests that it will be extraordinarily difficult to implement a privatization program large enough to seriously undermine the state's economic role (Cyril Lin 2000 ; Justin Lin, Fang Cai, and Zhou Li 1998; and Chong-en Bai, David Li, and Yijiang Wang 1997). The other special Asian case is India, which adopted a major economic reform and liberalization program in 1991, after being wedded to state-directed economic development for the first 44 years of its independence. India's reform program shares two key features with China's: it was adopted in response to highly disappointing SOE performance (Sumit Majumdar 1996), and privatization has thus far not figured prominently in the reform agenda.

On the other hand, Latin America has truly embraced privatization. Chile's program is particularly important, both because it was Latin America's first and because the 1990 Telefonos de Chile privatization, which used a large American depository receipt (ADR) share tranche targeted toward U.S. investors, opened the first important pathway for developing countries to directly tap western capital markets.

Mexico's program was both vast in scope and remarkably successful at reducing the state's role in what had been an interventionist economy. La Porta and López-de-Silanes (1999) report that in 1982, Mexican SOEs produced 14 percent of GDP, received net transfers and subsidies equal to 12.7 percent of

GDP, and accounted for 38 percent of fixed capital investment. By June 1992, the government had privatized 361 of its roughly 1,200 SOEs, and the need for subsidies had been virtually eliminated.

Several other countries in Latin America have also executed large divestment programs (Pablo Gottret 1999). For example, Bolivia's innovative "capitalization" scheme has been widely acclaimed. However, the most important program in the region is Brazil's. Given the size of Brazil's economy and its privatization program, and the fact that the Cardoso government was able to sell several very large SOEs (CVRD in 1997 and Telebras in 1998) in spite of significant political opposition, this country's program is likely to remain very influential.

Privatization in sub-Saharan Africa has been something of a stealth economic policy. Few governments have openly adopted an explicit SOE divestment strategy, but Bennell (1997) shows that there has been substantially more privatization in the region than is commonly believed. For example, Steven Jones, Megginson, Robert Nash and Netter (1999) show that Nigeria has been one of the most frequent sellers of SOEs, using public share offerings, although they were very small. The experience of the African National Congress after it came to power in South Africa also shows the policy realities that governments with interventionist instincts face in this new era. Though nationalization and redistribution of wealth have been central planks of ANC ideology for decades, the Mandela and Mbeki governments have almost totally refrained from nationalization and have even sold off several SOEs (though use of the word "privatization" remains taboo).

The last major region to adopt privatization programs comprises the former Soviet-bloc countries of central and eastern Europe. These countries began privatizing SOEs as part of a broader effort to transform themselves from command to market economies. Therefore, they faced the most difficult challenges and had the most restricted set of policy choices. After the collapse of communism in 1989–91, all of the newly elected governments of the region were under pressure to create something resembling a market economy as quickly as possible. However, political considerations essentially required these governments to significantly limit foreign purchases of divested assets.

Since the region had little financial savings, these twin imperatives compelled many—though not all—governments throughout the region to launch "mass privatization" programs. These programs generally involved distributing vouchers to the population, which citizens could then use to bid for shares in companies being privatized. The programs resulted in a massive reduction of state ownership and were initially popular politically, but became unpopular in many countries (especially Russia) because of the largely correct perception that they were robbery by the old elite and the new oligarchs. The net effects have been disappointing in some cases, but have varied widely. We discuss the empirical evidence on voucher privatization in section 5.

Although different regions have embraced privatization at varying speeds, governments have found the lure of revenue from sales of SOEs to be attractive—which is one reason the policy has spread so rapidly. According to *Privatisation International* (Henry Gibbon 1998, 2000), the cumulative value of proceeds raised by privatizing governments exceeded $1 trillion sometime during the second half of 1999. As an added benefit, this revenue has come to governments without raising taxes or

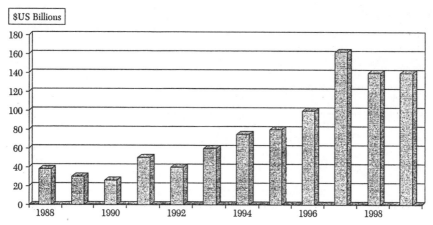

Figure 1. Annual Privatization Revenues for Divesting Governments, 1988–99

Source: *Privatisation International.*

cutting other government services. Annual proceeds grew steadily before peaking at over $160 billion in 1997. Since then, proceeds seem to have leveled off at an annual rate of about $140 billion. Figure 1 shows the annual revenues governments have received from privatizations from 1988 through 1999. Ladan Mahboobi (2000) reports similar figures classified by privatizations in OECD and non-OECD countries. He reports that since 1990 privatization in OECD countries has raised over $600 billion, approximately two-thirds of global privatization activity. Western Europe has accounted for over half of these proceeds. Finally, Jeffry Davis, Rolando Ossowski, Thomas Richardson, and Steven Barnett (2000) report for a sample of transition and non-transition countries that privatization proceeds were an average of one and three-quarters percent of GDP.

The historical discussion suggests that state ownership has been substantially reduced since 1979, and in most countries this has in fact occurred. Using data from Eytan Sheshinski and Luis Felipe López-Calva (1999), figure 2 demonstrates

the role of state-owned enterprises in the economies of high-income (industrialized) countries has declined significantly, from about 8.5 percent of GDP in 1984 to less than 6 percent in 1991. Data presented in James Schmitz (1996), Mahboobi (2000), and Bernado Bortolotti, Marcella Fantini, and Domenico Siniscalco (1999a), as well as our own empirical work on share issue privatizations suggests that the SOE share of industrialized-country GDP has continued to decline since 1991, and is now probably below 5 percent.

The low-income countries show an even more dramatic reduction in state ownership. From a high point of almost 16 percent of GDP, the average SOE share of national output dropped to barely 7 percent in 1995, and has probably dropped to about 5 percent since then. The middle-income countries also experienced significant reductions in state ownership during the 1990s. Since the upper- and lower-middle-income groups include the transition economies of central and eastern Europe, this decline was expected, given the extremely

328   *Journal of Economic Literature, Vol. XXXIX (June 2001)*

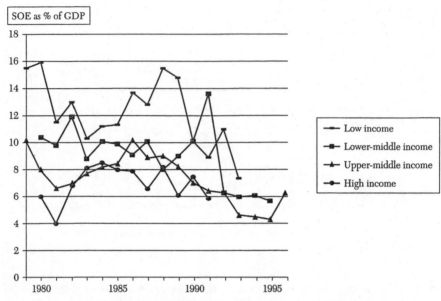

Figure 2. SOE Share of GDP by State of National Development, 1979–96

Source: World Bank, as reported in Sheshinski and López-Calva (1999).

high beginning levels of state ownership. For example, Nemat Shafik (1995) reports that the Czechoslovakian government owned 98 percent of all property in 1989.

3. Why Have Governments Embraced Privatization?

3.1 Efficiency of State vs Private Ownership: Theory

Throughout history, scholars, including economists, have debated the role of government in the economy.[8] Among

[8] For example, Friedrich von Hayek's (1994) passionate critiques of the welfare state and collectivism, exemplified in the 1944 book *The Road to Serfdom*, had a direct impact on policymakers in developing a motive for privatization. Yergin and Stanislaw (1998, pp. 98–107) discuss how Hayek's work was the intellectual basis for Keith Joseph and then Thatcher and the Tory politicians who began the intellectual campaign against statism in the U.K. that triggered the worldwide privatization movement.

economists, this debate now spans many areas, including welfare economics, public choice, public finance, industrial organization, law and economics, corporate finance, and macroeconomics. In this section, we summarize some of the important theoretical issues that arise in the study of privatization and that are needed to analyze the empirical evidence we review in the rest of the paper. We concentrate on empirical evidence because, as Jean-Jacques Laffont and Jean Tirole (1993) say after presenting their model analyzing trade-offs between government and private ownership in promoting efficiency, "theory alone is thus unlikely to be conclusive in this respect." There are also several excellent articles that discuss the theory of privatization and review the literature, including Anthony Boardman and Aidan Vining (1989), John Vickers and George Yarrow (1991), Shleifer (1998), Oleh Havrylyshyn and Donald McGettigan (2000), John Nellis (1999, 2000), Sheshinski and López-Calva (1999), Simeon Djankov and Peter Murrell (2000a,b) and Shirley and Patrick Walsh (2000).

The economic theory of privatization is a subset of the large literature on the economics of ownership and the role for government ownership (or regulation) of productive resources. An initial question to be asked is "what is the proper role of government?" Implicitly, we assume that the goal of government is to promote efficiency. Thus, we discuss the efficiency implications of government ownership and, more importantly, the movement from government ownership to privatization. To a large extent we ignore the arguments regarding the importance of equitable concerns such as income distribution, because they are beyond the scope of this review. The effects of privatization on productive efficiency, or at least observable variables that are proxies for productive efficiency, is the focus of most of the empirical literature we review here.

The theoretical arguments for the advantages of private ownership of the means of production are based on a fundamental theorem of welfare economics: Under strong assumptions, a competitive equilibrium is pareto optimal. However, the assumptions include requirements that there are no externalities in production or consumption, that the product is not a public good, that the market is not monopolistic in structure, and that information costs are low. Thus, a theoretical argument for government intervention based on efficiency grounds rests on an argument that markets have failed in some way, one or more of these assumptions do not hold, and that the government can resolve the market failure.

Intellectual arguments for government intervention based on efficiency considerations have been made in many areas. Governments perceive the need to regulate (or own) natural monopolies or other monopolies, intervene in the case of externalities (such as regulating pollution), and help provide public goods (such as providing national defense and education, or in areas where there is a public good aspect to providing information). The arguments for government intervention become more complicated when they extend to distributional concerns. For example, some argue that the role of government is to act as a "welfare state" (A. Briggs 1961), using state intervention in the market economy to modify the actions of the market.[9] Thus, the arguments for state ownership or control rest on some actual or perceived market failure, and countries have often responded to market failure with state ownership. Privatization, in turn, is a response to the failings of state ownership. Some theoretical arguments that have arisen in the privatization debate are discussed next.

3.1.1. *The impact of privatization depends on the degree of market failure.* As noted above, welfare theory (ignoring the theory of second best) argues that privatization tends to have the greatest positive impact in cases where the role for government in lessening market failure is the weakest, i.e., for SOEs in competitive markets or markets that can readily become competitive. Sheshinski and López-Calva (1999), in summarizing the theoretical literature, argue that there should be ". . . important efficiency gains from changes to private ownership in

---

[9] I. Gough (1989) notes that Briggs (1961) claims that Archbishop Temple first used the term in wartime Britain to differentiate Britain from the "warfare" state of Nazi Germany.

competitive structures." In fact, the effects of competition can be so strong that SOEs, in an increasingly global environment, may be forced to respond to pressures that maximize productive efficiency without the ownership change of privatization. (Shirley and Walsh 2000 provide additional discussion of the effects of competition on the privatization decision.)

In contrast, the justification for privatization is less compelling in markets for public goods and natural monopolies where competitive considerations are weaker. However, Shleifer (1998) and others have argued that even in those markets, government-owned firms are rarely the appropriate solution, for many of the reasons discussed below.

3.1.2. *Contracting ability impacts the efficiency of state and private ownership.* Government ownership of firms results in problems in defining the goals of the firm. While the shareholder-wealth-maximizing model of corporate organization is becoming increasingly dominant in part because of the advantages of having a well-defined corporate goal (see Henry Hansmann and Reinier Kraakman 2000), governments have other objectives than profit or shareholder-wealth maximization. Further, these objectives can change from one administration to the next. Government's inability to credibly commit to a policy can significantly reduce the efficiency of an SOE's operations and governance. Even if the government does attempt to maximize social welfare, for example, welfare is a difficult thing to measure and use in guiding policy.[10] In addition,

the government's goals can be inconsistent with efficiency and maximizing social welfare, or even malevolent (see Laffont and Tirole 1993; Shleifer 1998).

In addition, even if the government and the nation's citizens agree that profit maximization is the goal of the firm, it is difficult to write complete contracts that adequately tie managers' incentives to that goal. Shleifer (1998) argues that the owners of public firms (the nation's citizens) are less able to write complete contracts with their managers because of diffuse ownership, making it difficult to tie the managers' incentives to the returns from their decisions. This is a subset of the broader arguments, based on property rights and agency costs, that there will be differences in performance between government and privately held firms because there is a broader range of monitoring devices under private ownership.[11]

3.1.3. *Ownership structure affects the ease with which government can intervene in firm operations.* Governments can intervene in the operations of any firm, either public or private. However, the government's transaction costs of intervening in production arrangements and other decisions of the firm are greater when firms are privately owned. Thus, to the extent that government intervention has greater costs than benefits, private ownership is preferred to public ownership (see David Sappington and Joseph Stiglitz 1987).

3.1.4. *A major source of inefficiency in public firms stems from less-prosperous firms being allowed to rely on the*

---

[10] Stiglitz (1998) provides an insightful analysis, based on personal experience, of the difficulty governments face in implementing pareto-efficient improvements due to information costs and the problems of commitment and dynamic bargaining. These arguments apply to both government regulation (the main case Stiglitz analyzes) and to state ownership.

[11] Armen Alchain (1977, p. 36) notes, "behavior under [public and private] ownership is different, not because the objectives sought by organizations under each form are different, but, instead, because even with the same explicit organization goals, the costs-rewards system impinging on the employees and the 'owners' of the organization are different."

government for funding, leading to "soft" budget constraints. The state is unlikely to allow a large SOE to face bankruptcy. Thus the discipline enforced on private firms by capital markets and the threat of financial distress is less important for state-owned firms. János Kornai (1988, 1993, 2000), Eric Berglof and Gérard Roland (1998), and Roman Frydman, Cheryl Gray, Marek Hessel, and Andrzej Rapaczynski (2000) all suggest that soft budget constraints were a major source of inefficiency in communist firms. They also note that supposedly "hard" budget constraints imposed on SOEs by government are not very effective either.

3.1.5. *Privatization can impact efficiency through its effect on government fiscal conditions.* As noted in section 1, governments have raised huge amounts of money by selling SOEs. Such sales have helped reduce the fiscal deficit in many countries. Though important, examining the efficiency effects of reducing government deficits is beyond the scope of this paper. Davis et al. (2000) review the evidence on the macroeconomic effects of privatization, discuss the difficulties of using macroeconomic privatization data and report some evidence on the effects from eighteen developing countries. They find evidence that the proceeds from privatization are saved by governments and not used to increase government spending.

3.1.6. *At a macroeconomic level, privatization can help develop product and security markets and institutions.* One important motivation for privatization is to help develop factor and product markets, as well as security markets. As discussed above, welfare economics argues that efficiency is achieved through competitive markets. Thus, to the extent that privatization promotes competition, privatization can have important efficiency effects. Inevitably, the effec-

tiveness of privatization programs and markets themselves are simultaneously determined. It has been clear in the transition economies that the success of privatization depends on the strength of the markets within the economies, and vice versa. Thus, the impact of privatization will differ across countries depending on the strength of the existing private sector. Similarly, evidence suggests that the effectiveness of privatization depends on institutional factors such as the protection of investors. However, privatization can also stimulate the development of institutions that improve market operations.

3.2 *Summary of Privatization Theory*

Theoretical work that examines privatization offers many reasons why, even in the case of market failure, state ownership has important weaknesses. As Shleifer (1998) sums up much of the literature, ". . . a good government that wants to further 'social goals' would rarely own producers to meet its objectives." A question for the post-privatization world is the role of the public sector in the economy and in the regulation of firms. The alternative to state ownership is rarely purely private, unregulated firms. State ownership is only one form of the continuum of governance structures that reflect the level of state regulation of public and privately owned firms (Laffont and Tirole 1993). Many of the theoretical arguments for privatization are based on the premise that the harmful effects of state intervention have a greater impact under state ownership than under state regulation, not that the harmful effects can be eliminated through privatization. However, in this paper we leave to others the continuing debate on the proper role of regulation in a market-oriented economy. Instead, we analyze recent empirical literature examining the relative effectiveness of state versus private ownership.[12]

3.3 *Efficiency of State vs Private Ownership: Empirical Evidence*

Comparing the performance of government-owned to privately owned firms is one method through which the impact of government ownership on firm performance can be analyzed.[13] In section 5 we present a more complete discussion of the potential problems in all empirical work in this area, which includes lack of data and bad data, omitted variables, endogeneity, and selection bias. There are two methodological difficulties that are especially pronounced in attempts to isolate the impact of ownership on performance. First, in comparing SOEs to privately owned firms, it is difficult, if not impossible, to determine the appropriate set of comparison firms or benchmarks, especially in developing economies with limited private sectors. Second, there are generally fundamental reasons why certain firms are government owned and others are privately owned, including the de-

---

[12] The opinions of policymakers throughout the world have been moving closer to those expressed by Ronald Coase in his classic 1960 article, "The Problem of Social Cost." In analyzing market failure, Coase says, "All solutions have costs, and there is no reason to suppose that governmental regulation is called for simply because the problem is not handled well by the market or the firm." James Brickley, Clifford Smith, and Jerold Zimmerman (2001, p. 54), in a more recent analysis, say markets have worked better because, "First, the price system motivates better use of knowledge and information in economic decisions. Second, it provides stronger incentives for individuals to make productive decisions."

[13] A related literature that we do not review analyzes the relative performance of nonprofit firms and for-profit firms. James Brickley and R. Lawrence Van Horn (2000), in an analysis of large hospitals, argue that the evidence suggests there is little distinction between the behavior of nonprofit and for-profit hospitals. Their results suggest the similarities in behavior are due to the effects of competition and not identical objective functions of the managers.

gree of perceived market failure within the particular industry. These factors that determine whether the firm is publicly or privately owned likely also have significant effects on performance. Thus, it is difficult to evaluate the effects of government ownership where the ownership structure is itself endogenous to the system that includes both political and performance goals. Despite these problems, researchers have compared SOE and private firm performance in several cases with some success. We summarize the papers included here in table 1.

Given the above noted limitations, Issac Ehrlich, George Gallais-Hamonno, Zhiqiang Liu, and Randall Lutter (1994) provide good evidence on productivity differences between state-owned and privately owned firms. They use a sample of 23 comparable international airlines of different (and in some cases changing) ownership categories over the period 1973–83 for which they are able to obtain good and comparable cost, output, and ownership data. They develop a model of endogenous, firm-specific productivity growth as a function of firm-specific capital and use the model as a basis for their fixed-effects regressions estimating a cost function in a simultaneous framework with input-demand equations. They argue that they are able to separate the impact of ownership changes on short-term levels of productivity changes from the long-term effects on the rate of productivity growth, improving on earlier studies that concentrated on static rather than dynamic effects of, and changes in, state ownership. Further, they suggest they are able to isolate the effects of ownership from other factors impacting the productivity growth rate, including market conditions and exogenous technical changes.

Ehrlich et al. (1994) find a significant

TABLE 1
RECENT EMPIRICAL STUDIES ON PUBLIC VS PRIVATE OWNERSHIP

Study	Sample description, study period, and methodology	Summary of findings and conclusions
Boardman and Vining 1989	Examines economic performance of 500 largest non-US firms in 1983, classified by ownership structure as SOE, private, or mixed (ME). Employs 4 profitability ratios and 2 measures of X-efficiency.	SOEs and MEs are significantly less profitable and productive than private firms. MEs are no more profitable than pure SOEs—so full private ownership is required to gain efficiency.
Vining and Boardman 1992	Asks whether ownership "matters" in determining efficiency of SOEs, or if only the degree of competition is important. Estimates performance model using 1986 data from 500 largest nonfinancial Canadian firms, including 12 SOEs and 93 MEs.	After controlling for size, market share and other factors, private firms are significantly more profitable and efficient than MEs and SOEs, though now find that MEs outperform SOEs. Thus, ownership has an effect separable from competition alone.
Pinto, Belka, and Krajewski 1993	Tests whether privatization is required to improve performance of SOEs by examining how Polish state sector responded in the 3 years after "Big Bang" reforms of Jan. 1990, which liberalized prices, tightened fiscal/monetary policy and introduced competition, without privatization.	Significant performance improvement due to macroeconomic stabilization package, even without privatization; mostly due to hard budget constraints, tight bank lending policies, enhanced credibility of government's "no bailout" pledge.
Ehrlich, Gallais-Hamonno, Liu, Lutter 1994	Examines impact of state ownership on long-run rate of productivity growth and/or cost decline for 23 international airlines during 1973–83.	State ownership can lower long-run annual rate of productivity growth by 1.6–2.0% and rate of unit cost by 1.7–1.9%. Ownership effects not affected by degree of competition.
Majumdar 1996	Using industry-level survey data, compares performance of SOEs, MEs, and private Indian firms for 1973–89. SOEs and MEs account for 37% of employment and 66% of capital investment in India in 1989.	Documents efficiency scores averaging 0.975 for private firms, significantly higher than averages of 0.912 for MEs and 0.638 for SOEs. State sector efficiency improves during "efficiency drives" but declines afterwards.
Kole and Mulherin 1997	Tests whether postwar performance of 17 firms partly owned by US government due to seizure of "enemy" property during WWII differs significantly from performance of private US firms.	Though these firms experience abnormally high turnover among boards of directors, manager tenure is stable, and SOE performance is not significantly different from private firms.
Dewenter and Malatesta 2001	Tests whether profitability, labor intensity, and debt levels of SOEs listed among 500 largest non-US firms in 1975, 1985, and 1995 differ from private firms on same lists.	After controlling for business cycles, finds private firms significantly (often dramatically) more profitable, have significantly less debt, and less labor intensive production processes than SOEs.
LaPorta, Lopez-de-Silanes, and Shleifer 2000a	Using data from 92 countries, examines whether state ownership of banks impacts financial system development and growth rates of economy and productivity.	Extensive state ownership, especially in poorest countries, retards financial system development and restricts economic growth rates, mostly due to impact on productivity.
Tian 2000	Studies relation between state shareholding and firm performance of 825 publicly traded Chinese firms in 1998. 413 had some government ownership, 312 had none.	Performance of "private" enterprises significantly superior to "mixed" enterprises. Corporate value generally declines with state ownership, then increases after state share passes 45%.
Karpoff 2001	Examines 35 government financed and 57 privately funded expeditions to the Arctic from 1819–1909.	Private expeditions performed better using several measures of performance. More major discoveries were made by private expeditions; most tragedies occurred on government-sponsored expeditions. Robust results in regressions explaining expedition outcomes.

link between ownership and firm-specific rates of productivity growth. Their results suggest that private ownership leads to higher rates of productivity growth and declining costs in the long run, and these differences are not affected by the degree of market competition or regulation. Their estimates suggest that the short-run effects of changes from state to private ownership on productivity and costs are ambiguous, providing a possible explanation for some of the anomalous results in studies. However, their point estimates indicate that the change from complete state to private ownership in the long run would increase productivity growth by 1.6 to 2 percent a year, while costs would decline by 1.7 to 1.9 percent. Their empirics also suggest that a partial change from state to private ownership has little effect on long-run productivity growth—the benefits are based on complete privatization of the firm.

This paper has advantages over much of the other work in the area due to the good data, as well as guidance from a well-developed literature in estimating the determinants of productivity. The authors perform some of the more sophisticated econometric analysis of papers in this area. For example, they replicate their results with a subset of firms that did not experience any within-firm changes in ownership, enabling the authors to be sure that their time-ownership interaction term captures only between-firm variations in ownership. Ehrlich et al. also perform various other robustness checks using different specifications and subsamples, as well as controlling for the special characteristics of their sample period (oil price shocks and deregulation in the United States), and find that their results are robust. Finally, they consider the potential for simultaneity effects

between ownership and productivity, and find that causality goes from ownership to productivity, and not vice versa. The weakness in the work is that it is based on one industry with relatively old data. The authors also note that they make the implicit assumption that all firms are cost minimizing, but if state-owned enterprises have other objectives, it is difficult to interpret the meaning of differences in costs.

Sumit Majumdar (1996) examines differences in efficiency between government-owned, mixed, and private-sector firms in India. He finds support for the superior efficiency of private and mixed-sector firms over SOEs. Using aggregate, industry-level survey data, Majumdar finds that SOEs owned by the central and state governments have average efficiency scores of 0.658 and 0.638, respectively, over the period 1973–89. Mixed enterprises score 0.92, and private enterprises score 0.975. A concern with Majumdar's study is that the aggregated nature of the data, along with problems arising from the reliance on survey data, limits his ability to identify any specific areas where private versus state ownership works best, and whether there are simultaneity and selection bias problems in trying to estimate the effects of ownership and productivity. In addition, he can provide little insight into the reasons for the efficiency differences between the sectors.

George Tian (2000) offers another country-specific study. He examines 825 companies listed on the Shanghai Stock Exchange, with 513 mixed-ownership firms and 312 private firms. He finds that private firms perform better than mixed ownership firms. In addition, he examines the valuation of the companies and finds that corporate value with small government shareholdings decreases with the fraction of state shareholding but rises when the government is a large shareholder.

Another approach to studying the effects of government ownership on efficiency relies on a multi-industry, multi-national, time-series methodology. While cross-sectional time series studies suffer from methodological problems we discuss later, they are able to capture differences that are not apparent in single-country or single-industry studies. An influential paper taking this approach is Anthony Boardman and Aidan R. Vining (1989) who examine the economic performance of the 500 largest non-U.S. industrial firms in 1983. Using four profitability ratios and two measures of X-efficiency, they show that state-owned and mixed (state and private) ownership enterprises are significantly less profitable and productive than are privately owned firms. They also find that mixed enterprises are no more profitable than SOEs, suggesting that full private control, not just partial ownership, is essential to achieving performance improvement. In a later study, Vining and Boardman (1992) use a sample of Canadian firms to re-examine the state versus private ownership question. Their results are qualitatively similar to their earlier findings. In addition, the Canadian study finds that mixed enterprises are more profitable than SOEs, though they fall far short of private-firm levels.

Kathryn Dewenter and Paul Malatesta (2001) follow the general approach of Boardman and Vining (1989) using more recent data. They test whether the profitability, labor intensity, and debt levels of SOEs in the 500 largest international companies, as reported in *Fortune* for 1975, 1985, and 1995, differ from privately owned firms in the same samples. Their data have 1,369 total firm years, of which 147 represent government-owned firms. Since *Fortune* excluded

U.S. firms until 1995, the data are mainly international. After controlling for firm size, location, industry, and business-cycle effects, Dewenter and Malatesta find robust evidence that private companies are significantly (often dramatically) more profitable than SOEs, and also have lower levels of indebtedness and fewer labor-intensive production processes than do their state-owned counterparts.

Finally, Frydman, Gray, Hessel, and Rapaczynski (1999) compare the performance of privatized and state firms in the transition economies of Central Europe, and explicitly try to control for selection bias.[14] Using survey data for 506 midsize manufacturing firms in the Czech Republic, Hungary, and Poland in 1994, they compare four measures of firm performance—sales revenues, employment, labor productivity (revenue per employee) and material costs per unit of revenue. They compare the privatized group to the nonprivatized group with panel data, controlling for potential pre-privatization differences between the two groups. Frydman, Gray, Hessel, and Rapaczynski find that the average effect of privatization is that it works—privatized firms perform better than the state owned firms. However, the performance improvement is concentrated in revenue improvement (not cost reduction) in firms privatized to outside owners.

Frydman et al. (1999) make two important contributions. First, they show that while privatization improves performance, the effect is limited to certain measures of performance and cases where the SOE is sold to outside owners. Second, they attempt to control for the effects of selection bias in examining

[14] Frydman et al. also compare the performance of the privatized firms to that of the firms when they were SOEs. Thus, we also discuss the paper in section 5 and it is summarized in table 5.

the effects of privatization in several ways. They use a fixed effects model to control for selection bias caused by unobserved firm characteristics correlated with performance outcomes that are fixed over time. Further, they contrast the performance of firms privatized in one period with those privatized in another for two different time periods to compare the privatized firms with how they would have performed without privatization. Finally, to control partially for the possibility that better firms are selected for privatization, they contrast the pre-privatization performance of managerially controlled firms with those controlled by other owners. Thus, the paper does an excellent job of controlling for potential biases, though it necessarily depends on survey data.

We conclude this section with two studies that use unique situations to analyze the effects of government versus private ownership. Stacey Kole and J. Harold Mulherin (1997) set out to answer the basic question in the public versus private debate as posed by Sam Peltzman (1971), "If a privately owned firm is socialized, and nothing else happens, how will the ownership alone affect the firm's behavior?" Kole and Mulherin study seventeen firms with significant German or Japanese ownership when the United States entered World War II. The U.S. government assumed ownership of the foreign stock in these firms and ended up holding between 35 and 100 percent of the common stock for up to 23 years during and after World War II. Kole and Mulherin find industry controls for five firms, comprising 61 percent of the book value of the seventeen firms, and compare the performance of the government-owned firms. They find no significant difference between the performance of their sample with the private-sector

firms and state "the preceding results stand in contrast to the typical results regarding the inefficiency of government enterprise." The authors argue that the fact that these firms were operating in competitive industries forced them to operate efficiently.

The Kole and Mulherin (1997) results are evidence that in a competitive environment, where the government has no agenda other than as a passive investor, factors other than ownership determine firm performance. Many of the firms were involved in the war effort, so the government had an incentive to run them efficiently. In addition, all the firms were eventually reprivatized, so the government was also concerned with running them efficiently to maximize the later sale value. Kole and Mulherin admit that their sample and the period they study is novel, limiting its generality. Further, their results are based on only five firms. Still, their findings do illustrate the importance of factors other than ownership in determining firm performance.

In a paper featuring a very interesting natural experiment, Jonathan Karpoff (2001) studies a comprehensive sample of 35 government-funded and 57 privately-funded expeditions to the Arctic from 1818 to 1909 seeking to locate and navigate a northwest passage, discover the North Pole, and make other discoveries in arctic regions. Karpoff finds that the private expeditions performed better using several measures of performance. He shows most major arctic discoveries were made by private expeditions, while most tragedies (lost ships and lives) were on publicly funded expeditions. He notes the fact that the public expeditions had greater losses could mean the public expeditions took greater risks, but then the public expeditions would have had a greater share of discoveries, which did not occur. He also estimates regressions explaining outcomes in several ways (crew deaths, ships lost, tonnage of ships lost, incidence of scurvy, level of expedition accomplishment), controlling for exploratory objectives sought, country of origin, the leader's previous arctic experience, or the decade in which the expedition occurred. In essentially every regression, the dummy variable for private expedition is significant with a sign indicating that the private expedition performed better. Karpoff concludes that the incentives were better aligned in the private expeditions, leading to systematic differences in the ways public and private expeditions were organized. While the uniqueness of the sample limits its generality, he provides an interesting illustration of the impact of ownership on the performance of an organization.[15]

3.4 Policy Alternatives to Privatization

As discussed earlier, some argue that competition and deregulation are more important than privatization or governance changes in improving performance of firms (George Yarrow 1986; John Kay and D. J. Thompson 1986; Matthew Bishop and Kay 1989; John Vickers and Yarrow 1991; Franklin Allen and Douglas Gale 1999).

Others maintain that privatization is necessary for significant performance improvements (Vining and Boardman 1992; Maxim Boycko, Shleifer, and Robert Vishny 1994, 1996a,b; John Nellis 1994; Josef Brada 1996; and Shleifer 1998). Although much of this debate is outside the scope of this paper, there are a few empirical studies that examine countries where economic reform has

been implemented instead of, or prior to, full privatization.[16]

Brian Pinto, Merek Belka, and Stefan Krajewski (1993) examine the way in which the Polish state sector responded in the three years following Poland's "Big Bang" reforms of January 1990. These reforms deregulated prices, introduced foreign competition to many industries, and signaled that tight monetary and fiscal policies would be pursued. However, the Polish government did not immediately launch a large-scale privatization program. The authors document significant performance improvements on the part of most manufacturing firms. They conclude that these improvements were due to the imposition of hard budget constraints reinforced by tighter bank lending behavior, consistency in the government's "no bailout signal," import competition, and reputational concerns of SOE managers.

The use of incentive contracts for management and workers is potentially the best way to improve performance in SOEs (Leroy Jones 1991). The World Bank endorsed these contracts in the 1980s. China has undergone widespread economic reform with minimal privatization through the use of these incentive contracts and offers a natural setting in which to study their impact.

Theodore Groves, Yongmiao Hong, John McMillan, and Barry Naughton (1995) discuss the ways incentives were added to the Chinese managerial labor market by the late 1980s, including replacement after poor performance and linking managerial pay to profits. Further, managers were selected by auctions, where the auction process

---

[15] Kelly Olds (1994) also uses data from the 1800s to show that after the privatization of the tax-supported Congregationalist churches in New England, demand for preachers and church membership rose dramatically.

[16] Majumdar (1996) also suggests that reform can improve SOE performance by showing that the gap between the private and public firms' performance partly closes during those periods when governments are pushing reform agendas.

revealed information about the managers that in a market economy could have come from observations of their performance. Groves, Hong, McMillan, and Naughton (1994) show that after 1978, when Chinese firms were given more autonomy and allowed to retain more profits and to increase workers' incentives through bonuses and differing work contracts, there were increases in workers' incomes (though not of managers') and in investment in the firms.

Wei Li (1997) documents marked improvements in the marginal and total factor productivity of 272 Chinese SOEs over the period 1980–89 as a result of economic reforms in China, including the increased use of incentives. He finds evidence of substantial increases in productivity over the reform period, much of which can be attributed to the reform. In addition, his evidence suggests that 87 percent of the growth in productivity was due to improved incentives and compensation. Li notes, however, the potential for selection bias in his study both in the firms selected for the survey and in the responses to the survey.

Shirley and Lixin Xu (1998) come to the opposite conclusion concerning the ability of incentive contracts to improve firm performance. They analyze the effects of these contracts in twelve monopoly SOEs, and find that the incentive contracts have no effect on profitability or labor productivity; they also find some evidence of negative effects on growth in total factor productivity. They attribute the failure of the contracts to the inability of governments to follow through on promised actions and the inability of supervisory agencies to negotiate and monitor the contracts effectively. It must be noted, however, that the study is based on a small sample, limiting the ability to draw conclusions,

especially in light of the evidence from the studies of Chinese firms.

The evidence from China suggests that enterprise restructuring, concentrating on improving the allocation of property rights and incentives can yield large benefits even without privatization.[17] Naturally, this begs the question whether economic reform coupled with privatization could lead to even greater performance improvements. Unfortunately, this is little evidence on this question and it would be very difficult to develop such evidence. Note also that the evidence on the benefits of reform without privatization comes primarily from one country where country-specific factors may play an important but unidentified role. One thing we can say is that, as we note later in the paper, the evidence demonstrating the benefits of privatization is weakest for countries in eastern Europe, where privatization was implemented rapidly. This may suggest that privatization should have proceeded along a more gradual path. We address that question later on.

4. How Do Countries Privatize?

A key decision to be made by the privatizing government is on the method of transferring the state-owned asset to private ownership. This decision is difficult because, in addition to the economic factors such as valuing the assets, privatizations are generally part of an ongoing, highly politicized process. Some of the factors that influence the privatization method include: (1) the history of the asset's ownership, (2) the financial and competitive position of the SOE, (3) the government's ideological view of markets and regulation,

---

[17] This is consistent with the findings of Brickley and Van Horn (2000) that the managers of nonprofit hospitals face similar incentives to the managers of for-profit hospitals and behave in a similar manner.

(4) the past, present, and potential future regulatory structure in the country, (5) the need to pay off important interest groups in the privatization, (6) the government's ability to credibly commit itself to respect investors' property rights after divestiture, (7) the capital market conditions and existing institutional framework for corporate governance in the country, (8) the sophistication of potential investors, and (9) the government's willingness to let foreigners own divested assets.

The complexity of goals means that countries have used various methods for privatizing different types of assets. Although financial economists have learned much about selling assets in well-developed capital markets, we still have a limited understanding of the determinants and implications of the privatization method for state-owned assets. Theoreticians have modeled some aspects of the privatization process, but to be tractable, their models must ignore important factors. Empirical evidence on the determinants of privatization is also limited by the complexity of the goals of the privatization process.

4.1 Methods of Privatization

Brada (1996) presents an excellent taxonomy of privatization methods. Although the context of his paper is central and eastern Europe, his classification of four principal divestment methods is quite general. In addition, he provides a review of the successes and failures of each of these general approaches in central and eastern Europe. Of course, there are many variations within each of his categories, and he shows that many privatizations use combinations of different methods.

Brada's first category is *privatization through restitution*. This method is appropriate when land or other easily identifiable property that was expropri-

ated in years past can be returned to either the original owners or to their heirs. This method is rarely observed outside eastern Europe, though it has been important there. For example, Brada (1996) reports that up to 10 percent of the value of state property in the Czech Republic consisted of restitution claims. The major difficulty with this method is that the records needed to prove ownership are often inadequate or conflicting.

The second method is *privatization through sale of state property*, where a government trades its ownership claim for an explicit cash payment. This category takes two important forms. The first is *direct sales* (or asset sales) of state-owned enterprises (or some parts thereof) to an individual, an existing corporation, or a group of investors. The second form is *share issue privatizations* (SIPs), in which some or all of a government's stake in an SOE is sold to investors through a public share offering. These are similar to IPOs in the private sector, but where private IPOs are structured primarily to raise revenue, SIPs are structured to raise money and to respond to some of the political factors mentioned earlier.

Brada's third category is *mass* or *voucher privatization*, whereby eligible citizens can use vouchers that are distributed free or at nominal cost to bid for stakes in SOEs or other assets. This method has been used only in the transition economies of central and eastern Europe, where it has brought about fundamental changes in the ownership of business assets in those countries, although it has not always changed effective control. Longer descriptions of the issues that these governments have confronted when designing voucher privatization programs are provided in Morris Bornstein (1994, 1999), Melinda Alexandrowicz (1994), Bernard Drum (1994) and Shafik (1995).

The final method is *privatization from below*, through the startup of new private businesses in formerly socialist countries. Havrylyshyn and McGettigan (2000) stress the importance of this type of economic growth in the transition economies. Although privatization from below has progressed rapidly in many regions (including China, the transition economies of central and eastern Europe, Latin America, and sub-Saharan Africa), a survey of this phenomenon is beyond the scope of our paper.

There are many other methods besides the four described above that governments can use to increase private-sector participation. For example, the term "privatization" in the United States means something different from any of these strategies. As López-de-Silanes, Shleifer, and Vishny (1997) show, the privatization debate in the United States refers to the choice between provision of goods and services by (state and local) government employees and the contracting out of that production to private firms. Their empirical study finds that the more binding are state fiscal constraints and the less powerful are public-sector unions, the greater the likelihood of privatization.

4.2 *The Choice of Sale Method*

Henry Gibbon (1997) provides one of the most helpful delineations of the decisions facing a government that wants to privatize through cash sales. Gibbon discusses the steps such a government must take in developing a divestment program. These include setting up a structure for privatization (including legislation, if necessary), providing adequate performance records for SOEs being sold (generating believable accounting data), developing any necessary new regulatory structures, and determining the appropriate post-sale relationship between the firm and the government. Others who examine non-pricing issues relating to actual divestment contracts include Carliss Baldwin and Sugato Bhattacharya (1991), Rondinelli and Iacono (1996), Klaus Schmidt (1996), Shafik (1996), and Francesca Cornelli and David Li (1997).

Two empirical papers analyze the choice of privatization method. One explicitly studies the choice between an asset sale and a share issue privatization. Using a sample of 1,992 privatizations that raised $720 billion in 92 countries, Megginson, Nash, Netter, and Annette Poulsen (2000) examine why 767 firms were divested using share offerings (in public capital markets), but 1225 companies were privatized via direct sales (in private markets). They find robust results that the choice is influenced by capital market, political, and firm-specific factors, and report that SIPs are more likely to be used when capital markets are less developed, presumably as a way to develop capital markets, and when there is less income inequality. SIPs are also more likely the larger the size of the offering and the more profitable the SOE. On the other hand, governments with greater ability to commit to property rights are more likely to privatize via asset sales. Perhaps the most interesting result is that governments choose to privatize the more profitable SOEs through SIPs—evidence supporting the possibility of sample selection bias in studies of performance of privatized firms. In the second paper, Bernardo Bortolotti, Marcella Fantini, and Domenico Siniscalco (1999a) estimate the determinants of the fraction of privatization revenues that come from public offerings (SIPs) for privatizations in 49 countries. They find that the greater the selling government's deficit and the more conservative the selling government, the more likely it is that privatization will occur through public offerings. However, SIPs are less likely in French civil law countries. Bortolotti, Fantini, and Carlo Scapa (2000) examine factors that lead countries to sell shares in SOEs abroad.

4.3 Restructuring SOEs, and Sequencing and Staging of Sales

Some of the most complex issues involve the interrelated questions of when to privatize and at what pace, what order to follow in privatizing (sequencing), whether to sell an SOE all at once or in stages (staging), whether to restructure an SOE prior to sale, and the role of macroeconomic reform in privatization. Since these are complex issues that involve factors outside the scope of this article (especially macroeconomic reform which we do not discuss) we do not spend much time on them. Further, their complexity has limited empirical work in this area.

Several authors have theoretically modeled the sequencing and staging of SOE sales, including Barbara Katz and Joel Owen (1993, 1995), Boycko, Shleifer, and Vishny (1996b), Francesca Cornelli and David Li (1997), Enrico Perotti (1995), and Bruno Biais and Perotti (2000). The models illustrate the importance of sequencing and staging to build reputational capital with investors by the privatizing government, building domestic support for the program, and identifying bidders that will maximize the efficiency of the firm. While the complexities of these interrelationships have limited empiricists' ability to identify factors in sequencing and staging, several articles that empirically examine them are Perotti and Serhat Guney (1993), Dewenter and Malatesta (1997), Jones, Megginson, Nash, and Netter (1999),

and Megginson, Nash, Netter, and Poulsen (2000).

A related practical question about privatization is whether governments should restructure SOEs (e.g., lay off redundant workers) prior to selling or leave this to the new owners. This is related to questions discussed in section 3.4: can governments reform SOEs (including reform without privatization) and should reform and privatization proceed quickly or slowly? Early advice from the World Bank (John Nellis and Sunita Kikeri 1989) was that governments should restructure SOEs prior to divestment, since governments are better able than private owners to cushion the financial blow to displaced workers by using unemployment payments or pensions. Government-led restructuring can thus provide a private buyer of the SOE with a "clean slate." Preparing companies for privatization was standard practice in the United Kingdom during the 1980s, in part to smooth the transition with the trade unions. However, by 1992, the same authors (Kikeri, Nellis, and Shirley 1992) had become more nuanced in their interpretation of the optimal strategy. They said (p. 54) that small and medium-sized SOEs "should be sold 'as is' at the best price possible, as quickly as possible." They also noted that in all cases (p. 60) new investments "should be left to private owners once a decision has been made to privatise the enterprise."

Two empirical papers that examine SOE reform prior to privatization are López-de-Silanes (1997) and Dewenter and Malatesta (2000). López-de-Silanes examines whether prior government restructuring of SOEs improves the net price received for the company, and finds evidence that it does not. He shows that prices would have increased by 71 cents per dollar of assets if the only restructuring step taken had been to fire the CEO and if the assets had been divested an average of one year earlier. He argues that other restructuring steps slow down the process and consume too many resources to be worthwhile. The 71 cents per dollar in added value would be a significant improvement on the average 54 cents per dollar of assets actually received. However, this evidence is based on a small sample of banks, which limits its usefulness. Dewenter and Malatesta (2001) find some evidence that the improvements brought about by privatization occur before the SOE is privatized.

4.4 *Pricing and Allocation of Control and Ownership*

Although mass or voucher privatization programs have attracted a great deal of academic interest, asset sales and SIPs account for most of the value of assets that have been divested by governments in the past two decades.[18] Thus we focus on the latter two methods.

4.4.1 *Pricing Decisions in Asset Sales*

Four papers study the revenue impact of SOE direct sale pricing decisions. At a theoretical level, Jeremy Bulow and Paul Klemperer (1996) ask whether it is more profitable to sell a company through an auction with no reserve price or by using an optimally structured direct negotiation with one less bidder. They show that under most conditions, a simple competitive auction with N + 1 bidders will yield more expected revenue than a seller could expect to earn by fully exploiting his or her monopoly selling position against N bidders. López-de-Silanes' (1997) study

of Mexican privatizations empirically supports this theoretical conclusion that maximizing the number of bidders in an open auction is usually the best way to maximize revenues.[19] He finds that prices received are sensitive to the level of competition in the auction process but that the Mexican government frequently restricted participation (particularly by foreigners) in spite of this fact. Nonetheless, the amount of revenue generated was the main criteria in selecting the winning bidder for more than 98 percent of the SOEs sold.

Rondinelli and Iacono (1996) examine auctions in central and eastern Europe, where thousands of small businesses have been auctioned off, as well as in Latin America and Russia, where larger SOEs have been sold. Many types of auctions have been used, including English, Dutch, first price, second price, double, and pro-rata sales. Auctions have been used to sell both lease rights and ownership rights. In other cases, governments have sold SOEs directly to groups of private investors or firms, setting prices and terms by negotiation. In some cases, the groups of investors consist of management or employees. In other cases, the government has liquidated the SOE and sold physical assets to a group of investors.

Archana Hingorani, Kenneth Lehn, and Anil Makhija (1997) examine an actual voucher privatization program, the first round of the Czech Republic's mass privatization in 1991. Because the mechanics of how companies are divested by this government are actually more similar to an asset sale than to any other method, we discuss their work here. Hingorani, Lehn, and Makhija test whether the level of share demand,

---

[18] However, it is also true that a much larger *number* of companies were transferred to private ownership through mass privatization programs. It is also likely that more employees were from firms that were transferred in mass schemes than from firms that were sold in SIPs. We thank John Nellis for pointing this out to us.

[19] The Mexican program relied almost exclusively on direct sales, rather than SIPs, as its principal divestment technique.

as measured by voucher redemptions by Czech citizens, effectively predicts the actual level of stock prices in the secondary market. The authors confirm the predictive power of share demand, and also document that share demand is positively related to the level of insider shareholdings and the extent of foreign ownership in a company being sold. They find that share demand is positively related to the level of past profitability, which itself shows that even imperfect accounting statements convey useful information. Additionally, they find that share demand is inversely related to the firm's market risk, which they measure as the post-offering coefficient of variation of stock prices.[20]

4.4.2 *Pricing and Share and Control Allocation in SIPs*

Any government that intends to privatize SOEs using public share offerings faces three sets of interrelated decisions: (1) how to transfer control, (2) how to price the offer, and (3) how to allocate shares. *The control transfer decision* includes whether to sell the SOE all at once or through a series of partial sales. If the government chooses the latter course, then it must determine how large a fraction of the company's shares to issue in the initial versus subsequent offers. The government must also decide whether to insert any postprivatization restrictions on corporate control. *The pricing decision* requires that the government determine the amount of underpricing, and whether the offer price should be set by a tender

offer, a book-building exercise, or at a fixed price. If the latter, the government must decide whether the offering price should be set immediately prior to the offer or many weeks in advance. *The share allocation decision* requires the government to choose whether to favor one group of potential investors over another (i.e., domestic investors, SOE employees, or both, over foreign and institutional investors). It also requires deciding whether to use the best available investment banker as lead underwriter (regardless of nationality) or to favor a national champion.

Several papers empirically examine the choices governments make in designing SIP programs. Kojo Menyah and Krishna Paudyal (1996) and Menyah, Paudyal, and Charles Inyangete (1995) investigate how the aims and objectives of privatization influence the procedures and incentives used in the sale of state-owned shares on the London Stock Exchange by the U.K. government. Jones, Megginson, Nash, and Netter (1999), Qi Huang and Richard Levich (1998), and Dewenter and Malatesta (1997) present comprehensive studies of the pricing and share and control allocation decisions made by governments disposing of SOEs through public share offering. The results are broadly similar, so we concentrate on the paper by Jones et al. (1999) since it has the largest sample.

Jones et al. (1999), whose results are summarized in table 2, provide evidence on the way political factors impact the offer pricing, share allocation, and other terms in SIPs. They analyze a large sample of 630 SIPs from 59 countries made over the period June 1977 to July 1997.[21] One result they document

---

[20] Stijn Claessens (1997) examines the relation between ownership concentration and equity share prices from the voucher bidding rounds and the secondary market prices for the 1491 firms that emerged from the mass privatization voucher scheme in the Czech and Slovak Republics. He finds that the prices are related to the resulting ownership structure, with more concentrated ownership associated with higher prices.

[21] Though Jones et al. rely primarily on *Privatisation International* for the data used in this study; one of the authors has also developed from secondary sources (primarily the *Financial Times*,

TABLE 2
PRICING, SHARE ALLOCATION, AND CONTROL ALLOCATION PATTERNS IN SIPs

Sample of 630 share issue privatizations (SIPs) executed by 59 national governments during 1977–97. Measures are broken down for the 417 initial public offerings of SIP shares and the 213 seasoned SIP offerings.

Measure	Initial SIPS			Seasoned Offers		
	Mean	Median	Number	Mean	Median	Number
Pricing Variables						
Issue size (US$ million)	555.7	104.0	417	1,068.9	311.0	172
Initial return[1]	34.1	12.4	242	9.4	3.3	55
Percent of offer at fixed price[2]	85.0	100.0	273	61.0	100.0	77
Cost of sales as a percent of issue[3]	4.4	3.3	178	2.5	2.6	61
Share Allocation Variables						
Percent of offer allocated to employees	8.5	7.0	255	4.8	2.6	76
Fraction of offers with some allocation to employees	91.0		255	65.8		76
Percent of offer allocated to foreigners	28.4	11.5	348	35.9	32.5	142
Percent of offers with some allocation to foreigners	57.1		348	67.6		142
Control Allocation Variables						
Percent of capital sold in offer[4]	43.9	35.0	384	22.7	18.1	154
Percent of offers where 100% of capital sold	11.5		384	0		154
Percent of capital where 50% or more of capital sold	28.9		384	8.4		154

Source: Jones, Megginson, Nash, and Netter (1999).
Notes:
[1] also known as initial underpricing, the return an investor who bought shares at the offering price could earn by reselling those shares at end of the first day's trading.
[2] measures the fraction of an issue offered to investors at a predetermined, fixed price rather than an auction-determined price.
[3] a measure of the sum of cash expenses and underwriter discount charged by the investment banking syndicate managing the issue.
[4] measures the fraction of a firm's total common equity (which is not necessarily synonymous with total voting rights) sold in an offering.

is the sheer size of SIP offers—the mean (median) size of initial SIPs is $555.7 million ($104.0 million) and the mean size of seasoned issues is $1.069 *billion* (median $311.0 million), much larger than typical stock offerings. They also find that SIPs are significantly underpriced by government sellers. The mean level of underpricing for initial

but also publications such as Price Waterhouse 1989b) an appendix that details similar information for an additional 500 SIPs. This appendix can be obtained upon request by contacting *wmegginson@ou.edu.*

SIPs is 34.1 percent (median 12.4 percent). Even seasoned SIP offers are underpriced by an average of 9.4 percent (median 3.3 percent). We return to this issue in section 6.

The evidence of Jones et al. on allocation of control in SIPs supports a political interpretation of divesting governments' motives. Jones et al. find that nearly all SIPs are essentially secondary offerings, in which only the government sells its shares and no money flows to the firm itself. Since the divesting government sells an average (median) of

43.9 percent (35.0 percent) of the SOE's capital in initial offers and 22.7 percent (18.1 percent) in seasoned issues, the offers represent significant reductions in direct government stock ownership. Although governments typically surrender day-to-day operating control of the SOE to private owners in the initial SIP, they retain effective veto power through a variety of techniques. The most common technique is government retention of a "golden share," which gives it the power to veto certain actions, such as foreign takeovers.[22]

4.5 *Voucher Privatizations*

Voucher privatization has been the most controversial method of divesting state-owned assets. Boycko, Shleifer, and Vishny (1994) show that the decision to pursue mass privatization, and even the specific program design, is largely dictated by politics. The privatization programs practiced in western Europe and elsewhere were politically difficult to execute in eastern Europe, although Hungary, Estonia, and Poland used case-by-case privatizations, which have been successful at a macro level. Nonetheless, voucher privatization schemes can be made attractive from an economic perspective, since they maximize value, foster free and efficient markets, and promote effective corporate governance. Barbara Katz and Joel Owen (1997)

[22] Though golden shares have been widely adopted, they are in fact almost never used to affect control contests (Patrick McCurry 2000). The EU is trying to block new adoptions of golden shares and roll back those already in place, charging they are designed to discourage free cross-border competition for corporate control. At a recent OECD conference, the director of Italy's privatization program, Vittorio Grilli, pointed out an additional political problem with exercising a golden share: When a government uses its share to veto a takeover bid, this is equivalent to publicly stating it does not approve of the bidder. Such a statement is awkward at best, and could cause an international incident if the bidder is a foreign company.

investigate what they call the "voucher portfolio problem." This problem arises whenever the proportion of ownership resulting from a given voucher bid is unknown, but the post-privatization performance of a divested company largely depends on the skills of the new owners and their respective ownership stakes. Katz and Owen also provide a good discussion of the philosophical differences between the Czech program, which relied heavily on vouchers and prohibited post-sale trading of stock, and the Russian program, which privatized relatively small (29 percent on average) stakes in most firms and allowed unrestricted trading of vouchers.

Although most countries' actual experience with vouchers has been poor, none has been quite as dismal as Russia's. Although a variety of factors have played a role, Frydman, Katharina Pistor, and Rapaczynski (1996) show that insider control of privatized firms has been by far the most important impediment to effective reform. Initially, the Russian government had high hopes that the "voucher privatization funds" (VPFs) formed during the initial voucher distributions might be able to overcome the collective action problem inherent in mass privatization programs. Such funds might use their concentrated ownership in privatized firms to force managers to restructure. Though most funds attempted to exercise their "voice" in corporate boardrooms, insider dominance completely blocked their efforts. The VPFs turned instead to their "exit" option and sold shares on the secondary market.

Pistor and Andrew Spicer (1996) also examine the early promise and subsequent failure of privatization investment funds in Russia and the Czech Republic. In both countries, citizens have become owners of the worst performing privatized assets, while the "crown jewels" have all come under insider control. As the authors say, ". . . establishing property rights is a longer and more complicated process than allocating title." Olivier Blanchard and Phillipe Aghion (1996) also conclude that privatization is proceeding slowly in eastern Europe, largely because insiders, who currently have control of firms but no property rights, oppose outsider privatization. Given this reality, Blanchard and Aghion examine whether privatization would proceed more rapidly if governments were simply to allocate property rights to insiders (insider privatization). However, they find there is a wedge between the private value of the firm to insiders and its value to an outsider, and that this difference might well preclude value-increasing exchanges. Given the actual experience with insider dominance of most voucher privatizations, we conclude that this wedge is in fact alive, well, and fully operational.

5. Has Privatization Improved Performance?

Since privatization has been part of government policy tool kits for almost two decades now, academic researchers have had enough time to execute many empirical studies of the effect of divestment on the performance of former SOEs. However, there are difficult methodological problems with research in this area.[23] An important problem is data availability and consistency. The amount of information that must be disclosed is much less in most countries than in the United States, and these

standards vary from country to country as well as within countries over time. A large literature in accounting has shown that management can manipulate U.S. accounting data, and this problem is probably greater for international firms. Furthermore, the possibility of sample selection bias can arise from several sources, including governments' desire to make privatization "look good" by privatizing the healthiest firms first. Another sample selection problem is that data availability tends to be greater in the more developed countries (and perhaps for the better performing firms within countries), so developed countries (and better performing firms) are overrepresented in empirical analysis. For example, in cross-sectional regressions using fixed effects, estimation will probably rely mainly on data from developed countries.

There are also many problems in measuring performance changes that arise from using accounting or stock data. We discuss the problems with stock return data in section 6; the problems with accounting data are more important since many empirical studies employ primarily accounting information. These problems include determining the correct measure of operating performance, selecting an appropriate benchmark with which to compare performance, and determining the appropriate statistical tests to use (Ahmed Galal, Leroy Jones, Pankaj Tandon, and Ingo Vogelsang 1994; and Brad Barber and John Lyon 1996). The finance literature has not reached a consensus on the ways to deal with these problems for U.S. companies, much less privatized international firms. Barber and Lyon (1996) argue that test statistics designed to determine whether there is abnormal performance using accounting data are misspecified when the sample firms have performed unusually well or

[23] Many of the difficulties are similar to those discussed in Jonathan Temple (1999), who surveys cross-country research on the determinants of growth. Temple discusses the substantial problems that arise in estimating and interpreting cross-country regressions. James Tybout (2000) also discusses the difficulties with data in attempting to assess the performance of manufacturing firms in developing countries.

poorly. They suggest that sample firms must be matched to control firms with similar pre-event performance, which is especially difficult in studies of privatized firms.

Therefore, the results of each of the studies we discuss must be kept in perspective. We also note that the studies of post-performance rarely examine the welfare effects on consumers. Most important, few studies control for the possible use of market power by the privatized firms; that is, performance improvements could be due to greater exploitation of monopoly power, which has harmful effects on allocative efficiency, rather than productive efficiency. Many of the studies on performance changes after privatization examine the effects of divestiture on groups such as workers, but few examine the effect of privatization on consumers. On the other hand, one of the principal reasons for launching privatizations, particularly of monopoly utilities, is consumer dissatisfaction with a firm's service. Furthermore, the studies cited here almost unanimously report increases in performance associated with privatization.[24] This consistency is perhaps the most telling result we report—privatization appears to improve performance measured in many different ways, in many different countries.[25]

With the above caveats in mind, this section evaluates the results of 38 studies that employ accounting and/or real output data to examine the impact of privatization on the operating efficiency, ownership structure, and/or financial performance of former SOEs in developed, developing, and transition economies. Though all these studies are detailed in the accompanying tables, and most are discussed at least briefly in the text, we also specify which studies we think are the most important—and why we think this is so. To effectively synthesize such a large number of empirical studies, we first categorize papers according to whether they examine privatization in transition or non-transition economies. The latter studies are evaluated in section 5.1, while the transition economies are examined in section 5.2. This dichotomization is necessary, since both direct observation and published research suggest that reforming transition economies invariably requires embracing a great many economic and political changes simultaneously, whereas privatization (and attendant regulatory changes) is often the sole major component of reform processes in non-transition economies. A further organizational step is to present, in tables 3 through 7, summary information for each of the studies we examine. Presenting this information in tabular form saves us from having to sequentially discuss each paper's sample construction methodology, estimation procedure, and empirical results in the section's text. Instead, we can identify key findings that appear in many different studies, and can discuss methodological pros and cons for entire groups of studies, rather than for each paper in turn.

5.1 *Empirical Studies of Non-Transition Economies*

We separate non-transition studies by empirical methodology, depending upon how the papers compare performance

---

[24] A cynic might say that all of the gains researchers have documented after privatization are due to selection bias. However, while there is some evidence discussed elsewhere that the better firms are privatized first, at least in SIPs the evidence is still strong that performance improves after privatization. Further, the paper that does the best job of controlling for selection bias, Frydman, Gray, Hessel, and Rapaczynski (1999), finds privatized firms perform better than SOEs.

[25] Temple (1999) also notes the importance of both historical case studies and cross-sectional analysis in assessing recent developments in the economic theory of growth.

348   *Journal of Economic Literature, Vol. XXXIX (June 2001)*

changes resulting from privatization. The first set of papers examines a single industry, a single country, or one or a small number of individual firms. While these studies employ a variety of empirical techniques, most compare post-privatization performance changes with either a comparison group of non-privatized firms or with a "counterfactual" expectation of what would have occurred if the privatized firms had remained state-owned. The second set of studies examines only firms divested through public share offerings, and measures privatization-related performance changes by comparing the three-year mean or median operating and financial performance of divested firms to their own mean or median performance during their last three years as state-owned firms.

5.1.1 *Case, Single-Industry, and Single-Country Studies*

The studies we examine in this section are summarized in table 3. The first study listed merits detailed analysis because it has proven so influential, both due to the rigor of its methodology and because it was sponsored by the World Bank. Galal, Jones, Tandon, and Vogelsang (1994) compare the actual post-privatization performance of twelve large firms—mostly airlines and regulated utilities—in Britain, Chile, Malaysia, and Mexico to the predicted performance of these firms had they not been divested. Using this counterfactual approach, the authors document net welfare gains in eleven of the twelve cases considered which equal, on average, 26 percent of the firms' pre-divestiture sales. They find no case where workers are made significantly worse off, and three where workers significantly benefit. David Newberry and Michael Pollitt (1997) perform a similar counterfactual analysis of the 1990 restructuring and

privatization of the U.K.'s Central Electricity Generating Board (CEGB), and document significant post-privatization performance improvements. However, they find that the producers and their shareholders capture all of the financial rewards of this improvement and more, whereas the government and consumers lose out. The authors conclude that CEGB's restructuring and privatization was in fact "worth it," but could have been implemented more efficiently and with greater concern for the public's welfare.[26]

Two of the studies described in table 3 examine national privatization experiences. Stephen Martin and David Parker (1995) find that, after adjusting for business cycle effects, less than half the British firms they study perform better after being privatized. The authors do, however, find evidence of a "shake-out" effect, where several firms improve performance prior to being privatized (but not afterward). The results of the second national study are far less ambiguous. La Porta and López-de-Silanes (1999) find that the former Mexican SOEs they study rapidly close a large performance gap with industry-matched private firms that had existed prior to divestment. These firms go from being highly unprofitable before privatization to being very profitable thereafter. Output increases 54.3 percent, in spite of a reduced level of investment spending, and sales per employee roughly double. The privatized firms reduce (blue- and white-collar)

---

[26] The privatization and liberalization of the British electricity industry is also discussed at length in David Newberry (1997) and Vickers and Yarrow (1991), while the regulatory regime adopted for earlier utility privatizations is described in M. E. Beesley and S. C. Littlechild (1989). None of these works showers the Thatcher government with praise for its policy decisions, though Beesley and Littlechild do find the RPI-X price regulation system adopted in the U.K. is superior to the U.S. rate of return regulatory regime.

TABLE 3
CASE STUDIES, COUNTRY AND INDUSTRY-SPECIFIC EMPIRICAL STUDIES: NON-TRANSITION ECONOMIES

Study	Sample description, study period, and methodology	Summary of findings and conclusions
Galal, Jones, Tandon, and Vogelsang 1994	Compares actual post-privatization performance of 12 large firms (mostly airlines and regulated utilities) in UK, Chile, Malaysia, Mexico to predicted performance if the firms remained SOEs.	Documents net welfare gains in 11 of the 12 cases which equal, on average, 26% of the firms' pre-divestiture sales. Find no case where workers were made worse off, and 3 where workers were made significantly better off.
Martin and Parker 1995	Using 2 measures (ROR on capital employed and annual growth in value-added per employee-hour), examines whether 11 UK firms privatized in 1981–88 improved performance after divestment. Attempts to control for business cycle effects.	Mixed results. Outright performance improvements after privatization found in less than half of firm-measures studied. Several firms improved prior to divestiture, indicating an initial "shake-out" effect upon privatization announcement.
Ramamurti 1996	Surveys studies of 4 telecom, 2 airline, and 1 toll-road privatization programs in Latin America during 1987–91. Discusses political economic issues, methods used to overcome bureaucratic/ideological opposition to divestiture.	Concludes privatization very positive for telecoms, partly due to scope for technology, capital investment, and attractiveness of offer terms. Much less scope for productivity improvements for airlines and roads, and little improvement observed.
Boles de Boer and Evans 1996	Estimates impact of 1987 deregulation and 1990 privatization of Telecom New Zealand on price and quality of telephone services. Examines whether investors benefited.	Documents significant declines in price of phone services, due mostly to productivity growth that cut costs at a 5.6% annual rate, and significant improvement in service levels. Shareholders also benefited significantly.
Petrazzini and Clark 1996	Using International Telecommunications Union (ITU) data through 1994, tests whether deregulation and privatization impact level and growth in teledensity (main lines per 100 people), prices, service quality, and employment by telecoms in 26 developing countries.	Deregulation and privatization both are associated with significant improvements in level and growth in teledensity, but have no consistent impact on service quality. Deregulation associated with lower prices and increased employment; privatization has the opposite effect.
Ramamurti 1997	Examines restructuring and privatization of Ferrocarilla Argentinos, the national railroad, in 1990. Tests whether productivity, employment, and need for operating subsidies (equal to 1% of GDP in 1990) change significantly after divestiture.	Documents a 370% improvement in labor productivity and a 78.7% decline in employment (from 92,000 to 19,682). Services were expanded and improved, and delivered at lower cost to consumers. Need for operating subsidies largely eliminated.
Eckel, Eckel, and Singal 1997	Examines effect of British Airways' privatization on competitors' stock prices. Tests whether fares on competitive routes decline after privatization.	Stock prices of US competitors' decline on average 7% upon BA's privatization, and fares on routes served by BA and competitors fall by 14.3%. Compensation of BA executives increases and becomes more performance-contingent.
Newberry and Pollitt 1997	Performs cost-benefit analysis of the 1990 restructuring and privatization of Central Electricity Generating Board (CEGB). Compares actual performance of privatized firms to a counterfactual assuming CEGB remained state-owned.	Restructuring/privatization of CEGB resulted in permanent cost reduction of 5% per year. Producers and shareholders capture all this benefit and more. Consumers and government lose. Shows that alternative fuel purchases involve unnecessarily high costs and wealth flows out of country.
Ros 1999	Uses ITU data and panel data regression methodology to examine effects of privatization and competition on network expansion and efficiency in 110 countries over 1986–95.	Countries with at least 50% private ownership of main telecom firm have significantly higher teledensity levels and growth rates. Both privatization and competition increase efficiency, but only privatization is positively associated with network expansion.
La Porta and López-de-Silanes 1999	Tests whether performance of 218 Mexican SOEs privatized through June 1992 improves after divestment. Compares performance with industry-matched firms, and splits improvements documented between industry and firm-specific influences.	Output of privatized firms increased 54.3%; employment declined by half (though wages for remaining workers increased). Firms achieved a 24% point increase in operating profitability, eliminating need for subsidies equal to 12.7% of GDP. Higher product prices explain 5% of improvement; transfers from laid-off workers, 31%, and incentive-related productivity gains account for remaining 64%.

TABLE 3 *(Cont.)*

Study	Sample description, study period, and methodology	Summary of findings and conclusions
Wallsten 2000a	Performs econometric analysis of effects of tele-communications reforms in developing countries. Using panel dataset of 30 African and Latin American countries from 1984–97, explores effects of privatization, competition and regulation on telecommunications performance.	Competition is significantly associated with increases in per capita access and decreases in cost. Privatization is helpful only if coupled with effective, independent regulation. Increasing competition is single best reform; competition in combination with privatization is best. Privatizing a monopoly without regulatory reforms should be avoided.
Laurin and Bozec 2000	Compares productivity and profitability of 2 large Canadian rail carriers, before and after 1995 privatization of Canadian National (CN). Compares accounting ratios for 17-year period 1981–97 and 3 sub-periods: the fully state-owned era (1981–91), pre-privatization (1992–95), and post-privatization. Compares stock returns from 1995–98. Creates 6-firm comparison group of Canadian privatizations and computes accounting ratios and stock returns for these firms.	Total factor productivity of CN much lower than that of privately owned Canadian Pacific (CP) during 1981–91, but became as efficient during pre-privatization (1992–95), exceeded it after 1995. CN stock price outperformed CP, the transportation industry, and the Canadian market after 1995. Both firms shed workers after 1992, but CN's employment declined more (34% vs 18%) as average productivity almost doubled (97% increase). CN's capital spending increased significantly, though CP's increased more. Six-firm Canadian privatization comparison group experienced significant increases in investment spending and productivity and decline in employment.
Boylaud and Nicoletti 2000	Uses factor analysis and database on market structure and regulation to investigate effects of liberalization and privatization on productivity, prices and quality of long-distance and cellular telephone services in 23 OECD countries over 1991–97.	Prospective and actual competition both bring about productivity and quality improvements and lower prices in telecom services, but no clear effect was found for privatization.

employment by half, but those workers who remain are paid significantly more. The authors attribute most of the performance improvement to productivity gains resulting from better incentives, with at most one-third of the improvement being attributable to lower employment costs.

Three of the papers described in table 3 are essentially case studies of individual privatized companies, though two of the articles benchmark performance changes with respect to one or more private companies. Catherine Eckel, Doug Eckel, and Vijay Singal (1997) examine the effect of British Airways' (BA) 1987 privatization on *competitors'* stock prices and on fares charged in those routes where BA competes directly with foreign airlines. They find that the stock prices of U.S. competitors fall, as do airfares in markets served by BA; both findings suggest that stock traders anticipated a much more competitive

BA would result from the divestiture.[27] Claude Laurin and Yves Bozec (2000) compare the productivity and profitability of two large Canadian rail carriers (one state-owned and one private-sector), both before and after the 1995 privatization of Canadian National (CN). They find that CN's relatively poor performance during the "fully state-owned period" (1981–91) rapidly converges on Canadian Pacific's performance levels during the pre-privatization but post-announcement period (1992–95), and then surpasses it thereafter. These

[27] Eckel, Eckel, and Singal also examine the two-stage privatization of Air Canada (from 100 percent state ownership to 57 percent, then to zero). Unlike BA, Air Canada does not compete with U.S. carriers on many routes, so there is no significant competitor stock price effect resulting from its divestiture. Air Canada's fares do not fall after the first, partial privatization, but fall a significant 13.7 percent after the final, complete divestiture of state ownership.

findings suggest two separable impacts of privatization on firm performance: an "anticipation" effect prior to divestiture and a "follow through" effect subsequently. The final case study, Ravi Ramamurti (1997), examines the 1990 restructuring and privatization of Ferrocarilla Argentino, the Argentine national freight and passenger railway system. The author documents a nearly incredible 370 percent improvement in labor productivity and an equally striking (and not unrelated) 78.7 percent decline in employment—from 92,000 to 18,682 workers.[28] Operating subsidies declined almost to zero, and consumers benefited from expanded (and better quality) service and lower costs. Ramamurti concludes that these performance improvements could not have been achieved without privatization.

No less than six of the studies detailed in table 3 examine the telecommunications industry, which has been transformed by the twin forces of technological change and deregulation (including privatization) since 1984—the year when the AT&T monopoly was broken up in the United States and the Thatcher government began privatizing British Telecom. Five of these are empirical studies, while Ramamurti (1996) provides a simple, though highly readable, summary of empirical studies examining four telecom privatizations in Latin America. Ramamurti concludes that all were judged to be political and economic success stories. Unfortunately, the empirical studies tell somewhat conflicting stories, probably due in part to differences in the nations covered and methodology employed. Ben Petrazini and Theodore Clark (1996), Agustin Ros (1999), and Scott Wallsten (2000a) examine developing countries exclusively or as separate subsamples, while Ros (1999) and Olivier Boylaud and Giuseppe Nicoletti (2000) provide similar coverage of OECD countries, and David Boles de Boer and Lewis Evans (1996) study the deregulation and privatization of Telecom New Zealand. Though Ros, Wallsten, and Boylaud and Nicoletti all use some variant of panel data methodology, they arrive at slightly different conclusions regarding the relative importance of deregulation/liberalization and privatization in promoting expanded teledensity (number of main lines per 100 population) and operating efficiency of national telecom companies, and the quality and pricing of telecom services. On balance, these studies generally indicate that deregulation and liberalization of telecom services are associated with significant growth in teledensity and operating efficiency, and significant improvements in the quality and price of telecom services. The impact of privatization, per se, is somewhat less clear-cut, but most studies agree that the combination of privatization and deregulation/liberalization is associated with significant telecommunications improvements. This is certainly the result predicted by Noll (2000) in his analysis of the political economy of telecom reform in developing countries. The Juliet D'Souza and Megginson (2000) study's findings—described in the following section—also support the idea that telecom privatization yields net benefits.[29]

[28] Ramamurti (1997) details the intense political maneuvering that accompanied the attempt to restructure and slim down FA. The generous severance payments awarded to displaced workers were instrumental in winning union acquiescence in the restructuring plan, while the presence of effective road transport competition for rail traffic reduced the threat of a potentially crippling strike weapon.

[29] Though they do not quite fit into our empirical classification scheme, six related studies deserve mention here. Peter Smith and Björn Wellenius (1999) and Wellenius (2000) present normative analyses of telecom regulation in developing countries, while Walter Wasserfallen and Stefan Müller (1998) discuss the privatization and

5.1.2 *Pre- vs Post-Privatization Performance for SIPs*

The studies summarized in table 4 all examine how privatization affects firm performance by comparing pre- and post-divestment data for companies privatized via public share offering. Since the first study to be published using this methodology is Megginson, Nash, and van Randenborgh (1994), we will refer to this as the MNR methodology. This empirical procedure has several obvious economic and econometric drawbacks. Of these, selection bias probably causes the greatest concern, since by definition a sample of SIPs will be biased towards the very largest companies sold during any nation's privatization program. Furthermore, since governments have a natural tendency to privatize the "easiest" firms first, those SOEs sold via share offerings (particularly those sold early in the process) may well be among the healthiest state-owned firms.[30] Another drawback of the

MNR methodology is its need to examine only simple, universally available accounting variables (such as assets, sales, and net income) or physical units such as number of employees. Obviously, researchers must be careful when comparing accounting information generated at different times in many different countries. Most of the studies cited here also ignore (or, at best, imperfectly account for) changes in the macroeconomy or industry over the seven-year event window during which they compute pre- versus post-privatization performance changes. Finally, the studies cannot account for the impact on privatized firms of any regulatory or market-opening initiatives that often are launched simultaneously with or immediately after major privatization programs.

In spite of these drawbacks, studies employing the MNR methodology have two key advantages. First, they are the only studies that can examine and directly compare large samples of economically significant firms, from different industries, privatized in different countries, over different time periods. Since each firm is compared to itself (a few years earlier) using simple, inflation-adjusted sales and income data (that produce results in simple percentages), this methodology allows one to efficiently aggregate multinational, multi-industry results. This point is made clear in table 5, which summarizes the results of three studies that use precisely the same empirical proxies and test methodology—and can thus be aggregated and directly compared—yet examine non-overlapping samples. In total, these three studies examine seven performance criteria for 204 companies from 41 countries. Second, while focusing on SIPs yields a selection bias, it also yields samples that encompass the largest and most politically influential

---

deregulation of western Europe's telecom industry. Michael Pollitt (1997) analyzes the impact of liberalization on the performance of the international electric supply industry, and Bortolotti, Fantini, and Siniscalso (1999b) document that effective regulation is a crucial institutional variable in electric utility privatization. Establishing such a regulatory regime allows governments to increase the pace of privatization, sell higher stakes, and maximize offering proceeds. Finally, Wallsten (2000b) shows that exclusivity periods, which are usually granted to telecom monopolies as they are being privatized, are economically harmful to consumers and do not achieve the efficiency objectives assigned to them at the time of divestment. Exclusivity periods do, however, raise the price that investors are willing to pay for privatized telecoms, which largely explains why they are employed.

[30] Megginson, Nash, Netter, and Poulsen (2000) find that governments selling SOEs tend to sell the more profitable SOEs in the public capital markets and the less profitable in the less transparent private markets. Those sold in the public capital markets are the firms that appear in studies of performance. Dewenter and Malatesta (2001) also show performance improvements before privatization in firms that are being privatized.

TABLE 4

EMPIRICAL STUDIES ON PERFORMANCE CHANGES FOR FIRMS PRIVATIZED VIA PUBLIC SHARE OFFERINGS: NON-TRANSITION ECONOMIES

These studies each employ samples from more than one country and more than one industry.

Study	Sample description, study period, and methodology	Summary of findings and conclusions
Megginson, Nash, van Randenborgh 1994	Compares 3-year average post-privatization performance ratios to 3-year pre-privatization values for 61 firms from 18 countries and 32 industries from 1961–89. Tests significance of median changes in post pre-privatization periods. Binomial tests for percent of firms changing as predicted.	Documents economically and statistically significant post-privatization increases in output (real sales), operating efficiency, profitability, capital investment spending, and dividend payments; significant decreases in leverage; no evidence of employment declines, but significant changes in firm directors.
Macquieira and Zurita 1996	Compares pre- versus post-privatization performance of 22 Chilean firms privatized over 1984–89. Uses Megginson, Nash and van Randenborgh (MNR) methodology to analyze first without adjusting for overall market movements (as in MNR), then with adjustment for contemporaneous changes.	Unadjusted results virtually identical to MNR: significant increases in output, profitability, employment, investment, dividend payments. After adjusting for market movements, changes in output, employment, and liquidity are no longer significant, and leverage increases significantly.
Boubakri and Cosset 1998	Compares 3-year average post-privatization performance ratios to 3-year pre-privatization values for 79 firms from 21 developing countries and 32 industries over 1980–92. Tests for significance of median changes in ratio values post- versus pre-privatization. Binomial tests for percentage of firms changing as predicted.	Documents significant post-privatization increases in output (real sales), operating efficiency, profitability, capital investment spending, dividend payments, employment; significant decreases in leverage. Performance improvements are generally larger than those documented by MNR.
D'Souza and Megginson 1999	Documents offering terms, sale methods, and ownership structure resulting from privatization of 78 firms from 10 developing and 15 developed countries over 1990–94. Compares 3-year average post-privatization performance ratios to 3-year pre-privatization values for subsample of 26 firms. Tests for significance of median changes in ratio values post-vs pre-privatization. Binomial tests for percent of firms changing as predicted.	Documents significant post-privatization increases in output (real sales), operating efficiency, and profitability, and significant decreases in leverage. Capital investment spending increases insignificantly, while employment declines significantly. More of the firms privitized in the 1990s are from telecoms and other regulated industries.
Verbrugge, Megginson, Owens 2000	Study offering terms and share ownership results for 65 banks fully or partially privatized from 1981 to 1996. Then compare pre- and post-privatization performance changes for 32 banks in OECD countries and 5 in developing countries.	Documents moderate performance improvements in OECD countries. Ratios proxying for profitability, fee income (noninterest income as fraction of total), and capital adequacy increase significantly; leverage ratio declines significantly. Documents large, ongoing state ownership, and significantly positive initial returns to IPO investors.
Boubakri and Cosset 1999	Examine pre- versus post-privatization performance of 16 African firms privatized through public share offering during 1989–96. Also summarize findings of three other studies pertaining to privatization in developing countries.	Document significantly increased capital spending by privatized firms, but find only insignificant changes in profitability, efficiency, output and leverage.
D'Souza and Megginson 2000	Examines pre- versus post-privatization performance changes for 17 national telecom companies privatized through share offerings during 1981–94.	Profitability, output, operating efficiency, capital spending, number of access lines, and average salary per employee all increase significantly after privatization. Leverage declines significantly; employment declines insignificantly.
Dewenter and Malatesta 2001	Compares pre- versus post-privatization performance of 63 large, high-information companies divested during 1981–94 over both short-term [(+1 to +3) versus (−3 to −1)] and long-term [(+1 to +5) versus (−10 to −1)] horizons. Examines long-run stock return performance of privatized firms and compares relative performance of a large sample (1,500 firm-years) of state and privately owned firms during 1975, 1985, and 1995.	Documents significant increases in profitability (using net income) and significant decreases in leverage and labor intensity (employees ÷ sales) over short- and long-term horizons. Operating profits increase *prior to* privatization, but not after. Significantly positive long-term (1–5 years) abnormal stock returns, mostly in Hungary, Poland, and UK. Results strongly indicate that private firms outperform SOEs.

TABLE 4 *(Cont.)*

Study	Sample description, study period, and methodology	Summary of findings and conclusions
Boardman, Laurin, and Vining 2000	Compares 3-year average post-privatization performance ratios to 5-year pre-privatization values for 9 Canadian firms privatized during 1988–95. Computes long-run (up to 5 years) stock returns for divested firms.	Profitability, measured as return on sales or assets, more than doubles after privatization; efficiency and sales increase significantly (though less drastically). Leverage and employment decline significantly; capital spending increases significantly. Privatized firms significantly outperform Canadian stock market over all long-term holding periods.

privatizations. As discussed in section 4, SIPs account for more than two-thirds of the $1 trillion of total revenues raised by governments since 1977. With these methodological caveats in mind, we turn to a summary of the findings of studies using the MNR technique.

All of these studies offer at least limited support for the proposition that privatization is associated with significant improvements in the operating and financial performance of SOEs divested via public share offering. Two of these studies focus on specific industries: banking (James Verbrugge, Wanda Owens, and Megginson 2000) and telecommunications (D'Souza and Megginson 2000); one examines data from a single country, Chile (Carlos Macquieira and Salvador Zurita 1996); and the other six employ multi-industry, multinational samples. Five of these studies—MNR (1994), Narjess Boubakri and Jean-Claude Cosset (1998), D'Souza and Megginson (1999, 2000), and Boardman, Laurin and Vining (2000)—document economically and statistically significant post-privatization increases in real sales (output), profitability, efficiency (sales per employee), and capital spending, coupled with significant declines in leverage. Macquieira and Zurita find similar results for Chilean firms using data that is not adjusted for changes experienced by other Chilean

firms over the study period, but many of these improvements cease to be statistically significant once such adjustments are made. Verbrugge et al. (2000) document significant, though modest, increases in the profitability and capital adequacy of commercial banks privatized in OECD countries, as well as significant declines in leverage, but they also find substantial ongoing state involvement in these banks' affairs. Consistent with the result that state connections matter in bank operations, Philip Hersch, David Kemme, and Netter (1997) find that in Hungary the banks made it much easier for firms headed by former members of the nomenklatura to get loans than other firms.

Finally, Dewenter and Malatesta (2000) estimate the effects of government ownership and privatization using a sample of large firms from three separate time periods (1975, 1985, and 1995) compiled by *Fortune*. They estimate regressions explaining profitability controlling for firm size, location, industry, and the business cycle. They find that net income-based profitability measures increase significantly after privatization, but operating income-based measures do not. Instead, they find that operating profits increase prior to divestiture, once more supporting the idea that privatization can have a significant anticipation effect.

TABLE 5
PERFORMANCE OF NEWLY PRIVATIZED FIRMS

Results of three empirical studies comparing three-year average operating and financial performance of a combined sample of 211 privatized firms with average performance of those firms during their last three years as SOEs. The studies employ the Wilcoxon rank sum test (with its z-statistic) to test for change in median value, and multiple proxies for most economic variables being measured. This table summarizes one proxy per topic, and emphasizes the one highlighted in the studies (usually the variable that uses either physical measures, such as number of employees, or financial ratios using current-dollar measures in the numerator or denominator, or both). Efficiency and output measures are index values, with the value during the year of privatization defined as 1.000; inflation-adjusted sales figures are used in efficiency and output measures.

Variables and Studies Cited	Number of Observations	Mean Value before Privatization	Mean Value after Privatization	Mean Change due to Privatization	Z-Statistic for Difference in Performance	% of Firms with Improved Performance	Z-Statistic for Significance of % Change
Profitability (%) net income ÷ sales							
Megginson, Nash, and van Randenborgh 1994	55	0.0552 (0.0442)	0.0799 (0.0611)	0.249 (0.0140)	3.15***	69.1	3.06***
Boubakri and Cosset 1998	78	0.0493 (0.0460)	0.1098 (0.0799)	0.0605 (0.0181)	3.16***	62.8	2.29**
D'Souza and Megginson 1999	78	0.14 (0.05)	0.17 (0.08)	0.03 (0.03)	3.92***	71	4.17***
Weighted Average	*218*[a]	*0.0862*	*0.1257*	*0.0396*		*67.6*	
Efficiency (real sales per employee)							
Megginson, Nash, and van Randenborgh 1994	51	0.956 (0.942)	1.062 (1.055)	0.1064 (0.1157)	3.66***	85.7	6.03***
Boubakri and Cosset 1998	56	0.9224 (0.9056)	1.1703 (1.1265)	0.2479 (0.2414)	4.79***	80.4	4.60***
D'Souza and Megginson 1999	63	1.02 (0.87)	1.23 (1.16)	0.21 (0.29)	4.87***	79	5.76***
Weighted Average	*170*	*0.9733*	*1.1599*	*0.1914*		*81.5*	
Investment (%) capital expenditures ÷ sales							
Megginson, Nash, and van Randenborgh 1994	43	0.1169 (0.0668)	0.1689 (0.1221)	0.0521 (0.0159)	2.35**	67.4	2.44**
Boubakri and Cosset 1998	48	0.1052 (0.0649)	0.2375 (0.1043)	0.1322 (0.0137)	2.28**	62.5	1.74*
D'Souza and Megginson 1999	66	0.18 (0.11)	0.17 (0.10)	−0.01 (−0.01)	0.80	55	0.81
Weighted Average	*154*	*0.1405*	*0.1900*	*0.0493*		*60.6*	
Output (real sales, adjusted by cpi)							
Megginson, Nash, and van Randenborgh 1994	57	0.899 (0.890)	1.140 (1.105)	0.241 (0.190)	4.77***	75.4	4.46***
Boubakri and Cosset 1998	78	0.9691 (0.9165)	1.220 (1.123)	0.2530 (0.1892)	5.19***	75.6	4.58***
D'Souza and Megginson 1999	85	0.93 (0.76)	2.70 (1.86)	1.76 (1.11)	7.30***	88	10.94***
Weighted Average	*209*[a]	*0.9358*	*1.7211*	*0.8321*		*80.3*	
Employment (total employees)							
Megginson, Nash, and van Randenborgh 1994	39	40,850 (19,360)	43,200 (23,720)	2,346 (276)	0.96	64.1	1.84*
Boubakri and Cosset 1998	57	10,672 (3,388)	10,811 (3,745)	139 (104)	1.48	57.9	1.19
D'Souza and Megginson 1999	66	22,941 (9,876)	22,136 (9,106)	−805 (−770)	−1.62	36	−2.14**
Weighted Average	*162*	*22,936*	*23,222*	*286*		*49.5*	

356   Journal of Economic Literature, Vol. XXXIX (June 2001)

TABLE 5 *(Cont.)*

Variables and Studies Cited	Number of Observa- tions	Mean Value before Privatiza- tion	Mean Value after Privatiza- tion	Mean Change due to Privatiza- tion	Z-Statistic for Difference in Perfor- mance	% of Firms with Improved Perfor- mance	Z-Statistic for Significance of % Change
Leverage (%)							
total debt ÷ total assets							
Megginson, Nash and van	53	0.6622	0.6379	−0.0243	−2.41**	71.7	3.51***
Randenborgh 1994		(0.7039)	(0.6618)	(−0.0234)			
Boubakri and Cosset	65	0.5495	0.4986	−0.508	−2.48**	73.1	2.11**
1998		(0.5575)	(0.4789)	(−0.0162)			
D'Souza and Megginson	72	0.29	0.23	−0.06	−3.08***	67	3.05***
1999		(0.26)	(0.18)	(−0.08)			
Weighted Average	*188*	*0.4826*	*0.4357*	*−0.0469*		*67.0*	
Dividends (%)							
cash dividends ÷ sales							
Megginson, Nash and van	39	0.0128	0.0300	0.0172	4.63***	89.7	8.18***
Randenborgh 1994		(0.0054)	(0.0223)	(0.0121)			
Boubakri and Cosset	67	0.0284	0.0528	0.0244	4.37***	76.1	4.28***
1998		(0.0089)	(0.0305)	(0.0130)			
D'Souza and Megginson	51	0.015	0.04	0.025	4.98***	79	5.24***
1999		(0.00)	(0.02)	(0.02)			
Weighted Average	*106*	*0.0202*	*0.0655*	*0.0228*		*80.4*	

[a] Number exceeds 211 because of overlapping firms in different samples.
*** Indicates significance at the 1 percent level
 ** Indicates significance at the 5 percent level
  * Indicates significance at the 10 percent level

5.1.3 *Summary and Analysis*

These 22 studies from non-transition economies offer at least limited support for the proposition that privatization is associated with improvements in the operating and financial performance of divested firms. Several of the studies offer strong support for this proposition, and only Martin and Parker (1995) document outright performance declines (for six of eleven British firms) after privatization. Almost all studies that examine post-privatization changes in output, efficiency, profitability, capital investment spending, and leverage document significant increases in the first four and significant declines in leverage.

The studies examined here are far less unanimous regarding the impact of privatization on employment levels in privatized firms. All governments fear that privatization will cause former SOEs to shed workers, and the key question in virtually every case is whether the divested firm's sales will increase enough after privatization to offset the dramatically higher levels of per-worker productivity. Three studies document significant *increases* in employment (Galal et al. 1994; Megginson, Nash, and van Randenborgh 1994; and Boubakri and Cosset 1998), two find insignificant changes (Macquieira and Zurita 1996; and D'Souza and Megginson 2000) while the remaining five document significant—sometimes massive—employment declines (Ramamurti 1997; La Porta and López-de-Silanes 1999; Laurin and Bozec 2000; D'Souza and Megginson 1999; and Boardman, Laurin, and Vining 2000). These conflicting results could be due to differences in methodology, sample size and make-up, or omitted factors. However, it is more likely that the studies reflect real differences in post-privatization employment changes between countries and between industries. In other words, there is no "standard" outcome. Perhaps the safest conclusion we can assert is that privatization does not automatically mean employment reductions in divested firms—though this will likely occur unless sales can increase fast enough after divestiture to offset very large productivity gains.

In our opinion, the Galal et al. (1994), La Porta and López-de-Silanes (1999), Dewenter and Malatesta (2001), and the three articles summarized in D'Souza and Megginson (1999) are the most persuasive studies examined in this section. As mentioned, the main strength of Galal et al. is its construction and use of a clear "counterfactual" that (virtually uniquely) allows both the financial and welfare gains from privatization to be measured. La Porta and López-de-Silanes execute what we consider the best single-country study, since it examines almost the entire population of Mexican privatizations and compares performance changes to industry-matched private firms. Dewenter and Malatesta both contrast the performance of private-sector and state-owned firms over three non-overlapping periods and study how the performance of privatized firms changes over an extended time period. Finally, D'Souza and Megginson's summary and comparison of three studies that use the same methodology—but non-overlapping samples—provides compelling evidence that the operating and financial gains to privatization are pervasive.

Since the empirical studies discussed in this section generally document performance improvements after privatiza-tion, a natural follow-on question is to ask *why* performance improves. As we will discuss in the next section, a key determinant of performance improvement in transition economies is bringing in new managers after privatization. No study explicitly documents systematic evidence of this occurring in non-transition economies, but Catherine Wolfram (1998) and Michael Cragg and I. J. Alexander Dyck (1999a,b) show that the compensation and pay-performance sensitivity of managers of privatized U.K. firms increases significantly after divestment. The only study that explicitly addresses the sources of post-privatization performance improvement using data from multiple non-transition economies, D'Souza et al. (2000), finds stronger efficiency gains for firms in developing countries, in regulated industries, in firms that restructure operations after privatization, and in countries providing greater amounts of shareholder protection.

We now turn to an examination of research findings about privatization's impact in transition economies. Privatization is both more difficult and more all-encompassing in these countries than it is in either industrialized or non-transition developing countries. This is because in transition economies, privatization is only part of the massive changes in the economy as countries move from communism to more market oriented methods of allocating resources and organizing production.

5.2 Privatization in Transition Economies

We categorize the empirical studies that examine privatization in transition economies into more manageable groups. Both direct observation and the findings of these studies suggest that a logical classification scheme is to evaluate separately studies that examine

358 *Journal of Economic Literature, Vol. XXXIX (June 2001)*

firms privatized in central and eastern Europe and those which study the privatization programs of Russia and the other republics of the former Soviet Union. These categories are evaluated in sections 5.2.1 and 5.2.2, respectively. We then conclude section 5 with a brief overview of China's liberalization and privatization program.

Note that testing for the effects of privatization on firm performance is even more difficult in transition economies than in non-transition economies. As mentioned above, privatization in these countries occurs at the same time as, and is part of, other massive economy-wide changes. Thus, isolating the effects of privatization itself is problematic. Further, as discussed by Djankov and Murrell (2000b, p. 9) "mis-reporting and accounting difficulties are rife in transition economies." In general, the data from transition economies is much worse and much more limited than from non-transition economies. Finally, the transition economies are undergoing many other major changes in their political and economic environments. The number of firms privatized in some way in transition is much greater than in non-transition economies (Djankov and Murrell 2000a report over 150,000 large firms in 27 transition economies faced the revolutionary changes of transition). However, we do not have good data or even any data on many of these firms. The data that do exist often come from surveys rather than mandated disclosure. Thus, the studies of privatization in transition economies has greater problems with significant selection bias, as well as omitted variables, than in the studies of non-transition economies.

5.2.1 *Privatization in Central and Eastern Europe*

The empirical studies that examine privatization programs in central and eastern Europe are summarized in table 6. These countries employed varying methods of privatizing SOEs, including asset sales (Hungary and eastern Germany), voucher privatizations (the Czech Republic and early Polish divestitures), "spontaneous privatizations" (Slovenia), share offerings (later Polish sales), or a combination of techniques. The studies also cover differing event periods during the 1990s, employ differing empirical methodologies, and ask somewhat different questions—though all directly or indirectly ask how privatization impacts firm-level operating performance. Additionally, all of these studies must contend with the fact that output typically fell dramatically in every central and eastern European country during the period immediately after the collapse of socialism in 1989–91, though in most cases output later snapped back smartly.[31] These studies must therefore examine whether, for example, the output of privatized firms contracted less than did the output of firms that remained state-owned. These and other econometric challenges that must be faced in disentangling the effects of privatization, ownership structure changes, and other influences on the post-divestment performance of privatized firms in transition settings are discussed at length in Andrew Weiss and Georgiy Nikitin (1998) and Frydman, Gray, Hessel, and Rapaczynski—hereafter FGHR—(1999).

In spite of all the caveats spelled out above, the studies summarized in table 6 yield surprisingly consistent results

---

[31] This "U-shape" pattern of aggregate output in 26 transition economies is documented and examined econometrically in Andrew Berg, Eduardo Borensztein, Ratna Sahay and Jeromin Zettelmeyer (1999). They find that structural reforms—including privatization—are critically important in promoting rapid recovery from the initial economic decline. Taken as a whole, their results strongly support a "radical" approach to reforms.

TABLE 6

SUMMARY OF EMPIRICAL STUDIES OF PRIVATIZATION IN TRANSITION ECONOMIES: CENTRAL AND EASTERN EUROPE

Study	Sample description, study period, and methodology	Summary of empirical findings and conclusions
Claessens, Djankov, and Pohl 1997	Examines determinants of performance improvements for 706 Czech firms privatized during 1992–95. Using Tobins-Q, tests whether concentrated ownership structure or outside monitor (bank or investment fund) improves Q more than dispersed ownership.	Privatized firms do prosper, primarily because of resulting concentrated ownership structure. The more concentrated the post-privatization ownership structure the higher the firm's profitability and market valuation. Large stakes owned by bank-sponsored funds and strategic investors are particularly value-enhancing.
Pohl, Anderson, Claessens, and Djankov 1997	Compares extent of restructuring of over 6,300 private and state-owned firms in 7 east European countries during 1992–95. Uses 6 measures to examine which strategies improve performance the most.	Privatization dramatically increases restructuring likelihood and success. Firms privatized for 4 years will increase productivity 3–5 times more than similar SOEs. Little difference in performance based on method of privatization, but ownership and financing effects impact restructuring.
Smith, Cin and Vodopivec 1997	Using a sample with 22,735 firm-years of data drawn from period of "spontaneous privatization" in Slovenia (1989–92), examines impact of foreign and employee ownership on firms.	Percentage point increase in foreign ownership is associated with a 3.9% increase in value added, and for employee ownership with a 1.4% increase. Firms with higher revenues, profits, and exports are more likely to exhibit foreign and employee ownership.
Dyck 1997	Develops and tests an adverse selection model to explain Treuhand's role in restructuring and privatizing east Germany's SOEs. In less than 5 years, Treuhand privatized more than 13,800 firms and parts of firms and, uniquely, had resources to pay for restructuring itself—but almost never chose to do so. Instead, it emphasized speed and sales to existing western firms over giveaways and sales to capital funds. Paper rationalizes Treuhand's approach.	Privatized east German firms were more likely to put western (usually German) managers in key positions than were companies that remained state-owned. Treuhand emphasized sales open to all buyers rather than favoring east Germans. Principal message: privatization programs must carefully consider when and how to affect managerial replacement in firms. Plans open to western buyers and which allow management change are most likely to improve firm performance.
Frydman, Gray, Hessel and Rapaczynski 1999	Compares performance of privatized and state-owned firms in central European transition economies, and asks "when does privatization work?" Examines influence of ownership structure on performance using a sample of 90 state-owned and 128 privatized companies in Czech Republic, Hungary, and Poland. Employs panel data regression methods to isolate ownership effects.	Privatization "works," but only when firm is controlled by outside owners (other than managers or employees). Privatization adds over 18 percentage points to annual growth rate of firm sold to domestic financial firm, and 12 percentage points when sold to a foreign buyer. Privatization to an outside owner also adds about 9 percentage points to productivity growth. Gain does not come at expense of higher unemployment; insider controlled firms are less likely to restructure, but outsider-controlled firms grow faster. Shows the importance of entrepreneurship in reviving sales growth.
Weiss and Nikitin 1998	Analyzes effects of ownership by investment funds on performance of 125 privatized Czech firms during 1993–95. Assesses these effects by measuring relationship between changes in performance and in composition of ownership at the start of privatization. Uses robust estimation techniques, in addition to OLS, since data strongly reject normality.	Ownership concentration and composition jointly affect performance of privatized firms. Concentration in the hands of a large shareholder, other than an investment fund or company, is associated with significant improvements for all measures of performance. Concentrated ownership by funds did not improve performance. Preliminary post-1996 data suggests changes in investment fund legislation may improve their performance.
Claessens and Djankov 1999a	Studies effect of management turnover on changes in financial and operating performance of 706 privatized Czech firms over the period 1993–97. Examines changes in profitability and labor productivity.	Finds that the appointment of new managers is associated with significant improvements in profit margins and labor productivity, particularly if the managers are selected by private owners. New managers appointed by the National Property Fund also improve performance, though not by as much.

TABLE 6 *(Cont.)*

Study	Sample description, study period, and methodology	Summary of empirical findings and conclusions
Claessens and Djankov 1999b	Examines the relationship between ownership concentration and corporate performance for 706 privatized Czech firms during the period 1992–97. Use profitability and labor productivity as indicators of corporate performance.	Finds that concentrated ownership is associated with higher profitability and labor productivity. Also finds that foreign strategic owners and non-bank-sponsored investment funds improve performance more than bank-sponsored funds.
Frydman, Gray, Hessel and Rapaczynski 2000	Examines whether the imposition of hard budget constraints is alone sufficient to improve corporate performance in the Czech Republic, Hungary, and Poland. Employs a sample of 216 firms, split between state-owned (31%), privatized (43%), and private (26%) firms.	Finds privatization alone added nearly 10 percentage points to the revenue growth of a firm sold to outside owners. Most importantly, finds that the threat of hard budget constraints for poorly performing SOEs falters, since governments are unwilling to allow these firms to fail. The brunt of SOEs' lower creditworthiness falls on state creditors.
Frydman, Hessel and Rapaczynski 2000	Examines whether privatized central European firms controlled by outside investors are more entrepreneurial—in terms of ability to increase revenues—than firms controlled by insiders or the state. Study employs survey data from a sample of 506 manufacturing firms in the Czech Republic, Hungary, and Poland.	Documents that all state and privatized firms engage in similar types of restructuring, but that product restructuring by firms owned by outside investors is significantly more effiective, in terms of revenue generation, than by firms with other types of ownership. Concludes the more entrepreneurial behavior of outsider-owned firms is due to incentive effects, rather than human capital effects, of privatization—specifically greater readiness to take risks.
Harper 2000	Examines the effects of privatization on the financial and operating performance of 174 firms privatized in the first—and 380 firms divested in the second—wave of the Czech Republic's voucher privatizations of 1992 and 1994. Compares results for privatized firms to those which remain state-owned. Employs Megginson, Nash and van Randenborgh methodology and variables to measure changes.	Finds that the first wave of privatization yielded disappointing results. Real sales, profitability, efficiency and employment all declined dramatically (and significantly). However, second wave firms experienced significant increases in efficiency and profitability and the decline in employment—though still significant—was much less drastic than after first wave (−17% vs −41%).
Lizal, Singer, and Svejnar 2000	Examines the performance effects of the wave of break-ups of Czechoslovak SOEs on the subsequent performance of the master firm and the spin-offs. The regressions use data for 373 firms in 1991 and 262 firms in 1992.	There was an immediate (in 1991) positive effect on the efficiency and profitability of small and medium size firms (both master and spin-offs) and negative for the larger firms. The results for 1992 are similar but not statistically significant.

regarding the impact of privatization on the performance of divested central and eastern European firms. This is especially true of the five studies—Dyck (1997), Weiss and Nikitin (1998), Claessens and Djankov (1999b), Lubomir Lizal, Miroslav Singer, Jan Svejnar (2000), and Frydman, Hessel, and Rapaczynski (2000)—we consider the most persuasive due to sample size, period of coverage and/or methodological rigor. All but one (Joel Harper 2000) of the studies detailed in table 6 explicitly test whether the type of ownership structure that emerges from the process is

related to post-privatization performance, and these studies document consistent and significant relationships. Other things equal:

i) Private ownership is associated with better firm-level performance than is continued state ownership. Concentrated private ownership is associated with greater improvement than is diffuse ownership.

ii) Foreign ownership, where allowed, is associated with greater post-privatization performance improvement than is purely domestic ownership.[32] Majority ownership by outside (non-employee) investors is associated with significantly greater improvement than is any form of insider control.

iii) Firm-level restructuring is associated with significant (sometimes dramatic) post-privatization performance improvements, and this is a key advantage of outsider control—firms controlled by non-employee investors are much more likely to restructure.

iv) Most studies document that performance improves more when new managers are brought in to run a firm after it is privatized than when the original managers are retained. The precise reason for this is unclear, though FGHR (2000) find that the more entrepreneurial behavior of outsider-owned firms is due to incentive rather than human capital effects.

v) The role of investment funds in promoting efficiency improvements in privatized Czech firms is ambiguous. FGHR (1999) find selling an SOE to a domestic financial company significantly increases the growth rate of the enterprise, while Weiss and Nikitin (1998) find that concentrated ownership by investment funds is not associated with improvement. Claessens and Djankov (1999b) document greater improvement for companies controlled by non-bank-sponsored investment funds than by bank-sponsored funds.

vi) There is evidence that while performance improves especially for smaller firms, the performance improvement declines over time. Lizal, Singer, and Svejnar (2000) find that for Czech firms there is an improvement in performance among SOE firms that are broken up, which declines over time—perhaps due to increased competition or managers siphoning off profits.

vii) The impact of privatization on employment is also ambiguous, primarily because employment falls for virtually all firms in transition economies after reforms are initiated. Harper (2000) documents employment declines following the first Czech mass privatization wave in 1992, but not after the second wave in 1994. FGHR (1999) is the only study that explicitly examined employment changes—after accounting for ownership structure changes—and found that sales grow fast enough in outsider-controlled firms to offset the significant increase in labor productivity.

viii) There is little evidence that governments have been able to impose hard budget constraints on firms that remain state-owned after reforms begin. FGHR (2000) find that the threat of hard budget constraints falters for poorly performing SOEs, since governments are unwilling to allow these firms to fail. However, both FGHR and Mark Schaffer (1998) show that the burden of lower SOE creditworthiness falls on the state (as deferred taxes) or on state creditors, rather than on private creditors or suppliers.

5.2.2 *Privatization in the Former Soviet Union*

Table 7 summarizes the results of six empirical studies that examine

---

[32] In his analysis of the reasons why Hungary's privatization program has proven to be so much more successful than those in most other central and eastern European countries, Peter Mihályi (2000) emphasizes the importance of selling SOEs directly to western transnational companies, and thus plugging them into the global trading system. Other countries stressed domestic over foreign ownership, and thus missed out on the opportunity of using privatization as a way of attracting foreign direct investment.

TABLE 7
SUMMARY OF EMPIRICAL STUDIES OF PRIVATIZATION IN TRANSITION ECONOMIES:
RUSSIA AND FORMER SOVIET REPUBLICS

Study	Sample description, study period, and methodology	Summary of empirical findings and conclusions
Barberis, Boycko, Shleifer, and Tsukanova 1996	Surveys 452 Russian shops sold in early 1990s to measure importance of alternative channels through which privatization promotes restructuring.	Documents that new owners and managers raise likelihood of value-increasing restructuring. Finds equity incentives do not improve performance; instead points to importance of new human capital in economic transformation.
Earle 1998	Investigates impact of ownership structure on (labor) productivity of Russian industrial firms. Using 1994 survey data, examines differential impact of insider, outsider, or state ownership on performance of 430 firms, of which 86 remained 100% state-owned, 299 were partially privatized, and 45 were newly created. Adjusts empirical methods to account for tendency of insiders to claim dominant ownership in the best firms being divested.	OLS regressions show positive impact of private (relative to state) share ownership on labor productivity, primarily due to managerial ownership. After adjusting for selection bias, finds that only outsider ownership is significantly associated with productivity improvements. Stresses that leaving insiders in control of firms, while politically expedient, has negative long-term implications for restructuring of Russian industry.
Earle and Estrin 1998	Using a sample similar to that used by Earle (1998), examines whether privatization, competition and hardening budget constraints enhance efficiency in Russia.	Finds a 10 percentage-point increase in private share ownership raises real sales per employee by 3–5%. Subsidies (soft budget constraints) reduce pace of restructuring in SOEs, but the effect is small and often insignificant.
Djankov 1999a	Investigates relation between ownership structure and enterprise restructuring for 960 firms privatized in 6 newly independent states between 1995–97. Employs survey data collected by World Bank in late 1997 from Georgia, Kazakhstan, Kyrgyz Republic, Moldova, Russia, and Ukraine.	Shows that foreign ownership is positively associated with enterprise restructuring at high ownership levels (>30%), while managerial ownership is positively related to restructuring at low (<10%) or high levels, but negative at intermediate levels. Employee ownership is beneficial to labor productivity at low ownership levels, but is otherwise insignificant.
Djankov 1999b	Using same survey data as Djankov (1999a), studies effects of different privatization modalities on restructuring process in Georgia (92 firms) and Moldova (149 firms). Georgia employed voucher privatization, while the majority of Moldovan firms were acquired by investment funds—and numerous others were sold to managers for cash.	Privatization through management buy-outs is positively associated with enterprise restructuring, while voucher privatized firms do not restructure more rapidly than state-owned firms. Implies that managers who gain ownership for free may have less incentive to restructure, as their income is not solely based on success of the enterprise.
Black, Kraakman, and Tarassova 2000	Surveys the history of privatization in Russia. While mostly descriptive, several case studies are analyzed.	Authors conclude that Russian privatization has created a "kleptocracy" and has essentially failed. Stresses importance of minimizing incentives for self-dealing in design of privatization programs.

privatization programs in Russia and the other republics of the former Soviet Union. It is very difficult to reach a simple conclusion regarding privatization's impact in the former Soviet Union in general, and Russia in particular, for four principal reasons. First, the transition from socialism to capitalism was much more difficult and painful in the former Soviet Union republics than anywhere else in the world, both be-

cause these republics were under communist rule the longest and because the transition to capitalism also coincided with dissolution of the Soviet Union. Breaking up any continental-scale nation would likely prove traumatic; breaking up a country that was also an economic system proved doubly so. Second, the contraction in output that occurred in the former Soviet Union after 1991 was far greater than anywhere else—and there is as yet no upturn—making it very difficult to document any kind of relative performance improvement, or to assign causality to any improvement that is found. Third, it seems clear that the former Soviet Union republics—especially Russia—took a decided turn for the worse economically after 1997, so competently executed studies examining privatization's impact in the same country, but at different times, might well reach radically different conclusions. Finally, all five studies that examine Russia's experience rely either on survey data or anecdotal evidence, so the "raw material" for empirical analysis is of much poorer quality here than in other regions. For these reasons, we believe that no truly persuasive empirical study of privatization in the former Soviet Union has yet been performed, nor is one likely until these economies stabilize and several years of reliable accounting (not survey) data become available.

In spite of the difficulties (and caveats) spelled out above, the studies summarized in table 7 do yield consistent conclusions. Certainly the most important result all these studies find is that insider privatization has been a failure throughout the former Soviet Union, especially in Russia, and that the concentrated managerial ownership structure that characterizes almost all privatized firms will likely hamper these economies for many years. As described in Bornstein (1994), John Earle (1998), Earle and Saul Estrin (1998), and Bernard Black, Reinier Kraakman, and Anna Tarassova (2000), Russian reformers considered rapid privatization to be an imperative, and for this reason they opted for the politically expedient technique of favoring incumbent managers and employees with allocations of controlling shareholdings during the initial mass privatization waves of 1992–93.

The investment funds created during this program proved ineffective, due primarily to insider control and poor legal protection of (outside) shareholder voting rights. In spite of this, Nicholas Barberis, Boycko, Shleifer, and Natalia Tsukanova (1996), Earle (1998), and Earle and Estrin (1998) document that privatization was associated with performance improvements in firms that were divested during the mass privatization program of the early 1990s. However, all three studies, as well as Djankov (1999a,b), find that post-privatization performance improves the most (or only) for firms that are outsider controlled, and all the studies stress the importance of bringing in new management. Additionally, Djankov (1999a) finds that foreign share ownership is associated with significantly greater performance improvement than is purely domestic ownership, and Djankov (1999b) shows that managers who actually pay for divested firms (through management buy-outs) improve performance more than do managers who are effectively given control (through voucher schemes).

Russia provides an example of what can go wrong with privatizations in the 1995 "loans for shares" scheme, which transferred control of twelve natural resource firms to a small group of "oligarchs" at very low prices. Black et al. (2000) argue this was a corrupt and nontransparent transfer of assets that precipitated widespread insider expropriation. Further, it contributed to the political unpopularity of privatization in Russia. It provides a cautionary note that privatization is not an economic panacea.[33]

[33] The Czech Republic's market collapse of 1997, described in Jack Coffee (1999), and the Lithuanian government's tortuous privatization of the Mazheikiu Nafta refinery in early 2000, described by Val Samonis (2000), are also examples of what can go wrong in privatization programs.

Black et al. also argue that a poorly designed privatization program is worse than none at all. However, Nellis (1999) and other commentators point out that many of Russia's problems resulted from a collapse of central governmental authority and would thus not likely be solved by renationalization. Perhaps the best long-term hope for economic revitalization in the former Soviet Union republics is the type of *de novo* private development described in Havrylyshyn and McGettigan (2000).

5.2.3 *Summary of Evidence*

Review articles by Djankov and Murrell (2000a,b) and a macroeconomic study by Jeffrey Sachs, Clifford Zinnes, and Yair Eilat (2000) examine the effects of privatization in transition economies. Djankov and Murrell review the empirical results of studies of privatization in transition economies and attempt to synthesize the results across the studies. They conclude that the evidence shows that: in most countries, privately owned firms perform better than state-owned firms, usually significantly better statistically; there is little evidence privatization has hurt firm performance even in Russia and other Commonwealth of Independent States (CIS) countries; much better outcomes occur when the new owners are concentrated; and privatization has had a larger positive impact in non-CIS countries, eastern and central Europe, and the Baltic states than in the CIS countries. They interpret the last result to be caused by institutional factors, including the choice of privatization method. They suggest the best empirical proxy for how well the institutions performed was the length of time the country had spent under communism—the shorter the time the better the performance of the institutions.

Empirically, at a macro level, Sachs,

Zinnes, and Eilat (2000) examine the relationship between privatization, institutional reforms, and overall economic performance (measured by change in GDP from before transition, foreign direct investment, and exports) in transition economies. They find that change in ownership is not enough to improve macroeconomic performance. The gains from privatization come from change in ownership combined with other reforms such as institutions to address incentive and contracting issues, hardened budget constraints, removal of barriers to entry, and an effective legal and regulatory framework. While this is a macroeconomic study, the changes they report must come from the operations of individual firms.

Our reading of the evidence from transition economies is very similar. Privatization improves performance but various factors impact the success of the privatization. Most important is that allowing incumbent managers to gain control of privatized firms, through whatever means, will yield disappointing results. Whenever possible, firms should be privatized, for cash, in as transparent a method as possible, and through an auction or sale process that is open to the broadest possible cross-section of potential buyers (including foreigners). Finally, institutional factors matter, and we discuss their implications in a later section.

5.2.4 *Economic Reform in China*

China, one of the most important transition economies, has been vigorously pursuing economic reform since 1978. It has dramatically increased the total factor productivity (Li 1997) of Chinese SOEs, largely by improving incentives (Groves, Hong, McMillan, and Naughton 1994, 1995) and decentralizing economic decision making (Yuanzheng Cao, Yingyi Qian, and Barry

Weingast 1999; Lawrence Lau, Qian, and Gerard Roland 2000). Lau, Qian, and Roland (2000) show theoretically and empirically that the Chinese have successfully followed a dual-track approach to market liberalization, as a method of implementing an efficient Pareto-improving reform. The idea was to continually enforce the existing plan, while liberalizing the market to make implicit transfers to compensate losers under reform.

The Chinese Communist Party recently committed the country to a massive privatization program (Lin 2000) under the slogan "seize the large, release the small," which roughly translates as privatizing all but the largest 300 or so SOEs. Assuming this plan is even partially implemented, the result will be a privatization program of unprecedented scale. Furthermore, the World Trade Organization accord negotiated between China and the United States in November 1999 (and subsequently with the European Union in early 2000) may ultimately lead to China's accession to the WTO. If this occurs, broad swathes of heretofore protected Chinese industry—including telecommunications, automobile production, and financial services—will be opened to international competition for the first time. This process will almost certainly increase the pressure on China to fully privatize its industry.

On the other hand, there are reasons to believe that China's "privatization" program will do little to lessen the state's role in economic decision making, either at the macro- or micro-economic levels. For one thing, the ownership structure of Chinese stock companies is unique. As described by Xiaonian Xu and Yang Wang (1997), Tian (2000), and Lin (2000), only one-third of the stock in China's publicly listed former SOEs can be owned by in-

dividuals; the remaining two-thirds of a company's shares must be owned by the state and by domestic (usually financial) institutions—which are invariably state-owned. So-called "A-shares" may be owned and traded only by Chinese citizens, while B-shares are stocks listed in Shanghai or Shenzhen that may be owned and traded only by foreigners. Other shares are listed in Hong Kong (H-shares) or New York (N-shares), and these are also restricted to foreigners. The net effect of this fractionalization of ownership is that, even in publicly listed former SOEs, control is never really contestable, and the long-term financial performance of "privatized" Chinese companies has been quite poor. This is particularly true for the "Red Chip" (PRC-controlled companies incorporated and listed in Hong Kong) and H-shares sold in Hong Kong.[34]

These ownership restrictions could, however, be rescinded by government fiat at any time. Perhaps the key constraint on privatization in China is the fact that SOEs, rather than the government itself, serve as the country's social safety net. As described in Bai, Li, and Wang (1997) and Lin, Cai, and Li (1998), Chinese SOEs are burdened with many social welfare responsibilities. Thus it is difficult to imagine the government adopting a privatization program that would either grant these firms discretion over staffing levels or subject them to truly enterprise-threatening competition. In sum, the long-term prognosis for privatization in China is unclear; there is great scope for such a program to have a dramatic impact, coupled with great danger of social turmoil if handled (or sequenced) incorrectly.

[34] We thank Cyril Lin, Samuel Huang, and George Tian for helping us understand Chinese listing procedures. See *http://www.csrc.gov.cn/ CSRCsite/eng/elaws/elaws.htm* for an English-language summary of Chinese securities laws.

366   *Journal of Economic Literature, Vol. XXXIX (June 2001)*

We now shift our emphasis from transition economies to examining whether investors who participate in share issue privatizations have, on average, benefited from these investments—both initially (first day) and longer term (up to five years).

6. *Do Investors Benefit from Privatization?*

6.1 *Initial Returns from SIPs*

As noted earlier, governments generally rely on share offerings as the best method of privatizing large state-owned enterprises, and they routinely adopt highly politicized offer terms in order to achieve political objectives. Offering terms that differ fundamentally from those observed in private-sector offerings, plus the very large average size of privatization issues, have motivated many researchers to examine the initial and long-term returns earned by SIP investors. Table 8 summarizes the results of ten studies examining initial returns. Most of these studies evaluate whether investors who purchase privatization initial public offerings (PIPOs) at the offering price, and then sell these shares on the first day of open market trading, earn returns that are significantly different from zero. These studies test whether PIPOs are "underpriced." A few also test whether PIPOs yield initial returns that are materially different from the significantly positive first-day returns earned by investors in private-sector IPOs, as documented in a vast number of articles using both U.S. and international data. The U.S. market experience is summarized in Roger Ibbotson, Jody Sindelar, and Jay Ritter (1994), and international IPO underpricing studies are surveyed in Tim Loughran, Ritter, and Kristian Rydqvist (1994).

Five of the studies in table 8 examine PIPO returns from individual countries. All five studies document significant, often massive, average levels of underpricing, ranging from 39.6 percent for the forty British PIPOs studied by Menyah and Paudyal (1996) to *940 percent* for the 308 Chinese PIPOs Class A issues (domestic issuance) examined by Dongwei Su and Belton Fleisher (1999). Menyah and Paudyal, and Paudyal, B. Saadouni, and R. Briston (1998) find that U.K. and Malaysian PIPOs are significantly more underpriced than their private-sector counterparts, and Wolfgang Ausenegg (2000) finds the same result for Polish PIPOs. Hungarian PIPOs are also more underpriced than private IPOs, but the difference is not significant (Ranko Jelic and Richard Briston 2000b). Since there are as yet few truly comparable private-sector IPOs in China, Su and Fleisher cannot test whether private offerings also have the incredible underpricing they document for PIPOs. They do find that Class B shares, issued internationally, are much less underpriced (37 percent mean initial return). Unlike almost any comparable group of IPOs, over 90 percent of Chinese PIPOs do in fact execute seasoned equity offerings within a short time after the PIPO. Further, the probability of a seasoned offer occurring is positively related to the level of the initial offer underpricing, which is consistent with various signalling models, including Ivo Welch (1989).

The other five studies in table 8 examine multinational samples of PIPOs, generally using offering data from *Privatisation International* and stock returns from *Datastream*. The number of countries studied ranges from eight in Dewenter and Malatesta (1997) to 61 in Alexander Ljungqvist, Tim Jenkinson, and William Wilhelm (2000), though the studies' main results are similar. All these studies document economically

TABLE 8

SUMMARY OF EMPIRICAL STUDIES EXAMINING INITIAL RETURNS TO INVESTORS IN SHARE ISSUE PRIVATIZATION

(Return earned by investors who buy shares in SIPs at the offer price and sell the shares immediately after trading begins.)

Study	Sample description, study period, and methodology	Summary of empirical findings and conclusions
Menyah and Paudyal 1996	Examines initial and long-term returns for 40 UK privatization IPOs (PIPOs) and 75 private-sector IPOs on London Stock Exchange between 1981–91.	PIPOs offer a market-adjusted initial return of 39.6%, compared to private sector IPO initial return of 3.5%. Regression analysis explains up to 64% of variation in PIPO initial returns.
Dewenter and Malatesta 1997	Tests whether privatization IPOs (PIPOs) are more or less underpriced than private sector IPOs in 8 countries. Compares actual initial returns for 109 companies from Canada, France, Hungary, Japan, Malaysia, Poland, Thailand and UK with national average initial returns reported in Loughran, Ritter, and Rydqvist 1994.	Mixed results. Initial returns to privatization issues are higher than to private sector IPOs in unregulated industries and in UK. Privatization IPOs are lower than private offers in Canada and Malaysia; but there is no systematic tendency to underprice PIPOs on the part of all governments.
Huang and Levich 1998	Studies offering terms and initial returns to investors in 507 privatization share offerings from 39 countries during 1979–96; tests alternative explanations for observed underpricing.	Average initial returns of 32.2% for PIPOs and 7.17% for seasoned privatization offerings. SIPs from non-OECD countries are more underpriced than OECD offers, but there is no evidence PIPOs are underpriced more than private IPOs.
Paudyal, Saadouni, and Briston 1998	Examines initial and long-term returns offered to investors in 18 PIPOs and 77 private sector IPOs in Malaysia from 1984–95. Provides details of offering terms and share allocation patterns.	Malaysia PIPOs offer market-adjusted initial returns of 103.5% (median 79.9%), significantly greater than the private sector IPO initial returns of 52.5% (29.4%).
Jones, Megginson, Nash, and Netter 1999	Examines how political and economic factors influence initial returns, and share and control allocation patterns, for a sample of 630 SIPs from 59 countries during 1977–97.	Governments deliberately underprice both PIPOs (mean 34.1%, median 12.4%) and seasoned SIPs (9.4% and 3.3%). Share and control allocation patterns are best explained by political factors. Support predictions of Biais and Perotti (2000) theoretical model.
Su and Fleisher 1999	Studies cross-sectional pattern of underpricing of 308 Chinese PIPOs from 1987–95. Tests whether observed underpricing for domestic shares can be explained using a signalling model.	Massive underpricing, with average initial return of 940% on A shares (issued domestically). Findings consistent with a signalling model, since 91% of all firms subsequently execute seasoned equity offerings. Less underpricing for B shares (international).
Jelic and Briston 2000b	Examines initial and long-term returns for 25 PIPOs and 24 other IPOs in Hungary during 1990–98.	PIPOs are much larger and have higher market-adjusted initial returns than other IPOs (44% mean and 9% median vs 40% and 5%, respectively), but return differences are insignificant.
Jelic and Briston 2000a	Examines initial and long-term returns for 55 PIPOs and 110 other IPOs in Poland during 1990–98.	Using first-day opening prices (not offer prices), finds small, significant positive mean abnormal initial returns (1.16%) for PIPOs and insignificant mean abnormal initial returns (0.22%) for other IPOs. The difference is insignificant.
Ausenegg 2000	Examines initial and long-term returns for 52 PIPOs and 107 other IPOs in Poland during 1990–98.	Significantly positive initial abnormal return for PIPOs (60.4% mean, 19.8% median) and other IPOs (19.8% and 12.9%), though difference is insignificant. Without Bank Slaski, mean PIPO initial return cut roughly in half.
Choi and Nam 2000	Compares initial returns of 185 PIPOs from 30 countries during 1981–97 to those of private sector IPOs from same countries, using mean national initial returns reported in Loughran, Ritter, and Rydqvist 1994.	PIPOs tend to be more underpriced than private sector IPOs (mean 31% vs 24.6%), and underpricing for PIPOs is positively related to the stake sold and to degree of uncertainty in ex-ante value of newly privatized firms.
Ljungqvist, Jenkinson, and Wilhelm 2000	Analyzes direct and indirect costs (associated with underpricing) of 2,051 IPOs, including 185 PIPOs, in 61 non-US markets during 1992–99. Primarily a private-sector, underwriting study.	PIPOs are significantly more underpriced (by about 9 percentage points) than are private-sector IPOs, and underwriter spreads are a significant 61 basis points lower.

and statistically significant underpricing of PIPOs, averaging about 30 percent in the large-sample studies. The two that examine seasoned SIPs (Huang and Levich 1998; and Jones, Megginson, Nash, and Netter 1999) find these are significantly underpriced as well, though much less so than are PIPOs. Four of these studies—Dewenter and Malatesta (1997), Huang and Levich (1998), Seung-Doo Choi and Sang-Koo Nam (2000), and Ljungqvist et al. (2000)—also test whether PIPOs are significantly more underpriced than private-sector IPOs. The first three studies find no systematic evidence that PIPOs are significantly more or less underpriced than private IPOs; instead all three suggest that results vary by country. However, the Ljungqvist et al. study performs the most convincing analysis of the relative underpricing of IPOs and PIPOs, since they use regression methodology and a privatization dummy variable to examine underpricing for a sample of 2,051 IPOs—including 185 PIPOs—from 61 non-U.S. markets. They document that PIPOs are significantly more underpriced (by about 9 percentage points) than are private sector IPOs. They also find that the underwriting spreads on PIPOs are significantly lower (by a mean 61 basis points) than on IPOs.

The principal objective of the Jones et al. (1999) study differs from the others in that it tests whether government issuers are attempting to maximize SIP offering proceeds or are instead trying to achieve multiple political and economic objectives, even at the cost of revenue maximization. Jones et al. (1999) test the underpricing models of Perotti (1995) and Biais and Perotti (2000). Both models predict that governments that are ideologically committed to privatization and economic reform will deliberately underprice SIPs

and will privatize in stages, to signal their commitment to protecting investor property rights. "Populist" governments pursuing privatization strictly as a means of raising revenue will be unwilling to underprice as much as will committed governments. Populist governments will also try to sell larger stakes in SOEs. Jones et al. (1999) find that initial returns (underpricing) are significantly positively related to the fraction of the firm's capital sold and to the degree of income inequality (Gini coefficient) in a country. They also find that initial returns are negatively related to the level of government spending as a fraction of GDP (a proxy for how socialist a society is) and to a dummy variable indicating that more than 50 percent of a company's stock is being sold. Collectively, these findings strongly support the predictions of Perotti (1995) and Biais and Perotti (2000).

6.2 *Long-Run Returns from SIPs*

Since the seminal article by Jay Ritter (1991), financial economists have paid close attention to estimating the long-run returns earned by investors who purchase unseasoned and seasoned issues. Most of these papers find significantly negative long-term returns, whether they examine U.S. offerings or international stock issues, though a few studies document insignificantly positive long-term performance.[35]

There is a major debate in the empirical finance literature on methodological issues in estimating long-run

---

[35] Early long-run return studies, using both U.S. and international data, are summarized in Loughran, Ritter, and Rydqvist (1994). Later studies employing U.S. data and finding negative long-run returns include Tim Loughran and Ritter (1995, 1997), Katherine Spiess and John Affleck-Graves (1995), and Richard Carter, Frederick Dark, and Ajai Singh (1998). Only a few U.S. studies, including Alon Brav and Paul Gompers (1997), find (insignificantly) positive long-term returns.

returns. This is not surprising, since findings of significant negative (or positive) long-run returns can be interpreted as evidence contradicting the efficient market hypothesis, a fundamental concept in finance. The debate centers on how to calculate long-run returns and how to construct test statistics. For example, Mark Mitchell and Erik Stafford (2000) argue that most corporate actions are not random events. They contend that after controlling for cross-correlation of abnormal returns, most statistical evidence of abnormal performance disappears. John Lyon, Brad Barber, and Chih-Ling Tsai (1999), drawing on the work of S. P. Kothari and Jerold Warner (1997) and Barber and Lyon (1997), note five reasons for misspecification in test statistics designed to detect long-run returns. There are three sources of bias—a new listing bias, a rebalancing bias, and a skewness bias—as well as cross-sectional dependence in sample observations and a poorly specified asset-pricing model. Lyon, Barber, and Tsai, among others, suggest several methods to control for misspecification, but there is no one correct method. They conclude that the "analysis of long-run returns is treacherous." Linda Canina, Roni Michaely, Richard Thaler, and Kent Womack (1998) present another approach to dealing with long-run returns, and Fama (1998) argues bad model problems are "unavoidable . . . and more serious in tests on long-term returns." Two other papers that do an excellent job of analyzing the problems with estimating long-run returns are Alon Brav, Christopher Geczy, and Paul Gompers (2000), and B. Espen Eckbo, Ronald Masulis, and Øyvind Norli (2000).

Since the methodological problems identified with estimates of long-run returns have not been resolved for U.S.

firms, they have not been resolved for privatizations that are subject to the additional problems of scarce data and the lack of liquid markets. Nevertheless, the fact that most of the studies of long-run returns following privatizations—using different methodologies and focusing on different countries—find similar results lessens some of the methodological concerns.

We discuss fifteen studies that examine the returns earned by investors who buy and hold privatization share issues, and the number of such studies appears to be growing rapidly. The papers are summarized in table 9. Eight of these focus on either a single country or a single market for issues, and the other seven examine multinational samples. Mario Levis (1993) and Menyah, Paudyal, and Inganyete (1995) examine the British experience, and both document significantly positive long-run abnormal returns for SIP investors. However, Reena Aggarwal, Ricardo Leal, and Leonardo Hernandez (1993) find the opposite result for their sample of nine Chilean SIPs. Ranko Jelic and Richard Briston (2000b) find that 25 Hungarian PIPOs yield large but insignificantly positive long-run returns (peaking at 21.3 percent in month 15), though they do find that these cumulative returns are significantly higher than the highly negative returns (reaching –70 percent by month 30) earned on 24 private-sector IPOs. Jelic and Briston (2000a) document significantly positive one-, three-, and five-year excess returns for Polish PIPOs, but Ausenegg (2000) finds insignificant long-term returns for essentially the same sample. Given the differing estimation methodologies employed in these two studies, it is not clear whether Polish PIPOs earn significantly higher long-run returns than IPOs. Stephen Foerster and G. Andrew Karolyi (2000) find insignificant long-run

TABLE 9
EMPIRICAL STUDIES OF LONG-RUN RETURNS TO INVESTORS IN SHARE ISSUE PRIVATIZATIONS
1–5 year returns earned by investors who buy and hold offerings. Unless otherwise noted, long-run return
excludes first-day return to issue date.

Study	Sample description, study period, and methodology	Summary of empirical findings and conclusions
Levis 1993	Examines long-run return to 806 British IPOs from 1980–88. Sample includes 12 PIPOs, accounting for 76% of total IPO value.	Private sector IPOs underperformed the market by +10% over 3 years, PIPOs outperformed the market by +15%.
Aggarwal, Leal and Hernandez 1993	Examines long-run (1-year) returns for Latin American IPOs, including 9 Chilean PIPOs from 1982–90.	Using returns from offer price, finds significant negative 1-year market-adjusted returns for PIPOs averaging –29.9% (median –32.4%) vs –9.8% (–23.0%) for private sector IPOs.
Menyah, Paudyal and Inganyete 1995	Examines initial and long-term returns for 40 British PIPOs and 75 private sector IPOs executed on London Stock Exchange 1981–91.	Significant positive 33% market-adjusted 400-day (80-week) return for PIPO vs insignificant 3.5% return for private sector IPOs.
Davidson 1998	Studies 1, 3, 5, and 10-year market adjusted returns for SIPs from 5 European countries (Austria, France, Italy, Spain, UK) through March 1997.	After long period of underperformance, averaging 1–1.5% per year, finds SIPs outperformed European market averages in previous 12 months.
Foerster and Karolyi 2000	Examines long-run return for 333 non-US firms that list stock on US markets in the form of ADRs in 1982–96. Compares returns for 77 SIPs (38 IPOs, 39 seasoned offers) with private offers.	Insignificantly positive 4.1% 3-year abnormal returns for SIPs vs insignificantly negative returns of –1.7% for full sample.
Paudyal, Saadouni, and Briston 1998	Examines initial and long-term returns offered to investors in 18 PIPOs and 77 private sector IPOs in Malaysia 1984–95. Provides details of offering terms and share allocation patterns.	PIPOs and private sector IPOs yield normal returns (insignificantly different from overall market) over 1, 3, and 5-year holding periods.
Boubakri and Cosset 2000	Evaluates long-term returns to investors in 120 SIPs from 26 developing countries during 1982–95.	Significant 3-year raw returns (112% mean, 30% median), but insignificant mean (37–46%) and median (–7% to 13%) market-adjusted returns, due to weighting of SIPs in stock market indices. Significant positive long-run returns after adjusting for impact of SIP size on index.
Jelic and Briston 2000	Examines initial and long-term returns for 25 PIPOs and 24 other IPOs in Hungary during 1990–98.	PIPOs yield insignificantly positive market-adjusted returns over 1, 2, and 3-year holding periods, peaking at 21.3% in month 15; private-sector IPOs yield significantly negative returns.
Jelic and Briston 2000b	Examines initial and long-term returns for 55 PIPOs and 110 other IPOs in Poland during 1990–98.	PIPO investors earn positive 1, 3, and 5-year market-adjusted returns; other IPO investors earn negative returns. Significant differences for most holding periods.
Ausenegg 1000	Examines initial and long-term returns for 52 PIPOs and 107 other IPOs in Poland during 1990–99.	PIPO and private-sector IPO investors earn negative—often significant—abnormal returns over 1, 3, and 5-year holding periods.
Perotti and Oijen 2000	Develops a theoretical model suggesting that long-run returns to investors in developing-country SIPs will earn excess returns if/when political risk is resolved. Tests the model using data from 22 countries with active privatization programs during 1988–95.	Their proxy for political risk declines by an annual average of 3.6% during the course of a privatization program, and stock markets develop rapidly. Decline in risk leads to positive excess returns for SIPs of about 6% per year.
Choi, Nam, and Ryu 2000	Computes buy-and-hold returns of 204 PIPOs from 37 countries in 1977–97.	Significantly positive market-adjusted returns to SIPs over 1, 3, and 5-year holding periods.
Megginson, Nash, Netter, and Schwartz 2000	Examines long-run (1, 3, and 5-yr.) returns for 158 PIPOs from 33 countries from 1981–97. Computes local-currency and $ returns vs national and international indices, and vs matching firms.	Economically and statistically positive holding-period returns in both local currency and $, and vs all market indices. 5-year excess returns exceeding 80% are found for most comparisons.

TABLE 9 (Cont.)

Study	Sample description, study period, and methodology	Summary of empirical findings and conclusions
Dewenter and Mala-testa 2001	Examines long-run returns to investors in 102 SIPs from developed and developing countries over 1981–94. Examines long-run stock returns of privatized firms and compares relative performance of large sample (1,500 firm-years) of state- and privately owned firms in 1975, 1985, and 1995.	Significant positive long-term (1–5 years) abnormal stock returns, mostly concentrated in Hungary, Poland, and UK.
Boardman and Laurin 2000	Examines factors influencing long-run returns of 99 SIPs in 1980–95. Tests effect of relative size, fraction retained (by government), presence of golden share, initial return, and timing on 3-year buy-and-hold returns. Examines whether UK utility SIPs earned "excessive" returns.	Significant positive abnormal returns to all SIPs over 1 (9.2%), 2 (13.5%) and 3-year (37.4%) holding periods. UK SIPs are higher than non-UK issues, and UK utilities have highest returns (60.6% 3-year excess returns), but 3-year non-UK SIP returns also significant. Excess returns are positively related to fraction retained and initial period return; negatively related to relative size and presence of golden share.

returns for privatization stocks listing in the United States in the form of American depository receipts (ADRs) compared to local benchmarks. The returns are significantly negative compared to U.S. benchmarks. Paudyal, Saadouni, and Briston (1998) find that investors earn insignificant long-term returns on eighteen Malaysian PIPOs, as well as on 77 private-sector IPOs.

Two of the multinational studies described in table 9 focus on long-run returns earned by investors in SIPs from developing countries. A third examines only western European offerings. Narjess Boubakri and Jean-Claude Cosset (2000) study returns from 120 SIPs from 26 developing countries, while Enrico Perotti and Pieter Oijen (2000) develop and test a model of long-term returns using data from twenty developing nations. Both studies document large, highly significant long-run returns, though the mean 112 percent three-year return found by Boubakri and Cosset is not significant once the returns from national markets over the corresponding time periods are subtracted (the absolute returns are converted into market-adjusted or excess returns). This is primarily due to the ex-

tremely large weightings that SIPs themselves have in most developing-country national stock market indices. Once these size biases are accounted for, SIPs significantly outperform most national market indices. Perotti and Oijen document significantly positive market-adjusted returns, and argue that this results from a progressive resolution of political risk as governments refrain from expropriating investors' wealth in privatized firms, which had been feared. Their proxy for political risk declines by an average of 3.6 percent annually during the course of a privatization program, and this leads to positive excess returns for SIPs of about 6 percent per year. Richard Davidson (1998) documents that large European SIPs began to outperform market indices in five countries during the mid-1990s. However, these SIPs did so only after an extended period of sub-par performance.

The remaining four long-run return studies employ multinational samples that cover a large number of countries and regions. For this reason, and because all the studies are recent enough to employ state-of-the-art techniques for computing net-of-market returns,

372   *Journal of Economic Literature, Vol. XXXIX (June 2001)*

we consider these the most persuasive evidence on long-term excess returns earned by SIP investors. Megginson, Nash, Netter, and Adam Schwartz (2000) examine the long-run buy-and-hold returns earned by domestic, international, and U.S. investors who purchase shares at the first open-market price in 158 SIPs from 33 countries during the period 1981–97. They use several benchmarks and compute one, three, and five-year local currency and U.S. dollar net returns with respect to domestic, international, U.S. market indices, and industry-matched comparison samples. They find statistically significant positive net returns for the 158 unseasoned SIPs for all holding periods and versus all benchmarks. Boardman and Laurin (2000), Choi, Nam, and Gui-Youl Ryu (2000), and Dewenter and Malatesta (2000) find similar results. All four studies document significantly positive market-adjusted returns over holding periods of up to five years. In general, British privatizations yield higher long-run returns than do non-U.K. initial and seasoned SIPs, and British utilities yield the highest returns among the U.K. offerings. However, the net return is significantly positive for most non-U.K. subsamples as well.

These studies, and those cited earlier, support the conclusion that the average long-term, market-adjusted return earned by international investors in share issue privatizations is economically and significantly positive. Apart from Perotti and Oijen, however, few of these studies can offer any convincing explanation of precisely *why* SIP issues outperform over time, and isolating one or more specific cause-and-effect relationships is likely to prove extremely difficult. Most likely, these excess returns result from a gradual resolution of uncertainty on the part of investors regarding both the microeconomic suc-

cess of privatization programs and the ability of governments to resist the temptation to expropriate shareholder wealth in privatized firms through direct intervention or targeted regulation or taxation. If so, an important implication is that returns on SIPs are likely to be much lower in the future than they have been historically, since investors will no longer demand a political risk premium to purchase shares. The determinants of the long-run returns will be an interesting source of future research.

7. Privatization's Impact on Financial Market Development

7.1 Stock Market Capitalization and Trading

There is no doubt that privatization has had a major impact on capital markets. Table 10 describes the growth in the total market capitalization, and in the value of shares traded, on the world's stock exchanges from 1983 to 1999. This was a period of rapid growth in the capitalization of markets in every country except Japan, which suffered a four-year, 70 percent decline in total market capitalization after reaching a value of $4.4 trillion in 1989. At year-end 1999, Japan's market was eight times as valuable in dollar terms (and less than four times as valuable in yen terms) as it was in 1983. By contrast, total world market capitalization increased over tenfold (to $35.0 trillion) between 1983 and 1999, and the total capitalization of the U.S. market increased almost ninefold (from $1.9 trillion to $16.6 trillion) over the same period. The growth in markets outside the United States was even greater. It is also in these markets that privatization's impact has been greatest, since there have been only two significant SIPs in the United States in the modern era (Conrail in 1987 and U.S. Enrichment

TABLE 10
THE GROWTH OF WORLD STOCK MARKET CAPITALIZATION AND TRADING VOLUME, 1983–99

Aggregate market capitalization and trading volume in $US millions

	1983	1986	1989	1992	1995	1998	1999
Market Capitalization[a]							
Developed countries	3,301,117	6,378,234	10,957,463	9,921,841	15,842,152	24,530,692	32,820,474
United States	1,898,063	2,636,598	3,505,686	4,485,040	6,857,622	12,926,177	16,642,462
Japan	565,164	1,841,785	4,392,597	2,399,004	3,667,292	2,495,757	4,554,886
United Kingdom	225,800	439,500	826,598	927,129	1,407,737	2,372,738	2,855,351
Developing countries	83,222	135,056	755,210	1,000,014	1,939,919	1,908,258	2,184,899
Total World	3,384,339	6,513,290	11,712,673	10,921,855	17,782,071	26,519,773	35,005,373
World, ex. US	1,486,276	3,876,692	8,206,987	6,436,815	10,924,449	13,593,596	18,362,911
US as % of world	56.1%	40.5%	29.9%	41.1%	38.6%	48.7%	47.5%
Trading Volume[b]							
Developed countries	1,202,546	3,495,708	6,297,069	4,151,573	9,169,761	20,917,462	35,187,632
United States	797,123	1,795,998	2,015,544	2,081,658	5,108,591	13,148,480	19,993,439
Japan	230,906	1,145,615	2,800,695	635,261	1,231,552	948,522	1,891,654
United Kingdom	42,544	132,912	320,268	382,996	510,131	1,167,382	3,399,381
Developing countries	25,215	77,972	1,170,928	631,277	1,046,546	1,956,858	2,320,891
Total world	1,227,761	3,573,680	7,467,997	4,782,850	10,216,307	22,874,320	37,508,523
World, ex. US	430,638	1,777,682	5,452,453	2,701,192	5,107,716	9,725,840	17,515,084
US as % of world	64.9%	50.3%	27.0%	43.5%	50.0%	57.5%	53.3%

Sources: Data sources: 1983–98, the World Bank's *Emerging Markets Fact Book* (various issues); 1999 data from Statistics section of the International Federation of Stock Exchange's website (*www.fibv.com*).
[a] Year-end values, translated from local currencies into US$ at the contemporaneous exchange rate.
[b] Total value of all trades executed during the year.

Corporation in 1999). Between 1983 and 1999, the total capitalization of non-U.S. stock markets increased from $1.49 trillion to $18.36 trillion. The total market capitalization of developing country stock exchanges increased by 26 times during these sixteen years, even after declining significantly from 1997's peak value of $2.5 trillion to $2.2 trillion in 1999.

Though the rise in market capitalization has been impressive, trading volumes have increased even more. The total value of shares traded worldwide between 1983 and 1999 rose from $1.2 trillion to more than $37.5 trillion. As before, non-U.S. markets experienced the greatest increases. The value of shares traded on markets in developing countries rose from $25 billion in 1983 to more than $2.3 trillion in 1999. This rise in market liquidity was probably due in large part to the increasing popularity of "emerging market" investing among western investors, particularly institutional investors such as pension and mutual funds.

What role has privatization played in this remarkable growth in market capitalization and trading volume? At the end of 1983, the total market capitalization of the handful of British, Chilean, and Singaporean firms that had been privatized was less than $50 billion. By the middle of 2000, the 152 privatized firms listed in either the *Business Week* "Global 1000" ranking of the most valuable companies in developed-nation stock markets or the *Business Week* "Top 200 Emerging Market Companies" ranking had a total market capitalization of $3.31 trillion. This equals approximately 13 percent of the combined market capitalization of the firms

TABLE 11
MARKET VALUES OF 25 LARGEST PUBLICLY TRADED PRIVATIZED FIRMS

Company	Country	Global 1000 Rank	Country Rank	Market Value US $mil[c]	Market Value as % of National Market Capitalization
NTT DoCoMo	Japan	8	1	247,237	5.4
BP Amoco	UK	12	2	207,506	7.3
Nippon Telegraph & Telephone	Japan	15	2	189,156	4.2
Deutsche Telekom	Germany	16	1	187,247	13.1
France Telecom	France	25	1	148,711	9.9
TotalFinaElf	France	33	2	116,318	7.7
China Telecom	China	42[a]	1	102,464	16.8[b]
British Telecom	UK	45	4	93,701	3.3
Telecom Italia	Italy	54	1	85,258	11.7
TIM (Telecom Italia Mobiliare)	Italy	60	2	75,917	10.4
Telefonica	Spain	72	1	66,571	15.4
ING Groep	Netherlands	92	3	57,474	8.3
ENEL	Italy	98	3	53,418	7.3
STMicroelectronics	France	101	6	51,324	3.4
Telstra	Australia	108	1	49,915	11.7
Cable & Wireless	UK	121	10	45,941	1.6
Banco Bilbao Vizcaya Argentaria	Spain	127	2	43,359	10.1
ENI	Italy	128	4	43,058	5.9
BNP Paribas	France	139	10	40,390	2.7
Sonera	Finland	147	2	37,199	10.6
Telefonos de Mexico	Mexico	151[a]	1	36,383	23.6
CGNU	UK	164	14	33,957	1.2
SK Telecom	Korea	186	2	30,388	9.9
Cable & Wireless HKT	Hong Kong	195	2	27,780	4.6
Swisscom	Switzerland	206	8	25,732	3.7

Source: Data are from Morgan Stanley Capital International, as reported in "The Business Week Global 1000," *Business Week* (July 10, 2000). Global 1000 Rank refers to a company's global ranking based on market valuation, while Country Rank refers to its relative position among firms from its country on the Global 1000 List.
[a] These firms are from a companion "Top 200 Emerging-Market Companies" ranking in the same *Business Week* issue, and they are given the rankings they would have if this list was included in the "Global 1000" list.
[b] Expressed as a percentage of the Hong Kong market's total capitalization.
[c] Stock market value, total sales, and total profits (in US $mil. translated at contemporaneous exchange rate) of the 25 most valuable publicly traded privatized firms as of May 31, 2000.

on the two lists, and is more than 27 percent of the non-U.S. total. (American firms accounted for 484 of the "Global 1000" firms, and $13.1 trillion of the $23.9 trillion "Global 1000" total capitalization.)

An examination of the historical evolution of non-U.S. stock markets since 1980 suggests that large SIPs played a key role in the growth of capital mar-

kets almost everywhere, especially because they are generally among the largest firms in national markets. Using the *Business Week* 2000 "Global 1000" and "Top 200" data, table 11 details the total market value and relative size of the world's 25 most valuable privatized firms. Columns 1 and 2 give the company names and domicile countries.

Column 3 shows each firm's ranking in the "Global 1000" list (firms from the "Top 200 Emerging Markets" list are given the ranking they would have if included in the "Global 1000" ranking). Column 4 gives the firm's ranking within its home market, and column 5 lists the firm's total market capitalization. Column 6 expresses the single firm's market capitalization as a percentage of the entire national market's year-end 1999 capitalization.

Table 11 plus data reported in Maria Boutchkova and Megginson (2000) reveal the relative importance of SIPs in most non-U.S. stock exchanges. Privatized firms are the most valuable companies in Japan, Germany, France, Italy, Spain, Australia, Mexico, Singapore, China, Denmark, New Zealand, Portugal, Russia, Argentina, Brazil, Greece, Malaysia, Poland, the Czech Republic, Hungary, Turkey, Indonesia, Egypt, and Peru. They are the second-most valuable firms in many other countries, including Britain, Finland, Hong Kong, Korea, Chile, and the Philippines. Privatized companies are the first and second-most valuable companies in Japan, France, Spain, Argentina, and Indonesia, and they occupy the three top slots in Italy, Portugal, Russia, and Greece. Table 11 shows that the largest privatized firms often account for sizeable fractions of the total capitalization of national stock markets, even in advanced countries such as Germany (13.1 percent), Italy (11.7 percent), Spain (15.4 percent), and Australia (11.7 percent). In developing countries such as Korea (9.9 percent) and Mexico (23.6 percent), individual privatized firms also account for large fractions of the total market capitalization.

Another way to measure the impact of privatized firms on capital market development is to see how important SIPs have been as security offerings, and

here the impact is even greater. As table 12 shows, the ten largest, and thirty of the 35 largest, share offerings in history have been privatizations. Ten SIPs have been larger than the biggest U.S. share offering, the $10.6 billion AT&T Wireless tracking stock offering in April 2000. Jones, Megginson, Nash, and Netter (1999) show that, between 1984 and 1997, 112 SIPs raised at least $1 billion, a stock offering size rarely observed in the United States. Twenty-five SIPs have raised more than $7 billion, a feat no private-sector issuer achieved prior to April 2000, and governments have raised a total of more than $700 billion through some 750 public share offerings since 1977. Outside of the entire U.S. corporate sector, this is an unprecedented volume of common equity issuance, and it has fundamentally changed the nature of global stock market trading and investment.

Why should we care about privatization's impact on the development of capital markets? Obviously, new share listings can directly create some net new wealth and a handful of new (albeit well-paying) jobs, but the principal economic payoff from increasingly efficient and liquid capital markets comes from the financing opportunities and monitoring possibilities they provide. Several studies (Ross Levine 1997; Asli Demirgüç-Kunt and Yojislav Maksimovic 1998; Levine and Sara Zervos 1998; Rajan and Luigi Zingales 1998; Avandhar Subrahmanyam and Sheridan Titman 1999; Thorsten Beck, Levine, and Norman Loayza 2000; Geert Bekaert and Campbell Harvey 2000; Jeffrey Wurgler 2000; and Peter Blair Henry 2000a,b) document that efficient capital markets promote economic growth and allow individual firms to fund investment opportunities they otherwise would have to forgo. Therefore, privatization

TABLE 12
WORLD'S LARGEST SHARE OFFERING
Share offerings raising over $5 billion as of August 15, 2000. Offers reported in nominal amounts (not inflation-adjusted), and translated into millions of US dollars using the contemporaneous exchange rate.

Date	Company	Country	Amount ($mil)	IPO[a]/SEO[b]
Nov 87	Nippon Telegraph & Telephone	Japan	40,260	SEO
Oct 88	Nippon Telegraph & Telephone	Japan	22,400	SEO
Nov 99	ENEL	Italy	18,900	IPO
Oct 98	NTT DoCoMo	Japan	18,000	IPO
Oct 97	Telecom Italia	Italy	15,500	SEO
Feb 87	Nippon Telegraph & Telephone	Japan	15,097	IPO
Nov 99	Nippon Telegraph & Telephone	Japan	15,000	SEO
Jun 00	Deutsche Telekom	Germany	14,760	SEO
Nov 96	Deutsche Telekom	Germany	13,300	IPO
Oct 87	British Petroleum	United Kingdom	12,430	SEO
Apr 00	ATT Wireless (tracking stock)[c]	United States	10,600	IPO
Nov 98	France Telecom	France	10,500	SEO
Nov 97	Telstra	Australia	10,530	IPO
Oct 99	Telstra	Australia	10,400	SEO
Jun 99	Deutsche Telekom	Germany	10,200	SEO
Dec 90	Regional Electricity Companies[d]	United Kingdom	9,995	IPO
Dec 91	British Telecom	United Kingdom	9,927	SEO
Jun 00	Telia	Sweden	8,800	IPO
Dec 89	UK Water Authorities[d]	United Kingdom	8,679	IPO
Dec 86	British Gas	United Kingdom	8,012	IPO
Jun 98	Endesa	Spain	8,000	SEO
Jul 97	ENI	Italy	7,800	SEO
Apr 00	Oracle Japan[c]	Japan	7,500	IPO
Jul 93	British Telecom	United Kingdom	7,360	SEO
Oct 93	Japan Railroad East	Japan	7,312	IPO
Dec 98	Nippon Telegraph & Telephone	Japan	7,300	SEO
Oct 97	France Telecom	France	7,080	IPO
Jul 99	Credit Lyonnais	France	6,960	IPO
Feb 94	Elf Acquitaine	France	6,823	SEO
Jun 97	Halifax Building Society[c]	United Kingdom	6,813	IPO
Jun 98	ENI	Italy	6,740	SEO
May 94	Autoliv Sverige[c]	Sweden	5,818	IPO
Oct 96	ENI	Italy	5,864	SEO
Oct 98	Swisscom	Switzerland	5,600	IPO
Jul 99	United Parcel Service[c]	USA	5,500	IPO

Amounts reported for share issue privatization (SIP) offers are as described in the *Financial Times* at the time of the issue.
[a] initial public offering.
[b] seasoned equity offering.
[c] private-sector offering; amounts are from the Securities Data Corporation file.
[d] group offering of multiple companies that trade separately after the IPO.

deserves credit for whatever direct role it has played in promoting stock market development (through new share offerings), and for the indirect role it has played in bond market development. This catalytic role can be assumed because several of the aforementioned studies find development of one market also promotes development of related markets.

8. Privatization's Impact on International Corporate Governance Practices

It would be an understatement to assert that interest in corporate governance issues has been growing recently among policy makers and academic economists. A nation's corporate governance system can be defined as the set of laws, institutions, practices, and regulations that determine how limited-liability companies will be run, and in whose interest. Evidence of the professional interest in corporate governance is not hard to find. Several countries and multilateral agencies have recently published "codes" or "principles" of good corporate governance practices, such as OECD (1999). In the academic arena, one of the recent growth areas in corporate finance has been the interaction between law and finance, highlighted by cross-sectional studies of the determinants and effects of international differences in securities law and corporate governance. Studies have examined governance practices in developed countries (Shleifer and Vishny 1997; LaPorta, López-de-Silanes, Shleifer, and Vishny 1997, 1998, 1999, 2000b,c; Maria Maher and Thomas Andersson 1999; and Dyck 2000b); transition economies (Berglof and von Thadden 1999; Coffee 1999; and Dyck 2000a); and individual countries such as Russia (Black, Kraakman, and Tarassova 2000) and China (Xu and Wang 1997; and Lin 2000). However, the study of the impact of law and corporate finance has been expanded into studies of their effects on macroeconomics (such as currency crisis), investment, innovation, and financing (Rajan 2000 discusses these areas of study).

While a survey of this research is outside the scope of this paper (Megginson 2000 is a more complete survey of the effects of corporate governance), we need to mention several findings because they impact the interpretation of the effects of privatization. There are several reasons analysis of international patterns in corporate governance and securities laws has become increasingly important. These include the large increase in the total value of security issues on global capital markets, and a comparable increase in the total value of mergers and acquisitions worldwide.[36] Until recently, relying on securities markets for corporate financing and resorting to (often hostile) public takeovers to effect changes in control of corporate assets were American practices, but both trends have now "gone global." In particular, the adoption of the euro in January 1999 has been accompanied by the value of European mergers and acquisitions roughly doubling to $1.22 trillion in 1999 versus 1998 (itself a record year). Another reason for the interest in corporate governance today is the important role that poor governance practices are perceived to have played in the East Asian economic contraction that began in July 1997 (Claessens, Djankov, S. Fan, and Larry Lang 2000; and Simon Johnson, Peter Boone, Alasdair Breach, and Eric Friedman 2000).

Finally, academic research by La Porta, López-de-Silanes, and Shleifer (1999), and La Porta, López-de-Silanes, Shleifer, and Vishny (1997, 1998, 1999, 2000a,c) presents evidence that corporate governance generally, and corporate legal systems specifically, significantly influence capital market size, ownership structure, and efficiency. Most importantly, La Porta et al. argue in their articles that there are differences

[36] The data are taken from the *Investment Dealers Digest*. Each January, *IDD* details the prior year's total worldwide security issuance and mergers and acquisitions volume.

between countries in the degree to which the legal system protects investors, which in turn affects the development and operation of external capital markets. It appears that capital markets have developed better in countries where the legal system had a common law origin than in countries with a civil law basis. Rajan (2000), however, suggests that some other factor that is correlated with the origin of the legal system likely explains the above findings. In any event, the framework and operation of a country's legal system impacts the operation of financial markets and corporate governance in that country.

Similarly, the structure and operation of a country's legal system will affect the impact of privatization. Privatization is a major change in the governance structure of a firm. Thus, how well the legal system protects investors is presumably a determinant of the success of privatization in improving firm performance (Sachs, Zinnes, and Eilat 2000; and Djankov and Murrell 2000a,b present evidence this is the case in transition economies). Further, privatization usually accompanies changes in a country's legal system. For example, industrialized-country governments that implement large-scale SIP programs often need to significantly change their corporate governance systems, while governments from the transition economies of China and central and eastern Europe must create such a system almost from scratch. As we mentioned above, this has an implication for most of the studies we discuss in this paper. Since the privatizations are occurring at the same time as other major changes, including the legal system, it is impossible to completely isolate the impact of privatization on firm operations from the other changes affecting the firm.

In addition, privatization impacts the patterns of the changes in the legal system in many countries. One of the distinctive aspects of SIP programs is the tendency of governments to sell shares to large numbers of citizens, often one million or more. Democratic governments are usually acutely aware of the political fallout that could result if small investors suffer losses on their SIP investments because of inadequate shareholder protection or insider dealings. Thus, at the same time they launch the first large SIPs, most governments establish (or augment) a regulatory body similar to the U.S. Securities and Exchange Commission. Since utilities comprise many of the important privatizations and since many utilities are natural monopolies, most privatizing governments establish regulatory bodies for these firms as well. In addition, national stock exchanges are often illiquid and nontransparent at the beginning of large SIP programs. Governments must establish the listing and other regulations that will assure potential investors that the market is a reputable place in which to invest and trade.

There is some literature that examines the actual corporate governance provisions of privatized firms. In their study of SIPs, Jones, Megginson, Nash, and Netter (1999) find that governments tend to retain some sort of decisive voting rights in privatized firms even after a majority of the income rights have been sold. In many countries, the government retains a golden share (90 percent of U.K. SIPs have such a feature). This special share held by the government enables it to veto mergers, liquidations, asset sales, and other major corporate events. An alternative method of retaining ultimate control is for the government to insert some control restrictions directly into the SIP's charter.

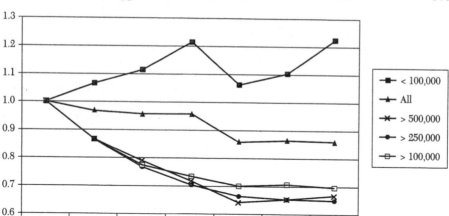

Figure 3. Changes in the Number of Shareholders in Privatized Firms over Years +1 to +6

Notes: This figure represents the dynamics of share ownership of a sample of privatized firms, where the number of shareholders in Year 0 is normalized to 1 and in subsequent years shows the change with respect to Year 0. The companies with less than 100,000 initial shareholders exhibit increasing numbers of shareholders, and the companies with more than 100,000, more than 250,000 and more than 500,000 initial shareholders exhibit strong declines that pull the whole sample to a significant decrease in the number of shareholders over the whole period.

8.1 Individual Share Ownership in Privatized Companies

Boutchkova and Megginson (2000) study the evolution of share ownership in large SIPs. They look at how many individual stockholders are created in a sample of large privatization share offerings, as well as how these highly atomistic ownership structures evolve over time. They compare the numbers of stockholders in the privatized firms in the 1999 *Business Week* "Global 1000" and "Top 200 Emerging Markets" lists to capitalization-matched private sector firms from the same markets, obtaining useable data for 97 of the 153 privatized companies and for 99 of the matching privately owned firms. For most of the cases with data available for both the privatized and the matching firm, the privatized company has a larger number of shareholders. This result holds despite the fact that in most cases governments retain sizable

stakes in these firms, thus reducing their effective total capitalization since these stakes have not yet been sold to private investors. Boutchkova and Megginson conclude that the number of shareholders in the privatized companies is significantly higher than the number of shareholders in the matching private-sector (non-privatized) sample companies.

Boutchkova and Megginson (2000) also examine how the total number of shareholders in a company evolves during the years subsequent to an SIP. They demonstrate that the extremely large numbers of shareholders created by many SIPs are not a stable pattern of corporate ownership. Figure 3 shows the dynamics in share ownership in privatized firms. For SIPs with less than 100,000 initial investors, the number of shareholders increases steadily from one year to four years after the privatization. However, for the 39 SIPs that initially have more than 100,000

380   *Journal of Economic Literature, Vol. XXXIX (June 2001)*

shareholders, the total number of share-holders declines steadily. In the largest privatizations (those with 500,000 or more initial investors) the total number of shareholders declines by 33 percent within five years of the share offering.

The implications of this finding for government efforts to develop an effective corporate governance system or equity culture are unclear. Many new stockholders do not retain the shares they purchase. Other evidence suggests that retail investors in privatizations generally own only that one stock, hardly indicative of a class of well-diversified stockholders. On the other hand, since the long-run returns to investors in SIPs are generally positive, the first experience of these new retail investors in stock market trading is a positive one. Furthermore, the fact that governments are able to entice large numbers of investors to return for subsequent share offerings suggests that these programs are indeed creating (at least minimally) effective governance systems and stock markets capable of absorbing large new stock issues.

9. The "Lessons" of Privatization Research

9.1 Some Thoughts on the Current Literature

Our reading of the extant literature on privatization suggests the following conclusions:

1. The privatization programs of the last twenty years have significantly reduced the role of state-owned enterprises in the economic life of most countries. Most of this reduction has happened in developing countries only during the 1990s. The SOE share of "global GDP" has declined

from more than 10 percent in 1979 to less than 6 percent today.[37]

2. Research now supports the proposition that privately owned firms are more efficient and more profitable than otherwise-comparable state-owned firms. There is limited empirical evidence, especially from China, that suggests that non-privatizing reform measures, such as price deregulation, market liberalization, and increased use of incentives, can improve the efficiency of SOEs, but it also seems likely that these reforms would be even more effective if coupled with privatization.

3. Governments use three basic techniques to privatize their SOEs: share issue privatizations (SIPs), asset sales, and voucher or mass privatizations. We are beginning to understand the determinants of the method selected in specific circumstances. However, there is great variation within all the techniques, because privatization is a complex process involving a host of political and economic factors. Voucher privatizations are the least economically productive divestment technique, but those governments that use it generally have few other realistic options.

4. Governments attempt to craft the offering terms of SIPs to balance competing economic, political, and financial objectives. Most governments underprice share offerings (particularly initial offerings) and then use targeted share allocations to favor domestic over foreign investors. SOE employees are particularly favored, receiving preferential allocations in 91 percent of offers. Governments

---

[37] These figures are based on the study findings discussed in section 2, and on the observation that OECD countries represent about three-quarters of world GDP and developing countries account for the remaining 25 percent.

frequently retain golden shares that give them veto power over certain control changes, and also insert various other control restrictions into the corporate charters of privatized firms.

5. We know that privatization "works," in the sense that divested firms almost always become more efficient, more profitable, and financially healthier, and increase their capital investment spending. These results hold for both transition and non-transition economies, though the results vary more in the transition economies. The question of whether privatization generally costs at least some SOE workers their jobs is still unresolved. The answer is ultimately based on whether sales increase faster than productivity in privatized firms. Most studies find that employment in privatized firms usually does fall, though three large-sample studies document employment increases. What is clear is that whenever employment is cut, there is almost invariably a large compensating performance improvement. Several studies also highlight the need to bring new entrepreneurial management into privatized firms to maximize performance improvements. However, there is little empirical evidence on how privatization affects consumers.

6. Investors who purchase initial SIP shares at the offering price and then sell those shares at the first post-issue trading price earn significantly positive excess (market-adjusted) returns. Additionally, there is now convincing evidence that initial returns on privatization IPOs are significantly higher than the initial returns earned on private-sector IPOs. Investors who purchase privatization IPO shares at their first post-offer trading price,

and then retain those shares for one-, three-, or five-year holding periods, also earn significantly positive net returns.

7. Though it is difficult to pinpoint causality, it appears that countries that have launched large-scale SIP programs have experienced rapid growth in their national stock market capitalization and trading volume. Countries (other than the United States) that have either not launched major privatization programs or have emphasized asset sales and vouchers over public share offerings appear to lag behind in market development. Privatized firms are one of the two or three most valuable companies in most non-U.S. markets, and the ten largest (and thirty of the 35 largest) share issues in financial history have all been privatizations.

8. Emerging (largely anecdotal) evidence suggests that adopting a large-scale SIP program is often a major spur to modernizing a nation's corporate governance system. Transition economies that launch privatization programs must create such systems largely from scratch, and the record of success here is decidedly mixed. Many governments try to develop an equity culture among their citizenry through SIP programs, also with mixed results. Share ownership has dramatically increased in most non-transition countries over the past fifteen years, but the share ownership patterns that are created when SIPs are sold to large numbers of investors (often one million or more) are not stable. However, it seems clear that privatization programs lead to significant improvements in securities market regulation, information disclosure rules, and other required components of modern financial systems.

9.2 Avenues for Further Research

While much has indeed been learned about the effectiveness of privatization as a political and economic policy, there are several important areas that need further research. We believe that, in particular, there are three aspects of privatization that need to be understood much better for public policy reasons. First, researchers need to more closely examine the sequencing and staging of privatization, and conclusively document whether reforms other than government divestiture can effectively serve as a substitute (or precursor) for privatization. Responsible policy makers are understandably reluctant to "bet their economies" on a rapid, and essentially irreversible, privatization program without some assurance that all necessary prerequisite policies have been put into place. Until these policies are identified, and the interactions between various policy options are established, launching large-scale privatization programs will remain a leap of faith.

The second vital area of research is to conclusively document the labor economics of privatization programs. Do most such programs actually cost SOE workers jobs? Are there gender-specific impacts relating to the total commercialization of state-owned enterprises, as might happen if privatization caused SOEs to shut down child care or other social services? Are worker training/retraining programs effective methods of dealing with worker redundancies, or should governments emphasize lump-sum severance packages when lay-offs are required? Do privatization programs create more jobs economy-wide than they destroy? These questions are not only vitally important to policy makers, they are inherently interesting in their own right.

Finally, what role can privatization play in equipping companies and countries to meet the challenges posed by major economic forces such as globalization and the rapid growth of information-based business? Technological breakthroughs have transformed the global telecommunications industry during the past decade, and privatized telecom companies have been at the forefront of this revolution. Indeed, it is unlikely that this most dynamic of industries would have been able to grow nearly as rapidly under the former state ownership model. But how important will privatization be for the global oil and gas industry's development in the future, and for the energy-based utilities that are now being impacted by technological and regulatory changes similar to those that hit telecommunications during the 1990s? How can developing countries structure privatization programs to most effectively attract foreign direct investment from multinational companies? How will privatization impact the worldwide shift from commercial bank-based systems of corporate finance to capital market-based finance? All of these questions can, and should, be answered using the tools of economic analysis, and it is hard to imagine an area of research more intrinsically interesting to economists than analyzing the optimal role of government in the business of nations.

REFERENCES

Aggarwal, Reena; Ricardo Leal, and Leonardo Hernandez. 1993. "The Aftermarket Performance of Initial Public Offerings in Latin America, *Finan. Manage.* 22, pp. 43–53.

Alexandrowicz, Melinda Roth. 1994. "Mass Privatization Programs," *FPD Note No. 4*, Washington, DC: World Bank.

Alchain, Armen. 1977. "Some Economics of Property Rights," in *Economic Forces at Work*. Armen Alchain, ed. Indianapolis: Liberty Press, pp. 127–149.

Allen, Franklin and Douglas Gale. 1999. "Corporate Governance and Competition," working paper, Wharton School, U. Pennsylvania.

Aussenegg, Wolfgang. 2000. "Privatization versus

Private Sector Initial Public Offerings in Poland," working paper, Vienna U. Technology.

Bai, Chong-en; David D. Li and Yijiaiang Wang. 1997. "Enterprise Productivity and Efficiency: When Is Up Really Down?" *J. Comp. Econ.* 24, pp. 265–80.

Baldwin, Carliss Y. and Sugato Bhattacharya. 1991. "Choosing the Method of Sale: A Clinical Study of Conrail," *J. Finan. Econ.* 30, pp. 69–98.

Barber, Brad and John Lyon. 1996. "Detecting Abnormal Operating Performance: The Empirical Power and Specification of Test Statistics," *J. Finan. Econ.* 41, pp. 359–99.

————. 1997. "Detecting Long-Run Abnormal Stock Returns: The Empirical Power and Specification of Test Statistics," *J. Finan. Econ.* 43, pp. 341–72.

Barberis, Nicholas; Maxim Boycko, Andrei Shleifer and Natalia Tsukanova. 1996. "How Does Privatization Work? Evidence from the Russian Shops," *J. Polit. Econ.* 104, pp. 764–90.

Beck, Thorsten; Ross Levine, and Norman Loayza. 2000. "Finance and the Sources of Growth," *J. Finan. Econ.* 58, pp. 261–300.

Beesley, M. E. and S. C. Littlefield. 1989. "The Regulation of Privatized Monopolies in the United Kingdom," *Rand J. Econ.* 20, pp. 454–73.

Bekaert, Geert and Campbell Harvey. 2000. "Foreign Speculators and Emerging Equity Markets," *J. Fin.* 55, pp. 565–613.

Bennell, Paul. 1997. "Privatization in Sub-Saharan Africa: Progress and Prospects during the 1990s," *World Develop.* 25, pp. 1785–803.

Berg, Andrew; Eduardo Borensztein, Ratna Sahay, and Jeromin Zettelmeyer. 1999. "The Evolution of Output in Transition Economies: Explaining the Differences," IMF working paper WP/99/73.

Berglof, Eric and Gérard Roland. 1998. "Soft Budget Constraints and Banking in Transition Economies," *J. Comp. Econ.* 26, pp. 18–40.

Berglof, Eric and Ernst-Ludwig von Thadden. 1999. "The Changing Corporate Governance Paradigm: Implications for Transitional and Developing Countries," SITE working paper, Stockholm School of Economics.

Biais, Bruno and Enrico Perotti. 2000. "Machiavellian Privatization," forthcoming, *Amer. Econ. Rev.*

Bishop, Matthew R. and John A. Kay. 1989. "Privatization in the United Kingdom: Lessons from Experience," *World Develop.* 17, pp. 643–57.

Black, Bernard; Reinier Kraakman, and Anna Tarassova. 2000. "Russian Privatization and Corporate Governance: What Went Wrong?" *Stanford Law Rev.* 52, forthcoming.

Blanchard, Olivier and Philippe Aghion. 1996. "On Insider Privatization," *Europ. Econ. Rev.* 40, pp. 759–66.

Boardman, Anthony E. and Claude Laurin. 2000. "Factors Affecting the Stock Price Performance of Share Issue Privatizations," *Applied Econ.* forthcoming.

Boardman, Anthony E.; Claude Laurin and Aidan Vining. 2000. "Privatization in Canada: Operating, Financial and Stock Price Performance with International Comparisons," working paper, U. British Columbia, Vancouver.

Boardman, Anthony and Aidan R. Vining. 1989. "Ownership and Performance in Competitive Environments: A Comparison of the Performance of Private, Mixed, and State-Owned Enterprises," *J. Law Econ.* 32:1, pp. 1–33.

Boles de Boer, David and Lewis Evans. 1996. "The Economic Efficiency of Telecommunications in a Deregulated Market: The Case of New Zealand," *Econ. Record* 72, pp. 24–35.

Bornstein, Morris. 1994. "Russia's Mass Privatization Program," *Communist Economies Econ. Transformation*, 6:4, pp. 419–57.

————. 1999. "Framework Issues in the Privatization Strategies of the Czech Republic, Hungary and Poland," *Post-Communist Econ.* 11:1, pp. 47–77.

Bortolotti, Bernardo; Marcella Fantini, and Carlo Scarpa. 2000. "Why Do Governments Sell Privatised Companies Abroad?" working paper, Fondazione ENI-Enrico Mattei (FEEM), Milan.

Bortolotti, Bernardo; Marcella Fantini, and Domenico Siniscalco. 1999a. "Privatisation: Politics, Institutions, and Financial Markets," working paper, FEEM, Milan.

————. 1999b. "Regulation and Privatisation: The Case of Electricity," working paper, FEEM, Milan.

Boubakri, Narjess and Jean-Claude Cosset. 1998. "The Financial and Operating Performance of Newly-Privatized Firms: Evidence from Developing Countries," *J. Fin.* 53, pp. 1081–110.

————. 1999. "Does Privatization Meet the Expectations? Evidence from African Countries," working paper, Ecole des HEC, Montreal.

————. 2000. "The Aftermarket Performance of Privatization Offerings in Developing Countries," working paper, Ecole des HEC, Montreal.

Boutchkova, Maria K. and William L. Megginson. 2000. "The Impact of Privatization on Capital Market Development and Individual Share Ownership," *Finan. Manage.* 29:1, pp. 67–77.

Boycko, Maxim; Andrei Shleifer, and Robert W. Vishny. 1994. "Voucher Privatization," *J. Finan. Econ.* 35, pp. 249–66.

————. 1996a. "A Theory of Privatisation," *Econ. J.* 106, pp. 309–19.

————. 1996b. "Second-Best Economic Policy for a Divided Government," *Europ. Econ. Rev.* 40, pp. 767–74.

Boylaud, Olivier and Giuseppe Nicoletti. 2000. "Regulation, Market Structure and Performance in Telecommunications," OECD Econ. Dept. working paper 237, Paris.

Brada, Josef C. 1996. "Privatization Is Transition—Or Is It?" *J. Econ. Perspect.* 10, pp. 67–86.

Brav, Alon and Paul A. Gompers. 1997. "Myth or Reality? The Long-Run Underperformance of

Initial Public Offerings: Evidence from Venture- and Non-Venture Capital-Backed Companies," *J. Fin.* 52, pp. 1791–821.

Brav, Alon; Christopher Geczy, and Paul Gompers. 2000. "Is the Abnormal Return Following Equity Issuances Abnormal?" *J. Finan. Econ.* 56, pp. 209–49.

Brickley, James A.; Clifford W. Smith, and Jerold L. Zimmerman. 2001. *Managerial Economics and Organizational Architecture.* 2nd ed. Chicago: Irwin.

Brickley, James A. and R. Lawrence Van Horn. 2000. "Incentives in Nonprofit Organizations: Evidence from Hospitals," working paper, U. Rochester.

Briggs, A. 1961. "The Welfare State in Historical Perspective," *Archives Europ. Sociologie* 2:2, pp. 221–59.

Bulow, Jeremy and Paul Klemperer. 1996. "Auctions versus Negotiations," *Amer. Econ. Rev.* 86, pp. 180–94.

Canina, Linda; Roni Michaely, Richard Thaler, and Kent Womack. 1998. "Caveat Compounder: A Warning about Using the Daily CRSP Equal-Weighted Index to Compute Long-Run Excess Returns," *J. Fin.* 53, pp. 403–16.

Cao, Yuanzheng; Yingyi Qian, and Barry R. Weingast. 1999. "From Federalism, Chinese Style to Privatization, Chinese Style," *Econ. Transition* 7:1, pp. 103–31.

Carter, Richard B.; Frederick H. Dark, and Ajai K. Singh. 1998. "Underwriter Reputation, Initial Returns, and the Long-Run Performance of IPO Stocks," *J. Fin.* 53, pp. 285–311.

Choi, Seung-Doo and Sang-Koo Nam. 2000. "The Short-Run Performance of IPOs of Privately and Publicly Owned Firms: International Evidence," *Multinat. Finance J.* forthcoming.

Choi, Seung-Doo; Sang-Koo Nam, and Gui-Youl Ryu. 2000. "Do Privatization IPOs Outperform the Market? International Evidence," working paper, Korea U., Seoul.

Claessens, Stijn. 1997. "Corporate Governance and Equity Prices: Evidence from the Czech and Slovak Republics," *J. Fin.* 52, pp. 1641–58.

Claessens, Stijn and Simeon Djankov. 1999a. "Enterprise Performance and Management Turnover in the Czech Republic," *Europ. Econ. Rev.* 43, pp. 1115–24.

———. 1999b. "Ownership Concentration and Corporate Performance in the Czech Republic," *J. Comp. Econ.* 27, pp. 498–513.

Claessens, Stijn; Simeon Djankov, S. Fan, and Larry Lang. 2000. "Expropriation of Minority Shareholders: Evidence from East Asia," World Bank Policy Research Paper 2088.

Claessens, Stijn; Simeon Djankov, and Gerhard Pohl. 1997. "Ownership and Corporate Governance: Evidence from the Czech Republic," World Bank Policy Research Paper 1737.

Coase, Ronald. 1960. "The Problem of Social Cost," *J. Law Econ.* 1, pp. 1–44.

Coffee, Jack C. Jr. 1999. "Privatization and Corporate Governance: The Lessons From Securities Market Failure," *J. Corporat. Law* 25, pp. 1–39.

Cornelli, Francesca and David D. Li. 1997. "Large Shareholders, Private Benefits of Control, and Optimal Schemes of Privatization," *Rand J. Econ.* 28, pp. 585–604.

Cragg, Michael I. and I. J. Alexander Dyck. 1999a. "Management Control and Privatization in the United Kingdom," *Rand J. Econ.* 30:3, pp. 475–497.

———. 1999b. "Privatization, Compensation and Management Incentives: Evidence From the United Kingdom," working paper, Harvard Business School.

Davidson, Richard. 1998. "Market Analysis: Underperformance Over?" *Privatisation International Yearbook.* London: IFR Publishing.

Davis, Jeffry; Rolando Ossowski, Thomas Richardson, and Steven Barnett. 2000. "Fiscal and Macroeconomic Aspects of Privatization," IMF Occasional Paper 194.

Demirgüç-Kunt, Asli and Vojislav Maksimovic. 1998. "Law, Finance, and Firm Growth," *J. Fin.* 53, pp. 2107–39.

Dewenter, Kathryn and Paul H. Malatesta. 1997. "Public Offerings of State-Owned and Privately Owned Enterprises: An International Comparison," *J. Fin.* 52, pp. 1659–79.

———. 2001. "State-Owned and Privately-Owned Firms: An Empirical Analysis of Profitability, Leverage, and Labour Intensity," *Amer. Econ. Rev.* 91, pp. 320–34.

Djankov, Simeon. 1999a. "Ownership Structure and Enterprise Restructuring in Six Newly Independent States," *Comp. Econ. Stud.* 41:1, pp. 75–95.

———. 1999b. "The Restructuring of Insider-Dominated Firms: A Comparative Analysis," *Econ. Transition* 7:2, pp. 467–79.

Djankov, Simeon and Peter Murrell. 2000a. "The Determinants of Enterprise Restructuring in Transition: An Assessment of the Evidence," working paper, U. Maryland.

———. 2000b. "Enterprise Restructuring in Transition: A Quantitative Survey," working paper, U. Maryland.

Drum, Bernard. 1994. "Mass Privatization in Ukraine," FPD Note No. 8, World Bank.

D'Souza, Juliet and William L. Megginson. 1999. "The Financial and Operating Performance of Newly Privatized Firms in the 1990s," *J. Fin.* 54, pp. 1397–438.

———. 2000. "Sources of Performance Improvement in Privatized Firms: A Clinical Study of the Global Telecommunications Industry," working paper, U. Oklahoma.

D'Souza, Juliet; Robert Nash, and William L. Megginson. 2000. "Determinants of Performance Improvement in Newly-Privatized Firms: Does Restructuring and Corporate Governance Matter?" working paper, U. Oklahoma.

Dyck, I. J. Alexander. 1997. "Privatization in Eastern Germany: Management Selection and Economic Transition," *Amer. Econ. Rev.* 87, pp. 565–97.

———. 2000a. "Ownership Structure, Legal Protections and Corporate Governance," working paper, Harvard Business School.

———. 2000b. "Privatization and Corporate Governance: Principles, Evidence and Future Challenges," working paper, Harvard Business School.

Earle, John. 1998. "Post-Privatization Ownership and Productivity in Russian Industrial Enterprises," SITE working paper 127, Stockholm School of Economics.

Earle, John and Saul Estrin 1998. "Privatization, Competition and Budget Constraints: Disciplining Enterprises in Russia," SITE working paper 128, Stockholm School of Economics.

Eckbo, B. Espen, Ronald Masulis and Øyvind Norli. 2000. "Seasoned Public Offerings: Resolution of the "New Issues Puzzle," *J. Finan. Econ.* 56, pp. 251–91.

Eckel, Catherine; Doug Eckel, and Vijay Singal. 1997. "Privatization and Efficiency: Industry Effects of the Sale of British Airways," *J. Finan. Econ.* 43, pp. 275–98.

Ehrlich, Isaac; Georges Gallais-Hamonno, Zhiqiang Liu, and Randall Lutter. 1994. "Productivity Growth and Firm Ownership: An Empirical Investigation," *J. Polit. Econ.* 102, pp. 1006–38.

Fama, Eugene F. 1998. "Market Efficiency, Long-Term Returns, and Behavioral Finance," *J. Finan. Econ.* 49, pp. 283–306.

Foerster, Stephen R. and G. Andrew Karolyi. 2000. "The Long-Run Performance of Global Equity Offerings," *J. Finan. Quant. Anal.* forthcoming.

Frydman, Roman; Cheryl W. Gray, Marek Hessel, and Andrzej Rapaczynski. 1999. "When Does Privatization Work? The Impact of Private Ownership on Corporate Performance in Transition Economies," *Quart. J. Econ.* 114:4, pp. 1153–91.

———. 2000. "The Limits of Discipline: Ownership and Hard Budget Constraints in the Transition Economies," C. V. Starr Center for Applied Econ. working paper, NYU.

Frydman, Roman; Marek Hessel, and Andrzej Rapaczynski. 2000. "Why Ownership Matters: Entrepreneurship and the Restructuring of Enterprises in Central Europe," C. V. Starr Center for Applied Econ. working paper, NYU.

Frydman, Roman; Katharina Pistor, and Andrzej Rapaczynski. 1996. "Exit and Voice After Mass Privatization: The Case of Russia," *Europ. Econ. Rev.* 40, pp. 581–588.

Galal, Ahmed; Leroy Jones, Pankaj Tandon, and Ingo Vogelsang. 1994. *Welfare Consequences of Selling Public Enterprises*. Oxford: Oxford U. Press.

Gibbon, Henry. 1997. "A Seller's Manual: Guidelines for Selling State-Owned Enterprises," *Privatisation Yearbook, Privatisation Int.* pp. 16–26.

———. 1998. "Worldwide Economic Orthodoxy," *Privatisation Int.* 123, pp. 4–5.

———. 2000. "Editor's Letter," *Privatisation Yearbook*, London: Thomson Financial, p. 1.

Gottret, Pablo. 1999. "Bolivia: Capitalisation, Pension Reform, and Their Impact on Capital Markets," working paper, OECD, Paris.

Gough, I. 1989. "The Welfare State," in *The New Palgrave Social Economics*. NY: W. W. Norton, pp. 276–81.

Groves, Theodore; Yongmiao Hong, John McMillan, and Barry Naughton. 1994. "Autonomy and Incentives in Chinese State Enterprises," *Quart. J. Econ.* 109:1, pp. 183–209.

———. 1995. "China's Evolving Managerial Labor Market," *J. Polit. Econ.* 103:4, pp. 873–92.

Hansmann, Henry and Reinier Kraakman. 2000. "The End of History for Corporate Law," working paper, NYU and Harvard Law School.

Harper, Joel T. 2000. "The Performance of Privatized Firms in the Czech Republic," working paper, Florida Atlantic U., Boca Raton.

Havrylyshyn, Oleh and Donald McGettigan. 2000. "Privatisation in Transition Countries," *Post Soviet Affairs* 16, pp. 257–86.

Hayek, Friedrich von. 1994. *The Road to Serfdom*. Chicago: U. Chicago Press.

Henry, Peter. 2000a. "Do Stock Market Liberalizations Cause Investment Booms?" *J. Finan. Econ.* 58, pp. 301–34.

———. 2000b. "Stock Market Liberalization, Economic Reform, and Emerging Market Equity Prices," *J. Fin.* 55, pp. 529–64

Hersch, Philip; David Kemme, and Jeffry Netter. 1997. "Access to Bank Loans in a Transition Economy: The Case of Hungary," *J. Comp. Econ.* 24, pp. 79–89.

Hingorani, Archana; Kenneth Lehn, and Anil Makhija. 1997. "Investor Behavior in Mass Privatization: The Case of the Czech Voucher Scheme," *J. Finan. Econ.* 44, pp. 349–96.

Huang, Qi and Richard M. Levich. 1998. "Underpricing of New Equity Offerings by Privatized Firms: An International Test," working paper, NYU.

Ibbotson, Roger; Jody Sindelar, and Jay Ritter. 1994. "The Market's Problem with the Pricing of Initial Public Offerings," *J. App. Corp. Fin.* 7, pp. 66–74.

Jelic, Ranko and Richard Briston. 2000a. "Privatisation Initial Public Offerings: The Polish Experience," working paper, U. Birmingham, U.K.

———. 2000b. "Hungarian Privatisation Strategy and Financial Performance of Privatised Companies," *J. Bus. Fin. Acc.* forthcoming.

Jenkinson, Timothy and Colin Mayer. 1988. "The Privatisation Process in France and the U.K." *Europ. Econ. Rev.* 32, pp. 482–90.

Johnson, Simon; Peter Boone, Alasdair Breach, and Eric Friedman. 2000. "Corporate Governance in the Asian Financial Crisis," *J. Finan. Econ.* 58, pp. 141–86.

Jones, Leroy P. 1991, "Performance Evaluation for Public Enterprises," World Bank Discussion Paper 122, Washington DC.

Jones, Steven L.; William L. Megginson, Robert C. Nash, and Jeffry M. Netter. 1999. "Share Issue Privatizations as Financial Means to Political and Economic Ends," *J. Finan. Econ.* 53, pp. 217–53.

Karpoff, Jonathan. 2001. "Public versus Private Initiative in Arctic Exploration: The Effects of Incentives and Organizational Form," *J. Polit. Econ.* 109, pp. 38–78.

Katz, Barbara G. and Joel Owen. 1993. "Privatization: Choosing the Optimal Time Path," *J. Compar. Econ.* 17, pp. 715–36.

———. 1995. "Designing the Optimal Privatization Plan for Restructuring Firms and Industries in Transition," *J. Compar. Econ.* 21, pp. 1–28.

———. 1997. "Optimal Voucher Privatization Fund Bids when Bidding Affects Firm Performance," *J. Compar. Econ.* 24, pp. 25–43.

Kay, J. A. and D. J. Thompson. 1986. "Privatisation: A Policy in Search of a Rationale," *Econ. J.* 96, pp. 18–32.

Kikeri, Sunita; John Nellis, and Mary Shirley. 1992. *Privatization: The Lessons of Experience.* Washington, DC: World Bank.

Kole, Stacey R. and J. Harold Mulherin. 1997. "The Government as a Shareholder: A Case from the United States," *J. Law Econ.* 40, pp. 1–22.

Kornai, János. 1988. "Individual Freedom and Reform of the Socialist Economy," *Europ. Econ. Rev.* 32, pp. 233–67.

———. 1993. "The Evolution of Financial Discipline under the Postsocialist System," *Kyklos* 46:3, pp. 315–36.

———. 2000. "Ten Years after 'The Road to a Free Economy': The Author's Self Evaluation," working paper, Harvard U.

Kothari, S. P. and Jerold B. Warner. 1997. "Measuring Long-Horizon Security Price Performance," *J. Finan. Econ.* 43, pp. 301–40.

La Porta, Rafael and Florencio López-de-Silanes. 1999. "Benefits of Privatization—Evidence From Mexico," *Quart. J. Econ.* 114:4, pp. 1193–242.

La Porta, Rafael; Florencio López-de-Silanes, and Andrei Shleifer. 2000a. "Government Ownership of Banks," NBER Working Paper 7620, Cambridge, MA.

———. 2000b. "Investor Protection and Corporate Governance," *J. Finan. Econ.* 58, pp. 3–27.

La Porta, Rafael; Florencio López-de-Silanes, Andrei Shleifer, and Robert Vishny. 1997. "Legal Determinants of External Finance," *J. Fin.* 52, pp. 1131–50.

———. 1998. "Law and Finance," *J. Polit. Econ.* 106, 1113–1150.

———. 1999. "The Quality of Government," *J. Law Econ. Org.* 15:1, pp. 222–79.

———. 2000. "Investor Protection and Corporate Valuation," NBER Working Paper 7403, Cambridge, MA.

Laffont, Jean-Jacques and Jean Tirole. 1993. *A Theory of Incentives in Procurement and Regulation.* Cambridge, MA: MIT Press.

Lau, Lawrence J. Yingyi Qian, and Gerard Roland. 2000. "Reform Without Losers: An Interpretation of China's Dual-Track Approach to Transition," *J. Polit. Econ.* 108, pp. 120–143.

Laurin, Claude and Yves Bozec. 2000. "Privatization and Productivity Improvement: The Case of Canadian National (CN)," working paper, Ecoles de HEC, Montreal.

Levine, Ross. 1997. "Financial Development and Economic Growth: Views and Agenda," *J. Econ. Lit.* 35, pp. 688–726.

Levine, Ross and Sara Zervos. 1998. "Stock Markets, Banks, and Economic Growth," *Amer. Econ. Rev.* 88, pp. 537–558.

Levis, Mario. 1993. "The Long-Run Performance of Initial Public Offerings: The U.K. Experience 1980–88," *Finan. Manag.* 22, pp. 28–41.

Li, Wei. 1997. "The Impact of Economic Reform on the Performance of Chinese State Enterprises, 1980–1989," *J. Polit. Econ.* 105, pp. 1080–106.

Lin, Cyril. 2000. "Corporate Governance of State-Owned Enterprises in China," working paper, Asian Development Bank, Manila.

Lin, Justin Yifu; Fang Cai, and Zhou Li. 1998. "Competition, Policy Burdens, and State-Owned Enterprise Reform," *Amer. Econ. Rev.* 88, pp. 422–27.

Lizal, Lubomir; Miroslav Singer, and Jan Svejnar, 2000, "Enterprise Break-ups and Performance During the Transition from Plan to Market," *Rev. Econ. Statist.* forthcoming.

Ljungqvist, Alexander P.; Tim Jenkinson, and William J. Wilhelm, Jr. 2000. "Has the Introduction of Bookbuilding Increased the Efficiency of International IPOs?" working paper, Stern School of Business, NYU.

López-de-Silanes, Florencio. 1997. "Determinants of Privatization Prices," *Quart. J. Econ.* 112, pp. 965–1025.

López-de-Silanes, Florencio; Andrei Shleifer, and Robert W. Vishny. 1997. "Privatization in the United States," *Rand J. Econ.* 28, pp. 447–71.

Loughran, Tim and Jay R. Ritter. 1995. "The New Issues Puzzle," *J. Fin.* 50, pp. 23–51.

———. 1997. "The Operating Performance of Firms Conducting Seasoned Equity Offerings," *J. Finance* 52, pp. 1823–50.

Loughran, Tim; Jay Ritter, and Kristian Rydqvist. 1994. "Initial Public Offerings: International Insight," *Pacific-Basin Finan. J.* 2, pp. 165–99.

Lyon, John; Brad Barber, and Chih-Ling Tsai. 1999. "Improved Methods for Tests of Long-Run Abnormal Stock Returns," *J. Finance* 54, pp. 165–201.

Macquieira, Carlos and Salvador Zurita. 1996. "Privatizaciones en Chile: Eficiencia y Politicas Financieras," *Estudios de Administracion* 3:2, pp. 1–36.

Mahboobi, Ladan. 2000. "Recent Privatisation Trends," OECD *Financial Market Trends*, No. 76, pp. 43–64.

Maher, Maria and Thomas Andersson. 1999,

"Corporate Governance: Effects on Firm Performance and Economic Growth," working paper, OECD, Paris.

Majumdar, Sumit K. 1996. "Assessing Comparative Efficiency of the State-Owned, Mixed, and Private Sectors in Indian Industry," *Public Choice* 96, pp. 1–24.

Martin, Stephen and David Parker. 1995. "Privatization and Economic Performance Throughout the UK Business Cycle," *Manag. Decis. Econ.* 16, pp. 225–37.

McCurry, Patrick. 2000. "Golden Shares Fail to Shine," *Privatisation Int.* 136, pp. 41–43.

Megginson, William. 2000. "Corporate Governance in Publicly Quoted Companies," working paper, OECD, Paris.

Megginson, William; Robert Nash, Jeffry Netter, and Annette Poulsen. 2000. "The Choice between Private and Public Markets: Evidence from Privatizations," working paper, U. Georgia.

Megginson, William; Robert. Nash, Jeffry Netter, and Adam Schwartz. 2000. "The Long Term Return to Investors in Share Issue Privatizations," *Finan. Manag.* 29, pp. 67–77.

Megginson, William; Robert Nash, and Matthias van Randenborgh. 1994. "The Financial and Operating Performance of Newly Privatized Firms: An International Empirical Analysis," *J. Finance* 49, pp. 403–52.

Menyah, Kojo and Krishna Paudyal. 1996. "Share Issue Privatisations: The UK Experience," in *Empirical Issues in Raising Equity Capital*. Mario Levis, ed. Amsterdam: Elsevier Science.

Menyah, Kojo; Krishna Paudyal, and Charles Inyangete. 1995. "Subscriber Return, Underpricing, and Long-Term Performance of U.K. Privatization Initial Public Offers," *J. Econ. Bus.* 47, pp. 473–95.

Mihályi, Peter. 2000. "FDI Through Cross-Border M&A—The Post-Communist Privatization Story Reconsidered," working paper, UNCTAD, New York.

Mitchell, Mark and Erik Stafford. 2000. "Managerial Decisions and Long-Term Stock Price Performance," *J. Bus.* 73, pp. 287–329.

Nellis, John. 1994. "Is Privatization Necessary?" *Viewpoint Note 17*, Washington DC: World Bank.

———. 1999. "Time to Rethink Privatization in Transition Economies?" IFC Discussion Paper 38, World Bank Group.

———. 2000. "Privatization in Transition Economies: What Next?" working paper, World Bank.

Nellis, John and Sunita Kikeri. 1989. "Public Enterprise Reform: Privatization and the World Bank," *World Devel.* 17, pp. 659–72.

Newbery, David. 1997. "Privatization and Liberalisation of Network Utilities," *Europ. Econ. Rev.* 41, pp. 357–83.

Newbery, David and Michael G. Pollitt. 1997. "The Restructuring and Privatization of Britain's CEGB—Was It Worth It?," *J. Indust. Econ.* 45, pp. 269–303.

Noll, Roger G. 2000. "Telecommunications Reform in Developing Countries," in *Economic Policy Reform: The Second Stage*. Anne O. Kreuger, ed. Chicago: U. Chicago Press.

Olds, Kelly, 1994. "Privatizing the Church: Disestablishment in Connecticut and Massachusetts," *J. Polit. Econ.* 102, pp. 277–97.

Organization of Economic Cooperation and Development. 1999. *OECD Principles of Corporate Governance*, Paris: OECD.

Paudyal, K.; B. Saadouni and R. J. Briston. 1998. "Privatization Initial Public Offerings in Malaysia: Initial Premium and Long-Term Performance," *Pacific Basin Fin. J.* 6. pp. 427–51.

Peltzman, Sam. 1971. "Pricing in Public and Private Enterprises: Electric Utilities in the United States," *J. Law Econ.* 14, pp. 109–47.

Perotti, Enrico. 1995. "Credible Privatization," *Amer. Econ. Rev.* 85, pp. 847–59.

Perotti, Enrico and Serhat E. Guney. 1993. "Successful Privatization Plans: Enhanced Credibility Through Timing and Pricing of Sales," *Fin. Manage.* 22, pp. 84–98.

Perotti, Enrico and Pieter van Oijen. 2000. "Privatization, Political Risk and Stock Market Development in Emerging Economies," *J. Int. Money Fin.* forthcoming.

Petrazzini, Ben A. and Theodore H. Clark. 1996. "Costs and Benefits of Telecommunications Liberalization in Developing Countries," working paper, Hong Kong U. Science Technology.

Pinto, Brian; Merek Belka, and Stefan Krajewski. 1993. "Transforming State Enterprises in Poland: Evidence on Adjustment by Manufacturing Firms," *Brookings Papers Econ. Act.* 0:1, pp. 213–61.

Pistor, Katharina and Andrew Spicer. 1996. "Investment Funds in Mass Privatization and Beyond: Evidence from the Czech Republic and Russia," *Private Sector* 7, World Bank, pp. 33–36.

Pohl, Gerhard; Robert E. Anderson, Stijn Claessens, and Simeon Djankov. 1997. "Privatization and Restructuring in Central and Eastern Europe: Evidence and Policy Options," World Bank Technical Paper 368.

Pollitt, Michael G. 1997. "The Impact of Liberalization on the Performance of the Electric Supply Industry: An International Survey," *J. Energy Lit.* 3:2, pp. 3–31.

Price Waterhouse. 1989a. *Privatization: Learning the Lessons from the U.K. Experience.* London: Price Waterhouse.

———. 1989b. *Privatization: The Facts.* London: Price Waterhouse.

Rajan, Raghuram. 2000. NBER Program Report: Corporate Finance." *NBER Reporter, Spring 2000*, pp. 1–5.

Rajan, Raghuram G. and Luigi Zingales. 1998. "Financial Dependence and Growth," *Amer. Econ. Rev.* 88, pp. 559–86.

Ramamurti, Ravi. 1996. "The New Frontier of Privatization," in *Privatizing Monopolies: Lessons from the Telecommunications and Transport*

Sectors in Latin America. Ravi Ramamurti, ed. Baltimore: Johns Hopkins U. Press, pp. 1–45.

———. 1997. "Testing the Limits of Privatization: Argentine Railroads," *World Develop*. 25, pp. 1973–93.

Ritter, Jay R. 1991. "The Long-Run Performance of Initial Public Offerings," *J. Fin*. 46, pp. 3–27.

Rondinelli, Dennis and Max Iacono. 1996. *Policies and Institutions for Managing Privatization*. International Training Centre, ILO, Turin, Italy.

Ros, Agustin J. 1999. "Does Ownership or Competition Matter? The Effects of Telecommunications Reform on Network Expansion and Efficiency," *J. Reg. Econ*. 15, pp. 65–92.

Sachs, Jeffrey; Clifford Zinnes, and Yair Eilat. 2000. "The Gains from Privatization in Transition Economies: Is 'Change of Ownership' Enough?" CAER II Discussion paper 63, HIID, Harvard.

Samonis, Val. 2000. "Mergers and Acquisitions in Transition Economies: 'Williams' Lithuania Deal Decomposed," working paper, Center for European Integration Studies, Bonn, Germany.

Sappington, David E.M. and Joseph E. Stiglitz. 1987. "Privatization, Information and Incentives," *J. Pol. Anal. Manage*. 6, pp. 567–82.

Schaffer, Mark E. 1998. "Do Firms in Transition Economies Have Soft Budget Constraints? A Reconsideration of Concepts and Evidence," *J. Comp. Econ*. 26, pp. 80–103.

Schmidt, Klaus. 1996. "The Costs and Benefits of Privatization: An Incomplete Contracts Approach," *J. Law Econ. Org*. 12:1, pp. 1–24.

Schmitz, James A. Jr. 1996. "The Role of Public Enterprises: How Much Does It Differ across Countries?" *Fed. Reserve Bank of Minneapolis Quart. Rev*. 20, pp. 2–15.

Shafik, Nemat. 1995. "Making a Market: Mass Privatization in the Czech and Slovak Republics," *World Develop*. 23, pp. 1143–56.

———. 1996. "Selling Privatization Politically," *Columbia J. World Bus*. 31, pp. 20–29.

Sheshinski, Eytan and Luis Felipe López-Calva. 1999. "Privatization and its Benefits: Theory and Evidence," HIID Discussion Paper 698, Harvard U.

Shirley, Mary M. 1999. "Bureaucrats in Business: The Role of Privatization in State Owned Enterprise Reform," *World Develop*. 27:1, pp. 115–36.

Shirley, Mary and John Nellis, 1991, "Public Enterprise Reform: The Lessons of Experience," Publication 9800, World Bank, Washington, DC.

Shirley, Mary and Patrick Walsh. 2000. "Public vs. Private Ownership: The Current State of the Debate," working paper, World Bank, Washington, DC.

Shirley, Mary M. and Lixin Colin Xu. 1998. "Information, Incentives and Commitment: An Empirical Analysis of Contracts between Government and State Enterprises," *J. Law Econ. Org*. 14:2, pp. 358–78.

Shleifer, Andrei. 1998. "State versus Private Ownership," *J. Econ. Perspect*. 12, pp. 133–50.

Shleifer, Andrei and Robert W. Vishny. 1997. "A Survey of Corporate Governance," *J. Finance* 52, pp. 737–83.

Smith, Peter L. and Björn Wellenius. 1999. "Mitigating Regulatory Risk in Telecommunications," *Private Sector*, World Bank, pp. 33–44.

Smith, Stephen C.; Beon-Cheol Cin, and Milan Vodopivec. 1997. "Privatization Incidence, Ownership Forms, and Firm Performance: Evidence from Slovenia," *J. Comp. Econ*. 25, pp. 158–79.

Sobel, Robert. 1999. *The Pursuit of Wealth*. New York: McGraw Hill.

Spiess, D. Katherine and John Affleck-Graves. 1995. "Underperformance in Long-run Stock Returns Following Seasoned Equity Offerings," *J. Finan. Econ*. 38, pp. 243–67.

Stigliz, Joseph. 1998. "The Private Uses of Public Interests: Incentives and Institutions," *J. Econ. Perspect*. 12, pp. 3–22.

Su, Dongwei and Belton M. Fleisher. 1999. "An Empirical Investigation of Underpricing in Chinese IPOs," *Pacific Basin Fin. J*. 7, pp. 173–202.

Subrahmanyam, Avanidhar and Sheridan Titman. 1999. "The Going Public Decision and the Development of Financial Markets," *J. Finance* 54, pp. 1045–82.

Temple, Jonathan. 1999. "The New Growth Evidence," *J. Econ. Lit*. 37, pp. 112–156.

Tian, George Lihui. 2000. "State Shareholding and Corporate Performance: A Study of a Unique Chinese Data Set," working paper, London Business School.

Tybout, James. 2000. "Manufacturing Firms in Developing Countries: How Well Do They Do and Why?" *J. Econ. Lit*. 38, pp. 11–44.

Verbrugge, James; Wanda Owens, and William Megginson. 2000. "State Ownership and the Financial Performance of Privatized Banks: An Empirical Analysis," *Proceedings of a Policy Research Workshop at the World Bank, March 15–16, 1999*. Dallas: Fed. Reserve Bank Dallas.

Vickers, John and George Yarrow. 1991. "Economic Perspectives on Privatization," *J. Econ. Perspect*. 5, pp. 111–32.

Vining, Aidan R. and Anthony E. Boardman. 1992. "Ownership Versus Competition: Efficiency in Public Enterprise, *Pub. Choice*, 73, pp. 205–39.

Wallsten, Scott J. 2000a. "An Econometric Analysis of Telecommunications Competition, Privatization, and Regulation in Africa and Latin America," *J. Indust. Econ*. forthcoming.

———. 2000b. "Telecommunications Privatization in Developing Countries: The Real Effects of Exclusivity Periods," working paper, Stanford U.

Wasserfallen, Walter and Stefan Müller. 1998. "Deregulation and Privatization: Evidence from the Telecommunications Industry in Europe and Implications for Switzerland," working paper, Studienzentrum Gerzensee, Switzerland.

Weiss, Andrew and Georgiy Nikitin. 1998. "Effects of Ownership by Investment Funds on the Performance of Czech Firms," working paper, Boston U.

Welch, Ivo. 1989. "Seasoned Offerings, Imitation Costs, and the Underpricing of Initial Public Offerings," *J. Finance* 44, pp. 421–49.

Wellenius, Björn. 2000. "Extending Telecommunications beyond the Market: Towards Universal Service in Competitive Environments," in *Private Sector* 21, World Bank, pp. 5–18.

Wolfram, Catherine D. 1998. "Increases in Executive Pay Following Privatization," *J. Econ. Manag. Strat.* 7:3, pp. 327–61.

World Bank. 1995. *Bureaucrats in Business.* Washington, DC: Oxford U. Press for the World Bank.

Wurgler, Jeffrey. 2000. "Financial Markets and the Allocation of Capital," *J. Finan. Econ.* 58, pp. 187–214.

Xu, Xiaonian and Yan Wang. 1997. "Ownership Structure, Corporate Governance, and Firms' Performance: The Case of Chinese Stock Companies," working paper, World Bank.

Yarrow, George. 1986. "Privatization in Theory and Practice," *Econ. Pol.* 2, pp. 324–64.

Yergin, Daniel and Joseph Stanislaw. 1998. *The Commanding Heights: The Battle between Government and the Marketplace That Is Remaking the Modern World.* NY: Simon & Schuster.

Yotopoulos, Pan A. 1989. "The (Rip)tide of Privatization: Lessons from Chile," *World Develop.* 17, pp. 683–702.

[19]

ELSEVIER   European Economic Review 42 (1998) 1177–1201

EUROPEAN
ECONOMIC
REVIEW

Privatization under political interference: Evidence from Eastern Germany

Harald Hau*

ESSEC, School of Management, 95021 Cergy Pontoise Cedex, France

Accepted 20 July 1997

Abstract

Can privatization authority be successfully delegated to a privatization agency? To address this question we examine the liquidation policy of the German privatization agency. The theoretical part develops a dynamic model of optimal liquidation under incomplete political insulation of the privatization agency. We explore how external political interference affects its liquidation policy and derive testable implications for the distribution of liquidation decisions and privatization prices. The empirical part uses micro data on 1804 privatization contracts and 1097 liquidation decisions to verify the model predictions. The data confirm the view that political liquidation constraints are an important determinant of privatization outcomes. © 1998 Elsevier Science B.V. All rights reserved.

JEL classification: D8; P2; P3

Keywords: Privatization; Political uncertainty; Timing of liquidation decisions

1. Introduction

Can the authority to privatize state-owned enterprises be successfully delegated to an independent agency similar to the delegation of monetary authority to an independent central bank? The German privatization agency Treuhandanstalt with its independent statute has more than once been compared to the

---

*Tel.: + 33 1 34 43 32 39; e-mail: hhau@edu.essec.fr.

1178 *H. Hau / European Economic Review 42 (1998) 1177 1201*

Bundesbank.[1] Opposing testimony argues that its position to withstand political interference was in fact weak and that it usually had to give in to large sales subsidies once the liquidation option became politically obsolete.

The theoretical part of the paper undertakes an analysis of the optimal liquidation policy of a privatization agency under incomplete political insulation. How should the privatization agency adjust its liquidation policy to the risk of political interference and a sequential loss of its decision autonomy? This paper develops a fully dynamic framework which can address this question. The framework implies various testable implications for the intertemporal distribution of the liquidation decisions and the distribution of privatization prices.

In the empirical part, we confront the model implications with new micro data on 1804 German privatization contracts and 1097 liquidation decisions. The data support the model implications. We conclude that liquidation constraints played an important role in the privatization process and is crucial for understanding the distribution of privatization outcomes. We find in particular that large firms and firms in industries with high sectorial unemployment profited disproportionately from liquidation constraints and could only be sold with large sales subsidies. This subsidy bias towards large state-owned enterprises (SOEs) increased over time and suggests a sequential erosion of the agency's decision autonomy. We also find evidence that political intervention risk accelerated the liquidation process and increased the dispersion of privatization outcomes by frequently suspending the quality threshold for privatization.

An important debate of the privatization literature concerns the optimal speed of economic transition. A fast transition in Eastern Germany was partly achieved by a policy of swift and massive liquidation.[2] Aghion et al. (1994) criticize the speed of transition as too fast because of the job losses it implied. By contrast, the model presented here can rationalize such a policy. A privatization agency facing an erosion of its decision autonomy will try to accelerate the liquidation process in order to preempt high sales subsidies in a later stage of the privatization when liquidation is no longer politically feasible.

The paper also relates to a larger literature that emphasizes political insulation as an important comparative advantage of private over public ownership (Sappington and Stiglitz, 1987; Shapiro and Willig, 1990; Willig, 1993). The dynamic perspective in our model highlights transition problems that exist before private ownership is established. Different privatization methods and institutional structures provide varying degrees of insulation during the transition. 'State-led restructuring' as advocated by Carlin and Mayer (1994)

---

[1] See, e.g., Czada (1993, p. 156).

[2] Treuhandanstalt decided to liquidate approximately 30% of all SOEs. See also Economist (May, 1994, pp. 75 76).

H. Hau / European Economic Review 42 (1998) 1177–1201   1179

faces the risk that the political process distorts the investment and restructuring process.[3] The problem of political insulation appears particularly acute for countries in both economic and political transition. As Boycko et al. (1993) pointed out, the main benefit of voucher privatization in Russia was its commitment value and the loss of control that it entailed for the state bureaucracy.

Compared to other Central and Eastern European countries, Germany offers a best case scenario for the political autonomy of the privatization agency. Partial political insulation could be reached by a strong representation of West German industry managers in the privatization agency.[4] Generous unemployment benefits were used to soften the resistance to firm liquidation. Nevertheless, Czada (1993) finds direct evidence for increasing 'external constraints' on the decision process of the privatization agency in a survey of 300 executive managers. Czada's survey data suggest that the external pressure on the internal decision making process was initially small, but increased over time. To what extent these external constraints are reflected in the privatization outcomes remains an open question and the subject of our analysis.

The rest of this paper is organized as follows. We first review the privatization and liquidation process in the German privatization program in Section 2. Section 3 develops a dynamic model of optimal liquidation under political intervention risk. We characterize the dynamically optimal liquidation decision and summarize the empirical implications in four testable propositions. New contractual data are discussed in Section 4.1, and Section 4.2 describes the methodology. The empirical implications are examined in Sections 4.3, 4.4, 4.5 and 4.6. Section 5 concludes.

2. The German wholesale program: privatization vs. liquidation

In March 1990 the privatization agency Treuhandanstalt (THA) was created by the East German government prior to German unification. The agency received an independent statute in the unification treaty and was formally supervised by the Federal Ministry of Finance. The THA was directed by a 23-member supervisory board that included the five prime ministers of the new 'Bundesländer', trade-unionists, and prominent business people. The board of

---

[3] The potential for state-led restructuring has also been questioned by Dyck (1995) in a model that accounts for the information problem faced by state-led restructuring. For an early warning against political interference, see Bös (1992). Sales subsidies were strongly criticized by the Deutsches Institut für Wirtschaftsforschung (1991, 1992).

[4] According to Seibel (1993, p. 138), all regional chief executive officers (Niederlassungsleiter), all industry directors (Branchendirektoren), and 61.5 percent of all divisional directors (Abteilungsleiter) of the privatization agency were recruited from private industry.

Table 1
Summary statistics

Quarter	Privatizations		Restitutions	Liquidations[a]
	All	Sample		
1990 : 4		30		77
1991 : 1	1670[b]	167	491[b]	160
1991 : 2		252		173
1991 : 3	931	216	140	222
1991 : 4	696	178	239	281
1992 : 1	715	169	152	351
1992 : 2	591	207	170	331
1992 : 3	614	176	212	209
1992 : 4	311	164	136	5
1993 : 1	240	78	92	3
1993 : 2	133	56	157	0
1993 : 3	178	51	98	0
1993 : 4	166	60	33	0
Total	6245	1804	1920	1812

Source : Central controlling division of the THA and BVS.
[a] Exclusive of the liquidation of holding companies (Restliquidationen).
[b] Combined total for 1990 : 4, 1991 : 1 and 1991 : 2.

directors and the executive officers were largely recruited from the West German business community.

The THA adopted a wholesale method for privatization. Potential buyers submitted their entire entrepreneurial plan for firm development and a bid was approved based on the entire business plan rather than on the basis of maximum sales proceeds alone (Priewe, 1993).[5] The sales contracts typically specified investment and employment pledges of the investor. In most cases contractual penalties were specified for violation of the pledges.

Table 1 presents summary statistics for the German privatization program. The privatization process gained momentum after the German unification in October 1990 and proceeded at high speed. Up to January 1994, a total of 6245 SOEs had been sold, and 3219 had been liquidated. Many liquidations included those of holding companies after their major assets had been sold (Rest-liquidationen). Excluding the liquidation of holdings reduces the number of liquidation decisions to 1812. In 1920 cases the SOEs had been returned to

---

[5] To allow for a clear model exposition in Section 3.1, we abstract from heterogenous managerial abilities of the bidder and assume that the privatization agency maximizes revenue. For a framework which accounts for heterogenous managerial ability, see Dyck (1995).

previous owners or to local government. A portfolio of 951 SOEs was left for sale at the end of our sample period in January 1994. We can compare the liquidation decisions to successful sales. The quarterly sales of SOEs decreased from 931 privatizations in the third quarter of 1991 to 166 privatizations in the fourth quarter of 1993. The number of liquidations peaked with 351 cases in the first quarter of 1992 with few liquidation decisions after third quarter of 1992. Most liquidation decisions were made in an early phase of the privatization program.

When should the privatization agency liquidate a SOE? Liquidating a SOE in an early stage of the privatization process implies that the chance of finding a buyer are severely reduced since buyer search and matching requires time. Prolonged search on the other hand implies two countervailing risks. In the absence of a buyer, who can restructure the firm, its profitability is likely to deteriorate. The accumulating losses have to be absorbed by the privatization agency. A second risk may results from imperfect political insulation of the privatization agency. In a prolonged buyer search a SOE is more likely to find external political support against its liquidation and the privatization agency is likely to lose its liquidation option.

3. Privatization under political interference

How should the privatization agency react to its sequential loss of decision autonomy? The following section provides an analysis of the decision problem of the privatization agency with respect to optimal timing of liquidation decisions. We examine in particular how political risk of losing liquidation options due to political interference affects the policy of the privatization agency. The empirical implications are summarized in four testable propositions about the cross-sectional and intertemporal distribution of privatization prices and firm liquidations.

3.1. The model

The privatization agency faces three types of uncertainty: about the profitability of SOEs, about future selling opportunities, and about its ability to liquidate SOEs. First, profit uncertainty is a common assumption in models of optimal investment decisions.[6] But it appears as particularly important for a period of economic transition when firms undergo extensive restructuring. Second, uncertainty about selling opportunities represents the randomness in matching

---

[6] For a survey of dynamic investment models see Dixit and Pindyck (1994).

a buyer and a SOE. Potential buyers have to engage in an extensive search efforts prior to the acquisition of a SOE. This search process may be complicated by the lack of reliable accounting data and legal uncertainty due to unspecified ownership rights.[7] Third, the privatization agency faces political uncertainty about its ability to undertake firm liquidations. Soaring unemployment in the economic transition can lead to political intervention and restrictions on the agency's decision autonomy.

To obtain a tractable analytical framework, we make specific assumptions about the stochastic processes that govern each type of uncertainty. The profit flow of a SOE under continued public ownership is denoted by Π_t and can be decomposed into a non-stochastic lower loss limit $\overline{\Pi} < 0$ and a stochastic component Ψ_t. The stochastic component follows a geometric Brownian motion with a drift parameter α and a variance parameter σ:

$$\Pi_t = \overline{\Pi}_t + \Psi_t,$$

$$\mathrm{d}\Psi_t = \alpha \Psi_t \, \mathrm{d}t + \sigma \Psi_t \, \mathrm{d}w_t. \tag{1}$$

To assure a finite present firm value, we assume that the discount rate exceeds the drift parameter α for the profit growth ($r > \alpha$). The initial profit flow at the beginning of the privatization program is denoted by $\Pi_0 = \overline{\Pi} + \Psi_0$. It is convenient to assume that the profit flow follows a geometric Brownian motion. This allows for an analytical solution to the optimal liquidation policy. The negative lower bound $\overline{\Pi} < 0$ implies that the firm value can become negative. The privatization agency influences the profit flow of the SOE only through liquidation decisions.[8] A firm liquidation terminates the firm's profit flow at a fixed liquidation cost $C_L > 0$. It is assumed that the liquidation cost does not exceed the present value of the SOE for the lowest possible profit level, that is $- C_L > \overline{\Pi}/r$.

The availability of the liquidation option is jeopardized by an exogenous political process. For simplicity, we model political intervention as an independent Poisson process, I_t^p, with a constant probability p that the liquidation option is eliminated. Let T_P denote the time when the liquidation option is lost.

$$I_t^p = \begin{cases} 1, & p \, \mathrm{d}t, \\ 0, & 1 - p \, \mathrm{d}t. \end{cases} \tag{2}$$

---

[7] Legal uncertainty about ownership existed in the German privatization process for firms whose former owners were dispossessed by the communist government. Former owners could claim restitution of their ownership rights. Uncertainty about the validity of such claims interfered with the privatization procedures.

[8] This appears as a realistic assumption for mass privatizations, in which the privatization agency cannot influence operational business decisions of SOEs for administrative and informational constraints. In the German privatization, additional liability considerations impaired such interference. For details on the restructuring management, see Schwalbach (1993, pp. 189–193).

H. Hau / European Economic Review 42 (1998) 1177–1201   1183

The privatization agency chooses a liquidation time T_L for those SOEs without liquidation constraint. The optimal choice of the liquidation time maximizes the present value of the expected cash flow. Assuming that the discount rate r is constant, we can write the reservation value of the privatization agency for a SOE as

$$F(\Psi_t, I_t^p) = \max_{\{T_L\}} \; E_t[(1 - I_t^p)V_t^0 + I_t^p V_t^1],$$

$$V_t^0 \equiv \int_t^{T_L} e^{-r(s-t)}\Pi_s \, ds - e^{-r(T_L - t)}C_L,$$

$$V_t^1 \equiv \int_t^{\infty} e^{-r(s-t)}\Pi_s \, ds. \tag{3}$$

with stochastic transitions Eqs. (1) and (2). The reservation value of the privatization agency is given either by the firm value V_t^0 for an optimal liquidation policy or by the firm value V_t^1 in the absence of the liquidation option.

We assume that potential buyers arrive sequentially. The matching of a SOE and a potential buyer is modeled as an independent Poisson process:

$$I_t^m = \begin{cases} 1. & m \, dt, \\ 0, & 1 - m \, dt, \end{cases} \tag{4}$$

where m denotes the matching probability. The time of the successful matching is denoted by T_M. Potential buyers have a comparative advantage in restructuring a SOE, and the firm's profit flow under private ownerships exceeds the profit flow under continued state ownership. We assume an asymmetric bargaining situation in which the buyer can make an offer and the privatization agency accepts or rejects it. The buyer then bids the reservation value $F(\Psi_t, I_t^p)$ of the privatization agency and the privatization agency accepts the bid. Under this asymmetric bargaining situation, the entire surplus of ownership transfer goes to the buyer. While this assumption might seem somewhat extreme, considerable bargaining asymmetry is plausible for a mass privatization program in which the privatization agency confronts severe administrative constraints.[9] Under tight administrative constraints the privatization agency may have to restrict its sales efforts to approving buyer offers.[10]

---

[9] For a discussion of tight administrative constraints in the German privatization process, see Kloepfer (1993, pp. 55–57).

[10] A negotiating team of the THA sold up to three firms a week and relied heavily on information provided by the buyer.

Let the switching time $T^{\min} \equiv \min\{T_M, T_P, T_L\}$ be defined as the time of the first event of either matching, intervention, or liquidation. The privatization revenue for the firm then follows as

$$
R(\Psi_t, I_t^p, I_t^m) = \begin{cases} F(\Psi_{T_M}, 0) & \text{for } T_M = T^{\min}, \\ -C_L & \text{for } T_L = T^{\min}, \\ F(\Psi_{T_M}, 1) & \text{for } T_P = T^{\min}. \end{cases}
$$

The buyer will offer the reservation value $F(\Psi_{T_M}, 0)$ for a SOE that can still be liquidated. SOEs for which the privatization agency lost the liquidation option only yield $F(\Psi_{T_M}, 1)$. If no buyer is found until the optimal liquidation time T_L, the SOE is liquidated at a cost $-C_L$.

3.2. Dynamic optimization

The dynamic optimization problem of the privatization agency implies the following Bellman equation:[11]

$$
rF(\Psi_t, 0)dt = \max_{\{T_L\}} \{\Pi_t \, dt + E_t[dF(\Psi_t, 0)]\}
$$

$$
E_t[dF(\Psi_t, 0)] = p[F(\Psi_t, 1) - F(\Psi_t, 0)]dt + \alpha \Psi_t F_\Psi(\Psi_t, 0)dt
$$

$$
+ \tfrac{1}{2}\sigma^2 \Psi_t^2 F_{\Psi\Psi}(\Psi_t, 0)dt. \tag{5}
$$

The Bellman equation has a straightforward economic interpretation. If the privatization agency discounts capital at rate r, the left-hand side of Eq. (5) represents its required mean return from public ownership over the time interval dt. The right-hand side denotes the expected return of continued ownership. It consists of the profit flow Π_t and the expected change in the reservation value $E_t[dF(\Psi_t, 0)]$. The expected change in the reservation value can be decomposed into the expected cost of a loss of the liquidation option $p[F(\Psi_t, 0) - F(\Psi_t, 1)] \, dt$, the expected change in the reservation value $\alpha \Psi_t F_\Psi(\Psi_t, 0) \, dt$

---

[11] In the time interval dt, $F(\Psi_t, 0)$ changes to $F(\Psi_t + d\Psi_t, 0)$ with the probability $1 - p \, dt$ and to $F(\Psi_t + d\Psi_t, 1)$ with probability $p \, dt$. Thus

$$
F(\Psi_t, 0) = \Pi_t dt + e^{-r \, dt}\{(1 - p \, dt)E[F(\Psi_t + d\Psi_t, 0)] + p \, dt \, E[F(\Psi_t + d\Psi_t, 1)]\}.
$$

Expanding the right-hand side using Ito's Lemma and retaining only terms of order dt, we obtain Eq. (5).

H. Hau / European Economic Review 42 (1998) 1177–1201   1185

due to profit flow changes, and the usual second derivative term of order dt. Optimality requires that the expected return equals the required mean return.

The reservation value after political intervention can be calculated directly as

$$F(\Psi_t, 1) = \mathrm{E}[V_t^1] = \frac{\overline{\Pi}}{r} + \frac{\Psi_t}{r - \alpha}. \tag{6}$$

Substituting Eq. (6) into the Bellman Eq. (5) yields a linear second-order differential equation with the following general solution:

$$F(\Psi_t, 0) = \frac{\overline{\Pi}}{r} + \frac{\Psi_t}{r - \alpha} + B_1 \Psi_t^{\beta_1} + B_2 \Psi_t^{\beta_2}, \tag{7}$$

where B_1 and B_2 are undetermined coefficients. The characteristic roots β_1 and β_2 are given by the quadratic equation

$$\mathcal{Q} = \tfrac{1}{2}\sigma^2 \beta(1 - \beta) + \alpha\beta - (r + p) = 0. \tag{8}$$

The quadratic equation has one positive root $\beta_1 > 1$, and the second root β_2 is negative. The solution for the two coefficients B_1 and B_2 and the quality threshold Ψ_{T_L}, at which the privatization agency undertakes the firm liquidation, are determined by Eq. (7) and the following three boundary conditions:

$$\lim_{\Psi_{t \to \infty}} F(\Psi_t, 0) = \lim_{\Psi_{t \to \infty}} F(\Psi_t, 1), \tag{9}$$

$$F(\Psi_{T_L}, 0) = -C_L, \tag{10}$$

$$F_\psi(\Psi_{T_L}, 0) = 0. \tag{11}$$

The boundary condition, Eq. (9), requires that for arbitrarily high profit flows the liquidation option has no value as its exercise is never desired. Eq. (10) states that the reservation value of the agency at the optimal liquidation time T_L equals the (negative) liquidation cost. The so-called smooth pasting condition is expressed in Eq. (11). For the optimal liquidation time T_L, local variations in the realization of the state variable Ψ_t do not change the reservation value for the firm.[12]

3.3. Optimal timing of liquidation decisions

Using Eqs. (7)–(11) we can now solve for the quality threshold Ψ_{T_L} at which the privatization agency stops the search process for a buyer and liquidates the

---

[12] For a no-arbitrage interpretation of the smooth pasting condition, see Dixit and Pindyck (1994, pp. 130–133).

SOE. We ask in particular how political risk affects the required quality threshold $\Pi_{T_L} = \overline{\Pi} + \Psi_{T_L}$ above which a SOE qualifies for continued buyer search.

The boundary condition, Eq. (9), implies $B_1 = 0$ for the coefficient of the positive root β_1. Eqs. (10) and (11) jointly determine the liquidation threshold for the profit process as

$$\Psi_{T_L} = \frac{\beta_2(r - \alpha)}{1 - \beta_2}\left(C_L + \frac{\overline{\Pi}}{r}\right) > 0. \tag{12}$$

The optimal liquidation time T_L is implicitly defined as the time when the stochastic component Ψ_t of the profit process reaches the value Ψ_{T_L}. For a firm profit flow lower than $\Pi_{T_L} = \overline{\Pi} + \Psi_{T_L}$, continued search for a buyer is not optimal. The boundary conditions of Eqs. (10) and (11) determine the coefficient B_2 in Eq. (7). The reservation value of the privatization agency with a liquidation option follows as

$$F(\Psi_t, 0) = \frac{\overline{\Pi}}{r} + \frac{\Psi_t}{r - \alpha} + \frac{(-\beta_2)^{-\beta_2}(r - \alpha)^{-\beta_2}}{(1 - \beta_2)^{1 - \beta_2}}\left(-C_L - \frac{\overline{\Pi}}{r}\right)^{1 - \beta_2}\Psi_t^{\beta_2}. \tag{13}$$

The first two terms in Eq. (13) characterize the present value of the future profit flow without the liquidation option. The third term denotes the increase in the reservation value for the SOE if liquidation is an option. The value of the liquidation option depends on the difference between the profit loss under liquidation, $-C_L$, and the present value $\overline{\Pi}/r$ of the maximal loss flow. Higher liquidation costs decrease the value of the liquidation option.

Determining the effect of political intervention risk on the optimal liquidation policy is straightforward. According to Eq. (8), the negative root β_2 decreases if the probability of intervention p increases. Eq. (12) implies that the liquidation threshold Ψ_{T_L} for the profit process increases. Thus,

$$\frac{\partial \beta_2}{\partial p} < 0, \qquad \frac{\partial \Psi_{T_L}}{\partial p} > 0.$$

The expected return of continued operation on the right-hand side of Eq. (5) is depressed by the additional risk of the loss of the liquidation option. Fig. 1 graphs the value function of a firm for two different levels of political intervention risk. The firm's reservation value in the case of higher political risk is lower for any level of the profit flow. Political risk, therefore, decreases the agency's reservation price and the privatization revenue even for firms that can still be liquidated, but might acquire political protection in the future. The reservation price of the privatization agency has to account for the risk of losing the liquidation option if the search for a buyer continues. If a SOE obtains political protection against liquidation, the reservation value of the privatization agency

H. Hau / European Economic Review 42 (1998) 1177–1201   1187

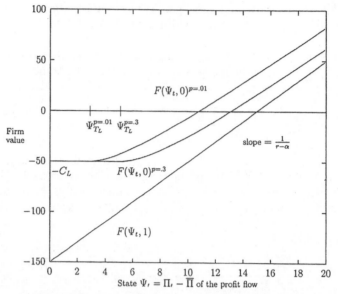

Fig. 1. Firm value $F(\Psi_t, 0)$ for two levels of political risk and the firm value $F(\Psi_t, 1)$ for a SOE under liquidation constraints. The parameters are $\overline{\Pi} = -15$, $C_L = 50$, $r = 0.1$, $\alpha = 0$, $\sigma^2 = 0.4$.

decreases to the linear schedule given by $F(\Psi_t, 1)$. The firm price can now fall below the liquidation cost $-C_L$ and large sales subsidies are a possible privatization outcome.

The negative effect of political intervention on privatization revenue has been named the Kvaerner effect. During the German privatization program, the Norwegian company Kvaerner lowered its offer and demanded particularly high subsidies for buying an East German shipyard following political intervention against the shipyard's liquidation (Schmidt, 1993, p. 230).

3.4. Revenue implications

The model has specific implications for the price patterns in different groups of SOEs. Higher political risk lowers the reservation price of the privatization agency along the time path of possible sales. However, political risk has a relatively minor influence on firms with a high profit flow $\overline{\Pi} + \Psi_t$ for which the liquidation option is unlikely to be exercised. The difference in the reservation price becomes substantial between firms with and without liquidation options as we consider low quality firms. This is evident from the widening gap between $F(\Psi_t, 0)$ and $F(\Psi_t, 1)$ for a decreasing profit flow parameter Ψ_t. As long as the privatization agency retains the liquidation option, the $F(\Psi_t, 0)$ schedule determines the privatization price. Frequent political intervention with its loss of the liquidation option implies lower privatization prices on the $F(\Psi_t, 1)$ schedule. Large sales subsidies below the liquidation costs $- C_L$ become more likely under higher political risk. We summarize these considerations in the following statement:

Implication 1 (Subsidy patterns). Groups of SOEs with frequent political intervention should be characterized by high sales subsidies for low-quality firms.

Implication 1 concerns the cross-sectional privatization pattern. Incomplete political insulation of the privatization agency is reflected in a subsidy bias towards low-quality firms in industry groups with high political intervention risk. But differences in the political intervention risk also affect the time series behavior of the privatization revenue. As the loss of political insulation occurs as a dynamic process, industries with a higher intervention risk encounter a stronger decrease in the average privatization revenue. Eqs. (5) and (6) imply that the expected change in the reservation value decreases in the risk parameter p for an unprotected SOE and is constant for a protected SOE:

$$\frac{\mathrm{d}}{\mathrm{d}p} \mathrm{E}_t[\mathrm{d}F(\Psi_t, 0)] < 0, \qquad \frac{\mathrm{d}}{\mathrm{d}p} \mathrm{E}_t[\mathrm{d}F(\Psi_t, 1)] = 0.$$

By assumption investors bid the reservation price of the privatization agency. Dynamically eroding decision autonomy implies that the average sales price should decrease over time and this decrease should be stronger for groups of SOEs with higher political risk. We summarize as follows:

Implication 2 (Time patterns). Groups of SOEs with frequent political intervention should show a steeper intertemporal decrease of their average sales price.

3.5. The liquidation density

The eroding political insulation of the privatization agency influences the liquidation behavior of the privatization agency. Higher political risk increases the liquidation threshold and firms are liquidated earlier than they would be in the absence of political intervention. We can determine a closed form solution for the distribution of the time interval until liquidation is undertaken. We first determine the so-called *passage time* until a geometric Brownian motion Ψ_t reaches the liquidation threshold Ψ_{T_L}. Consider a firm with an initial profit flow $\Pi_0 = \overline{\Pi} + \Psi_0$ at time t_0 and let $n(.)$ denote the density function of a normal

H. Hau / European Economic Review 42 (1998) 1177–1201   1189

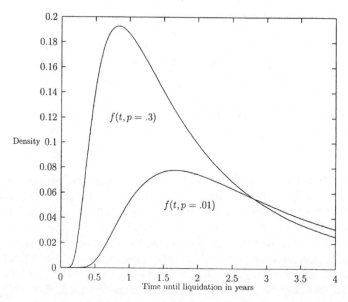

Fig. 2. Liquidation density plotted for two levels of political risk. The parameters are $\Pi_0 = 15$, $\bar{\Pi} = -15$, $C_L = 50$, $r = 0.1$, $\alpha = 0$ and $\sigma^2 = 0.4$.

distribution. The distribution of the passage time $g(t, p)$ until liquidation can be calculated as[13]

$$g(t, p) = x_0 [\sigma^2(t - t_0)^3]^{-1/2} \, n \left[\frac{x_0 + (\alpha - \frac{1}{2}\sigma^2)(t - t_0)}{\sigma \sqrt{t - t_0}} \right],$$

where $x_0 \equiv \ln(\Psi_0) - \ln(\Psi_{T_L})$. The distribution of the passage time states probabilities for a firm that does not face the possibility of a buyer match. Since the matching process prior to liquidation is an independent Poisson process, the liquidation density follows as

$$f(t, p, m) = e^{-m(t - t_0)} g(t, p). \tag{14}$$

The liquidation density accounts for the possibility that a SOEs escapes liquidation through a buyer match. Fig. 2 graphs the liquidation density for two

---

[13]To arrive at the solution for the passage time, we define a Brownian motion process as $W_t = \ln(\Psi_t)$. The drift of W_t follows as $\alpha_w = \alpha - \frac{1}{2}\sigma^2$. A Brownian motion reaches an absorption barrier at a distance $x_0 \equiv \ln(\Psi_0) - \ln(\Psi_{T_L})$ below the initial value in a passage time whose distribution is derived by Ingersoll (1987, pp. 351–353).

different levels of risk. Higher political risk shifts the liquidation density to the left and moves the average liquidation date forward. The privatization agency accelerates the liquidation process in rational anticipation of the risk to lose the liquidation option. A lower matching rate m moves the average liquidation date backward. If we assume that the intervention risk and the matching rate are negatively correlated across groups of SOEs, cross-sectional comparisons in the intervention risk may produce ambiguous results for the average liquidation date.

In order to isolate the role of political risk, it is more useful to estimate the average passage time, which is independent of the matching rate. We denote by $L(j)$ the set of liquidated SOEs of group j, by $\#L(j)$ the number of set elements and by $T_L(i,j)$ the liquidation time of a firm i. For an estimate $\hat{m}(j)$ of the matching rate in group j, we determine the average passage time $PT(j)$ from the liquidation distribution in Eq. (14) as

$$PT(j) = \frac{1}{\#L(j)} \sum_{i \in L(j)} e^{\hat{m}(j)[T_L(i,\,j) - t_0]}[T_L(i,j) - t_0]. \tag{15}$$

The model prediction is summarized as follows:

Implication 3 (*Liquidation pattern*). Groups of SOEs with higher political risk should face liquidation relatively faster with a lower passage time until liquidation.

The ability of the privatization agency to preempt political interference by faster liquidations renders such interventions counterproductive. Political interest groups should therefore be expected to challenge the mandate and the role of the privatization agency and not only lobby for protection of a particular industry. The delegation of privatization authority not only accelerates the privatization process but also polarizes the political conflict.

3.6. The variance effect of political interference

The following section explores the model implications for the second moment of the revenue distribution across different industries. Both the risk of losing the liquidation option and its loss imply a lower reservation value of the privatization agency. As pointed out before, groups of SOEs with higher rates of political intervention should therefore be characterized by a lower average privatization price due to more privatizations of low quality firms. The suspension of the liquidation option increases at the same time the variance of the revenue distribution in groups with frequent political interference. Variations in the level of political interference across different industries thus induce a

H. Hau / European Economic Review 42 (1998) 1177–1201   1191

negative correlation between average privatization price in a group of SOEs and the intra-group price variance.

Formally, let $N(j)$ denote the set of privatized firms in group j and $R(i,j)$ the privatization price of firm i. The average privatization price of group j then follows as

$$R(j) = \frac{1}{\# N(j)} \sum_{i \in N(j)} R(i,j)$$

and the intra-group price variance is given by

$$\text{VAR}(j) = \frac{1}{\# N(j)} \sum_{i \in N(j)} [R(i,j) - R(j)]^2.$$

A higher political intervention rate p decreases the average group price and increases the intra-group price variance. A lower matching rate tends to have the same effect. The slower stock reduction allows for a larger dispersion of the state variable Ψ_t and provides time for more political interventions. A negative correlation between intervention risk and the matching rate reinforces the variance effect of political intervention summarized in implication 4:

Implication 4 (Variance effect). Groups of SOEs with higher political intervention risk should be characterized by both lower average privatization prices and a higher intra-group price variance.

4. Evidence on privatization outcomes

The following empirical part of the paper confronts the model implications with micro data on privatization prices and the liquidation decisions of the German privatization agency. First, we discuss the data. Second, we justify our method of grouping SOEs according to their political risk. The following sections examine the empirical validity of each of the model implications.

4.1. Data

The contract-controlling division of the THA provided micro data on individual sales contracts. A second data set was obtained from the BVS (Bundesanstalt für Vereinigungsbedingte Sonderaufgaben)[14] with information about the timing of liquidation decisions.

---

[14] The BVS is the successor organization of the THA.

The contractual data contain privatization contracts from 17 major industries and include only those cases in which the entire company was sold.[15] Complete privatization accounted for a total of 2614 contracts. Of these, 1804 contained legally binding employment pledges, and 1614 had both employment and investment pledges. The contract-controlling division recorded pledges only when pledges constituted legal claims against the investors. Pledges went unrecorded whenever promises of investors represented a mere statement of intent. Contracts with unrecorded employment pledges are excluded from the sample.

The contractual data allow the calculation of a sales price for each SOE. The price calculation has to account for the various side payments implied by the contractual arrangement. Financial restructuring prior to privatization included the creation of balance sheets and the injection of equity capital to obtain a positive capital stock (Ausgleichsverbindlichkeiten) for viable SOEs. All financial arrangements that changed this equity assignment in the last balance sheet prior to the sale were counted as side payments such as additional debt redemption or capital injection. The price calculation does not include any debt that SOEs had prior to the German monetary union of July 1990 (Altkredite). This preexisting debt is treated as a liability of the THA. In cases where the buyer agreed to take over such old debt, it is counted as revenue for the THA.

The second data set on 1812 liquidated SOEs allows us to document the timing of liquidation decision. It records all liquidations in which the entire SOEs was subject to the liquidation procedure and excludes liquidations of holding companies without remaining assets.[16] The liquidation date is the day on which the board of directors (Vorstand) of the privatization agency took a liquidation decision. The data set reduces to 1097 observations if we concentrate on SOEs in the 17 major industries for which we have contract data.

4.2. Methodology

To make the privatization prices comparable across SOEs of different size and quality, we form the ratio of the price to the employment pledge (future employment as of 1994) specified in the contract. This ratio is referred to as the per capita price (PCP) of a SOE. The employment pledges represent a forward-looking measure of plant size. Similarly, the investment pledges are divided by

---

[15] Excluded are SOEs of which the buyer acquired only some company divisions while the remaining divisions were liquidated by the THA.

[16] The liquidation of holding companies is usually referred to as 'Mantelliquidation' or 'Restliquidation' and accounts for 1904 cases.

Table 2
Privatization contracts

	Obs.	Average PCP[a]	Average PE[b]	Average PCI[a]
Chemicals	71	11.0	0.49	83.5
Plastics	41	− 10.1	0.49	63.5
Ceramics	108	− 5.6	0.55	74.8
Light metal	61	− 24.1	0.52	47.3
Steel	48	12.3	0.54	35.5
Machinery	289	4.4	0.41	40.6
Cars	99	12.5	0.54	57.3
Electrical	85	4.0	0.50	29.3
Optical	15	− 17.7	0.33	28.5
Consumer	65	− 24.3	0.43	40.3
Wood	125	− 24.6	0.53	42.5
Paper	78	13.3	0.53	56.9
Leather	25	− 13.8	0.37	45.7
Textile	77	− 29.8	0.37	41.8
Food	233	13.8	0.52	69.9
Construction	331	13.7	0.66	24.6
Constr. supply	53	13.3	0.62	22.2
Total	1804	2.03	0.52	46.5

[a] In thousands of DM per employee.
[b] In percent of employment in 1990.

the employment pledges and denoted as the per capita investment (PCI). Finally, the role of employment preservation in the privatization contracts is measured by the ratio of employment pledges to original employment in 1990 and denoted as preserved employment (PE).

Table 2 presents summary statistics of these three contractual variables for 17 industries. The data show considerable variation for the average PCP across industries. The average price for a workshop position ranges from a negative sales price (subsidy) of DM − 29 800 in the textile industry to a revenue of DM 13 700 in the construction industry. Seven industries show negative average sales prices. The PE in SOEs is particularly low in the optical industry at only 33%.[17] The variable PE measures the preserved employment only for firms that were successfully privatized and excludes SOEs that were liquidated. PE therefore understates the industry-specific employment loss.

---

[17] Schmidt (1993) reports that the council of experts of the THA (Leitungsausschuß) proposed liquidation of the entire microelectronic and optical industry. This proposal met with protest from the federal state governments of Saxony, Thuringia, and Brandenburg and was abandoned.

An important parameter of our model is the probability $p(j)$ of a SOE in group j to obtain political protection against its liquidation. This parameter is not directly measurable. The following analysis assumes that large firms find it easier to obtain political protection. Economies of scale in the rent-seeking competition between small and large firms may justify this assumption. We divide firms into three size groups, with small firms having less than 50 employees, the medium size with between 50 and 500 employees and large firms with more than 500 employees in 1990. It is assumed that $p(j)$ increases with each size groups.

Second, the ability to obtain political protection will generally increase with the level of sectorial unemployment that pertains to a certain industry. We therefore divide firms into a group A with low, a group B with average and a group C with high sectorial unemployment. Group A is composed of the construction and construction supply industry, group C of the textile, leather and optical industry. All other sectors form group B. We assume that the parameter $p(j)$ is low for group A and high for group C. This industry sorting is largely independent of the firm size sorting. Group A (group B, group C) comprises 16.93 (22.41, 17.09) % small, 65.36 (62.16, 63.25) % medium and 17.71 (15.43, 19.66) % large SOEs.

4.3. Implication 1: Subsidy patterns

The theoretical part of the model predicts that industry groups with frequent political intervention should be marked by a frequent privatization of low-quality SOEs that sell only at the cost of high subsidies. To examine this model implication, we first divide each size group and each industry group into four price quantiles. Quantile 1 contains the 25% of SOEs with the highest PCP, Quantile 4 the 25% with the lowest PCP, and Quantile 2 and 3 the two 25% groups in between. Table 3 shows the average PCP, PCI and PE for each price quantile for small, medium and large firms.

The two higher price quantiles show no clear size effect for the PCP. In the highest price quantile the average PCP increases from DM 50 300 for small firms to DM 61 000 for the group of large firms. For the lowest price quantile, however, we find a substantial subsidy bias toward large SOEs. The (negative) price for the lowest price quantile decreases from DM $-28\,500$ per employee for small SOEs to DM $-114\,600$ in the case of large SOEs. The PE decreases as the size of the SOE increases for all price quantiles. Thus, large SOEs had the more severe reductions in their workforce.

The quantile analysis is repeated for the industry groups with different sectorial unemployment. Table 4 reports the average PCP, PCI and PE for each price quantile in group A, B and C. Again the variation in the average PCP is small for high quality firms. A substantial difference emerges for the low quality

H. Hau / European Economic Review 42 (1998) 1177–1201

Table 3
Firm size and subsidy

Firm size	Quantile 1	Quantile 2	Quantile 3	Quantile 4
(a) *Average per capita price (PCP)*[a]				
Small firms	50.3	15.7	5.2	− 28.5
Medium firms	66.4	17.3	1.8	− 73.8
Large firms	61.0	14.1	− 12.2	− 114.6
(b) *Average per capita investment (PCI)*[a]				
Small firms	50.4	38.3	30.5	53.3
Medium firms	60.0	35.3	35.1	53.3
Large firms	62.3	41.9	44.9	62.6
(c) *Average preserved employment (PE)*[b]				
Small firms	0.65	0.76	0.74	0.56
Medium firms	0.50	0.61	0.56	0.36
Large firms	0.43	0.50	0.35	0.22

[a] In thousands of DM per employee.
[b] In percent of employment in 1990.

Table 4
Industry group and subsidy

Industry	Quantile 1	Quantile 2	Quantile 3	Quantile 4
(a) *Average per capita price (PCP)*[a]				
Group A	43.6	18.0	6.8	− 13.9
Group B	69.3	17.2	− 0.1	− 82.6
Group C	38.0	1.8	− 20.6	− 120.7
(b) *Average per capita investment (PCI)*[a]				
Group A	31.7	23.3	18.2	23.7
Group B	65.6	43.2	43.8	61.6
Group C	58.4	27.9	33.5	43.2
(c) *Average preserved employment (PE)*[b]				
Group A	0.62	0.72	0.70	0.60
Group B	0.49	0.60	0.54	0.34
Group C	0.41	0.46	0.38	0.20

[a] In thousands of DM per employee.
[b] In percent of employment in 1990.

quantile. The average PCP falls from DM − 13.900 to DM in group A to − 120.700 in group C. The most subsidized firms again have the lowest percentage of employment retention. Only 20% of the employees are retained in the low quality quantile of group C compared to 60% in group A.

1196   *H. Hau / European Economic Review 42 (1998) 1177–1201*

In summary the data confirm the model implications concerning the subsidy pattern. Both the magnitude of the sales subsidies and the subsidy bias toward large SOEs and industries with large sectorial unemployment support the claim that liquidation constraints played an important role in the German privatization process. Large SOEs and SOEs in industries with large sectorial unemployment appear to have benefited from liquidation constraints more frequently than small SOEs. Political intervention risk differed across firm types.

4.4. Implication 2: Time patterns

We assume that the privatization agency faced a continuous decrease in its decision autonomy with respect to liquidation decision. The theoretical analysis in Section 3.4 predicts a steeper decrease of the average revenue for firms with higher political risk $p(j)$ than for those that cannot procure political protection. Did the subsidy problem deteriorate over time as described by the model?

To examine the implied time pattern, the size and industry groups are divided into six half-year intervals from January 1991 to December 1993. Table 5 reports the average PCP of the six groups for each time interval. We observe an intertemporal decrease in the average PCP for all six groups. Second, we find that firm groups with higher political risk show indeed a steeper revenue decline. The difference in the slope is statistically significant at a 1% level for both the size groups and the industry groups.

The intertemporal decrease in the average PCP as such is not very surprising. Better SOEs could be sold first or the quality of unsold SOEs may have deteriorated in the absence of a buyer. But self-selection and quality deterioration do not explain the systematic difference in the price decrease across groups

Table 5
Time pattern

	Average quarterly per capita price (PCP)[a]					
	1991 : 1	1991 : 2	1992 : 1	1992 : 2	1993 : 1	1993 : 2
Small firms	19.3	17.7	8.7	− 1.7	− 22.6	− 16.1
Medium firms	20.4	22.9	1.3	− 11.1	− 30.8	− 46.5
Large firms	20.6	11.1	0.0	− 11.0	− 80.0	− 66.9
Group A	19.1	15.4	11.3	6.1	3.4	− 9.9
Group B	20.5	21.9	3.1	− 9.3	− 46.3	− 50.8
Group C	22.1	11.1	− 29.0	− 27.0	− 44.9	− 80.1

[a] In thousands of DM per employee.

Table 6
Liquidation pattern

	Privat.	Liquid.	Av. matching rate[a] $\hat{m}(j)$	Av. passage time[b] $PT(j)$
Small firms	944	577	0.0395	581
Medium firms	1301	428	0.0404	612
Large firms	368	92	0.0367	502
Group A	522	62	0.0625	792
Group B	1933	777	0.0390	580
Group C	158	258	0.0139	410

[a] Average monthly rate for the period 1991 : 1 to 1992 : 12.
[b] In days since 1 January 1991.

unless they apply particularly to large SOEs or SOEs in industry group C. Firm specific political intervention risk and the dynamic erosion of the THA's ability to liquidate can account for the observed time pattern.

4.5. Implication 3: Liquidation patterns

Did the privatization agency accelerate firm liquidations in industries with higher intervention risk? To address this question, we estimated the average passage time according to Eq. (15). We calculated a monthly matching rate as the ratio of the number of privatizations and the stock of SOEs at the beginning of each month and averaged this matching rate for the 24 months from January 1991 to December 1992. Table 6 documents the average monthly matching rates for the size and industry groups. SOEs in group A had a monthly matching chance of 6.25% relative to 1.39% for group C. The matching rates are similar across size groups.

The passage time is measured in days relative to the reference date of 1 January 1991. In accordance with our model, large SOEs and SOEs in group C show a lower average passage time until liquidation. The time differences to small SOEs and SOEs in group A are 79 and 382 days, respectively. Conditional on the absence of a matching buyer, large SOEs and SOEs in group C tended to be liquidated early.

We emphasize that a lower relative average passage time does not imply an earlier relative average liquidation date unless the matching rates are equal across size and industry groups. The passage time distribution gives liquidation probabilities conditional on the absence of a buyer match, while the liquidation density measures these probabilities for a firm that may escape liquidation by a buyer match. The higher the matching rate, the earlier should be the average liquidation date relative to the average passage time. Small (medium, large) SOEs were liquidated on average after only 319 (343, 307) days and SOEs in group A (group B, group C) after 310 (326, 335) days.

The low average liquidation date highlights the overall speed with which liquidation decisions were undertaken. The privatization agency became fully operational only after the German unification in November 1990. A year later the board of directors had taken more than half of all liquidation decisions. The policy of fast liquidation was plausibly motivated by rational foresight of future liquidation constraints.

4.6. Implication 4: variance effect

The variance effect predicts that groups of SOEs with high political risk show a lower average privatization price and a higher intra-group price variance. Again we measure privatization price by the PCP. It is instructive to look first at evidence for the size and industry groups. Table 7 reports the average per capita price in group j, PCP(j), and the intra-group variance of the per capita price, VAR(j). The first moment of the PCP decreases with firm size. This is not surprising given the evidence on the subsidy bias for large firms in Section 4.3. Associated with this subsidy pattern is a substantial increase in the second moment. The variance of the PCP in the group of large SOEs is more than three times higher than in the group of small SOEs. If we sort the SOEs according to sectorial unemployment, a similar variance effect is evident. Between group A and group C the intra-group variance increases by a factor 6.5.

Formally testing for the variance effect requires a sufficient number of firm groups. To increase the number of observations we thus divided SOEs within each of the 17 industry sectors into a group of large firms with more than 100 employees and a group of small firms with less than 100 employees

Table 7
Variance effect I

	Average group price PCP(j)	Intra-group price variance VAR(j)
Small firms	10.8	1450
Medium firms	3.0	4217
Large firms	− 13.0	5537
Group A	13.6	718
Group B	1.0	4667
Group C	− 28.8	4706

H. Hau / European Economic Review 42 (1998) 1177–1201   1199

in 1990. Only the two industry sectors with the lowest number of firms, namely the leather and optical industries, are not split into subsamples to guarantee enough observations in each firm group. Altogether, we obtained 32 firm groups.

The results of a linear OLS regression are shown in Table 8. Fig. 3 plots the 32 observations. The coefficient β_1 is negative and significant at a 3% level. The difference in the price variance across groups is substantial. The seven groups with the highest price variance have a more than 5 times larger intra-industry PCP variance than the seven groups with the lowest PCP variance.

Table 8
Variance effect II

Parameter	$PCP(j) = \beta_0 + \beta_1 \, VAR(j)$	
	OLS estimate	*T*-value
β_0	8.4822	(1.645)
β_1	− 0.0028	(− 2.316)

Adjusted $R^2 = 0.12$.

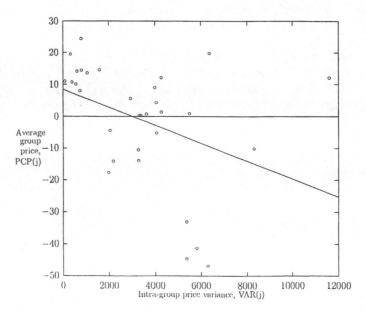

Fig. 3. Average group revenue and intra-group revenue variance.

The group of large chemical firms has a distinctly higher variance than other groups. This might be explained by the fact that sales contracts for this industry occasionally included ownership in valuable gas and oil pipelines. The large intra-industry variance for the chemical industry might be traced to the firm-specific inclusion or exclusion of such network assets rather than differences in the respective liquidation policy. Excluding large chemical firms from our sample implies that the *t*-value for the coefficient β_1 increases to 3.766. We conclude that the data confirms the variance effect of firm-specific political risk.

5. Conclusion

Can privatization authority be successfully delegated? We explored this question from the vantage point of a privatization agency, which faces a dynamic decision problem about liquidation decisions under incomplete political insulation. The model implications were confronted with micro data from the German privatization process.

The micro data confirms several cross-sectional and intertemporal model predictions resulting from the political constraints of the agency. In particular we find a subsidy bias towards large firms and industries with large sectorial unemployment and interpret this as evidence for incomplete insulation of the German privatization agency. The relative increase of this subsidy bias suggests that the agency's insulation problem deteriorated over time. Our model also predicts that a privatization agency faced with eroding decision autonomy should accelerate the liquidation process. Cross-sectional evidence for six groups of SOEs suggests that the passage time until liquidation was shorter for the groups with higher political intervention risk. We also emphasize that the overall speed of the liquidation decisions is supportive of the acceleration hypothesis. Finally, the variance enhancing effect of political intervention risk for the revenue distribution can be identified in the data.

On a more general level, our analysis illustrates that the degree of political insulation of a privatization agency is an important determinant for privatization outcomes. A successful institutional design must pay particular attention to the political insulation of the privatization agency.

Acknowledgements

I thank Dirk Bergemann, Igal Hendel, Charles Jones, Kenneth Rogoff, Marcel Thum, François Bourguignon and the two referees for their comments. Financial support was provided by Center for International Studies at Princeton University, the Hermann-Schlosser-Stiftung and the Bradley Foundation. I am thankful to the THA and the BVS for data access. All errors are my own.

References

Aghion, P., Blanchard, O., Carlin, W., 1994. The economics of enterprise restructuring in central and eastern Europe. Discussion paper, no. 1058. Center for Economic Policy Research, London.

Bös, D., 1992. Privatization in East Germany. IMF, Fiscal affairs department, Washington DC.

Boycko, M., Shleifer, A., Vishny, R., 1993. Privatizing Russia. Brookings Papers on Economic Activity 93 (2), 139–181.

Carlin, W., Mayer, C., 1994. The Treuhandanstalt: Privatization by the state and market. In: Blanchard, O., Froot, K., Sachs, J. (Eds.), The Transition in Eastern Europe, vol. 2. University of Chicago Press, Chicago, IL.

Czada, R., 1993. Die Treuhandanstalt im Umfeld von Politik und Verbänden. In: Fischer, W., Hax, H., Schneider, H.K. (Eds.), Treuhandanstalt – Das Unmögliche wagen. Akademie Verlag, Berlin.

Deutsches Institut für Wirtschaftsforschung, 1991. Subventionierung und Privatisierung durch die Treuhandanstalt: Kurswechsel erforderlich. DIW-Wochenbericht, No. 41, 575–580.

Deutsches Institut für Wirtschaftsforschung, 1992. Analyse der strukturellen Entwicklung der deutschen Wirtschaft. Strukturberichterstattung, Berlin.

Dixit, A., Pindyck, R.S., 1994. Investment under Uncertainty. Princeton University Press, Princeton, NJ.

Dyck, A., 1995. Privatization in Eastern Germany: Management selection and economic transition. Working paper, no. 95/030. Harvard Business School, Cambridge, MA.

East German privatization: Fast and loose. Economist, May 1994, 75–76.

Ingersoll, J.E., 1987. Theory of Financial Decision Making. Rowman and Littlefield, New York.

Kloepfer, M., 1993. Öffentlich-rechtliche Vorgaben für die Treuhand. In: Fischer, W., Hax, H., Schneider, H.K. (Eds.), Treuhandanstalt – Das Unmögliche wagen. Akademie Verlag, Berlin.

Priewe, J., 1993. Privatization of the industrial sector: The function and the activities of the Treuhandanstalt. Cambridge Journal of Economics 17 (3), 333–348.

Sappington, D., Stiglitz, J., 1987. Privatization, information and incentives. Journal of Policy Analysis and Management 6, 567–582.

Schmidt, K.-D., 1993. Strategien der Privatisierung. In: Fischer, W., Hax, H., Schneider, H.K. (Eds.), Treuhandanstalt – Das Unmögliche wagen. Akademie Verlag, Berlin.

Schwalbach, J., 1993. Begleitung sanierungsfähiger Unternehmen auf dem Weg zur Privatisierung. In: Fischer, W., Hax, H., Schneider, H.K. (Eds.), Treuhandanstalt – Das Unmögliche wagen. Akademie Verlag, Berlin.

Seibel, W., 1993. Die organisatorische Entwicklung der Treuhandanstalt. In: Fischer, W., Hax, H., Schneider, H.K. (Eds.), Treuhandanstalt – Das Unmögliche wagen. Akademie Verlag, Berlin.

Shapiro, C., Willig, R., 1990. Economic rationales for the scope of privatization. Discussion paper 41. Princeton University, Princeton, NJ.

Willig, R., 1993. Public versus regulated private enterprise. In: Bruno, M., Pleskovic, B. (Eds.), Proceedings of the World Bank Annual Conference on Development Economics 1993. World Bank, Washington DC.

[20]

PERGAMON

Long Range Planning 33 (2000) 201–219

LRP long range planning
www.elsevier.com/locate/lrp

PowerGen: The Development of Corporate Planning in a Privatized Utility

David Jennings

Following privatization in 1991, PowerGen has developed from being a UK electricity generator to become a diversified international energy company. This article looks at the development of PowerGen's corporate planning process to meet the extensive and continuing changes that have taken place in the company's environment, strategy and organization. The development of the company's planning process indicates that planning systems can be reconfigured, perhaps frequently, to maintain consistency with the organization's changing strategy and structure. The current planning process is discussed, and its ability to balance autonomy and adaptation by the business units with co-ordination and the realization of financial expectations. In conclusion, effective planning activity requires: appropriate reconfiguration of the planning process to meet contextual change; clear expression of central management intent concerning business unit performance; an organizational structure that facilitates the communication and negotiation of business unit planning guidelines; and organization-wide commitment to the planning process and its agreed outputs. © 2000 Elsevier Science Ltd. All rights reserved.

Planning: process and context

While there has been speculation concerning the 'fall' of planning,[1] there is evidence that the practice of formal corporate planning is becoming more prevalent. Houlden[2] has found, between 1985 and 1992, a doubling of the number of organizations employing corporate planning units.

Planning processes are potentially affected by a range of contextual factors. The reconfiguration of planning systems to reflect contextual change is an important assumption with implications for both the effectiveness of the planning process and

Dr David Jennings is a principal lecturer in strategic management at Nottingham Business School. Corresponding address: Nottingham Business School, Nottingham Trent University, Department of Strategic Management and Marketing, Burton Street, Nottingham NG1 4BU, UK. E-mail: david.jennings@ntu.ac.uk

its role. However, appropriate reconfiguration may not take place. Chakravarthy's survey of senior executives in a wide range of industries found planning systems to be, for the most part, lacking in both external and internal fit (in matching the characteristics of proposed ideal systems).[3] Failure to reflect the planning system's particular context can be expected to result in a system that is ineffective, with the planning process assuming the role of an organizational ritual.

Within the literature of corporate planning a range of contextual factors has been identified as affecting the configuration of the planning process.

External context

The nature of the organization's external environment has relevance for the characteristics of the planning process. Planning systems in more complex environments have been found to be more flexible, with plans reviewed more frequently and with shorter horizons. Greater environmental complexity may also increase the number of decision areas to which strategic planning is applied and planning stages undertaken.[4] However, the effect of environmental complexity upon planning characteristics may be more strongly related to senior management perceptions of the environment than to objective measures of complexity.[5,6]

The relationship between planning characteristics and environmental uncertainty is less well established. Lindsay and Rue[7] found a positive relationship between the scope of planning and planning stages undertaken, and the complexity and instability of the business environment. Later studies[6,8] have concluded that environmental uncertainty and volatility do not have a consistent effect upon planning characteristics and may be moderated by top management's interpretation of the environment.[9] However, Kukalis[10] found shorter plan horizons to be particularly related to more turbulent environments. A similar relationship is found by Yasai-Ardekani and Haug,[11] with highly competitive environments being associated with shorter planning horizons and greater involvement of top management teams.

Internal context

An organization's complexity (diversity and interdependence between business units) may partly determine its need for corporate planning[12] and may be critical to the extensiveness of the planning process.[4,11] For organizations structured into divisions, strategic planning can act as an integrative device,[10] with planning systems having greater scope and formality within diversified, divisionally structured companies.[13]

The nature of the organization's core technology may also be an important consideration. The vulnerability of the core technology through the length of the investment gestation period or technological inflexibility has been associated with higher planning effort and sophistication,[4,13] with the planning process

> *Failure to reflect the planning system's particular context can be expected to result in a system that is ineffective*

acting to protect core technologies from environmental pertur-bations.[11]

Central management's perception of the type of performance improvement that is needed (strategic versus more immediate financial improvement) presents a pressure for performance improvement that may be expected to affect the characteristics of the corporate planning system. Chakravarthy and Lor-ange[3,14,15] propose that a firm's planning system needs to achieve a balance between adaptation (promoting creativity and the identification of environmental threats and opportunities) and integration (emphasizing control and the co-ordination of internal resources). An adaptive orientation may require parti-cipative goal setting and a loose link between long-term finan-cial plans and business unit budgets. Integration implies a top-down approach to goal setting, an emphasis upon operating rather than strategic budgets and a tight linkage between long-term financial plans and budgets. Pressure for strategic develop-ment requires a planning system characterized by an adaptive approach; financial pressure requires integration. The two pressures may be simultaneously present, with their influence dependent upon the views of the organization's senior manage-ment concerning performance. For a particular organization, integration and adaptive orientations need not be mutually exclusive; a balanced approach has been found to be associated with greater long-term financial success.[16]

integration and adaptive orientations need not be mutually exclusive

The rapid rate of environmental and organizational change that has become a characteristic of many industries[17] poses a difficult challenge to the practice of formal corporate planning. Planning can serve a number of important organizational roles: enabling organization-wide response to environmental change; protecting core technologies through helping to recognize and address uncertainties; providing an integrative device and act-ing as a basis for divisional and business control.[13] The signifi-cance of these roles may require a continuing commitment to planning; however, that process may also need to be adapted to meet contextual change.

PowerGen

As a privatized company PowerGen has moved abruptly from the context of a nationalized industry to a more complex and changing environment, characterized by increasing competition and changing regulatory and government policy. These factors affect both the profitability of the core market and, at times, the strategic initiatives that the company is able to undertake (for example, through governmental restrictions on merger and capacity development). Within this context PowerGen has achieved a diversification of the company into other energy-re-lated industries and has established overseas undertakings in Australia, Germany, Portugal, Indonesia and India, while main-taining financial performance. During 1999 the company's divi-dend yield was 70% higher than its larger privatized rival,

Exhibit 1. PowerGen today

PowerGen was created as part of the UK government's programme for the privatization of the electricity generation and supply industry. The company was privatized in 1991 as a generating company, vested with twenty-one power stations, providing approximately 30% of the electricity supplied to the transmission and distribution networks in England and Wales.

The company now operates gas and electricity generating, trading and supply businesses within the UK, serving the industrial and domestic customer. Group and associated undertakings include the following:

- **PowerGen CHP Ltd.** Sale of energy services involving the construction of combined heat and power plant

- **PowerGen North Sea Ltd.** Oil and gas related activities

- **Kinetica Ltd.** Transportation and marketing of natural gas in the UK

- **Wavedriver Ltd.** Development of electric vehicle-related technology

- **Csepel Power Company** Hungary; generation and sale of electricity

- **Yallourn Energy Pty.** Australia; mining of brown coal and production and sale of electricity from coal-fired power station

- **Saale Energie** Germany; holding and management company for the Group's interest in Schkopau power station

- **MIBRAG GmbH and MIBRAG BV.** Germany and Netherlands; mining and sale of brown coal and generation and sale of electricity

- **Turbogas Produtora Energetica** Portugal; construction of gas-fired power station plant

- **PT Jawa Power** Indonesia; construction of coal-fired power station plant

- **Gujarat Torrent Energy Corporation** India; construction of gas-fired power station plant

- **Cottam Development Centre** UK; construction and operation of gas-fired power station plant to develop, test and commercially operate the next generation of gas-power plant technology (a joint venture with Siemens)

In 1998 PowerGen acquired East Midland Electricity, a regional electricity supply company, from Dominion Resources, an American utility. Group turnover exceeds £3bn, with a market value of £5bn.

National Power. Exhibit 1 shows PowerGen's current position and holdings.

PowerGen has pursued a long-term vision of strategic development[18] with planning as an integral part of its management process. The company's experience provides insight into both the reconfiguration of the planning process to meet changes in context and the operation of planning in a diversified utility. The case methodology on which this study is based is described in the Appendix.

Strategy, organization and planning pre-privatization

Prior to the privatization of the electricity industry in England and Wales, the Central Electricity Generating Board (CEGB) was responsible for the generation and transmission of electricity. In 1989 the CEGB's non-nuclear generating capacity was divided to form two organizations, namely National Power and PowerGen. PowerGen's functions were conferred in March 1990 and it was privatized in March 1991.

The aim of the CEGB had been to achieve the highest level of generating plant availability at lowest cost while working within given limits on new investment. By the late 1980s the CEGB had adopted a functional structure within which a centralized planning process helped to determine the funds available to the power stations in order for them to deliver their particular generating requirements. Each power station was required to produce a five-year plan for its own operations. The planning process commenced with the issue of corporate guidance for the power stations and took a year to complete. However, the process sometimes experienced delays and on occasion a new planning cycle commenced before the previous cycle was complete. A central planning team provided the overall co-ordination of planning activity and developed an extensive set of forecasts with which to estimate growth in the demand for electricity. The power stations received detailed guidance for their planning, with a central staff group determining each station's fuel strategy and production requirements. The resulting plans followed a centrally determined format and contained a considerable amount of detail.

New strategic initiatives

The situation in which PowerGen was to operate differed considerably from that of the nationalized CEGB. The generators were to sell electricity into a competitive electricity pool and a progressively liberalized and competitive electricity market, meet the expectations of shareholders, and operate within a

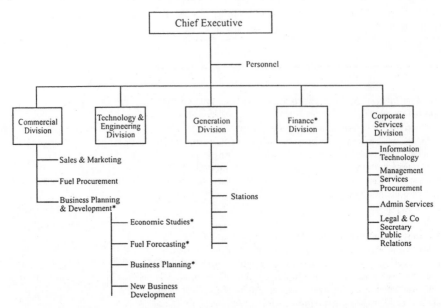

Figure 1. Organization structure 1990 (asterisks denote those involved in managing the planning process)

developing economic and environmental regulatory framework. In addition, the company faced difficult demand and supply conditions, with the total demand for electricity for the period 1990–1997 forecast to grow at only 0.6% per year and a significant level of industry overcapacity.

Within this context PowerGen adopted a number of strategic objectives. Recognizing the inefficiencies of the pre-privatization industry and the demands of the new competitive environment, there was a need to become a world-class low-cost electricity producer. It was accepted that through competition, and possibly regulation, the company would suffer an inevitable loss of market share and that medium and longer term growth would require the establishment of new income streams in other energy-related areas where the company's core competencies could create value. The increasing international demand for power and the opening up of electricity markets to foreign investment presented opportunities for PowerGen's diversification overseas. PowerGen would also seek the opportunity to re-integrate generation with supply.[6]

At an early stage the company developed a joint venture with Conoco, both to address its own growing needs for gas supply and to supply outside customers. Further developments focused upon gas field development and production, gas retailing and transportation, electricity sales to the competitive industrial and commercial market, the operation and development of combined heat and power schemes and international

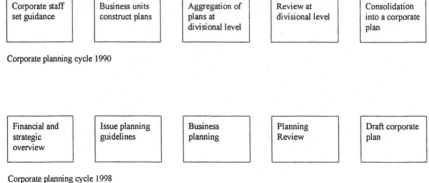

Corporate planning cycle 1990

Corporate planning cycle 1998

Figure 2. Corporate planning cycle, 1990 and 1998

power developments in India, the Asia Pacific region and
Europe.

The development of corporate planning

Prior to privatization, the services of the McKinsey consulting
company had been engaged to help develop PowerGen's strategy and organizational structure. A structure was proposed that
was based upon well-defined functional responsibilities and few
layers of management, with each function forming a division.
(See Figure 1, where an asterisk indicates those involved in
managing the planning process.)

Post-privatization planning

The McKinsey review considered the planning process, recommending a five-stage process that was introduced in 1990 along
with the new organization structure (see Figure 2). The planning process was to be led and managed by the Commercial
Division, within which a large group of planners assisted the
development of the company's corporate strategy and its diversification through the New Business Development unit.

The planning process retained a high degree of centrality.
Staff in the Business Planning and Development Department
constructed a number of scenarios for the core business, the
Generation Division. These scenarios focused upon market
share, pool prices and competitor analysis. The decisions that
could be made by each business unit (each power station) were
essentially those that had been available to them within the
CEGB. The focus of planning remained, as with the CEGB,
upon developing the resource implications of a centrally determined strategy. The role of units in the other divisions was primarily to forecast costs within the scenarios that had been
developed by the Business Planning staff. The plans from the
business units were aggregated to provide divisional plans.

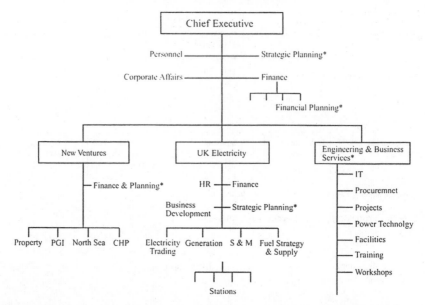

Figure 3. Organization structure 1992 (asterisks denote those involved in managing the planning process)

Financial projections from these exercises were consolidated by the Finance Division.

Devolution

The centralized approach to planning associated with the CEGB became increasingly less relevant with the opening of the market for electricity, the wholesale Electricity Pool, at the start of April 1990. The operation of the Pool became the focus of PowerGen's strategy, requiring the development of both a strong commercial orientation and increased operational flexibility.

In 1992 PowerGen introduced a number of organizational changes that were to result in the devolution of the planning process. The company was reorganized (see Figure 3) from a functional form into three divisions: New Ventures (containing PowerGen International, North Sea, and Combined Heat and Power); UK Electricity (UK Generation, including sales and marketing); and an Engineering and Business Services Division. Each division was given its own managing director.

Reorganization was accompanied by changes in the planning process. The existing large, central planning team was replaced by planning staff within the divisions. A much smaller central Strategic Planning function was introduced with responsibility for both corporate strategy and corporate planning. All business units became either profit or cost centres with the scope of options available to the business units considerably widened and provided with a stronger commercial focus. In addition the level of detail required in business unit plans was reduced to provide a plan that could be expressed on a few sheets of paper. The time required to carry out the corporate planning process also changed, from a year or more to a nine-month process.

The changes to the planning process were consistent with the developing planning needs of PowerGen; the growth in the significance of the new businesses and their need for greater autonomy to achieve adaptation to their own particular competitive environments and, in the core generation business, the need for increased flexibility and wider exploitation of the opportunities for cost reduction to meet market and competitive conditions.

Planning problems: 1993–1994

From 1993 to 1994 several developments occurred that would affect the future profitability of the core business, UK Electricity. These included an agreement with the industry regulator to cap wholesale prices in the Electricity Pool, and also for PowerGen to sell 2 GW of power plant. The effect on profit forecasts was compounded by an unexpected increase in electricity supplied by Nuclear Electric.

For any organization, planning is inherently an iterative process, but during the 1993–1994 planning cycle, presentation of the corporate plan to the Board was delayed by the need for substantial reworking of the plan to more fully reflect Power-Gen's financial priorities. The 1993 planning cycle revealed a rift between strategic decisions and the group's financial requirements. In part the problem was seen as a result of the way in which planning responsibilities had been assigned within the company. The company's Strategic Planner, reporting to the Chief Executive, was responsible for both the development of corporate strategy and production of the corporate plan, an arrangement that limited the influence of the Finance Department in shaping the corporate plan early on in the planning cycle. Responsibility for the plan and for managing the corporate planning process was passed to the Director of Finance, effectively increasing the influence of financial considerations in the planning process.

The planning difficulties also reflected a failure by the centre to fully communicate scenario information. The centre had considered that such an event as 'price capping' could occur, but had not communicated that early enough for it to become a part of the assumptions for business planning. PowerGen adopted the practice that scenarios should be developed by the business managers and planners; the plans that followed were to be robust to the possibilities identified by the scenarios.

The difficulties experienced in the 1993–1994 planning cycle were added to by the divisional form of organization which PowerGen had adopted in 1992. From the perspective of managing the planning process, the divisions added a level of bu-

PowerGen adopted the practice that scenarios should be developed by the business managers and planners

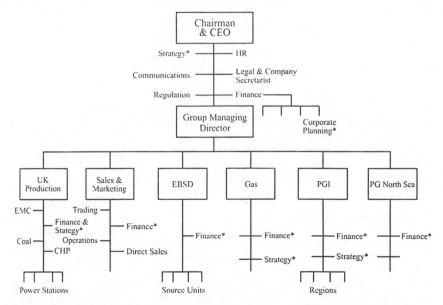

Figure 4. Organization structure 1996 (asterisks denote those involved in managing the planning process)

reaucracy and affected communication with the business units. Priorities and issues that were identified at corporate level were filtered, and often new arguments added, before being addressed by business unit planners.

Encouraging adaptation and integration

By 1996 several of the diversification initiatives within the New Venture Division had developed to a stage where they justified their own management, on a level with that of the company's core business, UK Electricity. Within the core business, the signalled liberalization of the electricity market (1998) argued for sales and marketing to be given greater autonomy and separated from generation. In September 1996 PowerGen underwent a further reorganization that reflected these developments and replaced the divisional form of organization with new clusters of business units, each cluster headed by a managing director, with a Group Managing Director addressing the overall development and co-ordination of the businesses (see Figure 4).

The reorganization improved the focus of unit managers upon the particular circumstances associated with their businesses, and also enabled corporate staff involved in planning to develop targets that more exactly addressed the role and potential of the individual businesses.

The planning system encouraged initiatives by the business units within a corporate context; it also addressed the need for coordination between a number of the business units. In the

UK PowerGen was seeking to build an integrated gas and electricity business. The businesses that made up the UK electricity and gas value chain required the co-ordination of their strategies and objectives. There was also a need for co-ordination between UK activities and the developing overseas operations which were supported by PowerGen's core skills in electricity and fuel trading, power station construction and operation.

The planning process in 1998
Scenarios and the business environment

Since privatization a number of developments have increased the environmental complexity and uncertainty facing PowerGen. These include industrial and geographic diversification, increased competition in the UK generation industry (the core business for revenue) and the actions and reactions occurring at the interface between the company, regulator and government.

Under the CEGB considerable effort had been put into the development of its own forecasts concerning the demand for electricity and the factors, such as GDP, upon which demand was based. Following privatization scenario construction was increasingly used as a way of exploring the possibilities presented by an environment where forecasts were often unreliable in predicting the price of gas, oil and coal, and inappropriate for anticipating changes in regulatory conditions.

PowerGen has adopted the practice of developing a number of scenarios prior to the commencement of the planning cycle. The principal scenario exercises concern the inputs and outputs of PowerGen's businesses, the markets and prices for gas, coal and electricity. Scenario production takes the form of a devolved process, carried out by the business units with assistance from the corporate strategy staff. For each scenario exercise a team is drawn from a number of functions and businesses representing the various groups with a significant interest in the output from the scenario. The team is led by a representative of the unit that either has the most expertise or involvement in the area on which the scenario is focused.

Information from the scenario exercises is incorporated into the planning guidelines. While scenarios can be seen as facilitating the adaptive role of planning, their joint construction and acceptance by business units also acts to facilitate co-ordination between those units. Figure 2 shows the main stages in PowerGen's current planning process.

Scenario production takes the form of a devolved process

Financial and strategic overview

Strategy debates take place within PowerGen to consider issues and opportunities as they arise. As part of this process the corporate strategy and planning staff meet with business unit managers as need dictates. The corporate strategy team uses a range of techniques to assist in the examination of situations and issues, including Porter's techniques for analysing competitive position and the profit drivers in an industry, portfolio techniques and the analysis of core competencies, skills and resources. In developing and appraising options, the business units may use whatever strategic techniques they believe appropriate. This partly reflects the considerable resources that PowerGen has invested in management education and development, but it also reflects the belief that technique is secondary to the quality of the debate achieved. Consequently, when examining strategic issues people are involved from across the different businesses, calling upon as wide a range of experience as possible. The ongoing examination of business unit strategy by business and corporate staff makes it unnecessary to have a comprehensive review prior to the planning cycle.

During the initial overview stage of the planning process each business unit provides an update of its plan for the previous year, taking account of developments in strategy and the market context, together with the options that the business believes are open to it. A base case for the business unit's plan is agreed, forming the option which is expected to be developed in the subsequent business plan. Business unit strategy is established before developing detailed planning guidance. Partly this reflects the need for inter-business co-ordination. However, there is scope for flexibility as issues affecting business unit strategies often emerge and have to be addressed within the subsequent stages of the corporate planning process, prior to Board approval.

technique is secondary to the quality of the debate achieved

Consolidation of this information provides a strategic and financial overview that is examined for its strategic fit with the overall priorities of the company and the acceptability of the projected balance sheet and profitability. Conclusions from this comparison support the development of the guidelines, the corporate context of strategic and financial priorities and targets agreed with each business unit within which business planning is conducted.

Planning guidelines

Typically, the development of planning guidelines involves a great deal of discussion and lobbying between the corporate strategy and planning staff and business unit managers before the resulting guidelines are formally agreed.

The guidelines differ between business groups and are further developed within each group before becoming a basis for business unit plans. Within UK Production, the guidance for each of the business units (power stations) specifies financial and environmental constraints, generation allocations and an indicative running regime. Particular attention is given to short-term profit. For PowerGen International, the objectives include the size of developments and when they are to occur, the plant capacity to be achieved in each country, the profit level in five to ten years' time, and the number of projects to be delivered each year to achieve those objectives. More immediate targets would also typically refer to the human resource development that is required to underpin the longer term achievements.

Business planning

All units, including corporate staff units, produce a plan with a five-year horizon. Typically, a plan is a brief document clearly stating the business unit's objectives and how it expects to meet them, the key issues facing the business, how the business is going to develop and the expected financial performance.

Planning review

The plan review stage involves the corporate planning staff, business planners and business directors. Once business units have submitted their individual plans, the team examines the overall financial picture that the plans present and whether in total they meet the group requirements. This leads to feedback into the business reviews where the Group Managing Director and Financial Director review the plans of individual business units with each unit's managing director.

Performance review

Following the presentation of the plan to the Board, the performance of the managing directors of the various businesses is reviewed. The reward scheme is based upon business and corporate performance. While corporate performance typically involves earnings per share, business performance includes the year's contribution to achieving the longer term key achievements that the business aims to deliver over the next five years. All of the financial and strategic targets will have been specified in the previous year's plan.

Continuity and change in corporate planning

Following privatization, PowerGen has retained a commitment to corporate planning. A number of factors may explain this continuing commitment. The acceptance of a planning discipline may represent a continuation within PowerGen of part of the pre-privatization CEGB culture. In turn, the cultural acceptance of planning can assist the effectiveness of a planning process,[19] helping to sustain the continuation of the process.

Other reasons for the continuation of planning can be found in the company's need for planning. PowerGen's core technologies typically require investments with a long gestation period, and the resulting plant is inflexible in the type of product that it can be used to deliver. Such investments create a particular need for planning as a means of addressing and reducing uncertainty. Similarly, the emphasis in PowerGen's strategy upon the integration of activities, typified by the linkages between gas and generating activities, UK operations and overseas initiatives, creates a need for the co-ordinative function of corporate planning.

Since privatization PowerGen's planning process has retained

the emphasis in PowerGen's strategy upon the integration of activities, typified by the linkages between gas and generating activities, creates a need for the co-ordinative function of corporate planning

Table 1. Changes in the planning process

CEGB pre-1990	PowerGen 1998
Large central planning unit	Small central planning staff
Central forecasts	Scenarios developed on a devolved and cross-business basis
Technical and resource-based focus	Financial and strategic focus
Narrow scope for (business) unit options	Wider and more strategic range of business unit options, degree of freedom varying between units
Detailed business plans following a prescribed format	Brief plans, discretionary format
Twelve-month planning cycle (or more)	Six-month cycle

a number of fundamental characteristics. The corporate planning process remains formal and extensive and plans still have a five-year horizon. But there has also been a number of significant changes in the operation of the process (see Table 1). Planning at PowerGen has become a more devolved process with a greater emphasis on commercial and strategic concerns. The organization's planning staff have largely been redistributed to the business units leaving small corporate planning and strategy functions (three staff in Strategy, four in Corporate Planning). The greater involvement of business units in exploring the uncertainties facing them has been achieved through participation in cross-organization scenario exercises. Business plans have become shorter, commercially orientated and based upon a wider range of business unit options. In addition the planning cycle is completed in a shorter period of time, a development that is consistent with the increased uncertainty of the company's business environment.[10,11]

Performance pressures and planning system characteristics

The development of PowerGen's corporate planning system can be seen as embodying change in the system's orientation between adaptation and integration. Pre-privatization, and until the reorganization of 1992, the system demonstrated an emphasis upon integration and control, with PowerGen operating as a functionally organized entity within which a centralized planning process provided a highly constrained role for business unit planning. The limited scope of PowerGen's initial portfolio, a single business, was consistent with a centralized approach to planning.[20] In addition, centralized initiatives and the 'top-down' setting of goals are necessary to initiate diversification.[3]

The devolved planning system (1992) represents a move to an adaptive orientation. The competitive pressures presented by the operation of the electricity market required greater innovation and flexibility at business unit level in the reduction of costs. Similarly the further development of the new businesses required a less centralized approach. The devolution of the company encouraged business units to identify and exploit the opportunities available to them. Within the core business, namely generation, the result was often to provide greater cost reductions than those that had been targeted.

A third phase was initiated by concern during the 1993–1994 planning cycle that an imbalance was occurring between the organization's strategic development and more immediate financial performance. Central management responsibilities were reassigned, with responsibility for corporate planning becoming located within the finance function, providing greater control of the financial implications of plans. In addition it was recognized that the organizational structure required modification to provide more effective communication of the centre's views concerning the priorities and issues that business unit managers were to address. This development, however, does not simply represent a return to earlier centralization. The performance guidelines, directing business unit plans, are developed in a manner that facilitates an adaptive response by business units. Guidelines developed for the business clusters are limited to reflect corporate priorities and cross-group concerns. The guidelines are further developed within the business clusters before being addressed by the business units. The development of guidelines also provides flexibility through the upward feeding of information concerning market conditions facing the business units and the process of negotiation. As a result business unit strategy can, on occasion, become a driver for corporate strategy through the presentation of further opportunities to the central strategy and planning staff.

Recognition of the potential for developing linkages between activities to achieve synergies within the UK businesses and between UK activities and diversification in other countries required the planning system to also serve an integrative role, the need for co-ordination being addressed through a number of mechanisms including the monthly meeting of a Business Executive (representing all of the company's businesses), cross-organization scenario development and through the planning guidance agreed with each business unit.

PowerGen's experience supports the view that the overall orientation of a planning system can be changed to address central management's perceptions concerning the need for an adaptive response by business units or an alternative emphasis upon control and integration. The orientation can also be varied between business units. The businesses that constitute a diversified company can be assigned different missions,[21] with the emphasis upon adaptation and integration being varied between businesses by framing and negotiating guidelines for performance that reflect central managers' intentions for each particular business unit. PowerGen International's longer term financial targets and broad indicators for strategic development facilitate a more adaptive approach by those business units. For UK Production, the emphasis is upon shorter term profit

the result was often to provide greater cost reductions than those that had been targeted

achieved within centrally determined constraints upon fuel buying and revenue achievement.

The role given to planning is part of an organization's corporate management style, by which central management attempts to add value to the diversified company's businesses.[22] The style of an organization may be determined by factors that are constant across the organization, including the personality of the CEO, senior management's skills, the financial condition of the organization and the shape of the portfolio of businesses,[22] with the implication that a particular style (such as that of strategic planning or financial control) operates company-wide. However, the adopted corporate management style also needs to be appropriate to the nature of the individual business, as must planning. The changes in the design and operation of PowerGen's planning system indicate that aspects of corporate style can flex to accommodate changes in context and be varied between business units.

Conclusions

PowerGen's experience provides an example of the reconfiguration of a planning system to accommodate changes in strategic and organizational context, thereby helping to maintain the relevance of planning activity. The company's experience suggests a number of principles necessary for effective planning activity.

- Planning processes should be reconfigured, perhaps frequently, in order to maintain their consistency with the organization's changing strategy and structure.
- Developments in corporate expectations concerning financial and strategic performance need to be expressed through a clear central management intent that may be varied between business units.
- An organizational structure is required that facilitates the communication of priorities and issues to the business units and is in turn able to facilitate the negotiation and fine-tuning of planning guidelines between central and business-level management, with an accepted framework for resolving associated conflicts within the planning process.
- Planning requires commitment throughout the organization, both to participation in the planning process and to the agreed outputs of that process. Commitment can be based upon cultural factors, making planning decisions into formally accepted agreements and by linking planned financial and strategic targets to performance review and reward.

Planning systems need to be seen as open to redesign, with senior management adopting a proactive approach to the development of the corporate planning process. PowerGen's experience suggests that a number of factors may facilitate such adaptation, including organization-wide commitment to planning and the integration of planning outputs into other organizational processes, such as human resource planning, budgeting and review and reward systems. Such integration may not only help to realize the benefits of planning,[23,24] but may also facilitate the development of the planning system through the promotion of consistency with changes in other aspects of the organization.

Appendix A

Research method
This article is based upon longitudinal case research. The rationale for employing a case approach was justified by the complexity of planning processes.[25] While studies of planning have tended to use a survey-based approach,[26] survey instruments may not capture the richness of a planning system or its context.[3]

This study took the form of an embedded, single case design,[27] covering the recent development of the organization's corporate planning process. Research data was primarily gained through tape-recorded interviews. A series of in-depth interviews was conducted with the heads of Corporate and Financial Planning and Strategic Planning. Several interviews were also conducted with business-level planners. All interviews were conducted between late 1997 and early 1998. Analysis was conducted through the writing of a case study and by the use of tabular displays based upon factors suggested by the literature and the primary information.[28]

Retrospective accounts may be open to a number of sources of inaccuracy.[29] To minimize these effects, use was made of multiple respondents and documentary evidence. The construction of a single case assisted in the evaluation of consistency between respondents' accounts. The independent review of that case by all respondents and by two non-interviewed personnel with relevant knowledge of the planning process helped to verify the accuracy and completeness of the case information.

References

1. H. Mintzberg, *The Rise and Fall of Strategic Planning*, Prentice Hall, New York (1994).
2. B. T. Houlden, How corporate planning adapts and survives, *Long Range Planning* 28(4), 99–108 (1995).
3. B. S. Chakravarthy, On tailoring a strategic planning system to its context: some empirical evidence, *Strategic Management Journal* 8, 517–534 (1987).
4. S. Kukalis, Determinants of strategic planning systems in large organizations: a contingency approach, *Journal of Management Studies* 28(2), 143–160 (1991).
5. R. Y. Odom and W. R. Boxx, Environment, planning processes, and organizational performance of churches, *Strategic Management Journal* 9, 197–205 (1988).

6. L. C. Rhyne, The relationship of information usage characteristics to planning system sophistication; an empirical examination, *Strategic Management Journal* **6**, 319–337 (1985).

7. W. M. Lindsay and L. W. Rue, Impact of the organization environment on the long range planning process: a contingency view, *Academy of Management Journal* **23**(3), 385–404 (1980).

8. W. R. Boulton, W. M. Lindsay, S. G. Franklin and L. W. Rue, Strategic planning: determining the impact of environmental characteristics and uncertainty, *Academy of Management Journal* **25**(3), 500–509 (1982).

9. M. Javidan, The impact of environmental uncertainty on long range planning practices of the US savings and loans industry, *Strategic Management Journal* **5**, 381–392 (1984).

10. S. Kukalis, Strategic planning in large US corporations—a survey, *Omega* **16**(5), 393–404 (1988).

11. M. Yasai-Ardekani and R. S. Haug, Contextual determinants of strategic planning processes, *Journal of Management Studies* **34**(5), 729–768 (1997).

12. B. T. Houlden, Survival of the corporate planner, *Long Range Planning* **18**(5), 49–54 (1985).

13. P. Grinyer, S. Al-Bazzaz and M. Yasai-Ardekani, Towards a contingency theory of corporate planning: findings in 48 UK companies, *Strategic Management Journal* **7**, 3–28 (1986).

14. B. S. Chakravarthy and P. Lorange, Adapting strategic planning to the changing needs of a business, *Journal of Organizational Change Management* **4**(2), 6–18 (1991).

15. B. S. Chakravarthy and P. Lorange, Managing strategic adaptation: options in administrative systems, *Interfaces* **14**(1), 34–46 (1984).

16. L. C. Rhyne, Contrasting planning systems in high, medium and low performance companies, *Journal of Management Studies* **24**(4), 363–385 (1987).

17. R. A. D'Aveni, Coping with hypercompetition: utilizing the new 7Ss framework, *Academy of Management Executive* **9**(3), 45–56 (1995).

18. E. A. Wallis, Managing privatization at PowerGen, *Long Range Planning* **28**(6), 10–18 (1995).

19. V. Ramanujam and N. Venkatraman, Planning system characteristics and planning effectiveness, *Strategic Management Journal* **8**, 453–468 (1987).

20. R. Rumelt, *Strategy, Structure and the Financial Performance of the Fortune 500*, Harvard University Press, Cambridge, MA (1974).

21. P. Hasperlagh, Portfolio planning: uses and limits, *Harvard Business Review* **January/February**, 58–73 (1982).

22. M. Goold and A. Campbell, *Strategies and Styles*, Basil Blackwell, Oxford (1987).

23. I. Bonn and C. Christodoulou, From strategic planning to

strategic management, *Long Range Planning* **29**(4), 543–551 (1996).

24. D. M. Reid, Operationalizing strategic planning, *Strategic Management Journal* **10**, 553–567 (1989).

25. B. K. Boyd, Strategic planning and financial performance: a meta-analytic review, *Journal of Management Studies* **28**(4), 353–374 (1991).

26. A. S. Hutt and R. K. Reger, A review of strategy process research, *Journal of Management* **13**(2), 211–236 (1987).

27. R. K. Yin, *Case Study Research, Design and Method*, Sage, London (1989).

28. K. M. Eisenhardt, Building theories from case study research, *Academy of Management Review* **14**(4), 532–550 (1989).

29. C. C. Miller, L. B. Cardinal and W. H. Glick, Retrospective reports in organizational research: a re-examination of recent evidence, *Academy of Management Journal* **40**(1), 189–204 (1997).

© *Academy of Management Journal*
1999, Vol. 42, No. 5, 526–538.

CORPORATE PERFORMANCE AND STAKEHOLDER MANAGEMENT: BALANCING SHAREHOLDER AND CUSTOMER INTERESTS IN THE U.K. PRIVATIZED WATER INDUSTRY

STUART OGDEN
University of Leeds

ROBERT WATSON
University of Strathclyde

This study examined a major contention of stakeholder theory: namely, that a firm can simultaneously enhance the interests of its shareholders and other relevant stakeholders. Financial data relating to the U.K. water supply industry and the customer service performance indicators introduced after privatization in 1989 to protect customer interests provided the basis of our empirical analysis. The results show that, although improving relative customer service performance is costly for firms in terms of current profits, shareholder returns respond in a significantly positive manner to such improvements. We interpret this finding as being consistent with stakeholder theory.

Privatization has been a significant feature of the political and economic scene in the United Kingdom since 1980. Privatization refers to the transfer of ownership and control of an economic activity previously undertaken by nationally or locally government-controlled agencies to private-sector, profit-seeking organizations. In various forms, privatization has also become increasingly popular in the rest of western Europe (Vickers & Wright, 1989), in the formerly centrally planned economies (Ash, Hare, & Canning, 1994), in less developed countries (Price, 1994), and in Canada and Australia (Richardson, 1990). Privatization of publicly owned utilities is of particular interest from the perspective of stakeholder management. The transfer from public to private ownership not only involves significant changes in the composition of stakeholders, but also requires consideration of how the interests of the different stakeholders are to be balanced by the managers of the privatized utility. This is highlighted in the case of the recently privatized U.K. water industry, where, by virtue of the essential nature of the product, managers could not be left to pursue the interests of the new shareholders exclusively. The need to ensure that account was taken of customer interests has led to the development, by an independent government-appointed regula-

tor, of performance measures of customer service. These measures provide an opportunity to empirically examine a key contention of stakeholder theory, namely, that companies practicing stakeholder management will, other things being equal, be relatively successful in conventional financial performance terms (cf. Donaldson & Preston, 1995).

Privatization in 1989 resulted in the ten state-owned regional water companies becoming public limited companies, each with a full London Stock Exchange listing of its shares. Despite the government's claim that private-sector provision of goods and services subject to the disciplines of market forces would be more efficient than public-sector provision (Department of the Environment, 1986), there had been scant opportunity to develop market competition in the water industry (Littlechild, 1986). Consequently, privatization left the monopoly character of the industry largely unchanged. Each of the ten water companies continued to operate as a regional monopolist controlling the supply of an essential commodity. Privatization, therefore, required the U.K. government to design a regulatory system that would ensure that the managers of the ten water companies had, in addition to legal obligations regarding water quality and other public health matters, incentives to maintain a satisfactory balance between the potentially conflicting interests of two key stakeholders: the new shareholders, and customers. The regulatory system, though primarily based upon price controls, also provides strong financial incentives for firms to be cost-efficient while encouraging them to in-

We thank the editors of this *AMJ* special research forum and the two anonymous reviewers for their helpful comments on a draft of this article and Helen Short of the University of Leeds for her invaluable research assistance. Both authors contributed equally to this work.

vest resources on improvements in customer service. Thus, the regulatory system provides an opportunity to empirically test stakeholder notions whereby the proper objectives and responsibilities of firms extend beyond the maximization of shareholder returns (cf. Freeman, 1984; Freeman & Evan, 1990).

The purposes of this study were, first, to examine how the potential conflicts of interest between shareholders and customers were intended to be reconciled through the system of regulation and, second, to determine whether any empirical evidence suggested that the system of regulation actually achieved its main purpose. We empirically investigated the performance of the privatized water companies in terms of both financial measures (that is, relative shareholder returns and profitability) and customer service performance measures. These latter performance measures, which are monitored and published by the water industry regulator annually, constitute an important criterion for determining the maximum allowable price increase for each water company. In addition, a water company's high score on customer service measures both reduces the probability of its experiencing adverse regulatory interventions and enhances its reputation with potential purchasers of nonregulated services. Consequently, attaining high levels of customer service can be expected to have a positive effect upon anticipated future income streams. This expectation in turn is an incentive for water company executives to ensure that their organizations perform well on these customer service measures.

It is hypothesized that although discretionary expenditures made to improve customer service will be costly in terms of current reported profits, they will be associated with higher shareholder returns since investors will perceive that future profit levels and risk exposure will be improved. Our empirical results are consistent with the above hypotheses. We found that performance on customer service measures is significantly, negatively correlated with current profits but significantly, positively correlated with shareholder returns measures.

STAKEHOLDER THEORY AND THE REGULATION OF THE PRIVATIZED WATER INDUSTRY

Stakeholder models of the firm have attracted considerable support in recent years (e.g., Donaldson & Preston, 1995), not only because of ethical dissatisfaction with the exclusive privileging of shareholder interests, but also on the grounds of economic efficiency. The "incomplete contracting" literature (Ezzamel & Watson, 1997; Garvey & Swan, 1994; Hart, 1995; Kay & Silberston, 1995), for example, contains the argument that economic efficiency frequently requires firms' executives to exercise their discretion in a way favoring the interests of other stakeholders, such as customers and suppliers. The executives do so because, if other stakeholders perceived that managerial discretion was always being exercised in favor of one particular party—for instance, shareholders or the executives themselves—they would be unwilling to do business with the firms. From this perspective, an economically successful firm will necessarily be one in which senior management adopts corporate governance strategies and policies that facilitate the maintenance of an appropriate balance between different stakeholder interests.

Though this argument is conceptually clear, it has proved difficult in practice to evaluate specific institutional arrangements for incorporating non-shareholder interests, particularly in terms of their effect on economic performance. Indeed, the ease with which shareholders can be identified and the ready availability of shareholder wealth and financial performance measures in part explain the continuing primacy attached to shareholder interests. Defining who other stakeholders are, determining how their interests are best served, and developing performance indicators that measure a company's degree of success in doing so are complex issues not easily resolved in practice. Donaldson and Preston, for example, commented that testing a simple hypothesis, such as the statement that corporations whose managers adopt stakeholder principles and practices will perform better financially than those that do not, "involves some formidable challenges" (1995: 77). Not surprisingly, they noted a dearth of empirical tests of such hypotheses and cited the work of Clarkson (Clarkson, Deck, & Shiner, 1992; cf. Clarkson, 1995) as the only significant example known to them.

In the case of the U.K. privatized water companies, these problems of defining stakeholder interests and measuring how well those interests are served are much reduced. The regulatory system for the water industry requires an explicit articulation of the interests to be served by regulation and the measures by which its effectiveness may be assessed. The water companies therefore provide an interesting research site for empirically examining some of the issues raised by a stakeholder view of the firm. Although managers had for the first time to consider the interests of shareholders after water privatization, maximizing shareholder returns could not be pursued without constraint.

528   *Academy of Management Journal*   October

Given the nature of the product, managers had also to satisfy a number of public health and safety concerns and to meet standards set for water quality and customer service. In this context, the water companies presented a strong prima facie case for arguing that managers were required to take a stakeholder perspective on their performance. The appropriateness of this was widely acknowledged. Kay and Silberston (1995), for example, writing from an incomplete contracting perspective, commented that, given the nature of water as a product, no sensible person would wish to have water supplied by a company that invariably put the interests of its shareholders ahead of those of its customers!

The essence of the U.K. water company regulatory system is contained in the duties prescribed for the director general of the Office of Water Services (OFWAT). According to the 1991 Water Industry Act, he[1] has a primary duty to ensure that the functions of water and sewerage undertakers are properly carried out and that companies are able (in particular, by securing reasonable returns on their capital) to finance the proper carrying out of their functions. The director general also has the secondary duties of protecting the interests of customers in respect to the level of charges, the quality of services, promoting economy and efficiency and, where possible, facilitating competition between the water companies.

Economic regulation operates through price controls, based on the so-called RPI + k formula. The first component of the pricing formula is designed to allow each firm to recover general rises in prices outside of its control, or inflation, as measured by the retail price index (RPI), and the second component is an adjustment factor *(k)* that is separately negotiated between each company and the director general of OFWAT. The individual k-factors, which are subject to periodic review, are based on an assessment of each company's inherited infrastructure and the new investment it needs to achieve the requisite water quality and service standards, other unique local factors that impact upon costs (such as geology and climate), and an efficiency target. The director general assesses the scope for improved efficiency in terms of both the individual operating circumstances of each company and comparisons with the costs incurred by the most efficient of the other companies for similar activities (the so-called yardstick or benchmark cost basis). Where appropriate, the director general determines the speed with which a firm can reasonably be expected to get its costs down to the levels of the most efficient

supplier while still providing a reasonable return to investors (Cowan, 1994; Littlechild, 1986). This partial adjustment process promotes cost efficiency by providing firms with an incentive to achieve greater-than-anticipated cost savings, since the resulting increase in profitability represents a recurring annual windfall gain until the k-factor is renegotiated.

An exclusive focus on providing incentives for firms to reduce costs may, however, result in managers reducing expenditures on activities related to customer service. Indeed, Littlechild, in his official report for the Department of the Environment on the regulatory framework for the privatized industry, questioned whether "a privatized Water Authority [would] have any incentive to set and meet challenging levels of service targets which do not contribute directly to profits" (1986: 18). Public awareness of the obvious conflict of interests between shareholders' desire to have increases in profits and customer service requirements was high. Consequently, in establishing the new regulatory framework, the government claimed that it would "be designed to ensure that the benefits of greater efficiency are systematically passed on to customers in the form of lower prices and better service than would otherwise have occurred" (Department of the Environment, 1986: 3). This claim is reflected in OFWAT's aim, stated in an information leaflet distributed to the public: "to ensure that the companies provide customers with a good quality and efficient service at a fair price" (Office of Water Services, 1998).

To allow companies to finance their provision of water services and to encourage them to improve customer service levels, the regulator is able to allow all or part of the costs involved to be recovered from customers through adjustments to the k-factor in the pricing formula. Customer service improvements have typically involved reducing problems of low water pressure, improving the security of the water supply, reducing the need for restrictions in periods of low rainfall, and improving the handling of contacts with customers, such as billing complaints. In determining whether to allow the costs of new investment to improve customer service levels, the director general of OFWAT has first to decide whether a planned investment is appropriate and second, what proportion of these costs may be passed on to customers. In considering this, he takes into account the quality of service already provided, the levels of service provided by the other water companies, cost comparisons with other companies, and the scope for improvements in internal efficiency. Insofar as the director general allows costs (including a reason-

---

[1] One man has held this office since its inception.

1999   *Ogden and Watson*   529

able return on capital) to be passed on to customers, a firm may enhance its future profits, although clearly, its current-year profits would be reduced by the costs of the improvements.

However, there are penalties as well as incentives in the privatized system. The director general annually scrutinizes each company's progress toward meeting its quality obligations and its performance in delivering services to customers. He may penalize companies whose performance is poor by, for example, making punitive adjustments to the *k*-factor, or by requiring a company to engage in additional expenditure to make good performance shortfalls without taking any compensating allowance for the costs incurred (cf. Office of Water Services, 1997). The director general is likely to be particularly severe to companies in which investment programs are not on track for delivering the targeted service improvements allowed for in price limits. Investigations (Office of Water Services, 1996) of three companies' failure to meet agreed-upon outputs resulted in one company, Yorkshire Water, having to agree not to raise charges by more than the rate of inflation from April 1, 1998, until March 2000. The benefit to Yorkshire Water's customers has been estimated to be approximately £44 million. Ultimately, of course, the director general may seek to have a company's appointment to provide water services terminated. Consequently, performing well in delivering services to customers is of critical importance to the water companies.

MEASURES OF CUSTOMER SERVICE

OFWAT has developed seven indicators of levels of service to monitor the quality of service the U.K. water companies provide to their customers. These are the adequacy of water resources, the pressure of water mains, interruptions to the supply, water use restrictions, properties at risk of sewer flooding, the total number of written and telephoned queries about billing and the time taken to respond to them and, finally, the total number of written complaints received about any aspect of service and the time taken to respond to them. These measures are seen by OFWAT as "important output measures" (Office of Water Services, 1990: 1). Each year all the companies are required to report to OFWAT on the quality of the delivery of their services in terms of these seven indicators (e.g., Office of Water Services, 1991). The reporting period covered by the customer service measures coincides with the firms' accounting year, which runs from April 1 to March 31. Firms are required to supply the regulator with the necessary data in July. OFWAT's as-

sessments of company performance are then published in late November or early December.

OFWAT has noted, however, that only four of the measures of service—water pressure, interruptions of supply, responses to billing queries, and responses to written complaints—currently allow for comparisons between companies (see Table 1). OFWAT views the number of properties at risk for sewer flooding as unsuitable for comparative purposes because the data currently available lack consistency. The adequacy of the water supply and restrictions on water use are also considered unsuitable as they are largely influenced by climatic and weather patterns (Office of Water Services, 1994). Also, reliable comparable data have only been available since 1991 for two of the measures that can be compared, pressure and interruptions.

Another initiative to protect customers' interests involved the establishment of ten customer services committees (CSCs). Each covers a geographic area approximately equivalent to the boundaries of one of the old water authorities. The committees are independent of the water companies, and the chair and members (usually 12) of each customer service committee are all appointed by the director general. Their mission statement, as set out in an annual report, is the following: "The CSC will represent the interest of customers of the water and sewerage companies in its region and will advise and support the DG in regulating the water industry to secure for customers the combination of service and price they would have in a competitive market" (Office of Water Services National Customer Council, 1998). One of the CSCs' principal tasks is to investigate and resolve complaints made to them about the water companies. These are reported, as a percentage of each company's customer base, each year in the CSCs' annual reports and are highlighted in OFWAT's annual reports. The complaints to the customer service committees provide an important additional measure of customer service; see Table 1, where this measure appears as "complaints to OFWAT."

INCENTIVES FOR BALANCING SHAREHOLDER AND CUSTOMER INTERESTS

The water company executives have had to take OFWAT's disciplinary powers and the regulatory penalties for poor or substandard performance seriously, particularly since the director general has declared his intention to take into account each company's performance on customer service in his periodic review of prices and *k*-factors (Office of Water Services, 1993). Consequently, the managers have been keen to achieve quality improvements to

530   *Academy of Management Journal*   October

TABLE 1
Descriptive Statistics by Year [a]

Variable	1992	1993	1994	1995	1996	1997
Financial characteristics and firm performance						
Total sales [b]	332.40 (179.20)	393.30 (233.70)	467.80 (279.80)	524.50 (314.90)	584.40 (326.40)	627.20 (350.20)
Total capital employed [b]	1,243.20 (505.60)	1,505.50 (607.70)	1,700.60 (671.80)	1,891.80 (773.10)	2,034.30 (837.40)	2,210.10 (962.70)
Debt/equity [c]	0.13 (0.07)	0.29 (0.08)	0.35 (0.12)	0.38 (0.16)	0.38 (0.18)	0.68 (0.72)
Posttax profit/equity [d]	12.10 (2.30)	12.70 (1.90)	12.50 (1.70)	11.90 (1.60)	12.40 (1.30)	14.20 (2.20)
Annual shareholder returns (April–March) [d]	30.60 (7.60)	0.80 (2.50)	55.50 (3.90)	8.30 (4.40)	−0.30 (13.30)	27.00 (7.10)
Shareholder returns for profits announcement month (May–June) [d]	−0.04 (0.03)	−0.03 (0.02)	−0.05 (0.03)	0.05 (0.03)	0.08 (0.03)	0.04 (0.10)
Shareholder returns for customer service performance announcement month (November–December) [d]	−0.06 (0.02)	0.05 (0.02)	−0.04 (0.03)	0.06 (0.02)	0.02 (0.03)	0.02 (0.03)
Customer service performance measures						
Complaints to OFWAT	1.80 (0.80)	4.80 (3.60)	6.60 (4.50)	6.50 (4.60)	5.20 (3.00)	5.50 (2.70)
Inadequate water pressure [d]	0.90 (1.00)	1.00 (0.80)	1.00 (0.80)	0.80 (0.70)	0.60 (0.50)	0.80 (0.90)
Supply interruptions [d]	0.40 (0.40)	0.20 (0.20)	0.30 (0.30)	0.40 (0.50)	0.30 (0.40)	0.70 (0.90)
Responses to billing queries [e]	2.20 (1.20)	2.90 (1.20)	2.90 (1.30)	3.80 (1.20)	4.40 (0.70)	4.80 (0.40)
Responses to written complaints	1.90 (1.00)	1.90 (0.90)	3.20 (1.40)	3.90 (1.70)	4.80 (0.40)	4.90 (0.30)

[a] Statistics are means and standard deviations (in parentheses). $N = 10$ (observations per year).
[b] Millions of U.K. pounds.
[c] Proportions.
[d] Percentages.
[e] Ratings on a five-point scale, where 1 was "very poor" and 5 was "very good."

customer service within declared time scales and budgets and have, on occasion, volunteered to provide additional improvements in customer service. Companies have variously offered customers rebates or abatements of the available price increase allowed for in their *k*-factors, and they have introduced customer service initiatives that went beyond statutory requirements in areas such as compensation for missed appointments (Office of Water Services, 1997). These improvements were designed to secure the goodwill of the director general as well as to benefit customers. However, all these "voluntary" provisions have entailed significant amounts of expenditure, which have on occasion caused concern to shareholders. Certainly investment analysts have been conscious that the water companies could spend too much money on achieving high standards of customer service, as well as too little (Ogden, 1997).

Senior managers of the water companies have had reasons beyond regulatory considerations for pursuing improvements in customer service. In the first instance, managers were keen to distinguish their newly privatized companies from the old public sector companies. They were also anxious to counter the many critics of the water privatization process (Ogden, 1991). On both counts, there is little doubt that managers believed that being responsive to customer needs and providing good service to customers was part of the definition of a successful private sector company. From the perspective of resource dependency theory (e.g., Pfeffer & Salancik, 1978), a creditable demonstration of commitment to customer service was simply seen as a condition of their continued survival. This is particularly evident in the mission statements made by the boards of the water companies in their statutory annual reports. The Northumbrian Water Group's 1994 annual report provides a typical example: "At the heart of our new vision of the Group's future is the need for us all within Northumbrian Water to focus our efforts ever more intensely on the needs and desires of our customers."

Furthermore, managers were conscious that improved customer service could serve as a source of legitimacy for their new private-sector status. Managers' pursuit of legitimacy may be considered as reflecting strategic initiatives (cf. Ashforth & Gibbs, 1990; Pfeffer & Salancik, 1978; Suchman, 1995) to instrumentally deploy and manipulate their newfound commitment to customer service and thus to garner support for their new private-sector status. It may also be considered as an example of an institutional response to cultural pressures for enterprise and consumer sovereignty that underpinned the government's whole privatization project (Ogden, 1997).

Managers were also aware that comparisons of performance made possible by OFWAT's measures of levels of service were used by other audiences, most notably the City and financial analysts. Analysts' reports on individual water company performance, although primarily concerned with financial performance, have considered performance on customer service as an important indicator of managerial competence and company success. Analysts have also incorporated the levels of service performance into assessments of a company's exposure to regulatory risk and the likelihood of any company's having to remedy some shortfall in performance expected by the regulator, with all its attendant cost implications and reputational damage (e.g., Charterhouse Tilney Equity Research, 1993; Warburg Securities, 1991).

Finally, senior managers have seen commercial potential in achieving good performance on customer service measures that extends beyond the regulatory sphere of OFWAT. Establishing a reputation as a customer-focused organization, particularly when doing so may be externally validated by an independent body such as OFWAT, is valued as a resource in exploiting business opportunities outside the regulated activities of water services. The importance of this, and the resource-based view of the firm it reflects (e.g., Hall, 1992), should not be underestimated. To date, the two main areas of diversification for the water companies have been waste management services and international contracts for providing water services. Further support for this consideration can be drawn from the marketing literature (e.g., Kotler, 1984). In particular, Narver and Slater's study (1990) indicates that business performance may be enhanced in the longer term by increasing market orientation, particularly in terms of the attention given to customers' current and future needs. This effect appears to apply whatever the degree of competition within a company's environment (Slater & Narver, 1994), a finding of particular relevance to the water companies since they remain regional monopolists in regard to the provision of water services.

From the above, it can be argued that the privatization of the U.K. water industry provides a potentially rich research setting for examining many of the implications and actual consequences that arise in the practical application of stakeholder conceptions of the firm. Our primary concern here was to investigate whether any empirical evidence suggested that the postprivatization regulatory system actually produced significant benefits to both shareholders and customers. Positive results are not a forgone conclusion since the history of utility regulation is replete with examples of "regulatory capture" (for a review, see Self [1993]). The many statements in OFWAT and water company publications affirming the importance of customer service may have simply constituted marketing hype and/or self-serving rhetoric declaimed by the interested parties to legitimate their current policies and practices. What would count as evidence that the regulator and the water companies were taking improvements in customer service seriously would be (1) evidence that customer service performance (assessed in terms of the published measures) was improving over time coupled with (2) evidence that customer service performance was also economically significant in relation to reported profits and shareholder wealth measures.

Given the possibility that the published customer service measures might simply reflect the regulator's and the water companies' joint desire to be seen to be attending to customer interests, a plausible null hypothesis was that results on these measures would not be related in any economically meaningful manner to either the companies' profits or their returns (dividend payments and capital gains) to their shareholders. The following two alternative hypotheses suggest themselves:

Hypothesis 1. The customer service performance of the United Kingdom's privatized water companies, as measured by published customer service levels, will be negatively related to the companies' contemporaneous reported profitability.

Hypothesis 2. The customer service performance of the United Kingdom's privatized water companies, as measured by published customer service levels, can be expected to have a positive impact on future profitability and will therefore be positively related to current-period shareholder returns.

We tested the first hypothesis to establish whether or not differences between companies in terms of the published measures of customer service were related to differences in profits. Supportive results would indicate that the water companies were prepared to commit real resources, which

532   *Academy of Management Journal*   October

would have otherwise accrued to their shareholders, to improving their customer service. We tested the second hypothesis to ascertain whether these customer service results had any consequences for shareholder wealth. If the regulator allowed companies to recoup all or most of their costs (plus a profit margin) through higher charges to customers, then external capital markets would interpret better-than-average customer service levels as value-enhancing. In these circumstances, the customer service indicators could be expected to be positively related to current-period relative shareholder returns.

It is by no means certain that managers' decisions about expenditures to improve customer service will inexorably enhance future profitability. Considerable pressures and risks influence managers' judgments about how best to balance shareholder and customer interests. On the one hand, there is, of course, the regulatory imperative to achieve minimum standards of customer service. There is regulatory risk if not enough is achieved. Managers may also enhance the legitimacy of their companies as private-sector actors and secure reputational benefits that can be commercially exploited in other markets. On the other hand, achieving improved customer service entails considerable expenditure. Moreover, managers may be too ambitious in their plans for customer service, be inefficient in carrying out those plans, or fail to secure enough recompense through the k-factor determined by the director general, all of which would have adverse consequences for their companies' financial performance. Despite these potential difficulties, the regulator can be expected to have confidence in the reliability of his own system for determining customer service levels and to therefore reward the water companies with high scores on these measures.

EMPIRICAL MODELING OF THE RELATIONSHIPS BETWEEN SHAREHOLDER WEALTH, PROFITS, AND CUSTOMER SERVICE LEVELS

Our empirical testing of Hypotheses 1 and 2 needed to take account of the character of the water industry and the panel nature of our data, which consisted of six annual cross sections of ten observations, each representing one water company. As we were analyzing regulated enterprises supplying an identical basic product, but with very different inherited cost bases and local operating conditions, there was likely to be very little intertemporal variation in the ranking of companies in terms of their profitability. In addition to these time-invariant,

firm-specific fixed effects, both the average profit levels and shareholder returns of the sample were influenced by common economy- or sector-wide factors. In testing our hypotheses, therefore, we needed to be able to control for these time-varying and firm-level fixed effects in order to isolate the influence of different customer service performance levels on profitability and changes in shareholder wealth (returns). In both the profits and shareholder returns models described below, the dependent variables are expressed in terms of the deviation of company i's profits (or returns) at time t from the sector's average profits (or returns) for the same period. This method effectively overcame the problem of time-specific effects.[2] As for the firm-level fixed effects, these were only likely to be of any importance in respect to the profit model because, in an informationally efficient market, share prices will rapidly incorporate the financial consequences of any anticipated firm-level fixed effects (see Malkiel [1996] for a review). Hence, we estimated only the relative profits models controlling for fixed effects.[3]

Finally, given the combination of price regulation and highly stable operating and cost conditions that give rise to fixed effects with respect to relative profitability, one of the few ways open to an individual water company to significantly improve its posttax profitability ranking is to increase its debt-to-equity ratio. For any positive level of operating profits, taking on more debt and/or reducing the equity base (through, for instance, share repurchases) has the effect of increasing the posttax return per unit of equity. Hence, because capital structure changes could be expected to have a significant impact on our relative profits measure, our empirical analysis also had to include controls for this factor.

Relative Profits Model

We controlled for common time period influences on company profits by defining our depen-

---

[2] We also reestimated each of the empirical models including five dummy variables relating to the time period of the observations (the number of years covered by our panel data minus one, which is represented by the constant term). However, as expected, the dummies' inclusion did not result in any improvement in the explanatory power of the estimates.

[3] All of the shareholder returns models were also reestimated with controls for fixed effects included. However, as expected, the fixed effects models did not result in any statistically significant improvement in the explanatory power of the estimates.

dent variable in terms of the relative profits available for distribution to shareholders (that is, posttax profits or, in U.S. accounting terminology, net income). To obtain an accounting-based measure of the return to shareholders, we needed to control for differences in the sizes of the companies' equity bases by deflating the profit measure by the book value of shareholders' equity (issued share capital plus reserves). The dependent variable, the sector-relative profit of company *i* over time *t* (a year) was therefore defined as follows:

$$Relative\ profits_{it} = (profits/equity)_{it}$$
$$-(sector\text{-}average\ profits/equity)_t.$$

Our estimating equation for explaining the differences in relative profitability became:

$$Relative\ profits_{it} = \Sigma\ \alpha_i$$
$$+\beta\ log\ (book\ value\ of\ capital\ employed_{it})$$
$$+\beta(debt/equity)_{it}$$
$$+\beta(customer\ service\ performance_{it})+u_{it},$$

where $\Sigma\ \alpha_i$ represents firm-specific fixed effects[4] and u_{it} is an error term.

Three alternative specifications of the above profit model were estimated. Model 1, our benchmark, did not include any customer service variables. Models 2 and 3 both included customer service measures. Model 2 included five customer service variables, which consisted of the standardized values of five individual measures, and model 3 had a single composite customer service variable. Thus, the difference between models 2 and 3 was this: in model 2, the individual slope coefficients could differ, but in the more restrictive model 3, the slope coefficients on the individual customer service variables were of equal sign and magnitude.

Shareholder Returns Model

As for the relative profits models, for the shareholder returns model we isolated the common external influences upon shareholder returns from the firm-specific factors in each period. Our dependent variable, relative shareholder returns for firm *i* over time *t*, was thus defined as follows:

$$Relative\ returns_{it} = returns_{it}$$
$$- sector\text{-}average\ returns_t$$

---

[4] See chapter 2 of Baltagi (1995) for an exposition of the methods used to control for fixed effects.

Our empirical equation thus was:

$$Relative\ returns_{it}$$
$$= \Sigma\ \beta(firm\text{-}specific\ factors)_{it} + u_{it}.$$

Because we assumed an informationally efficient capital market, the vector of firm-specific factors assumed to influence returns included only information (news) received by the market within time period *t* that could have been expected to have altered investor expectations regarding the level and riskiness of an individual firm's anticipated future profits. The two items of firm-specific information incorporated into our empirical models that would have been released to the market during a one-year period were relative profits and measures of customer service performance.

A major difficulty in any analysis of the impact of an economic variable upon shareholder returns is determining the most appropriate time frame for observing such an impact. All ten privatized water companies had accounting year-ends on March 31, and the financial accounts for each year were all published in late May or early June. To date, the director general has published results on the customer service performance measures between late November and early December of each year. To test Hypothesis 2, we measured returns over two different periods. We assessed announcement or news effects by measuring returns over the month in which the regulator released the customer service findings. Only the customer service variable or variables were included in this customer service announcement month model. Then, to compare the relative announcement impacts upon share prices of profits and of the performance variables, we also estimated a profit announcement month model.

To test the possibility that investors inferred some financial and customer service performance information from other sources prior to the information's actual release by the regulator, and to allow for the possibility that investors may have taken some time to appreciate the impact of such information on future profitability, we also measured returns for the subsequent one-year period, from April 1 to March 31. The resulting annual returns model included both relative profits and customer service as explanatory variables since both items were released during the year covered by the dependent variable.

To ensure that the values associated with all five of the indicator variables were all positively associated with improvements in customer service levels, we expressed three of them (complaints to OFWAT, inadequate water pressure, and supply interruptions) as 100 percent minus the reported

TABLE 2
Estimation of Relative Profits Function 1991–92 to 1996–97 [a]

Independent Variable	Model 1	Model 2	Model 3
Book value of capital employed$_{it}$ [b]	−0.013 (1.39)	−0.010 (1.39)	−0.012 (1.41)
(Debt/equity)$_{it}$	0.012 (2.58)**	0.011 (2.88)**	0.012 (2.68)**
F for constant and firm-level fixed effects	15.570**	18.180**	17.520**
Complaints to OFWAT$_{it}$		2.802E-3 (1.26)	
Inadequate water pressure$_{it}$ [c]		−7.804E-3 (3.60)**	
Supply interruptions$_{it}$ [c]		−4.269E-3 (2.83)**	
Responses to billing queries$_{it}$ [c]		0.325E-3 (0.21)	
Responses to written complaints$_{it}$ [c]		−3.281E-3 (2.33)*	
Customer service$_{it}$ [c]			−2.150E-3 (2.79)**
F for new variables		4.06**	6.26**
Adjusted R^2	72.00	78.80	74.80
Equation F	14.79**	14.68**	15.57**

[a] The dependent variable was calculated as $(profits/equity)_{it} - (sector\text{-}average\ profits/equity)_t$. $N = 60$. White's (1980) heteroskedasticity-adjusted *t*-values are shown in parentheses.
[b] Logarithm.
[c] Standardized measure.
* $p \leq .05$
** $p \leq .01$

percentages published by OFWAT (and shown in Table 1). The five variables could not, however, be simply aggregated to provide a summary overall measure of customer service levels because the measurement units differed: the three just noted were percentages, but the variables measuring responses to billing queries and to written complaints were expressed as integer values on a five-point scale. In order to aggregate the five indicator variables, we thus transformed each variable into an annual standardized value.

These standardized relative measures of customer service were individually entered into the model 2 relative profits estimate.[5] Standardization also enabled us to aggregate these five measures to produce a single composite indicator of relative customer service performance, *customer service*, in which each indicator had equal weight (that is, the indicators were added together).

In order to summarize each firms' customer service performance, the regulator had to have constructed a similar composite measure.[6] We entered

---

[5] The individual standardized customer service variables were also entered into the shareholder returns models. However, none of the individual variables were of any statistical significance and, consequently, these results are not reported here.

[6] Moreover, given the relatively few degrees of freedom associated with our data set and the "pairwise" correlations between the individual nonfinancial indica-

our composite measure into the relative profits (model 3) and shareholder returns models. A statistically significant, negative coefficient on this variable in the profits model would imply that performing on customer service was costly in terms of current reported profitability, as stated by Hypothesis 1. However, although such an effect was expected to depress profits, the costs associated with improvements in customer service are costs that the regulator may allow to be passed on to customers. Hence, as stated by Hypothesis 2, a statistically positive coefficient on this variable was to be expected when it was entered into the (announcement month and annual) shareholder returns models, since thus passing costs on implies higher future profits, which is good news to shareholders.

RESULTS

Table 2 presents our estimates relating to Hypothesis 1. As stated above, we made three alternative estimates of our relative profits model. Model 1, which includes controls for the unobservable firm-level fixed effects, firm size, and differences in capital structure, is able to explain a high proportion of the cross-sectional variability in relative profits. As anticipated, the firm-level fixed effects are highly significant—indeed, on their own, they

---

tors, this composite variable was also likely to provide a more efficient statistical estimator of their influence.

TABLE 3
Relative Shareholder Returns Functions 1991–92 to 1996–97 [a]

Independent Variable	Earnings Announcement Month Returns	Customer Service Announcement Month Returns	Annual Returns
(Profit/equity)$_{it}$	0.125 (0.28)		0.121 (0.16)
Customer service$_{it}$		2.611E-3 (2.29)*	10.045E-3 (2.46)*
Constant	0.014 (1.93)[†]	−0.069E-3 (0.02)	0.288E-3 (0.03)
Adjusted R^2	−1.6	6.3	7.5
Equation F	0.09	4.96*	3.40*

[a] The dependent variable was calculated as *relative returns*$_{it}$ = *returns*$_{it}$ − *sector-average returns*$_t$. The returns for each company and the sector-average returns were calculated as natural logarithms. $N = 60$. White's (1980) heteroskedasticity-adjusted t-values are shown in parentheses.
[†] $p \leq .10$
* $p \leq .05$

account for some 70 percent of the cross-sectional variation in profitability. Also, the debt-to-equity ratio is, as expected, positive and statistically significant at the 1 percent confidence level.

Model 2 includes the five individual standardized customer service variables (complaints to OFWAT, inadequate water pressure, supply interruptions, and responses to billing queries and written complaints). The incremental impact of these five measures is statistically significant at the 1 percent confidence level. However, although only three of the five variables are negative, all three are statistically significant at 5 percent or better levels of confidence. Model 3 includes only the aggregate variable customer service, which thereby constrains all five variables to have the same slope coefficients. Despite this restriction, model 3 appears to be well specified: the composite variable is negative and statistically significant at a 1 percent level of confidence, though there is a slight decrease in the overall explanatory power of the model relative to model 2.

These results provide strong empirical support for our first hypothesis. As can be seen from Table 2, in both models that include customer service measures, the variables are negatively related to the dependent variable at a 1 percent confidence level. These results imply that, despite the negative consequences of customer service increases for current reported profits, managers are prepared to expend resources to improve such service. We now consider whether such expenditures appear to also be in the interests of shareholders.

Table 3 presents our empirical estimates of the shareholder returns functions used to test Hypothesis 2, which predicts that the customer service measures will be positively related to current-

period shareholder returns. We made this prediction because some or all of the costs associated with improvements in customer service can likely be subsequently passed on to customers, thus increasing future profits and current value.

Though in both the annual returns and announcement month returns models the relative profits measure has a positive coefficient, neither of these coefficients is statistically significant at a 5 percent level. These results imply that the revelation of the profit figures to the capital markets did not appear to be regarded as news in that there is no statistical evidence that this information systematically altered the existing perceptions of investors regarding the current values of the firms.[7] Of course, given the huge fixed effects in relation to relative profits shown in Table 2, this finding should not be too surprising. These firm-level fixed effects reflect the highly regulated nature of the industry's pricing policies, the inherited infrastructure, the location-specific cost structures of individual firms, and the limited scope for increasing sales of their price-regulated product. In an informationally efficient market, share prices should already reflect any anticipated intertemporal profitability rankings. Hence, much of the information contained in the financial statements regarding relative profitability would not constitute news and, therefore, no share

---

[7] After obtaining the results presented in this article, we reestimated the shareholder return models using different time horizons for the measurement of the dependent variable. These additional estimates did not, however, produce significantly different results from those presented here.

price reaction should occur at the time of its release.

The situation in regard to the customer service performance measures is, however, somewhat different. Table 2 shows that the estimated positive coefficient on the customer service variables, for both the announcement and annual returns versions of the model, is statistically significant at better than 5 percent confidence levels. This pattern appears to indicate that our composite customer service variable is of some statistical importance in explaining both relative annual shareholder returns and relative shareholder returns for the month immediately surrounding revelation of this information to the market. These results imply, for example, that a firm that performs one standard deviation better than the mean on customer service in any period will earn an approximately 1 percent higher-than-average return for its shareholders. Although this positive relationship between relative shareholder returns and relative performance in terms of customer service measures is not particularly large, it does nevertheless appear to constitute an important form of value-relevant information to equity investors. Indeed, it appears to be much more important to shareholders than information releases regarding relative profitability over the same period.

DISCUSSION AND CONCLUSIONS

The empirical results presented in this article provide statistical evidence indicating that it is possible, to some extent, to align the apparently conflicting concerns of different stakeholder groups. Our findings support both the plausibility of the stakeholder model of the firm and the possibility of quantifying and empirically testing propositions and predictions grounded on the stakeholder model.

Opportunities to test these propositions further could be explored in other regulated and/or privatized utilities. In the United Kingdom, for example, customer service standards have been incorporated into the regulatory frameworks for British Telecom and the privatized gas and electricity industries. However, it is important to note that the use of measures of customer service in these regulatory processes is still at an early stage of development. With all the privatized utilities, including water, a number of issues remain unresolved. Principal among these is the question of who determines what customer service standards are to be, how they are to be measured, and their adequacy in reflecting customer needs.

Nevertheless, from the evidence presented here, it is apparent that in some circumstances a system of regulation that provides a relatively high degree of discretion to the regulator can, when coupled with market-based incentives and trust, result in mutual benefits for different stakeholder groups with apparently conflicting economic interests. Clearly, the effectiveness of this regulatory system relies very heavily on how the regulator exercises its discretion and on the quality of the relationships between the regulator and water company executives. Without a high level of mutual trust between the parties, the system would be beset with legal challenges to the regulator's decisions. The fact that, in the nine years since privatization, only one of the ten privatized water companies has sought judicial review of any of the regulator's decisions suggests that the required high level of mutual trust exists. Southwest Water appealed to the Monopolies and Mergers Commission over the OFWAT director general's determination of its efficiency target (that is, its k-factor) following its 1994 periodic review. The outcome of this appeal for the company was, in fact, a more demanding k-factor than that originally proposed by the director general (Monopolies and Mergers Commission, 1995).

The role of trust identified here echoes the importance Jones (1995) attached more generally to trust in developing an instrumental theory of stakeholder management. He argued that "trusting and cooperative relationships help solve problems related to opportunism" (Jones, 1995: 432) and that because "the costs of opportunism and of preventing or reducing opportunism are significant, firms that contract on the basis of trust and cooperation will have a competitive advantage over those that do not use such criteria" (1995: 432). Seeking this advantage, he concludes, provides not only an explanation for altruistic firm behaviors, but also a basis for an instrumental theory of stakeholder management.

Our discussion of the respective roles of managers and regulator in balancing competing stakeholder interests also has implications for debates about the basis of stakeholder theory. Although instrumental justifications for stakeholder theory are well established (Freeman, 1984; Freeman & Evan, 1990), some commentators have argued that these are inadequate as a basis for stakeholder theory. Donaldson and Preston (1995), for example, suggested that even if it is prudent for managers to pay attention to stakeholder interests, there is no guarantee that they will do so. Stakeholders have no assurance that their interests will be properly considered or that managers will not behave opportunistically at their expense. Donaldson and Preston argued instead for a normative basis for stakeholder theory, which, they suggested, resides in managers' recognition that all stakeholders' interests have intrinsic value. The ultimate managerial implication of stakeholder theory is that, rather than treat stakeholders' interests instrumentally, managers "should acknowledge the validity of diverse stakeholder interests and should attempt to respond to them within a mutually supportive framework, because that is a moral requirement for the legitimacy of the management function" (Donaldson & Preston, 1995: 87). Our evidence indicates, however, that such a basis for managerial behavior is still far from being realized. It could be expected, given the essential nature of their product, that managers in the water industry would take due account of all stakeholders' interests in their decision making. However, the regulatory system presumes the opposite. The responsibility for ensuring that customer interests are adequately attended to is located with the regulator. Moreover, the incentives and sanctions at its disposal are designed to operate on the assumption that managers will act instrumentally.

One limitation of our study is that it was restricted to one industry. Moreover, given the changes occasioned by that industry's recent privatization, the small number of companies operating within it, and its regulatory environment, the U.K. water industry can by no means be considered typical. Another limitation of the study concerns the measures of customer service. Although we used the measures employed by the U.K. Office of Water Services, only four of the seven measures lent themselves to comparison. As regards our empirical analysis of the data, the power of the tests of the shareholder returns models might be improved if daily share data were used instead of monthly data. Further, although the estimation problems would be complex, there might be benefits from undertaking a more detailed analysis of the cash flow consequences directly associated with each customer service indicator.

Beyond the confines of regulated utilities, our research has two major implications for stakeholder theory. The first of these is reiteration of the importance of the abilities to define stakeholders' interests and to measure and monitor those interests. The second is to emphasize the need for the measurement and monitoring of companies' performance in regard to stakeholders' interests to be transparent. Such transparency would facilitate independent substantive evaluation of companies' treatment of stakeholders and avoid the reliance on companies' own assessment of their performance. Companies that believe that they already take serious account of stakeholder interests may welcome such evaluation, because it would provide an opportunity to demonstrate the validity of their claims about serving stakeholders.

REFERENCES

Ash, T., Hare, P., & Canning, A. 1994. Privatisation in the former centrally planned economies. In P. M. Jackson & C. M. Price (Eds.), *Privatisation and regulation:* 213–236. London: Longman.

Ashforth, B. E., & Gibbs, B. W. 1990. The double-edge of organizational legitimation. *Organization Science.* 1: 177–194.

Baltagi, B. H. 1995. *Econometric analysis of panel data.* Chichester: Wiley.

Charterhouse Tilney Equity Research. 1993. *Water sector review* (mimeo). London: Charterhouse Tilney Equity Research.

Clarkson, M. B. E. 1995. A stakeholder framework for analyzing and evaluating corporate social performance. *Academy of Management Review.* 20: 92–117.

Clarkson, M. B. E., Deck, M. C., & Shiner, N. J. 1992. *The stakeholder management model in practice.* Paper presented at the annual meeting of the Academy of Management, Las Vegas.

Cowan, S. 1994. Privatisation and regulation of the water industry in England and Wales. In M. Bishop, J. Kay, C. Mayer, & D. Thompson (Eds.), *Privatisation and economic performance:* 112–136. Oxford: Oxford University Press.

Department of the Environment. 1986. *Privatisation of the water authorities in England and Wales* (cmnd. 9734). London: Her Majesty's Stationery Office.

Donaldson, T., & Preston, L. E. 1995. The stakeholder theory of the corporation: Concepts, evidence, and implications. *Academy of Management Review.* 20: 65–91.

Ezzamel, M., & Watson, R. 1997. Wearing two hats: The conflicting control and management roles of non-executive directors. In K. Keasey, S. Thompson, & M. Wright (Eds.), *Corporate governance:* 54–79. Oxford: Oxford University Press.

Freeman, R.E. 1984. *Strategic management: A stakeholder approach.* Boston: Pitman.

Freeman, R. E., & Evan, W. M. 1990. Corporate governance: A stakeholder interpretation. *Journal of Behavioral Economics,* 19: 337–359.

Garvey, G., & Swan, P. 1994. The economics of corporate governance. *Journal of Corporate Finance,* 1: 139–174.

Hall, R. 1992. The strategic analysis of intangible resources. *Strategic Management Journal,* 13: 135–144.

Hart, O. 1995. Corporate governance: Some theory and implications. *Economic Journal,* 105: 678–689.

538   *Academy of Management Journal*   October

Jones, T. M. 1995. Instrumental stakeholder theory: A synthesis of ethics and economics. *Academy of Management Review,* 20: 404–437.

Kay, J., & Silberston, A. 1995. Corporate governance. *National Institute Economic Review,* 3(August): 84–97.

Kotler, P. 1984. *Marketing management: Analysis, planning and control.* Englewood Cliffs, NJ: Prentice-Hall.

Littlechild, S. 1986. *Economic regulation of privatised water authorities:* A report to the Department of the Environment. London: Her Majesty's Stationery Office.

Malkiel, B. G. 1996. *A random walk down Wall Street* (6th ed.). New York: Norton.

Monopolies and Mergers Commission. 1995. *South West Water Services Ltd: A report on the determination of adjustment factors and infrastructure charges for South West Water Services Ltd.* London: Her Majesty's Stationery Office.

Narver, J. C., & Slater, S. F. 1990. The effect of market orientation on business profitability. *Journal of Marketing,* 54: 20–35.

Office of Water Services. 1990. *The water industry of England and Wales: Levels of service information 1989/90.* Birmingham: Office of Water Services.

Office of Water Services. 1991. *Annual report 1990.* London: Her Majesty's Stationery Office.

Office of Water Services. 1992. *Levels of service report for the water industry of England and Wales 1991/2.* Birmingham: Office of Water Services.

Office of Water Services. 1993. *Annual report 1992.* London: Her Majesty's Stationery Office.

Office of Water Services. 1994. *Levels of service report for the water industry of England and Wales 1993/4.* Birmingham: Office of Water Services.

Office of Water Services. 1996. *The director general's annual report 1995.* London: Her Majesty's Stationery Office.

Office of Water Services. 1997. *The director general's annual report 1996.* London: Her Majesty's Stationery Office.

Office of Water Services. 1998. *OFWAT complaints procedure: How we can help you if you have a complaint about a water company.* Birmingham: Office of Water Services.

Office of Water Services National Customer Council. 1998. *Representing water customers: The 1997–98 annual report of the OFWAT National Customer Council and the ten regional Customer Service Committees.* Birmingham: Office of Water Services.

Ogden, S. G. 1997. Accounting for organizational performance: The construction of the customer in the privatized water industry. *Accounting, Organizations and Society.* 22: 529–556.

Ogden, S. G., & Anderson, F. 1995. Representing customer interests: The case of the UK privatized water industry. *Public Administration,* 73: 535–559.

Pfeffer, J., & Salancik, G. 1978. *The external control of organizations: A resource dependence perspective.* New York: Harper & Row.

Price, C. M. 1994. Privatization in less developed countries. In P. J. Jackson & C. M. Price (Eds.), *Privatization and regulation:* 237–254. London: Longman.

Richardson, J. (Ed.). 1990. *Privatisation and deregulation in Canada and Britain.* Aldershot: Dartmouth.

Self, P. 1993. *Government by the market?* London: Macmillan.

Slater, S. F., & Narver, J. C. 1994. Does competitive environment moderate the market orientation-performance relationship? *Journal of Marketing,* 58: 46–55.

Suchman, M.C. 1995. Managing legitimacy: Strategic and institutional approaches. *Academy of Management Review,* 20: 571–610.

Vickers, J., & Wright, V. 1989. *The politics of industrial privatization in Western Europe.* London: Cass.

Warburg Securities. 1993. *Analyst's report on the water industry* (mimeo). London: S.G. Warburg Securities.

White, H. 1980. A heteroskedasticity-consistent covariance matrix estimator and a direct test of heteroskedasticity. *Econometrica,* 48: 817–838.

Stuart Ogden is a professor of accounting and organizational analysis at the University of Leeds. He received his M.A. in industrial relations at the University of Warwick. His current research interests are privatization and processes of organizational change, corporate governance and executive compensation, and management competences.

Robert Watson is a professor of finance and accounting at the University of Strathclyde. He received his Ph.D. in finance at the University of Manchester. His current research interests are corporate governance and executive compensation, managerial labor markets, and financial statement analysis.

[22]

Pergamon

www.elsevier.com/locate/worlddev

World Development Vol. 29, No. 7, pp. 1179–1198, 2001
© 2001 Elsevier Science Ltd. All rights reserved
Printed in Great Britain
0305-750X/01/$ - see front matter

PII: S0305-750X(01)00034-1

Utilities Privatization and the Poor: Lessons and Evidence from Latin America

ANTONIO ESTACHE

The World Bank, Washington, DC, USA and Universite de Bruxelles, Bruxelles, Belgium

ANDRES GOMEZ-LOBO

University of Chile, Santiago, Chile

and

DANNY LEIPZIGER *

The World Bank, Washington, DC, USA

Summary. — The perception that privatization hurts the poor is growing and creating a backlash against the private provision of basic infrastructure services. At the same time, governments are finding themselves fiscally strapped, searching for ways to finance the large investments needed to expand services to the poor. In Latin America, a laboratory for privatization, evidence exists which sheds light on the privatization experience. This paper analyzes the channels through which the poor might either lose or gain from privatization, examines the evidence accumulated on what has actually happened, and then discusses the policy options available to decision-makers who want to increase efficiency while at the same time dealing with the infrastructure needs of the poor that have been identified as being important for their welfare. In that context, the issue of whether welfare considerations should form part of the regulatory approach to privatized services is examined. The paper's major aims are to shed light on the issue of who can and does benefit from privatization of utilities, and to guide policy-makers in the choices. © 2001 Elsevier Science Ltd. All rights reserved.

Key words — Latin America, privatization, infrastructure, utilities, poverty, private sector

1. INTRODUCTION

The number of countries in Latin America pursuing utility sector liberalization policies and that rely on increased private sector participation in the sector has grown dramatically in the last decade. These reforms have generated total (private plus linked government) investments of US$236.5 billion during 1990–98 in Latin America, almost half of all the investment in developing countries. While this is significant, it initially tended to be concentrated in the largest southern cone economies, Argentina, Bolivia, Brazil, Chile and Mexico— although Central America and the Caribbean are now having their own privatization phase.

Moreover, while this represents only a fraction of the infrastructure needs in Latin America, it

_____

* A preliminary version of the paper was presented at the "Infrastructure for Development: Private Solutions and the Poor" Conference, held in London, 31 May–2 June 2000. We would like to thank Ian Alexander, Penelope Brook, Vivien Foster, Luis Guasch, Neil Roger, Anna Wellenstein, Dale Whittington, Quentin Wodon, MarianneFay, and anonymous referees for useful discussions/suggestions/comments. The usual disclaimers apply, namely, that the views expressed do not necessarily reflect those of the World Bank or any other institution affiliated with the authors. Final revision accepted: 8 February 2001.

detracts from the overriding need to increase productive public investment levels as part of a renewed growth strategy in the region. [1]

Of equal importance is the fact that the increased role of the private sector in infrastructure is producing secondary distributional effects that have been too often underestimated or ignored by policy-makers pressed by the concern to attract private capital to address fiscal problems. The emergence of the distributional issue often stems from the fact that many of the improvements in potential access are combined with changes in pricing and financing rules under which the private providers operate. [2] Even when costs go down as a result of greater productive efficiency, improved technology or more effective uses of scale economies, direct subsidies or cross-subsidies tend to disappear, either as an explicit government decision for resource allocation reasons or as a natural consequence of market forces acting in a liberalized market.

While average nominal tariffs have declined with privatization in many instances, the need to raise the effective tariffs or fares for some user groups follows from the need to guarantee the financial viability of service providers and their incentive to expand service coverage where it is the most needed. In the process, however, it may increase the financial burden imposed on some groups of vulnerable households. This is a real concern since the private investment figure quoted earlier is equivalent to UScts15/day/inhabitant which the investors will somehow want to recover. [3] Balance that against the fact that according to a household survey of 12 large countries accounting for 71% of the population of the region, one-third of the population lives on less than US$2/day, a standard definition of poverty. [4] This simple arithmetic exercise clearly illustrates the potential conflict and social problems that can arise as a result of the legitimate needs of operators to recover their investments and the poor who naturally feel privatization should improve services at an affordable price.

The paper provides a *tour d'horizon* of the "utilities privatization" experience in Latin America, focusing on some outstanding issues surrounding its impact on the poor, and delves into the reasons why its benefits may be undervalued by some, especially the poor. [5] The idea is to take stock but also to help policy-makers improve the integration of social dimensions in the reform of their infrastructure sectors and the education of the voters on the

extent to which this integration is taking place. The perception that privatization policies hurt the poor is widespread in the popular press and is an important factor determining the political sensitivity of the reform agenda. This is why it is important to document the real impact on the poor of sectoral policies in the infrastructure arena. One of the main points we want to argue here is that, in view of the weakness of the general welfare systems in most reforming countries, there is a need to integrate the social dimension explicitly in the utility reform process.

We address the following specific questions:
—How and when can the poor lose from infrastructure privatization?
—How to mainstream the measurement of the expected effects of reforms in the context of utilities privatization?
—Is there a case for a special short- to medium-run "infrastructure specific welfare policy" while a country gets its act together in putting together a more encompassing welfare policy?
—How can this overview help in drawing guidelines for a policy advisor to minimize the risks of losses by the poor from the privatization of utilities given that not all countries face similar circumstances?

2. CAN THE POOR LOSE FROM INFRASTRUCTURE PRIVATIZATION?

There is a widespread impression that infrastructure privatization has hurt the poor in Latin America—even if there are many examples where governments have been able to benefit the poor through increased private sector participation. Three stylized facts lead us to question a naive acceptance of the proposition that equates privatization with harm for the more vulnerable in society.

The first (stylized fact 1) is that infrastructure privatizations are generally part of a wider set of reforms and the status of the poor reflects the interactions of multiple policy factors. A series of studies of Argentina—a country that undertook an encompassing privatization process—points to the limits of such blanket statements. Relying on a general equilibrium framework which models the main interactions across markets resulting from reforms, Chisari, Estache, and Romero (1999) and Navajas (2000) show that, if anything, infrastructure privatization hurt the middle class relatively more through a redirection or suppression of existing subsidies (stylized fact 2) and may have even benefited the truly poor by increasing access to services (stylized fact 3).

The second stylized fact is well illustrated by Colombia in a study by Vélez (1996). A careful study of its public subsidies in 1992 showed that 38% of all public sector subsidies (including health, education, housing and other public services) were, in fact, spent on utility services representing 1.4% of GNP. Of these 80% were spent in the electricity sector where the study found that these subsidies benefited mostly middle-income households. Subsidies in the water sector were more focused on poor households, but were still not particularly progressive. More recent evidence shows that the distributional impacts of these subsidies have not improved much since 1992. [6] The main effect of this type of subsidy is often to increase rather than decrease inequality. The suppression or the redesign of this subsidy thus offers the potential to help the poor.

The third stylized fact is that privatization, if designed and implemented properly, provides an opportunity to end the exclusion of the poor, perpetuated by many cash strapped public utilities. Indeed, in many Latin American countries, the very poor did not have access to utility services before privatization and generally did not benefit from service expansions. Privatization, however, has the potential to change this. This point is illustrated by the Chilean case where in 1988, 2% of households in the lowest two income deciles had access to electricity and 3% had access to telephones. A decade later, only 5.5% of the very poor households lacked electricity and 60% lacked telephone access. [7] For Bolivia, Ajwad and Wodon (2000) show that access to water is the only service for which the poor benefit as much as the non-poor from an expansion of the service. In all other cases (sewage, electricity, garbage collection, and telephone), the non-poor benefit more than the poor from a service expansion.

(a) *Microeconomic linkages*

Starting with microeconomic linkages, it may be worth highlighting that privatization can affect the actual costs faced by poor households through several channels, as summarized in Table 1.

(i) *Losing from joining the formal economy and paying a higher effective tariff?*

Any type of private participation is likely to increase substantially the effectiveness of revenue collection. If poorer households were not billed prior to the reform or informal connections to the service were tolerated, the actual payments of these households is likely to increase after the reform. [8] This will occur even if nominal tariffs do not change (or even decrease), since these households would have to actually pay for the service whereas before they paid nothing.

There are also examples of countries in which the poorest formally unconnected users get illegal connections from illegal providers and pay these illegal providers for services equivalent to those offered by the formal operators. In the Dominican Republic, for instance, flat fees are commonly paid by the poorest for illegal connections. The introduction of a formal operator concerned with cost recovery may simply provide the poor with an option, and it may generate competition between the privatized operator and the informal operator at the retail level which can end up cutting costs for the poorest, as seen in evidence from Guatemala and Paraguay. [9] The evidence of deaths in the Dominican Republic related to improper handling of wires by users and the informal connected shows that in the case of electricity, informal connections also pose a safety threat to the household and the surrounding community. [10] Therefore, even if the formalization of the service and the concomitant increase in expenditure ends up being a higher financial cost to the household, this impact may be compensated by the increased safety. In the water sector this may also be the case when, due to an illegal connection, there is a serious reduction in the quality of the water that reaches the household. [11]

More generally, the co-existence of informal and formal providers is often the result of inefficient management by public utility companies—which are unable to identify and incorporate their implicit customers—rather than a strategy pursued by poorer households to obtain free services. In fact, there is mounting evidence from Willingness-to-Pay surveys undertaken in Central and South America indicating that even very poor households would prefer to pay a reasonable bill in order to have a formal connection to piped water services than maintain an informal connection. [12] This is partly due to the uncertainty

Table 1. *Summary of microeconomic linkages between increased private sector participation in infrastructure and welfare of the poor*[a]

Side effects of privatization	Possible sources of increase in cost burden for the poor	Possible mitigating factors and welfare gains for the poor
The cost of increasing formality	Revenue collection and discouragement of informal connections are likely to be more effective and result in increase in effective price paid	—A formal connection, even at a cost, may be a true aspiration of vulnerable households —Safety likely to increase with the formalization of connections —Informal connection may have been more expensive —Reform can bring technology choices that lower costs
The cost of tariff level adjustments	Average tariff levels can increase, due to cost recovery requirements and need to finance quality related investments	—Increase in average tariffs depends on pre-reform price levels and the distribution of the benefits of private participation between stakeholders —Reform can cut cost significantly enough through improvements in efficiency or new technologies
The costs of tariff structure adjustments	Tariff structures likely to be reformed in ways which could increase the marginal tariff faced by a poor household	—Competition likely to decrease average tariffs and may also compensate for any tariff rebalancing that affects the poor
The costs of increasing the price of substitutes	Privatization may restrict access to some alternative services, especially if connection to public network is mandatory	—Access to other types of alternative services will not be affected if foreseen in contracts —Availability of communal services may increase as a result of privatization
The costs of increasing the price of complements	The cost of obtaining a connection to the infrastructure service is likely to increase substantially	—The cost of obtaining other complementary equipment is likely to be unaffected by privatization, but will remain high
The costs of improved quality of service	Quality of service likely to improve, but this may make network services unaffordable for the poor	—There is considerable evidence showing that poor households are willing to pay reasonable amounts to improve quality of service

[a] *Source*: Adapted from Foster (1999).

regarding the continuation of access to the service faced by a household that is informally or illegally connected. In other cases, being a formal customer of a utility, certified by the presentation of a water or electricity bill, may be necessary in order to obtain other state benefits or in order to proceed with bureaucratic processes within the state apparatus. For urban households who live in recently created shanty towns without proper land titles, a formal connection to a utility, even at a cost, may be a first step in the direction of formal ownership of the property.

(ii) *Losing from changes in the tariff level and structure?*

The inclusion of users into the commercial cadastre of the companies is only the most

obvious way in which the poorest can be affected. Their situation may also be influenced by the increase in average tariffs that can stem from privatization. This is usually the result of the need to make the utility providers financially self-sufficient. Prior to reform, many utility companies do not charge the true cost of the service and the resulting financial deficit of this implicit universal subsidy is funded from government budgetary resources. Since one of the motivating forces for reform is often the reduction in fiscal deficits, privatization will usually be accompanied by a rise in tariffs in order to cover costs.

Privatization, however, does not always increase effective tariffs. The impact of a reform process on prices will depend on the pre-reform tariff level and pricing formula as well as on how the benefits of privatization are distributed between stakeholders. In particular, who receives the financial compensation for the assets sold or concessioned depends on the tendering mechanism used to award the contracts or utility company. When one of the main objectives of the reform is to reduce the fiscal deficit, governments may be tempted to set a high tariff level and award the service to the private investor who offers the highest upfront or annual transfer to the government. In some respects, high tariffs in this case can be viewed as a tax on consumers to fund the fiscal deficit through a high sale value of the company. If it hurts the poor disproportionately, it can be viewed as the result of regressive taxation rather than privatization *per se*. On the other hand, if a company is privatized to the bidder that offers to charge the lowest tariff, then consumers would receive more of the financial rewards of the reforms. This effect may even result in a reduction of average tariffs.

There is evidence from a survey of 600 concession contracts from around the world that in most cases contracts are tendered for the highest transfer or annual fee, suggesting that governments tend to use the auction to address more immediate fiscal concerns rather than to address efficiency concerns which would more directly meet the need of the final users (Guasch, 2000). Some cases illustrate how other stakeholders, and in particular consumers, can gain from lower tariffs when the contracts are tendered according to this variable. In 1992, the water and sanitation services in the Buenos Aires Metropolitan Region were concessioned for 30 years. The investment commitments were of the order of US$4,000 million during the period of the concession. The contract was awarded to the company that offered the lowest tariff. As a result, tariffs were reduced on average by 26.9%. A few years into the concession there was a renegotiation process that resulted in an increase in tariffs of 13.5% due to the need to bring forward the investment plans and increase quality of service. The net result was still a drop in average tariffs after services were concessioned which benefited all clients, including the poorest connected customers.

Generally, competition and effective regulation should serve to lower costs and tariffs. The evidence from a General Equilibrium Model for Argentina shows that the indirect gains from effective regulation of the utility industries

tended to benefit the poorest income groups relatively more. [13] While privatization itself tends to benefit the new owners and hence the richest, the effective regulation of the new "private" monopolies cuts tariffs to their efficient levels, cutting costs to other sectors of the economy, increasing demand for their outputs and generating additional demand for key labor inputs, including employment for the poor.

To the extent that privatization introduces competition, private sector participation may have substantial effects in reducing tariffs. In Chile, when the long-distance telecommunications market was liberalized in 1994, call prices dropped more than 50% (80% for large clients). A drop in prices of a similar magnitude occurred in 1998 in the mobile telephony industry when the Personal Communication Services (PCS) system was introduced and the number of mobile telephone companies increased from two to four. In the electricity sector, generating prices fell by 50% during 1988–98. This was due primarily to the arrival of natural gas from Argentina to fuel new Combined Cycle Power plants and, therefore, cannot be attributed directly to the privatization process. Retail electricity tariffs have not fallen by the same magnitude as generating prices—during 1988–98 they only fell by 25%—because competition in generation exceeds competition in distribution; specifically the vertical integration problem has meant that all the gains from generation have not been passed through to end-users (Bitran, Estache, Guasch, & Serven, 1999; Serra, 2000). In Argentina, the effectiveness of the restructuring process and the success of the introduction of competition was such that the wholesale price of electricity in Argentina dropped by 50% in the five-year period after privatization due to the intense competition in the generation sector after the entry of 21 new generators. Residential customers enjoyed a 40% drop in the five years after privatization (1992–97) (Estache & Rodriguez-Pardina, 2000; FIEL, 2000). In all of the cases we examined, the critical variable seems to be competition. Privatization is generally a pre-condition for competition for political reasons but is not the key factor in cutting tariffs. Competition, however, is.

Tariff structures may also change in ways that may be detrimental to some vulnerable groups and not only in poor countries. Tariffs can be differentiated along at least two dimensions, the category of clients and the quantity

Table 2. *Substitutes for private household connections to infrastructure services*[a]

	Energy	Telecommunications	Water
Self-supply	Collection of firewood		Collection of river water Construction of wells
Communal supply		Public telephones	Stand-pipes
Alternative nonnetwork suppliers	Kerosene Bottled gas	Resale of telephone services	Tanker supplies Bottled water Resale of piped water
Alternative network suppliers	Informal networks	Pagers Mobile telephones Voice mail services	Informal networks

[a] *Source*: Foster (1999).

consumed by an individual client. In the first case, pre-reform tariffs will usually (but not always) contain an element of cross-subsidy, either from commercial or industrial customers to domestic customers or from more affluent customers to less affluent ones (usually through the geographic differentiation of tariffs). On the quantity dimension, tariffs may contain some type of lifeline rate or rising block structure to reduce bills of low-consumption households. In some instances, tariffs do not include fixed charges in order to protect households with low consumption. In the water sector, where increasing block tariffs have been known to have disappointing effects, practitioners are now considering the use of uniform price with rebate designs in which a volumetric charge set equal to marginal cost is complemented by a fixed monthly rebate (or a negative fixed charge); this can be targeted to the poorest and can be set to generate enough, but not excessive, revenue while preserving marginal cost pricing. [14]

(iii) *Losing from changes in the prices and availability of substitutes and complements?*

An unexpected effect of privatization on the poor is related to the prices and availability of substitute and complementary goods. Substitute goods are those that provide alternative forms of energy, water, light or communication. Table 2 provides some examples for each of the utility services. It is ironic that in many cases, due to the shortcomings of public utility providers, the poor only have access to utility services through these alternative goods, which for the most part are provided by the private sector. Therefore, for many of these households privatization is not so much a transition from

public sector to private sector provision, as a transition from informal private sector provision to formal private sector provision.

In general, privatization should be neutral with respect to the availability of substitute goods or even increase the options and availability of communal supply. Throughout Latin America, private operators are promoting the use of alternative technologies in the power sector. Renewable energy sources are the upshot of a public–private partnership in an increasing number of countries. Cooperative arrangements have been introduced by some of the private distribution companies in poor neighborhoods to increase the number of shared connections (see World Bank, 1995). The main exception has been in the water sector when reforms are accompanied by a legal requirement prohibiting self-supply and the resale of piped water and where residential units are obliged to connect to the formal public network. This was initially a problem in the Aguas Argentinas concession, where the need to reduce losses in the network led the private operator to end informal agreements for the use of less reliable connections in the poorest neighborhoods, allowed by the public provider prior to privatization.

Note that the end of the need to rely on substitutes may be good news for many poor households. Consider some figures on the price ratio between what poor unconnected urban households are paying water vendors compared to the price charged by the public utility companies. They provide a stark illustration of how the status quo in many utility industries does not benefit the poor and that the poor are willing to pay quite significant amounts to access utilities. Table 3 shows that poor

Table 3. *Comparing prices paid by water vendors and charges at public utilities*[a]

Country	City	Ratio of prices paid to vendor to public utilities tariffs
Colombia	Cali	10
Ecuador	Guayaquil	20
Haiti	Port-au-Prince	17–100
Honduras	Tegucigalpa	16–34
Peru	Lima	17

[a] *Source*: Garn (1993) cited by Tynan (2000).

households often pay over 10 or 20 times the price paid by connected households with regular service, thus highlighting the benefits reaped by these households if services are expanded as a result of privatization.

Finally, the importance of the complementarity between some goods can be underestimated. To begin with, it is worth noting that in many countries urban water is pumped to the apartments in most buildings. This means that the access to water depends on the availability of electricity. In fact, increased reliability and lower prices in electricity are a major determinant of improved and cheaper services in water. [15] But there is a second dimension to complementarity. When investment is required to connect to the network, privatization may have an adverse effect on the poor if households are legally required to connect to the network and there are no connection subsidies or credit facilities that reduce the large up-front costs that households must incur in order to connect. This is a critical issue in the water sector where connection costs can be several hundreds of dollars. [16]

(iv) *Losing discretion in quality decisions*

Finally, privatization will also affect the quality of service. This may have beneficial effects on poorer households if the pre-reform quality was inadequate, especially as regards the continuity of service. Privatization, especially if accompanied by the introduction of competition, may also spur more diversity in the types of services offered, some of which may be more closely tailored to the needs of poorer households. Quality improvements may also be costly and will thus be reflected in higher tariffs, which may hurt the poor. The balance between quality and tariffs imposed by the regulator on a private provider may be based on standards relevant for the average customer and may not be the adequate balance for poorer households.

In many instances, the benefits poor households derive from improved service provision may more than compensate for the impact on tariffs. This depends on the exact magnitude of the tariff increase, although the evidence shows that poor households are usually willing to pay substantially more for a reliable service than the pre-reform tariffs. For instance, during 1995–98, ESA Consultores of Honduras undertook several WTP (willingness to pay) surveys in Central and South America trying to measure households attitudes and valuations regarding water and sanitation services. [17] The main conclusions from these studies included:

—Where households are not connected there is a high willingness to pay for a connection to the public network.

—Usually these households spend a significant amount of resources for alternative low-quality supplies and are willing to pay to be connected. [18]

—When users are receiving minimal coverage, they are willing to pay more for uninterrupted service. [19]

—Where the quality of service is relatively good, households are willing to increase their monthly expenditure in order to reverse a deterioration of the service. [20]

—Therefore, the fact that the poor end up paying more post privatization may not be welfare reducing.

(b) *Macroeconomic linkages*

The macroeconomic linkages between increased private sector participation and poverty are mostly indirect as seen in Table 4. To the extent that additional privately financed infrastructure promotes economic growth, it will be beneficial to the poor (see Kraay & Dollar, 2000; Leipziger, 2001). In addition, if the reforms reduce the fiscal deficit, more resources can be allocated to better targeted public expenditure programs. The magnitude and sign of the above effects will depend on the counterfactual considered. That is, how much would the growth rate be without privatization and how would extra fiscal resources be spent? The difficult problems arise during the transition. Significant changes in relative prices throughout the economy needed to unleash growth can be very damaging to the least prepared segments of the population. Managing the effects of privatization on the relative price of public services is one of the purposes of safety nets.

Table 4. *Summary of macroeconomic linkages*[a]

Macroeconomic effect	Areas of potential loss to the poor	Ameliorating factors
Economic growth	Relative price changes for infra-structure services can influence consumption baskets especially where no safety nets are in place to address specifically the needs of the poor	—Over the medium run, increased private sector participation in infra-structure should contribute to growth which in turn tends to reduce poverty levels
Reduction in employment	—Workforce often reduced soon after privatization —Wages may also decrease for some of the workers during a transition period	—Depends to what extent poor households were employed by public enterprises, on the nature of the compensation provided to workers laid-off, and labor market's ability to generate new jobs
Reallocation of public expenditure	—Reduction in overall subsidy allocation during transition as a result of fiscal adjustment may reflect lower priorities for privatized utilities	—"Privatization revenue" and better targeting may ease financing of the needs of the real poor

[a] *Source*: Adapted from Foster (1999).

A second and more direct effect might be the reduction in employment associated with the privatization of a public utility company. Both theory and evidence point to a significant reduction in employment after privatization—although there is also growing evidence, in the Argentine and Mexican transport sectors for instance, that in some sectors, employment will eventually rebound. In addition, wages may also be reduced. It is not possible, however, to make any general assertion regarding these effects since they will depend not only on the employment structure of the company, but also on the flexibility of the labor market and on the relative wages in the utility and outside. Chisari *et al.* (1999), for instance, show that much of the unemployment increase that occurred during the implementation of the privatization of Argentina's utilities could best be explained by the rationing of the credit market which prevented the adjustment needed to absorb excess labor.

Finally, it may be worth pointing out that changes in subsidy policies may be intended to help the poor but may also cause damage during the transition. It is quite common that a key companion of a privatization policy is fiscal adjustment. Most fiscal adjustments end up reducing subsidies. This cut in subsidy is commonly handled in a way to keep matters simple, favoring cuts across-the-board. This lack of discrimination is a potential concern for the poorest (*viz.*, even if they only get a modest share of these subsidies it may account for a larger share of household income), and is often a high price to pay to achieve the longer run gains of reform.

3. MEASURING THE EXPECTED EFFECTS OF REFORM

Regrettably, there are no quantitative rules that guide policy-makers, essentially since the effects of privatization on the poor will depend on the particular situation of a country and the details of the reform process. Nevertheless, as a first step, policy-makers should try to ascertain and measure the potential impacts of the reforms on the poor. This would entail trying to answer quite specifically the following two main questions:

—*Who is benefiting from status quo implicit and explicit subsidies? Are they poor?* We have seen that many of the studies of the effectiveness of targeting prior to privatization suggest that the poor are not the main beneficiaries. Therefore a successful privatization program for water or electricity must measure the likely distributional impact of changes including changes to subsidy designs and programs. This requires an analysis of the tariff structure, implicit subsidies and explicit subsidies of the current service provider and a socioeconomic assessment of the status of the benefited households. [21]

—*Are the poorer households connected to the service?* This is a crucial question that needs to be addressed in order to clarify the potential impacts of the reform process on the poor. If not, are they paying informally? What is the true economic value of access, taking into account social benefits or externalities?

Ideally the answer to these two questions would entail a comparison of the welfare of the poor with and without reform. At least in principle, the welfare impacts can be measured using a simple consumer surplus framework. But this is not just an academic exercise. Generating the information serves two purposes. First, it can be used to inform public opinion regarding the true effects of the privatization process. Second, it can generate the information needed to design the policy to counter any undesirable social impacts of the reform.

Why then is it that some of the most creative and politically astute governments in the developing world have not measured these impacts in order to better inform their electorate and better help their poor. Whereas in the initial round of reforms, governments might have been either genuinely or cynically unaware of distributional concerns, this is no longer likely. While we cannot rule out the interplay of some political economy factors (including potentially thorny issues regarding the relative political strength of winners and losers), the reality that gains take time has unfortunately led some reform actors and their advisors to underestimate publicly the distributional consequences. On the other hand, even the best-intentioned policy-makers have faced difficulties in assessing their options simply because they do not have the basic information needed to consider policy tradeoffs. In this respect, the main obstacle is the *weakness of the data* available to evaluate the relationship between infrastructure provision and the poor. To measure the microeconomic impacts, ideally a researcher would need a data set that contains:

—household level observations on a wide range of socioeconomic variables;
—information on expenditure and *physical* consumption of utility services; and
—information on households not connected or informally connected to services.

These data would permit the simulation of the welfare impacts of different tariffs, subsidy and connection policies related to reform. For example, rising block tariffs might be proposed as a way to harmonize distributive objectives with economic efficiency and financial sustainability of the service provider. The unit price of the service would be cheaper for the first units of consumption, up to the level considered sufficient for the basic needs of a poor household. All users benefit from this cheap tariff. Consumption in subsequent blocks could then be charged at its true economic cost or higher. The efficiency and effectiveness of these types of social tariffs will depend on the correlation between household physical consumption and household poverty levels. In order to evaluate this relationship—so that the exact size of the first block can be established fairly—a database which records for each household both socioeconomic variables and *physical* consumption of utility services is required. This approach has been adopted for water services in Cartagena, Colombia—where in 1998, the maximum rate is about seven time larger than the first block rate—and in Panama City where the tariff differentiation is done by type of users: social, residential or commercial.

More generally, such a household level database would be an extremely useful tool for calibrating impacts and evaluating designs. Such a database is rarely available, however, even in developed countries. Most countries undertake household level surveys—many following the Living Standards Measurement Survey (LSMS) methodology sponsored by the World Bank—which are valuable instruments to measure poverty, evaluate impacts of different social programs and design well targeted subsidy schemes. As regards the infrastructure sectors, however, these surveys have some serious shortcomings. [22] LSMS records a large number of socioeconomic variables which can be used to ascertain the poverty level of the sampled households. As regards water usage, all surveys incorporate a question on the amount the household spent on water services during the last month or the last payment period, although they do not tend to record the volume of water consumed. [23] As such, the only way that physical water use can be inferred from the information collected in the LSMS is to transform the monetary expenditure into a physical consumption variable by applying the corresponding tariff structure to the household's declared water bill.

The deficiencies with the LSMS methodology as regards the infrastructure sectors can be illustrated in the case of water in Panama where a conscious effort was made to anticipate the needs of the poor in the preparation of privatization. Experience with this approach revealed that the expenditure information was deficient in a number of respects, which made it very difficult to draw reliable inferences about the physical volume of consumption. Shortcomings included:

—the fact that there are multiple tariff structures applied to residential customers and that the survey did not contain any information on which tariff applied to which household.

—the absence of a variable identifying whether the household had measured water supply. Therefore, it is impossible to know whether the expenditure transformation gave actual or imputed water consumption.

—the quality of the expenditure data can be poor, e.g., where the household was not able to produce a recent water bill, the estimate is based on memory. In these cases, it is not always clear whether the estimated consumption included the charge for refuse collection, which in the case of Panama is billed together with the water service.

To illustrate this point, consider findings of Gómez-Lobo *et al.* (1999) concerning the quality of the water expenditure data of the 1997 LSMS for Panama. In order to gauge how substantial the divergence might be between actual water expenditure and that reported in the survey, histograms were plotted comparing the frequency distribution of expenditure in the survey as against the client database of the Panama water utility, IDAAN. The resulting distributions for the standard residential tariff and the special social tariff showed such wide variation that they appear to come from widely disparate distributions.

Fortunately, these deficiencies can be eliminated by relatively inexpensive changes to the survey design and implementation. [24] Until that is done, however, there will be a lack of suitable data to analyze the social impacts of sectoral reforms in the infrastructure sector. There is still much that a creative analyst can do to try to answer the questions posed at the beginning of this section, even if only poor or incomplete data are available. Komives, Whittington, and Wu (2000) show how to squeeze as much information as possible from these LSMS. But more needs to be done. Foster (2000) suggests an expansion of the standard questionnaires used to collect the required information—and provides some guidelines as to how to go about it—but this collection is impossible without a political commitment that may be harder to achieve in view of the stakes for some of the beneficiaries of the existing policies.

4. IS THERE A CASE FOR A SPECIAL WELFARE POLICY FOR INFRASTRUCTURE?

To motivate the discussion, it may be useful to see how the potential costs of not having a special welfare policy work out in practice with the help of a recent crisis in Argentina. In 1995 the water and sanitation services for the Province of Tucuman in Argentina were concessioned to a consortium of Compagnie Generale des Eaux and a local investor for 30 years. To fund the required investment program, the concessionaire bid a tariff increase of 68%. The tariff increase would be immediate and would affect all customer groups equally in a population with a significant share of urban and rural poor. With hindsight, this last characteristic of the winning bid was probably a misjudgment. The tariff increase proved very unpopular and was considered unjust by low-consumption users. The situation deteriorated with a series of episodes of turbid water. The result was a nonpayment campaign by consumers which provoked a financial crises for the concessionaire. Provincial elections brought to power a new administration which was much more hostile to the concession program. At first the authorities and the concessionaire began negotiating the contract. One initiative was to introduce a special tariff for low-income users and a system of rising block tariffs for regular customers. The negotiations did not prosper, however, and the case ended in international arbitration.

This example illustrates the challenges of addressing social issues in the context of privatization. Although the causes of the failure of the Tucuman water concession are many and complex, perhaps earlier attention to the social and distributive issues related to the tariff increases would have increased the chances of success or an explicit subsidy program would have helped diffuse the explosive situation. The main problem may have been, however, that the government had not addressed the poverty issue as part of its general welfare program and was trying to get the job done through the renegotiation of the design of the concession.

A key question is whether as a matter of principle, the linkages between poverty and infrastructure in general should simply be viewed as just another manifestation of poverty generally and, as such, should be tackled through the general welfare system? The Pareto-optimal answer is yes, but we live in an imperfect world. Therefore, the more pressing question is: given the unlikely prospect of a general welfare policy in most countries, if analysis raises concerns regarding the impact of reforms on the poor, is there a real case for welfare policies in the infrastructure? In short, are the "fuel poor"—a term used in the United Kingdom to refer to vulnerable households that underconsume energy resources—any different from the "general poor"? [25]

Unfortunately, linking welfare programs to changes in the utility industries is quite complex. First, it is quite difficult to isolate the effects on the poor of changes in utilities from the effects of other simultaneous policy changes. For example, it is not uncommon for privatization to raise tariffs faced by poor households, but other changes in the economy (possibly indirectly linked to the privatization process, such as higher economic growth) may compensate for this effect. Second, welfare programs aimed at utility consumers would not reach the unconnected poor, which in some cases can be a substantial proportion of vulnerable households. An alternative is to consider more general poverty alleviation programs which may be more efficient in their overall net impact on vulnerable households. This seems promising but hard to implement.

This discussion begs the recognition of a basic issue. Once social objectives have been recognized as important and once the limits of general welfare systems have been recognized, should utility regulators have social and welfare objectives in their statutory duties? Some critics, such as Vickers (1998), argue that "the advantages of regulators having discretion to pursue distributional ends are outweighed by disadvantages of capture, influence activities, uncertainty and unaccountability. Regulators, perhaps like central bankers, should have narrow objectives." At first then, it would seem that the distributional impacts of utility reform should be tackled through more general welfare policies aimed at alleviating poverty, and therefore should not be addressed directly in the utility industries nor should they be part of the concerns of the regulator.

Before looking into the options available to rely on utilities to implement the focused objectives chosen by politicians, it is worth revisiting a question currently haunting many reformers: how realistic is it to expect that the government will be able to put together general welfare policies which will support privatization policies.

Traditional economic wisdom is to let the government take care of the poor. Conventional public economics suggests that the most efficient tax/benefit system would be one based on lump-sum transfers. This assumes that governments have the ability to not only raise taxes without distorting resource allocation decisions but that, in addition, they know exactly who the poor are and how to reach them. In most developing countries, the tax system is usually quite inefficient and unable to raise resources at a low enough cost to enable sufficient funding of a welfare system. While distortions in raising taxes and transferring income are difficult to avoid, taxes should be introduced where they cause the lowest welfare loss. The rule of thumb is that distortions should be applied to goods and activities with low demand or supply elasticities—known as the Ramsey pricing rule. On the demand side, this can be quite dramatic since the poorest often are likely to have few reasonable alternatives to the services offered by the utilities and hence social and efficiency considerations would conflict.

To decide how much to rely on the general welfare system to address the need of the poorest in the infrastructure sector, it is worth considering the cost of public funds—a measure of the efficiency of the tax system. The cost of public funds is the welfare loss that occurs when an additional unit of tax is raised to fund an expenditure program. It is positive because taxes tend to distort some resource allocation decisions in the economy. [26] Most developed countries have costs of public funds between 0.15 and 0.35, meaning that to raise one additional dollar in taxes costs the economy US\$1.15–US\$1.35. The higher this cost, the more a welfare program funded through utility prices is likely to be the way forward. Indeed, while long-term efforts should be geared to improve the welfare system, addressing poverty problems directly in the infrastructure sectors may well be more efficient in a second-best sense than relying on the current welfare structure in many countries.

A new approach could be to make the utilities take care of the poor. The common practice of using two-part tariffs in utility industries opens up the possibility of following a Ramsey recipe. The connection and disconnection elasticity for utility services is probably very inelastic for a broad range of the income distribution. Therefore, taxing and transferring income through the design of tariffs and in particular through the design of the fixed charges of utility bills may well be very efficient, at least for some limited range of tax values. Fixed charges in utility tariffs will be very close to true "lump sum" taxes if the disconnection elasticity is low, which is probably the case for most households. Therefore, implementing welfare programs through a transparent cross-subsidy in the utility rates, especially if under-taken such that only fixed charges are affected, may well be more efficient than a general poverty alleviation program undertaken with general tax funds.

This has implications not only for the effi-cient design of utility subsidy programs—where taxes or transfers should be based on the fixed charges of tariffs as much as possible—but it also opens up the possibility of using this vehicle for other poverty alleviation programs. [27] Indeed, tailoring welfare programs to the utility industries allows bene-fits to be linked or conditioned on the consumption of utility services. At first, this may seem suboptimal, given that unconditional cash transfers, such as raising the minimum wage or increasing benefit payments from other poverty alleviation programs, should increase the utility of households, since they are then free to spend the extra resources as they freely wish. There are several possible reasons why benefits in the utility industries should be linked to the actual consumption of the services.

First, policy-makers may be interested in guaranteeing that households *consume* a mini-mum amount of a service rather than simply guarantee that they have sufficient resources to purchase the service. This argument may be relevant where individual consumption provides important social externalities, such as the public health benefits of water and sanita-tion. It is probably less relevant for electricity and gas. Another type of consumption exter-nality occurs in the telecommunications indus-try, where the value of the service to all users increases with the aggregate number of users. In these cases, the social value of consumption (or connection in the case of telecommunica-tions) is higher than the private value. [28] Therefore, welfare transfers linked directly to observed consumption may be preferable to unconditional transfers to vulnerable house-holds.

Second, as mentioned in Serra (2000), it may be that the consumption of certain goods by poor households enter directly the social welfare function of society. [29] In other words,

the general public may care about the actual consumption of certain goods by poor house-holds, not necessarily their income level. Therefore, equivalent cash transfers would not be a perfect substitute from a social point of view. This situation may also determine the way vulnerable groups articulate their welfare demands, since a petition for subsidies directly linked to utility services may have more politi-cal resonance than cash transfers.

Third, introducing distributive consider-ations into a reform process, perhaps by designing a special welfare program, may be unavoidable for political reasons. The success of the privatization process may depend on such a policy, even when strict welfare consid-erations may not justify it. This approach to welfare policy design may not be very recom-mendable since it risks generating public transfers that benefit particular interest groups and not necessarily the most needy. As the experience in Tucuman suggests, however, disregarding social issues altogether can be a very risky strategy for a reform process.

In summary, there is a case for adverse distributional effects to be addressed directly in the utility industries with measures aimed at lowering the financial burden on vulnerable households that consume the services. But, this does not necessarily entail that a utility regu-lator designs or even administers the welfare program. On the contrary, it is advisable that as far as possible these programs be integrated into the general welfare and poverty alleviation policies of a government, thus maintaining coherence with complementary poverty reduc-tion efforts and to guarantee efficient and encompassing eligibility assessments. The Chilean water subsidy scheme and the Colom-bian residential utility subsidy provide two examples of designs in which policies in the utility industry are integrated successfully with more general welfare policies of a govern-ment. [30]

5. GUIDELINES TO PROTECT THE POOR

Recognizing that social issues should be an integral part of a successful privatization strategy in the utility sector, what would be some of the guidelines that policy-makers should consider when designing reforms? The first task is to generate the needed information to make an informed judgement. Armed with this knowledge, it is possible to distinguish the groups affected, characterize the nature of the impact and devise effective and efficient counter measures. For possible policy actions, three broad spheres of public policy can be distinguished: the privatization strategy, regulatory policy and social policy. These three areas should be viewed as complementary, although the timing and institutional responsibility may be different in each case. Privatization policy and social policy actions have to be considered early in the reform process and will probably be the task of institutions distinct from the regulatory agency but they need to be specified first to ensure that the regulatory concerns are consistent with the privatization and social goals. Any future changes in policies and social priorities should also be anticipated and regulatory rules providing guidelines to address this kind of situation are likely to be part of the more general rules regarding renegotiation of the commitments made to the private operator at the time of privatization. [31]

(a) *Privatization strategy*

Evidence shows that, in general, competition is good for all consumers, including the poor. This reinforces the need to undertake reforms that promote competition, such as vertical and horizontal separation, elimination of exclusivity clauses in contracts and laws, and the development of a regulatory "culture" that promotes competition. These recommendations are also worthy from a strict efficiency viewpoint, a case where efficiency considerations and welfare considerations coincide. The only drawback that competition may have is that it forces the elimination of cross-subsidies, which may hurt the poor. But, the impact of the general drop in tariffs or the availability of services which usually accompanies competition may more than compensate for the effects of the elimination of cross-subsidies. Furthermore, it is still possible to maintain internally generated cross-subsidies, even in the face of competition through the creation of a universal welfare fund or to use Chilean-style targeted subsidies outside of the tariff formula. [32]

Another area which deserves careful attention is the investment and quality targets that are set at the time of privatization, especially in a concession contract as part of the definition of the service obligations imposed on the operators. It will often be the case that poorer households are not connected to the service; therefore, the connection targets set prior to

privatization may have an important impact on the poor. If tariffs are sufficiently high so that it is profitable to serve poorer households, then a private company should extend services to these households out of self-interest—as happened in the residential telecommunications market in Chile, for example. But, if the economics from the viewpoint of the operators make it unprofitable to serve more vulnerable households, then it may be convenient to specify investment targets in the contract. These connection targets must specify the geographic area or the type of customer to be reached. In the La Paz-El Alto water concession there is an explicit number of new connections mandated for water, with specific neighborhood targets in fringe areas. There are percentage coverage targets for sewerage. In Monteria, Colombia, specific water and sewerage expansion targets were set and monitored similar targets can be found throughout Latin American concessions. [33]

The setting of quality standards also impacts on the poor. The recommendation is to avoid setting targets based on developed country benchmarks that may make the service too expensive for poorer households. This means leaving some flexibility in the contract to allow the company, the regulator and users in the future to agree to a different price/quality combination when it is convenient. This does not imply that quality standards should not be set in the contract, which may give an incentive for a company to reduce cost by eroding quality. It suggests rather, leaving the door open to allow, in certain specific circumstances (for example, when the representative leaders of a community demand it), the company, with due sanction from the regulator, to alter the price/quality combination for that community to improve efficiency within the same cost parameters. [34]

It is important to eliminate any legal obstacle that may prevent more innovative or alternative projects from being implemented. Although it may be the task of the future regulator to promote such projects, it is important to avoid at the outset any legal constraint in the contract which may limit this type of initiative in the future. One way of doing so is the inclusion of the clear specification of the universal service obligations (USO) in the scope of responsibilities of the monopolies. USO is an obligation imposed on the provider of infrastructure services. It ensures anyone in their service area the access to an affordable minimum level of a standard quality service bundle. This does not mean that the provider has to deliver access to the infrastructure network which would be a more specific requirement. This distinction is important in the case of water, for instance, where alternative technologies can provide more effective ways of meeting the needs of the poor. But this requires more flexibility than most large utilities are typically willing to offer. One of the best known successful examples is the condominium system adopted in the Northeast of Brazil for the delivery of sanitation services. It is essentially a negotiated co-ownership agreement for a small community of users of local public services. The negotiation allows the adjustment of preferences to the form of supply of the service which explains why very different sewer systems can co-exist in cities such as Fortaleza or Recife. [35]

A major source of concern for potential investors is that sometimes "affordable" means at a price that may not necessarily cover the cost of delivering the service. Moreover, the precise definition of the range of services to be covered through the obligation varies by sector and country. In addition, who the main beneficiaries of the USO are can vary. USO obligations may address spatial or geographical differences, specifying for instance that rural areas or inner cities are to be serviced just like richer urban areas. The USO is then said to be aiming at benefiting high-cost customers. It can also be focusing on criteria more related to the income level of the potential users or to specific demographic or institutional characteristics (retirees, schools, hospitals). Low-income groups, for instance, cannot necessarily afford the connection costs to a water main at prices that other income groups can afford. Moreover, they typically cannot borrow either—because of capital market imperfections in many developing countries—which further limits their access to these services.

Attention should also be paid to the way a contract or company is tendered in the privatization process. As mentioned earlier, the variable chosen to award the company or contract will determine the distribution of benefits between all stakeholders, including poor users. Choosing a tendering mechanism is a complex issue, which should cover many considerations. As regards the poor, however, the following rule of thumb should be borne in mind: if poor households are connected to the service, then they will benefit more if tariffs are chosen as the competitive variable, while if they are unconnected, then choosing investment commitments as the tendering variable has a higher potential of benefiting the poor.

(b) *Regulatory policy*

Earlier we argued that it would be theoretically best that the regulator's duties did not include distributional or welfare objectives. Practically as well, we have little evidence that the governance of regulatory agencies exceeds those of national governments in a political economy sense. But, there are actions and decisions within the traditional sphere of activities of a regulatory agency that can enhance the benefits that poorer households can obtain from utility reform. There is merit in strict regulatory rules (that are enforceable) due to their higher predictability and lower susceptibility to corruption. Greater discretion granted to the regulator may, however, provide some margin in tariff design between, say, price- quality mixes, that can benefit the poor. [36] On the margin, therefore, regulators can make pro-poor decisions, if they are so motivated and if their mandate allows. Once these margins become too large, however, it is best to place decisions in the hands of policymakers.

Regulators should also be reasonably open to new and innovative approaches to solve investment and operational issues related to poorer users. These include, for example, community participation in the construction and operation of networks which may reduce their cost, the supply of communal services, or even permitting small-scale private vendors or networks in certain circumstances. This is the case of *aguateros* in Paraguay. There are hundreds of small-scale private service providers of water services, including relatively large companies supplying as many as 800 connections (Solo and Snell, 1998; cited in Ehrhardt, 2000). Another example is the telecommunications micro-entrepreneurs in Peru, who turn regular cell phones into mobile pay phones by charging a mark-up over the normal tariff, and who are often seen in public gatherings wearing brightly colored hats or clothes (Melo, 2000). These activities should not be suppressed by a regulator provided that they cater to an underserved market segment.

Perhaps the most effective means that a regulator has, however, to benefit lower income users is to promote competition in the services where this is possible. Besides its impact on tariffs, competition will increase the range of available goods and services, often generating services specifically tailored to the needs of poorer households. A clear example was the introduction of a "calling party pays" system for cellular telephones by the telecommunication regulator in Chile. The introduction by telephone companies of cellular telephones based on the use of pre-paid cards together with the above regulatory decision has prompted an accelerated increase in the access of poorer households to cellular telephony. These households do not have the credit record to access more traditional credit plans and usually favor pre-payment methods which allow them to have a strict budgetary control over their expenditure. Thus, this system is especially attractive to poorer households. In Peru, pre-payment cellular users account for over 60% of cellular clients (Melo, 2000). The private sector may also develop other services which may be attractive to poorer users, such as special voice messaging services which can be accessed from any telephone (including a pay phone).

Besides promoting competition, a regulator can also allow and even promote the use of new and innovative tariff structures which may benefit low-income users. Ideally services should be offered as an optional or menu choice to users. Optional, or menu tariffs, have the advantage that users can decide what is the best choice for themselves and thus reduces the informational requirements of the regulator when it comes to deciding the best quality or service standards. Aguas de Illimani in Bolivia, for example, offers households a choice between the regular connection fee for the water service or a lower fee provided households supply their own labor for the connection activities (Komives, 1999 cited in Ehrhardt, 2000). In Peru, companies offer "popular lines" in the telecommunication sector, which have no initial connection fee, only a flat monthly rate has to be paid, but monthly traffic is limited (Melo, 2000). This may be an attractive service for some poor (and even non-poor) households with low-telephone usage. By offering this service as an option, users can self-select the option which is best suited for them and could be an attractive way to overcome the obstacle posed by high connection charges for poorer households.

(c) *Social policy*

If there is an overriding social concern regarding the impact on the poor of a reform process, then special measures can be introduced through the welfare system. It was argued above that there is a case for special welfare programs in the utility industries, although this does not necessarily mean that it should be administered by the sectoral regulator. Although the optimal design of a subsidy scheme goes beyond the limits of this paper, we attempt to give some criteria that may be useful to consider if special welfare programs are to be created. All subsidies, including implicit ones, can be classified according to: (i) the source of the funding, (ii) the eligibility criteria used to identify beneficiaries, and (iii) the good or service being subsidized.

The funding of subsidies can come from a variety of sources. First, governments can provide the funds from general tax revenues. This is quite typical in the case of urban transport and "negative concessions" as those awarded for many toll roads. Second, they can be raised by charging certain customers a price higher than the cost of service. This has been quite standard for public utilities in Latin America and is likely to continue to be common for private utilities when governments cannot make credible commitments to finance subsidies. Third, a fund can be established whereby all companies must make a contribution according to some proportional rule (e.g., proportional to the number of customers that each company serves or proportional to each company's revenues). Companies might still charge a price cost markup on customers in order to pay for this contribution. Unlike the second case, however, the company would be free to decide which prices and which customer to charge. In Argentina, a sector-specific levy finances the expansion needs in electricity distribution and transmission in the poorest provinces but the telecoms sector is the one in which subsidies are most commonly funded out of sector specific funds or fees as in various Central American countries. [37]

The eligibility for a subsidy can be determined according to some categorical variable, geographical zones, or directly through means testing. Argentina has subsidies benefiting specific groups (e.g., pensioner or students), and Chisari and Estache (1999) show that while the intended categories benefit, many others do also. As mentioned earlier, in Colombia, a geographic subsidy has consumers taxed/subsidized in their utility bills according to a national socioeconomic classification system based on neighborhood characteristics. It is a consumption subsidy funded by price cost margins over some consumers, although an important part of the subsidy is also funded by transfers from central government. Vélez (1996) has shown that, while intended, in Colombia, the subsidy is not well focused on the poor. Rather it is neutral in terms of its impact on income groups. In general, in spite of the fact that they are easier to implement, categorical and geographic subsidies have major drawbacks. They will incur higher errors of exclusion (poor customers that should be eligible are not chosen) and inclusion (relatively wealthier households are erroneously deemed eligible) than a means-tested subsidy. [38]

Finally, once the specific type of subsidy has been decided, its object has to be picked as well and a criteria must be followed to avoid mistakes. Subsidies can be classified according to the good or service which is the object of the subsidy. In utility industries, this can either be the consumption of a utility service or the connection costs to the network. Ideally, the subsidy scheme should be directed to those goods with the highest difference between willingness to pay and costs. There is a strong presumption that in Latin America at least this would indicate that connections or network expansion subsidies should be favored over consumption subsidies. This is because the capital market failures have a stronger impact on connections. Indeed, while the willingness to pay for a connection is quite high—it is almost impossible to borrow to pay for this connection. [39]

6. CONCLUSIONS

The main conclusions of this paper are that:

—It is a myth to believe that *status quo* arrangements in the utility industries (i.e. public provision) are beneficial to poor households. Indeed, many poor would benefit from the service expansion that may be possible through privatization and which would allow them to avoid the high costs of alternative sources.

—It is a myth that existing subsidies benefit the poor; the middle class tends to be the main beneficiary.

—It is a myth that poor households are not willing or able to pay for a regular and reliable service. Many of these households currently pay much more for a deficient service from private vendors (in the case of water) or alternative sources (in the case of energy) than they would from a public provider.

—It is a myth that there is no role for government once the private sector takes over utilities services. The way markets are restructured, the way competition is introduced and maintained, and the way regulatory commitments are implemented determine whether privatization is beneficial to poor households.

—The weaker the regulatory structure, the less likely it is that the concerns of the poor will be accommodated in public policy decisions.

—With stronger governance and clear political support to social policy comes innovative reform—e.g., Chilean water subsidies that are targeted and support minimum usage or concession contracts that mandate access to rural electricity or phones, awarded to the lowest bidders for public subsidies.

What is really needed is not only a political commitment to privatize, but also institutional and regulatory reforms that make the poor better off as a result. *If pre-privatization policy on expenditure incidence was poor, unless something is explicitly done, it will be weak post-privatization as well. Privatization is not a substitute for responsible, redistributive welfare policies.* Welfare discussions are complex, especially interhousehold welfare discussions. Moreover, welfare options open up the possible, but not much more. Policies leading to *potential* welfare gains abound in economics. Policies leading to real welfare gains are a much rarer commodity. Whether a policy achieves a real gain consistent with its potential depends on its design, its implementation and, in particular, the political commitment behind it.

NOTES

1. See Leipziger (2000) or Canning, Fay, and Perotti (1992), for instance.

2. While in most sectors (with the exception of power generation) service concessions tends to be the norm and there is seldom a transfer of ownership of assets to the private operators, policy-makers, academic and casual observers continue to talk about privatization. This broad concept of privatization is the one retained throughout the paper.

3. This back of the envelope result is obtained by dividing the average daily investment made during 1990–98 and dividing it by the 1998 population.

4. Wodon (2000), including a detailed survey of recent studies on the topic.

5. See Sheshinski and Lopez-Calva (1999) for a recent survey of the more general linkages between privatization and poverty. See also Estache, Foster, Wodon, and Wellenstein (1999).

6. This observation is also documented by Benitez, Chisari, and Estache (2000) for Argentina for all utilities, by Wodon (2000) for electricity subsidies in Honduras and by Foster, Gómez-Lobo, and Halpern (1999) for Panama for water subsidies.

7. See Contreras and Gómez-Lobo (2000).

8. The evidence suggests that illegal or informal connections are much more common among poor households and therefore the implicit subsidy from nonpayment is bound to be progressive. For example, Vélez (1996) estimates that the implicit subsidy from nonpayment by informal or illegal connection in the main urban centers of Colombia in 1992 accounted for 6% of all subsidies in the electricity sector and 24% of all subsidies in water and sanitation. In the gas sector, whereas formally connected households paid a surcharge over costs, nonpaying households received an implicit subsidy. Overall, close to 9% of all subsidies in the gas, electricity and water sector distributed in 1992 were accounted for by illegal connections or nonpayment. Furthermore, the distribution of this subsidy was highly progressive with more than 72% and 73% of the subsidy benefiting households in the five poorest deciles of the income distribution in the electricity and water sector, respectively (with close to 20% of the subsidy in each sector benefiting households in the first decile). The elimination of this implicit subsidy could have a negative effect on poor households if it is not compensated by other measures.

9. Solo (1999).

10. Estache (2000).

11. The crucial point in this argument is whether the household is aware and values the extra safety and health benefits of a formal connection. If this is the case then the household would presumably be willing to pay for a formal service. If the household does not value these benefits, however, then it is a public health concern which may justify some type of subsidy for the service.

12. Walker, Ordonez, Serrano, and Halpern (2000).

13. See Chisari *et al.* (1999).

14. See Boland and Whittington (2000), for more details.

15. Arguably, a privatization process may even be beneficial to the poor if reform promotes the development of a more dynamic and productive industry for these complementary goods. As such, privatization may increase the availability of low-cost durable goods for poor households.

16. In Buenos Aires for instance, the concession contract charged new customers the cost of the connection plus part of the cost of expanding the secondary network, which totaled between $1,100 and $1,500 per connection. The operator was allowed to recover its investments in two years. Many unconnected customers were in areas with an average household income of about US$245 a month, i.e. among the poorest, and were being asked to contribute almost 20% of their income to these complementary investments.

17. The cities and dates of these studies are: Honduras—Tegucigalpa (marginal neighborhoods), 1995; Nicaragua—Managua (marginal neighborhoods), 1996; Venezuela—Caracas, Barquisimeto, Mérida (all the population), 1996; Guatemala—Guatemala City (marginal neighborhoods), 1997; Venezuela—Caracas (marginal neighborhoods), 1997; Panama—Panama City and Colon (entire population), 1998.

18. For example, in Tegucigalpa, in 1995, unconnected households spent an average of $10 a month for 3.7 m^3 of water. This expenditure represented 7% of household income for a volume that is significantly below the recommended minimum of monthly basic consumption of 15 m^3. These households could reduce their expenditure and increase their consumption if connected to the public supply network.

19. Households in marginal sectors that were connected but did not receive a daily service, were willing to pay $4.50 per month for a daily 4 h service. That represents 3% of average household income and is three times higher than the tariff they paid at the time ($1.50). Similar WTP results were found in the other cities.

20. In Caracas, for example, households were willing to pay up to three times their tariffs at the time to maintain the quality of service.

21. For a study in this direction see Gómez-Lobo, Foster, and Halpern (2000) where an analysis of the impacts of current subsidies was undertaken for the Panamanian public water supplier.

22. See, for example, Gómez-Lobo, Foster, and Halpern (1999) for an analysis of the problems of the LSMS surveys related to water and sanitation.

23. Other water-related questions in LSMS include the source of water supply, the average number of hours a day in which a dwelling receives water, and whether there is a sewerage connection. Other questions that are sometimes included are the distance of the dwelling to the water supply, location of the tap, and other characteristics of the water and sewerage services.

24. See Gómez-Lobo *et al.* (1999).

25. It may also be worth wondering if the special treatment to be granted to the fuel poor is based on society's judgement that access to utilities is desirable from a more "philosophical" viewpoint—a merit good argument in the public finance literature—or is it based on more technical assessments of the needs of the poor since this would have to influence the design of the privatization strategy since the valuation of the activities are no longer based on commercial or social criteria alone.

26. A common source of distortion influencing the opportunity cost of public funds arises in capital markets because the financing of an expenditure program may end up crowding out private investments. The percentage difference between the present value of the stream of consumption that the private investment would have yielded and the present value of the consumption allowed by the expenditure program is one way of measuring the deadweight loss of a specific program. More "macro" measures are also used in the literature. For a more detailed discussion, see Boadway and Wildasin (1984), Ahmad and Stern (1991) or Sandmo (1998).

27. See Waddams-Price (2000) for a recent review.

28. This argument also justifies the imposition of universal service obligation considered now to be a standard to address the needs of the poor (see Chisari & Estache, 1999 for a discussion of the design of these obligations).

29. Arguably, this may just be another case of consumption externality, where the consumption of one household enters the utility function of another directly.

30. In Chile, the Ministry of Planning (MIDEPLAN), the social welfare ministry, and not the water regulator who determines the number of subsidies allocated to each region. This allocation is based on yearly household surveys that portray the socioeconomic conditions of each zone, the water tariff in each area, and fiscal budgetary constraints. This evaluation is better undertaken at a central level by an organism with expertise in poverty and social issues. Once the number of subsidies is determined at an aggregate level, it is up to the municipalities in each region to distribute these subsidies to eligible households. This is undertaken using the same socioeconomic assessment instrument as any other public subsidy, a "poverty score." This is a numerical synthesis of a poverty assessment exercise based on a household interview by a social worker. A household's poverty score is used to determine eligibility to almost all public subsidies and therefore guarantees that all poverty alleviation measures are correctly targeted. In Colombia, households receive a subsidy (or a tax in the case of wealthier households) for all utility services based on the geographic location of a dwelling. There are six categories depending on the characteristics of neighborhoods. The important point to note is that the category of each zone is determined by the Secretariat of Planning based on census data and other information. This means that one prerequisite for using the tariff for redistributive purposes is an accurate poverty mapping. This is, however, proving to be a challenging task as discussed later.

31. The arrival of the Blair administration resulted in such changes and an increase in social concerns and these were addressed without changing the financial equation faced by the private operators. Similar changes are occurring in Argentina and Chile with the arrival of Presidents De la Rua and Lagos, respectively, and a UK-type strategy to introduce the changes is likely being considered in both countries.

32. A recent report by Cremer, Gasmi, and Laffont (1998) provide detailed examples from many OECD countries in all sectors. For a longer discussion of universal social funds, see Chisari and Estache (1999).

33. Mandatory connection requirements in the sectoral laws should also be given careful thought. This is usually an issue in the water and sanitation sector, where public health considerations make this a reasonable requirement. However, connection charges, unless subsidized, could be an enormous financial obstacle for poorer households. See Esrey (1996).

34. Community preferences will have to be considered along with public goods aspects of the service of course.

35. Lyonnaise des Eaux (1998).

36. It is important that regulators be careful in sanctioning subaverage quality standards only when there is a real social expression from the community in this respect and not as a way for a private company to increase its profitability by reducing quality. But, of course, communities can be myopic or not anxious to pay full costs, including externalities.

37. Which type of funding is more convenient will depend in part on the efficiency, equity and administra-

tive costs associated with the distortions created by the general tax system (the cost of public funds). When the tax financed subsidies are too costly to enforce and tax reform is not a realistic option, it may be more efficient to raise funds from the utility industry, especially if done through the fixed charge part of utility tariffs. The specific system selected should, however, depend on its sustainability in a competitive environment. Unlike general taxation which is quite neutral for the utility industry, cross-subsidies in a competitive environment will create incentives for "cream skimming" high-paying customers and ignoring low-paying customers. The third alternative avoids this last problem since all companies will have the same proportional responsibility in the funding of the subsidy scheme—although this may also allow for implicit and less transparent subsidies across operational zones.

38. While subsidies in utility industries generally account for a small proportion of household income, means tested subsidies have the undesirable consequence of affecting incentives, especially with respect to labor market participation. This is sometimes labeled the "poverty trap" problem in the welfare system. Geographic subsidies also have secondary economic effects that are often ignored. Such subsidies, for example, may alter the housing value or rental price of properties in the benefited areas, thus reducing the purported benefits of the scheme for those living in those areas.

39. In fact the net present value of the benefits from—and the willingness to pay for—a connection are for many poor and for society is, in many cases, likely to be higher than the amount of the loan which would be needed to finance the connection. An efficient capital market would be willing to provide this loan.

REFERENCES

Ahmad, E., & Stern, N. (1991). *The theory and practice of tax reform in developing countries*. Cambridge: Cambridge University Press.

Ajwad, I., & Wodon, Q. (2000). *Do local governments maximize access rates to public services across areas? A test based on marginal benefit incidence analysis*. Mimeo, Washington, DC: The World Bank.

Benitez, D., Chisari, O., & Estache, A. (2000). *Measuring the fiscal-efficiency-distribution trade-offs in Argentina's utilities privatization*. Mimeo, Washington, DC: World Bank.

Bitran, E., Estache, A., Guasch, J. L., & Serven, P. (1999). Privatizing and regulating Chile's utilities, 1974–2000. In G. Perry, & D. M. Leipziger (Eds.),

Chile: Recent policy lessons and emerging challenges. Washington, DC: World Bank.

Boland, J., & Whittington, D. (2000). The political economy of water tariff design in developing countries: Increasing block tariffs versus uniform price with rebate. In A. Dinar (Ed.), *The political economy of water pricing reforms*. New York: Oxford University Press.

Boadway, R., & Wildasin, A. (1984). *Public sector economics* (2nd ed.). Boston: Little Brown.

Canning, D., Fay, M., & Perotti, R. (1992). Infrastructure and growth. *Rivista di Politica economica, 82*, 113–147.

Chisari, O., Estache, A., & Romero, C. (1999). Winners and losers from privatization and regulation of utilities: Lessons from a general equilibrium model of Argentina. *The World Bank Economic Review, 13*(2), 357–378.

Chisari, O., & Estache, A. (1999). *Universal service obligations in Argentina.* Mimeo, Washington, DC: World Bank.

Contreras, D., & Gómez-Lobo, A. (2000) *Privatization of telecommunications and electricity in Chile: How did the poor fare?.* Mimeo, Washington, DC: World Bank.

Cremer, H., Gasmi, F., & Laffont, J. J. (1998). *Universal service definition, cost and financing: The EEC experience.* Mimeo, Toulouse: IDEI.

Ehrhardt, D. (2000). *Using market structure reforms to improve options for the poor.* Mimeo, Washington, DC: World Bank.

Esrey, S. (1996). Water, waste and well-being: A multi-country study. *American Journal of Epidemiology, 43*(6), 608–623.

Estache, A., Foster, V., Wodon, Q., & Wellenstein, A. (1999). *Infrastructure and Poverty in Latin America.* Mimeo, Washington, DC: World Bank.

Estache, A., & Rodriguez-Pardina, M. (2000). Light and lightning at the end of the public tunnel. In L. Manzetti (Ed.), *Regulatory policy in Latin America: post-privatization realities.* Miami: North–South Center Press, University of Miami.

Estache, A. (2000). *Notes on the social consequences of electricity reform in the Dominican Republic.* Mimeo, Washington, DC: World Bank.

FIEL (2000). *Subsidies in Chilean public utilities.* Mimeo, Washington, DC: World Bank.

Foster, V. (1999). *Literature review for regional studies project on privatization and infrastructure services of the urban poor.* Mimeo, Washington, DC: World Bank.

Foster, V., Gómez-Lobo, A., & Halpern, J. (1999). *Designing water subsidies in Panama.* Policy Research Working Paper No. 2344, Washington, DC: World Bank.

Foster, V. (2000). Measuring the impact of reform and private participation in infrastructure on the poor, presented at a World Bank workshop on poverty and infrastructure privatization, PSD Group.

Garn, H. A. (1993). *Pricing and demand management: A theme paper on managing water resources to meet megacity needs.* Washington, DC: World Bank.

Gómez-Lobo, A., Foster, V., & Halpern, J. (1999). *Informational and modeling issues related to water subsidy design.* Mimeo, Washington, DC: World Bank.

Gómez-Lobo, A., Foster, V., Halpern, J. (2000). Better household surveys for better design of infrastructure subsidies. *Viewpoint* Note No. 213, Washington, DC: World Bank.

Guasch, J. L. (2000). *The impact on performance and renegotiation of concession design: Lessons from an empirical analysis of ten years of concession experience.* Mimeo, Washington, DC: World Bank.

Komives, K., Whittington, D., & Wu, X. (2000). *Infrastructure coverage and the poor: A global perspective.* Mimeo, Washington, DC: World Bank.

Kraay, A., & Dollar, D. (2000). *Growth is good for the poor.* Mimeo, Washington, DC: World Bank.

Leipziger, D. (2000). Achieving social and political consensus, The World Bank. *Development outreach, 2*(1), 18–23.

Leipziger, D. (2001). Why is Latin America lagging behind. *Finance & Development,* Washington, DC: International Monetary Fund, March.

Eaux, Lyonnaise des (1998). *Alternative solutions for water supply and sanitation in areas with limited financial resources.* France: Nanterre.

Melo, J. R. (2000). *Telecoms reform and the poor.* Mimeo, Washington, DC: World Bank.

Navajas (2000). El Impacto Distributivo de los Cambios en los Precios Relativos en la Argentina Entre 1988–98 y los Efectos de las Privatizaciones y la Desregulación Económica. In *Fundación de Investigaciones Económicas Latinoamericanas,* La Distribución del Ingreso en la Argentina.

Sandmo, A. (1998). Redistribution and the marginal cost of public funds. *Journal of Public Economics (Netherlands), 70,* 365–382.

Serra, P. (2000). *Subsidies in Chilean public utilities.* Mimeo, Washington, DC: World Bank.

Sheshinski, E., & Lopez-Calva, L.-P. (1999). *Privatization and poverty.* Mimeo, Cambridge, MA: Harvard Institute of International Development.

Solo, T. M. (1999), Competition in water and sanitation and the role of small-scale entrepreneurs. *Viewpoint,* Washington, DC: World Bank.

Tynan, N. (2000). *Private participation in infrastructure and the poor: Water and sanitation.* Mimeo, Washington, DC: World Bank.

Vélez, C. E. (1996). *Gasto social y desigualdad logros y desafíos: estudio de la incidencia del gasto público social en Colombia.* República de Colombia: Departamento de Planeación Nacional.

Vickers, J. (1998). Regulation, competition and the structure of prices. In Dieter Helm, & Tim Jenkinson (Eds.), *Competition in regulated industries.* New York: Oxford University Press.

Waddams-Price, C. (2000). *Rethinking subsidies for infrastructure.* Mimeo, Washington, DC: World Bank and University of Warwick.

Walker, I., Ordonez, F., Serrano, P., & Halpern, J. (2000). *Pricing, subsidies, and the poor: demand for improved water services in Central America.* Policy Research Working Paper No. 2468, Washington, DC: World Bank.

Wodon, Q. (Ed.) (2000). *Poverty and policy in Latin America and the Caribbean.* Technical Paper 467, Washington, DC: World Bank.

World Bank (1995). *Reforming provincial utilities in Argentina.* Mimeo, Washington, DC: World Bank.

[23]

Equity Valuation in the Czech Voucher Privatization Auctions

Raj Aggarwal and Joel T. Harper*

This is a study of the determinants of share pricing and demand in the path-breaking Czech voucher-based multiple-round mass privatization auction. The results presented here document that share valuation and demand in this auction were based on firm characteristics such as return on sales, sales growth, and ownership structure in the early rounds. However, such information declined in importance while auction results on share prices and trading volumes from prior rounds increased in importance as determinants of share prices and demand in later rounds. While share prices overshot or undershot in the early rounds, by round four they had stabilized and the market cleared successfully by the fifth and final round. These results are new evidence on the price discovery process in the Czech privatization auction and confirm the success of this auction in the efficient pricing and equitable distribution of enterprise shares.

Several formerly socialist countries have used mass privatizations to transform public sector enterprises into private business firms in the 1990s. These transfers of ownership have been unprecedented in scale and scope and have been major mechanisms for these formerly socialist countries to move from planned to market directed economies. The mass privatization carried out by Czechoslovakia (and subsequently the Czech Republic) was the earliest and one of the largest and most successful such programs (e.g., Gray, 1996). The first wave of Czech voucher mass privatization occurred in 1992 (a subsequent smaller auction occurred in 1994) and by the end of the voucher privatization about 85% of the state's assets had been privatized. This successful Czech voucher-based mass privatization not only transferred a large fraction of the Czech economy to private hands, it also created over six million shareholders. However, this privatization program had to overcome a number of challenges.

For instance, mass privatizations face a difficult "Catch 22" type of problem, i.e., how do you sell off major parts of an economy without well-developed financial markets and with inadequate domestic ability to make these purchases, but avoid selling significant proportions of domestic assets to foreigners at fire sale prices. Voucher mass privatizations were developed as a solution to this Catch 22 problem. In voucher mass privatizations, such as the one in the Czech Republic, state owned assets are distributed to a large proportion of the population generally through an auction using inexpensive widely available vouchers.[1]

---

[1]While the Czech voucher-based mass privatization is the best known, other countries that have used vouchers in one form or another include Poland, Russia, Romania, Bulgaria, Armenia, Kazakhstan, Kyrgyz Republic, Latvia, Lithuania and the Ukraine. However, vouchers were not used similarly in each country. For example, Byoko, Shleifer, and Vishny (1994) describe differences in voucher plans for Russia, Poland, and Czechoslovakia.

The authors are grateful for comments from two anonymous reviewers, Karyn Williams, Nikhil Varaiya, Petr Kucera, and other participants in the research seminars where earlier versions were presented, and for research support from Florida Atlantic University, John Carroll University, and the Mellen Foundation, but are solely responsible for the contents of this paper.

Raj Aggarwal is Firestone Chair at Kent State University. Joel T. Harper is an Assistant Professor at Florida Atlantic University.

For mass privatizations to be successful, formerly state owned firms must be valued fairly. But, enterprise valuation in mass privatization is a significant problem due, in part, to the fact that there is generally little verifiable information that is useful for asset valuation. Further, because the assets to be sold were managed with socialist procedures and goals, accounting and other firm level data, commonly used by investors for valuing firms, are perceived to be unreliable and are often inaccurate. In addition, there usually is considerable confusion about property rights, much macroeconomic uncertainty, and rapidly changing industry and competitive structures.

Under these conditions, and in the absence of a well-developed equity market, how do mass privatizations price the assets for sale fairly? One approach has been to use multiple round auctions to assist the price discovery process, especially as only limited information useful for enterprise valuation is available in an ex-socialist economy. In such cases, how do share prices and demand change in each round of the auction process and what are the determinants of such changes? This study examines how public assets were priced and the determinants of the price discovery process in *each round* of the 1992 Czech voucher-based mass privatization auction.

This study finds that while equity prices were based on company characteristics such as return on sales, sales growth, and other ownership characteristics in the early rounds, pricing in subsequent auction rounds was determined more by prior round outcomes regarding share prices and trading volumes and decreasingly by firm-specific information. In addition, the results presented here document that, in spite of some over- and under-shooting as in a cobweb model, most share prices stabilized by the third or fourth rounds. These results indicate that this Czech mass privatization priced shares efficiently especially as the ascending auction process effectively cleared the market by the fifth and last round.

Next, this paper reviews relevant prior literature and describes the Czech voucher auction for mass privatization. The subsequent section presents our pricing and trading volume models, the research design, and describes the data. Following that, empirical results on the determinants of share pricing and trading volumes in this ascending auction mass privatization are presented and discussed, and the final section provides some concluding remarks.

I. Economic Reform, Mass Privatization, and Share Valuation

Given the rapidly changing industrial structure, the lack of reliable firm level data, or useful equity market signals, the valuation of firms to be privatized is indeed a daunting task. Useful prior literature covers both the macroeconomics of the privatization process and how firms may be valued in such cases. In countries with developed capital markets, the process that comes closest is the valuation of initial public offerings (IPOs). Finally, the few studies related to firm valuation in privatization in developed and emerging markets are also reviewed for insights useful in understanding the Czech voucher privatization auctions.

A. Economic Reform and Privatization

Privatization of state owned firms is a major aspect of the recent global move to more market oriented economies. Indeed, privatized firms represent over 20% of the total non-US capitalization of the largest 1,000 firms, and privatized firms are the most valuable publicly traded firms in many countries including Australia, Brazil, China, France, Germany, Italy, Japan, Mexico, Singapore, and Spain (Boutchkova and Megginson, 2000). Further, privatization generally seems to have been beneficial for the firms involved. The effects of privatization on firm performance are investigated by Boubakri and Cosset (1998), Claessens and Djankov (1998), Megginson, Nash, and van Randenborgh (1994), and Boutchkova and Megginson (2000). These studies test performance changes in firms after privatization and, while none of the companies studied were from the former Soviet Bloc, these studies find that privatized firms from industrial, ex-socialist, and developing countries show improved operating efficiency, profitability, and capital spending. These beneficial changes are traced to changes in ownership and greater responsiveness to financial markets and consumers. These studies confirm other case studies, such as Al-Obaidan and Scully (1992), who find that private oil firms are more efficient than state-owned oil firms. Gleason, Mathur, and Mathur (1999) find that acquisitions of former state owned enterprises adds value to investing firms. As a result, privatization of state firms is considered an important part of economic reform in ex-socialist nations.

However, former communist countries faced many different problems and challenges in their economic reform programs. Besides privatization, some of these challenges include price and trade liberalization, reform of the banking systems, and the simultaneous development of capital markets. Much of this literature focuses on the order of privatization, e.g., among the many macroeconomic reforms contemplated, which ones should precede privatization, which industries should be privatized first, should firms be restructured before privatization, and what methods should be used to privatize state owned firms (e.g., Aggarwal and Mejstrik, 1992; Aghion, 1993; Brainard, 1991; Djankov, 1998; Murphy, Shleifer, and Vishny, 1992; Roland, 1993; Sachs, 1993)?

Another theme has to do with the speed of reform. Conventional economic thought and literature recommends a slow transformation from a state economy to a market economy. Slow transformation allows countries to continually evaluate the progress of policies and privatized firms and make necessary changes and adjustments. The disadvantages to a slower process are that it becomes more politicized and there is a threat of a start-stop process with changes in economic policies and in governments (e.g., Sachs, 1993). Consequently, several countries in Eastern Europe, such as Hungary, Poland, and Russia, chose a fast, "big-bang" approach to economic reform and privatization. These countries feared that a slow process would take too long and would be too easily reversed. Arguably, the fastest reform policies were these of Czechoslovakia and the succeeding Czech Republic (Mertlik, 1997).

B. Share Valuation and Privatizations as IPOs

In one branch of the previous literature, privatization has been compared to an IPO, an initial public offering (e.g., Dewenter and Malatesta, 1997; Perotti and Guney, 1993). It has been widely noted that the valuation of newly public firms is an inexact science even in countries with well-developed and mature financial markets. The pervasive underpricing found in IPOs in most countries is one indication of the difficulty of pricing new issues (see Ibbotson, 1975; Kunz and Aggarwal, 1994; Logue, 1973; and Miller and Reilly, 1987). Indeed, Jenkins and Meyers (1994) and Morgan Stanley (1997) document that privatization IPO underpricing has been larger than in typical private firm IPOs.[2]

Perotti and Guney (1993) examine privatizations as corporate IPOs issued by governments of countries with well-developed capital markets and they suggest that because relatively more information is known about the public firms about to be privatized, the underpricing

---

[2] Although privatizations may be similar to IPOs, Jones, Megginson, Nash, and Netter (1999) find that their sample of share issue privatizations are much larger than traditional IPOs and reflect much older firms. Comparing Czech firms privatized by vouchers with those in the Ibbotson, Sindelar, and Ritter's (1994) study of IPOs, the Czech firms are about the same size but reflect considerably older firms.

80   *Financial Management* • Winter 2000

should not be as great. Instead, they find that underpricing is generally greater in privatizations than in other IPOs. However, Dewenter and Malatesta (1997) do not support these findings and find that underpricing in privatizations is not systematically different than that in IPOs. Perotti (1995) theorizes that a government committed to the complete eventual transfer of control to private owners for a firm initially being partially privatized, may use underpricing as a credible signal of its promises. There may also be other reasons why governments may underprice privatization IPOs. For example, they may do so to ensure the political success of privatization programs, to reflect the asymmetric information advantage of the government, and to reflect the risk aversion and higher capital costs of private investors (e.g., Bel, 1998). Jones et al. (1999) find that most governments operate under a constrained revenue maximization objective when privatizing firms. This objective leads to some underpricing of shares, favors the use of a fixed price offerings, the selection of domestic investment bankers, and the distribution of shares to employees and domestic investors to achieve political goals in a privatization.

These studies mostly address privatization pricing and distribution in countries with well-developed capital markets and few studies address privatization in countries without well-developed capital markets. More specifically, there are very few studies of the conditions in the Czech mass privatizations where many firms are being privatized simultaneously with an auction process in an environment of relatively little reliable business information. Nevertheless, even this limited literature may provide some guidelines in selecting variables that may be useful in understanding the price and demand characteristics of enterprise shares in the Czech voucher privatization and similar auctions.

C. Share Pricing in Mass Privatizations

The literature on the financial and price discovery aspects of the privatization auctions still seems to be relatively sparse, especially with respect to voucher mass privatization plans. In a pioneering study, Hingorani, Lehn, and Makhija (1997) document that share demand in the Czech mass privatization auction was related to inside ownership, measures of financial distress, and proxies for agency costs. Claessens (1997) and Claessens, Djankov, and Pohl (1997) found that for the Czech mass privatization program, a more concentrated ownership structure was related to higher privatization and post-privatization share valuations, return on assets, and Tobin's Q. However, Harper (2001) finds that operating efficiency and profitability decreases following privatization in the auction process. Similarly, Dewenter and Malatesta (2000) find that much of the firm performance improvements occurs over the three years prior to the privatization and performance measures are lower in the five years following privatization. As this brief review indicates, there is much need for additional research on privatization. Indeed, prior research does not address how pricing and trading volume might change in the various rounds of the Czech mass privatization auction process even though price discovery and informational content of trades in the developed capital markets have been a major focus of recent research.[3]

Using an expanded set of firm characteristics and outcomes of *each* of the sequential auction rounds as independent variables, this study contributes to the literature by focusing on the determinants of share prices and trading volumes in each of the auction rounds on a

---

[3]See for example, studies such as O'Hara and Oldfield (1986), Stein (1992), Domowitz (1993), and Hasbrouck (1995) develop models and provide empirical evidence that shows that price formation is not only a function of supply and demand, but also a function of expectations, return generating processes, and information revealed in previous trades.

"frame by frame" basis in the Czech mass privatization program. Although the number of trades that occur in this setting is smaller than in most microstructure studies, much greater detail on each auction round is available, allowing special insights into the price formation process. This study uses specific information revealed in each round of a sequential auction, the Czech mass privatization voucher auction, to examine price formation in a series of trades. Thus, this study not only adds to our understanding of the pricing of firms in privatizations, but it also provides insights on the microstructure of the price discovery process in a multiple round auction.

II. Czech Voucher Privatization Auction

The mass privatization program of the Czech and Slovak Federal Republic (CSFR) and the subsequent Czech Republic was not an economic experiment held in a vacuum. The politics of the country helped shape the economic policy and the form of privatization. The finance minister of the CSFR, Vaclav Klaus, who later became the Prime Minister of the Czech Republic, advocated strong free market reforms. His ideas won out over rivals that advocated slower paced reform and less radical transformation. These differences about the pace of reform and economic policy were echoed in the election of leaders in the Czech Parliament and the Slovak Parliament. The Czechs elected market reform minded leaders while the Slovaks elected officials that favored slower reforms and more social democratic ideals. These differences eventually came to a head in the middle of 1992 (during the voucher auction) and led to the "velvet divorce" and the separation of the CSFR into two independent countries beginning January 1, 1993. Table I presents a timeline of the voucher auction and political events surrounding the auction.

As Finance Minister, Klaus began a series of economic reforms, which included price liberalization, opening of markets, and a restrictive fiscal policy. As a result, inflation increased, growth slowed, and the economy entered into a recession. In addition to these traditional reforms, the Czech system used privatization as the centerpiece of these economic reforms. During 1990 and 1991, many small firms were restored to their original owners or sold to other owners, and managers of large state owned firms (especially those slated to be privatized) were given more discretion in running the state owned enterprises with profits becoming a primary concern for these businesses (e.g., Aggarwal and Mejstrik, 1992).

Firms in the first wave of voucher privatization typically had clearer property rights and liability claims. Firms with more significant problems, such as significant unresolved restitutional or bankruptcy claims, firms with unapproved privatization plans, and firms in industries such as pharmaceuticals, mining, and chemicals were scheduled to be privatized in later waves. For firms privatized in the first wave, managers would continue to have autonomy and decision making power after privatization. Soft budget constraints could possibly continue in the form of bad debts, but subsidies did not continue after privatization (Mertlik, 1997).

A. Czech Auction Process

Auctions have been shown to efficiently allocate resources and assets. Auction processes are used in stock exchanges, and in markets for Treasury securities, foreign exchange, debt instruments, and other commodities (McAfee and McMillan, 1987; Klemperer, 1999). A recent and innovative use of an auction process was implemented

82   *Financial Management* • Winter 2000

Table I. Timeline of the Czech Voucher Auction and Related Political Events

1991, October 31	Preliminary List of Companies to be Privatized Approved
1991, November 1	Registration for Vouchers Begins
1992, February	Investment Privatization Funds Registered and Published
1992, March	Financial Information is distributed in *Kuponova Privatizace*
1992, March 1 – April 26	Individuals Assign Vouchers to Funds
1992, May 18 – June 8	First Round of Bidding for Shares
1992, June 7 & 8	Parliamentary Elections, Klaus and Meciar elected as Premiers of the Czech Republic and Slovakia
1992, June 20	Klaus and Meciar agree to dissolve the CSFR and form independent republics
1992, July 7 – July 28	Second Round of Bidding for Shares
1992, August 26– September 15	Third Round
1992, October 14 – 27	Fourth Round
1992, Nov. 23 – Dec. 4	Fifth Round (Final Round of Bidding)
1992, November 26	Parliament Approves Separation of Czech Republic and Slovakia
1993, January 1	Czech Republic Gains Independence
1993, May 24	Shares Passed to New Owners

Source: Kortba, 1995, and news sources

by the Czech Republic (with Slovakia) in their mass privatization program. This unique voucher auction designed to privatize large firms included all citizens that wished to participate and included multiple rounds with shares (equity claims on assets) for many firms and many bidders. While similar to auctions that take place in security markets, the Czech mass privatization auction also had some unique characteristics and was one of the first mass privatization auctions in ex-communist countries (e.g., Boycko, Schleifer, and Vishny, 1994; Mejstrik, 1997).

As discussed above and elsewhere, there are many limitations in traditional privatization methods when applied to former communist countries (e.g., Lipton and Sachs, 1990). Such limitations include little or no reliable information useful in determining firm value and limited resources among citizens to buy the firms offered in privatization. As one of the first ex-socialist countries to address these issues effectively, the Czech voucher auction had to innovate in several aspects of pricing and distribution of shares.

The first unique aspect of the Czech voucher auction was the cost to participate and the nature of units used in the auction process. To participate in the auction, you had to be a Czech citizen and at least 18 years old. Instead of using currency to bid for shares, participants bought (and were limited to) 1,000 voucher points for 1,000 Czech Crowns (Kc), about \$35, a fifth of the average monthly salary. This was a minimal cost to individuals and was not designed to raise revenue for the state. This is in contrast to traditional privatization programs and auction markets where the goal is to maximize revenue.[4] The voucher points could be used to directly bid for and purchase shares in the firms that were being privatized (shares bought in the privatization auction could not be resold immediately). The vouchers could also be given to investment (mutual fund) companies in return for shares in the investment company funds. Individuals assigned over 70% of the vouchers to investment funds (with

---

[4]See Jones et al. (1999) for further discussion of constrained and unconstrained revenue maximization in privatizations.

some questionable results, e.g., Ellerman, 1998).[5]

The second unique aspect of the Czech auction was its goals. The goal of the auction was to distribute all shares in the privatizing firms and use up all voucher points while obtaining prices that accurately reflected relative market values. The political goal of distributing all shares and using all the points may at times conflict with the economic goal of obtaining accurate and fair relative market values. Hingorani et. al. (1997) and Hillion and Young (1996) find evidence that these goals do conflict and leads to some mispricing in the auction. Thus, it is important to note that the auction process was not designed to transfer funds to the firms or raise revenue for the government. The process was designed to equitably distribute all available shares at fair relative market values to the citizens. Indeed, over 90% of those eligible participated, and the Czech voucher privatization constituted a significant windfall of approximately US$13 billion that averaged two months salary for the participants (e.g., Svejnar, 1995).

Of course, the auctioned firms were not guaranteed to succeed after privatization. In the privatization program, the Czech government took the position that the market could better and more quickly reform state owned firms than could the government. In addition, government time and resources would not have to be used to reform underperfoming or bankrupt companies. Thus, this process put investors at risk of investing in potentially bankrupt companies or firms that were in poor financial condition. As indicated above, managers controlled the firms to be privatized before the privatization began and subsidies did not continue after privatization.

The first and the major wave of Czech large scale privatization began in 1992. Out of 1,491 firms to be so privatized in Czechoslovakia, 988 were located in the Czech Republic. Actual bidding in the first round of the auction began in May 1992 and lasted three weeks (to June 8). After bidding ended, the second round started about a month later (July 7) and lasted for another three weeks. The process continued using about the same time frame for each round and the fifth and final round bidding ended on December 4, 1992.

A government agency, the Center for Coupon (Voucher) Privatization (CKP), published and distributed information about the firms available for privatization. This information was collected by the State Statistical Office and was published in the form of a special newspaper that included sales, profits, employees and bank loans for the previous three years, equity and asset values, and other share distribution (besides the voucher auction). This newspaper also provided information about the auction process and other share distribution methods that were being used by each firm. This was the only information provided to investors by the CKP for valuing a firm and for developing an appropriate bidding strategy in the multiple round voucher auction. The companies themselves did not distribute any information to the public.

Orders were taken for shares in these firms in each round. If the amount of orders was close to the number of shares being offered (within the boundary conditions given below), shares were distributed at that price. If any shares remained, then a new price was listed and orders were taken for a second round. If the number of shares ordered at the price was too large or too small compared to the number of shares being offered (outside the boundary condition), then no shares would be distributed and the price would be changed for the next round. Before each round, the results from the previous round (number of shares offered, price, percent demanded, number distributed) were published as was the new number of

---

[5]While there were over 400 funds at the beginning of the privatization auction, the 10 largest held over 50% of the vouchers. These funds bought more shares in earlier rounds while the relatively less informed individual investors became more active in later rounds as more information was revealed. For details see Hillion and Young (1996), Hingorani, Lehn and Makhija (1997) and Hanousek and Kroch (1998).

84 *Financial Management* • Winter 2000

shares being offered (total shares offered - shares distributed) and the new offering price. The number of auction rounds was not known with certainty at the beginning of the auction, but it was believed that the auction would last between four and six rounds (the privatization process actually had five rounds).

Thus, in the Czech five round privatization auction process, in each round the price was set and the demand was determined for each firm. While the price is known in each round, it is uncertain if and how many shares will be sold at that price. In contrast, in traditional auctions, the price is determined by the demand in a single round where all shares are distributed.

Formally, the Czech privatization auction can be described by the following rules:

1. There are M firms with N shares of each firm for a total of MxN shares in the auction. These shares are offered in rounds r (r = 1...i). The shares offered in each round is $S_{m,r}$ ($S_{m,1} = N_{m,1}$) at price $p_{m,r}$. In the first round, all prices (but not book value) are equal for all firms. At the beginning of each round, orders are taken for each firm at price $p_{m,r}$ and number of shares $n_{m,r}$. The sum of shares ordered from all investors in each round for each firm is given by:

$$D_{m,r} = \sum_{n=1}^{N} n_{m,r}$$

2. The number of vouchers is known and no new coupons enter the auction after the first round has begun.

3. Trading occurs when the following conditions hold:

$\alpha S_{m,r} < D_{m,r} < \gamma S_{m,r}$, $\alpha < 1$ and $\gamma > 1$

$\alpha < \dfrac{D_{m,r}}{S_{m,r}} < \gamma$, remaining shares, $S_{m,r} - D_{m,r}$, proceed to next round.

If demand is lower than the boundary condition, $D_{m,r} < \alpha S_{m,r}$, then no shares are sold and the price is lowered for the next round, $p_{m,r}+1 = f(\alpha S_{m,r}/D_{m,r})$. If demand is greater than supply, then no shares are issued and the price is raised for the next round. That is if $D_{m,r} > \gamma S_{m,r}$, then $p_{m,r}+1 = f(\gamma S_{m,r}/D_{m,r})$. If $S_{m,r} < D_{m,r} < \gamma S_{m,r}$, then shares are prorated. α and γ are constant, but are not known initially. The equilibrium price is $D_m/S_m = 1$. After the auction began, these boundary conditions remained constant and were known to be $\alpha = 0$ and $\gamma = 1.25$.

As the rules regarding how many shares are sold in each round and how the offer price is set for the next round indicate, the Czech privatization auction with its five rounds of bidding combined the distributional and efficiency advantages of ascending auctions with some of the revenue advantages of sealed bid auctions within each round. In an ascending auction, the process of price adjustment may be somewhat inefficient and in spite of some over- and under-shooting. Because of learning from public information (e.g., number of shares sold) released after each round, share prices eventually adjust as in a cobweb model to efficient market prices (e.g., Stein, 1992). As noted in earlier literature, while ascending auctions may not be robust against revenue reducing collusion among bidders, such auctions are less vulnerable to corruption, minimize the winners curse, and the iterative price discovery process is apt to maximize revenue and generate reliable market prices. The next section describes the development and estimation of the empirical models for the determinants of share demand

and prices in each auction round.

III. Research Design and Data

We use multivariate regression and a limited dependent variable model (a probit analysis) to determine what information available to the CKP and to investors was significant in determining share prices and trading volumes in each round of the auction. In each round a new voucher price is set for each firm using market information (demand) from the previous round(s) in the auction. Thus, we also analyze the importance of information revealed during prior auction rounds, such as market demand at that round's price, and the change in the auction price from the prior round.

A. Fundamental Firm Variables

The variables used in this study reflect fundamental firm characteristics including size, profitability, growth opportunities, types of ownership, and industry effects. We proxy the firm's size by using 1991 sales (production). We use sales instead of assets because sales is a more current measure whereas asset value depends upon the time it was purchased, depreciation methods, and other accounting policies, and may not reflect the actual value or size of the firm (especially in an ex-socialist economy).

To proxy profitability, we use 1991 profit margin (return on sales, ROS) measured by profit/ sales. Again, this study favors ROS instead of return on assets as the measure of profitability because of the problems and distortions associated with determining the book value of assets and the effects of inflation. Since sales and profit are measured in the same real currency value, such distortions in ROS, if any, are likely to be much lower. We proxy operating efficiency by using sales efficiency (Sales Eff) which is the 1991 sales per employee. We expect that the profitability and efficiency measures are positively related to the auction price of the firm (although not in the first round, as the first round value is not a market value but is simply the book value). The net effect of size is hard to predict. We might expect a large firm with better name and product recognition to have higher demand than a smaller firm, which would lead to positive relationships between size and share value and demand. This positive size effect is likely to be offset as larger firms in Czechoslovakia tended to be less profitable and efficient than smaller firms (Hingorani et al. do indeed find that this initial value is negatively related to firm size). The growth measure used here is the nominal sales growth from 1989 to 1991. Firms had increasing control over production and sales during this time period, and firms with positive growth in sales would signal continuing opportunities and should have a positive association with equity value.

In addition to profitability and growth, another important financial variable is the debt ratio. The debt ratio measures financial distress, but may also reflect an additional source of firm monitoring. While many banks were privatized, the government still retained major stakes and still influenced bank decisions. In addition, many of the major banks sponsored investment privatization funds that bought shares of the companies to which the banks had loans outstanding (e.g., Claessens, 1997). There are two possible measures of the debt ratio, total liabilities to total assets and bank credit to total assets. Total debt ratio includes bank loans and other sources of debt, mainly from the government. As it is likely to be more reliable, this study uses the total debt to total assets ratio (DEBT) as a measure of financial leverage.

Ownership structure can also be expected to be important. The relinquishment of control and the distribution choice of shares (domestic, foreign, direct sale, or transfer to a municipal government) are political choices within the auction. These choices regarding ownership, control, and distribution of shares reflect the government's commitment to privatization and economic reform (Perotti, 1995). They also reflect the constraints placed on the government during privatization (Jones et al., 1999). The inclusion of these explanatory variables helps describe the impact of these choices on the share valuation and the demand for these shares.

The categories used by the CKP in classifying share ownership are also used here. Every firm had 3% of shares withheld by the government for future restitution. Other share distributions (all measured in percents of the total) included shares temporarily held by the government for future distribution (TempGov) or shares transferred to local governments and municipalities or held by the national government for longer periods (PermGov). In addition, the government may have special voting rights (the so-called "golden share") in privatized firms, such as veto power over future plans. The variable GovVote is a dummy variable equal to 1 if there are special voting rights retained by the government and equal to 0 otherwise. Continued significant long-term government ownership or voting rights could be viewed as a negative sign because of past government mismanagement. Temporary holdings may be viewed as a positive signal because the government may benefit from its preferential access to information especially if its stake appreciates and the government is sending a signal of committed privatization (Perotti, 1995).

Other ownership variables include the percentage of shares sold directly to private investors or given to the private sector for restitution purposes (PrvtOwn). This transfer of shares includes sale to domestic investors, foreign investors, shares sold through intermediaries and shares distributed to satisfy restitution claims. We expect a positive relationship between equity values and private ownership. We also include a dummy variable if there was a foreign investor (ForOwn) and expect a positive relationship with value as such ownership was perceived to give a firm value-enhancing preferential access to capital and technology (Lam, 1997).[6]

Industry effects are captured by using a dummy variable for manufacturing firms. The variable Industrial is equal to 1 if the firm is a manufacturing firm, 0 otherwise.[7] It is expected that Industrial will have a negative relationship to value and demand. This is because manufacturing firms have higher fixed costs and operating leverage and have a different competitive environment and industry structure compared to non-manufacturing firms. Consistent with the findings of Claessens (1997) and Hingorani et al. (1997), manufacturing firms will probably be more difficult to restructure.

B. Transactions Variables

For the first auction round, all shares for every firm were offered at a price of 3 shares/100 vouchers (33.33 vouchers per share). Although this was the initial auction value, each firm actually had different per share book values and numbers of shares offered in the voucher process. Thus, instead of using 33.33 vouchers for the first round price as is done in prior studies, we compute and use the actual first round share valuations based on the book value

---

[6]Disaggregated data on varying categories of private ownership other than foreign versus domestic is not available and all other studies in this area use variations on the broad definition used here. For example, "inside owners" in Hingorani et al (1997) seems to refer to domestic ownership. Further, as Frydman et al note, "..the Czech privatization programs gave no special concessions to employees and tended to exclude them from ownership."

[7]The composition of our Industry variable seems to be largely the same as the consensus on the composition of "strategic industries" (e.g. Manzetti, 1994). The only difference seems to be our inclusion of food and beverage production companies as manufacturing companies.

per share for each firm. The book value of shares in the auction for each firm was measured as the percent of the total shares available in the auction (after deducting shares distributed by other methods) multiplied by the total book value of the firm. The first round per-share book value, R1VR, was then computed by taking this available book value divided by the number of shares available for voucher auctions. While most shares were priced near 1,000 Kc per share, the mean book equity value for the firms being privatized was found to be 983 Kc with a standard deviation of 258 Kc.

The CKP collects all bids and determines the demand schedule for shares of each firm in each round. For the second and subsequent auction rounds, the CKP has information about the valuation and demand for each firm in the prior round. So, in determining the price for the second and each subsequent round, the CKP considered firm financial information in addition to the previous round's valuation and the share demand. As indicated earlier, if demand is so high that the shares are considered to be oversubscribed, it will cause no shares to be issued in that round and offer prices will be raised in the following round. This process continues for all five rounds of bidding. However, shares with no demand and excess demand are recorded as zero shares sold. To avoid this confounding problem in our models, we created an excess demand variable, ED. ED is 1 if the share price increases in the following round and equal to 0 if there is no price change or there is a decrease in price. Thus, firms that sold no shares because of excess demand will have percent of shares sold equal to 0, but ED equal to 1 while firms that have no demand will have both variables equal to 0. ED1 to ED4 are excess demand variables for a firm's shares in rounds 1 to 4 (since no voucher prices exist after round 5, we do not have ED5). Share demand variables for each firm reflect the percent of offered shares that were sold in each round, R1S to R5S.[8] High values of these variables indicate high demand for the voucher price quoted. If no shares were sold, it is due to either excess or no demand (captured by the ED variables described above). We expect a positive relationship between EDn and R(n+1)VR.

Information revealed in each of the auction rounds is captured in valuation variables and in demand variables. In this study, limited information about specific companies that may have been released while the bidding took place is reflected in the bids submitted for each firm. The auction prices per share in voucher terms in the first round, R1VR, is also the book equity value per share in the first round. R2VR to R5VR are the share prices (vouchers per share) in rounds two through five.

C. Empirical Models

Based on the above discussion and in prior literature, it is hypothesized here that R1VR, the first round valuation, depends on fundamental firm characteristics, ownership structure, and the industry classification of the firm. The valuation model then takes the form:

$$R1VR = \alpha_0 + \Sigma\,\beta_i\,FV_i + \Sigma\beta_i OV_i + \Sigma\beta_i Ind_i + \varepsilon_i \qquad (1)$$

where FV are the fundamental firm variables, OV are the alternative ownership variables and control for political objectives through ownership distribution, Ind is the industry dummy variable, and ε_i is the error term. Adding terms for the price and quantity information revealed in the first round, the second round valuation model takes the form:

---

[8] R5S is not always 1 as all shares were not sold even after round 5 with about 7% of all the shares to be sold in this wave of privatization being held in a trust to be sold later by the government.

$$R2VR = \alpha_0 + \Sigma \beta_i FV_i + \Sigma \beta_i OV_i + \Sigma \beta_i Ind_i + \beta_i ED1 + \beta_i R1VR + \beta_i R1S + \varepsilon_i \qquad (2)$$

Each subsequent round's valuation model continues to add the three independent variables in each round reflecting the auction results of each of the previous rounds. Financial, ownership, and industry variables can be expected to decline in importance in the later rounds of the auction as they would be considered historical information. The share price and demand variables generated in each prior auction rounds should become the most important in later rounds. The excess demand (ED) variables should be positively related to the share valuation as the existence of excess demand requires an increase in the offer price.

A regression model is also used to measure the percentage of available shares sold (trading volume) in each round. At the beginning of the first round, each investor has the financial information for each firm and the coupon price for each firm, but the CKP has the additional information on the total demand for each firm before making sales (distribution) decisions. At the beginning of the second round, each investor has the information that he had at the beginning of the prior round and new information about the demand for the firms' shares at the first round price, and a new offer price. This process continues for the subsequent rounds. Building on the share pricing models, the first round shares sold (trading volume) model is:

$$R1S = \alpha_0 + \Sigma \beta_i FV_i + \Sigma \beta_i OV_i + \Sigma \beta_i Ind_i + \beta_i ED1 + \beta_i R1VR + \varepsilon_i \qquad (3)$$

The second round shares sold (trading volume) model adds the new market information to the equation:

$$R2S = \alpha_0 + \Sigma \beta_i FV_i + \Sigma \beta_i OV_i + \Sigma \beta_i Ind_i + \beta_i ED1 + \beta_i R1VR + \beta_i R1S + \beta_i ED2 + \beta_i R2VR + \varepsilon_i \quad (4)$$

It is worth noting here that in contrast to the share valuation model described above, this trading volume model includes the demand and price variables from the same round. While the excess demand variables are ex post in terms of measurement, they are ex ante with respect to the information known to the CKP when making decisions pertaining to share distributions.[9] For example, in determining share prices for each round, the CKP has no demand information for that round. However, in determining share sales (trading volume) for each round, the CKP does know the demand for such shares.[10]

A probit analysis using only firms that sold shares in a particular round may provide useful additional insights as this set of firms has more complete information about share demand than does the full set of firms that includes firms with no trading in a round. We compare firms with low percentage of shares sold to those firms that sold the greatest percentage in each round. For the probit analysis, R1S is defined to be equal to 0, if the firm is in the lower quartile of percentage of shares sold and equal to 1 if it is in the upper quartile

[9]An anonymous referee notes that these equations also describe the political process of distribution in addition to the market demand for shares.

[10]We also estimate the share demand models excluding the ED variables, which occur in the same round. This estimation would be from the viewpoint of the investor who is not making the distribution decision and excludes any seemingly ex post information in the model. The results from this estimation are consistent with the ones presented in the paper.

[11]Firms with no share sales represent both no demand and excess demand conditions. Consequently, firms with no sales were excluded in order to have the two extreme quartiles represent more accurately firms with high versus low share demand. The results from the probit model can be expected to be different from the results of the regression model as the probit model emphasizes relative differences in share demand among firms while less differences are less important in the regression model.

of shares sold. Once again, valuation ratios and the percent sold for each firm in previous rounds were used as independent variables for these equations in later rounds.[11]

We hypothesize that firm value initially depends mostly on the book value of the firm and demand for shares depends initially on firm specific information such as past profitability and performance and ownership characteristics. However, in the succeeding auction rounds, such "historical" data should become less important and outcomes of prior auction rounds such as demand and share prices in each round should become more important in determining share prices and trading volumes. Also, the excess demand variables should be negatively related to the percentage sold in each round as the existence of excess demand would decrease the probability that any shares were sold in that round.

The source of the data for each of the 988 Czech firms in the privatization program is the Ministry of Finance's Center for Coupon Privatization division, the CKP (*Kuponova Privatizace Prvni Vlna* and *Kuponova Privatizace Noviny*). These publications contained information on the number of shares per vouchers for each round (price), the number of shares available for sale in each round, the number of shares sold and the number of shares demanded in the previous round. This information was originally distributed as an insert in newspapers after each round. Before the auction began, the CKP also distributed information about each firm including the previous three years sales, profit, bank credits, and number of employees. Other financial information included the previous year's assets and net business equity and the types of share ownership. Of the 988 firms in the first wave, four firms had missing information about the number of employees, assets, profit, or net business equity for 1991; 171 firms did not have all three years of sales information, so the sales growth variable, Sales Gr, could not be computed. In addition, there were 79 firms that did not have industry information available. The remaining 734 firms analyzed in this study are about 75% of the firms that were privatized in the first wave. Based on these data on the firms privatized by the Czech Republic, the auction models developed in this study are estimated and used to examine empirically the determinants of firm value and trading volume in the various rounds of the privatization auction process.

Table II lists the variables used in this study, and Table III provides some descriptive statistics on selected variables. Sales, ROS, Sales Eff, and Sales Gr are independent fundamental valuation variables measuring the size, efficiency, profitability, and growth of the firm. The alternative share distribution variables, TempGov, PermGov, PrvtOwn, ForOwn, and GovVote, give information on other owners, share distributions, or other controlling factors such as voting rights. The industry dummy variable for manufacturing firms is Industrial. As can be expected in such groups, the data in Table III confirm the disproportional impact of large firms on the mean values of many variables.

IV. Empirical Results

Descriptive information about trading volumes and share prices and their dispersion through the five rounds is presented in Figure I. As demonstrated in Figure Ia, the range of auction prices increases greatly in the third round with a jump in the standard deviation of those prices in the fourth round as is shown by Figure Ib. The large increase in standard deviation in the fourth round is due mainly to an increase in the proportion of firms with very high and very low values. As shown in Figure Ic, trading volume declined in each succeeding round but attained a fairly steady level for rounds three through five. Figure Id shows the mean proportions of firm shares sold and their standard deviations.

Table II. Definitions of the Variables Used in this Paper

Size	is the 1991 sales amount.
ROS	is the 1991 return on sales; = 1991 profit / 1991 sales.
SalesEff.	is the 1991 sales efficiency; = 1991 sales / # of employees in 1991.
Sales Gr.	is the % compounded nominal annual sales growth from 1989 to 1991.
Debt	is the debt ratio using total liabilities to total assets in 1991.
TempGov	is percent of shares temporary held by the government to be distributed at a later time.
PermGov	is the percent of shares held permanently by national or municipal government.
PrvtOwn	is the percent of shares sold directly to domestic or foreign investors distributed for restitution or sold through intermediaries.
ForOwn	percentage sold directly to foreign investors.
GovVote	dummy variable that is 1 if the government has special voting rights in the privatized firm, 0 otherwise.
Industrial	industry dummy variable that is 1 if the firm is in manufacturing, 0 otherwise.
VSP	is the percent of shares available for voucher sales.
NEqV	is the book value of the firm available in the voucher sale; = VSP*Book Value.
R1VR	is the first round value ratio; = NEqV / Number of shares offered in voucher auction.
R1S	is the percentage of shares sold that was offered in round 1.
R2VR - R5VR	is the valuation ratio, the auction price for the firm in terms of vouchers, for rounds 2 through 5.
R2S - R5S	is the percentage of shares sold that was offered in rounds 2 to 5.
ED1 - ED4	is a dummy variable that represents excess demand for shares in each round. Excess demand exists if the price is greater in the following round, so that ED = 1 if excess demand, 0 otherwise (price decrease or no price change in the following round). Excess demand cannot be measured in the last round since there were no more price changes and excess demand cannot be measured.

A. Share Valuation

Results from the multivariate regression valuation models corrected for autocorrelation and heteroskedasticity using White's procedure are presented in Table IV.[12] As these results show, the first round valuation of the firms being privatized are not related to any ownership variables, but positively related to the industry dummy variable. Round 1 valuation is also positively related not only to return on sales but also somewhat surprisingly to the debt ratio. In spite of these significant variables, the model only explains one percent of the variation in first round firm valuation. This is due to the fact that in this first round, many firms had valuation ratios close to one and, thus, the intercept closely replicates the valuation. As expected, model R-squares generally increase in the succeeding rounds (with the exception of round four when the share valuation standard deviation increases greatly).[13]

[12]These and subsequent empirical estimates presented in this paper are robust to alternative measures of efficiency, profitability, leverage (e.g. return on assets, net income per employee, and bank debt to total assets), nominal versus real measures of variables such as sales growth, or ownership (private versus domestic). Similarly the results did not change significantly when a dummy (0, 1) location variable (for Prague) was added to the estimated equations.

[13]While the inter-quartile range did not change much, the standard deviation of share prices increased greatly in round 4 with the highest share price increasing from 800 points in round 3 to over 10,000 points in round 4.

Table III. Selected Descriptors of Independent And Dependent Variables

This table presents descriptive data for the first round of the first wave of the Czech voucher auction (Currency Value in thousands of US Dollars (32Kc/$). Please see Table II for definitions of variables.

Variable	Mean	Median	Std. Dev.
Shares Available	215,045	82,294	606,734
Net Worth	10,988	3,271	53,748
Total Assets	13,314	3,787	64,282
Sales	17,750	5,307	71,146
Profit	2,656	322	25,962
Bank Credit	4,977	1,079	20,404
Liabilities	31,645	2,042	31,645
Employees	914	428	1,853
ROS	0.0877	0.0725	0.4079
Sales Eff.	18.57	10.70	24.9
RIVR	0.9831	0.9661	0.2583

After round 1, the CKP set a new price for each firm using the demand from the previous round(s) and the remaining share supply. In the round 2 model, the voucher price is significantly positively related to private ownership and demand (R1S and ED1) from the previous round. It is also positively related to growth opportunities (Sales Gr) at the 0.10 level. These coefficients all have the expected signs. However, second round valuation is negatively related to the debt ratio and industry variable, which is a reversal of the previous round. The sign for Debt is now consistent with an increased risk of financial distress and bankruptcy and, this sign persists in the third round. The negative coefficient for the manufacturing firms indicates higher costs and risks in restructuring "smoke-stack" firms.

In the final three rounds, the main determinants of value were the most recent auction variables in the model. Historical financial information is no longer important in determining value, indicating that this information is already reflected in round 2 values. Consistent with the Perotti (1995) contention regarding signals of future government interference, temporary government ownership has a significant negative impact on share values. This negative impact of government ownership on value may be an indication that market participants are not fully convinced that this is a temporary holding.

The economic effects of these variables on share valuation are interesting. For example, in round 3, firms that had excess demand in the prior round experienced an average increase of 61 coupons per share. In addition, for every percentage increase in shares sold in round 2, the price per share increased by an average of almost 40 coupons. However, compared to round 2, industrial firms lost an average of 6 coupons per share. As another example, the very large coefficients for round 4 estimation reflect the dramatic changes in prices and is supported by the graphical display of prices in Figure I.

The impact of price and trading volume information revealed prior to each round in the auction is also interesting. As expected of a downward sloping demand curve, share demand (RS and ED) positively impacts the offer price. It also appears that share prices overshot and undershot in successive rounds as in a cobweb model of adjustment in this ascending

Figure I. Dispersion of Prices and Trading Volumes by Auction Round

A. Quartile Prices for the Sample in Each of the Five Auction Rounds

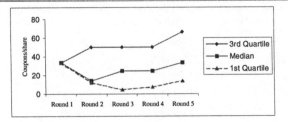

B. Mean Prices and Standard Deviations for Sample Firms in Each of the Five Auction Rounds

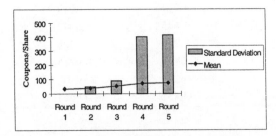

C. Percent of Total Shares Sold in the Five Auction Rounds

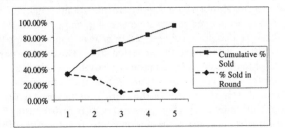

D. Mean Percent of Available Shares Sold and Standard Deviation of Sales for Sample Firms in the Round

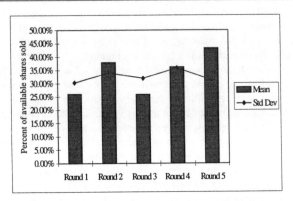

Table IV. Regression Model for the Determinants of Equity Valuation in Each Auction Round

Variable	Round 1 Estimated Coefficient	Round 1 T-Ratio	Round 2 Estimated Coefficient	Round 2 T-Ratio	Round 3 Estimated Coefficient	Round 3 T-Ratio	Round 4 Estimated Coefficient	Round 4 T-Ratio	Round 5 Estimated Coefficient	Round 5 T-Ratio
Intercept	0.969	89.22 ***	15.261	3.76 ***	-44.321	-6.03 ***	-129.170	-1.78 *	-95.302	-2.20 **
Sales	0.000	0.36	0.000	-0.87	0.000	2.36 **	0.000	-1.46	0.000	0.39
ROS	0.017	2.77 ***	2.031	0.95	-2.632	-0.92	11.329	0.74	-1.580	-1.01
Sales Eff.	0.000	-0.14	0.003	0.83	0.002	0.42	-0.043	-1.19	-0.003	-0.86
Sales Gr.	-0.003	-1.06	5.194	1.79 *	-3.732	-1.33	-17.976	-0.71	-2.033	-0.68
Debt	0.003	3.15 ***	-1.567	-2.49 **	0.270	0.26	-3.885	-0.95	0.573	0.68
TempGov	-0.034	-0.55	9.683	1.03	-25.359	-2.07 **	18.487	0.55	21.787	0.63
PermGov	0.016	0.10	-38.177	-1.49	32.511	0.87	-2.015	-0.02	-10.668	-0.09
PrvtOwn	-0.060	-1.28	36.543	2.00 **	12.690	0.56	310.250	1.11	9.199	0.47
ForOwn	-0.006	-0.33	23.631	1.46	-17.676	-1.37	-171.820	-0.96	-2.259	-0.13
GovVote	-0.010	-0.92	-5.938	-1.23	10.190	1.61	-14.572	-0.65	-3.434	-0.37
Industrial	0.029	1.99 ***	-8.973	-3.27 ***	-6.104	-2.07	-1.061	-0.11	0.778	0.27
R1VR			-2.182	-0.86	-0.412	-0.10	15.370	0.81	49.576	1.16
R1S			15.961	2.58 ***	20.175	1.65	-32.220	-0.57	16.740	1.37
ED1			63.432	15.89 ***	-23.510	-2.43 **	-134.100	-1.07	30.924	2.10 **
R2VR					1.600	10.43 ***	1.633	1.14	-0.261	-0.62
R2S					40.124	5.10 ***	46.834	1.47	-9.522	-1.13
ED2					60.686	13.82 ***	19.912	0.65	17.111	1.14
R3VR							1.751	2.20 **	-0.004	-0.03
R3S							135.830	1.87 *	15.193	1.17
ED3							114.840	1.97 **	-1.008	-0.10
R4VR									1.001	159.00 ***
R4S									16.631	3.67 ***
ED4									50.954	4.34 ***
	N=734		N=717		N=675		N=653		N=609	
R-Squared	0.01		0.55		0.80		0.27		0.98	

***Significant at the 0.01 level.
**Significant at the 0.05 level.
*Significant at the 0.10 level.

auction (e.g., Stein, 1992). However, by the third round the CKP had obtained enough information to determine with some degree of accuracy the firms' share value, and share prices stabilized with only minor adjustments to prices in the fourth and fifth rounds. The coefficient of almost one and the very large t-statistic for the R4VR in the valuation of the fifth round indicates that prices changed only slightly from the fourth to the fifth round.

The somewhat surprising drop in R-square in Round 4 is due to the very large increase in share price standard deviation and range from Round 3 to Round 4. This increased variance of share prices indicates that Round 4 may have been influenced more by political goals regarding share distributions. It appears that as there was only one more round after the fourth round, prices in this fourth round may have been set to sell as many shares as possible, especially since share sales were particularly low in round 3.[14] While such pricing may not have temporarily been wholly consistent with the economic objective of obtaining accurate relative market valuations, it is consistent with the distributional objectives of the voucher auction and mass privatization. This pricing action is also consistent with the cobweb model where share prices may over- and under-shoot in an ascending auction but progressively get closer to their economic values. Any remaining deviations from economic values can be expected to be corrected in the fifth and final round.

B. Trading Volume

Results for the multivariate regression for the trading volume (shares sold) model are presented in Table V. Round 1 demand is positively related to sales growth. As expected, special government voting rights had a negative impact on demand and the round 1 valuation ratio (R1VR) had a significant positive effect on demand. Since all shares had the same nominal price, we find that firms with higher equity book value have greater demand.

As expected, the excess demand variables are negatively related to the shares sold in each round. While the existence of excess demand for a firm prohibits such shares from being traded in a round, the excess demand from the previous round has a positive effect. For example, the percent of shares sold in the second round is negatively related to excess demand in the second round (as no shares were sold for such firms), but positively related to the excess demand of the first round. Consistent with a cobweb model, this switching of signs indicates an effort by the CKP to move offer prices towards an economic equilibrium price (from a price that was too low in a round, to a price that may be too high in the next round, and then lower in the subsequent round). Once again, these results also show that this process of adjustment essentially ended in round four for most firms, indicating that an equilibrium price had nearly been reached, with only minor adjustments made thereafter.

For the most part, these estimates indicate that while corporate financial information did not have an effect on the percentage of shares sold in each round, the major influence on the number of shares sold in each round was the previous rounds' trading volume and auction price. The influence of fundamental firm characteristics including ownership information on demand declined with each subsequent round.

C. Probit Models

Table VI presents for each of the five rounds the results of the probit model designed to

---

[14]Shares sold as a percentage of shares available for sale were 33%, 42%, 25%, 41%, and 67% in rounds 1 through 5, respectively (note that not all shares were sold even after round 5 with about 7% of all shares to be sold ending up in a trust to be sold later by the government. Hingorani, Lehn and Makhija (1997) confirm our contention that share mispricing was greatest in round 4.

Table V. Regression Model for the Determinants of the Percent of Shares Sold in Each Round

Variable	Round 1		Round 2		Round 3		Round 4		Round 5	
	Estimated Coefficient	T-Ratio	Estimated Coefficient	T-Ratio	Estimated Coefficient	T-Ratio	Estimated Coefficient	T-Ratio	Estimated Coefficient	T-Ratio
Intercept	0.295	12.65***	0.459	14.00***	0.251	3.42***	0.340	4.78***	0.508	3.19***
Sales	0.000	0.97	0.000	0.72	0.000	-0.54	0.000	0.09	0.000	-0.51
ROS	-0.002	-0.07	0.023	1.77*	0.006	0.34	0.001	0.08	-0.011	-0.99
Sales Eff.	0.000	-0.39	0.000	-0.21	0.000	0.35	0.000	0.84	0.000	0.16
Sales Gr.	0.027	2.13**	0.019	1.24	0.016	1.34	0.006	0.44	0.007	0.75
Debt	-0.002	-0.58	0.007	1.46	-0.006	-1.15	-0.010	-1.54	0.006	1.13
TempGov	0.132	1.67	-0.050	-0.68	-0.176	-2.62***	0.194	2.06**	-0.033	-0.36
PermGov	0.297	1.34	-0.235	-0.82	0.628	1.84*	0.250	0.60	-0.032	-0.12
PrvtGov	0.035	0.50	-0.028	-0.31	0.144	1.41	0.130	1.21	-0.162	-2.04**
ForOwn	-0.025	-0.51	-0.022	-0.40	-0.018	-0.20	-0.105	-1.35	0.035	0.60
GovVote	-0.074	-2.24**	-0.014	-0.24	-0.063	-1.29	0.115	1.53	-0.008	-0.13
Industrial	0.008	0.36	-0.025	-1.04	0.023	0.96	0.041	1.38	-0.049	-2.11**
R1VR	0.047	3.60***	-0.002	-0.11	0.001	0.03	0.083	3.31***	0.042	0.29
ED1	-0.296	-11.83***	0.253	6.70***	0.016	0.29	-0.014	-0.28	-0.049	-1.24
R1S			-0.175	-3.04***	-0.134	-2.40**	0.028	0.45	-0.083	-1.55
R2VR			-0.001	-1.78	0.001	0.91	0.000	0.19	0.000	0.46
ED2			-0.215	-7.23***	0.188	3.80***	-0.085	-1.63	-0.069	-1.75*
R2S					-0.086	-1.91*	0.124	2.33**	-0.004	-0.10
R3VR					0.000	-0.90	-0.001	-2.15**	0.000	-0.59
ED3					-0.106	-2.12**	0.007	0.16	0.084	2.65***
R3S							-0.059	-1.27	-0.066	-1.79*
R4VR							0.000	4.82***	0.000	-0.88
ED4							-0.137	-3.58***	0.116	3.76***
R4S									-0.239	-6.05***
R5VR									0.000	0.76
	N=734		N=717		N=675		N=653		N=609	
R-Squared	0.22		0.30		0.20		0.08		0.28	

***Significant at the 0.01 level.
**Significant at the 0.05 level.
*Significant at the 0.10 level.

Table VI. Probit Analysis of the Determinants of Lower and Upper Quartile of the Shares Sold in Each Round

Variable	Round One		Round Two		Round Three		Round Four		Round Five	
	Est. Coeff.	T-Ratio	Est. Coeff.	T-Ratio	Est. Coeff.	T-Ratio	Est. Coeff.	T-Ratio	Est. Coeff.	T-Ratio
Intercept	-1.110	-1.89*	-0.713	-0.61	6.323	2.87***	-2.140	-0.95	-1.251	-0.76
Sales	0.000	0.22	0.000	0.11	0.000	1.02	0.000	1.96**	0.000	1.09
ROS	-0.127	-1.05	1.265	1.33	0.148	0.95	-0.161	-0.67	-3.289	-2.61***
Sales Eff.	0.000	1.79*	0.000	0.34	0.000	-0.48	0.000	0.67	0.000	-0.89
Sales Gr.	0.527	2.59***	0.275	1.34	0.217	1.26	0.750	2.99***	0.137	0.86
Debt	-0.126	-1.34	0.174	1.27	-0.065	-0.91	-0.078	-0.30	0.139	2.31**
TempGov	1.517	1.89*	-0.912	-1.08	-0.738	-0.69	-6.316	-2.34**	-0.227	-0.24
PermGov	3.589	1.32	-0.761	-0.30	2.108	0.67	0.104	0.15	-4.312	-0.66
PrvtOwn	11.495	2.67**	-0.944	-0.76	1.732	1.83*	-4.190	-2.10**	-3.020	-2.39**
ForOwn	2.563	0.12	-0.957	-1.15	-0.656	-1.26	1.296	1.04	0.741	0.99
GovVote	-0.587	-0.83	-0.060	-0.13	0.244	0.34	0.636	0.49	0.229	0.33
Industrial	0.275	1.28	-0.126	-0.54	0.199	0.69	-0.013	-0.25	-0.205	-0.76
R1VR	0.416	0.75	-0.612	-0.53	-5.100	-2.34**	2.664	1.31	1.257	0.85
ED1	4.800	0.44	3.153	7.36***	-0.980	-2.00**	0.783	0.79	-0.679	-1.42
R1UQ			4.277	5.46***	-2.425	-4.19***	-0.071	-0.68	-0.555	-1.06
R2VR			-0.017	-4.04***	-0.006	-1.13	0.016	1.06	0.003	0.43
ED2			1.903	4.22***	-0.393	-1.03	-1.293	-1.66	-0.620	-1.41
R2UQ					-0.290	-0.48	1.036	1.07	0.423	0.86
R3VR					-0.002	-0.60	-0.023	-1.52	0.000	0.66
ED3					2.334	4.29***	1.125	1.47	0.737	1.82*
R3UQ							-0.591	-0.52	-0.693	-1.30
R4VR							-0.012	-0.97	-0.005	-0.75
ED4							4.447	3.77***	1.233	3.68***
R4UQ									-0.103	-0.25
R5VR									0.005	1.05
	N = 250		N = 251		N = 192		N = 231		N = 276	
Chow R^2	0.25		0.52		0.53		0.88		0.68	
% of Correct Predictions	0.70		0.81		0.84		0.97		0.90	

***Significant at the 0.01 level.

**Significant at the 0.05 level.

*Significant at the 0.10 level.

distinguish between firms in the highest versus the lowest quartiles in terms of the percentage of shares sold. These models generally fit well, explaining about 25% to 88% of the category choices of low and high demand and have prediction rates that range from 70% to 97%. The main factors that contributed to the success of trading in round 1 (the likelihood of trades taking place) are private ownership (either foreign or domestic) and sales growth. In addition, temporary government ownership and sales efficiency are positive and significant at the 0.10 level. This indicates that investors analyzed the fundamental firm information provided by the CKP to make initial selections based on firm efficiency and growth, and did not seek out firms in any one sector of the economy. This confirms the results from the valuation and trading volume regressions that in round 1 fundamental corporate characteristics were important determinants of share values.

After the first round, the major factor in determining if a trade took place was the extent of demand at the price set for that auction round. Historical information generally played less of a role in each succeeding auction round, but some fundamental valuation measures such as sales growth continued to have a positive impact on demand. Ownership variables also had an impact in some rounds, but this impact is not consistent with respect to its sign. The explanatory power (R2) of the probit estimates go up dramatically in rounds 4 and 5. These increases are consistent with the wider ranges of prices and volumes in these rounds.

V. Conclusions

Mass privatization of state owned companies is a challenge given that domestic financial markets are under-developed or non-existent. Not only is there little private capital for investment in these companies, but the lack of financial markets also means the lack of useful asset pricing signals. Further, there is generally also a lack of appropriately trained analysts and other professionals necessary for valuing companies being privatized. The auction process used in the Czech voucher-based mass privatization process was designed to overcome these limitations. It was unique when it was implemented and it was widely considered to be a success in distributing Czech state owned companies. This paper presents the results of an empirical analysis using regression and probit models of the determinants of share demand and prices in each of the five rounds of the 1992 Czech voucher mass privatization auction.

The results presented here show that while specific firm characteristics such as return on sales, sales growth, and ownership characteristics were important in the early rounds, in the later auction rounds, the role of firm specific characteristics declined while prior round share prices and trading volumes became more important. While there was some undershooting and overshooting in the early rounds as in a cobweb model, share prices were generally near their final equilibrium by the fourth round and only minor adjustments in share prices were made in the fifth and final auction round. Interestingly, the extent of residual government ownership generally had a negative impact on share prices while foreign ownership had a positive impact on share prices. The findings presented here suggest that the Czech mass privatization process allocated shares to investors efficiently and distributed privatization assets equitably.

This study contributes to the literature by examining the determinants of value in each round of the auction process. This "frame-by-frame" study of the Czech mass privatization auction provides useful information not only on the use of an ascending auction but also provides some insights on the microstructure of the price formation process in auction markets. Consistent with microstructure and other literature, the findings presented here indicate that market generated information such as prices and trade volumes can contribute to further changes in asset prices and volatility.

This research could be extended not only to the analysis of the second wave of the Czech mass privatization, but also to the analysis of privatization in other former communist countries. A number of other countries, such as Russia and Poland, have also used various forms of voucher mass privatization (while others such as Hungary have used more direct sales). The results presented here may also be of interest in understanding infant capital markets, especially as many equity exchanges began as call markets. ■

References

Aggarwal, R. and M. Majstrik, 1992, "Privatization and Capital Market Development in Eastern Europe: Lessons from the Czechoslovak Experience," CERGE Working Paper No. 14, Center for Economic Research and Graduate Education, Charles University, Prague (September).

Aghion, P., 1993, "Economic Reform in Eastern Europe: Can Theory Help?," *European Economic Review* 37(2/3), 525-532.

Al-Obaidan, A.M., and G.W. Scully, 1992, "Efficiency Differences Between Private and State-Owned Enterprises in the International Petroleum Industry," *Applied Economics* 58(1), 237-246.

Bel, G., 1998, "Privatization in the Stock Market: Sale in One Go or Sale in Tranches?," *Economics Letters* 58(1), 113-117.

Boubakri, N. and J.C. Cosset, 1998, "The Financial and Operating Performance of Newly Privatized Firms: Evidence from Developing Countries," *Journal of Finance* 53(3), 1081-1110.

Boycko, M., A. Shleifer, and R.W. Vishny, 1994, "Voucher Privatizations," *Journal of Financial Economics* 76(1), 249-266.

Brainard, L.J., 1991, "Reform in Eastern Europe: Creating a Capital Market," *Federal Reserve Bank of Kansas City Economic Review* 76(1), 48-58.

Claessens, S., 1997, "Corporate Governance and Equity Prices: Evidence from the Czech and Slovak Republics," *Journal of Finance* 52(4), 1641-1659.

Claessens, S. and S. Djankov, 1998, "Politicians and Firms in Seven Eastern European Countries," World Bank Working Paper No. 1954, Washington, DC (August).

Claessens, S., S. Djankov, and G. Pohl, 1997, "Ownership and Corporate Governance: Evidence from the Czech Republic," World Bank Working Paper No. 1737, Washington, DC (March).

Cramton, P., 1998, "Ascending Auctions," *European Economic Review* 42(2/3), 745-756.

Dewenter, K.L., and P.H. Malatesta, 1997, "Public Offerings of State-Owned and Privately-Owned Enterprises: An International Comparison," *Journal of Finance* 52(4), 1659-1680.

Dewenter, K.L., and P.H. Malatesta, 2000, "State Owned and and Privately-Owned Firms: An Empirical Analysis of Profitability, Leverage, and Labor Intensity," *American Economic Review* (Forthcoming).

Djankov, S., 1998, "Enterprise Isolation Programs in Transition Economies," World Bank Working Paper No. 1952, Washington, DC, August.

Domowitz, I., 1993, "Automating the Price Discovery Process: Some International Comparisons and Regulatory Implications," *Journal of Financial Services Research* 6(4), 305-326.

Ellerman, D., 1998, "Voucher Privatization with Investment Funds," World Bank Working Paper No. 1924, Washington, DC, May.

Gray, C. W., 1996, "In Search of Owners: Privatization and Corporate Governance in Transition Economics," *World Bank Research Observer* 11(2), 179-197

Gleason, K.C., I. Mathur and L.K. Mathur, 1999, "Shareholders' Gains from Corporate Expansion to the Republics of the Former Soviet Union," *Financial Management* 28(1), 61-74.

Hanousek, J. and E.A. Kroch, 1998, "The Two Waves of Voucher Privatization in the Czech Republic: A Model of Learning in Sequential Bidding," *Applied Economics* 30(1) 133-143.

Harper, J.T., 2001, "Short-Term Effects of Privatization on Operating Performance in the Czech Republic," *Journal of Financial Research* (forthcoming).

Hasbrouck, J., 1995, "One Security, Many Markets: Determining the Contributions to Price Discovery," *Journal of Finance* 50(4), 1175-1199.

Hillion, P., and D.S. Young, 1996, "The Czechoslovak Privatization Auction: An Empirical Analysis," Working Paper, INSEAD (September).

Hingorani, A., K. Lehn, and A. Makhija, 1997, "Investor Behavior in Mass Privatization: The Case of the Czech Voucher Scheme," *Journal of Financial Economics* 44(3), 348-396.

Ibbotson, R., 1975, "Price Performance of Common Stock New Issues," *Journal of Financial Economics* 2(3), 235-272.

Ibbotson, R., J. Sindelar, and J. Ritter, 1994, "Market Problems with the Pricing of Initial Public Offerings," *Journal of Applied Corporate Finance* 7(1), 66-74.

Jenkinson, T. and C. Mayer, 1994, "The Cost of Privatization in the U.K. and France," in M. Bishop, J. A. Kay, and C. Mayer (eds.), *Privatization and Economic Performance* New York, NY, Oxford University Press, 290-298.

Jones, S.L., W.L. Megginson, R. C. Nash, and J.M. Netter, 1999, "Share Issue Privatizations as Financial Means to Political and Economic Ends," *Journal of Financial Economics* 53(2), 217-253.

Klemperer, P., 1999, "Auction Theory: A Guide to the Literature," *Journal of Economic Surveys* 13(3), 152-189.

Kortba, J., 1995, "Privatization Process in the Czech Republic: Players and Winners," in J. Svejnar, Ed., *The Czech Republic and Economic Transition in Eastern Europe*, San Diego, CA, Academic Press, 159-198.

Kunz, R.M. and R. Aggarwal, 1994, "Why Initial Public Offerings Are Underpriced: Evidence from Switzerland," *Journal of Banking and Finance* 18(4), 705-723.

Lam, S.S., 1997, "Control Versus Firm Value: The Impact of Restrictions on Foreign Share Ownership," *Financial Management* 26(1), 48-61.

Lipton, D., and J. Sachs, 1990, "Privatization in Eastern Europe: The Case of Poland," *Brookings Papers on Economic Activity* 2, 293-304.

Logue, D.E., 1973, "On the Pricing of Unseasoned Equity Offerings: 1965-69," *Journal of Financial and Quantitative Analysis* 8(1), 91-103.

Manzetti, L., 1994, "The Politics of Privatization and Deregulation in Latin America," *Quarterly Review of Economics and Finance* 34(Special Issue), 43-76.

McAfee, P. and J. McMillan, 1987, "Auctions and Bidding," *Journal of Economic Literature* 25(2), 699-738.

Megginson, W.L., R.C. Nash, and M. van Randenborgh, 1994, "The Financial and Operating Performance of Newly Privatized Firms: An International Perspective," *Journal of Finance* 49(2), 403-452.

Mejstrik, M., (ed.), 1997, *Privatization Process in East-Central Europe: Evolutionary Process of Czech Privatization*, Boston, MA, Kluwer Academic Publishers.

Mertik, P., 1997, "Czech Privatization," *Eastern European Economics* 35(2), 64-83.

Miller, R.E. and F.K. Reilly, 1987, "An Examination of Mispricing, Returns, and Uncertainty for Initial Public Offerings," *Financial Management* 16(2), 33-38.

Morgan Stanley, 1997, "Privatized Companies: Undervaluation Over?," London, The Company.

Murphy, K.M., A. Shleifer, and R.W. Vishny, 1992, "The Transition to a Market Economy: Pitfalls of Partial Reform," *Quarterly Journal of Economics* 107(3), 293-315.

O'Hara, M., and G.S. Oldfield, 1986, "The Microeconomics of Market Making," *Journal of Financial and Quantitative Analysis* 21(4), 361-376.

Perotti, E.C., and S.E. Guney, 1993, "The Structure of Privatization Plans," *Financial Management* 22(1), 84-98.

Perotti, E.C., 1995, "Credible Privatization," *American Economic Review* 85(4), 847-859.

Roland, G., 1993, "The Political Economy of Restructuring and Privatization in Eastern Europe," *European Economic Review* 37(2/3), 533-540.

Sachs, J., 1993, *Poland's Jump to the Market Economy*, Cambridge, MA, MIT Press.

Stein, J. L., 1992, "Price Discovery Processes," *Economic Record* (Supplement) 34-45.

Svejnar, J., Ed., 1995, *The Czech Republic and Economic Transition in Eastern Europe*, San Diego, CA, Academic Press.

White, H., 1980, "A Heteroskedasticity-Consistent Covariance Matrix Estimator and a Direct Test for Heteroskedasticity," *Econometrica* (May), 817-838.

PERGAMON

Telecommunications Policy 25 (2001) 381–407

TELECOMMUNICATIONS
P O L I C Y

www.elsevier.com/locate/telpol

Competitive dynamics in Polish telecommunications, 1990–2000: growth, regulation, and privatization of an infrastructural multi-network

David Dornisch*

Global Transmedia Communications Corporation, 1 University Plaza, Suite 208 Hackensack, NJ 07601, USA

Abstract

This paper analyzes the relationship between governmental regulatory policies and competitive dynamics amongst private operators and the national monopolist, TP SA, in three network segments of the Polish telecommunications sector. Special attention is paid to the evolution of organizational strategies in a regulatory environment characterized by constant strategic indecision and reorientations of national policy makers. The paper finds that regulatory/competition coevolution has taken diverse forms in the three network subsegments, with asymmetric duopoly operating in the local fixed network, hidden competition at work in the long-distance fixed network, and oligopolistic technology-driven competition characterizing the high-growth cellular network. The conclusion reached is that Polish telecommunications to date has been stuck in a broad stage of pre-competitive market maneuverings by domestic and international capital, in preparation for privatization of the national operator and for full liberalization as part of EU integration. © 2001 Elsevier Science Ltd. All rights reserved.

Keywords: Poland; Competitive dynamics; Coevolution; Development; Investment; Regulation; Convergence; TP SA

1. Introduction: post-socialist sectoral development

Telecommunications is a sector whose development is pivotal for the effective functioning of economies, on local, national, and global scales. Telecommunications enables the reduction of transaction costs at a macro-economic scale through the rapid, efficient flow of information. In micro-economic terms it supports the formation of strategic alliances tying together diverse, remote organizations into joint projects. Telecommunications is also a vital developmental force in its own right. It is a site of rapid technological innovation, reflected in the constant emergence

*Corresponding author. Tel.: + 1-201-343-7546.

E-mail addresses: d_dornisch@yahoo.com (D. Dornisch).

0308-5961/01/$ - see front matter © 2001 Elsevier Science Ltd. All rights reserved.
PII: S 0 3 0 8 - 5 9 6 1 (0 1) 0 0 0 1 3 - 1

382   *D. Dornisch / Telecommunications Policy 25 (2001) 381–407*

of new products and services. This technological and competitive whirlwind accounts for an increasing percentage of the gross national product of most advanced and developing countries.

In Poland, pressures to develop telecommunications products and services are becoming increasingly evident in the country's post-socialist economic transformation. As the experiences of western countries show, modernization of industrial, finance, service, and educational sectors is predicated on incorporation of up-to-date telecommunications technologies. There is now general agreement that the collapse of state socialism in countries like Poland resulted in no small part from their inability to build up the telecommunications infrastructure that became a sine qua non for economic growth beginning in the 1980s.

Since 1990, Poland has entered into an intensive, national-scale project to modernize its telecommunications infrastructure. Significant changes have occurred as demonstrated by a number of basic indicators. First, the public telephone system in Poland has undergone a process of basic overhaul and expansion, reflected in the sustained investment efforts of the dominant Polish telecommunications operator, Telekomunikacja Polska S.A. (TP SA). This is reflected most fundamentally by the data given in Table 1.

These steadily increasing indicators of the size of the basic fixed telephone network in Poland are mirrored in the investment indicators given in Table 2. Here we see that pronounced growth in the size of TP SA's investment outlays has occurred alongside an increase in the share of income allocated to investments.

Table 1
TP SA-operated public network[a]

Year	Customers	Growth in # customers	TP SA teledensity (lines per 100 inhabitants)
1992	3,938,144	372,850	10.25
1993	4,415,751	477,607	11.47
1994	5,006,094	590,343	12.98
1995	5,728,497	722,403	14.85
1996	6,538,581	810,084	16.94
1997	7,470,000	931,419	19.30
1998	8,500,000	1,030,000	22.00
1999	9,550,000	1,050,000	22.45

[a] Source: Bielański (1998a, p. 22); Kulisiewicz (2000, p. 12, 18).

Table 2
Income and investments in TP SA (in million PZl)[a]

Year	1992	1993	1994	1995	1996	1997
Income	1910	2730	3670	5012	6432	8338
Profit	449	687	664	841	750	970
Investments	715	1210	1435	2146	3150	4254
Relation of investments to income (%)	37.4	44.3	39.1	42.8	49.0	51.0

[a] Source: Bielański (1998a, p. 23).

Growth of the public network has also been accompanied by marked improvements in the quality of service. The waiting time for a new line, for example, has dropped markedly from 167 months in 1989, to 48 months in 1994, and finally to 33 months in 1999 (Kontkiewicz-Chachulska & Kubasik, 1997). Modernization is reflected in TP SA's systematic replacement of old analog equipment and cable technologies with digital ones; along with this there has been pronounced movement to fiber optics cables and automatic digital switches.

This general expansion of the size and quality of the basic public telephone network built and serviced by TP SA has also been enhanced by the emergence of a whole set of new operators competing with and complementing TP SA's efforts. The appearance of these operators underlies a fundamental transformation of Polish telecommunications involving the slow emergence of a *network of networks* (Economides, 1995), or multi-network, that extends well beyond the previous unified public network dominated by TP SA. The basic components of this multi-network include

1. Local subnetworks complementary to the main TP SA-operated public network.
2. Private national-level long-distance fiber-optic networks.
3. Cellular/mobile telephone networks.
4. Data transmission networks.
5. Radiocommunications networks.
6. Satellite networks.

With the expansion and diversification implied in the above, Poland has become a part of important changes in telecommunications occurring internationally. But despite these undeniable signs of progress, there are a number of evident shortcomings plaguing the development of the telecommunications sector in Poland. Most evidently, clear problems with the quality and quantity of telecommunications services remain in evidence in Poland. Broken or failed connections, poor reception, overloading of networks due to limited infrastructural capacity during high usage periods, limited choice in selection of products and services, and little flexibility in prices all continue to be in evidence. One telling indicator of the present imbalances in the telecommunications sector is the large divergence in the density of telephone networks between urban and rural areas. As Table 3 shows, urban areas outstrip rural areas in the density of telephone connections per inhabitant by well over 100%.

Table 3
Customers per 100 inhabitants (including private operators)[a]

Year	Total	City	Village
1992	10.25	14.29	3.62
1993	11.47	16.08	4.00
1994	12.98	18.15	4.58
1995	14.85	20.63	5.46
1996	16.94	23.23	6.74
1997	19.72	26.49	8.71
1998	22.79	29.82	11.42
1999	26.08	33.03	14.81

[a] Source: Różyński (1997, p. 14); Kulisiewicz (2000, p. 12).

384 *D. Dornisch / Telecommunications Policy 25 (2001) 381–407*

Table 4
Basic telecommunications indicators in the OECD and Central Europe (1989)[a]

Country	Number of main lines ('000s)	Number of lines per 100 inhabitants	New main lines 1980–89 ('000s)	Average yearly growth 1980–89
OECD	*345,898.31*	*43.08*	*93,137.14*	*3.55*
Bulgaria	1994.00	22.23	1034.00	8.46
Czechoslovakia	2226.39	14.26	577.39	3.39
Yugoslavia	3560.08	15.06	2048.08	9.98
Poland	3121.37	8.22	1178.37	5.41
Romania	2161.31	9.42	738.31	4.75
Hungary	916.00	8.64	299.00	4.49
Eastern Europe	*13,979.15*	*11.67*	*5875.15*	*6.25*

[a] Source: Kontkiewicz-Chachulska and Kubasik (1997, p. 239).

In comparative terms, Poland continues to find itself in an unfavorable situation. Poland began the post-socialist transformation far down the list in the international ranking of advancement of the telecommunications sector. Table 4 provides this ranking in cross-national perspective in 1989.

Poland's relative position in this ranking has changed little, despite the changes in absolute numbers given previously. Poland as of 1995 compared negatively with all countries of the European Community, to which it presently aspires. Whereas Poland in 1995 had a telephone density of 14.85 customers out of every 100 inhabitants (1997—19.3; see above), in 1995 it was 49.8 in Germany, 56.0 in France, and 45.72 in Belgium. In comparison with other East European countries, while it has moved beyond the ostensible losers in levels (Romania) and in rates (Bulgaria), Poland continues to compare unfavorably with its primary competitors, Hungary and the Czech Republic (with the former at teledensity of 35 and the latter at 37).[1]

Generally, Poland is experiencing continued difficulties in keeping up with the frantic pace of telecommunications innovation, competition, and market activity apparent in most advanced capitalist countries. Despite its impressive absolute rates, Poland, with $16 invested in telecommunications per inhabitant in 1995, compares unfavorably with European Union countries, such as Germany ($183.2), Luxembourg ($166.7), France ($107.8), Portugal ($57.4), Greece ($60.9), and Great Britain ($70.9) (Gawron, 1996, p. 26). Collectively, Poland lags behind the European Union ($97.5) in terms of telecommunications investments per inhabitant by a measure of 6. Even comparisons with the least developed countries are strongly unfavorable for Poland, with the most striking case being Portugal, which in 1994 invested in telecommunications 3.5 times more per inhabitant than Poland.

From the above, a basic paradox arises in considering Polish telecommunications. On the one hand, in comparison with its previous state, Poland has since 1989 greatly improved its telecommunications infrastructure, with marked intensification of investment and

---

[1] See the ESIS Knowledge database at http://www.eu-esis.org.

modernization efforts. At the same time, Poland continues to lag both its near neighbors and more distant western countries in the rate of telecommunications investments, growth, and innovation.

In the remainder of this paper, the basis for this paradox is examined in more detail. In doing so, the objective is to look under the broad trends outlined above and explore the effects of the regulatory environment and competitive dynamics on growth in the Polish telecommunications sector. The point of entry is the emerging consensus that telecommunications has on a global scale shifted from being a sector dominated by large national-level monopolies and extensive governmental regulation to one characterized by the increasing withdrawal of the state and by intense competition amongst entrepreneurial and multi-national corporations of all shapes and sizes. This shift has in turn became the basis for a high degree of technological innovation, the rapid development of powerful new telecommunications infrastructures, the convergence of multiple media platforms (data, voice, video), intense merger and alliance activity, and improved productivity at the sectoral and economy-wide levels (Bar et al., 2000; Jamison, 1998; Communications International, 1998; Davies, 1994).

This paper evaluates the extent to which Poland has moved toward this new model of competitive dynamics. In the first section the coevolution[2] of regulatory policy at the governmental level and competition at the sectoral level is analyzed in three segments of the Polish multi-network: fixed local, fixed inter-city (long-distance), and mobile. This involves an effort to establish the extent to which governmental policy-making has supported the emergence of competitive conditions in the three network segments and the ways in which firms have responded to those policies and to each other in their investment and strategic behavior. This section also explores the extent to which governmental competition policy has supported sectoral development and the extent to which development has occurred in the sector *in spite of* what has typically been inconsistent and opaque governmental policy.

After examining regulatory and competitive configurations in the three network segments the focus shifts in the second section to the prospects for intensified competition and enhanced growth of Polish telecommunications in the middle- to long-term. This section explores the significance for future development of a set of emerging factors, including (1) privatization of the national operator, (2) transformation of the legal and regulatory regime governing telecommunications; (3) accession to and integration with the European Community; (4) consolidation of private firms and new technological/organizational trends.

2. Regulatory and competitive configurations in Polish telecommunications networks

A fact that emerges from even a cursory examination of the Polish multi-network is that different segments of that network vary strongly in their regulatory environments and competitive dynamics. Moreover, during various periods, different segments have shown greater competitive

---

[2] For useful overviews of this concept see the section on coevolution in Baum and Singh (1994) and the special edition on coevolution in *Organization Studies* from September 1999.

386   *D. Dornisch / Telecommunications Policy 25 (2001) 381–407*

Table 5
TP SA local switches[a]

| Year | Number of switches | | | | Number of lines added on to particular types of switches ('000) | | | |
	Manual	Automatic	In that: digital	Total	Manual	Automatic	In that: digital	Total
1991	2279	3947	—	6226	332.2	3677.6	—	4009.8
1992	2052	4248	34	6300	337.6	4219.3	210.1	4556.8
1993	1817	4520	305	6337	325.2	5003.2	791.9	5328.4
1994	1492	4757	600	6250	287.9	5597.2	1291.7	5885.1
1995	1217	5115	1070	6332	242.7	6508.1	2234.5	6750.8

[a] Source: Kontkiewicz-Chachulska and Kubasik (1997).

and developmental dynamism than others. The three most dynamic segments, the fixed local network, the fixed inter-city (long-distance) network, and the mobile network,[3] are analyzed here.

2.1. Fixed telephony networks

We can differentiate three hierarchical levels of competition in the fixed network: local (or city), national (or inter-city), and international. I focus on the first two of these.

2.1.1. Local networks: asymmetric duopoly

The Polish national operator, TP SA, has made a concentrated effort to upgrade its local network infrastructure on a nationwide scale since 1992, when TP SA was divided off as a commercialized entity separate from the state socialist structure which had combined postal, telegraph, and telephony services in one enterprise (PPTiT, of Polska Poczta, Telegraf i Telefon). General data on the development of the TP SA-governed fixed network (measured in terms of changes in network density) have been presented in Table 1. The expansion of new lines has grown steadily from a rate of 8.3% in 1992 (in relation to the number of lines existing in 1991) to 14.3% in 1997 (TP SA, 1998, p. 7). This has been accompanied by the earlier-mentioned improvements in the waiting time for installment of new lines by TP SA. Technological development has involved phasing out analog and particularly manual switches in favor of digital switches, as shown in Table 5.

TP SA's investment activity has been accompanied by the entry of a substantial number of new, smaller private operators into the local telephony market. At the end of 1999, the local network was the only level of the fixed network in which competition was allowed, in keeping with the *Telecommunications Law* of 1990 (amended in 1995). The Telecommunications Law and subsequent administrative directives of the Ministry of Telecommunications specifies *duopoly* as the form which competition should take in local communications markets. This means that in addition to TP SA, whose network presently covers the entire country, on every local market one

---

[3] Because competition has yet to occur in the fixed international network, with TP SA possessing a legal monopoly until 2003, a separate section for this market is not included. Instead, the focus is on the parts of the multi-network that are most dynamically changing. Some analysis of emerging data transmission networks also appears, but in the context of analysis of inter-city networks. The fixed local network receives the most detailed analysis, as it has had the longest and most complex post-socialist competition history.

other competitor may operate. Realization of this duopoly policy, as reflected in Ministerial policy, on the one hand, and firm/market-level responses, on the other, has, over time, taken different shapes. We can identify two primary periods of local duopoly in Poland.

Stage 1. Bottom–up locality-specific telephony initiatives. The first period of market evolution (1990–1995), which began in the early 1990s, can be described as one of *bottom–up entrepreneurship* in local fixed markets. At this early stage, the Ministry's policy in awarding rights to investment/operation was to let duopoly competition take shape on its own without central steering. Here, on a location-by-location basis, private operators (or private entrepreneurs aspiring to this designation) could select their own site for development of independent telecommunications infrastructure. If their proposal to the Ministry, typically agreed in advance with the local self-governments of the communities in which investment was to take place, was accepted, they received a permit (*zezwolenie*) for operation. The motivation for this policy was to promote the development of telecommunications infrastructure in the most poorly developed parts of the TP SA network; most of the projects proposed were directed to small towns and villages suffering severe infrastructural shortcomings. Simultaneously, as a by-product, policy-makers hoped this would place greater competitive pressure on TP SA, forcing it to pay more attention to these underdeveloped regions of the network (Gospodarek, 1997; Rutkowski, 1993).

At this early stage, there was little precedent legally, procedurally, and organizationally in the organization of these bottom–up undertakings. Correspondingly, there was high variation in the types of entities motivating them. Examples of firms sponsoring these bottom–up undertakings include the following: a limited liability company, PT 'Centrala,' Ltd. operating in Mielec; telecommunation cooperatives in Zbąszyń and Łańcut; a regional development agency 'Arreks' SA operating in Kleszczów and surrounding townships; and a coal mine 'Bogdanka' SA in the Lublin area (Kontkiewicz-Chachulska & Kubasik, 1997; Margas, 1999a).

Stage 2. Bureaucratic allocation of market territory. With time, it became increasingly evident that the existing policy was not providing a sufficiently fast pace of development of alternative private networks. The telecommunications needs of local Poland could not be met on a wide scale through the bottom–up approach. The scale of this activity was simply too limited and too localized. To stimulate more dynamic development of the fixed infrastructure—and to gain greater control over the process—the Ministry fundamentally altered its policy. In particular, the Ministry shifted from the use of site-specific permits granted on the basis of local bottom–up initiatives to holding organized competitions, or public tenders (*przetargi*) for operating concessions (*koncesje*), in which independent telephony companies submitted proposals for developing particular localities (*gminy*), sets of localities, and provinces[4] (*voivodships, or województwa*).[5]

With this shift in policy, reflected in the 1995 amendment of the 1990 Telecommunications Law,[6] came a fundamental shift in the character of the operating permits granted. Tenders

---

[4] Important to recognize here is that the new period *cannot* be represented as a period of "top–down" ministerial fiat, in opposition to the earlier bottom–up entrepreneurship. The Ministry is able to exercise only limited control over private operators via the concessioning mechanism. Its primary instrument for controlling firms' activities once they receive concessions is through indirect regulation and certification of projects and services.

[5] Voivodship is the anglicized term for the Polish province, or województwo. I will in the remainder of this paper use the term voivodship.

[6] For more on the political and economic context of the amendment, see Gospodarek (1997).

388   *D. Dornisch | Telecommunications Policy 25 (2001) 381–407*

announced in 1995 and 1996 generally were for larger areas than the licenses granted to bottom–up entrepreneurs in the previous stage). In particular, the Ministry successively auctioned off investment and operation rights to specific provinces, or voivodships (under the pre-1999 administrative division of the country), awarding each voivodship to an individual private operator (though with the important initial exception that larger regional capitol cities were excluded from the tenders).[7] This process of assignment of territories was completed at the end of 1998 with the awarding of the urban centers excluded from the earlier full-voivodship tenders to private operators, and in particular with the awarding of Warsaw to the firm El-Net in December of 1998.

This policy shift has led not only to a more consistent assignment of territories to operators, but has also changed the firm composition of the sector of private operators. With the completion of the concessioning process at the end of 1998, 43 nominally independent operators had been granted a total of 90 concessions to invest in and operate specific local networks (Margas, 1999a). Before 1995 the overwhelming majority of private operators were confined to small, bounded localities. After 1995 the average size of the territory on which private operators function has expanded significantly. Prior to 1995 the 23 existing operators were limited to individual localities (district, village, or town) or to several such localities (2 of the 23). Subsequently, the 20 new operators (some of which were affiliated with each other through capital relations or joint holding membership) appearing as a result of ministerial concessioning functioned either on the territory of a whole voivodship (of which there were 49 in the country at the time) or in several voivodships (10 in both cases) (Margas, 1999a). Appendix A provides customer totals possessed by private operators nationally and in city and village categories as of the end of 1999.

Although the policy change of 1995 was effective in accelerating the allocation of market territory to private operators, it was much less effective in assuring them favorable conditions for functioning. The initiation of investments and operations has occurred in a fragmented manner. Of all concessions granted to the present point in time, only a minority has led to the actual undertaking of investments, with an even smaller number resulting in actual operation (Margas, 1999a; Gospodarek, 1997).

The number of customers serviced by private clients at the end of 1996 was 54,464. That number increased threefold by the end of 1997 to 180,000. Significant, though comparatively slower, growth was noted as well for 1998, when the number reached 290,000 (Margas, 1999b), and for 1999, with 530,000 customers. But a comparison of these numbers with those of TP SA (see Table 1)—1996: 6.54 million; 1997: 7.47 million; 1998: 8.3 million; 1999: 9.6 million——indicates a very limited share of private operators in the market.[8] At the present rates, it would take two decades for private operators to reach the absolute numbers of clients possessed by TP SA. The development of the market of private operators has occurred at a slower rate than that initially projected by the Ministry at the time of the 1995 amendment. The Ministry's 1998

---

[7] Note that in addition to the new concessions granted, many of the licenses awarded in the previous stage were redefined as concessions under this amendment.

[8] The difficulties operators have in mobilizing networks operationally is reflected in the following rough calculation: taking the 1999 total of 580,000 customers of private operators and dividing that by 5000 (an average number of customers serviced by any local township-based operator; my estimation) gives 116; in other words, about 116 townships are presently being served, out of a total of several thousand, throughout all of Poland, by private operators competing with TP SA.

expectation of 3 million customers (requiring 4.5 billion USD investment) serviced by the year 2000 by private operators has proven unrealistic given the existing tempo of private investments.

While the formal conditions for constitution of competitive local duopolies have been created via the Ministry's concessioning activities, monopoly conditions still exist de facto in the majority of locations. A number of factors explain the slowness of private operators' development. The first is economic: the small and medium-sized operators populating the local telephony markets have had great difficulty in marshalling the technical and financial resources necessary to first build and then mobilize local networks. Such enterprises have greater difficulty than large firms in obtaining the large sums of capital necessary to undertake even small-scale telecommunications investments. Until only very recently, this scale deficit has applied across all private operators, as even the largest of them, Netia SA, has employment of only 1000.[9]

The second problem which private operators have faced in starting up concerns the bureaucratic and regulatory environment. Bureaucratic slowness in authorizing initiation of network construction is endemic. Ministerial approval of the technical standards of operators' equipment has been notoriously inefficient (Włodarczyk, 1997; Grupa Warsztatowa, 1996). Of particular importance is the fact that the Ministry has been, by most accounts, unable to fashion a fair interconnection policy making it possible for private operators to economically integrate their new local networks with TP SA's (Burak, 2000). Instead, the lack of a clear policy has made TP SA the de facto policy-maker in the sphere of interconnection (Kontkiewicz-Chachulska & Kubasik, 1998); TP SA has by and large maintained the status quo discriminatory interconnection policy contained in the 1990 Telecommunications Law and continued in the 1995 amendment (Burak, 2000).

Third, private operators have been plagued by TP SA monopoly practices. TP SA has intentionally delayed interconnection agreements and actions so as to damage the sensitive financial/competitive position of private operators (Fronczak, 1998; Grupa Warsztatowa IV, 1996). After investments have been made, it has refused to approve operators' homologization and technological compatibility standards so as to block their initiation of network service. Most importantly, TP SA has maintained a highly unbalanced tariff structure that has made private operators unable to rationalize their pricing policies. This discriminatory pricing policy of TP SA's involves cross-subsidization of very low local prices through the maintenance of high long-distance prices (Fedorowicz & Świderek, 2001). As private operators to date have not been able to also compete in long-distance networks, the low local tariffs are the prices against which they are forced to compete. This causes severe limitations in their income-generation possibilities, with negative consequences for their ability to invest and grow (Kulisiewicz, 1999, 2000; Meth-Cohn, 1999).

TP SA's anti-competitive practices have been the objects of frequent sanctions reflected in successive decisions of the Polish Anti-Monopoly Bureau (Streżyńska, 1997; Fedorowicz & Świderek, 2001). Its decisions have produced important changes in the degree of TP SA's cross-subsidization practices in recent years. While in 1994 the ratio between long-distance and local calls was 36 : 1, this has been successively diminished since then, from 18 : 1, 15 : 1, to 12 : 1 in 1998.

---

[9] An added financial burden for the private operators is the concession fees they have had to pay to obtain the rights to operate in a given region. These fees for operation, running into the tens of millions of dollars, are not required of TP SA by the Ministry and constitute a de facto start-up penalty for the small private operators.

390   *D. Dornisch / Telecommunications Policy 25 (2001) 381–407*

Nevertheless, this still greatly exceeds the average ratio of 7 : 1 found in OECD countries (see Kontkiewicz-Chachulska & Kubasik, 1998). More generally, however, the actions of the Anti-Monopoly Bureau have had only limited effects in opening the telecommunications sector to competition. Its institutional-legal possibilities for shaping competitive dynamics are limited, as it operates in a primarily ex-post fashion, altering and sanctioning anti-competitive practices after they appear through typically lengthy legal actions (Grupa Warsztatowa IV, 1996; Streżyńska, 1997).

In contrast, the Ministry of Communications which, conceivably, could take a more proactive, ex ante role in shaping competition, has been lax in preempting TP SA's monopoly practices. In large part, this stems from a fundamental contradiction in its institutional role, where it is simultaneously both regulator of the sector and owner of the national operator.[10] The Ministry has as yet to realize its oft-repeated promises to consistently fight the national operator's monopolist tendencies in order to produce greater competition. Most commentators assert that the primary reason for the delays in deregulation has been the preparations for the sell-off via public tender of 35% of TP SA in 2000 (initially scheduled for 1999, but then delayed because of bureaucratic and political complications).[11] Because of the fiscal and political pressures for obtaining a high price for the sale of the national operator, the Ministry has been unable to impose restrictions that would diminish TP SA's financial standing and thus its salability under eventual privatization.

2.1.1.1. Further prospects for competition and development. Despite the ongoing limitations, the local fixed markets are presently moving into a third stage of development, in which the possibility for increased competition is becoming more realistic. In particular, a clear consolidation of the private operator market has occurred in 1997–99 with the emergence of several dominant private operators. The organizational form that these operators have employed to drive this development has been the multi-firm alliance or holding grouping together several subordinate enterprises (investment projects) dispersed amongst the voivodships of a given macro-region or throughout the whole of Poland. Typically, these alliances are sponsored by foreign and/or large domestic corporate investors, with the largest amongst them being Netia (main investor: the Swedish national operator, Telia), Elektrim (numerous international institutional shareholders), Poland Telecom Operators (Creditanstalt and American Pension Funds), Telefonia Lokalna (KGHM Poland Copper and PSE Polish Energy Networks) and Telefonia Polska-Zachód (Bresnan Partners International). This increasing consolidation amongst private operators is reflected in the "group" column of Appendix A, where 18 of the 25 largest individual private operators are members of one of the three primary holding groups.

These emerging alliances have had some success in overcoming financial barriers to development and in intensifying investments, though despite continued large financial losses

---

[10] Note that there is some ambiguity about the ownership function as nominally it is the Ministry of the Treasury, rather than the Ministry of Communications that exercises formal state ownership under the 1995 amendment. Nevertheless, in practice, it has been the Ministry of Communications which has been the state organ interacting most frequently with TP SA. Strong personal and institutional ties, some held over from the state socialist period, continue to characterize the relationship between the two.

[11] This view has been expressed by numerous commentators in both scientific and media accounts (see, for example. Guz, 1999; Rutkowski, 1999; Grupa Warsztatowa, 1996; Kontkiewicz-Chachulska & Kubasik, 1997, 1998).

D. Dornisch / Telecommunications Policy 25 (2001) 381–407 391

(Kulisiewicz, 1998a, b). Strong ties to international capital and sources of know-how, in addition to the economies of scale coming with consolidation, have enabled them to more effectively raise needed capital than their small, locality-specific competitors. Due to their size, they have also been able to place stronger pressure for institutional change on policy-makers and regulators through national-level lobbying. In some localities, these alliances have moved from the investment to the operation phase. In the city of Lublin and in outlying smaller towns, for example, Netia SA has established itself as a significant competitor to TP SA (Brzuszkiewicz, 1999).

Despite the continued activity of private operators in Poland, the years 1999 and, particularly, 2000 have been characterized by increasing stagnation in the local fixed telephony markets. Increasing financial pressures, TP SA blocking action, and continued regulatory inaction in opening markets have inhibited network build-out investments by the private operators. For intensification of local market development and competition to occur clear external changes in the status of TP SA and the regulatory environment appear necessary (see Section 2). Convergence of varied types of communications (local, long-distance, data, voice, and mobile) and further consolidation of operators not only within, but also *across* borders of market segments may also stimulate the development of local telephony markets (see inter-city analysis and conclusion).

2.1.2. Inter-city (long-distance) network. A dual face: monopoly vs. hidden competition

TP SA's program of investment in the inter-city network has marked a significant increase on previous levels. Table 6 details the rate of modernization and replacement of inter-city switches and connections. Here we see increases in the numbers of both automatic and, especially, digital switches and connections, with accelerated replacement of manual technologies. In addition to these data, the number of fiberoptics lines (which are primarily, though not solely, inter-city; precise data here are not available) increased markedly. Despite these modest increases, however, TP SA's inter-city efforts have lagged far behind the intensity of its local network modernization. TP SA invested 198 million PZl in 1995, 249 million in 1996, and 243 million in 1997 in inter-city telephony, amounting to 9%, 8%, and 6% of total company investments in each of the respective years. The rate of increase in inter-city investment outlays has been considerably smaller than in local telephony, where 1.7 billion (79% of total), 2.5 billion (81%), and 3.7 (85%) was invested in these three years (Telekomunikacja Polska SA Prospekt Emisyjny, 1998, p. 13).

Table 6
Long-distance (inter-city) switches[a]

	Number of switches				Number of connections	
	Manual	Automatic	In that: digital	Total	Automatic	In that: digital
1991	291	17	—	308	2312	—
1992	272	30	2	302	42,222	17,180
1993	257	28	17	285	66,320	51,390
1994	217	52	38	269	258,532	219,230
1995	172	64	50	236	310,134	270,832

[a] Source: Kontkiewicz-Chachulska and Kubasik (1997, p. 245).

392   *D. Dornisch / Telecommunications Policy 25 (2001) 381–407*

Also in contrast to the fixed local market, TP SA held a monopoly on fixed inter-city telephony through the 1990s. Under the Telecommunications Law from 1990 (and its 1995 amendment) and according to ministerial policy statements, competition was to begin in the inter-city market only in 1999. That date was subsequently delayed to 2000, as it was not until late 1999 (October) that the first public tenders for inter-city operators were announced by the Ministry. These were concluded in the first half of 2000 (see below for details).

Despite the delays in the formal introduction of competition, through the 1990s there has been a large amount of pre-competitive movement by prospective entrants to the inter-city market. This has taken a number of forms. The first of these is represented by the preliminary investments in inter-city fiberoptics backbone networks undertaken by two firms in particular, Tel-Energo and Kolpak, the telecommunications subsidiaries of the national energy provider, PSE SA, and the national rail operator, PKP, respectively. Since 1993, these two entities have constructed long-distance networks amounting to 7000 km (Tel-Energo) and 5000 km (Kolpak). The initial purpose of these networks was to meet the communications needs of the energy complex and rail system by providing a faster, more reliable alternative to the existing TP SA backbone network. At the same time, these companies also had a broader long-term strategic purpose of positioning themselves for entry into the lucrative telecommunications service sector and the provision of connections and services to external clients.

The second important pre-market development in the inter-city network has been the creation of a set of data transmission networks, in addition to that operated by TP SA. In recent years, the Ministry has granted a series of concessions for the development of independent data transmission networks to private or non-profit entities. These include the following:[12]

1. *Telbank*—A network owned, developed, and operated by a consortium of Polish banks. Intended initially for the data transfer needs of the Polish banking system, this firm has recently begun to expand its operations by leasing lines, and providing switching and services to external entities.
2. *NASK*—A non-profit entity that has developed a network to provide internet and other data transmission to academic institutions on a national scale.
3. *Pol-34*—A second, enhanced, university-based network.
4. In the summer of 1999, *Tel-Energo* received a concession from the Ministry for provision of data transmission services.

These two sets of undertakings are particularly significant because they have resulted in a high degree of hidden competition in the inter-city network. *The network has a dual face*, in which, on the one hand, monopoly conditions on the public side of the network are maintained, while a *hidden competition* on the private side of the network is emerging. The self-provisioning activities of corporate entities like Tel-Energo, Kolpak, and Telbank all represent attempts to bypass the TP SA monopoly to provide more efficient communications systems for particular infrastructural sectors (energy, rail, and banking). The infrastructural and intracorporate networks being built, while they are not directly impinging on the TP SA monopoly in inter-city voice communications,

---

[12] Note that these data transmission firms do not have rights to develop voice telephony services. In this sense they differ from the Kolpak and Tel-Energo networks, which received concessions explicitly for meeting their own internal voice telephony needs.

have clear indirect effects on this monopoly, for two reasons. First, in the private spheres within which such networks have been built, they have been used for providing internal voice telephony services. This is evidently the case for Tel-Energo and Kolpak, but also so for Telbank, despite the fact that it did not receive a concession for provision of voice communications.[13] Second, these operators have begun to extend their networks to external agents. Most significantly here, private operators, such as Netia, Telefonia Lokalna, Retel, and Szeptel (see Appendix A) are integrating their local networks not with the TP SA network but with, in particular, the backbone network of Tel-Energo (Zwierzchowski, 1998, 1999) by renting connections from it. This activity is authorized by the Ministry because it ostensibly does not affect the inter-city monopoly of TP SA. Nevertheless, it provides a means for local operators to bypass the TP SA network and to service telephone voice communication at an ambiguous extra-local, inter-zone level.

2.1.2.1. Further prospects for competition and development. Given the diverse set of undertakings noted above, pronounced competition in the inter-city market could begin immediately, a claim often made by representatives of various private operators (Guz, 1999; Zwierzchowski, 1998, 1999). Ongoing developments indicate the strongly artificial nature of the inter-city monopoly. As is increasingly recognized, the technological distance between voice telephony services and the provision of data transmission services is quickly narrowing, as platforms (e.g. IP, ATM, Frame Relay, DSL, and other broadband solutions) developed by western operators now involve efforts to combine the two into one package. Combining these two services on the existing alternative inter-city backbone and data transmission (which themselves are inter-city) networks is primarily a question of technology development and further investment financing. Moreover, it is only a short jump from the operation of a closed private network (data transmission and/or voice) to the integration of these private networks with the public inter-city network and the provision of services to businesses and consumers. In Poland the primary limitations to the extension of existing private networks to the public and of their integration with the TP SA network are formal, involving the need for liberalized competition policy and for equitable interconnection and access standards for operators and customers.

At present, the possibility for breaking down the monopoly and for the rectification of the relative neglect of inter-city infrastructure and services is emerging. The first ministerial tenders for inter-city investment/operation concessions were announced in October 1999. The result of these tenders has been the selection in February 2000 of a set of three investment consortia composed of existing and prospective telecommunications investors (both foreign and domestic). In announcing this competition, the Ministry specified that all applicants must be consortia of cooperating firms, rather than individual entities. The purpose of this, as indicated by the Ministry, was to ensure sufficient degrees of technological know-how, local market knowledge, and financing capability. The three consortia selected were the following (Margas, 1999b, 2000a, b; Różyński, 2000):

1. *Netia 1 Ltd.*: Composed of Netia, Netia's Swedish co-owner Telia, Warsaw-based energy plant Stoen (German-financed), and the Polish banks BRE (Export Development Bank) and PKO BP;

---

[13] According to a respondent in Tel-Energo, while formally such activity is not permitted, the central authorities have neither the bureaucratic nor technical ability to monitor or control this activity.

394 *D. Dornisch / Telecommunications Policy 25 (2001) 381–407*

2. *NG Rail Telecommunications Ltd.* (NG Koleje Telekomunikacja sp. z o.o.): Composed of PKP (Polish Rail Enterprise), the British energy concern National Grid (via its Polish subsidiary Energies), and Centrala Ltd. (part of the Polish Telecom Operators local operator holding);

3. *Independent Interzone Operator* (Niezależny Operator Międzystrefowy): Composed of Tel-Energo (the telecommunications subsidiary of PSE, the national energy network company) and PKN (the Polish Petroleum Concern, or Polski Koncern Naftowy).

The selection and introduction of these three operators may substantially change the dynamic of competition and investment in the inter-city market. A number of developments can be expected to result from this in the medium term. First, given the already advanced state of existing inter-city network investment projects, a marked movement toward price competition amongst the new private operators and TP SA may occur. Under such a change, TP SA will likely be unable to maintain the presently artificially high prices for inter-city communications that it has maintained through the 1990s by virtue of its long-distance services monopoly. Prices will almost surely decrease under such circumstances. Though note that, while this is the expectation, as of January 2001, this had not happened (Fedorowicz & Świderek, 2001).

More generally, the new concessions have not only the potential to provide alternative sources of inter-city investment to those of TP SA's, but will also place increased pressure on TP SA to further intensify its inter-city investment efforts, which have been relatively limited to date. In addition, however, introduction of competition on the inter-city market has the potential to generate competition and development beyond that segment. First, as TP SA lowers its inter-city prices, it will be forced to make up for this by increasing its local prices, which will improve the revenue-generating capabilities of the local operators, who will be able to intensify their investment efforts. Second, the new inter-city consortia, being constituted of groups of inter-city voice and data transmission service providers, existing and potential local private operators, and domestic and foreign strategic investors, can stimulate a process of consolidation amongst operators in different segments of the telecommunications sector. By extension, the emergence of competition in the inter-city market appears to have the potential of stimulating intensified investment dynamics throughout all market segments of the whole telecommunications sector.

2.2. Mobile network: technology-driven competition

In the market for mobile telephony services free and open competition has emerged more quickly than in the fixed market. At present, this competition is characterized by greater intensity and clarity, despite the relative newness of mobile telephone technologies in comparison with fixed technologies. The lack of early TP SA domination in this market and its inexperience with the new mobile technologies explains this more transparent situation, and this in turn has made it possible for the Ministry to pursue a more open, straightforward concessioning policy than in the fixed market.[14]

---

[14] Generally speaking, the regulation of the mobile market has been less hamstrung by the constraints of legal precedent and by parliamentary concern over the status of the national operator within it than the fixed market. It has also received less attention from the Ministry than the fixed market and, at least, until recently, has been allowed to develop largely on its own without pronounced regulatory interventions.

D. Dornisch / Telecommunications Policy 25 (2001) 381–407 395

The mobile network is characterized by high levels of investment and market expansion. According to Bielański (1998b), the largest investment outlays in 1990s Poland have occurred in the cellular telephony sector. This trend began in 1992, when the first concession for mobile networks using the *Nordic Mobile Telephone System* (NMT) technology was granted to Centertel SA, the cellular subsidiary of TP SA. It picked up speed with the granting of two more concessions in 1996 for mobile networks using the GSM-900 technology. A fourth concession was granted to Polkomtel for the DCS (or GSM-1800) technology in 1997. The following table presents the basic contours of the process of mobile network development in 1990's Poland (Table 7).

Development of the mobile telephony network has been the primary process driving the development of the telecommunications market in the latter half of the 1990s. The market opening that occurred in 1996 made possible the introduction of two new GSM systems and the simultaneous elimination of the high connection and calling prices maintained to that point by the monopolist Centertel (Kontkiewicz-Chachulska & Kubasik, 1997: 283). As of mid-1999, the size of the cellular market (2.5 million clients in mid-1999) has reached 25% of the size of the fixed market (approx. 9 million in mid-1999) (Margas & Świderek, 1999). The two private cellular operators have become the main competition for TP SA, both directly, with respect to its cellular subsidiary, Centertel, and indirectly, through intermodal competition with TP SA itself.

The rules of competition have been more open in the mobile network than in the fixed network, but actual competitive pressures amongst cellular operators have been relatively weak. Firms have been able to develop their client bases and generate high revenues without pursuing differentiated strategic campaigns. Until now the high ongoing demand for new, fashionable cellular products (telephones, valued-added services, pricing packages) has been the primary reason for the expansion of firms. *Competition is thus technology-driven in the mobile telephony market.* As in other reforming countries, cellular technologies have proven particularly valuable to Polish customers because of the underdeveloped fixed network (see Gruber, 1999). Amongst cellular firms, differences in financial results derive from differentiated demand and cost structures characterizing particular technologies. In 1998 both GSM operators generated 66% greater

Table 7
Development of the mobile network in Poland measured in number of customers ('000s)[a]

Cellular technology (operator)	Year							
	1992	1993	1994	1995	1996	1997	1998	1999
NMT 450 (PTK-Centertel)	2.1	13.6	39	75	151	250	220	180[b]
Era GSM (PTC)	—	—	—	—	30	300	780	1800[b]
Plus GSM (Polkomtel)	—	—	—	—	40	300	800	1550[b]
DCS 1800 (PTK-Centertel)	—	—	—	—	—	—	200	600[b]
Total	2.1	13.6	39	75	221	850	2000	4080

[a] Source: Kontkiewicz-Chachulska and Kubasik (1997, p. 264); Margas and Świderek (1999); TP SA abbreviated stock emissions prospectus (1998, p. 11); Kulisiewicz (2000).
[b] Estimate.

396   *D. Dornisch / Telecommunications Policy 25 (2001) 381–407*

revenues than Centertel, which serviced the outmoded NMT system and had only begun to develop its DCS system (Kulisiewicz, 1999). This difference resulted from the high demand for the more advanced GSM technologies, under conditions of similar activization and connection prices for both systems.

2.1.2.2. Further prospects for competition and development. In the immediate future this technology-driven competition should continue. Competition may intensify somewhat, but it is not likely to become cutthroat. As Bielański (1998a, b, p. 40) notes, "Prices will fall further, although firms are avoiding a destructive price war. It can be expected that firms will stay with their existing service rates; concerning telephone sales, when pressured to do so, they will periodically organize more aggressive, but short, sales promotions." It also appears that the dynamic growth of the sector will continue for the near future, as by most accounts the Polish cellular market has not reached the saturation point (Margas & Świderek, 1999).

Yet there exist several factors that potentially may influence the quality and intensity of competition. One of these is the leveling of the technological profiles of the three cellular operators resulting from recent ministerial concessioning decisions. In particular, since mid-1999 the Ministry of Communications granted TP SA's Centertel a new concession for operating a GSM-900 network, thus making it the first bi-modal operator functioning with a combined GSM/DCS system (in addition to the NMT technology, which it is presently phasing out). After several months of bureaucratic wrangling, the other two mobile operators, Polkomtel and PTC, were granted DCS concessions in late summer 1999, thus creating in total a market of three bi-modal operators.

As a result of this technological evening, greater strategic differentiation amongst the operators can be expected. Even before the concessioning events of late 1999, differentiation in the strategies of the GSM operators PTC (Era system) and Polkomtel (Plus system) had become evident. According to Margas and Świderek (1999), Plus had begun into 1999 to concentrate more and more on attracting business clients, while Era had increasingly focused on individual clients. This has also begun to result in increasing divergence in the revenue and profits of the two operators, with Plus showing higher earnings in 1999 and 2000 (Kulisiewicz, 2000; Ronin, 2000).

For several reasons operators on the emerging bi-modal cellular market may be forced to pursue more active strategies. First, competition for customers may intensify with the reconfiguration of the market to three equal bimodal competitors; this may in turn make it more difficult for the operators to recoup the large investment outlays they have made through network service revenues. Second, while DCS technologies have carrying capacities three times those of GSM, there are some indications that increasing effort will become necessary to expand the customer base, because at some point saturation of the urban markets in which the GSM operators have primarily developed will occur. Third, expanding into less lucrative rural and small town regions may require more nuanced strategies on the part of operators.[15]

---

[15] According to a manager of one of the private operators interviewed in fall 1999, the dynamics of cellular telephony consumer markets are opaque to the operators themselves. First, the rate of expansion of the market has greatly exceeded all expectations. Second, despite continued high expansion rates no signs exist at present that the pace of this is likely to wane in the near future.

3. Enhancing competition and development in polish telecommunications: three factors

While there is considerable competitive movement in each of the three network segments analyzed in the previous section, there is also high ambiguity in their present and future development. There are two factors that, in different ways in each of the three segments, appear to constitute a continued drag on the ability of the Polish telecommunications sector to generate the types of competitiveness and growth characterizing Western Europe and North America.

The first of these is the continued de facto dominance of the national operator, TP SA, at a sectoral level. This dominance, and the imbalance it produces in the market, is reflected in the stark differences in earnings results between TP SA and its competitors. As Table 8 shows, TP SA through 1999 and into 2000 has continued to account for a disproportionate share of profits in the sector. TP SA generated profits of 1.08 billion PZl in 1999, while the sector as a whole generated profits of 760 million PZl; in other words, the 34 firms making up the sector in addition to TP SA operated at a loss of 300 million PZl. Moreover, the gap between TP SA's and the sector's earning performance has increased every year since 1997 (see Table 8). This condition applies to all three market segments analyzed here. It also applies to all of the larger private telecommunications companies which throughout the 1990s operated at a year-by-year loss with one exception—Polkomtel Plus generated a small profit in 1999 (Ronin, 2000; on Netia, see Świderek, 1999).

The second factor causing serious friction in the ability of the Polish telecommunications sector to dynamically develop is the continued strategic inconsistency of ministerial and governmental policy-makers. Polish policy-makers' decisions resemble an intricate game of first giving and then taking away from operators resources crucial to their ability to actively develop their networks and operations. This was evident most recently in (1) the Warsaw concessioning case (fixed local market), where bureaucratic wrangling lasted for nearly 16 months through 1999 and into 2000

Table 8
Telecommunications and internet services in Poland 1997–99[a]

	Income from network services and operations		Sales income ('000 PZl)	Net profit ('000 PZl)	Profitability (net income/ sales) (%)	Employment
	Total ('000 PZl)	Growth on previous year ('000 PZl)				
1997 (36 firms)						
Sector	10,777,538	3,608,296	11,733,045	957,952	9.5	79,886
TP SA	8,254,766	1,886,388	8,338,148	969,838	11.6	72,749
1998 (68 firms)						
Sector	14,225,849	3,448,311	15,621,766	718,245	5.0	82,435
TP SA	10,053,657	1,798,891	10,127,185	1,020,813	10.1	72,900
1999 (35 firms)						
Sector	18,918,144	4,838,826	19,573,310	760,026	4.0	N/A
TP SA	12,312,399	2,258,742	12,384,084	1,079,248	8.7	72,180

[a] Source: Kulisiewicz (1998a, b, 1999, 2000).

398   *D. Dornisch / Telecommunications Policy 25 (2001) 381–407*

(Bień, Kasprów, Margas, & Marszalek, 2000); (2) the aftermath of the inter-city concessioning decisions, where the Ministry through 2000 continued to neglect to take the executive decisions needed for the chosen inter-city consortia to begin operations (Burak, 2000); and (3) the third-generation wireless UMTS licensing debacle of late 2000, where the public tender had to be called off due to investors' accusations of unfairness (Świderek, 2000).

This section looks more closely at the possibilities for overcoming these two evident drags on the accelerated growth of the sector. In 2000, movements in three areas have occurred which may alter the conditions for development of the Polish telecommunications sector: privatization of TP SA, enactment of a new Telecommunications Law, and Polish accession to the EU.

3.1. Privatization of TP SA

The privatization of the Polish national operator has been delayed in comparison with its nearest East European competitors. The Czech government in 1995 sold 27% of SPT Telecom to a Swiss–Dutch consortium for $1.45 billion. The state retained 51% of the shares, while 19% passed to small domestic shareholders as part of the national mass privatization program in the form of vouchers (conditions as of 1997) (Welfens & Wiegert, 1997; Graack, 1997). Hungary sold 27.5% of the shares of its national operator Matav to the Magyar consortium (Ameritech and Deutsche Telekom) in 1993. By the end of 1998 these strategic investors had increased their stake to 59.58%. Other shareholders at this time were APV Rt. (the state holding agency responsible for privatization) with 5.75% and individual stockholders with 34.67% (Graack, 1997; Matav, 1999).

In Poland, by contrast, the first stage of privatization was not conducted until 1998, when 15% of shares were sold to small individual shareholders as part of a public stock flotation. The second stage, involving the sale of 35–50% of TP SA shares to a strategic foreign investor was initially planned for the end of 1999. This sale was delayed to 2000, however, as the initial public tender met with insufficient interest on the part of foreign investors, due to a poorly conducted invitation-to-offer process. A new public tender was announced at the end of 1999, and the Ministry received four new offers by late-February of 2000, the deadline for submitting. The transaction was consummated in June of 2000, with 35% of TP SA stock sold to France Telecom.

For some analysts and policy-makers, the main chance for intensified telecommunications competition and development is seen in the privatization of the Polish national operator, TP SA. According to them, with privatization, problems of inefficient management and monopoly practices will be eliminated. This occurs through the lessening of the state's ownership role in enterprise governance and through the introduction of rational decision-making which is market-based rather than political. Under this *simple privatization argument*, present sector-level problems of limited competition and hampered development result directly from the presence of state ownership in TP SA. Correspondingly, efforts to streamline competition and regulatory mechanisms in support of development should be subordinated to the overarching privatization imperative.

Two points can be made in response to this argument. First, while privatization itself may be a crucial step in the sector's evolution, the *preparations* for privatization have hampered its evolution. State policy-makers have used the privatization argument to justify neglect of competitive regulations and, simultaneously, to disguise their primary imperative, maximizing TP SA stock price and thus the budgetary windfall from privatization.

The second reservation is that private monopolies can be equally as ineffective as public monopolies. Such an eventuality is a distinct possibility in light of the frequent demands made by foreign investors for guarantees of monopoly position in Poland for a number of years.[16] The danger exists that privatization may, in fact, as work by Schamis (1998) on Mexico and other Latin American countries shows, become a tool serving to maintain the domination of particular international and domestic interest groups over lucrative strategic and infrastructural sectors.

The presence of strong market competition can constitute a crucial external factor stimulating changes internal to TP SA even after privatization. In Polish conditions privatization in itself does not guarantee intensified competition and development. Privatization can bring positive effects only when the regulatory system assures transparent rules of the competitive game. Privatization and regulatory change must occur simultaneously, with one supporting the other.

3.2. The new telecommunications law

The second factor conditioning transformations of Polish telecommunications is changes in telecommunications law and in regulatory mechanisms. Such changes should be driven by the overriding imperatives of investment, innovation, and development. Here, then, neither privatization nor streamlined competition regulations are ends in themselves, but rather tools to realize developmental imperatives.

Several such issues stand out as particularly relevant strategically and politically:

1. *Withdrawing the requirement that the state own a majority share* in all inter-city and mobile telephony ventures and in the national operator.
2. *Separation of the national operator ownership and sectoral regulation functions*, presently both filled by the Ministry of Communications through the creation of a separate regulatory body, the Telecommunications Regulatory Office (Urząd Regulacji Telekomunikacji).[17]
3. *Instituting a level playing field* for all operators. At present, private operators are clearly discriminated in multiple ways. Most necessary here are changes in the rules governing network

---

[16] This seems to have been at play in the recent stock sale of TP SA to France Telecom which, by some accounts, forced changes in the newly enacted Telecommunications Law of 2000 further delaying the opening of the telephony market, particularly in the area of interconnection, as a condition for its investment (see Świderek, 2000; Margas, 2000b).

[17] Numerous analysts have pointed to the evident conflicts of interest arising from this within the Ministry (Piątek, 1997; Stachów, 1998). Two regulatory bodies have been active in the telecommunications sector to date: Polska Inspekcja Telefonii i Poczty (PITiP) (Polish Telephone and Post Inspectorate) and Urząd Ochrony Konsumentów i Konkurencji (UAKK; earlier Urząd Antymonopolowy, or Anti-Monopoly Office). The first of these is fully subordinated to the Ministry. As noted earlier, the second is dependent of the Ministry, but has to date acted as a competition rear guard, acting post hoc to limit or reverse ongoing anti-competitive practices of TP SA (Grupa Warsztatowa IV, 1996). According to most analysts of the regulatory situation, what is needed is an additional regulatory institution, both independent of the Ministry *and* proactively and ex ante able to guard the market from unfair practices (Piątek, 1997; Metaxas, 1998).

400   *D. Dornisch / Telecommunications Policy 25 (2001) 381–407*

interconnection through the introduction of cost-based interconnection tariffs and the limitation of time-consuming and bureaucratic concessioning procedures.

After years of bureaucratic and legislative delay, a new telecommunications law was finally enacted in April of 2000. This law was created by combining elements of two previous projects, one developed by a parliamentary committee and the other governmental in origin. According to most legal commentators, the new project is a clear step forward from those projects as well as from the amended law from 1995 (see Winiecki, 1999; Harris, 1999). It introduces improvements in all three of the above-noted areas. At the same time, ambiguity remains as to how this law will be implemented and which elements will be followed through on in practice, given the notorious inefficiency of the existing national telecommunications administration.

3.3. EU expectations in telecommunications and accession

In the short-term it can be expected that despite the progress in enacting a new law and in privatizing TP SA ambiguity in governmental strategy regarding the telecommunications sector will continue. Regardless of these difficulties, in the medium to long-term strong pressures to reform the sector will persist due to Poland's aspirations to European Community accession, particularly in the areas of legislation and regulatory institutions. The European Community's primary expectations concern two spheres (Piątek, 1997): (1) technological homologization; (2) competitive opening of markets.

Given the almost exclusive use by operators in the Polish telecommunications sector of equipment, designs, and know-how taken from western corporate sponsors and investors, the first issue is relatively unproblematic. The second, however, is more problematic. As depicted in Table 9, the new Telecommunications Law contains a series of provisions that may lead to substantial change in crucial areas of market activity. Commentators on the new Law (see Winiecki, 1999), however, have expressed preliminary reservations regarding two aspects of these provisions: (1) *lack of clarity*—the involved items do not unambiguously place alternative private operators on an even legal footing with the national incumbent, TP SA; (2) *implementation*—as post-socialist legal practice has repeatedly demonstrated, realization of newly enacted legal frameworks often exceeds the capacity of existing administrative, legal, and political institutions.

The character of the new Telecommunications Law directly reflects the agreements resulting from the successful completion of the initial EU negotiation phase for telecommunications

Table 9
Telecommunications Law of May 2000. Liberalization and harmonization with EU Policy: intended endpoints

1. Interconnection	Inter-operator arbitrage; principle of open access to TP SA network
2. Operator entry	Open public operator entry contingent on meeting of licensing requirement
3. Foreign investment	No limitations on ownership levels and entry
4. Price-rebalancing/cross-subsidization	Narrowing of local/long-distance price ratios
5. Regulation	Creation of Telecommunications Regulation Office (URT) independent of Ministry of Communications

(during the summer of 1999). This, however, is only an initial step in the process of harmonizing the competitive regime in Polish telecommunications with EU law. New complications will surely arise as actual implementation begins. Legal, competitive and institutional practices will likely turn out to vary substantially from the initial agreements reached through negotiation.

4. Conclusion

Privatization, the new law, and European Integration are likely to produce fundamental changes in the structure and functioning of the telecommunications sector in Poland. Privatization of the national operator (sale of TP SA to France Telecom), despite the evident delays, will create a new developmental dynamic that we are only seeing the beginnings of at present. Enactment of the new legislation, likewise delayed for political and technical reasons, will introduce a series of essential changes into the regulatory environment. European accession, although the most distant in time, has and will continue to have an increasing influence on telecommunications in Poland through the formal and informal pressures it exerts on the government, institutions, and firms.

These are all longer term processes which will likely meet with frequent delays and setbacks, for political, legal, and financial reasons. Not waiting for the expected transformations in the above three areas, network operators in all market segments are presently undertaking initiatives that may on their own fundamentally alter the functioning of the sector. In particular, they have begun to join forces through a number of emerging strategic alliances, first to generate more developmental dynamism, and second to constitute a counterweight to the economic and political strength of TP SA (Błaszczak, 1999). Most importantly, 1999 and 2000 brought a major campaign by the Polish corporation Elektrim to diversify into telecommunications by building a powerful consortium of telecommunications operators in various market segments and allying itself with international telecommunications actors Vivendi and, most recently, Deutsche Telekom. Tel-Energo has, for its part, undertaken a campaign of building up the technical capabilities of its backbone fiberoptics network and has concluded a serious of cooperation agreements with a wide range of operators in the local and inter-city networks. The new inter-city (long-distance) consortia appear to have the potential to fundamentally alter the conditions of competition throughout all market segments. Obviously, this process of operator self-alignment will meet with problems, represented, for example, in limitations in financing such ambitious undertakings in increasingly tight financial markets and in the existence of an atmosphere of evident mistrust amongst many private operators. Nevertheless, the process of consolidation may lead to a situation in which groups of strongly tied operators will radically change the competitive environment despite ongoing ministerial indecision and slowness of institutional change.[18] This could potentially create conditions for a new equilibrium favoring intensified levels of investment

---

[18] Appendix B depicts the emerging alliance structure of the Polish telecommunications sector, identifying the linkages between domestic and foreign investors, on the one hand, and concrete telecommunications ventures and operators, on the other.

402   *D. Dornisch / Telecommunications Policy 25 (2001) 381–407*

and meeting the "huge unmet demand in the Polish [telecommunications] market" noted in a recent World Bank technical paper (Bruce, Kessides, and Kneifel, 2000).

It is not likely that the next few years in Poland will bring a situation similar to the British one, where liberal market conditions are actively guarded by the state and its regulatory agencies (Oftel and the Department of Trade and Industry) (Vogel, 1996). Nevertheless, changes in the sector are presently occurring at such a fast rate that policy-makers will be forced to frequently reorient their positions. In the statements of some of the representatives of the Ministry of Communications (Płachecki, 1999) and TP SA (Rzepka, 1999), one can observe an increasing awareness of the fact that telecommunications has become a sector whose development is dependent on effective provision of services to demanding customers. They have recognized that the old model of treating telecommunications as a purely infrastructural sector, whose activity is oriented to maintaining its own internal stability and whose flexibility in responding to customer wishes is a secondary issue, is a thing of the past. Such changes provide hope for the activization of competition and the acceleration of development in the Polish telecommunications sector.

Acknowledgements

In Poland, I would like to express my deep appreciation for their comments and advice to Ewa Balcerowicz, Barbara Błaszczyk, Hanna Kontkiewicz-Chachulska, Andrzej Cylwik, Jerzy Gospodarek, Tadeusz Skoczny, and Zofia Włodarczyk. I especially appreciated the comments and advice of Andrzej Baniak at the Central European University in Budapest, Robin Mansell and Nick von Tunzelmann at the Science and Technology Policy Research Institute at Brighton University, and Slavo Radosevic at the University College London.

Appendix A. Independent local operators in Poland (as of 12/31/99) (Source: Kulisiewicz, 2000, p. 12).

	Operator	Group	Customers			
			Total	%	Town	Village
Total			530,192	100	381,179	149,013
1	Netia Telekom Silesia	Netia	82,374	15.5	82,374	0
2	Netia Telekom Telmedia	Netia	58,824	11.1	50,969	7855
3	El-Net	Elektrim	33,107	6.2	16,948	16,159
4	Netia Telekom Toruń	Netia	27,988	5.3	25,402	2586
5	Netia Telekom Kalisz	Netia	23,479	4.4	22,426	1053
6	Telekomunikacja Dębicka	Poland Telecom Operators	19,280	3.6	7177	12,103
7	Pilicka Telefonia		19,087	3.6	8992	101,095
8	Telefony Brzeskie	PTO	19,003	3.6	4086	14.917
9	Telefonia Lokalna Dialog		18,403	3.5	18,107	296
10	Netia Telekom Lublin	Netia	18,252	3.4	17,811	441
11	Retel	PTO	15,917	3.0	4647	11,270
12	Cuprum		14,378		13,705	673
13	Netia Telekom Mazowsze	Netia	13,357		9622	3735

Appendix A (*Continued*)

	Operator	Group	Customers			
			Total	%	Town	Village
14	Telefony Rzeszowskie Teler	PTO	13,084		1489	11,595
15	Netia Telekom Włocławek	Netia	12,452		12,452	0
16	Netia Telekom Ostrowiec	Netia	12,329		10,621	1708
17	Szeptel		12,031		2700	9331
18	Telefony Podlaskie		11,467		5344	6123
19	Elektrim TV-Tel	Elektrim	10,498		4536	5962
20	Netia Telekom Świdnik	Netia	10,356		9549	807
21	Telefonia Polska-Zachód	Elektrim	9385		9385	0
22	Netia Telekom Pila	Netia	9089		9089	0
23	Central-West Polish Telephones	PTO	8047		1920	6127
24	District Telephone Cooperative in Tyczyn		6960		1082	5878
25	Petrotel		6190		4985	1205
26	Telephone Cooperative Wist		5553		321	5232
27	Netia Telekom Warszawa	Netia	5262		3537	1725
28	Coal Company Rybnik		5259		5055	204
29	Telefony Opalenickie		4980		2289	2691
30	Centrala PT		4319		4319	0
31	Township Union of Wieluń Lands		3110		475	2635
32	Netia Telekom Modlin	Netia	2438		2242	196
33	Elterix		2141		1853	288
34	Intertel		1782		1373	409
35	Hard Coal Mine Bełchatów		1757		0	1757
36	Telecommunications Co-op Zbąszyń		1601		940	661
37	Telgram PT		1246		973	273
38	Hydroplant Żarnowiec		1120		0	1120
39	Regional Development Agency Arreks		1021		0	1021
40	Ertel		892		892	0
41	Hard Coal Mine Bogdanka		806		60	746
42	Telefonia Regionalna		678		678	0
43	COIG		476		476	0
44	Telbeskid		414		278	136

404   *D. Dornisch / Telecommunications Policy 25 (2001) 381–407*

Appendix B

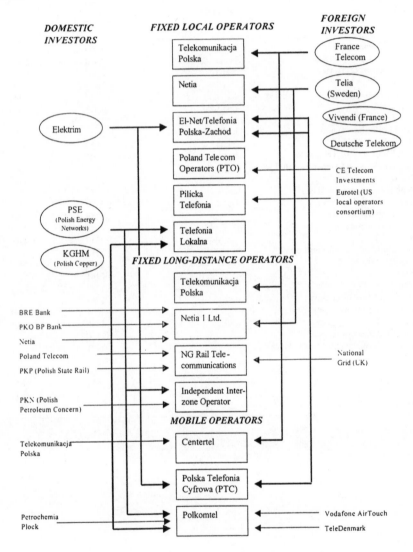

References

Bar, F., Cohen, S., Cowhey, P., DeLong, B., Kleeman, M., & Zysman, J. (2000). Access and innovation policy for the third-generation internet. *Telecommunications Policy, 24*(6/7).

Baum, J., Singh. I. (Eds.) (1994). Evolutionary dynamics of organizations. New York: Oxford University Press.

Bielański, P. J. (1998a). Telefony na sprzedaż. (Telephones for sale.). *Raport Teleinfo, 7*(3), 14–23.

Bielański, P. J. (1998b). Stuknał milion komórek. (One million cellular customers.). *Raport Teleinfo, 7*(3), 34–43.

Bień, K., Kasprów, R., Margas, D., & Marszałek, A. (2000). Walka o warszawski rynek. (The battle for the Warsaw market.) *Rzeczpospolita* (20.V).

Blaszczak, A. (1999). Jest pomysł i grupa, będą pieniądze. (There's an idea and a group, and the money's coming.) *Rzeczpospolita* (12.III).

Bruce, R., Kessides, I., & Kneifel, L. (2000). Overcoming obstacles to liberalization of the Telecom sector in Estonia, Poland, the Czech Republic, Slovenia, and Hungary. World Bank Technical Paper No. 440, The World Bank, Washington.

Brzuszkiewicz, J. (1999). Telefoniczna wojna małego z dużym. (The telephone war of the big versus the small.) *Gazeta w Lublinie* (7.IV).

Burak, A. (2000). Monopol trzyma się mocno. (The monopoly holds on strong.) *Rzeczpospolita* (26.VIII).

Communications International. (1998). *Telecoms liberalisation in Europe.* London: Communications International.

Davies, A. (1994). *Telecommunications and politics: The decentralised alternative.* London: Pinter Publishers.

Economides, N. (1995). Principles of interconnection. Paper submitted to the New Zealand Ministry of Commerce (http://www.stern.nyu.edu/networks/principl.pdf).

Fedorowicz. H., & Świderek, T. (2001). Prawie 55 mln zł kary dla TP SA. (55 million Zloty fine for TP SA.) *Rzeczpospolita* (30.I).

Fronczak, K. (1998). Mam mnóstwo pytań—rozmowa z Meirem Srebernikiem, prezesem zarządu Netii SA. (I have many questions—discussion with Meir Srebernik, Chairman of the Board, Netia, Inc.) *Nowe Życie Gospodarcze* (Nr. 48. 29.XI), 11–13.

Gawron. P. (1996). Prywatyzacja Giganta. (Privatizing the giant.) *Życie Gospodarcze* (16.VIII), 24–26.

Gospodarek. J. (1997). Ustawa o łączności z 1990 r. i jej zmiany na drodze Polski do Unii Europejskiej. (The Telecommunications Law of 1990 and its modification on the road to the European Union.) In: P. Jasiński & T. Skoczny. *Telekomunikacja*, Warsaw: Regulatory Policy Research Centre, Oxford University and Centrum Europejskie Uniwersytetu Warszawskiego.

Graack, C. (1997). Infrastructure investments and regulation in telecommmunications. Discussion Paper 31, Europäisches Institut für internationale Wirtschaftsbeziehungen (EIIW), Potsdam.

Gruber, H. (1999). Competition and innovation: The diffusion of mobile telecommunications in Central and Eastern Europe. Draft, European Investment Bank.

Grupa Warsztatowa, IV. (1996). Praktyki monopolistyczne Telekomunikacji Polskiej S.A. na przykładzie dopuszczania na rynek innych operatorów (1994–1995). (Monopoly practices of TP SA in the area of new operator entry.) Unpublished manuscript, Warszawa: Krajowa Szkoła Administracji Publicznej.

Guz, J. (1999). Ewolucja rynku telekomunikacyjnego w Polsce. (Evolution of the telecommunications market in Poland.) *Presented at the seminar Deregulacja monopoli naturalnych na przykładzie rynku telekomunikacyjnego. (Deregulation of natural monopolies: The example of telecommunications.)* Warsaw, June 21.

Harris, R. (1999). Regulacje prawne Unii Europejskiej dla telekomunikacji. (European Union legal regulations in telecommunications.) *Presented at the seminar Deregulacja monopoli naturalnych na przykładzie rynku telekomunikacyjnego. (Deregulation of natural monopolies: The example of telecommunications.)* Warsaw, June 21.

Jamison, M. A. (1998). Emerging patterns in global telecommunications alliances and mergers. *Industrial and Corporate Change. 7*(4), 695–714.

Kontkiewicz-Chachulska, H., Kubasik, J. (1997). Przemiany w sektorze telekomunikacyjnym w Polsce po roku 1989. (Changes in the Polish Telecommunications Sector after 1989.) In: P. Jasiński & T. Skoczny, *Telekomunikacja*. Warsaw: Regulatory Policy Research Centre, Oxford University and Centrum Europejskie Uniwersytetu Warszawskiego.

Kontkiewicz-Chachulska, H., & Kubasik, J. (1998). Emerging liberalised telecommmunications market: Interconnection and tariff policy in Poland. Draft.

Kulisiewicz, T. (1998a). Polski rynek telekomunikacyjny w 1997 roku. (The Polish telecommunications market in 1997.). *Teleinfo, 500*, 138–150.

Kulisiewicz, T. (1998b). Niełatwe zadania: rozmowa z Andrzejem Zielińskim, Ministrem Łączności w latach 1993–97. (A difficult task: Discussion with Andrzej Zieliński, Minister of Communications, 1993–97.). *Raport Teleinfo, 7*(3), 4–9.

Kulisiewicz, T. (1999). Telekomunikacja przed eksplozją. (Telecommunications before the explosion.). *Teleinfo, 500*, 182–199.

Kulisiewicz, T. (2000). Polski rynek telekomunikacyjny w 1999 roku. (The Polish telecommunications market in 1999.). *Teleinfo, 500*, 2–23.

Margas, D. (1999a). Operatorzy łączcie się. (Operators unite.) *Rzeczpospolita* (10.II).

Margas, D. (1999b). Wpłynęły trzy oferty. (Three offers in.) *Rzeczpospolita* (26.XI).

Margas, D. (2000a). Trzy nowe firmy. (Three new firms.) *Rzeczpospolita* (28.I).

Margas, D. (2000b). Konieczne pośrednictwo TP SA. (TP SA's mediation necessary.) *Rzeczpospolita* (13.V).

Margas, D., & Świderek, T. (1999). Trzeci operator GSM. (The third GSM operator) *Rzeczpospolita* (22.IV).

Matav. (1999). *1999 Annual report*. Budapest.

Metaxas, G. (1998). Regulacja polskiego runku telekomunikacyjnego—porównanie z liberalizacją w UE. (Regulation of the Polish telecommunications market—comparisons with liberalization in the EU.). In S. Umiński (Ed.), *Wykorzystanie Doswiadczeń Unii Europejskiej w Procesie Liberalizacji Sektora Telekomunikacyjnego w Polsce*. *Transformacja Gospodarki #98*. Gdańsk: Instytut Badań nad Gospodarką Rynkową.

Meth-Cohn, D. (1999). High stakes. *Business Central Europe* (September).

Piatek, S. (1997). Nowe prawo telekomunikacyjne. (The new telecommunications law.) In: P. Jasiński, & T. Skoczny, *Telekomunikacja*. Warsaw: Regulatory Policy Research Centre, Oxford University and Centrum Europejskie Uniwersytetu Warszawskiego.

Plachecki, A. (1999). Rozwój telekomunikacji jako czynnik stymulujący wzrost gospodarczy oraz wzrost dochodów budżetu państwa. (The development of telecommunications as a factor stimulating economic growth and the growth of state budgetary revenues.) *Presented at the seminar Deregulacja monopoli naturalnych na przykładzie rynku telekomunikacyjnego. (Deregulation of natural monopolies: The example of telecommunications.)* Warsaw, June 21.

Ronin, M. (2000). Plus na plusie, Era ze stratą. (Plus in the black, Era with a loss) *Teleinfo* 36 (4.IX).

Różyński, P. (1997). Operator numer 1. (Operator number 1.). *Raport Teleinfo, 6*(7), 13–16.

Różyński, P. (2000). Czysta formalność. (A pure formality.) *Teleinfo* 6, http:www.teleinfo.com.pl/ti/2000/06/t10.html.

Rutkowski, P. (1993) Własny telefon. (Your own telephone.) *Rzeczpospolita* (28.VII).

Rutkowski, P. (1999). Deregulacja rynku telekomunikacyjnego w polityce gospodarczej. (Deregulation of the telecommunications market in economic policy) *Presented at the seminar Deregulacja monopoli naturalnych na przykładzie rynku telekomunikacyjnego. (Deregulation of natural monopolies: The example of telecommunications.)* Warsaw, June 21.

Rzepka, P. (1999). Tworzenie rynku telekomunikacyjnego—deregulacja monopolisty szansą czy zagrożeniem dla rozwoju sektora? (Creating the telecommunications market—deregulation of a monopolist: Chance or threat for sectoral development?) *Presented at the seminar Deregulacja monopoli naturalnych na przykładzie rynku telekomunikacyjnego. (Deregulation of natural monopolies: The example of telecommunications.)* Warsaw, June 21.

Schamis, H. (1998). The politics of economic reform: Distributional coalitions and policy change in Latin America. Kellogg Institute Paper #250. University of Notre Dame.

Stachów, L. (1998). Projekt urzędu nieżaleinego regulatora telekomunikacyjnego w Polsce. (Project for an Independent Telecommunications Regulatory Body in Poland.) In: S. Umiński, *Wykorzystanie Doswiadczeń Unii Europejskiej w Procesie Liberalizacji Sektora Telekomunikacyjnego w Polsce*. Transformacja Gospodarki #98. Gdańsk: Instytut Badań nad Gospodarką Rynkową.

Streżyńska, A. (1997). Przeciwdziałanie praktykom monopolistycznym w telekomunikacji w latach 1990–1996. (Counteracting monopoly practices in telecommunications, 1990–96.). In P. Jasiński, & T. Skoczny (Eds.), *Telekomunikacja* (pp. 12–24). Warsaw: Regulatory Policy Research Centre, Oxford University and Centrum Europejskie Uniwersytetu Warszawskiego.

Świderek, T. (1999). Wzrost przychodów i straty: wyniki roczne Netia holdings. (Income gains and losses: Netia's yearly economic results.) *Rzeczpospolita* (15.III).

Świderek, T. (2000). Obniżki kosztów nie będzie. (No price reductions.) *Rzeczpospolita* (15.VII).

Telekomunikacja Polska, S. A. (1998). Skrócona wersja Prospektu Sprzedaży Akcji. (Shortened version of stock emission prospectus.) *Gazeta Wyborcza* (5.X).

Vogel, S. (1996). *Freer markets, more rules.* Ithaca, NY: Cornell University Press.

Welfens, P., & Wiegert, R. (1997). Transformation policies, regulation of telecommunications and foreign direct investment in transforming economies. Discussion Paper 32, Europäisches Institut für internationale Wirtschafts-beziehungen (EIIW), Potsdam.

Winiecki, J. (1999). Projekt Ustawy: 'Prawo Telekomunikacyjne'. (Project of draft legislation: Telecommunications Law.) Towarzystwo Ekonomistów Polskich, Ośrodek Monitorowania Inicjatyw Legislacyjnych. Raport nr 18/99.

Włodarczyk, Z. (1997). Polityka telekomunikacyjna a polityka konkurencji. (Telecommunications policy and competition policy.) In: P. Jasiński, & T. Skoczny, *Telekomunikacja.* (pp. 12–24) Warsaw: Regulatory Policy Research Centre, Oxford University and Centrum Europejskie Uniwersytetu Warszawskiego.

Zwierzchowski, Z. (1998). Tel-Energo i Kolpak. *Raport Teleinfo*, 7(3), 48–51.

Zwierzchowski, Z. (1999). Łączność z pradem i koleją. (Communications in energy and the rail system.) *Rzeczpospolita* (11.III).

[25]

How Does Privatization Work? Evidence from the Russian Shops

Nicholas Barberis

Harvard University

Maxim Boycko

Russian Privatization Center

Andrei Shleifer

Harvard University

Natalia Tsukanova

Boston Consulting Group

We use a survey of 452 Russian shops, most of which were privatized between 1992 and 1993, to measure the importance of alternative channels through which privatization promotes restructuring. Restructuring is measured as major renovation, a change in suppliers, an increase in hours stores stay open, and layoffs. There is strong evidence that the presence of new owners and new managers raises the likelihood of restructuring. In contrast, there is no evidence that equity incentives of old managers promote restructuring. The evidence points to the critical role new human capital plays in economic transformation.

We are grateful to Anna Ackerman for research assistance; to Gary Becker, Bengt Holmstrom, Larry Katz, Kevin M. Murphy, Jim Poterba, Sherwin Rosen, Robert Vishny, two anonymous referees, and seminar participants at Chicago, Harvard, the National Bureau of Economic Research, and Stanford for many helpful comments; and to the National Science Foundation for support of this research.

[*Journal of Political Economy*, 1996, vol. 104, no. 4]

I. Introduction

A number of recent studies have testified to the benefits of private as opposed to state ownership of firms. One research strand compares private and state firms in the same line of activity, such as air transport or railroads, and finds the former to be more efficient (see Vining and Boardman [1992] for a survey). A second strand reveals the improvements in a given company's operations following privatization (see Megginson, Nash, and van Randenborgh 1994). A third strand documents the lower cost of contracting public services to private suppliers than providing it publicly (see Donahue 1989). This research makes a convincing case for the greater efficiency of private ownership.

It is less clear from the existing research exactly how private ownership leads to greater efficiency. One commonly accepted view is that private owners have stronger incentives than government appointees to maximize profits because they own equity and so bear the financial consequences of their decisions. Empirically, however, the case for incentives as the reason for greater efficiency of private ownership has not yet been established.

A second theory suggests that privatization works insofar as it selects owners and managers who are better at running firms efficiently. Managers of state firms are selected for their ability to get along with politicians, address political concerns, and lobby for assistance. In contrast, managers of private firms are selected for their ability to run them efficiently. In the short run, entrepreneurs buy privatizing firms precisely to restructure them and increase profits. In the long run, privatization changes selection criteria for new managers from political acceptability to market skills. On that theory, privatization works when it brings such new and different people to run firms.

The two theories, of course, are not mutually exclusive, but it is useful to know how much explanatory power each of them has. To this end, we have designed and conducted a survey of 452 shops in seven Russian cities.[1] Of these shops, 413 were privatized in 1992 and 1993 and will be the focus of our analysis. In addition, we surveyed 38 state shops and, by accident, one newly started private shop. The traditional Soviet shops were famous for their inefficiency. They stocked very few and very low quality goods, used much more space than they needed, provided horrible service, closed early, and hardly ever upgraded their appearance. All these shops needed restructuring, and they needed it fast. In 1992 and 1993, Russia privatized

---

[1] A related survey was conducted around the same time in Eastern Europe by Earle et al. (1994).

most of its shops. For this reason, the Russian shops present a good laboratory for testing theories of how privatization works.

The survey was conducted in 1992 and 1993 and asked questions on restructuring steps taken at these shops following privatization. The four restructuring steps that we analyze in this paper reflect the most obvious changes that socialist stores needed: major renovation, a change in suppliers to get different goods, an increase in working hours, and employee layoffs. The survey also contained questions on changes in ownership and management and on the structure of shareholdings. Finally, the survey looked at the method of privatization. This information is used here to shed light on the theories of how privatization works.

Understanding how privatization works has some interest for at least three reasons. First, it may help shed light on the successes and failures of privatization. As we describe below, in many instances privatization of shops in Russia has led to no changes at all, and it is not obvious, at first sight, what exactly accounts for the failures. Second, the analysis may shed light on the two theories we outlined, namely incentives (Holmstrom 1979) and human capital (Rosen 1992). Third, the analysis in this paper may help design future privatization programs and modify the ones that have already been put in place. If, for example, we discovered that incentives play a critical role, then the transfer of state property to insiders, such as the workers and the managers, which is always politically the easiest, would be attractive as long as insiders received cash flow incentives. If, in contrast, the data showed that new owners are critical, then the design of a privatization program should focus on management turnover both in the process of and after privatization, which makes transfers to insiders look less attractive. A good privatization program in this case would rely on insider incentives to the smallest politically feasible extent and would encourage competitive transfers of control via auctions and similar mechanisms.

Section II describes our survey. Section III presents basic empirical results on the effects of human capital and incentives on the postprivatization restructuring of shops. Section IV presents a conclusion.

II. Description of the Data

The analysis in this paper is based on responses to a survey of managers of 452 shops located in seven Russian cities. The cities are in all parts of Russia; they include Krasnodar (49 shops), Moscow (47), Nizhni Novgorod (61), Omsk (102), Smolensk (80), Voronezh (43), and Yaroslavl (70). The privatized shops were selected randomly from a comprehensive list of such shops offered by privatization officials in that city; the state shops were selected randomly from a similar list of shops that have not yet been privatized. The survey was conducted by us between June 1992 and August 1993. The privatization of shops in Russia started in April 1992, but almost 70 percent of the shops in our sample were privatized between October 1992 and March 1993. Because the survey was conducted so soon after the shops were privatized, we measured only the short-run restructuring effects of privatization. In the longer run, learning, product market competition, and further ownership changes might bring about further restructuring. Nonetheless, our approach is useful if one wants to understand how particular privatization strategies can have immediate effects.

Of the shops in the sample, 80 percent were food retail, 11 percent were other retail, and 9 percent were other services, such as barbers. Half of the shops had under 20 employees, with an average of 25 employees. We have no reason to believe that our sample of privatized shops is in any way unrepresentative.

The Russian law provides for two methods of privatizing shops. The first is an auction, conducted either by outcry or as a tender, in which the party that offers the highest price wins. The second is a competition, where various participants submit bids and criteria other than price, such as preservation of shop profile or employment, can be used to determine the winners. In addition, in some cities, especially Moscow, shops were illegally privatized via a noncompetitive sale to their managers and workers. Most cities have used a combination of privatization methods, although proportions differed across cities. In our sample, 35 percent of the privatized shops were sold to the workers, 25 percent in auctions, and 40 percent in competitions, although the workers could have also won an auction or a competition. Both auctions and competitions were highly competitive, with the median number of 11 participants.

Three-quarters of the privatization contracts contained some restrictions on the future activities of the shop. Of the privatization contracts that had restrictions, 96 percent restricted the future profile of activities for 3–5 years (e.g., a food shop could not be converted to an electronics shop for a certain period of time); 67 percent restricted layoffs, typically for only 1 year; and 12 percent required continued sale of goods to the poor at subsidized prices. Except for restrictions on layoffs and on prices to the poor, the vast majority of the surveyed shop managers did not consider the restrictions to be binding. In particular, as any recent visitor to Russia can testify, profile restrictions rarely bind since shops can always devote a small fraction of floor space to the original business and sell whatever they want in the rest of the space.

Our measures of shop restructuring were limited by two considerations. First, the survey had to be short so that busy shop managers would agree to be interviewed during the business day. In fact, the survey contained 41 questions and took about half an hour to administer. Second, as we learned from pilot surveys, we could not ask questions about sales, profits, wages, or any other parameters that could be interpreted by shop managers as coming from the government tax authorities. These two considerations prevented us from asking detailed questions from which we could infer changes in shop productivity. Rather, we opted for asking whether shops undertook particular restructuring steps and getting quick yes or no answers. The one exception to that is that we have a bit more information on how many suppliers shops changed.

We focus on four measures of shop restructuring, which represent the most tangible steps that could be taken in the first few months after privatization. The first measure is whether the shop has made a major renovation (*kapitalny remont*), which a Russian manager would have clearly interpreted as a major redesign and rebuilding of premises.[2] Major renovation has the advantage of being a significant step, but it also has the problem of requiring capital. Since new owners might just have better access to capital, as opposed to better human capital, major renovation under new owners is not conclusive evidence of the importance of human capital for restructuring. Moreover, new owners may renovate shops simply to suit their personal tastes, much like new owners in the West renovate shops (or houses) that worked perfectly well under old ownership. In this case, renovation under new ownership would not be evidence of efficiency improvements. Our additional measures of restructuring do not suffer from these alternative interpretations.

The second measure is whether the shop has changed over half of its suppliers. The shift from the traditional state suppliers to new private, or even state, suppliers is a significant step toward increasing the variety and quality of goods sold in a shop. Moreover, changing suppliers does not require physical capital and is unlikely to reflect solely the tastes of the new owners. The third measure—which also does not suffer from the problems of the major renovation variable—is whether the shop stays open longer than it did before. Finally, the fourth measure, which is probably the least informative about restructuring, is whether a shop has laid off employees. Privatized shops often experience an increase in business, and thus absence

---

[2] We also asked whether a shop had a minor renovation (*kosmetichesky remont*), which was a much more common restructuring measure than major renovation, but not one correlated with any of the determinants of restructuring investigated in this paper.

of employee layoffs does not represent a failure to restructure. Moreover, given that the workers are at least partial owners in many cases, wages are very low, and politicians are extremely hostile to unemployment, layoffs in many cases are not the wisest restructuring strategy, quite aside from the fact that they are restricted.

In our sample of 452 shops, 14.5 percent of the shops made a major renovation. In addition, 44 percent of the shops have changed at least a half of their suppliers. The principal reasons given for changing suppliers were access to new goods (78 percent of the answers), better service (45 percent), and lower prices (52 percent). Only 32 percent reported being abandoned by the old suppliers. A quarter of the shops reported that all their suppliers belonged to the private sector, and 40 percent stated that over half of the suppliers were private. Only 15.9 percent of the shops reported staying open longer hours, although 73 percent said that the work was more intensive. Finally, 44 percent of the shops reported that employees were dismissed, whereas only 19 percent reported that managers were dismissed. Far and away the dominant reason given for worker dismissal was inadequate qualifications (45 percent). Only 3 percent of the shops stated decreased demand as a reason, and 15 percent mentioned increased productivity.

Before asking how privatization affects restructuring, we can use our small sample of 38 state firms to ask *whether* privatization affects restructuring. In our sample, 16 percent of privatized firms had a major renovation, compared to 0 percent of state firms. The likelihood of major renovation indeed rises sharply as a result of privatization, confirming its validity as a restructuring measure. With other measures, the difference is not as drastic. The likelihood of changing over 50 percent of suppliers is 43 percent for privatized firms and 49 percent for state firms. Among privatized shops, 16.2 percent reported longer hours, compared to 13 percent of state shops. Finally, 44 percent of privatized shops have laid off employees, compared to 47 percent of state shops. These results can be interpreted in two ways. They may be suggesting that capital renovation and longer hours are the better restructuring measures since they are more closely associated with privatization. Alternatively—and we tend to favor this interpretation on the basis of our experience in Russia—these results may mean that badly done privatizations, of which there are many in this sample, may be no more effective in bringing about restructuring than state ownership.

Much of our analysis uses ownership information generated by the survey. We divided the potential owners after privatization into the workers, the old management, the new management, and two kinds of outside investor: a physical person and a legal entity. The difference between the last two categories of owners is not substantive since there usually are entrepreneurs even behind legal entities that are buying the shops. Of the 413 privatized shops, 353 specified their ownership structure. In almost 70 percent of these shops, old employees and managers retained some ownership, whereas a new manager appeared as an owner in 6 percent of the shops, an individual outside investor in 14 percent, and a firm-investor in 29 percent of the shops. The ownership structures fell into three distinct groups. In 183 cases (52 percent of the total), the shop was owned entirely by the workers and old managers, some of whom won it in an auction or competition. In 107 cases (30 percent of the total), the shop was owned entirely by new managers and outside investors. Only 63 cases (18 percent) had a mixed ownership structure.

Among shops owned by their workers and old managers, managers, on average, owned 56 percent of equity and workers owned 44 percent. Among shops owned entirely by new people, the shop was almost always owned 100 percent by only one category of owner (the manager, the individual investor, or the firm-investor). In 6 percent of the cases, this owner was the new manager; in 89 percent of the cases, the owner is an outside investor; and in only 5 percent of the cases, both the new investor and the new manager have ownership. Finally, in the residual category of 63 firms with both old and new owners, the dominant pattern was a combination of old workers and managers and an outside investor.

We use these ownership data in two ways. First, we use them to define measures of change in human capital of the owners of the shop. We identify new human capital with having 100 percent of the shop owned by a combination of a new manager, an individual investor, and a legal entity–investor. That is, we conclude that decisions are made by individuals with different human capital only if employees and old managers have no ownership in a shop. According to this measure, 30 percent of the shops were run with new human capital. We have experimented with defining new human capital if new people own 50 percent of the shares; the empirical results were similar but weaker.

We try to distinguish new ownership from new management. In this survey, management change is identified by an affirmative answer to the question of whether the shop had management layoffs. This measure is not perfect since it points to new management not only when the top manager was replaced by an outsider, but also when the top manager stayed but some of his subordinates were laid off, or when the top manager was laid off and replaced by his deputy. However, this is the only measure of new management we have. In our sample, management was changed at least partially in 19 percent of the cases. There is a substantial overlap between ownership change and management change. In fact, management changed in 39 percent of the cases in which ownership changed but in only 11 percent of the cases in which ownership did not change. As we mentioned, management layoffs did not necessarily lead to entirely new blood at the helm. In 31 percent of the cases in which a manager was laid off, the firm was still entirely owned by old managers and workers, whereas in 59 percent of the cases it was owned entirely by new people. Keeping this reservation in mind, we examine the effect of new management on restructuring.

The second purpose to which we put the ownership data is to test incentive theories. For that, we simply use information on management ownership and outside investor ownership. It is interesting that new managers were very rarely given ownership stakes. There are only six cases of new managers who are the sole owners and seven cases of new managers who own shares together with investors. These facts are surprising if ownership incentives were needed to motivate managers.

A fundamental problem we need to address is that the acquisition of shops by new owners, as well as the actual distribution of equity, might be endogenous: new owners and the distribution of equity might be selected optimally according to privatizing shops' needs. For example, if only some shops need major renovation and only new owners can provide capital for such renovation, then new owners would acquire only the shops that require renovation, creating a spurious correlation between new ownership and restructuring. Similarly, the distribution of equity might be endogenously determined by the characteristics of a given shop (see Demsetz and Lehn 1985). If this endogeneity problem drives our results, we cannot draw conclusions about the roles of human capital and equity incentives for restructuring.

To address this problem, we use the method of privatization and a measure of whether the shop was sold together with its premises as instruments for change in ownership and management, as well as for equity stakes. The idea is that the method and the procedure of privatization were determined before the actual winners emerged. These may be bad instruments if, for example, only the shops that needed restructuring were put up for auction and hence were likely to get new owners. However, it is very difficult to argue that our instruments do not work for supplier change and longer hours as measures of restructuring, since the method of privatization was in all likelihood not determined with these restructuring steps in mind. Thus, for at least some of our restructuring measures, we have adequate instruments to test the theories.

Finally, our hypotheses on the determinants of restructuring presume that the ownership structure and human capital allocation emerging from privatization matter. But if privatized shops can always be resold or equity stakes can always be redivided, then as long as privatization puts the shop in the private sector, who owns it does not matter. A consequence of this view is that some firms do not restructure not because they have managers with wrong human capital or bad incentives, but because it does not pay to attract managers with good human capital and incentives to these shops. Fortunately for our paper, this view is inconsistent with the facts. As of the time of the surveys, resale of Russian shops was virtually impossible and never happened in our sample. When shops were turned over to their workers, the contract typically restricted resale explicitly, allegedly to prevent speculation. Even in arm's-length privatizations, restrictions on land and real estate transfers prevented resale of shops. For these reasons, the ownership structures and human capital allocations that emerged from privatizations were not necessarily efficient and could not be easily altered. As a result, the theories we look at are actually testable with the data we have.

In sum, we have some measures of shop restructuring and its potential determinants. We also have some instruments for these determinants. In the next section, we examine the hypotheses concerning the role of human capital and incentives in restructuring empirically.

III. Evidence

This section is divided into three parts. First, we provide a simple overview of the results using conditional means of our restructuring variables. Second, we present ordinary least squares (OLS) regressions of our restructuring variables on measures of human capital change and incentives. Although our dependent variables are discrete, we use OLS with heteroskedasticity-corrected standard errors rather than probits to make the comparison of regressions and instrumental variable results easier. We have performed probits as well (and reported them in an earlier draft of the paper); the implied probabilities from probits are extremely close to OLS parameter estimates. The last subsection presents the instrumental variable estimates of the effects of human capital and incentives on restructuring.

Overview

The empirical work in our paper uses a somewhat smaller sample of firms than some of the raw statistics we described. The reason is that we need privatized firms for which we have data on both ownership

TABLE 1

PROBABILITY OF RESTRUCTURING

Variable	Renovation ($N = 331$)	Supplier Change ($N = 336$)	Longer Hours ($N = 334$)	Employee Layoffs ($N = 266$)
Unrestricted mean	.1360	.4524	.1647	.4624
Complete ownership change:				
No	.1026	.3849	.1555	.4639
Yes	.2165	.6186	.1875	.4583
Management layoffs:				
No	.1074	.4066	.125	.3973
Yes	.2623	.6508	.3387	.766
Management ownership:				
<23%	.1091	.4881	.1446	.3511
>23%	.1627	.4167	.1845	.5701
Outside investor ownership:				
=0	.1141	.369	.1658	.549
>0	.1633	.557	.1633	.3451
Shop owns its premises:				
No	.1131	.4533	.1518	.5054
Yes	.1818	.4505	.1909	.3625
Competitive sale method:				
No	.1197	.3058	.1441	.5169
Yes	.1355	.5209	.1745	.4206

NOTE.—Unconditional and conditional means of four measures of restructuring: renovation, one if capital renovation was done, and zero otherwise; supplier change, one if more than 50 percent of the suppliers were changed, zero otherwise; longer hours, one if longer hours were worked, zero otherwise; and employee layoffs, one if layoffs were made, zero otherwise. Complete ownership change is one if 100 percent of the owners are new to the firm, zero otherwise. Management layoffs is one if managers were laid off, zero otherwise. Management ownership is the percentage of the shop owned by the management, whether old or new. Outside investor ownership is the percentage of the shop owned by outsiders, whether physical or legal entities. A shop is sold in a competitive sale method if it is sold by auction or competition.

change and management layoffs. We are also restricted by incomplete responses to the questions about restructuring. With these cuts in the sample, we have 331 privatized shops for which we have data on renovation, 336 with data on supplier change, 334 with data on increases in hours the shop is open, and 266 with data on employee layoffs and on employment restrictions. In these four samples, major renovation occurs in 13.6 percent of the shops, a change in suppliers in 45.2 percent, an increase in hours in 16.5 percent, and a layoff in 46.2 percent, respectively.

Table 1 presents the probabilities of restructuring as a function of its potential determinants. The likelihood of renovation in firms without complete ownership change is 10 percent, compared to 22 percent for firms with complete ownership change. Similarly, complete ownership change raises the probability of a change in suppliers from 38 to 62 percent and that of an increase in hours from 15.5 to 19 percent. In contrast, complete ownership change has no effect on the likelihood of layoffs. Management change sharply raises the likelihood of renovation, supplier change, and increase in shop hours. It also raises the likelihood of layoffs considerably, although this result may simply mean that managers are laid off at the same time as the workers. The importance of management and ownership change for restructuring is the key result of this study.

Next, we divide shops into those in which the manager share is above the median of 23 percent and those in which it is below the median. Higher management ownership raises the likelihood of renovation, longer store hours, and layoffs, but not of supplier change. When we divide shops into those with zero and positive outside investor ownership, we find that positive investor ownership raises the odds of renovation and supplier change, though not of longer hours. In contrast, layoffs are more likely when outside investors own no shares. One problem with looking at conditional means is that higher management and investor ownership may be correlated with the presence of new managers and owners, who have an effect on restructuring because of their human capital.

Table 1 also shows that when the shops are auctioned or sold in a competition with criteria other than price alone, the likelihood of restructuring other than layoffs is higher than when they are sold to the old managers and workers at a low price. We argue below that the use of the auction method encourages restructuring in part because it facilitates human capital turnover.

Human Capital: OLS Results

The initial tests of the human capital theory are presented in table 2. We estimate regressions with four dependent variables: the renovation dummy, the change over half the suppliers dummy, the longer store hours dummy, and the employee layoffs dummy. The independent variables are the date of privatization relative to June 1992, in months (which can be negative), the complete change of ownership dummy, and the management layoff dummy. In the layoff regressions, we also control for layoff restrictions. We attempted to control for the city, the size of the shop, and the sector of the shop in the regressions, but these controls did not matter and so we did not use them in the results reported in this section and elsewhere in the paper.

Table 2 shows that restructuring takes time. Waiting 1 month gives a 1.4–1.6-percentage-point higher probability of renovation, a 1.9–2.2-percentage-point higher probability of a change in suppliers, a 1.2–1.6-percentage-point higher probability of longer store hours, and a 1.4–2.0-percentage-point higher probability of layoffs.

TABLE 2

RESTRUCTURING AS A FUNCTION OF HUMAN CAPITAL CHANGE

VARIABLE	RENOVATION (N = 331)			SUPPLIER CHANGE (N = 336)			LONGER HOURS (N = 334)			EMPLOYEE LAYOFFS (N = 266)		
	(1)	(2)	(3)	(4)	(5)	(6)	(7)	(8)	(9)	(10)	(11)	(12)
Constant	.265	.255	.238	.601	.597	.560	.317	.249	.26	.774	.641	.65
	(.067)	(.071)	(.070)	(.079)	(.082)	(.083)	(.067)	(.065)	(.066)	(.095)	(.098)	(.099)
Date	−.016	−.014	−.014	−.022	−.019	−.019	−.016	−.012	−.012	−.020	−.014	−.014
	(.006)	(.006)	(.006)	(.007)	(.007)	(.007)	(.006)	(.006)	(.005)	(.009)	(.008)	(.008)
Complete ownership change	.104		.071	.223		.178	.024		−.033	.025		−.093
	(.045)		(.051)	(.058)		(.071)	(.046)		(.045)	(.068)		(.080)
Management layoffs		.13	.087		.210	.125		.192	.2		.322	.329
		(.060)	(.088)		(.068)	(.103)		(.064)	(.099)		(.074)	(.102)
Complete ownership change × management layoff			.028			.033			.009			.05
			(.124)			(.139)			(.130)			(.149)
Layoff restrictions										−.172	−.142	−.122
										(.065)	(.063)	(.065)
Adjusted R^2	4.31	4.49	4.88	6.24	4.73	6.78	1.85	5.69	5.25	4.14	9.96	9.74

NOTE.—OLS regression estimates of the probability of four measures of restructuring as a function of the date since privatization and variables indicating human capital change. The measures of restructuring are renovation, one if capital renovation was done, and zero otherwise; supplier change, one if more than 50 percent of the suppliers were changed, zero otherwise; longer hours, one if longer hours were worked, zero otherwise; and employee layoffs, one if layoffs were made, zero otherwise. Date is the number of months after June 1992 that privatization occurred. Complete ownership change is one if 100 percent of the owners are new to the firm, zero otherwise. Management layoffs is one if managers were laid off, zero otherwise. The employee layoff regressions also control for layoff restrictions, one if restrictions were reported, zero otherwise. Heteroskedasticity-consistent standard errors are in parentheses.

Table 2 also shows that shops with completely new owners have a 10.4-percentage-point higher probability of renovation than shops without completely new owners, a large difference given that the overall likelihood of renovation in this subsample is only 13.6 percent. The comparable number for new managers is an even higher 13 percentage points. Both of these effects are statistically significant. In column 3, we include both new management and new ownership dummies as well as the interaction term. The incremental effect of new ownership on renovation when there is no management change is 7.1 percentage points and is not significant. The incremental effect of new management on renovation when there is no ownership change is 8.7 percentage points and is not significant either. However, the total effect of new management and ownership on the probability of renovation is 18.5 percentage points, with a t-statistic of 2.4. New human capital, measured by the combined management and ownership change, has a large effect on restructuring.

The increase in the probability of changing over half of the suppliers when owners change is a highly significant 22 percentage points, which is also quantitatively substantial given that the overall probability of supplier change is 45 percent. The increased probability of a change in suppliers when managers change is an also significant 21 percentage points. When we include both dummies and an interaction term in the regression, we continue getting a significant 17.8-percentage-point effect of new ownership without management change but an insignificant 12.5-percentage-point effect of new management without ownership change. The combined effect of new ownership and management is 33.6 percentage points, with a t-statistic of 4.2. Thus new owners together with new managers sharply raise the likelihood of changing over half of the suppliers.

For supplier change, we actually have more data, since we allowed shop managers to choose from four categories: changing no suppliers, changing over 90 percent of suppliers, changing about 25 percent of suppliers, and changing about 50 percent of suppliers. We have estimated the supplier change regression in table 2, as well as all the subsequent supplier change equations, using a more continuously defined measure of supplier change. Both in terms of parameter estimates and in terms of statistical significance, the results were similar to those we report.

The increase in the probability of longer hours is a statistically insignificant 2.4 percentage points and a statistically significant and large 19 percentage points when management changes. When both variables are included in the regression, the effect of new ownership is negative and insignificant, but the effect of new management is still a significant 20 percentage points. The combined effect of new human capital is 17.5 percentage points, with a *t*-statistic of 2.2.

The results are very different for employee layoffs. New ownership does not increase significantly the likelihood of layoffs. Perhaps the most plausible reason is that outside investors primarily buy shops in order to expand operations. In contrast, new management does increase the likelihood of layoffs by over 30 percentage points (which is large relative to the mean probability of layoffs of 44 percent). This result is highly statistically significant but has two interpretations. First, new managers may be more likely to lay off workers than old managers are. Second, old managers might get fired together with the workers, in which case management turnover is correlated with, but does not cause, employee layoffs. This difficulty of interpretation renders layoffs the least useful restructuring variable. The regression with both new ownership and new management confirms the insignificant net effect of the former and the significant net effect of the latter. The total incremental effect of new ownership and management is 29 percentage points, with a *t*-statistic of 3.1. The total effect comes from new management and hence has an ambiguous interpretation. Layoff restrictions do reduce the probability of layoffs by 12–17 percentage points, depending on specification.

In sum, new human capital, as measured by new ownership or new management, matters for restructuring, as measured by major shop renovations, supplier changes, and increases in store hours. The effects of these changes in human capital are quantitatively large and generally statistically significant. The results are more ambiguous for layoffs. The results are consistent with the human capital theory of how privatization works. Specifically, when new people acquire and control the shops, restructuring follows. In contrast, when old managers stay, as in the case in which shops are turned over to them and the workers, much less happens. Privatization works through turnover of human capital at the helm.

There is an alternative interpretation of the evidence on renovations, namely that new owners have money or access to loans, rather than skills, and hence can afford to renovate. Old managers and employees, in contrast, face capital market constraints. This story undoubtedly has some truth to it, but it does not explain the evidence on supplier changes and longer store hours, neither of which requires money but both of which are more likely with new owners. We thus continue to favor the human capital interpretation because it can explain the results for all three restructuring measures.

The more troublesome alternative story is that new ownership and management are endogenous. The shops in which the benefits of restructuring are the highest are the ones that attract new owners and managers. In contrast, the shops that do not need restructuring simply go to the managers and the workers. By this interpretation, shops with new owners restructure not because these owners have human capital suitable for restructuring, but because they are selected to be different shops. We take up this alternative story later in this section.

Incentives: OLS Results

Table 3 examines the effect of incentives on the likelihood of restructuring. As before, we run OLS using four measures of restructuring—renovation, change in suppliers, longer store hours, and employee layoffs—controlling for the date of privatization, which again shows up with both statistically significant and substantively large coefficients. We use two measures of incentives: total management ownership and total outside investor ownership. In layoff regressions, we control for restrictions on layoffs.

The likelihood of renovation is not significantly increased by higher management ownership. The coefficient in the regression with management ownership alone is in fact negative. When outside investor ownership is also included, the coefficient on management ownership becomes positive but still small and insignificant. The effect of outside investor ownership is also small and insignificant.

A better picture for incentives emerges from supplier change regressions. The coefficient on management ownership, when included alone, is again insignificant and "has the wrong sign." However, when outside investor ownership is also included, the regression implies a three-percentage-point rise in the probability of supplier change per 10-percentage-point increase in management ownership. Outside investor ownership is statistically significant both when included alone and in combination with management ownership. In the latter specification, the parameter estimate suggests a three-percentage-point increase in the probability of supplier change per 10-percentage-point rise in outside investor ownership. Outside investor ownership provides some incentives for supplier change, and perhaps management ownership does so as well.

The longer-hours regressions also suggest some effectiveness of equity ownership. Management ownership raises the likelihood of an hours increase by two percentage points per 10 percent increase in ownership—a relatively large effect. Outside investor ownership, when included alone, has no effect on this measure of restructuring. When both ownership variables are included, both coefficients are positive and significant, although quantitatively the effect of management ownership continues to be much larger. This result is not sur-

TABLE 3
RESTRUCTURING AS A FUNCTION OF CASH FLOW INCENTIVES

VARIABLE	RENOVATION (N = 353)			SUPPLIER CHANGE (N = 340)			LONGER HOURS (N = 338)			EMPLOYEE LAYOFFS (N = 266)		
	(1)	(2)	(3)	(4)	(5)	(6)	(7)	(8)	(9)	(10)	(11)	(12)
Constant	.393	.362	.304	.719	.607	.474	.257	.324	.151	.671	.786	.707
	(.076)	(.069)	(.090)	(.082)	(.077)	(.101)	(.066)	(.065)	(.077)	(.110)	(.093)	(.123)
Date	-.023	-.023	-.022	-.023	-.024	-.023	-.015	-.016	-.014	-.019	-.019	-.018
	(.006)	(.006)	(.006)	(.007)	(.007)	(.007)	(.005)	(.006)	(.005)	(.009)	(.008)	(.008)
Management ownership	-.000		.001	-.001		.003	.002		.003	.002		.002
	(.001)		(.001)	(.001)		(.001)	(.001)		(.001)	(.001)		(.002)
Outside investor ownership		.001	.001		.002	.003		-.000	.001		-.001	-.001
		(.000)	(.001)		(.001)	(.001)		(.000)	(.000)		(.001)	(.001)
Layoff restrictions										-.127	-.131	-.121
										(.068)	(.068)	(.068)
Adjusted R^2	4.34	4.99	5.06	2.41	5.74	6.48	3.43	1.75	4.66	5.39	5.20	5.18

NOTE.—OLS regression estimates of the probability of four measures of restructuring as a function of the date since privatization and variables measuring cash flow incentives. The measures of restructuring are renovation, one if capital renovation was done, and zero otherwise; supplier change, one if more than 50 percent of the suppliers were changed, zero otherwise; longer hours, one if longer hours were worked, zero otherwise; and employee layoffs, one if layoffs were made, zero otherwise. Date is the number of months after June 1992 that privatization occurred. Management ownership is the percentage of the shop owned by the management, whether old or new. Outside investor ownership is the percentage of the shop owned by outsiders, whether physical or legal entities. The employee layoffs regressions also control for layoff restrictions, one if restrictions were reported, zero otherwise. Heteroskedasticity-consistent standard errors are in parentheses.

TABLE 4

RESTRUCTURING AS A FUNCTION OF MANAGEMENT OWNERSHIP

VARIABLE	SUBSAMPLE: NO COMPLETE OWNERSHIP CHANGE AND NO MANAGEMENT LAYOFFS			
	Renovation (N = 172)	Supplier Change (N = 174)	Longer Hours (N = 174)	Employee Layoffs (N = 143)
Constant	.263	.456	1.866	.472
	(.095)	(.132)	(.088)	(.188)
Date	−.016	−.014	.008	−.019
	(.007)	(.010)	(.006)	(.012)
Management ownership	−.000	.001	−.002	.001
	(.001)	(.002)	(.001)	(.002)
Layoff restrictions				.117
				(.085)
Adjusted R^2	2.44	.14	1.30	1.83

NOTE.—OLS regression estimates of the probability of four measures of restructuring as a function of the date since privatization and management ownership, a variable measuring cash flow incentives, within a subsample in which no managers were laid off and people new to the shop own less than 50 percent of the shop. The measures of restructuring are renovation, one if capital renovation was done, and zero otherwise; supplier change, one if more than 50 percent of the suppliers were changed, zero otherwise; longer hours, one if longer hours were worked, zero otherwise; and employee layoffs, one if layoffs were made, zero otherwise. Date is the number of months after June 1992 that privatization occurred. Management ownership is the percentage of the shop owned by the management, whether old or new. The employee layoffs regressions also control for layoff restrictions, one if restrictions were reported, zero otherwise. Heteroskedasticity-consistent standard errors are in parentheses.

prising if store managers, rather than owners, are primarily responsible for keeping them open longer.

The evidence on employee layoffs is the least conclusive. There is a marginally significant but small effect of higher management ownership on the probability of layoffs, which becomes insignificant once outside investor ownership is controlled for. The coefficient on outside investor ownership is insignificant and has the wrong sign. Cash flow ownership does not provide a strong incentive to lay people off.

Although the results in table 3 offer some support for the role of cash flow incentives in raising the probability of restructuring, their interpretation is ambiguous. Specifically, new human capital variables and ownership variables are probably correlated, and high ownership might proxy for human capital change. One way to address this problem in our data is to focus on situations in which human capital is old. Specifically, we look at the subsample in which less than 50 percent of the shares are owned by new people *and* managers are not laid off, and we estimate the likelihood of restructuring as a function of old management ownership. These results, presented in table 4, show no evidence of a significant positive effect of higher management ownership on the likelihood of renovation, supplier change, or increase in store hours and a negative effect on layoffs. This result, in our opinion, is a setback for the view that equity ownership incentives, without human capital change, promote the restructuring of shops. What explains these results? We are aware of five possible interpretations.[3]

First, it is possible that, in shops, managerial effort is largely observable by owners, and hence there is no reason to rely on equity ownership as an incentive device. The fact that, when new owners hire new managers, they do not give them any equity is consistent with this view. Shops thus do not provide a useful laboratory for testing the role of equity incentives. While this view has some merit, we are not entirely convinced. The so-called sponsors who are the owners of shops are often entrepreneurs operating in many diverse lines of business. They are unlikely to keep an eye on managers intensively enough to be able to do without equity incentives.

Second, incentives may take the form of ex post settling up rather than ex ante ownership. The owner and the manager might simply reach an understanding that, if a shop does well, the owner will reward the manager. We are not fully persuaded by this argument either. After all, many of the new shop owners have earned their money in semilegal activities, and their reputations are not pristine. To a manager, equity should be a safer bet. Moreover, even if owners use other incentives, management equity ownership should provide, on the margin, an extra incentive for restructuring.

Third, it is possible that, by focusing on share ownership, we are looking at the wrong margin of incentives. Even if ownership incentives are strong, shops controlled by insiders may be less likely to be restructured simply because the effort cost of restructuring is too high for the workers, and they would rather continue their old working habits unless forced to change them by the new owners. Under this theory, new owners restructure not because they have the appropriate human capital, but because they do not fully bear the cost of higher worker effort. Thus, even if new owners pay higher wages for getting more work out of the old employees, they still can extract some of the rents from the workers. Because the workers pay the full effort cost of restructuring, they do not have an incentive to support the restructuring when they share control. This argument is similar to that made by Shleifer and Summers (1988) in the context of hostile takeovers.

This theory faces both theoretical and empirical difficulties. To get

---

[3] Following Morck, Shleifer, and Vishny (1988), we checked for a systematic nonlinear relationship between management ownership and the probability of restructuring, and we found none.

people to work harder, new owners must pay higher wages and so face the same cost of extracting higher effort as worker-owners do. If the workers were getting such large rents from their jobs before privatization, they would have tried to stop privatization of their shops or quit after new owners gained control. If anything, the evidence seems to be the reverse: resistance to small-scale privatization is low and few people quit (or are laid off) after new owners gain control. This theory also has trouble explaining why the old managers are not more likely to restructure when their ownership increases, even though the cost to them of extracting rents from the workers stays constant while benefits rise.

The fourth interpretation of the share ownership evidence is that equity incentives are not nearly as important as new human capital for the restructuring of shops. The old managers simply do not have the skills to restructure, at least in the short period of time over which we observe these shops. Even with incentives, one cannot teach an old dog new tricks.

Finally, the fifth possibility is endogeneity. In the case of ownership, this explanation would argue that shops are heterogeneous, and different ones require different management and outsider ownership to provide optimal incentives. In a cross section, then, there is no necessary relationship between equity ownership and performance, as in the argument made by Demsetz and Lehn (1985). Below we deal with the possibility of endogeneity of new owners and equity ownership.

Human Capital and Incentives: Two-Stage Least Squares Results

In this subsection, we try to address the selection argument. This argument is based fundamentally on unobserved heterogeneity of shops. It states that new owners and equity shares are selected endogenously to suit different needs of different shops. New owners and managers appear only in shops that need restructuring, and therefore the positive correlation between new ownership and restructuring is spurious. Optimal equity ownership differs across shops, and hence there is no obvious correlation between it and restructuring in equilibrium. Thus all of our evidence can be explained by these selection arguments.

Before we test the selection argument empirically, we want to stress that we find it ex ante quite unconvincing, for several reasons. First, even if one believed that new owners are selected endogenously for some shops, there is a question of *why* new owners are needed for restructuring of these shops. After all, insiders could always buy the shops a lot cheaper. One possibility is that new owners provide capital for restructuring, which is needed only in some shops, and which old owners do not have access to. But this possibility is inconsistent with our evidence that new owners are also more likely to change suppliers and to keep the shops open longer—the two restructuring strategies that do not require capital. An alternative possibility, of course, is that new owners are selected into shops that need restructuring because these owners have the appropriate human capital. This possibility is consistent with our view.

Second, it is not clear to us, on the basis of our experience in Russia, that the new owners actually do get the shops that need restructuring most. If anything, the shops that benefit the most from restructuring are the ones that workers and managers would lobby the hardest to keep for themselves. In the city of Moscow, such lobbying turned privatization of shops into outright giveaways to the insiders, and Moscow surely has some of the most valuable shops, which can benefit a lot from restructuring. The selection argument, then, is less appealing than it seems initially.

Nonetheless, we try to address this argument empirically as well. To this end, we use three instruments for the potentially endogenous variables: a dummy equal to one if the shop was sold in an auction, a dummy equal to one if the shop was sold in a competition, and a dummy equal to one if the shop was sold together with its premises. These variables are likely to be correlated with ownership and management change, as well as resulting ownership structure. The question is, Are they also uncorrelated with the unobserved urgency of restructuring shops? For the case of capital renovation, one could argue that we do not have adequate instruments. To attract new owners to those shops that need capital renovation, local officials might put up these shops for auctions and competitions, as well as include the premises in the privatization package. In this case, our instruments are correlated with the unobserved need for renovation. However, this argument is implausible for the longer store hours and supplier change variables. Local officials are unlikely to select for auctions the shops that could benefit from staying open longer or need to change some suppliers, and the shops that need capital renovation the most are unlikely to be the very same shops that most urgently require other restructuring measures. Thus, for supplier change and longer store hours, we do have theoretically plausible instruments.

Table 5 presents the results of the first-stage instrumental variable OLS regressions. The method of privatization has a very large and statistically significant effect on all the dependent variables: complete ownership change, management layoff, management ownership, and

Privatization and Globalization

TABLE 5

PREDICTING HUMAN CAPITAL CHANGE AND OWNERSHIP

Variable Being Instrumented	Complete Ownership Change (N = 327)	Management Layoffs (N = 327)	Management Ownership (N = 331)	Outside Investor Ownership (N = 331)
Constant	.108	.264	47.144	1.208
	(.058)	(.074)	(4.432)	(5.486)
Date	−.013	−.021	−.124	−.198
	(.006)	(.006)	(.372)	(.521)
Shop owns its premises	.109	.050	−9.166	15.156
	(.048)	(.045)	(2.797)	(4.332)
Auction dummy	.488	.266	−20.726	51.336
	(.056)	(.058)	(3.933)	(5.256)
Competition dummy	.387	.108	−24.241	49.500
	(.045)	(.041)	(2.745)	(4.264)
Adjusted R^2	23	10.9	21.1	32.5

NOTE.—First-stage results from a two-stage least squares procedure in which the variables measuring human capital change and the cash flow incentives are regressed on four instrumental variables. Complete ownership change is one if 100 percent of the owners are new to the firm, zero otherwise. Management layoffs is one if managers were laid off, zero otherwise. Management ownership is the percentage of the shop owned by the management, whether old or new. Outside investor ownership is the percentage of the shop owned by outsiders, whether physical or legal entities. The instrumental variables are date, the number of months since June 1992 that privatization occurred; a dummy variable taking the value one if shop owners also own the premises; a dummy variable taking the value one if the shop was sold off in an auction; and a dummy variable taking the value one if the shop was sold off in a competition. Heteroskedasticity-consistent standard errors are in parentheses.

outside investor ownership. Shops privatized through an auction or competition are more likely to change owners and managers, and to have low management and high outsider ownership, than shops turned over to the workers. These effects are not surprising, but suggest that we have good instruments.

More interesting, the inclusion of premises in the privatization significantly raises the likelihood of complete ownership change, as well as reduces management and raises outside shareholder ownership. It has no effect on the likelihood of management layoffs. The inclusion of premises may offer the buyer of a shop better property rights than a lease from the local government, which is the principal alternative way to get access to space. This greater security of property rights might therefore attract new owners who want to invest in the shop, consistent with the theories of Grossman and Hart (1986). In fact, our survey investigated a bit further the issue of security of access to space. In the sample, 33 percent of the shops owned their premises, and the remaining leased them from the local governments. Over 97 percent of the shop managers said that the terms of the rent were defined, 67 percent reported the duration of leases of over 10 years, and 72 percent said that their leases contained an option to buy. At the same time, 29 percent of the shop managers said that their rent changed every month, and 37 percent indicated that the rates of growth of rent were not defined, which suggests considerable residual power of the landlords. While we cannot vouch for the security of ownership of premises against regulatory expropriation by the bureaucrats, ownership still seems more secure than leasing. It is not surprising, therefore, that inclusion of premises attracts new owners, who own a lot of equity and give little to their managers.

Table 6 presents the second-stage results of the instrumental variable procedure. The magnitude of the effect of ownership change on the probability of renovation increases, although the effect is no longer statistically significant. The effect of management change on renovation remains marginally significant.[4] The effects of new ownership and new management on supplier change and increase in store hours are quantitatively larger than in OLS and still statistically significant. Complete ownership change raises the likelihood of supplier change by 56 percentage points and that of longer hours by 17 percentage points. The corresponding effects for management layoffs are 115 percentage points and 57 percentage points, respectively. The instrumental variable evidence thus confirms that new human capital encourages restructuring, consistent with our theoretical skepticism about the selection story.

Table 7 presents the second-stage regressions for the equity ownership variables. As in table 3, some, though by no means all, of the coefficients on the incentive variables are significant either statistically or substantively. However, we have the same problem as in table 3 of the correlation of high outside investor ownership and low management ownership with new owners and managers. Consequently, we need to look at the instrumental variable results for the subset of shops that did not change owners and managers, as in table 4. This is possible to do since in many cases insiders won an auction or a competition. Indeed, the first-stage regression shows that, in this subsample, management ownership is lower in shops privatized through auction or competition, as well as in shops that own their premises. The second-stage results, presented in table 8, are similar to those in table 4. They show no significant effects of (predicted) management ownership on the probability of any restructuring measure we analyze. This evidence, as before, is not supportive of the importance of equity ownership by the old managers for the restructuring of privatized shops.

---

[4] Even though we expressed a theoretical doubt concerning the validity of our instruments for the renovation equation, a $\chi^2(2)$ test fails to reject the null hypothesis that the instruments are exogenous.

TABLE 6

TWO-STAGE LEAST SQUARES ESTIMATES OF THE EFFECTS OF HUMAN CAPITAL CHANGE

VARIABLE	RENOVATION (N = 327)		SUPPLIER CHANGE (N = 332)		LONGER HOURS (N = 330)		EMPLOYEE LAYOFFS (N = 265)	
	(1)	(2)	(3)	(4)	(5)	(6)	(7)	(8)
Constant	.260	.164	.494	.206	.258	.088	.808	.928
	(.076)	(.108)	(.090)	(.161)	(.071)	(.107)	(.102)	(.174)
Date	−.017	−.010	−.021	.002	−.014	−.003	−.021	−.027
	(.006)	(.008)	(.008)	(.012)	(.006)	(.008)	(.009)	(.012)
Complete ownership change	.129		.557		.172		−.187	
	(.091)		(.116)		(.094)		(.181)	
Management layoffs		.360		1.158		.572		−.379
		(.194)		(.328)		(.213)		(.336)
Layoff restrictions							−.129	−.193
							(.074)	(.074)

NOTE.—Second-stage results of a two-stage least squares procedure in which four measures of restructuring are regressed on fitted values of the explanatory variables. The measures of restructuring are renovation, one if capital renovation was done, and zero otherwise; supplier change, one if more than 50 percent of the suppliers were changed, zero otherwise; longer hours, one if longer hours were worked, zero otherwise; and employee layoffs, one if layoffs were made, zero otherwise. The explanatory variables are date, the number of months after June 1992 that privatization occurred; complete ownership change, one if 100 percent of the owners are new to the firm, zero otherwise; and management layoffs, one if managers were laid off, zero otherwise. The employee layoffs regressions also control for layoff restrictions, one if restrictions were reported, zero otherwise. First-stage results are in table 5. Heteroskedasticity-consistent standard errors are in parentheses.

TABLE 7

TWO-STAGE LEAST SQUARES ESTIMATES OF THE EFFECTS OF INCENTIVES

VARIABLE	RENOVATION (N = 331)			SUPPLIER CHANGE (N = 336)			LONGER HOURS (N = 334)			EMPLOYEE LAYOFFS (N = 265)		
	(1)	(2)	(3)	(4)	(5)	(6)	(7)	(8)	(9)	(10)	(11)	(12)
Constant	.362	.272	−.225	.957	.538	−1.205	.370	.279	−1.171	.607	.777	−.775
	(.083)	(.071)	(.552)	(.110)	(.083)	(1.121)	(.087)	(.066)	(.878)	(.191)	(.096)	(2.239)
Date	−.018	−.018	−.015	−.028	−.026	−.016	−.016	−.016	−.008	−.017	−.018	−.013
	(.006)	(.006)	(.007)	(.008)	(.007)	(.015)	(.006)	(.006)	(.011)	(.009)	(.009)	(.016)
Management ownership	−.002		.010	−.008		.036	−.002		.030	.004		.032
	(.002)		(.011)	(.002)		(.023)	(.002)		(.018)	(.004)		(.045)
Outside investor ownership		.001	.006		.004	.022		.001	.015		−.001	.013
		(.001)	(.005)		(.001)	(.011)		(.000)	(.009)		(.002)	(.021)
Layoff restrictions										−.103	−.126	.027
										(.088)	(.079)	(.257)

NOTE.—Second-stage results of a two-stage least squares procedure in which four measures of restructuring are regressed on fitted values of the explanatory variables. The measures of restructuring are renovation, one if capital renovation was done, and zero otherwise; supplier change, one if more than 50 percent of the suppliers were changed, zero otherwise; longer hours, one if longer hours were worked, zero otherwise; and employee layoffs, one if layoffs were made, zero otherwise. The explanatory variables are date, the number of months after June 1992 that privatization occurred; management ownership, the percentage of the shop owned by the management, whether old or new; and outside investor ownership, the percentage of the shop owned by outsiders, whether physical or legal entities. The employee layoff regressions also control for layoff restrictions, one if restrictions were reported, zero otherwise. First-stage results are in table 5. Heteroskedasticity-consistent standard errors are in parentheses.

787

TABLE 8

TWO-STAGE LEAST SQUARES ESTIMATES OF THE EFFECTS OF INCENTIVES

	SUBSAMPLE: NO COMPLETE OWNERSHIP CHANGE AND NO MANAGEMENT LAYOFFS			
VARIABLE	Renovation ($N = 172$)	Supplier Change ($N = 174$)	Longer Hours ($N = 174$)	Employee Layoffs ($N = 143$)
Constant	−.060	1.599	1.644	.647
	(.305)	(.612)	(.331)	(.544)
Date	−.010	−.032	.012	−.022
	(.008)	(.016)	(.008)	(.015)
Management ownership	.006	−.022	.003	−.004
	(.006)	(.012)	(.007)	(.014)
Layoff restrictions				.149
				(.128)

NOTE.—Second-stage results of a two-stage least squares procedure in which four measures of restructuring are regressed on fitted values of the explanatory variables, within the subsample in which no managers were laid off and people new to the shop own less than 50 percent of the shop. The measures of restructuring are renovation, one if capital renovation was done, and zero otherwise; supplier change, one if more than 50 percent of the suppliers were changed, zero otherwise; longer hours, one if longer hours were worked, zero otherwise; and employee layoffs, one if layoffs were made, zero otherwise. The explanatory variables are date, the number of months after June 1992 that privatization occurred, and management ownership, the percentage of the shop owned by the management, whether old or new. The employee layoff regressions also control for layoff restrictions, one if restrictions were reported, zero otherwise. Instruments are described in table 5. Heteroskedasticity-consistent standard errors are in parentheses.

In sum, the two-stage least squares results confirm the OLS evidence that human capital change stimulates restructuring, but the effect of equity incentives in our data is not nearly as clear.

IV. Conclusion

The principal message we draw from our empirical evidence is that restructuring requires new people, who have new skills more suitable to a market economy. A secondary message is that, without new people, equity incentives for old people might not be particularly effective in bringing about significant change. These messages, of course, are subject to several caveats. First, we have surveyed the shops only a few months after they were privatized, and more restructuring was sure to come later. Moreover, the beneficial effects of equity incentives might take longer to work than those of new human capital. Second, equity incentives might not be the only, or even the dominant, form of incentives for shop managers. Ex post settling up and other pay-for-performance arrangements, such as bonuses, might be more common in shops. Third, the results for shops may not extend to industrial firms, especially since the latter rely less on ex post settling up and more on managerial equity ownership. All these criticisms have some validity, especially in suggesting caution in interpreting our results on incentives. Nonetheless, these criticisms do not significantly detract from the central positive message of the importance of new human capital for restructuring. In fact, to the extent that appropriate human capital is more essential for complicated industrial firms than for small shops, the central conclusion of this paper might be even more compelling for industrial firms.

Much of the design of privatization programs, including the work of some of the present authors on large-scale privatization in Russia (Boycko, Shleifer, and Vishny 1993, 1996), has focused on cash flow incentives. In many cases, insiders were given substantial ownership stakes in the privatizing firms. One reason for this was the political requirement to buy insider support for privatization, on the argument that even insider-dominated privatization is better than state ownership. But another reason was the idea that when insiders get ownership incentives, they become more interested in restructuring because they can benefit from higher profits. In the Russian and other recent privatizations, considerable effort was made to bring in large outside investors to provide both oversight of the managers and new ideas and capital. Nonetheless, in the vast majority of cases, insiders retained control.

If our results on human capital can be generalized to large-scale privatization, they suggest that continued control by old managers presents a problem for restructuring and that more attention should have been paid to management turnover as opposed to shareholder oversight over the existing managers. To some extent, large investors have begun to force old managers out: by some estimates, this happened in 10 percent of first shareholder meetings in Russia. Moreover, many old managers have been given enough wealth that they can afford to retire in peace and let a new generation take over. This, however, is probably not enough. Further reforms should facilitate director retirement (with large golden parachutes) as well as forced removals through proxy fights, bankruptcies, and other aggressive corporate control mechanisms. If privatization were designed from scratch, these strategies should have received more attention than they have.

A more general lesson of this limited study of Russian shops is that the success of reform depends significantly on the speed of turnover of political and economic leadership. Freely operating financial markets and governance mechanisms speed up this process in firms, whereas frequent elections do so in political markets. This view also points to the importance of developing new human capital through training.

In conclusion, we want to emphasize that our paper's finding that skills may matter more than incentives is relevant for labor markets in general. Recent research in labor economics, and especially in the analysis of executive pay, has stressed incentives and ignored "slotting" people into jobs[5] (Jensen and Murphy 1990). If finding the right person for the job is much more important than offering incentives on that job, then Jensen and Murphy's and other results of little responsiveness of pay to performance are not surprising. The diversity of people and of their talents would dominate the differences in productivities, much as it does in the Russian shops. At least when we started this project, this conclusion was by no means obvious.

References

Boycko, Maxim; Shleifer, Andrei; and Vishny, Robert W. "Privatizing Russia." *Brookings Papers Econ. Activity*, no. 2 (1993), pp. 139–81.
———. "A Theory of Privatization." *Econ. J.* 106 (March 1996): 309–19.
Demsetz, Harold, and Lehn, Kenneth. "The Structure of Corporate Ownership: Causes and Consequences." *J.P.E.* 93 (December 1985): 1155–77.
Donahue, John D. *The Privatization Decision: Public Ends, Private Means.* New York: Basic Books, 1989.
Earle, John S.; Frydman, Roman; Rapaczynski, Andrzej; and Turkewitz, Joel. *Small Privatization: The Transformation of Retail Trade and Consumer Services in the Czech Republic, Hungary, and Poland.* Budapest: Central European Univ. Press, 1994.
Grossman, Sanford J., and Hart, Oliver D. "The Costs and Benefits of Ownership: A Theory of Vertical and Lateral Integration." *J.P.E.* 94 (August 1986): 691–719.
Holmstrom, Bengt. "Moral Hazard and Observability." *Bell J. Econ.* 10 (Spring 1979): 74–91.
Jensen, Michael C., and Murphy, Kevin J. "Performance Pay and Top-Management Incentives." *J.P.E.* 98 (April 1990): 225–64.
Megginson, William L.; Nash, Robert C.; and van Randenborgh, Mathias. "The Financial and Operating Performance of Newly Privatized Firms: An International Empirical Analysis." *J. Finance* 49 (June 1994): 403–52.
Morck, Randall; Shleifer, Andrei; and Vishny, Robert W. "Management Ownership and Market Valuation: An Empirical Analysis." *J. Financial Econ.* 20 (January–March 1988): 293–315.
Rosen, Sherwin. "Contracts and the Market for Executives." In *Contract Economics*, edited by Lars Werin and Hans Wijkander. Oxford: Blackwell, 1992.
Shleifer, Andrei, and Summers, Lawrence H. "Breach of Trust in Hostile Takeovers." In *Corporate Takeovers: Causes and Consequences*, edited by Alan J. Auerbach. Chicago: Univ. Chicago Press (for NBER), 1988.
Vining, Aiden R., and Boardman, Anthony E. "Ownership versus Competition: Efficiency in Public Enterprise." *Public Choice* 73 (March 1992): 205–39.

[5] We owe this term to Gary S. Becker.

[26]

Academy of Management Executive, 1998, Vol. 12, No. 2

Carrying out a successful privatization: The YPF case

Robert Grosse and Juan Yañes

Executive Overview

The Argentine national oil company, YPF, was drastically restructured and sold to the public in an initial public offering during the early 1990s. This process of privatization was the most successful large-scale one in Argentina during the period, and it serves as a useful benchmark for other privatizations in other countries and contexts. The most important internal strategic factors that contributed to the success of this privatization were: (1) the redefinition of core businesses and elimination of non-core activities; (2) the restructuring of the organization and personnel to fit the core business; and (3) the positioning of the firm for sale to private-sector investors. The most important external factors that contributed to the success of this privatization were: (1) the government's firm and clear position on the issue, and the creation of a legal framework to permit privatization of YPF and deregulation of the industry; and (2) the identification of key pressure groups and defusing of their efforts to oppose the privatization.

The Argentine national oil company, Yacimientos Petroliferos Fiscales (YPF) was drastically restructured in the early 1990s. Nonstrategic assets were sold for slightly over $US 2 billion, then 45 percent of the company was sold to the public for approximately $US 3 billion in July of 1993, in what was said to be the year's largest global initial public offering (IPO). A few months later, another 15 percent of the company was sold to private Argentine investors in exchange for government long-term bonds, bringing the total privatization to 60 percent of YPF at a price of approximately $US 4 billion. Then and now about half of the ownership of YPF was in the hands of private foreign shareholders.

Numerous lessons are to be learned from the YPF privatization process, possibly the most successful major privatization to take place during the post-debt-crisis era in the developing countries. Although the lessons are not necessarily all applicable in other contexts today, key parts of the process will be of direct value in guiding prospective privatizations elsewhere.

The case of Argentina is particularly interesting, because the country had experienced repeated bouts of 1000-plus percent annual inflation during the mid- and late-1980s.[1] Moreover, Argentina had followed broadly inward-looking economic policies under a series of military governments since the 1930s. While Argentines had not been familiar with a market-driven, competitive economy for half a century, they were all too familiar with a slow-growing, inflation-plagued, and ineptly managed economy in recent years. The dramatic policy reform begun at the end of the 1980s is strikingly illustrated with this example of the YPF privatization.

The YPF case is not typical of privatizations in general, since it involves an oil company (a national treasure type of firm that has not often been privatized), and because the privatization has been extremely successful.[2] The YPF example is especially attractive because it reflects a government's willingness to make the crucial decisions that permit the privatization process to proceed effectively and a management team's willingness to learn from other world-class companies and their experiences.

Interestingly, YPF's transformation was part of one long process. From the outset, the State Reform Laws (1989),[3] which formed the backbone of broad deregulation across many industries, belonged to the same chain process as the other critical elements—societal positioning of privatization, company transformation,[4] dealing with pressure groups, corporate restructuring, and finally, YPF's initial public offering in 1993. The common objec-

52   *Academy of Management Executive*   May

tive throughout all of these phases was the total makeover of an unprofitable, poorly-managed, state-owned enterprise into a competitive international company.

Goals of Privatization

The goals of privatization programs are several, generally focusing on (1) the generation of funds for the government via the public offering of the

---

The YPF example is especially attractive because it reflects a government's willingness to make the crucial decisions that permit the privatization process to proceed effectively and a management team's willingness to learn from other world-class companies and their experiences.

---

company being privatized, and (2) the improvement of quality in the activity being undertaken (e.g., provision of telephone service, operation of a commercial bank, production and sale of a natural resource) by putting it in the hands of market-focused managers. Additional goals of privatization often include (3) demonstration that the government is serious about promoting the private sector (and often about allowing foreign investors to participate in these activities, as well as about deregulating markets); (4) undercutting powerful pressure groups that hinder economic development (such as workers' unions, subsidized clients, and influential politicians); (5) improvement of the balance of payments through attracting foreign direct investment and/or through generation of new exports; and (6) eliminating losing businesses from the government sector, thus helping to reduce the drain on the national treasury and perhaps reducing external debt as well.[5]

Since privatization is just a term for selling of government-owned assets, this idea is not new. However, beginning with the British government's decision in the early 1980s to actively push more and more economic activity into the private sector, the term privatization became more commonly used. The privatizations of British Petroleum, British Steel, British Telecom, British Gas, and British Airways corporations—all majority or wholly state-owned at the time—were a clear bellwether of this movement, which has continued into the 1990s.[6]

The fall of the Berlin Wall in 1989 and the demise

of the Soviet Union have likewise led to massive efforts in the former members of the Soviet bloc to sell off government-owned companies and to join the capitalist development process in western Europe.[7] The eastern European context is quite different from those in western Europe and Latin America. With no recent capitalist experience to fall back on, the eastern European countries are faced with the need to privatize massive numbers of firms at the same time. Also, without stock markets to facilitate the public offering of company shares, a major outlet for sale to the private sector is missing. Both of these features make a careful, systematic privatization process such as that of YPF difficult to copy.[8] In these contexts, the lessons from YPF can best be applied to small numbers of large state-owned enterprises, for which the returns to the government from using a systematic and time-consuming privatization process outweigh the costs.

In the case of YPF, the goals of Argentina's government were principally to attract investment into the oil sector that would permit the capital spending and the human and technological resources needed to make YPF competitive with international giants such as Exxon and Shell, and also to demonstrate the government's commitment to building the private sector, including the participation of foreign investors, as well as local ones. Underlying these specific goals were the general ones of generating funds for the government, improving the quality of management of the firm and the sector, and undercutting the powerful unions that pushed employment far above the competitive levels of the international oil companies. Thus, the YPF case fits the general model of denationalization of state-owned enterprises, and it had specific focus on making the company competitive with the global oil majors.

The Conditions Facing YPF and Argentina

Many countries in Latin America had experienced a strong fever of anti-American nationalism, ideologically stimulated by the Soviet Union during the 1950s and 1960s. This attitude was reinforced by the oil crises of the 1970s and the redistribution of economic power toward natural resource producers that occurred during that decade. With the dramatic drop of oil prices after 1981 and the external debt crisis that began in 1982, the power of Latin American countries declined markedly. The wave of privatizations in this region began at the end of the 1980s, as most of the countries in Latin America, weighed down by immense external debt burdens and by disastrous public service and infrastructure support, were encouraged to make both their public and private sectors more efficient.[9] The sell-off of state-owned enterprises was one of many specific steps in this direction, and it was used extensively first by Chile, then by Mexico and Argentina, and eventually by most of the countries in Latin America.

In Argentina, after 40 years of nationalist-populist rule and a weakening economy, the public clearly supported a process to transform the costly and inefficient state-owned enterprises into privately held businesses. In the early part of this century, Argentina's economy was among the ten strongest in the world. Remembering the efficiency and success of the private system in 1989, the Argentine people gave newly-elected President Carlos Menem a clear mandate to reverse the nationalization of many state-owned firms. He began this process with a highly-visible and rapid sequence of steps that produced the privatization of the national telephone company, ENTel. YPF was the largest company in the country, and the only major oil company worldwide to be losing money. Therefore, it was also an outstanding test case for the privatization plans of the new government.

The History of Privatization in Argentina

The sale of state-owned enterprises to private-sector purchasers began to be considered actively by the government of Argentina during the external debt crisis of the 1980s. As early as the end of the military regimes in 1983, World Bank and IMF project teams recommended wholesale reform of the public sector in Argentina as part of the steps toward regaining access to international financial resources. In response, the government of President Raul Alfonsin (1983–89) put together a list of enterprises to possibly be privatized, beginning with ENTel and Aerolineas Argentinas, the national airline.

As early as the end of the military regimes in 1983, World Bank and IMF project teams recommended wholesale reform of the public sector in Argentina as part of the steps toward regaining access to international financial resources.

These early efforts did not advance much from project definitions. First, Alfonsin's Radical Party itself had in the past been a strong advocate of the state as the owner of business, and therefore not enough leadership was provided. Second, the Peronist party was in the majority in Congress, with strong representation of labor union members, and it would not let the proposals that were submitted for approval progress to materialization. And, perhaps most importantly, a fundamental weakness in the overall process at this time was that there was no sequential link between the steps needed to carry out privatizations; that is, there was no set of common objectives and long-term vision that could successfully tie all of the phases together.

The first privatizations actually undertaken by Argentina were those of Aerolineas and ENTel. Although President Alfonsin's government began these processes, neither one was completed by his administration. They were quickly reinitiated by President Menem's team upon taking office, and completed within the first year of his term.

Dimensions of the Privatization Process

The more common analyses of privatizations have focused on economic costs and benefits of such experiences.[10] To give a full perspective of government concerns and company management issues, it is necessary to expand the terms of reference to include the industry structure and regulatory regime that accompany and follow privatization, as well as the corporate governance issues and organizational performance.[11]

The key conditions of privatization have three dimensions. The first dimension is the government perspective, which is evaluated in terms of such measures as financial impact of selling the state-owned firm and also regulatory effectiveness in the sector. Second, the society is discussed in terms of identifying the key groups affected by the privatization, the impacts on them, and the ways that their support or lack of opposition may be obtained.[12] The third dimension is the company, in which privatization is evaluated in terms of the firm's efficiency and other performance criteria before and after the event.

Figure 1 depicts the situation of YPF in the early 1990s as it undertook the process that led to privatization in July 1993.

The Government Dimension

During the first three decades of the century, Argentina was a model of liberal economy. Investments in infrastructure and social services poured into the country, and exports of grain and beef produced large surpluses of international reserves. All this changed in the 1930s with the emergence of military dictatorships—fascist-inspired

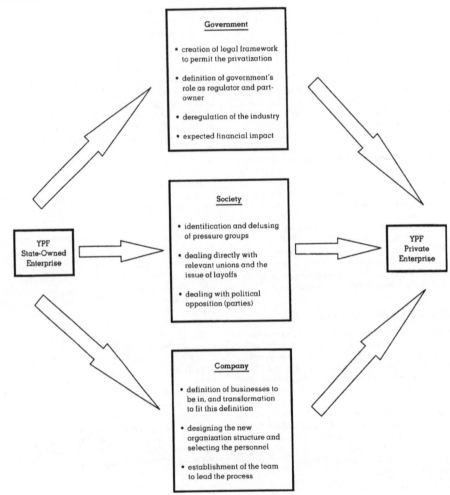

FIGURE 1
Dimensions of Successful Privatization—YPF

and populist in style—that took over and lasted until the Falklands War in 1982. During that half century, the state not only ran—very incompetently—the monetary and fiscal machine, but it also owned and poorly managed over half the overall economy. Railroads transported almost no freight nor fare-paying passengers. Ports, serving scarce freight, were ruled by corrupt union leaders and incompetent civil servants. Electricity, telephone and other utilities were poorly serviced and plagued with shut-offs and scarcities. With the economy in dramatically weak condition, it was clear to the civilian government that the easiest thing to do was return to the free capitalist market.

But the first civilian government (Alfonsin, 1983–89) still produced a disastrous handling of the economy. The only option at the end of the 1980s was to reverse the role of the state. The Menem government (1989-) was given an implicit popular mandate to pursue a wholesale reduction in state-owned business activity and a general opening of the economy to domestic and foreign competition. Several private firms, both domestic and foreign, were active in the oil industry, though rigidly controlled by the state oil company. They were subject to the state's monopolistic direction and were in the upstream segment subcontracted to YPF. There were also a few, small local independents that had been participating in the strongly regulated downstream segment of the oil industry.

Because of the severity of the economic situation at the time of the national elections in May 1989, Menem took office in July 1989, five months ahead of schedule.[13] Soon after his inauguration, Congress passed the State Reform Law, which declared 32 state-owned enterprises eligible for privatization. (See Appendix.) The privatization program was accompanied by a series of regulatory reforms designed to allow private companies to provide public services that previously had been regulated as natural monopolies.

During 1989, the Menem government deregulated many areas of the oil industry. Decree 1055/89 lifted the restrictions on the market for crude oil and provided for concessions of marginal areas,[14] joint ventures for the development of central areas, and unrestricted disposal of crude production. Decree 1212/89 deregulated down-stream activities, allowing for renegotiation of existing contracts, the lifting of price controls, the lifting of restrictions on the setting up of refineries, and the lifting of restrictions on the setting up and ownership of service stations. And Decree 1589/89 opened up the domestic market and legislated the unrestricted import and export of crude oil, the elimination of duties and tariffs, and the free disposability of crude oil for operators under the Houston Plan concessions. This plan, elaborated in the early 1980s by the government of Alfonsin, encouraged independent oil companies to invest in exploration and production, under contract with YPF. These three decrees effectively allowed other domestic and foreign oil companies to participate directly in all aspects of the industry except for ownership of the underground reservoir of crude oil resources of Argentina.[15]

The crucial nature of the industry deregulation program to this process cannot be overstated. Without deregulation there would not be competition, hence there would be no pressure to make the enterprise healthy on a continuing basis. The privatized business without deregulation could continue to behave like a monopoly, and management creativity would not grow strong enough to enable the firm to compete as a world-class business. In this situation it would be difficult to attract private investors, and so the cycle of problems would remain.

In December 1990, the Argentine government issued Decree 2248/90, which transformed YPF into a corporation. This rule created the legal form in which YPF could be sold to other investors.[16] But it was only in the spring of 1993, shortly before the

> **Without deregulation there would not be competition, hence there would be no pressure to make the enterprise healthy on a continuing basis.**

initial public offering, that Congress passed the Law of Privatization of YPF, which allowed the company to be divested by the government. The approval of this law had been delayed for two reasons. First, there was intensive lobbying by independent oil companies aiming to have a larger piece of YPF sold before the initial public offer. Second, the oil producing provinces of Argentina were demanding to receive a larger share of the company's ownership. President Menem had agreed to pursue the privatization even in 1990, but the company needed first to be put into condition for successful sale, and then the above problems slowed down the legal process.

As a result of these regulatory changes, the government of Argentina created the conditions needed to sell YPF to private investors and to operate the company competitively with other participants in the market. The incredible shift in policy embodied in these changes may not appear obvious: the country was selling the crown jewels to private investors, an idea never even considered during most of the previous half-century in Argentina. Despite the skepticism of disbelieving observers (who did not act to stop the process), rapid decisionmaking was able to allow YPF to reduce the opposition to selling the company.

The Social Dimension

Given the country's recent history of a strong, inward-looking government and fairly isolationist policies, on a superficial level it could be argued that the social conditions in Argentina seemed not to favor the process. This history belies the reality that a great majority of Argentines had become extremely disillusioned with the bureaucratic inefficiencies of the government, the negative impact on the economy of labor market rigidities caused by corrupt union leaders, and the country's social and economic decline from being a world leader in the 1930s to being an industrial laggard and virtually bankrupt economy in the 1980s. Social conditions actually were quite favorable toward the privatization and rationalization of YPF as a symbol of the new Argentina.

On the other hand, pressure groups such as labor unions, particularly the Union of Petroleum Workers of the State, actively opposed the sale of YPF. Labor relations were a very sensitive issue throughout the process of privatization and restructuring of YPF. As early as October 1990, YPF's management took the first step of renegotiating a labor contract, with Menem's support. The union was awarded generous benefits for layoffs, while at the same time YPF management was given the right to carry out such layoffs. Many employees whose jobs were terminated were encouraged to organize their own private firms, with YPF contracting to buy their services from them for as long as two years. These arrangements, called *emprendimientos*, covered more than five thousand of YPF's workers who were laid off.

Other employees accepted the assignment to attend courses for retraining and developing additional skills for one year with full pay, after which they were required to find new employment elsewhere. After this training, the employees were discharged with generous severance payments. A large number of employees remained with the non-core businesses, and thus they disengaged themselves from YPF after receiving severance benefits.

Of course, there was opposition from suppliers, competitors, dealers, and agents that took all forms. Suppliers pressed to maintain their long-privileged positions, their prices, and their volumes, against foreign competition. Competitors demanded plans for an even smaller YPF. Dealers and agents, a largely corrupted part of the system, demanded to maintain their privileged cash credit positions. Again, transparency, uniform treatment, and speed in the privatization process were the remedies used to smooth over the opposition.

The Company Dimension

The company's situation in the early 1990s was clearly ripe for a rationalization process. YPF demonstrated many of the characteristics of poorly-managed state-owned firms at that time:

- Overstaffed. YPF employed 39,000 direct employees and 13,000 contractees on a continuous, permanent basis—for an oil output of only 410,000 barrels per day (similar to current output of the properties retained after disengaging from its non-core reserves[17]) and mainly concentrated in upstream and refining operations.

- Losing money. YPF lost $US 576 million for the fiscal year 1990.
- Unfocused. YPF operated numerous unrelated activities such as hospitals, schools, housing, and utilities, and also many businesses of clearly low strategic value.
- Bureaucratic culture. YPF leaders were not cost/profit oriented but rather driven by activity levels and volume; the firm was overcentralized and hierarchical rather than strategic.
- Deteriorating assets. YPF was underinvesting in plant and equipment and delaying maintenance on vital facilities.

Change in these attributes was the central focus of the process leading up to public sale of the firm.

The Path of YPF's Privatization

While the previous section described the Argentine government's and society's concerns and actions during the privatization of YPF, the present section turns to the decisions made within or concerning the company itself. These are concerns and decisions of the managers responsible for running the company.

Defining the Business and Transforming the Company

As Menem's government tried to establish the plan for transforming YPF, McKinsey & Company, an international strategy consultant, was called in to assist. In 1990, the firm completed a study elaborating a strategic plan for the privatization effort. This plan highlighted both the businesses that were considered strategic to YPF's core activity, as well as those that were clearly not necessary for success in YPF's markets. Based on the consultants' analysis, YPF management estimated that the Argentine government would obtain, at best, about $US 3 billion for selling YPF in block on the open international market, a value that at closer look could be much improved. By transforming and restructuring the organization prior to a public offering, the value could be more than doubled to approximately $US 8 billion. Reducing YPF to a highly profitable, high value generating core, was the McKinsey prescription and the Government's decision.

To set the process in motion, Menem selected a visionary leader who appeared to possess the necessary capabilities of industry knowledge and management skills. He approached Jose Estenssoro, a former executive of Hughes Tool Company in Latin America and in 1990 an Argentine oil-industry entrepreneur, and asked him to take on the presidency of YPF. Estenssoro replied that he would indeed accept the task, but that the company needed to be privatized, and the industry needed to be deregulated. Estenssoro and Menem agreed to pursue this plan. Estenssoro defined the

---

Reducing YPF to a highly profitable, high value generating core, was the McKinsey prescription and the Government's decision.

---

task as a three-step process: (1) eliminating nonstrategic, unprofitable businesses; (2) restructuring the organization; and (3) offering the company to investors in national and foreign markets through an initial public offering. Estenssoro's three step plan covered a span of three years.

The first step of eliminating nonstrategic, unprofitable businesses was begun in 1990, as soon as Estenssoro accepted the challenge of transforming the organization. As became the norm throughout several other phases of the activity, Estenssoro delegated the task to external executives, in this case a high-powered team of former Hughes Tool associates. The first phase dealt with sorting out the long list of nonstrategic, noneconomic, underutilized assets. These assets—including marginal producing areas, obsolete refineries, tanker fleets, schools, hospitals, and airplanes, that YPF had amassed over the years—were put out for unrestricted bids, and were sold for a total sum of $US 2.1 billion.

Since speed was a critical factor and major political driver, the transformation process was to be carried out by the orchestration of multiple international consulting resources.[18] These consultants were all proven experts in complementary areas of corporate restructuring. This blend of external talent was financed in part by funds that YPF obtained from a World Bank loan in 1991.[19]

Restructuring the New YPF

The second step of the process of remaking YPF began in 1991. It involved both the massive downsizing of the firm and the reorganization of its human resources and operating structure. In fact, these two processes were largely unconnected with each other, because of the speed with which they were designed, implemented, and completed. The organization's grossly inflated levels of management had never been systematically evaluated, so Estenssoro and a team of external consult-

ants decided to eliminate all positions and start from a clean slate while building the new organizational frame. Since YPF was a state-owned enterprise that underpaid its personnel and offered few challenges, it was assumed that those who would elect to stay in a new, demanding environment would be the exceptions. The plan was simple and transparent: everyone from top to bottom was offered a clear and well-defined economic incentive to leave the company.

Two important lessons emerge from this part of the organizational restructuring. The first involved use of successfully mitigating labor relations. YPF was extremely generous to those employees who left. Severance options included early retirement with full benefits for those eligible, training and educational courses plus one year's salary for those interested in learning a new marketable skill, or an entrepreneurial option with a guaranteed contract from YPF (the so-called *emprendimientos* described above). Many of the workers at YPF were political appointees and family members who were hired without proper training, so their skills needed to be upgraded to become marketable. These generous severance packages, the cost of which exceeded $US 1 billion, are representative of YPF's visionary planning, as its leaders strived to help alleviate the situational unemployment that would result when 90 percent of the workers in the country's largest company would soon be out of a job.

The second lesson explains one aspect of YPF's success in downsizing. Had the company followed a more common but less successful model of leaving the restructuring to the new owners, the labor unions and other groups would have strongly obstructed the plans of YPF's new management. Since the mandate to transform came directly from the popularly elected Menem, Estenssoro's team was successful in renegotiating and terminating labor contracts with little interference. Moreover, it could be easily inferred that Menem made sure that the labor leaders learned that he was holding in his hands vital records questioning the severe mismanagement of their respective unions.

The cost was high, but so were the final returns. The head count balance showed that about 50,000 employees left YPF in just under two years. Close to 3,500 new employees, chosen after a rigorous professional evaluation process, were incorporated. The new force of somewhat less than 6,000 employees is a very different one. The average age dropped eleven years to 38 years, and the new employees are being trained for very demanding objectives.

Parallel to YPF's organizational rightsizing was

the step of organizing the new structure. The Arthur D. Little consulting firm was called in and assigned the task of redesigning the new structure, following the most modern concepts of reengineering. The resulting management structure was simple and compact: autonomous strategic business units that shared service/staff units. To fill key positions, an intensive executive selection process took place in which highly skilled, high-potential people were chosen, based on leadership, moral fortitude, intelligence and judgment, rather than only on the conventional qualities of education and experience.

As the new organization took shape, it became evident that new information technology was necessary for the implementation of the new organizational structure. A leaner YPF, with fewer middlemen in the decision ladder, was achievable only with a modern communication and information infrastructure.[20] Andersen Consulting, with its proven skill in information technology, was brought in to assist with the task of formulating new work processes and designing and linking the new information network with the most modern technology and systems. Given the importance of information technology to competitive positioning, the information technology phase of YPF's modernization lasted over four years. During its peak the company was using some 200 international experts simultaneously, mostly Andersen consultants.

The Initial Public Offering

The third and final step of the privatization process as identified by Estenssoro was the domestic and international sale of shares in YPF through an initial public offering. Once conditions had been established for the sell-off, the government proceeded to orchestrate the IPO. Price Waterhouse was retained to carry out a valuation of the firm, with the end of setting a price on the shares to be issued.

Next, a process of informing potential investors about the company was pursued. An intense, several-month-long preparation analysis, headed by CS First Boston and Merrill Lynch experts, preceded the public offering. Every phase of the business—including strategic and operating plans, financial balances, and organizational strengths and weaknesses—was tested. YPF and the investment bankers went on an elaborate road show through most of the prospective markets. On July 1, 1993, after the proper certifications with the stock exchanges were validated, 30 percent of the shares were put up for sale at a floor price of $US 19 per share in New York, London, and Buenos Aires. The issue was greatly oversubscribed.

In reviewing the features of the YPF privatization presented above, it is clear that the key company strategies that produced the highly successful results were:

1. redefinition of the core businesses and elimination of noncore activities;
2. restructuring of the organization and personnel to fit the core businesses;
3. positioning of the firm for public (or private placement) sale to private sector investors.

Outcome for the Government

As a result of the initial public offering, and a subsequent sale of another 15 percent of YPF shares in exchange for outstanding government bonds in the domestic market, 60 percent of YPF's 353 million shares were sold to private investors. The Federal government retained a direct 20 percent share in the company established in the Privatization Law. In addition, 10 percent of the shares were held by the government for an employee trust, and the remaining 10 percent were held on behalf of the five provincial governments. (The provincial governments sold approximately half of their shares during 1995, leaving 65 percent of total shares traded in the market. The shares in the employee trust reverted to the employees in 1997, and most of them have been traded into the market, leaving 75 percent of the shares now traded.)

As a result of the privatization and deregulation processes undertaken by the Argentine government, a range of other impacts occurred. The net financial results for the government from the privatization of YPF are shown in Table 1.

The first-year financial impact on the government was a net one-time positive flow of about $US 4.2 billion, along with a recurring positive flow of about $US 60 million per year in dividends that should continue indefinitely.[21] As long as ownership of the shares does not change, the Argentine government retains control of 20 percent of the firm (which was valued at about $US 7 billion for the entire firm at yearend 1995). From the nationalistic point of view, about 50 percent of the total ownership of YPF remains in Argentine hands, since 15 percent of the shares are traded in the Buenos Aires stock exchange.

YPF had continuing cash flows from:

• Tax revenues. These will improve from the situation of no income tax paid during the three

Table 1
Income Statements for the Years Ended December 31, 1990–1995

Category	1990	1991	1992	1993	1990–1993 % Change	1994	1995
Net Sales	4,584	4,159	3,867	3,956	-13.69	4,394	4,954
Cost of Sales	4,542	3,343	2,847	2,720	-40.10	2,970	3,225
Gross Profit	42	816	1,020	1,236	+2842.85	1,424	1,729
Selling & Administrative	547	451	428	418	-23.58	499	535
R&D Expenses	207	103	70	*	—	—	—
Net Income Before Taxes[†]	-494	253	256	734	—	576	883
Taxes	—	—	—	—	—	12	61
Preferred Stock Dividends	—	—	—	—	—	—	29
Other Adjustments	-82	—	—	-28	—	—	—
Net Income After Taxes	-576	253	256	706	—	564	793

(Amounts expressed in millions of constant Argentine pesos. 1993)

[*] Beginning in the second half of 1992, YPF discontinued its internally managed research and development activity, and switched to outside research centers under contract. Therefore R&D expenses are now part of business unit budgets.

[†] Net income before taxes does not equate to the line items above, because in 1990 there was $218 million of one-time income from selling non-core businesses, and subsequently through 1995 there were net outflows due to severance payments to employees.

Sources: 1996 YPF Company Statement was used for the years 1994 and 1995. 1993 YPF Company Statement was used for the years 1991, 1992, and 1993. The results for 1990 come from Arthur Anderson Internal Audit of the company derived from Worldscope Computer Services (Univ. of Miami).

years prior to privatization and through 1995 to about $US 200–300 million expected to be paid afterward.[22]

- Earnings on the government's shares in YPF. Net income after tax of about $US 0.5 billion after privatization, compared to low profits or losses before. This amount was largely held as retained earnings by YPF, so about $US 120 million was actually distributed as dividends each year. Shares increased from $19 per share to $32 per share during 1993–97.

One time items were:

- Revenues on the sales of non-strategic assets: $US 2.1 billion for sales of some refineries, company stores, supplier businesses, etc.
- Receipts for share sales: $US 4.0 billion from the initial IPO in Argentina and abroad, plus the subsequent sale of 15 percent of shares in exchange for outstanding government bonds in the market
- Social cost of dealing with unemployed ex-employees: severance costs of about $US 1.0 billion; then intangible improvement in lower future costs of health and benefits for employees

A Contrary Example: Aerolineas Argentinas

The case of Aerolineas Argentinas presents a sharp counterpoint to that of YPF. Aerolineas was privatized in 1990, with no transformation of the firm nor any restructuring of the personnel before the public offering. The sale was carried out through a bidding process in which qualified bidders were permitted to make their offers in a sealed auction. Out of this came only one formal bid, from a consortium of Iberia, the Spanish government-owned airline, and a group of Argentine entrepreneurs, including the owners of the competing domestic airline, Austral. Aerolineas Argentinas was sold to this consortium, which ran into labor strife when layoffs were attempted, financing problems when profitability failed to arrive, and management disagreements among the members of the consortium. Until 1995, domestic airline service was a virtual monopoly of Aerolineas, staffing was much higher per passenger mile than for competing international airlines, and the firm was losing hundreds of millions of dollars each year. Two additional aspects of the Aerolineas privatization that differentiate it from the YPF case are the lack of transparency in the public sale of the company, and the lack of strong leadership at the company, which was simply sold as is to the winning consortium of buyers. This situation is now changing: the government is now encouraging greater competition, and Aerolineas is negotiating a change in ownership. However, the early years could not provide a more striking contrast with YPF.[23]

Lessons from the YPF Experience

The lessons from the highly-successful privatization of YPF are numerous and yield a set of critical elements that can be followed sequentially to lead to successful privatization. They are presented in Table 2.

Table 2
Critical Elements of Privatization

1. Industry Deregulation (supervision still needed)
2. Societal Positioning of Privatization
3. Company Transformation (choice of businesses to be in)
4. Dealing with Pressure Groups (unions; government agencies)
5. Company Restructuring (downsizing; reengineering; development of human resources)
6. Company Sale (via IPO or private placement or other mechanism)
7. Review to Ensure Effective Competition

The steps may not be possible to carry out in the sequence listed, but this sequence helped to produce the highly-successful results in the YPF situation.

Another caveat regarding the application of the experience to other contexts is that YPF is a huge company, and Argentina is a country with a continuing participation of capitalist business in the economy. The YPF experience does not provide a fully-transferable model for privatizations of very small companies and for situations in formerly communist countries where hundreds or thousands of companies need to be denationalized rapidly. The costs and the time needed to carry out a privatization like YPF's will not be bearable in some contexts. By the same token, privatization of large state-owned enterprises in formerly-communist countries may very well benefit from following the sequence presented from the YPF experience. And privatizations in countries of Latin America and Asia, and perhaps Africa and the Middle East, should directly benefit from the lessons of YPF, tempered by concern for the costs involved.

The use of outside consultants to obtain needed expertise, for example, will be feasible when the market can value that expertise and pay for it. Establishment of a market price for the IPO is almost necessarily a task reserved for outside, impartial valuation. Similarly, the design and implementation of a modern management information system may best be done by an outside, specialist firm. The World Bank recommended consulting assistance routinely in Latin American economic reform programs during the late 1980s, and even partially funded the costs in many cases. In Argentina, the privatizations of large state-owned companies such as YPF, ENTel, and Aerolineas benefited from this assistance.

Likewise, the cost of transforming the firm into a focused and well-organized enterprise should be undertaken before sell-off to the private sector, *if* this cost can be more than recouped in the subsequent sale to the public. Clearly it is desirable to overcome the obstacles to restructuring and trans-

> ## Establishment of a market price for the IPO is almost necessarily a task reserved for outside, impartial valuation.

forming the firm before it leaves the political control of the government; but if the market will not pay for such a transformation, then it would be preferable to sell the firm first and leave redefinition of the organization and the strategy to the new owners. The time and expense needed to transform the business into a competitive form and to restructure personnel before privatization may outweigh the benefits in cases of small firms and also in cases in eastern Europe where massive numbers of privatizations are sought in a short time frame.[24]

The dimensions that were used to organize this paper may serve as a basis for assessing privatizations more broadly. In the present case we see that each of the three dimensions contained some critical features that contributed to the overall success of the venture.

At the government level, the key steps were first to recognize the need for moving YPF into the private sector and second to implement a process that facilitated this result. Not to be ignored is the prior step, taken in 1989, to deregulate the oil industry. This step meant that YPF needed to compete with other local and foreign oil companies (which implied an inflow of foreign direct investment) in its private-sector reincarnation, rather than just replacing a public monopoly with a private one. Finally, the government had to define a series of rules and policies that allowed YPF to be privatized under Argentine law.

At the level of society, the key needs were to communicate the decisions on YPF's transformation and sale to the public transparently and quickly, reducing the ability of pressure groups to mount effective campaigns to stop the process. At the same time it was very important to demonstrate to the public that the crown jewels were not being given away, but that YPF would remain in Argentine hands, its management virtually completely Argentine. Fortunately, the required expertise and leadership capabilities were found among nationals, so that the company has been remade successfully for its now-global owners, and it continues to be run by a group of capable Argentines.

At the company level, key steps were the selection of talented leaders, the transformation of the firm into a better-focused organization, and the restructuring of the organization to pursue the focal activities. Obviously, a strong and visionary management team was needed to carry out this process. Perhaps not as obviously, the team was assisted at all stages of the process by outside experts—for valuing the company, identifying the appropriate focus of the company's business, designing and implementing the restructuring of personnel, and finally for designing and carrying out the initial public offering. This willingness to call on massive external help for special knowledge and skills not possessed by the company was a vital part of the success story.

The importance of the dealing with all of the dimensions of the process cannot be overstated.[25] In another privatization only three years earlier, Argentina's government had experienced almost exactly opposite results in the case of Aerolineas Argentinas. That company had not been restructured, nor had the industry been deregulated, nor had marginal assets been eliminated, before the privatization took place. Subsequently, labor protests against layoffs and job restructuring caused tremendous problems for the airline, and the lack of domestic competition gave Aerolineas a monopoly that did not produce improvements in service and price as hoped.

The death of Estenssoro in a small plane crash in May 1995 raised the question of succession. Unquestionably, organizations need to identify and groom replacements for the current leaders. At YPF, where gray-haired cohort was brought in to carry out the privatization, the need for skilled and knowledgeable young internal candidates for promotion to the top spots was glaringly visible. The visionary leadership provided by Estenssoro could not easily be replicated. The challenges of competing in the global oil industry require that kind of leadership if YPF is to succeed into the 21st century. Eighteen months after Estenssoro's death, the personnel replacement table developed in YPF's new policies has proven to be solid. Good leaders are now being generated by the system of continuous training and rotational management.

After privatization, YPF became a competitor in the international oil industry. To build its position outside Argentina, the company in 1995 acquired Maxus Corporation, a U.S.-based oil producer with reserves in Ecuador, Bolivia, Venezuela, and Indonesia, and natural gas production in Texas. YPF took over management control and assigned Roberto Monti to restructure and lead Maxus, which in recent years had been losing money. By the end of 1996, Monti had turned around the company and produced positive profits. As a result, Monti was named chief executive officer of YPF, to begin with

the retirement of President Nels Leon in April 1997. Previously, in 1992, YPF had acquired the Argentine assets of AGIP, the Italian oil company, and incorporated them into its downstream business.

By the end of 1995 another concern arose. After the Mexican financial crisis of 1994 and its aftershocks, most Latin American stock markets dropped in dollar terms and were not producing the returns they had in the early 1990s. YPF's shares languished at about $US 20 per share, very near the pricing of the initial public offering in 1993. Dividend payouts had only been about $US 0.80 per share per year, so investors were not receiving the spectacular short-term returns that many had hoped for. On the other hand, by mid-year 1997, the ADR[26] price had risen to $US 32 per share, along with the broad bull market and rising oil prices.

An underlying issue for any privatization case is that the stock market will have its peaks and troughs. Therefore, the company needs to have a solid base of long-range investors. By demonstrating that a deep reservoir of talented decisionmakers is in place, ready to take charge when needed, a firm can attract such investors. Similarly, the firm needs to continue to demonstrate that it is not bound by internally-available skills, but that it will look outside for premium experience and capabilities when appropriate. World-class companies occupy such positions because they continue to invest in talent and experience to achieve excellence.

Endnotes

[1] Argentine inflation was approximately 800 percent in 1985, 3100 percent in 1989, and 2400 percent in 1990, according to consumer price indices reported by the International Monetary Fund in *International Financial Statistics*.

[2] Indeed, looking at all of the Argentine privatizations through 1993, Azpiazo and Vispo conclude that the majority were carried out quite imperfectly, too quickly, and with too little concern for deregulation of the various industrial sectors. See Azpiazo, Daniel, & Vispo, Adolfo. December 1994. Some lessons from the Argentine privatization process. *Cepal Review*, 129–147.

[3] Reforma del Estado: Law No. 23.696 was approved and sanctioned by the National Legislative Power one month after President Menem took office in July 1989. Among other objectives, this law set out to establish ad hoc legislation that would legalize drastic changes in the administrative structure of both government and state-owned agencies and authorize privatization. Additionally, there are a total of seven decrees and resolutions under which the Argentine petroleum industry was deregulated.

[4] We consistently use the term "transformation" to discuss the change of YPF from an unfocused enterprise with activities in oil, transportation, food service, etc., into a focused, integrated oil company. We then use the term "restructuring" consistently to refer to the internal reorganization and downsizing of personnel in the firm to meet the new organization's goals.

[5] These issues are explored in detail in Ramamurti & Vernon

(Eds.), *Privatization and control of state-owned enterprises.* Washington, D.C.: The World Bank, 1991, for developing countries; and in Vickers, and Yarrow, G. 1988. *Privatization: An economic analysis.* Cambridge, MA: MIT Press, for industrial countries, specifically the UK.

[5] See, for example, Caves, R. 1990. Lessons from privatization in Britain: State enterprise behavior, public choice, and corporate governance. *Journal of Economic Behavior and Organization,* 13; and Fraser, R. 1988. *Privatization: The UK experience and international trends.* London: Longman.

[6] See Samonis, V. 1994. Privatization in Eastern Europe. *Current Politics and Economics of Europe.*

[8] This context is described in detail by Targetti, F. *Privatization in Europe: West and East experiences.* Brookfield, VT: Dartmouth.

[9] See Ramamurti, R. (Ed.). 1995. *Privatization of infrastructure in Latin America.* Baltimore: Johns Hopkins University Press. On a more general level concerning economic restructuring in Latin America at the time, see Edwards, S. *Crisis and reform in Latin America.* Washington, D.C.: The World Bank.

[10] For example, Vickers, J. and Yarrow, G. 1988. *Privatization: An economic analysis.* Cambridge, Mass.: MIT Press; and Galal, A., Jones, L., Tandon, P., and Vogelsang, I. 1994. *Welfare consequences of selling public enterprises: An empirical analysis.* New York: Oxford University Press.

[11] Cf., Ramamurti and Vernon (Eds.), 1991; Parker, D. 1995. Privatization and agency status: Identifying the critical factors for performance improvement. *British Journal of Management.*

[12] A similar framework is presented in Rondinelli, D., and Iacono, M. 1996. *Policies and institutions for managing privatization.* Geneva: International Labour Office. They argue that privatizations can best be managed by: establishing high-level political commitment; gaining cooperation of important stakeholders; providing clear direction for privatization in the context of total public policy; and supporting the process by developing institutional and management capabilities. These dimensions clearly parallel the structure suggested here.

[13] For example, inflation in Argentina exceeded 197 percent per month in July of 1989.

[14] Marginal areas are those which, because of well location and geographical characteristics, have more value to competing producers with core reserves in the same area.

[15] More discussion of the beginning of the petroleum sector deregulation is found in Gerchunoff, Pablo, & Coloma, German. 1993. Privatization in Argentina. In Manuel Sanchez and Rossana Corona (Eds.), *Privatization in Latin America,* 282–290. Washington, D.C.: Interamerican Development Bank.

[16] The sources of these last two paragraphs are: YPF Oil Policy, 1992 Internal Document; and *Clarin,* November 3, 1990.

[17] Actual oil production was about 470,000 barrels per day in 1990, which is the same level as in 1996. About two-thirds of the original reserves that were in production at the beginning of the transformation process were sold as nonstrategic or noneconomic. From a manpower perspective in the downstream activities, it is estimated that the local affiliates of Exxon and Shell were three to four times more efficient than YPF.

[18] Speed, of course, is relative in the British privatizations of the 1980s, about four companies were privatized per year. In the Czech privatizations of 1994, about six to 10 companies were privatized per day. Speed in the YPF context meant achieving the whole process within two or three years.

[19] YPF's privatization was in part funded by the $US 300 million Public Enterprise and Adjustment Loan 1 (PERAL 1). A technical assistance loan was also made in a parallel move, providing an additional $US 23 million (Public Enterprise Reform Execution Loan—PEREL). These were the first of several World Bank loans to help Argentina restructure its economy. The sum of the loans totaled $US 1.5 billion. ("Privatizing Argentina's Public Sector"

OED Precis No. 100. World Bank, December 1995.) "Bank-assisted loans frequently require a wide range of consulting services. . . ." (*Guide to International Business Opportunities in Projects Funded by the World Bank.* World Bank).

[20] Without information technology to facilitate communications and streamline processes, middle managers' role was predominantly to be information providers. Now, those at the base of the organization are able to interface with all levels—management, clients, and suppliers—making their own decisions when necessary. Thus, several middle management layers were eliminated in the organizational design phase of YPF's restructuring, and the flatter structure is sustained through integrating better technology and systems.

[21] Ongoing dividends should continue at about the $US 120 million per year for the 40 percent share that has been government-owned. In 1995 the provincial Argentine governments sold about 5 percent of their 10 percent share of the company, so government dividends will decline as a percentage of total YPF dividends in the future.

[22] In fact, income tax was not paid by YPF for many years leading up to the privatization. The only taxes paid were asset taxes not related to income. In addition, tax revenues in 1993–95 were offset by other obligations of the Argentine government to YPF; so the first income tax paid by the privatized YPF that constituted an actual cash flow to the government occurred in 1996.

[23] The Aerolineas debacle is described in detail in Grosse, R. 1995. The privatization of Aerolineas Argentinas. In Ramamurti, R. (Ed.). 1995. *Privatization of infrastructure in Latin America.* Baltimore: Johns Hopkins University Press.

[24] By the same token, the results of the privatization program in Russia show that personnel restructuring was *not* carried out before moving the firms into the private sector—and the subsequent overstaffing of these firms is often a huge barrier to becoming competitive. In the Russian privatization scheme, company workers on average have gained about half of the shares of newly-private firms, though they tend to exercise much less control over activities of the firms. See, Filatotchev, I., et al. Winter 1996. Corporate restructuring in Russian privatizations. *California Management Review,* 87–104.

[25] These lessons parallel those listed in a recent study of privatizations throughout Latin America. See, Holden, P., and Rajapatirana, S. 1995. *Unshackling the private sector.* Washington, D.C.: World Bank.

[26] ADRs, or American Depositary Receipts, are derivative instruments based on shares of stock issued in the company's home country and then resold in dollars on a U.S. securities exchange. An intermediating bank buys and holds the stock shares (i.e., deposits them in the bank's vault), then issues the ADRs. Since the ADRs are based entirely on the underlying stock performance, their prices are determined essentially by the home-country share price translated through the exchange rate into dollars.

About the Authors

Robert Grosse is director of research and professor of world business at Thunderbird, the American Graduate School of International Management. He was director of the University of Miami's International Business & Banking Institute from 1986–93. He holds a BA degree from Princeton University and a doctorate from the University of North Carolina, both in international economics. Professor Grosse writes on financial and managerial strategy of international firms, and on government-business relations, especially in Latin America. He serves on the editorial board of the *Journal of International Business Studies.* He has written fourteen books, including his textbook, *International Business,* with Duane Kujawa (Irwin, 3rd edition,

1995). He has been examining the phenomenon of privatization of state-owned companies in Latin America, and has written articles about the sale of Aerolineas Argentinas and the sales of other public service firms in the region.

Juan Yañes is President of MAI Consulting in Coral Gables, Florida. MAI Consulting specializes in the evaluation of corporate change strategies, and the design of the corresponding organizational structure. MAI's most recent accomplishments include the comanagement of major restructuring projects for important petroleum companies in Latin America. Yañes graduated as a petroleum engineer at the Universidad de Cuyo in Argentina and received a master in International Studies from the Florida International University of Miami, Florida. He has over 50 years' experience in the petroleum industry, many of them in top management positions in the international organization of Exxon.

Appendix
Agentina's Privatization Program: 1990–1994

SECTOR/COMPANY	DATE	TERMS OF TRANSFER
Telephone	11/90	Sale of 60%
ENTEL	12/91	Sale of Telefonica de Argentina (30%)
	3/92	Sale of Telecom (30%)
Aviation Aerolineas Argentinas	11/90	Sale of 85%
Petrochemicals	10/90	Sale of 30%
Polisur		
Induclor	10/90	Sale of 30%
Monomeros Vinilicos	10/90	Sale of 30%
Petropol	10/90	Sale of 30%
Subsecretaria de Combustibles	10/90	Concession of 86 marginal areas
Television Channel 11	1/90	Concession for 15 years
Channel 13		
Water Works	12/92	Concession for 30 years
Obras Sanitarias de la Nacion		
6 Radio Stations	2/91	Concession
Railroads	11/91	Concession for 30 years
Ramal Rosario-Bahia Blanca		
Linea Mitre	8/92	Concession for 30 years
Ramal Delta Borges	9/92	Sociedad Comercial del Plata
		Concession for 30 years
Linea Urquiza	12/92	Concession for 30 years
Linea General Roca	12/92	Concession for 30 years
Linea San Martin	12/92	Concession for 30 years
Linea General Urquiza and Sub-Terraneos de Buenos Aires	12/92	Concession for 20 years
Linea Belgrano Norte	11/93	Concession for 10 years
Linea San Martin		Concession for 10 years
Hydroelectric	8/93	Sale of 59%
HIDRONOR	12/93	
Ship Repair	12/91	Sale
TANDANOR		
Electricity	10/92	Sale to the Distrilec Consortium and the Endesa-Electricito de France Consortium
SEGBA		
Agua y Energia Electrica	8/92	Sale
Oil and Gas	7/93	Sale of 45.3% to Private Investors
YPF		
Gas del Estado	12/92	Sale of 8 distributors and 2 transporters
Steel	10/92	Sale of 80%
SOMISA		
Altos Hornos Zapla	4/92	Sale
Horse Racing	11/92	Concession
Hipodromo Argentino		
Llao-Llao Hotel	5/91	Sale
Surplus State Property	1/91–1/94	Sale of 826 buildings
Fabrica Militar	2/93	Sale
Caja Nacional de Ahorro y Seguro	4/94	Sale of 60%
Highways	9/90	Concession of 10,000 KM

Sources: Ministerio de Economia de Argentina. 1994. *Privatization Update,* March 31. *Apertura* Business Magazine. 1993. Special Issue (Argentina) *Latin Finance.* Privatization Supplement, March 1994.

[27]

Black–White Earnings Differentials: Privatization versus Deregulation

By JAMES PEOPLES, JR., AND WAYNE K. TALLEY*

Over 40 years ago Gary Becker (1957) argued that competition helps mitigate the ability of firms to engage in wage and employment discrimination. Deregulated transportation industries, in particular, provide fertile ground to test the Becker hypothesis. The increase in competition from deregulation should make it increasingly costly for employers to exercise discriminatory preferences. Several studies of the deregulated trucking industry provide support for this hypothesis (Nancy L. Rose, 1987; Peoples and Lisa Saunders, 1993; John S. Heywood and Peoples, 1994).

This study also utilizes information on transportation industries to test the Becker hypothesis. It differs from the literature in that one of the transportation industries examined is privatized.[1] At question is whether the Becker hypothesis also holds for a publicly owned transportation industry in a privatized environment. This question is addressed by investigating privatization's effect on black–white earnings differentials of public-transit bus drivers. These results are then compared with deregulation's effect on black–white earnings differentials of private for-hire truck drivers. Such a comparison allows for analyzing differences in differential earnings for comparable occupations in privatization and deregulation regimes.

† *Discussants:* Abera Gelan, Alverno College; Solomon Mebratu, University of Wisconsin–Milwaukee; Gary Hoover, University of Alabama.

* Peoples: Department of Economics, University of Wisconsin, Milwaukee, WI 53201 (e-mail: peoples@uwm.edu); Talley: Department of Economics, Old Dominion University, Norfolk, VA 23529 (e-mail: wktalley@odu.edu).
[1] The one exception is the study by Peoples and Talley (2000).

I. Transportation Industries

A. *Public Transit*

An overview of the public-transit industry reveals a business environment that presented nontrivial employment opportunities for blacks before the civil-rights era. Prior to 1960, transit firms were generally privately owned, operating under exclusive franchises subject to government regulation of fares and routes. While such regulation does not necessarily discourage employment discrimination, barriers for blacks as transit bus drivers were relatively low by the 1960's. Successful black employment gains occurred, in part, because the labor-supply schedule for this occupation was (and remains) relatively elastic (Philip W. Jeffress, 1971). The changing demographics of transit riders also contributed to enhancing black transit employment for bus drivers. For instance, by 1960 transit systems serviced a disproportionate share of blacks who resided in densely populated areas. Such a clientele is not likely to object to the employment of minorities. Further, transit unions did not have a policy of restricting black employment. Transit unions were more likely to promote employment opportunities for minorities. The most powerful transit union, the Transport Workers Union of America (TWA), even created its own civil-rights committee to address unfair employment practices.

After 1960 changes in the transit industry's business environment indirectly improved the chances of blacks receiving high wages. The 1960's saw a sharp deterioration in transit ridership, resulting from rising incomes and private automobile use. Declining demand threatened the solvency of many transit firms and precipitated a trend of public takeover and growing government subsidization. Public-transit firms operating in densely populated areas received a large share of these subsidies. Transit subsidization helped finance higher earnings for workers in this industry, especially blacks who were disproportionately employed as transit workers in densely populated locations.

By 1980, changing attitudes toward the financing of transit services reduced the opportunity for black transit employees to receive high earnings. The Reagan Administration held the view that operating subsidies increased the cost of transit service by financing increases in labor earnings disproportionate to increases in productivity. While the Reagan Administration sought to eliminate federal operating subsidies, resistance from Congress allowed these subsidies to continue, though at significantly lower levels (American Public Transit Association, 1997).

Another effort to lower public-transit costs is depicted by the 1984 transit-privatization initiative of the Urban Mass Transportation Administration (UMTA). This initiative promoted the contracting-out of public-transit service to lower-cost private providers. UMTA's contracting-out privatization policy charged "localities with the responsibility of demonstrating that they were actively encouraging private firms to participate in the provision of new and restructured local services" as a condition for obtaining or retaining matching funds from the federal government (E. D. Sclar et al., 1989 p. 9). Greater emphasis on contracting-out to low-cost private establishments placed downward pressure on the earnings of public-transit workers. Black transit drivers were most vulnerable to this wage pressure, since they were disproportionately employed in public systems that rely on federal subsidies.

B. *For-Hire Trucking*

Regulation of entry and rates influenced racial employment in the trucking industry, but much differently than the regulation effect in the transit industry. The Motor Carrier Act of 1935 severely restricted entry into the lucrative less-than-truckload (LTL) sector of the for-hire trucking industry. The lack of competition in the highly organized LTL sector depicts a business environment that presents employers and unions with the latitude to restrict employment of workers from non-preferred groups. Evidence from past research reveals that blacks were one-fourth as likely to be employed in the lucrative segment of the for-hire industry compared to their employment in the rest of the industry (Richard Leone, 1970). Such employment disparities occurred even though truck drivers faced a highly elastic labor-supply curve (Rose, 1987). The lack of black truck drivers employed in the LTL sector was due in part to union seniority rules that relegated transfers to the bottom of the LTL seniority list. Barriers to black LTL employment is particularly significant because rate regulation based on cost mark-up pricing methods allowed payment of high wages to drivers in the LTL sector. The opportunity to negotiate high union wages was further enhanced by the Teamsters' control over the labor supply of LTL truck drivers.

Deregulation initiated by the Interstate Commerce Commission in 1978 and legislated by the 1980 Motor Carrier Act (MCA) profoundly changed the business environment in the for-hire trucking industry. Entry restrictions eased, and federal regulators relied more heavily on the market to set rates. Significant entry of low-cost nonunion carriers occurred following deregulation. This influx of new carriers contributed to the percentage of union drivers in the for-hire truck sector falling from 56.8 percent in 1978 to 24.9 percent in 1995. Trucking deregulation policy also had the unplanned effect of improving employment opportunities for black drivers. The share of for-hire jobs held by black drivers increased from 15.5 percent in 1978 to 24.3 percent in 1995 (Barry T. Hirsch and David A. Macpherson, 1998). Such employment patterns comport well with the view that union and trucking firms are less likely to indulge in employment discrimination when faced with stepped-up competition.

Evidence suggesting that black drivers experienced eroding employment barriers in the still-lucrative LTL sector is not as obvious as for the rest of the for-hire industry. High LTL start-up cost associated with necessary production inputs such as terminals and dock equipment creates a tremendous barrier to greater competition. High LTL barriers to entry contributed to an increasing share of the LTL freight hauled by the largest carriers in this sector. LTL carriers also remained highly organized. The lack of competition coupled with the union's control over the supply of drivers could still provide employers and unions with the latitude to exercise hiring preferences in the high-wage LTL segment of the for-hire industry. Empirical analysis is then required to examine the extent to which the racial earnings differential declined following deregulation.

II. Data and Earnings Model

Individual information for public-transit bus and private for-hire truck drivers is taken from Current Population Survey (CPS) files of the Bureau of the Census for the years 1973–1996 (excluding 1982) and used to examine black–white earnings differentials in the public-transit and private for-hire trucking industries. Data covering the observation periods from 1973–1981 were taken from May CPS files. Data for the 1983–1996 observation period were taken from 168 monthly CPS outgoing rotation group files for January 1983 through December 1996.[2] The year 1982 was omitted, because union-status information was not collected in the survey. The selected samples consist of full-time public-transit bus and private for-hire truck drivers, age 16–64, who reported information on their usual weekly earnings, usual hours worked, union status, and a set of demographic characteristics.[3]

The CPS public-transit bus and private truck driver samples are used to estimate the following earnings equations:

(1a) $\ln(\text{Earnings})_{j,t,\text{transit,union}}$

$$= \alpha_1(\text{Black})_{j,t} + \alpha_2(\text{Privatization})_{j,t}$$

$$+ \alpha_3(\text{Privatization} \times \text{Black})_{j,t}$$

$$+ \sum \beta_k X_{j,t,k} + \varepsilon_{j,t,\text{transit,union}}$$

(1b) $\ln(\text{Earnings})_{j,t,\text{truck,union}}$

$$= \alpha_1(\text{Black})_{j,t} + \alpha_2(\text{Deregulation})_{j,t}$$

$$+ \alpha_3(\text{Deregulation} \times \text{Black})_{j,t}$$

$$+ \sum \beta_k X_{j,t,k} + \varepsilon_{j,t,\text{truck,union}}$$

where j indexes individual drivers, t indexes the observation year, "transit" and "truck" index public-transit bus and private truck sectors, and "union" indexes union status (i.e., union vs. nonunion). The variable ln(Earnings) is the natural log of usual weekly earnings in 1983–1984 dollars.[4] The variable "Black" is a dummy equaling 1 if the driver is black. The industrial policy variables "Privatization" and "Deregulation" are dummies equaling 1 for the observation years 1984–1996 and 1979–1996, respectively. The control vector **X** includes a constant as well as the standard labor earnings determinants. In addition, the annual national unemployment rate is included as an earnings determinant to control for time-variant distortions such as changes in the business cycle.

The coefficients of particular interest to this study are α_1 and α_3. The coefficient α_1 measures the black–white log-earnings differential of drivers for the observation period prior to the industrial policy. The coefficient α_3 measures the change in the black–white log-earnings differentials of drivers for the observation period following the introduction of such policy.

III. Estimation Results

Estimates of equation (1a) for union and nonunion public transit bus drivers appear in columns (i) and (ii) of Table 1, and estimates of equation (1b) for union and nonunion private for-hire truck drivers appear in columns (iii) and (iv). The estimated coefficient on the "Black" dummy in column (i) indicates an 11.74-percent earnings premium for black union public-transit bus drivers in the pre-privatization period.[5] This finding is consistent with the view that black

---

[2] Twelve-month CPS files in which the union question was asked are not available prior to 1983.
[3] Truck drivers in the samples are employee drivers. Self-employed truck drivers (i.e., owner-operators) are not considered.

[4] Usual weekly earnings were deflated using the Consumer Price Index (CPI).
[5] Earnings differentials are calculated as $(e^\alpha - 1) \times 100$.

TABLE 1—PARTIAL RESULTS ON LOG WEEKLY EARNINGS

| Variable | Public-transit bus drivers | | Private for-hire truck drivers | |
	Union (i)	Nonunion (ii)	Union (iii)	Nonunion (iv)
Black	0.111	−0.0589	−0.155	−0.240
	(2.552)	(−0.661)	(−3.418)	(−3.717)
Privatization	0.045	0.082	—	—
	(1.293)	(1.296)		
Privatization × Black	−0.1407	0.1138	—	—
	(−2.29)	(1.010)		
Deregulation	—	—	−0.155	−0.129
			(−10.769)	(−6.444)
Deregulation × Black	—	—	0.062	0.225
			(1.291)	(3.403)
Sample size:	737	327	5,326	10,465

Notes: The control variables include age, age-squared, log of weekly hours worked, annual U.S. unemployment rate, and dummies for marital status, gender, five levels of educational attainment, and residence in three of the four U.S. geographic quadrants. Numbers in parentheses are t statistics. Complete results are available from the authors upon request.

union transit drivers benefited from the pre-privatization transit labor environment. This finding is also unique to union transit drivers in that the estimated coefficient on the "Black" dummy in column (ii) indicates that black non-union transit drivers received earnings 5.72-percent below those of their white counterparts in the pre-privatization period.

The results in column (i) support the Becker hypothesis that stepped-up competition is associated with smaller racial earnings differentials. For example, the estimated coefficient on the Privatization × Black interaction term indicates a 13.12-percent erosion of the black union earnings premium for the period. This erosion left black union transit drivers with earnings closely resembling those of their white counterparts. Further, the earnings disadvantage of black nonunion transit drivers eroded in the post-privatization period, with their earnings slightly exceeding those of their white counterparts.

Findings in column (iii) indicate that black union truck drivers received an earnings discount below that of their white counterparts in the pre-deregulation period. The estimated coefficient on the "Black" variable indicates that black union truck drivers received a 14.35-

percent discount in earnings. Findings in column (iv) indicate an even larger black discount for nonunion drivers. The estimated coefficient on the "Black" variable indicates that black nonunion truck drivers received earnings that were 21.33 percent below those of their white counterparts.

The estimated coefficient on the Deregulation × Black interaction term in column (iii) indicates a 6.4-percentage-point erosion of the earnings discount for black union truck driver earnings in the post-deregulation period. While this result supports the Becker hypothesis, the remaining 7.95-percent earnings advantage for white truck drivers is also consistent with the notion that a racial earnings differential can still persist without stepped-up competition in all segments of the for-hire trucking industry. The results in column (iv) indicate a complete erosion of the earnings disadvantage for black nonunion truck drivers in the post-deregulation period.

IV. Conclusion

Industrial policy over the last 25 years has emphasized greater reliance on competitive markets to enhance consumer welfare. Such policy may also have the unintended effect of reducing racial wage disparities. Support for this view has been reported for the deregulated trucking industry. This study finds that privatization in the public transit sector is associated with declines in the racial earnings differential that resemble those found in trucking. The privatization results are unique in that they reveal that it is the earnings advantage of blacks that erodes following the introduction of this policy. In sum, the results from this study suggest that Becker's hypothesis on competition and discrimination holds for publicly owned establishments in a privatized environment, at least when the occupation used for analysis requires modest training.

REFERENCES

American Public Transit Association. *Transit fact book.* Washington, DC: American Public Transit Association, 1997.

Becker, Gary S. *The economics of discrimination.* Chicago: University of Chicago Press, 1957.

Heywood, John S. and Peoples, James, Jr. "Deregulation and the Prevalence of Black Truck Drivers." *Journal of Law and Economics*, April 1994, *37*(1), pp. 133–55.

Hirsch, Barry T. and Macpherson, David A. "Earnings and Employment in Trucking: Deregulating a Naturally Competitive Industry," in J. Peoples, ed., *Regulatory reform and labor markets*. Boston, MA: Kluwer, 1998, pp. 61–112.

Jeffress, Philip W. "The Negro in the Urban Transit Industry," in H. R. Northrup, H. W. Risher, Jr., R. D. Leone, and P. W. Jeffress, eds., *Negro employment in land and air transport*. Philadelphia: University of Pennsylvania Press, 1971, pp. 1–101.

Leone, Richard. *The Negro in the trucking industry*. Philadelphia: University of Pennsylvania Press, 1970.

Peoples, James, Jr. and Saunders, Lisa. "Trucking Deregulation and the Black/White Wage Gap." *Industrial and Labor Relations Review*, October 1993, *47*(1), pp. 23–35.

Peoples, James, Jr. and Talley, Wayne K. "Privatization, City Residency, and Black–White Earnings Differentials: Evidence from the Public Transit Sector." Unpublished manuscript, University of Wisconsin–Milwaukee, 2000.

Rose, Nancy L. "Labor Rent Sharing and Regulation: Evidence from the Trucking Industry." *Journal of Political Economy*, December 1987, *95*(6), pp. 1146–78.

Sclar, E. D.; Schaeffer, K. H. and Brandwein, R. *The emperor's new clothes: Transit privatization and public policy*. Washington, DC: Economic Policy Institute, 1989.

Part V
Privatization and Business Strategy

[28]

© *Academy of Management Review*
2000, Vol. 25, No. 3, 509-524.

PRIVATIZATION AND ENTREPRENEURIAL TRANSFORMATION: EMERGING ISSUES AND A FUTURE RESEARCH AGENDA

SHAKER A. ZAHRA
Georgia State University

R. DUANE IRELAND
University of Richmond

ISABEL GUTIERREZ
Carlos III University

MICHAEL A. HITT
Texas A&M University

Privatization has become a popular strategy to promote economic development in emerging, developing, and developed economies. Despite its popularity, little attention has been devoted to examination of the organizational and managerial implications of privatization or to the effect of privatization on companies' ability to innovate and engage in entrepreneurial activities. In this article we discuss privatization's increasing importance and present a model that links privatization to a firm's entrepreneurial activities. We conclude with a discussion of issues that we believe deserve scholars' attention in theory development and subsequent empirical examination.

The global economic landscape is undergoing unprecedented change that is multifaceted and wide ranging in nature (Hitt, Harrison, & Ireland, in press b; Ireland & Hitt, 1999) and that is clearly evident in the adoption of privatization as a strategy on a worldwide basis. The primary purpose of this strategic option is to promote economic development in emerging, developing, and developed economies. Emerging economies and their markets, however, are characterized by economic, social, or political instability (Hitt, Dacin, Levitas, Arregle, & Borza, in press a). There are also substantial differences in the institutional infrastructure between emerging and developed economies (Newman, this issue). Given that the idiosyncratic characteristics of an economy's structure can profoundly affect the rules of exchange in its markets (North, 1990), these differences can have a

major effect on the outcomes that countries or companies can achieve through privatization.

Following decades of experimentation with various systems of state ownership and control, many nations have adopted privatization strategies as a centerpiece of their national policies—policies that aim to promote and support social progress and economic development or to initiate economic renewal. Over $700 billion in assets have been privatized in the world's economies in the last decade alone, approximately 40 percent of which has occurred in emerging economies (Ramamurti, this issue). Brazil is expected to privatize as much as $80 billion in assets before its ongoing conversion of public assets to private ownership is completed (Doh, this issue). Countries using privatization strategies as a primary policy tool to induce and promote economic growth represent most of the world's regions, including Africa, Asia, Latin America, and Europe.

By placing the means of production outside of state ownership and control, privatization unleashes the forces and discipline of the free mar-

---

Duane Ireland was on the faculty at Baylor University while working on this special topic forum.

510   *Academy of Management Review*   July

ket. The resulting pattern of action (i.e., privatization) and reaction (i.e., the forces of a free market economy) strongly influence the degree to which governments control their national economies (D'Souza & Megginson, 1999; Melloan, 2000). Privatization, therefore, has the potential to transform national economies, industries, and organizations by infusing a spirit of entrepreneurial risk taking. These changes are in process currently across the world's six major continents, making privatization an integral part of emerging, developing, and developed countries' twenty-first-century strategic agendas. Effective privatizations, however, where state-owned industries are privatized without creating significant unemployment and related disruptions, are difficult to achieve (Melloan, 2000). Consequently, some of the contributors in this special topic forum challenge us to proceed cautiously when forming expectations about privatization's outcomes.

When examining privatization as a change strategy, researchers are concerned with privatization's effects on the creation of wealth. To date, most privatization researchers have focused on the country as the unit of analysis, primarily examining the macroenvironmental conditions that lead to privatization (e.g., Filatotchev, Hoskisson, Buck, & Wright, 1996; Galal, Jones, Tandon, & Vogelsang, 1994; Grosse & Yanes, 1998). Researchers also have examined the factors that lead to the use of particular approaches to privatization (e.g., Miller, 1995; Minniti & Polutnik, 1999; Ramamurti, 1992). Most of this research has been grounded in economic or financial theories, leaving important organizational issues unexplored.

Further, in prior research scholars have not examined the major organizational transformations that occur following privatization. These transformations can be far reaching, possibly leading to the formation of new stakeholder groups and redefining the patterns of these stakeholders' interactions with the firm. The effects of these groups' interaction patterns on a firm may be significant, creating a need for extensive organizational and behavioral adjustments.

THE PURPOSE OF THE SPECIAL TOPIC FORUM

With this *Academy of Management Review* special topic forum, the authors seek to contribute to our understanding of the *potential* effects of privatization on organizational transformation. Organizational transformation includes changes in organizational values, cultures, systems, and strategies. Transformation centers on how a firm is organized, governed, and managed as it adjusts to the competitive realities of a market economy. Changes in cognitive, strategic, cultural, and structural dimensions that are required to support organizational transformation may induce or expand entrepreneurial actions, calculated risk taking, and innovation. Entrepreneurial activities are important for achieving efficiency, improving productivity, and creating wealth (Baumol, 1996). These activities foster innovation that leads to the introduction of a new product, process, technology, system, technique, resource, or capability to the firm or its markets (Covin & Miles, 1999). Innovation is the foundation for competitive advantage in the new global economy (Hitt, Nixon, Hoskisson, & Kochhar, 1999). An entrepreneurial transformation, in which the firm engages in more entrepreneurial activities, risk taking, and innovation, is key to an organization's transition from what is often a state-owned status to one of competing in a market-based economy.

Even though one reason to privatize firms is to promote entrepreneurial transformation, achieving such a transformation is more difficult in an emerging economy than in a developed economy. Typically, the sparse resources and capabilities previously state-owned enterprises possess are inadequate to support an entrepreneurial transformation. As a result, newly privatized firms in emerging economies often find it necessary to seek financial, technological, and managerial resources and capabilities from more richly endowed firms (Hitt et al., in press a).

To compete successfully in a market-based economy, privatized firms also must quickly learn how to use newly acquired resources (Zahra, Ireland, & Hitt, in press). Rapidly acquiring application-oriented and learning-based skills is oftentimes facilitated by the development of cooperative arrangements, such as joint ventures and equity strategic alliances (Hitt, Ireland, & Hoskisson, in press c). Some of these alliances are formed with companies that are outside the privatized firm's domestic market. Although such international joint ventures are a challenging organizational form, the rate of their formation continues to increase (Yan, 1998).

Regardless of the mode used to acquire and apply new skills, firms find how to use modern technologies and the related skills required to engage in successful commercial activities difficult without adequate levels of absorptive capacity (Cohen & Levinthal, 1990). This capacity allows privatized firms to assimilate and exploit new knowledge. Assimilation and exploitation of new knowledge can ignite innovation in privatized firms. Developing absorptive capacity can be difficult, given that firms from developed markets have learned how to buffer their core technologies from appropriation by other firms, even those with whom they form strategic alliances. Written contracts are a formal means of preventing appropriation, whereas interactions based on trust that have evolved over time are an informal yet equally effective means of protecting a firm's intellectual property.

Recent research results highlight the importance of these capabilities. Uhlenbruck and De-Castro (in press) found that acquisitions of newly privatized firms from emerging markets by companies from developed countries enhanced the acquired firm's performance. Transferring new technologies, managerial skills, and financial resources from the acquiring to the acquired firm led to higher performance. The transfer of skills facilitates the acquired and recently privatized firms' efforts to transform into viable competitors in a market-based economy (Hitt et al., in press b).

Focusing on the organizational transformation that may follow privatization and privatization's potential effects on entrepreneurial activities, this special topic forum is designed to improve our understanding of several phenomena, including (1) the factors that serve as a catalyst for privatization in countries at different stages of their economic development; (2) different privatization strategies and their unique characteristics; (3) the effect of privatization on the process of organizational transformation, particularly in promoting firm-level entrepreneurship; and (4) the implications of organizational transformation for the effective management of privatized firms. Our goal, indeed our hope, is to highlight the importance of privatization in creating a new set of organizational dynamics that promote innovation, risk taking, proactive management, and entrepreneurship. This emphasis is based on the fact that countries, industries, and organizations that foster entrepreneurship are well positioned to achieve technological and economic progress.

In the next section we examine the domain and importance of privatization. A model that links the antecedents and the process of privatization to entrepreneurial transformation follows this discussion. Thereafter, we review the key themes in the articles appearing in the special topic forum, highlighting their contributions. We also describe major areas for future research and challenges scholars face as they seek to build theories that are capable of effectively capturing the relationships between privatization and entrepreneurial transformation.

PRIVATIZATION: DOMAIN AND IMPORTANCE

To capture a complex phenomenon, in most definitions of privatization authors highlight the change in a firm's ownership and, as a consequence, the change in its governance and control systems (e.g., Ramamurti, 1992). Changes in firms' ownership occur in several ways (Ramamurti, this issue; Ramirez, 1998). These changes, however, typically produce a transfer of ownership of fully or partially owned public or state-owned enterprises to private parties. This transfer determines the appropriation of residual rents (profits) *and* the allocation of residual decision rights (ownership rights).

Ramamurti (this issue) notes that privatization can be defined in both a *narrow* and a *broad* sense. The different definitions indicate that as a process, privatization has many shapes (Doh, this issue). Viewed *broadly*, privatization is any action that increases the role of the private sector in the economy. In this broad sense, activities that would constitute privatization might include the sale of public assets, deregulation, opening state monopolies to greater competition, contracting out, the private provision of public services, joint capital projects using public and private finance, reduced subsidies, and increasing or introducing user charges (Jackson & Price, 1994).

From a *narrow* lens, privatization is any action that transfers some or all of the ownership and/or control of state-owned enterprises to the private sector. As Ramamurti (this issue) observes, privatization of one type does not necessarily imply privatization of the other type. For example, a nation might privatize some of its state-owned enterprises without deregulating

512   *Academy of Management Review*   July

the industry or the base economy in which those enterprises compete.

Another form of the narrow definition of privatization is the transfer of ownership and decision-making authority from federal, state, or municipal governments to the hands of private investors (DeCastro & Uhlenbruck, 1997; Ogden & Watson, 1999; Vickers & Yarrow, 1988). The potential effects of narrow and broad types of privatization provide an important research question. Although not the focus of the special topic forum, we revisit this issue in our discussion of future research directions.

The appropriation of residual rents (profits) can occur through private or public mechanisms. When it occurs through private mechanisms, profits go to private owners as rewards for risk taking, entrepreneurial activities, and efficient and innovative management (Jensen & Meckling, 1976). These profits also can be used in ways that benefit the public welfare, such as expanding companies' operations to create jobs and reduce unemployment (Hart, 1995). These actions should benefit the firm, its shareholders, and the general public welfare.

Allocation of ownership rights is another key dimension in understanding privatization. Ownership rights refer to the locus of authority for making strategic choices (Jensen & Meckling, 1976). These rights usually occur on a continuum, ranging from wholly public to totally private. Owners generally have the authority to decide the firm's strategic goals, develop its competitive strategy, and allocate its resources. Certainly, this is the case when private parties hold ownership.

When public managers, representing state owners or a specific constituency, control ownership and, hence, decision rights, the mandate embodied in their organizations' founding charters will be discharged. Public managers, therefore, often must address a set of complex—indeed, competing—goals that include creating employment opportunities, managing national resources, and ensuring social justice. Achieving these diverse goals frequently entails satisficing multiple political claims, which may result in significant deviations from market-based efficiency. Thus, considered from a micro level, these managers often operate from an institutionalized public sector template when encountering privatization. Johnson, Smith, and Codling (this issue) propose that at the onset of

privatization, this template may be deeply embedded, taken for granted, and oftentimes mindlessly enacted. To facilitate the privatization process, a firm is challenged to take actions through which a private sector template can be institutionalized within its managerial ranks. Therefore, Johnson and colleagues view privatization as a process of institutional change.

Figure 1 indicates that different types of privatization activities can be observed from linking the two dimensions of ownership rights and the appropriation of profits. In prior research scholars have failed to recognize the different types of privatization, thereby overlooking a major source of variation in the observed results of privatization.

Four types of organizational forms are evident in Figure 1. Cell 1 represents the "pure public firm," where ownership rights are in the hands of public owners and the appropriation of profits is used for the public good. This type of organization dominated many underdeveloped and socialist countries in the second half of the twentieth century. In cell 2 public owners control ownership (decision) rights while residual rents are appropriated through market (private) means. Here, two major organizational forms are prevalent: franchises and regulated firms. Both organizational forms have been used widely in developed and emerging economies. In cell 3 private owners hold ownership rights, but the appropriation of profits is performed for the public good. Such organizations typically are classified as "not-for-profit." Finally, in cell 4

FIGURE 1
Classification of Firms with Ownership Rights and Profit Orientation

		Ownership rights	
		Private	Public
Profit appropriation orientation	Yes	Pure private firm (4)	• Regulated • Franchises (2)
	No	Not-for-profit organization (3)	Pure public firm (1)

Source: Adapted from Salas (1998).

private owners to whom the profits are also disbursed hold the ownership rights. This cell, therefore, depicts the prototypical "pure private firm."

We suggest that multiple outcomes are possible when privatizing pure publicly owned firms (Figure 1). Most researchers readily recognize a firm's movement from pure public to pure private forms, but the other forms of organization require further study. For instance, the state might permit the private appropriation of residual rents, thereby moving the firm from cell 1 to cell 2. Franchising and management contracts can be used to achieve this change. A final type of privatization entails moving the public firm (cell 1) to a not-for-profit status (cell 3). The state might make this change to avoid the costly management of public firms while promoting efficiency and social good. Although theoretically interesting, management scholars have not systematically examined this type of privatization strategy.

As the above discussion suggests, privatization is a multidimensional construct that can affect different facets of organizational transformation in multiple ways. Similarly, several forces can influence these dimensions, affecting the overall gains that companies are able to achieve following privatization. Understanding how to achieve these gains, however, requires an appreciation of the antecedents of privatization and the resulting changes from privatization.

A MODEL OF PRIVATIZATION: ANTECEDENTS AND EFFECTS

As shown in Figure 2, a complex set of variables interacts to affect the mode and process of privatization (DeCastro & Uhlenbruck, 1997; Johnson & Loveman, 1995; Ogden & Watson, 1999). These variables, however, differ significantly between developed and emerging economies. Although in both types of economies governments aspire to curtail governmental control, promote competition, improve productivity, and induce market-based efficiency, in emerging economies other motives can significantly affect privatization efforts. Often, in emerging economies, privatization has been implemented in response to demands from the International Monetary Fund (IMF). Governments of emerging economies that seek loans to support economic development often have been required to introduce substantial economic liberalization policies (Hoskisson, Eden, Lau, & Wright, in press).

Thus, in these economies privatization is used as a means of transplanting a procapitalist political ideology by liberalizing the economy, promoting foreign investment, infusing new technology, and increasing national standards of living. In some emerging economies privatization is also used as a means to upgrade infrastructure and facilitate future industrial growth. An improved infrastructure supports companies' efforts to enhance the efficiency of their operations and also can facilitate the creation and

FIGURE 2
A Model of the Privatization Process and Outcomes

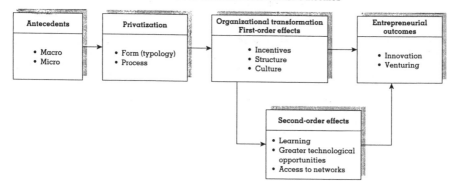

growth of new firms, which are the engine of economic and technological progress (Acs & Audretsch, 1993).

Macroenvironmental factors alone do not explain the selection of enterprises targeted for privatization. The importance of the enterprise to the national welfare or other sectors of the national economy plays a key role in the selection process (Shafik, 1996). The economic importance of an enterprise usually is determined by its potential contributions in fulfilling market demand, creating jobs, and meeting the needs of other sectors in the national economy. These evaluations, however, are also often based on the perceived importance of the enterprise for national sovereignty and identity. The greater the importance attached to national sovereignty, the less likely it is that an enterprise will be privatized.

Other factors that influence the selection of enterprises for privatization include their cost of operations, solvency, and track record in earning profits (Shafik, 1996; Shleifer & Vishny, 1994). For example, poorly performing public enterprises frequently are among the first to be privatized, perhaps to buffer the taxpayer from their operating costs. The decision to select an enterprise for privatization also depends on the availability of competent managerial leaders who can oversee the firm's transformation. This is a particularly difficult task in emerging economies, where the lack of qualified senior executives can make the transformation of a public enterprise into a private firm challenging (Ozkaya & Askari, 1999).

Most prior research on the antecedents of privatization has been descriptive in nature or based on case studies (Johnson & Loveman, 1995; Soulsby & Clark, 1996). Moreover, this research has not been well grounded in theory, making it difficult to draw solid conclusions about the relative importance of the different antecedent variables or to predict which firms are most likely to be privatized. Therefore, an important opportunity exists for management scholars to explore the determinants of privatization and their relative importance. It should be recognized that privatization decisions are not totally rational, because political factors affect the choice of companies to be privatized. Future research on privatization would also benefit from connecting the antecedent vari-

ables discussed earlier (Figure 2) to the types of privatization strategies followed.

PRIVATIZATION STRATEGIES: MODES AND PROCESSES

Privatization can be partial or full, occurring in ways that include the sale of a company's assets or shares (through public bidding or negotiated agreements) to domestic or foreign investors; the granting of leases, concessions, or management contracts; and employee or management buyouts (Djankov, 1999). Countries employ different strategies in privatizing their economies (Cuervo & Villalonga, this issue) and use different strategies in separate economic sectors, or apply different strategies within the same sector at different points in time. These differences reflect variations in political ideology, stage of development, national cultures, and long-term development plans (Filatotchev, Wright, Buck, & Dymonia, 1999a; Filatotchev, Wright, Buck, & Zhukov, 1999b).

Researchers have documented the frequency with which different modes of privatization have been used, as well as the resulting outcomes (success or the lack thereof; Djankov, 1999; D'Souza & Megginson, 1999; Welfens, 1992). Yet, as Cuervo and Villalonga (this issue) observe, little attention has been given to documenting the processes used to implement these strategies or to examining the relationship between them and subsequent changes in a company's structure or organizational culture. Still, there is anecdotal evidence that the process by which a firm is privatized could affect its future gains (Dean, Carlisle, & Baden-Fuller, 1999; Johnson & Loveman, 1995; Smith, Golden, & Pitcher, 1999). These observations are consistent with research indicating that the speed, direction, and magnitude of changes introduced to revise a company's business definition, strategy, or organizational structure can affect the outcomes of these efforts (Huber & Glick, 1995). As noted in Figure 2, we separate these outcomes into first- and second-order effects.

First-Order Effects of Privatization

Privatization also creates a new context in which firms must compete to survive and succeed. The transformation accompanying privatization changes the enterprise's structure and

2000 *Zahra, Ireland, Gutierrez, and Hitt* 515

the way it is managed, thereby leading to fundamental changes in the firm's culture (Johnson & Loveman, 1995). Privatization also changes managers' incentives (Wright, Hoskisson, Busenitz, & Dial, this issue). Below we examine changes in managerial incentives, as well as organizational structure and culture following privatization.

Managerial incentives. Managers of state-owned enterprises usually have limited discretion to initiate and implement strategic changes (Cragg & Dyck, 1999) and are constrained by bureaucratic controls that limit the scope of their activities and authority. Some of the controls are financial in nature, specifying performance quotas and targets. Financial controls typically reflect the objectives of political policy makers (Vickers & Yarrow, 1988). Commonly, financial controls stifle managerial efforts to think strategically about the organization's purpose and the actions to be taken to achieve it (Hitt et al., in press c). Central or governmental planning authorities often have the responsibility to establish public managers' compensation (Cragg & Dyck, 2000).

Following privatization, a new set of dynamics occurs. Notably, senior managers begin to plan and develop strategies based on analyses of industry and market conditions. Managers also have the discretion to redefine organizational goals to reflect the objectives of their key stakeholders (Yarrow, 1986). Furthermore, they have greater discretion in aligning resource allocations with the firm's objectives. Discretion is the capability through which managers select and support projects that they believe are vital to accomplish the firm's long-term goals. Resource allocation decisions, therefore, should reflect market realities and the managers' judgments about the strategic actions that have the highest probability of leading to firm profitability. Thus, after privatization, managerial discretion for resource allocation increases, improving the alignment among the firm's goals, resources, and capabilities. These observations are based on the assumption that managers are capable of operating effectively in a market economy and that they have the knowledge and skills required to develop and implement effective strategies.

After privatization, the firm and its management are subjected to market forces. The managers become accountable to shareholders,

compelling them to pursue strategies that increase shareholder wealth. Managers assume the burden of reorganizing the existing capital and labor stocks, establishing sales and marketing units, implementing new accounting and control systems, deciding new product strategies, and developing and implementing new investment programs (Sachs & Lipton, 1990). As a result, managers' reputations and compensation should be tied to the firm's performance, providing them with incentives to formulate and implement strategies that increase shareholder value (Zahra, 1996). There is evidence that managers' compensation increases following privatization and that the compensation of managers in privatized companies is similar to that of other publicly held corporations (Cragg & Dyck, 2000). Increased discretion and compensation can improve managers' willingness to take risks and support innovation (Hoskisson, Hitt, & Hill, 1993; Wright et al., this issue).

Organizational structure and culture. The freeing of prices, reduction in regulation, and increase in competition associated with economic transition highlight the inefficient organization of firms before the privatization process. For firms to survive economic liberalization, they often need to be restructured. Limited research exists in which authors have examined the changes in a firm's organizational structure and culture following privatization. The implications of these changes, if any, for managerial decision making have not been well documented (Cragg & Dyck, 1999, 2000). However, some research indicates that privatized companies often experience structural and cultural changes that affect their operations (Cuervo & Villalonga, this issue; Johnson & Loveman, 1995). For example, privatized firms become subject to market pressures and are forced to become more efficient and cost effective, which often requires employee attrition (D'Souza & Megginson, 1999). Privatized firms frequently downsize their employee base and provide the survivors of such layoffs with training to develop new skills and increase job performance. Employee pay and benefits often are revised to reflect labor market conditions, and incentive systems and other approaches are used to motivate employees and improve their performance.

Privatized companies also change their organizational structures to ensure faster decision making by eliminating layers of management and reducing bureaucratic rules (Cuervo & Vil-

516   *Academy of Management Review*   July

lalonga, this issue). Flatter organizational structures, therefore, are more common in privatized companies, and they usually facilitate communication between management and employees. Improved communication can strengthen employee commitment to the organization, encouraging employees to be more productive and innovative. When the organizational culture strengthens employee identification with the company, it promotes a willingness to take the types of risk that lead to product, process, and administrative innovations (Kanter, 1989).

Second-Order Effects of Privatization

Privatization also creates a set of national (macro) and organizational (micro) changes, as indicated in Figure 2. These changes, in turn, may stimulate organizational learning (Doh, this issue; Newman, this issue) and the acquisition of new skills. Learning capabilities and additional skills can provide the foundation for enhanced technological opportunities for firms, as well as the capabilities needed to gain access to different domestic and international networks (Zahra et al., in press). We refer to these three variables (learning, opportunities, and networks) as second-order privatization effects. We distinguish these effects from the more apparent changes within a firm following privatization.

Although more subtle than first-order effects, second-order effects are equally powerful in their potential impacts. Second-order privatization effects reflect the combined influences of internal (organizational) changes and external (macro) variables. Three potential second-order privatization effects are highlighted in Figure 2: improved organizational learning, increased technological opportunities, and gaining access to networks.

Improved organizational learning. Ideally, the first-order effects discussed above (Figure 2) will create an internal environment that encourages managers to experiment and explore new strategic alternatives. The changes privatization induces usually are so radical that a new organizational mindset is needed to comprehend and capitalize on the opportunities that become available to the firm (Smith et al., 1999). Thus, privatization can be viewed as a "frame-breaking" event that compels managers to envision and examine their industry, environment,

competition, and the firm from a different perspective (Dean et al., 1999). Frame-breaking change usually is conducive to experimentation and innovation, which, in turn, promote organizational learning (Newman, this issue).

Privatization also creates a business environment hospitable to foreign investments, particularly those involving the transfer of innovative technology, as well as modern management, production, and marketing techniques. Some foreign investors partner with privatized companies by forming strategic alliances, such as joint ventures. These alliances give the privatized companies opportunities to learn new skills and capabilities from their more resource-rich foreign partners (often from developed market countries; Hitt et al., in press a).

Learning new capabilities is likely to facilitate privatized companies' abilities to capitalize on market opportunities. The freedom to act independently because of privatization also spurs innovation that increases technological opportunities throughout an entire industry. As such, privatized firms can introduce new products and services to the market, unencumbered by government bureaucracy or political processes. Alternatively, privatized firms may initially attempt to license, copy, or imitate the technological skills of their advanced foreign partners or rivals.

These imitative processes are important, especially in the developmental stage, where privatized firms focus on building their skills and capabilities by learning from foreign partners or competitors. Appropriation by imitation is affected by the degree to which partners protect their proprietary technologies through formal mechanisms (e.g., contracts) or informal means (e.g., structural configurations influencing the nature of interactions between partners). Once they achieve technological proficiency, however, some privatized firms experiment with new R&D processes to develop innovations. Experimentation also enables privatized firms to develop a new set of routines that can be useful in making the transition from imitation to innovation (Kim, 1997).

Increased technological opportunities. We define technological opportunities as the potential for product and process innovation within an industry. As indicated in Figure 2, we expect these opportunities to increase subsequent to privatization. Privatization often encourages foreign investments (Filatotchev et al., 1999a) that facilitate or even promote technology transfer. Foreign partners may be willing to transfer the technology because of a potentially significant return on their investment over time. Also, foreign partners may learn new capabilities from the venture (Hitt et al., in press a; Zahra et al., in press). The flow of modern technology into a newly privatized economy can spark innovation as local entrepreneurs use this technology to pursue promising market opportunities. The transfer of technology also allows local entrepreneurs to integrate separate technologies imported from different countries. This process fuels experimentation and innovation, leading to higher productivity.

Following privatization, technological opportunities are likely to increase, because local entrepreneurs are more willing to take risks, either by forming their own companies or by forming joint ventures. This process is made easier by informal and formal sources of venture capital that increase following the liberalization of an economy, encouraging entrepreneurs to identify and pursue new market opportunities. Also, developmental financial institutions (DFIs) often play an important role in financing privatized companies' strategic actions or entrepreneurial efforts. George and Prabhu (this issue) describe DFIs and their roles in emerging economies. DFIs' role is similar to that of large institutional investors present in developed countries. These organizations provide long-term capital through loans or take equity positions in newly privatized firms. Some DFIs offer a range of other important services in addition to providing capital, such as serving in a consulting-type capacity. In this capacity DFIs assist in efforts to identify market opportunities, search for managerial talent, and conduct feasibility studies. These services and growing access to capital can increase the competitiveness of privatized firms (George & Prabhu, this issue).

The identification and pursuit of new technological opportunities vary across countries and economies. The speed of actions taken to identify and pursue these opportunities depends partially on the national economy's level of technological sophistication, as well as its absorptive capacity (ability to learn). A country's absorptive capacity is determined by its prior investments to acquire and assimilate technological skills (Mowery & Oxley, 1995). As the absorptive capacity of the country expands, its

ability to assimilate new technology increases. Assimilation increases the ease and speed of innovation diffusion, thereby igniting innovation. Given the interdependence of economic sectors, innovation in one industry can fuel innovation in other industries, thereby enhancing the total set of technological opportunities.

National culture is another factor that can determine the nature and size of emerging technological opportunities. Some research indicates that national cultural variables play a major role in determining the rates of innovation (Shane, 1995). In societies valuing risk taking and innovation, entrepreneurs are likely to seek and identify market opportunities that might have been overlooked prior to the liberalization of the economy. Further, coupled with the adoption of imported technologies, the effect of national cultures in these societies on creating technological opportunities will increase following privatization. These opportunities will expand as domestic entrepreneurs become connected to influential networks within and across their national borders.

Gaining access to networks. Liberalization of an economy and extensive privatization are also expected to link domestic producers and entrepreneurs to venture capitalists, investors, and technology providers outside their national borders. As stated previously, privatization often encourages foreign investments in the form of cooperative ventures and the increased availability of institutional capital. Following privatization, foreign investors become an important linkage between local firms and external sources of ideas, technology, and capital. Maturing relationships between domestic firms and foreign investors also build trust, thereby allowing a free flow of information and ideas leading to additional ventures. Of course, the development of trust and the learning that can occur as a result of its emergence can lead to additional cooperative ventures and enhanced innovation.

Domestic firms might develop their own trade associations or cooperative organizations to increase their chances of survival. As in developed countries, trade associations and other organizations that are framed around mutual interests disseminate information. The purpose of this information is to educate members regarding current market opportunities and possibilities, as well as the nature of different competitive strategies, and to provide the insights required to lobby local and state officials. Effective lobbying efforts are those through which firm representatives articulate common industry positions about issues of critical interest to trade association members. Cooperative associations also serve as a catalyst for further new venture partnerships among members (Doh, this issue).

ENTREPRENEURIAL OUTCOMES OF PRIVATIZATION

Our model highlights two key entrepreneurial outcomes of privatization: innovation and new ventures (or venturing; Figure 2). We refer to innovation as the creation of goods and services, where product innovation also includes upgrades and extensions of existing products (incremental innovation). It also includes radical new product development. Whether radically new or modified products, these innovations are necessary to capitalize on the technological opportunities created by liberalization of the economy and the resulting privatization. Product innovations help to meet the growing expectations of consumers who have discretionary incomes created through risk taking in the new economy. Process innovations or the introduction of new methods of producing goods or services also should flourish following privatization. Process innovations are necessary to assimilate foreign technologies in domestic industries and to build new and efficient manufacturing systems. Thus, process innovations contribute to the operational efficiencies and improved productivity levels often reported following privatization.

New ventures involving the creation of new business or a move into new domestic and international markets are perhaps the most visible changes following privatization. Favorable tax laws rewarding calculated risk-taking practices can encourage new business creation. Changes in property laws also accompany privatization, making it safer for individuals or groups of investors to create, own, and manage a new enterprise.

Domestic and international venturing are important means for developing new revenue sources (Zahra, 1996). Venturing is made possible by the emergence of supportive industries and services (e.g., international consultants), increased exposure to different economic systems, and access to networks. Domestic companies also join forces with international firms to penetrate new domestic and international markets.

Figure 2 indicates that the macro and micro changes discussed can directly influence privatization outcomes. In prior research scholars have linked changes in a firm's institutional context to increased innovation and venturing (Kirzner, 1973; Morris, 1998). Macroinstitutional changes are crucial in inducing strategic changes (Newman, this issue).

CAVEATS AND EXTENSIONS OF MODEL

The above discussion suggests that privatization can yield diverse but important outcomes that create wealth for nations and companies. Nonetheless, articles in this issue also indicate that the lack of institutional infrastructure might serve as a barrier to successful entrepreneurial efforts (see Newman and Spicer, McDermott, & Kogut, this issue).

Newman explains that although institutional change is necessary to promote the organizational changes desired, too much institutional change can inhibit second-order learning. When this occurs, some managers rely on obsolete or older inappropriate routines that lead to non-adaptive mimetic changes (Newman & Nollen, 1998). This type of institutional "upheaval," as Newman (this issue) calls it, has especially strong effects on firms that were embedded in the central planning systems in the former socialist countries. These firms did not possess sufficient entrepreneurial capabilities and are unable to operate effectively in a market-oriented economy without significant support.

Equally important, Johnson and colleagues (this issue) argue that public sector managers develop a mindset, through institutionalization processes, that is counterproductive with respect to effective privatization. These authors observe that privatization requires a shift from one institutional template to another. For these reasons and others, Spicer and colleagues (this issue) argue that entrepreneurship is better fostered through gradual privatization processes (as completed through negotiated property rights reform processes) rather than large-scale rapid privatizations. The gradual approach permits experimentation with infrastructure needs and institutions to determine the ones that are more effective as compared to an immediate change to a total market-based economy.

In addition to institutional barriers, privatized firms in emerging economies might experience unique agency costs. In these countries the corporate governance structures and laws governing ownership rights often are underdeveloped and/or weak (Dharwadkar, George, & Brandes, this issue). The weak governance structures and limited protection of minority shareholders often create the potential for significant agency problems. Managers in newly privatized firms might expropriate the firm's assets, grant themselves special privileges, and become entrenched, opposing change and innovation. Of course, these outcomes are antithetical to those expected from privatization, as described earlier. Dharwadkar and colleagues, therefore, suggest that stronger governance structures and protection of ownership rights are required to overcome the agency problems some privatized firms experience. These authors also propose that certain ownership, organizational, and capital structures are likely to be more effective in the emerging economy context. These structures can mitigate agency costs and improve firm performance.

Interestingly, firms in which DFIs are involved, by providing capital, are likely to have stronger governance mechanisms. In fact, George and Prabhu (this issue) argue that DFI involvement in firm governance increases value creation. DFIs usually encourage efficient resource utilization and act to prevent agency problems. However, DFIs might not become involved in the governance of a firm unless it is vital to the national economic interest or priorities. Thus, DFIs may help prevent or resolve some but not all of the potential agency problems in newly privatized firms.

Wright and colleagues (this issue) suggest that the agency problems can be mitigated with the right incentive structure. Specifically, a combination of appropriate ownership, organizational, and incentive structures, along with institutional investor involvement, can reduce the agency problems and increase the effectiveness of privatization. Outcomes such as these may become part of the negotiated processes that Spicer and colleagues (this issue) discuss.

Doh (this issue) argues that privatization takes many forms, as suggested earlier. More important, Doh emphasizes the benefits a firm gains by being a first mover in privatization. Interestingly, he says that the benefits of the first mover are greater when it partners with an incumbent. Second and third movers, Doh argues, are at a significant disadvantage in this

environment. Clearly, this is an empirical question. Indeed, Ramamurti (this issue) suggests that the causes of privatization and their effects are understood properly only through a dynamic—not a static—model: one that encompasses analyses of firm, industry, and country effects.

These works, coupled with all the issues addressed in the special topic forum, suggest several areas for future research.

FUTURE RESEARCH

The articles in this special topic forum provide a wealth of issues for scholars to examine as they conduct future studies on privatization. Table 1 summarizes the focus, level of analysis, economic context, theoretical basis, and variables examined in each of the contributions included in the special topic forum. The theoretical arguments the contributors articulate, as well as the propositions they offer, should be tested empirically.

Further, we suggest below other avenues for additional research. The area of privatization and entrepreneurial transformation is particularly rich in research opportunities. The increasing globalization of the world economy highlights the need for a greater appreciation and understanding of the effects of privatization on entrepreneurial transformation.

Several areas require further research. First, the effects of different types and levels of privatization should be explored. We believe that all privatization activities are unlikely to have the same outcomes; as such, more work must be done to identify the specific effects of each type and level of privatization to have a better theoretical understanding of the outcomes expected from privatization. Ramamurti's (this issue) suggestion of the difference between broad and narrow privatizations may be a framework through which some of these research questions could be explored.

Second, the increasing growth of cooperative arrangements (e.g., strategic alliances) among firms is another issue requiring study. Do alliances facilitate privatized firms' efforts to compete successfully in market-based economies? Are the most successful partnerships formed between newly privatized firms within the same economy or between a newly privatized firm and another company from a developed economy?

520   *Academy of Management Review*   July

TABLE 1
Articles in This Issue: Themes and Theoretical Bases

Author(s)	Economic Context	Level of Analysis	Theory Base	Ownership Structure	Dependent Variables
Ramamurti	Emerging economies	Multiple	Agency theory	• Partial ownership • Dispersed ownership • Employee stock ownership plans • Local groups • Multinational enterprises	Selection of firms to be privatized
Doh	Emerging economies	Firm	Integration of I/O and resource-based view	Not applicable	First mover advantage and entrepreneurial transformation
Johnson, Smith, & Codling	Emerging economies	Manager and firm	Microinstitutional perspective	Not applicable	Entrepreneurial mindset
Cuervo & Villalonga	Emerging and advanced economies	Firm	Agency theory and public choice theory	Not applicable	Company performance
Wright, Hoskisson, Busenitz, & Dial	Transition economies	Firm	Agency and cognition theory	Management ownership (through buyouts)	Managerial behavior and entrepreneurial activities
Newman	Transition economies	Firm	Organizational learning, institutional theory, and organizational change theory	Not applicable	Organizational transformation, learning, and entrepreneurial behavior
George & Prabhu	Emerging economies	Country and firm	Stakeholder theory and corporate governance	• Management and employee • Foreign firms • Domestic individuals and firms	Firm performance
Spicer, McDermott, & Kogut	Emerging economies	Firm	Institutional theory	Not applicable	Effective policies, focused on gradual restructuring, that foster entrepreneurship
Dharwadkar, George, & Brandes	Emerging economies	Firm	Agency theory	• Ownership dispersion (dominant vs. distributed) • Ownership type (outsider vs. insider)	Managerial behavior and firm performance

As Table 1 indicates, the authors of articles published in this special topic forum have used several theoretical bases, including industrial organization (I/O) economics, the resource-based view of the firm, and institutional theory, to describe newly privatized firms' behavior. Organizational learning and organizational change theories also have been applied to help us understand how newly privatized firms react to their changing environments. Finally, authors have analyzed agency theory and entrepreneur-

ial cognition theory to explain managerial behavior. Still, we need to understand how these theoretical perspectives can be integrated to develop a theory of privatized firm behavior. Which of these theoretical perspectives provide the most effective explanations of privatized firms and managerial behavior? Are there other potent theories that can help in understanding these important phenomena?

Beyond these points and theoretical issues is a specific set of research questions we believe scholars should address in future research. For example, research should be completed that will contribute to our understanding of how the institutional infrastructure affects the entrepreneurial potential of privatization. What steps can be taken to change the infrastructure simultaneously with privatization? How can privatization be successfully implemented?

Johnson and colleagues (this issue) argue that an entrepreneurial mindset is not common among managers in privatized firms, although this mindset likely is related positively to strong performance following privatization. We need more research on how to infuse an entrepreneurial mindset in managers within newly privatized firms. Moreover, what is the relationship between a global mindset (Hitt et al., 2001b) and an entrepreneurial one? Is a combination of the two mindsets one that would be even more facilitative of firm success while privatizing and following the completion of the privatization process? Perhaps managerial incentives are the answer, as suggested by Wright and colleagues (this issue), in that appropriate incentives might stimulate and support development of appropriate entrepreneurial mindsets.

We need empirical work, however, in which scholars examine this issue. Do the incentives reduce the agency problems identified by Dharwadkar and colleagues (this issue)? If not, why not, and what incentives might overcome agency problems? Can DFIs facilitate the formation of entrepreneurial mindsets by providing more effective governance of privatized firms? Are there better means of establishing effective governance in privatized firms? If so, do these means vary by the characteristics of unique national cultures?

Peng (in press) argues that changes in transitional economies to a free market system unleash the power of entrepreneurship. His arguments relate to general entrepreneurial ventures developed in the economy, as opposed to privatized firms. For example, Peng suggests that in Central and Eastern Europe, about 5 percent of the adult population has started a new venture—a figure similar to the percent of the population in the United States engaging in entrepreneurial ventures. McCarthy, Puffer, and Shekshnia (1993) also describe the resurgence of an entrepreneurial class in Russia. Therefore, while privatized firms may experience problems operating entrepreneurially in a free market, entrepreneurial ventures may flourish in the general population. Clearly, we need additional research to understand how the entrepreneurial mindset develops in the general population, as well as insights about why this mindset permits some to identify and exploit opportunities while others fail to do so (Shane & Venkataraman, 2000). Moreover, additional research should be conducted to isolate the outcomes of entrepreneurial ventures outside of privatized firms in transition economies.

There is a need to understand human resource management (HRM) requirements in newly privatized firms, especially in transition economies. How can employees' skills, motivation, and productivity be enhanced? What are the most effective ways in which explicit and tacit knowledge can be developed and transferred among the workforces of former state-owned enterprises? According to Welsh, Luthans, and Sommer (1993), the HRM challenges might be particularly significant in these firms.

CONCLUSIONS

Privatization is a frequently used strategic option in today's rapidly globalizing economy. Driving the popularity of this strategy is the desire of different nations' governments to spur the type of economic activity that will allow their countries to be productive participants in global markets—markets that, in many instances, are becoming more consistent with the forces of free market economies in their operational and legislative contexts. The popularity of privatization is evident in developing and developed, as well as emerging, markets. In developed markets, formerly state-controlled industries are being deregulated (e.g., utilities). Thus, privatization occurs in selected sectors, and because of an active free market in other sectors, there are many successful examples (best practices) of the newly deregulated firms to follow.

In emerging economies, however, it is common for many industries to be operated or controlled by the national or state governments. Furthermore, privatization might be required by external parties for the financing needed (e.g., IMF), encouraging these governments to liberalize their economies. In these cases there is mass, and oftentimes rapid, privatization. Mass privatization is intended to support a rapid privatization program, in which the state's role is minimized and the market's role maximized

(Spicer et al., this issue). The twin goals of mass privatization often may be speed and fairness (Newman & Nollen, 1998). Nonetheless, because infrastructures required to privatize enterprises in a "fair" manner might not be developed quickly during a mass privatization program or process, the fairness dimension in countries experiencing a rapid privatization process often becomes a subject of debate among citizens and their government representatives.

As this discussion and some of the articles included in the special topic forum indicate, there are few previous exemplars or models of privatization in the global economy. The privatized firms in developed markets frequently are resource rich, whereas those in emerging markets are resource poor. The emerging market context is more uncertain, with economic, social, and political instability (Hitt et al., in press a). These characteristics of the environment clearly affect the rules of exchange in markets (North, 1990). There are major differences in the institutional infrastructures between emerging and developed economy countries (Newman, this issue). Thus, the entrepreneurial outcomes are not as certain as suggested in the previous literature on the economic transformation in transition economies. The work published in this special topic forum provides some explanations and describes activities that might be necessary to promote more effective entrepreneurial efforts. The articles presented herein also offer an interesting set of answers to existing but complex questions, along with new research questions.

We are pleased to commend the authors' contributions to you. We hope these articles will stimulate interesting and productive analyses of important research questions about privatization and entrepreneurial transformations across multiple types of economic structures.

REFERENCES

Acs, Z., & Audretsch, D. (Eds.). 1993. *Small firms and entrepreneurship: An East-West comparison.* Cambridge, MA: Cambridge University Press.

Baumol, W. J. 1996. Entrepreneurship: Productive, unproductive, and destructive. *Journal of Business Venturing,* 11: 3–22.

Cohen, W. M., & Levinthal, D. A. 1990. Absorptive capacity: A new perspective on learning and innovation. *Administrative Science Quarterly,* 35: 128–152.

Covin, J. G., & Miles, M. P. 1999. Corporate entrepreneurship

and the pursuit of competitive advantage. *Entrepreneurship: Theory and Practice,* 23(3): 47–63.

Cragg, M. I., & Dyck, I. J. 1999. Management control and privatization in the United Kingdom. *Rand Journal of Economics,* 30: 475–497.

Cragg, M. I., & Dyck, I. J. 2000. Executive pay and UK privatization: The demise of "one country, two systems." *Journal of Business Research,* 47: 3–18.

Dean, A., Carlisle, Y., & Baden-Fuller, C. 1999. Punctuated and continuous change: The UK water industry. *British Journal of Management,* 10(1998 Conference Issue): S3–S18.

DeCastro, J., & Uhlenbruck, N. 1997. Characteristics of privatization: Evidence from developed, less-developed, and former communist countries. *Journal of International Business Studies,* 28: 123–143.

Djankov, S. 1999. Ownership structure and enterprise restructuring in six newly independent states. *Comparative Economic Studies,* 41(1): 75–95.

D'Souza, J., & Megginson, W. L. 1999. The financial and operating performance of privatized firms during the 1990s. *Journal of Finance,* 54: 1397–1438.

Filatotchev, I., Hoskisson, R. E., Buck, T., & Wright, M. 1996. Corporate restructuring in Russian privatization. *California Management Review,* 38(2): 87–105.

Filatotchev, I., Wright, M., Buck, T., & Dymonia, N. 1999a. Exporting and restructuring in privatized firms from Russia, Ukraine and Belarus. *World Economy,* 22: 1013–1037.

Filatotchev, I., Wright, M., Buck, T., & Zhukov, V. 1999b. Corporate entrepreneurs and privatized firms in Russia, Ukraine, and Belarus. *Journal of Business Venturing,* 14: 475–492.

Galal, A., Jones, L., Tandon, P., & Vogelsang, I. 1994. *Welfare consequences of selling public enterprises: An empirical analysis.* New York: Oxford University Press.

Grosse, R., & Yanes, J. 1998. Carrying out a successful privatization: The YPF case. *Academy of Management Executive,* 12(2): 51–63.

Hart, O. 1995. An economist's perspective on the theory of the firm. In O. E. Williamson (Ed.), *Organization theory: From Chester Barnard to the present and beyond:* 154–171. New York: Oxford University Press.

Hitt, M. A., Dacin, M. T., Levitas, E., Arregle, J.-L., & Borza, A. In press a. Partner selection in emerging and developed market contexts: Resource-based and organizational learning perspectives. *Academy of Management Journal.*

Hitt, M. A., Harrison, J. S., & Ireland, R. D. In press b. *Creating value through mergers and acquisitions: A complete guide to successful M&As.* New York: Oxford University Press.

Hitt, M. A., Ireland, R. D., & Hoskisson, R. E. In press c. *Strategic management: Competitiveness and globalization* (4th ed.). Cincinnati: South-Western Publishing.

Hitt, M. A., Nixon, R. D., Hoskisson, R. E., & Kochhar, R. 1999. Corporate entrepreneurship and cross-functional fertilization: Activation, process and disintegration of a new product design team. *Entrepreneurship: Theory and Practice,* 23(3): 145–167.

Hoskisson, R. E., Eden, L., Lau, C. M., & Wright, M. In press. Strategy in emerging economies. *Academy of Management Journal.*

Hoskisson, R. E., Hitt, M. A., & Hill, C. W. L. 1993. Managerial incentives and investment in R&D in large multiproduct firms. *Organization Science,* 4: 325–341.

Huber, G. P., & Glick, W. H. 1995. *Organizational change and redesign: Ideas and insights for improving performance.* New York: Oxford University Press.

Ireland, R. D., & Hitt, M. A. 1999. Achieving and maintaining strategic competitiveness in the 21st century: The role of strategic leadership. *Academy of Management Executive,* 13(1): 43–57.

Jackson, P., & Price, C. (Eds.). 1994. *Privatization and regulation: A review of the issues.* London: Longman.

Jensen, M. C., & Meckling, W. 1976. Theory of the firm: Managerial behavior, agency costs, and ownership structure. *Journal of Financial Economics,* 3: 305–360.

Johnson, S., & Loveman, G. 1995. Starting over: Poland after communism. *Harvard Business Review,* 73(2): 44–57.

Kanter, R. M. 1989. *When giants learn to dance.* New York: Simon and Schuster.

Kim, L. 1997. *Imitation to innovation: The dynamics of Korea's technological learning.* Boston: Harvard Business School Press.

Kirzner, I. 1973. *Competition and entrepreneurship.* Chicago: University of Chicago Press.

McCarthy, D., Puffer, S., & Shekshnia, S. 1993. The resurgence of an entrepreneurial class in Russia. *Journal of Management Inquiry,* 2: 125–137.

Melloan, G. 2000. Designing a foreign policy for the new millennium. *Wall Street Journal,* January 4: A23.

Miller, A. N. 1995. British privatization: Evaluating the results. *Columbia Journal of World Business,* 30(4): 82–98.

Minniti, M., & Polutnik, L. 1999. Financial development and small firms financing in Slovenia. *Comparative Economic Studies,* 41(2/3): 111–133.

Morris, M. H. 1998. *Entrepreneurial intensity: Sustainable advantages for individuals, organizations, and societies.* Westport, CT: Quorum.

Mowery, D. C., & Oxley, J. E. 1995. Inward technology transfer and competitiveness: The role of national innovation systems. *Cambridge Journal of Economics,* 19(1): 67–93.

Newman, K. L., & Nollen, S. 1998. *Managing radical organizational change.* Thousand Oaks, CA: Sage.

North, D. 1990. *Institutions, institutional change and economic performance.* New York: Cambridge University Press.

Ogden, S., & Watson, R. 1999. Corporate performance and stakeholder management: Balancing shareholder and customer interests in the U.K. privatized water industry. *Academy of Management Journal,* 42: 526–538.

Ozkaya, M., & Askari, H. 1999. Management of newly privatized companies: Its importance and how little we know. *World Development,* 27: 1097–1114.

Peng, M. W. In press. How do entrepreneurs create wealth in transition economies? *Academy of Management Executive.*

Ramamurti, R. 1992. Why are developing countries privatizing? *Journal of International Business Studies,* 23: 225–249.

Ramirez, M. D. 1998. Privatizing and regulatory reform in Mexico and Chile: A critical overview. *Quarterly Review of Economics and Finance,* 38: 421–439.

Sachs, J., & Lipton, D. 1990. Poland's economic reform. *Foreign Affairs,* 69(3): 47–66.

Salas, V. 1998. *Conceptualizing privatization.* Paper presented at the annual meeting of the Academy of Management, San Diego, CA.

Shafik, N. 1996. Selling privatization politically. *Columbia Journal of World Business,* 31(4): 21–29.

Shane, S. 1995. Uncertainty avoidance and the preference for innovation championing roles. *Journal of International Business Studies,* 26: 47–68.

Shane, S., & Venkataraman, S. 2000. The promise of entrepreneurship as a field of research. *Academy of Management Review,* 25: 217–226.

Shleifer, A., & Vishny, R. W. 1994. Politicians and firms. *Quarterly Journal of Economics,* 109: 995–1025.

Smith, A., Golden, P., & Pitcher, P. 1999. The clock is ticking: Surviving privatization and deregulation by utilizing the running time. *European Management Journal,* 17: 409–421.

Soulsby, A., & Clark, E. 1996. The emergence of post-communist management in the Czech Republic. *Organization Studies,* 17: 227–247.

Uhlenbruck, K., & DeCastro, J. In press. Foreign acquisitions in Central and Eastern Europe: Outcomes of privatization in transitional economies. *Academy of Management Journal.*

Vickers, J., & Yarrow, G. 1988. *Privatization: An economic analysis.* Cambridge, MA: MIT Press.

Welfens, P. J. J. 1992. Foreign investment in the East European transition. *Management International Review,* 32: 199–218.

Welsh, D. H. B., Luthans, F., & Sommer, S. B. 1993. Managing Russian factory workers: The impact of U.S. based behavioral and participative techniques. *Academy of Management Journal,* 36: 58–79.

Yan, A. 1998. Structural stability and reconfiguration of international joint ventures. *Journal of International Business Studies,* 29: 773–796.

Yarrow, G. 1986. Privatization in theory and practice. *Economic Policy,* 2: 324–377.

Zahra, S. 1996. Governance, ownership and corporate entrepreneurship: The moderating impact of industry technological opportunities. *Academy of Management Journal,* 39: 1713–1735.

Zahra, S. A., Ireland, R. D., & Hitt, M. A. In press. International expansion by new venture firms: International diversity, mode of market entry, technological learning and performance. *Academy of Management Journal.*

Shaker A. Zahra is professor of strategic management at the J. Mack Robinson College of Business at Georgia State University in Atlanta. He is also a visiting professor of entrepreneurship at Jonkoping International Business School in Sweden. His research centers on entrepreneurship in new ventures and established companies, technology management, and global strategy.

R. Duane Ireland is a professor of management and holds the W. David Robbins Chair in Business Policy at the University of Richmond. He received his Ph.D. from Texas Tech University. His research interests include corporate governance, factors influencing environmental search processes, strategy for entrepreneurial ventures and established organizations, and knowledge acquisition through strategic alliances.

Isabel Gutierrez is a professor of management at Carlos III University, Spain. She received her Ph.D. from the University of Seville. Her current research interests include localized competition, industry structure, and the dynamics of competitive interactions. She is also interested in the founding characteristics, strategy, and performance of entrepreneurial ventures.

Michael A. Hitt is a distinguished professor of management and holds the Paul M. and Rosalie Robertson Chair in Business Administration at Texas A&M University. He received his Ph.D. from the University of Colorado. His research interests focus on international strategic alliances, innovation, corporate governance, and the importance of human capital (knowledge) in the new economy.

[29]

© Academy of Management Review
2000, Vol. 25, No. 3, 551–571.

ENTREPRENEURIAL PRIVATIZATION STRATEGIES: ORDER OF ENTRY AND LOCAL PARTNER COLLABORATION AS SOURCES OF COMPETITIVE ADVANTAGE

JONATHAN P. DOH
American University
The George Washington University

Firm-level responses to privatization have not been widely studied. Drawing from industrial organization economics, the resource-based view, and interorganizational cooperative strategy, I develop an integrated theory to show how privatization encourages early entry; how delayed market liberalization reinforces first mover benefits; and how firms with specialized resources, an entrepreneurial orientation, and local partner collaborations gain postprivatization competitive advantage. I construct a model and provide case illustrations to support the theoretical development, discuss implications of the research, propose methods to test the model, and make suggestions for future inquiry.

Privatization has become a mantra of national economic policy makers, investment bankers, management consultants, and regional and local public administrators. A broad consensus has emerged within academic, public policy, and managerial circles that market-based approaches should be considered as potential responses to the social and economic failures of traditional government-owned enterprise and government-provided services. Privatization is now a pervasive and integral part of government management and organization and a significant force in the industrial structure of national and regional economies. Brazil alone is expected to auction off more than $80 billion in public assets before its latest round of privatization is over (Kambhato, 1998). To most researchers and analysts, privatization connotes the transfer (not necessarily sale) of assets, functions, or responsibilities from government to private hands or, in more limited examples, any form of private participation in government-owned enterprise or operations.

The specific approach, terms, and outcome of the privatization process, however, can have myriad forms. For example, in some instances a loss-making government corporation is given to a private firm or sold for a nominal fee. Other privatizations, especially those in Russia, the Newly Independent States, and Eastern Europe, have included the distribution of shares to the general public—the technical "owners" of capital when these economies were organized according to socialist principles. In other situations only a minority portion of the assets is distributed, with the majority shares remaining in government hands. In this article I deal with one of the most common privatization transactions: the competitive auctioning of state assets to private investors. In most instances investors bidding on these privatizations take the form of a consortium composed of international firms and local partners, one of which is typically the incumbent provider.

Privatization programs and policies have been studied at several levels. In most research scholars have focused on the economic and social rationale for privatization or on specific questions related to how governments can better achieve certain socioeconomic goals through alternate privatization structures and policies. In normative studies researchers have argued, on economic philosophy grounds, the advantages and benefits of privatization as a way to

I thank the special issue editors, especially Professor Duane Ireland, and the three anonymous reviewers for their insightful comments on earlier versions of this article. I also acknowledge Hildy Teegen, Douglas Sanford, Robert Weiner, Jeffrey Cummings, and Gary Jones, all at the George Washington University, for assistance with earlier stages of this research. Cooperation from a number of government agencies and private companies was instrumental in preparation of this article, as was the research assistance of Alison Kruchkowski. An earlier version of this work was presented at the 1999 annual meeting of the Academy of Management.

552   *Academy of Management Review*   July

minimize government involvement in areas where the social good or service justification for government provision is no longer defensible. Much of the contemporary literature on privatization has emanated from the economics and finance disciplines (e.g., Boubakri & Cosset, 1998; Caves, 1990; Dewenter & Malatesta, 1997; Megginson, Nash, & Van Randenborgh, 1994; Perotti & Guney, 1993; Vickers & Yarrow, 1991; Yarrow, 1986). In many of the economic studies, researchers have sought to determine the success of privatization as measured by efficiency and, in some instances, social welfare (Boubakri & Cosset, 1998; Megginson et al., 1994; Perotti & Guney, 1993). Some practitioner literature has emerged from management journals and multilateral development organizations in which scholars provide advice to governments as they wrestle with the challenge of integrating their economies into regional or global systems (Durschlag, Puri, & Rao, 1994; Galal & Shirley, 1994; Money & Griffith, 1993). Other researchers have offered helpful generalizations in reviewing past privatization (Hensley & White, 1993; Lieberman, 1990, 1993; World Bank, 1992).

Very few scholars have examined the strategies of private investors and developers in response to privatization programs. Uhlenbreck and DeCastro note that "empirical research and theory on direct investment into former SOEs, unfortunately, is scant" (1998: 620). An understanding of the unique set of factors influencing successful corporate responses to privatization, however, is becoming an integral component of the international strategies of private firms. This is especially the case for firms doing business in infrastructure industries, such as telecommunications, electric power, water, and rail and road transportation, as they seek to capitalize on massive divestitures.[1]

In this article I explore several factors that contribute to firm-level responses to privatization opportunities. To begin, a brief justification for an integrated theoretical framework for understanding firm-level responses to privatization is presented. I argue that the necessary antecedents for construction of such a theory can be found in the industrial organization (I/O) and resource-based strategy schools and suggest that specific conditions suggested by these theories—notably, first mover and order-of-entry effects, pioneering advantage, and firm-level entrepreneurial orientation—are particularly applicable to the circumstances surrounding privatization. I offer propositions to illustrate how these factors affect firm-level competitive positioning in response to privatization. Following this, in the next section I apply emerging literature on social network theory and interorganizational dynamics to privatization strategy. Specifically, I identify cooperative strategy, social network externalities, and strategic alliances and joint ventures with host country firms and other stakeholders as especially important in establishing a competitive privatization strategy. I then discuss the implications of this analysis using case illustrations and make suggestions for empirical methods that could be used to test the arguments presented here. I conclude with suggestions for further research, focusing on additional theoretical grounding that may be relevant in the case of privatization, and further study—conceptual, theoretical, and empirical—that could add to our understanding of firm-level responses to privatization. The principal contribution of this article is the development of an integrated theory of firm-level privatization strategy.

EARLY ENTRY AS A SOURCE OF COMPETITIVE ADVANTAGE IN PRIVATIZATION

In this section I review the limited research on corporate strategic response to privatization, ar-

---

[1] I am primarily concerned in this article with corporate strategic responses to emerging markets' privatization of infrastructure industries: telecommunications, oil and gas, electric power, water, and transportation. These industries constitute the majority of privatizations in recent years (approximately $75 billion of the $123 billion in emerging markets privatization from 1990 to 1996, according to the World Bank), and they share several common elements. First, because of historical approaches to industries featuring long-run declining average costs, these industries typically were organized as national, regional, or sectoral monopolies, either as a single government agency or government-owned corporation. Second, in some of these industries—notably,

telecommunications and electric power—privatization is followed by market liberalization, allowing other entrants to participate in the market post privatization. Often, a period of protection is provided the incumbent and its foreign and/or local partners. This "liberalization lag" poses interesting theoretical and practical questions that I explore later in the article.

guing for better-developed theoretical models to understand and inform this growing phenomenon. The theoretical basis for construction of such a model of corporate privatization strategy can be found in two established wings of strategic management—notably, the I/O economics and resource-based views of strategy. Early entry and entrepreneurial orientation are presented as the most relevant elements of these literature streams. I construct propositions to operationalize this theory in the particular case of privatization.

Privatization and Corporate Strategy

Research in which scholars have examined foreign investor response to privatization has been limited. In some managerial-oriented literature, researchers have provided advice and recommendations for investors and governments. The few existing studies have been focused primarily on the response by Western investors to privatization in Russia, the Newly Independent States, and Eastern Europe. Filatotchev, Hoskisson, Buck, and Wright (1996), for example, surveyed privatized Russian enterprises to determine the degree to which foreign investors and local partners were able to transform state-owned enterprise (SOE) ownership, human resource, and financial structures. These researchers found that despite structural, regulatory, and cultural constraints, U.S. investors were able to reform and restructure privatized enterprise. After 2 years of postprivatization experience, however, most firms had not demonstrated increased investment levels, reduced wages (an imputed measure of increased labor productivity), or improved trading relationships (Filatotchev et al., 1996).

DeCastro and Uhlenbruck (1997) examined differences between developed and developing country privatization programs and firm strategies. They found that privatization deals in less developed countries (LDCs) and former communist countries (FCCs) were more likely to include postprivatization conditions than deals in developed countries but that LDCs and FCCs were no more likely than developed countries to impose job, local ownership, and "other" conditions (DeCastro & Uhlenbruck, 1997). Further, privatization deals were more likely to be cross-border acquisitions in LDCs and FCCs than in developed countries (DeCastro & Uhlenbruck, 1997).

These findings are consistent with the "nascent capital markets" view of Perotti and Guney (1993) and Dewenter and Malatesta (1997) that presumes limitations in domestic capital for privatization investments. In a recent conceptual analysis of privatization from the investor perspective, Uhlenbruck and DeCastro (1998) examined privatization using mergers and acquisitions theory. These researchers suggested that firms evaluate the degree to which characteristics of the former state ministry or state-owned firm are compatible with the investors' interests and that a "strategic fit" is necessary for successful integration of foreign investors with local SOEs (Uhlenbruck & DeCastro, 1998).

Managerial and policy-oriented research has provided helpful guidance because of the implications it draws from past practice. Much of the literature, however, is atheoretical or does not include well-developed theory, the authors relying instead on stylized facts. Specifically, these researchers have rarely used established managerial theory to examine the strategies of foreign investors responding to privatization, with some notable exceptions (e.g., Uhlenbruck & DeCastro, 1998).

Corporate Privatization Strategy: I/O and Resource-Based Views

Two main frameworks for analyzing the determinants of corporate strategic advantage have prevailed over the past several decades. Proponents of the I/O view of strategy argue that firms earn supranormal returns primarily by exercising monopoly power (Bain, 1956). Monopoly power, in turn, exists to the extent that the firm or industry has erected barriers to entry that restrict competitive forces. Law and economics I/O economists, such as those studying utility economics (e.g., Kahn, 1988), examined the linkages among industry structure, conduct, and performance in order to derive public policies that promote competition (Demsetz, 1973). More recently, corporate strategic management researchers have adapted the industrial economics view of industry configuration to explore, from a managerial perspective, the impact of industry structure, dynamism, entry and exit barriers, and learning effects on the competitive position of the firm (Porter, 1980, 1981, 1985, 1986, 1990, 1991). The I/O approach to strategy emphasizes the advantages of entering markets in

554   *Academy of Management Review*   July

which competition is stifled, positioning the firm to influence the terms of such competition through the erection of mobility barriers and, in so doing, generating surplus rents (Caves & Porter, 1977; Porter, 1980). These conditions are especially acute in the case of privatization. Privatization presents a limited, abrupt market disruption, allowing entrants to shape the terms of competition for years to come through marketing, public policy, technological lockout, and other means.

Despite the widespread influence of I/O concepts on strategic thinking, scholars have also questioned their utility. In particular, the I/O school has been criticized for inattention to the dynamics of competition, the relative performance differences among firms within the same industry (Rumelt, 1991; Wernerfelt, 1989), and the influence of technology and technological change on the business environment (Nelson & Winter, 1982). In response to the emerging view that the I/O strategy school was incomplete as an explanation for strategy and competition, researchers began exploring the impact of the development, acquisition, and deployment of firm resources on successful corporate strategies. Building on earlier work by Penrose (1959) and Nelson and Winter (1982), proponents of the resource-based perspective examined the economic returns to resources that a firm owns, acquires, or develops (Barney, 1986, 1991, 1995; Nelson & Winter, 1992; Peteraf, 1993). Resources must demonstrate a specific set of characteristics in order to generate above-normal returns (Barney, 1991; Peteraf, 1993). They must be valuable in facilitating exploitation of an opportunity in the business environment or at least contribute to neutralizing a threat. They must also be scarce or must come together in a unique way as a result of how the firm packages or bundles them (Barney, 1991; Teece, 1986). In addition, resources must be immobile (Teece, 1986). Imperfectly immobile resources include those that are idiosyncratic to the firm (Williamson, 1979), those for which property rights are not well defined (Dierickx & Cool, 1989), or those that are cospecialized with other assets (Teece, 1986).

A related characteristic to that of imperfect mobility is imperfect imitation (Barney, 1991). Resources must provide some ex post limits to competition. Once a firm has gained an initial competitive advantage, there must be additional resources to freeze out competitors and

allow the firm to maintain rent-earning status for a period of time (Peteraf, 1993). For a firm to be in a position to exploit a valuable and rare resource, it must have a resource position barrier preventing imitation by other firms (Wernerfelt, 1989). Hence, sustaining a competitive advantage over a period of time requires the presence of isolating mechanisms that prevent imitation (Lippman & Rumelt, 1982).

Privatization involves the acquisition, stockpiling, and, most important, exchange of resources. The government must evaluate the revealed and tacit resources of the investing firm and decide how best to encourage the transfer of those resources to foster entrepreneurial transformation of the SOE and the broader market environment. The investor must evaluate the visible and tacit resources of the SOE, the government itself, and local firms with which the investor may partner. Both governments and investors seek a "strategic fit" through integration of resources among investor firms, host governments, and the SOE (Uhlenbruck & DeCastro, 1998). The monopoly concession typically provided as part of the privatization may itself be viewed as a resource or strategic asset that can be deployed and leveraged (Kay, 1995). The cost to acquire that very valuable resource, however, might include social goods provided by the investor beyond the narrow requirements of the privatization contract. Hence, intangible resources, such as political legitimacy and reputation, also might play a role in firm-level competitive positioning.

The I/O school and resource-based view are often contrasted as two antithetical approaches to strategy, yet proponents of these two views draw upon several common theoretical assumptions. First, although adherents to the resource-based view emphasize the importance of company-specific resources and competencies, they do so in the context of the competitive environment, especially with the extension of Black and Boal (1994) described later in this article. Both the I/O and resource-based view rely on economic reasoning. Followers of the resource-based view see capabilities as the core of a competitive position but tempered by the influence of fundamental market forces: demand (value), scarcity, and appropriability (Prahalad & Hamel, 1990). Further, although Porter focused almost exclusively on the industry environment, he also advocated specific approaches to respond to that environment with "focus" and "niche" strategies that acknowledge the importance of unique firm resources (Porter, 1980, 1985). When firms focus on a specialized market, they must possess some unique asset (resource) that allows them to exploit that market. Scholars working from a resource-based perspective commonly focus on resources that generate rents because they are unique or specialized. These include brand names, in-house knowledge or technology, and skilled personnel (Wernerfelt, 1989). These same resources, however, often are employed by the firm in differentiating its products, as Porter proposed (Porter, 1980).

The application of an integrated I/O and resource-based view of privatization strategy would appear to be an appropriate base upon which to build a theory of corporate privatization strategy. Privatization encourages strategies designed to shape and exploit market imperfections, garner monopolizing rents, collaborate with scarce partners, and exploit relationships with government officials. These are all approaches suggested in the I/O view of strategy (Porter, 1981). Moreover, these same strategies, especially when bolstered by firm-level technological prowess, entrepreneurial orientation, and the development of external network relationships, constitute resources that can be deployed to maximize competitive positioning in response to privatization.

Order of Entry, Pioneering Advantage, and Competitive Positioning in Privatization

Both the I/O economics and resource-based views of competition suggest that the order of entry of firms into a particular market is a relevant determinant of competitive advantage and that there are specific gains from status as a pioneer or first mover. Specifically, a research stream has emerged in which researchers assert that in some industries and economic environments, there are significant economies associated with first mover or early entry positioning.[2]

---

[2] In this article I review the literature on first mover, order-of-entry, and pioneering advantage as part of a single literature stream. Although there are some differences in this literature in terms of level of analysis (market versus industry versus firm), research questions, and perspectives on the relative importance of early versus later entry, it shares a common focus on the relevance of market entry timing and sequence in determining competitive position.

Broadly, early entrants have the potential to internalize advantages that might be difficult for later entrants to appropriate (Kerin, Varadarajan, & Peterson, 1992; Lieberman & Montgomery, 1988; Mascarenhas, 1992). Patterson defines a first mover as "an organization which is first to employ a particular strategy within the context of a specific scope" (1993: 760).

Researchers have argued for a range of benefits associated with first mover or early entry positioning. These include capturing learning effects for which timely deployment might be key to garnering market share, scale economies that accrue from opportunities for capturing that greater share, and development of alliances with the most attractive (or in some cases only) local partner. Lieberman and Montgomery (1988) have suggested that first mover advantages are best measured in terms of the firm's ability to earn positive economic profit. Three ways to achieve a first mover advantage are through attaining technological leadership, preempting scarce assets, and increasing buyer switching costs (Lieberman & Montgomery, 1988).

Technological leadership represents the potential for a company to gain an advantage by capturing and internalizing technological superiority, including harnessing research and development and garnering patent abilities. This leadership contributes to an "experience curve" effect: as a company becomes more experienced, it uses innovation to produce output at a lower production cost (Porter, 1985). From a resource-based view, technological leadership constitutes a firm-level resource that is idiosyncratic to the firm, immobile, and inimitable.

Preemption of scarce assets can include being the first to purchase input factors, move into a specific location, and invest in plant and equipment. A first mover could acquire such assets by having superior information and purchasing assets at market prices below those that would prevail later in the evolution of the market.

Porter (1980) focused on the power of buyers and the attractiveness of industries in which buyer switching costs are high. Lieberman and Montgomery (1988) subdivided the category into three types of switching costs: (1) financial transaction costs required to switch to new products from old ones, (2) time and money required to teach and learn how to use a new product; and (3) contractual costs, which are usually created by the seller.

556   *Academy of Management Review*   July

The definition of exactly which entity constitutes a first mover in a privatization transaction requires exploration and clarification. When discussing first mover advantages generically, one assumes firms enter a market in which there are no dominant incumbents and that the market itself is open to new entrants. In the case of privatization, however, it appears as if an adaptation of first mover theory is appropriate. In most cases an auction or tender takes place in which foreign firms are offered the opportunity to partner with the incumbent firm. When accorded the ability to serve both as a first mover and incumbent, market entrants reap benefits from both the pioneering position and the power of incumbency.

Privatization implies a radical, discontinuous change in marketplace conditions. When a SOE is sold, the transaction presents a one-time adjustment in the industry environment, inviting a restructuring in which there will be specific beneficiaries and losers. In particular, privatization creates an environment especially suitable for the erection and maintenance of high entry barriers and subsequent market closeout, making the stakes especially high for participation in the process as an early mover.

> *Assumption 1: Privatization generates strong first mover pressure.*

> *Proposition 1a: Privatization confers first mover benefits.*

> *Proposition 1b: First mover benefits are strengthened when the investor is able to integrate with the incumbent.*

First Movers, Market Liberalization, and Time/Benefit Contingency

The value of first mover status varies partly in relation to its sustainability—that is, the duration and longevity of the first mover barriers. Patterson (1993), in studying six industries, mapped an opportunity curve within which these strategic barriers dissipated, arguing that barriers conferring uniqueness are the most valuable tools for preserving first mover advantage. In the case of infrastructure privatization, first mover advantages, in theory, have great durability in that concessions often include the right to provide monopoly service indefinitely. In infrastructure privatizations, however, sale of

the SOE most often is followed later by market liberalization, providing the first mover a limited window in which to capitalize on that entry status before rivals are permitted to compete in the market.

> *Proposition 1c: First mover advantages will be strengthened when a privatization transaction includes a monopoly concession or purchase agreement that provides protection from market competition for a designated period.*

In the case of telecommunications, which constituted nearly a quarter of the value of all emerging markets' privatization in the period 1990 to 1996, privatization includes an initial sale of the state-owned or controlled monopoly, followed by market liberalization in which other investors are permitted to participate selectively in the newly privatized industry (Kambhato, 1998). Drawing from this World Bank analysis (Kambhato, 1998) and my own calculations, I show in Figure 1 the delay between the initial privatization of telecommunications monopolies in major countries around the world and the subsequent opening of long-distance markets in those same countries to competition from other private sector entrants. This is the period within which the initial entrant, partnered with the incumbent, is fully protected from competitive threats from subsequent market entrants. This figure illustrates the critical role played by government regulation on the structure and timing of postprivatization market opening.

First movers might create economies of scale, generate the ability to earn greater market shares, and erect barriers to entry (Patterson, 1993). A first mover can position itself to consume all future benefits if it can use temporal strategic barriers successfully. The later the followers, the greater the first mover advantage for the pioneering firm (Patterson, 1993). Or, as proponents of the resource-based perspective would suggest, there must be barriers to constrain the appropriation of resources acquired as part of early mover positioning (Barney, 1991). If the first mover can use temporal strategic barriers successfully, it should be able to achieve benefit flows through entering early, which will, in turn, discourage followers. As mentioned above, in infrastructure industries this notion incorporates the function of market liberalization, which in large part determines the length

FIGURE 1
**Telecommunications Privatization and "Liberalization Lag" Between Initial Privatization and
Opening of Long-Distance Market**

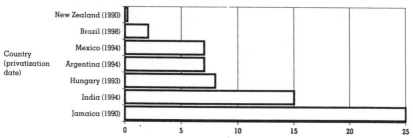

Country
(privatization
date)

New Zealand (1990)
Brazil (1998)
Mexico (1994)
Argentina (1994)
Hungary (1993)
India (1994)
Jamaica (1990)

Time delay between privatization and long-distance market opening (years)

Source: Kambhato (1998) and author's calculations.

of time a first mover will remain alone in a recently privatized market. According to the resource-based view, once a firm has used resources to gain a competitive advantage, there must also be resources to freeze out competitors and allow the firm to maintain a surplus rent-earning status for a period of time (Peteraf, 1993).

Proposition 1d: First mover competitive advantage will be lessened by the expected or actual liberalization of the newly privatized market; the sooner the market liberalizes, the less the first mover advantage will be.

Many privatizations are conducted in multiple stages, partly because of domestic capital market constraints (Dewenter & Malatesta, 1997; Perotti & Guney, 1993) and learning curve effects. This suggests there is another cycle of first mover advantages that persists well beyond the

initial period of monopoly protection, giving the first entrant an "insider" position in participating in subsequent rounds.

Proposition 1e: Participating in the first or early rounds of the multistaged privatization of a SOE increases post-privatization competitive advantage.

Figure 2 shows a simple, stylized representation of the relationship between privatization, first mover advantages, and market liberalization. As the "liberalization lag" between privatization and market liberalization lengthens, the value of the first mover position grows exponentially.

**Pioneering Advantage, Entrepreneurial
Orientation, and First Mover Characteristics**

Both the I/O and resource-based strategy schools suggest that certain types of firms are

FIGURE 2
Relationship Between Privatization, First Mover Advantage, and Time-to-Market Liberalization

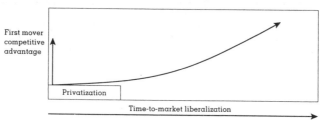

First mover
competitive
advantage

Privatization

Time-to-market liberalization

more capable of taking advantage of first mover opportunities than are others. Lieberman and Montgomery (1988) note that firms possessing technological and product superiority are in a better position to exploit first mover benefits because they possess resources and capabilities that can be used to achieve competitive advantage through market lockout. Firms possessing marketing prowess are better able to compete as second or later entrants because of their ability to learn from the experiences of the first mover and to attack first mover positions using marketing and sales-oriented strategies (Lieberman & Montgomery, 1988). Additional first mover benefits from these resources include reputational effects from benchmarking products, economic advantages from early attainment of critical sales volumes, and preemptive domination of distribution and communication channels (Lieberman & Montgomery, 1988). Lieberman and Montgomery (1988) also suggest that a firm's resource base tends to influence the likelihood and timing of entry.

Firm-level competitive strategy is influenced by entrepreneurial orientation. Barringer and Bluedorn (1999), for example, found a positive relationship between the intensity of corporate entrepreneurship and specific strategic management practices, such as scanning intensity, planning flexibility, locus of planning, and strategic controls. More specifically, pioneering advantage may be viewed as one element of firm-level entrepreneurial orientation (Cooper & Dunkelberg, 1986). Entrepreneurial firms are proactive, risk tolerant, and innovative (Covin & Slevin, 1989: 79), and they demonstrate flexibility and adaptability to changing environmental conditions (Barringer & Bluedorn, 1999). Proactivity includes the notion of developing an aggressive competitive orientation and the ability to identify and seize opportunities ahead of competitors (Covin & Slevin, 1989: 79). Lumpkin and Dess note that "the essential act of entrepreneurship is new entry . . . new entry is thus the central idea underlying the concept of entrepreneurship" (1996: 135). Elements of an entrepreneurial orientation might include "a propensity to act autonomously, a willingness to innovate and take risks, and a tendency to be aggressive toward competitors and proactive relative to marketplace opportunities" (Lumpkin & Dess, 1996: 135). Some researchers argue that early entry and other dimensions of entrepre-

neurial orientation are not necessarily corollaries but may vary independently (Cahill, 1995, 1996). In the case of privatization, one-time industry reconfiguration presents a unique, anomalous circumstance that generates pressures for firms either to participate or lose out on long-term rent streams derived from the privatization opportunity, as well as to array and deploy resources rapidly to take advantage of that market opportunity.

> *Proposition 1f: Firms with a more entrepreneurial orientation (risk tolerant, aggressively competitive, innovative) are more likely to be first movers. Hence, such firms will be more likely to take advantage of and benefit from privatization opportunities than will firms with a less entrepreneurial orientation.*

Firms that participate in early rounds of multi-industry or multifirm privatization may be in a position to deploy their first mover resources and increase the likelihood of success in subsequent rounds in the initial (focal) or other markets. The role of learning in multinational corporation (MNC) internationalization decisions suggests that an effective organization continuously develops new knowledge and incorporates that learning into strategic management decisions (Senge, 1990). The ability of an MNC to learn from experience in foreign markets and then transfer that knowledge to other markets is consistent with a range of research streams in the international business literature, especially studies of the organizational management of multibusiness, multinational firms and their subsidiaries (Prahalad & Doz, 1987; Stopford & Wells, 1972).

> *Proposition 1g: First mover status and learning in early rounds of multi-industry or multifirm privatization will strengthen the position of the first mover/incumbent in subsequent rounds and will enable it to compete more successfully in privatizations in other sectors and markets.*

Disadvantages of Early Entry

The positive aspects of being a first mover can be overshadowed. The most critical potential *disadvantage* of first mover status is the opportunity for later entrants to take advantage of the first mover's strategic errors (Kerin, Varadarajan, & Peterson, 1992). The negative attributes of being a pioneer in a market arguably can lead to complete failure—even the demise of the firm. These same disadvantages, however, generate advantages for subsequent firms. Early entrants might see these later entrants benefiting from a "free ride" on the first mover investments, from solutions made to technological problems or an unsure market, and from outdated technology providing a gateway to entry (Lieberman & Montgomery, 1988).

As proponents of both the I/O and resource-based schools have argued, and as Lieberman and Montgomery (1988) elaborate, early entry is most attractive when a firm can influence how market confidence will be resolved. Reliance by first movers/incumbents on outdated technology allows later entrants to become influential competitors in the market. Replacement technology often appears while the old technology is still growing, which could make it difficult for the incumbent to take adequate preventative measures. Incumbent inertia also can make later entry a more attractive alternative. This occurs when the incumbent firm is unable to adapt to changing market conditions because it is tied to past practices. It may have financial burdens or be reluctant to develop new products that could cannibalize its existing merchandise. The position of Telmex, the incumbent state-run telecommunications monopoly in the privatizing Mexican telecommunications market, described in a later section, is characterized by these conditions.

Tellis and Golder conclude that "market pioneering is neither necessary nor sufficient for long-term success and leadership . . . . a first strike may be desirable, but careful preparation for attack, counterattack, penetration, and consolidation are critical for success" (Tellis & Golder, 1996: 73). In their exploration of the theory of "competitive dynamics," which involves examining the way that firms act and react to one another, Smith, Grimm, and Gannon (1992) found that a slow second strategy for easy-to-imitate competitive actions might be preferable to first mover, fast second, slow third, and late mover strategies. Moreover, the "winners" in a competitive tender may purchase away the entirety of the first mover benefit, making it diffi-cult to later evaluate its worth and the ability of that particular firm to deploy resources to fully exploit the first mover position (Thaler, 1991). In sum, erection of barriers to entry has been identified as one of the main contributors to the value of first mover positioning in response to privatization.

> Proposition 1h: First mover positioning will be less advantageous when investor firms lack sufficient resources to erect barriers to entry post privatization or when the liberalization program does not allow for erection of such barriers.

Figure 3 presents an integrated model of the relationships among privatization, first mover pressures and advantages, and first mover firm strategy and competitive advantage. It also shows integration of the variables related to collaborative strategy and local partner alliances discussed in the next section.

In the following section I explore social network theory and interorganizational cooperation as additional theoretical motivations for privatization strategy. These theories and their application provide a complement to the order-of-entry and first mover effects described above. Specifically, I explore the role of local partners, including government agencies and other stakeholders, as resource-generating agents. These collaborations further reinforce the competitive advantages derived from early market entry, especially under the particular conditions of privatization followed by market liberalization.

RESOURCE NETWORKS, LOCAL PARTNER ALLIANCES, AND ORGANIZATIONAL LEARNING

First mover and pioneering status imply advantages to be gained from status as an early entrant into a market. Strategic alliances complement, strengthen, and reinforce the competitive position attained by first mover status. I/O and resource-based views of competitive strategy, as well as more recent work on network externalities and interorganizational competitive advantage, have highlighted the importance of learning and knowledge acquisition through network relationships external to the focal organization (Dyer & Singh, 1998). The interaction between early entry status and local

560 *Academy of Management Review* July

FIGURE 3
Model of Privatization Strategy: Entry Position, Market Structure, Firm Resources, and Competitive Success

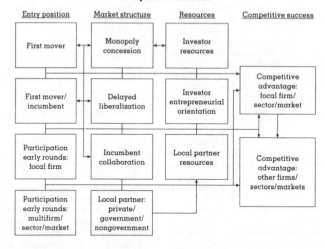

alliance relationships places the first mover in a powerful position to earn long-term rents from the initial privatization. Alliance partners are in a unique position to influence the postprivatization regulatory environment, particularly by encouraging the erection and maintenance of market entry barriers. Collaboration also might facilitate the early entrant's ability to compete as a "local" firm in subsequent rounds of privatization and to develop resources, capabilities, and knowledge (e.g., Barney, 1991; Black & Boal, 1994) that can be deployed in other privatizing markets.

Interorganizational Cooperation and International Strategic Alliances

In a rich and increasingly diverse literature, researchers have examined the motivations for collective action via collaborative strategies and alliance structures among firms. The description of international strategic alliances (ISAs) and the exploration of the conditions under which ISAs tend to be viewed by the firm as the preferred mode of entry have occupied a great deal of international business research effort (Buckley & Casson, 1988, 1996; Contractor

& Lorange, 1988a; Kogut, 1988; Root, 1988). More recently, researchers have begun to focus on more specific and more complex explanations of ISA formation. This includes research directed toward understanding the conditions that appear to lead to better or worse ISA performance and endurance and, of interest to this study, the primary motivations for entering into such relationships (Harrigan, 1988; Killing, 1988; Lyles & Salk, 1996; Madhok, 1997; Makino & Delios, 1996). Contractor and Lorange (1988b) have identified a range of rationales for firm-level cooperation, including faster entry and payback, economies of scale and rationalization, complementary technologies and patents, and co-opting or blocking competition. Of relevance to this study, many of these authors also point to the potential for freezing competition and establishing a beachhead position in the market through first mover–like positioning.

Complementing research on ISAs is recent work on interorganizational cooperation and the influence of network resources on firm capabilities. This work suggests that a narrow resource-based view of the firm misses the importance and value of resources that constitute part of a firm network (Dyer & Singh, 1998). Black and Boal (1994) have identified a critical shortcoming in the resource-based view—notably, that resources are evaluated from a "stand-alone viewpoint." Barney (1991) referred to bundles of resources, but those working within the resource-based view framework generally treat resources as singular items. Black and Boal (1994) have argued that resources could be separated into contained resources (simple networks of resource factors that can be monetarily valued) and system resources (created by a complex network of firm resources factors). Further, network theorists have illustrated how and when resources combine to add value and how networks facilitate resource exchanges (Thorelli, 1986). Other researchers have suggested that access to information about potential partners constitutes a resource and that such resources are an important catalyst for new alliances, partly because alliances entail considerable hazards (Gulati, 1999). Firms' capabilities with alliance formation and material resources are factors in their future alliance decisions (Gulati & Garguilo, 1999). Dyer and Singh (1998) have identified four potential sources of interorganizational competitive advantage from alliances: relation-specific assets, knowledge-sharing routines, complementary resources and capabilities, and effective governance. They argue that resources acquired through extrafirm or intraorganizational contacts are critical to competitive success (Dyer & Singh, 1998).

Powerful forces are set in motion by the proposed privatization of state-owned infrastructure industries, previously organized as national, regional, or sectoral monopolies. These forces generate intense pressures on firms to move early to take advantage of one-time ownership options that generate bountiful rent streams for years to come. These first mover pressures, in turn, increase the stakes associated with winning concessions and competing successfully post privatization, prompting firms to form alliances with local partners that can provide market and political/regulatory knowledge. Further, alliances with governments or other stakeholders can smooth the way toward favorable regulatory treatment as the market prepares for open competition and can help erect or maintain market entry barriers. Together, these alliances provide a powerful advantage to early entrants that are difficult for later followers to challenge.

Assumption 2: Privatization generates strong pressure for firms to collaborate in their efforts to participate in privatization opportunities.

Collaboration and Local Partner Advantage

Research in strategic alliances and joint ventures indicates a range of rationales for entering into collaborative partnerships. These include co-opting, blocking or freezing competition, and establishing a beachhead position in the privatizing market through first mover–like positioning (Contractor & Lorange, 1988b). As Filatotchev et al. note:

> Joint venture arrangements [can be used] as a stepping stone towards closer involvement with other enterprises. Such a route may be feasible where there are entrepreneurs who have links with other firms and where foreign interests without such links are likely to be resisted (1996: 93).

As Madhok (1997) has argued, ISAs facilitate rapid market entry, allow firms to share costs/risks, combine product/market complementarities, and reduce time to market. ISAs are preferable for firms possessing product knowledge but lacking market knowledge (Madhok, 1997). In the highly regulated infrastructure industries, knowledge about the market and regulatory environments is critical to overall strategic decisions about how to deploy or redeploy resources to compete post privatization. Hence, partnerships with local firms connected with regulatory organizations or possessing relationships with incumbent government monopolies will help firms to navigate the postprivatization market and regulatory environment.

Proposition 2a: Strategic alliances with local private partners will reinforce first mover benefits accorded early entrants in privatization transactions.

In addition to the strategic alliance and cooperative strategy literature summarized here, researchers have examined other types of cooperative strategies, such as buyer-supplier strategies and stakeholder alliances between firms and their external constituents. Alliance relationships—both traditional and alternate—appear to be on the rise, stimulated by a series of factors in the external environment that are creating turbulence and placing pressure on organizations to become more flexible, dynamic, responsive, and nimble. In particular, firms participating in the transition from government-controlled monopoly industries to regulated competition must develop alliances and collaborations with government (Baron, 1995; Boddewyn & Brewer, 1995) and nongovernment stakeholders (Freeman, 1984; Mitchell, Agle, & Wood, 1997).

> *Proposition 2b: Strategic alliances with local government or nongovernment partners will reinforce first mover benefits accorded early entrants in privatization transactions.*

Strategic Alliances and Joint Ventures: The Organizational Learning Motivation

Learning is a powerful motivating force and competitive advantage in firm-level strategic management. In the strategic alliance literature, several researchers have argued that learning can be an important determinant in the initial motivations for and ultimate success of international joint ventures (Hamel, 1991; Inkpen, 1995, 1996). Barkema and Vermeulen (1998) have applied a learning perspective to determine the conditions under which firms expand internationally, finding that a firm's multinational diversity leads to foreign start-ups, rather than acquisitions, whereas product diversity has a curvilinear effect on the tendency to use start-ups. Makino and Delios (1996) have argued that some kinds of local knowledge cannot be internalized simply as a result of a MNC operating in that market, but acquisition of that knowledge requires indigenous firm experience through partnerships or alliances. As noted above, knowledge of evolving regulatory conditions and how to respond to them is especially valuable to firms operating in infrastructure industries. Moreover, as Makino and Delios (1996) have argued, an understanding of the complex mix of regulations, industry structure, competitive dynamics, and business-government relationships is unlikely to be arrived at simply by operating in that marketplace, especially in the short run.

> *Proposition 2c: Local partners who provide tangible resources, such as specific knowledge about markets,*

> *regulatory expertise, and political connections, will provide greater competitive benefits than those lacking such resources.*

As was the case with first mover competitive advantage, the value of local collaboration resources will be less if the market opens early to new entrants. That is, the market liberalization timetable will influence the value of local partner collaboration.

> *Proposition 2d: Benefits from collaboration will be lessened by the expected or actual liberalization of the newly privatized market; the sooner the market opening, the less the benefit from local partner collaboration will be.*

As noted above, collaboration can yield other valuable information regarding the nature and direction of local market trends and regulatory policy, and it can provide knowledge acquisition opportunities that can be redeployed in other regions and even in other sectors. In Figure 3 the outcome variables include the competitive position of the first mover/incumbent not only in the initial host country market but also in subsequent privatizations in that market or others.

> *Proposition 2e: Collaboration with partners in the first or early rounds of the multistaged privatization of a SOE increases postprivatization competitive advantage.*

> *Proposition 2f: Collaboration with partners in early rounds of multiindustry or multifirm privatization will strengthen the position of the first mover/incumbent in subsequent rounds and will enable it to compete more successfully in privatizations in other sectors and markets.*

ILLUSTRATIONS, DISCUSSION, AND PROPOSED METHODS

In this section I provide some illustrations and applications of the theory constructed in the previous sections. In addition, I discuss the implications of the theory for understanding the relationship of first mover and early entry effects to successful firm-level privatization strategies.

Preliminary suggestions of methodologies that might be employed to test the relationships proposed here are also offered.

Contrasting First and Later Movers

It is premature to draw definitive generalizations regarding the potential applications of this theory to corporate privatization strategy, but some examples illustrate its relevance and validity. Specifically, a comparison between first movers and later followers may be useful in an initial determination of the insight offered by this theory.

Telmex privatization. In December 1990 the Mexican government accepted a $1.757 billion bid for a minority (20.4 percent) but controlling interest in Telmex from an international consortium composed of Grupo Carso; Southwestern Bell; and France Cable et Radio, an affiliate of France Telecom. In 1991 and 1992 two more public offerings were made, resulting in combined proceeds of $6.3 billion (Whitacre, 1994: S24). At the same time, the Mexican government was also in the process of opening the long-distance market to competition but provided for a period of time within which Telmex would maintain its monopoly in order to ready itself to compete against other market entrants. Under Mexican legislation Telmex's long-distance monopoly was due to expire in August 1996, when the government would open the market to international joint ventures in the domestic long-distance market (Trotta, 1996). As part of the North American Free Trade Agreement (NAFTA) negotiations, Mexico agreed to lift all restrictions on investment in the telecommunications services sector, and President Zedillo subsequently decided to waive all entrance fees for those companies applying for telephone concessions. It was hoped that liberalization would bring a more competitive and entrepreneurial telecommunications industry that would be demonstrated by technological advances, an expanding service sector, and greatly reduced telecommunications rates for the Mexican consumer.

After market opening, Telmex faced competitors in the long-distance market but maintained monopoly control over local networks. The ability to "bundle" local and long-distance service and to cross-market and cross-subsidize gave Telmex a strong initial advantage. Moreover, the Mexican government was responsive to providing the Telmex consortium protection and financial support for infrastructure investment,

and it did so partly by charging new carriers a combined U.S. $423 million to help Telmex pay for improvements needed on the long-distance network (Dombey, 1997).

Telmex was also able to charge interconnection fees that, based on international standards, were artificially high. For example, for 1998 the agreement on fees included a 39.5¢ charge to complete each call on the Telmex local network (*New York Times*, 1998). This fee was more than eight times the equivalent fee charged by U.S. carriers to complete in-bound international calls. The artificially high fee structure had a huge negative impact on revenue of the two principal competitors to Telmex: the MCI/Avantel and AT&T/Alestra joint ventures. Avantel stated that 70 percent of its revenues went to pay these interconnection fees (Friedland, 1998; *New York Times*, 1998). This fee schedule, which hurt both the MCI and AT&T joint ventures, was initiated by the government in 1996 after MCI's entry. According to MCI, the fee schedule was used to protect Telmex from the new competition that came in after the market was liberalized, resulting in MCI's curtailed investment in the market (*New York Times*, 1998). In the initial balloting under which consumers were permitted to switch long-distance carriers, Telmex retained a 60 to 80 percent market share, partly because the great majority of ballots went unreturned, leaving Telmex the default carrier (U.S. Department of State, 1998a,b). Table 1 presents a chronology of Mexican telecommunications privatization and market liberalization.

In the case of the Mexican privatization, despite the poor reputation of Telmex, write-offs associated with the peso devaluation, and the high cost of infrastructure investment necessary to modernize the network, it does appear that Telmex is slowly becoming a more dynamic and competitive organization. It also appears as if Southwestern Bell, in its partnership with Telmex, is garnering substantial first mover/incumbent benefits. Avantel and AT&T are having difficulty gaining market share in Mexico because of the relatively high interconnection fees described above. The *nominal* first mover and entrepreneurial entrant, MCI/Avantel, is suffering both from the power of the first mover/incumbent partnership and the brand and service reputation of the later mover, AT&T/Alestra.

In the case of the Telmex privatization in Mexico, one of the largest emerging market privat-

564   *Academy of Management Review*   July

TABLE 1
Mexican Telecommunications Privatization/Market Liberalization Time Line

Date	Development
December 1990	Government of Mexico sells 20 percent share in Telefonos de Mexico, the national operating company, to Grupo Carso, Southwestern Bell International, and France Telecom
December 1991	Telmex shares increase by 237 percent for the year
January 1994	NAFTA implementation begins; MCI and Banamex form Avantel
December 1994	Run on Mexican peso begins; AT&T and Grupo Alfa form Alestra
September 1995	Avantel receives official concession from the Mexican government
December 1995	Alestra receives official concession from the Mexican government
April 1996	Alestra merges operations with GTE, Bancomer, and Telefonica
August 1996	President Zedillo places ceremonial first telephone call over Avantel network, marking the opening to private line traffic
January 1997	Open competition for Mexican long distance begins
1997 through 1998	Ballots held throughout major Mexican cities, allowing customers to switch long-distance service; Telmex retains 60 to 80 percent market share

izations on record, the time delay between the initial privatization and market opening was approximately 6 years. The advantage accorded the first mover incumbent/international partnership, however, seemed to persist well beyond this time frame.

Embratel privatization. The first steps taken to liberalize the telecommunications sector in Brazil began in August 1995. From 1946 until 1995, the government held a monopoly in local, long-distance, and international telecommunications (Gullish, 1998). The telecommunications sector as a whole was inefficient and underdeveloped, with substantial backed-up demand and just eleven lines per one hundred inhabitants. Before privatization could occur, the Brazilian government needed to facilitate entry by foreign investors. As in many Latin American countries, laws prevented foreign ownership. A constitutional amendment in 1995 allowed the entrance of private domestic and foreign investors in the telecommunications sector (D'Almedia & Hirata, 1998). Although there was some liberalization in the period 1995 to 1997, it was only with the approval of the General Telecommunications Law in 1997 that conditions were set for privatization, including the establishment of the long-awaited regulatory entity, ANATEL. Prior to the sale of Telebras, the state telecommunications monopoly, the system was composed of a holding company and twenty-eight subsidiaries. Twenty-seven of those subsidiaries were responsible for local service and one, Embratel, operated intercity and international long-distance calls and provided forty other communications services, including satellite, high-speed data, and frame and

packet switch services (*Financial Times* Intelligence Wire, 1998).

After numerous delays, the sale of Telebras was completed on July 29, 1998. The long-distance portion of Telebras, Embratel, was purchased by MCI for $2.28 billion through its fully owned Brazilian subsidiary, Startel (*Financial Times* Intelligence Wire, 1998). MCI received 51.79 percent of the voting shares of Embratel, which had the only nationwide and international network connected to businesses customers (*Financial Times* Intelligence Wire, 1998). Embratel will remain the sole long-distance carrier until further licenses are awarded, but that will not occur before December 31, 2001.

In Brazil MCI partnered with the incumbent carrier, Embratel, after participating aggressively in a bidding competition with Sprint to attain that position. On the day that MCI publicly announced its interest in acquiring Embratel, MCI's Vice President for Global Strategy and Development said that the American company would aggressively pursue purchase of Embratel unless the terms of the future sale of concessions of "mirror" companies were altered to subsequent investors' advantage. This suggests that MCI viewed direct, early investment in Embratel as more advantageous than waiting to enter the market as a mirror company. MCI clearly had concerns about the potential disadvantages of becoming a later entrant into the Brazilian market. Its priority in developing new products and services in the Latin American market precluded the company from settling for later entry.

2000

Doh

565

Lieberman and Montgomery (1988) have suggested that early movers may be able to establish a reputation for quality that can be transferred to additional products through umbrella branding and other tactics. Published reports stating that the purchase of Embratel was partly based on MCI's decision to use Embratel "as a wedge to expand into local telephone service and the cellular markets" in Brazil reflect this potential competitive advantage (Mills, 1998).

Sprint's decision to bid until the very last moment with MCI for Embratel also may reflect first mover concerns. Sprint, like MCI, never had monopolistic advantages in its home U.S. market. For Sprint, a stake in the telecommunications market represented another fundamental step in expanding its reach in a global industry. Following the loss of Embratel to MCI, Sprint remained persistent in moving into the Brazilian long-distance market; proof of this was the company's decision to bid for the licenses for mirror long-distance companies (Barham, 1999). In February of 1999, Sprint took a 25 percent stake in the consortium that bought the first mirror license to compete against Embratel. Ironically, if the proposed MCI-Worldcom/Sprint merger is approved, the combined company likely will be forced to divest from this mirror company, because Brazilian law prevents a single firm from participation in both the primary and mirror long-distance service. Table 2 presents an illustration of the chronology of Bra-

zil's telecommunications privatization and market liberalization. In Brazil MCI partnered with the incumbent, Embratel, although the period in which MCI will profit from exclusive market positioning is unclear. It does appear as if MCI may have learned from its experience in Mexico, ensuring that it had a position within the Brazilian market prior to full market opening.

Regulations, Switching Costs, Time Benefits, and First Mover Characteristics

Regulations, switching costs, and other factors contribute to the first mover/incumbency advantage. Switching electric power, energy, water, or telecommunications carriers is, in theory, relatively unconstrained. But the way in which the balloting process was conducted in Mexico meant that Telmex was the beneficiary because the majority of households did not exercise a preference and, therefore, were automatically left with the default carrier—Telmex. (An alternative would have been to randomly or proportionately assign one of the carriers in order to fairly distribute service.)

First mover literature suggests that the first product on the market able to satisfy consumers' demand will gain a large portion of market share unless a "new" product provides some definitive advantage. Telephone users in Mexico expressed relative satisfaction with the in-

TABLE 2
Brazilian Telecommunications Privatization/Market Liberalization Time Line

Date	Development
1990	Private companies allowed to provide paging, value-added, and private network services in Brazil
1991	Embratel's monopoly in data and Internet communications terminated
August 1995	Congress amends constitution to remove mandated monopoly in telecommunications
November 1995	President Cardoso announces plan for expanding telecommunications system, including the privatization of state-owned companies
May 1996	Full competition permitted in value-added, cellular, and satellite services
April 1997	Licenses sold to operate "mirror" cellular services
July 1997	Telecommunications reform passed, removing all legislative restrictions to privatization
October 1997	New independent regulator, Agencia National de Telecomunicações, established
January 1998	Each of twenty-seven *state-level* telephone companies divided into two companies: a cellular company and a wireline telephone company
May 1998	Government gives potential buyers access to "data rooms," where information on individual companies to be privatized is available
July 29, 1998	Telebras system, which had been restructured into three wireline regional companies, eight cellular operators (Band A), and Embratel, sold to private investors for $19 billion
August 1998	Announcement of terms for sale of concession licenses to operate mirror companies in competition with recently privatized ones
2002	Full competition expected in all areas of the Brazilian telecommunications market

566   *Academy of Management Review*   July

cumbent carrier. MCI was the second overall mover in terms of all competitors but the first to compete against the incumbent. Nonetheless, it trailed AT&T in terms of market share, probably because AT&T's overall brand image obviated whatever earlier entry advantage the MCI consortium may have possessed (Torres, 1996). The first mover literature indicates that firms with high levels of product identification, brand imagery, and marketing and manufacturing prowess will be successful later movers—a view that seems to be supported when comparing the "earlier entrant" MCI/Avantel to the later one, AT&T/Alestra. That is, AT&T/Alestra, because of its name recognition and product identification, possessed advantages over MCI/Avantel, notwithstanding MCI's earlier market entry.

Organizational Learning and Experience Curve Effects

The impact of organizational learning and experience curve effects requires further exploration and application. As described below, AES's strategy in Latin America demonstrates how firms may benefit from participation in early rounds of privatization and use local partner relationships to compete in subsequent rounds in the initial market, in other markets, and even across industries.

AES, one of the largest independent power companies in the world, has pursued a first mover strategy and, in so doing, has built a virtual electricity network in Latin America. In 1997 AES purchased a 13.75 percent stake in the Sao Paulo electric utility Light Servicos de Eletricidade (Light). In addition to the AES stake, Electricité de France and Houston Industries Energy each took 11.35 percent of the utility in the transaction. In 1998 AES, together with The Southern Company and The Opportunity Fund, a Brazilian investment fund, acquired 14.41 percent of Companhia Energetica de Minas Gerais (Cemig), an integrated electric utility serving the State of Minas Gerais in Brazil (*Latin Finance*, 1998). Light recently paid $1.78 billion for a 28 percent equity stake of Sao Paulo power provider Eletropaulo Metropolitana, which includes control of 75 percent of the voting shares of the electricity distributor (*Energy Daily*, 1998). The purchase gives Light and, by extension, its three foreign partners responsibility for distributing electricity in Brazil's two largest metropol-

itan areas and for completing a value chain of electricity generation and distribution. This purchase would have been difficult had AES and Houston not had a relationship with the local power generator that served the distributor.

AES also has used its early experience in generation to pursue privatizations of electricity and gas distribution—a related, but different, industry segment. In June 1999 AES announced it was paying $350 million to Houston Industries and an Argentine construction company, Techint, for 90 percent of the shares of the Buenos Aires Province power distributor EDELAP. That purchase extends AES's influence in the Buenos Aires province electricity market, where last year it paid $330 million for controlling stakes in two neighboring distributors, EDEN and EDES. AES was also one of the bidders—via its Rio power distributor Light—in the July auction of Brazilian long-distance provider Embratel, but lost out in that bid to MCI (*Global Power Report*, 1999).

In the case of AES, first mover strategies appear to have allowed the firm to compete for subsequent privatization in Brazil and to benefit from positioning itself as a "local" firm in these deals. Moreover, the cumulative experience of competing for a series of privatizations appears to have allowed AES to apply knowledge from one market, region, and even industry to another. AES, however, also has experienced some of the costs of its entrepreneurial orientation and first mover strategy. Although AES posted record earnings of $311 million for 1998, it indicated its intention to take a charge against 1999 earnings in the first quarter because of Brazil's currency devaluation and economic problems. It estimated the write-off would be $105 million. AES also has said it will have to reduce stockholder equity by $760 million because of the lower value of the Brazilian assets (*Global Power Report*, 1998), illustrating some of the risks associated with maintaining an entrepreneurial orientation as a first mover in a risky, volatile market.

Proposed Methods

Although these illustrations provide some preliminary evidence supporting application of a first mover/collaborative approach to privatization, more sophisticated methods must be developed. One particular challenge is how to isolate the impact of first mover or early entry position—and the benefits of collaboration in conjunction with that pioneering advantage—from other market, industry, and firm-level factors. Privatization is a highly idiosyncratic phenomenon, and controlling for the range of variables necessary to isolate first mover and alliance influences will be difficult.

The privatization phenomenon presents substantial methodological challenges to determining first mover advantage. First, the population of privatization transactions and firms competing for concessions is relatively small. Further, as mentioned earlier, the "winners" in a competitive tender may purchase away the entirety of the first mover benefit, making it difficult to evaluate its value and the ability of that particular firm to deploy resources to exploit the first mover position fully. Finance theorists suggest that these winners might even overpay because high bidders consistently lose money, failing to account for the adverse selection problem inherent in winning the auction. The winner's curse is especially problematic in bidding for items of uncertain value, resulting in below normal or even negative average profits for bidders (Thaler, 1991). Although bidders may hold unbiased estimates of the auctioned item's value, this estimate can be overly optimistic, given that participants' bids are influenced by their estimates of value (Thaler, 1991). This phenomenon may confound the ability to separate the first mover benefits of a particular privatization transaction from the transaction itself.

In one recent effort to differentiate between first mover advantages and competitive benefits of firm-level attributes, researchers used data envelope analysis to determine whether the relationship between pioneering and market share is a result of researchers' inability to control for managerial skills (Murthi, Srinivasan, & Kalyanaram, 1996). To determine whether "efficient" firms have a greater pioneering advantage than inefficient firms, these researchers estimated a model with interaction terms between pioneering and efficiency variables. The interaction between manufacturing efficiency and order of entry was in the expected direction but not significant (Murthi et al., 1996). Hence, although pioneers possess superior managerial skills, the impact of pioneering alone on market share is itself quite significant (Murthi et al., 1996). These researchers also noted the difficulty of measuring subjective factors, such as managerial capability. They controlled for unob-

served firm-specific factors, including unmeasured managerial skills, as a way to minimize the variability in management skill that might be attributed mistakenly to pioneering advantage (Murthi et al., 1996).

In addition to the I/O and resource-based strategy routes, some first mover/pioneering advantage research has originated in the marketing literature (Cahill, 1995; Szymanski, Troy, & Bharadwaj, 1995). Hence, marketing research methods and techniques may be appropriate for testing the model. One potentially fruitful approach is the use of conjoint analysis to determine the relative importance of first mover positioning versus other firm-level or environmental conditions relevant to successful privatization strategies. Widely used in consumer marketing research, conjoint analysis, also known as trade-off analysis or assessment, allows respondents to assess and exchange ratings directly between attributes, thus permitting the researcher to identify and rank consumer values for various attributes (Green, Krieger, Agarwal, & Johnson, 1991; Green & Srinivasan, 1990). In the case of firm-level and transaction-specific characteristics of privatization, conjoint analysis may be used to reveal the latent importance assigned to early entry versus other contributors to competitive assessment, including other resources and industry factors.

Further research on firm-level response to privatization should be facilitated as the record of activity grows. Over the next several years, it has been estimated that an additional $50 to $70 billion will be spent in emerging market privatizations. As more countries and firms in more sectors are involved in privatization, the application of methods from strategic management, international business, and marketing should help to further inform what drives privatization strategies and competitive success.

CONCLUSIONS, LIMITATIONS, AND SUGGESTIONS FOR FURTHER RESEARCH

In this article I have drawn from two established schools of strategic management—the I/O and resource-based schools—to examine the role of first mover and pioneering advantage effects on the success of new, foreign market entrants in response to privatization opportunities. The major contribution of this discussion is the unique application and integration of first mover, order-of-entry, pioneering advantage, and collaborative strategy effects to the privatization phenomenon. Privatization presents a particularly powerful case supporting the competitive effects of first mover positioning. The theoretical development and case review suggest that first movers/incumbents possess a significant advantage over other pioneering firms, especially when market liberalization is delayed, first movers partner with the incumbent, and a complicit government provides incumbency protections. In these limited examples, however, the sequential order among those entering the markets *subsequent* to the initial investor is not a material factor in success. In other words, the initial entrant, partnered with the incumbent, reaps the bulk of first mover benefits while the second and third entrants vie for a very inferior position. Hence, the definition of first mover must be further refined under this circumstance to refer specifically to the first mover/incumbent partnership.

Another major contribution is the application of the time-benefit model to the common circumstance in which privatization is followed by liberalization or market opening (see Figures 1 and 2). Not only does this "lag" provide powerful benefits to the first mover/incumbent, but these benefits persist beyond the stated term of protection so that first movers establish a formidable dominance in the market that is difficult for later entrants to challenge. The opportunity to partner with a local firm or government agency appears to strengthen these relationships further and position first movers to participate in subsequent privatizations in the initial and other sectors and markets.

This discussion is limited in a number of respects. Many of the arguments offered here are relevant to the range of privatization phenomena, but I have intentionally delimited the subset of privatization under examination to competitively bid infrastructure privatizations. Although these constitute the bulk of privatizations in emerging markets over the last decade, there are other privatizations programs—for example, in financial services, for which the theories offered here might be less relevant. Further, I have introduced the notion of "liberalization lag" as an important intervening variable that strengthens the first mover pressure and benefits. Many but not all privatizations in infrastructure include this privatization-

market liberalization sequence. As in any conceptual/theoretical presentation, the ultimate value of the theory and application will be measured in future empirical testing. Although I have offered case examples and suggestions for methodological approaches to the research questions, it is only through subsequent empirical application that the value of the arguments will be tested. So far, the managerial implications are tentative, based primarily on ex post review of limited cases.

Further, I have intentionally excluded myriad other variables that could unilaterally influence successful privatization strategy—variables that might also interact with the constructs I have explored. As mentioned above, these include the range of market, industry, and firm-level characteristics that contribute to international corporate competitive position. Because of the idiosyncratic and stylized nature of privatization, it is hard to make generalizations at all, for conditions vary widely according to political, economic, cultural, and other circumstances. Of promise, however, is the growing record of "successful" privatizations and the apparent learning by government policy makers from experiences in other jurisdictions, as evidenced by Brazil's very sophisticated approach to privatization sequence, process, structure, and implementation in the Telebras privatization.

This discussion builds on prior research in I/O economics, the resource-based view of the firm, social network theory, foreign direct investment theory, internalization, international business strategy, and collaborative strategy and strategic alliances. The relevance to practitioners is potentially powerful: investors choosing between participation in early versus later rounds of privatization (i.e., the initial sale of the state monopoly versus subsequent entrants into a liberalized market) would be wise to consider the costs of missing out on the initial, and highly valuable, first mover position. Government policy makers could use this study and future empirical tests to structure privatization in a manner that does not shelter the incumbent so completely from competition, assuming the goal of these privatizations is to attain a more market-based, transparent pricing, and efficient postprivatization industry structure.

As noted above, in further research scholars should examine the relative contribution of entry order versus firm-level resources and competencies. Researchers also could explore the degree to which specific and relative resource capabilities and deficits of early entrants strengthen or weaken first mover advantages. The role of learning by firms participating in a series of privatizations also should be examined to uncover how firm strategies incorporate earlier experiences. Finally, first mover and pioneering advantage and alliance/learning motivations are undoubtedly affected by factors informed by other managerial theories and principles, such as transaction cost, agency, and the related problem of information asymmetries. Some of these theoretical approaches are examined in other articles in this special issue. Only through integration of a range of theoretical foundations can we fully explain the phenomenon of privatization and corporate strategic response and success, and the role of early entry status and collaborative strategies to that success.

REFERENCES

Bain, J. S. 1956. *Barriers to new competition.* Cambridge, MA: Harvard University Press.

Barham, J. 1999. Groups sign "mirror" phone deals in Brazil. *Financial Times,* January 16: 19.

Barkema, H. G., & Vermeulen, F. 1998. International expansion through start-up or acquisition: A learning perspective. *Academy of Management Journal,* 41: 7–26.

Barney, J. 1986. Organization culture: Can it be a source of sustained competitive advantage? *Academy of Management Review,* 11: 656–665.

Barney, J. 1991. Firm resources and sustained competitive advantage. *Journal of Management,* 17: 99–120.

Barney, J. 1995. Looking inside for competitive advantage. *Academy of Management Executive,* 9(4): 49–61.

Baron, D. P. 1995. Integrated strategy: Market and nonmarket components. *California Management Review,* 37(2): 47–65.

Barringer, B. R., & Bluedorn, A. C. 1999. The relationship between corporate entrepreneurship and strategic management. *Strategic Management Journal,* 20: 421–444.

Black, J. A., & Boal, K. B. 1994. Strategic resources: Traits, configurations and paths to sustainable competitive advantage. *Strategic Management Journal,* 15: 131–148.

Boddewyn, J. M., & Brewer, T. 1995. International-business political behavior: New theoretical directions. *Academy of Management Review,* 19: 119–143.

Boubakri, N., & Cosset, J. 1998. The financial and operating performance of newly privatized firms: Evidence from developing countries. *Journal of Finance,* 53: 1081–1097.

Buckley, P. J., & Casson, M. 1988. A theory of cooperation in international business? In F. Contractor & P. Lorange (Eds.), *Cooperative strategies in international business:* 31–53. Lexington, MA: Lexington Books.

Buckley, P. J., & Casson, M. 1996. An economic model of international joint venture strategy. *Journal of International Business Studies,* 27: 849–876.

Cahill, D. 1995. Review of managing imitation strategies. *Journal of Business & Industrial Marketing,* 10(5): 60–61.

Cahill, D. 1996. Entrepreneurial orientation or pioneer advantage. *Academy of Management Review,* 21: 603–605.

Caves, R. E. 1990. Lessons from privatization in Britain: State enterprise behavior, public choice, and corporate governance. *Journal of Economic Behavior and Organization,* 13: 145–169.

Caves, R. E., & Porter, M. E. 1977. From entry barriers to mobility barriers: Conjectural decisions and contrived deterrence to new competition. *Quarterly Journal of Economics,* 91: 241–262.

Contractor, F. J., & Lorange, P. (Eds.). 1988a. *Cooperative strategies in international business.* Lexington, MA: Lexington Books.

Contractor, F. J., & Lorange, P. 1988b. Why should firms cooperate? The strategy and economics basis for cooperative ventures. In F. Contractor & P. Lorange (Eds.), *Cooperative strategies in international business:* 3–30. Lexington, MA: Lexington Books.

Cooper, A. C., & Dunkelberg, W. C. 1986. Entrepreneurship and paths to business ownership. *Strategic Management Journal,* 7: 53–68.

Covin, J. G., & Slevin, D. P. 1989. Strategic management of small firms in hostile and benign environments. *Strategic Management Journal,* 10: 75–87.

D'Almedia, R., & Hirata, A. 1998. Public network telephone system. *Industry sector analysis.* Washington, DC: U.S. Department of Commerce.

DeCastro, J., & Uhlenbruck, N. 1997. Characteristics of privatization: Evidence from developed, less-developed, and former communist countries. *Journal of International Business Studies,* 28: 123–143.

Demsetz, H. 1973. Industry structure, market rivalry, and public policy. *Journal of Law and Economics,* 16: 1–9.

Dewenter, K. L., & Malatesta, P. H. 1997. Public offerings of state-owned and privately-owned enterprises: An international comparison. *Journal of Finance,* 52: 1659–1679.

Dierickx, I., & Cool, K. 1989. Asset stock accumulation and the sustainability of competitive advantage. *Management Science,* 35: 1504–1513.

Dombey, D. 1997. Telmex gets lion's share of long-distance. *Financial Times,* June 4: 1.

Durchslag, S., Puri, T., & Rao, A. 1994. The promise of infrastructure privatization. *McKinsey Quarterly,* 4(2): 3–19.

Dyer, J. H., & Singh, H. 1998. The relational view: Cooperative strategy and sources of interorganizational competitive advantage. *Academy of Management Review,* 23: 660–679.

Energy Daily. 1998. Houston Industries, AES, EDF boost Brazilian presence. April 20: 1.

Filatotchev, I., Hoskisson, R. E., Buck, T., & Wright, M. 1996. Corporate restructuring in Russian privatization: Implications for U.S. investors. *California Management Review*, 38(2): 87–98.

Financial Times Intelligence Wire. 1998. Brazil—telecommunications system privatization: An overview. *International Market Insight Reports*, October 20.

Freeman, R. E. 1984. *Strategic management: A stakeholder approach*. Boston: Pitman.

Friedland, J. 1998. US phone giants find Telmex can be a bruising competitor. *Wall Street Journal*, October 23: www.wsj.com

Galal, A., & Shirley, M. 1994. *Does privatization deliver? Highlights from a World Bank conference*. Washington, DC: World Bank.

Global Power Report. 1999. AES posts strong earnings in 1998, but prepares to take hit on Brazil. February 19: 4.

Green, P. E., Krieger, A. M., Agarwal, M. K., & Johnson, R. M. 1991. Adaptive conjoint analysis: Some caveats and suggestions; comment. *Journal of Marketing Research*, 28: 215–225.

Green, P. E., & Srinivasan, V. 1990. Conjoint analysis in marketing: New developments with implications for research and practice. *Journal of Marketing*, 54: 3–19.

Gulati, R. 1999. Network location and learning: The influence of network resources and firm capabilities on alliance formation. *Strategic Management Journal*, 20: 397–420.

Gulati, R., & Garguilo, M. 1999. Where do interorganizational networks come from? *American Journal of Sociology*, 104: 1439–1493.

Gullish, J. J. 1998. Telebra's privatization. *Brazilianist*, May 19: www.brazilianist.com/autumn97/gullish3.html

Hamel, G. 1991. Competition for competence and interpartner learning within international strategic alliances. *Strategic Management Journal*, 12(Special Issue): 83–104.

Harrigan, K. 1988. Strategic alliances and partner asymmetries. In F. Contractor & P. Lorange (Eds.), *Cooperative strategies in international business*: 205–226. Lexington, MA: Lexington Books.

Hensley, M. L., & White, E. P. 1993. The privatization experience in Malaysia: Integrating build-operate-own and build-operate-transfer techniques within the national privatization strategy. *Columbia Journal of World Business*, 28(1): 70–82.

Inkpen, A. C. 1995. *The management of international joint ventures: An organizational learning perspective*. London: Routledge.

Inkpen, A. C. 1996. Creating knowledge through collaboration. *California Management Review*, 39(1): 123–140.

Kahn, A. 1988. (First published in 1971.) *The economics of regulation*. Cambridge, MA: MIT Press.

Kambhato, P. 1998. The flagship role of telecommunications. In I. Lieberman & C. Kirkness (Eds.), *Privatization and emerging equity markets*: 88–103. Washington, DC: World Bank.

Kay, J. 1995. *Why firms succeed: Choosing assets and challenging competitors to create value*. Oxford: Oxford University Press.

Kerin, R. P., Varadarajan, R., & Peterson, R. A. 1992. First-mover advantage: A synthesis, conceptual framework, and research propositions. *Journal of Marketing*, 56(4): 33–52.

Killing, P. J. 1988. Understanding alliances: The role of task and organizational complexity. In F. Contractor & P. Lorange (Eds.), *Cooperative strategies in international business*: 55–95. Lexington, MA: Lexington Books.

Kogut, B. 1988. A study of the life cycle of joint ventures. In F. Contractor & P. Lorange (Eds.), *Cooperative strategies in international business*: 169–185. Lexington, MA: Lexington Books.

Latin Finance. 1998. The power and the glory: Postscript. September 1: 132.

Lieberman, I. 1990. *Industrial restructuring policy and practice*. Washington, DC: World Bank.

Lieberman, I. 1993. Privatization: The theme of the 1990s—an overview. *Columbia Journal of World Business*, 28(1): 8–17.

Lieberman, M., & Montgomery, D. 1988. First mover advantages. *Strategic Management Journal*, 9: 41–58.

Lippman, S. A., & Rumelt, R. 1982. Uncertain imitability: An analysis of interfirm differences in efficiency under competition. *Bell Journal of Economics*, 13: 418–438.

Lumpkin, G. T., & Dess, G. G. 1996. Clarifying the entrepreneurial orientation construct and linking it to performance. *Academy of Management Review*, 21: 135–172.

Lyles, M. A., & Salk, J. E. 1996. Knowledge acquisition from parents in international joint ventures: An empirical examination in the Hungarian context. *Journal of International Business Studies*, 27: 877–903.

Madhok, A. 1997. Economizing and strategizing in foreign market entry. In P. W. Beamish & J. P. Killing (Eds.), *Cooperative strategies: North American perspectives*: 25–50. San Francisco: New Lexington Press.

Makino, S., & Delios, A. 1996. Local knowledge transfer and performance: Implications for alliance formation in Asia. *Journal of International Business Studies*, 27: 905–927.

Mascarenhas, B. 1992. Order of entry and performance in international markets. *Strategic Management Journal*, 13: 499–510.

Megginson, W. L., Nash, R. C., & Van Randenborgh, M. 1994. The financial and operating performance of newly privatized firms: An international empirical analysis. *Journal of Finance*, 49: 403–452.

Mills, M. 1998. MCI a long-distance winner in Brazil. *Washington Post*, July 30: E1.

Mitchell, R. K., Agle, B. R., & Wood, D. J. 1997. Toward a theory of stakeholder identification and salience: Defining the principle of who and what really counts. *Academy of Management Review*, 22: 853–886.

Money, R. W., & Griffith, S. 1993. Privatizing a distressed state-owned enterprise: Lessons learned through privatization work in Argentina's steel sector. *Columbia Journal of World Business*, 28(1): 36–44.

Murthi, P. S., Srinivasan, K., & Kalyanaram, G. 1996. Controlling for observed and unobserved managerial skills in determining first-mover market share advantages. *Journal of Marketing Research*, 33: 329–407.

Nelson, R., & Winter, S. 1982. *An evolutionary theory of economic change.* Cambridge, MA: Harvard University Press.

New York Times. 1998. Joint-venture Mexico funds halted by MCI. February 6: D18.

Patterson, W. C. 1993. First-mover advantage: The opportunity curve. *Journal of Management Studies*, 30: 759–777.

Penrose, E. T. 1959. *The theory of growth of the firm.* London: Blackwell.

Perotti, E. C., & Guney, S. E. 1993. The structure of privatization plans. *Financial Management*, 22(1): 84–98.

Peteraf, M. 1993. The cornerstones of competitive advantage: A resource-based view. *Strategic Management Journal*, 14: 179–192.

Porter, M. E. 1980. *Competitive strategy: Techniques for analyzing industries and companies.* New York: Free Press.

Porter, M. E. 1981. The contribution of industrial organization to strategic management. *Academy of Management Review*, 6: 609–620.

Porter, M. E. 1985. *Competitive advantage: Creating and sustaining superior performance.* New York: Free Press.

Porter, M. E. 1986. Competition in global industries: A conceptual framework. In M. E. Porter (Ed.), *Competition in global industries:* 15–60. Boston: Harvard Business School Press.

Porter, M. E. 1990. *The competitive advantage of nations.* New York: Free Press.

Porter, M. E. 1991. Towards a dynamic theory of strategy. *Strategic Management Journal*, 12: 95–117.

Prahalad, C. K., & Doz, Y. 1987. *The multinational mission: Balancing local demands and global vision.* New York: Free Press.

Prahalad, C. K., & Hamel, G. 1990. The core competence of the corporation. *Harvard Business Review*, 68(3): 79–91.

Root, F. R. 1988. Some taxonomies of international cooperative arrangements. In F. Contractor & P. Lorange (Eds.), *Cooperative strategies in international business:* 69–80. Lexington, MA: Lexington Books.

Rumelt, R. P. 1991. How much does industry matter? *Strategic Management Journal*, 12: 167–185.

Senge, P. M. 1990. *The fifth discipline: The art and practice of the learning organization.* New York: Doubleday.

Smith, K. G., Grimm, C. M., & Gannon, M. J. 1992. *Dynamics of competitive strategy.* Newbury Park, CA: Sage.

Stopford, J. M., & Wells, L. T. 1972. *Managing the multinational enterprise.* New York: Basic Books.

Szymanski, D. M., Troy, L. C., & Bharadwaj, S. G. 1995. Order of entry and business performance: An empirical synthesis and reexamination. *Journal of Marketing*, 59(4): 17–33.

Teece, D. 1986. Firm boundaries, technological innovation, and strategic management. In L. G. Thomas, III (Ed.), *The economics of strategic planning:* 187–198. Lexington, MA: Lexington Books.

Tellis, G., & Golder, P. 1996. First to market, first to fail? Real causes of enduring market leadership. *Sloan Management Review*, 37(2): 65–77.

Thaler, R. H. 1991. *The winner's curse: Paradoxes and anomalies of economic life.* New York: Free Press.

Thorelli, H. B. 1986. Networks between markets and hierarchies. *Strategic Management Journal*, 7: 37–51.

Torres, C. 1996. Long distance call: Taking a gamble, MCI plunged into Mexico as AT&T hesitated. *Wall Street Journal*, November 18: A1.

Trotta, D. 1996. Avantel ends phone monopoly in Mexico. *Washington Times*, August 13: B6.

Uhlenbruck, N., & DeCastro, J. 1998. Privatization from the acquirer's perspective: A mergers and acquisitions based framework. *Journal of Management Studies*, 5: 619–629.

U.S. Department of State. 1998a. *Mexico: Opening the long distance telephone market.* Mexico City: U.S. Embassy.

U.S. Department of State. 1998b. *Mexican long distance telephone competition: Early results.* Mexico City: U.S. Embassy.

Vickers, J., & Yarrow, G. 1991. Economic perspectives on privatization. *Journal of Economic Perspectives*, 5(2): 111–132.

Wernerfelt, B. 1989. From critical resources to corporate strategy. *Journal of General Management*, 14: 4–12.

Whitacre, E. E. 1994. Keys to success: Privatization in the telecommunications industry. *Latin Finance*, March: S24.

Williamson, O. E. 1979. Transaction-cost economics: The governance of contractual relations. *Journal of Law and Economics*, 22: 233–261.

World Bank. 1992. *Privatization: The lessons of experience.* Washington, DC: World Bank.

Yarrow, G. 1986. Privatization in theory and practice. *Economic Policy*, 2: 324–364.

Jonathan P. Doh is academic director of the International Business and Trade Semester at American University, a doctoral candidate in strategic management/public policy and international business at The George Washington University, and an adjunct fellow at the Center for Strategic and International Studies. His research interests center on competitive rivalry, international entrepreneurship, corporate privatization strategy, strategic alliances and joint ventures, and international business-government relations.

[30]

CORPORATE ENTREPRENEURS AND PRIVATIZED FIRMS IN RUSSIA, UKRAINE, AND BELARUS

IGOR FILATOTCHEV

MIKE WRIGHT

TREVOR BUCK

VLADIMIR ZHUKOV

University of Nottingham Business School

EXECUTIVE SUMMARY

This paper provides a preliminary examination of the development of corporate entrepreneurship in privatized firms in Russia, Belarus, and Ukraine, three countries with a common background as part of the Soviet Union, but with different incentives and constraints on entrepreneurship since the beginning of transition. Using large-scale surveys of newly privatized companies, the paper shows that there are differences in the nature and extent of entrepreneurship in established businesses in the three countries. The paper utilizes representative samples of general directors in 105 privatized Russian enterprises, 100 privatized Ukranian enterprises, and 68 privatized enterprises in Belarus.

Evidence is presented that suggests that Russian privatized firms have lower insider stakes, greater outside ownership, less employee voice, and greater managerial power within the firm than is the case in Belarus and Ukraine. The active monitoring of managers by outsiders may be an important aspect of the transformation of Russian firms to efficient, commercially viable entities. In Ukraine and Belarus a lack of outside involvement in corporate governance may lead to managerial opportunism and low incentives to attract outside strategic investors, including foreign partners. Russia appears to be building a stronger platform for the future development and effectiveness of entrepreneurship than is the case in Ukraine and Belarus. The findings provide evidence of the importance of direct involvement and the

Address correspondence to Igor Filatotchev. University of Nottingham, School of Management and Finance, Nottingham, U.K.; Phone: 44-1159 515 265; Fax: 44-1159 515 252; E-mail: Igor.Filatotchev@Nottingham.ac.uk

The authors wish to thank the Department for International Development for financial support. Comments from the editor and two anonymous reviewers are acknowledged with gratitude.

Journal of Business Venturing **14**, 475–492
0883-9026/99/$–see front matter
PII S0883-9026(98)00028-7

development of relationships to counteract the shortcomings of the legal infrastructure and financial reporting mechanisms.

In general, the findings of the study for Russia show that in the current hostile and rapidly changing environment, entrepreneurial priorities and actions so far have primarily focused on controlling cash flow, seeking new markets, and redefining businesses through retrenchment and restructuring. Although it is, as yet, too early to examine the longer term effects of the changes in entrepreneurial conditions, the paper presents the first large-scale comparative evidence of the indications of a divergence in entrepreneurial development between the three countries. There was a greater incidence of turnover among the senior management team in Russia. Managers in Ukraine and Belarus had more diverse strategic objectives in contrast to those in Russia where managers have behaved in a more realistic fashion by focusing on retrenchment.

For academics, the study's findings suggest further research is needed to examine the longer term nature and effects of corporate entrepreneurship, compare entrepreneurship in new start-ups in the three countries, and compare with corporate entrepreneurship elsewhere in emerging markets and the barriers to the development of corporate entrepreneurship. For practitioners and policy makers, the study highlights the need to develop and enforce an appropriate regulatory framework which strengthens the rules of the game under which corporate entrepreneurship operates. © *1999 Elsevier Science Inc.*

INTRODUCTION

The literature on entrepreneurship has traditionally concentrated on new business start-ups, but more recently there has been growing attention to entrepreneurship in established businesses (Cooper and Dunkelberg 1986; Wright et al. 1992; Guth and Ginsberg 1990; Zahra 1995). In this paper we provide the first comparative large-scale analysis of such corporate entrepreneurship in privatized firms in the transition economies of Russia, Ukraine, and Belarus. In general, the findings of the study show that corporate entrepreneurship has primarily focused on controlling cash flow, seeking new markets, and redefining businesses through retrenchment and restructuring.

It is generally agreed that former centrally planned economies (CPEs) involved no significant legal role for individual entrepreneurs, and as a result CPEs ultimately suffered from low customer satisfaction and levels of innovation. Economic reforms were expected to create a solid foundation for the liberation of entrepreneurship. In the former USSR in particular, however, there was a long history of low levels of private business start-ups (Kantorovich 1998). Since 1991 new business start-ups have been mainly restricted to the service sector, such as trade, financial services, and consultancy. The former commanding heights of the former USSR in the manufacturing sector have seen few new private firms (EBRD 1997). Rather, the principal reforms of the manufacturing sector in the former USSR have comprised the gradual withdrawal of the State from enterprise decisions, price liberalization, and a mass privatization program that has generally put the ownership of enterprises into the hands of enterprise incumbents: managers and employees. Control has tended to follow ownership, and privatized manufacturing firms have been described as manager-controlled employee buy-outs (Earle and Estrin 1996).

Former republics of the USSR provide fertile ground for the study of entrepreneurial development under different regimes of economic reform, and in particular different patterns of enterprise ownership and control. To address these issues, this paper presents preliminary evidence from those former republics which were the main industrial regions of the USSR, now independent nations: Russia, Ukraine, and Belarus. From their common starting point as members of the Soviet Union with similar privatization methods in which incumbents obtained significant equity stakes, each country has experienced contrasting constraints on the development of entrepreneurial actions.

The purpose of this paper is to provide an exploratory examination of the nature and extent of corporate entrepreneurship in the former USSR, concentrating on outside influences from owners and lenders on the entrepreneurial decisions of incumbent managers. This analysis abstracts from the degree of product market competition facing firms, but this factor is addressed in the final section. Evidence is provided on the important ownership and control positions held by directors and the generally low involvement of outsiders; these features are particularly marked in Ukraine and Belarus. The paper examines the effects of the ownership changes following privatization on short- and long-term entrepreneurial strategies, but it is too early to examine the longer term effects of the changes in entrepreneurial conditions.

The paper has three parts. First, it outlines the main problems facing entrepreneurship in Russia, Ukraine, and Belarus, and in particular the influences of incentives and constraints on the actions of managers of newly privatized companies. This includes an analysis of the privatization programs in the manufacturing industries of the three countries. Second, the paper goes on to present evidence from a large-scale questionnaire survey of general directors of enterprises in the three countries which involves 105 privatized companies in Russia, 100 in Ukraine, and 68 in Belarus. Third, implications for academics and practitioners are outlined.

CORPORATE ENTREPRENEURSHIP IN THE FORMER SOVIET UNION

Entrepreneurship in the former Soviet Union (USSR) may develop either through the creation of new firms (start-ups, greenfield investment, etc.) or through the entrepreneurial transformation of privatized enterprises, that is, corporate entrepreneurship (Ners 1995). The literature on corporate entrepreneurship within existing corporations recognizes that it has two broad dimensions: innovations aimed at business creation and venturing and innovations concerned with strategic renewal (Block and MacMillan 1993; Guth and Ginsberg 1990; Stopford and Baden-Fuller 1994; Zahra 1993, 1996).

Major surveys by international agencies find that the creation of de novo businesses in the former USSR continues to lag behind the rate of new business creation in other former Communist countries in Central Europe, with the number of officially registered smaller businesses in Russia remaining at only around 1 million in 1997 (EBRD 1997). In contrast, the privatization of State-owned enterprises has been an important tool of economic reform in Russia, though to a much lesser extent in Ukraine and Belarus (Table 1). The form but not the scale of the Russian mass privatization model, involving the distribution of vouchers to citizens and eventual insider control (Boycko et al. 1993), was however, imitated in Belarus and Ukraine (Filatotchev et al. 1996).

A key issue concerns the extent to which managers in the former USSR, whether through starting a business or becoming owners as part of the privatization program, have the characteristics and expertise to engage in entrepreneurial actions. Entrepreneurship has been under-developed in these countries for a considerable period. Hisrich and Grachev (1993) in reviewing the historical development of entrepreneurship in the Russian Empire find that from the 16th to the 19th century, entrepreneurship was generally underdeveloped and entrepreneurs were considered as inferior individuals. During

TABLE 1 Privatization in Russia, Ukraine, and Belarus

	Russia	Ukraine	Belarus
Commencement of privatization program	1992	1994	1993
Coverage of program	All industry*	Selected, listed firms only	Selected, listed firms only
Target number of firms covered	20,000	8,000	8,500
Actual number of firms privatized by 1997	20,000	3,000	212**
Private companies' share of industrial output 1997	89%	40%	12%
Private companies' share of industrial employment 1997	81%	21%	8%

* Excluding certain "strategic" firms in the natural resource and defense-related sectors;
** Plus other so-called "privatized" firms where the State has retained a majority shareholding. Sources: European Bank for Reconstruction and Development, Transition Report 1997, London, EBRD. Belarussky Rinok, March 1997: 7, Minsk.

the period of central planning in the former USSR, most strategic decisions were made at the center with enterprises carrying out routine, planned operations. In effect, entrepreneurship was concentrated in the Ministries which tried to run the country as a single firm (USSR Inc.).

The nature of entrepreneurship, however, reflects the rules of the game (Baumol 1996) and in the former USSR it was often unproductive or even destructive. In practice, many designers and administrators of the plan at all levels diverted economic rents to their own individual benefit (Richman 1965). At the level of the individual enterprise, the actual outcome was described as "reverse entrepreneurship" (Filatotchev et al. 1992) whereby valuable inputs (especially raw materials) were extensively converted into finished goods of low value. Under state control, enterprises operated with soft budget constraints, where state agencies acted as a lender of last resort to enterprises over-demanding resources to reach ratcheted targets set by Ministries. Although under the central planning system there were few rewards for innovation nor penalties for failure, it was nevertheless possible to identify entrepreneurs outside the ministries (Hisrich and Grachev 1993). These individuals either emerged as entrepreneurs through the development of the shadow economy or were employed by factories as 'tolkachi' to identify and obtain scarce material inputs (Filatotchev et al. 1992).

The beginning of economic reforms in the former USSR dramatically changed the conditions in which companies produce and sell their outputs. Managers have to learn to run their companies in a situation where the state is gradually withdrawing from the system of control and funding of enterprises and free-market mechanisms are slowly evolving in all areas of a company's operations. To survive in this rapidly changing environment, there is a need for more entrepreneurial managers (Ernst et al. 1996).

Doubts have been raised about whether the psyche of managers in Russia compared to those in the West predisposes them to act entrepreneurially and make the changes necessary for survival in a market economy (Holt et al. 1994). At the start of the reform process there was a general absence of sufficiently skilled managers in existing businesses trained to compete in a market-based economy (Puffer 1994). Studies of the entrepreneurial characteristics of Russian entrepreneurs who have started a business have found that although they located control internally, they possessed significantly lower internal locus of control scores than entrepreneurs elsewhere (Kaufman et al. 1995) and perceive serious constraints on the starting of a viable business in the manufacturing sector in particular (McCarthy et al. 1993). Within existing enterprises, the so-called Red Directors of the former Soviet system tended to be all-powerful and experienced in dealing with routine functional problems, but were often inflexible regarding the adjustments required in a market economy. Although managers were generally technically excellent or had some relevant training, they were often inexperienced in such functions as marketing, finance, strategic planning, etc. (Linz 1997; Filatotchev et al. 1996b). As managers were chosen by the mainly negative selection of the former regime, they are less likely to display entrepreneurial drive. Moreover, Red Directors may have been so imbued with the modus operandi of the former system that they were unable to effect entrepreneurial actions following privatization (Linz 1996). Krueger (1995), however, argues that the former Red Directors, even the nomenklatura, are more entrepreneurial and have more savvy than is generally believed. Hard budget constraints are a new concept for managers in the former command economies, and time is required to adapt to these changes (Linz and Krueger 1996).

A long-standing importance has been attached to equity ownership as an important aspect of entrepreneurship since ownership rights are crucial to the generation of entrepreneurial profit through the coordination of resources in an uncertain environment (Hawley 1900; Gartner and Shane 1995). The introduction of equity ownership for managers following the privatization of enterprises in the former USSR may thus be expected to provide a stimulus to corporate entrepreneurship. It is expected that managers' acting as corporate entrepreneurs will seek to further concentrate ownership in their hands in all three countries in order to be in a more dominant position to effect longer term restructuring. However, the above problems may affect the willingness or ability of incumbent managers in existing business to undertake entrepreneurial actions, and attention turns to improving their quality using certain mechanisms involving outsiders as shareholders, outside lenders and monitors, and the role of product market competition.

The general reluctance of founders of entrepreneurial businesses to allow influence and involvement by outsiders is well-known (Ang 1991). In established businesses substantial managerial equity stakes may also increase the risk of entrenchment (Morck et al. 1988), with the added problem in the former USSR that managers may be able to prevent sales of their shares to outsiders (Filatotchev et al. 1996). The corollary is that important wealth creation may derive from new entrepreneurial ventures where close relationships are established between entrepreneurs and outside financiers to try and enhance a company's value through counseling and oversight (Bhide 1994). Early evidence suggested that an openness to outside equity finance and the contribution that outsiders can bring to new firms is positively associated with growth (Hutchinson 1975). A more recent literature and debate have developed concerning the financial and monitoring contributions of venture capitalists in entrepreneurial ventures (for example, Wright and Robbie (1998) for a review). This literature has shown that venture capitalists may adopt different approaches to monitoring investees according to circumstances (for example, Sapienza et al. 1996), but there is mixed evidence about investees' views concerning the contribution made by outsiders (Rosenstein et al. 1993). In the context of established businesses, a number of authors have emphasized the need to examine the link between governance and ownership systems and entrepreneurial activity (for example, Bull 1989; Wright et al. 1992; Zahra 1993, 1995, 1996). In particular, Zahra (1995) explicitly examines corporate entrepreneurship activities in management leveraged buy-outs. He points to the importance of the combination of managerial equity incentives and governance by outsiders in increasing attention to value-enhancing activities. These activities relate on the one hand to the reduction of opportunism, producing cost reductions, and on the other to an increase in managerial discretion leading to entrepreneurial actions.

There have been similar arguments concerning the potential benefits to be derived from outsiders' involvement in enterprises in the former USSR which would otherwise be dominated by insiders (for example, Frydman et al. 1993). Outside monitoring and control per se may be insufficient to promote entrepreneurial actions (that is, downsizing, modernization of production capacities, re-focusing, etc.) if they are not accompanied by changes in managerial attitudes and skills. A major criticism leveled at large-scale, rapid privatization is that although ownership changed, management largely did not, since the programs themselves were biased towards the acquisition of ownership by incumbents without the need for outside finance (Brada 1996). Outside shareholders may however, be more pre-disposed to achieve such changes by replacing existing inefficient managers with more able and better trained corporate entrepreneurs (Denis et al. 1997). To the extent that managers have greater equity stakes and outsiders have less influence, the degree of replacement of directors is expected to be significantly lower. In the light of Table 1, this suggests that the rate of replacement of managers will be lower in Belarus and Ukraine than it is Russia.

Restricted access to finance may introduce a further constraint on corporate entrepreneurial actions (see Zahra 1996, for a review of the issues). Privatized state-owned firms in the former USSR are likely to have high-investment finance needs and to experience major financial difficulties because of environmental uncertainties, yet at the time of privatization are likely to have access to insignificant amounts of extra capital (Frydman et al. 1993). The underdeveloped financial sector also means that access to equity finance is very limited. Creditors (mainly banks) have an opportunity to impose direct monitoring on managers using a wide variety of channels, such as board representation, performance-related provision of loans, indirect controls, etc. (see, for example, Jensen 1993; Kaplan 1997). However, the existence of under-capitalized banks and a general absence of monitoring skills by bank executives lead to an expectation that such monitoring will be thin.

The nature of corporate entrepreneurship may be influenced by the nature of ownership and control and the nature of the product market environments in which firms are operating (Zahra 1993). Zahra (1996) finds that in large U.S. companies, corporate entrepreneurship is positively associated with long-term institutional share ownership. In contrast, outside investors without this commitment may be associated with reduced corporate entrepreneurship where they use short-term financial rather than longer-term strategic controls. Managers in Russia, Ukraine, and Belarus may be hostile towards outside investors if they are perceived to be only concerned with short-term financial results rather than with longer term entrepreneurial actions involving strategic development and modernization. Earlier survey evidence from Russia suggests that managers of privatized enterprises perceive banks, investment funds, and other financial institutions to be primarily short-term portfolio speculators (Wright et al. 1998). It is, therefore, expected that incumbent managers will be reluctant to cede majority control and significant influence to outsiders.

Zahra (1993) shows that in hostile product market environments involving a reduction in demand and/or increased competition, entrepreneurial decisions by insiders are positively associated with retrenchment and a redefinition of the business through restructuring and a search for innovative ways to manage the hostility. In contrast, incumbent managers are more likely to investigate new business creation in dynamic and growing environments. Managers in the three countries examined here may recognize that products are not competitive on world markets and require considerable investment to achieve such a position. However, the generally hostile market conditions in the three countries lead to an expectation that retrenchment will be an important priority for corporate entrepreneurs. Downsizing and getting rid of less productive divisions and surplus labor may be required to address the problems caused by the high level of 'labor hoarding' which companies have inherited from their central planning past (see for example, Kornai 1980). Sharp falls in demand may also suggest that managers will give priority to seeking new markets.

Impediments to entrepreneurial actions may be exacerbated by the nature of the privatization program. First, the use of voucher privatization techniques enable employees generally to obtain a significant equity stake in privatized enterprises. As such, their already entrenched rights may be strengthened further, with the consequence that even where directors wish to undertake entrepreneurial actions they are frustrated from doing so. Second, differences in the political priority given to privatization programs may also have an impact on corporate entrepreneurship. Although all three countries used mass privatization schemes, privatization programs in Ukraine and Belarus were promoted by their national governments with far less vigor than in Russia. Table 1 shows that the impact of privatization has been greatest in Russia and least in Belarus, with Ukraine in an intermediate position. Indeed in Belarus, the privatization process has been halted since 1996, and in 1997 some privatized firms were re-nationalized as the State reintroduced many of the institutions of central planning. In Ukraine, the government has exhibited an intermediate, stop-start commitment to privatization. Moreover, it seems likely that in Ukraine and Belarus, companies to be privatized were carefully selected by incumbent managers with strong political contacts. Rather than engaging in entrepreneurial actions to improve efficiency, these managers may entrench themselves and resist reform by relying on their contacts in government and a continuing weak market system. This continuation of slack rules of the game (Baumol 1996) may mean that such managers initiate destructive entrepreneurship involving the personal appropriation of the firm's resources (Bim 1996).

DATA

For each of the three countries, a sample of medium- and large-sized industrial firms was sought, covering the main industrial regions, all types of privatized firms and different industrial sectors, concentrating on firms that had been privatized for more than 1 year. In Russia, 105 useable responses were collected, exactly 100 in Ukraine, and 68 in Belarus. Given the importance of synchronicity (Frydman et al. 1997), simultaneous surveys were made in each of the three countries from January to July 1997.

The same questionnaire was applied to each country after being piloted in Moscow and Minsk. The questionnaire design included a combination of two types of questions. The first type related to measurable company characteristics for the 1995–1997 period (employment, market structure, etc.) from companies' unpublished financial reports. The second type related to respondents' perceptions of current entrepreneurial strategies and attitudes with all responses being scaled on a 7-point Likert scale. This approach, and the targeting of General Directors as respondents at the center of strategic developments in their enterprises, was adopted to minimize the problems of respondent recall.

The questions proved to be easily understood by Russian managers, who generally gave full, rational responses. In Belarus and Ukraine, however, managers seemed rather unfamiliar with Western terminology, and it was decided here to invest more resources in the form of face-to-face interviews, using the same questionnaire (adjusted for national currencies, etc.) that was applied through a postal survey in Russia. In each of the three countries, a random 5% of returns were checked by at least two of the authors on a personal visit.

Assessing the representativeness of samples of privatized enterprises in the former USSR is problematical where data relating to the population is often unavailable. However, on the available criteria where it is possible to make comparisons, the samples appear to be reasonably representative. The ownership distribution of the Russian firms in our sample (see below) was compared with those reported in similar surveys of privatized conducted in Russia at approximately the same time (Blasi et al. 1997) and no significant differences were identified. Published statistics of the industry, size, and regional distributions of privatized enterprises in Russia are not available. Comparisons between the Russian sample in this paper and these characteristics of all Russian enterprises (that is, privatized, state-owned, and private) generally show a close match. As regards the distribution of the employment size of Russian firms surveyed there is, not surprisingly, a greater proportion of larger firms in the sample than is the case in the Russian economy as a whole; this is to be expected given the focus here on those enterprises coming within the scope of the main manufacturing enterprise privatization programs as opposed to the tender privatization program, which was mainly aimed at shops and smaller service enterprises, and new start-ups (see Appendix tables). The regional distribution of the sample was generally close to that for Russia as a whole. For Belarus, the representativeness of the sample is indicated by the fact that it comprises 32% of all industrial privatized firms in that country.

RESULTS

The results of these simultaneous surveys are now presented in relation to the different constraints and pressure on incumbent managers in the three countries and their patterns of entrepreneurial responses.

Ownership

The distribution of equity stakes in the three countries is given by Table 2, which also shows the results of tests on the equality of mean ownership distributions across the three countries. These tests indicate the existence of statistically significant differences between the three samples; the Russian sample, as expected, generally being significantly different from the sample for the other two countries. Clearly some market-based ownership restructuring is taking place in a situation where, although managers have significant stockholdings, other employees hold the majority of the equity. Ukraine and Belarus exhibit significantly higher levels of ownership by incumbents than in Russia. Ownership by non-managerial employees in Ukraine and Belarus is also relatively higher (at about 57.7% and 56.9%, respectively, compared with only 38.7% in Russia).

TABLE 2   Distribution of Voting Shares Among Shareholders (percentage of total)

Shareholders	Russia		Ukraine		Balarus		Anova[1]	
	1997	change, 1995–1997	1997	change, 1995–1997	1997	change, 1995–1997	1997	change, 1995–1997
Individual directors in total	15.9%	4.8%	12.2%	0.9%	11.9%	2%	1.2	2.4***
Individual workers in total	387	−5.9	577	−6.2	56.9	2	10.7*	5.7*
Insiders in total	54.6	−1	69.9	−5.3	68.8	4	5.1*	4.2**
Trading partners	4.1	0.5	0.1	0.1	1.1	0.4	3.0***	0.3
Investment funds	3.6	0.8	4.6	1.6	2	1.6	0.6	0.3
Banks	1.7	0.3	0	0	0.6	0.2	2.0	0.2
External private individuals	12.9	1.4	11.7	4.5	10.9	3	0.2	1.8
Holding companies	1.7	0.1	1.4	0	1.5	0	0.03	0.02
Foreign investors	0.6	0.3	1.6	0.5	1.9	1.9	0.9	1.8
Other organizations	15.1	0.4	5.1	1.4	1.7	0.4	7.0*	0.2
Outsiders in total	397	3.8	24.5	8.1	19.7	7.5	9.7*	1.9
The State	5.7	−2.7	5.6	−2.8	11.5	−11.5	1.7	8.8*

Russian sample reduced from 105 to 91 companies as 14 could not distinguish manager and other employee ownership. In Belarus and Ukraine there were 39 and 35 useable responses respectively. Significance Levels: * = $p < 0.01$; ** = $p < 0.05$; *** = $p < 0.1$; [1] Figures are F-ratios. Because of space constraints and for clarity of presentation, significance tests using Pearson chi-squared and Kruskal-Wallis ANOVA across the three countries and pair-wise tests for differences between countries are omitted. Data are available from the authors on request. The Pearson chi-squared and the Kruskal-Wallis tests produced the same significant differences as for the ANOVA. The pair-wise tests involving Russia against Ukraine and Belarus combined constantly show that the Russian mean score for each long run priority variable is significantly different from that for Ukraine/Belarus.

Since 1995 the average equity stake held by management has increased in each of the three countries. but most notably in Russia. In Russia and Ukraine this process of consolidating managerial share ownership has been accompanied by a gradual erosion of employees' stakes. Only in Belarus has employees' share ownership actually increased, by 2% on average. Our survey shows that a substantial proportion of managers in Russia (and less so in Belarus and Ukraine) are trying to promote further changes in the insiders' ownership structure of their companies. In 29.8% of cases, Russian managers have acquired shares from employees compared to 12.2% in Ukraine and 10.4% in Belarus. In almost a third of cases Russian managers have further intentions to purchase shares from employees (36.4% in Ukraine and 31.8% in Belarus).

Russian companies on average display significantly greater involvement by outsiders in their ownership structures than is the case in Ukraine and Belarus. Among outside investors, external private individual holdings account for the highest outside ownership stake in Russia and Ukraine, with the remaining equity being owned by a wide group of interests. In Belarus, the State is the largest outside shareholder. In all three countries, private institutional investors (banks, investment funds, etc.) are still in a minority as shareholders, although there is evidence of a gradual increase in their stakes in 1995–1997.

Outsider Influence on Corporate Entrepreneurship

The potential controlling role of different stakeholders in the decision-making process was identified by looking at the composition of companies' Boards. The survey results suggest a link between insiders' stock and internal voice, although there are striking differences between Russia and the other two countries. Russian managers hold not only significantly more stock on average than their Ukranian and Belarussian counterparts, they also exercise more voice as proxied by Board representation (89 Russian companies reported that managers are represented on the Board in 1997, compared with 59 and 38 in Ukraine and Belarus, respectively) (Table 3). On the other hand, during 1995–1997 there was a slight fall in the number of companies in Russia which had employees sitting on the Board, while in Ukraine and Belarus these numbers increased substantially. Combined with the dynamics of insider ownership patterns this evidence suggests that, as expected, Russian managers are more effectively taking control in the vast majority of companies than their Ukranian and Belarussian counterparts. This may be expected to impact on corporate entrepreneurship.

There are clear signs of the increasing involvement of outside equityholders in companies' Boards, in Russia in particular: 35 companies reported that they have external private individuals represented on the Board in 1997, and 24 companies had other industrial organizations among their Board members (Table 3). Such organizations as banks and investment funds are gradually consolidating their voice in newly privatized companies in Russia and Ukraine and to a much lesser extent in Belarus: 13 Russian companies mentioned investment funds among their Board members (10 cases in Ukraine and only 3 in Belarus), and 6 companies had bank representation (6 in Ukraine and 2 in Belarus). On the other hand, in Belarus, 32 companies had State representatives on the Board at the beginning of 1997, a substantial increase compared to 23 cases in 1995. This indicates that the active role of outsiders in Russia is slowly evolving towards that found in enterprises in the West, while in Belarus in particular, privatization has resulted in the creation of organizations where the State is directly involved in control. This implies again that corporate entrepreneurship should be relatively more active in Russia than in the other two countries.

There is evidence of senior managerial changes in all three countries (Table 4). In the period between 1995 and 1997, the general Director had been replaced in more than a third of cases (a quarter of cases in Ukraine and Belarus). In Russia and Belarus, in almost half of cases other members of the Directorate had been replaced too, with significantly less being replaced in Ukraine (Pearson chi-square = 3.35, $p < 0.1$). These differential response rates may again reflect relative outsider pressures on boards in the three countries.

However, there is a substantially lower average number of seats held by outside stakeholders on companies' Boards compared to insiders in all three countries, suggesting that their power is currently rather limited. Reflecting the deep mistrust of outsiders noted earlier, there remains a widespread reluctance to cede majority control (Table 5). Only one-third of senior directors in Belarus would agree to give majority control to outside strategic partners, even if they were to provide the capital necessary for restructuring the company, technological expertise and a marketing network. Managers in Russia and Ukraine are somewhat less entrenched than their Belarussian colleagues: almost half of all respondents would agree to swap their controlling stake for strategic investments.

Moreover, there is a direct link between the extent of insider control and managerial hostility to an outside take-over. The majority of directors in the three countries reported that they would seek to prevent an unexpected accumulation of shares especially by outside domestic and foreign investors, with there being no significant difference in this respect between the three countries. Obviously, their strategy is to keep and re-enforce insider voice in the governance mechanism, blocking the acquisition of controlling stakes by outsiders and reducing their ability to intervene.

TABLE 3 Shareholder Board Representation, 1995–1997 (total number of companies reporting a particular shareholder on the board)

Stakeholders	Russia			Ukraine			Belarus		
	1995	1997	change, 1995–1997	1995	1997	change, 1995–1997	1995	1997	change, 1995–1997
Banks	6 (1.2)[1]	6 (1.5)[1]	0 (0.3)	4 (1)[2]	6 (2.2)[2]	2 (1.2)	0 (0)[3]	2 (1.5)[3]	2 (1.5)
Investment funds	10 (1.9)	13 (2.5)	3 (0.6)	5 (2.4)	10 (2.1)	5 (−0.3)	1 (1)	3 (1.3)***	2 (0.3)
External private individuals	24 (1.8)	35 (2)	11 (0.2)	4 (3.2)	10 (1.6)	6 (−1.6)	4 (1.5)	11 (2.5)	7 (1)
Industrial organizations	20 (2.1)	24 (2.3)	4 (2.2)	1 (1)	3 (2)	2 (1)	4 (3)	9 (2.2)	5 (−1.2)
Foreign companies	1 (1.1)	2 (1)	1 (0)	2 (2)	1 (3)	−1 (1)	0 (0)	0 (0)	0 (0)
Managers	84 (3.4)*	89 (3.3)*	5 (−0.1)	40 (5.7)	59 (4.9)	19 (−0.8)	27 (6.1*)	38 (5.3)*	11 (−0.8)
Employees	57 (3.0)	56 (2.7)	−1 (−0.3)	21 (2.9)	32 (2.7)	11 (−0.2)	28 (3.3)	37 (3.0)	9 (−0.3)
The State	27 (1.4)	18 (1.3)	−9 (−0.1)	10 (1.9)	10 (1.8)	0 (−0.1)	23 (1.6)	32 (1.5)	9 (−0.1)

Average number of seats held by each particular shareholder is in brackets. Significance levels: * = $p < 0.01$; ** = $p < 0.05$; *** = $p < 0.1$; [1] Asterisks in columns relate to t-tests on probability of equality in Russian and Ukrainian population means; [2] Asterisks in columns relate to t-tests on probability of equality in Ukrainian and Belarusian population means; [3] Asterisks in columns relate to t-tests on probability of equality in Russian and Belarusian population means.

TABLE 4   Changes to the Directorate Since Privatization (percentage of companies responding 'yes')

	Russia	Ukraine	Belarus	Pearson chi-square
New General Director	35.2[1]	25[2]	27.9[3]	2.66
Replacement of other member of directorate	50***	37.5	47	3.35

Signifiance level: *** = p < 0.1; [1] Asterisks in columns relate to *t*-tests on probability of equality in Russian and Ukrainian population means; [2] Asterisks in columns relate to *t*-tests on probability of equality in Ukrainian and Belarusian population means; [3] Asterisks in columns relate to *t*-tests on probability of equality in Russian and Belarusian population means.

The survey results support expectations that the usual Western private financial lending channels have been largely inoperative, especially in Belarus: such sources of funding as issue of bonds and equity, selling/leasing of buildings and equipment hardly scored above 3 on average. Credits from domestic banks have been mentioned as the second most important source of funding in Russia and Belarus (average scores 4.5 and 4.3 respectively), and the third in Ukraine (average score 4.9). This may be a sign that privatized companies are gradually shifting to borrowings that are more consistent with market competition in financial provision or soft credits directed by the State.

When asked about banks' involvement, more than 90% of managers in the three countries scored as low influence all bank-related factors suggested in the questionnaire, such as banks appointing Directors, restricting the operational/strategic decisions of managers, and restricting directors remuneration. Among possible channels of banks' influence, only telephone contacts scored significantly on a 7-point scale where 7 = high importance (average score 4.4 in Russia, 4.2 in Belarus, and 3.4 in Ukraine). The second most important channel of control in Russia and Belarus was sending accounts to the bank on a regular basis (average scores 3.6 and 3.7, respectively). Such standard Western channels of bank monitoring and control as representation on a supervisory board (for example, Germany) and monitoring of debt covenants (for example, as in the U.K.) had very minor importance in all three countries. Our survey shows that there is not only a substantial laxity in banks' monitoring and control of industrial companies, but the banks also do not usually impose any serious penalties upon managers failing to meet payments of interest and capital.

Entrepreneurial Strategies

In the light of these influences on the penalties and reward facing corporate entrepreneurs, our survey results provide preliminary evidence on their different responses in privatized enterprises in three countries of the former USSR.

The overwhelming need for entrepreneurial action was revealed by survey questions concerning product quality. There is widespread recognition that products are not competitive on world markets and that considerable investment is required to achieve this position. Fewer than 25% of managers in all three countries consider their main products to be competitive on world markets in terms of price, build quality, design and packaging, and after-sales servicing, with design and after-sales servicing being the worst factors of all. In all three countries, managers' assessments of the most important actions required to achieve world standards were: investment in machinery and equipment (average score above 6 on a 7-point Likert scale where 7 = high importance),

TABLE 5 Managers' Attitudes to a Hostile Take-Over by Other Investors

	Russia	Ukraine	Belarus	Pearson chi-square
Employees	55.8[1]	59.7***[2]	43.9[3]	3.64
Outside domestic investors	68.9	60.9	68.8	1.31
Outside foreign investors	70.6	58.8	70.3	2.73

Percentages of companies answering 'yes' to the question: Will Directors try to prevent an unexpected accumulation of shares by the following investors?

Significance Level: *** = $p < 0.1$; [1] Asterisks in columns relate to t-tests on probability of equality in Russian and Ukrainian population means; [2] Asterisks in columns relate to t-tests on probability of equality in Ukrainian and Belarusian population means; [3] Asterisks in columns relate to t-tests on probability of equality in Russian and Belarusian population means.

followed by investment in marketing (average score above 5), and investment in research and development.

Some important national differences did emerge when enterprise directors were invited to score different entrepreneurial priorities on a 7-point second scale with 7 = 'high priority.' Table 6 shows that directors of privatized companies in all three countries surveyed placed a uniformly high and anticipated emphasis on short-run responses involving cash-flow monitoring and seeking domestic markets for existing products. Besides these ex ante priorities, however, other short-run responses were surveyed relating to the ex post retrenchment of employment levels and productive capacity. According to the surveys, Russian managers on average reduced gross employment levels by 23%, 1995–1997, compared with 19.5% in Ukraine and 14.3% in Belarus. Similarly, actual capacity reductions through the permanent closure of plant and workshops averaged 3.6% of output in Russia over the same period compared with only 2.1% in Belarus and Ukraine. These actual responses may reflect the relatively stronger outside pres-

TABLE 6 Mean Values of Directors' Enterpreneurial Properties (Responses on a 7-point Likert scale where 1 = not important and 7 = very important.[1] Rows ranked in terms of average Russian response)

	Russia (Mean score)	Ukraine (Mean score)	Belarus (Mean score)	ANOVA[2]
Short-term priorities				
Cash flow monitoring	6.1	5.9	5.9	0.6
Seeking new domestic markets, existing products	5.7	6.2	5.3	5.2*
Long-term priorities				
Development of new products for domestic market	5.2	6.0	5.9	4.0*
Seeking new outside investors	4.4	5.6	5.1	6.4*
Marketing and advertising	4.1	5.8	5.5	22.9*
Monitoring firm's return on investment	3.7	5.5	5.4	15.9*
Development of new products for export	3.0	5.6	5.4	32.7*
Seeking new export markets for existing products	2.7	5.6	5.6	52.4*

Significance Levels: * = $p < 0.1$; ** = $p < 0.05$; *** = $p < 0.01$;
[1] Cronbach's alpha for Russia = 0.79, Ukraine = 0.79, and Belarus 0.77; [2] Because of space constraints and for clarity of presentation, significance tests using Pearson chi-squared and Kruskal-Wallis ANOVA across the three countries and pair-wise tests for differences between countries are omitted. Data are available from the authors on request. The Pearson chi-squared and the Kruskal-Wallis tests produced the same significant differences as for the ANOVA. The pair-wise tests involving Russia against Ukraine and Belarus combined consistantly show that the Russian mean score for each long run priority variable is significantly different from that for Ukraine/Belarus.

sures faced by Russian managers. Uniform short-run entrepreneurial priorities should, however, also be interpreted in conjunction with long-run priorities.

Striking national variations were reported in relation to long-run managerial priorities, and this result was consistent with relatively weak corporate governance in Belarus and Ukraine (Table 6). Managers in both Ukraine and Belarus were prepared to disclose high priorities (average 5.6) for increased sales of existing products in export markets, despite the fact that more than 75% of all directors in the three countries had already admitted (see above) that their products in their current forms were uncompetitive on world markets, necessitating infeasibly high levels of investment. These responses suggest that directors in Belarus and Ukraine do not have a structurally focused approach to short-term and long-term stabilization and recovery strategies. This conclusion is reinforced by the comparisons of the long-run priorities listed in Table 6 between Russia and the scores for Belarus and Ukraine. The overall test for equality of mean scores identified significant differences between the three countries, and pair-wise comparisons between Russia and the combined Ukraine and Belarus scores consistently found there to be significant differences in long run priorities.

Russian managers in the middle of a short-run crisis have quite properly focussed on short-run entrepreneurial responses, and in Table 6 report significantly lower current priorities for all long-run factors. It is in this context that the high priorities also reported for short run strategies should be interpreted. Again, these differences in the apparent quality of entrepreneurial responses may be attributable to stronger external constraints on Russian managers. Weaker constraints in Belarus and Ukraine may have contributed to lower executive replacement rates, less retrenchment and a lack of appropriate entrepreneurial priorities compared with Russia.

DISCUSSION AND POLICY IMPLICATIONS

This study has provided preliminary comparative evidence concerning the development of entrepreneurship in privatized enterprises in three republics in the former USSR.

In terms of ownership structure and decision-making mechanisms, our survey evidence across the three countries emphasizes the important potential role of corporate entrepreneurs. However, the evidence indicates that although the three countries started from a common base, their subsequent reforms have not been homogeneous. Russian privatized firms have lower employee stakes, greater outside ownership, and greater managerial power within the firm (vis-a-vis employees) than is the case in Ukraine and Belarus. In Russia, corporate entrepreneurs are, therefore, subject to more outside influence as well as less internal influence from employees. The balance of power within enterprises in Ukraine and Belarus appears to lie very much with inside managers and employees, which may have negative implications for the exercising of corporate entrepreneurship where employees resist managers' attempts at restructuring. In this sense, Russia has arguably built a better platform for the liberation of latent entrepreneurial capacity. Managers of Russian firms are also relatively less hostile to outside investors, but in Belarus the State still represents a significant stakeholder influence. In Russia and Ukraine, firms have been actively using bank loans as a source of funding, but they are still not exposed to any effective scrutiny by the outside providers of finance.

Our preliminary survey results on post-privatization corporate entrepreneurship in the three countries show evidence of strategies aimed at securing enterprise survival in a rapidly changing and hostile market environment. The most obvious changes were in managerial tenure and directors' objectives. Russian enterprises experienced the highest replacement rate of directors, which may be associated with the greater presence of outside shareholders in these companies compared to their counterparts in Ukraine and Belarus. This arrival of new people in companies' decision-making centers may facilitate further long-term corporate entrepreneurship.

Generally, actual and proposed short-run managerial decisions and intended long-run priorities in Russia are consistent with less employee influence and the higher level of involvement of outsiders in Russian privatized firms. Russian managers have properly focussed on short-run priorities in a short-run crisis, while the high priority given to all short and long-run factors in Belarus and Ukraine implies unfocussed and unrealistic entrepreneurial attitudes among managers from these countries. In terms of actual short-run retrenchments, Russian managers have also achieved more.

It must of course be recognized that any improved corporate governance from outside owners and lenders can only be seen as a necessary, and not a sufficient, condition for improved corporate entrepreneurship, in the context of product markets that may not be competitive. Without competitive product markets, greater pressure from capital markets may even induce managerial incumbents to exercise any product market monopoly power they may enjoy, and simply exploit consumers more by raising product prices. To date, no evidence is available on relative product market conditions in the three countries, and important research remains to be done on this key issue.

The findings of the study suggest some implications for policymakers and practitioners. Corporate entrepreneurial behavior appears to be markedly affected by the prevailing conditions in the countries studied here and lower employee (and higher outsider) ownership and control seems to be associated with more realistic managerial decisions and priorities, but these need further support from the market environment.

The legislation essential to the functioning of a market economy, such as company and bankruptcy law, has been successfully enacted in all three countries surveyed (Appendix Tables A1, A2). However, in Russia, Ukraine, and Belarus such laws are often not enforced, and contractual obligations are sometimes ignored with impunity (Black 1996). The legal system in these countries is often replaced by private mechanisms of enforcing agreements and resolving disputes, including organized crime. This lack of law enforcement can mean that corporate entrepreneurial actions may be either destructive or unproductive and dysfunctional managers can remain in post. Hence, there is a need to address continuing shortcomings in the legal and regulatory environment that will strengthen the rules of the game promoting productive entrepreneurship. Western institutions, such as the U.K. Know-How Fund, USAID, KU, etc., could also play a more active role in providing technical assistance and training to emerging corporate entrepreneurs in the former USSR.

Our study also has implications for researchers. First, given the necessarily short period covered by surveys and the exploratory nature of the analysis, there is a need for longitudinal studies in order to compare both the development of corporate entrepreneurial strategies as well as outcomes (that is, performance and life-cycles of enterprises) as well as to consider more fully the different forces at play in each of the three countries examined in this study. Second, there is a need to compare the quality of entrepreneurship in existing firms with entrepreneurship in new ventures in the three countries. Third, there is scope for comparison of corporate entrepreneurship with other countries in Central and Eastern Europe.

Finally, our findings clearly suggest that ownership transformation by itself cannot

490 I. FILATOTCHEV ET AL.

be relied upon to create extensive long term corporate entrepreneurship and further work remains to be done on the importance of product market competitive conditions and their interplay with corporate governance changes. Privatization is just the beginning of a long-term process. The development of corporate entrepreneurship and the liberation of latent entrepreneurial talents in privatized companies will not happen by itself, over a short period of time. An important role is likely to be played by supportive and robust corporate governance mechanisms combined with the strengthening of the legal framework and the liberalization of capital and product markets.

REFERENCES

Ang, J. 1991. Small business uniqueness and the theory of financial management. *Journal of Small Business Finance* 1(1):1–13.

Baumol, W. 1996. Entrepreneurship: productive, unproductive and destructive. *Journal of Business Venturing* 11(1):3–22.

Bhide, A. 1994. Efficient markets, inefficient governance. *Harvard Business Review* 94(6): 128–139.

Bim, A. 1996. Ownership and control of Russian enterprises and strategies of shareholders. *Communist Economics and Economic Transformation* 8(4):471–500.

Black, B., Kraakman, R., and Hay, J. 1996. Corporate law from scratch: In R. Frydman, C.W. Gray, and A. Rapaczynski, eds., *Corporate Governance in Central Europe and Russia*, vol. 2. Budapest: Central European University Press.

Blasi, J., Kroumova, M., and Kruse, D. 1997. *Kremlin Capitalism. Privatizing the Russian Economy.* Ithaca and London: Cornell University Press.

Block, Z., and MacMillan, I. 1993. *Corporate Venturing,* Boston, MA: Harvard Business School Press.

Boycko, M., Shleifer, A., and Vishny, R. 1993. *Privatizing Russia.* Cambridge, MA: The MIT Press.

Brada, J. 1996. Privatization is transition: or is it? *Journal of Economic Perspectives* 10(2):67–86.

Bull, I. 1989. Financial performance of leveraged buy-outs. *Journal of Business Venturing* 4(4):263–279.

Cooper, A., and Dunkelberg, W. 1986. Entrepreneurship and paths to business ownership. *Strategic Management Journal* 7(1):53–56.

Denis, D., Denis, D. K., and Sarin, A. 1997. Ownership structure and top executive turnover. *Journal of Financial Economics* 45(2):193–221.

Earle, J., and Estrin, S. 1996. Employee ownership in transition. In R. Frydman, C.W. Gray, and A. Rapaczynski, eds., vol. 2, *Corporate Governance in Central Europe and Russia.* Budapest: Central European University Press.

EBRD. 1997. *Transition Report.* London: European Bank for Reconstruction and Development.

Ernst, M., Alexeev, M., and Marer, P. 1996. *Transforming The Core: Restructuring Industrial Enterprises in Russia and Central Europe.* Boulder, CO: Westview Press.

Filatotchev, I., Buck, T., and Wright, M. 1992. Privatization and entrepreneurship in the break-up of the USSR. *World Economy* 15(4):505–524.

Filatotchev, I., Buck, T., Wright, M., and Van Frausum, Y. 1996. Privatization and industrial restructuring in Ukraine. *Communist Economies and Economic Transformation* 8(2):185–203.

Filatotchev, I., Hoskisson, R., Buck, T., and Wright, M. 1996. Corporate restructuring in Russian privatizations: Implications for US investors. *California Management Review* 38(2):87–105.

Frydman, R., Phelps, E., Rapaczyaski, A. and Shleifer, A. 1993. Needed mechanisms of corporate governance and finance in Eastern Europe. *Economics of Transition*; 1(2):171–207.

Frydman, R., Gray, C., Hessel, M., and Rapaczynski, A. 1997. *Private Ownership And Corporate Performance: Some Lessons From Transition Economies.* New York: New York University.

Gartner, W., and Shane, S. 1995. Measuring entrepreneurship over time. *Journal of Business Venturing* 10(4):283–301.

Guth, W., and Ginsberg, A. 1990. Guest editors' introduction: corporate entrepreneurship. *Strategic Management Journal* 11(S):5–15.

Hawley, F. 1900. Enterprise and profit. *Quarterly Journal of Economics* 15(1):75–105.

Hisrich, R., and Grachev, M. 1993. The Russian entrepreneur. *Journal of Business Venturing* 8(6):487–497.

Holt, D., Ralston, D., and Terpstra, R. 1994. Constraints on capitalism in Russia: The managerial psyche, social infrastructure and ideology. *California Management Review* 36(3):124–141.

Hutchinson, P., Piper, J., and Ray, G. 1975. The financing of rapid growth firms up to flotation. *Accounting and Business Research* 5(18):145–151.

Jensen, M. 1993. The modern industrial revolution, exit, and failure of internal control systems. *Journal of Finance* 48(3):831–880.

Kantorovich, V. 1998. New business creation and Russian economic recovery. *Paper presented at the 6th Annual Meeting of the Association for Comparative Economic Studies.* Chicago, Jan. 5th.

Kaplan, S. 1997. Corporate governance and corporate performance: a comparison of Germany, Japan and the US. *Journal of Applied Corporate Finance* 9(4):86–93.

Kaufman, P., Welsh, D., and Bushmarin, N. 1995. Locus of control and entrepreneurship in the Russian Republic. *Entrepreneurship: Theory and Practice* 20(1):43–56.

Kornai, J. 1980. *The Economics of Shortage.* Volumes A and B, Amsterdam: North Holland.

Krueger, G. 1995. Transition strategies of former state-owned enterprises in Russia. *Comparative Economic Studies* 37(4):89–110.

Linz, S. 1996. Red executives in Russia's transition economy. *Post-Soviet Geography and Economics* 37(10):633–651.

Linz, S. 1997. Russian firms in transition: champions, challengers and chaff. *Comparative Economic Studies* 39(2):1–36.

Linz, S., and Krueger, G. 1996. Russia's managers in transition: pilferers or paladins? *Post-Soviet Geography and Economics* 37(7):397–425.

McCarthy, D., Puffer, S., and Shekshnia, S. 1993. The resurgence of an entrepreneurial class in Russia. *Journal of Management Inquiry* 2(2):125–137.

Morck, R., Shleifer, A., and Vishny, R. 1988. Management ownership and market valuation: An empirical analysis. *Journal of Financial Economics* 20(1):293–316.

Ners, K. 1995. Privatization (from above, below or mass privatization) versus generic private enterprise building. *Communist Economies and Economic Transformation* 7(1):105–116.

Puffer, S. 1994. Understanding the bear: A portrait of Russian business leaders. *Academy of Management Executive* 8(1):41–54.

Richman, B. 1965. *Soviet Management*, Englewood Cliffs, NJ: Prentice Hall.

Rosenstein, J., Bruno, A., Bygrave, W., and Taylor, N. 1993. The CEO, venture capitalists, and the board. *Journal of Business Venturing* 8(2):99–113.

Sapienza, H., Manigart, S., and Vermeir, C. 1996. Venture capitalists' governance and value added in four countries. *Journal of Business Venturing* 11(6):439–470.

Stopford, J., and Baden-Fuller, C. 1994. Creating corporate entrepreneurship. *Strategic Management Journal* 15(7):521–536.

World Bank 1996. *Mass Privatization in Ukraine.* State Property Fund of Ukraine, Meeting with World Bank Representatives. Washington, DC.

Wright, M., and Robbie, K. 1998. Venture capital and private equity: a review and synthesis. *Journal of Business Finance and Accounting* 25(5/6):521–570.

Wright, M., Thompson, S., and Robbie, K. 1992. Venture capital and management-led leveraged buyouts: a European perspective. *Journal of Business Venturing* 7(1):47–72.

Wright, M., Filatotchev, I., and Buck, T. 1996. Entrepreneurship and privatized firms in Russia and Ukraine: Evidence on performance. In *Frontiers of Entrepreneurship Research*, Proceedings of the 16th Annual Entrepreneurship Conference, Seattle, USA, March 1996. Babson College, MA: Center for Entrepreneurial Studies.

Wright, M., Filatotchev, I., Hoskisson, R., and Buck, T. 1998. Revitalizing privatized Russian enterprises. *Academy of Management Executive* 12(2):74–85.

Zahra, S. 1993. Environment, corporate entrepreneurship and financial performance: A taxonomic approach. *Journal of Business Venturing* 8(4):319–340.

Zahra, S. 1995. Corporate entrepreneurship and financial performance: The case of management leveraged buy-outs. *Journal of Business Venturing* 10(3):225–248.

Zahra, S. 1996. Governance, ownership and corporate entrepreneurship: the moderating impact of industrial technological opportunities. *Academy of Management Journal* 39(6):1713–1735.

APPENDIX: SAMPLE CHARACTERISTICS (RUSSIAN SAMPLE)

TABLE A1   Industrial Structure of Privatized Firms

Industry	Share in Total Non-State Russian Industrial Firms' Employment (%)[1]	Share in the Total Sample in This Survey (%)
Metallurgy	10.95	22.07
Chemical and petrochemical	7.14	2.21
Engineering	41.46	41.23
Timber, forestry, pulp, and paper	10.54	11.94
Building materials	7.44	6.35
Light industries	10.56	10.39
Food	11.92	5.81
Total	100.00	100.00

In 1995; Non-state firms include both privatized and de novo firms where data on the number of privatized firms are not available. Sources: Goskomstat Russia (1996), Promishlennost Rossii, pp. 30–1, 80–1.

TABLE A2   Employment Distribution

Number of Employees	Share in Total Russian Industrial Output (%)[1]	Share in Total Sample in This Survey's Sales (%)
Less than 200	10.8	4.69
200–499	13.4	10.52
500 or more	75.8	84.79
Total	100.0	100.0

[1] In 1995, excluding Far East. Source: Goskomstat Russia (1996), Promishlennost Rossii, p.18.

Part VI
Re-appearing Statization

[31]

Russia's Retreat to Statization and the Implications for Business

Daniel J. McCarthy   Sheila M. Puffer
Alexander I. Naumov

Despite the many problems that emerged during Russia's experiment with a market economy in the 1990s, Western firms are not likely to forego the lure that still exists in that market of 150 million people. Understanding the economic and political developments of that decade, and their effects upon business, can provide insights into the potential for business opportunities in the coming years. This article is based on a longitudinal field study of the political and economic environment for businesses in Russia, supplemented by statistical data and other information from published sources. We analyze the major economic and political developments during the 1990s and classify them in four stages —commercialization, privatization, nomenklatura, and statization. A scenario is then presented in which the statization stage, a period of increased state involvement in the economy, will likely continue in the next decade. An enlarged state role, however, is expected to coexist with a still evolving private sector. The article concludes with implications for Western firms doing business in Russia's mixed economy.

R ussia's march to a market-based economy, which was foreseen by many at the start of the 1990s as con-

Daniel J. McCarthy, Professor of Strategic Management and High Technology Management, Northeastern University, 313 Hayden Hall, Boston, MA 02115, USA. Tel.: +1-617-373-4758; Fax: +1-617-373-8628.
Sheila M. Puffer, Professor of International Business and Human Resources Management, Northeastern University, 325 Hayden Hall, Boston, MA 02115, USA. Tel.: 1-617-373-5249; Fax: +1-617-373-2491.
Alexander Naumov, Deputy Director, School of Business Administration, Moscow State University, Moscow, Russia. Tel.:+7-095-939-0897; Fax: +7-095-939-0877.

tinuing indefinitely, had clearly ended by the close of the decade with a marked increase in the state's involvement in the economy and business. This trend, concurrent with the continued development of entrepreneurships and other businesses with mixed private and governmental ownership, could well be the reality of the next decade. Western companies that would do business in Russia as the 21st century begins will likely have to adjust to a changing set of opportunities and obstacles in the new mixed economy.

In this article we introduce and analyze four stages that we have identified as representing the country's evolution during the 1990s. These stages track the changing conditions in the political, legal, and economic landscapes that led Russia to retreat to its familiar past of strong state influence on the economy. The article also documents the positive developments of that period, which some observers expect could form the foundation of a new type of mixed economy, albeit one with a renewed state influence. Western managers interested in doing business in Russia can incorporate an understanding of the four stages of the 1990s capitalist decade into a road map for managing their operations in that country.

FOUR STAGES OF THE 1990S RUSSIAN ECONOMY

Emerging from seven decades of central planning and state-owned enterprises, the country experienced several significant economic, legal, and political developments during the 1990s that deeply affected business. These developments led to four stages, which we have labeled commercialization, privatization, nomenklatura, and statization (Puffer, McCarthy, & Naumov, 2000).

The first stage, commercialization, was the beginning of a fledgling market economy, and was followed by the privatization stage that saw the ownership of many state enterprises pass into private hands. Obstacles to achieving the objectives of these market-oriented periods, however, occurred with the excesses of inept and corrupt members of

the Yeltsin government and well-placed business people. The most notorious of these, but relatively few in number, were the oligarchs who headed major financial and business conglomerates, and who often acted in concert with government officials for mutual personal gain. This greed defined a third stage, the nomenklatura period, and led to a major financial crisis in mid-1998. The oligarchs were blamed by many for the crisis, but to attribute the period's problems solely to this relatively small group would be inaccurate. Thousands of other business and government officials at all levels were involved in plundering the country's wealth. Thus, to emphasize the large size of this privileged group, we called the period the nomenklatura stage, adopting the term used for elites during earlier times. One result of the nomenklatura period was increased government involvement and intervention in the economic arena, including the freezing of company assets held in banks, a moratorium on government debt payments, and a major devaluation of the ruble. Although these were obvious interventions by the government into the economy and the affairs of business, the first signs of such events heralding a new fourth stage, statization, had actually begun to develop some time before the crisis. The move toward large business-financial conglomerates headed by the oligarchs, coupled with their close relationship with key government officials of the Yeltsin administration, had already set the course for more state involvement in the economy.

Entering 2000, President Yeltsin resigned after what many viewed as years of neglect, corruption, and confusing changes for the economy and business, and appointed Vladimir Putin as his successor. Still a virtual unknown, especially with regard to economic policy when elected president in March 2000, Putin quickly went on record as favoring increased state involvement in business and the economy. Although he was likely to renationalize some key industries and probably expand the list of enterprises exempt from privatization, such actions would not necessarily lead to a wholesale renationalization of privatized enterprises. In fact, of Russia's 3 million businesses, only 342,600 were state-owned enterprises, whereas 2,251,000 were privately owned in early 2000 (*Economic Newsletter*, February 2000). Nationalizing large numbers of these private companies would be nearly unthinkable. Instead, Putin's policy would likely result in a gradual continuation of more government involvement in economic affairs. After a decade of experimentation with a market economy, Russia had clearly begun a retreat, in part at least, to a more familiar position that was likely to embrace many practices of its earlier centralized economy (Starobin & Fairlamb, 2000).

This section analyzes the four stages that culminated in this reversal of direction. The country had started on a new economic course that could see the return of viable commercial opportunities for Western companies. A plausible scenario would be a mixed economy involving a relatively strong hand on the part of the state. This state role, however, could coexist with a more vibrant commercial sector driven by entrepreneurs, and possibly by hybrid organizations, including joint ventures

owned by private parties and the state. The private-sector owners might be Russian or international. Such a scenario would not be very different from the one that developed in China over the last decade (Peng & Heath, 1996). Insights as to the viability of this relatively positive scenario can be gained by reviewing key events of the four stages of Russia's economic and political evolution during the 1990s.

COMMERCIALIZATION STAGE—LATE 1980s THROUGH 1992

The Commercialization stage began when the government established policies encouraging the creation of cooperatives, small businesses, and joint ventures (Blasi et al., 1997). The objective was to help alleviate the inefficiencies of state organizations in such areas as consumer goods and services. Gorbachev's reforms in the second half of the 1980s paved the way for a fuller transition to a market economy. This transition was unleashed further with Yeltsin's market reforms coupled with the fall of the Soviet Union in late 1991 (McCarthy & Puffer, 1997). This period was fruitful for entrepreneurs and others who welcomed the freedom to start and manage their own businesses (Zhuplev et al., 1998). During this phase, managers were able to establish entrepreneurships and acquire more decision-making authority in state-owned enterprises (Vlachoutsicos & Lawrence, 1996). They were also able to establish objectives of achieving profitability and serving the emerging needs of the new industrial and consumer markets. To many managers, the opportunities seemed unlimited.

The government hoped that commercialization would reduce the inefficiency of state organizations and central planning by developing more flexible and rapid responses to changing market needs. It was not expected to totally and immediately destroy state ownership, which in fact coexisted throughout the period with private commercial activity. To foster private enterprise, it was clear that a commercial banking system was required, and the government took several measures that led to its rapid development. In the late 1980s, the government also established legislation encouraging cooperatives and joint ventures, which represented the earliest types of private and quasi-private enterprises. Although some of these organizations were private, governments at various levels, such as the Moscow city government, often participated in ownership and management. The Commercialization stage thus marked the beginning of a market-oriented economy as well as private enterprises, but with the simultaneous and pervasive involvement of the government in the economy. This stage can be divided into two periods: the Gorbachev period that began in the late 1980s and prevailed until late 1991, and the initial Yeltsin period which started in late 1991 and lasted until the beginning of the Privatization phase in early 1992.

The Gorbachev Era

Perestroika, the policy of economic restructuring, was initiated in 1985 by then-Communist Party Secretary

Mikhail Gorbachev and was intensified during his term as President of the USSR from 1988 to 1991. This policy ushered in enormous changes in the economic system. The Law on Soviet State Enterprises of 1987, for instance, introduced many features of a market-oriented economy, including foreign joint-venture partners and self-financing by enterprises. Managers were also permitted to select customers and suppliers, to have greater flexibility in workforce management, and to exercise far greater freedom in product and production decisions. Another pathbreaking piece of legislation was the New Enterprise Law of June 1990, which virtually dismantled the Soviet central ministries (McCarthy & Puffer, 1992; Shama & Sementsov, 1992).

The government's main goal during this period was to foster a more open economy to better prepare the country for the subsequent Privatization stage. Yet, policies initiated at the time also gave rise to a class of wealthy and influential individuals, sometimes called New Russians. The term referred to people who prospered personally from the changes that occurred with the liberalization of the economy. Many of these individuals were able to divert, for their own gain, resources allocated by the government to prepare state enterprises for privatization.

The Yeltsin Era

Boris Yeltsin's rise to power in mid-1991 radically changed the development of private and commercialized state organizations, and accelerated the transition to a market-oriented economy. Two major events occurred at the beginning of 1992. The first was the government's freeing of prices of most goods from state control. The second was the cancellation of many state orders to enterprises, coupled with the substitution of a freer, decentralized method for orders and procurement of goods and services. These and other related changes precipitated rampant inflation, with prices rising sharply to near world levels, with the exception of raw materials. In 1992, for instance, prices rose by 2,400%, wages by 1,200%, and incomes by 900% (*Economic Newsletter*, March 1993). What followed was the commercialization of many state organizations, primarily through the creation of open and closed stock companies, depending upon the conditions for share ownership. Thus, preparation for the next stage, privatization, was underway.

PRIVATIZATION STAGE—1993 THROUGH MID-1994

The economic situation remained unstable as the country entered 1993. Industrial production in January compared to January 1992 showed a decrease of 14% in oil and natural gas output, 12% in coal, and 16% in steel production, and predictions for the remainder of the year called for even further decreases (*Economic Newsletter*, March 1993). It was in this relatively negative environment that privatization of state enterprises began.

The first phase of privatization, called voucher privatization, began in early 1993 and consisted of issuing vouchers representing ownership shares in enterprises and organizations that were formerly owned by the state (Boycko et al., 1995; McCarthy & Puffer, 1995). This stage was associated with Anatoly Chubais who headed the State Property Commission that was responsible for the privatization process. The idea behind the commission's system of voucher privatization was that every Russian citizen was to obtain some ownership of the enterprises to be privatized. But, although ownership was redistributed into private hands, no new capital was infused into the enterprises.

By the end of privatization's first phase in mid-1994, more than 19,000 of the 29,000 designated enterprises had been privatized (*Economic Newsletter*, June 1994), stock had accrued to over 40 million citizens, and more than 60% of the labor force was employed in the private sector (Sachs, 1995). Moreover, virtually all the smaller and medium-sized organizations that were formerly state-owned were at least partially in private hands by the end of 1993. New entrepreneurships began to flourish, and many adapted to the freer environment more quickly and successfully than did larger formerly state-owned organizations. By many accounts, the privatization program was considered quite successful at the time.

Mixed Results

It appeared at first glance that privatization was moving in a positive direction. Yet, in many privatized organizations, the state remained a partial owner, and the former senior managers continued to operate overstaffed and inefficient organizations. Some analysts reported that more than 70% of the shares of privatized companies had ended up in the hands of enterprise workers and managers. Also, the objectives of many top-level managers had little to do with generating profits for reinvestment in their enterprises. They were often more concerned with satisfying workers' demands for job security, and in accumulating enterprise shares for themselves. Many workers expected that they would start earning dividends shortly after receiving shares of their enterprises, and while an attractive prospect, this positive outcome rarely materialized.

Some managers were able to initiate effective market strategies, and restructure and reorient the activities of their enterprises in new directions. Yet, many former state enterprise directors were interested in adopting only the form of privatization that would allow the largest portion of shares to be distributed to them and their workers. Many bought large percentages of shares very cheaply and eventually became the primary owners of their enterprises, but then stripped the firms of their assets. Many senior managers thus ended up owning shares of enterprises that were destitute and virtually incapable of producing anything. Although 70% of large former state-owned enterprises had been declared privatized by mid-1994 (*Economic Newsletter*, August 1994), many observers recognized that little had actually changed. Most privatized firms were still operating in essentially the same way that state-owned enterprises had for decades. Few changed their product offerings in re-

sponse to market needs, and continued to produce for inventory to maintain employment, even though workers were often not paid on time for their labor. With sales withering, such enterprises were unable to invest in new plant and technology, and still relied upon government subsidies for continued operation. It was estimated that the total value of credits received by enterprises during the summer of 1994 exceeded 13 trillion rubles. The percentage of enterprises receiving subsidies was greatest in the defense sector in which less than half of the major organizations had been privatized.

Some analysts argued that what had occurred was not privatization, but destatization. Although a large percentage of state enterprises had supposedly been privatized, 43% of industrial production came from enterprises where the state was still the sole owner. An additional 40% came from firms where the state continued to own a significant share. Few improvements occurred, and industrial production for the first 10 months of 1994 shrank by 22% compared to the same period in 1993 (*Economic Newsletter*, July 1994).

Overall, the results of privatization's first stage turned out to be less successful than expected. Although much ownership had been redistributed into private hands, little new capital had been infused into the enterprises. Another important requirement for progress, a change of management, also failed to occur. The same people continued to run the newly privatized enterprises, except that many of the best managers left to work in private business. Thus, managers who were in charge when their enterprises had reached a state of crisis during the communist and postcommunist periods remained in charge. The decline in industrial production continued, unemployment grew, and the public expressed increasing dissatisfaction with the privatization process. Although the negative consequences of privatization would seem to label the program a failure, some Western experts argued that the government's willingness to allow managers and others to gain control of enterprises constituted the only politically feasible process (Shleifer & Treisman, 2000).

NOMENKLATURA STAGE—MID-1994 THROUGH 1997

Begun During Privatization's Second Phase

The Nomenklatura stage began in mid-1994 with the start of privatization's second phase, which had the objective of infusing fresh capital into newly privatized Russian enterprises. Government officials believed that such funds would enable former state-owned enterprises to operate as private firms. The specific objective was to find strategic investors for the most economically important enterprises, primarily in the natural resources, metallurgy, telecommunications, high technology, and food sectors. In contrast to the earlier period of voucher privatization, shares at this stage were sold for money to the highest bidder in open auctions. However, many observers expressed skepticism about the openness and honesty of the auction process.

Because of the government's onerous taxation policies and restrictive foreign investment measures, new funds for enterprise investment under privatization's second phase did not materialize to any significant extent. Additional hindrances to capital infusion were problems caused by the government's freeing of the ruble, and President Yeltsin's announcement in mid-1994 that the role of government institutions in regulating the market should be strengthened. These events resulted in increasing uncertainty about the government's real objectives, and gave rise to questions about whether it had a clear policy on privatization.

Inconsistent Government Policy

Some government officials argued that the market had not yet developed to the point where it could significantly influence changes in the behavior of enterprise managers and workers, which might increase their effectiveness. Many in the government, therefore, saw it necessary to become more actively involved in regulating the economy. It appeared to many observers that the government was trying to move in two directions simultaneously—liberalizing market transactions, while also increasing government controls. There was a rapid increase in barter caused by the government's uncertain directions and onerous tax policies, and some reports indicated that nearly three-quarters of transactions during 1996 and 1997 were conducted on a nonmonetary basis.

The New Nomenklatura

Probably the most serious deterrent to successful privatization was that funds received by enterprises were often appropriated by the senior managers for their own gain. Enterprise managers, government bureaucrats, and former communist party officials, who engaged in these and other questionable activities in business-government circles, were referred to as the nomenklatura (Mikheyev, 1997). Within this new elite were found the leaders of large commercial organizations as well as a significant number of high-level state and local bureaucrats. The most influential of these cooperated in building a new group of oligopolies with powerful former state enterprises as the foundations. These large conglomerates became known as FIGs, financial and industrial groups. Under the friendly eye of the state, they were able to conduct business without real oversight or competition. This situation was most egregious in five or six large conglomerates such as Menatep, which had major holdings in banks, enterprises, and natural resources. The leaders of the largest financial-industrial enterprise groups became known as oligarchs who, with their government allies, gained substantial control over the economy. In 1993 the first FIG was registered consisting of 20 industrial enterprises and one bank, and the number increased dramatically by the end of the Nomenklatura period. The rise of FIGs and other powerful commercial banks was a major force that eventually contributed to restraining the development of a market economy.

Gaining control of large amounts of fixed assets, however, actually increased the need of these institutions for additional capital. Lacking resources to finance their growing businesses, they tried to attract large quantities of foreign capital. One of the most outstanding illustrations is found in the activities of Vladimir Potanin. In mid-1997, he convinced the international financier George Soros to put up $980 million to assist him in buying 25% of Svyazinvest, the state-owned telecommunications company. Additionally, he borrowed over $600 million through syndicated loans from foreign banks and through Eurobonds, and in late 1997 British Petroleum paid Potanin $571 million for a 10-percent stake in Sidanko, Russia's third largest oil producer (Kranz, 1999). Other very large financial-industrial groups that emerged included Onexim, Menatep, Inkombank, and Alfa.

Business and Government Became Mutually Dependent

Transactions using money from the state budget turned out to be very profitable for FIGs and powerful banks. One such activity was the purchase of treasury bills from the government. Called GKOs and OFZs, these treasury bills were issued by the government to finance the state budget, because tax collections proved insufficient. This practice began at a modest level in 1993 and 1994, but by 1998 such financial instruments amounted to over 15% of the country's GNP. These government obligations often carried annual interest rates of over 200%, and by the end of

1997, 35% of all banking assets were held in the form of GKOs, and they produced 41% of all bank earnings. Thus, these banks and the new private enterprises to which they made loans became closely linked to the state budget. And the government's voracious appetite for bank loans also severely limited funds for the entrepreneurial sector. Finally, many state enterprises, as well as semiprivatized firms whose controlling share packages still belonged to the government, deposited their funds in the commercial banks to earn high interest rates (*Economic Newsletter*, October 1998).

Although many bankers, industrialists, and government officials were reaping enormous profits from these financial transactions, little was reinvested in developing the country's economic potential. Instead, huge amounts of capital were spirited out of the country to personal accounts and investments abroad. According to a conservative World Bank estimate, $88.7 billion fled Russia from 1993 through 1996, and a later study by a team of Canadian and Russian academic economists estimated the figure to be $140 billion from 1992 to 1997 (Reddaway, 1998). The primary reason for this capital flight was that key Yeltsin government officials had become highly dependent on close ties to the oligarchs and other powerful figures. These officials no longer had the power to prevent such activities nor to continue with progressive reforms in the national interest (Reddaway, 1998). Thus, these self-serving activities occurred while the government, under phase two of privatization, was ostensibly trying to attract strategic investors to newly privatized enterprises.

Some Positive Signs

In contrast to the deterioration of large enterprises, which experienced a decrease of 10 million workers from 1994 to 1997, the number of employees in small businesses grew by 600,000 from 1995 to 1997. The entrepreneurial sector therefore seemed to be growing successfully, and one source predicted that, "if there is any hope for growth in the economy, it will have to come from that sector" (*Economic Newsletter*, December 1998). The same source noted that the number of new businesses rose by about 20,000 from 1996 to 1997, and Russian statistics estimated that 2.7 million such businesses were operating in 1997.

Although the privatization process did not improve the performance of most large enterprises, the economy was on a fairly even keel for 1997, with GDP increasing 0.4% and industrial output, 1.9%. Inflation seemed to be under control, with prices rising only 11% during the year (*Economic Newsletter*, February 1999). It was apparent, however, that the economy was still very fragile. Foreign investors, as well as Russian managers and workers, needed to show patience and systematically develop their businesses using effective long-term strategies to become more competitive.

Storm Signals

This perspective, however, did not seem to be the disposition or objective of any of these parties, nor of many government officials during the Nomenklatura period. Many managers and their government allies were more interested in solidifying their power and wealth by accumulating ownership in the assets of former state-owned enterprises. In many cases, they sold off these assets, or created their own companies to shelter such assets. Other serious problems also prevented privatization's objectives from being achieved. One source noted that "any money that reaches Russia from abroad risks being siphoned off by organized crime, in cahoots with the state" (*The Economist*, 1999, p. 19). Another survey reported that dealing with corrupt government officials was even more harmful to business than threats from the mafia (*Economic Newsletter*, July 1999).

In retrospect, both phases of privatization, the latter of which included the Nomenklatura stage, were assessed by most analysts as failing to achieve their goals. The hoped-for infusion of new capital into enterprises, through the sale of additional stock, did not materialize to any great extent because of continuing political, legal, and economic instability. The initially positive view of Phase One's accomplishments changed over the years as ownership of shares became consolidated in the hands of a few individuals, specifically senior enterprise executives, and the oligarchs or leaders of large conglomerates. Such developments contributed to the reluctance of new investors to purchase shares in these closely-held organizations. Instead, many large foreign companies, especially from North America and Western Europe, chose the route of direct investment in their own Russian subsidiaries, as well as selective participation in partnerships with Russian en-

terprises and government organizations (Puffer, McCarthy, & Zhuplev, 1998).

STATIZATION STAGE—1998 THROUGH THE END OF THE DECADE

The government had vacillated during the decade between loosening and tightening its grip on the economy, but in early 1998, significantly tighter controls were imposed when President Yeltsin announced that the deteriorating economic situation made it necessary for the government to become more deeply involved in regulating the economy. GDP, in fact, had begun to decline in May of 1998, after a period of relative stability.

August 1998 Financial Crisis

The downward trend continued so that by August, when the financial crisis occurred, GDP for that month was down more than 8% and industrial production by 11.5% compared to a year earlier. For 1998 as a whole, both GDP and industrial output had declined approximately 5% relative to 1997. Inflation had also become a major problem, with prices having risen 84% during the year. Another signal of economic deterioration was foreign capital investment which, in the first 6 months of 1998, was equal only to the corresponding period for 1997. By contrast, in 1996 foreign investment had increased by 2.3 times over 1995, and further increased in 1997 by 1.8 times over 1996 (*Economic Newsletter*, January 1999).

The financial crisis of August 1998, which saw the government default on its internal and international debts, ended any semblance of financial stability and confidence in a free-market economy. The IMF postponed a $4.3 billion payment of a $22.6 billion rescue package, after the Russian government defaulted on $40 billion of its domestic debt in August and also allowed the ruble to devalue precipitously. Without such relief, according to the Russian finance ministry, the economy could contract by 5 to 7% in 1999. Some Western and Russian analysts believed that it was the ill-conceived policies of the Western-controlled world financial institutions that had caused the crisis in the first place, with their large infusions of cash without proper controls and accountability (Reddaway, 1998). To facilitate the government's plans to take a leading role in bolstering the economy, a policy was formulated of using the oligopolies instead of developing small business. This move toward favoring large enterprises, coupled with the close relationships between the oligarchs and government officials, set a clear course for increased state involvement in the economy.

Problems Persist

The country's deteriorating financial situation was exacerbated by the mid-February 1999 disclosure that the Central Bank had channeled $50 million into an offshore account in the U.K. (*Economic Newsletter*, February 1999). PricewaterhouseCoopers, the international accounting firm retained by the International Monetary Fund to audit the Bank's policies and accounts, uncovered this violation when auditing the bank's activities with the offshore institution, Financial Management Company. The auditors also found that the Central Bank was keeping double books for transactions with this organization. Further allegations of wrongdoing and money laundering surfaced in September 1999. American, British, and Russian investigators announced that there was "strong evidence" that 780 Russian officials used a bond-selling scheme to send billions of dollars out of the country in 1998, a few hours after the IMF deposited a $4.8 billion loan into the Central Bank. The investigators also suspected that the Russian mafia and Kremlin authorities had siphoned as much as $15 billion out of the country through the Bank of New York and other financial institutions.

One source reported Russia's debt to be $150.6 billion, of which $16 billion was obligated to be serviced in 1999. Despite such staggering liabilities, tax collections were reported to be only $1 billion in January 1999. It seemed likely that Russia would be able to pay off no more than $7 billion of its debt, putting enormous pressure on the government to reschedule its obligations (*Economic Newsletter*, February 1999). Many analysts believed the government itself was largely responsible for the crisis and the events leading up to it. Others also blamed the self-serving oligarchs, and some laid the blame directly on the President.

Government Reacts

Given these circumstances, the Statization stage was perhaps the logical culmination of the Privatization and Nomenklatura stages. With power being heavily concentrated in fewer and fewer interlocking hands, and the economy rapidly deteriorating, a return to a more pervasive role of government was virtually inevitable. The country's difficult situation was exacerbated by Yeltsin's ineffectiveness at governing, as well as by constant changes in government officials and policies, growing resentment and discontent among citizens, and the increasing power of the communists in parliament. The September 1998 appointment as prime minister of Evgeny Primakov, a 68-year-old Soviet-era cabinet minister, confirmed in the eyes of most observers that a return to increased state control and involvement in the economy was inevitable. He himself announced: "State intervention in economic life is essential to establish economic order" (Thornhill, 1998). In a volatile environment, Primakov's appointment had added an element of stability, but many saw his lack of a clear economic direction as a sign that the country would not make any significant economic progress.

The West, particularly the IMF and the World Bank, had demanded a plan of austerity and tough measures, such as cutting federal spending, to bring the economy back from the brink. External pressures notwithstanding, Primakov's initial plans showed none of the toughness needed to improve the country's projected $5 billion deficit. It was considered by many as a vague and inconsistent plan that retreated from market principles. One authority commented that the country had reached a stage of "stalled transition" that could restart in a number of different directions, most negative, but some positive (Colton, 1999).

Yeltsin's Capricious Decisions

Primakov's lack of a credible plan was one reason given by Yeltsin for replacing him in May 1999 with Sergei Stepashin. Some observers, however, believed that Primakov's ouster was the result of his endorsing the arrest of the oligarch Boris Berezovsky, a close friend of Yeltsin's daughter (Goldman, 1999). Almost concurrent with this dispute, Yeltsin named his fourth prime minister in 17 months. His August 10, 1999 appointment to the prime minister's post of Federal Security Service chief, Vladimir Putin, was seen by many experts as purely a survival strategy on Yeltsin's part. But despite the many erratic decisions by Yeltsin, the IMF had seen it necessary to approve a $4.5 billion loan program for Russia in July 1999 to help stabilize the economy.

Some Good News

In a surprising turn of events, the crisis of mid-1998 actually helped the country's economy, because the 75% devaluation of the ruble made imports far too expensive for most Russians. Ironically, the devaluation spurred investment in plant and equipment on the part of Western companies, as well as many domestic firms. Russian companies were reported by a long-involved Western executive as becoming more aggressive in their investments to take advantage of what they saw as a window of opportunity against foreign investors (Tappan, 1998). Among the multinationals, the same observer found in an informal survey in late 1998 that 97% of the foreign executives he interviewed said they planned to stay in Russia despite the problems. Other sources noted that Danone of France had committed to building a $100 million plant in Moscow, Nestle of Switzerland planned a $30 to $50 million plant, and Cadbury of the U.K., IKEA of Sweden, and H. J. Heinz, Procter & Gamble, and Gillette of the U.S. were among multinationals that planned major capital investments to ensure their market positions (*Economic Newsletter*, July 1999; Matlack, 1999).

Although serious problems persisted in the economy, such investment was one of a number of relatively positive indicators in 1999. The economy had, in fact, shown some signs of recovery during the first and second quarters, particularly in the area of natural resources such as oil, gas, and metals. GDP turned remarkably positive with a year-to-year increase of 6% in May 1999 over May 1998, 9% in June, and 11% in July. By January 2000, the monthly increase of 10% over a year earlier was the strongest since the collapse of the Soviet Union in 1991. More importantly, the recovery was widespread with one study of 50 industries noting that 80% showed increases in production (*Economic Newsletter*, March 2000). The solid basis for this improvement was noted some time earlier by a British expert on key Russian industries (Hill, 1998).

The ruble's devaluation contributed to substantial increases in exports of many products, especially petroleum, nonferrous metals, and semifinished products, and in fact, Russia had a trade surplus with the U.S. of nearly $4 billion in 1999. The Russian stock market, although still considered very risky, rebounded strongly and showed a remarkably strong increase during the first quarter of 2000. Germany continued to be the largest investor in Russia as well as its major trading partner, whereas the United States followed closely behind. Direct investment in the country rose 4.5% in 1999, and although not as large an increase as in 1997, it was far more positive than the decline of 6.7% during 1998. And although consumer prices continued to rise, they did so at a slower pace. (*Economic Newsletter*, June, July, August, 1999; March 2000).

So although the Statization period marked an increasing government involvement in the economy, its activity was relatively benign during the last year of the decade. The country had continued to edge its way out of the mid-1998 crisis, albeit at a relatively slow rate. Still, the signs of a potential turnaround, or at least a cessation of the downward spiral, had begun to emerge by early 1999. A parallel positive development was the increasing investment activity by Western multinationals, as well as the U.S.-Russia Investment Fund sponsored by the U.S. government, which adjusted its strategy. After temporarily halting lending and investments following the August 1998 financial crisis, it reinstated its programs by the end of the year. It was even clearer by mid-1999 that the international community would continue to support Russia, but not without imposing conditions given the inherent risks. Such support, as well as the devaluation of the ruble, had allowed improvements in the economy and in some Russian businesses, and the country entered the new decade with renewed hope.

A Scenario: Toward Statist Capitalism and a Mixed Economy

Considering the outcomes of the four stages of Russia's attempts to develop a market-oriented economy during the 1990s, our research leads us to the conclusion that the country will continue in the basic direction that was being followed as the decade ended. To provide more confidence to those who would invest in the country's future, however, clarification by the government is needed regarding the economy's direction under an increased state presence. A likely scenario at this point would be a mixed economy, or what might be called statist capitalism.

The Unknown Putin

President Putin has presented himself as a strong leader cast in the mold of many prior leaders familiar to the Russian population. For this and other reasons, he will likely exert even more government influence over the economy. He has to realize that the Russian public is highly disillusioned with the failures of capitalism and a market economy, and a government advocating a strong commitment to that direction would quickly fall from favor. Also, the excesses of the oligarchs and government officials during the decade, which included gaining control of state-enterprise assets, triggering the flight of capital to safe offshore havens, and

other flagrant abuses of power, added to the public outcry for change.

Putin must commit to strong actions to counteract the effects of years of corruption, neglect, and confusion under Yeltsin that culminated in the nomenklatura period and the financial crisis. As the decade ended, however, a major question still remained as to how Putin would deal with the oligarchs, and where his loyalties lay. A positive early sign was his dismissal of Yeltsin's daughter, Tatiana, from her government post, but it was not clear how much his power depended upon the oligarchs and Yeltsin's inner circle. To effect real change, Putin would have to distance himself from these forces and provide the leadership needed to recharge the economy.

Need for Change

President Putin must also provide clear signals as to government policies after years of confusing and conflicting changes that offered no possible continuity for business decision making. More clarity and continuity must be provided, particularly in areas such as taxation, business legislation, property rights, and economic infrastructure (Koretz, 2000; Shleifer & Treisman, 2000). Putin had put forth a plan that included a government-run industrial policy (Starobin & Fairlamb, 2000), and in February 2000, his finance minister proposed to slash personal income tax rates from 30 to 20%. Putin also pledged to protect property rights and require Russian companies to adopt international accounting standards (Starobin & Tavernise, 2000). Motivations to take such actions included Putin's awareness that the country's GDP of $190 billion was one-fiftieth that of the U.S., and that its per capita GDP of $1,800 was about one-sixth that of Portugal, and one-eighth that of Spain. However, the last quarter of the decade did see some improvements in the economy compared to earlier periods. Real investment, for instance, grew by one percentage compared to the prior year, and this relatively small gain looked promising when compared to the 16-percent average annual decline during the decade (Koretz, 2000).

Change is Likely

Putin's varied experiences and public statements seemed to indicate that he was likely to favor a mixed economy in which the state maintained a strong hand concurrently with a more market-based private sector. He became somewhat familiar with a market economy during his security assignments in Germany in the 1990s, and a former policy advisor to German chancellor Shroeder said of Putin: "He knows that Russia needs a fully functioning, well-regulated, private-sector economy to survive" (Starobin & Fairlamb, 2000, p. 48). It would not be surprising though, to see the state control, or even renationalize the energy sector, as well as other key natural-resource-based companies. The temptation would be hard to resist, because doing so would ensure government access to hard currencies that the export of such products generates (McCarthy & Puffer, 1995). Early in 2000, world oil prices were very strong, and coordinated efforts by the

world oil cartel seemed likely to perpetuate the situation for some time.

Putin was sure to recognize also that, due to the ruble's devaluation, some Russian companies were recovering. The country's GDP actually grew by 1.5% during 1999, and output increased in almost all sectors of the economy (*Economic Newsletter*, February 2000). And if the currency strengthened, the government would likely take action to protect the fragile progress of its industry. Another benefit of a weak ruble was an increasing number of Western companies adding to their investments in the country. McDonald's, for instance, which employed 5,000 people at the end of 1999, planned to open 10 new restaurants during 2000. Most of its supplies of food and materials came from its own Russian-based farms and processing plant, or from Russian companies. Its low-cost structure had even allowed McDonald's to export from Russia to its operations in Western and Eastern Europe (Shekshnia, Puffer, & McCarthy, 2000). Such signs of progress would likely encourage the continuation of private enterprise, concurrent with a government policy that would simultaneously increase state involvement in the economy.

Other arguments abounded for continuing to foster the positive aspects of the fragile market economy of the 1990s. A vibrant entrepreneurial sector, for instance, had contributed strongly to employment, as well as to production of goods and services during the decade. And, in a tentative vote of confidence for Putin's early signals, the flight of capital from the country to offshore havens was predicted to slow considerably in 2000 to an estimated $15 billion compared to $20 billion in 1999 (Starobin & Tavernise, 2000). Also, mixed ownership such as in hybrid enterprises had shown marked promise for carrying out projects during the 1990s, especially those with a social orientation. Additionally, Russia will continue to need foreign investment to help rebuild its economy and infrastructure, some of which would almost surely have to be private. Such investments had already begun to increase during 1999 with $613 million in the third quarter, compared to $411 million in the same quarter a year earlier (Starobin & Tavernise, 2000). Importantly, the IMF and World Bank would likely continue putting pressure on the government to maintain aspects of openness, free markets, and competition.

Finally, numerous segments of the Russian population did not want to return to the past. Those groups included young adults who have grown up during this decade, as well as others in an emerging middle class. Even more nefarious groups within the country such as corrupt business and government officials, and former communists who accumulated a relatively high level of material wealth, would be unlikely to want a return to conditions of earlier times. It would be difficult for Putin or any Russian leader to ignore these realities as the country entered the new century. Still, the excesses of the decade and the resulting popular disenchantment with the evolving market economy would also lead to a stronger role for the state.

IMPLICATIONS FOR WESTERN MANAGERS

Although it is always difficult to predict the future, and especially so for Russia, firms investing and doing business in such turbulent environments need to develop plans (Holden, Cooper, & Carr, 1998). Understanding more about such situations can help managers in that process. This article has attempted to provide background by analyzing Russia's capitalist decade of the 1990s, and then developing a plausible scenario for the foreseeable future. These conditions suggest a number of important implications for Western business managers.

Four Economic Stages Show Trends and Opportunities

An analysis of the four stages that occurred during Russia's attempted transition to a market economy provides insights into positive and negative causes and results of that rocky evolution. It is reasonable to conclude from such a study that the country will not likely return to its central-planning mode, but that the state is likely to take a stronger, more proactive role in the economy than it did during the 1990s. The resulting resurgence of statization, however, will likely be accompanied by the parallel development of the private sector that had a promising emergence during the decade. It is this mixed economy, then, that seems to be the most plausible scenario for Russia's foreseeable future, and a number of opportunities for Western businesses can be envisioned under these circumstances.

The Market is Still There

The country may be going in the direction of China, which is attracting large amounts of foreign investment, so Western firms should not give up on exploring opportunities in Russia. The market of 150 million people includes many who have been exposed to and who have come to prefer Western products and business practices. This sizable market also explains why many Western firms took advantage of this opportunity in earlier decades (Puffer, McCarthy, & Zhuplev, 1998).

Investment Opportunities Exist

The weakness of the ruble inhibits exporting to Russia for the foreseeable future, and the currency is likely to stay weak relative to Western currencies. Companies from those countries should consider investing in plant and equipment in Russia in order to capitalize on the low cost of production such as McDonald's has done, or in well-positioned Russian companies. The impressive increase in foreign investment late in 1999 indicated that more Western companies were seeing the Russian economy in an increasingly positive light. Another opportunity for Western businesses investing there might be found in exporting lower cost products from Russia to other European countries. Firms should also consider pricing products at a level accessible to larger segments of the domestic population. Major Russian companies were themselves increasing their capital investments, including Surgutneftegaz, Russia's second largest oil producer which planned to double its capital investment

over its 1999 figure of $500 million (Starobin & Tavernise, 2000).

Infrastructure Needs Rebuilding

Opportunities may reopen for some firms to be involved in the development of a business infrastructure, such as telecommunications and the Internet. Many companies may want to invest in Russian firms with a strong market position, as did the Swedish national phone company, Telia, which invested $81 million for a 15% stake in the St. Petersburg-based Telecom Invest (Starobin & Tavernise, 2000). A focus on infrastructure could well be a priority of a new administration because it can stimulate business development as well as employment. Putin is likely to take action in this area to improve the economy and the lives of Russian citizens after a chaotic decade of widespread deprivation and disillusionment.

Early Signs of Encouragement

It is likely that new tax laws as well as other legislation affecting foreign companies, such as those dealing with private property, will be government priorities in the near future. One of Putin's first actions as acting president was to convene a group of Western-minded liberal economists to develop a new tax system, including the revision of the payroll tax with its huge 40-percent impact on workers' wages. Companies like McDonald's had already developed plans to lobby the government for a reduction of such tax burdens. And in early 2000, Putin had already put forth a plan calling for tax reductions, as well as pledging to protect property rights.

The Risk Remains

Investing in Russia, as in other questionable situations, calls for considerable risk management, which argues for flexibility in a firm's investment approach (McCarthy & Puffer, 1997). Although companies with manufacturing operations might have to commit substantial resources relatively early in their operations, service businesses will often be able to invest on an incremental basis. Many Western companies have shown willingness over the years, even at the end of the 1990s, to tolerate the risk and increase their investments in what could become a highly profitable market for them. Given the country's history of unpredictability, however, only companies willing and able to deal with substantial risk are likely to have the staying power to weather the inevitable turbulence.

Unresolved Questions

If Putin is truly to act as a strong leader with some measure of independence from Yeltsin's inner circle, he must seriously address the excesses of vested political interests, the oligarchs, and criminal elements that seriously injured the Russian economy, especially during the second half of the 1990s. Such actions would provide a far more positive business environment for multinationals as well as for Russian companies. Putin's early statements and actions indicated such intentions, but time will tell whether he has the resolve to follow through.

Conclusion

As Russia's new president, Vladimir Putin hopefully has learned from both the positive and negative experiences of the government's attempts in the 1990s to create a market economy (Shleifer & Treisman, 2000). Although the country has entered the 21st century as a mixed economy with substantial state involvement, it can still be a fruitful area for investment by Western companies. Those willing to take the risk may well position themselves for a return that justifies their confidence and patient pursuit of profit.

References

Blasi, J. R., Kroumova, M., & Kruse, D. (1997). *Kremlin capitalism: Privatizing the Russian economy.* Ithaca, NY: Cornell University Press.

Boycko, M., Shleifer, A., & Vishy, R. (1995). *Privatizing Russia.* Cambridge: MIT Press.

Colton, T. J. (1999). Russia stalled; The uncertain transition from Communism. *Harvard Magazine*, (March/April):, 33–35.

Economic Newsletter (1993, 1994, 1998, 1999, 2000). Cambridge, MA: Harvard University, Davis Center for Russian Studies. March; 1993; June, July, August 1994, October, December 1998; January, February, June, July, August, December 1999; March 2000.

Goldman, M. I. (1999). Russia's mixed-up moves reveal its dangerous divide. *The Washington Post*, June, 20: B1, B5.

Hill, M. R. (1998). From Soviet giants to Russian survivors. *Leadership and Organization Development, 19*(6): 325–331.

Holden, N., Cooper, C., & Carr, J. (1998). *Dealing with the new Russia.* Chichester: Wiley.

Koretz, G. (2000). Russia's revival may be shaky. *Business Week*, March, 13: 28.

Kranz, P. (1999). Fall of an oligarch: Can Vladimir Potanin save his empire? *Business Week*, March, *1*: 44, 45.

Matlack, C. (1999). Betting on a new label: Made in Russia. *Business Week*, April 12: 122.

McCarthy, D. J. & Puffer, S. M. (1992). Perestroika at the plant level: Managers' job attitudes and views of decision-making in the former USSR. *Columbia Journal of World Business*, 27(1): 86–99.

McCarthy, D. J. & Puffer, S. M. (1995). "Diamonds and Rust" on Russia's road to privatization: The profits and pitfalls for Western managers. *Columbia Journal of World Business*, 30(3): 56–69.

McCarthy, D. J. & Puffer, S. M. (1997). Strategic investment flexibility for MNE success in Russia. *Journal of World Business*, 32(4): 293–319.

Mikheyev, D. (1997). *Russia transformed*. Indianapolis: Hudson Institute.

Peng, M. & Heath, P. (1996). The growth of the firm in planned economies in transition. *Academy of Management Review*, 21: 492–528.

Puffer, S. M., McCarthy, D. J., & Naumov, A. I. (2000). *The Russian capitalist experiment: From state-owned organizations to entrepreneurships*. Cheltenham, U.K. and Northampton, MA: Edward Elgar.

Puffer, S. M., McCarthy, D. J., & Zhuplev, A. V. (1998). Doing business in Russia: Lessons from early entrants. *Thunderbird International Business Review*, 40(5): 461–484.

Reddaway, P. (1998). The roots of Russia's crisis: The Soviet legacy, IMF/G7 policies, and Yeltsin's authoritarianism: Where is the crisis now leading? *Russia Business Watch*, 6: 12–15.

Sachs, J. (1995). What have we learned about rule of law and economic reform in Russia? Seminar, Russian Research Center, Harvard University, May 9.

Shama, A. & Sementsov, S. (1992). The collapse of the Soviet ministries: Economic and legal transformation. *The International Executive*, 34(2): 131–150.

Shekshnia, S. V., Puffer, S. M., & McCarthy, D. J. (2000). Labour relations in the Russian fast-food industry. In T. Royle & B. Towers (Eds.), *Labour relations in the global fast-food industry*. London: Routledge.

Shleifer, A. & Treisman, D. (2000). *Without a map: Political tactics and economic reform in Russia*. Cambridge: MIT Press.

Starobin, P. & Fairlamb, D. (2000). Putin's Russia: Can the former KGB spymaster succeed where Yeltsin failed? *Business Week*, January 17: 48–50.

Starobin, P. & Tavernise, S. (2000). A new home for Russian capital—Russia: The flight of capital seems to be abating as faith builds in Putin. *Business Week*, March 6: 58.

The Economist. (1999). Russian organised crime: Crime without punishment. August 28: 17–19.

Tappan, M. A. (1998). Grassroots business recovery in Russia. *Harriman Review*, Special issue on the Russian economy in crisis. December: 12, 13.

Thornhill, J. (1998). Parliamentary chiefs back Primakov's strategy. *Financial Times*, November, *3*: 3.

Vlachoutsicos, C. A. & Lawrence, P. R. (1996). How managerial learning can assist economic transformation in Russia. *Organization Studies*, 17(2): 311–325.

Zhuplev, A., Kon'kov, A., & Kiesner, F. (1998). Russian and American small business: Motivations and obstacles. *European Management Journal*, 16(4): 505–516.

Name Index